NOAA DIVING MANUAL
Diving for Science and Technology

Fourth Edition

James T. Joiner
EDITOR

NATIONAL OCEANIC AND ATMOSPHERIC ADMINISTRATION
D. James Baker, Under Secretary for Oceans and Atmosphere
OFFICE OF OCEANIC AND ATMOSPHERIC RESEARCH
David L. Evans, Assistant Administrator
NATIONAL UNDERSEA RESEARCH PROGRAM
Barbara Moore, Director
OFFICE OF MARINE AND AVIATION OPERATIONS
Rear Admiral Evelyn J. Fields, Director
NOAA DIVING PROGRAM
David A. Dinsmore, Director

Published   - 1977
Second Edition - 1979
Third Edition   - 1991
Fourth Edition - 2001

ISBN: 0-941332-70-5
Library of Congress Catalog Card Number: 98-96829

Library of Congress cataloging in publication data
    United States.
    National Oceanic and Atmospheric Administration.
    National Undersea Research Program (NURP).

    Includes bibliographies and Index

1. Diving, Scientific	2. Hyperbaric Physiology	
3. Diving, Research	4. Nitrox Diving	5. Underwater Diving
I. Title	II. Joiner, Jim	

Publisher
Best Publishing Company
2355 North Steves Boulevard
P.O. Box 30100
Flagstaff, AZ, USA 86003-0100

TABLE OF CONTENTS

FOREWORD

The National Oceanic and Atmospheric Administration has a broad mission to describe and predict changes in the Earth's environment, and conserve and manage wisely our coastal and marine resources to ensure sustainable economic opportunities. As the population grows, it places increasing demands on our oceans and resources. Conserving and managing the oceans have become critical challenges. Important fisheries have declined, coastal habitats destroyed, and our waters polluted. Among NOAA's many responsibilities is to research and monitor our oceans, coasts, and Great Lakes.

With over 70 percent of our planet covered by water and largely unexplored, our oceans and inland seas are a vast source of unique plants and animals, food and recreation, minerals, and potential medicines. In order to better understand our water environment and resources, NOAA operates satellites, ships, and submersibles, as well as the world's only underwater laboratory. To add a uniquely human dimension to ocean research and marine services, NOAA conducts wet diving operations wherever our agency is involved in marine operations and scientific studies.

NOAA has the largest diving complement of any civil federal agency—more than 300 men and women. This number does not include those civilian scientists, engineers, and technicians who dive under the auspices of NOAA-sponsored research grants, a factor that significantly increases that number. In order to successfully conduct various missions, these divers include scientists, engineers, technicians, and officers in the NOAA Corps.

Because the tasks NOAA divers carry out are as varied as those of any group of underwater workers in the world, this version of the *NOAA Diving Manual*—greatly expanded and revised—contains instructions, recommendations, and general guidance on the broadest possible range of underwater living conditions and dive situations. Thus, while the manual is directed toward NOAA, it will be useful, as were previous editions, to working divers who have other affiliations and to those who dive for recreation.

Under authority delegated by the Secretary of Commerce, NOAA is charged with the mandate under Section 21(e) of the Outer Continental Shelf Lands Act Amendments of 1978 to "conduct studies of underwater diving techniques and equipment suitable for protection of human safety and improvement in diver performance." NOAA is proud of its record of safe diving and the assistance it has provided to the diving community. For example, the decompression sickness rate in the past ten years has been 0.015 percent. Safety is our number one priority.

I wish to convey my appreciation to the many individuals and groups that made possible this 4th Edition of the *NOAA Diving Manual*. The editor obtained recommendations from leading divers, medical and scientific authorities, equipment manufacturers, and others in the diving community. To those who contributed, I express, on behalf of NOAA, my thanks for their assistance in making this revision possible.

D. James Baker

D. James Baker
Under Secretary for Oceans and Atmosphere
National Oceanic and Atmospheric Administration

PREFACE

In 1970, when the National Oceanic and Atmospheric Administration (NOAA) came into existence, its divers were volunteers who were concerned with scientific accomplishments and with the physical biological technology required to improve the nation's capability in one of the harshest environments on Earth. This group of pioneers was determined to continually seek better and safer ways to explore, perform research, and undertake analysis of the underwater realm. Since that time, NOAA has been recognized as one of the major authorities on diving and underwater technology.

Today, thousands of professional research scientists, graduate students, technicians, and undergraduates around the world have carried out scientific diving using scuba, surface-supplied diving equipment, and underwater habitats. NOAA's goal under the National Undersea Research Program (NURP) is to advance undersea exploration and experimentation to help mankind learn about and protect the world's largest natural resource. NURP researchers, with the aid of diving, are able to study such important coastal problems and processes relating to fisheries, water quality, coral reefs, seamounts, and volcanoes that bear on our economic, social, and environmental well being. The value of the fishing industry alone is enormous — $3.7 billion dockside with a resulting $38 billion annual impact on the economy.

The first *NOAA Diving Manual* was produced in 1977. There have been two revisions since then. The *NOAA Diving Manual* addresses the needs of scientific and research divers and also recognizes that the manual is useful for others who dive because it contains a wealth of information on applied diving technology. The manual has made diving techniques safer by improving procedures for certification, training standards, technical diving with special emphasis on decompression, and mixed-gas diving.

In preparing the 4th Edition, the foremost objectives were to provide guidance on safe diving practices under varying experimental and environmental conditions, make recommendations for safe diving practices using different breathing gases and systems, and introduce the myriad scientific and technical developments that have occurred since the last manual update in 1991. While these primary goals are far from new or even original, combined they form a synergistic effect that will bring an in-depth understanding of diving and the diver to a new level.

The development of this manual was a three-year-long process. It began with the initial planning team who determined what information should be included in the new manual so that it would offer a set of guiding principles for the conduct and administration of safe and efficient diving in a variety of environmental conditions. This group, whose names appear on the Contributors and Reviewers page, also decided which chapters should be merged, added, revised, or eliminated so that the new manual would utilize the most recent knowledge of diving physiology, hyperbaric medicine, underwater scientific methodology, as well as the development of new equipment and operational techniques. Individually, and collectively, they are to be praised for their vision and insight as well as their energy and personal involvement.

The multidisciplinary nature of diving is such that the planners of this new edition knew it would need the input and assistance of numerous experts to cover the wide variety of diving-related specialties. The decision was to assemble several experts on each subject who would volunteer their expertise and talent to produce a new, totally revised chapter. It was further decided that these experts would serve as a writing team, using an interactive process that required several reviews of the same material to ensure that all of the authors were satisfied their respective chapter contained the latest material available on their subject area.

Two NOAA offices were instrumental for the development of the 4th Edition of the *NOAA Diving Manual*. The NOAA Diving Program was responsible for reviewing and editing all material in the manual for technical accuracy and compliance with NOAA standards and procedures. The NOAA Diving Program determined the contents and also wrote significant portions of the book. NOAA's National Undersea Research Program served as NOAA's lead in the interagency agreement with the National Technical Information Service of the Department of Commerce. In this role, NURP assisted in selecting the publisher, and also provided guidance and conducted reviews of the materials.

The diverse panel of diving experts provided a cross-pollination of information, special knowledge, and philosophies that has made this 4th Edition of the *NOAA Diving Manual* a unique accumulation of instructions, recommendations, and general guidance on dive procedures, equipment, and safety measures. It is designed specially for the research and scientific diver, but offers a wealth of information for the entire diving community, including commercial and recreational divers, military, and those involved in the instructional area of diving.

The individual contributions for these experts are too numerous to list, but their assistance and dedication has elevated this *NOAA Diving Manual* to new heights. As the Senior Editor for this project, I am extremely grateful to all those who have utilized their knowledge, experience, and judgment to contribute information to the manual, and who, in addition, donated thousands of hours to the successful completion of the project.

James T. Joiner
Editor

CONTRIBUTORS AND REVIEWERS

As with every project, there are some people who need special recognition for their untiring devotion to a project. In addition to those contributing to the manual in a technical sense, the production and assembly of a document of this size, duration, and diversity would not be possible without the assistance of a number of people who worked behind the scenes. First, we would like to recognize those Best Publishing Company employees who have worked and reworked the material in the manual for the past three years. In addition, special recognition is given to:

Arrington, Steve
Auerbach, Paul
Averill, Harry
Bachman, Leonard
Barnea, Nir
Barsky, Kristine
Barsky, Steven
Bennett, Peter
Bookspan, Jolie
Brylske, Alex
Carpenter, Tom
Carson, Daryl
Chapin, Julie Ann
Clarke, Richard E.
Clinchy, Richard A. III
Cobb, Bill
Collie, Marcia
Cooper, Craig
Cote, Christopher
Cotter, Patrick
Craynock, Jules
Crosson, Dudley
Dinsmore, David A.
Dovenbarger, Joel
Edmonds, Carl
Egstrom, Glen
Emmerman, Michael N.
Eng, Doug
Fahres, Tom
Flagg, Marco
Forman, Will
Fryburg, Richard
Galerne, Andre
Goldberg, Lawrence

Goldman, Jana
Guastaferro, Jan
Hamilton, R.W. (Bill)
Heine, John N.
High, William L. (Bill)
Hines, Anson H.
Hoshlyk, Michael
Junker, David
Kakuk, Brian
Kalvaitis, Al
Kelly, Michael
Kesling, Doug
Koblick, Ian
Kushner, Steve
Lambertsen, Christian J.
Lang, Michael A.
Lanphier, Edward H.
Lawler, David
Littler, Diane S.
Littler, Mark M.
Lenihan, Dan
Maines, Gary
Maney, Ted
McClain, Forrest
Miller, James W.
Moon, Richard
Moore, Barbara
Myers, Ed
Nadler, Jeff
Newell, Cliff
Nord, Dan
Nordoff, Andy
Orr, Betty
Orr, Dan

Patrick, Jim
Peterson, Russell
Reimers, Steve
Richardson, Drew
Roller, Milka Pejoric
Rosner, John
Ryan, Ron
Sack, Richard
Santi, Giunio G.
Saxon, Ross
Shreeves, Karl
Silverstein, Joel D.
Smith, James P.
Smith, Leann G.
Stockhausen, Patricia A.
Stolp, Brent
Thombs, Paul A.
Urick, Steve
Valley, William
Van Liew, Hugh D.
Vasquez, Joie
Viders, Hillary
Walker, Kimberley
Wallace, Carla
Ward, Mike
Wells, Morgan
Weydig, Kathy A.
White, Dan
Wienke, Bruce
Wood, Frank
Workman, Ian
Workman, W.T. (Tom)
Yount, David E.
Zahorniak, Richard

CONTRIBUTORS AND REVIEWERS

Former Contributors

Bachrach, Arthur J.
Bangasser, Susan
Barsky, Steven
Bassett, Bruce
Bauer, Judy
Bell, George C.
Bell, Richard
Bennett, Peter
Berey, Richard W.
Black, Stan
Bornmann, Robert
Bove, Alfred
Busby, Frank
Butler, Glenn
Clark, James D.
Clarke, Richard E
Clifton, H. Edward
Cobb, William F.
Corry, James A.
Crosson, Dudley J.
Daugherty, C. Gordon
Davis, Jefferson C.
Desautels, David
Dingler, John R.
Dinsmore, David A.
Eckenhoff, Roderic G.
Edel, Peter
Egstrom, Glen
Emmerman, Michael
Farmer, Joseph C., Jr.
Feldman, Bruce A.
Fife, William
Flynn, Edward T.

Francis, Art, Lt.
Graver, Dennis
Halstead, Bruce W.
Hamner, William M.
Hamilton, R.W.
Heine, John N.
Hendrick, Walter, Jr.
Hennessy, T. R.
High, William L.
Hobson, Edmund
Hollien, Harry
Hubbard, Dennis
Hussey, Nancy R.
Jenkins, Wallace T.
Kent, Marthe B.
Kinney, Jo Ann S.
Lambertsen, Christian J.
Lanphier, Edward H.
Lewbel, George
Loewenherz, James W.
Long, Richard W.
Macintyre, Ian G.
Mathewson, R. Duncan, III
Mayers, Douglas
McCarthy, James
Miller, James W.
Miller, John N.
Murray, Rusty
Murru, Frank
Newell, Cliff
Norquist, David S.
Orr, Dan
Pegnato, Paul

Pelissier, Michael
Peterson, David H.
Peterson, Russell
Phoel, William C.
Reimers, Steve
Robinson, Jill
Rogers, Wayne
Roman, Charles M.
Rounds, Richard
Rutkowski, Richard I.
Schane, William
Schroeder, William W.
Somers, Lee
Spaur, William
Staehle, Michael
Stanley, Chet
Stewart, James R.
Stewart, Joan, Ph.D.
Stone, Richard B.
Strauss, Michael B.
Swan, George
Thompson, Terry
Thornton, J. Scott
Valentine, Page
Vorosmarti, James, Jr.
Walsh, Michael
Waterman, Stanton A.
Webb, Paul
Wells, Morgan
Wicklund, Robert I.
Wilkie, Donald W.
Williscroft, Robert
Workman, Ian

Acknowledgements

We wish to convey our thanks to the many organizations who helped make this publication possible, for the invaluable contributions and support they so generously made.

ASSOCIATION OF DIVING CONTRACTORS INTERNATIONAL
AMERICAN COLLEGE OF PREHOSPITAL MEDICINE
BROCO
DELTA P
DESERT STAR SYSTEMS
DIVERS ALERT NETWORK (DAN)
DIVING SYSTEMS INTERNATIONAL
GOLD FAMILY TRUST
GREENSTONE FAMILY TRUST
HAMILTON RESEARCH, LTD.
HIGH-TECH DIVING & SAFETY
INSTRUCTIONAL TECHNOLOGIES
KOBLICK MARINE CENTER
LIFEGUARD SYSTEMS, INC.
MARINE MARKETING AND CONSULTING
MICHIGAN STATE POLICE U/W RECOVERY UNIT
MOSS LANDING MARINE LABORATORY
NATIONAL ASSOCIATION OF UNDERWATER INSTRUCTORS
NATIONAL MUSEUM OF NATURAL HISTORY
NATIONAL TECHNICAL INFORMATION SERVICE
NATIONAL UNDERSEA RESEARCH PROGRAM
NAVY EXPERIMENTAL DIVING UNIT
NOAA DIVING PROGRAM
OCEAN NEWS
OCEAN ROYALE
OCEANEERING INTERNATIONAL
PADI AMERICAS
PROFESSIONAL SCUBA INSPECTORS INC.
RICHLAND MEMORIAL HOSPITAL
SCUBA TRAINING AND TECHNOLOGY CO.
SCUBAPRO
SEA TEST SERVICES
SEA QUEST
SEARIOUS FUN INC.
SMITHSONIAN INSTITUTION
SOUTHWEST ENTERPRISES
SUBSALVE
TOMSKY FAMILY TRUST
UNDERSEA RESEARCH FOUNDATION
UNIVERSITY OF HAWAII
UNIVERSITY OF NORTH CAROLINA AT WILMINGTON
UNIVERSITY OF PENNSYLVANIA
U.S. ARMY CORP OF ENGINEERS
U.S. ENVIRONMENTAL PROTECTION AGENCY
U.S. GEOLOGICAL SURVEY
U.S. NAVY

Technical Information

The 4th Edition of the *NOAA Diving Manual* is the result of a collaborative partnership between Best Publishing Company and the Department of Commerce's National Oceanic and Atmospheric Administration (NOAA) and the National Technical Information Service.

NOAA Diving Program
7600 Sand Point Way NE, Seattle, WA 98115
Phone: (206) 526-6196
www.ndc.noaa.gov

The NOAA Diving Program is responsible for overseeing and managing all NOAA diving personnel, equipment, and activities and ensuring that all diving is performed in a safe and efficient manner. The NOAA Diving Program trains and certifies NOAA scientists, engineers, and technicians to carry out a broad variety of underwater tasks to meet NOAA's goals for data acquisition. The focus of training at the NOAA Diving Center is preparing students to meet the mental and physical challenges that face them as working divers. With more than 300 active divers, NOAA has the largest complement of divers of any civilian federal agency. Averaging more than 9,000 dives per year, the NOAA Diving Program has consistently maintained an excellent diving safety record (99.985% safe dive statistic).

National Undersea Research Program
SSMC3, R/NURP, Room 11359, 1315 East-West Highway, Silver Spring, MD 20910
Phone: (301) 713-2427
www.nurp.noaa.gov

The National Undersea Research Program (NURP) within NOAA provides a unique national service by providing scientists with the tools and expertise they need to work in the undersea environment. NURP equips scientists with submersibles, remotely operated or autonomous underwater vehicles, mixed gas diving gear, underwater laboratories, and observatories. NURP serves NOAA's mission to describe and predict changes in the Earth's environment and to conserve and manage wisely the nation's coastal and marine resources. Advanced undersea technologies and techniques are used to explore, describe, study, and understand the vast ocean environments and resources that are critical to our planet's survival.

National Technical Information Service
U.S. Department of Commerce, 5285 Port Royal Road, Springfield, VA 22161
Phone: (800) 553-6847 or (703) 605-6000
Online ordering: www.ntis.gov or www.ntis.gov/product/noaadive.htm

The National Technical Information Service of the Department of Commerce is the federal government's central source for the sale of scientific, technical, engineering, and related business information produced by or for the U.S. Government and complementary material from international sources. Nearly three million products are available from NTIS in a variety of formats, including microfiche, paper, diskette, audiovisual, CD-ROM, and online.

Best Publishing Company
P.O. Box 30100, Flagstaff, AZ 86003-0100
Phone: (800) 468-1055 or (520) 527-1055
www.bestpub.com

Best Publishing Company, founded in 1966, is one of the largest publishers of technical books on diving. Best Publishing Company promotes their expertise in publishing titles in several categories: commercial diving, military diving, recreational scuba diving, scientific diving, history of diving, and also diving medicine with a special emphasis on hyperbaric medicine. Distributed nationally and internationally, Best Publishing Company has become a leader in the world of publishing titles that are intended to promote safety and conservation for all levels of divers while pursuing and advancing their interest in the underwater environment. For more information and any issued errata or updates to this 4th Edition, complete registration card at the back of this manual.

History of Diving & NOAA Contributions

History of Diving & NOAA Contributions

1.0 GENERAL

Divers have penetrated the oceans throughout the centuries for purposes identical to those of modern diving: to acquire food, search for treasure, carry out military operations, perform scientific research and exploration, and enjoy the aquatic environment. In a brief history of diving, Arthur Bachrach identified major principal periods in the history of diving: free (or breath-hold) diving, bell diving, surface support or helmet (hard-hat) diving, scuba diving, and saturation diving (Bachrach 1982). This chapter also describes the formation and contributions of NOAA's Diving Program and the National Undersea Research Program.

1.1 FREE (BREATH-HOLD) DIVING

Free diving, or breath-hold diving, is the earliest of all diving techniques, and it has played a historic role in the search for food and treasure. The Hae-Nyu and Ama pearl

FIGURE 1.1
Female Ama Diver

divers of Korea and Japan (see Figure 1.1) are among the better-known breath-hold divers. In his book, *Half Mile Down*, William Beebe (1934) reports finding several mother-of-pearl inlays in the course of conducting an archeological dig at a Mesopotamia site that dated back to 4500 B.C. These shells must have been gathered by divers and then fashioned into inlays by artisans of the period. Beebe also describes the extensive use of pearl shells among people from other ancient cultures. The Emperor of China, for example, received an oyster pearl tribute around 2250 B.C. Free divers were also used in military operations, as the Greek historian Thucydides reports. Divers participated in an Athenian attack in which they cut through underwater barriers that had been built to obstruct and damage the Greek ships. Free or breath-hold divers sometimes used hollow reeds as breathing tubes, which allowed them to remain submerged for longer periods; this type of primitive snorkel was useful in military operations.

1.2 DIVING BELLS

The second principal historical mode of diving is bell diving. One of the earliest reports of the use of a device that enabled a diver to enter the water with some degree of protection and a supply of air involved the diving bell *Colimpha* used in Alexander the Great's descent in approximately 330 B.C. Aristotle described diving systems in use in his time: "They contrive a means of respiration for divers, by means of a container sent down to them; naturally the container is not filled with water, but air, which constantly assists the submerged man."

In the 1500 years following this period, very few developments occurred in diving. It was not until 1535 that an Italian developed a device that can be considered a true diving bell. This open bell designed by Guglielmo de Lorena actually worked. A diver worked for about an hour exploring the bottom of Lake Nemi, Italy, for the purpose of locating Trajan's pleasure barges. In 1551, Nicholas Tartaglia published an ingenious but impracticable design (see Figure 1.2) for a diving apparatus considered to be an open bell. It consisted of a wooden frame like

FIGURE 1.2
Open-Water Diving Bell
(Circa 1551)

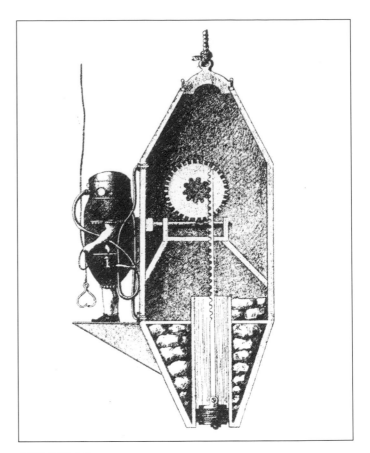

FIGURE 1.3
Klingert's Apparatus (Circa 1797)

that of a gigantic hour-glass to which a heavy weight was attached by a rope. A man standing in the frame, with his head enclosed in a large glass ball, open only at the bottom, was to wind himself down to the sea-floor by turning a windlass on which the rope was coiled. What he could do when he got there is not very clear.

In 1691, the astronomer Sir Edmund Halley, then Secretary of the Royal Society, built and patented a forerunner of the modern diving bell, which he later described in a report to the Society. As Sir Edmund described it, the bell was made of wood coated with lead, was approximately 60 cubic feet (1.7 cubic meters) in volume, and had glass at the top to allow light to enter; there was also a valve to vent the air and a barrel to provide replenished air. It has been thought that Halley undoubtedly knew of a development reported by a physicist, Denis Papin, who in 1689 had proposed a plan to provide air from the surface to a diving bell under pressure. Papin proposed to use force pumps or bellows to provide air and to maintain a constant pressure within the bell. There was speculation that Halley's choice of the barrel rather than the forced air method of replenishment may have reflected Halley's concern that Papin, also a Fellow of the Royal Society, would accuse him of stealing his concept. Halley's method was used for over a century until John Smeaton introduced a successful forcing pump in 1788. In 1799, Smeaton dived with his "diving chests," which used a forcing pump to replenish the air supply.

Diving bells are used today as part of modern diving systems, providing a method of transporting divers to their work sites while under pressure and, once at the site, of supplying breathing gas while the diver works. Both modern-day open (or "wet") and closed bells are clearly the successors of these ancient systems.

1.3 HELMET (HARD-HAT) DIVING

Although these early diving bells provided some protection and an air supply, they limited the mobility of the diver. In the seventeenth and eighteenth centuries, a number of devices were developed to provide air to divers and to afford greater mobility. For example, a German named Klingert published in 1797 a design for a complete diving helmet and dress (see Figure 1.3). The diving helmet obtained air by means of a twin breathing-pipe led into the helmet opposite the diver's mouth and was supported at the surface by a float. However, no details were given on how the air was "pumped" to the diver at depth. Unfortunately, most of these devices were not successful because they relied on long tubes from the surface to provide air to the diver and thus did not deal with the problem of equalizing pressure at depth.

The first real step toward the development of a surface-supported diving technique occurred when the French scientist Sieur Freminet devised a system in which air was pumped from the surface with a bellows, allowing a constant flow of air to pass through a hose to the diver in the water. This system is considered by many to be the first true helmet-hose diving apparatus. Freminet has been credited with diving in 1774 with this device to a depth of 50 feet (15 meters), where he remained for a period of one hour.

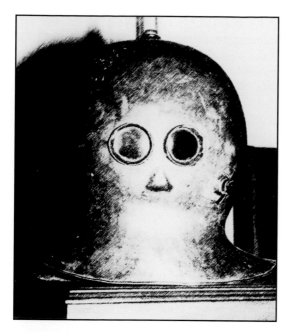

FIGURE 1.4
Earliest Functional Helmet (Circa 1823)

The first major breakthrough in surface-support diving systems occurred with Augustus Siebe's invention of the diving dress in 1819. Around the same time, John and Charles Deane were working on a design for a "smoke apparatus," a suit that would allow firefighters to work in burning buildings. They received a patent for this system in 1823, and later modified it to "Deane's Patent Diving Dress," consisting of a protective suit and a separate helmet with ports and hose connections for surface-supplied air (see Figure 1.4). Siebe's diving dress consisted of a waist-length jacket with a metal helmet sealed to the collar. Divers received air under pressure from the surface by force pump; the air subsequently escaped freely at the diver's waist. In 1837, Siebe modified this open dress, which allowed the air to escape, into the closed type of dress. The closed suit retained the attached helmet but, by venting the air via a valve, provided the diver with a full-body air-tight suit. This suit served as the basis for modern hard-hat diving gear. Siebe's diving suit was tested and found to be successful in 1839 when the British started the salvage of the ship *Royal George* at a depth of 65 feet (19.8 meters).

No major developments occurred in hard-hat gear until the twentieth century, when mixed breathing gases, helium-oxygen in particular, were developed. The first major open-sea use of helium and oxygen as a breathing mixture occurred in the salvage of the submarine, *USS Squalus*, in 1939. The breathing of mixed gases such as helium-oxygen permitted divers to dive to greater depths for longer periods than had been possible with air mixtures. The surface-supported diving technique is probably still the most widely used commercial diving method. The use of mixed gas and the development of improved decompression tables have extended the diver's capability to work in these depths. Although surface-supported diving has several advantages in terms of stability, gas supply, and length of work period, a major problem with this type of gear is that it severely limits the diver's mobility. This limitation has been overcome in certain dive situations by the development of the self-contained underwater breathing apparatus (scuba).

1.4 SCUBA DIVING

The development of the self-contained underwater breathing apparatus (scuba) provided the free-moving diver with a portable air supply which, although finite in comparison with the unlimited air supply available to the helmet diver, allowed for mobility. Scuba diving is the most frequently used mode in recreational diving and, in various forms, is also widely used to perform underwater work for military, scientific, and commercial purposes.

There were many steps in the development of a successful self-contained underwater system. In 1808, Freiderich von Drieberg invented a bellows-in-a-box device that was worn on the diver's back and delivered compressed air from the surface. This device, named Triton, did not actually work, but it did serve to suggest that compressed air could be used in diving, an idea initially conceived of by Halley in 1716. In 1865, two French inventors, Rouquayrol and Denayrouse, developed a suit described as "self-contained." In fact, their suit was not self-contained but consisted of a helmet using a surface-supported system with an air reservoir that was carried on the diver's back and was sufficient to provide one breathing cycle on demand. The demand valve regulator was used with surface supply largely because tanks of adequate strength were not yet available to handle air at high pressure. This system's demand valve, which was automatically controlled, represented a major breakthrough because it permitted the diver to have a breath of air when needed in an emergency.

The demand valve played a critical part in the later development of one form of scuba apparatus. However, since divers using scuba gear exhaled directly into the surrounding water, much air was wasted. One solution to this problem was advanced by Henry Fleuss, a merchant seaman who invented a closed-circuit breathing apparatus in 1879 that used pure oxygen compressed to 450 psig for the breathing gas supply and caustic potash to purify the exhaled oxygen. Although his rebreather could be used under certain conditions, the depth limitations associated with the use of pure oxygen directed most attention to compressed air as a breathing mixture.

In the 1920s, a French naval officer, Captain Yves Le Prieur, began work on a self-contained air diving apparatus that resulted in the award of a patent in 1926, shared with his countryman Fernez. This device was a steel cylinder containing compressed air that was worn on the diver's back and had an air hose connected to a mouthpiece; the diver wore a nose clip and air-tight goggles that undoubtedly were protective and an aid to vision, but did not permit pressure equalization. The major problem with Le Prieur's apparatus was the lack of a demand valve, which necessitated a continuous flow, and thus a waste of gas.

In 1939, Dr. Christian Lambertsen began the development of a series of three patented forms of oxygen rebreathing equipment for neutral buoyancy underwater swimming, which became the first self-contained underwater breathing apparatus successfully used by a large number of divers. The Lambertsen Amphibious Respiratory Unit (LARU) formed the basis for the establishment of U.S. military self-contained diving.

This apparatus was designated "scuba" by its users. An equivalent self-contained apparatus was used by the military forces of Italy and Great Britain during World War II and continues today. The rebreathing principle, which avoids waste of gas supply, has been extended to include forms of scuba that allow the use of mixed gas (nitrogen-oxygen or helium-oxygen mixtures) to increase depth and duration beyond the practical limits of air or pure oxygen breathing.

A major development in mobility in diving occurred during the 1930s when French inventor, de Corlieu developed a set of swim fins, the first to be produced since Borelli designed a pair of claw-like fins in 1680. When used with Le Prieur's tanks, goggles, and nose clip, de Carlieu's fins enabled divers to move horizontally through the water like true swimmers, instead of being lowered vertically in a diving bell or in hard-hat gear. The later use of a single-lens face mask, which allowed better visibility as well as pressure equalization, also increased the comfort and depth range of diving equipment.

In 1943, two other French inventors, Emile Gagnan and Captain Jacques-Yves Cousteau, demonstrated their "Aqua Lung." This apparatus used a demand intake valve drawing from two or three cylinders, each containing over 2,500 psi. Thus the demand regulator, invented over 70 years earlier and extensively used in aviation, came into use in a self-contained breathing apparatus that did not emit a wasteful flow of air during inhalation. This application made possible the development of modern open-circuit scuba gear.

Scuba added a major working tool to the systems available to divers; it allowed divers greater freedom of movement and required much less burdensome support equipment. Scuba also enriched the world of sport diving by permitting recreational divers to go beyond goggles and breath-hold diving to more extended dives at greater depths.

1.5 SATURATION DIVING

Although the development of surface-supplied diving permitted divers to spend a considerable amount of working time under water, divers using such systems for deep and/or long dives incurred a substantial decompression obligation. The initial development of saturation diving by the U.S. Navy in the late 1950s and its extension by naval, civilian government, university, and commercial laboratories revolutionized scientific, commercial, and military diving. This technique provided a method for divers to remain at pressures equivalent to depths of up to 2,000 feet (610 meters) for periods of days or weeks without incurring a proportional decompression obligation.

Divers operating in the saturation mode work out of a pressurized facility, such as a diving bell, seafloor habitat, or diver lock-out submersible. These subsea facilities are maintained at the pressure of the depth at which the diver will be working; this depth is termed the saturation or storage depth.

The historical development of saturation diving depended both on technological and scientific advances. Engineers developed the technology essential to support the saturated diver, and physiologists and other scientists defined the respiratory and other physiological capabilities and limits of this mode of diving. Many researchers played essential roles in the development of the saturation concept, but the U.S. Navy team working at the U.S. Submarine Medical Research Laboratory in New London, Connecticut, is generally given credit for making the major initial breakthrough in this field. This team was led by two U.S. Navy diving medical officers, George Bond and Robert Workman, who, in the period from the mid-1950s to 1962, supervised the painstaking animal tests and volunteer human dives that provided the scientific evidence necessary to confirm the validity of the saturation concept.

1.5.1 Saturation Diving Systems

The earliest saturation dive performed in the open sea was conducted by Edwin Link (founding father of Harbor Branch Oceanographic Institution) and his associates and involved the use of a diving bell for diving and for decompression. Initial Navy efforts involved placing a saturation habitat on the seafloor. In 1964, Edwin Link, Christian Lambertsen, and James Lawrie developed the first deck decompression chamber, which allowed divers in a sealed bell to be locked into a pressurized environment at the surface for the slow decompression from saturation. The first commercial application of this form of saturation diving took place on the Smith Mountain Dam project in 1965 and involved the use of a personnel transfer capsule. The techniques pioneered at Smith Mountain have since become standard in commercial diving operations; saturated divers live under pressure in the deck decompression chamber on board a surface vessel, and are then transferred to the underwater worksite in a pressurized personnel transfer chamber, also called a surface decompression chamber. Although saturation diving systems are the most widely used saturation systems in commercial diving today, two other diving technologies have also taken advantage of the principle of saturation, namely, habitats and lock-out submersibles.

1.5.2 Habitats

Habitats are seafloor laboratories in which saturated diver-scientists live and work under pressure for extended periods of time. Habitat divers dive from the surface and enter the habitat, or they may be compressed in a pressure vessel on the surface to the pressure of the habitat's storage depth and then be transferred to the habitat. Decompression may take place on the seafloor or in a surface decompression chamber after the completion of the divers' work. The most famous and widely used habitat was NOAA's *Hydrolab* which was based in the Bahamas and Caribbean from 1972 to 1985 and provided a base for more than 600 researchers from nine countries during that time. *Hydrolab* now resides at the NOAA campus in Silver Spring, Maryland. The *Aquarius*, a more flexible and technologically advanced habitat system, has replaced the *Hydrolab* as NOAA's principal undersea research laboratory and is presently deployed in the Florida Keys National Marine Sanctuary.

1.5.3 Lock-Out Submersibles

Lock-out submersibles provide an alternative method for diver-scientists to gain access to the underwater environment. Lock-out submersibles are dual-purpose vehicles that permit the submersible's pilot and crew to remain at surface pressure, while the diver-scientist is pressurized in a separate compartment to the pressure of the depth at which he or she will be working. The lock-out compartment thus serves as a personnel transfer capsule, transporting the diver to and from the seafloor. Lock-out submersibles have seen limited use since the 1980s.

1.6 NOAA'S DIVING PROGRAM

For over 40 years, NOAA and its predecessors have played a significant role in the development and support of scientific diving. Prior to the formation of NOAA in 1970, most of the non-defense dive activities centered in the United States Coast and Geodetic Survey (C&GS) and the Department of Interior's Bureau of Commercial Fisheries (BCF).

When NOAA was formed in October 1970, the C&GS and BCF became two of NOAA's major line components with C&GS renamed the National Ocean Service and the BCF became the National Marine Fisheries Service

(NMFS). A new NOAA component was created that formed a series of Environmental Research Laboratories. In May 1971, these NOAA line offices met to develop operational and reporting requirements to promote safety and establish uniform diving regulations.

A critical step to improve safety and versatility of manned undersea operations was the 1971 establishment of the Manned Undersea Science and Technology Program (MUS&T) to achieve a better understanding, assessment, and use of the marine environment. The major objectives included developing a NOAA civilian diving program as well as advanced ocean floor observatories and submersible systems. The MUS&T Program assumed responsibility for all NOAA diving activities including planning, administering, and overseeing the NOAA Diving Program (NDP). Significant accomplishments included the establishment of NOAA's Diving Regulations, a Diving Safety Board, a Medical Review Board, and the preparation and publication of the first edition of the *NOAA Diving Manual* in 1975. A program was initiated in 1973 to develop fully equipped field centers of diving expertise which included recompression chambers for emergency treatment and medical training.

Although the NOAA Diving Office was detached from the MUS&T program in 1979, the internal structure has been essentially unchanged. Present facilities include the NOAA Dive Center in Seattle, Washington, that has several recompression chambers and a 40,000 gallon controlled tank for equipment testing and training. Significant accomplishments include the development of a NOAA diver database to allow close monitoring of diver activity relating to certification maintenance. A standardized equipment program integrated with this diver database has resulted in dramatic cost savings and improved quality control and safety.

Other significant developments included diving safety, physiology, and biomedical programs with the U.S. Navy, underwater fatality statistics studies and accident response programs, polluted water diving research, and hot water diving studies. A major innovation by NOAA was the 1977 introduction of nitrogen-oxygen (nitrox) breathing mixtures and decompression tables to the diving community. Nitrox maximizes bottom time for scuba diving investigators. The NDP also developed a system for preparing nitrox in the field.

The NOAA Diving Program plays a critical role in the development and support of scientific diving for NOAA and the United States. NOAA has more than 300 divers at 40 locations and on 14 ships and has the largest complement of divers of any civilian government agency. Averaging 10,000 dives annually, its exemplary safety record is attributed to thorough training, adherence to established standards and procedures, and the use of quality, well-maintained equipment.

1.7 UNDERSEA AND DIVING RESEARCH

The creation of what is now known as the National Undersea Research Program (NURP) was initiated with the 1977 genesis of NOAA's Undersea Laboratory System (NULS), under the Manned Undersea Science and Technology (MUS&T) Program, to provide staffed underwater facilities and other research support. Later that year, NULS deployed an undersea research habitat, Hydrolab, to allow science missions off St. Croix, Virgin Island.

In 1980, the MUS&T office was reorganized under NOAA's Office of Undersea Research and became the Office of Undersea Research (OUR) which evolved into NURP. At present, NURP supports extramural research programs through scientists from marine and academic institutes carried out primarily through six National Undersea Research Centers.

NURP is a comprehensive underwater research program that places scientists under water directly, through the use of submersibles, underwater laboratories, and scuba diving, or indirectly by using remotely operated vehicles (ROVs) and observatories. The *in situ* (in place) approach allows acquisition of otherwise unobtainable observations, samples, and experimentation related to NOAA priority research objectives such as building sustainable fisheries and sustaining healthy coasts. NURP also provides access for the United States research community to civilian, military, and international undersea technology. In the past decade, NURP has annually supported nearly 8,000 air, nitrox, and mixed-gas scuba dives addressing issues relating to ecosystem health, coastal processes, and fisheries.

NOAA has traditionally sponsored R&D programs to improve diver performance. Dive tables and training requirements developed by these programs are now worldwide standards. NOAA is the only federal program with statutory responsibility to improve the safety and performance of divers. Examples of NOAA's diving research program include fundamental hyperbaric physiological research, operational procedures, safety, medical aspects, environmental impacts on divers, technology development, and data dissemination. Active international programs include the U.S.-Japan Cooperative Program on National Resources (UJNR) Panel on Diving Physiology and Technology and the U.S./France Cooperative Program of Oceanography.

1.8 SUMMARY

Humans have explored the ocean depths at least since the fifth millennium B.C., and the development of the diving techniques and systems described in this section reflects a human drive for mastery over all aspects of the environment. The search for methods that will allow humans to live comfortably in the marine biosphere for long periods of time continues today, as engineers and scientists work together to make access to the sea safer, easier, and more economical.

Physics of Diving

2

SECTION	PAGE

Physics of Diving

2.0 GENERAL

In all diving operations, safety is the primary consideration. One key to safety is a clear understanding of the physics of diving. Physics is the field of science dealing with matter and energy and their interactions. This chapter explores physical laws and principles that pertain to the diving environment and its influence on the diver. Gravity is passive, vision and hearing may be misleading, color perception changes at varying depth, and breathing dynamics are ever changing. The principles of physics provide the keystone for understanding the reasons for employing various diving procedures and the operation of associated equipment. Many of these principles receive further elaboration in other sections of the NOAA Diving Manual.

2.1 PRESSURE

Pressure is force acting on a unit area. Stated mathematically,

$$\text{Pressure} = \text{force/area} \quad P = F/A$$

In the United States, pressure is typically measured in pounds per square inch (psi). Under water, two kinds of pressure affect a person, the weight of the surrounding water and the weight of the atmosphere over that water. One concept that must be remembered at all times is: a diver, at any depth, must be in pressure balance with the forces at that depth.

At all depths, the diver must compensate for the pressure exerted by the atmosphere, by the water, and by the gases being used for breathing under water. This compensation must always be thought of in terms of attaining and maintaining a balance between the pressure inside the body and the external pressure.

2.1.1 Atmospheric Pressure

Atmospheric pressure is the pressure exerted by the earth's atmosphere; it decreases with altitude above sea level. At sea level, atmospheric pressure is equal to 14.7 pounds per square inch (psi) or one atmosphere (atm). The higher the altitude above sea level, the lower the atmospheric pressure. For example, at 18,000 ft. (5,486 m), atmospheric pressure is 7.35 psi, or half that at sea level (see Figure 2.1). At sea level, atmospheric pressure is considered constant and universal; that is, anywhere on the earth at sea level, the pressure is 14.7 psi. The pressure inside a person's lungs is the same as the pressure outside.

2.1.2 Hydrostatic Pressure

Pressure due to the weight of water is called "hydrostatic pressure." The weight of water is cumulative; the deeper the dive, the more water there is above the diver and the greater the weight of that water. This weight affects a diver from all sides equally and increases at a rate of 0.445 psi per foot of seawater. Thus, at a depth of 33 ft. (10.1 m) of seawater (fsw), the hydrostatic pressure is 14.7 psi, or one atmosphere, the same pressure as atmospheric pressure at sea level. In freshwater, 34 ft. (10.4 m) equals 14.7 psi or 0.432 psi per foot of freshwater (ffw). Thereafter, for every 34 ft. of additional depth in freshwater, the hydrostatic pressure increases by one atmosphere (see Figure 2.1).

2.1.3 Absolute Pressure

The sum of atmospheric pressure plus hydrostatic pressure is called the "absolute pressure." Absolute pressure can be expressed in many ways, including "pounds per square inch absolute" **(psia)**, "atmospheres absolute" **(ata)**, feet of seawater absolute **(fswa)**, feet of freshwater absolute **(ffwa)**, or millimeters of mercury absolute **(mmHga)**.

To understand the effects of absolute pressure on a diver, consider this: the feet of a 6-foot tall man standing under water will be exposed to pressure that is almost three pounds per square inch greater than that exerted at his head.

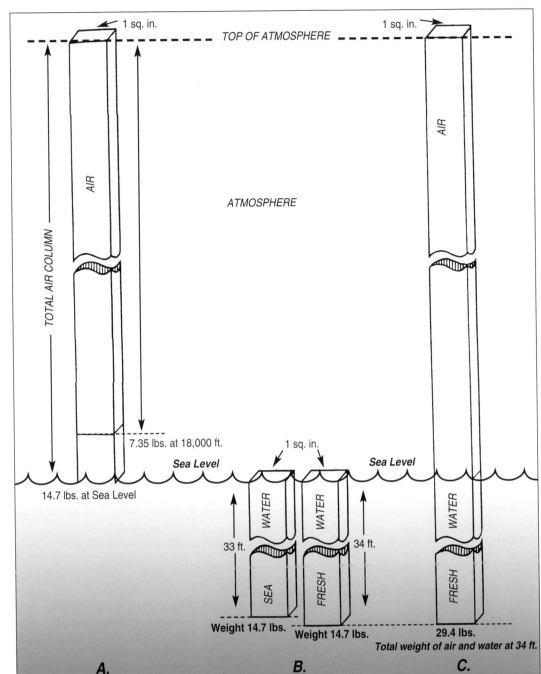

A. A one square inch column of air extending from sea level to the top of the atmosphere weighs 14.7 lbs. One half of the weight is contained in the first 18,000 ft. (5,486 m or 3 1/2 miles) of the column.

B. A one-inch square column of seawater 33 ft. (10.1 m) deep and a column of freshwater 34 ft.(10.4 m) deep each weigh 14.7 lbs.

C. At a depth of 34 ft. (10.4 m) of freshwater, the sum of atmospheric and hydrostatic pressures equal 29.4 lbs.

FIGURE 2.1
Weight of Air and Water

2.1.4 Gauge Pressure

The difference between atmospheric pressure and the pressure being measured is "gauge pressure." Consider the pressure gauge on a scuba tank, for instance. The zero reading on the gauge before it is attached actually represents the ambient atmospheric pressure. To put it another way, at sea level, the zero on the tank gauge actually represents 14.7 psia. Thus, the pressure in the tank is referred to in terms of "pounds per square inch gauge" (psig). To convert gauge pressure to absolute pressure, add 14.7.

2.1.5 Partial Pressure

In a mixture of gases, the proportion of the total pressure contributed by each gas in the mixture is called the "partial pressure." Although traces of other gases are also present in atmospheric air, for our discussion here, we can approximate that atmospheric air is composed of 21% oxygen and 79% nitrogen, for a total of 100%, or one atmosphere absolute. The impact of partial pressures upon the diver is explained in detail later in this chapter under Dalton's Law.

The body can function normally only when the pressure difference between the inside of the body and the outside is very small.

2.2 DENSITY

Density can be defined as weight per unit volume. Expressed mathematically,

Density = Weight/Volume or D = W/V

Density is expressed in pounds per cubic foot (lbs/ft³) or in grams per cubic centimeter (g/cm³).

Gas density is related to absolute pressure. As depth increases, the density of the breathing gas increases and becomes heavier per unit volume. High gas density increases the effort required to breathe and limits a diver's ability to ventilate the lungs adequately, especially during strenuous exercise and at deeper depths (see Table 2.1).

Freshwater has a density of 62.4 pounds per cubic foot. Seawater has a density of 64.0 pounds per cubic foot (see Figure 2.2). As a result, freshwater floats on top

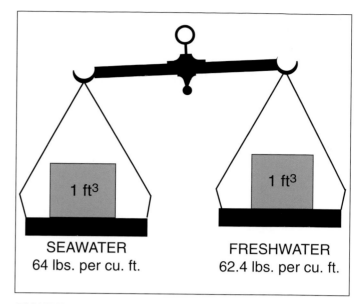

FIGURE 2.2
Seawater and Freshwater Density

of seawater and a diver floats easier in seawater than in freshwater.

2.2.1 Specific Gravity

Specific gravity is the ratio of the weight of a given volume of a substance (density) to that of an equal volume of another substance (water [for liquids and solids] and air [for gases] are used as standards). Water has a specific gravity of 1.0 at 39.2°F (4C). Substances that are more dense than freshwater have a specific gravity greater than 1.0. Thus, the specific gravity of seawater is 64.0/62.4 = 1.026.

2.3 WATER

Physical laws that act upon a person above the surface of water also apply below the surface. As a diver descends into the water, those forces increase; the diver should be aware of these effects.

2.3.1 Freshwater

Water, H_2O, is a major constituent of all living matter. It is an odorless, tasteless, very slightly compressible liquid oxide of hydrogen, which freezes at 32°F (0C), and boils at 212°F (100C). In its purest form, water is a poor conductor of electricity.

2.3.2 Seawater

Seawater contains just about every substance known. Sodium chloride (common table salt) is the most abundant chemical. Because of its components, seawater is a good conductor of electricity.

TABLE 2.1
Pressure Chart

Depth	Pressure		Gas Volume	Gas Density
Sea Level	14.7 psia	1 ata	1ft³	1x
33 feet	29.4 psia	2 ata	1/2 ft³	2×
66 feet	44.1 psia	3 ata	1/3 ft³	3×
99 feet	58.8 psia	4 ata	1/4 ft³	4×
132 feet	73.5 psia	5 ata	1/5 ft³	5×
165 feet	88.2 psia	6 ata	1/6 ft³	6×
297 feet	147.0 psia	10 ata	1/10 ft³	10×

1. Pressure of each atmosphere is equal to approximately 15 psi, i.e., at three atmospheres of pressure it is approximately 45 psi, at six atmospheres it is approximately 90 psi, etc.

2. Gas volume is inversely proportional to the depth in atmospheres absolute (ata), i.e., any gas volume at four ata is one-fourth of the sea level volume; at six ata it is one-sixth, etc.

3. Gas density is directly proportional to the pressure in atmospheres absolute (ata), i.e., when a gas mixture at sea level is taken to two atmospheres absolute, each gas in the mixture is twice as dense; at three atmospheres absolute it is three times as dense, etc.

psia = pounds per square inch absolute
ata = atmospheres absolute

2.3.3 pH

The pH of an aqueous solution expresses the level of acids or alkalis present. The pH of a liquid can range from 0 (strongly acidic) to 14 (strongly alkaline), with a value of seven representing neutrality. The pH balance in blood signals to the brain the need to breathe. Too much carbon dioxide in the blood causes the pH level in the blood to change, making it more acidic. One of the ways the body can reduce the acidity of the blood is to increase ventilation, which reduces the CO_2 level and thus reduces the acidity. The importance of pH in diving is covered in Chapter 3, Diving Physiology.

2.4 UNITS OF MEASUREMENT

How much air do we have? How deep are we? How much longer can we stay on the bottom? Divers must have a common system of communicating the answers to these questions.

There are two systems for specifying force, length, and time: the English System and the International System of Units (SI), also known as the Metric System. The English System is based on the pound, the foot, and the second, and is widely used in the United States. The International System of Units is used virtually everywhere else, and is based on the kilogram, the meter, and the second. Every diver will eventually encounter the International System of Units and should be able to convert units of measurement from one system to the other (see Tables 2.2, 2.3, and 2.4).

2.4.1 Length

The principle SI unit of length is the meter (39.37 inches). Smaller lengths are measured in centimeters (cm) or millimeters (mm). Greater lengths are measured in kilometers (km).

$$39.37 \text{ in} \times 1 \text{ ft}/12 \text{ in} = 3.28 \text{ ft} = 1 \text{ m}$$

Example: Convert 10 feet to meters.
Solution: 10 ft × 1 m/3.28 ft = 3.05 m

Example: Convert 10 meters to feet.
Solution: 10 m × 3.28 ft/1 m = 32.8 ft

2.4.2 Area

In both the English and International System of Units (SI), area is expressed as a length squared. For example, a room that is 12 feet by 10 feet would have an area that is 120 square feet (12 ft x 10 ft).

2.4.3 Volume

Volume is expressed in units of length cubed. Using the room example from paragraph 2.4.2 but adding a third dimension—an eight-foot ceiling would result in a volume of 960 cubic feet (120 ft^2 x 8 ft). The English System, in addition to using cubic feet, uses other units of volume such as gallons. The International System of Units (SI) uses the liter (1). A liter equals 1000 cubic centimeters (cm^3) or 0.001 cubic meters (m^3), which is one milliliter (ml).

2.4.4 Weight

The pound is the standard measure of weight in the English System. The kilogram is the standard measure of weight in the International System of Units. One liter of water at 4C weighs one kilogram or almost 2.2 lbs.

$$1 \text{ liter(l)} = 1 \text{ kg} = 2.2 \text{ lbs.}$$

Example: Convert 180 pounds to kilograms.
Solution: 180 lbs × 1 kg/2.2 lbs = 81.8 kg

Example: Convert 82 kilograms to pounds.
Solution: 82 kg × 2.2 lbs/1 kg = 180.4 lbs

2.5 TEMPERATURE

Body temperature is a measure of the heat retained in the human body. Heat is associated with the motion of molecules. The more rapidly the molecules move, the higher the temperature.

Temperature is usually measured either with the Fahrenheit (°F) scale or with the Celsius, or Centigrade, (C) scale.

Temperatures must be converted to absolute when the gas laws are used. The absolute temperature scales, which use Rankine (R) or Kelvin (K), are based upon the absolute zero (the lowest temperature that could possibly be reached) (see Figure 2.3). Note that the degree symbol (°) is used only with Fahrenheit temperatures.

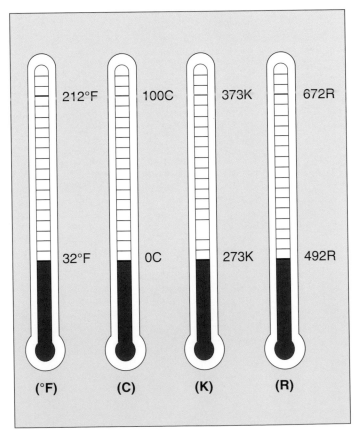

FIGURE 2.3
Freezing and Boiling Points of Water

TABLE 2.2
Conversion Factors, Metric to English Units

To Convert From SI Units	To English Units	Multiply By
PRESSURE		
1 gm/cm^2	inches of freshwater	0.394
1kg/cm^2	pounds/square inch (psi)	14.22
1kg/cm^2	feet of freshwater (ffw)	32.8
1kg/cm^2	inches of mercury (in. Hg)	28.96
1 cm Hg	pounds/square inch	0.193
1 cm Hg	foot of freshwater (ffw)	0.447
1 cm Hg	foot of seawater (fsw)	0.434
1 cm Hg	inches of mercury	0.394
1 cm of freshwater	inch of freshwater	0.394
VOLUME AND CAPACITY		
1 cc or ml	cubic inch (in^3)	0.061
1 m^3	cubic feet (ft^3)	35.31
1 liter	cubic inches	61.02
1 liter	cubic foot	0.035
1 liter	fluid ounces (fl oz)	33.81
1 liter	quarts (qt)	1.057

To Convert From SI Units	To English Units	Multiply By
WEIGHT		
1 gram	ounce (oz)	0.035
1 kg	ounces	35.27
1 kg	pounds (lb)	2.205
LENGTH		
1 cm	inch	0.394
1 meter	inches	39.37
1 meter	feet	3.28
1 km	mile	0.621
AREA		
1 cm^2	square inch	0.155
1 m^2	square feet	10.76
1 km^2	square mile	0.386

TABLE 2.3
Conversion Table for Barometric Pressure Units

		atm	N/m^2 or Pa	bars	mb	kg/cm^2	gm/cm$_2$ (cm H$_2$O)	mm Hg	in. Hg	lb/in^2 (psi)
1 atmosphere	=	1	1.013X10^5	1.013	1013	1.033	1033	760	29.92	14.70
1 Newton (N)/m$_2$ or Pascal (Pa)	=	.9869X10^{-5}	1	10^{-5}	.01	1.02X10^{-5}	.0102	.0075	.2953X10^{-3}	.1451X10^{-3}
1 bar	=	.9869	10^5	1	1000	1.02	1020	750.1	29.53	14.51
1 millibar (mb)	=	.9869X10^{-3}	100	.001	1	.00102	1.02	.7501	.02953	.01451
1 kg/cm^2	=	.9681	.9807X10^5	.9807	980.7	1	1000	735	28.94	14.22
1 gm/cm^2 (1 cm H$_2$O)	=	968.1	98.07	.9807X10^{-3}	.9807	.001	1	.735	.02894	.01422
1 mm Hg	=	.001316	133.3	.001333	1.333	.00136	1.36	1	.03937	.01934
1 in. Hg	=	.0334	3386	.03386	33.86	.03453	34.53	25.4	1	.4910
1 lb/in^2 (psi)	=	.06804	6895	.06895	68.95	.0703	70.3	51.70	2.035	1

TABLE 2.4
Barometric Pressure Conversions

Units	psig	psia	atm	ata	fsw	fswa	ffw	ffwa
psig →		Add 14.7	Divide 14.7	Add 14.7, Divide 14.7	Divide .445	Divide .445 Add 33	Divide .432	Divide .432 Add 34
psia →	Minus 14.7		Minus 14.7 Divide 14.7	Divide 14.7	Minus 14.7 Divide .445	Divide .445	Minus 14.7 Divide .432	Divide .432
atm →	Times 14.7	Times 14.7 Add 14.7		Add 1	Times 33	Times 33 Add 33	Times 34	Times 34 Add 34
ata →	Minus 1 Times 14.7	Times 14.7	Minus 1		Times 33 Minus 33	Times 33	Times 34 Minus 34	Times 34
fsw →	Times .445	Times .445 Add 14.7	Divide 33	Add 33 Divide 33		Add 33	Times 1.03	Times 1.03 Add 34
fswa →	Minus 33 Times .445	Times .445	Minus 33 Divide 33	Divide 33	Minus 33		Minus 33 Times 1.03	Times 1.03
ffw →	Times .432	Times .432 Add 14.7	Divide 34	Add 34 Divide 34	Times .97	Add 34 Times .97		Add 34
ffwa →	Minus 34 Times .432	Times .432	Minus 34 Divide 34	Divide 34	Minus 34 Times .97	Times .97	Minus 34	

Either of the absolute temperature scales, Rankine or Kelvin, may be used in gas law calculations.

To convert from Fahrenheit to absolute temperature Rankine, use the following equation:

$$°F + 460 = R$$

To convert from Celsius, or Centigrade, to absolute temperature Kelvin, use the following equation:

$$C + 273 = K$$

The Fahrenheit (°F) and Rankine (R) temperature scales are used in the English System. The Celsius (C) and Kelvin (K) temperature scales are used in the International System of Units. The Celsius and Fahrenheit scales are based on the temperature of melting ice as 0C (32°F) and the temperature of boiling water as 100C (212°F).

To convert from Fahrenheit to Celsius, use the following equation:

$$C = 5/9 \times (°F - 32) \quad or \quad C = .56 \times (°F - 32)$$

To convert from Celsius to Fahrenheit, use the following equation:

$$°F = (9/5 \times C) + 32 \quad or \quad °F = (1.8 \times C) + 32$$

2.5.1 Heat

Water temperature is an important consideration in all diving operations. Human beings function effectively within a narrow range of internal temperatures, becoming chilled when the water temperature drops below 75°F (23.9C) and overheated when body temperature rises above 98.6°F (37C). Below that temperature, body heat loss occurs faster than it can be replaced. A person who has become chilled cannot work efficiently or think clearly and may be more susceptible to decompression sickness.

A cellular neoprene wet suit loses a portion of its insulating property as depth increases and the material is compressed (see Figure 2.4). As a consequence, it is often necessary to employ a thicker suit, a dry suit, or a hot water suit to compensate for extended exposures to cold water.

2.6 BUOYANCY (Archimedes' Principle)

A Greek mathematician named Archimedes determined why things float 2000 years ago. He established that *"Any object wholly or partly immersed in a fluid is buoyed up by a force equal to the weight of the fluid displaced by the object."* This explains why a steel ship floats, but its anchor does not. The more water displaced, the greater the buoyancy (see Figure 2.5).

If the weight of the displaced water (total displacement) is greater than the weight of the submerged body,

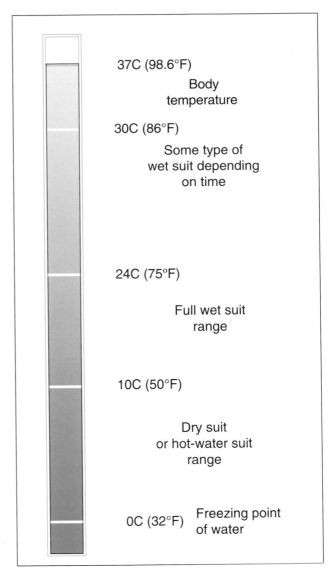

FIGURE 2.4
Recommended Thermal Protection

the buoyancy is **positive** and the object floats. If the weight of the displaced water is less than the weight of the object, then the buoyancy is **negative** and the object sinks. If the weight of the object is equal to the weight of the displaced water, then buoyancy is **neutral** and the object is suspended. Neutral buoyancy is the state frequently used when diving.

Buoyancy is dependent upon the density of the surrounding liquid. Seawater has a density of 64.0 pounds per cubic foot, compared to 62.4 pounds per cubic foot for freshwater. Therefore, each cubic foot of seawater that is displaced by a volume of air in a container has a lifting force of 64 pounds. The greater the density, the greater the buoyancy force. Thus, it is easier to float in seawater than in a freshwater lake.

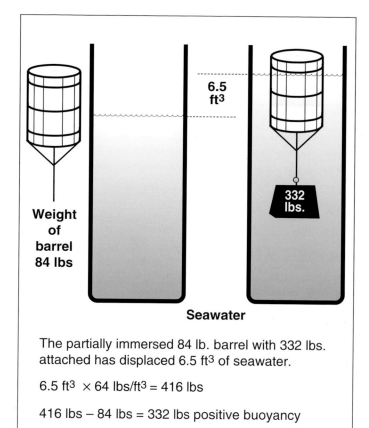

The partially immersed 84 lb. barrel with 332 lbs. attached has displaced 6.5 ft³ of seawater.

6.5 ft³ × 64 lbs/ft³ = 416 lbs

416 lbs − 84 lbs = 332 lbs positive buoyancy

FIGURE 2.5
Archimedes' Principle

An understanding of buoyancy serves the diver in a number of ways. By using weights, by expanding the air in a buoyancy compensator, or by increasing the size of a variable-volume diving suit, a diver can manipulate his buoyancy to meet operational needs. When working on the bottom, for example, a slightly negative buoyancy provides better traction and more stability on the sea floor. Buoyancy is also an invaluable aid to lifting heavy items in salvage operations.

2.7 GASES USED IN DIVING

Air breathed on the surface (atmospheric air) is also the most common gas breathed under water. Gases react in specific ways to the effects of pressure, volume, and temperature.

2.7.1 Atmospheric Air

The components of dry atmospheric air are given in Table 2.5. Depending upon the location and weather conditions, atmospheric air may also contain industrial pollutants. The most common pollutant is carbon monoxide, often present around the exhaust outlets of internal-combustion engines. Diving safety is jeopardized if pollutants are not filtered from compressed air prior to diving.

TABLE 2.5
Components of Dry Atmospheric Air

Component	Concentration	
	Percent by Volume	Parts per Million (ppm)
Nitrogen	78.084	
Oxygen	20.946	
Argon	0.934	
Carbon Dioxide	0.033	
Rare Gases	0.003	30.00*
Neon		18.18*
Helium		5.24*
Carbon Monoxide		2.36*
Methane		2.0 *
Krypton		1.14*
Hydrogen		0.5 *
Nitrous Oxide		0.5 *
Xenon		0.08*
		*Approximate

Besides atmospheric air, divers use various mixtures of oxygen, nitrogen, and helium. In some diving applications, special mixtures of one or more of the gases may be blended with oxygen. The physiological effects of each gas alone, or in combination with other gases, must be taken into account to insure that no harm is done to body organs and functions. The so-called "inert" gases breathed from the atmosphere, or those in gas mixtures we breathe when diving, serve only to dilute and mix with oxygen.

2.7.2 Oxygen (O_2)

Oxygen is the most important of all gases and is one of the most abundant elements on earth. Fire cannot burn without oxygen and people cannot survive without oxygen. Atmospheric air contains approximately 21% oxygen, which exists freely in a diatomic state (two atoms paired off to make one molecule). This colorless, odorless, tasteless, and active gas readily combines with other elements. From the air we breathe, only oxygen is actually used by the body. The other 79% of the air serves to dilute the oxygen. Pure 100% oxygen is often used for breathing in hospitals, aircraft, and hyperbaric medical treatment facilities. Sometimes 100% oxygen is used in shallow diving and in certain phases of diving. For storage in saturation and for deeper diving the percentage may be less; in fact, it may be too low to be safely breathed at sea level. Mixtures low in oxygen require special labeling and handling to ensure that they are not breathed unintentionally. Breathing a mixture with no oxygen will result in unconsciousness, brain damage, and death within a few minutes. Besides its essential metabolic role, oxygen is fundamental to decompression. Still, the gas can also be toxic. Breathing pure oxygen under pressure may affect the central nervous system in short exposures, and various other parts of the body and nervous system, particularly the lungs, from longer exposures.

Oxygen is the agent responsible for most oxidation that takes place on this planet. The gas itself does not bum, nor does it explode. In order for combustion to take place there has to be oxygen, fuel, and a source of ignition. Material burns more vigorously in an oxygen-enriched environment, and a great deal faster and more intensely in pure oxygen. With several methods for mixing gases, it is necessary to handle pure oxygen appropriately.

Oxygen comes in three basic grades: aviator's oxygen (Grade A), medical/industrial oxygen (Grade B or USP grade [Medical Grade]), and technical oxygen (Grade C). Aviator's oxygen is ultra-dry in order to prevent freezing of regulators, but otherwise it is the same as medical oxygen. Technical (welding) oxygen comes from the same source as medical, but the containers may not be evacuated prior to filling and may contain pre-existing contaminants and objectionable odors; accordingly, it is not recommended for diving. However, if this is the only oxygen available in a case where decompression sickness needs to be treated, it is far better to use technical oxygen than not to breathe oxygen when it is needed. Significant contamination in oxygen is quite rare. Oxygen cylinders should never be completely emptied, but should be maintained with a minimum of 25 psi cylinder pressure to prevent contamination from entering the cylinder.

In the United States, oxygen is shipped in gas cylinders that are color-coded green. This is the only gas for which there is a uniform color-coding, and this green color applies only in the U.S. Color-coding should never be relied upon to make positive identification of the gas in any cylinder. If the oxygen is Grade A or B, the label on the cylinder should clearly state this; Grade C may have no identification other than that it is oxygen.

2.7.3 Nitrogen (N₂)

Nitrogen gas, which forms the largest proportion of the air we breathe, is also taken through the lungs into the blood stream, but it plays no part in metabolism. In breathing air under pressure it is the nitrogen portion that plays the major role in decompression. For diving, nitrogen may be used to dilute oxygen, but it has several disadvantages compared with other gases. When breathed at increased partial pressures, typically at least 100 ft. (31m) or deeper, it has a distinct anesthetic effect, producing an intoxicated state characterized by a loss of judgment and disorientation called *nitrogen narcosis.*

2.7.4 Helium (He)

Helium is used extensively in deep diving as a diluting agent for oxygen. Helium has a lower density than nitrogen and it does not cause the same problems associated with nitrogen narcosis. A lower-density gas, in deep diving, reduces breathing resistance (see Section 2.2).

However, helium does have several disadvantages. Breathing helium-oxygen mixtures impairs voice communication when diving by creating the "Donald Duck" voice. Helium also has a high thermal conductivity, which can cause rapid heat loss from the body, especially via the respiratory system.

2.7.5 Carbon Dioxide (CO₂)

Carbon dioxide is a natural by-product of metabolism that is eliminated from the body by breathing. Although generally not considered poisonous, excessive carbon dioxide can cause unconsciousness that can be fatal for divers. The two major concerns with carbon dioxide are control of the quantity in the breathing supply, and its removal after exhalation. Elevated carbon dioxide levels may further predispose a diver to nitrogen narcosis, oxygen toxicity, and decompression sickness.

Carbon dioxide is considered biologically "active" since it directly influences the pH level of blood. In addition, recent advances in medicine indicate that carbon dioxide may be involved chemically in changes with dilation of blood vessels.

With divers using closed or semi-closed breathing systems, it is absolutely essential to remove carbon dioxide from the breathing gas.

2.7.6 Carbon Monoxide (CO)

Carbon monoxide is a poisonous gas which interferes with the blood's ability to carry oxygen. Because it is colorless, odorless, and tasteless, it is difficult to detect and it acts as a cellular poison. It is produced by the incomplete combustion of fuels and is most commonly found in the exhaust of internal-combustion engines, and by overheated oil-lubricated compressors.

The usual carbon monoxide problem for divers is contamination of the air supply because the compressor intake is too close to the compressor-motor exhaust. The exhaust gases, including carbon monoxide, are sucked in with the air at the intake of the compressor. The effects can be lethal.

2.7.7 Argon (Ar), Neon (Ne), Hydrogen (H₂)

Argon, neon, and hydrogen have been used experimentally to dilute oxygen in breathing-gas mixtures, but normally these gases are not used in diving operations. Argon has narcotic properties and a density that make it inappropriate for use as a breathing gas. However, it is frequently used for inflation of variable-volume dry suits for warmth, because its higher density reduces the conduction of heat.

Neon causes less voice distortion than helium and has lower thermal conductivity. As a breathing gas, however, neon is expensive and causes increased breathing resistance at moderate or heavy workloads.

Hydrogen has two important advantages as a breathing gas: it is readily available and it produces less breathing resistance at depth than other gases. However, the explosive properties of hydrogen are a significant disadvantage.

2.8 GAS LAWS

Definitions have been provided of terms, units of measurement, and the properties of the gases divers use under water. What follows are various physical laws that directly and indirectly affect underwater activity.

Gases are subject to three interrelated factors: pressure, volume, and temperature. A change in one results in a measurable change in the others. This is true whether we are dealing with a pure gas or with a gas mixture. The relationships among these three factors have been defined as the gas laws.

A diver needs a basic understanding of the gas laws. As a diver moves up and down the water column, pressure changes affect the air in dive equipment and in the diver's lungs. It is also essential to determine whether the air compressor on deck has the capacity to deliver an adequate supply of air to a proposed operating depth, and to be able to interpret the reading on the depth gauge of the pneumofathometer hose as conditions of temperature and depth vary.

2.8.1 Boyle's Law

"For any gas at a constant temperature, the volume of the gas will vary inversely with the pressure." If an inverted bucket is filled with air at the surface where the pressure is one atmosphere (14.7 psi), and then taken under water to a depth of 33 fsw (10.1 msw), or two atmospheres (29.4 psi), it will be only half full of air. Any compressible air space, whether it is in a diver's body or in a flexible container, will change its volume during descent and ascent. Ear and sinus clearing, diving mask volume, changes in buoyancy, functioning of a scuba regulator, descent or ascent, air consumption, decompression—all are governed by Boyle's Law (see Figure 2.6).

Examples of Boyle's Law

An open-bottom diving bell with a volume of 24 cubic feet is lowered into the water from a surface support ship. No air is supplied to or lost from the bell. Calculate the volume of the air space in the bell at depths of 33, 66, and 99 fsw (10.1, 20.3, and 30.4 msw, respectively).

Boyle's Equation:

$$P_1 V_1 = P_2 V_2$$

P_1 = initial pressure surface absolute
V_1 = initial volume in cubic feet (ft^3)
P_2 = final pressure absolute
V_2 = final volume in cubic feet (ft^3)

Example 1 - Boyle's Law

Transposing to determine the volume (V_2) at 33 ft.:

$$V_2 = \frac{P_1 V_1}{P_2}$$

P_1 = 1 ata
P_2 = 2 ata
V_1 = 24 ft^3

$$V_2 = \frac{1 \text{ ata} \times 24 \text{ ft}^3}{2 \text{ ata}}$$

$$V_2 = 12 \text{ ft}^3$$

NOTE: The volume of air in the open bell has been compressed from 24 to 12 ft^3 in the first 33 ft. of water.

Example 2 - Boyle's Law

Using the method illustrated above to determine the air volume at 66 ft.:

$$V_3 = \frac{P_1 V_1}{P_3}$$

P_3 = 3 ata

$$V_3 = \frac{1 \text{ ata} \times 24 \text{ ft}^3}{3 \text{ ata}}$$

$$V_3 = 8 \text{ ft}^3$$

NOTE: The volume of air in the open bell has been compressed from 24 to 8 ft^3 at 66 ft.

Example 3 - Boyle's Law

For the 99 ft. depth, using the method illustrated previously, the air volume would be:

$$V_4 = \frac{P_1 V_1}{P_4}$$

P_4 = 4 ata

$$V_4 = \frac{1 \text{ ata} \times 24 \text{ ft}^3}{4 \text{ ata}}$$

$$V_4 = 6 \text{ ft}^3$$

How is it that a breath-hold diver can return to the surface from a depth of several hundred feet with no problem, but a scuba diver at a very shallow depth who comes to the surface holding his breath may develop an air embolism and die?

Assume that a breath-hold diver is going from the surface down to 99 ft. During descent, the gas in his lungs will be compressed, until at 99 ft. it will be reduced to one-fourth the original volume. As he ascends, the volume of gas in his lungs expands back to the original amount, thus there is no change in the original volume.

A scuba diver at 99 ft. is in a pressure/volume balance with his environment. He takes a breath of air, discards his

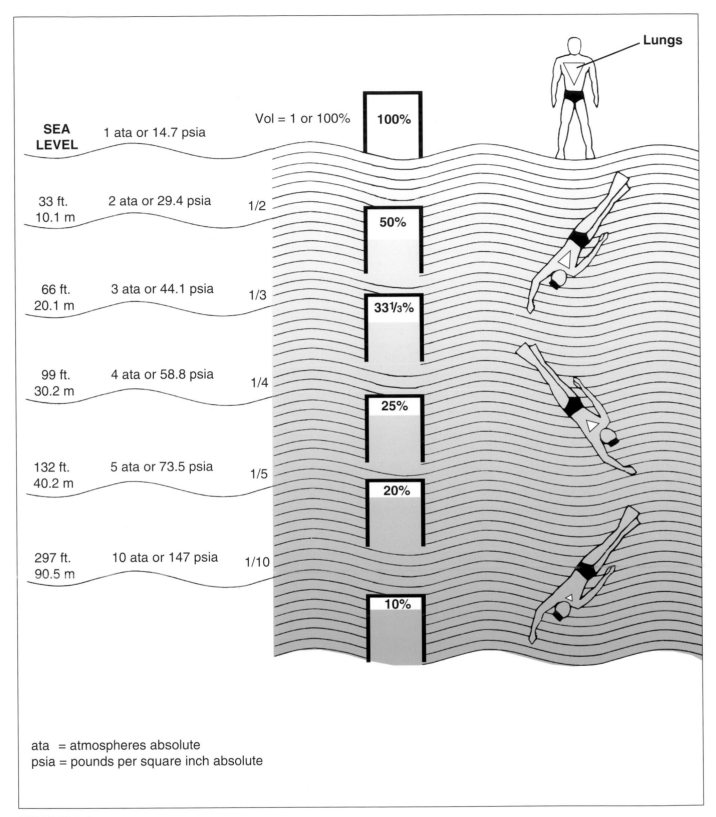

FIGURE 2.6
Boyle's Law Applied to Depth Versus Volume and Pressure

scuba gear and ascends holding his breath. As he ascends, his body is affected by Boyle's Law. By the time he reaches 33 ft., the air in his lungs will have increased in volume to match the decrease in water pressure. If he continues to ascend without releasing air from his lungs, the effect of increasing volume in his lungs may actually rupture the lungs with fatal consequences.

2.8.2 Charles'/Gay-Lussac's Law

Temperature has an effect on the pressure and volume of a gas. It is essential to know the effect of temperature since temperature at depth is often different from that at the surface.

"For any gas at a constant pressure, the volume of the gas will vary directly with the absolute temperature or for any gas at a constant volume, the pressure of the gas will vary directly with the absolute temperature."

Example 1: Charles' Law – <u>Volume Change</u>

To illustrate Charles' Law, consider a balloon with the capacity of 24 ft³ of air which is lowered into the water to a depth of 99 ft. At the surface the temperature is 80°F, at depth the temperature is 45°F. What is the volume of the gas at 99 ft?

From Example 3 in the illustration of Boyle's Law above, we know that the volume of the gas (24 ft³) was compressed to six cubic feet when lowered to the 99 ft. level. The application of Charles' equation illustrates the further reduction of volume due to temperature effects.

Charles' Equation:

$$\frac{V_1}{V_2} = \frac{T_1}{T_2} \quad \text{(pressure remains constant)}$$

where

V_1 = volume at 99 ft. = 6 ft³
T_1 = 80°F + 460 = 540 Rankine
T_2 = 45°F + 460 = 505 Rankine
V_2 = unknown

Transposing:

$$V_2 = \frac{V_1 T_2}{T_1}$$

$$V_2 = \frac{6 \text{ ft}^3 \times 505 \text{ R}}{540 \text{ R}}$$

$$V_2 = 5.61 \text{ ft}^3$$

NOTE: The volume within the balloon at 99 ft. was reduced further due to the drop in temperature.

Example 2: Gay-Lussac's Law – <u>Pressure Change</u>

A scuba cylinder contains 3,000 psig (3,014.7 psia) at 64°F. It is left on the boat deck on a hot summer day. What will the cylinder pressure be if the temperature of the air inside reaches 102°F?

Stated mathematically:

$$\frac{P_1}{P_2} = \frac{T_1}{T_2} \quad \text{(volume constant)}$$

P_1 = 3,014.7 psia
T_1 = 64°F + 460 = 524 Rankine
T_2 = 102°F + 460 = 562 Rankine
P_2 = Unknown

Transposing:

$$P_2 = \frac{P_1 T_2}{T_1}$$

$$P_2 = \frac{3,014.7 \text{ psia} \times 562 \text{ R}}{524 \text{ R}}$$

$$P_2 = 3,233.3 \text{ psia}$$

Converting to gauge pressure yields:

3,233.3 psia - 14.7 psi = 3,218.6 psig

Note that a scuba cylinder is a non-flexible, constant-volume container. As kinetic energy increases with increased temperature, the molecules travel faster. They hit the vessel walls harder and more often. This means pressure within the cylinder increases as the temperature is raised, and there is an increase in pressure associated with heating a scuba cylinder. To prevent this increase in pressure (and possible rupture of the scuba valve safety disc), it is especially important to store full scuba cylinders in a cool place.

2.8.3 Dalton's Law

The human body has a wide range of reactions to various gases or mixtures under different conditions of pressures. Dalton's Law is used to compute the partial pressure differences between breathing at the surface and breathing at various depths in the water.

"The total pressure exerted by a mixture of gases is equal to the sum of the pressures of each of the different gases making up the mixture, with each gas acting as if it alone was present and occupied the total volume." In other words, the whole is equal to the sum of the parts, and each part is not affected by any of the other parts.

According to Dalton's Law, the total pressure of a mixture of gases is the sum of the partial pressures of the components of the mixture.

Stated mathematically:

$$P_t = PP_1 + PP_2 + PP_3, \text{ etc}$$

P_t = Total Pressure
PP_1, etc. = Partial Pressure of the first gas, etc.

Partial pressure of a given quantity of a particular gas is the pressure it would exert if it alone occupied the total volume. The figure P_x is used to indicate partial pressure. The subscript x represents the specific gas (i.e. PO_2 for the partial pressure of oxygen). To determine the partial pressure of a gas in a mixture, use the following equation:

Partial Pressure = (Percent of Component) × (Total Pressure [absolute])

Stated mathematically:

$$P_x = Gas\ \% \times P_t$$

(The pressure can be stated in psi, atm, etc.)
Gas % = Percent of Component (decimal)
P_t = Total Pressure
P_x = Partial Pressure of Gas

Imagine a container at atmospheric pressure (1 atm or 14.7 psi). If the container is filled with oxygen alone, the partial pressure of the oxygen will be 14.7 psi (1 atm). If the container is filled with dry atmospheric air, the total pressure will also be 14.7 psi (1 atm), as the partial pressures of all the constituent gases contribute to the total pressure (see Table 2.6).

Example 1: Dalton's Law
Calculate the partial pressure of nitrogen in a total mixture as follows:

$$P_x = Gas\ \%\ (decimal) \times P_t$$

$$PN_2 = .7808 \times 14.7\ psi\ = 11.478\ psi$$

or in atmospheres:

$$PN_2 = .7808 \times 1.0\ atm\ = .7808\ atm$$

If a scuba cylinder is filled to 2,000 psi with atmospheric air, the partial pressure of the various components will reflect the increased pressure in the same proportion as their percentage of the gas (see Table 2.7).

Example 2: Dalton's Law
What is the partial pressure of nitrogen within the scuba cylinder filled to 2,000 psi?

$$P_x = Gas\ \%\ (decimal) \times P_t$$

$$PN_2 = .7808 \times 2,000\ psi\ = 1,561.6\ psi$$

or in atmospheres:

$$PN_2 = 2,000\ psi \times 1\ atm/14.7\ psi = 136.05\ atm$$

$$PN_2 = .7808 \times 136.05\ atm\ = 106.23\ atm$$

Observe in Tables 2.6 and 2.7 that, while the partial pressures of some constituents of the air (particularly CO_2) were negligible at 14.7 psi, these partial pressures have increased to significant levels at 2,000 psi.

The implications for divers are important. If surface air is contaminated with 2% (PCO_2 .02 ata) of carbon dioxide, a level a person can easily accommodate at one atm, the partial pressure at depth will be dangerously high.

The Dalton's Law correlation in gas density with oxygen and nitrogen richness is illustrated in Figure 2.7.

2.8.4 Henry's Law
"The amount of any given gas that will dissolve in a liquid at a given temperature is proportional to the partial pressure of that gas in equilibrium with the liquid and the solubility coefficient of the gas in the particular liquid." If one unit of gas is dissolved at one atm, then two units will be dissolved at two atm, three units at three atm, etc.

Henry's Law stated mathematically:

$$\frac{VG}{VL} = \propto P_1$$

where
VG = Volume of gas dissolved at STPD
  (standard temperature pressure dry)

VL = Volume of the liquid

$\propto$ = Solubility coefficient at specified temperatures

P_1 = Partial pressure of that gas above the liquid

When a gas-free liquid is first exposed to a gas mixture, gas molecules will diffuse into the solution, pushed by the partial pressure of each individual gas. As the gas molecules enter the liquid, they add to a state of "gas tension," a way of identifying the partial pressure of the gas in the liquid. The difference between the gas tension and the partial pressure of the gas outside the liquid is called the pressure gradient, which gives an indication of the net rate at which the gas tends to enter or leave the solution. When the gradient for diffusion into tissue is high, with low tension and high partial pressure, the rate of absorption into the liquid is high. As the number of gas molecules in the liquid increases, the gas tension increases until it reaches an equilibrium value equal to the outside partial pressure. At that point, the liquid is "saturated" with the gas molecules, and the pressure gradient is zero. Unless there is some change in temperature or pressure, the net rate at which gas molecules enter or leave the liquid will be zero, and the two states will remain in balance.

How does this phenomenon apply to divers? To begin with, a large percentage of the human body is water. Whenever a gas is in contact with a liquid, a portion of the gas will dissolve in the liquid until equilibrium is reached.

TABLE 2.6
Air at 14.7 psi (1 atm)

Air	Percent of component	Partial Pressure atm	Partial Pressure psi
N_2	78.08%	.7808 atm	11.478 psi
O_2	20.95%	.2095 atm	3.080 psi
CO_2	.03%	.0003 atm	.004 psi
Other	.94%	.0094 atm	.138 psi
Total	100.00%	1.000 atm	14.700 psi

TABLE 2.7
Air at 2,000 psi (136.05 atm)

Air	Percent of component	Partial Pressure atm	Partial Pressure psi
N_2	78.08%	106.23 atm	1561.6 psi
O_2	20.95%	28.50 atm	419.0 psi
CO_2	.03%	.04 atm	.6 psi
Other	.94%	1.28 atm	18.8 psi
Total	100.00%	136.05 atm	2000.0 psi

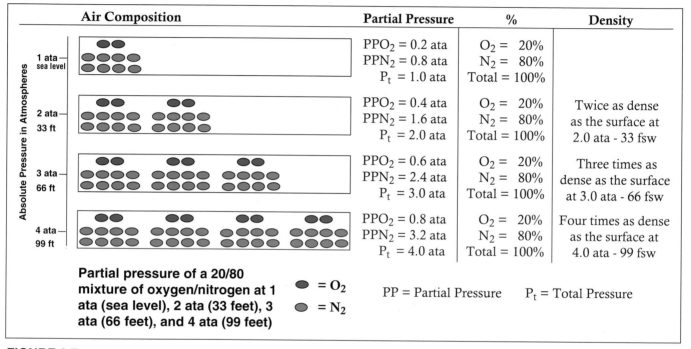

Partial pressure of a 20/80 mixture of oxygen/nitrogen at 1 ata (sea level), 2 ata (33 feet), 3 ata (66 feet), and 4 ata (99 feet)

FIGURE 2.7
Partial Pressure

Gas can dissolve in water and fat in the human body as they make up a large percentage of the body's total mass. The deeper one dives, the greater the pressure exerted upon the body, and the higher the total pressure of the breathing gas. It follows that more gas will dissolve in the body tissues. During ascent, the dissolved gases will begin to be released.

If a diver's rate of ascent (including decompression stops) is controlled properly, the dissolved gas will be carried to the lungs by the tissue's blood supply and will be exhaled before it accumulates and forms bubbles in the tissues. If, on the other hand, ascent is too rapid and/or decompression stops are missed or reduced so that the pressure is reduced at a rate higher than the body can accommodate, gas bubbles may form, disrupting body tissues and systems, and producing a condition known as decompression sickness (the bends).

The various gases are dissolved in the body in proportion to the partial pressure of each gas in the breathing medium.

The amount of gas dissolved is also governed by the length of time and the pressure at which you breathe it. However, as gases vary in their solubility, the exact amount dissolved depends on the specific gas in question. If a diver breathes a gas long enough, his body will become saturated; but this occurs slowly. Depending on the gas, it will take anywhere from 8 to 24 hours.

Some gases are more soluble than others and some liquids are better solvents than other liquids. For example, nitrogen is five times more soluble (on a weight-for-weight basis) in fat than in water. These facts and the differences in blood supply have led to the postulate of tissues with different saturation halftimes (5-minute tissues, 10-minute tissues, 20-, 40-, 75-, etc.). This serves as the basis for calculating decompression tables.

2.8.5 General Gas Law

Pressure, volume, and temperature are interrelated. A change in one factor must be balanced by a change in one

Physics of Diving

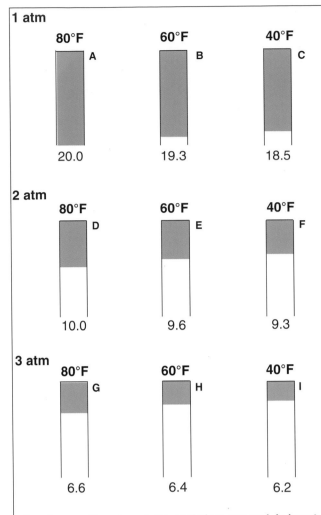

Imagine a uniform-bore tube, sealed on one end, is inverted in a container of water at 80°F and one atmosphere. The volume of air in the tube will be affected by changes in temperature and pressure in accordance to the following gas laws:

Charles' Law:
(A, B, C) (D, E, F) (G, H, I) illustrate the reduction in volume caused by a reduction temperature at a constant pressure.

Boyle's Law:
(A, D, G) (B, E, H) (C, F, I) illustrate the reduction in volume caused by an increased pressure at a constant temperature.

The General Gas Law (Charles' and Boyle's Laws Combined):
(A, E, I) (C, E, G) illustrate that a change in either volume, temperature, or pressure causes changes to the others.

FIGURE 2.8
Gas Laws

or both of the remaining factors. The General Gas Law (also known as the Ideal Gas Law) is a convenient combination of Charles' and Boyle's laws. It is used to predict the behavior of a given quantity of gas when changes may be expected in any or all of the variables (see Figure 2.8).

The general gas law is stated mathematically as follows:

$$\frac{P_1 V_1}{T_1} = \frac{P_2 V_2}{T_2}$$

where
P1 = initial pressure (absolute)
V1 = initial volume
T1 = initial temperature (absolute)

and
P2 = final pressure (absolute)
V2 = final volume
T2 = final temperature (absolute)

Example of General Gas Law:
Consider the open diving bell of 24 ft³ capacity lowered to 99 ft. in seawater. Surface temperature is 80°F and depth temperature is 45°F. Determine the volume of the gas in the bell at depth.

The General Gas Law states:

$$\frac{P_1 V_1}{T_1} = \frac{P_2 V_2}{T_2}$$

P_1 = 14.7 psia
V_1 = 24 ft³
T_1 = 80°F + 460 = 540 Rankine
P_2 = 58.8 psia
T_2 = 45°F + 460 = 505 Rankine
V_2 = Unknown

Transposing:
$$V_2 = \frac{P_1 V_1 T_2}{T_1 P_2}$$

$$V_2 = \frac{(14.7 \text{ psia}) (24 \text{ ft}^3) (505 \text{ R})}{(540 \text{ R}) (58.8 \text{ psia})}$$

$$V_2 = 5.61 \text{ ft}^3$$

NOTE: The volume was reduced, due to the drop in temperature and the increase in outside pressure.

2.9 MOISTURE IN BREATHING GAS

Breathing gas should have sufficient moisture for comfort. Too much moisture in a system can increase breathing resistance and produce lung congestion; too little can cause an uncomfortable sensation of dryness in the mouth, throat, nasal passages, and sinus cavities. Air or other breathing gases supplied from surface compressors or tanks can be assumed to be dry. This dryness can be reduced by removing the mouthpiece and rinsing the mouth with water or by introducing a small amount of water inside a full-face mask. It can be dangerous to use gum or candy to reduce dryness while diving. Do not remove your mouthpiece in seawater or freshwater that may be polluted.

2.9.1 Humidity

Water vapor (a gas) behaves in accordance with the gas laws. However, because water vapor condenses at temperatures we are likely to encounter while diving, the effects of humidity are important considerations.

2.9.2 Condensation in Breathing Hoses or Mask

Exhaled gas contains moisture that may condense in breathing hoses of a rebreather or in your mask. This water is easily blown out through the exhaust valve and, in general, presents no problem. However, in very cold water, this condensation may freeze, disrupting normal functioning of a scuba regulator. The dive should be aborted if such a condition occurs.

2.9.3 Fogging of the Mask

Masks become fogged because of the moisture in exhaled breath, or because of evaporation through facial skin. This fogging can be prevented by moistening the face plate with saliva, liquid soap, or commercial anti-fogging products. Exhalation through the mouth, instead of the nose, will reduce face mask fogging.

2.10 LIGHT

The sense of sight allows perception of electromagnetic energy (light). Human beings can perceive only the very narrow range of wave lengths from 380 to 800 nanometers (see Chapter 3). Eyes function by collecting light that is emitted or reflected by an object. Some light is absorbed by the object, making the object appear colored. The energy waves that are received by the eye are turned to electrical impulses in nerves and sent to the brain via the optic nerve. The brain interprets the signals and we "see."

Under water, the eyes continue to function by collecting light reflected off objects, but the light itself changes. Water slows the speed at which light travels. As light enters or leaves water, this change in speed causes light rays to bend, or refract (see Figure 2.9 and 2.10). That is why a pencil in a glass of water looks bent. Seen through a diving mask, refraction affects close vision, creating distortions that affect eye-hand coordination and the ability to grasp objects under water.

By placing a pocket of air (i.e., a facemask) between the water and the eyes, the light rays are refracted twice – once when they enter the air from the water and again as they enter the eyes; a clearer image is now focused on the retina. Due to imperfect correction, however, the retinal image is larger. Objects may now appear approximately 25% larger because of the larger-than-normal retinal image.

The visual distortions caused by the mask vary considerably with the viewing distance. For example, at distances

of less than four feet (1.2 m), objects appear closer than they actually are. However, overestimation occurs at distances greater than four feet, and this degree of error increases in turbid or muddy water. Other perceptual distortions are also apparent. Stationary objects appear to move when the head is turned from side to side.

Turbidity is another factor affecting underwater visibility. Turbidity refers to the clarity of the water, and depends on the quantity of particulates in suspension. Muddy water is more turbid than clear water. Turbidity can cause overestimation of the distance of an underwater object.

It is important to remember that underwater distance perception is very likely to be inaccurate and that errors of both underestimation and overestimation may occur. As a rule of thumb, the closer the object, the more likely it will appear to be closer than it really is. Additionally the more turbid the water, the more likely it will appear farther than it really is.

2.10.1 Colors

Water absorbs light according to its wavelength. The deeper the light penetrates the water, the more light wavelengths are absorbed. Absorption begins at the red end of the spectrum. Orange is the next color to be lost, followed by yellow, and then green. In very deep water, the only colors visible are blue and violet. Turbidity affects the ability to see colors because the suspended particles diffuse and scatter light. Turbid water gives greatest transparency to wavelengths in the green range. Thus, very clear water is blue, while turbid water is usually green.

Three feet of distilled water absorbs twelve percent of the red, but only one percent of the blue rays. Therefore at 65 ft. (19.8 m), even in very clear water, red is not visible, and the intensity of yellow has decreased by about 95 percent. At the

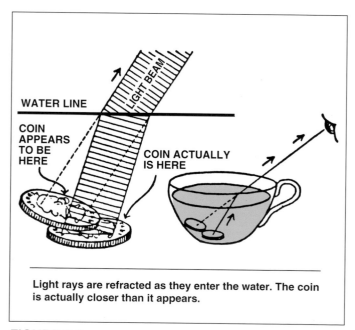

Light rays are refracted as they enter the water. The coin is actually closer than it appears.

FIGURE 2.9
Refraction

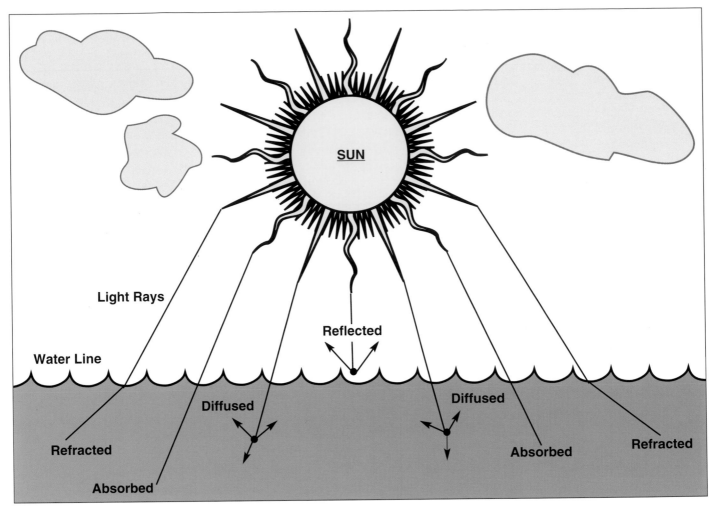

FIGURE 2.10
Sunlight In Air And Water

same depth, however, blue appears with 40 to 50 percent of its initial surface intensity. Some sunlight may penetrate to as deep as 2,000 ft. (610 m) (Kinney 1985).

Turbidity also affects the ability to see colors because the suspended particles diffuse and scatter light.

In general, as depth increases, the ability to discern colors decreases, until visible objects are distinguishable only by differences in brightness. At deeper depths, contrast becomes the most important factor in visibility. Fluorescent paint does aid visibility (see Table 2.8).

2.11 SOUND

Although light and sound both travel in waves, the nature of these two waves is different. Light waves are electromagnetic. Sound is produced by pressure waves triggered by vibration. As the medium containing the pressure wave comes into contact with another medium, a sympathetic vibration occurs. This transfers the wave pattern to the second medium. As an example, a sound is produced and the disturbance travels through the air as a pressure wave striking

our eardrums. This sets off a sympathetic vibration in the eardrums. The inner ear turns this mechanical vibration of the eardrum into a nerve impulse. The impulses are sent to our brain for interpretation.

The more dense the medium through which sound travels, the faster the speed of sound. In dense media, molecules are packed close together, allowing easier transmission of the wave motion. The speed of sound through air is 1,125 ft. (343 m) per second; the speed of sound through seawater is 5,023 ft. (1,531 m) per second; and the speed of sound through steel is 16,600 ft. (5,060 m) per second. The speed of transmission of sound in water depends on the temperature of the water (colder water is denser, thereby allowing it to transmit sound faster) and salinity (seawater allows sound to travel faster than freshwater, again because it is more dense).

Because the speed of sound depends on the density of the medium it travels through, interesting acoustical effects occur in water that has several temperature layers (known as thermoclines). The density of water varies according to its temperature. When sound waves transfer from water of one temperature/density to another, as when they

TABLE 2.8
Colors That Give Best Visibility Against a Water Background

Water Condition	Natural Illumination	Incandescent Illumination	Mercury Light
Murky, turbid water of low visibility (rivers, harbors, etc.)	Fluorescent yellow, orange, and red	Yellow, orange, red, and white (no advantage in fluorescent paint)	Fluorescent yellow-green and yellow-orange
	Regular yellow, orange, and white		Regular yellow, white
Moderately turbid water (sounds, bays, coastal water)	Any fluorescence in the yellows, oranges, or reds	Any fluorescence in the yellows, oranges, or reds	Fluorescent yellow-green or yellow-orange
	Regular paint of yellow, orange, and white	Regular paint of yellow, orange, and white	Regular yellow, white
Clear water (southern water, deep water offshore, etc. See note.)	Fluorescent paint	Fluorescent paint	Fluorescent paint

NOTE: With any type of illumination, fluorescent paints are superior.
  a. With long viewing distances, fluorescent green and yellow-green are excellent.
  b. With short viewing distances, fluorescent orange is excellent.

encounter a thermocline, substantial energy is lost. This tends to isolate sound within water of a consistent temperature. Interestingly, a diver who is not in the same thermocline range as the source of a sound often cannot hear that sound, even though it is coming from only a few feet away.

Hearing under water is affected in important ways. It is almost impossible to determine from which direction a sound originates. On land, sound reaches one ear before the other; thus, the direction of the source can be determined. Under water, sound travels so quickly it reaches both ears without an appreciable interval. The sound seems to originate from all directions. Sound travels faster, seems non-directional, and is more easily heard under water.

NOTES

Diving Physiology

Diving Physiology

3.0 GENERAL

This section provides an overview of how the human body responds to the varied conditions of diving. Diving physics, explained in the previous chapter, does not directly determine how the body reacts to forces on it. Despite many external physical forces, the body normally maintains internal functions within healthy ranges. Past a point, however, the body cannot maintain healthy physiology, which may result in medical problems. A knowledge of diving physiology contributes to diving safety and enables a diver to describe diving-related medical symptoms when problems occur.

3.1 SYSTEMS OF THE BODY

The body tissues and organs are organized into various systems, each with a specific job. These systems are as follows:

3.1.1 Musculoskeletal System

Bones provide the basic structure around which the body is formed (see Figure 3.1). They give strength to the

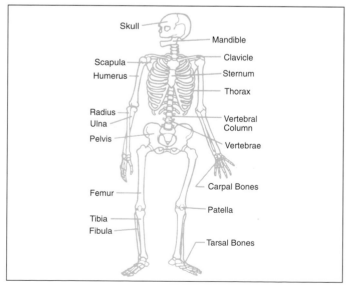

FIGURE 3.1
Skeletal System

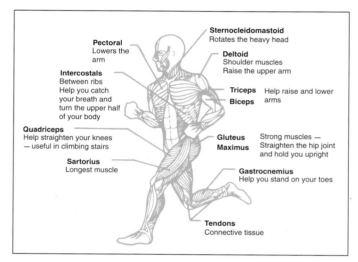

FIGURE 3.2
Muscular System

body and protection to the organs. Bones are the last tissues to become saturated with inert gases. The muscles make the body move — every movement from the blinking of an eyelid to breathing (see Figure 3.2). Additionally, muscles offer protection to the vital organs. Some muscles are controlled consciously, while others, like the heart, function automatically.

3.1.2 Nervous System

The nervous system includes the brain, spinal cord, and a complex network of nerves. Collectively, the brain and spinal cord are called the central nervous system (CNS). All nerves originate in the brain or spinal cord. The basic unit of the nervous system is the neuron (see Figure 3.3), which has the ability to transmit electrochemical signals as quickly as 350 feet per second. There are over ten billion nerve cells in the body, the largest of which has fibers that reach all the way from the spinal cord to the big toe (three feet or more). The brain uses approximately 20% of the available oxygen supply in the blood, at a rate ten times faster than other tissues, and its cells will begin to die within four to six minutes if deprived of that oxygen supply.

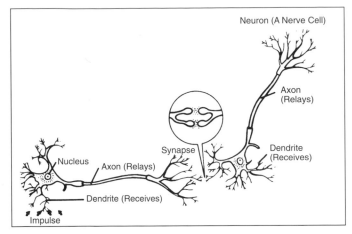

FIGURE 3.3
A Nerve Cell

3.1.3 Digestive System

The digestive system consists of the stomach, small and large intestine, the salivary glands, pancreas, liver, and gall bladder (see Figure 3.4). The digestive system converts food to a form that can be transported to and utilized by the cells. Through a combination of mechanical, chemical, and bacteriological actions, the digestive system reduces food into soluble basic materials such as amino acids, fatty acids, sugars, and water. These materials diffuse into the blood and are carried by the circulatory system to all of the cells in the body. Non-digested material passes out of the body as feces.

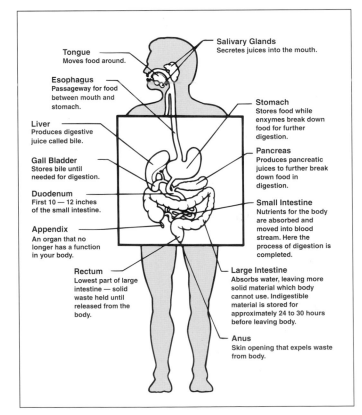

FIGURE 3.4
Digestive System

3.2 RESPIRATION AND CIRCULATION

Two body processes most noticeably affected during diving are respiration and circulation (see Figure 3.5).

3.2.1 Process of Respiration

Respiration is the process of getting oxygen (O_2) into the body, and carbon dioxide (CO_2) out. Inspired air is warmed as it passes through the nose, mouth, and throat. This warm air continues down the trachea, into two bronchi at the top of each lung. These bronchi divide and re-divide into ten bronchopulmonary branches which make up the five lobes of the lungs: three for the right lung; the left lung has only two lobes to allow room for the heart. In each lobe, the branches divide into even smaller tubes called bronchioles. The purpose of all these branches is to provide a large amount of gas-transfer tissue in a small area. Unfolded, the bronchio-pulmonary branches would be enormous—between 750 and 860 square feet each (70 and 80 square meters).

The larger bronchioles have a muscular lining that can squeeze or relax to regulate how much air can pass. Special cells lining the bronchioles secrete mucus to lubricate and moisten the lungs so that breathing doesn't dry them, and to trap dust and other particles. Trapped particles are then removed by coughing or swallowing. Irritating stimuli trigger the secretion of too much mucus into the bronchioles; this congests air passages, creating respiratory conditions that cause problems when diving. Other stimuli can trigger bronchiole-muscle spasms, reducing the amount of air breathed in a given time. When spasms occur frequently, asthma is suspected.

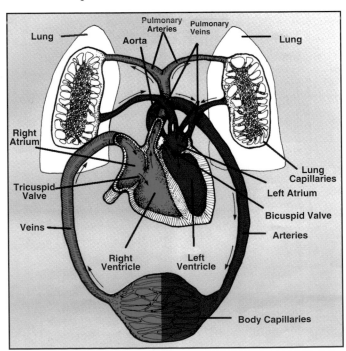

FIGURE 3.5
Respiratory and Circulatory System

NOAA Diving Manual

The bronchioles are honeycombed with pouches, each containing a cluster of tiny air sacs called alveoli. Each alveolus is less than .04 inch (1mm) wide. Surrounding each alveolus is a network of tiny blood vessels called capillaries. It is in the capillaries that dissolved oxygen and carbon dioxide are exchanged between the lungs and the bloodstream. The walls of alveoli and their capillaries are only one cell thick, semi-permeable, and close together so gas transfers easily. There are about 300 million alveoli in each lung, so gas transfers quickly. This process is shown in Figures 3.6 and 3.7.

3.2.2 Mechanics of Respiration

The volume of air breathed in and out is called tidal volume; like the tide, it comes in and goes out. Tidal volume at rest averages about 0.5 liter.

Normal inhalation requires the contraction of the inspiratory rib muscles (external intercostals) and the diaphragm muscle below the lungs. As the chest cavity enlarges, it pulls on the double membrane around the lungs called the pleura. In turn, the pleura pulls on the lungs, enlarging them. As lung volume increases, pressure within decreases allowing air to flow into the lungs to equalize pressure. To exhale, the diaphragm and inspiratory muscles relax, pushing on the lungs by elastic recoil and pushing air out.

Normal inspiration can be increased by adding contraction of some of the neck muscles (accessory muscles), and more rib muscles. Exhalation can be increased by contracting the abdominal wall and the expiratory muscles of the chest (internal intercostals).

Vital capacity refers to the largest volume exhaled after maximum inhalation. This volume is usually determined by size and age; larger individuals usually have higher vital capacity. Vital capacity alone does not determine capacity for exercise, the ability to breathe adequately during exertion, or the ability to deliver oxygen to the blood.

Additional air that can be inhaled after a normal inspiration is the inspiratory reserve. Inspiratory reserve averages three liters. After exhaling normally, one can forceably exhale another liter or so of air, called the expiratory reserve. Even after forcefully expelling all the air possible, there is still just over a liter in the lungs. This residual volume keeps the lungs from collapsing.

Besides exchanging oxygen and carbon dioxide, lungs have several other interesting functions, including filtering. Lungs are directly exposed to all the pollutants, dust, smoke, bacteria, and viruses in the air. Particles not trapped by bronchiole mucus enter the alveoli. There, special cells called alveolar macrophages engulf or destroy them. Lungs also filter the blood supply, removing harmful particles, such as fat globules and small blood clots. Special cells and enzymes break down and remove the trapped particles. The lungs even filter gas bubbles generated during diving ascents, preventing bubbles, in most cases, from going back to the heart and being pumped from there to the rest of the body. However, too many bubbles will overwhelm this pulmonary filter.

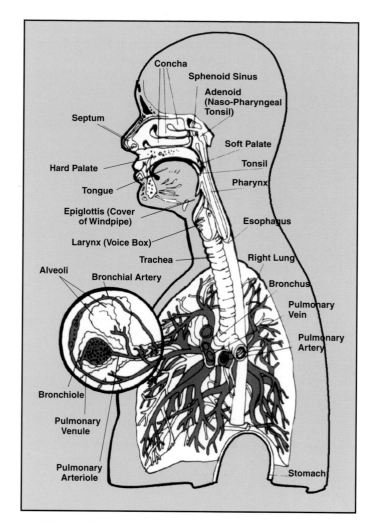

FIGURE 3.6
Process of Respiration

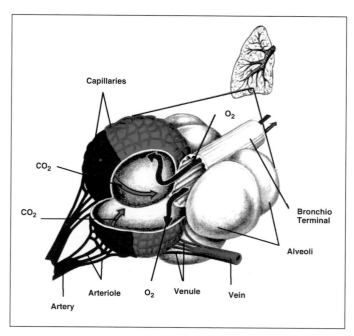

FIGURE 3.7
Lung Air Sacs (Aveoli)

Diving Physiology

3.2.3 Control of Respiration

At rest, a person normally breathes about a 0.5 liter of air, 12 to 20 times a minute. During exertion or emotional stress, rate and volume increase many times. The rate slows during rest and deep relaxation.

The body has many self-regulatory mechanisms to keep internal levels of oxygen and carbon dioxide the same, even during heavy exercise. Although tissues use oxygen during exertion, net blood levels do not fall. Although the body produces carbon dioxide during exercise, levels do not ordinarily rise. The body makes the necessary adjustments by changing breathing patterns.

What is called "the respiratory center" is several separate groups of nerve cells in the brain stem, each regulating different respiratory events. Every few seconds, bursts of impulses from these main nerve centers signal the respiratory muscles, and separately determine rate, pattern, and depth of inspiration and expiration.

As the primary stimulus during exercise, rising production of CO_2 stimulates receptors in the respiratory center, resulting in greatly increased inspiratory and expiratory signals to the respiratory muscles. Ventilation increases to remove ("blow off") CO_2; this immediately restores the blood CO_2 level to normal and keeps it there throughout exercise.

Oxygen, as the secondary stimulus, does not directly affect the respiratory center to any great degree. Oxygen acts on cells called chemoreceptors in two places in the heart. These chemoreceptors transmit signals to the brain's respiratory controls.

An excessive ventilatory rate during emotional stress such as fear, or during deliberate hyperventilation, can lower CO_2 too far. Low CO_2 reduces the drive to breathe, sometimes so low that one can become oxygen deficient (hypoxia), or even unconscious (see Section 3.2.6.3). An insufficient ventilatory rate may occur when breathing resistance is high or there is a high partial pressure of oxygen, both found in certain diving situations. These can contribute to carbon dioxide toxicity (hypercapnia) (see Section 3.2.6.2).

3.2.4 Circulation

Oxygen from air in the lungs needs to get to the tissue, and carbon dioxide from the tissue needs to get back to the lungs. Oxygen in the alveoli dissolves and transfers into the blood through the millions of alveolar capillaries. These capillaries join, forming fewer but larger venules; the venules join, forming the large pulmonary vein; and the pulmonary vein carries the oxygenated blood to the left side of the heart.

The left side of the heart pumps blood into the aorta, and through a series of large muscular blood vessels called arteries (see Figure 3.8). Arteries branch into many progressively smaller arterioles. The muscular arteriole walls squeeze or relax to regulate how much blood can pass. Arterial constriction and dilation is useful to direct blood

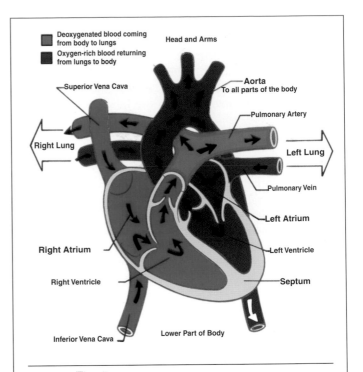

De-oxygenated blood entering the inferior and superior vena cava, flows into the right atrium, right ventricle, to the lungs via the pulmonary artery, O_2/CO_2 exchange in the pulmonary capillary bed, back to the left atrium through the pulmonary vein, left ventricle, and back into the systemic circulation through the ascending and descending aorta. It is interesting to note that this circulatory loop takes only 90 seconds, which explains why a bubble which is introduced into the arterial circulation due to a lung overpressure accident can quickly cause an arterial gas embolism.

FIGURE 3.8
Flow of Blood Through the Heart

into needed areas, away from others, and to increase and decrease resistance to blood flow, which is a factor in controlling blood pressure. Arterial pressure also contributes to the force that distributes blood through the body.

Arterioles increase in number and decrease in size until they become capillaries—the human body has nearly 60,000 miles (100,000 km) of them. Capillaries are so narrow that blood cells can only go through them single file. The number of capillaries in any particular part of the body depends on how metabolically active that part is. Muscles may have approximately 240,000 capillaries per square centimeter. The lens of the eye has none. Only about five to ten percent of capillaries flow with blood at any given time. The body contains a finite amount of blood, therefore it must be regulated to meet the body's varying needs. When there is insufficient blood to meet the body's needs, problems arise. For example, if blood fluid volume depletes from dehydration or can't keep up with the competing demands of exercise and cooling in the heat, the body is adversely affected.

NOAA Diving Manual

Dissolved oxygen transfers easily through the capillary walls to the cells, and carbon dioxide transfers from cells to capillaries. The CO_2-loaded blood continues through all the capillaries, onward to venules, then veins, and back to the heart. The heart pumps the blood to the lungs where CO_2 is removed and more oxygen is received. A small amount of oxygen and nutrient-rich blood reaches the lungs directly from the left side of the heart; the lungs, like all other tissues, need oxygen to function.

Another part of the circulatory system is the lymph system. As blood passes through capillary networks, pressure inside capillaries pushes fluid out of the capillaries. About one percent of the liquid is not resorbed and remains in the spaces between capillaries and cells. The lymph system drains this extra fluid so it can return to the blood vessels to maintain proper blood volume. The lymph system also filters cell debris and foreign substances in the blood, and makes and stores infection-fighting white cells (lymphocytes) in bean-shaped storage bodies called lymph nodes. Whenever lymphocytes collect to fight invaders, the swollen piles of them can be felt in the lymph nodes.

3.2.4.1 Blood Transport of Oxygen and Carbon Dioxide

Blood transports food, water, disease-fighting cells, chemicals, messages, waste, and repair kits throughout the body. This section focuses on the blood's role in bringing oxygen to the body and carbon dioxide back to the lungs.

Blood is mostly water. Oxygen and carbon dioxide don't dissolve well in water, particularly in warm water, as in the body. As a result, at sea level pressure, only a small amount of oxygen dissolves in blood plasma (the part of blood without cells). The oxygen-carrying problem is solved with a red protein molecule called hemoglobin found inside red blood cells. Red blood cells carry far more oxygen with hemoglobin than they could without it. Up to four oxygen molecules loosely attach to each hemoglobin molecule to form oxyhemoglobin. At sea level, about 98 percent of the oxygen in blood is carried by hemoglobin.

A hemoglobin molecule with four oxygen molecules bound to it looks red, while hemoglobin without bound oxygen is so dark-red that it looks blue. This is why oxygenated (arterial) blood looks red, and deoxygenated (venous) blood looks blue. It is also why, if all of the blood is deoxygenating from a serious injury or disease process, the victim can look blue; this is called cyanosis, from the word root *cyan*, meaning blue.

Carbon dioxide is easier to transport in the blood than oxygen; it can be transported in higher quantity, and in more ways (see Figure 3.9). Dissolved CO_2 diffuses out of cells into capillary blood. A small amount stays in the dissolved state in blood plasma all the way to the lung. Hemoglobin can loosely bond a small amount, and when combined, it is called carbaminohemoglobin. An even smaller amount of CO_2 can bond with plasma proteins. These three ways are minor and slow.

The bulk of CO_2 (about 70%) reacts quickly with water inside red blood cells to form first the weak, unstable

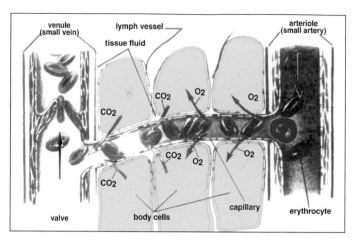

FIGURE 3.9
Carbon Dioxide Exchange

carbonic acid (H_2CO_3), and then, just as quickly (another small fraction of a second) loses hydrogens to become bicarbonate ions (H_2CO3), many of which diffuse into the plasma where it is transported to the lungs. Bicarbonate is alkaline, and so it is a buffering agent in the blood against acids, such as carbonic acid. Hemoglobin also functions as a powerful acid-base buffer and scavenges the acidic hydrogen ions. These are useful reactions in the body. Acid from carbon dioxide and its reactions may form in great quantities, yet still not build to unhealthy levels.

Ordinarily, the reaction of changing carbonic acid to bicarbonate ions would take seconds to minutes—too slow to be useful, so an enzyme called carbonic anhydrase inside red blood cells decreases the reaction time by a factor of 5,000 times so that great amounts of CO_2 can react with water, even before blood leaves the capillaries on the way back to the lung. Drugs called carbonic anhydrase inhibitors block the reaction of carbonic anhydrase, slowing CO_2 transport so that tissue levels rise. Carbonic anhydrase inhibitors are used to combat glaucoma, fluid retention, and altitude sickness.

Carbonic acid is used to carbonate soft drinks. Just as bicarbonate in soda releases carbon dioxide gas when a pop can is opened, bicarbonate in blood becomes carbonic acid again, releasing carbon dioxide into the alveoli so that CO_2 can be exhaled. The difference between the soft drink and the body is that the reaction to release carbon dioxide in soda has no catalyst to speed it up. Though seemingly fast, it is far too slow to keep one alive if it occurred at the same rate in the body. The lungs have enzymes to speed the reaction.

Carbon dioxide is also released in the lung by hemoglobin. When hemoglobin arrives in the alveolar capillaries with excess carbon dioxide, it first wants to pick up new oxygen. The oxygen makes the hemoglobin a stronger acid. Having just become more acidic, hemoglobin does not want the existing acid from the acidic carbon dioxide any more, so it releases it. This effect, called the Haldane Effect, means that picking up oxygen in the lung promotes releasing carbon dioxide. The reverse is also true—as hemoglobin picks up carbon dioxide in the body, it makes the hemoglobin more acid, so it wants to release its stores of oxygen right then, which is an important factor in oxygen delivery to the cells. The Haldane Effect is named for Scottish-born British physiologist John Scott Haldane, who also co-developed the first algorithm to estimate amounts of inert gas absorbed and released by the body. Many modern decompression tables are based on his work.

3.2.4.2 Tissue Gas Exchange

Blood flow is not the only determinant of how much oxygen reaches the body. How much oxygen the blood releases to cells, and how much carbon dioxide it removes, is determined by variable, yet tightly regulated processes.

Cells withdraw oxygen from the blood. By the time blood returns to the lungs, oxygen pressure is low. Oxygen in the air in the lungs travels toward the blood through a simple gradient of higher to lower pressure. Now it is blood with higher oxygen pressure. Oxygenated blood travels back to oxygen-depleted tissues. Gas transfers via that pressure gradient to the lower pressure areas of the body.

Meanwhile, cells have been producing carbon dioxide. Body CO_2 concentration is higher than blood concentration. CO_2 travels from tissue to blood, then blood to lungs, down its own gradient. Gas exchange of carbon dioxide and oxygen occurs quickly and easily, so that tissue levels remain in set ranges, even though blood rushes through the body, and even with the high demands of exercise.

The body also controls oxygen delivery; it does not simply accept all the oxygen provided by the gradient. One regulation mechanism involves the small blood vessels. Oxygen is a vasoconstrictor. With high oxygen pressures during diving, small blood vessels constrict, thus reducing the oxygen delivered through vascular beds.

Another control mechanism is the hemoglobin-oxygen buffer system. Hemoglobin does not just carry oxygen and blindly deliver it to the cells. Hemoglobin regulates how much oxygen it releases. With low surrounding oxygen partial pressure, at altitude or other low oxygen states, for example, hemoglobin releases more than usual. With increased oxygen pressure, as during diving, hemoglobin releases less. Within limits (though one breathes higher or lower than normal pressure oxygen), hemoglobin still delivers oxygen to the body tissues at almost normal pressure. The lungs get exposed to too much or too little oxygen, but the rest of the body does not.

However, above and below a range of about half normal pressure at moderate altitude to many times normal at depth, the body can't compensate. See Section 3.3.3.3 on Oxygen Toxicity for effects of excess oxygen.

3.2.4.3 Tissue Use of Oxygen

The body uses some of the oxygen supplied to it, but not all, even during heavy exercise. At rest, the body inhales approximately 21 percent oxygen, and exhales about 16 percent. This is why mouth-to-mouth resuscitation can work. Exhaled air has sufficient O_2 to benefit the hypoxic victim. During exercise, working muscles need more oxygen; so, the blood vessels redistribute blood flow, the blood releases more oxygen, and the working cells extract more of the oxygen from the blood supply (see Figure 3.10). The better shape one is in, the more oxygen the body can deliver and extract. The amount of oxygen taken up by the body, the oxygen consumption, is a means of measuring the body's metabolism and energy production. Usually about 25% of the oxygen used by the body is available for muscular activity; the balance produces heat and supports other metabolic functions.

During exercise, heart rate and the force of the heart beat increase. Blood pressure rises. Hemoglobin distributes nitric oxide, which controls the width of the blood vessels. Blood vessels constrict in areas of the body not using as much, such as the digestive tract, spleen, liver, and non-working muscles. Contraction of arteriolar muscles constricts the arteriole, reducing the amount of blood entering the capillary bed. Arteriolar smooth muscle cells form sphincters, called precapillary sphincters, at selected places in the capillary bed to shut off blood flow. Every capillary bed has one capillary with no sphincter, called the thoroughfare channel. It stays open all the time, allowing some blood passage to maintain normal functioning.

Blood expelled from low-demand areas increases blood flow to areas with high demand for oxygen supply and for carbon dioxide and waste removal. In these areas, the arteriolar muscular lining relaxes to allow more blood to enter.

Unlike other areas of the body with varying blood supply, the brain always needs a steady supply of oxygen. If circulation slows or stops, consciousness may be lost in seconds, and irreparable brain damage may occur within four to six minutes (see Section 3.2.6.1).

Aerobic fitness is the ability of lungs, heart, and blood vessels to deliver oxygen, and the ability of the muscles and other cells to extract and use it. Aerobically fit people can deliver, extract, and use more oxygen when exercising and are able to do more aerobic exercise. Average exercise increases the amount of oxygen needed by the active tissues by about ten times. Heavy exercise can increase it to around twenty times, depending on the aerobic fitness. The better aerobic shape one is in, the more work the body can do without reaching its own maximum oxygen-processing ability. World-class athletes have reached over 30 times their resting rate. Merely breathing in more oxygen does not affect how much one can use for exercise. One has to increase their ability to deliver, extract, and use oxygen. Supplying more oxygen does not improve one's fitness. Only regular aerobic exercise will make the necessary changes in the body.

NOAA Diving Manual

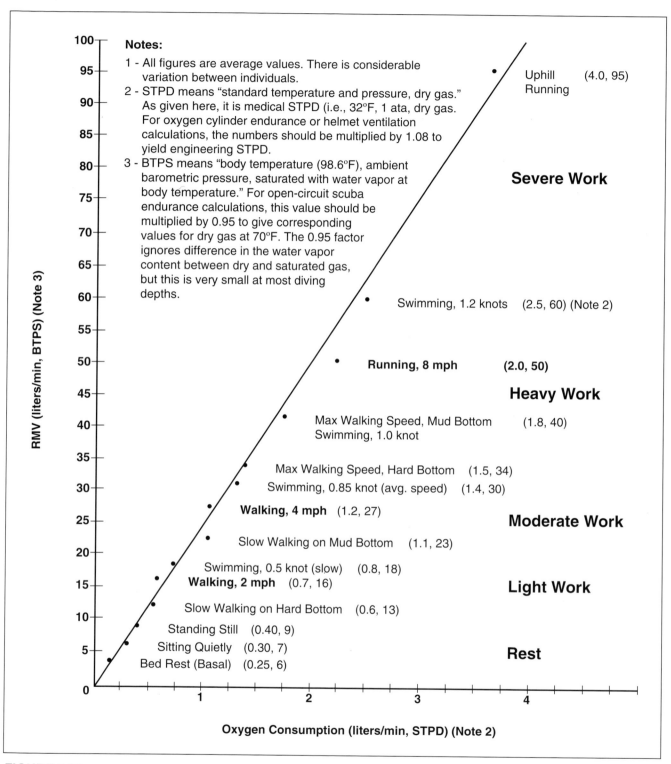

Notes:

1 - All figures are average values. There is considerable variation between individuals.
2 - STPD means "standard temperature and pressure, dry gas." As given here, it is medical STPD (i.e., 32°F, 1 ata, dry gas. For oxygen cylinder endurance or helmet ventilation calculations, the numbers should be multiplied by 1.08 to yield engineering STPD.
3 - BTPS means "body temperature (98.6°F), ambient barometric pressure, saturated with water vapor at body temperature." For open-circuit scuba endurance calculations, this value should be multiplied by 0.95 to give corresponding values for dry gas at 70°F. The 0.95 factor ignores difference in the water vapor content between dry and saturated gas, but this is very small at most diving depths.

Uphill Running (4.0, 95)

Severe Work

Swimming, 1.2 knots (2.5, 60) (Note 2)

Running, 8 mph **(2.0, 50)**

Heavy Work

Max Walking Speed, Mud Bottom (1.8, 40)
Swimming, 1.0 knot

Max Walking Speed, Hard Bottom (1.5, 34)
Swimming, 0.85 knot (avg. speed) (1.4, 30)

Walking, 4 mph (1.2, 27)

Moderate Work

Slow Walking on Mud Bottom (1.1, 23)

Swimming, 0.5 knot (slow) (0.8, 18)
Walking, 2 mph (0.7, 16)

Light Work

Slow Walking on Hard Bottom (0.6, 13)

Standing Still (0.40, 9)

Sitting Quietly (0.30, 7)

Bed Rest (Basal) (0.25, 6)

Rest

RMV (liters/min, BTPS) (Note 3)

Oxygen Consumption (liters/min, STPD) (Note 2)

FIGURE 3.10
Oxygen Consumption and RMV at Different Work Rates

Aerobic fitness is not the only fitness needed for life activities. In rapid-onset, short duration, and intense activity, the body uses special stored fuel and glucose, not oxygen. Because these two fuels are not oxygen-using (aerobic) systems, they are called anaerobic. These two anaerobic systems are utilized for breath-hold diving, swimming against strong currents, sprints, hauling out of the water in full gear, or rescuing a heavy buddy. Regularly exercising at high speed and intensity for short bouts improves one's anaerobic capacity.

3.2.5 Summary of Respiration and Circulation Processes

The processes of respiration and circulation include six important, continuous phases:

1. Breathing air into the lungs (ventilation)
2. Oxygen and carbon dioxide exchange between air in the lung alveoli and blood
3. Oxygen transport by blood to the body tissue
4. Releasing oxygen by blood to cells, and extraction by body cells
5. Use of oxygen in the cells by combining oxygen with fat and carbohydrates to generate energy and produce waste products including carbon dioxide
6. Carbon dioxide transport by blood back to the heart, then lungs, where it diffuses into the lungs and is breathed out of the body

3.2.6 Respiratory Problems
3.2.6.1 Hypoxia

The brain requires constant oxygen to maintain consciousness, and ultimately, life. The brain is subject to damage when it is deprived of oxygen for more than four to six minutes, as can happen in heart failure when the blood supply to the brain is interrupted, in drowning, asphyxia, if breathing stops and the lungs receive no oxygen, or if the oxygen partial pressure in the lungs is insufficient. An inadequate supply of oxygen is known as hypoxia, which means low oxygen and can mean any situation where cells have insufficient oxygen. Hypoxia may result from several situations:

- Breathing mixtures that may be low in oxygen such as in seafloor or surface-based saturation systems or rebreathers
- Ascending to high elevation
- Convulsing under water from an oxygen-toxicity event
- Breathing the wrong gas; for example, mistaking the argon supply for dry suits for a breathing gas supply
- Breathing gas from a scuba cylinder that has been stored with a little water in it for long periods — the oxidation reaction (misting) can, over time, consume nearly all of the oxygen in the cylinder
- Inadequate purging of breathing bags in closed or semiclosed breathing apparatus

In terms of inspired oxygen percentage at one atmosphere or at equivalent oxygen partial pressures, there are usually no perceptible effects down to about 16% oxygen (PO_2 of 0.16 ata). At 12-14%, most people will not notice the first symptoms of tingling, numb lips, and tunnel vision. These symptoms become more prominent at 9-10%, with the onset of dizziness; collapse is imminent for some. At levels much below this, some people can stay conscious with great effort but most will become unconscious. There is a significant variation between individuals in susceptibility and symptoms; an adaptation to altitude can greatly increase one's tolerance to hypoxia. Fitness helps, but individual physiology is a more prominent factor. Typical responses are included in Table 3.1, which shows both the range of hypoxic effects and higher ranges of oxygen uses.

Hypoxia decreases the ability to think, orient, see properly, or perform tasks. Of all the cells in the body, brain cells are the most vulnerable to hypoxia. Unconsciousness and death can occur in brain cells before the

TABLE 3.1
Effects of Different Levels of Oxygen Partial Pressure

PO_2 (atm)	Application and Effect
<0.08	Coma to ultimate death
<0.08-0.10	Unconsciousness in most people
0.09-0.10	Serious signs/symptoms of hypoxia
0.14-0.16	Initial signs/symptoms of hypoxia
0.21	Normal environment oxygen (sea level air)
0.35-0.40	Normal saturation dive PO_2 level
0.50	Threshold for whole-body effects; maximum saturation dive exposure
1.6	NOAA limit for maximum exposure for a working diver
2.2	Commercial/military "Sur-D" chamber surface decompression, 100% O_2 at 40 fsw pressure
2.4	60% N_2/40% O_2 nitrox recompression treatment gas at six ata (165 fsw)
2.8	100% O_2 recompression treatment gas at 2.8 ata (60 fsw)
3.0	50/50 nitrox recompression treatment gas for use in the chamber at six ata

effects of hypoxia are apparent in other cells. The victims of hypoxia do not usually understand what is occurring, and they may even experience a feeling of well-being.

Signs and Symptoms:
- Frequently none (the diver may simply lapse into sudden unconsciousness)
- Mental changes similar to those of alcohol intoxication
- Confusion, clumsiness, slowing of response
- Foolish behavior
- Cyanosis (bluish discoloration of the lips, nailbeds, and skin)
- In severe cases, cessation of breathing

Prevention:
- Avoid excessive hyperventilation before a breath-hold dive.
- When diving with a rebreather, flush the breathing circuit with fresh gas mixture before ascending.
- Always know the amount of oxygen in gas mixtures being breathed.

Treatment:
- Get the victim to the surface and into fresh air.
- If under water and using a rebreather, manually add oxygen to the breathing circuit and begin ascent immediately; if manual adjustments are made incorrectly, oxygen toxicity may result.
- If the victim is still breathing, supplying a breathing gas with sufficient oxygen usually causes a rapid reversal of symptoms.
- An unconscious victim should be treated as if he is suffering from gas embolism.
- Cardiopulmonary resuscitation should be administered if necessary and should be continued after the victim is in the recompression chamber.

3.2.6.2 Carbon Dioxide Toxicity

In diving, carbon dioxide excess (hypercapnia) occurs either from too much carbon dioxide in the breathing medium or because carbon dioxide produced by the body is not eliminated properly by the equipment or by the diver.

The breathing mixture itself may contain a higher than normal level of CO_2, or the equipment may allow exhaled CO_2 to be rebreathed.

Failure of the carbon dioxide absorption system of closed or semi-closed circuit breathing systems allows the build up of high CO_2 levels in any space where exhaled air accumulates and can be re-inhaled. Too much of this "dead space" in diving helmets or masks and in overly-large snorkels allows exhaled CO_2 to collect and be rebreathed.

Some full-face masks have as much as 0.5 liter of dead space. Free-flow helmets generally do not have dead space problems unless the flow rate is maintained at a low volume for an extended period. Oral-nasal masks inside full-face masks/helmets are also effective in reducing the amount of dead space.

A well-designed system has little dead space. Dead space volume cannot be determined by visual examination; special equipment is needed to determine how much exhaled gas is rebreathed.

Normally, the body keeps arterial CO_2 levels the same (within 3 mmHg), even with heavy exercise. With exercise, the body produces more CO_2, but the breathing rate automatically increases to eliminate the excess. The more production, the greater the sensation of shortness of breath occurs, and the greater the ventilatory effort. However, it is also true that large differences exist in individual responses to increases in carbon dioxide.

It is unknown why some divers do not increase ventilation sufficiently. Other divers deliberately breathe slowly, or they skip breathe—pausing after each breath to conserve cylinder air. In these cases, CO_2 may not be removed in a normal fashion, and carbon dioxide levels may rise (hypercapnia).

Another factor elevating CO_2 is the increased effort of breathing at depth. To a smaller extent, high oxygen partial pressure decreases ventilation in some situations; the body has enough oxygen and does not need to breathe as much, so it does not get rid of CO_2 as fast.

WARNING
SKIP-BREATHING IS NOT A SAFE PROCEDURE. CARBON DIOXIDE TOXICITY OCCURS WITH LITTLE OR NO WARNING.

Signs and Symptoms:

Occasionally, CO_2 poisoning produces no symptoms, although it is usually accompanied by an overwhelming urge to breathe and noticeable air starvation. There may be headache, dizziness, weakness, perspiration, nausea, a slowing of responses, confusion, clumsiness, flushed skin, and unconsciousness. In extreme cases, muscle twitching and convulsions may occur. The progressive nature of CO_2 poisoning is shown in Figure 3.11.

Zone I: At these concentrations and durations, no perceptible physiological effects are observed.

Zone II: Small threshold hearing losses have been found and there is a perceptible doubling in the depth of respiration.

Zone III: Discomfort, mental depression, headache, dizziness, nausea, "air hunger," and decrease in visual discrimination.

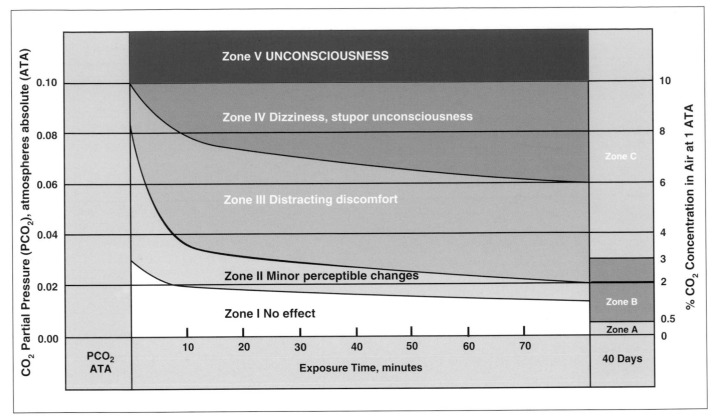

FIGURE 3.11
The Relationship of Physiological Effects in Carbon Dioxide Concentration and Exposure Periods

Zone IV: Marked physical distress, dizziness, stupor, inability to take steps for self-preservation.

Zone V: Unconsciousness. Above a CO_2 partial pressure (PCO_2) of 0.15 ata, muscle spasms, rigidity, and death can occur. The bar graph at the right of Figure 3.11 extends the period of exposure to 40 days.

Zone A: Concentrations between 0.5 and 3.0% (0.005-0.03 ata partial pressure), no biochemical or other effects.

Zone B: Above 3% (0.03 ata partial pressure). Adaptive biochemical changes, which may be considered a mild physiological strain.

Zone C: Pathological changes in basic physiological functions. For normal diving operations, ventilation rates should be maintained so that carbon dioxide partial pressures are maintained in Zones I and II for short-term exposures and in Zones A and B for long-term exposures.

Treatment:
Divers who are aware that they are experiencing carbon dioxide buildup should stop, rest, breathe deeply, and ventilate themselves and their apparatus. Fresh breathing gas usually relieves all symptoms quickly, although any

headache caused by the buildup may persist even after surfacing. If a diver becomes unconscious, he should be treated in accordance with the procedure described in Chapter 21.

3.2.6.3 Hyperventilation
Hyperventilation includes several conditions that have the end result of lowering the blood carbon dioxide levels through overbreathing. In diving, hyperventilation means short-term, rapid, deep breathing beyond the amount needed for the activity. Divers may hyperventilate unintentionally during high-stress situations, from various health problems, or intentionally to extend breath-holding time.

Hyperventilation lowers CO_2 levels below normal, a condition known alternately as hypocapnia or hypocarbia. Without enough CO_2, normal, needed carbonic acid levels are not achieved, pushing body chemistry to the alkaline. The resulting alkalosis initially produces tingling fingers and limbs and lightheadedness. Over a longer period, it may produce weakness, faintness, headache, and blurred vision.

Slowing breathing will correct this, but divers may not be aware of why symptoms are occurring and not take corrective measures.

Divers who notice that they are excessively hyperventilating should take immediate steps to slow their breathing

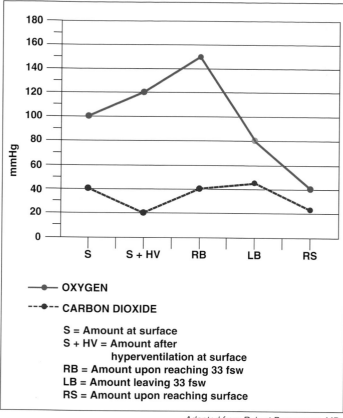

Adapted from Robert Bumgarner, MD,
"Diving Medicine - Shallow Water Blackout," Skin Diver, November 1990.

FIGURE 3.12
Partial Pressure – mmHg

oxygen in the blood. Expressed as partial pressure of oxygen in the arterial blood, it is below a level of approximately 40–50 mmHg that an individual is exposed to the risk of sudden loss of consciousness (syncope).

Figure 3.12 depicts the changes in partial pressures of oxygen and carbon dioxide in the arterial blood on a free dive to 33 fsw (2 ata) and subsequent return to the surface. At "S" (surface), the chart illustrates that the arterial tension of CO_2 is 40 mmHg and O_2 at 100 mmHg. These are normal values for a healthy human at sea level. After hyperventilation (S + HV) the carbon dioxide is decreased to 1/2 its normal value (20 mmHg) and partial pressure of oxygen (120 mmHg) increases slightly.

In the healthy individual, it is the carbon dioxide level that stimulates one to breathe. At 33 fsw (RB) oxygen has been used up and there has been little or no real increase in CO_2. However, due to the increase in ambient pressure to 2 ata, the actual partial pressure of the carbon dioxide has doubled to 40 mmHg. Oxygen, though consumed to the equivalent of 80 mmHg at sea level, is 150 mmHg at the 33 fsw, so there is no oxygen-deprivation distress at depth.

Eventually, the carbon dioxide rises slightly to 44 mmHg (LB), a level sufficient to stimulate the diver to want to breathe or in this case return to the surface. While at depth (2 ata) the partial pressure of the oxygen (80 mmHg) is sufficient to maintain consciousness. However, a significant amount of oxygen has been utilized. When the diver returns to the surface (RS), the partial pressures of the gases are cut in half by the reduction in ambient pressure to 1 ata. The net effect is that O_2 partial pressure falls to 40 mmHg, or below the level necessary to remain conscious and the diver "blacks out."

3.2.6.5 Carbon Monoxide Poisoning

Carbon monoxide (CO) is a poisonous gas, directly toxic to the body. It used to be popular to describe carbon-monoxide toxicity as simply a matter of carbon monoxide combining with hemoglobin to make carboxyhemoglobin, which blocked hemoglobin from carrying oxygen and produced hypoxia (oxygen deficiency). Although that is one of the effects, the situation is far more serious.

Carbon monoxide combines strongly with myoglobin, the oxygen-transporting and storage protein of muscle, and with the respiratory enzymes necessary for oxygen use in cells, directly stopping vital cellular functions. The entire oxygen process of transport, uptake, and utilization is disrupted. Carbon monoxide also blocks hemoglobin from removing carbon dioxide. Effects of CO increase with depth. The increased pressure of oxygen at depth does not offset carbon monoxide toxicity. Because of cellular toxicity, hypoxia occurs even if the air being breathed has sufficient oxygen.

CO exposure can result in pounding headache, nausea, and vomiting. High concentrations may cause sudden loss of consciousness.

rate, notify their buddies, and, if feasible, ascend promptly. After reaching the surface, they should establish positive buoyancy inflating their buoyancy compensators or variable-volume dry suits. Hyperventilating divers should not attempt to swim to a boat or the shore unaided because they may lose consciousness in the attempt.

During surface-supplied diving, the tender should continuously monitor the sound of diver's breathing for signs of hyperventilation. Divers starting to hyperventilate should be instructed to stop work, rest, try to control their breathing rate, and ventilate their mask/helmet. Once on the surface, slowing breathing, breathing into a paper bag to rebreathe air with a higher level of carbon dioxide, or even holding the breath for short periods will restore CO_2 to normal levels.

3.2.6.4 Shallow Water Blackout

Hyperventilation prior to a surface dive used to be popular with free divers to extend their breath-hold time. It is still used today by some who have the distorted view that it will improve their diving capabilities. Unfortunately, upon ascending, the process may also lead to unconsciousness on or before returning to the surface.

It is important to understand that for a human being to remain conscious there has to be a certain concentration of

Diving Physiology

TABLE 3.2
Carboxyhemoglobin Relative to CO Exposure

Continuous Exposure Level of CO	HbCO in Blood
50 ppm	8.4 %
40 ppm	6.7 %
30 ppm	5.0 %
20 ppm	3.3 %
10 ppm	1.7 %
—	0.5 % (non-smoker)

Hemoglobin binds with CO 200 to 300 times more readily than O_2, rendering it difficult and time consuming to eliminate from the body once inhaled. CO behaves in half-time fashion, like nitrogen. At sea level breathing regular air, 5 1/2 hours pass before half the CO leaves the body; another 5 1/2 hours must pass for the next 25 percent to leave, and so on. Breathing 100 percent oxygen at the surface reduces the half-time to just under 1 1/2 hours. At three ata (66 ft.) in a hyperbaric chamber, the half-time is about 23 minutes.

Contamination of a scuba cylinder of air with CO can come from fumes drawn into the compressor intake. These fumes can come from the exhaust of an internal combustion engine or from partial combustion of lubricating oil in a compressor not properly operated or maintained. Air intakes on compressors must be protected to avoid carbon monoxide contamination. Use oil with an appropriate flash point if using an oil-lubricated compressor.

Smoking cigarettes creates carboxyhemoglobin in the blood. The exhaled breath of a smoker can contain more carbon monoxide than NOAA allows in its compressed air for diving (see Table 3.2). Diving-industry standards call for air suppliers to adhere to air-quality standards.

Signs and Symptoms:

Carbon monoxide poisoning usually produces no symptoms until the victim loses consciousness. Some victims experience headache, nausea, dizziness, weakness, a feeling of tightness in the head, confusion, or clumsiness, while others may be unresponsive or display poor judgement. Rapid deep breathing may progress to cessation of breathing. There may be abnormal redness or blueness of lips, nailbeds, or skin. The classic sign of CO poisoning, "cherry-red" lips, may or may not occur and is therefore not a reliable diagnostic aid.

Treatment:

The victim should be given fresh air and, if available, oxygen. Some effects, such as headache or nausea, may persist after the exposure has ended. An unconscious victim should be treated in accordance with the procedures outlined in Chapter 21. The treatment of choice is hyperbaric oxygen therapy in a recompression chamber.

3.2.6.6 Excessive Resistance to Breathing

"Work-of-breathing" is the amount of effort involved with inhaling against the elastic resistance of the chest walls, the resistive forces from restrictions in and lengths of the airways, and those of supplemental breathing apparatuses. If breathing resistance is high, it makes breathing more difficult, particularly during hard work.

Work-of-breathing increases with high resistance to gas flow in poorly tuned scuba regulators, valves, and hoses, and from tight equipment and exposure suits, or from an air supply in which the supply valve is not wide open. Breathing resistance can increase with gas density, which increases with depth. Some regulators are not designed to handle deep depths or high breathing needs. Well-designed, fitting, and maintained equipment minimizes resistance to the flow of breathing gas. Resistance increases to the square of the increased flow rate. That is, doubling the flow rate increases breathing resistance by four times. Rapid breathing patterns increase turbulence which, past a point, can increase breathing resistance. Small-bore snorkels, small-diameter exhaust valves, breathing hoses, and mouthpieces may increase turbulent flow to the point of increasing work-of-breathing.

The body compensates for high breathing resistance by reducing ventilation—easily demonstrated by breathing through a narrow tube. As work-of-breathing increases, the body reaches a limit; it will accept increased carbon dioxide rather than perform the increased respiratory work required to maintain a normal CO_2 level in the tissues. Excess breathing resistance has been implicated in some diving accidents.

To reduce work-of-breathing, breathe normally. Keep equipment well tuned and serviced regularly.

3.2.6.7 Lipoid Pneumonia

Lipoid pneumonia can result if a diver breathes gas containing suspended petroleum vapor. Once petroleum particles enter the lungs they remain there for a long time. This condition is commonly known as "black lung" and is prevented by not allowing oil vapor in the diver's breathing gas and by ensuring that only approved oil is used in diving compressors.

<u>NOTE</u>
Oil of any kind is dangerous if breathed into the diver's lungs.

3.3 EFFECTS OF PRESSURE

Effects of pressure may be arbitrarily divided into two main categories:

1.   Direct, mechanical effects during descent and ascent.
2.   Effects from changes in the partial pressure of inspired gases during descent and ascent.

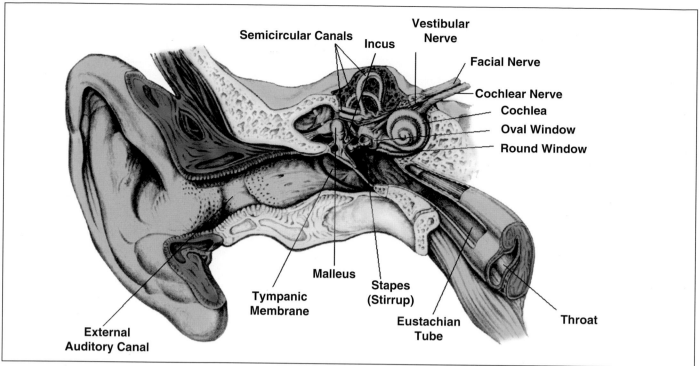

FIGURE 3.13
Principle Parts of the Ear

3.3.1 Direct Effects of Pressure During Descent

The body can withstand great hydrostatic pressure. Divers have made open-sea dives to over 1,500 fsw (682 psia); in experimental situations, divers have been exposed to pressures equivalent to 2,250 fsw (1,016 psia). Pressure increases do not affect the liquid areas of the body which are essentially incompressible and do not change shape or distort. Air spaces are not affected as long as pressure inside the air space is the same as pressure outside. If openings to the air space are blocked on descent or ascent preventing pressure equalization, the air spaces can be mechanically distorted and injured. Injury from pressure change is called barotrauma. The Greek word *baros*, means weight or pressure, and *trauma* means injury.

This section covers barotrauma during descent, as pressure increases on the air spaces of the ears, sinuses, lungs, and in certain pieces of diving equipment.

3.3.1.1 Ears

The ear has three divisions: outer, middle, and inner (see Figures 3.13). Each division functions separately to convert sound waves into nerve impulses going to the brain.

The outer ear is comprised of the outer projecting portion and the ear canal. The outer ear collects sound waves and channels them through the ear canal to the ear drum which begins the middle ear (see Figure 3.14). The middle ear is a tiny air cavity in the temporal bone on both sides of the skull. It is a closed air space; when pressure increases volume decreases, making the middle

ear susceptible to pressure problems. The middle ear has three small bones (malleus, incus, stapes) which intensify sound waves from the ear drum and transforms them into mechanical vibrations going to the inner ear through a small, delicate, oval membrane called the oval window. The last of the three middle ear bones, the stirrup,

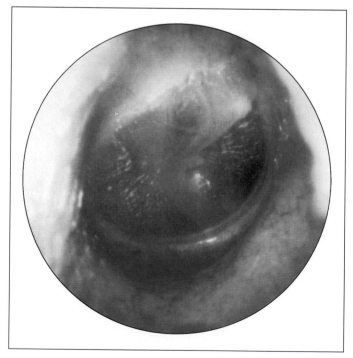

FIGURE 3.14
Tympanic Membrane (Ear Drum)

Diving Physiology

attaches directly to the oval window. The oval window is 20 times smaller than the ear drum, so pressure changes on the ear drum from sound waves or diving amplify greatly on the oval window. Another delicate structure separating middle and inner ear is the round window.

WARNING
MIDDLE EAR SQUEEZE, OR TOO VIGOROUS AUTO INFLATION OF THE MIDDLE EAR SPACE USING A VALSALVA MANEUVER (ATTEMPTING TO EXHALE THROUGH CLOSED NOSTRILS), CAN TRANSFER PRESSURE AGAINST OVAL OR ROUND WINDOWS, OR EVEN RUPTURE THEM, LEADING TO VERTIGO AND SOMETIMES PERMANENT HEARING LOSS.

The middle ears connect to the throat by the eustachian tubes, allowing air to enter the middle ears for pressure equalization. The eustachian tube is about 1.5 inches (3.8 cm) long in the adult. Pressure equalization of the middle ear is ongoing, whether diving, flying, or while on dry land. The eustachian tubes open as middle-ear volume changes when swallowing and chewing, allowing air to pass and equalize pressure.

The closed, fluid-filled inner ear has two parts. Both have intricate shapes, called labyrinths. Receptor cells in the inner ear receive mechanical vibrations, change them to neural impulses, and transmit them to the brain. The second, separate function of the inner ear pertains to location, motion, and balance.

During descent, water pressure increases against the ear drum. The ear drum bows inward, compressing air in the middle ear, initially equalizing pressure; however, the ear drum can stretch only so far. As water pressure increases relative to middle ear pressure, it creates an uncomfortable relative vacuum in the middle ear. This is "middle-ear squeeze," or barotitis media. Ear squeeze is common among divers, but easily preventable.

Successful methods of equalizing middle-ear pressure are swallowing, yawning, or gently blowing against a closed mouth and nostrils, which allows air from the throat to enter the middle ear through the eustachian tube. If one does not equalize pressure, negative pressure in the middle ear continues to stress the eardrum, expanding the blood vessels of the eardrum and middle-ear lining. Either the ear drum will rupture, allowing air or water to enter the middle ear and equalize the pressure, or the blood vessels will leak and rupture to allow enough bleeding in the middle ear to equalize pressure. Inner-ear injury may occur from rupture of the round window. Round-window rupture requires surgical repair. Injuries to the eardrum or inner ear may occur with as little as three pounds of pressure differential and can happen at any depth. It's usually more difficult to equalize during descent than ascent because the air passes out of the middle ear through the eustachian tube more easily than into the middle ear.

WARNING
BECAUSE OF THE DANGER OF EAR DAMAGE, DO NOT DO A <u>FORCEFUL</u> VALSALVA MANEUVER BEFORE OR DURING DESCENT OR ASCENT.

Upper respiratory infection (URI) may reduce or prevent equalization. Conditions contributing to stuffiness include acute or chronic inflammatory illness, allergy, irritation from smoking, and prolonged use of nasal spray. If one has difficulty equalizing on the surface, don't dive. If one has an upper respiratory infection of any kind, don't dive until the infection has cleared.

Systemic and topical drugs may improve nasal and sinus function and middle-ear equalization. Use them cautiously because a rebound phenomenon can occur, particularly with nasal spray. When the drug wears off, greater congestion and equalization problems can reoccur.

If you have chronic nasal obstruction, frequent upper-respiratory infections, nasal allergies, mastoid or ear disease, or chronic sinus trouble, see an ear, nose, and throat specialist.

Signs and Symptoms:
- Fullness or pressure in region of the external ear canals
- Squeaking sound
- Pain
- Blood or fluid from external ear
- Rupture of ear drum

Prevention:
- Use of solid ear plugs are prohibited in diving.
- Fit of diving hoods and earphones should be adjusted so that they do not completely cover or seal the external ear canal during ascent or descent.
- Accumulated wax that can obstruct the ear canal should be removed by gently irrigating the canal with a lukewarm water solution, using a rubber bulb syringe. Care should be taken before irrigation to guarantee that there is no ear drum perforation behind the obstructing wax.
- Descend feet first, preferably down the anchor line or descent line. Membranes line the airways in the head, and gravity affects blood in the vessels within the membranes. When you are upside down in water, the membranes of the air passages swell and narrow.
- Don't wait for ear pain to start before equalizing. Start equalizing as soon as pressure is felt, or before.
- Equalize gently. Avoid forceful blowing.
- Stop descent if ear blockage or fullness develops. Ascend until symptoms resolve, even if you must return to the surface.

Treatment:
Ear drum rupture should be treated according to the procedures for treating middle ear barotrauma. See a physician.

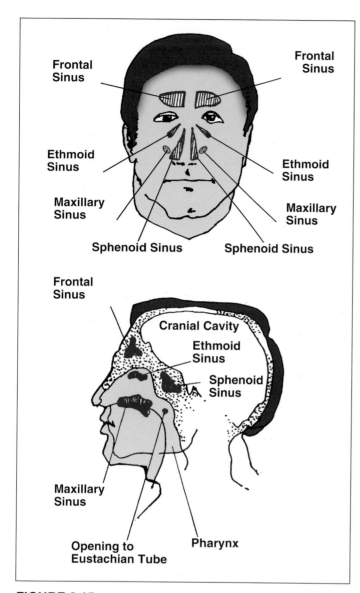

FIGURE 3.15
Sinus Cavities in the Head

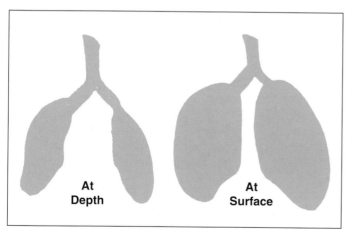

FIGURE 3.16
Effect of Descent/Ascent on Lungs

3.3.1.2 Sinuses

The term "sinus" can mean any channel, hollow space, or cavity in a bone, or a dilated area in a blood vessel or soft tissue; most often sinus refers to the four, paired, mucus-lined, air cavities in the facial bones of the head. Sinus cavities are shown in Figure 3.15.

The same kind of membrane lines the sinuses and nose, so nasal infections spread easily to the sinuses. In sinusitis, mucous membranes inflame and swell, closing sinus openings and preventing infected material from draining. If nasal inflammation, congestion, deformities, or masses block sinus openings, the sinus lining swells and inflames, absorbing pre-existing gas which forms negative pressure. When blockage occurs during descent, the relative vacuum in the sinus increases the risk of damage. Hemorrhage into the sinus may occur.

Don't dive if you have congested sinuses. Various over-the-counter and prescription medications open sinus passages. If a decongestant wears off during your dive, the sinuses become closed spaces (rebound effect) containing high pressure air. This can lead to a reverse block on ascent. Sinus barotrauma can also occur during ascent if blockage of a one-way valve of the sinus, by inflamed mucosa, cysts, or polyps, allows equalization on descent, but impairs it on ascent.

Signs and Symptoms:
- Sensation of fullness or pain in the vicinity of the involved sinus or in the upper teeth
- Numbness of the front of the face
- Bleeding from the nose

Treatment:

The treatment of sinus squeeze may involve the use of nasal decongestants, vasoconstrictors, and antihistamines taken by mouth. These medications will promote nasal mucosal shrinkage and opening of the sinus. Most of the symptoms of paranasal sinus barotrauma disappear within five to ten days without serious complications. Divers who have symptoms for longer periods should see a specialist. If severe pain and nasal bleeding are present or if there is a yellow or greenish nasal discharge, with or without fever, a specialist should be seen promptly. Individuals with a history of nasal or sinus problems should have a complete otolaryngologic evaluation before beginning to dive.

3.3.1.3 Lungs

On a breath-hold dive, there is no compressed air supply. So lung pressure cannot be equalized with ambient-pressure. Lung spaces compress with increasing depth (see Figure 3.16). It used to be thought that the lungs compress by the simple pressure-volume relationship of Boyle's Law; that is at five times surface pressure (132 ft. or 40 m) lung volume would compress to 1/5 volume, which can become less than residual volume, depending on the size of the lungs. At such low volume, a condition called thoracic squeeze would develop, including pulmonary congestion, swelling, and hemorrhage of the lung tissue.

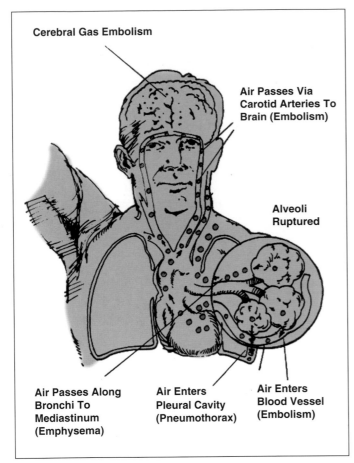

FIGURE 3.17
Consequences of Overinflation of the Lungs

However, the body has many self-regulatory abilities. Thoracic squeeze does not readily occur, even at far greater depths. Compression during descent shifts blood from the extremities and abdomen into thoracic blood vessels, maintaining a larger than predicted lung volume. Lung volume can fall below residual volume without the damage previously thought. Record free dives to over 400 ft. (122 m) have been successful. Such dives are not without other dangers; they should not be attempted without extraordinary preparation and training.

Signs and Symptoms:
- Feeling of chest compression during descent
- Pain in the chest
- Difficulty in breathing on return to the surface
- Bloody sputum

Treatment:
In severe cases of lung squeeze, the diver requires assistance to the surface. The diver should be placed face down, and blood should be cleared from the mouth. If breathing has ceased, cardiopulmonary resuscitation with oxygen should be administered. Attendants should be alert for symptoms of shock, and treatment for shock should be instituted, if necessary. The dive accident management plan should be initiated.

3.3.1.4 Eyes
Non-compressible fluids fill the eyes, protecting them against direct water pressure. Use of a mask preserves underwater vision, but introduces an air-space around the eyes that must be equalized with ambient pressure during descent. Without equalization, negative pressure in the mask space creates suction on the eyes and lids. Swelling, bruising, and bleeding can occur in the mucous membrane lining the eyelid (conjunctiva). A more serious injury can also occur — blood in the anterior chamber of the eye, called hyphema. To prevent mask squeeze, mask pressure is equalized by exhaling through the nose during descent. During ascent, air vents harmlessly out of the mask.

Signs and Symptoms:
- Sensation of suction on the face, or of mask being forced into face
- Pain or a squeezing sensation
- Face swollen or bruised
- Whites of eyes bright red

Treatment:
Ice packs should be applied to the damaged tissues and pain relievers may be administered if required. In serious cases, the services of a physician knowledgeable in diving medicine should be obtained.

3.3.2 Direct Effects of Pressure During Ascent
During ascent, ambient pressure decreases and air in the body's air spaces expands. When this air vents freely, there is no problem. When expanding air is blocked from venting, overinflation occurs and increases the possibility of overpressurization injury.

This section covers barotrauma during ascent, as decreasing pressure affects the lungs, gastrointestinal tract, teeth, and the space behind contact lenses.

3.3.2.1 Lungs—Pneumothorax
If breathing is normal and there are not any lung lesions or conditions that obstruct air flow, lungs will vent expanding air on ascent without problem. If expanding air is blocked from exiting, the lungs will overinflate, thus damaging the alveoli and bronchial passages. Breath-holding or insufficient exhalation can create general lung barotrauma; obstruction from chronic or acute respiratory diseases, or bronchospasm with asthma, can result in localized lung overpressure and barotrauma. If expanding air ruptures the lung, air escapes into the small, normally airless area between lungs and chest wall (see Figure 3.17). This injury is called pneumothorax.

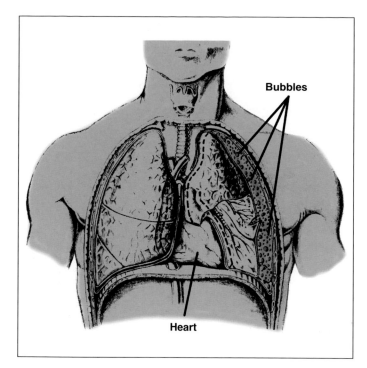

FIGURE 3.18
Lungs — Pneumothorax

The lungs are attached to the chest wall by a thin, paired membrane called the pleura. The two pleural membranes lie so close to each other that they touch. A watery fluid lubricates the layer between them, making a suction between the layers, which holds open the lungs. Air rupturing the lung walls vents air into the pleural cavity, breaking the suction. There are two types of pneumothorax; simple and tension. A simple pneumothorax is a one time leaking of air into the pleura cavity. A tension pneumothorax is a repeated leaking of air from the lungs into the pleural cavity with each successive breath, thus progressively enlarging the air pocket. A large amount of air between pleural membranes prevents the lungs from expanding. Trapped intrapleural gas expands as ascent continues, increasing pressure in the chest cavity. A lung may collapse, and the heart may push out of normal position, causing sudden severe pain, difficulty breathing, and, rarely, coughing frothy blood or death from shock (see Figure 3.18).

Signs and Symptoms:
- Difficulty or rapid breathing
- Leaning toward affected side
- Hypotension
- Cyanosis and shock
- Chest pain (deep breath hurts)
- Shortness of breath
- Decreased or absent lung sounds on affected side
- Rapid, shallow breathing
- Death

Treatment:

Simple Pneumothorax
- Normally improves with time as air is reabsorbed.
- Monitor for signs of tension pneumothorax.
- Monitor ABC (airway, breathing, and circulation) and administer 100 percent oxygen.
- Transport to nearest medical facility.

Tension Pneumothorax
- Position patient on injured side.
- ABC.
- Treat for shock and administer 100 percent oxygen.
- Transport immediately to nearest medical facility (air must be vented from chest cavity).

WARNING
DO NOT HOLD BREATH WHEN ASCENDING USING SCUBA OR SURFACE-SUPPLIED EQUIPMENT.

WARNING
A DIVER WHO HAS HAD AN OVERPRESSURE ACCIDENT MUST BE EXAMINED IMMEDIATELY BY A DIVING MEDICAL DOCTOR.

3.3.2.2 Lungs—Mediastinal Emphysema

Emphysema, in general, means an abnormal distention of body tissues from retention of air. The most familiar type of emphysema usually results from smoking or other lung pollution, and permanently overexpands and damages alveoli. In mediastinal emphysema, air escapes from a lung overpressurization into tissues around the heart, major blood vessels, and trachea (windpipe). This gas expands on ascent, causing pain under the sternum (breast-bone), shortness of breath, or, in extreme cases, fainting from impaired blood return to the heart (see Figure 3.19).

Signs and Symptoms:
- Pain under the breastbone that may radiate to the neck, collarbone, or shoulder
- Shortness of breath
- Faintness
- Blueness (cyanosis) of the skin, lips, or nailbeds
- Difficulty in breathing
- Shock
- Swelling around the neck
- A brassy quality to the voice
- A sensation of pressure on the windpipe
- Cough
- Deviation of adams apple to affected side

Treatment:
- ABC
- Administer oxygen and monitor for shock
- Examine diver for other signs of pulmonary barotrauma

Diving Physiology

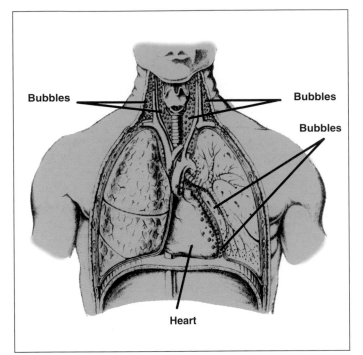

FIGURE 3.19
Lungs — Mediastinal Emphysema and Subcutaneous Emphysema

- Mediastinal emphysema causing respiratory or circulatory impairment may require recompression.
- Transport to the nearest medical facility.

3.3.2.3 Lungs—Subcutaneous Emphysema

Subcutaneous emphysema results from air forced into tissues beneath the skin of the neck. It can be associated with mediastinal emphysema or can occur alone (see Figure 3.19).

Signs and Symptoms:
- Feeling of fullness in the neck area
- Swelling or inflation around the neck and upper chest
- Crackling sensation when skin is palpated
- Change in sound of voice
- Cough

Treatment:
Unless complicated by gas embolism, recompression is not normally required. The services of a physician should be obtained and oxygen should be administered if breathing is impaired.

3.3.2.4 Arterial Gas Embolism

An arterial gas embolism occurs when a bubble of gas (or air) causes a blockage of the blood supply to the heart, brain, or other vital tissue (see Figure 3.20). Arterial gas embolism may be abbreviated AGE. A cerebral (brain) arterial gas embolism is abbreviated CAGE.

The bubble tends to increase in size as the pressure decreases (Boyle's Law), which makes the blockage worse.

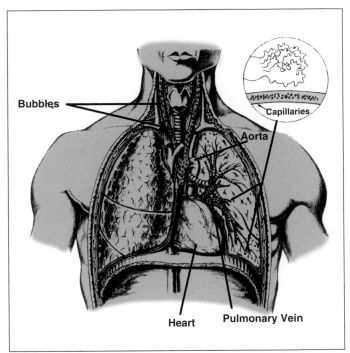

FIGURE 3.20
Arterial Gas Embolism

When a diver holds his breath or has local air trapped in his lungs during ascent, the volume of gas in the lungs increases due to a reduction in ambient pressure. Alveoli can rupture or air can be forced across apparently intact alveoli. If air bubbles enter the pulmonary veins, they travel to the left side of the heart muscle, and then commonly on through the carotid arteries to embolize the brain. As the bubbles pass into smaller arteries, they reach a point where they can move no further, and here they stop circulation. Deprived of oxygen, those tissues die.

Arterial gas embolism may occur quickly after surfacing with damage depending on the area involved. There is no way to predict which area will be affected. Symptoms of arterial gas embolism usually occur immediately or within five minutes of surfacing. Prompt recompression is the only treatment for gas embolism.

One, a few, or all of the symptoms listed below may be present.

Signs and Symptoms:
- Chest pain
- Cough or shortness of breath
- Bloody, frothy sputum
- Headache
- Visual disturbances including blindness, partial or complete
- Numbness or tingling (paresthesias)
- Weakness or paralysis
- Loss of, or change in, sensation over part of body
- Dizziness

- Confusion
- Sudden unconsciousness (usually immediately after surfacing, but sometimes before surfacing)
- Respiratory arrest
- Death

WARNING
ARTERIAL GAS EMBOLISM IS LIFE THREATENING AND REQUIRES IMMEDIATE TREATMENT.

Prevention:
- Never hold your breath when diving with compressed gases
- Ascend slowly (30 feet per minute)
- Do not dive with a chest cold or obstructed air passages
- Maintain good physical fitness, nutrition, and hydration
- Carry sufficient quantities of gas to complete the dive

Treatment:
- Establish and maintain ABC, and initiate cardiopulmonary resuscitation, if necessary
- Administer 100 percent oxygen with the injured diver supine or in recovery position
- Transport to nearest medical facility and initiate recompression treatment ASAP
- Perform a physical examination, including neurological examination, as soon as situation permits
- Provide additional life support measures
- Reassess diver's condition regularly

Rescuers and attendants must be aware that many embolism patients are also near-drowning victims. Position the injured diver in a supine or the recovery position. Injured diver position should not be allowed to interfere with the immediate administration of CPR. Administer 100 percent oxygen with a tight-fitting oronasal mask by demand/positive-pressure valve or non-rebreather mask at 15-lpm, and transport the patient as rapidly as possible to a medical facility for recompression treatment. A gas embolism case is a minute-to-minute emergency transfer. The chances of full recovery decrease with each minute lost in returning the patient to pressure. If air transportation is required, the patient must not be exposed to decreased cabin pressure during transit; consequently, aircraft capable of being pressurized to sea level must be used. A helicopter or unpressurized aircraft must be flown as low as is safely possible. Despite the decreased chance of recovery if therapy is delayed, patients have responded even after several hours delay. Victims should not be taken back into the water for treatment.

3.3.2.5 Stomach and Intestine

Only a small amount of gas is normally present in the small intestine at any time. Although gas enters or forms in larger quantities, most is usually absorbed back through the intestinal mucosa. Any air remaining in the stomach and large intestine compresses with descent and returns to normal volume on ascent. The intestines are surrounded by soft tissue so compression and expansion are, normally, neither hazardous nor noticeable.

If you add enough gas to the system while under water, the gas will expand on ascent. These gases can be generated by swallowing air, or within the intestine from carbon dioxide liberated by reactions between gastric and pancreatic juices, or a prior gas-producing meal. Ambient pressure pushing on a stomach full of gas can cause belching or back flow of stomach contents (heartburn). Severe injury is rare. With a hernia, expanding gas trapped in a loop of bowel could make the hernia irreducible.

To prevent gastrointestinal (GI) barotrauma, breathe normally, don't swallow air, and avoid large meals and gas-producing food and drink before diving. Should GI distress occur on ascent, descend to relieve discomfort, and slowly re-ascend. It may help to keep the legs moving. If surfacing is necessary before relieving pressure, try various over-the-counter, anti-gas preparations. In extreme cases, get medical attention.

3.3.2.6 Teeth

Barodontalgia means "tooth pain." It occurs when a small pocket of gas collected in a tooth during the dive expands on ascent. Tooth pain has been reported during air travel as well.

The air space may be generated by decay resulting in an area for gas to collect under a filling. Other causes of tooth squeeze include recent extractions, gum infections that have formed periodontal pockets, large areas of decay where the pulp is infected, abscesses, recent fillings, and recent root canal therapy. Part of the root canal procedure is to dry and temporarily seal the canal between treatments with a material designed for pressure of one atmosphere. Exposure to higher pressures can produce small leaks that cannot release air fast enough during ascent. Trapped air can shatter full porcelain crowns in teeth where the cement bond is failing. Gas accumulated slowly during a saturation dive has been known to (rarely) cause tooth cracking and even explosion.

Tooth squeeze is not common, but prevention is worth keeping in mind. Keep teeth clean, have cavities filled and ill-fitting crowns replaced. Complete endodontic therapy before diving. Before undergoing any dental work, inform the dentist of diving status.

3.3.2.7 Contact Lenses

Bubbles have been found in the precorneal film of tears beneath hard contact lenses after ascent. Affected divers

TABLE 3.3
Narcotic Effects of Compressed Air Diving

Guideline Depths		
Feet	**Meters**	**Effect**
0-100	0-30.5	Mild impairment of performance on unpracticed tasks. Mild euphoria.
100	30.5	Reasoning and immediate memory affected more than motor coordination and choice reactions. Delayed response to visual and auditory stimuli.
100-165	30.5-50-3	Laughter and loquacity may be overcome by self control. Idea fixation and overconfidence. Calculation errors.
165	50.3	Sleepiness, hallucinations, impaired judgment.
165-230	50.3-70.1	Convivial group atmosphere. May be terror reaction in some. Talkative. Dizziness reported occasionally. Uncontrolled laughter approaching hysteria in some.
230	70.1	Severe impairment of intellectual performance. Manual dexterity less affected.
230-300	70.1-91.5	Gross delay in response to stimuli. Diminished concentration. Mental confusion. Increased auditory sensitivity, i.e. sounds seem louder.
300	91.5	Stupefaction. Severe impairment of practical activity and judgment. Mental abnormalities and memory defects. Deterioration in handwriting, euphoria, hyperexcitablity. Almost total loss of intellectual and perceptive faculties.
300	91.5	Hallucinations (similar to those caused by hallucinogenic drugs rather than alcohol).

experienced soreness, decreased visual acuity, and the appearance of halos around lights for about two hours after ascent. Divers who wear contact lenses should use either soft lenses or hard fenestrated lenses (hard lenses with a special hole drilled). Consult with an ophthalmologist.

3.3.3 Indirect Effects of Pressure During Descent

Indirect effects of pressure occur from changes in the partial pressure of the gases in the breathing mix. This section covers inert gas narcosis, high pressure nervous syndrome (HPNS), and oxygen toxicity.

3.3.3.1 Inert Gas Narcosis

Inert gas narcosis is a condition of confusion or stupor resulting from increased pressure of dissolved inert gas. The most common inert gas narcosis is nitrogen narcosis.

The gases producing narcosis have no effect if they are not breathed under pressure. High pressure dissolves gas in the protein coverings of nerve cell membranes, depressing nerve excitability and interfering with signals. Of course, there are other factors involved in this complex and incompletely understood phenomenon.

Although often portrayed as such, narcosis is not always rapturous or intoxicating. Effects can be unpleasant or frightening, particularly in limited visibility or cold water. Even if pleasant, narcosis impairs intellectual capacities, short-term memory, time perception, orientation, judgment, reasoning, and the ability to perform mental functions, making it difficult to monitor time, depth, air supply, or the location of a buddy. Dive plan information may be forgotten. Spatial orientation may become a matter of complete indifference. Severe narcosis can produce hallucinations, bizarre behavior, or loss of consciousness. Physical problems include decreased motor ability and slowed reaction time. Because it decreases perceptions of cold and decreases heat production, narcosis may play an important role in diving hypothermia. Despite the popular belief, narcosis does not slow respiration. Narcosis is dangerous because it increases the risk of an accident while diminishing the ability to cope with one.

Impairment increases with depth. Narcosis is often first noticed at approximately 100 feet (31 m) when breathing compressed air. Wide variations in susceptibility occur; although, at greater depths, most compressed-air divers are affected (see Table 3.3).

Helium causes minimal narcosis, making it useful at depths where nitrogen narcosis would incapacitate a diver. Two other inert gases used in experimental diving are neon and argon. Neon is not narcotic; however, argon is narcotic at deeper depths. Interestingly, it appears that too high an oxygen level can leave some oxygen in the tissues unmetabolized. To the extent that it is present in certain tissues, oxygen may also act as an inert gas and produce narcosis (Bennett and Elliott 1993).

Several factors can compound the effects of narcosis: CO_2, fatigue, anxiety, cold, alcohol, and hangovers. Medications that might cause drowsiness or reduce alertness, such as motion sickness remedies and sedatives, or sedating recreational drugs, also contribute to narcosis. This is consistent with the view that narcosis depresses the central nervous system (CNS). Narcosis rapidly reverses with ascent, though divers who have experienced narcosis may not remember events occurring at depth.

Signs and Symptoms:
- Loss of judgment and skill
- A false feeling of well being
- Lack of concern for job or safety
- Inappropriate laughter
- Euphoria

Prevention and Treatment:

There is no specific treatment for nitrogen narcosis. A diver experiencing narcosis must be brought to a shallower depth, where the effects will be reversed.

3.3.3.2 High Pressure Nervous Syndrome (HPNS)

High pressure nervous syndrome (HPNS) occurs at depths greater than 400 fsw (123 msw). First noted in the 1960s, HPNS was initially thought to be an effect of breathing helium, so it was called helium tremors. At that time, helium was the most commonly used diluent gas for diving at deeper depths. HPNS becomes worse with increasing pressure and rate of compression.

HPNS is characterized by dizziness, nausea, vomiting, postural and intention tremors, fatigue and somnolence, sudden muscle twitching (called myoclonic jerking), stomach cramps, intellectual and psychomotor performance decrements, and poor sleep with nightmares.

Adding a small amount (5-10%) of nitrogen into the breathing mix reduces HPNS. At high pressure, nitrogen is a neural depressant. Other methods of preventing or reducing HPNS include slow, steady compression, stage compression with long intervals, exponential compression rates, and careful personnel selection.

3.3.3.3 Oxygen Toxicity

Given oxygen's metabolic effects, it should be no great surprise that in excess it can be toxic. In fact, all living things have enzymes and other mechanisms that protect against oxygen's toxicities. There are two types of oxygen poisoning for which divers must be concerned: those affecting the central nervous system (CNS), and those affecting many other parts of the body more generally, particularly the lungs.

Con	– Convulsion
V	– Visual disturbances, including tunnel vision
E	– Ear ringing
N	– Nausea
T	– Tingling, twitching or muscle spasms, especially of the face and lips
I	– Irritability, restlessness, euphoria, anxiety
D	– Dizziness, dyspnea

FIGURE 3.21
CNS Oxygen Toxicity Signs and Symptoms

3.3.3.3.1 CNS: Central Nervous System

CNS oxygen toxicity can occur at the high end of PO_2 levels, even after short exposures. Typically, it can develop within a few to many minutes on exposure to partial pressures of oxygen above 1.6 atm (roughly 5 to 50 min, but this is highly variable) (Lambertsen 1978). The end result may be an epileptic-like convulsion that is not damaging in itself, but can result in drowning or physical injury. The acronym *CONVENTID* (see Figure 3.21) is a simple way to remember all the signs and symptoms of CNS oxygen toxicity. It is important to note that these symptoms may come in any order.

There are other signs and symptoms of CNS toxicity. Not onerous in themselves, they are justification to stop a dive. They include twitching of lips and facial muscles, visual or hearing disturbances, nausea, dizziness, difficulty in breathing (dyspnea), anxiety, confusion, poor coordination, and unusual fatigue. These may warn of an impending convulsion; however, a convulsion is just as likely to occur without any warning. Divers have been known to "black out" or go unconscious without a convulsion; this may be a manifestation of oxygen toxicity.

3.3.3.3.2 Lung and "Whole-Body"

Slower developing oxygen toxicities may follow exposure to lower levels of oxygen for longer times. The lung is the principal organ affected, but many other parts of the body can be affected as well. Therefore, the term "whole-body" toxicity is used to include the affected parts of the body other than the CNS.

A classical symptom of whole-body toxicity is pulmonary irritation, the result of oxygen's effect on the lung. Such a symptom usually takes hours or longer to develop from exposure levels that may be lower than those that cause CNS symptoms. Whole-body oxygen toxicity is generally of little concern to divers doing no-stop dives, even when breathing oxygen-enriched mixtures, but it may be seen during intensive diving operations or during long oxygen treatments for decompression sickness in a hyperbaric chamber. Symptoms are chest pain or discomfort, coughing, inability to take a deep breath without pain or coughing, a development of fluid in the lungs, and a reduction in vital capacity. Non-pulmonary symptoms of "whole-body" oxygen toxicity include skin numbness and itching, headache, dizziness, nausea, effects on the eyes, and a dramatic reduction of aerobic capacity during exercise.

3.3.3.3.3 Variations in Tolerance

There is wide variation in susceptibility to oxygen toxicity among individuals, and a significant variation in a single individual at different times. Part of this latter variation is due to unknown causes, but a large part can be attributed to known environmental and physiological circumstances. Susceptibility to CNS toxicity is increased by certain factors, particularly those that cause an increase in internal PCO_2, such as exercise, breathing dense gas, or breathing against a resistance. Immersion, dramatic changes of temperature, and physical exertion also increases ones susceptibility to CNS oxygen toxicity. These differences make it difficult to predict the occurrence of CNS oxygen toxicity.

3.3.3.3.4 Benefits of Intermittent Exposure

Oxygen poisoning can be reduced or postponed by interrupting the exposure time (U.S.Navy Diving Manual 1999). If "breaks" in periods of low oxygen are taken during oxygen breathing, tolerance is greatly improved. In the U.S.N. tables for treatment of decompression sickness using oxygen, breaks of five minutes of air breathing are taken every 20 or 30 minutes of oxygen breathing at high PO_2 levels. This avoids oxygen convulsions in all but very rare cases and also postpones pulmonary toxicity. In situations where supplemental oxygen or high oxygen content mixtures are used for decompression, it is strongly recommended that a five minute "air" break be taken every 20 minutes to minimize the risk of oxygen poisoning.

3.3.3.3.5 Concepts of Oxygen Exposure Management

The traditional method used for prevention of CNS oxygen toxicity is to stay within exposure durations that are based on the oxygen level, or PO_2, to which the diver is exposed (U.S.Navy Diving Manual 1999). These limits allow a certain time at each PO_2 range. Such an approach has been practiced by the U.S. Navy and by NOAA for many years in their procedures for mixed gas and oxygen diving.

As with decompression, a limit appears to be implemented as if it were a solid line dividing "no problems" from "guaranteed problems." Actually, a limit is a solid line drawn through a wide gray area of gradually increasing risk. The limits given here and in other limit-based algorithms (such as a decompression table) are recommended guidelines for use under normal conditions. They have been proven in practice. They work for most people most of the time, but they are not guaranteed to work for all people all of the time under all circumstances. They may need to be more conservative when conditions are more stressful.

Diving with procedures described in this chapter imposes a relatively low risk of oxygen toxicity. The exposures are short and outside the limits that are expected to cause problems.

3.3.3.3.6 Prevention of CNS Poisoning

With the help of experts, NOAA developed estimated oxygen exposure limits that were published in the 1991 version of the *NOAA Diving Manual*. These limits are shown in Table 3.4. They are intended for a diver doing dives for research, sampling, inspection, observation, and light to moderate work at the higher PO_2 levels. The lower levels can be used for heavier and more stressful types of work.

For each level of oxygen, the chart shows an allowable time for a single exposure and also an accumulated time at that level over a full day.

If more than one dive is made to the maximum exposure of a PO_2 of 1.6 ata, a suggested surface interval of at least 90 minutes is advised between dives (three dives of 45 minutes each would theoretically be possible within the 150-minutes daily total allowed at 1.6 ata PO_2). This helps lower the accumulated oxygen dose. This only applies to the exposure at 1.6 ata, because only one maximal dive can be done in a single day with lower oxygen exposure levels.

If, however, one or more dives in a 24-hour period have reached or exceeded the limits for a normal single exposure, the diver should spend a minimum of two hours at a normoxic PO_2 (such as on the surface breathing air) before resuming diving. If diving in a 24-hour period reaches the Maximum 24-hour Limit, the diver must spend a minimum of 12 hours at normoxic PO_2 before diving again.

3.3.3.3.7 The "Oxygen Clock" or "O_2 Limit Fraction"

These exposure limits are sometimes referred to as the "oxygen clock" in percentage of the allowable limit, or the "O_2 limit fraction" as a decimal fraction of the limit (Hamilton 1988). For single dives to a single depth (square profile), calculating the percentage of oxygen exposure is as simple as dividing the minutes of the exposure by the maximum allowable exposure time at a given PO_2. However, it is rare that a diver is ever at one depth for the entire dive. Although the principle has not been verified experimentally, it is customary to add the percentages or fractions of exposure for different parts of the dive to calculate an estimated total oxygen exposure for a given dive.

It is not necessary to have a dive computer to track these exposures if the dive can be separated into segments

TABLE 3.4
NOAA Oxygen Exposure Limits

PO2 (atm)	Maximum Single Exposure (minutes)	Maximum per 24 hr (minutes)
1.60	45	150
1.55	83	165
1.50	120	180
1.45	135	180
1.40	150	180
1.35	165	195
1.30	180	210
1.25	195	225
1.20	210	240
1.10	240	270
1.00	300	300
0.90	360	360
0.80	450	450
0.70	570	570
0.60	720	720

that have a predominant or average level. The times spent at each depth or exposure level can be assigned a fraction or percentage of the "allowable" limit, and these can simply be added together. Table 3.5 allows these segments to be determined from a chart.

For multilevel dives or more than one dive of less than maximum allowed duration, it is possible to interpolate the limit values. That is to say, at any level the full limit on the oxygen clock is 100 percent of the limit, or an O_2 limit fraction of 1.0. Exposures at all levels are totaled. For example, at 1.4 atm the allowable exposure time is 150 minutes (see Figure 3.22). If a diver has an exposure to that level for 75 minutes, half the allowable time, this would run the oxygen clock to 50 percent of the limit or the limit fraction to 0.5. If there is additional exposure on the same dive, for example, 60 minutes at 1.3 PO_2, for which the allowable time is 180 minutes, an additional one-third, 33 percent or 0.33 is added, giving an oxygen clock now of 83 percent or a limit fraction of 0.83. When the total reaches 100 percent or 1.0, the diver is considered to have reached the allowable limit, and further exposure to elevated oxygen is at increased risk. Diving beyond the limit is not recommended.

Although there has been no specific laboratory validation of this technique of interpolating the exposure times, it appears to work in practice. The NOAA oxygen exposure limits have been shown to be reasonable limits through extensive use.

TABLE 3.5
CNS Oxygen Exposure Table

Oxygen PO2 (atm)	Single Dive Limit (minutes)	Bottom Time Values (minutes)											
		5	10	15	20	25	30	35	40	45	50	55	60
1.20	210	2%	5%	7%	10%	12%	14%	17%	19%	21%	24%	26%	29%
1.25	195	3%	5%	8%	10%	13%	15%	18%	21%	23%	26%	28%	31%
1.30	180	3%	6%	8%	11%	14%	17%	19%	22%	25%	28%	31%	33%
1.35	165	3%	6%	9%	12%	15%	18%	21%	24%	27%	30%	33%	36%
1.40	150	3%	7%	10%	13%	17%	20%	23%	27%	30%	33%	37%	40%
1.45	135	4%	7%	11%	15%	19%	22%	26%	30%	33%	37%	41%	44%
1.50	120	4%	8%	13%	17%	21%	25%	29%	33%	38%	42%	46%	50%
1.55	82	6%	12%	18%	24%	30%	36%	42%	48%	55%	61%	67%	73%
1.60	45	11%	22%	33%	44%	56%	67%	78%	89%	100%	111%	122%	133%

Note: Oxygen exposure is a percentage of NOAA's allowable limits. The 1.60 atm PO2 level; the "oxygen clock" runs more than three times as fast at 1.60 atm than at a PO2 level of 1.40 atm. Values for intermediate "0.05" PO2 values are linearly interpolated. Values in table are normally rounded. Highlighted percentages indicate times exceeding the NOAA oxygen exposure limits.

Oxygen PO_2	Single Dive Limit	Actual Dive Time	% Limit
1.40 atm	150 min	75 min	50%
1.30 atm	180 min	60 min	33%
	Totals:	135 min	88%

FIGURE 3.22
Multi-Level Dive Oxygen Exposure

3.3.3.3.8 Prevention of Lung or Whole-Body Toxicity

Other parts of the body are sensitive to excess oxygen, especially the lungs. Pulmonary oxygen toxicity, and in due course other whole-body aspects, can become a problem in extended or repeated oxygen-based decompressions, and in treatments in a recompression chamber. These conditions are unlikely to be encountered in nitrox diving; in fact, they are not significantly more likely than in ordinary scuba diving with air. However, procedures have been developed for managing this toxicity, and it is helpful for the diver to be acquainted with the general methods and terminology (U.S. Navy Diving Manual 1999).

On continued exposure to above normal PO_2, generally at levels below those causing CNS toxicity but above a PO_2 of 0.5 atm, the lungs may show symptoms and a reduction in vital capacity. Vital capacity is the maximum amount of gas that a person can exhale after taking a full inspiration. Although it takes training to get reproducible data, vital capacity is relatively easy to measure; it has been used as the primary indicator for pulmonary toxicity. At the laboratory of Dr. C.J. Lambertsen at the University of Pennsylvania, empirical methods were developed in the early 1970s to use vital capacity as a monitor for pulmonary effects of oxygen exposure. Among the developments was a "unit" for measuring and tracking oxygen exposure, the UPTD or Unit Pulmonary Toxicity Dose, as a function of PO_2 and time.

The dose measure was conceived around a basic unit of exposure equivalent to one minute of breathing 100 percent oxygen at a pressure of one atm. At PO_2 levels above this, the dose increases more rapidly as the PO_2 increases. This toxicity appears to have a threshold at 0.5 atm PO_2 below which toxicity development is insignificant. The unit dose for different exposure levels was determined by fitting a curve to empirical data, then deriving an equation to describe the curve. This equation is available in several references, including the *Underwater Handbook*, (Shilling et al. 1976, p. 158), which includes "look-up" tables for deriving doses from exposure data. The method also used an additional dose term, CPTD, a measure of the Cumulative Pulmonary Toxicity Dose. The method does not include a means of calculating recovery when exposure is below 0.5 atm PO_2.

A more recent approach, designated the Repex method, allows doses to be calculated or tabulated the same way using the same equation but calls the single dose unit, OTU or Oxygen Tolerance Unit (see Table 3.6).

The Repex method provides procedures for avoiding toxic effects during extended operational exposures and takes recovery into account.

Tracking OTUs is not of great importance when the dives are of a no-stop nature. It is when the diver will be conducting many dives over more than three days, and where the exposures get lengthy, that OTU tracking will be of significant value.

Table 3.6 gives the empirically determined Repex limits for whole-body oxygen exposure. The Repex limits allow a greater exposure for a diver who has not been exposed recently, but the allowable daily dose decreases as exposure days increase. The total for a given "mission" or exposure period is given in the third column. Table 3.7 facilitates calculating OTU or UPTD per minute for a range of PO_2s.

3.3.4 Indirect Effects of Pressure During Ascent

This section covers inert gas elimination, decompression sickness, counterdiffusion, and aseptic bone necrosis (dysbaric osteonecrosis).

3.3.4.1 Inert Gas Elimination

Even on land there is pressure on the body. This pressure comes from the atmosphere and dissolves nitrogen everywhere in the body until the internal nitrogen pressure reaches about the same as nitrogen pressure in the blood. It is not exactly the same as the ambient nitrogen pressure because water vapor and carbon dioxide from the body "dilutes" the air breathed. Subtracting the small water vapor pressure and arterial CO_2 values gives the blood nitrogen tension. This, more or less, is the starting nitrogen tension.

At depth, water pressure increases the nitrogen dissolved in the body. Upon ascent, or at increased elevation on land, extra nitrogen begins coming back out of the body. Ascend slowly enough and the nitrogen passes into the bloodstream, still dissolved, then travels to the lungs where it is exhaled. This process continues until the internal nitrogen pressure is again equal to ambient. Come up too fast and nitrogen can't stay dissolved. It begins to become a gas again before it can be exhaled and forms bubbles inside the body. This triggers a cascade of problems that become decompression sickness (see Section 3.3.4.2).

Taking up inert gas by the body is called absorption or on-gassing. Giving up gas is called elimination or off-gassing. Nitrogen and carbon monoxide enter and leave the body in real and measurable units of time. The units are called half-times. Half-times refer to the time in minutes necessary to uptake or eliminate enough nitrogen to fill or empty half the area with gas. A half-time is the same as a half-life of radioactivity, which is the time needed for half the nuclei in a specific isotopic to decay.

Half-times describe real biological processes, not just theoretical numbers. How fast the body areas equilibrate with ambient pressure depends on the volume of blood flow and the capacity of the area to absorb the dissolved gas. Different areas of the body are made of different materials

TABLE 3.6
REPEX Oxygen Exposure Chart for Tolerable Multiple Day Exposures

Exposure Days	OTU Average Dose	OTU Total Dose
1	850	850
2	700	1400
3	620	1860
4	525	2100
5	460	2300
6	420	2520
7	380	2660
8	350	2800
9	330	2970
10	310	3100
11	300	3300
12	300	3600
13	300	3900
14	300	4200
15-30	300	as required

TABLE 3.7
OTU Calculation Table

PO_2 (atm)	OTU Per Minute
0.50	0
0.55	0.15
0.60	0.27
0.65	0.37
0.70	0.47
0.75	0.56
0.80	0.65
0.85	0.74
0.90	0.83
0.95	0.92
1.00	1.00
1.05	1.08
1.10	1.16
1.15	1.24
1.20	1.32
1.25	1.40
1.30	1.48
1.35	1.55
1.40	1.63
1.45	1.70
1.50	1.78
1.55	1.85
1.60	1.92
1.65	2.00
1.70	2.07
1.75	2.14
1.80	2.21
1.85	2.28
1.90	2.35
1.95	2.42
2.00	2.49

and have varying blood supplies, so some take up nitrogen slowly, while others do it faster. These are called the slow and fast compartments, or tissues. In decompression, the term "tissue" or "compartment" means the different body areas that on-gas and off-gas at the same rate. The areas that are grouped into each compartment designation might be scattered all over the body. For example, fatty tissues hold more gas than watery tissues, and take longer than watery tissues to absorb and eliminate inert gas; these are called "slow" compartments. Fast compartments usually build higher amounts of nitrogen after a dive than slower ones because they on-gas more in the same period of time.

When a compartment fills to capacity, it is called saturated. Given enough time, the pressure of nitrogen in all the different compartments will eventually equal ambient pressure, and thus, the entire body is saturated. On most dives, there is not enough time for total saturation. Faster compartments may be saturated, while slow compartments may be practically empty, while other compartments attain middling pressure.

Differences in solubility and rates of gas diffusion give different gases different half-times. Helium is much less soluble in tissues than nitrogen, but it diffuses faster, so helium equilibration occurs faster than for nitrogen. Still, the basic principles of absorption and elimination apply for any inert gas breathed. On ascent, for example, the diver's tissues, especially the slow compartments, may continue to absorb nitrogen. During most dives, there isn't time for slower compartments to equilibrate with ambient pressure; these compartments have a lower pressure than the surrounding water. During ascent, ambient pressure can drive nitrogen into slow tissues, even as higher pressure, fast compartments off-gas. Not all nitrogen passes directly back into the blood stream for direct off-gassing by exhalation. Nitrogen may pass from the higher pressure in one part of the body to the lower pressure in an adjacent one (Hamilton, pers. com. 2000).

Fast tissues not only on-gas quickly, they also off-gas quickly. Decompression or safety stops taken near the surface on a recreational-type dive are favorable. They allow some extra gas to be taken up by the slow tissues, but allow more gas to be given off by the faster tissues, while holding at a pressure slightly greater than the surface (Hamilton, pers. com. 2000).

After ascending to the surface (or to a shallower level), equilibration at the new level may require 24 hours or so, even though the dive was far shorter in duration. Half-time gas elimination is the reason. It takes six half-times before a compartment can fill or empty. No matter how much gas a compartment starts with, it takes six half-times to empty. A 60-minute compartment will half fill (or empty) with nitrogen in 60 minutes. After another 60 minutes, or two hours total, the compartment will be 3/4 or 75 percent full (or depleted). It will take another 60 minutes for the remaining 1/4 to move, making the compartment 7/8 or 87.5 percent full (or empty) in three hours (1/2 + 1/4 + 1/8 = 7/8). In four hours, the compartment will be 93.8 percent exchanged and in five hours it will be 97.0 percent. It takes six half-times for any compartment to become about 99 percent full or empty. For practical purposes 99 percent is completely saturated or de-saturated. This means a 60-minute compartment is full or empty in six hours, since six half-times x 60 minutes = 360 minutes or six hours. A fast compartment like a five-minute compartment fills or empties in only 30 minutes (6 half-times x 5 minutes = 30 minutes). The slow 120-minute compartment fills and empties in 12 hours (6 half-times x 120 minutes = 720 minutes or 12 hours).

Several complicated factors can slow the release of nitrogen from the body. However, for practical applications like calculating decompression tables, off-gassing is considered to proceed at the same half-time rate as on-gassing. This means that after any dive, it takes six hours for the 60-minute compartment to return to its starting amount of nitrogen, and 12 hours for the 120-minute half-time compartment to return to starting pressure—equilibration with ambient pressure on land.

From another perspective, oxygen can significantly enhance decompression. Decompression requirements are dictated by the on-gassing of inert gases. By breathing 100 percent oxygen, the inert gas gradient is significantly increased, thus increasing inert gas elimination from the body. For example, pure oxygen can be used to shorten decompression on the 20 and 10 fsw stops. In addition, high oxygen content mixtures can also be used to shorten decompression from the 30 fsw stop and deeper. Mixes rich in oxygen have proven to substantially improve decompression outcome when used as a supplemental decompression gas from both air and nitrox dives.

3.3.4.2 Decompression Sickness

Decompression sickness (DCS, also known as "the bends") is the result of inadequate decompression following exposure to increased pressure. During a dive, the diver's body tissues absorb nitrogen from the breathing gas in proportion to the surrounding pressure. If the diver ascends too quickly, the nitrogen may come out of solution and form bubbles in the body's fluids and tissues.

WARNING
ALTHOUGH DECOMPRESSION SICKNESS MAY OCCUR AS A RESULT OF VIOLATING ACCEPTED SAFE DIVING PRACTICES, IT CAN ALSO OCCUR EVEN WHEN THE ACCEPTED GUIDELINES ARE BEING FOLLOWED PRECISELY.

Bubbles form after many dives, often with no symptoms; these are called silent bubbles. It's probably not true that asymptomatic bubbles form after every dive; however, they are not uncommon. Bubbles cause damage in several ways: they can block blood and lymph circulation, depriving vital areas of oxygen and waste removal; extravascular bubbles can compress and stretch blood vessels and nerves creating pain, damage, and disability; as foreign invaders to the body, bubbles can provoke a cascade of defenses including blood coagulation, release of vasoactive substances from cells lining the blood vessels, and the body's immune system reacts by coating the bubbles with lipoproteins, which then denature and release circulating fat emboli. Bubbles do not pass from body tissues into veins, unless the veins are already torn. Bubbles, even though tiny, are too big to pass directly through blood vessel walls. They may redissolve for passage through vessel walls then reform into bubbles, but they do not drain into vessels intact. Although bubbles are a good explanation for many decompression problems, they may not be the sole precursor of decompression problems. Pressure may have direct effects of its own on blood cells and other body areas (Bookspan 1995).

It is not easy to detect bubbles in tissue, but they can be detected in circulating blood because they are moving. This is done with a device called a Doppler ultrasonic bubble detector. Ultrasonic sound waves at too high a frequency to be heard are used in various ways in medical diagnosis. Using Doppler electronics, only waves reflected from moving objects are detected. Bubbles can be "heard" moving through the circulation on the way to the lungs. Doppler bubble detectors have shown that normal and otherwise benign dives may create a few circulating bubbles in some divers. These are called "silent bubbles" because they do not cause overt symptoms. In fact, the bubbles detected in the venous blood are "on their way out" and are not likely to be involved in decompression sickness. Doppler bubble detection in venous blood has not proven to be useful for predicting DCS in a given diver, but dive profiles that cause a lot of bubbles also tend to cause a substantial number of DCS cases.

Major determinants of risk of DCS are depth, time at depth, ascent rate, and multiple dives. Individual variation is also a factor. The same depth and time profile, or "dose" of nitrogen, varies in effect on different people, just as the same dose of medication can vary in effect. Individual factors have been explored but are not well understood, leaving these variables open to sometimes wild conjecture. Other factors that may predispose to DCS include fatigue, dehydration, smoking, alcohol consumption, and carbon dioxide retention. Environmental factors include chilling at the end of a dive, heavy work, and the use of heated suits.

WARNING
DECOMPRESSION SICKNESS MAY OCCUR EVEN IF DECOMPRESSION TABLES OR COMPUTERS ARE PROPERLY USED. ALTHOUGH IT IS UNCOMMON FOR DCS TO OCCUR ON NO-DECOMPRESSION DIVES, IT CAN HAPPEN.

There was early speculation, now dismissed, that birth control pills or menstruation might increase risk for women. Given the dearth of comparative DCS studies, there is no substantive evidence that gender plays a role in DCS (Bookspan 1995). Most medical experts today agree that decompression sickness is the result of complex individual, not sex specific, factors. However, we still do not have definitive answers and additional research is needed.

WARNING
THE MAJOR DETERMINANTS OF THE RISK OF DECOMPRESSION SICKNESS ARE DEPTH, TIME AT DEPTH, ASCENT RATE, AND MULTIPLE DIVES.

Decompression sickness was formerly divided into Type I, Type II, and Type III. Type I DCS included skin itching or marbling; brief, mild pain called "niggles," which resolved typically within ten minutes; joint pain; and lymphatic swelling. Extreme fatigue was sometimes grouped into Type I. Type II DCS was considered to be respiratory symptoms, hypo-volemic shock, cardiopulmonary problems, and central or peripheral nervous system involvement. Type III grouped DCS and arterial gas embolism together, also called decompression illness (DCI). Arterial gas embolism is covered in Section 3.3.2.4. It is now more common to categorize decompression sickness by area involved and severity of symptom.

Limb Bends. A common symptom of DCS is pain, usually in the elbow, shoulder, hip, or knee. DCS pain is often described as dull, throbbing, and deep in the joint or tissue. Pain onset is usually gradual and, in the early stages, the diver may not recognize the pain as DCS. Pain slowly intensifies, however, and, in severe cases, interferes with limb strength. In divers, upper limbs are affected about three times as often as lower limbs. In caisson workers, lower limbs are more often affected.

Central Nervous System (CNS) Decompression Sickness may cause muscular weakness, numbness, "pins and needles," paralysis, loss of sensation, loss of sphincter control, and, in extreme cases, death. Often, the symptoms do not follow typical nerve distribution and are unstable in position and type during the early stages—different from the usual history of traumatic nerve injuries. Strange neurological complaints or findings should not be dismissed as imaginary.

Cerebral Decompression Sickness is decompression sickness occurring in the brain. It may produce almost any symptom: headache or visual disturbance, dizziness, tunnel vision, tinnitus (buzzing or ringing in the ears), partial deafness, confusion, disorientation, emotional, even psychotic symptoms, paralysis, and unconsciousness. Cerebral DCS is more common than previously thought and may account for a portion of symptoms formerly attributed to spinal-cord DCS. There is some discussion whether, and to what extent, long-term brain changes occur with repeated exposure to decompression stress, even decompression stress that does not result in known decompression sickness.

Pulmonary DCS, or *"Chokes"* occurs in about two percent of DCS cases. It is characterized by pain under the breastbone (sternum) on inhalation, coughing that can become paroxysmal, and severe respiratory distress that can end in death.

Skin Bends come in two forms: harmless simple itchy skin after hyperbaric chamber exposure, or rashy marbling on the torso, called cutis marmorata, that may warn of serious decompression sickness.

Inner-Ear Decompression Sickness (vestibular decompression sickness, or labyrinthine decompression sickness) produces vertigo, ringing in the ears, nausea, or vomiting. Inner ear DCS is also called "staggers" because of difficulty maintaining balance. Vestibular decompression sickness occurs more after deep helium-oxygen dives, particularly after switching to air in the later stages of decompression, although it also has occurred in shallower air diving.

It should be assumed that any diver with ear symptoms during descent is experiencing inner ear barotrauma, including possible rupture of the oval and round windows; *this diver should not be recompressed.* Recompression would again subject the diver to unequal middle-ear pressures. Even without inner ear DCS or barotrauma, hearing impairment can result from diving. Divers should have periodic audiometric examinations.

First Aid. Secure the victim's ABC (airway, breathing and circulation). Give 100 percent O_2 through a demand/positive-pressure type mask. If necessary, CPR should begin immediately. Make the victim comfortable and place him in a supine position, take notes and record vital signs every fifteen minutes, continually monitor the victim's level of consciousness, check for neurological deficits, conduct an interview with both the diver and his buddy regarding the cause of the accident including the diver's profile within the last 24 hours and any pertinent medical information, collect the patient's diving equipment and send it with the diver to the medical facility/recompression chamber. Also, the diver should only be given fluids by mouth if he is fully conscious, able to tolerate liquids, and intravenous (IV) therapy is not available. The treatment of choice for re-hydration is Ringers® Solution administered by IV. Mild hypovolemia may be more common in diving than generally realized. DCS treatment is less effective if hypovolemia is uncorrected. Transport without delay to a hyperbaric treatment facility. If transporting by air, ascend to an altitude or equivalent pressure of no greater than 1,000 feet. Prompt recompression treatment increases the likelihood of a favorable outcome. Several treatments may be needed. Complete resolution of symptoms is not guaranteed.

Do not treat by returning the diver to the water. In-water recompression can be hazardous and should not be attempted unless circumstances are extraordinary, for example, in isolated areas with no medical treatment options, and with specific equipment and rehearsed procedures in place for a system of surplus air, oxygen cylinders, added personnel, extra thermal protection, and land support.

NOTE
Taking vital signs and/or interviewing the injured diver must not interrupt oxygen breathing. NOAA requires that an oxygen kit capable of ventilating an unconscious victim be on site during all diving operations.

Prevention:
- Make safety stops (when conditions permit)
- Ascend slowly (30 feet per minute)
- Use longer surface intervals
- Plan the dive well and have a backup plan
- Maintain good physical fitness, nutrition, and hydration

Treatment:
- If condition permits, perform quick neurological examination before recompression to ensure that case is pain only.
- Administer 100 percent oxygen, if possible, via tight-fitting oronasal mask by demand/positive-pressure valve or non-rebreather mask at 15-lpm constant flow with the injured diver positioned supine or in recover position.
- Enter chamber, put diver on oxygen, pressurize chamber to 60 fsw, and initiate recompression on appropriate treatment table.
- Reassess diver regularly.

Remember, Divers Alert Network (DAN) provides 24 hour emergency services to assist injured divers. If assistance is required, a DAN medical professional (hyperbarically-trained physician or paramedic) can be reached at (919) 684-8111 (24 hrs).

WARNING
WHEN PLANNING DIVES, CHECK AVAILABILITY OF EMERGENCY OXYGEN/FIRST AID EQUIPMENT, CONTACT INFORMATION FOR LOCAL/REGIONAL EMERGENCY MEDICAL ASSISTANCE AND TREATMENT FACILITY, AND DEVELOP AN EMERGENCY ASSISTANCE PLAN. ANY DELAY IN SYMPTOM RECOGNITION, FIRST AID, AND TREATMENT CAN RESULT IN PERMANENT INJURY.

3.3.4.3 Treatment Tables

The primary treatment for decompression sickness is recompression. Hyperbaric oxygen therapy treatment tables include U.S.N. Treatment Tables 1, 2A, 3, 4, 5, 6, 6A, 7, 8, and 9. These tables are shown in Appendix VI, along with Accident Treatment Flow Charts to be followed when selecting a treatment strategy. The first step in any treatment involves diagnosing the condition properly. The Accident Treatment Flow Charts are diagnostic aids designed to ensure the selection of an appropriate table. Once a treatment table has been chosen, treatment is conducted in accordance with the recompression procedures specified for that table. If complications occur during or after treatment, the procedures shown in the Accident Treatment Flow Charts will help determine the appropriate course of action.

3.3.4.4 Failures of Treatment

Four major complications may affect the recompression treatment of a patient. These are:

- Worsening of the patient's condition during treatment
- Recurrence of the patient's original symptoms or development of new symptoms *during* treatment
- Recurrence of the patient's original symptoms or development of new symptoms *after* treatment
- Failure of symptoms of decompression sickness or gas embolism to resolve despite all efforts using standard treatment procedures

Alternative treatment procedures have been developed and used successfully when standard treatment procedures have failed. These special procedures may involve the use of saturation diving decompression schedules; cases of this type occur more frequently when a significant period of time has elapsed between the onset of symptoms and the initial recompression. Although it is important to know that alternative procedures are available, it is equally important to note that they have not been standardized. The use of an oxygen-nitrogen saturation therapy may be the only course of action when the situation involves a paralyzed diver already at depth whose condition is deteriorating. It is therefore essential that the advice of experts in the field of hyperbaric medicine, such as Divers Alert Network (DAN), be obtained early in the treatment process.

3.3.4.5 Counterdiffusion

Divers breathing one gas mixture while surrounded by another can develop serious skin lesions, nausea, vomiting, and vestibular problems, even with no change in ambient pressure. Problems can also occur after switching from breathing nitrogen-oxygen mix to breathing heliox while still under pressure. Different gases have different diffusion rates. Helium, for example, diffuses faster than nitrogen; in other words, helium moves into tissues from blood faster than nitrogen moves out. Total inert gas partial pressure in the body increases even though depth has not changed. This increased inert gas partial pressure can result in bubble formation. The inner ear seems particularly susceptible, resulting in vestibular symptoms. Because two different gases can go in opposite directions in the body at the same ambient pressure, it is termed isobaric counterdiffusion or isobaric counterexchange.

Interestingly, cases of inner-ear DCS have occurred after diving heliox, then switching to air. Although it would be expected that helium in tissues moves into blood faster than nitrogen in breathing air moves into tissues, which would reduce gas load and risk of DCS, it's possible that the middle ear (and other structures) fill with heliox during the dive. During the switch to air during decompression, partial pressure of helium in blood falls quickly, but the middle ear and other structures remain full of heliox, and the total inner ear inert-gas partial pressure rises.

3.3.4.6 Aseptic Bone Necrosis (Dysbaric Osteonecrosis)

Months to years after prolonged pressure exposure, joint surfaces of the long-bone ends can die. The hip and shoulder are most often affected, resulting in pain, spasm around the joint, and finally, disabling arthritis. This condition is called avascular necrosis of bone, caisson disease of bone, aseptic bone necrosis, or dysbaric bone necrosis. The word "necrosis" means death of cells in an area. Bone necrosis, and its crippling effects, was first noted in 1888 in caisson workers (Kindwall 1972).

Aseptic bone necrosis seems to involve several mechanisms of damage: bubbles formed during decompression obstruct blood vessels in the bone ends, platelets, fat, and blood cells clump and obstruct blood flow, and blood vessels themselves narrow in reaction to bubble damage. Bone ends seem to be vulnerable because supersaturation in fatty bone marrow may generate fat emboli that occlude vessels, the surrounding bone tissue is not elastic with minimal margin for foreign body accumulation, and bone collects uranium 238 which might promote nucleation and subsequent gas bubble formation.

Bone necrosis seems to be a significant occupational hazard of professional divers, caisson workers, and others who spend great amounts of time compressing and decompressing at depth. There seems to be a definite relationship between length of time exposed to depth and bone lesions, although cases have occurred with minimal exposure. Other factors may include cases of bends, and the adequacy and promptness of recompression treatment.

Bone necrosis is seldom seen in the elbows, wrists, or ankles, and lesions that occur in the shafts of the long bones rarely cause symptoms or disability. Lesions that occur in the head of the femur (long leg bone) or humerus (upper arm bone) weaken bone underlying the cartilage covering the joint, causing the joint surface to break down. Lesions often are bilateral, resulting in the collapse of both femoral heads. Severe disability is the result. The only treatment known to have any degree of success is surgical repair or replacement of the joint.

3.3.4.7 Patent Foramen Ovale

The foramen ovale is a flap-like opening in the septum wall which separates the right and left atria of the heart. The foramen ovale is normally open in a developing fetus, because the fetus derives its oxygen and nutritional supply directly from its mother via the umbilical circulation. Upon birth, when the neonate's lungs become functional the foramen ovale functionally closes. Within a year after birth, the foramen ovale structurally closes. However, in an estimated 20 percent to 30 percent of the general population, the foramen ovale remains partially or fully open (patent "PFO"). In normal activities at sea level, a PFO does not induce any detrimental effects, and most people with PFOs are not aware of the anomaly. PFOs can be detected by means of a specialized echocardiogram, but this is an expensive and complex test which is not recommended for the general population. However, PFO can cause severe problems for divers (Bove 1997). In divers with a partially or fully open foramen ovale, performing a forceful valsalva maneuver may shift the pressure gradient so as to open the foramen ovale and allow bubbles to shunt. If the bubbles accumulated during a dive bypass the lungs and are shunted directly into the diver's systemic circulation, they can block cartoid or coronary arteries, leading to arterial gas embolism. Depending on where these shunted bubbles lodge, they may also induce DCS. PFOs have been implicated in a number of otherwise unexplained cases of decompression illness.

3.3.4.8 Pregnancy and Diving

The consensus of diving medical experts agrees that women should not dive during pregnancy. Given the limited existing data, however, it is difficult to extract specific safety guidelines. This is because animal studies may not accurately enough simulate human physiology, and anecdotal diving surveys of pregnant female divers, whose data relies on subjective reporting, is often not scientifically accurate. Additionally, because of the potential dire consequences, it is unethical and illegal to conduct experiments which purposely induce decompression illness in pregnant women and their fetuses. Nevertheless, from the existing experiences of humans and animal studies, there are risks associated with diving during pregnancy, both for the mother and her fetus (Bove 1997).

3.4 HYPOTHERMIA/HYPERTHERMIA

The body maintains internal temperature well, despite functioning in a wide range of cold environments. The body produces and loses heat several ways. By itself, the heat loss process is not a problem as long as heat is restored. Otherwise chilling results.

The body's inner, or core, temperature is the familiar 37C/98.6°F. Skin temperature is usually much lower, close to ambient temperature, and variable. It used to be popular to refer to any downward variation of body temperature as hypothermia. However, core temperature normally falls several degrees during sleep, for example, and is not hypothermia, and skin temperature drops dramatically with falling ambient temperature to protect the core against hypothermia. True clinical hypothermia is reduction of core temperature (not skin temperature) below 35C/95°F. Hypothermia is not the most common danger of cold. A diver can become incapacitated by chilling without ever becoming hypothermic.

3.4.1 Effects of Cold

Chilling, even if not life-threatening in itself, increases fatigue and reduces dexterity and sense of touch, making it difficult to do useful work or to control diving equipment such as weight belts and buoyancy compensators. Short-term memory and ability to think clearly may be seriously affected. Shivering further reduces coordination and may make it difficult to hold the mouthpiece. By the time shivering becomes uncontrollable, oxygen consumption has increased greatly. A diver may become helpless even before reaching moderate hypothermia (see Table 3.8).

Many factors interact in susceptibility to chilling. Water temperature and duration of exposure are obvious factors. Thermal protection by protective garments and the body's heat-producing and heat-saving abilities are covered in the following Section 3.4.3. Nitrogen narcosis reduces perception of cold and inhibits central neural structures involved in temperature regulation and heat production. Narcosis seems to be a large contributor to hypothermia in compressed-air divers. Susceptibility to chilling increases with dehydration, fatigue, hunger, and illness. If a diver is out of shape, underweight, a smoker, or has been using drugs or alcohol, he is at risk of chilling.

Gradual heat loss over a long period, such as multiple dives in warm water over days, often will not cause shivering; however, the accumulated slow cooling can result in impaired performance and fatigue similar to that accompanying cold water chilling.

Terminate a dive and begin rewarming if any of the following signs and symptoms are present:

Signs and Symptoms:
- Loss of dexterity and grip strength
- Difficulty performing routine tasks, confusion, or repeating tasks or procedures
- Intermittent shivering, even though routine tasks can still be performed
- Behavioral changes in a buddy that may indicate existing or approaching hypothermia

3.4.2 First Aid for Hypothermia
Treatment:

The best help that fellow divers can render at the scene of the accident is:

- ABC (airway, breathing, and circulation)
- Handle the victim extremely gently
- Prevent further heat loss
- Activate the EMS system immediately

WARNING
SEVERE HYPOTHERMIA IS A LIFE-THREATENING CONDITION AND NEEDS TO BE TREATED BY TRAINED MEDICAL PERSONNEL.

ABC. As in any medical emergency, protecting the ABC is the utmost priority. In addition to securing and monitoring the victim's airway, breathing, and circulation, it is also important to determine the victim's temperature.

Treat the Victim Gently. A victim of severe hypothermia must be carefully removed from the water in as horizontal a position as possible to reduce the possibility of hypotension (reduced blood pressure) and shock. The victim should be removed from the cold environment, and sheltered. The victim should be kept lying down in a supine position, but not in direct contact with the cold ground or metal objects, and should always be handled very gently.

Prevent Further Heat Loss. To prevent further heat loss, rescuers should remove the victim's wet clothes, and cover him with blankets, particularly around the areas of highest heat loss—the head, neck, armpits, chest, and groin. Never attempt to rewarm a severely hypothermic diver in

TABLE 3.8
Signs and Symptoms of Dropping Core Temperature

Core Temperature °F	C	Symptoms
Below 98.6	37	*CHILLING* Cold sensations, skin vasoconstriction, increased muscle tension, increased oxygen consumption
97	36	Sporadic shivering suppressed by voluntary movements, gross shivering in bouts, further increase in oxygen consumption, uncontrollable shivering
95	35	*MODERATE HYPOTHERMIA* Voluntary tolerance limit in laboratory experiments; mental confusion, impairment of rational thought, possible drowning, decreased will to struggle
93	34	Loss of memory, speech impairment, sensory function impairment, motor performance impairment
91	33	Hallucinations, delusions, partial loss of consciousness; in shipwrecks and survival history, 50% do not survive; shivering impaired
90	32	*SEVERE HYPOTHERMIA* Heart rhythm irregularities, motor performance grossly impaired
88	31	Shivering stopped, failure to recognize familiar people
86	30	Muscles rigid, no response to pain
84	29	Loss of consciousness
80	27	Ventricular fibrillation (ineffective heartbeat), muscles flaccid
79	26	Death

the field. Ideally, hypothermia victims should be stabilized in a hospital setting and carefully rewarmed under medical supervision.

It is widely debated whether and by which method even trained medics should attempt field rewarming, because rapid or aggressive rewarming may precipitate a phenomenon known as "afterdrop," in which the core temperature continues to drop even when rewarming has begun. Afterdrop is believed to occur when cold blood in the periphery circulates to the central core as vessels in the skin dilate from the warm environment. The heart of a severely hypothermic person is extremely vulnerable, and afterdrop can induce ventricular fibrillation (uncontrolled, irregular heart beats). Well-intentioned "remedies" such as rigorous rubbing of the victim's extremities, heat packs, hot drinks, hot baths, alcoholic beverages, even a cigarette, therefore, can be lethal.

Activate the EMS System. Divers should always have a dive accident management plan, which includes information and equipment for contacting the local EMS and U.S. Coast Guard.

Fortunately, divers rarely have to deal with severe hypothermia. It is more likely that a diver will appear cold or complain of being cold, will be shivering and/or have slightly impaired speech and dexterity. Other divers or the diving supervisor should remove this diver from the water and wind immediately, remove wet clothing, and dry him off. As long as the diver is not shivering uncontrollably, is conscious, has a core temperature of 95°F (35C) or more, and can swallow, he can be given warm drinks that contain no alcohol or caffeine, and should be wrapped in warm blankets or an exposure bag. A chilled person can warm up by taking a warm bath or shower.

Often a lay rescuer cannot distinguish between the various categories of hypothermia, as signs and symptoms may overlap. Good indicators are the diver's level of consciousness, temperature, and intensity of shivering (or lack of shivering). If unsure, a lay rescuer should refrain from aggressive rewarming.

WARNING
DO NOT TAKE HOT BATHS OR SHOWERS AFTER COMPLETING DECOMPRESSION DIVES (OR DIVES NEAR DECOMPRESSION LIMITS). HEAT MAY STIMULATE BUBBLE FORMATION.

3.4.3 Thermal Protection

A variety of diving suits are available, from standard foam neoprene wet suits and dry suits to specially heated suits.

NOTE
A wet suit does not stop heat loss, it merely slows it.

Diving in water temperature below 50°F usually requires a dry suit, which provides insulation by maintaining a dry air space between the suit and the diver's skin.

However, if flooded, the suit loses its insulating value and can become a severe thermal hazard. Protective suits create an interesting complication. The body's defense is reduced by the thermal barrier of the clothing. This complication, long known, is only just being recognized as an important contributor to designing protective systems.

Body fat, ability to generate heat, ability to constrict blood vessels in the limbs to shunt and save heat for the core, physical conditioning, and regular cold exposure are important contributors to cold tolerance and protection.

There is evidence that vasoconstriction, a heat-preservation response, may be highly efficient in women. During vasoconstriction, blood vessels in the shell narrow and restrict cutaneous blood flow, thereby decreasing convective heat transfer from core to skin and subsequent loss to the environment and shunt the warm blood to the vital organs.

Vasoconstriction, however, is only one of many factors involved in thermal stress. Each diver will respond to the cold water environment based on his own specific physiological makeup, level of training and conditioning, and the environmental factors in that particular situation.

Prevention of Hypothermia:
- Check air and water temperature conditions before the dive.
- Wear adequate thermal protection for the dive.
- After a dive, get out of wet clothes.
- Move to a warm, protected area.
- Dry your hair.
- Wear a hat.
- Drink warm liquids in between dives.
- When considering adequate thermal protection, factor in the duration of decompression or safety stops.
- Be adequately nourished, stay well hydrated, and avoid alcohol and caffeine.
- Repetitive dives should not be made until diver is completely rewarmed.
- For maximum cold water performance, divers should swim in cold water on a regular basis to improve cold tolerance.

3.4.4 Thermal Stress Irrespective of Ambient Temperature

Hypothermia is not a problem only in frigid environments and can occur irrespective of ambient temperature. Similarly, divers may also suffer extremes of hot and cold thermal stress simultaneously during the same dive. There have been documented cases of severe heat exhaustion in Arctic waters by commercial divers as a result of wearing thick, occlusive dry suits, aggravated by dehydration from breathing dry compressed gas and perspiring from prolonged underwater swimming or heavy underwater work. Perspiration from excessive or from predive overheating can also cause the diver's dry suit underwear to lose insulation, thus predisposing him to hypothermia.

Warm Water Hypothermia. Divers also have to be wary of hypothermia in warm environments. A phenomenon called "warm water hypothermia" can occur even in the tropics, especially during long dives and repetitive dives made without adequate rewarming between dives. In warm water hypothermia, long slow cooling can take place in water temperatures as warm as 82°–91°F (27–33C). Although warm water hypothermia is not as easily recognized as its cold water counterpart, it definitely warrants attention. The physiological mechanisms of warm water hypothermia have been demonstrated in various medical studies, but they still are not clearly understood. The victim in this situation may not shiver, because the drop in core temperature may not be rapid enough to activate the body's thermoregulator defense mechanism. There may be a discrepancy between the input of the receptors in the body's shell and core, making the diver's skin feel warm while his core is cooling. Warm water hypothermia can cause confusion, fatigue, apathy, incoordination, delayed reaction time, and sudden anxiety. These mental and physical disabilities, especially when concurrent with any problems during the dive itself, can result in panic, embolization, and drowning.

3.4.5 Survival in Cold Water

When diving, wear thermal protection appropriate for the water temperature. Although exercise increases heat transfer to the water, it is not always the case that the only outcome of swimming or other movement is net heat loss. Heavy exercise can generate enough heat to match heat loss in cold water. Because it is more common to chill in very cold water even with exercise, the common recommendation is to remain still, not swim in very cold water.

If ship abandonment is necessary, specific procedures increase chance of survival. Ship sinkings, even in worst cases, usually require, at minimum, 15 to 30 minutes, affording valuable preparation time. Being prepared and practiced makes best use of this time:

- Don a personal flotation device immediately.
- Wear several layers of clothing because the trapped air provides insulation. Even in the water, extra layers of clothing reduce the rate of body heat loss.
- Board a lifeboat or raft as soon as possible to avoid wetting insulating clothing and losing body heat.
- If it is necessary to enter the water, enter slowly to minimize likelihood of increasing breathing rate, swallowing water, wetting the face and head, shock, and death.
- Once in the water, orient to lifeboats, floating objects, etc. Button up, turn on signal lights immediately, before manual dexterity is lost.
- Keep head and neck out of the water. Protect head, neck, groin, and the sides of the chest—these are areas of rapid heat loss.
- In extremely cold water, do not attempt to swim except to a nearby craft, fellow survivor, or floating object.

- To conserve body heat, hold knees against chest, arms around the side of chest. This is called the Heat Escape Lessening Position (HELP). If others are nearby, huddle together and maintain maximum body contact.
- Keep a positive attitude. Will to live makes a difference.

3.4.6 Overheating and Hyperthermia

The body's adaptation to overheating involves complex integrations between the circulatory, neurologic, endocrine, and exocrine functions. As it does in response to cold stress, when exposed to ambient heat, the body's core temperature is regulated by the control center in the hypothalamus, which reacts to changes in the temperature of the circulating blood and to impulses from thermal receptors in the body's shell. Whenever core temperature rises above normal, the heat-promoting center in the hypothalamus is inhibited.Concurrently, the heat-loss center in the brain is stimulated, resulting in vasodilation. Through vasodilation, heat is dissipated from the shell through conduction, convection, and radiation. If the external environment is so hot or the body is so overheated that heat cannot be lost by conduction, the sudorific (sweating) mechanism is activated, allowing heat to escape as the sweat evaporates. At high ambient temperatures and during exercise, sweating provides the major physiologic defense against overheating. As sweating causes the body to lose fluid and electrolytes, hormonal adjustments begin. Vasopressin or antidiuretic hormone is released by the pituitary gland and the hormone aldosterone, which helps conserve sodium, is released from the adrenal cortex.

As core temperature continues to rise beyond the homeostatic range (100°F/37.8C), the body's natural heat loss processes become ineffective, the hypothalamus is depressed, biochemical reactions are impaired, and proteins begin to degrade. At 106°F (41C), most people go into convulsions. The outside limit for human life is 108°F (43C).

3.4.7 Types of Heat Stress

Heat syncope is the sudden loss of consciousness due to heat. It is usually experienced by individuals undergoing prolonged exposure to a hot environment to which they are not acclimatized, or by individuals who have been moving about in extreme heat while dressed in heavy garments (i.e., tenders on long duty, fully dressed scuba divers).

Heat cramps are a mild response to heat stress, and are manifested by muscle cramps. Cramping usually occurs in the legs, arms, or abdomen, and may occur several hours after exercise. If unaccompanied by serious complications, heat cramps are best treated by rest, oral fluids, cooling down, ice, and stretching and massaging the muscles. For severe cramping, electrolyte replacement drinks or salt tablets may be indicated.

Heat exhaustion is a serious problem in which hypovolemia (low blood volume) develops as a result of fluid loss. Heat exhaustion often develops in unacclimatized people and is evidenced by profuse sweating, nausea, vomiting, a weak and rapid pulse, ataxia, low blood pressure, headache, dizziness, altered mental state, and general weakness, and may require medical attention. Victims of severe heat exhaustion should be given IV fluids, cooled aggressively (e.g. with an ice bath), and possibly transported to an emergency medical facility.

Heat stroke, the most serious and complex heat disorder, is a serious, life-threatening medical emergency. When hyperthermia has progressed to heat stroke, the body's thermoregulatory mechanism, or capacity to cool itself by sweating, has failed and core temperatures can soar to above 105°F, leading to convulsions, delirium, and coma. The skin becomes hot and dry. As the temperature spirals upward, permanent brain damage may occur. If left untreated, heat stroke can result in death due to circulatory collapse and damage to the central nervous system. Victims of heat stroke must be stabilized, removed from the hot environment immediately, cooled aggressively, put in the shock position (legs slightly elevated), given IV fluid replacement, and be transported to an emergency medical facility.

Unlike chilling, overheating rarely results from immersion in water. However, if water temperature is high, around 86°F (29.4C), there is little or no difference between the skin and water temperature; heat has no gradient to transfer to the water. Any exercise under such conditions can end in overheating. Even in cooler water, heavy exercise can generate more heat than is lost, and the diver can become warm. However, hyperthermia under water has only recently been a subject of attention, and primarily by military and commercial dive operations that put divers in waters near the Equator, the Persian Gulf, etc., or in hazardous warm environments (nuclear reactor coolant pools) that require dry suits for protection.

To reduce the risk of overheating, drink water and juices liberally. Drink before thirsty. Avoid alcohol, coffee, and other fluids which act as diuretics. Avoid drugs that increase susceptibility to overheating. To acclimate to the climatic conditions, gradually and regularly increase heat exposure. Get into good physical condition—it will greatly extend heat tolerance.

The prevention of hyperthermia in these specialized dive situations involves a number of strategies, including heat acclimatization, specialized equipment (i.e. suit-undersuit or SUS), ice vests, pre-cooling, etc. Other suggestions to add to those for preventing hyperthermia are:

- Dive buddy teams should suit up in sync, particularly on a hot day, to minimize time spent above the water enclosed in a dry suit or wet suit. If divers

- cannot suit up together, the first buddy to get dressed should wait in the water and cool off.
- Wear a hat or visor, and use a high SPF broad-spectrum sunscreen before and after diving.
- Ingest salt only if needed. Individuals who tend to sweat copiously can use salt with meals, but should avoid salt tablets, which can cause excessive body salt levels.

Protective dress required for diving in contaminated water can lead to overheating and/or hypothermia in warm water situations (see Chapter 13, Polluted-Water Diving).

3.5 DRUGS AND DIVING

The use of prescription and over-the-counter medications while diving is a complex issue. Drug interaction is an enormous topic; it is difficult to know all the variables, all the possible drugs, and effects or changes caused by diving. Individual variability, existing medical and physical conditions, and the mental and physical requirements of the specific dive are additional variables.

3.5.1 Prescription Drugs

The hyperbaric environment of diving may change how some drugs act in the body. Specific concerns include:

- How the body absorbs, metabolizes, and excretes the drug.
- Possible physical effects of the type of breathing gas, increased density of the gases, water temperature, and other environmental factors.
- Side effects; on the surface, side effects, like drowsiness from antihistamines, may be acceptable. Under water, as with the operation of machinery on land, any impairment of cognitive function, neuromuscular strength, coordination, or integration of thought and action may lead to accidents.

There are several commonly used drugs that may affect diver safety, performance, and the diver's ability to thermoregulate. These drugs include beta blockers, motion sickness remedies, antihistamines, amphetamines, tranquilizers, sedatives, hypertensive drugs, and decongestants. Before diving, consult with your physician and ask the following questions:

- What is the underlying condition/illness/disease? Is it relative or absolute contraindication to diving?
- What is the half-life of the drug, and how long before or after use would it be prudent to avoid a high-pressure environment?
- What are any side effects that might increase risk of diving?
- Does the drug interfere with physical performance or exercise tolerance?
- Does the drug interfere with consciousness or cause alteration in decision-making ability?
- Does the drug produce rebound phenomena?

Divers and their physicians have an obligation to communicate with each other. The clinician has the responsibility to explain the nature of treatment to the diver, and the diver has the responsibility to inform the physician that diving exposure is anticipated, and what other drugs they may be taking.

3.5.2 Smoking

Cigarette smoke contains poisons in gas and particulate form, including hydrogen cyanide, nitrogen oxides, and carbon monoxide. Smoking directly affects the respiratory and cardiovascular systems; it creates toxic effects throughout the body ranging from bone-cell destruction to cancerous changes. Additionally, smoking is addictive.

In the respiratory system, poisons deposit on the mucous lining of the airways and lungs. Over time, they irritate the air spaces, scar the lungs, and damage the cilia (thousands of microscopic hairs lining the airways). Cilia normally move mucus, and the pollutants that accumulate in the mucus, out of the lungs to the throat. The mucus is usually swallowed or blown out the nose. Smoking paralyzes the cilia; pollutants stay in the lungs, increasing the smoker's risk of bronchitis, influenza, and other respiratory infections. The accumulation of secretions can make equalizing ear and sinus pressure difficult. Smoking eventually produces structural weakness in the lung, such as irreversibly enlarged and useless alveoli, leading to a lung disease called emphysema.

Smoking affects the cardiovascular system, accelerating atherosclerotic changes in blood vessels, damaging heart tissue, and limiting the oxygen-carrying ability of red blood cells. Inhaled nicotine and carbon monoxide increase stickiness of blood platelets, causing clumping that can block blood flow in the small vessels. It is speculated that increased clumping increases susceptibility to decompression sickness. Cigarette smoke is directly toxic to bone cells and the discs in the back, increasing risk of back pain and disc degeneration.

The dose of carbon monoxide a smoker receives from smoking is toxic; it causes fatigue, headache, irritability, dizziness, and disturbed sleep, as well as changes in neurologic reflexes, psychomotor test results, sensory discrimination, and electrocardiograms. Carbon monoxide concentration inhaled from smoking one cigarette averages 400 to 500 ppm, producing up to ten percent carboxyhemoglobin (HbCO) (see Table 3.9). The level in non-smokers is generally 0.5 percent.

The HbCO level in the blood of divers who smoke is higher than it would be if they were exposed to 20 ppm carbon monoxide for 12 hours (maximum carbon monoxide level allowed in divers' breathing air by NOAA).

A heavy smoker takes approximately eight hours to eliminate 75 percent of the carbon monoxide inhaled.

TABLE 3.9
**Carboxyhemoglobin
as a Function of Smoking**

Smoking Habits	Median HbCO Level, %	Expired CO, ppm
Light smoker (less than 1/2 pack/day)	3.8	17.1
Moderate smoker (more than 1/2 pack/day and less than 2 packs/day)	5.9	27.5
Heavy smoker (2 packs or more/day)	6.9	32.4

The HbCO level, even for a light smoker diving eight hours after the last cigarette (0.95%), is almost twice that of a non-smoker (0.50%). The carboxyhemoglobin level of a person who does not smoke, but is exposed to the smoke of others (passive smoke), can rise to five percent after exposure.

Epidemiologists have discovered that smoking is implicated not only in fatal lung disorders and coronary artery disease, but also in strokes, bladder cancer, cervical cancer, hearing deficits, and is a serious risk factor during pregnancy.

Each cubic centimeter of tobacco smoke contains over five million particles, including chemicals which are so dangerous that they are on the Environmental Protection Agency's list of substances which are illegal to dispose of in the environment. According to the American Lung Association, "cigarette smoke in its gaseous and particulate phases contains 4,700 compounds, including 43 known carcinogens, which can damage tissues and cause disease."

For divers, the respiratory deficits caused by smoking can be especially dangerous if the diving activities involve deep exposures which create breathing resistance, thermal stress, swimming against strong currents or a number of factors which necessitate optimal aerobic capacity and increased supply of oxygen. Intuitively, it seems likely that carboxyhemoglobin may not be able to carry as much CO_2 as normal hemoglobin does. If so, carbon dioxide toxicity and decompression sickness (CO_2 is believed to be a predisposing factor to DCS) cannot be ruled out. There is yet another hazard associated with carbon monoxide, one which pathologists do not yet fully understand. Long term exposure to CO results in the CO binding to the cellular enzyme cytochrome oxidase, an enzyme necessary for the transfer of oxygen from the blood to the inside of the cells.

Even a moderate smoker will have about six to eight percent of his hemoglobin tied up with carbon monoxide, and therefore will have the oxygen-carrying capacity of the blood reduced by that amount. Carbon monoxide has a 220 to 290-fold greater affinity for hemoglobin than oxygen does, and therefore readily combines with this vital component of the blood to produce carboxyhemoglobin. For every molecule of carbon monoxide in the blood, the blood can carry one less molecule of oxygen. For heavy chronic smokers, the oxygen-carrying capacity of blood can be reduced by as much as ten percent. Anyone with a history of unconsciousness, or anyone exhibiting confusion or other neurological signs, no matter how good they look upon admission, must be treated with hyperbaric oxygen (Kindwall 1999).

3.5.3 Illicit Drugs and Alcohol

Psychoactive agents impair cognitive and motor performance, the very basis of their use.

Alcohol, barbiturates, and marijuana are commonly abused nervous system depressants. Depressed motor function is hazardous under water. Risk of cold injury and nitrogen narcosis increases, and, as blood glucose falls, which is another side effect of these drugs, weakness and confusion increase. Because of its diuretic action, alcohol can contribute to dehydration, particularly in the tropics. Drugs take time to leave the system, meaning their hazards may persist even days after taking them.

Cocaine and the many other commonly abused central nervous system stimulants render a diver incapable of responding properly to life-threatening emergencies. These drugs are often combined with alcohol or marijuana, thus compounding problems. Cocaine increases the likelihood of an oxygen toxicity seizure; it can trigger abnormal heart beats, sudden heart attack, even in a young person, and heart illness.

Other Important Facts About Alcohol. Alcohol interferes with the body's ability to replenish the energy the body needs after diving, and it causes a dramatic drop in blood-glucose level, leading to hypoglycemia which can cause weakness, confusion, irritability, interference with temperature maintenance, and fainting. According to the American College of Sports Medicine, because alcohol is a depressant of the central nervous system, even a small amount can disrupt a wide variety of psychomotor skills, reaction time, hand-eye coordination, alertness, accuracy, balance, and complex coordination. Because of these detriments, alcohol is banned by various federations within the International Olympic Committee. Diving under these circumstances can be even more hazardous.

Alcohol by itself causes acutely diminished mental and physical faculties; alcohol consumption combined with breathing compressed gas may accelerate and multiply the effects of nitrogen narcosis.

Alcohol can enhance exercise fatigue by increasing lactic acid production, which will make even non-stressful swimming and diving much more difficult.

Diving Physiology

The decreased strength, power, local muscular, and overall cardiovascular endurance caused by alcohol may become life-threatening detriments in an emergency diving situation. For a diver who drinks and dives, an unexpected problem (i.e., having to swim a great distance on the surface, struggling against a strong current, rescuing another diver, etc.) may intensify into a diving accident or fatality.

Alcohol is considered a factor in many drownings and diving accidents. In analysis of large numbers of drownings in the U.S. and Australia, about 80 percent of the adult victims had elevated blood alcohol levels (BAL). According to DAN Accident Report data, approximately one-third of the reported diving accident victims had consumed alcohol within 12 hours before or after diving. Tests have also shown that some individuals still have a BAL above the legal limit for driving 24 hours after their last drink (Plueckhahn 1984). There are some divers, therefore, who ideally should refrain from drinking alcohol 24 hours before and after a dive.

It's important to drink a lot of fluids before and after diving, but those fluids should be water and fruit juices, not alcoholic beverages. Alcohol is a diuretic, i.e., a substance that causes greater loss of fluids than it contains. Not only fluid, but essential minerals and electrolytes are lost through diuresis (urination). Alcohol inhibits the brain hormone ADH (Antidiuretic Hormone), creating a vicious cycle whereby the more alcohol a person drinks, the more he urinates, which leads to further dehydration. When the brain becomes dehydrated, the individual experiences dizziness, headache, and a "hangover" feeling.

For divers, dehydration resulting from alcohol consumption poses a number of problems. Dehydration creates hypovolemia (thicker blood volume), resulting in slower off-gassing of nitrogen. This makes alcohol a major risk factor in decompression sickness, particularly bends with serious neurological deficits. According to DAN, there appears to be a relationship between an increased number of drinks and the severity of decompression illness. In a study on alcohol and bends, it was reported that alcohol can reduce the surface tension, a force which limits bubble growth, and therefore may encourage bubble formation (Edmonds, Lowry, and Pennefather 1992). Additionally, the vasodilation of capillaries caused by alcohol may allow nitrogen to escape too rapidly, increasing chances of decompression sickness (DCS) even more.

Alcohol also predisposes a diver to thermal stress. As alcohol dilates the peripheral blood vessels, circulation is diverted to the skin and heat escapes. In cold climates, this impairment in thermoregulation may deteriorate into a life-threatening state of hypothermia.

One of the first signs of hypothermia is shivering, which concurrently promotes a faster rate of nitrogen elimination. In hot environments, alcohol can increase sweating, which leads to further dehydration, and precipitates hyperthermia, a state of elevated body core temperature, which can progress to heat stroke.

Air Diving and Decompression

4

Air Diving and Decompression

4.0 GENERAL

As explained in previous sections concerning the physics and physiology of diving, body tissues absorb additional nitrogen from the air breathed during dives and release this excess nitrogen during ascent. After surfacing, body tissue continues to release excess nitrogen until the level of nitrogen dissolved in the tissue returns to normal.

By keeping the amount of nitrogen being absorbed and released within acceptable limits, the risk of a serious diving malady known as decompression sickness, or DCS, is reduced. Divers have many tools at their disposal to help plan and make dives in which the risk of DCS remains within acceptable levels. These tools include dive tables and dive computers.

Even when divers use computers as their primary dive planning tool, it is important to have a working knowledge of dive tables. Dive tables can provide an important back-up in case of computer failure or operator error. They can even help divers pre-plan a series of two or more dives—which is something that is generally beyond the capabilities of dive computers.

There is a wide variety of dive tables available, including versions by the U.S. Navy, other foreign governments, and recreational training organizations. For military and selected scientific and commercial divers in the United States, the standard dive tables are those appearing in the *U.S. Navy Diving Manual*. A complete set of the U.S. Navy Dive Tables can be found in Appendix IV.

This section of the *NOAA Diving Manual* is devoted to the proper use of U.S. Navy Dive Tables for relatively shallow, scientific and research diving. A working knowledge of U.S. Navy dive table usage will also make it easier to understand and use other dive tables as well.

4.1 DECOMPRESSION TABLE DEVELOPMENT

4.1.1 Table Computation Prediction

The most common method used for predicting if a profile (of pressure and gas as functions of time) will cause DCS dates back to around the turn of the century, when physiologist J.S. Haldane developed a hypothetical method for tracking gas in the body and showed how to develop decompression profiles or "tables." At the outset, it is important to realize that this "model" proposed by Haldane, and later modified by others, is hypothetical. It is not what really happens in the body, nor was it intended to be; but, it does afford a method of moving from yesterday's dive experience to tomorrow's new decompression tables. This was the first such model; many others have followed, and many are offshoots of the Haldane method. A well-developed computational method similar to Haldane's was published by the late Swiss cardiologist, Prof. A.A. Bühlmann, and it has been widely used by others.

At today's state of knowledge, the only sound criterion for the preparation of useful decompression tables is empirical experience. As models improve, prediction capability will continue to improve, but the judgment as to whether a model is right is how well it actually works, not how sophisticated the math may be.

4.1.2 Computing Decompression Tables

Experience has shown that certain profiles, and presumably the hypothetical gas loadings produced by such profiles, have or have not produced DCS. With enough experience (data) it is possible to assign limits to various ascents from depth. With these tools, table developers calculate suitably slow ascent rates for a variety of exposure profiles; the results of these calculations are decompression tables.

The limits just mentioned are in terms of the gas loading that can be tolerated in each compartment at each depth during ascent. Ascent limits are normally considered in 10 fsw or 3 msw increments, and are known as "M-values" (where M stands for "maximum"), the maximum permitted gas loading at that depth in that compartment. To calculate a decompression table, the developer needs a set of M-values, usually determined from experience. The calculated gas loadings in each compartment are compared with the M-values, and ascent is adjusted to keep the loadings below the limits. The diver's ascent is halted, with "stops" at specified depths, to wait until the hypothetical gas loadings have "decayed" to below the limits for that depth; the diver then ascends to the next stop and the process is repeated.

The J.S. Haldane decompression model goes back nearly a century, but by using it with continuously updated experience, it can be used to produce reliable decompression tables. It is not quite correct to consider this a 'theory" of how the human body works. Rather, it is a computational tool that allows prediction of tomorrow's dive from yesterday's experience. The A.A. Bühlmann model uses the same equations for on-gassing, but calculates the ascent limits in a different way; it, too, is firmly based on experience.

4.1.3 Reliability of Tables

Virtually any exposure to pressure imposes an obligation for decompression, and even when it is done correctly it will create some probability of symptoms of a decompression disorder. For this reason, it is preferable not to use the word "safe" to describe a decompression procedure. In the sense that "safe" means "an acceptable level of risk" the word may be applicable, but too many people perceive that as meaning no risk at all, which is not the case. Satisfactory decompression tables can be referred to as being "reliable." The NOAA and U.S. Navy Dive Tables in this manual are considered reliable.

The limits of a decompression procedure do not represent a hard line between developing or not developing decompression sickness symptoms, but rather a fuzzy boundary of "acceptable risk." Accordingly, one should always consider DCS as a possibility. Be prepared for it psychologically and have a plan for dealing with it.

There is a wide variation in the physical makeup of divers, and part of this variation is in susceptibility to decompression disorders. There are differences among individuals, and in one person at different times. There are also environmental effects. Immersion, exercise, and warmth increase gas uptake and elimination; cold and dehydration reduce them. Depending on where in the dive these conditions occur, they may be either beneficial or detrimental to the decompression.

Because of the variations, a given schedule is not "safe" or "unsafe;" rather, DCS has a certain probability of occurring, therefore, decompression data is analyzed statistically. The U.S. Navy and other decompression researchers have developed means of analyzing past dives using statistics, one form of which is called "maximum likelihood." With it, the probability of DCS can be predicted from a given profile by comparing it with a collection of past dives of the same general type.

4.1.4 Dive Planning Software

In recent years there has been a remarkable development in the field of decompression technology; the development and marketing of commercially available computer programs for generating decompression tables. For decades it has been felt that only decompression specialists were qualified to produce decompression tables, and that all tables needed extensive testing before operational use.

Several entrepreneurs have prepared and distributed computer programs that can be used to generate decompression tables. This has been possible because of publications by Prof. Bühlmann that outline tested and accepted algorithms for computing tables. Most programs available are based, at least fundamentally, on Prof. Bühlmann's algorithms.

The different programs manage the algorithm in different ways, especially with regard to introducing extra conservatism into the computations. These differences make it difficult to compare programs and to really understand the affects of the conservatism. As with dive computers, many of these programs allow oxygen exposure to be tracked and signals the user when limits are exceeded. It is up to the user to know the meaning of the oxygen calculations and the limits used.

The warning remains, however; producing proper decompression tables in a safe manner requires a substantial knowledge of decompression practice. The user should have a firm idea of what to expect, and should be able to recognize if things are not right. The NOAA Diving Program has used one or more of these computer programs to produce custom decompression tables required for special diving operations beyond the scope of the U.S. Navy Dive Tables.

4.2 USING THE U.S. NAVY DIVE TABLES TO MAKE SINGLE DIVES

The simplest and easiest application of the information the U.S. Navy Dive Tables provide comes when you make what are known as single dives.

4.2.1 Single Versus Repetitive Dives

Dives will be either single or repetitive dives:

- A single dive is any dive made more than 12 hours following a previous dive.
- A repetitive dive is any dive made less than 12 hours after surfacing from a prior dive.

Why this distinction? Normally, body tissue is saturated with nitrogen at a partial pressure equal to that of the nitrogen found in atmospheric air. During a dive, body tissues absorb additional nitrogen from the air breathed under pressure.

As Figure 4.1 shows, after surfacing from a dive, some of this excess nitrogen will remain in body tissues for a period of time. The amount of excess nitrogen present will vary, depending on factors such as the depth and duration of the dive.

During time spent on the surface between dives, the amount of excess nitrogen present in tissue will decrease. As Figure 4.2 shows, no matter how much excess nitrogen

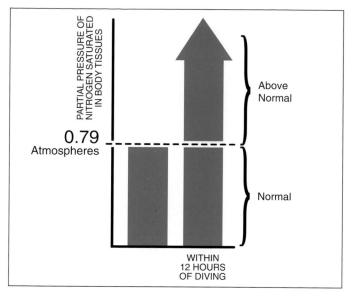

FIGURE 4.1
Excess Nitrogen Following Dive

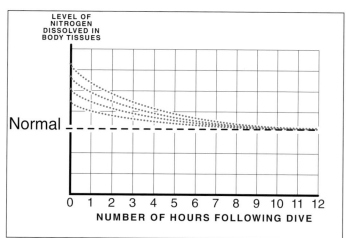

FIGURE 4.2
Nitrogen Off-Gases in Approximately 12 Hours

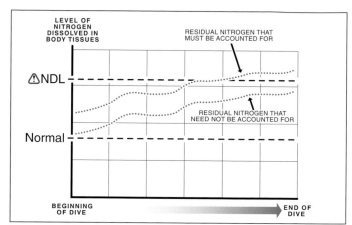

FIGURE 4.3
Risk of Exceeding U.S. Navy No-Decompression Limits

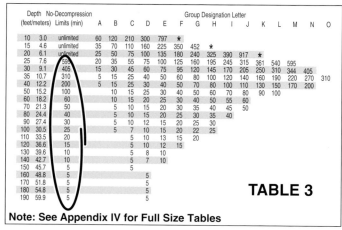

Note: See Appendix IV for Full Size Tables

TABLE 3

FIGURE 4.4
U.S. Navy No-Decompression Limits

is present following a dive, the vast majority of this nitrogen will off-gas within 12 hours of surfacing.

What this means is that, if a dive is made more than 12 hours after surfacing from a previous one, there is no need to worry about residual excess nitrogen. If, on the other hand, a dive is made less than 12 hours after surfacing from a previous dive, the body must account for the excess nitrogen remaining in tissue. If this is not done, as Figure 4.3 shows, there is the risk of exceeding the U.S. Navy Dive Tables' No-Decompression Limits (NDLs).

In summary:

- On single no-decompression dives, it is assumed that any excess nitrogen remaining in body tissues following the dive is not significant.

- On repetitive dives, it is assumed that the excess or residual nitrogen remaining in body tissues following previous dives is significant and must be accounted for to determine if decompression is required.

4.2.2 Planning Single Dives

Planning single dives is comparatively easy. Simply make certain that the Actual Bottom Time (ABT) of the dive remains well within the U.S. Navy's No-Decompression Limits.

As Figure 4.4 shows, the No-Decompression Limits are listed in the third column of Table 3 of the U.S. Navy Dive Tables.

To use the No-Decompression Limits, the diver must understand the U.S. Navy table definitions for (Actual) Bottom Time and Depth, as well as the term "dive schedule."

Air Diving and Decompression

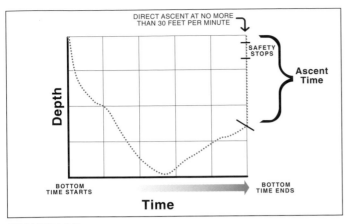

FIGURE 4.5
Actual Bottom Time (ABT)

In summary:

- As Figure 4.5 shows, Actual Bottom Time starts when the diver leaves the surface and ends when the diver begins a direct, uninterrupted ascent to the surface at a rate of no more than 30 feet per minute. (Note: The U.S. Navy Dive Tables allow for momentary variations in ascent rate of plus or minus 10 feet per minute.)
- Depth is defined as the maximum depth reached during any point during the dive—even if divers remain at this depth only momentarily.
- The term "dive schedule" refers to the combination of Actual Bottom Time and Depth, as they appear on the U.S. Navy Dive Tables.

Depths on the U.S. Navy Dive Tables appear in ten-foot/3.1-meter increments. It is unusual for divers to reach a maximum depth that is a precise multiple of ten feet. Therefore, round the actual depth to the next *greater* depth increment (making a 63-fsw dive a 70-fsw dive, as far as the U.S. Navy Dive Tables are concerned). When using the U.S. Navy Dive Tables, consistently round depth and time values in the more conservative direction, going to the next deeper depth or next greater time. Doing so increases the margin of safety.

Example 1:

Here is an example that better illustrates how to find the applicable U.S. Navy No-Decompression Limits for a particular dive:

Dive team #1 is engaged in a water-sampling study. Their task is to replace the charcoal trap at a sampling station on the bottom of a lake once every day. The sampling station is at an equivalent saltwater depth of 93 feet. It takes a maximum of 15 minutes for the divers to descend, locate the sampling station, collect the old trap and replace it with a new one, then begin their ascent.

Can they make this dive while remaining within the No-Decompression Limits?

To find the answer:

- Insofar as 93 fsw is a depth value that does not appear on Table 3, the divers must round this number to the next greater depth and consider the maximum depth of their dive to be 100 fsw.
- As Figure 4.6 shows, by consulting Table 3, the divers discover that the NDL for 100 fsw is 25 minutes.

Thus, it appears that, so long as they do not exceed a dive schedule of 100 fsw for 25 minutes, the divers can make this single dive each day, throughout the project, while remaining well within the U.S. Navy Dive Table No-Decompression Limits.

Practice Problem 1:

This is a practice problem that will illustrate how to find the applicable single-dive No-Decompression Limits on the U.S. Navy Dive Tables:

Depth (feet/meters)		No-Decompression Limits (min)
10	3.0	unlimited
15	4.6	unlimited
20	6.1	unlimited
25	7.6	595
30	9.1	405
35	10.7	310
40	12.2	200
50	15.2	100
60	18.2	60
70	21.3	50
80	24.4	40
90	27.4	
100	30.5	25
	33.5	
120	36.6	15
130	39.6	10
140	42.7	10
150	45.7	5
160	48.8	5
170	51.8	5
180	54.8	5
190	59.9	5

PART OF TABLE 3

FIGURE 4.6
No-Decompression Limit (NDL) for 100 fsw/30.5 msw

Depth (feet/meters)		No-Decompression Limits (min)
10	3.0	unlimited
15	4.6	unlimited
20	6.1	unlimited
25	7.6	595
30	9.1	405
35	10.7	310
40	12.2	200
50	15.2	?
60	18.2	60
70	21.3	50
80	24.4	40
90	27.4	30
100	30.5	25
110	33.5	20
120	36.6	15
130	39.6	10
140	42.7	10
150	45.7	5
160	48.8	5
170	51.8	5
180	54.8	5
190	59.9	5

PART OF TABLE 3

FIGURE 4.7
Answer to Practice Problem 1

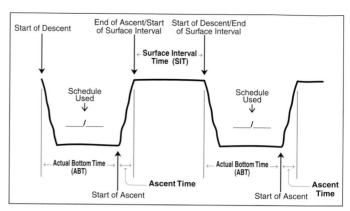

FIGURE 4.8
Diagram of Repetitive Dive Data

Your dive team must recover a sampling device located in a bay whose depth, at high tide, does not exceed 53 fsw. At this depth, how long do you have to search for and recover this device, without exceeding the U.S. Navy No-Decompression Limits?

For exposures of 51 to 60 fsw, the U.S. Navy No-Decompression limit is 60 minutes (see Figure 4.7).

4.3 USING THE U.S. NAVY DIVE TABLES TO MAKE REPETITIVE DIVES

Using the U.S. Navy Dive Tables to plan and make repetitive dives is a somewhat more complex process than for single dives. Nevertheless, with practice, you will find that this process is both easy to understand and easy to follow. To do so, you will need two things:

First, because this process involves more steps and more data than most divers can easily commit to memory, you will need a simple, written means of recording information pertaining to the dives you plan and make.

Second, you will need dive table information that accounts for the residual nitrogen present in your body from previous dives, and how that nitrogen will impact subsequent dives.

4.3.1 Recording Repetitive Dive Data

Divers have at their disposal a number of worksheets, logs, and other tools for planning and recording repetitive dive data. Among the simplest and most frequently used means of doing so is a simple, hand-drawn diagram, similar to the one appearing in Figure 4.8.

This particular approach to recording repetitive dive data has several advantages, including:

- All that is needed to create such a diagram is a pen or pencil, and a piece of paper.
- The design is highly intuitive, providing a visual representation of elements such as descents, bottom times, ascents and surface intervals—one that divers have little difficulty understanding.

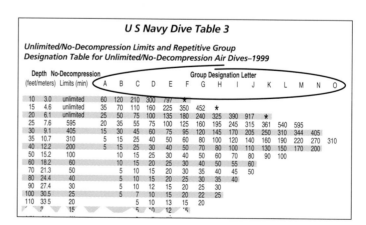

FIGURE 4.9
Repetitive Group Designation Letters

TABLE 4

Locate the diver's repetitive group designation from his previous dive along the diagonal line above the table. Read horizontally to the interval in which the diver's surface interval lies.

Next read vertically downward to the new repetitive group designation. Continue downward in this same column to the row which represents the depth of the repetitive dive. The time given at the intersection is residual nitrogen time, in minutes, to be applied to the repetitive dive.

* Dives following surface intervals of more than 12 hours are not repetitive dives. Use actual bottom times in the Standard Air Decompression Tables to compute decompression for such dives.

** If no Residual Nitrogen Time is given, then the repetitive group does not change.

Repetitive group at the beginning of the surface interval

Group	Surface interval ranges
A	0:10 / 12:00*
B	0:10 3:21 / 3:20 12:00*
C	0:10 1:40 4:50 / 1:39 4:49 12:00*
D	0:10 1:10 2:39 5:49 / 1:09 2:38 5:48 12:00*
E	0:10 0:55 1:58 3:25 6:35 / 0:54 1:57 3:24 6:34 12:00*
F	0:10 0:46 1:30 2:29 3:58 7:06 / 0:45 1:29 2:28 3:57 7:05 12:00*
G	0:10 0:41 1:16 2:00 2:59 4:26 7:36 / 0:40 1:15 1:59 2:58 4:25 7:35 12:00*
H	0:10 0:37 1:07 1:42 2:24 3:21 4:50 8:00 / 0:36 1:06 1:41 2:23 3:20 4:49 7:59 12:00*
I	0:10 0:34 1:00 1:30 2:03 2:45 3:44 5:13 8:22 / 0:33 0:59 1:29 2:02 2:44 3:43 5:12 8:21 12:00*
J	0:10 0:32 0:55 1:20 1:48 2:21 3:05 4:03 5:41 8:51 / 0:31 0:54 1:19 1:47 2:20 3:04 4:02 5:40 8:50 12:00*
K	0:10 0:29 0:50 1:12 1:36 2:04 2:39 3:22 4:20 5:49 8:59 / 0:28 0:49 1:11 1:35 2:03 2:38 3:21 4:19 5:48 8:58 12:00*
L	0:10 0:27 0:46 1:05 1:26 1:50 2:20 2:54 3:37 4:36 6:03 9:13 / 0:26 0:45 1:04 1:25 1:49 2:19 2:53 3:36 4:35 6:02 9:12 12:00*
M	0:10 0:26 0:43 1:00 1:19 1:40 2:06 2:35 3:09 3:53 4:50 6:19 9:29 / 0:25 0:42 0:59 1:18 1:39 2:05 2:34 3:08 3:52 4:49 6:18 9:28 12:00*
N	0:10 0:25 0:40 0:55 1:12 1:31 1:54 2:19 2:48 3:23 4:05 5:04 6:33 9:44 / 0:24 0:39 0:54 1:11 1:30 1:53 2:18 2:47 3:22 4:04 5:03 6:32 9:43 12:00*
O	0:10 0:24 0:37 0:52 1:08 1:25 1:44 2:05 2:30 3:00 3:34 4:18 5:17 6:45 9:55 / 0:23 0:36 0:51 1:07 1:24 1:43 2:04 2:29 2:59 3:33 4:17 5:16 6:44 9:54 12:00*
Z	0:10 0:23 0:35 0:49 1:03 1:19 1:37 1:56 2:18 2:43 3:11 3:46 4:30 5:28 6:57 10:06 / 0:22 0:34 0:48 1:02 1:18 1:36 1:55 2:17 2:42 3:10 3:45 4:29 5:27 6:56 10:05 12:00*

NEW GROUP DESIGNATION

Repetitive Dive Depth feet/meters	Z	O	N	M	L	K	J	I	H	G	F	E	D	C	B	A
10 3.0	**	**	**	**	**	**	**	**	**	**	**	797	279	159	88	39
20 6.1	**	**	**	**	**	**	917	399	279	208	159	120	88	62	39	18
30 9.1	**	**	469	349	279	229	190	159	132	109	88	70	54	39	25	12
40 12.2	257	241	213	187	161	138	116	101	87	73	61	49	37	25	17	7
50 15.2	169	160	142	124	111	99	87	76	66	56	47	38	29	21	13	6
60 18.2	122	117	107	97	88	79	70	61	52	44	36	30	24	17	11	5
70 21.3	100	96	87	80	72	64	57	50	43	37	31	26	20	15	9	4
80 24.4	84	80	73	68	61	54	48	43	38	32	28	23	18	13	8	4
90 27.4	73	70	64	58	53	47	43	38	33	29	24	20	16	11	7	3
100 30.5	64	62	57	52	48	43	38	34	30	26	22	18	14	10	7	3
110 33.5	57	55	51	47	42	38	34	31	27	24	20	16	13	10	6	3
120 36.6	52	50	46	43	39	35	32	28	25	21	18	15	12	9	6	3
130 39.6	46	44	40	38	35	31	28	25	22	19	16	13	11	8	6	3
140 42.7	42	40	38	35	32	29	26	23	20	18	15	12	10	7	5	2
150 45.7	40	38	35	32	30	27	24	22	19	17	14	12	9	7	5	2
160 48.8	37	36	33	31	28	26	23	20	18	16	13	11	9	6	4	2
170 51.8	35	34	31	29	26	24	22	19	17	15	13	10	8	6	4	2
180 54.8	32	31	29	27	25	22	20	18	16	14	12	10	8	6	4	2
190 59.9	31	30	28	26	24	21	19	17	15	13	11	10	8	6	4	2

FIGURE 4.10
Residual Nitrogen Timetable for Repetitive Air Dives

Throughout the balance of this section, this type of diagram will be used to explain the process of planning and recording repetitive dives.

4.3.2 Accounting for Residual Nitrogen

To account for the residual nitrogen present in the body from previous dives, and how that nitrogen will impact subsequent dives, the U.S. Navy Dive Tables provides two tools:

- Table 3, (see Figure 4.9), provides what are known as Repetitive Group Designations or, more commonly, Repetitive Group Letters. These "letters" represent the overall level of excess or residual nitrogen present in tissue following the end of any no-decompression dive. Higher letters (i.e., closer to the end of the alphabet) represent a greater overall level of residual nitrogen.

- Table 4, shown in Figure 4.10, actually provides a combination of two tables. The upper table depicts how the level of residual nitrogen decreases, the longer the surface interval. The lower table shows how divers must account for this excess nitrogen on subsequent dives.

In the balance of this section, a number of examples and problems are presented that show how to use these

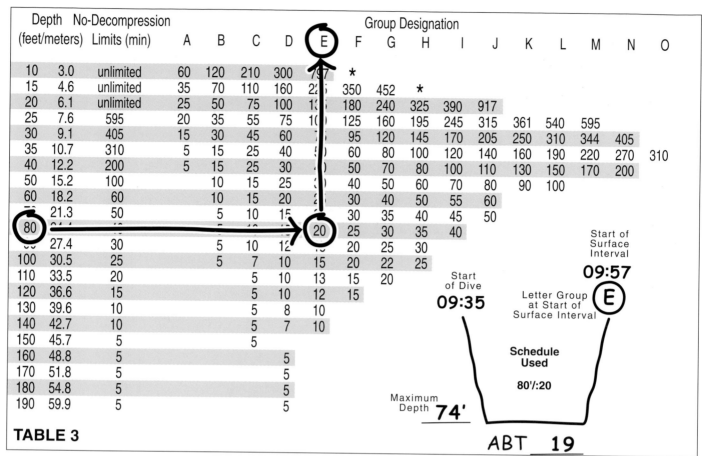

FIGURE 4.11
Calculation of a Repetitive Group Designation

tables to plan and make no-decompression, and repetitive dives.

4.3.3 Finding Repetitive Group Designations Following Single, No-Decompression Dives

If a repetitive dive takes place at least 12 hours following any previous exposures to elevated partial pressures of nitrogen, treat the first dive in any series of repetitive dives as a single dive. As outlined earlier in this chapter, all a diver must do is make sure that their Actual Bottom Time (ABT) for such dives does not exceed the U.S. Navy's No-Decompression Limits.

When such a dive is the first in a series of repetitive dives, the diver must take an additional step. That is, the diver must determine the Repetitive Group Designation (Letter Group) at the end of the dive.

Example 2:

Following is an example that illustrates how to find the applicable Letter Group at the end of a single dive.

Dive team #2 is conducting an aquatic-life census in a quiet, saltwater estuary. During the first dive of the day, they begin their descent at 9:35 am and reach a maximum depth of 74 fsw (23 msw). At 9:54 am they begin their ascent (surfacing at 9:57 am), making the

Actual Bottom Time for this dive 19 minutes. What is their Repetitive Group Designation (Letter Group) at the end of this first dive?

The answer appears in Figure 4.11.

Figure 4.11 reveals:

- Because a depth of 74 fsw does not appear on Table 3, the divers use the next greater depth, which is 80 fsw.
- Because a value of 19 minutes does not appear in the 80-foot row, they use the next greater time, which is 20 minutes.
- Table 3 shows that, for a single dive schedule of 80 fsw for 20 minutes, the Repetitive Group Designation at the beginning of the diver's surface interval is E.

Practice Problem 2:

Following is a problem to illustrate how to find the correct Letter Group following a no-decompression dive.

At 10:13 am, dive team #3 descends to conduct an inspection of their research vessel's running gear. During the course of the inspection, they accidentally drop a dive light. The vessel is at anchor and the hard, sandy bottom is only 47-fsw deep, and the water is relatively clear.

Air Diving and Decompression

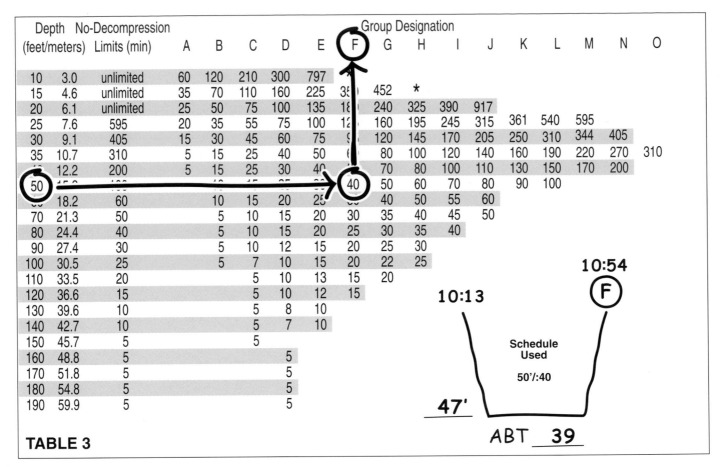

FIGURE 4.12
Answer to Practice Problem 2

Insofar as recovering the light poses little risk, the divers do so. With the light recovered and the inspection complete, they begin their ascent at 10:52 am and surface at 10:54 am. What is the Letter Group at the end of the dive?

The answer appears in Figure 4.12.

Figure 4.12 reveals:
- Because a depth of 47 fsw does not appear on Table 3, the divers use the next greater depth, which is 50 fsw.
- Because a value of 39 minutes does not appear in the 50-foot row, they use the next greater time, which is 40 minutes.
- Moving vertically up from the 40 minute time we find that the Repetitive Group Designation at the end of the dive (beginning of our surface interval) is F.

4.3.4 Determining a Repetitive Group Designation Following a Surface Interval

The longer the diver remains on the surface following a dive, the less residual nitrogen will be present in body tissues at the beginning of subsequent dives. This directly affects how long the diver can remain under water on these repetitive dives, without exceeding the U.S. Navy's No-Decompression Limits.

Example 3:

To determine how much residual nitrogen is present following a Surface Interval (SI) between dives, use the upper portion of Table 4. The best way to explain how to do so is with an example:

Dive team #2 plans to make an afternoon dive to complete the aquatic-life census they started in the morning. The divers had surfaced from the day's first dive at 9:57 am, and determined that, following this dive, their Repetitive Group Designation (Letter Group) was E. They anticipate re-entering the water at approximately 3:00 pm. What will their Letter Group be at the beginning of this next dive?

The answer appears in Figure 4.13.

Figure 4.13 reveals:
- The first step in this process is to determine the length of the Surface Interval. This is also known as Surface Interval Time or SIT (literally, time spent SITting on the surface). In this case, the interval between 9:57 am and 3:00 pm is five hours, three minutes (5:03).
- The next step is to enter Table 4 from the left, starting with the Repetitive Group Designation at the beginning of the Surface Interval, which in this case is E.

NOAA Diving Manual

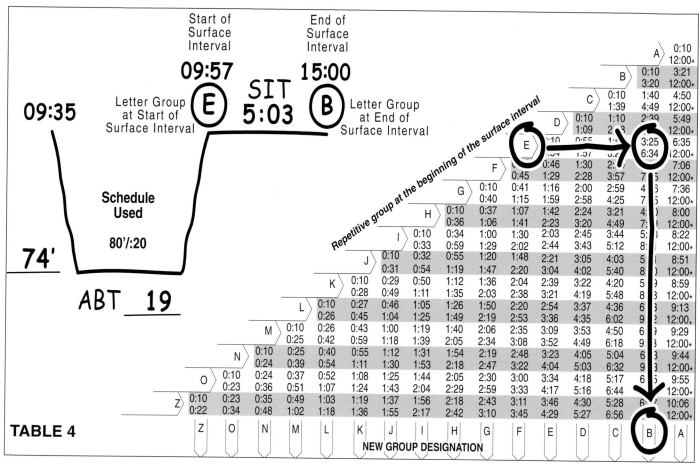

FIGURE 4.13
Answer to Example 3

- From here, the divers continue across the table until they find a range of times into which the Surface Interval of five hours, three minutes falls. This appears in the second column from the right.
- Moving down this column, they arrive at the new Repetitive Group Designation of B.

Practice Problem 3:

Following is a practice problem that illustrates of how to find the correct Letter Group following a Surface Interval:

Continuing the scenario presented in Practice Problem 2, while dive team #3 was retrieving the dive light they accidentally dropped during their morning dive, they discovered an apparently abandoned anchor with no surface float. Since the anchor appeared to be in good condition, they reported it to their divemaster. He, in turn, asked them to make a second dive, to further inspect the anchor and see if it could be of use to the vessel.

The divers surfaced from their morning dive at 10:54 am. At that time, their Repetitive Group Designation was F. They anticipate re-entering the water at 1:45 pm. What will their new Letter Group be at the end of this Surface Interval?

The answer appears in Figure 4.14.

Figure 4.14 reveals:

- The Surface Interval Time that elapsed between 10:54 am and 1:45 pm is two hours, 51 minutes (2:51).
- As before, the divers enter Table 4 from the left, starting at the Repetitive Group Designation which, in this case is F.
- They continue across the table until they find a range of times into which the Surface Interval of two hours, 51 minutes falls. This appears in the third column from the right.
- Moving down this column, they arrive at the new Letter Group C.

4.3.5 Determining Adjusted No-Decompression Limits for Repetitive Dives

As discussed earlier in this section, finding the allowable No-Decompression Limits for single dives is relatively easy. All a diver needs to do is consult the third column of Table 3. However, because divers must account for residual nitrogen remaining in their bodies' tissues from previous dives, determining the allowable No-Decompression Limit for repetitive dives is a somewhat more complex process. To do so, divers must consult the lower portion of Table 4 to see how their Repetitive Group Designation equates to time spent under water at a particular depth,

Air Diving and Decompression

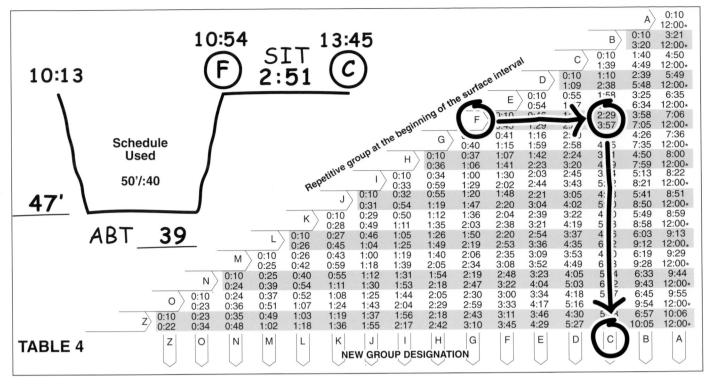

FIGURE 4.14
Answer to Practice Problem 3

then deduct this time from the single-dive No-Decompression Limit for this depth that appears on Table 3.

Example 4:

Following is an example of how to use Tables 3 and 4 (see Appendix V) to determine the adjusted No-Decompression Limit for a repetitive dive:

Continuing with the example of the divers conducting the aquatic-life census, it is now 3:00 pm. Team #2 is now ready to enter the water to finish the balance of their aquatic-life census. They finished their first dive of the day with a Repetitive Group Designation (Letter Group) of E. After five hours and three minutes on the surface, their new Letter Group is B. Having completed the deepest portion of their survey in the morning, they do not expect to exceed a maximum depth of 60 fsw (18.4 msw) on their second dive. What is their adjusted No-Decompression Limit for this depth?

The answer appears in Figure 4.15.

Figure 4.15 reveals:
- The divers begin this process by consulting Table 4. At the start of the dive, the divers' Repetitive Group Designation is B. Moving down the "B" column, they look for its intersection with the 60-foot row.
- At this intersection point, they find a Residual Nitrogen Time (RNT) of 11 minutes. What this means is that, according to the mathematical model that

underlies the U.S. Navy Dive Tables, the amount of residual nitrogen present in the divers' bodies at the start of their second dive is roughly equal to that which would be present in their systems 11 minutes into a single dive to a depth of 60 fsw.
- To determine the adjusted No-Decompression Limit, they deduct 11 minutes from the U.S. Navy Dive Tables' single-dive No-Decompression Limit of 60 minutes found in Table 3. Doing so results in a time of 49 minutes.

Thus, if the divers keep the Actual Bottom Time (ABT) of their second dive within a limit of 49 minutes, and do not exceed a maximum depth of 60 fsw, they will remain within the U.S. Navy Dive Tables' No-Decompression Limit.

Practice Problem 4:

The following practice problem will help illustrate how to determine adjusted No-Decompression Limits for repetitive dives:

Further continuing the scenario in Practice Problem 3, dive team #3 is preparing to perform an inspection of an anchor they discovered during their morning dive. They have already determined that their Repetitive Group Designation (Letter Group) at the start of this dive will be C. They also know that the depth of the upcoming dive will approach, but not exceed, 50 fsw. What is the maximum time they can spend on this dive without exceeding the U.S. Navy Dive Tables' No-Decompression Limit?

NOAA Diving Manual

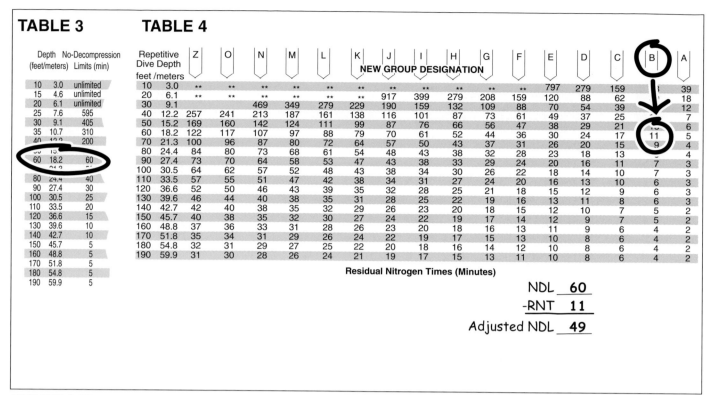

FIGURE 4.15
Answer to Example 4

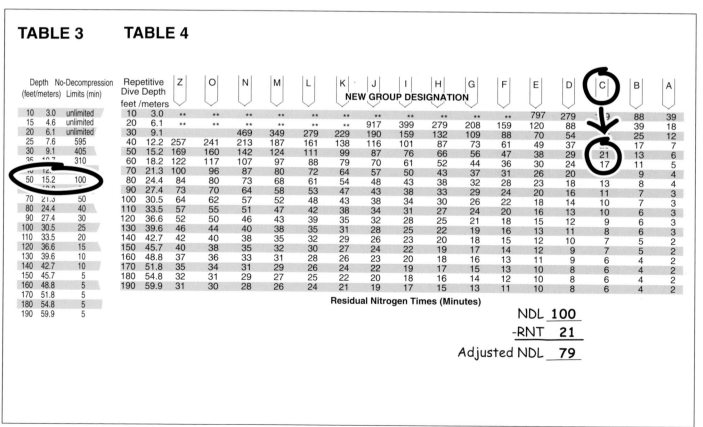

FIGURE 4.16
Answer to Practice Problem 4

Air Diving and Decompression

Ⓐ	Ⓑ	Ⓒ	Ⓓ	Ⓔ	Ⓕ	Ⓖ	Ⓗ	Ⓘ	Ⓙ	Ⓚ	Ⓛ	Ⓜ	Ⓝ	Ⓞ	LETTER GROUP
7	17	25	37	49	61	73	87	101	116	138	161	187	213	241	**40**
193	183	175	163	151	139	127	113	99	84						
6	13	21	29	38	47	56	66	76	87	99	111	124	142	160	**50**
94	87	79	71	62	53	44	34								
5	11	17	24	30	36	44	52	61	70	79	88	97	107	117	**60**
55	49	43	36	30	24	16									
4	9	15	20	26	31	37	43	50	57	64	72	80	87	96	**70**
46	41	35	30	24	19	13									
4	8	13	18	23	28	32	38	43	48	54	61	68	73	80	**80**
36	32	27	22	17	12										
3	7	11	16	20	24	29	33	38	43	47	53	58	64	70	**90**
27	23	19	14	10	6										
3	7	10	14	18	22	26	30	34	38	43	48	52	57	62	**100**
22	18	15	11	7											
3	6	10	13	16	20	24	27	31	34	38	42	47	51	55	**110**
17	14	10	7												
3	6	9	12	15	18	21	25	28	32	35	39	43	46	50	**120**
12	9	6													
3	6	8	11	13	16	19	22	25	28	31	35	38	40	44	**130**
7															
2	5	7	10	12	15	18	20	23	26	29	32	35	38	40	**140**
8															
RESIDUAL NITROGEN TIMES (RNT)															**DEPTH**
ADJUSTED NO-STOP DIVE TIMES (MAXIMUM)															

FIGURE 4.17
Commercially Produced Version of the U.S. Navy Dive Tables

The answer appears in Figure 4.16.

Figure 4.16 reveals:
- The divers start by entering Table 4 in the column for Letter Group C. Moving downward, they look for this column's intersection with the row for a depth of 50 fsw. This gives them a Residual Nitrogen Time (RNT) of 21 minutes.
- Deducting 21 minutes RNT from the U.S. Navy Dive Tables' single-dive No-Decompression Limit (NDL) of 100 minutes (Table 3), they arrive at an adjusted NDL of 79 minutes.

In regard to determining adjusted No-Decompression Limits for repetitive dives, there are two more points of which divers should be aware:

- Insofar as the adjusted No-Decompression Limits for any combination of Repetitive Group Designation and depth never changes, most commercially produced versions of the U.S. Navy and similar dive tables simply provide this information, as shown in Figure 4.17. This figure provides both the RNT and adjusted no-stop dive times at each depth interval, thus eliminating the requirement to subtract the RNT from the no-decompression limit to obtain the ABT. The top number is the RNT in minutes and the bottom number is the adjusted no-stop dive time in minutes. Having this information provided can greatly simplify the planning of repetitive dives.
- Because the diver cannot always be certain of the maximum depth that may be reached during any

dive, it is a good idea to calculate and record the adjusted No-Decompression Limits for all possible maximum depths on a plastic slate and carry this during the dive. As an alternative, take along commercially produced plastic versions of the U.S. Navy Dive Tables that contain this information.

4.3.6 Determining Repetitive Group Designations Following Repetitive Dives

Just as the U.S. Navy Dive Tables can provide a Repetitive Group Designation (Letter Group) following single dives, they can also do so following repetitive dives. However, as with determining adjusted no-decompression limits, the process for doing so is slightly more complex.

Example 5:

Following is an example showing how to use Tables 3 and 4 (see Figure 4.18) to determine the applicable Letter Group at the end of any repetitive dive:

Continuing with an earlier example, at 3:00 pm dive team #2 enters the water to finish the balance of their aquatic-life census. Their Letter Group at the beginning of this dive is B. They reach a maximum depth of 51 fsw and begin their ascent 42 minutes after initiating their descent. What is their Repetitive Group Designation (Letter Group) at the end of this dive?

The answer appears in Figure 4.18.

Figure 4.18 reveals:
- The divers know from the previous example that, for a dive in which team #2 starts in Letter Group B, and

TABLE 4

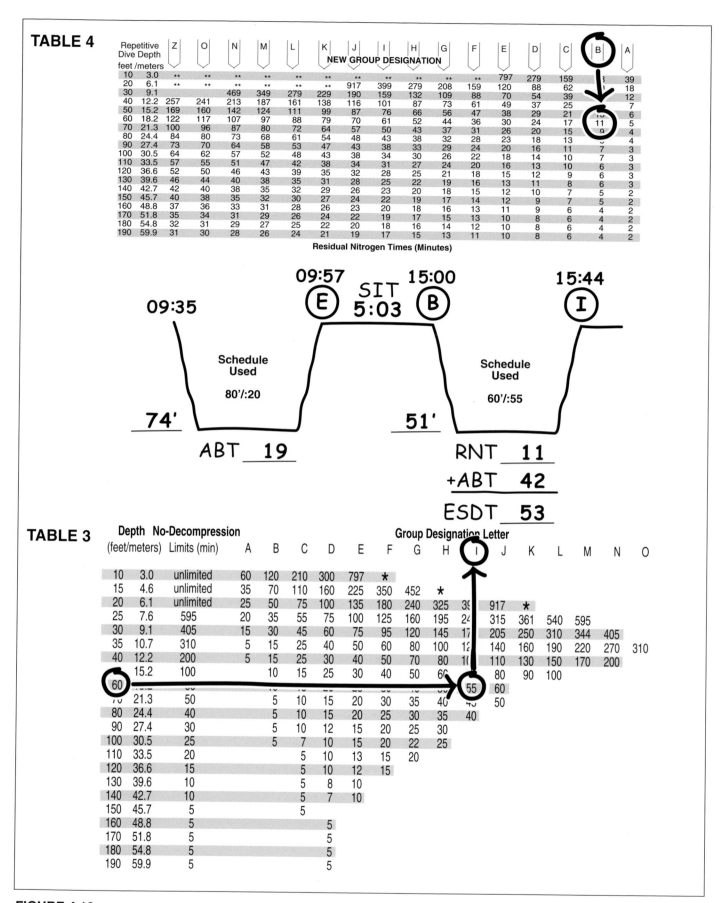

Repetitive Dive Depth feet/meters	Z	O	N	M	L	K	J	I	H	G	F	E	D	C	B	A
						NEW GROUP DESIGNATION										
10 3.0	**	**	**	**	**	**	**	**	**	**	**	797	279	159	B	39
20 6.1	**	**	**	**	**	**	917	399	279	208	159	120	88	62		18
30 9.1			469	349	279	229	190	159	132	109	88	70	54	39		12
40 12.2	257	241	213	187	161	138	116	101	87	73	61	49	37	25		7
50 15.2	169	160	142	124	111	99	87	76	66	56	47	38	29	21	15	6
60 18.2	122	117	107	97	88	79	70	61	52	44	36	30	24	17	11	5
70 21.3	100	96	87	80	72	64	57	50	43	37	31	26	20	15	9	4
80 24.4	84	80	73	68	61	54	48	43	38	32	28	23	18	13	8	4
90 27.4	73	70	64	58	53	47	43	38	33	29	24	20	16	11	7	3
100 30.5	64	62	57	52	48	43	38	34	30	26	22	18	14	10	7	3
110 33.5	57	55	51	47	42	38	34	31	27	24	20	16	13	10	6	3
120 36.6	52	50	46	43	39	35	32	28	25	21	18	15	12	9	6	3
130 39.6	46	44	40	38	35	31	28	25	22	19	16	13	11	8	6	3
140 42.7	42	40	38	35	32	29	26	23	20	18	15	12	10	7	5	2
150 45.7	40	38	35	32	30	27	24	22	19	17	14	12	9	7	5	2
160 48.8	37	36	33	31	28	26	23	20	18	16	13	11	9	6	4	2
170 51.8	35	34	31	29	26	24	22	19	17	15	13	10	8	6	4	2
180 54.8	32	31	29	27	25	22	20	18	16	14	12	10	8	6	4	2
190 59.9	31	30	28	26	24	21	19	17	15	13	11	10	8	6	4	2

Residual Nitrogen Times (Minutes)

09:57 (E)   SIT 5:03   15:00 (B)   15:44 (I)

09:35   Schedule Used   80'/:20   Schedule Used   60'/:55

74'   ABT __19__   51'   RNT __11__
                                   +ABT __42__
                                   ESDT __53__

TABLE 3

Depth (feet/meters)	No-Decompression Limits (min)	A	B	C	D	E	F	G	H	I	J	K	L	M	N	O
10 3.0	unlimited	60	120	210	300	797	*									
15 4.6	unlimited	35	70	110	160	225	350	452	*							
20 6.1	unlimited	25	50	75	100	135	180	240	325	39	917	*				
25 7.6	595	20	35	55	75	100	125	160	195	24	315	361	540	595		
30 9.1	405	15	30	45	60	75	95	120	145	17	205	250	310	344	405	
35 10.7	310	5	15	25	40	50	60	80	100	12	140	160	190	220	270	310
40 12.2	200	5	15	25	30	40	50	70	80	10	110	130	150	170	200	
15.2	100		10	15	25	30	40	50	66		80	90	100			
60										55	60					
70 21.3	50		5	10	15	20	30	35	40		50					
80 24.4	40		5	10	15	20	25	30	35	40						
90 27.4	30		5	10	12	15	20	25	30							
100 30.5	25		5	7	10	15	20	22	25							
110 33.5	20			5	10	13	15	20								
120 36.6	15			5	10	12	15									
130 39.6	10			5	8	10										
140 42.7	10			5	7	10										
150 45.7	5			5												
160 48.8	5					5										
170 51.8	5					5										
180 54.8	5					5										
190 59.9	5					5										

FIGURE 4.18
Answer to Example 5

Air Diving and Decompression

reach a maximum depth of between 51 and 60 fsw, their Residual Nitrogen Time (RNT) will be 11 minutes.
- By adding this RNT to the diver's Actual Bottom Time (ABT) of 42 minutes, they obtain an Equivalent Single Dive Time (ESDT) of 53 minutes.
- The divers treat this repetitive dive as though it were a single dive to 51 fsw for 53 minutes. Using the procedures outlined earlier, they use Table 3 to obtain a Repetitive Group Designation (Letter Group) of I.

Practice Problem 5:

The following practice problem will illustrate how to determine Repetitive Group Designations (Letter Groups) following repetitive dives:

Again continuing the scenario presented in Practice Problems 2 through 4, dive team #3 makes a mid-afternoon dive to inspect the anchor discovered during their morning dive. They have already determined that their Repetitive Group Designation (Letter Group) at the start of this repetitive dive will be C. The divers complete the inspection and begin their ascent 13 minutes after initiating descent. During the dive, they reach a maximum depth of 46 fsw. What is their Letter Group at the end of this dive?

The answer appears in Figure 4.19.

Figure 4.19 reveals:
- The divers already know from the previous problem that, for a dive in which they start in Letter Group C, and reach a maximum depth of between 41 and 50 fsw, their Residual Nitrogen Time (RNT) will be 21 minutes.
- Adding this RNT to their Actual Bottom Time (ABT) of 13 minutes, they obtain an Equivalent Single Dive Time (ESDT) of 34 minutes.
- Treating this repetitive dive as the equivalent of a single dive to 46 fsw for 34 minutes, the divers consult Table 3 to obtain a Repetitive Group Designation (Letter Group) of F.

4.3.7 Why Repetitive Group Designations Are Important

If divers never made more than one repetitive dive in any 12-hour period, determining the Repetitive Group Designation at the end of such dives might be of little value. However, as Figure 4.20 shows, it is possible to make several such dives in succession—in which case, determining the Letter Groups for the beginning and end of every dive becomes vital to divers who wish to use the U.S. Navy Dive Tables to help avoid decompression sickness (DCS).

Theoretically, it is possible for divers to make an infinite number of repetitive dives, and to track their Repetitive Group status while doing so. In the real world, working divers seldom make more than two to three dives in a single, 12-hour period. Nevertheless, the ability to accurately plan and record these dives using the U.S. Navy Dive Tables is important.

4.3.8 Determining the Minimum Allowable Surface Interval Between Dives

There are times when a diver may need to use the U.S. Navy Dive Tables to determine what is the minimum surface time needed before making a repetitive dive to a particular depth, for a specific amount of time.

Example 6:

Following is an example to illustrate why a diver might want to determine a minimum Surface Interval, and how to do so.

Let's say that dive team #2, from earlier examples, wants to complete their aquatic-life census as quickly as possible, to avoid being in the water when a forecast afternoon thunderstorm arrives. They surfaced from their first dive at 9:57 am, with a Repetitive Group Designation (Letter Group) of E. The divers' second dive will be to a depth of no more than 60 fsw, and they estimate they will need a maximum of 40 minutes to complete their survey. What is the soonest the divers can make their second dive?

The answer appears in Figure 4.21.

Figure 4.21 reveals:
- The first step in determining a minimum allowable surface interval between two dives is to establish what the maximum allowable Equivalent Single Dive Time (ESDT) will be for the second dive. When making a no-decompression dive, the ESDT will be the same as the No-Decompression Limit for the second dive's maximum possible depth. In this case, dive team #2 plans to go no deeper than 60 fsw; the U.S. Navy Dive Tables' No-Decompression Limit for 60 fsw is 60 minutes. Thus, their ESDT for the second dive must be equal to or less than 60 minutes.
- Next, the divers deduct the planned maximum Actual Bottom Time (ABT) for the maximum allowable Total Bottom Time (ESDT). In this instance, subtracting the maximum ABT of 40 minutes from the maximum ESDT of 60 minutes reveals that the Residual Nitrogen Time (RNT) at the beginning of the second dive must be equal to or less than 20 minutes.
- The third step is to consult Table 4 to find out what Repetitive Group Designation (Letter Group) will give the divers an RNT equal to or less than 20 minutes at 60 fsw. In this case, the divers discover that Letter Group C will give them an RNT of 17 minutes—a value that most closely approaches the desired 20 minutes, without exceeding it.
- The final step in this process is to find out the minimum amount of time needed to reach Letter Group C from Letter Group E. Consulting Table 4, it is clear that the divers must wait a minimum of one hour, 58 minutes to reach Group C, having surfaced in Group E. Thus, the divers will re-enter the water

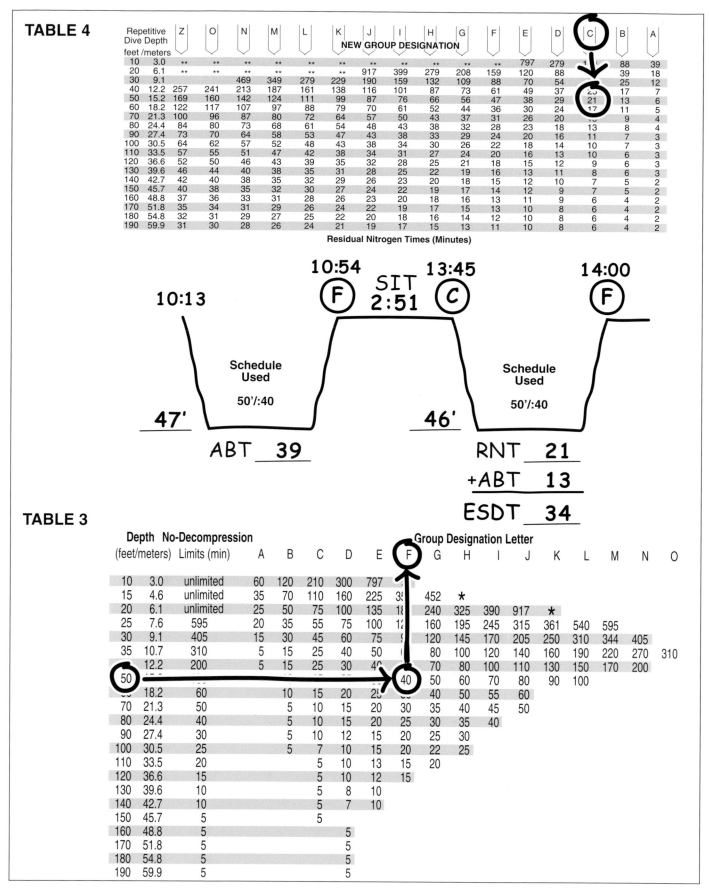

FIGURE 4.19
Answer to Practice Problem 5

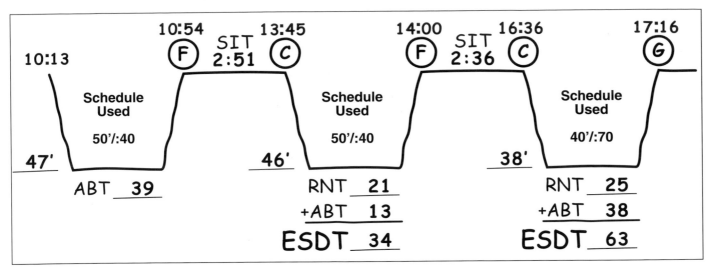

FIGURE 4.20
Record of Several Successive Repetitive Dives

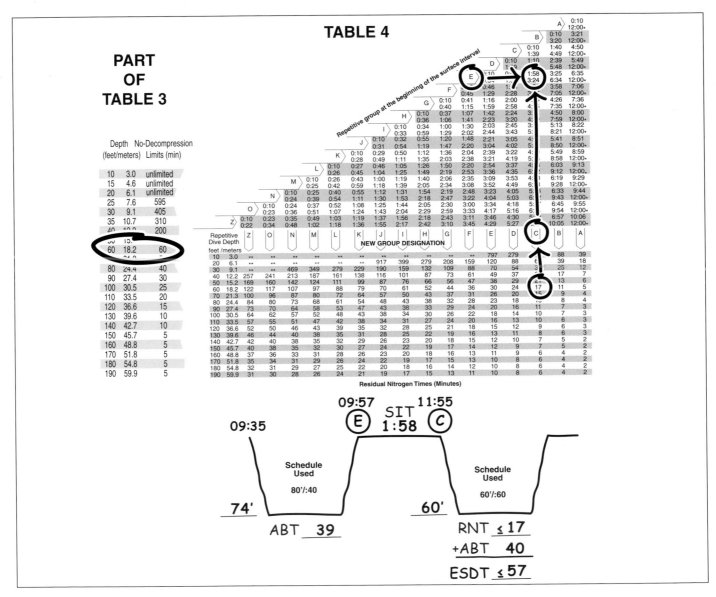

FIGURE 4.21
Answer to Example 6

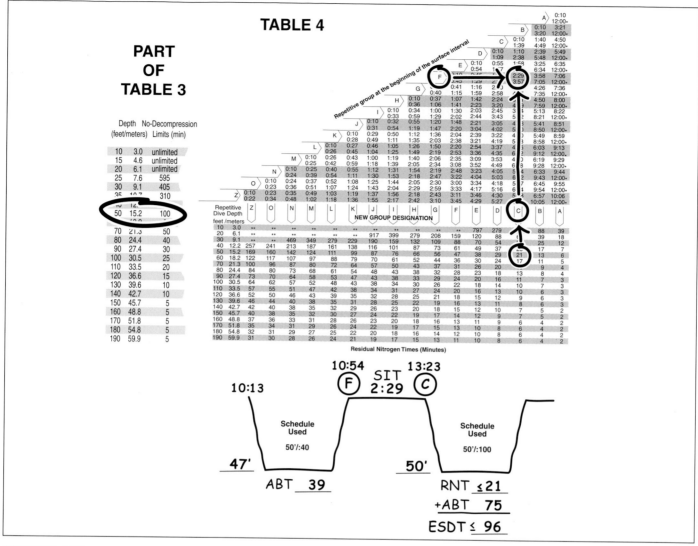

FIGURE 4.22
Answer to Practice Problem 6

at 11:55 am—and surface in time to avoid the forecast afternoon storm.

Practice Problem 6:

Following is a practice problem to show how to determine a minimum allowable Surface Interval:

In a variation on earlier problems, the divemaster not only wants dive team #3 to inspect the anchor they discovered on their first dive of the day but, if serviceable, tie a line to it for retrieval. Further, the divemaster wants the divers to do so as soon as possible, so that the vessel can then proceed to its next assignment. The divers know that the depth for this dive will not exceed 50 fsw. They also know from previous experience that, if the anchor is still useable, they will need approximately one hour, 15 minutes (:75) to inspect and prepare the anchor for recovery. With this in mind, how soon can they re-enter the water?

The answer appears in Figure 4.22.

Figure 4.22 reveals:
- Start by determining the maximum allowable Equivalent Single Dive Time (ESDT) for a repetitive dive to 50 fsw. This is the No-Decompression Limit for this depth, or 100 minutes.
- Next, deduct the planned maximum Actual Bottom Time (ABT) of 75 minutes from the maximum allowable ESDT. Doing so reveals that the Residual Nitrogen Time (RNT) for the second dive must be equal to or less than 25 minutes.
- Consulting Table 4, a Repetitive Group Designation of C will give them a RNT of 21 minutes for a depth of 50 fsw—the closest they can get to the desired RNT of 25 minutes, without exceeding it.
- Finally, examine Table 4 to find the minimum amount of time the divers must wait to get from Letter Group F to Letter Group C. This turns out to be two

Air Diving and Decompression

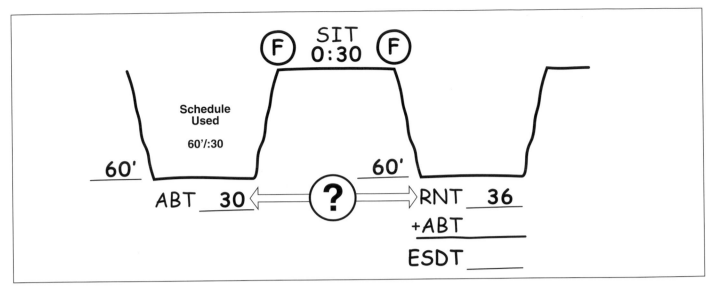

FIGURE 4.23
Contrary to Logic

hours, 29 minutes, putting them back in the water at 1:23 pm.

4.3.9 Exceptions to Normal Repetitive Dive Planning

There is a notable exception to normal U.S. Navy Dive Table planning procedures that may be applicable when making a repetitive dive to the same depth or deeper than the previous one, with a relatively short Surface Interval between the two. An example of just such a situation appears in Figure 4.23.

Figure 4.23 reveals:
- Begin by making a 60-foot dive with an Actual Bottom Time (ABT) of 30 minutes. Upon surfacing from this dive, Table 3 indicates the Repetitive Group Designation (Letter Group) is F.
- Before making the second dive, the divers spend a Surface Interval of 30 minutes off-gassing. According to Table 4, the Letter Group at the beginning of the second dive will still be F.
- Consulting Table 4 (the lower portion), the Residual Nitrogen Time (RNT) for a depth of 60 fsw is 36 minutes.

This appears to be contrary to logic. What the tables appear to be saying is that, after diving to 60 fsw for 30 minutes, then off-gassing for an additional 30 minutes at the surface, the amount of excess nitrogen remaining in tissues is roughly the same as it would be had the divers spent more time under water than they actually did. How can this be?

The answer is that the U.S. Navy Dive Tables are designed primarily for dives to varying depths, with longer Surface Intervals in between them than this example depicts. When making dives to comparable depths, with short Surface Intervals between them, this apparent anomaly appears.

Two methods a diver can use to deal with these situation follow:

- One approach is to simply ignore the apparent anomaly and continue to use the U.S. Navy Dive Tables exactly as designed. Doing so does not increase the overall risk and actually adds a degree of conservatism to a second dive. It does, however, diminish some additional bottom time.
- The other approach is to ignore the Residual Nitrogen Time (RNT) that Table 2 gives, and use the shorter Actual Bottom Time (ABT) from the first dive in its place. When doing so the diver is, in essence, considering both dives to be the same as one long dive to the same depth, with the Actual Bottom Times from each dive added together.

Bear in mind, this exception is only applicable when making a repetitive dive to the *same depth* or *deeper* than the dive preceding it (see Section 4.6.3.1 on Reverse Profile Dives).

4.3.10 Dealing With Surface Intervals of Less Than Ten Minutes

A somewhat similar situation to the one just outlined arises when making dives that are less than ten minutes apart. Notice that Table 4 does not provide information for Surface Intervals of less than ten minutes. This is because the U.S. Navy Dive Tables consider dives that are less than ten minutes apart to be part of the same dive. Thus, add the Actual Bottom Times from both dives together, and consider the deepest depth reached during either portion of the dive to be the maximum depth for the combined dive.

In general, however, experts recommend against this sort of "bounce" diving, as it may increase the risk of decompression sickness (DCS). Instead, whenever feasible, divers should remain at the surface for as long as possible between dives.

4.4 USING THE U.S. NAVY DIVE TABLES TO MAKE STAGED DECOMPRESSION DIVES

There are also U.S. Navy decompression tables covering dives that exceed the No-Decompression Limits (NDLs) and which require divers to stop at predetermined depths during ascent to decompress. Although the majority of dives conducted by NOAA divers do not involve staged decompression, it is important to understand how to do so, as a contingency procedure for unforeseen circumstances.

4.4.1 What Is Decompression?

The word "decompression" has two different meanings in diving. The first is the dictionary definition, the second is the act of doing it in a controlled way.

The dictionary definition of decompression is the reduction of pressure or release from compression. In the context of a pressure vessel, this meaning is more or less obvious, reducing the pressure is decompressing the vessel. It might well be called depressurizing. In the context of a diver ascending, the ascent takes the diver to a place where the pressure is lower, and this too is decompressing. Decompression is something that occurs on the ascent from every dive.

However, although divers occasionally use the word as defined, they also use the word "decompression" to mean the release or reduction of pressure in a controlled or planned way to avoid bubble formation and decompression sickness (DCS). The latter is an outcome of decompression when the pressure release is not done properly. So, it is in the best interest of the submerged diver to "decompress" in order to reach surface pressure. "Decompression" in this sense means the diver is required to follow a specific time, depth, and breathing gas profile. This profile, which may be called a decompression table or decompression schedule, is designed to allow a diver to ascend to the surface without incidence or symptoms. It may involve stops, or only require a specific ascent rate without stops.

The process of ascending to the surface is decompression in both senses. Ascending without stops is still decompressing. The important point is that every ascent is a decompression. Further, every dive of any consequence involves a certain decompression obligation. As far as diving is concerned, decompression can include:

Ascents: Because the ambient pressure decreases during ascent, ascents are a form of decompression. Slow ascents generally result in the formation of fewer gas bubbles in body tissues than faster ascents do. This is why the U.S. Navy Dive Tables require an ascent rate of no more than 30 feet per minute.

Precautionary Decompression Stops: Commonly known as "safety stops," these are stops made during ascent, even though the U.S. Navy Dive Tables do not require them. NOAA "no-stop" dive procedures recommends the divers make a safety stop of three to five minutes in the range of 10 to 20 fsw, nominally 15 fsw, for all no-stop dives conducted 60 fsw or deeper, plus all repetitive dives. The safety stop has been shown experimentally to reduce the level of ultrasonically-detected bubbles, and should therefore, reduce the likelihood of decompression sickness. In any event, the safety stop also requires the diver to have good buoyancy control in order to slow the ascent before surfacing and this is an all-around safety factor. Time spent at a safety stop is not part of bottom time or SIT and does not affect the divers repetitive group letter designation following the dive.

Note that most electronic dive timers record dive time from the time the diver enters the water to the time the diver surfaces without separating bottom time and ascent time. Therefore, the diver should note the time leaving the bottom for the ascent. The ascent time and safety stop time are not included in total bottom time. However, if the diver neglects to record when he actually left the bottom, then bottom time can be assumed to be the total dive time. This will make the repetitive group letter designation more conservative.

Mandatory Decompression Stops: These are stops that are required by the tables. Depending on the dive schedule, mandatory decompression may entail remaining at a depth of 10 fsw for just a few minutes—or it may require that divers make stops at deeper depths as well, and that the time divers must remain at these stops be substantially longer.

4.4.2 Decompression Diving Considerations

There is no such thing as a casual decompression dive; it requires additional planning and considerations above that required for no-decompression dives. Dives requiring mandatory decompression stops:

Entail Greater Risk:

As will be discussed later in this section, experts believe that remaining well within the No-Decompression Limits helps reduce the risk of decompression sickness (DCS). In contrast, experts generally believe that dives that exceed these limits—even when participants make the required decompression stops—pose a substantially greater risk of DCS.

Have Substantially Greater Logistical Requirements:

Making dives that require stage decompression entails considerably more in the way of equipment and support than no-decompression dives. Among these requirements:

- Participants must ensure that they not only have sufficient breathing gas for the dive itself, but also for the necessary decompression stops.

- The breathing gas used during the dive is generally not the best possible media to breathe during decompression. This may necessitate having a separate gas supply (usually oxygen or an oxygen-rich gas mixture) for decompression.
- Participants must be able to maintain specific depths during decompression. This may involve the use of ascent lines, decompression bars or platforms, lift or marking bags, etc.

Consider the plight of divers who find themselves having to make mandatory decompression stops in open-ocean conditions with no prior planning or preparation:

- They may be constantly monitoring their pressure gauges, hoping that their dwindling gas supply is sufficient to complete the necessary stops.
- They may be struggling to maintain a constant depth, as mandated by the tables, despite large waves passing over head and lack of an ascent line to hang on to.
- They may also find themselves drifting in a current, wondering when they are finally able to surface, and whether their support vessel will be able to find them.

Decompression Dives

Decompression diving is rarely conducted by NOAA scuba divers. However, there are occasions where decompression dives are done; for those there are specific procedures. NOAA diving activities that exceed the limits of no-stop dives are permitted only under the following conditions:

- A detailed dive plan has been approved by the NOAA Diving Safety Board.
- The project leader must demonstrate that the divemaster and all members of the diving team have a thorough knowledge of decompression and repetitive dive principles and practices.
- A decompression dive team must be composed of no fewer than three divers (two divers and a fully suited standby diver on the surface).
- Each participant must wear appropriate gear and thermal protection for the dive, including appropriate breathing gas cylinders, a timing device, depth gauge, and have on hand a decompression schedule for the maximum proposed depth of dive.
- A recompression chamber should be within two hours travel time from the dive site or diving vessel, if one is not on-site.

4.4.3 Making Mandatory Decompression Stops

As stated early, unforeseen circumstances may force a diver into a decompression profile. Therefore, all divers should know how to use the U.S. Navy Standard Air Decompression Tables.

Example 7:

Here is an example of just such a situation.

Dive team #3 plans a repetitive dive to 60 fsw. They base their dive plan on the assumption that their Actual Bottom Time (ABT) and Residual Nitrogen Time (RNT) together will not exceed the U.S. Navy No-Decompression Limit (NDL) for 60 fsw which is 60 minutes. Just prior to ascending, however, the divers decide to re-check their calculations. They discover—much to their horror—that they misread Table 4 and that their Total Bottom Time (TBT) for this dive is now the equivalent of having made a single dive to 60 fsw for 80 minutes. This is well in excess of the 60-minute NDL upon which they based their dive plan. Now what do they do?

The answer appears in Figure 4.24.

To find this information, the divers will need to consult the U.S. Navy Standard Air Decompression Table 5 (see Figure 4.25 or Appendix IV). Using this table, look up the values appearing for an 80-minute dive to a depth of between 51 and 60 fsw. Among the columns of data you will see:

- Time to First Stop: Based on an ascent rate of 30 feet per minute (fpm), the ascent time from 60 ft. to 10 ft. is 1:40 minutes.
- Time at Stop Depth: Columns are provided for stop depths of up to 40 fsw. In this instance, the tables require a 7-minute stop at 10 fsw.
- Total Ascent Time: The total of stop time plus ascent time is 9:00 minutes.
- Repetitive Group: The Repetitive Group Designation at the end of the dive is letter group L.

Armed with this information, the divers now know that they should ascend at a rate of 30 fpm to a depth of 10 fsw, wait there for seven minutes, then surface. Time to the first stop should be one minute and 40 seconds. The total time of ascent should be nine minutes. The RGD after surfacing will be group L. During their stop, the divers should keep their mouth as close to a depth of 10 fsw as possible.

It is worth noting that, even though Table 5 provides end-of-dive Repetitive Group information, making additional

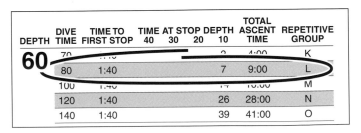

FIGURE 4.24
Answer to Example 7

Table 5. U.S. Navy Standard Air Decompression Table – 1999

Depth feet/meters	Bottom time (min)	Time first stop (min:sec)	Decompression stops (feet/meters) 50 15.2	40 12.1	30 9.1	20 6.0	10 3.0	Total decompression time (min:sec)	Repetitive group
40 12.1	200						0	1:20	*
	210	1:00					2	3:20	N
	230	1:00					7	8:20	N
	250	1:00					11	12:20	O
	270	1:00					15	16:20	O
	300	1:00					19	20:20	Z
					Exceptional Exposure				
	360	1:00					23	24:20	**
	480	1:00					41	42:20	**
	720	1:00					69	70:20	**
50 15.2	100						0	1:40	*
	110	1:20					3	4:40	L
	120	1:20					5	6:40	M
	140	1:20					10	11:40	M
	160	1:20					21	22:40	N
	180	1:20					29	30:40	O
	200	1:20					35	36:40	O
	220	1:20					40	41:40	Z
	240	1:20					47	48:40	Z
60 18.2	60						0	2:00	*
	70	1:40					2	4:00	K
	80	1:40					7	9:00	L
	100	1:40					14	16:00	M
	120	1:40					26	28:00	N
	140	1:40					39	41:00	O
	160	1:40					48	50:00	Z
	180	1:40					56	58:00	Z
	200	1:20				1	69	72:00	Z
					Exceptional Exposure				
	240	1:20				2	79	83:00	**
	360	1:20				20	119	141:00	**
	480	1:20				44	148	194:00	**
	720	1:20				78	187	267:00	**
70 21.3	50						0	2:20	*
	60	2:00					8	10:20	K
	70	2:00					14	16:20	L
	80	2:00					18	20:20	M
	90	2:00					23	25:20	N
	100	2:00					33	35:20	N
	110	1:40				2	41	45:20	O
	120	1:40				4	47	53:20	O
	130	1:40				6	52	60:20	O
	140	1:40				8	56	66:20	Z
	150	1:40				9	61	72:20	Z
	160	1:40				13	72	87:20	Z
	170	1:40				19	79	100:20	Z

* See No-Decompression Table 3 for Repetitive Groups
** Repetitive Dives may <u>not</u> follow Exceptional Exposure Dives

FIGURE 4.25
U.S. Navy Dive Table 5—Depth 40 to 70 fsw

Air Diving and Decompression

Table 5. U.S. Navy Standard Air Decompression Table – 1999 (Continued)

Depth feet/meters	Bottom time (min)	Time first stop (min:sec)	Decompression stops (feet/meters) 50 / 15.2	40 / 12.1	30 / 9.1	20 / 6.0	10 / 3.0	Total decompression time (min:sec)	Repetitive group
80 / 24.3	40						0	2:40	*
	50	2:20					10	12:40	K
	60	2:20					17	19:40	L
	70	2:20					23	25:40	M
	80	2:00				2	31	35:40	N
	90	2:00				7	39	48:40	N
	100	2:00				11	46	59:40	O
	110	2:00				13	53	68:40	O
	120	2:00				17	56	75:40	Z
	130	2:00				19	63	84:40	Z
	140	2:00				26	69	97:40	Z
	150	2:00				32	77	111:40	Z
	Exceptional Exposure								
	180	2:00				35	85	122:40	**
	240	1:40			6	52	120	180:40	**
	360	1:40			29	90	160	281:40	**
	480	1:40			59	107	187	355:40	**
	720	1:20		17	108	142	187	456:40	**
90 / 28.7	30						0	3:00	*
	40	2:40					7	10:00	J
	50	2:40					18	21:00	L
	60	2:40					25	28:00	M
	70	2:20				7	30	40:00	N
	80	2:20				13	40	56:00	N
	90	2:20				18	48	69:00	O
	100	2:20				21	54	78:00	Z
	110	2:20				24	61	88:00	Z
	120	2:20				32	68	103:00	Z
	130	2:00			5	36	74	118:00	Z
100 / 30.4	25						0	3:20	*
	30	3:00					3	6:20	I
	40	3:00					15	18:20	K
	50	2:40				2	24	29:20	L
	60	2:40				9	28	40:20	N
	70	2:40				17	39	59:20	O
	80	2:40				23	48	74:20	O
	90	2:20			3	23	57	86:20	Z
	100	2:20			7	23	66	99:20	Z
	110	2:20			10	34	72	119:20	Z
	120	2:20			12	41	78	134:20	Z
	Exceptional Exposure								
	180	2:00		1	29	53	118	204:20	**
	240	2:00		14	42	84	142	285:20	**
	360	1:40	2	42	73	111	187	418:20	**
	480	1:40	21	61	91	142	187	505:20	**
	720	1:40	55	106	122	142	187	615:20	**

* See No-Decompression Table 3 for Repetitive Groups
** Repetitive Dives may <u>not</u> follow Exceptional Exposure Dives

FIGURE 4.25
U.S. Navy Dive Table 5—Depth 80 to 100 fsw

dives following an exposure that requires mandatory stage decompression is not advised. Experts believe that doing so might pose a substantially greater risk of decompression sickness than such dives normally would. Instead, in instances in which a diver accidentally exceeds the No-Decompression Limits, he is best off remaining out of the water for at least 12 hours.

4.4.4 Omitted Decompression

In situations such as an uncontrolled ascent, loss of air supply, bodily injury, or other emergencies, a diver may be required to surface prematurely, without taking the required decompression. If a diver has omitted the required decompression and shows any symptom of embolism or decompression sickness after surfacing, immediate treatment using the appropriate treatment table should be instituted. Treatment in a recompression chamber is essential for these omitted decompression accidents.

4.4.4.1 Omitted Decompression 1

Should a diver realize that he has exceeded the no-decompression limits prior to reaching the surface, and he does not have access to U.S.N. Decompression Tables to determine required in-water decompression time, the diver should take the following precautions:

- Stop at 10 to 15 fsw for a minimum of 15 minutes or until he reaches 300 psi in their cylinder, whichever comes first.
- Once on the surface, the diver should consult the U.S. Navy Standard Air Decompression Tables to see if the amount of time spent at 10–15 feet met or exceeded the amount of decompression time required by the Tables.
- If the time spent at 10–15 feet did not equal or exceed the required time, the diver should be placed on oxygen for a minimum of 30 minutes, observed, and restricted from diving for 12 hours.
- If symptoms occur during or after breathing oxygen for 30 minutes, he should be transported (on oxygen) to the nearest medical facility for treatment.

4.4.4.2 Omitted Decompression 2

Should a diver not realize that he has exceeded the no-decompression limits prior to reaching the surface, or he has insufficient gas to perform in-water decompression, he should take the following precautions:

- Proceed to the surface at a normal rate of ascent.
- Once on the surface, he should notify the divemaster of omitted decompression.
- If asymptomatic, and he can be returned safely to the water within five minutes after surfacing, he should return to the depth of the missed decompression stops (with a dive buddy) and remain for 1 1/2 times the required decompression stop time.

- If he cannot be returned to the water within five minutes after surfacing, he should be placed on oxygen for a minimum of 60 minutes.
- If asymptomatic after breathing oxygen for 60 minutes, he should be observed for a minimum of 12 hours for signs and symptoms of DCS and restricted from diving during this observational period.
- If symptoms occur during or after breathing oxygen for 60 minutes, he should be transported (on oxygen) to the nearest medical facility for treatment.

NOTE
If a diver is asymptomatic but unable to return to the water to complete omitted decompression, and a recompression chamber is available within one hour travel, the diver should be transported to the chamber for possible treatment.

4.4.4.3 Use of Oxygen During Decompression

Oxygen can significantly enhance decompression. Decompression requirements are dictated by the uptake of inert gases. By breathing 100% oxygen, the inert gas gradient is significantly increased, thus increasing inert gas elimination from the body.

For example, pure oxygen can be used to shorten decompression on the 20 and 10 fsw stops. In addition, high oxygen content mixtures can also be used to shorten decompression from the 30 fsw stop and deeper. Mixes rich in oxygen have proven to substantially improve decompression outcome when used as a supplemental decompression gas from both air and nitrox dives.

4.5 DEALING WITH CHANGES IN ALTITUDE

The U.S. Navy Dive Tables make the following assumptions regarding altitude:

- The altitude at the surface of the water in which the dive is made is no more than 1,000 ft. (305 m) above sea level.
- For at least 12 hours following any dive, the divers will remain at an altitude no higher than 1,000 ft. above sea level.

Whenever a dive is made at altitudes more than 1,000 ft. above sea level, or travel to such an altitude following a dive, there are additional factors to take into consideration.

4.5.1 Diving at Altitude

When a dive is performed in a body of water at an altitude well above sea level, several things are different, and some of these must be considered in planning the decompression. First, the barometric or ambient pressure at the surface of the lake (dam) is less than that at sea level. The surface acts as the reference point for tables, and since that pressure is different, some compensation is needed in using standard air or nitrox decompression tables. The relative change in pressure on descent in the water will be greater than as sea level, requiring the tables to be adjusted for altitude.

Because of the reduced atmospheric pressure, dives conducted at altitude require more decompression than identical dives conducted at sea level. Standard air decompression tables, therefore, cannot be used as written. Some organizations calculate specific decompression tables for use at each altitude. An alternative approach is to correct the altitude dive to obtain an equivalent sea level dive, then determine the decompression requirement using standard tables. This procedure is commonly known as the "Cross Correction" technique and always yields a sea level dive that is deeper than the actual dive at altitude. A deeper sea level equivalent dive provides the extra decompression needed to offset effects of diving at altitude.

4.5.1.1 Altitude Correction Procedure

To apply the "Cross Correction" technique, the actual dive depth must first be corrected to determine the sea level equivalent depth. Strictly speaking, ascent rate should also be corrected, but this correction can safely be ignored.

4.5.1.2 Correction of Depth of Dive

Though fresh water is less dense than sea water, all dives will be assumed to be conducted in sea water, thus no corrections will be made based on water salinity. Enter Table 4.1 directly with the depth indicated on the line or fathometer.

Depth of a sea level equivalent dive is determined by multiplying the depth of the dive at altitude by a ratio of atmospheric pressure at sea level (14.7 psi) to atmospheric pressure at altitude (see Table 4.2). Using pounds per square inch (psi) as a unit for expressing atmospheric pressure at altitude equivalent depth is then:

Equivalent Depth (fsw) =
$$\text{Altitude Depth (fsw)} \times \frac{\text{Pressure at Sea Level (psi)}}{\text{Pressure at Altitude (psi)}}$$

Example:

A diver makes a dive to 60 fsw at an altitude of 5,000 ft. Using Table 4.2 we find that the atmospheric pressure measured at 5,000 ft. is 12.23 psia. Atmospheric pressure at sea level is 14.7 psi. Sea level equivalent depth is then:

Equivalent Depth (fsw) =
$$60 \text{ fsw} \times \frac{14.7 \text{ psi}}{12.23 \text{ psi}} = 72.1 \text{ fsw}$$

4.5.1.3 Correction for Decompression Stop Depths

Depth of the corrected stop at altitude is calculated by multiplying depth of a sea level equivalent stop by a ratio of atmospheric pressure at altitude to atmospheric pressure at sea level. [Note: This ratio is inverse to the ratio in the formula above.]

Altitude Stop Depth (fsw) =
$$\text{Sea Level Stop Depth (fsw)} \times \frac{\text{Pressure at Altitude (psi)}}{\text{Pressure at Sea Level (psi)}}$$

Example:

A NOAA diver makes a no-decompression dive at an altitude of 5,000 ft. and wants to perform a precautionary safety stop at 20 fsw. Stop depth used at altitude is then:

Altitude Stop Depth (fsw) =
$$20 \text{ fsw} \times \frac{12.23 \text{ psi}}{14.7 \text{ psi}} = 16.6 \text{ fsw}$$

To simplify calculations, Table 4.1 gives corrected sea level equivalent depths and equivalent stops depths for dives from 10-190 ft and for altitudes from 1,000 to 10,000 ft in 1,000 ft. increments.

4.5.1.4 Need for Correction

No correction is required for dives conducted at altitudes between sea level and 300 ft. The additional risk associated with these dives is minimal. At altitudes between 300 and 1,000 ft., correction is required for dives deeper than 145 fsw (actual depth). At altitudes above 1,000 ft., correction is required for all dives.

4.5.1.5 Depth Measurement at Altitude

The preferred method for measuring depth at altitude is a mechanical or electronic gauge that can be re-zeroed at the dive site. Once re-zeroed, no further correction of the reading is required.

Most mechanical depth gauges carried by divers have a sealed one-atmosphere reference and cannot be adjusted for altitude, thus they will read low throughout a dive at altitude. A correction factor of 1 fsw for every 1,000 ft. of altitude should be added to the reading of a sealed reference gauge before entering Table 4.1.

A sounding line or fathometer may be used to measure the depth if a suitable depth gauge is not available. These devices measure the linear distance below the surface of the water, not the water pressure.

4.5.1.6 Correction of Depth Gauges

Neither oil-filled nor capillary depth gauges provide accurate depth indications when used at altitude. Oil-filled depth gauges are designed to read 0 ft. at a pressure of one ata. At reduced atmospheric pressure, the gauge will read less than zero (unless there is a pin that stops the needle at zero); in the water, such a gauge will give a reading that is shallower than the actual depth. The depth readings can be corrected by adding a depth that is equal to the difference between the atmospheric pressure at the altitude site and one ata. Table 4.2 shows mean atmospheric pressures at various altitudes and the corrections necessary for oil-filled gauges.

Because of the reduced density of the air trapped in the capillary gauge at altitude, less water pressure is required than at sea level to compress the air to a given volume. As a result, the capillary gauge will indicate a depth greater than the actual depth. Because of the question about the accuracy of these gauges, a measured downline should be used.

TABLE 4.1
Sea Level Equivalent Depth (fsw)

Actual Depth (fsw)	Altitude (feet)									
	1,000	2,000	3,000	4,000	5,000	6,000	7,000	8,000	9,000	10,000
10	10	15	15	15	15	15	15	15	15	15
15	15	20	20	20	20	20	20	25	25	25
20	20	25	25	25	25	25	30	30	30	30
25	25	30	30	30	35	35	35	35	35	40
30	30	35	35	35	40	40	40	50	50	50
35	35	40	40	50	50	50	50	50	50	60
40	40	50	50	50	50	50	60	60	60	60
45	45	50	60	60	60	60	60	70	70	70
50	50	60	60	60	70	70	70	70	70	80
55	55	60	70	70	70	70	80	80	80	80
60	60	70	70	70	80	80	80	90	90	90
65	65	70	80	80	80	90	90	90	100	100
70	70	80	80	90	90	90	100	100	100	110
75	75	90	90	90	100	100	100	110	110	110
80	80	90	90	100	100	100	110	110	120	120
85	85	100	100	100	110	110	120	120	120	130
90	90	100	110	110	110	120	120	130	130	140
95	95	110	110	110	120	120	130	130	140	140
100	100	110	120	120	130	130	130	140	140	150
105	105	120	120	130	130	140	140	150	150	160
110	110	120	130	130	140	140	150	150	160	160
115	115	130	130	140	140	150	150	160	170	170
120	120	130	140	140	150	150	160	170	170	180
125	125	140	140	150	160	160	170	170	180	190
130	130	140	150	160	160	170	170	180	190	190
135	135	150	160	160	170	170	180	190	190	**200**
140	140	160	160	170	170	180	190	190	**200**	**210**
145	145	160	170	170	180	190	190	**200**	**210**	
150	160	170	170	180	190	190	**200**	**210**		
155	170	170	180	180	190	200	**210**			
160	170	180	180	190	**200**	**200**				
165	180	180	190	200	**200**					
170	180	190	190	**200**						
175	190	190	**200**							
180	190	**200**	**210**							
185	**200**	**200**								
190	**200**									

Note: Numbers below this bar ⌐ are Exceptional Exposure Limits

Table Water Stops	Equivalent Stop Depths (fsw)									
10	10	9	9	9	8	8	8	7	7	7
20	19	19	18	17	17	16	15	15	14	14
30	29	28	27	26	25	24	23	22	21	21
40	39	37	36	35	33	32	31	30	29	28
50	48	47	45	43	42	40	39	37	36	34
60	58	56	54	52	50	48	46	45	43	41

Air Diving and Decompression

4.5.1.7 Hypoxia During Altitude Diving

A diver surfacing from an altitude dive is moving from a breathing gas in which the oxygen partial pressure is relatively high to an atmosphere in which it is low. As a result, the diver may experience symptoms of hypoxia and breathing difficulty for a period after the dive.

4.5.1.8 Altitude Sickness

This is a real problem above 13,125 ft. (4,003 m), although it has been known to occur as low as 8,093 ft. (2,468 m). Altitude sickness can be prevented with proper acclimatization. All divers on high-altitude dives should be familiar with the symptoms and treatment of altitude sickness (Hackett 1988). Most divers will not find themselves under these conditions.

4.5.1.9 Breathing Gases

Seek expert guidance on the use of compressed air and other breathing gases at high altitude. Pure oxygen has been used successfully during no-stop decompression diving at 6,000 m altitude. The probable advantages of nitrox have not yet been fully explored, but use of nitrox and standard air tables corrected for altitude should introduce an extra level of safety. Special altitude nitrox tables can be calculated from variable gas-mixture algorithms. Allow for expansion of the gas with decreasing atmospheric pressure if filling is carried out substantially lower than the dive.

4.5.1.10 Equilibration at Altitude

Upon ascent to altitude, two things happen. The body off-gases excess nitrogen to come into equilibrium with the lower partial pressure of nitrogen in the atmosphere. It also begins a series of complicated adjustments to the lower partial pressure of oxygen. The first process is called equilibration; the second is called acclimatization. Twelve hours at altitude is required for equilibration. A longer period is required for full acclimatization.

If a diver begins a dive at altitude less than 12 hours after arrival, the residual nitrogen left over from sea level must be taken into account. In effect, the initial dive at altitude can be considered a repetitive dive, with the first dive being the ascent from sea level to altitude. Table 4.2 gives the repetitive group associated with an initial ascent to altitude. Using this group and the time at altitude before diving, enter the Residual Nitrogen Timetable for Repetitive Air Dives (see Appendix IV, Table 4) to determine a new repetitive group designator associated with that period of equilibration. Determine sea level equivalent depth for the planned dive using Table 4.1. From the new repetitive group and sea level equivalent depth, determine the residual nitrogen time associated with the dive. Add this time to the actual bottom time of the dive.

Example:

A diver ascends to 6,000 ft. in a helicopter and begins a dive to 100 ft. 90 minutes later. How much residual nitrogen time should be added to the dive?

TABLE 4.2
Pressure Variations with Altitude

Altitude, ft	Pressure, mmHg	Pressure, psi	Pressure, atm*	Repetitive Group	Oil-filled Gauge Correction, ft
0	760.0	14.70	1.000		0
1000	732.9	14.17	0.964	A	1.22
2000	706.7	13.67	0.930	B	2.37
3000	681.2	13.17	0.896	B	3.53
4000	656.4	12.70	0.864	C	4.61
5000	632.4	12.23	0.832	D	5.70
6000	609.1	11.78	0.801	E	6.75
7000	586.5	11.35	0.772	E	7.73
8000	584.6	10.92	0.743	F	8.72
9000	543.3	10.51	0.715	G	9.67
10000	522.8	10.11	0.588	H	10.58
11000	502.8	9.73	0.662		11.47
12000	483.5	9.35	0.636		12.35
13000	464.8	8.99	0.612		13.15
14000	446.6	8.64	0.588		13.98
15000	429.1	8.31	0.565		14.76
16000	412.1	7.97	0.542		15.54
17000	395.7	7.66	0.521		16.25
18000	379.8	7.35	0.500		16.96
19000	364.4	7.04	0.479		17.67
20000	349.5	6.76	0.461		18.28

* U.S. standard atmosphere.

Solution:

From Table 4.2, repetitive group upon arrival at 6,000 ft. is Group E. During 90 minutes at altitude, the diver will desaturate to Group D (Appendix IV, Table 4). From Table 4.1, sea level equivalent depth for a 100 ft. dive is 130 fsw. From Table 4, Appendix IV, residual nitrogen time for a 130 fsw dive in Group D is 11 minutes. The diver should add 11 minutes to bottom time.

Table 4.3 can also be used when a diver who is fully equilibrated at one altitude ascends to and dives at a higher altitude. Enter Table 4.2 with the difference between the two altitudes to determine an initial repetitive group.

Example:

Divers equilibrated at a base camp altitude of 6,000 ft., fly by helicopter to the dive site at 10,000 ft. What would be the starting repetitive group letter upon arrival at 10,000 feet?

Solution:

The difference between the altitudes is 4,000 ft. Entering Table 4.2 at 4,000 feet, the initial repetitive group to be used at 10,000 ft. is Group C.

WARNING
DIVING AT ALTITUDES ABOVE 10,000 FEET IMPOSES SERIOUS STRESS ON THE BODY AND IS STRONGLY DISCOURAGED.

Example:

Five hours after arriving at an altitude of 7,750 ft., divers make a 20-minute air dive to 62 ft. Depth was measured with a boat-mounted pneumofathometer and verified. The U.S. Navy No-Decompression Tables will be used for decompression. What is the proper decompression schedule?

Solution:

The altitude is first rounded up to 8,000 ft. Table 4.1 is entered at depth of 65 ft. The Sea Level Equivalent Depth for 8,000 ft. of altitude is 90 fsw. The repetitive group upon arrival at altitude is Group F (see Table 4.2). This decays to Group B during the five hours at altitude predive (see Table 4, Appendix IV). The residual nitrogen time for Group B at 90 fsw is seven minutes. The Equivalent Single Dive Time therefore is 27 minutes. The appropriate decompression schedule from the U.S. Navy Surface Decompression Table is 90 fsw for 30 minutes. The repetitive group designation at the end of the dive will be letter H.

4.5.1.11 Repetitive Dives

Repetitive dives may be conducted at altitude. The procedure is identical to that at sea level, with the exception that the sea level equivalent dive depth is always used to replace the actual dive depth.

Example:

Fourteen hours after ascending to an altitude of 4,850 ft., divers make a dive to 82 ft. for 20 minutes using the U.S. Navy No-Decompression Tables. Depth was measured prior to the dive with a sounding line. After two hours and ten minutes on the surface, they make a second dive to 75 ft. for 20 minutes and decompress on the Standard Decompression Table. What is the proper decompression schedule for the second dive?

Solution:

The altitude is first rounded up to 5,000 ft. Table 4.1 is entered at a depth of 85 ft. The Sea Level Equivalent Depth for the first dive is 110 fsw. Since the dive was conducted more than 12 hours after arriving at altitude, no residual nitrogen needs to be added to the bottom time. The repetitive group designation upon completion of the 20 minute dive is Group G. This decays to Group D during the two hours ten minutes surface interval.

The depth of the second dive is 75 ft. Table 4.1 is entered at an actual depth of 75 ft. The Sea Level Equivalent Depth for the second dive is 100 fsw. The residual nitrogen time for Group D at 100 is 14 minutes. The equivalent single dive time therefore is 34 minutes. The appropriate decompression schedule from the Standard Decompression Table is 100 fsw for 40 min. A 15-minute stop at ten ft. is required by the schedule. Table 4.1 is consulted to determine the altitude stop depth for 10 fsw, which is 8 ft. The ending group is letter K.

4.5.1.12 Ascent to Altitude After Diving/
Flying After Diving

Leaving the dive site may require temporary ascent to a higher altitude. For example, divers may drive over a mountain pass at higher altitude or leave the dive site by air.

Ascent to altitude after diving increases the risk of decompression sickness because of the additional reduction in atmospheric pressure. The higher the altitude, the greater the risk. (Pressurized commercial airline flights are addressed in Note 3 of Table 4.3).

Table 4.3 gives the surface interval (hours:minutes) required before making a further ascent to altitude. The surface interval depends on the planned increase in altitude and the highest repetitive group designator obtained in the previous 24-hour period. Enter the table with the highest repetitive group designator obtained in the previous 24-hour period. Read the required surface interval from the column for the planned change in altitude.

Example:

A diver surfaces from a 60 ft. for 60 minutes no-decompression dive at sea level in Repetitive Group J. After a surface interval of six hours ten minutes, the diver makes a second dive to 30 ft. for 20 minutes placing him in Repetitive Group C. He plans to fly home in a commercial aircraft in which the cabin pressure is controlled at 8,000 ft. What is the required surface interval before flying?

Solution:

The planned increase in altitude is 8,000 ft. Because the diver has made two dives in the previous 24-hour period, he must use the highest Repetitive Group Designator obtained during the two dives which was J. Enter Table 4.3 at 8,000 ft. and read down to Repetitive Group J. The diver must wait 17 hours and 35 minutes after completion of the second dive before flying.

Example:

Upon completion of a dive at an altitude of 4,000 ft., the diver plans to ascend to 7,500 ft. in order to cross a mountain pass. The diver's repetitive group upon surfacing is Group G. What is the required surface interval before crossing the pass?

Solution:

The planned increase in altitude is 3,500 ft (7,500–4,000 ft.). Enter Table 4.3 at 4,000 ft. (rounded up from 3,500 ft.) and read down to Repetitive Group G. The diver must delay one hour and 23 minutes before crossing the pass.

Example:

Upon completion of a dive at 2,000 ft., the diver plans to fly home in an unpressurized aircraft at 5,000 ft. The diver's repetitive group designator upon surfacing is Group K. What is the required surface interval before flying?

Solution:

The planned increase in altitude is 3,000 ft. (5,000–2,000 ft.). Enter Table 4.3 at 3,000 ft. and read down to Repetitive Group K. The diver must delay six hours and 25 minutes before taking the flight.

TABLE 4.3

Required Surface Interval Before Ascent to Altitude After Diving

Repetitive Group Designator	Altitude									
	1,000	2,000	3,000	4,000	5,000	6,000	7,000	8,000	9,000	10,000
A	0:00	0:00	0:00	0:00	0:00	0:00	0:00	0:00	0:00	0:00
B	0:00	0:00	0:00	0:00	0:00	0:00	0:00	0:00	0:00	2:11
C	0:00	0:00	0:00	0:00	0:00	0:00	0:00	0:00	3:06	8:26
D	0:00	0:00	0:00	0:00	0:00	0:00	0:09	3:28	7:33	12:52
E	0:00	0:00	0:00	0:00	0:00	0:51	3:35	6:54	10:59	16:18
F	0:00	0:00	0:00	0:00	1:12	3:40	6:23	9:43	13:47	19:07
G	0:00	0:00	0:00	1:23	3:34	6:02	8:46	12:05	16:10	21:29
H	0:00	0:00	1:31	3:26	5:37	8:05	10:49	14:09	18:13	23:33
I	0:00	1:32	3:20	5:15	7:26	9:54	12:38	15:58	20:02	24:00
J	1:32	3:09	4:57	6:52	9:04	11:32	14:16	17:35	21:39	24:00
K	3:00	4:37	6:25	8:20	10:32	13:00	15:44	19:03	23:07	24:00
L	4:21	5:57	7:46	9:41	11:52	14:20	17:04	20:23	24:00	24:00
M	5:35	7:11	9:00	10:55	13:06	15:34	18:18	21:37	24:00	24:00
N	6:43	8:20	10:08	12:03	14:14	16:42	19:26	22:46	24:00	24:00
O	7:47	9:24	11:12	13:07	15:18	17:46	20:30	23:49	24:00	24:00
Z	8:17	9:54	11:42	13:37	15:49	18:17	21:01	24:00	24:00	24:00

Exceptional Exposure   Wait 48 hours before flying

NOTE 1   When using Table 4-3, use the highest repetitive group designator obtained in the previous 24-hour period.

NOTE 2   Table 4-3 may only be used when the maximum altitude achieved is 10,000 ft. or less. For ascents above 10,000 ft., consult NOAA Diving Program for guidance.

NOTE 3   The cabin pressure in commercial aircraft is maintained at a constant value regardless of the actual altitude of the flight. Though cabin pressure varies somewhat with aircraft type, the nominal value is 8,000 feet to compute the required surface interval before flying.

NOTE 4   No surface interval is required before taking a commercial flight if the dive site is at 8,000 ft. or higher. In this case, flying results in an increase in atmospheric pressure rather than a decrease.

NOTE 5   No repetitive group is given for air dives with surface decompression on oxygen or air. For these surface decompression dives, enter the standard air table with the sea level equivalent depth and bottom time of the dive to obtain the appropriate repetitive group designator to be used.

NOTE 6   For ascent to altitude following a non-saturation helium-oxygen dive, wait 12 hours if the dive was a no-decompression dive. Wait 24 hours if the dive was a decompression dive.

4.6 BUILDING ADDITIONAL SAFETY FACTORS INTO DIVE TABLE USAGE

The U.S. Navy Dive Tables have no magical ability to protect users from decompression sickness. As with other dive tables and dive computers, the U.S. Navy Dive Tables are based on a mathematical model designed to emulate how most human bodies absorb and release nitrogen. They cannot take into account the wide range of human body and tissue types, nor the factors that may make a particular diver more or less susceptible to decompression sickness (DCS) at any given time. Researchers still know surprisingly little about the exact causes and nature of DCS. Therefore, it is important to remember that no dive table or dive computer can provide a guarantee of protection against decompression sickness. Even when using these items correctly, there is always a risk of DCS.

Fortunately, the U.S. Navy Dive Tables have a fairly good track record when it comes to helping divers avoid DCS. Still, there are many steps experts believe can be taken to further reduce the risk of decompression sickness. This section discusses several of these steps.

4.6.1 Remaining Well Within No-Decompression and Other Limits

Many experts believe that the closer one comes to the no-decompression limits, the greater the risk of DCS. For this reason, wise divers choose to remain well within dive table or dive computer limits. Several recreational diver training organizations go so far as to publish dive tables with no-decompression limits that are more conservative than those of the U.S. Navy.

Earlier in this section, examples were presented of how one would go about finding the minimum allowable Surface Interval between dives. Bear in mind, however, that the examples provided were based on extenuating circumstances. Wise divers avoid "pushing" dive table or dive computer limits unless absolutely necessary. This involves not only staying well within the no-decompression limits but also avoiding minimum Surface Intervals.

4.6.2 Making Slow Ascents and Safety Stops

As discussed earlier, slow ascents and precautionary decompression ("safety") stops help reduce the size and quantity of gas bubbles formed in body tissues as divers ascend. Many researchers believe that such asymptomatic or "silent" bubbles are a precursor to decompression sickness and that by reducing the size and quantity of such bubbles, we help reduce the risk of DCS.

To make safety stops even safer, a diver can add the time spent making such stops to Actual Bottom Time (ABT). Doing so further increases the safety margin. It also means that the ABT will more closely match the time recorded by the dive computer or automatic timing device, which typically records bottom time as being from the beginning of descent until the end of ascent.

4.6.3 Taking Advantage of the Dive Table's Inherent Margin of Safety on Multi-Level Dives

The U.S. Navy Dive Tables are based on the assumption that users will make what are known as square profile dives—dives in which participants descend almost immediately to their maximum depth and remain at this depth until beginning their ascent.

Many dives, however, are what are known as multi-level dives—in which participants will be at a variety of depths throughout the dive. Dive computers automatically account for multi-level diving, providing computer users with no additional margin of safety. Dive tables, in contrast, assume that the deepest depth reached during the dive was the actual depth for the entire dive. Thus, divers who make multi-level dives, yet use the U.S. Navy or similar dive tables correctly, may enjoy an additional margin of safety that computer users do not (see Figure 4.26).

4.6.3.1 Reverse Profile Dives

A reverse profile can refer to a series of repetitive dives during which the deepest dive is not the first in the series, or to a single multi-level dive during which the diver goes deeper after completing a shallower phase.

There is no convincing evidence that reverse dive profiles within the no-decompression limits subject a diver to a measurable increase in the risk of DCS.

Reverse profile dives should be conducted within the following parameters:

- No-decompression dives in less than 130 fsw (40 msw)
- Depth differentials of less than 40 fsw (12 msw)

Regardless of the dive profile, it is safest to be in the shallowest phase late in the dive when air supplies are low.

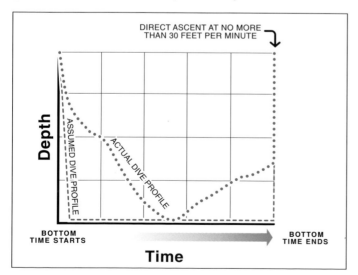

FIGURE 4.26
Actual Dive Profile Versus an Assumed Dive Profile

Air Diving and Decompression

4.6.4 Following Recommendations Concerning Cold and Arduous Dives

Unfortunately, many research and other working dives fall into the category of square-profile diving, and thus fail to afford dive-table users the additional margin of safety they enjoy when making multi-level dives. Additionally, such dives often take place in cold water and require divers to exert themselves—both factors that experts believe may contribute to the onset of decompression sickness.

Under these circumstances, divers should follow the U.S. Navy's recommendation for cold/arduous dives; that is, consider that the dive has been made to the next greater time increment appearing on the tables.

For example, a dive is made to a depth of 65 fsw for 40 minutes in 48°F water temperature. Normally decompression would be based on a 70 fsw/40 minutes schedule. However, because of the cold water temperature, decompression is based on 70 fsw/45 minutes schedule.

4.6.5 Managing Additional Risk Factors That May Contribute to Decompression Sickness

There are additional factors that experts believe may contribute to the risk of DCS over which divers have control. It makes sense to manage these risks intelligently, whenever possible. Among the ways to do so:

- Avoid factors such as cold, dehydration, and fatigue. Wise divers will wear adequate exposure protection both above and below the water. They will drink plenty of fluids (while avoiding coffee and alcohol, as these can lead to dehydration). They will further plan dives in such a manner as to require the least possible exertion.
- Maintain a high level of personal fitness. There are factors that may contribute to the risk of DCS, such as age over which we have little control, other than to allow additional safety margins. Divers can control their levels of health and fitness. Being fit benefits divers in a number of ways. Lean tissue absorbs less nitrogen than fat tissue. Increased personal fitness tends to lead to increased respiratory efficiency, which helps in the off-gassing of nitrogen. Fit divers also tend to have a lower overall level of carbon dioxide in their systems at any time, further reducing the risk of DCS.

4.7 NOAA NO-DECOMPRESSION DIVE CHARTS

NOAA has developed an abbreviated no-decompression dive table based upon the U.S. Navy Dive Tables titled NOAA No-Decompression Air Dive Table, see Table 4.4 and Appendix III.

4.7.1 General

The NOAA No-Decompression Charts are based upon the U.S. Navy Air Decompression Tables and presented in a format designed by the National Association of Underwater Instructors (NAUI) for recreational diving. The charts are configured so that each of three charts flows into the next. You begin with Chart 1, which is called the "Dive Times with End-of-Dive Group Letter" chart. Chart 1 provides maximum dive time information for dives between 40 and 130 ft. (12–40 m) and the group letter designation at the end of a dive. Look at Chart 1 (see Table 4.5) and note that maximum times are circled for each depth.

Chart 1 is entered horizontally from the left. The numbers on the chart represent bottom time in minutes. Find the row for the appropriate depth and move to the right along the line until you find a bottom time that meets or exceeds your dive time. Now follow that column downward, exit the chart, and find the group letter designation that indicates the amount of nitrogen remaining in your system following a dive. For example, a person who dives to 50 ft. (15 m) for 30 minutes would have an "E" group letter designation.

The longer you remain out of the water, the more excess nitrogen you eliminate. Crediting you with the loss of that nitrogen is the purpose of Chart 2, (see Table 4.6) the "Surface Interval Time" (SIT) chart. It consists of blocks containing two numbers which represent the minimum and maximum times for assignment to a particular group letter. The times are expressed as hours and minutes (Hours:Minutes).

The SIT chart is entered vertically coming down the column from Chart 1 and followed downward until you find a range of times into which the length of your surface interval falls. Then follow that row horizontally to the left, exit the chart, and receive a new letter designation. For example, if you enter the chart with an "E" group letter and have a surface interval of three hours, you will exit the chart on the third horizontal line and end up with a new group letter of "C." Note that the maximum time in the chart is 12 hours, so a dive after that amount of time is not a repetitive dive.

Chart 3 is the "Repetitive Dive Time." It tells your Residual Nitrogen Time (RNT) based on your current group letter and your planned depth and provides Maximum Dive Times that are reduced by the amount of your RNT. Your Actual Bottom Time (ABT) must not exceed the Adjusted Maximum Dive Time (AMDT). Your Residual Nitrogen Time (RNT) must be added to your ABT to obtain your Equivalent Single Dive Time (ESDT). This formula (RNT + ABT = ESDT) is illustrated in the upper left corner, see Appendix III, page III-1.

To use Chart 3, (see Table 4.7) enter it horizontally from the right on the row representing your group letter designation after your SIT and move to the left until you intersect the column corresponding to the depth of your

NOAA NO-DECOMPRESSION AIR DIVE TABLE

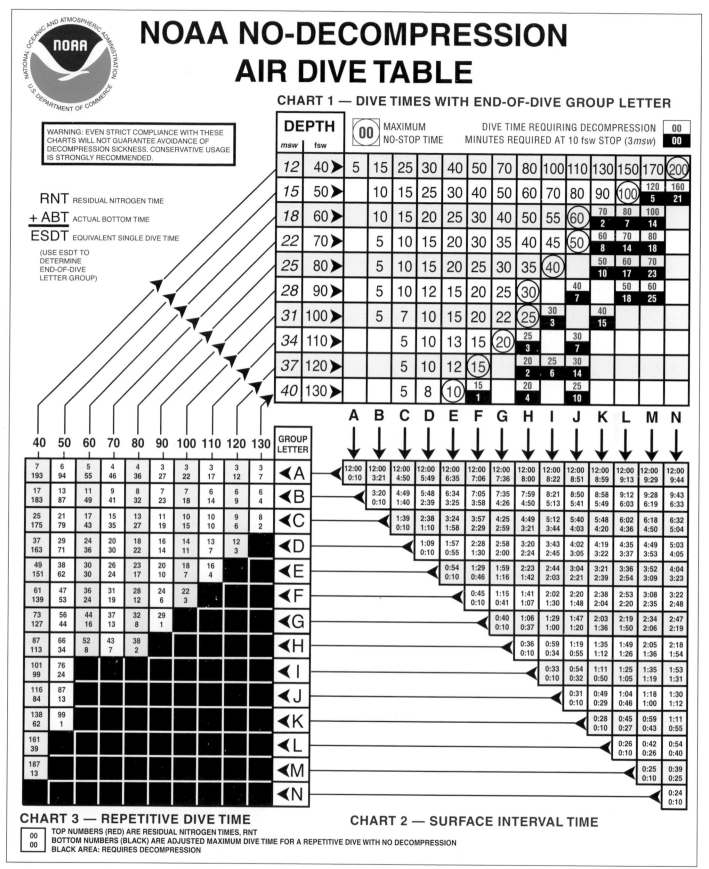

TABLE 4.4
No-Decompression Air Dive Table

planned repetitive dive. Depths are listed across the top of the chart. At the intersection of the depth and the group letter you will find two numbers. The top number represents RNT for that depth; the bottom number represents the Adjusted Maximum Dive Time (AMDT) for the depth. If you compare the totals of the AMDT and the Residual Nitrogen Times for any depth, you will find they all total the Maximum Dive Time Limit for that depth in Chart 1. The AMDT is found by simply subtracting RNT from Maximum Dive Time for a given depth. Chart 3 has already done the work for you. Your Actual Dive Time must not exceed your AMDT during a repetitive Dive.

An example of the use of Chart 3 is a "C" group letter diver planning a dive to 50 feet, you find the number 21 over the number 79. This means the diver has 21 minutes of RNT and the duration of the ABT must not exceed 79 minutes. The diver proceeds with the dive, keeping the ABT within the 79 minute Adjusted Maximum Dive Time, then adds the ABT to the 21 minutes of RNT and uses the dive schedule of 50 feet (15 m)/ESDT to re-enter Chart 1 and obtain an End-of-Dive group letter. Note how the cycle has been completed with the three charts.

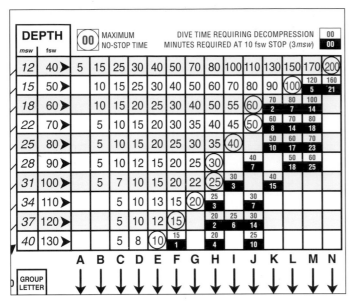

TABLE 4.5
Chart 1—Dive Times with End-of-Dive Group Letter

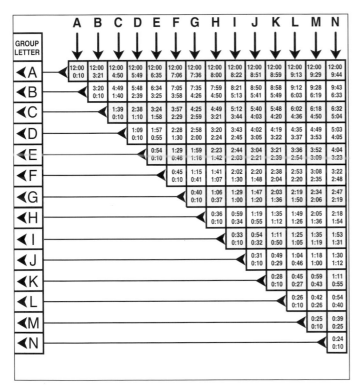

TABLE 4.6
Chart 2—Surface Interval Time

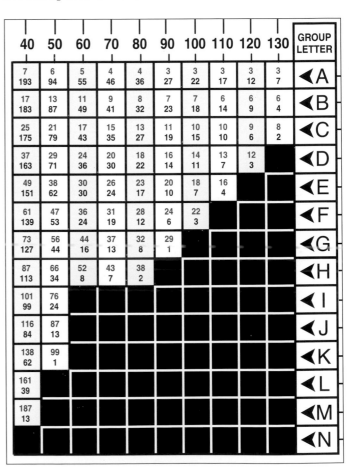

TABLE 4.7
Chart 3—Repetitive Dive Time

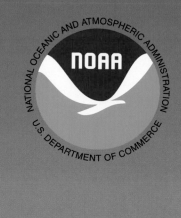

Diver and Diving Support Equipment

5

Diver and Diving Support Equipment

5.0 GENERAL

The type of diving equipment the diver wears has a tremendous impact on the diver's ability to work comfortably, safely, and efficiently (Bachrach and Egstrom 1986). Although equipment is a big factor in diver performance, equipment alone cannot make up for a diver's lack of ability in the water. A good diver must have a high level of fitness and must be comfortable in the water.

A competent diver should be able to dive with most any type of equipment provided he has been trained to use it. Selecting the right dive gear for a scientific dive is a matter of defining the objectives of the dive and the location. For some work, snorkeling equipment may be all that is required, while for other jobs surface-supplied gear may be the best choice. A diver must become totally familiar with new equipment before entering a working situation.

With all diving equipment, remember that streamlining is an essential factor in making it easy for the diver to swim and maneuver under water. The more equipment the diver wears, the more drag and change of center of gravity will be created. Each piece of equipment should have a definite purpose on a particular dive; and if it is not going to be used, it should not be carried. Streamlining is crucial to productivity for the scientific diver.

Given the durability of most diving gear, making the right selection at the time of purchase is critical, since it is hard to justify equipment replacement if the equipment is not worn out. By talking with diving officers and other scientific divers, the preferred models of gear for a particular location and type of diving are easily identified.

The NOAA Diving Program has a standardized equipment program whereby all active NOAA divers are issued dive equipment. The program, which includes yearly maintenance and testing of all scuba regulators, pressure and depth gauges by a factory-trained NOAA technician, provides standardization of equipment for all NOAA divers and helps ensure quality control.

FIGURE 5.1
Dive Mask with Nose Pocket

5.1 BASIC EQUIPMENT

5.1.1 Face Masks

Face masks for scuba diving are designed to cover the eyes and nose. The nose must be included inside the mask to allow the diver to equalize the pressure inside the mask by exhaling through his nostrils. This is one of the reasons that goggles that cover only the eyes are not acceptable for diving.

A critical issue in selecting a mask is the fit. The mask must fit comfortably and not leak. To test the fit, the diver places the mask against his face as he would when wearing it normally, but without using the strap to hold the mask in place. The diver then inhales through his nose, holds his breath, and attempts to make the mask seal against his face. If no air leaks into the mask and the mask stays in position, it can be considered to be a good fit, as long as it is comfortable. Divers with mustaches having difficulty achieving a mask seal may have to use some type of substance such as Vaseline® on their mustaches to achieve a proper seal.

Many divers find that a nose "pocket" is a useful feature of a mask in that it provides a means for the diver to pinch his nostrils closed in order to aid in equalizing the pressure in his ears (see Figure 5.1). Other features include purge valves and double feather edge seals. A purge is a one-way valve through which water can be expelled that enters the mask. Water can also be removed from a mask without a purge. A double feather edge is a type of sealing (double) edge on the material that fits against the face.

Once it is determined that the mask fits properly, the next most critical feature is visibility. Side windows in the masks can enhance peripheral vision (Egstrom 1982), but can sometimes produce a "rear view effect." Mask windows are made from safety-tempered glass. Additionally, some masks have downward lenses or optical devices that will help the diver see more of the equipment mounted on his chest and waist.

For divers who require glasses, prescription lenses are available that will fit many popular dive masks. For divers who have a common prescription and do not need bifocals, many dive stores stock lenses for their more popular mask styles. Divers who have an unusual prescription will need to order specially prepared lenses for their masks.

The lenses of new masks need to be washed with a mild liquid detergent, such as dishwashing detergent, to help remove any chemicals that may remain from manufacturing and may cause the mask to fog.

5.1.2 Snorkels

A snorkel is an indispensable piece of equipment for the open water scuba diver using self-contained open circuit gear (see Figure 5.2). The purpose of the snorkel is to allow the diver to swim more easily on the surface without consuming the compressed gas in his cylinder.

Ideally, the snorkel should not exceed 14 inches in length and should have the minimum number of bends possible. If the snorkel has a corrugated hose, allowing it to bend easily, the inside bore of the hose must be smooth, not ribbed. Small diameter snorkels, and those with corrugated hoses with internal ribs, produce high breathing resistance, add substantially to equipment dead air space (where no gas exchange takes place), and a corrugated hose also makes elimination of all water in the snorkel all but impossible.

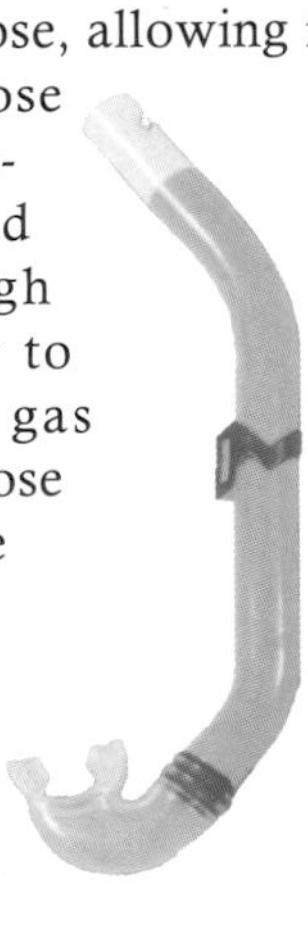

FIGURE 5.2
Snorkel with Attached Snorkel Holder

Many snorkels today are available with top mounted valves that help to keep water out of the snorkel while surface swimming. These valves are not designed to seal the snorkel under water but to keep spray from flooding the snorkel while the diver swims on the surface. These can be extremely effective and make surface swimming much easier.

Most modern snorkels use plastic rings or attachment devices to connect the snorkel to the diver's mask. These rings allow the snorkel to be easily removed from the mask, so that the mask can be stored in a protective box for transport to and from the dive site or during airline travel.

In the United States, the snorkel is traditionally mounted on the left side of the diver's head, since the regulator is routed over the diver's right shoulder. In Europe, the opposite arrangement is sometimes employed since the regulator may be directed over the diver's left shoulder.

5.1.3 Fins

Fins for scuba diving are usually much more rugged and have larger blades than those used for snorkeling or swimming. The fins provide propulsion for divers who are heavily encumbered with equipment and make underwater swimming much easier. Human leg muscles are very efficient for underwater propulsion when properly equipped.

When divers are fully geared up, it may not be possible for them to use their hands for swimming purposes, since straps and thermal protection suits inhibit normal arm movement. In addition, scientific divers are usually carrying instruments, slates, or other equipment that make it impractical to use their arms for swimming.

The human leg provides propulsion under water by moving the levers of the body, i.e. the femur and tibia, to provide thrust through the use of the fins. Since these bones are of different lengths in each individual, providing a different mechanical advantage for each diver, there is no one fin that will work best for each person. A fin that works very

FIGURE 5.3
Adjustable Heel Strap Fins

FIGURE 5.4
Full-foot Fins

FIGURE 5.5
Booties

well for one diver may not work satisfactorily for another; therefore, divers may have to try several different types and sizes before finding the best set of fins for their use.

Fins come in two styles, the open heel adjustable fin and the full-foot pocket fin (see Figures 5.3, 5.4). Fins are made from either rubber or graphite and are available in different foot pocket sizes. While full-foot fins, without booties, are frequently used in the tropics, they are rarely used in colder waters. One of the disadvantages to the full-foot fin is that when the foot pocket wears out, the fin cannot be repaired.

The open heel adjustable fin is normally worn with neoprene booties (see Figure 5.5). The major advantage to this type of fin is that if the heel strap breaks, it can be replaced.

5.2 THERMAL PROTECTION

The type of thermal protection will be determined by the water temperature, the diver's work load, personal physiology, and any contaminants that may be present in the water. Each of these factors is important, but it is essential for the diver to pay attention to his own comfort level in the water. While a large male may be comfortable in a six millimeter wet suit in 62°F water, a small female may be extremely uncomfortable.

5.2.1 Dive Skins

There are many different types of thin suits available that provide sun protection as well as protection from coral cuts, scrapes, and stinging creatures such as jellyfish. These suits are form fitting, have good stretch, and are generally referred to as "dive skins" or just "skins."

Skins made from Lycra® provide good protection from the sun but do not provide any thermal protection. There are also suits made from Lycra® combined with additional materials such as polyolefin microfibers which provide good wind resistance.

Dive skins may be worn in tropical waters when the diver's activity level is relatively high. During warm water dives where the diver will remain relatively inactive, a wet suit or Polartec® skin, which provides insulation equivalent to a 2-millimeter suit without the same buoyant properties of a wet suit, is recommended. In some cases where buoyancy is desirable, wet suits made from rubber are recommended.

5.2.2 Wet Suits

Wet suits are made from foam neoprene, a synthetic material with thousands of tiny closed cells that are filled with nitrogen gas (see Figure 5.6). The suits are designed to allow water to enter the area between the diver's skin and the suit. Ideally, a wet suit should fit snugly, allowing only a minimum of water inside the suit. This thin layer of water is warmed up by the diver's body and provides reasonable comfort at moderate temperatures. A cold water wet suit usually provides a double layer of insulation over the torso.

Wet suits come in a variety of thicknesses, one millimeter up to seven millimeters. They also come in numerous designs, including shorty suits, one-piece suits, and multi-piece suits.

For warm waters, above 80°F (26.7C), a one-piece suit, two to three millimeters thick, may be all that is necessary for most divers. As the water temperature drops, thicker suits and multiple layers of insulation become necessary. For example, in Southern California, the preferred wet suit is usually six or seven millimeters thick with a "farmer john" set of bib overalls and a jacket of the same material with an attached hood.

The use of zippers in wet suits is a personal preference of the diver. While zippers make it easier to don a suit, they also increase the cost of the suit, decrease reliability, and allow more water to enter the suit.

Most wet suits have a nylon exterior coating to help reduce abrasion to the rubber and a nylon interior to make it easier to don the suit. Some divers prefer a suit without a nylon lining and use a diluted solution of hair conditioner or talcum powder to make the neoprene surface slippery enough to slide easily over their skin.

Wet suits are very buoyant on the surface. For this reason, divers usually wear a weight belt when wearing this type of thermal protection. However, as the diver descends and the suit compresses at depth, buoyancy

FIGURE 5.6
Cold Water Wet Suit

TABLE 5.1
Efficiency of Wet Suits vs. Dry Suits

Water Temperature	Wetsuit			Drysuit		
	1st Dive	2nd Dive	3rd Dive	1st Dive	2nd Dive	3rd Dive
70°F	100%	100%	100%	100%	100%	100%
60°F	100%	90%	80%	100%	100%	100%
50°F	80%	70%	50%	100%	100%	100%
40°F	50%	25%	*	100%	85%	75%
32°F	*	*	*	100%	75%	55%

Table is based upon 30-minute dives at 50 fsw, with one hour surface intervals between dives. The * indicates an exposure not recommended unless involved in a contingency situation.

decreases and the diver must adjust for this change of buoyancy. Between dives, the water that has been trapped inside the wet suit normally leaks out. This causes a loss in body heat. In addition, divers wearing wet suits are subjected to evaporative cooling as the wind blows over their suit and the water on its surface vaporizes.

The cells of the material that provide the insulation for the wet suit begin to break down over time due to age and use. When this happens, the suit loses much of its insulation value.

Wet suits are most effective at water temperatures above 60°F (15.6C); in colder waters, a dry suit is generally recommended (see Table 5.1).

5.2.2.1 Maintenance of Wet Suits

Proper care of wet suits, like all dive gear, is critical to ensure long life and reliability. After each day of diving, the suit must be thoroughly rinsed with fresh, clean water and allowed to dry. Avoid hanging the suit in the sun to dry for long periods or for permanent storage. Heat and ultraviolet rays from the sun will deteriorate neoprene; therefore, store the suit in a cool, dark, and dry location.

5.2.3 Dry Suits

Dry suits are the most efficient form of passive thermal protection for the diver. Dry suits are designed as one-piece suits with a waterproof zipper for entering the suit, attached boots, and seals at the diver's wrists and neck. The suits are normally designed so that insulating undergarments may be worn beneath them. These undergarments trap a layer of air that provides primary protection against cold.

By varying the amount of underwear (insulation) worn underneath the dry suit, it is possible to dive in a wide variety of water temperatures. When purchasing a suit, the diver should try the suit on with the thickest underwear he anticipates using to ensure a proper fit.

Dry suits can increase a diver's bottom time dramatically, since the diver's body doesn't need to "burn" as many calories to keep warm. Keeping the diver warm will enhance his performance and lower the risk of hypothermia.

Dry suits are made from a variety of materials, including foam neoprene, crushed or compressed neoprene, tri-laminates, urethane-coated fabrics, and vulcanized rubber. Each type of material has advantages and disadvantages. A heavy duty suit made of vulcanized rubber, for example, is worn with cold water undergarments and is available with mating yokes to accommodate various diving helmets (see Figure 5.7).

Foam neoprene (wet suit material) is the least expensive type of dry suit. It has good stretch and thermal characteristics, but tends to develop leaks over time as cracks occur in the neoprene bubble layers and water migrates through the material (see Figure 5.8).

FIGURE 5.7
Heavy Duty Suit Made of Vulcanized Rubber

**FIGURE 5.8
Foam Neoprene Dry Suit**

Crushed and compressed neoprene are rugged dry-suit materials that have good stretch and some inherent insulation. The disadvantages to this type of suit are its relatively heavy weight and higher cost.

TLS stands for tri-laminate suit. This is an extremely lightweight material originally developed for chemical warfare. The material is very flexible and reasonably rugged. The disadvantage of suits made from this material is that they don't stretch.

Urethane-coated nylon material is similar in appearance to TLS but not nearly as flexible nor as reliable. The advantage to urethane-coated nylon dry suits is low cost.

Vulcanized rubber material has some stretch, but not nearly as much as crushed or compressed neoprene or foam neoprene. Vulcanized rubber dries quickly and is quick and easy to repair. One disadvantage of vulcanized rubber suits is that they cannot be tailored to be as form fitting as crushed neoprene or TLS suits. They are also relatively heavy suits when compared to TLS or urethane. Vulcanized rubber suits are preferred for diving in contaminated water because they are the easiest of all dry-suit types to decontaminate.

NOTE
Polluted-water diving requires specialized equipment and training (see Chapter 13 for more information).

The two main styles of dry suits are shoulder-entry suits and self-donning suits. Again, both types of suits have their advantages and disadvantages. Also, dry suits are designed with boots with either hard or soft soles.

With a shoulder-entry suit the diver gets into the suit through the back by opening the waterproof zipper. The disadvantage of a shoulder-entry suit is that it requires assistance to get in and out of the suit.

Self-donning dry suits have the major advantage of allowing the diver to get in and out of the suit by himself. The disadvantage is that self-donning suits are usually more expensive than a similar shoulder-entry suit.

5.2.3.1 Dry-Suit Valves
Most dry suits today have separate inflator and exhaust valves. This is the preferred arrangement to avoid getting water in the suit and for the most precise buoyancy control.

The most common location for the inflator valve is the middle of the diver's chest. Inflator valves must never be covered by the diver's buoyancy compensator, which can make it difficult to access the valve and lead to runaway inflation accidents. This can occur when the buoyancy compensator (BC) bladder pushes on the suit valve causing the valve to inflate the suit. As the suit inflates, it pushes the valve against the BC, which causes it to continue to inflate.

The inflator valve is supplied with air from a low pressure hose that connects to the first stage of the diver's regulator. The hose must only be connected to a low-pressure port. High-pressure breathing gas entering the hose will cause the hose to fail.

The inflator hose must be equipped with a quick disconnect fitting so that the hose can be immediately released from the valve in the event the valve sticks in the open position. The quick disconnect must be easy to operate so that it can be removed, or reconnected, even if the diver is wearing thick gloves or three-finger mitts.

Divers working in very cold water or using helium-oxygen gas mixtures sometimes use a suit inflation system that is independent of their breathing gas supply. In these situations, the preferred suit inflation gas is argon, which is normally supplied from a small cylinder mounted on the thigh of the diver's suit (Barsky et al. 1998). When this type of system is used the inflator valve will usually be mounted on the thigh as well.

No empirical data exists on the effects of argon absorbed transdermally on a diver's decompression obligation. For this reason, divers should be conservative in using this type of system.

The exhaust valve should be a low-profile valve that can be vented either automatically or manually during ascent. The most common location for the exhaust valve is on the left arm on the outside although a chest mounted valve is not uncommon. The exhaust valve must vent air faster than the inflator valve can supply it to the suit.

Different models of valves vent at different rates. A faster exhaust is better since it allows a diver to dump the air from his suit more quickly (Barsky, Long, and Stinton 1996). Even the same models of valves will not always vent at the same rate due to differences in manufacturing tolerances, wear, maintenance, etc.

5.2.3.2 Dry-Suit Seals and Accessories
Dry suits are equipped with seals at the wrists and neck. These seals can be either latex or neoprene.

Latex seals are the softest, thinnest, most flexible seals available and can be cut to fit the individual diver. However, latex seals are not as rugged as neoprene seals and are more prone to damage if mishandled. In areas with heavy smog, latex seals usually only last about a year before they must be replaced due to rubber deterioration.

Latex seals can be ordered in different thicknesses. Thicker latex seals last longer and are more reliable, but can be troublesome to don and remove. Some dry suits come with or may be adapted for use with a cuff ring system that allows change of cuff rings, seals, and the use of dry gloves.

Diver and Diving Support Equipment

Both latex and neoprene seals should be dusted with pure talcum powder prior to donning. Do not use scented talcs which contain oils and can damage the seals. If no talcum powder is available, soapy water may be used as an alternative. Neoprene seals are more rugged than latex seals and can last for several years. The negative side of neoprene seals is that they tend to leak more than latex seals.

Proper donning of suit cuffs is absolutely critical to a dry dive. Jewelry, rings, etc., should be removed when donning neck and wrist seals to avoid damage to the seals.

5.2.3.3 Dry-Suit Zippers

The waterproof, pressure-proof zipper is what made the modern dry suit possible. These zippers are very similar to the zippers used in space suits.

Just as a heavier latex seal is more reliable, the heavier the zipper the more rugged and damage resistant it will be. The most heavy-duty zippers have individually pinned "teeth" which can be replaced if broken. Lighter weight zippers must be completely replaced when damaged.

Special care must be taken to ensure that no dry-suit underwear, hair, or other foreign material is caught in the zipper when it is closed. Not only would this cause the zipper to leak, it may also cause the zipper to break. Damage/wear to zipper teeth can be minimized by not twisting the zipper at angles oblique to the normal linear direction during donning and removing the suit.

Dry-suit zippers should be lubricated with bee's wax prior to closing. The lubrication should only be applied to the outside of the zipper, never on the inside. Paraffin wax may also be used and even a bar of soap can be used if no other lubricant is available.

Silicone spray should never be used to lubricate a dry-suit zipper, or any other part of the suit. Silicone spray works its way into the fabric of the suit, making it difficult to get a good bond between the suit and replacement parts that must be glued to the suit when it is time to make repairs.

5.2.3.4 Dry-Suit Use

All divers who use dry suits must be trained to use them properly. Although dry suits are not difficult to use, accidents have occurred when divers who were untrained have attempted to use them.

Under normal conditions, dry-suit divers control their buoyancy under water by introducing air into the suit or buoyancy compensator, if a BC is worn. The air is also used to offset the effects of pressure to prevent suit squeeze. To control buoyancy upon ascent, the air must be vented out of the suit as it expands. Dry-suit divers should keep a thin layer of air in the suit at all times for thermal insulation. This may mean adding weight to the weight belt to compensate for the additional buoyancy.

The dry suit worn by the diver must never be used as a lifting device to lift heavy objects under water. If the diver loses control of the object, he will become positively buoyant, which can lead to a rapid ascent. Rapid ascents are dangerous and can cause lung over-pressure injuries and omitted decompression.

Some manufacturers recommend the use of buoyancy compensators with dry suits. The buoyancy compensator is used primarily for surface flotation and as a back-up device in the event of a catastrophic dry-suit failure. Divers who are more heavily weighted with multiple cylinders may need to use the buoyancy compensator in conjunction with the suit under water. Controlling two independent flotation systems (the dry suit and the buoyancy compensator) at the same time is considered an advanced skill and requires additional training and practice.

5.2.3.5 Dry-Suit Underwear

Several different types of dry-suit underwear are available in different thicknesses. The three most popular types of material used are Thinsulate®, Polartec®, and synthetic fleece.

Thinsulate® is made from polyolefin microfibers. The most important feature of Thinsulate® is that it is water resistant and maintains most of its insulating capabilities even when it is wet. Undergarments made of Thinsulate® have more bulk than most other types of dry-suit underwear. They also do not stretch or breathe and are not as comfortable to wear as some other types of undergarments.

Polartec® is another synthetic material that is widely used as dry-suit underwear. Polartec® is easy to don and the material has excellent stretch, which makes it easy to swim and move. The material has good insulation characteristics with very little bulk, but it does not maintain its insulation capabilities once it is wet. For this reason, it is not recommended for critical applications such as diving under the ice.

Synthetic fleeces are comfortable to wear but do not offer the insulating capabilities of either Thinsulate® or Polartec®. They also do not have the stretch capabilities of Polartec®.

As the diver varies his insulation, his buoyancy will change. Thinner dry-suit underwear traps less air and requires less weight than thicker material. This must be considered as the diver makes changes in his insulation with the season, when traveling to another location with different conditions, or with his work rate.

5.2.3.6 Dry Suits and Dry-Suit Underwear Maintenance

Dry suits require more maintenance than wet suits to ensure consistent performance. The seals, zipper, valves, and suit itself must receive regular attention.

At the end of each diving day, the exterior of the suit, including the valves, zippers, and seals, must be rinsed thoroughly with fresh water. If the diver has perspired inside the suit, the interior of the suit will need to be rinsed as well.

Check inside the suit for perspiration or moisture by reaching all the way down inside the suit to the boots. If the boots feel damp inside the suit, the inside of the suit needs rinsing.

The suit should be dried by hanging it to dry over a line or bar out of the sun. Do not use a hanger. If the suit has been rinsed inside, the suit must be turned inside out to dry the interior, too. The entire suit, both inside and outside, must be completely dry prior to storage.

Latex seals need to be washed periodically with a diluted solution of dishwashing soap and water. This will remove any body oils or other substances (i.e., gasoline, petroleum products, creosote) the suit may have been exposed to in the water which will cause the seals to deteriorate. When the seals begin to crack or appear sticky, they will need to be replaced by an authorized repair facility.

Aside from lubricating the zipper prior to every dive, the zipper should be cleaned regularly with soap and water and a toothbrush. This will help to remove corrosion from the zipper and keep it operating smoothly.

A small shot of silicone spray should be applied to the opening of the nipple of the inflator valve and the valve should be operated several times. The valve must work smoothly and not stick.

Dry suits should be stored rolled up, in a bag, in a cool, dry place, away from sources of ozone, such as hot-water heaters or electric motors. Several days prior to any dive the suit should be removed from storage and inspected to ensure it is in good condition for diving. Dry suits should be leak-checked prior to initial use each year. This is done by plugging the seals, inflating the suit, and brushing it with a diluted soap solution.

Dry-suit underwear needs to be laundered periodically to remove body oils, stains, and dirt. Divers must check the instructions supplied with the garment to determine proper laundry procedures. Improper laundering can ruin some garments, especially Thinsulate®.

5.2.4 Hot-Water Suits and Systems

Hot-water suit systems are the most effective way of keeping a surface-supplied diver warm in cold water (see Figure 5.9). The system consists of a surface heater, a mixing manifold, a hot-water hose that delivers heated water from the topside unit to the diver, and a special hot-water suit.

In most cases, these systems will be equipped with a suction pump that will draw raw sea water from over the side and supply it to the heating system. On a large ship, it may be possible to plumb the sea water intake on the surface heater directly into the ship's raw water supply.

The topside hot-water system can heat the water using a variety of different methods. The location and logistics of the site will usually determine which heating method is most practical. On a large ship or barge, steam is frequently

FIGURE 5.9
Hot-Water Suits

available, and this is usually the most reliable method for heating the water supply. Diesel and electrical powered units, as well as "Piggyback" units that draw their heat from the low-pressure air compressor that supplies the air for the surface-supplied diver, are also available.

The water supply to the diver is controlled using a mixing unit similar to that in a household fixture, but on a much larger scale. This mixing unit is normally located at the dive control station topside where the diving supervisor can monitor both temperature and water flow. The manufacturer for the hot-water system will normally provide charts that suggest the appropriate water temperature to supply to the diver based upon the flow rate, the length of hot-water hose in use, and the bottom temperature where the diver is working.

The hot-water hose is a heavy, insulated hose that is bundled into the diver's umbilical. This hose will usually be the thickest hose in the umbilical. This hose may connect to a thinner hose three to four foot prior to its termination at the diver to provide greater flexibility and freedom of movement for the diver.

The hose connects to the diver's suit with a quick disconnect fitting at a valve located on the suit at the waist. The valve is normally a simple, quarter-turn ball valve.

Hot-water suits are usually made from crushed neoprene or another non-compressible suit material. The suit should fit loosely. Inside the suit, there are perforated tubes that run down the diver's chest, back, legs, and arms. Hot water is distributed throughout the suit by these tubes. The water exits the suit at the ankles, wrists, neck, and through the zipper. The hot water continuously flushes through the suit.

It is recommended that the diver wear a thin (two–three mm) shorty wet suit under the hot-water suit. The shorty suit serves several important purposes. First, it provides some buoyancy, since most surface-supplied diving outfits do not include a buoyancy compensator. Second, in the event that the mixing valve fails and scalding hot water is accidentally sent to the diver, the shorty suit will provide some protection from burns. Finally, if several divers are sharing the same suit, wearing a shorty suit can help prevent fungal infections being passed from diver to diver.

5.2.5 Suit Accessories
5.2.5.1 Gloves

Gloves are worn by most divers to protect the hands from cuts in warm water and for thermal protection in cold water (see Figure 5.10). Gloves are made in a variety of styles and from different materials. Cold-water

FIGURE 5.10
Protective Diving Glove

FIGURE 5.11
Examples of Three-Finger Foam Neoprene Gloves

gloves are normally made from foam neoprene. Three-finger gloves may be worn in colder waters to provide better thermal protection (see Figure 5.11).

5.2.5.2 Hoods

A hood is required if the water is cold enough to warrant. Standard neoprene wet-suit hoods can be used with some dry suits; however, a more preferred hood is one made especially to seal against the neck seal of the dry suit. These hoods usually have a short neck, and use skin-in neoprene around the neck, and sometimes around the face, to provide a good seal against water intrusion. There are also dry hoods made out of neoprene or latex that can be attached directly to the dry suit. The latex hood uses an insulated liner, and works well in extremely cold environments. They generally do not seal against beards, or on people with very thin faces. Their features include:

- Neoprene or rubber (if rubber, an insulating skull cap made of fleece may be worn under the hood)
- May be permanently attached to suit
- May have a one-way valve at the very top to allow air to escape (otherwise it will balloon-up)

Regardless of the type of hood worn, divers must be able to equalize pressure in their outer ears to avoid an ear squeeze. Equalization requires allowing water to enter the hood and fill the outer ear canal. The same requirement can be achieved by allowing air from a full-face mask to flow into the hood and thus, reach the outer ear canal and ultimately the ear drum.

5.3 OPEN CIRCUIT SCUBA REGULATORS

The function of the open circuit scuba regulator is to reduce the high-pressure breathing gas supplied by the scuba cylinder to the ambient pressure at the diver. This is accomplished in two steps. The first stage of the regulator, which attaches to the cylinder valve, reduces the high pressure to an intermediate pressure that is usually about 140 psi over ambient pressure (see Figure 5.12). This intermediate pressure fills the low-pressure hose which connects the first stage and the second stage. The second stage reduces the intermediate pressure to ambient pressure.

The open circuit regulator in use today is known as a "demand regulator" because it only supplies air when the diver inhales or "demands" it. When the diver is not inhaling, no gas flows through the regulator.

The two most common designs for first stages are the piston and diaphragm models. First stages may be produced in either of two configurations: "balanced" or "unbalanced" models. Generally speaking, balanced regulators offer higher performance than unbalanced models and are the most common design found today.

The first stage of the regulator may be environmentally sealed to help keep contaminants out and prevent freeze-up during ice diving operations. Some regulators are supplied from the factory this way, while others may be equipped with this option after purchase.

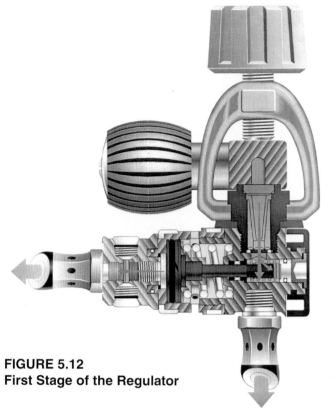

FIGURE 5.12
First Stage of the Regulator

FIGURE 5.14
Open High-Pressure (HP) and Low-Pressure (LP) Ports

is designed to work at higher pressures. With a DIN regulator and valve system, the first stage actually threads into the valve body. The principle behind the DIN fittings is known as a "captured O-ring" because once the regulator is screwed into the valve, it is almost impossible for an O-ring failure to cause a loss of breathing gas. For this reason, DIN fittings are preferred for all overhead environment dives such as wreck penetrations, ice diving, cave diving, and "virtual" overhead environments, such as decompression diving (Palmer 1994).

The first stage of the regulator must be equipped with a sufficient number of high- and low-pressure ports to allow attachment of all of the accessories the diver will need (see Figure 5.14). These may include an additional second stage hose, a low-pressure inflator for a buoyancy compensator, a low-pressure hose for a dry suit, and a high-pressure hose for a submersible pressure gauge. Ideally, the first stage will have enough ports so that the optimal routing for each hose can be achieved. Sharp bends or kinks in hoses must be avoided to prevent gas flow restrictions and premature hose failures.

Some first stage regulators are equipped with swivels that will permit the hoses to turn to help achieve a better angle for hose routing (see Figure 5.15). This is a desirable feature

The types of cylinder connections available are the traditional yoke connection and the European DIN connection. Yoke connectors are intended for high-pressure service not to exceed 3,000 psi. DIN connections are used for cylinders and regulators that operate at pressures up to 4,500 psi. (see Figure 5.13).

DIN is an acronym which stands for "Deutsches Institut fuer Normung," which is a European association of engineers and manufacturers that sets standards for compressed gas cylinders and valves. Valves manufactured to these standards are known as "DIN fittings" or "DIN valves."

The DIN connection for regulators and valves is a more reliable connection than the more common yoke fitting and

FIGURE 5.13
DIN System Threaded Valve Body

FIGURE 5.15
Hose Swivels

Diver and Diving Support Equipment

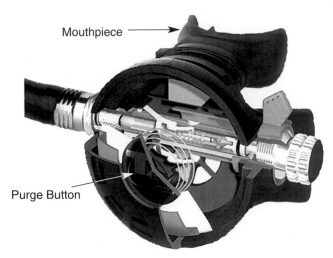

Mouthpiece

Purge Button

FIGURE 5.16
Cutaway of Second Stage Regulator

for divers who have many accessories connected to their regulators.

The second stage regulator includes the mouthpiece and purge button (see Figure 5.16). When the diver inhales, a lower pressure inside the second stage is created, which causes the diaphragm to depress, moving towards the diver's mouth and actuating a lever. The lever opens the valve that allows air to pass into the second stage and supply air to the diver. When the diver exhales, the diaphragm moves away from the diver's mouth and the exhaled gas exits the second stage through the exhaust valve.

If the diver depresses the purge button to expel water from the second stage, this action pushes directly on the diaphragm which activates the lever and allows gas to flow through the second stage as long as the button is pushed. If sand or other debris has accumulated in the second stage, or if the regulator is out of adjustment, the regulator may

vent gas vigorously on its own. This loss of gas is commonly referred to as a "free flow."

Most regulator second stages today are either downstream valves or pilot valves. Downstream valves tend to be more common and are usually simpler than pilot valves (see Figure 5.17).

To achieve higher performance, the regulator may be equipped with a "venturi" mechanism, which promotes higher gas flows. The venturi increases gas velocity and lowers pressure making breathing easier.

Pilot valve regulators offer high performance but tend to be more expensive than downstream designs. Most pilot valve regulators are extremely compact and lightweight. In a pilot valve regulator, the demand lever opens the pilot valve first. The pilot valve then opens the larger main valve that provides the breathing gas.

Pilot valve second stages and more traditional designs may have diver-operated adjustments that are designed to enhance breathing. In many cases, pilot valve second stages may be equipped with a "predive" and "dive" switch that changes the breathing characteristics to prevent air loss while surface swimming on snorkel when the regulator is not in use. Similarly, some regulators are equipped with adjustment knobs that can be set to make breathing easier at depth (see Figure 5.18).

Some second stages have also been engineered for ice diving operations and have special vanes or other devices in them to capture the heat from the diver's exhaled breath to help prevent freeze-up. These designs are recommended for divers who regularly conduct work under the ice.

Regulators can be equipped with an additional second stage, known as an "octopus" rig that can be used to supply air to an out-of-air diver in an emergency (see Figure 5.19). This system eliminates the need for two divers to share a single mouthpiece and is usually compact and

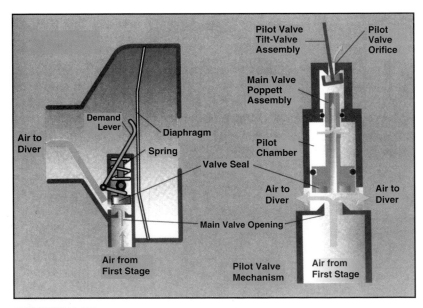

FIGURE 5.17
Downstream Second Stage

FIGURE 5.18
Adjustment Knob to Ease Diver's Breathing

helps to streamline the diver. The additional second hose with the second stage can be purchased in a right or left configuration. This allows the second hose to be positioned under either the diver's left or right arm.

5.3.1 Maintenance

All regulators should be rinsed promptly with fresh, clean water at the end of each day of diving, particularly after exposure to salt water. The preferred method of performing this task is to have the regulator connected to the cylinder with the pressure on. Water should be directed over the first stage, the hose, and both inside and outside of the second stage.

In the event that it is not possible to rinse the regulator while it is connected and pressurized, it may be rinsed with the dust cap in place over the high-pressure filter on the first stage. Failure to secure the dust cap in position prior to rinsing will allow water to enter the first stage which can lead to corrosion. Similarly, if the regulator is not connected, it is essential to avoid pressing the purge button on the second stage while rinsing. Pressing the purge button will also allow water to flow back through the hose and enter the first stage.

NOAA requires that all their scuba regulators be inspected and serviced by an authorized repair technician annually (see Figure 5.20). Regulators that are used daily will need to be inspected and serviced more frequently, as often as every quarter, depending on the environment and care. Prior to each dive, the diver should routinely do a predive inspection of regulator, hoses, mouthpieces, test breathing, leaks, etc.

FIGURE 5.20
NOAA Technician Inspecting and Repairing Regulators

5.4 EMERGENCY AIR SUPPLY

To cope with a complete loss of breathing gas, some divers prefer to carry an independent breathing gas supply, complete with its own regulator. Special compact systems are available with integrated regulators that have been designed for this purpose. Another option is to carry a small (usually 13 cu. ft.) "bail-out" cylinder with its own regulator (see Figure 5.21). The size of the cylinder should be determined by the distance and/or time that separates the diver from a direct access to the surface. The cylinder may also be referred to as a "pony bottle" or "reserve gas breathing supply."

5.5 COMPRESSED AIR

Compressed air is the most frequently used diver's breathing medium. In its natural state at sea level pressure, compressed air consists of nitrogen, oxygen, argon, carbon

FIGURE 5.19
Octopus Regulators

FIGURE 5.21
A Bail-Out Cylinder

Diver and Diving Support Equipment

dioxide, and trace amounts of other gases. Table 5.2 shows the natural composition of air and purity standards.

All ambient air does not meet the standards of purity necessary for use as a diver's breathing medium. For example, in urban areas the carbon monoxide concentration in the air may be high, and in some cases it may reach a concentration of 50-100 parts per million (ppm) (.005 - .01%). Ambient air may also contain dust, sulfur, oxides, and other impurities. These contaminants derive from industrial sources and engine exhausts and must be avoided in the breathing air supplied to a diver.

Scuba cylinders should not be filled from an ambient air source when an air pollution alert is in effect. The Environmental Protection Agency (EPA) monitors ozone and other oxidants in metropolitan areas, and the local EPA office should be consulted before a diving operation is undertaken in an area suspected of having high pollutant levels.

In addition to airborne pollutants, the air compressor machinery and storage system themselves may introduce contaminants, including lubricating oil and its vapor, into the breathing medium. Additionally, the temperature of the gas being compressed can be high enough at each successive stage to cause pyrolytic decomposition of any hydrocarbon compounds present. This is particularly true if the compressor's interstage coolers are not functioning properly. Intercooler malfunction can be caused by excessive condensate, impaired cooling water circulation, or, in the case of air radiator coolers, by loss of cooling air flow caused by debris, dirt, or lint getting into the radiator fins.

The free air intake of the compressor must be located to draw air from an area where there are no contaminants. Potential contaminants include engine or ventilation exhaust, fumes or vapors from stored chemicals, fuel, or paint, and excess moisture.

No compressor should be allowed to operate with its intake or first-stage suction blocked because this will produce a vacuum within the cylinders that can rapidly draw lubricating oil or oil vapor from the compressor crankcase into the air system. Some effective methods of preventing the intake of contaminated air are discussed below.

5.5.1 General Safety Precautions

There are three primary safety concerns associated with the use of compressed air or any compressed gas:

- Gas is sufficiently pure and appropriate for its intended use
- Compressed gas cylinders or storage cylinders are properly labeled and handled
- Cylinders are protected from fire and other hazards

Compressed air is available from many sources. Most of it, however, is produced for industrial purposes and is, therefore, not of the purity necessary for use as a diver's breathing medium. When compressed air is purchased from a manufacturer, it is essential that the gas is of high purity, free of oil contaminants, and suitable for breathing. It should be labeled "breathing air." Compressed air suspected of being contaminated should not be used for diving until tested and found safe.

Proper identification and careful handling of compressed gas cylinders are essential to safety. Compressed gas cylinders used to transport gas under pressure are subject to Department of Transportation (DOT) regulations. These regulations include design, material, inspection, and marking requirements. Compressed gas cylinders can be extremely hazardous if mishandled and should be stored securely in a rack, preferably in the upright position.

When in transit, cylinders should be secured from rolling. Standing an unsecured cylinder on end or allowing it to roll unsecured could result in the explosive rupture of the cylinder. Cylinders can become deadly projectiles capable of penetrating a wall, and they can propel themselves at great speeds over long distances.

Scuba cylinders are often fitted with a rubber or plastic boot that has holes in it to permit draining. These boots fit over the base of the cylinder and help to keep the cylinder in an upright position. However, cylinders equipped with such boots should not be left unsecured in an upright position, because the boot alone does not provide sufficient protection against falling.

NOTE
Cylinder boots should be removed frequently and the cylinder checked for evidence of corrosion.

Compressed gas cylinders are protected against excessive overpressure by a rupture disk on the cylinder valve. Because regulators or gauges may fail when a cylinder valve is opened to check the cylinder pressure, it is important to stand to the side rather than in the line of discharge to avoid the blast effect in case of failure.

WARNING
DO NOT STAND IN THE LINE OF DISCHARGE WHEN OPENING A HIGH-PRESSURE CYLINDER.

If a cylinder valve is suspected of having a thread or seal leak, it should be completely discharged before any attempt is made to repair the leak. Leaks can sometimes be detected by painting a 20 percent detergent soap solution (called "Snoop®") over the external parts of the valve with a brush. Even small leaks will be obvious because they will cause a froth of bubbles to form. After the leak has been repaired, the soap solution used for leak detection must be removed completely with fresh water and the valve dried carefully before reassembly.

With the exception of scuba cylinders used for nitrox, scuba cylinders generally are not color-coded or labeled as

TABLE 5.2
Air Purity Standards

LIMITING CHARACTERISTICS	OGA COMMODITY SPEC. FOR AIR ANSI/OGA G-7.1-1997 GRADE D	OGA COMMODITY SPEC. FOR AIR ANSI/OGA G-7.1-1997 GRADE D & -50°F DEWPOINT	OGA COMMODITY SPEC. FOR AIR ANSI/OGA G-7.1-1997 GRADE D & L	OGA COMMODITY SPEC. FOR AIR ANSI/OGA G-7.1-1997 GRADE E	OGA COMMODITY SPEC. FOR AIR ANSI/OGA G-7.1-1997 GRADE N	NAVSEA 0994-001-9010 US NAVY DIVING MANUAL APPENDIX N TABLE E N-1 NAUMED P-5112 US NAVY DIVER'S AIR SAMPLING	PROFESSIONAL ASSOCIATION OF DIVING INSTRUCTORS PADI PURE AIR PROGRAM	NATIONAL FIRE PROTECTION ASSOCIATION NFPA 1500, 1996 EDITION FIRE DEPARTMENT OCCUPATIONAL SAFETY AND HEALTH PROGRAM PAGE 1500-16, PAR 5-3.7 NFPA 1500	TEXAS COMMISSION ON FIRE PROTECTION CHAPTER 435 - FIREFIGHTER SAFETY TEXAS COMMISSION ON FIRE PROTECTION
Percent Oxygen Balance Predominantly Nitrogen	19.5-23.5	19.5-23.5	19.5-23.5	20-22	19.5-23.5	20-22	20-22	19.5-23.5	19.5-23.5
Water, ppm	Not Specified	63 ppm	24 ppm	Not Specified	Not Specified	Not Specified	Not Specified	25 ppm	25 ppm
Dewpoint (degrees °F)	Not Specified	-50°F	-65°F	Not Specified	Not Specified	Not Specified	Not Specified	-65°F	-65°F
Oil (condensed) (mg/m³ at NTP)	5	5	5	5	None	5	5	5	5
Particulates mg/m³	Not Specified	Not Specified	Not Specified	Not Specified	Not Specified	Not Specified	Not Specified	5	Not Specified
Carbon Monoxide ppm	10	10	10	10	10	20	10	10	10
Odor	None	None	None	None	None	None	None	None	None
Carbon Dioxide ppm	1,000	1,000	1,000	1,000	500	1,000	1,000	1,000	1,000
Total Volatile Hydrocarbons (less methane) ppm	Not Specified	Not Specified	Not Specified	25	Not Specified	25	25	Not Specified	Not Specified
Nitrogen Dioxide ppm	Not Specified	Not Specified	Not Specified	Not Specified	25	Not Specified	Not Specified	Not Specified	Not Specified
Nitric Oxide ppm	Not Specified	Not Specified	Not Specified	Not Specified		Not Specified	Not Specified	Not Specified	Not Specified
Sulfur Dioxide ppm	Not Specified	Not Specified	Not Specified	Not Specified	5	Not Specified	Not Specified	Not Specified	Not Specified
Halogenated Solvents ppm	Not Specified	Not Specified	Not Specified	Not Specified	Not Specified	Not Specified	Not Specified	Not Specified	Not Specified
Frequency Required (Times per year)	Not Specified	Not Specified	Not Specified	Not Specified	Not Specified	x2 NOL x4 OL	x4	x4	x2
TRI's Air Standard Code	02	71 or 72	68	06	27	01	05	15	20
Typical Uses	Manufacturing Firefighting	Manufacturing Firefighting Airline Respirators	Manufacturing	Diving	Hospital Manufacturing	Diving	Diving	Firefighting HAZ-MAT	Firefighting HAZ-MAT

Diver and Diving Support Equipment

to type of gas contained; however, large gas cylinders may be color-coded and labeled. The label should be used to identify the contents of a gas cylinder, because color-coding is not standardized. The safest way to verify gas content is via an analyzer.

WARNING
BECAUSE COLORS VARY AMONG MANUFACTURERS, THE CONTENT OF LARGE CYLINDERS SHOULD ALWAYS BE IDENTIFIED BY LABELS—DO NOT RELY ON CYLINDER COLOR.

Several special safety precautions to be observed when using compressed gas are noted on the label of gas cylinders. In general, these precautions concern the flammability of the gas and its ability to support combustion. Although not in itself flammable, compressed air does support combustion and should, therefore, not be used or stored in an area where open flames, hot work, or flammable gases are present.

5.6 AIR COMPRESSORS AND FILTERING SYSTEMS

Air compressors are the most common source of diver's breathing air. The compressor used for umbilical diving is generally backed up by a bank of high-pressure gas storage cylinders to reduce the possibility of interrupting the diver's breathing gas supply because of loss of power or compressor malfunction.

There are two main types of compressors: high-pressure, low-volume, for use in filling scuba cylinders; and low-pressure, high-volume, used for umbilical diving. A compressor is rated at the pressure at which it will unload or at which the unloading switches will activate. A compressor must have the output volume to provide a sufficient quantity of breathing medium and to provide pressure above the range equivalent to the ambient pressure the diver will experience at depth. When evaluating compressor capacity, the difference over bottom pressure and volume requirements of different types of underwater breathing apparatus and/or helmets must be considered, as well as umbilical length and diameter.

Any air compressor used for a diver's surface-supplied system must have an accumulator (volume cylinder) as an integral part of the system. The accumulator will provide a limited emergency supply of air if the compressor fails.

As the number of scientific and recreational divers increases, there is a concurrent rise in the number and variety of air compressors being used to supply breathing air. Operators should become thoroughly familiar with the requirements associated with the production of breathing air. To ensure proper maintenance and care, organizations using compressors should assign the responsibility for the operation of compressors to a specific individual.

Air compressors are generally rated by two parameters: the maximum pressure (measured in pounds per square inch gauge, or psig) they can deliver and the output volume (measured in standard cubic feet per minute, or scfm) that can be delivered at that pressure. To be effective, both the output volume and pressure must be equal to or exceed the requirements of the system they supply.

Air compressors commonly used to provide divers breathing air may be classified in the following groups:

- *Low-Pressure, High Volume Air Compressors:*
  These compressors are most often used to support surface-supplied diving operations or to supply hyperbaric chambers. They are generally found at sites where large-scale diving operations are being conducted or aboard surface platforms outfitted for diving. Units commonly used have output volumes of between 50 and 200 scfm at maximum discharge pressures of between 150 and 300 psig. These units may be either permanently installed or portable. Portable units are generally built into a skid assembly along with a power source (diesel engine, gasoline engine, or electric motor), volume tank, filter assembly, distribution manifold for divers' air, and a rack for storing divers' umbilical assemblies.
- *High-Pressure, Low Volume Air Compressors:*
  These compressors are used for filling scuba cylinders and high-pressure air storage systems. Portable units used for filling scuba cylinders are commonly available with a volumetric capacity of two to six scfm at a discharge pressure adequate to fully charge the cylinders (2,250 or 3,000 psig, depending on the type of cylinder).

Large, high-pressure cylinders are advantageous to use as a source of breathing gas when there is convenient access to a high-pressure compressor for recharging. Using cylinders as the gas source reduces the chance of losing the primary supply, since the entire volume of gas needed for a dive is compressed and stored before the dive. Most lock-out submersibles carry the divers' gas supply in high-pressure cylinders incorporated into the system. Compressed gas cylinders are also generally mounted on the exteriors of underwater habitats, submersibles, and diving bells to provide a backup gas supply in case of emergency. Divers using the habitat as a base can refill their scuba cylinders from these mounted cylinders.

Many types of compressors are available: centrifugal, rotary screw, axial flow, and reciprocating. The most commonly used type in the diving industry is the reciprocating, or piston-in-cylinder type. These compressors are further classified as "oil-lubricated" or "non-oil-lubricated," depending on whether or not they require lubrication of their compression cylinders.

In an oil-lubricated compressor, the oil in the crankcase assembly also lubricates the pistons and cylinder walls. As a result, some of the oil may come into direct contact with the air being compressed. The lubricants used in machines that provide breathing air must be of the quality specified for breathing air and be so designated by the equipment manufacturer. One lubricant should not be substituted for another unless the manufacturer's directions so specify. Chlorinated lubricants, non-synthetics, or phosphate esters (either pure or in a mixture) should never be used.

Oil-free compressors usually employ a standard oil-lubricated crankcase assembly similar to that of oil-lubricated machines; however, the pumping chambers in oil-free machines are designed to run either with water lubrication or with no lubrication at all using teflon rings on the pistons. For this reason, some manufacturers describe their machines as oil-free, even though the breakdown of such compressors could still result in oily breathing air. The mechanical connections between the pumping chambers and the crankcase on truly oil-free machines are carefully designed to prevent the migration of crankcase oil into the pumping chambers. The all-purpose crankcase lubricant recommended by the manufacturer can usually be used for oil-free compressors. The compressors used to provide breathing air in hospitals are of the oil-free type, but these machines are not widely used in operational diving.

In a typical three-stage compressor, the air is taken from ambient pressure to approximately 2,250 psi. Compressors typically use a ratio of 6:1, although this may vary with different makes and models of compressors. Each succeeding cylinder is proportionately smaller in volume than the previous one. Some efficiency (approximately ten percent) is lost because of the volume of the intercoolers and residual cylinder volumes; this factor is called volumetric efficiency. Intercoolers cool the air before further recompression and cause water and oil vapor to condense and collect as the air passes through the air/liquid separator at the discharge end of the intercooler.

Air leaving a compressor must be cooled and passed through an air/liquid separator to remove any condensed water and oil vapors before storage or immediate use. The separator is fitted with a drain valve that must be opened periodically to drain accumulated liquids. Air from an oil-free compressor does not generally require any further treatment unless the application requires that it be further dried or there is concern about possible contamination of the intake air. Air from an oil-lubricated compressor must be carefully filtered to remove any possible oil mist, oil vapors, possible by-products from oil oxidation in the compressor (predominantly carbon monoxide), or odors. Several types of filtration systems are available. To use most filtration agents properly, it is necessary to place them in the filtration system in a specific order. To do this, the direction of the air flow through the filter system must be known, and, if there is any doubt, it should be checked. Like other high-pressure components, filter canisters should be inspected visually for corrosion damage (High 1987).

For purposes of dehydration and adsorption, substances known as molecular sieves are often used. A molecular sieve is a material having an extremely large surface area to enhance its capacity for adsorption. Since it removes harmful contaminants by causing them to adhere to its surface, the sieve itself remains inert and virtually unchanged physically during the purification process. With appropriate periodic regeneration processes, most molecular sieves are capable of removing a wide range of contaminants, including carbon dioxide and most odors. However, the most effective way to remove hydrocarbons and odors is still with the use of activated carbon, which acts much like a molecular sieve.

Another popular filtration system involves the following components, which are used in the sequence shown:

1. Coalescing section to remove oil mist
2. Dessicant section to remove water vapor, nitrogen dioxide, hydrocarbons, and other contaminants removable by adsorption
3. Activated charcoal section for removal of residual odors and tastes
4. Hopcalite® section for carbon monoxide removal

The Hopcalite® oxidizes the carbon monoxide to carbon dioxide. Hopcalite® is a true catalyst in this reaction and is neither consumed nor exhausted in the process. The amount of carbon dioxide produced by the catalytic action is so small as to be physiologically insignificant. The amount of oxygen consumed is approximately 0.5 parts of oxygen per million parts of carbon monoxide, which has no appreciable effect on the air produced. The lifetime of this system is usually determined by the lifetime of the dessicant, since Hopcalite® is quickly "poisoned" and rendered ineffective by excessive water vapor. An aspect of this process that is not widely understood is that the carbon monoxide oxidation process releases substantial quantities of heat. If a Hopcalite® filter becomes extremely hot or shows signs of discoloration, the compressor output air should be checked for elevated carbon monoxide levels.

In addition to Hopcalite®, the use of activated alumina in combination with Multi-sorb® is also widespread. No matter what technique is employed, the location of the compressor intake with respect to possible sources of contamination is an important factor in ensuring satisfactory air quality. Compressors should not be operated near the exhausts of internal combustion engines, sewer manholes, sandblasting or painting operations, electric arcs, or sources of smoke. Plastic containers of volatile liquids can give off fumes even when they are tightly closed and thus should be kept clear of compressor intakes. Intakes must be provided with filters for removing dust and other particles. Proper orientation to wind direction is also critical in setting up air compressor systems.

The final step in the production of pure air is the filling station, usually located in a dive shop, on board ship, or near a diving installation. It is important for the diver to inspect the filling station to ensure that proper safety precautions are being observed and that federal, state, and local regulations are being followed. Figure 5.22 is a schematic of the processing of air from the intake to the

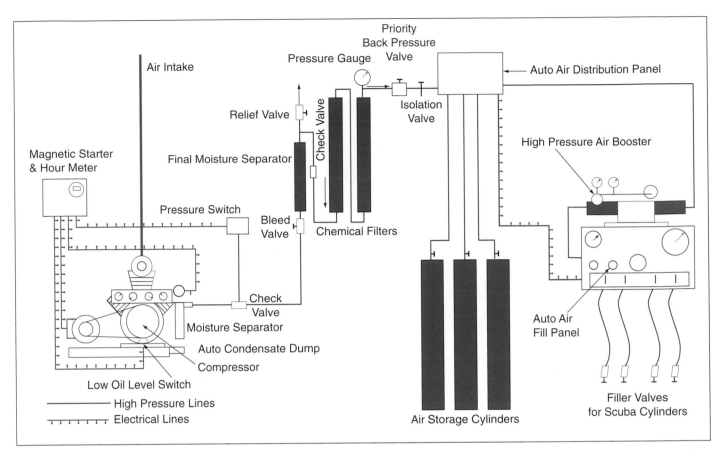

FIGURE 5.22
Schematic of the Production of Diver's Breathing Air

scuba cylinder. (Note that the system depicted in Figure 5.22 includes a high-pressure booster pump, which can increase the efficiency of cylinder filling operations by providing air at the filling station at a pressure above that of the air storage cylinder.)

For some diving operations, air is supplied by the manufacturer in banks of high-pressure cylinders. These cylinder banks are fitted with specific valves according to the type of gas contained and may be used to provide breathing air in surface-supplied diving operations and for filling scuba cylinders.

5.6.1 Maintenance

Both the compressor and filter system must be maintained properly. When running, the compressor must be cooled adequately, because the primary factor causing the breakdown of lubricants and contamination of the compressed air is high temperature in the compressor cylinder. Cylinder heads may be cooled by air blowers or water spray systems or by cooling systems integral to the compressor machinery. A cylinder head temperature controller is valuable in eliminating the possibility of excessive cylinder temperatures. Particular attention should be paid to draining the inter-stage and final-stage separators. Compressors and filters are usually given routine maintenance

on either an hours-of-operation or time basis. Filters have a recommended shelf life and, therefore, should be examined and replaced in accordance with the manufacturer's specifications. The compressor lubricant and mechanical parts should be replaced on a rigorous schedule, based on the manufacturer's recommendations or the results of an air analysis. Analysis of the output air from compressor systems should be performed twice a year. Oil mist analysis is difficult to perform and requires careful collection techniques as well as qualified laboratory analysis of the samples. Although carbon monoxide analysis, by far the most important test to be conducted on diver's breathing gas, can be performed in the field using colorimetric tubes, it is not a substitute for accurate analysis by a reputable testing laboratory.

A log should be kept for each compressor. The log should record all time in service, maintenance, and air analysis information.

5.6.2 Carbon Monoxide Monitoring Device

Deadly aldehydes can create false positive readings for carbon monoxide. The human body has a zero tolerance for aldehydes, and they have been proven to cause cancer in laboratory animals. They are also associated with leukemia in human beings.

In response to environmental concerns, refineries have reformulated common gasoline; the emission from engine exhaust contains aldehydes from methyl tertiary butyl ether (MTBE). Aldehydes and all single-carbon units like hydrogen, formic acid, formaldehydes, and methanol will identify as carbon monoxide on a monitoring device.

Whereas carbon monoxide tends to settle out on the ground, aldehydes migrate upward and can contaminate intakes in close proximity of a combustible type engine. Therefore, in the placement of compressor intakes, lateral distance from the compressor exhaust fumes, or any other combustible type engine, is now more critical than vertical distance.

5.6.3 Lubricants

Oil-lubricated compressors have a small amount of oil on the interior of the cylinder's walls which mixes with the air being compressed. This oil is filtered out by the compressor's filtering system. Because an improperly functioning filter can raise temperatures sufficiently to decompose or ignite the oil, it is important to carefully select oil to be used as a lubricant.

The oil's flashpoint (the temperature of the liquid oil at which sufficient vapors are given off to produce a flash when a flame is applied) and auto-ignition point (the temperature at which the oil, when mixed with air, will burn without an ignition source) are both important considerations. The most desirable compressor lubricants have higher-than-average flashpoints and low volatility. The oils recommended by the manufacturer of the compressor are generally the safest and most efficient lubricants for this equipment.

5.6.4 Duties and Responsibilities

All divers have a considerable responsibility for scuba cylinder safety. Approximately 90 percent of all cylinder explosions occur during the fill process. Fill station operators must have federally mandated hazardous materials (HAZ-MAT) training and re-training every three years (4.9 CFR 172.700). In addition, OSHA requires all cylinders to be inspected (29 CFR 1910.101 (A)).

The fill station itself should be made safe by incorporating whatever protective materials or procedures that can reasonably be incorporated into the system. While not all of the following items are relevant to every fill station, one should consider:

- Placing the fill station away from work areas
- Consulting with an engineer before constructing a cylinder diversion device
- Configuring controls away from the cylinder fill area
- Securing high-pressure hoses and fittings at close intervals
- Keeping the fill station away from critical building structural support and walls and providing a physical barrier between fill station operator and cylinder during fill

- Using an energy deflector to send explosive force in a safe direction
- Regularly inspecting compressor filters and piping
- Allowing only trained, authorized persons to work at the fill station
- Posting operating procedures and safety instructions
- Having schematic diagrams of all system components including proper labeling of all valves, gauges, etc.

A pre-fill visual inspection determines if the cylinder appears to be safe and meets legal requirements. Whenever a problem is noted, the cylinder should be set aside for a formal inspection by a trained technician.

5.7 COMPRESSED GAS CYLINDERS

Scuba cylinders contain the compressed breathing gas to be used by a diver. Most cylinders for diving are of steel or aluminum alloy construction, specially designed and manufactured to contain compressed air safely at service pressures usually from 2,250 to 3,500 psig or greater.

5.7.1 Cylinder Markings

Regardless of cylinder type, data describing the cylinder must be clearly stamped into the shoulder of the cylinder. Scuba cylinders must be manufactured in accordance with the precise specifications dictated by the Interstate Commerce Commission (ICC) (until 1970), thereafter by the DOT, and most recently reflected on aluminum cylinders as TC/DOT, which indicates equivalency with requirements of the Transport Canada (High 1987).

Regulatory changes in the more than 35 years since scuba cylinders entered service in the United States have produced a variety of code markings. Typically, steel cylinders carry the code *DOT* (or ICC), 3AA (steel type), and a *service pressure* of 2,250 psig (158 kg/cm^2) or higher on the first line. These marks are followed by the *serial number, cylinder manufacturer's symbol* (before 1982, the symbol of the user or equipment distributor), the original *hydrostatic test date* with testor's symbol, and a plus (+) mark, which indicates that a ten percent fill over-service-pressure is allowed for the five-year period of the original hydrostatic test.

Additional hydrostatic test dates, with the testor's codes, will be added on successful retest at required five-year or shorter intervals. However, since hydrostatic test facilities rarely retest scuba cylinders appropriately to permit inclusion of the plus mark (+) for continued ten percent overfill, few steel cylinders are filled in excess of the designated service pressure after the initial period. Figure 5.23 shows steel scuba cylinder markings. The Pressed Steel Tank Company (PST) produces cylinders in several volumes under the DOT exemption E9791 having a service pressure of 3,500 psig. Japanese cylinders sold by ASAHI were introduced in the U.S. in 1999. Those cylinders have the DOT authorization number E.

Aluminum alloy scuba cylinders entered U.S. commercial service in 1971 and are code-marked in a somewhat different manner than steel cylinders. Initially, DOT issued

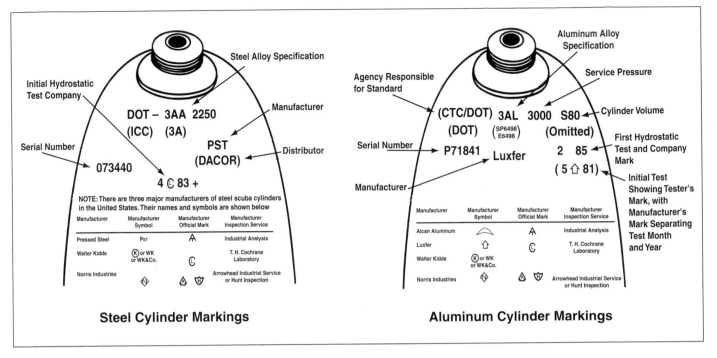

Steel Cylinder Markings

Aluminum Cylinder Markings

FIGURE 5.23
Cylinder Markings

special permits or exemptions for the manufacture of aluminum cylinders. These are indicated in some code markings as SP6498 or E6498, followed by the service pressure, which typically ranges from 2,475 to 3,000 psi (174 to 211 kg/cm²). No plus (+) or overfill allowance is used with aluminum alloy cylinders. Since 1982, aluminum cylinders reflect DOT and TC equivalency, the material designation (3AL), the service pressure, and a mark indicating volume and that the cylinder is intended for scuba service (S80), as shown in Figure 5.23.

> **NOTE**
> **Aluminum alloy cylinders should never be filled in excess of marked service pressure, and steel cylinders without a plus (+) after the current hydrostatic test date should also not be filled over their marked service pressure.**

The internal volume of a cylinder is a function of its physical dimensions and may be expressed in cubic inches or cubic feet. Of more interest is the capacity of the cylinder, which is the quantity of gas at surface pressure that can be compressed into the cylinder at its rated pressure. The capacity usually is expressed in standard cubic feet or standard liters of gas. Cylinders of various capacities are commercially available. Steel scuba cylinders generally have a rated working pressure of 2,250 psig (158 kg/cm² or 153 atm) to 3,500 psig. Cylinders with capacities from 26 standard cubic feet (742 standard liters) to over 100 standard cubic feet (2,857 standard liters) are used for scuba diving.

> **NOTE**
> **For long-term storage (i.e., more than 90 days), cylinders should be bled to approximately 20 psig and stored with valves closed to reduce internal corrosion.**

5.7.2 High-Pressure Cylinders

High-pressure cylinders are usually made from steel or aluminum, although prototypes of stainless steel and fiber wound composites have appeared. Carbon steel, used in early cylinders, has been replaced with chrome molybdenum steel. Aluminum is alloyed with other metals, such as magnesium and titanium. Steel cylinders were introduced in the late 1940s, and aluminum cylinders became popular in the 1970s, although the first aluminum cylinders were imported from France in 1950. Table 5.3 summarizes cylinder characteristics for a number of rated steel and aluminum cylinders. Steel cylinders are generally heavier and exhibit negative buoyancy when filled with air. Aluminum cylinders are lighter and tend to exhibit positive buoyancy before all cylinder air is depleted. To recover the buoyancy characteristics of steel cylinders, aluminum cylinders of the same size must have thicker walls, increasing their weight but not their displacement.

5.7.3 Cylinder Inspection and Maintenance

The exteriors of most steel cylinders are protected against corrosion by galvanized metal (zinc), epoxy paint, or vinyl-plastic coating. The zinc bonds to the cylinder and protects it from air and water. It is recommended that exteriors of steel cylinders be galvanized for protection against corrosion. Some cylinders, however, were painted with epoxy paints or plastics in lieu of galvanizing. A problem arises when the

TABLE 5.3
Cylinder Specifications

Material	Volume (ft³)	Pressure (psi)	Length (in)	Diameter (in)	Weight (lbs)	Buoyancy (lbs)
Steel	15	3300	13.80	4.00	7.5	-1.30
Aluminum	14	2015	16.60	4.40	5.4	3.22
Aluminum	50	3000	19.00	6.90	21.5	2.25
Steel	50	1980	22.50	6.80	20.8	2.43
Steel	72	2475	25.00	6.80	29.5	3.48
Aluminum	72	3000	26.00	6.90	28.5	3.60
Aluminum	80	3000	26.40	7.25	33.3	4.00
Aluminum	80	3000	27.00	7.25	34.5	4.12
Steel	95	3300	25.00	7.00	39.1	-6.11

painted coating is scratched or chipped, exposing the bare metal underneath to water resulting in oxidation (corrosion). Consequently, non-galvanized steel cylinders should not be used. Epoxy paint or plastic over zinc-galvanized surfaces is acceptable, however, because it reduces electrolytic corrosion of the zinc by salt water and imparts an attractive appearance. With proper preventive maintenance, electrolytic corrosion is relatively insignificant on bare zinc coating.

Since internal corrosion is a problem, manufacturers formerly applied protective linings on the interiors of steel cylinders. The use of internal coatings has only been relatively successful, because even a small flaw in the lining allows moisture in the cylinder to penetrate to bare metal. Corrosion under the lining cannot be seen or assessed. Also, the lining becomes unbonded and, in some cases, the resulting flakes clogged the valve or the regulator. Damaged linings must be removed.

A corrosion-inhibiting epoxy-polyester finish is usually applied to the exterior of aluminum cylinders both to protect them and to give them an attractive color. If this coating scrapes off, an oxide layer forms that tends to protect the cylinder from further corrosion. In the past, the interiors of some aluminum cylinders received a protective layer over the base metal, such as Alrock® or Irridite®, which was applied during the fabrication process. Aluminum scuba cylinders no longer receive any interior treatment.

Air cylinders and high-pressure manifolds should be rinsed thoroughly with fresh water after each use to remove traces of salt and other deposits. The exterior of the cylinder should be visually inspected for abrasion, dents, and corrosion. If the cylinder has deep abrasions or dents, it should be examined by a trained inspector before refilling; external corrosion should be removed and a protective coating applied to prevent further deterioration of the cylinder wall. Care also must be taken to prevent moisture accumulation inside high-pressure cylinders. Cylinders used under water as a source of air for power tools or for lift bags often become contaminated by moisture returning through the valve. Any cylinder allowed to bleed pressure to zero in the water should not be refilled until it is inspected by a trained technician. Cylinders should be stored with a minimum of 20 psi of air remaining in the cylinder to keep moisture from entering the cylinder.

Cylinders should not be placed in a water bath for filling. The risk of water entering a cylinder while immersed in water and the resulting corrosion is potentially more hazardous than the risk of over-heating during filling. Moisture in a cylinder often can be detected by (1) the presence of a whitish mist when the valve is opened; (2) the sound of sloshing water when the cylinder is tipped back and forth; or (3) a damp or metallic odor to the air in the cylinder. Water in a cylinder can create a particularly dangerous condition in cold water diving, since ice can form in the first stage or in the hose prior to the second stage valve, causing the flow of air to the diver to be interrupted.

Both steel and aluminum cylinders should be inspected internally by a trained technician at least once a year for damage and corrosion. Cylinders should be inspected more frequently if they are used in a tropical climate, if they receive especially hard service, or if flooding is suspected. A special rod-type low-voltage light that illuminates the entire inside of the cylinder should be used for internal visual inspection (see Figure 5.24). Standards and procedures for the visual inspection of compressed gas cylinders are discussed in detail in High (1987).

Two forms of inspection are used, depending on the interval since the previous inspection or the nature of the suspected problem. An *informal inspection* is a cursory look at a scuba cylinder's exterior and interior to determine if there is a reason to examine it further. A *formal inspection* is a complete evaluation against standards, in which a judgment is reached and evidence of the inspection is affixed to the cylinder in the form of a sticker that attests to the cylinder's suitability for continued use. The sticker should indicate the standard used, the date of inspection, and the person conducting the inspection.

The visual cylinder inspection procedure is neither complex nor time consuming, but should be performed only by persons properly trained and using appropriate tools.

In general, the cylinder exterior should be compared to standards for:

- Cuts, gouges, corrosion (general, pitting line), and stress lines
- Dents or bulges
- Signs of heat damage
- General abuse
- Condition of coating
- Current hydrostatic test date

Interior cylinder evaluations to standards should assess:

- Type and amount of cylinder contents (if any)
- Magnitude of general pitting or line corrosion
- Thread integrity
- Defects in interior coating (if any)
- Sign(s) of substantial material removal
- Internal neck cracks (aluminum cylinders)

There are several methods of hydrostatic testing of cylinders, including direct expansion, pressure recession, and the

Diver and Diving Support Equipment

**FIGURE 5.24
Internal Inspection
of a Scuba Cylinder**

(i.e., 90 days), cylinders should be bled to 20 psig and stored with valves closed to reduce internal corrosion. There is a potential for moist ambient air to pass through the open valve into an empty cylinder as air temperatures change. If there is moisture in the cylinder, air at the higher pressure (higher partial pressure of oxygen) accelerates corrosion.

However, a greater danger exists when partially filled aluminum cylinders are exposed to heat, as might occur during a building fire. The metal can soften before the temperature-raised pressure reaches that necessary to burst the frangible safety disk. An explosion may occur well below the cylinder service pressure.

Rules for the use of scuba cylinders:

1. Do not fill high-pressure cylinders if the date of the last hydrostatic test has expired (five years for steel and aluminum cylinders) or if more than one year has passed since the last formal visual inspection.
2. Charge cylinder at 300-600 psig/min to prevent excessive heat buildup.
3. Never exceed the maximum allowable pressure for any particular cylinder.
4. Never perform maintenance or repairs on a cylinder valve while the cylinder is charged.
5. Handle charged cylinders carefully. Handling by the valve or body is preferred. Handling by straps or backpack may allow the cylinder to slip or drop.
6. Store charged cylinders in an upright position in a cool, shady place to prevent overheating.
7. Secure cylinders properly to prevent falling or rolling.
8. Internal inspections, hydrostatic tests, and repair work should be performed only by trained technicians.
9. Have cylinders visually inspected for interior deterioration annually (or more frequently, depending on use).
10. Inspect cylinders externally before and after each dive for signs of general pitting or line corrosion, dents, cracks, or other damage. Never use a welded, fire-damaged, uninspected, gouged, or scarred cylinder.
11. Remove cylinder boot frequently to inspect for corrosion. Boots that inhibit rapid draining and drying should not be used because they allow water to remain in contact with the cylinder, forming corrosion.
12. Do not completely drain the cylinder of air during dives. Some residual air pressure prevents moisture from entering the cylinder.

water jacket method. The most common method is the water jacket method, which involves filling the cylinder with water, placing it in a water-filled pressure chamber, raising the pressure inside the cylinder with a hydraulic pump, and measuring the amount of cylinder expansion in terms of water column displacement. The pressure is increased to 5/3 the rated pressure of the cylinder, except for PST steel cylinders manufactured under the E9791 permit. These 3,500 psig cylinders are tested to 3/2 service pressure. According to DOT regulations, a permanent expansion of 10% or more of the total expansion indicates that the cylinder is unsafe for use and should be condemned.

Scuba cylinders may be stored at full pressure for short periods of time. However, for long-term storage

**WARNING
ALUMINUM CYLINDERS THAT HAVE BEEN
EXPOSED TO HEAT ABOVE 350°F (177C) SHOULD
BE REMOVED FROM SERVICE.**

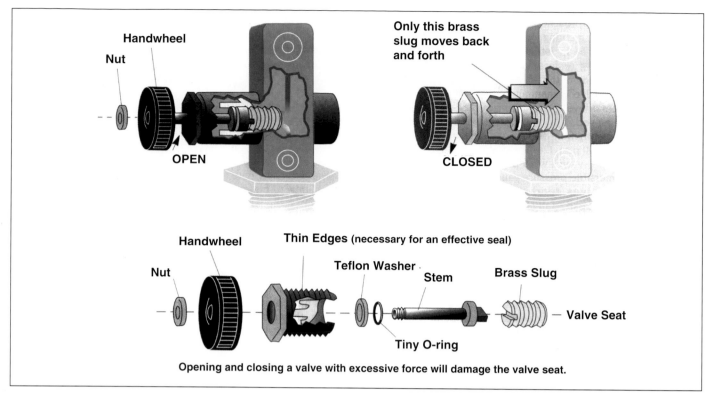

FIGURE 5.25
Valve Seats

5.7.4 Sustained Load Cracking (SLC) in 6351 Aluminum Alloy Cylinders

Sustained Load Cracking, a metallurgical anomaly, occasionally develops in high-pressure aluminum cylinders made from 6351-alloy and may lead to explosive rupture. Both Walter Kidde and Luxfer (1972 to June, 1988) used 6351-alloy. The standard inspection method to examine the cylinder thread area for cracks or corrosion damage uses a magnifying mirror and light source. Although most flawed cylinders with SLC have been identified by this method, a means to verify findings was desired.

In 1996 an eddy-current device was introduced as an additional tool for inspectors to detect occasional early, difficult-to-observe SLC. Sold under the brand name Visual Plus, it was followed in 1999 by a nearly identical unit, Visual Eddy. A third design is sold under the brand name Simple Eddy.

Each device is capable of locating early cracking but also may produce false positive readings when improperly operated or when the cylinder thread areas being tested are inadequately cleaned. These devices should not be used on steel cylinders nor are they required for aluminum cylinders made from 6061-alloy.

Another recently developed auxiliary tool, the Tank Inspection Pipe (TIP) (see Figure 5.24, bottom), is an excellent way to examine magnified, brightly lit cylinder threads.

Cylinder inspectors should communicate with cylinder manufacturers to ensure they have the most current cylinder service and safety notices.

5.7.5 Cylinder Valve and Manifold Assembly

Open-circuit scuba cylinders are normally worn on a diver's back with the manifold/valve assembly up. The demand valve or second stage of the single-hose regulator is positioned at the diver's mouth, regardless of cylinder orientation. The first stage must be kept in close proximity to the diver's lungs to ensure a minimum hydrostatic pressure differential between demand valve and respiratory organs, regardless of diver orientation. If this is not achieved, the diver's respiratory system must work harder than necessary to overcome this differential during inhalation (or exhalation, depending on orientation).

If the diver's air is to be supplied by two or more cylinders simultaneously, a manifold assembly is employed to join the cylinders and provide a common outlet. The manifold consists of sections of high-pressure piping and appropriate fittings specially configured and threaded to incorporate two or more cylinders, a valve and frangible burst disk into a single functional unit.

The cylinder valve assembly is a simple, manually operated, multiple-turn valve that controls the flow of high-pressure gas from the scuba cylinder (see Figure 5.25). It also is the point of attachment for the demand regulator. After the regulator has been attached to the cylinder valve and just before using the apparatus, the valve is opened fully and then backed off one-fourth of a turn. It remains open throughout the dive. On completion of the dive, the cylinder valve is closed and should be bled to atmospheric pressure, which prevents the O-ring from blowing out when the regulator is removed.

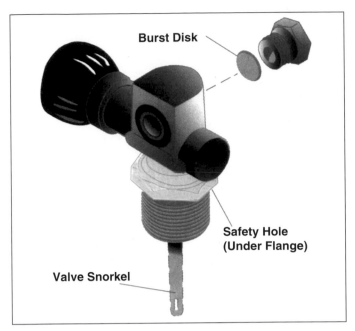

FIGURE 5.26
Cylinder Valve Safety Features

FIGURE 5.27
K-Valve and J-Valve

When a single cylinder supplies diver's air, the cylinder valve unit is generally sealed directly into the neck of the cylinder by a straight-threaded male connection containing a neoprene O-ring on the valve body. Most cylinders placed in service before 1960 were fitted with a valve having a 0.5-inch tapered thread without O-rings. When a single cylinder is utilized, the cylinder valve assembly houses a high-pressure burst disk as a safety feature to prevent cylinder pressure from reaching a critical level during charging or under conditions of elevated temperature. Old-style lead-filled blowout plugs must be replaced with modern frangible disk assemblies (see Figure 5.26). When twin cylinders are used, two separate burst disc assemblies must be installed in the manifold. Valve manufacturers use burst disks designed to rupture around the cylinder's hydrostatic test pressure. The rating may be stamped on the face of the burst disk assembly to prevent confusion, and disks of different pressure ratings must not be used interchangeably. Valves are not interchangeable between cylinders having different service pressures unless their respective burst disk assemblies are also interchanged.

5.7.6 Reserve Valve

The reserve valve (also called a J-valve), illustrated in Figure 5.27, is a spring-loaded check valve that begins to close as the cylinder pressure approaches a predetermined level, generally 300 or 500 psi (23 or 30 kg/cm^2). Until this pressure is approached, the reserve valve permits an unrestricted flow of air to the regulator throughout the dive. At the predetermined pressure, a spring forces a flow check against the port orifice and restricts the air flow, causing increased breathing resistance. This is followed by total obstruction of air flow if the reserve air is not manually released. The remaining or reserve air can be released by manually overriding the spring-loaded check valve. The K-valve is an open-closed valve with no reserve mechanism.

> **NOTE**
> **The reserve valve lever must be in the "down" position when charging cylinders.**

When a diver depresses the cylinder valve/manifold-mounted reserve lever, a plunger pin within the reserve valve advances, forcing the flow check to back off the orifice against the action of the spring. The remaining 300 or 500 psi (23 or 30 kg/cm^2) of air is then made available to the diver.

Divers should be aware that the availability and duration of the reserve air supplied through a reserve valve are dependent on the number of cylinders carried, the depth of the dive and the diver's RMV. The 300 psi (23 kg/cm^2) reserve available is at actual cylinder pressure; it is not 300 psi above ambient pressure. Thus, at a depth of 100 ft. (ambient pressure of approximately 50 psi), only 250 psi (17 kg/cm^2) is available until the diver starts to ascend. Also, the reserve valve mechanism retains a reserve air supply only in one cylinder of a twin set of cylinders; the other cylinder or cylinders are at a lower pressure when the reserve valve trips. When the reserve mechanism is activated, the reserve air distributes itself proportionately in all cylinders. For this reason, the reserve valve mechanism employed with twin cylinders must be set to provide a 500-psi reserve. Unfortunately, though generally reliable, the reserve valve mechanism is subject to physical damage or mechanical failure and, if moved as little as 1/8" to 1/4", may be tripped inadvertently early in the dive, which allows the reserve air to be exhausted without the diver's knowledge. Thus, the diver should continuously monitor his reserve valve and submersible pressure gauge during the dive.

> **NOTE**
> **Reserve valves should be inspected annually for defects or whenever a malfunction is suspected.**

NOAA Diving Manual

FIGURE 5.28
Air Fill Control Panel With Fill Hoses

FIGURE 5.29
Fill Station

TABLE 5.4
Typical Fill Times

FROM PRESSURE IN STORAGE (AFTER EQUALIZING IN DIVE TANK)	TO NOMINAL TANK SIZE AND PRESSURE			
	83 cu. ft. to 3,000 psi	71.2 cu. ft. to 2,475 psi	71.2 cu. ft. to 2,250 psi	80 cu. ft. to 4,400 psi
2,500 psi	12 sec.			60 sec.
2,250 psi	28 sec.	14 sec.		90 sec.
2,000 psi	39 sec.	22 sec.	12 sec.	
1,500 psi	75 sec.	50 sec.	35 sec.	

5.8 HIGH-PRESSURE AIR STORAGE SYSTEMS

For some scientific surface-supplied diving operations, a high-pressure air storage system may be better than a low-pressure compressor system. In some cases, the size of the surface support platform dictates the type of gas supply system to use. A high-pressure system can be tailored conveniently to the requirements of a particular operation, and offers the additional advantage of reduced noise and improved communication. The planning factors that influence the configuration of a high-pressure air storage system include:

- Depth of the planned dive
- Number of divers to be supplied and the anticipated exertion level
- Type of breathing apparatus (free flow or demand)
- Size of the surface support platform

A complete system includes high-pressure cylinders (200–350 standard cubic foot size), the necessary piping and manifolds, a pressure-reduction regulator, and a volume tank (at least one cubic foot volume) (see Figures 5.28, 5.29). A high-pressure filter should always be incorporated into or be located just upstream of each pressure regulator. Filter elements should be of the woven-metal cloth type and should have a collapse pressure rating greater than the maximum possible pressure differential. A high-pressure gauge must be located ahead of the pressure reduction regulator, and a low-pressure gauge must be connected to the volume cylinder. The volume tank must be fitted with an overpressure relief valve. A manually controlled regulator by-pass valve or a redundant regulator with its own filter also should be included in the system.

NOTE
If cylinder banks are used as a back-up to a compressor supply, the bank must be manifolded with the primary source so that an immediate switch from primary to secondary air is possible.

5.9 BREATHING GAS BOOSTER PUMPS

Booster pumps "boost" medium pressure storage gas (air, nitrox, oxygen) directly into dive cylinders to higher pressures rapidly. An example would be taking a pressure of 2,250 psi to 4,400 psi in a 80 cu. ft. cylinder in 60 seconds (see Table 5.4 and Figures 5.30, 5.31). This system of increasing pressure to a higher range provides cooler operation on medium pressure compressors which will extend time between overhauls of compressors. Gas booster pump benefits:

- Cooler operation to extend time between overhauls by thousands of hours regardless of compressor nameplate rating
- Lower cost storage cylinders, purifier units, compressors, motors and piping
- Provides 2,500 psi up to 5,000 psi scuba cylinder fills

WARNING
HIGH-PRESSURE GAS CAN BE DANGEROUS IF IMPROPERLY HANDLED.

NOTE
Maximum "net" boost is 2,250 psig. In practice (for reasonable fill speed), consider 2,000 psi as maximum "net." For example, storage pressure should be no less than 1,000 psi to top off 3,000 scuba cylinders or 2,400 psi to top off 4,400 psi scuba cylinders.

Diver and Diving Support Equipment

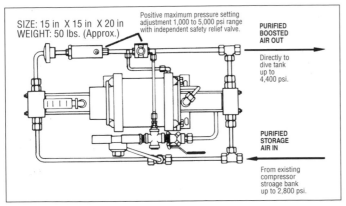

FIGURE 5.30
Pressure and Safety Controls on Booster Pump

5.10 SUBMERSIBLE PRESSURE GAUGES

Two styles of pressure gauges can be used to determine the amount of air in a scuba cylinder. A surface cylinder pressure gauge is used to check the amount of air in a cylinder on the surface. This type of gauge fits over the cylinder manifold outlet, attaches in the same manner as a regulator, and provides a discrete check of the pressure in a cylinder. A pressure release valve is installed on the gauge so that air trapped in the gauge can be relieved after a reading has been taken and the cylinder has been closed. These small dial gauge movements are designed with an accuracy of ± 100 psi but may become less accurate with use.

The submersible cylinder pressure gauge attaches directly to the first stage of a scuba regulator by a length of high-pressure rubber hose. These gauges provide divers

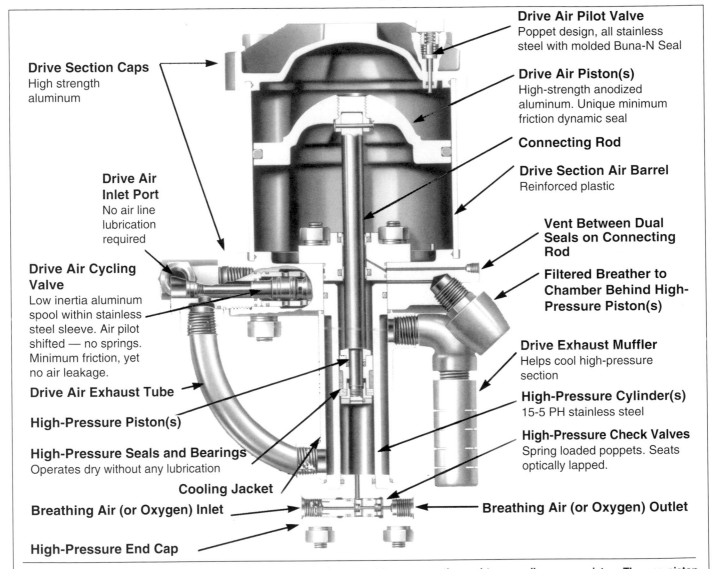

Boosters consist of a large area reciprocating air-drive directly coupled by a connecting rod to a small area gas piston. The gas piston operates in a high-pressure gas barrel section. Each gas barrel end cap contains high-pressure inlet and outlet check valves. The air-drive section includes a cycling spool and pilot valves that provide continuous reciprocating action when air is supplied to the air-drive inlet. Isolation of the gas compression chambers from the air-drive section is provided by three sets of dynamic seals. The intervening two chambers are vented to atmosphere. This design prevents air-drive contamination from entering the gas stream. Cooling is provided by routing the cold exhausted drive air through an individual jacket surrounding the gas barrel and also through an intercooler on the interstage line.

FIGURE 5.31
Oil-Free Air-Driven Gas Booster

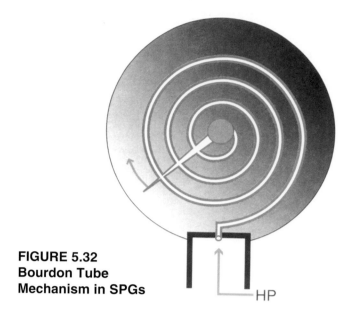

FIGURE 5.32
Bourdon Tube
Mechanism in SPGs

FIGURE 5.34
Submersible Pressure Gauge
Console

they are not precision laboratory instruments.

The gauge dial face should be easy to read and should have high-contrast markings. Most mechanical gauges have a luminous dial that is easy to read at night. Electronic gauges frequently have a back-light feature that can be turned on momentarily when needed.

Miniature submersible pressure gauges are available that connect directly to the first stage of a regulator without an intervening high-pressure hose (see Figure 5.33). These gauges are ideal for use with a bail-out cylinder or in other situations where a hoseless gauge is desirable.

The only maintenance that a submersible pressure gauge needs is a freshwater rinse after use. To prevent internal deterioration and corrosion of a surface gauge, the dust cap that covers the high-pressure inlet must be firmly in place. Submersible pressure gauges should be handled with care, should be stored securely when not in use, and should be tested annually by a qualified testing technician.

with a continual readout of their remaining air. Many units have a console that holds the compass, depth gauge, and cylinder pressure gauge. These consoles free the diver's arms from encumbrances.

Some type of submersible pressure gauge, whether it is mechanical or electronic, is essential for diving. In many cases today, manufacturers are offering air integrated dive computers that monitor both air pressure and bottom time to compute remaining dive time. However, some divers prefer to keep their instruments separate so that if one device fails, the other is not compromised.

Inside the mechanical submersible pressure gauge, one end of the pressure reading tube is sealed and is allowed to move; the other end is held fixed and is connected to a high-pressure air supply. As the air pressure increases, the bourdon tube tends to straighten out or to uncurl slightly (see Figure 5.32). This movement causes the needle on the gauge face to turn. Although gauges currently in use are designed to be accurate and reliable,

5.10.1 Use of Submersible Pressure Gauge

Use of a submersible cylinder pressure gauge (see Figure 5.34) is a requirement in nearly all recreational and scientific diving. These gauges have largely replaced constant reserve valves and audio systems. When reading a gauge is difficult, as is the case in low-visibility conditions, a reserve "J" valve can be carried as well. In addition, dial faces that glow in the dark increase gauge readability under marginal light conditions. Some newer gauges are able to provide data on the amount of time remaining for the dive at the current breathing gas consumption rate. This feature calculates the pressure drop in the cylinder over time and predicts the amount of air time remaining, assuming a continued constant rate of use. However, divers should be aware that changing their respiration rates can dramatically alter the amount of time remaining at low cylinder pressures or when diving at deep depths.

The use of consoles that allow other types of gauges to be added to the submersible pressure gauge has increased the amount of information that can be obtained when a diver monitors the submersible cylinder pressure gauge. Maximum depth indicators, bottom timers, and compasses are now commonly associated with pressure gauges. However, this use of console gauge holders has added considerably to the mass of the high-pressure hose end, and the

FIGURE 5.33
Miniature Submersible
Pressure Gauges

hose and gauge must be positioned carefully as a result; the high-pressure hose can be run inside the waist strap on the back pack so that the gauges are located on the thigh in a readable position. When worn improperly, a submersible pressure gauge positioned at the end of a 2- to 3-foot (0.6 to 0.9 m) length of high-pressure hose can increase the chance that a diver will foul on bottom debris or become entangled with equipment. The gauge supply hose must be connected to a high-pressure port with compatible threads or be used with an adapter.

The high-pressure hose normally has chrome-plated brass fittings with a restricting orifice. Should the high-pressure hose rupture, this orifice prevents rapid loss of cylinder air and allows the diver time to abort the dive and surface. Care must be taken to keep water from getting into the first stage of the regulator before the cylinder valve is opened, because otherwise water could be blown into the submersible pressure gauge and other regulator parts. Divers also should never submerge their scuba cylinders when the valve is off and there is no pressure in the attached regulator.

Gauge readings that err by as much as 300 psi (23 kg/cm^2) or more may occur because gauge accuracy declines with use, especially if small amounts of water have entered the mechanism. Divers should compare their gauges to known cylinder pressures regularly; gauges should be checked at various pressures. Professional dive facilities often use gauges in their high-pressure air systems that are accurate to one or two percent so they can make cylinders with known pressures available to their customers for comparison. All submersible pressure gauges (see Figure 5.35) used by NOAA divers are inspected and tested yearly by a trained technician.

WARNING
DO NOT LOOK DIRECTLY AT THE FACE OF ANY PRESSURE GAUGE WHEN TURNING ON THE CYLINDER BECAUSE OF THE POSSIBILITY OF A BLOWOUT.

Because the accuracy of the slow indicator needle declines during normal use, the needle on a defective unit might stick, which could cause the pressure reading to be higher than it actually is. Divers in the field can assess the adequacy of submersible gauge needle function by releasing pressure from the gauge over a three-minute period while they observe the needle for erratic movement. Defective gauges must be serviced for replacement of parts.

5.11 BUOYANCY COMPENSATORS
The buoyancy compensator, frequently referred to as a "BC" or "BCD" (buoyancy control device), was designed to allow the diver to make adjustments to his buoyancy. This can be done under water or on the surface.

The buoyancy compensator is not a lifesaving device and cannot be relied upon to float the diver face up in the water. In addition, any buoyancy compensator may fail to hold air due to damage or lack of maintenance. For a diver wearing a weight belt and weights, in an emergency, the only reasonably certain way to increase positive buoyancy is to drop the weight belt.

The buoyancy compensator is critical to making buoyancy adjustments throughout each dive. Prior to the dive, the diver should perform a predive inspection of functionality of the BC, including hoses, connections, over-pressurization valve, power inflator, etc. For surface swimming, the diver will normally want to have just enough air in the buoyancy compensator to be positively buoyant. At the start of the descent, the diver releases just enough air from the buoyancy compensator to start to sink. While swimming under water, the amount of air in the buoyancy compensator is adjusted to make the diver neutrally buoyant. While working on the bottom, the diver will frequently want to be negatively buoyant for added stability while taking photographs or writing on an underwater slate.

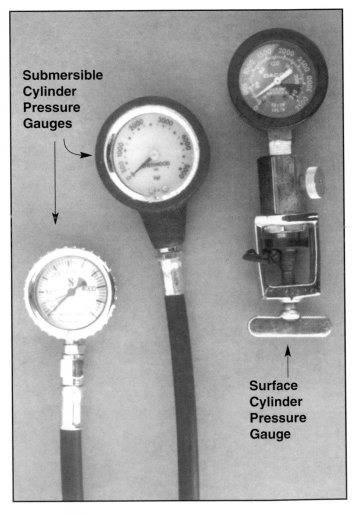

FIGURE 5.35
Gauges

Almost all buoyancy compensators include the following components in their design:

- An air bladder, or "air cell," which can be inflated or deflated
- An airway or corrugated inflator hose
- A mouthpiece for adding air orally and venting air
- A power inflator for adding low pressure air from the regulator
- A safety harness and buckles, or straps, for attaching the buoyancy compensator to the diver's body
- An overpressure relief valve for relieving air pressure

Buoyancy compensators vary widely in design, but most conform to either the "jacket" style, which wraps the diver in buoyancy or the "back-mounted" design, and places all of the buoyancy behind the diver. Nearly all buoyancy compensators, with the exception of the "horse-collar" design, include a cylinder band for mounting the scuba cylinder.

Original buoyancy compensators (see Figure 5.36), developed in the late 1960s, were of the "horse-collar" design. The horse-collar design places all of the buoyancy in front of the diver and can usually be relied upon to float the diver face up in most situations. This design makes it more difficult for the diver who is trying to swim horizontally or work vertically under water because the buoyancy of the unit tends to roll the diver backwards. If a horsecollar BC is used, the diver must use a separate backpack to support and secure the cylinder on his back.

Back-mounted buoyancy compensators put the air bladder behind the diver, leaving fewer straps and obstructions on the diver's chest. Many back-mounted BCs are made using a stretchy material to constrict the

FIGURE 5.37
Back-Mounted Buoyancy Compensator

air bladder. The bladder collapses when the air is vented from it, reducing it to an extremely compact size that renders very little drag.

The back-mounted buoyancy compensator (also referred to as "wings") is good for working in a vertical position in the water or swimming horizontally (see Figure 5.37). On the surface, a back-mounted BC will tend to push the diver into a face down position.

Jacket-style buoyancy compensators usually include a bladder that places some of the buoyancy in front of the diver around his waist and some of the buoyancy behind the diver (see Figure 5.38). This design is very comfortable to wear and offers good stability. It is a good compromise for allowing the diver to work comfortably in a variety of positions. Jacket-style buoyancy compensators tend to have more drag than back-mounted buoyancy compensators.

The cylinder band that secures the cylinder to the buoyancy compensator may attach to a metal or hard plastic plate, or it may connect directly to the soft fabric of the BC itself. In any case, the cylinder band is almost always made of stiff nylon webbing. The webbing must be threaded correctly through the buckle to prevent the cylinder from slipping out of the band. The webbing and BC must be soaked in water prior to adjusting the band to hold the cylinder or the band will loosen once it becomes wet and the cylinder

FIGURE 5.36
Original Horsecollar Buoyancy Compensator

FIGURE 5.38
Jacket-style Buoyancy Compensator

will fall out of the band. Instructions for threading the cylinder band are usually attached to the band itself.

Some models of buoyancy compensators include integrated weight systems, where the weights are contained in pockets in the BC. This design eliminates the need for a separate weight belt. One advantage to the weight integrated BC is that it prevents the buoyancy compensator from floating up on the diver's body.

Some divers find an integrated weight system more comfortable than wearing a weight belt because it helps eliminate the bruising that may occur from contact with the weights. Integrated weight systems also transfer the weight from the diver's hips to his shoulders, which helps to reduce back stress. For transporting the BC, it may be desirable to remove the weights from the BC rather than dealing with the combined weight of the BC, cylinder, and weights.

Some divers who use integrated BCs prefer to split their weights between the BC and weight belt, placing a small amount of weight in the BC and the balance on their belt. This reduced weight will usually still hold the BC down, without the bulk that sometimes occurs by filling the BC with the total compliment of weights normally used to dive.

Integrated weight systems are usually supplied with either a single point release (see Figure 5.39) or a dual point release. With a single point release, one pull will normally ditch all of the weights contained in the BC. Advantages to this design are that ditching the weights is extremely rapid and ditching can be accomplished with one hand.

Dual point release mechanisms usually require both hands and only ditch half the weights which are normally distributed on the left and right sides of the diver's body (see Figure 5.40). The value of this design is that in many cases, only half the weights may need to be ditched in order to establish positive buoyancy. When only half the weights are ditched, the diver's ascent will usually not be as rapid as when all the weights are ditched. Dual point release mechanisms should only be used by experienced divers with advanced training.

FIGURE 5.40
Dual Point Release
System

Some models of buoyancy compensators come in standard sizes, such as x-small, small, medium, large, and x-large. Others may be customized with different size components or widely adjustable waist belts and shoulder straps. Customization will usually provide a better fit but is usually more expensive.

Certain models of BCs are equipped with stainless steel D-rings which can be used as an attachment point for lights, instruments, and tools. Almost every BC also has an accessory pocket where small items may be stored.

Many BCs are equipped with a remote exhaust mechanism which is activated by a stainless steel cable running on the inside of the corrugated inflator hose. The remote exhaust is positioned on the shoulder end of the inflator hose. By pulling down on the inflator hose, the stainless cable is pulled and opens the remote exhaust that vents the buoyancy compensator.

The question frequently arises as to how much lift is needed for a buoyancy compensator. In most situations, the diver needs very little lift, beyond that needed to establish positive buoyancy for himself when fully geared up. For the average diver who is properly weighted and using a single cylinder, the diver normally does not need more than 20-30 pounds of lift. However, cold water divers wearing thick wet suits, or dry suits, and multiple high-pressure cylinders may need considerably more lift.

FIGURE 5.39
Back-Mounted
Buoyancy
Compensator
With Single
Point Weight
System

Buoyancy Testing

- Initial (predive) test: Adjust weight to float at eye level after exhalation and with no air in BC (and dry suit)

- Final (end-of-dive) test: Adjust weights to be able to remain motionless at a depth of 15 ft. with no air in BC (and dry suit) and 500 psi of air in cylinder

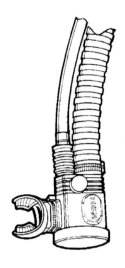

FIGURE 5.41
Power Inflator Integrated With a Regulator

Under no circumstances should the diver use his buoyancy compensator as a lifting device for retrieving heavy objects (over ten pounds) from the bottom. If the object is more than ten pounds negatively buoyant, a separate lift bag should be used to raise the object to the surface. The danger in using the BC as a lifting device is that, should the diver lose control of the object, he will become instantly positively buoyant and can suffer a rapid ascent. Rapid ascents are dangerous and can cause lung over-pressure injuries and omitted decompression.

5.11.1 Power Inflator Mechanisms

Almost all buoyancy compensators today are equipped with some type of low pressure power inflator (see Figures 5.41, 5.42) that uses air from the scuba cylinder to inflate the buoyancy compensator. Without the power inflator, it is necessary for the diver to remove the regulator from his mouth under water to blow air into the BC to achieve neutral buoyancy. This is undesirable.

The simplest power inflators are designed to solely add air to the buoyancy compensator and provide oral inflation and venting capabilities. They are normally equipped with a quick disconnect hose, similar to those used on a dry suit.

More sophisticated power inflators are available that also serve as an alternate air source for sharing air with a diving partner. They combine both functions into a single unit. This eliminates the need for two divers to attempt to share a single mouthpiece by passing it back and forth, a technique that is known as "buddy-breathing." It also eliminates the need for a separate dedicated "octopus" second stage.

Another design that is also popular utilizes a compact second stage that plugs in between the low pressure hose from the regulator and the quick disconnect fitting on the power inflator. These low profile regulators are true regulators and in some cases can be disconnected from the power inflator and still function independently.

5.11.2 Maintenance of Buoyancy Compensators

After diving, buoyancy compensators should be given a thorough rinse in fresh, clean water. If possible, the entire BC should be submerged in a tub of water and agitated vigorously.

Water should be run into the mouthpiece of the power inflator to remove any salt and sand that may have entered it. The exhaust button on the mouthpiece should be held open and water run inside the BC until it is at least 1/3 full. Following this, the BC should be turned upside down and rotated completely several times to ensure full circulation of the water inside it.

Once the water has been flushed through the BC, it should be turned upside down again and the exhaust button on the mouthpiece should be held open until all the water runs out of the BC. This procedure will help to clean out any water that entered the BC while diving. It may be necessary to repeat this procedure several times to thoroughly rinse the interior of the BC. Dirty water that is allowed to remain in the BC will cause bacterial growth.

The BC should be dried by inflating it fully and hanging it in a location with good air circulation that is out of direct sun light and other heat sources. The diver should check to see that air has not leaked out of the BC before it is deflated for storage. Prior to deflating, the BC should be turned upside down one more time and the exhaust button on the mouthpiece should be depressed to drain any water that has pooled inside of the BC.

5.11.3 Weight Belts and Weights

To offset the buoyancy of the diver's body and other equipment, a weight belt is usually worn while diving. The amount of weight worn will vary from diver to diver depending on the diver's personal physique, the type of equipment he is wearing, and any instruments he may be carrying.

Weights come in several different forms including lead shot, molded weights, and molded weights with plastic coatings (see Figure 5.43). Larger molded weights, over six pounds, are normally curved to conform to the shape of the human body. These curved weights are referred to as "hip weights."

Lead shot (small, round pellets) is normally supplied in sealed bags made of mesh or other materials, which are used in belts with pouches or in integrated weight systems

FIGURE 5.42
In-Line Compact Second Stage Combined With BC Inflator

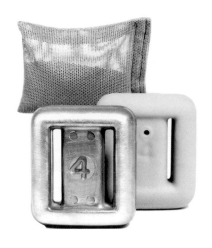

FIGURE 5.43
Shot Filled Bag and
Molded Weights

FIGURE 5.45
Weight Keepers

(see Figure 5.44). Molded weights are slotted so that they may be threaded onto belts made from nylon webbing.

To assemble a weight belt using molded weights and nylon webbing, the belt is fed from the back of each weight, through one of the two slots, over the top of the weight, and down through the second slot. To prevent the weights from sliding, "weight keepers" may be used on either side or center of each weight. "Weight keepers" are made from metal or plastic and are used to prevent molded weights from sliding on the belt (see Figure 5.45). The use of keepers can be avoided by putting a half twist in the belt webbing after it has been fed through the first slot but before it is inserted in the second slot. Weight keepers are not essential, but they are inexpensive and using them makes the belt more compact and requires less webbing.

Another alternative to the conventional weight belt is the weight safety harness (see Figure 5.46). By wearing a safety harness, the weights are supported on the diver's shoulders. If this type of system is used, it must be equipped with a mechanism to ditch the weights quickly and easily, without removing the entire safety harness. Divers can usually carry more weight by using a safety harness than they can carry comfortably on a weight belt.

Whatever type of weight system is used, the weights should be balanced on both sides of the diver's body. Putting more weight on one side or the other will cause the diver to "list" to one side. Positioning more weights closer to the diver's stomach will tend to cause the diver to assume a face-down position. Adjusting the weights closer to the diver's back will tend to roll the diver onto his back.

5.11.4 Safety Harnesses

The safety harness used by surface-supplied divers is an upper torso safety harness that serves the purpose of keeping umbilical stress distributed evenly against the diver. The safety harness is also a convenient hanger for tools and devices that the diver may be required to carry with him, but great care should be taken in hanging items from the safety harness because of the dangers of fouling.

A typical surface-supplied divers' safety harness is made of nylon webbing and is stitched, with rivets added at stress points. D-rings are used for securing the umbilical and fastening the safety harness across the diver's chest. D-rings should be stainless steel.

Many diving umbilicals incorporate a snap shackle; others incorporate a D-ring on the diver's end of the umbilical and leave it to the diver to supply his own snap shackle, which is moused onto the left side D-ring of the safety harness.

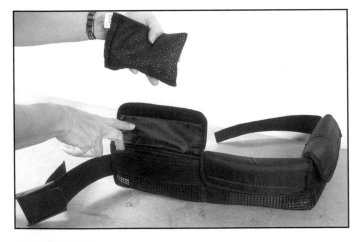

FIGURE 5.44
Weight Belt with Pouches

FIGURE 5.46
Weight Safety Harness

NOAA Diving Manual

Snap shackles (see Figure 5.47) should be stainless steel or brass, should be positive-lock, and should have a small lanyard attached to the opening pin. This lanyard should be no longer than the width of the diver's fist, should be small in diameter, and should be smooth and free of knobs or loops that could catch on underwater objects and inadvertently disengage the diver from his umbilical.

The safety harness and snap shackle should be rinsed in fresh water after each dive. Every couple of months the safety harness should be cleaned with soap and water to remove accumulated oils that will speed the deterioration of threads. Rinse it well. Inspect the safety harness and snap shackle frequently for signs of deterioration and repair or replace as necessary.

FIGURE 5.47
Snap Shackle

5.11.5 Safety Harness and Bail-Out Cylinder

The surface-supplied diver must be equipped with a safety harness (see Figure 5.48) and bail-out cylinder. The bail-out cylinder worn on the safety harness consist of a scuba cylinder with a first stage regulator and a low-pressure hose running to an emergency valve on the diver's headgear.

The bail-out cylinder provides an emergency source of breathing gas in the event the topside supply is cut off. The regulator used with the bail-out cylinder must be equipped with an over-pressure relief valve to vent pressure should the first stage develop a leak (see Figure 5.49). Without this valve, the low pressure hose supplying the bail-out gas to the helmet or mask would rupture if the first stage leaks.

FIGURE 5.49
Over-Pressure Relief Valve

5.12 SURFACE-SUPPLIED DIVING EQUIPMENT

Surface-supplied diving is an alternative to using self contained equipment. In this diving mode, the diver's breathing gas is supplied from topside via a diving hose (umbilical). For certain applications, surface-supplied diving is a superior method of working under water. Surface-supplied gear works best when the diver is working in a relatively restricted area especially on deep or extended dives. It is generally not recommended when the diver must cover large areas of the bottom (*U.S. Navy Diving Manual* Rev 4 1999).

The minimum equipment required for surface-supplied diving includes the following:

- Topside breathing gas source
- Dive control manifold
- Communications box
- Umbilical
- Safety harness
- Full-face mask or helmet
- Thermal protection
- Reserve breathing supply (bail-out cylinder)

5.12.1 Topside Breathing Gas Source

The topside breathing gas supply for surface-supplied diving can be either a low pressure compressor (see Figure 5.50) or multiple cylinders of high-pressure breathing gas (reduced to low pressure) (see Figure 5.51), or a combination of the two. There are many combinations of gas sources that can be used.

FIGURE 5.48
Diving Safety Harness

FIGURE 5.50
Low-Pressure Compressor

HP REGULATOR WITH UPSTREAM AND DOWNSTREAM PRESSURE GAUGES

FIGURE 5.51
Typical Manifolding for a HP Quad

If air is the only breathing medium required, the entire dive can be run using a single source, although it is much safer if multiple sources are available. The optimum arrangement is a low pressure compressor with a diesel engine as the power source and high-pressure cylinders as the back-up. If a low-pressure compressor is used, it must be equipped with a volume tank (which acts as a reserve and a moisture trap) and adequate filtration.

If mixed gas is being used, the system may include multiple cylinders of different mixtures. If high-pressure sources of oxygen are to be used during the dive, then the entire system must be oxygen cleaned and compatible (see Chapter 15).

5.12.2 Diver Control Manifold

Surface-supplied diving is normally conducted using some type of breathing gas manifold that is used to monitor and control the supply and pressure of gas to the diver. The manifold can be used to switch breathing gases supplied to the diver. Ideally, the manifold should be capable of supporting two divers.

Diver control manifolds designed exclusively for use with compressed air are typically the least complex and easiest to operate. They may be designed to handle only low-pressure air or may support both high-pressure and low-pressure air. If high-pressure air is used, the manifold will include a pressure-reducing regulator that is used to control the intermediate pressure supplied to the diver. In some cases where high-pressure air is used, scuba cylinders can be used as the air supply.

A pressure-reducing regulator is adjusted manually to the correct over-bottom helmet pressure for the depth of the diver. This regulator must be adjusted by topside personnel as the diver moves deeper or shallower. An ordinary scuba first-stage regulator mounted topside will not work properly because it cannot sense the pressure at the diver's depth.

Mixed gas manifolds are slightly more complex than air diving manifolds. They normally include multiple pressure-reducing regulators and a manual metering valve that can be used in an emergency if the regulators fail. Most mixed gas manifolds will accept breathing gas from a minimum of three sources.

Regardless of the type of manifold used, they normally are equipped with a "pneumofathometer," a device that is used to measure the diver's depth. The pneumofathometer consists of a large, highly accurate depth gauge with a needle valve connected between it and the air supply for the diver. A "T" fitting then connects to an open-ended hose which is bundled in the diver's umbilical, appropriately named the pneumofathometer hose.

To take a depth reading, the manifold operator opens the needle valve until the hose is filled with air and the diver reports that air is bubbling out the end of the hose. The manifold operator closes the valve and the back pressure trapped in the hose provides a highly accurate reading of the diver's depth on the gauge.

A manifold is a device that distributes gases in different directions. Diving manifolds are used in a variety of ways to distribute gases (which in motion have the properties of fluids). They may be blocks of steel with internally bored holes to provide various pathways for the gases, or co-fitted together, or combinations of hoses and fittings and mated together to distribute the gases. Manifolds may be fabricated on-site with available materials or purchased from supply houses.

High-pressure compressed gases, including air, are often stored and transported in steel frames that hold about 16 cylinders, standing upright or stacked on their sides all pointing in the same direction. Instead of moving a regulator from cylinder to cylinder as they are used, the cylinders are manifolded together so that new cylinders can be brought on line as needed, just by opening the cylinder valve and/or a manifold valve (see Figure 5.51). These are HP manifolds and are commonly fabricated using stainless steel tubing or flexible hoses and fittings, and high-pressure valves. Divers may be required to fabricate or repair such a manifold.

WARNING
NEVER WORK ON A HP MANIFOLD OR OTHER SYSTEM COMPONENT UNDER PRESSURE. REMEMBER TO OPEN HP VALVES S-L-O-W-L-Y.

Do not forget to close empty cylinders before opening full ones, or the contents of the full cylinder will be transferred into the empty cylinders. The volume of usable gas will remain the same, but the pressure drop may be counterproductive.

Manifolds are commonly fabricated and attached to compressor frames and volume tanks to distribute the air to different places. These manifolds are constructed using a combination of fittings and ball valves plumbed to accomplish the desired distribution. All valves should be properly labeled indicating their intended purpose.

FIGURE 5.52
Dive Station Volume Tank

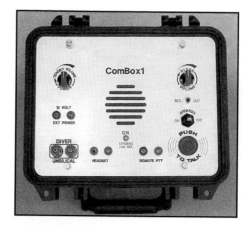

FIGURE 5.54
Communications Box

Manifolds are not considered pressure vessels but are, of course, subjected to the same pressures as the lines that feed them, and therefore they need to be maintained properly.

"Deck manifolds" are fabricated for special purposes to distribute gases at some point between the volume tanks (see Figure 5.52) and the divers. Usually they are small and portable and either sit among the hoses on deck or are hung on a bulkhead or railing. Label all valves and hoses as to purpose.

"Manifold rack boxes" are either purchased commercially or fabricated in-house, and are more than just manifolds (see Figure 5.53). One such manifold is called a "rack box" which not only distributes gases directly to the divers (their dive umbilicals are attached to the rack box) but has fittings for pneumofathometer hoses and depth gauges to monitor the divers' depths. Some commercial rack boxes also contain a built-in diver's radio.

5.12.3 Communication Box

Communications in surface-supplied diving are supported with a hardwire communications system that permits two-way speech. This is a more reliable system than wireless communications. The system consists of a topside communications box with a power supply, a cable,

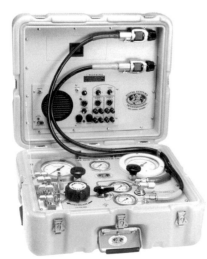

FIGURE 5.53
Air Manifold Box

waterproof connectors at the diver's mask or helmet, and earphones and a microphone inside the helmet (see Figure 5.54). The system works much like a telephone.

There are two types of hardwire communications systems; two-wire systems which are more commonly referred to as "push-to-talk," and four-wire systems which are known as "round robin." Either system is acceptable, but both systems require discipline in use.

In a push-to-talk system, only one person can speak at a time. The two wires must carry the signal one way at a time either up or down. This requires special care on the part of the topside operator, since when the button is depressed for topside to speak to the diver, the diver cannot be heard. When the diver speaks to topside, there is no button to push, he merely speaks into the helmet. In a four-wire system, two wires carry the signal down to the diver, and two wires carry the signal back up to the surface. Thus, both topside and the diver can speak at the same time. This system is more like using a telephone but still requires one person to speak at a time so each person can be understood clearly.

Deep diving with mixed gas requires using special communication systems with "helium unscramblers" to render the diver's speech intelligible. Without the use of the unscrambler the diver's speech is high pitched and difficult to understand.

5.12.4 Umbilical

The umbilical is a bundle of hoses and cables that are taped or twisted together. At a minimum, the umbilical will usually consist of the diver's air supply hose, communications wire, pneumofathometer hose, and a strength member. Other components may include a hot-water supply hose and a video cable.

The umbilical bundle can either float or sink, depending on the type of hose specified at the time of purchase. Most scientific divers will probably find a floating hose easier to work with, especially when the bottom is rocky or there are obstructions.

Diver and Diving Support Equipment

FIGURE 5.55
Full-Face Masks
With Voice
Communicators

FIGURE 5.56
Diving Helmet

The breathing gas hose must not kink and must be approved for breathing gas purposes. Hoses that are not especially designed for diving can give off toxic fumes that can be harmful to divers. The normal hose diameter for surface-supplied diving is 3/8 inch I.D. (internal diameter) hose.

The breathing gas hose is normally fitted with #6 JIC (Joint Industrial Conference) hose fittings or oxygen fittings. Either type is acceptable provided they are compatible with the fittings on the divers' mask or helmet and the breathing gas manifold. However, oxygen fittings cannot be joined to JIC fittings and vise versa.

The pneumofathometer hose is usually a soft, flexible hose with a 1/4 inch internal diameter. The hose is open-ended at the diver and normally fitted with a #4 JIC fitting on the topside end.

Communications wire should be constructed with a heavy plastic jacket that resists abrasion and punctures. In some cases, the communications wire may be strong enough to act as a strength member without a separate line for this purpose.

If a strength member is included in the umbilical it can be either 3/8" inch braided nylon or 3/8" inch polypropylene line. Manila, which is a fiber rope, should never be used because it does not have the strength of the synthetics and will eventually deteriorate and need to be replaced. Polypropylene floats and can help to make the umbilical more positively buoyant.

5.12.5 Full-Face Masks and Helmets

The mask or helmet provides breathing capability but also includes an oral/nasal cavity (small internal mask covering the nose and mouth) for speech. There is no mouthpiece in this gear for the diver to grip with his teeth, and the diver can breathe through both his nose and mouth.

The oral/nasal mask also helps to reduce carbon dioxide build-up inside the helmet.

Most diving masks and helmets today incorporate a demand regulator as well as a free-flow air system. Helmets that do not include a demand regulator may be impractical for scientific diving since they require a high-volume of low-pressure air to adequately supply breathing air to the diver. Free-flow helmets can only be used with high volume, low-pressure air compressors which are large, heavy, and expensive.

For shallow water diving and diving in relatively warm water under good conditions, a full-face mask is usually sufficient (see Figure 5.55). Deeper dives, as well as dives in cold, dangerously polluted waters, or areas with penetrating obstructions, warrant the use of a full coverage diving helmet (see Figure 5.56).

Masks and helmets used for surface-supplied diving should be equipped with adjustable regulators to allow the diver to tune the breathing effort based on the diver's workload. In addition, there should be a free-flow valve included so that a high volume of breathing gas can be supplied to clear the unit if it is flooded and to adequately ventilate the unit of carbon dioxide.

The buoyancy and balance of the helmet are critical to the diver's comfort. Head gear that is too buoyant will place a strain on the diver's jaw, while head gear that is too heavy will result in a sore neck. A helmet that is out of balance can throw the diver's head to one side. In most cases, small weights, such as bicycle wheel weights, can be glued inside the helmet, using silicone sealant, to adjust the balance of the helmet.

All full-face masks and helmets should be equipped with an equalizing device that will allow the diver to block his nose to equalize the pressure in his ears. The diver must be able to operate this device with a gloved hand.

Every mask and helmet must include a valve system that allows a bail-out cylinder to be plumbed directly into the breathing system with a shut-off knob. In the event that topside gas supply is interrupted, the diver need only open the emergency valve to access the bail-out supply.

FIGURE 5.57
Hookah Diver With Second Stage and Lifeline Attached

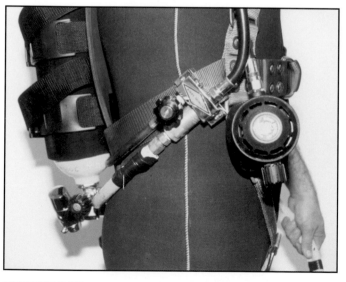

FIGURE 5.58
Emergency Air Cylinder Integrated With the Air Hose

5.12.6 Maintenance of Surface-Supplied Gear

In a surface-supplied system, there are more pieces of equipment to be maintained than when dealing with open circuit scuba. Gear that doesn't go in the water, such as the breathing gas manifold, requires little more than a wipe down with a damp cloth. Helmets, masks, and umbilicals require more extensive maintenance.

The inside of the umbilical must be blown dry if used with a low-pressure compressor that pumps moisture into the hose. This may not be necessary if the only breathing gas source was high-pressure cylinders. The ends of the umbilical must be taped or capped after each day of diving to eliminate contamination of the hose.

The umbilical must be properly coiled while diving and at the end of each day. It can be coiled in a "figure eight," which is the easiest method for most people to learn, or it can coiled over and under, which takes up far less space on a crowded deck. Once the umbilical is properly coiled, it should be tied with several pieces of line so it stays coiled during transport. If possible, the umbilical should be hung up for storage to prevent other objects from being stored on top of it or dropped on it.

Low-pressure compressor systems will need to have their volume tanks drained of moisture hourly during operations and again at the end of each diving day. The oil used to lubricate the compressor should be checked and topped off at the start of each day of operation. A log must be kept of compressor hours to ensure that oil and filter changes occur on schedule. Air samples should be taken from all high- and low-pressure compressors and analyzed at least once every 6 months.

5.13 HOOKAH

A very simple type of demand-mode diving known as hookah has been in use for over 50 years (see Figures 5.57, 5.58). Hookah diving can be a safe, inexpensive, and effective system for shallow water diving (generally 20 feet or less), where the user needs the security of an umbilical and lifeline, limitless gas supply, and good mobility. Typical uses include boat hull scrubbing or repair, dock and pier work, dredging, shallow water recovery, archeological work, and so on. With a hookah system, the diver uses a standard half mask, fins, and weight belt. Instead of diver-worn cylinders, a standard second stage demand regulator is coupled to a low-pressure air supply hose that is fed from a compressor on the surface. Another common system employs the use of high-pressure cylinders with an adjustable regulator to supply the breathing air to the demand regulator in lieu of the compressor. In the early days of scuba, many two-stage double hose regulators came standard with a fitting for attaching a low-pressure air source for hookah diving.

Today, simple hookah systems consist of a standard scuba second stage demand regulator coupled to a manifold block. The manifold block allows for attachment to a belt or harness assembly, which holds the system secure to the user. The manifold block also has provisions for integrating a small emergency air cylinder in the event the airline gets pinched or the surface supply is interrupted. The emergency cylinder is usually worn on the back or chest. Another feature of the manifold block is an integrated one-way valve (air non-return valve) located on the inlet side of the block. This valve is extremely important as it will prevent air from flowing up the umbilical due to a hose rupture or broken fitting near the surface. If a fitting or the air hose failed on or near the surface, the sudden lowering of pressure within the umbilical can, in some cases, draw lips or mouth tissues into the demand valve causing serious injury. Hookah air supply hose is usually a 1/4" to 3/8" inside diameter low-pressure hose with a minimum working pressure of 250 psig and is usually less than 50 ft. in length overall.

Hookahs are generally limited to relatively shallow water work, 20 ft. or less, because most lightweight portable low-pressure compressors cannot achieve the volume and pressures needed to provide good breathing performance much deeper. Performance and depth can be increased using a larger compressor or high-pressure storage cylinders and a pressure-reducing regulator, but at this point cost and complexity are on par with the use of lightweight full-face masks that offer greater safety, performance, and the option of voice communications. For optimal breathing performance with any hookah system, the air supply hose should be kept as short as possible and the supply pressure as high as possible above the minimum recommended by the manufacturer for the demand regulator. Use a good quality second stage demand regulator that is of a balanced design and/or has an adjustable spring biasing device that allows the user to adjust for varying supply pressures.

5.14 DEPTH GAUGES

Depth gauges are small, portable, pressure-sensitive meters that are calibrated in feet (or meters) and allow divers to determine their depth while submerged (see Figure 5.59). Depth gauges are delicate instruments and must be treated carefully to avoid damage. Accuracy is extremely important and should be checked annually. Only a few models of depth gauges can be calibrated in the field; most models must be returned to the manufacturer if repairs are needed.

Most commercially available depth gauges operate either on the capillary, diaphragm, or bourdon tube principle. Capillary depth gauges consist of a clear plastic tube that is open to the water at one end and is attached to a display that is calibrated in feet. As depth increases, the volume of air trapped in the tube decreases and the depth is read from the water level in the tube.

The diaphragm model has a sealed case, one side of which is a flexible diaphragm. As pressure increases, the diaphragm is distorted, which causes the needle to which it is linked to move.

Bourdon tube depth gauges are the most fragile of these types of gauges; they require more frequent calibration than

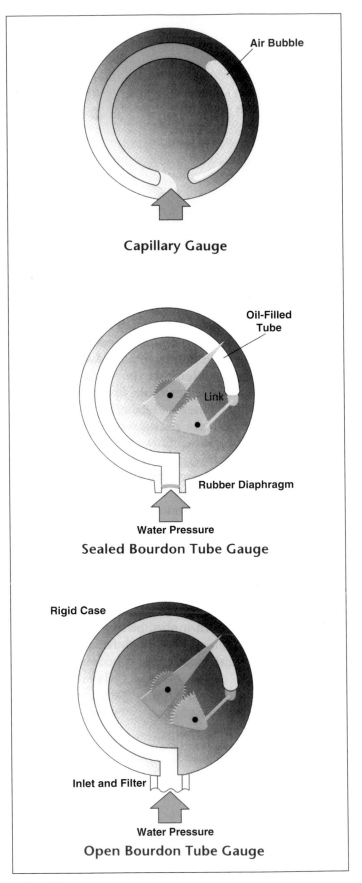

FIGURE 5.59
Three Types of Depth Gauges

NOAA Diving Manual

the other types. With bourdon tubes, water pressure causes a distortion of the tube, which in turn moves a needle that indicates depth. Both bourdon tube and diaphragm depth gauges are available in models that are sealed and oil-filled for smooth, reliable operation.

Open bourdon tube gauges tend to retain salt water in the tube, which may cause salt deposition or corrosion. To prevent this, the gauge should be stored in a jar of distilled water between dives.

Depth gauges are delicate, finely-tuned instruments and must be used, stored, and maintained with great care. Most dive computers today combine the functions of the watch and depth gauge into one unit that automatically performs decompression calculations and tracks surface intervals.

5.15 WIRELESS COMMUNICATIONS

Wireless communications systems provide an alternative to surface-supplied equipment when communications are needed by scuba divers. These systems can provide both diver-to-diver and diver-to-surface communications.

The basic components of an electronic underwater communications system include some type of full-face mask or "half mask," oral/nasal cavity and electronics (see Figures 5.60, 5.61). The electronics are carried in a small waterproof housing. There are connections for the microphone and earphones.

To get the highest level of intelligibility from a wireless system, a full-face mask is preferred. Since the half mask must seal in the space between the upper lip and the nose, where the scuba mask must also seal, most divers find it easier and more comfortable to wear the full-face mask. Although there are also systems that use a special mouthpiece to permit speech, the highest level of intelligibility of the diver's speech will occur when the nose and mouth are in the same cavity as is the case with full-face masks.

Wireless communications work best in open areas where there are relatively few underwater obstructions.

FIGURE 5.60
Half Mask Which Permits Speech

FIGURE 5.61
Wireless Unit Mounted to the Head Safety Harness

They do not work well in a swimming pool, thick kelp, or if two divers are separated by an obstruction. Water density differences such as those caused by thermoclines can also affect the range of a wireless system. Other factors can affect communications:

- Gas density of the diver's breathing gas
- Diver's underwater work level
- Nitrogen narcosis (if the diver is breathing air)
- Bubble noise
- Regulator noise
- Size and shape of the speaking cavity in the diver's mask
- Type of microphone
- Restrictions created by the diver's hood, mask, and straps
- Loss of natural feedback since the diver can't hear himself speak under water
- Lack of practice
- RF interference

Communications are especially recommended when two divers must work together on a common task. The ability to talk to each other makes it much easier to get the job done.

Critical features that should be evaluated in selecting a wireless system include:

- VOX: Systems that include VOX do not require the diver to push a switch to transmit. This may be critical for the scientific diver.
- Output Power: Generally speaking, the more powerful the system, the greater the range.

- Range: Long range is not critical for two divers using the buddy system, but becomes more important if the divers must communicate with other teams or a surface support station at a distance.
- Controls: Configuration and ease of use.
- Automatic On/Off Control versus Manual On/Off.
- Noise-cancelling microphone.
- Automatic Gain Control (AGC): The system should automatically adjust itself so the volume of another diver's voice is the same whether he is two feet away or 200 feet.
- Weight: Lighter and smaller systems are easier to use.
- Battery Life: Battery life is critical; the longer the better.
- Operating Depth: Most units on the market will operate to at least 130 ft. (39.6 m).

The diver must ensure that the wireless system has a good attachment point and that the wires are routed to avoid snags. Excess lengths of wire should be bundled together.

The wireless box should never be attached to the diver's weight belt. If the diver needs to ditch his belt, and the electronics are attached to it, he could find himself in a dangerous position. Also the transducer/receiver should not be mounted where it is covered by other equipment. Some of the systems are equipped with "lollipop" style earphones/speakers, designed to be worn under or over a diving hood. These speakers should never be placed directly over the ear opening but, instead, in front of or behind the ear. Placing the speakers directly over the ear opening could result in an outer ear squeeze.

When using wireless communications, it is important to speak slowly and distinctly in a normal tone of voice. It should not be necessary to shout while communicating. Exhalations should be minimized while sending or receiving a signal, but the diver must never hold his breath at any time while under water.

5.16 KNIVES

Dive knives are used as tools, not as defensive weapons against sharks or other underwater creatures (see Figure 5.62). There are many different types of knives and the diver should select the one most appropriate to his work.

Most diving knives are made from stainless steel with a corrosion resistant handle of some type of plastic. Ideally,

the steel of the blade should extend all the way through the length of the handle as one piece, or the knife will be prone to break.

If the diver must pry objects under water, a blunt tip knife is probably the best choice. The knife should have a sharp blade for cutting lines and nets that could entangle the diver.

Large knives should be worn in a sheath that can be mounted on the weight belt or the inside of the calf. Either of these locations will not pose a problem if the weight belt must be dropped. Smaller knives are also available that can be mounted on the diver's buoyancy compensator straps or even on a submersible pressure gauge hose.

After use, all dive knives should be rinsed with fresh water, dried, and sprayed with a corrosion inhibitor or light coat of oil. Additionally, medic shears are quite popular items that can be easily stowed to cut and "snip" through light line and medium line.

5.17 DIVE LIGHTS

A water/pressure-proof diving light is an important item of equipment when divers are operating in areas of low light (see Figure 5.63). Lights are used most frequently for photography, night diving, cave diving, wreck diving, exploring holes and crevices, or diving under ice. They are also of value at deeper depths if it is important to see the true colors of marine life, wreckage, etc. Regardless of the power of an underwater light, it will have only limited value in murky, dirty waters where visibility is restricted by suspended matter.

When selecting a light, there are several factors to consider, such as brightness and beam coverage, type of batteries (disposable or rechargeable), size and shape, and burn time. Ideally, a dive light should be neutral or just slightly negatively buoyant. Although floating lights are less likely to be lost, they are more awkward to handle under water, especially if they are not in constant use during the dive. In addition, it is impossible to place a floating light down on the bottom without having it drift away.

As with all other pieces of diving equipment, lights should be washed with fresh water after every use. The O-ring should be lubricated with a silicone grease and should be checked for debris every time the light is assembled. When not in use, the batteries should be removed and

**FIGURE 5.62
Dive Knives
With Serrated
Edges**

**FIGURE 5.63
Dive Light**

stored separately. Before a diving light is used, it should be checked thoroughly to ensure proper operation. The batteries should be replaced any time they show any signs of running low, and spare light bulbs and batteries should be available at the dive site.

Some lights today have dual bulbs that can be individually selected under water if one bulb burns out. This is a desirable feature.

5.18 COMPASSES AND NAVIGATION

An underwater compass consists of a small magnetic compass that is housed in a water/pressure-proof case and is worn attached to a diver's wrist by a band, attached by a clip to the BC, or mounted in the diver's console (see Figure 5.64), or integrated in the diver's console. Compasses are useful for underwater navigation, especially in conditions of reduced visibility.

Conventional mechanical compasses do not provide precise bearings, but they do provide a convenient, reliable directional reference point. Digital compasses are now available that are highly accurate and can be used to plan complex courses and automatically compute reciprocals. To limit magnetic interference, compasses should be worn on the wrist opposite from the diver's watch or other instruments.

Compass models are available with side viewing windows that allow a diver to read them while holding them horizontally in front of them when swimming. Compasses do not have to be recalibrated and the only maintenance needed is a fresh-water rinse after use. Electronic compasses will need their batteries replaced according to use.

Underwater GPS (Global Positioning System) units are now available which can help locate a diver's position on the bottom with great precision. The Global Positioning System is a satellite network that circles the world and provides very precise navigation information to receivers on the surface of the earth and at sea. GPS receivers are very common in airplanes, aboard boats, and increasingly, in automobiles. GPS for under water use will undoubtedly become more

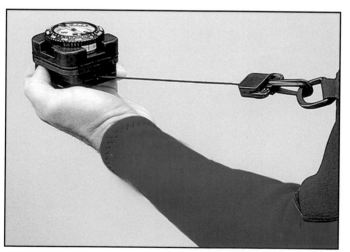

FIGURE 5.64
Compass Attached to Mechanical Retractor

common, especially for use on scientific diving projects. At the time of this writing, GPS units for diving are not self-contained, but require surface transponders to beam the signal to the diver under water (see Chapter 10).

5.19 SIGNAL DEVICES

For divers working at great distances from shore or in strong currents, signaling devices are considered essential pieces of safety equipment. Under heavy and even light sea conditions, it is difficult or impossible to spot a solo diver on the surface. The human voice does not carry very far, especially above the sound of strong winds, compressors, or outboard motors.

The simplest and least expensive visual signaling device is a mirror, but ordinary glass mirrors can break and are unsafe to carry while diving. Several diving equipment manufacturers make waterproof, unbreakable mirrors that can be carried in the pocket of a buoyancy compensator. Another simple signaling device is the inflatable tube that can be rolled up and stored in the BC pocket (see Figure 5.65). The tubes are made of PVC, urethane, or nylon and feature either oral or mechanical inflators. Before purchasing any inflatable signaling device, it should be tested to determine if it can be inflated to the point that it will be rigid enough to be seen above the waves. A device that is too short or can't be properly inflated is of no value.

Electronic strobes are the next step up from the simplicity of a mirror or inflatable tube. Strobes have the added advantage that they can be used at night as well as during the day. Strobes can also be used to mark an anchor line under water when visibility is good.

For signaling at greater distances with more visual impact, flares are another option that may be considered (see Figure 5.66). Various manufacturers produce flares that are specifically designed for divers. It must be remembered that, even if the flares aren't taken in the water, all flares have a shelflife and must be replaced at their expiration date. Flares can be extremely dangerous if used improperly and can cause severe personal injury.

Sound signaling devices have the advantage of gaining the divemaster's attention even if he is not looking in the direction of the diver when the device is operated. However, the diver must be close enough for the device to be heard; whereas, a visual device may be seen at a greater distance than some sounds may be heard.

FIGURE 5.65
Inflatable Tube

FIGURE 5.66
Packaged Flare

FIGURE 5.67
Air-Powered Horns
Connected to the
Low-Pressure Power Inflator

A whistle is the simplest sound signaling device. Any whistle that is to be used in the water must be waterproof. Whistles have a limited range compared to other more powerful sound generating devices. Some models of whistles will actually produce sound under water that can be heard for short distances.

Several devices are now available that use low pressure air from the diver's cylinder to operate an air horn (see Figure 5.67). These devices connect between the diver's low pressure inflator hose and BC power or dry-suit inflators. Most will work with almost any power inflator on the market and can be heard up to a mile away. Several mechanical models allow the diver to signal effectively under water.

5.20 SCOOTERS

Electrically powered scooters, also known as diver propulsion vehicles (DPVs), are available that can help make exploration and survey work much more productive for the free swimming scuba diver (see Figure 5.68). With a scooter, a diver can cover much more ground without fatigue than is possible under his own leg power.

Care must be taken when using scooters to avoid descents or ascents which are too rapid. Ideally, the scooter will be fitted with a compass and depth gauge so that the diver can see this information at a glance while operating the scooter rather than having to stop to check his position. If the scooter does not float on its own, it should be fitted with an inflatable collar that will provide buoyancy in the event the scooter loses power.

5.21 SHARK DEFENSE

Although any large animal under water can injure a diver, sharks are not nearly the threat that divers once thought. Certainly the potential for danger always exists when working with sharks, but most sharks, with a few exceptions, are not interested in human beings.

Most of the emphasis today in working with sharks is on defensive strategies, rather than offensive weaponry to kill sharks. There are several devices that can be used effectively, in most cases, to prevent injury if sharks are aggressive.

The simplest tool used for protection is the "shark billy." A stick similar in length to a broomstick that is used to butt an inquisitive shark that approaches.

Another form of protection is the "shark suit." The suit resembles the chain mail worn by medieval knights and provides protection from shark bites from most sharks. There are different styles of suits available depending on the type of shark the diver expects to encounter. Some suits are backed with Kevlar® plates to distribute the pressure of bites from large sharks to help avoid bone breakage. The advantage to this type of suit is that it is portable and moves with the diver. The disadvantage is that it is heavy and is approximately 20 pounds negative in the water.

Shark cages (see Figure 5.69) are available today that are much lighter and portable compared to previous models. Cages offer better protection than a suit, but they do not permit the diver to swim to different observation points. In Australia some abalone divers are using a motorized version of the shark cage to allow coverage of a greater area under a safer condition.

FIGURE 5.68
Underwater Scooter

**FIGURE 5.69
A Shark Cage
and Shark
Suit**

**FIGURE 5.71
Underwater Slate Used for Note-Taking**

Electrical shark deterrent devices (see Figure 5.70) are available that surround a diver with an electrical current that discourage most sharks, including white sharks, from approaching. These devices consist of an electronic package that attaches to the diver's cylinder, a control unit worn on the arm, and a probe which attaches to the diver's fin or thigh.

The advantages to electrical shark deterrent devices are that they will not harm the shark or the diver and they allow the diver to swim. The disadvantage is that they require battery power and will operate for a maximum of 75 minutes before they must be recharged.

Offensive devices that are used to kill sharks are not recommended unless there is no other alternative. Sharks are long-lived creatures that are slow to reproduce, and some species of sharks in certain areas are protected by law. In addition, killing a shark in the wild can be extremely difficult. It takes skill to use offensive devices properly to get a clean kill and avoid accidents that may injure the diver handling the device or his partner.

5.22 UNDERWATER SLATES

A slate is a useful piece of equipment when underwater observations are to be recorded or when divers need a means of communication beyond hand signals. A simple and useful slate can be constructed from a 1/8 or 1/4 inch (0.3 or 0.6 cm) thick piece of acrylic plastic that has been lightly sand-papered on both sides; these slates can be used with an ordinary lead or grease pencils (see Figure 5.71).

Semi-matte plastic sheets can be placed on a clip board, in a ring binder, or there are slates specifically designed to be worn on the diver's forearm. These sheets (about 1/32 in., [0.01 cm] thick) may be purchased in sizes up to 6 x 10 ft. (1.8 x 3.0 m). They may be cut as needed, and no sanding is required. Ordinary lead pencils can be used, and marks can be erased or wiped off with a rubber eraser or an abrasive cleanser. Some divers customize their underwater slates by equipping them with a compass, depth gauge, and watch that are mounted across the top. When slates are used, they should be attached to the diver with a loop or lanyard made of sturdy line to keep them from being lost.

5.23 SURFACE SUPPORT/MARKER FLOAT

If divers are working off the beach, rather than from a boat, some type of surface support float is recommended. Surface support floats are useful for many purposes including providing a place to rest while on the surface, a support station for gear, and a place to hoist a diver's down flag (the red and white striped dive flag in North America or the blue and white "Alpha" flag used internationally).

The surface support float can take many forms, depending upon the needs of the operation. Popular surface support floats include kayaks, paddle boards, body surfing boards, inner tubes, and buoys. These can be fitted with small anchors and waterproof compartments for storing accessories. When towed, surface marker floats provide an excellent means of tracking divers from the surface.

**FIGURE 5.70
Electrical Shark Deterrent Device**

Diver and Diving Support Equipment

5.24 DIVE COMPUTERS

Dive computers are electronic devices that are used to track a diver's depth and time and make calculations that provide a diver with information regarding impending or actual decompression obligations. In addition, they may also provide other information including such measures as ascent rate, breathing gas consumption rate, water temperature, and oxygen exposure. Some computers will track all of these parameters and automatically adjust the diver's decompression obligation based on a complex formula that takes these factors into account. For some divers, dive computers have replaced the use of a watch, depth gauge, and decompression tables for computing no-decompression times or actual decompression obligations.

Dive computers are based on mathematical models or "algorithms," which are an attempt to describe the absorption and elimination of the nitrogen within the human body (see Figures 5.72, 5.73). It must be remembered, however, that the computer cannot determine exactly what is happening within the body of an individual diver during a dive. The dive computer cannot make adjustments for a diver who is particularly cold, tired, out of shape, dehydrated, or has

**FIGURE 5.72
Air-Integrated
Hoseless Dive
Computer**

**FIGURE 5.73
Dive Computer
Console**

other factors that may affect his decompression obligation. In addition, a diver may make dives that violate the computer model and good diving practice, and most computers will still continue to function, even though such a dive or series of dives is more likely to lead to decompression sickness.

It is always possible for the diver to suffer from decompression sickness while using a dive computer, just as it is possible for this to happen while using dive tables. For this reason, divers should be conservative in the way they use a dive computer. If the diver "rides" the computer right up to the no-decompression limits, and some event causes the diver to make an emergency ascent, decompression sickness is more likely to occur. Even if the diver uses the computer properly, and follows a conservative dive profile, decompression sickness can still occur.

It is essential for the diver to read and understand the manual supplied with the dive computer in order to use it properly. Even if the diver is familiar with one type of dive computer, if a different model is used it will usually work quite differently from the computer previously used.

Different computers are based on distinct algorithms that vary in how "aggressive" or "conservative" they are in regards to decompression. Aggressive computers tend to allow for longer bottom times, shorter surface intervals, and shorter "no-fly" times after diving. More conservative computers provide shorter bottom times, longer surface intervals, and longer waits before flying in an aircraft after diving. Some computers can actually be adjusted by the diver to be either more conservative or liberal.

Most dive computers include the following components at a minimum (see Figure 5.74):

- A pressure transducer that senses the depth
- An analog to digital converter that converts the depth or pressure information into digital information
- A power supply, that may have a variety of battery configurations
- An internal clock to keep track of time (some computers will also track the date)
- A microprocessor to perform the calculations
- ROM or Read Only Memory that provides the instructions to the microprocessor
- RAM or Random Access Memory, that contains the current information for the dive or series of dives in progress
- A display that gives the diver the visual information of the status of his dive

Some computers must be turned on by pushing a button or bridging a set of contacts on the case. Other computers turn on automatically as soon as the computer is submerged in the water.

Once the computer is on, it will track the diver from the moment he descends below a specific depth (normally 4-6 ft.)

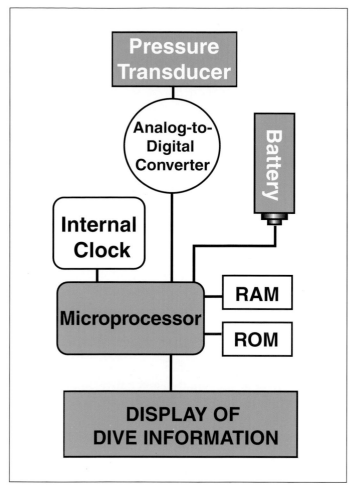

FIGURE 5.74
Schematic of Dive Computer Components

continuous depth. However, computers are typically much more liberal in calculating maximum dive times on multi-level dives and will provide the diver with a longer overall dive than the tables will usually allow.

Another major advantage to using a dive computer is that the computer does not make mistakes in making its mathematical calculations as people are prone to do. In addition, should the diver need to deviate from his planned dive, or accidentally overshoot his maximum depth, the computer will automatically make the calculations for his new dive profile. The computer also eliminates the need for carrying multiple instruments for time and depth measurement.

Dive computers are programmed for very slow ascent rates and will warn the diver when an ascent rate violation is taking place. When decompression is required, the computer will display a "ceiling" or a minimum depth to which the diver must ascend to start decompression. The computer will show a progressively shallower ceiling that the diver must adhere to in order to successfully complete his decompression. Should the diver violate the maximum depth capability of the computer or the required decompression, most computers will go into another type of violation mode, which may "lock" the diver out from using the computer for 24 hours.

There are numerous types of computers available and almost all are extremely compact. There are computers that are designed solely for air diving, as well as computers that can be used for nitrox or other gas mixtures.

Some computers today are integrated with an electronic submersible pressure gauge so that the computer not only performs decompression calculations but also displays the diver's cylinder pressure digitally. This type of computer will typically monitor the diver's breathing gas consumption rate. It may also show remaining dive time based upon the amount of gas remaining in the dive cylinder if this is less than the allowable bottom time for decompression purposes. The advantage of this type of computer is that it provides more information, and further integrates the diver's instruments into a single package. The disadvantage is that if the computer fails, all of the diver's instrumentation is lost.

Another variation on the breathing gas integrated dive computer is that some models are now available that are "hoseless." They use a transmitter to send the pressure information from the first stage regulator to the computer, which can be worn on the diver's wrist or attached to the diver's safety harness (see Figure 5.75). This type of system helps eliminate hose clutter. It should be noted that these systems can be sensitive to the signal from an electronic underwater strobe which may temporarily interrupt the transmission of cylinder pressure information.

Most of the computers on the market today can be adjusted for altitude diving. Some make these adjustments automatically, while others must be set by the diver.

Many dive computers today can be connected to a personal computer and the entire dive can be downloaded and printed out for a permanent record. This is especially useful

and throughout his dive. The computer will take a reading of the diver's depth every few seconds or minutes and continuously calculate the allowable remaining bottom time. As the diver moves deeper or shallower, the computer feeds this new information into the microprocessor and automatically calculates the remaining time for the new depth.

The dive computer does not calculate bottom times based on depth readings taken in ten foot intervals like most dive tables do. The computer will track the diver's depth to the foot and will continuously calculate nitrogen absorption and elimination for multi-level dives. When decompression calculations are based on traditional decompression tables, the diver must assume that his entire dive took place at the deepest depth. Although conservative, this assumption imposes a penalty on the diver in regards to his bottom time, especially during multi-level dives where nitrogen elimination takes place as the diver moves progressively shallower.

Most dive computers are actually more conservative in their allowance for maximum bottom time than the decompression tables are for a dive that takes place at one

**FIGURE 5.75
Hoseless Dive
Computers**

**FIGURE 5.76
Digital Depth Gauge**

in diving accidents for tracking the exact sequence of the dive(s) that may have caused the accident.

Dive computers are used for all types of diving, but they are especially useful for deep, repetitive dives or dives made over multiple days. In these situations, it is strongly recommended that each diver be equipped with a primary and a back-up computer.

The American Academy of Underwater Sciences (Lang and Hamilton eds. 1989) has developed a number of guidelines for dive computer use. A partial list of these recommendations is listed below:

1. Each diver relying on a dive computer to plan dives and indicate or determine decompression status must have his own unit.
2. On any given dive, the divers must follow the most conservative dive computer.
3. If the dive computer fails at any time during the dive, the dive must be terminated and appropriate surfacing procedures should be initiated immediately.
4. A diver should not dive for 18 hours before activating a dive computer to use it to control his diving.
5. Once the dive computer is in use, it must not be switched off until it indicates complete outgassing has occurred or 18 hours have elapsed, whichever comes first.
6. When using a dive computer, non-emergency ascents are to be made at the rate specified for the make and model of dive computer being used.
7. Whenever practical, divers using a dive computer should make a stop between 10 and 30 ft. (3.0 and 9.1 m) for five minutes, especially for dives below 60 ft. (18.3 m), at the completion of the dive.
8. Only one dive on the dive computer in which the NDL of the tables or the dive computer has been exceeded may be made in any 18-hour period.
9. For repetitive and multi-level dives, start the dive, or series of dives, at the maximum planned depth, followed by subsequent dives of shallower exposures.
10. Multiple deep dives require special consideration.

5.25 BOTTOM TIMERS

In lieu of a dive computer, some divers use a similar instrument that tracks and displays a diver's depth and bottom time, as well as displays the essential information that's required for the calculation of the dive (see Figure 5.76). The instrument compiles an enormous amount of data into a compact information center. The instrument turns itself on automatically when it is immersed and tracks the diver's depth, displays maximum depth, elapsed dive time, ascent rate (displayed as a percentage of the allowable ascent rate for any given depth), and water temperature. If ascent is too rapid, the diver is advised to slow down. On the surface it provides a record of the pertinent data from the last nine dives. In surface mode it continues to display the surface interval and temperature from the last dive until the next dive or until 24 hours have elapsed.

5.26 UNDERWATER PHOTOGRAPHY AND VIDEO

Underwater photography and video are two of the most important tools available to the diving scientist (see Figure 5.77). These data-recording techniques provide permanent visual records that can be used to document species, archaeological sites, geological features, effects of pollution, or other important items. Visual records can then be incorporated into scientific papers, conference presentations, books, interactive displays, or other media.

The integration of photography and video with the personal computer has allowed scientists to use this data in ways never before possible. For example, photographs can now be integrated with databases to provide a quick visual reference for each record in the database. Photographs can also be digitally enhanced, transmitted over

FIGURE 5.77
Underwater Video Camera

the Internet, or digitally archived for convenient storage. Low-cost video editing allows schools to produce professional-looking training videos at a fraction of the cost to have them produced outside.

This section is intended as an introduction to underwater photography and video to help the diving scientist understand which equipment to select for a particular project. There are numerous books that explain how to create photographs with particular camera systems. It is highly recommended that any diver who needs to create underwater photographs take a course in the subject which includes actual dives under the supervision of a competent underwater photography instructor. It takes dedication and practice to produce good quality still underwater photographs.

5.26.1 Still Photography vs. Video

Both still photography and video have their place on most scientific projects. In many cases, there will be applications for both techniques, although for specific tasks, one is usually better suited than the other.

Still photography is usually best suited for documenting individual creatures, artifacts, or small features of a specific site. No special equipment is needed to view a still

photographic print. Prints (or prints from transparencies/slides) can be included in scientific papers or books or can be enlarged for display purposes.

Video is best suited to dynamic events and situations. For example, documenting animal behavior is best done with video, as is conveying the expanse and spatial relationships between features of a large shipwreck.

Today, there are cameras available that can record live action video, as well as produce individual still digital images. It is also possible to "grab" a single frame of video from a recording for print purposes. While the quality of the still image produced by most video cameras is generally not very high at the time of this writing, it will undoubtedly improve steadily.

It takes practice and skill to produce high quality still underwater photographs. Conversely, capturing subjects on underwater video is usually much easier than producing quality still images. This is true because the video camera sees much better than the still camera (or human eye) does under water and is far more light sensitive. It is possible to record satisfactory underwater video in most instances without the use of any auxiliary lighting system, while still photography almost always requires some additional lighting.

5.26.2 Types of Underwater Camera Systems for Still Photography

There are two main types of underwater camera systems for still photography. These include: self-contained underwater cameras, and housings for land cameras (see Figure 5.78). Each type has advantages and limitations and is suited to particular applications.

Self-contained underwater cameras are generally the smallest underwater still camera systems (see Figure 5.79). The camera body is made watertight by a series of O-rings that seal the film compartment, the lens, and all the controls. The compact nature of self-contained underwater cameras is a major advantage when traveling, or when diving in strong currents or tight quarters, such as the interior of a shipwreck. In addition, the sharpness of the lenses for some of these cameras exceeds that available when using a land camera in a housing.

FIGURE 5.78
Typical Camera Housing

Diver and Diving Support Equipment

FIGURE 5.79
Self-Contained
Underwater Cameras

The disadvantage of self-contained underwater cameras is that the selection of lenses available for these cameras is usually quite limited, and these cameras are usually rangefinders, which do not allow you to see your exact composition through the lens. The limited lens selection means that the self-contained camera does not normally produce high quality photographs topside.

Underwater camera housings are available for many different types of topside cameras, from 35 mm through medium format. These housings may be made from plastic or aluminum.

With a housing, the underwater photographer has an almost unlimited number of lenses that can be used, provided there is a lens port that will accommodate the particular lens desired. Fortunately, this is rarely a problem since most underwater photography is done with either wide angle lenses, medium telephoto, or macro lenses, and the ports for these are normally readily available.

Housings are larger and heavier than self-contained underwater cameras. However, a properly constructed housing may be completely neutrally buoyant under water. Still, housings are bulkier and larger than the self-contained systems.

An increasing number of housings are available for digital cameras and video systems. One drawback to these systems is that the manufacturers of digital and video cameras tend to obsolete their products very quickly, which can make a housing worthless if the camera breaks and cannot be repaired or has been discontinued.

5.26.3 Light and Color

With conventional still photography using film, there must be light to produce an acceptable underwater photograph. To be successful in underwater photography, the scientist must understand how to use the available light and balance it with artificial light to produce photographs that reveal both color and detail in a subject.

As explained in the chapter on diving physics, colors "disappear" as the diver descends and the first colors to go are the reds and yellows. When color detail is important, artificial lighting is essential.

For dives deeper than 20 fsw (6.1 msw) in clear water or in turbid water or at night, some electronic underwater flash is almost always required for still underwater photography.

One of the most difficult tasks in producing a usable underwater photograph is to frame the subject so that there is contrast between the subject and the background. The best way to do this with larger subjects is to shoot at an upward angle, so that the subject is backlit. To use this technique effectively the diver must use electronic flash.

5.26.4 Electronic Flash

Electronic flash is the most economical and portable method of providing light for still underwater photographs (see Figure 5.80). There are several manufacturers of underwater flash systems (or strobes) that make compact units that provide sufficient light for most underwater photography situations.

Electronic flash units are rated according to their power, which almost always relates directly to the size of the flash. In most cases, the larger the flash unit, the more power, i.e., light, it delivers. However, beyond distances of 6 ft. (1.8 m), even with the most powerful flash systems, colors will usually appear muted and washed out.

FIGURE 5.80
Electronic Flash for Underwater Cameras

The amount of light needed to take a picture will be determined by the size of the subject to be photographed, the camera-to-subject distance, the type of film being used, and, to a lesser extent, the amount of available natural light. With the efficiency of today's underwater flash systems, even many of the smaller underwater flash systems will provide more than enough light for most photographic situations.

Many of the flash systems on the market today are designed to work in the TTL, or "through the lens," mode. These units "talk" to the electronics inside the camera and automatically regulate the amount of light produced by the flash. These systems can help make underwater photography simpler for the novice.

Experienced underwater photographers will often prefer to use their cameras and flash systems in the manual mode, which provides greater control. In addition, in certain situations, the TTL system in most cameras can be "fooled" by certain lighting situations, leaving the underwater photographer with an improperly exposed photo. Finally, should the TTL system fail, the only way to produce photos will be in the manual mode.

In selecting an electronic underwater flash, ideally the system will be capable of both TTL and manual exposures. In the manual mode, more versatile flash systems will be equipped with variable power settings.

Most experienced photographers use more than one flash to provide evenly balanced lighting with no shadows or dark areas in the image. The main flash may be more powerful than the second smaller flash which is used for "fill."

Some type of cable system is normally required to connect the flash to the camera. If possible, a user detachable cable is preferred so that in the event the cable fails the entire flash need not be returned to the manufacturer for repair. At least one spare cable should be carried on any dive trip so that diving operations need not be suspended in the event of a cable failure.

5.26.5 Trays and Flash Arms

It is impossible to juggle multiple flash units and a camera without some method of connecting them all together. To do this effectively, most underwater photographers use some type of specially designed tray to mount the camera and which provides a mounting point for the underwater flash units. The most popular systems for this type of work are articulated "arms" with multiple joints and connectors.

To avoid "backscatter," or light reflecting off particulate matter in the water, each of the flash heads should be no closer than 18 inches to the lens of the camera for still photography. The flash is usually either pointed straight ahead or even slightly away from the subject. Using two electronic strobes, this will create a cone of light that illuminates only the subject, but not the particles suspended in the water between the subject and the camera.

5.26.6 The Image Capture Medium: Prints, Slides, and Digital

In underwater still photography, the photographer should know how the images will be used to help choose the most effective way to produce an image. Each method of capturing an image has its applications.

To produce photographic prints for a museum exhibit, the best way to record an image is with color negative film. This film has the widest exposure latitude, which means that the exposure can vary over quite a range yet still produce an acceptable print. High-speed color negative films, such as ISO 400-800, will produce sharp, contrasty, colorful prints.

Color transparencies, or slides, are the most versatile type of images, but require more photographic skill to produce an acceptable exposure. Transparencies can be projected and used at scientific conferences or made into large backlit images for display purposes. Publishers of books and magazines prefer transparencies to produce the color separations used in printing. Color transparencies can also be used to make color prints or black and white prints.

Producing a good color transparency requires more skill on the photographer's part because the film has a narrow exposure latitude. This means that the film must be precisely exposed to get an acceptable image. There is little room for error when using transparency film. To shoot macro images, i.e., extreme close-ups of small creatures like snails or nudibranchs, a relatively slow speed film is used, such as ISO 64. Shooting wide angle shots or fast action will require a higher speed film, such as ISO 100 or ISO 200. Faster films are available but should only be used when absolutely necessary, since the images they produce will have a "grainy" appearance.

To get consistent results it is important to stick with one type of film and learn its characteristics. Photographers who switch film constantly will have a more difficult time producing acceptable images.

Digital images can be used to produce photographic prints, projected using a laptop computer and projection system, or be used to produce images in books, magazines, web sites, or journals. The big advantage to a digital image is that it can theoretically be stored forever with no loss in image quality when compared to a print or transparency.

Digital cameras have an extremely narrow exposure range, making correct exposures with digital cameras even more critical than with a conventional camera with transparency film. With a digital camera, a dark shadow area or an extreme highlight will produce almost no usable information.

To use digital images in print, the images must be fairly high resolution, which means large files must be stored in the computer system. High resolution color image files such as those used in books and magazines are extremely large.

5.26.7 Basic Techniques for Still Photography

To be successful in creating photographs to record scientific information under water, good diving skills are essential. Good buoyancy control and a high degree of comfort in the water are fundamental in underwater photography, as they are in any other aspect of data collection in scientific diving.

Probably the single most important aspect in still underwater photography is proper maintenance and set-up of the underwater camera system. Systems that are improperly prepared or maintained can ruin the chances of capturing a good underwater image at the very start of the dive. Underwater camera systems are somewhat delicate pieces of equipment that require careful postdive maintenance and meticulous predive preparation.

To produce a vibrant, properly exposed image, it is important to get as close as possible to the subject of the photograph. Ideally, the subject should fill the frame of the image.

Getting detail in an underwater photograph can be difficult if the subject is not positioned against a background that provides contrast. The greater the contrast there is between the subject and the background, the more definition will be seen in the subject. A blue fish photographed in front of a yellow sponge will be easily seen, but a yellow fish in front of a yellow sponge will be difficult to make out.

Shooting at an extreme upward angle will help to provide contrast and eliminate particulate matter in photographs. This technique will provide back lighting, leaving the subject in shadow with details that must be "filled in" with electronic flash (see Figure 5.81).

Tall subjects, such as people or kelp forests should usually be photographed vertically rather than horizontally. This will allow photographers to fill the frame with the subject.

To speed up the learning curve with new or unfamiliar photographic equipment, it is wise to keep a log of each exposure including shutter speed, f-stop, and flash setting and compare it against the results. This is the best way to learn to make proper exposures. This can be referred back to when photographing under similar conditions to produce more dependable results.

5.26.8 Video Cameras and Housings

Video is a dynamic tool that can be extremely useful to the diving scientist (see Figure 5.82). It is an extremely powerful medium that can be used to illustrate a concept or event in a way that words and still photographs cannot always match.

There are limitations to using video, however, which should be considered in selecting which tool is most appropriate for a particular project. To be effective, video must be edited, which takes considerable time and additional equipment. In addition, it takes time to sit and watch a video, compared to a still photograph which can be viewed

FIGURE 5.81
Upward Angle Shot Utilizing Natural Light

at a glance. Video is also not as portable as still photographs; watching video requires a VCR and monitor.

New video cameras and recording modes are constantly being developed. The current cameras on the market are extremely compact and user friendly. In many cases, the cameras and housings for video today are as compact or smaller than the underwater camera systems for still photography.

Most video housings are made of aluminum, although some fiberglass and plastic housings are also available. Any of these materials is considered acceptable.

Many of the housings that are currently available for video use external magnetically controlled switches to operate the camera mechanism rather than mechanically linked controls that physically penetrate the housing. This is a preferable arrangement because it helps eliminate potential leaks that could flood the housing and ruin the camera.

Some video systems have optics that permit the scientist to select either wide angle or macro images on the same dive without having to surface to change lenses or ports. These systems provide tremendous versatility.

FIGURE 5.82
Video Camera System

5.26.9 Basic Video Techniques

Shooting video under water is much simpler than shooting still photographs. In most cases, the camera will do almost everything for the diver automatically, once the camera has been properly installed in the housing. With most systems there is little more to do than hit the record button and zoom the lens. Even a novice underwater photographer can capture acceptable underwater video images with little or no experience.

The most fundamental instruction for the novice underwater videographer is to move the camera very slowly. When the camera is moved too quickly it becomes difficult for the viewer to follow the action.

As in underwater still photography, in most cases, the closer the camera is to the subject, the better the image will be.

If it isn't possible to get close to a subject, it may be necessary to use the zoom, but zooms should be used sparingly.

Unlike using a still camera, video cameras must always be held horizontally. To completely frame a tall subject the camera operator must move away from the object.

5.26.10 Camera Maintenance

The maintenance procedures for self-contained underwater cameras and housings are basically the same. Following every dive, especially in salt water, the camera should be soaked in a tub of clean, fresh water for a minimum of 20 minutes, longer if possible. Rinsing the camera with a hose is not an adequate method of removing the salts that can accumulate down inside the space between the controls and the camera body or housing.

While the camera is soaking in fresh water, each of the camera controls and adjustments should be operated for at least a minute to ensure that the salt water is displaced by fresh water. If this is not done and the camera is allowed to dry, the salts will solidify and cause the camera to corrode. In addition, when salts solidify, the crystals are quite hard and can cut O-rings, causing the camera or housing to leak.

After the camera has been rinsed and thoroughly dried, it must be opened to remove the film, disk, or media card. With a conventional film camera, the film must be rewound prior to opening the camera body. Never use compressed air to blow water off the camera body or housing because this technique can blow water past the O-rings and into the camera body. Use a soft towel or cloth to dry the camera or housing prior to opening it.

Always open the camera or housing back with the lens of the camera facing up, so that any water that is trapped by the O-ring in the camera or housing door will not run down inside the camera body. After the film or other media has been removed, remove the O-ring from the body door and dry the O-ring grove with a soft cloth or paper towel. Remove any other user serviceable O-rings and soak them in a pan of fresh water.

Between dive trips, store the O-rings in a sealed plastic bag, away from heat and UV light sources. Remove any batteries from the camera between trips.

Prior to diving, the camera must be reloaded with film or media, batteries must be installed, and the O-rings must be lubricated with O-ring grease and installed. Only a thin film of grease should be applied to the O-rings, and each of the seals and their grooves must be clean of hair, dirt, sand, or other debris. It is essential to follow the instructions provided by the manufacturer for the correct assembly of any housing or self-contained underwater camera.

NOTES

Surface-Supplied Diving

6

Surface-Supplied Diving

6.0 GENERAL

One of the diving modes of choice for underwater work that requires the diver to remain submerged for extended periods of time is surface-supplied diving. This section describes some of the techniques and procedures used by scientific divers engaged in routine underwater work operations using surface-supplied equipment.

6.1 SURFACE-SUPPLIED DIVING PROCEDURES

The surface-supplied air diving mode is used by divers because it gives them the flexibility they need to perform many different underwater tasks. In surface-supplied diving, the diver's breathing mixture is supplied from the surface by means of a flexible hose; thus, divers using this mode have a continuous supply of breathing gas.

The surface-supplied mode is generally used when divers need to remain under water for an extended period of time to accomplish the dive's objectives. The advantages of surface-supplied diving over scuba diving are that it:

- Provides a direct physical link to the diver
- Permits hard-wire communication between the diver and the surface
- Provides an assured continuous breathing gas supply and thus, longer bottom time
- Provides depth control

Another advantage of the surface-supplied mode is that it can be launched from a variety of support platforms (see Figure 6.1), including piers, small boats, barges, ships, and from the beach. The disadvantages of this mode, compared with the scuba mode are:

- The surface-supplied diver's mobility and operational range are restricted by the length of the umbilical.
- The drag weight of the umbilical.
- The large amount of equipment required to support surface-supplied diving.

FIGURE 6.1
Support Platform

6.1.1 Planning the Dive

The success of any dive depends on careful predive planning, which must consider the objectives of the dive, the tasks involved in achieving these goals, environmental conditions (both surface and under water), hazardous activities that may be taking place in the area of the diving operation, the personnel needed to carry out the dive, the schedule for the dive, the equipment needed to conduct the dive safely and efficiently, and the availability of emergency assistance. Figure 6.2 is a checklist that can be used to evaluate environmental conditions that may affect the dive.

For every surface-supplied dive, the dive supervisor should complete this checklist (or one adapted to the specific conditions of a particular dive) before deciding on personnel and equipment needs. Different environmental conditions affect members of the dive team differently. For example, divers are generally not affected by surface waves or swells except when entering or exiting the water; however, divers operating in very shallow waters, in surf, or in exceptionally large waves can be affected by wave action, surge condition, and currents.

WARNING
FOR AREAS WITH HIGH MARINE TRAFFIC, AN APPROPRIATE WARNING DISPLAY SHALL BE EXHIBITED NEAR THE WORK SITE IN CLEAR SIGHT OF ALL PERSONNEL IN THE NEAR VICINITY. THIS MAY INCLUDE, BUT IS NOT LIMITED TO SHAPES, LIGHTS, FLAGS, OR PLACARDS. A RIGID REPLICA OF THE INTERNATIONAL CODE FLAG "A" NOT LESS THAN ONE METER IN HEIGHT SHOULD BE EXHIBITED DURING ALL DIVING OPERATIONS.

Air temperature and wind conditions at the surface may also have a greater effect on the tender and other surface support personnel than on the diver because these individuals are more exposed than the diver to surface conditions. It is important to remember, however, that the surface crew should be able to operate with maximum efficiency throughout the dive; reductions in the performance of topside personnel could endanger the diver.

The underwater environment can influence many aspects of a dive, from crew selection to choice of diving equipment. All diving operations must consider:

- Depth
- Bottom type
- Temperature of the water
- Underwater visibility
- Tides and currents
- Marine life
- Support crew
- Cost of equipment
- Gas requirements
- Emergency assistance and treatment

In addition, the presence of contaminants in the water (see Chapter 13), underwater obstacles, ice, or other unusual environmental conditions can affect planning for some dives. Dive depth must be determined before the dive begins. To obtain an accurate depth profile of the area of the dive, a

SURFACE

ATMOSPHERE

Visibility _____

Sunrise/Set _____
Moonrise/Set _____
Temperature (air) _____
Humidity _____
Barometer_____
Precipitation_____
Cloud Description/Cover ____
Wind Direction/Force _____
Other: _____

_____

_____

SEA SURFACE

Sea State_____

_____

Wave Action:
  Height _____
  Length _____
  Direction_____
Current:
  Direction _____
  Velocity _____
  Type _____
  Visibility_____
Water Temperature _____

UNDER WATER

DEPTH CONDITIONS

Water Temperature:
_____ degrees at _____ depth
_____ degrees at _____ depth
_____ degrees at _____ depth
_____ degrees at bottom

Thermoclines:

at _____ depth
at _____ depth
Current:
  Direction _____
  Source _____
  Velocity _____
  Pattern _____
Tides:
  High Water ____/____ time
  Low Water ____/____ time
Ebb Direction _____
Flood Direction _____

Underwater Visibility:
_____ feet at _____ depth
_____ feet at _____ depth
_____ feet at _____ depth
At the Bottom
_____ feet at _____ depth

Bottom Type:
_____
_____

Obstructions:
_____
_____

Marine Life:
_____
_____

Other: _____
_____
Velocity _____
Velocity _____

FIGURE 6.2
Predive Environmental Checklist

series of depth measurements must be plotted. Methods of measuring depth that may be used include lead line sounding, pneumofathometer, high-resolution sonar, or ship-mounted fathometer. Depth readings on maps or charts are useful for general screening purposes, but are not sufficiently accurate to be used to measure dive depths. One of the more accurate methods is the diver's pneumo-hose.

Samples should be taken of the bottom in the general area of the dive; in some instances, observations can be made before the dive using remote sensing devices. Bottom conditions affect a diver's mobility and visibility under water; a sandy bottom allows maximum mobility, and the diver's movements do not stir up so much sediment that visibility is restricted. By comparison, working in an area with a muddy and silty bottom can be dangerous; the diver may become entrapped in the mud and usually generates sufficient silt to interfere substantially with visibility.

Currents must be considered in dive planning, whether the surface-supplied scientist diver is working in a river or the ocean. The direction and velocity of river, ocean, and tidal currents vary with such factors as the time of year, phase of the tide, bottom conditions, depth, and weather.

Underwater visibility and water temperature also have a major influence on dive planning.

6.1.2 Selecting the Dive Team

The number of dive team personnel necessary to conduct surface-supplied operations depends on many factors: type of equipment being used, environmental conditions, dive depth, platform being used, how the diver/divers will be deployed and retrieved, and the number of divers that will be deployed. As an example, to safely deploy one surface-supplied diver on an open ocean dive would usually require a minimum of six people: the working diver, dive tender, dive supervisor, standby diver, standby diver tender, and timekeeper. Keep in mind, one of the biggest problems is removing an unconscious diver from the water. If a diver is injured and unconscious there must be a plan and the resources available to render aid. In many surface-supplied diving operations, the minimum of six personnel would be inadequate or inefficient unless all persons were qualified in all duties to allow for rotation of personnel assignments. If all members of the team are fully trained and qualified, a job rotation can be set up to maximize the potential of the dive team and allow much greater in-water time. Whenever possible, it is desirable to have extra personnel available, if for no other reason than coiling umbilicals or being available in the event an injured or disabled diver needs to be pulled from the water.

The dive supervisor is responsible for planning, organizing, and managing all dive operations. The dive supervisor must remain at the dive site at all times. This individual determines equipment requirements, inspects the equipment before the dive, selects team members, ensures that emergency procedures and first aid supplies are available, conducts predive briefings, monitors the progress of the dive, debriefs the divers, checks equipment and diver logs at the completion of the dive, and prepares reports of the dive.

The diver(s) must be qualified and trained in the equipment and diving techniques needed for the dive. During the course of the dive, the diver must keep surface personnel informed of the progress of the dive, bottom conditions, and any problems (actual or potential). Every diver is responsible for ensuring that his diving gear is complete, in good repair, and ready for use. In addition, all divers must know both line pull signals and voice signals, and must respond to and comply with instructions from surface personnel.

The standby diver must be as well trained and qualified as the diver he is supporting; a standby is required for all surface-supplied operations, regardless of size. It is the responsibility of the standby diver to be ready to provide emergency or backup support to the diver any time the diver is in the water.

The tender is normally a qualified surface-supply diver or has received the specialized training required to be a competent tender. The tender is responsible for dressing the diver and tending his umbilical, and must work in unison with the diver. Every surface-supplied diver must have at least one tender in control of the umbilical at all times. Before the diver enters the water, the tender:

- Checks the diver's equipment
- Checks the air supply
- Helps the diver get dressed
- Helps the diver to the water entry point

Once the diver is in the water, the tender takes care of the diver's umbilical to ensure that no excess slack or tension is on the line. In addition, the tender maintains communication with the diver and keeps the diving supervisor informed of the diver's progress.

On complex and long dives, a standby tender may be needed. The standby tender must also be fully qualified as a tender and should attend all briefings and be kept fully aware of what is going on with the dive. It is the standby tender's job to assist the primary tender or replace the primary tender at any time.

A timekeeper may be designated to keep the diver's time during the job. The timekeeper's responsibilities include keeping an accurate record of dive times, depths, and noting all of the important details of the dive. During dives involving a limited number of dive team members, the tender may also serve as the timekeeper. On some dives, the dive supervisor may act as the timekeeper.

6.1.3 Preparing for the Dive

Normally, the dive team personnel will set up the dive station. The supervisor will ensure the dive station has been properly set up. To accomplish this, the supervisor uses a status board or status list to log gas pressures and system configurations. The status board is normally tailored specifically to each surface-supported diving system or configuration. The tenders normally assist the divers in donning their wet suits, dry suits, or hot water suits, as well as the safety harness, emergency gas supply, and helmet or mask. In many cases, the diver will dress to the point where he or she can rest comfortably while the safety harness, umbilical, and ancillary equipment can be donned. Usually the helmet or mask is the last item to be donned. A predive checklist should be used by the supervisor during the final dressing phase of the diver. The checklist assists the supervisor in ensuring that the diver is properly dressed prior to deployment, and aids in identifying and correcting potential problems. The diving supervisor checks the diver as well as the standby diver. A typical supervisor's predive checklist consists of the following as a minimum:

- Check to ensure the suit is donned properly
- Check diver's safety harness and emergency bailout system for proper fit and accessibility

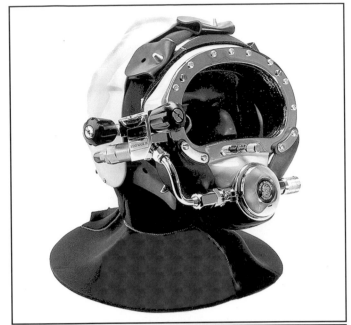

FIGURE 6.3
Lightweight Surface-Supplied Masks

- Check diver's weighting
- Check and log emergency bailout system cylinder pressure
- Check and log emergency bailout system gas mixture if diving mixed gas or nitrox
- Check primary and secondary gas bank and supply pressures
- Ensure gas flow to the mask or helmet
- Check function of the emergency gas system
- Check proper function of helmet or mask breathing components (i.e., demand regulator adjustment, purge, steady flow)
- Perform communications check

FIGURE 6.4
Surface-Supplied Diver Wearing a Lightweight Mask and Wet Suit

Once the diver is deployed, he should stop just under the surface and:

- Adjust the demand regulator air supply
- Check the function of the emergency supply valve and free-flow valve
- Complete a communications check with the surface

Figure 6.3 shows two types of lightweight surface-supplied masks and Figure 6.4 shows a surface-supplied diver ready to dive in a wet suit and lightweight mask. Figures 6.5 and 6.6 shows surface-supplied divers with lightweight helmets. Figure 6.7 shows the key features of diving helmets.

6.1.4 Tending the Surface-Supplied Diver

Contact between the tender and the diver must be maintained throughout the dive operation. The tender should always keep a hand on the diver, fully dressed with a mask and helmet, as the diver moves to or from the water entry point. The tender maintains physical control of the diver as the diver enters or leaves the water. As the diver descends, the tender pays out slack according to the descent rate, but never faster than is needed by the diver.

FIGURE 6.5
Lightweight Surface-Supplied Helmet

FIGURE 6.6
Surface-Supplied Diver in a Dry Suit

The tender should always be able to feel the diver. Once on the bottom, the diver and tender should work as a team. The tender should only give the diver enough slack in the umbilical so as not to hinder the diver's work; usually, this is about 2–3 ft. If intercom communications are lost, the tender and diver must be able to communicate through line-pull signals. All communications between the diver and tender should be passed on to the diving supervisor. If at any time voice or line pull communications are lost, the tender must immediately notify the diving supervisor. If voice communications are not used, the tender periodically signals the diver (using line-pulls) to check the diver's condition. If the diver fails to respond after several attempts to contact him, the situation should be treated as an emergency and the supervisor must be notified immediately.

6.1.5 The Dive

Once the diver is dressed and ready for the dive, the tender helps the diver to prepare for water entry. The entry technique used depends on the staging area and type of vessel involved in the operation. If a stage is used for the diver's entry, the diver should stand or sit squarely on the stage platform and maintain a good grip on the rails. If the diver makes a jump entry into the water, he must maintain a grip on the diving mask while the tender maintains sufficient slack on the umbilical.

When the diver is positioned for descent, the following actions, as appropriate, should be taken by various members of the dive team:

- The diver should check his buoyancy. Whether the diver is weighted neutrally or negatively will depend on the dive's objectives.
- The supervisor should verify that the air supply system, helmet (or mask), and communications are functioning properly. If not, corrections must be made before the diver's descent. The tender should check for any leaks in the air supply fittings or suit and also should look for air bubbles. No diver should dive with malfunctioning equipment.
- The supervisor should also verify with the diver that all equipment is functioning satisfactorily.
- The diving supervisor should give the diver permission to descend.
- The diver should descend down a descent or "shot" line. The descent rate used depends on the diver; however, it should not exceed 75 ft/min (22.9 m/min).
- The diver must equalize pressure in both ears during descent. If equalization is not possible, the dive must be terminated.

Surface-Supplied Diving

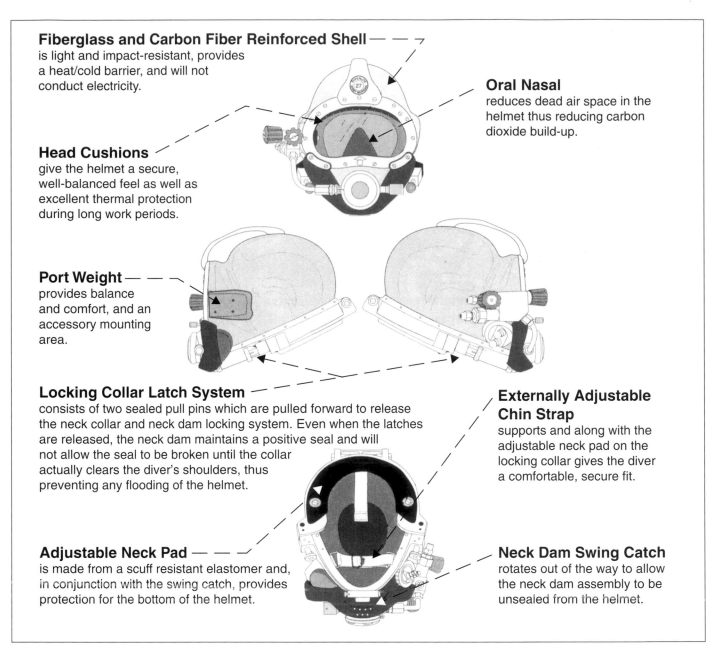

Fiberglass and Carbon Fiber Reinforced Shell
is light and impact-resistant, provides a heat/cold barrier, and will not conduct electricity.

Oral Nasal
reduces dead air space in the helmet thus reducing carbon dioxide build-up.

Head Cushions
give the helmet a secure, well-balanced feel as well as excellent thermal protection during long work periods.

Port Weight
provides balance and comfort, and an accessory mounting area.

Locking Collar Latch System
consists of two sealed pull pins which are pulled forward to release the neck collar and neck dam locking system. Even when the latches are released, the neck dam maintains a positive seal and will not allow the seal to be broken until the collar actually clears the diver's shoulders, thus preventing any flooding of the helmet.

Externally Adjustable Chin Strap
supports and along with the adjustable neck pad on the locking collar gives the diver a comfortable, secure fit.

Adjustable Neck Pad
is made from a scuff resistant elastomer and, in conjunction with the swing catch, provides protection for the bottom of the helmet.

Neck Dam Swing Catch
rotates out of the way to allow the neck dam assembly to be unsealed from the helmet.

FIGURE 6.7
Key Features of Diving Helmets

- When the diver reaches the bottom, the tender should be informed of the diver's status and the diver should ensure that the umbilical assembly is not fouled around the descent line.
- The diver may choose to attach a travel line and then proceed to the work area. A travel line should be used when visibility is extremely poor and the diver cannot see the descent line from a distance. In lieu of a travel line, the diver can pass his umbilical through the bail of the stage or bell before proceeding to the work site.
- After leaving the descent line, the diver should proceed slowly to conserve energy. It is advisable for

divers to carry one turn of the umbilical hose in the hand to allow for unexpected pulls on the hose.
- The diver should pass over, not under, wreckage and obstructions.
- If moving against a current, it may be necessary for the diver to assume a crawling position.
- If the diver is required to enter wreckage, tunnels, etc., a second diver must be on the bottom to tend the umbilical hose at the entrance to the confined space.
- The diver should be notified a few minutes in advance of termination of the dive so that the task can be completed and preparations made for ascent.

6.1.5.1 Ventilation

If the diver experiences rapid breathing, panting or shortness of breath, abnormal perspiration, or an unusual sensation of warmth, dizziness, or blurred vision, or if the helmet/mask viewport becomes foggy, there is probably an excess of carbon dioxide in the headgear. To eliminate excess CO_2 in a free-flow helmet or mask, the diver must ventilate the helmet or mask by significantly increasing the flow for a minimum of 15–20 seconds. In demand mode masks, CO_2 retention is not as common, but can be present if the diver does not breathe normally, or has the regulator adjustment device set too heavy, or does not moderate his work rate. To ventilate a demand mode helmet or mask, the free-flow or demand regulator purge valve can be used for five to ten seconds, this will normally flush any excess CO_2 from the oral nasal, or face cavity.

6.1.6 Diver Emergencies
6.1.6.1 Fouling

A surface-supplied diver's umbilical may become fouled in mooring lines, wreckage, or underwater structures, or the diver may be trapped by the cave-in of a tunnel, or by the shifting of heavy objects under water. In such emergencies, surface-supplied divers are in a better position to survive than scuba divers, because they have a virtually unlimited air supply and can communicate with the surface, both of which facilitate rescue operations. Fouling may result in fatigue, exposure, and prolonged submergence, and it may also necessitate an extended decompression. Divers who are fouled should:

- Remain calm and control breathing
- Think clearly
- Describe the situation to topside
- Determine the cause of fouling and, if possible, clear themselves
- Be careful to avoid cutting portions of the umbilical assembly when using a knife

If efforts to clear themselves are unsuccessful, divers should call for the standby diver and then wait calmly for his arrival. Struggling and other panicky actions might make the situation worse by further complicating the entanglement.

6.1.6.2 Blowup

Blowup is the uncontrolled ascent of a diver from depth. This is a hazard for divers using either a constant-volume dry suit (lightweight helmet connected to a dry suit) or variable-volume dry suit. A blowup occurs when the diving suit becomes over inflated, or the diver loses hold of the bottom or descending line and is buoyed up to the surface. A blowup is defined as the unexpected or uncontrolled ascent of the diver. A blowup can be caused by entanglement in rigging which causes the diver to be pulled to a shallower depth, but is usually a result of improper buoyancy control of a variable-volume dry suit. An excessive drag on the umbilical by the current can sweep a diver to the surface. Normally, a blowup occurs when the suit is over inflated or the diver loses hold of the descending line and is buoyed to the surface. During blowup, the diver typically exceeds the correct rate of ascent 30 ft/min (9.1 m/min) that must be maintained for a safe ascent. Accidental inversion of the diver, which causes the legs of the suit to fill with the breathing gas, also may result in an uncontrolled blowup. Accidental blowup can cause:

- Arterial gas embolism
- Decompression sickness
- Missed decompression stops
- Physical injury (if the diver on ascent strikes an object, such as the bottom of a ship or platform)

Before beginning a dive, the diver must be certain that all suit exhaust valves are functioning properly. The diving suit should fit the diver well to avoid leaving excessive space in the legs in which air can accumulate; air in the legs of the suit presents a serious hazard, particularly with variable-volume suits. Divers must be trained under controlled conditions, preferably in a training tank, in the use of all constant-volume dry suits, regardless of their previous experience with other types of suits. Using a constant-volume dry suit to assist in ascending is not recommended because losing control of the rate of ascent can be fatal.

After surfacing, blowup victims should not be allowed to resume diving. If a diver who has experienced a blowup appears to have no ill effects and is still within the no decompression range prescribed by the tables, he should return to a depth of 10 feet (3.0 m) and decompress for the amount of time that would normally have been required for ascent from the dive's working depth. The diver should then surface; after which, he should be observed for at least an hour for signs of delayed-onset decompression sickness or other injuries.

Blowup victims who are close to the no decompression limit, or who require decompression, may be able to follow surface decompression procedures; however, if unable to meet the criteria for surface decompression, the victim should be recompressed in a chamber to 60 ft. (18.3 m) and evaluated. Oxygen shall be available for breathing at 60 ft. Once at depth, the diver's condition should be evaluated for signs or symptoms of air embolism or decompression sickness, possibly requiring further descent in the chamber. The diving supervisor should consult with a qualified hyperbaric physician regarding the specific table to use for the treatment. If no chamber is available, conscious victims should be treated in accordance with recompression procedures for interrupted or omitted decompression; unconscious victims should be handled according to the recompression table, and treatment procedures that are designed for cases of air embolism or serious decompression sickness should be used.

6.1.6.3 Loss of Primary Air Supply

Although losing the primary air supply is an infrequent occurrence with most surface-supplied systems, it does occur occasionally. In the unlikely event gas supply to the gas control console is lost, the gas control operator should immediately switch to the secondary gas supply, notify the diving supervisor, and stand by for instructions. The diving supervisor will order the loss investigated and will immediately make preparations to abort the dive. The diving supervisor will have the tender remove all slack from the umbilical, and then will order the diver to check that the umbilical is clear and prepare to leave the bottom. Having the diver ensure the umbilical is clear is important. If the diver does not clear the umbilical and starts the ascent, he may not make it very far; at which point, the diver will have to return to the bottom in order to free the umbilical. If the primary gas supply cannot be restored by the time the diver is ready to ascend, the dive should be aborted. In many cases, the primary gas will be immediately restored and the dive will continue; however, it is always good practice to immediately prepare to abort whenever a potentially serious situation like this arises.

Sometimes the diver may report that his gas flow is low or the helmet or mask is breathing hard. A check of the supply console may reveal that the diver has the proper gas pressure. In this case, it is very possible that the diver's umbilical is being pinched or squeezed by a heavy object, or by rigging. The diver should switch to the emergency gas supply (bail-out) and see if the gas flow returns. If the diver now has adequate gas flow, the diver should immediately check to ensure that the umbilical is clear. The diving supervisor will have the tender remove the slack from the umbilical. Usually during the course of these two procedures, the source of the umbilical restriction will be found. If the umbilical cannot be freed, the standby diver should be deployed with a spare umbilical and the necessary tools to switch out the fouled umbilical, and the dive should be aborted. Loss of primary gas supply can be very serious. Never continue a dive with only one gas source.

6.1.6.4 Loss of Communication or Contact with the Diver

If contact with the diver is lost, the following procedure should be used:

1. If hard-wire voice communication is lost, the tender should immediately attempt to communicate with the diver by line-pull signals (see Table 8.2) and abort the dive.
2. Depending on diving conditions and the arrangements made during dive planning, the dive may either be terminated or continued to completion (using line-pull signals for communication). In research diving, it is generally best to terminate the dive so that the problem can be resolved and the dive plan revised.

3. If the tender does not receive an immediate line-pull signal reply from the diver, greater strain should be taken on the line and the signal should be sent again. Considerable resistance to the tender's pull may indicate that the umbilical line is fouled, in which case a standby diver may need to be dispatched.
4. If the tender feels sufficient tension on the line to conclude that it is still attached to the diver, but continues to receive no reply to line-pull signals, the diver should be assumed to be unconscious. In this event, the standby diver should be dispatched immediately.
5. If the diver is found to be not breathing, a check of the helmet or mask should be made to make sure breathing gas is available through the diver's apparatus. The diver's umbilical should be cleared and the diver brought to the surface.

6.1.6.5 Loss from View of Descent or Distance Line

Occasionally, a diver will lose sight of the descent line or lose contact with the distance line. If the distance line is lost, the diver should search carefully within arm's reach or within his immediate vicinity. If the water is less than 40 ft. (12.2 m) deep, the tender should be informed and should haul in the umbilical assembly and attempt to guide the diver back to the descending line. In this situation, the diver may be hauled a short distance off the bottom. When contact with the descent line is regained, the diver should signal the tender to be lowered to the bottom again. In water deeper than 40 ft. (12.2 m), the tender should guide the diver to the descent line in a systematic fashion using search procedures (see Chapter 10).

6.1.6.6 Falling

Falling is an especially serious hazard for divers using free-flow helmets or masks, with or without variable-volume dry suits. The principal danger is the sudden increase in ambient pressure; this can result in a squeeze if the diver cannot immediately compensate by adding gas to both the suit and the helmet or mask. With a demand helmet or facemask, the demand valve will automatically add gas as the ambient pressure increases; however, if the diver is wearing a variable-volume dry suit, a squeeze would still be possible. Squeezes can be very serious. The diver and tender must always be alert to the possibility of a fall. If the diver should start to fall, the tender should take a strain on the umbilical to stop the diver's descent.

6.1.6.7 Ascent

When the diver's bottom time has expired or the task has been completed, the diving supervisor will order the diver back to the stage/bell or descent line. The supervisor will have the tender remove any excess slack in the umbilical, and will ensure the diver's umbilical is clear and the diver is ready to ascend. The following procedure should be used:

1. The tender should exert a slight strain on the umbilical assembly.
2. The tender should exert a slow, steady pull, as directed by the diving supervisor.
3. The diving supervisor should start timing the ascent as soon as the diver indicates he has left the bottom.
4. The diving supervisor is responsible for ensuring the proper ascent rate (generally 30 ft/min 9.1 m/min).
5. The console operator will relay to the diving supervisor the depth (generally every ten feet) as read from the pneumofathometer.
6. If diving in a dry suit, the diver will bleed gas as necessary during ascent to avoid an accidental blowup.
7. Generally, the supervisor will inform the diver well in advance of decompression requirements.
8. When the diver surfaces, the tender and topside personnel help the diver to the dressing bench where the helmet or mask is removed followed by their remaining equipment.

6.1.7 Postdive Procedures

After the diver has removed all his equipment and been checked by the diving supervisor, the diver should remain in the general vicinity for at least 30 minutes. If diving operations have been concluded, the following procedure is recommended:

1. Clean the helmet or mask and emergency gas system; rinse thoroughly, and blow down with air.
2. Secure the air supply to the helmet or mask; disconnect and cap, or bag exposed fittings.
3. Clean and rinse all diving equipment.
4. Blow down the diver's umbilicals, disconnect, and stow.
5. Ensure the dive system has been properly secured.

Postdive maintenance should be performed according to manufacturer recommendations. Clean the interior of the full face mask or helmet oral cavity, or oral-nasal mask, and/or mouth piece, with a solution of poloxamer-iodine cleansing solution. Poloxamer-iodine solution is available from medical supply outlets and is intended for disinfecting and cleaning components to minimize the transmission of germs. Polaxamer-iodine is not an antiseptic; it is a disinfectant. The solution should be mixed at a ratio of 1/2 oz. polaxamer-iodine to one gallon of fresh water. The solution may be applied by sponge or brush, and the area being cleaned should be thoroughly brushed or scrubbed with the solution, and should remain in contact with the parts being cleaned for a full five minutes; then, all traces of the solution should be thoroughly rinsed with fresh water. All masks and helmets should be blown dry to ensure all trapped water is removed from the inlet valve and gas train components. Air dry all equipment thoroughly before storing.

6.1.8 Umbilical Diving from Small Boats

Although most surface-supplied diving is conducted from large vessels or fixed platforms, the umbilical system can be adapted readily to small boat operations that are anchored and secured. When working from a small boat with surface-supplied gear, it is best to have the boat anchored in a minimum of a two-point moor to help prevent the craft from entangling the diver. When diving surface-supplied from a small craft, a bank of high-pressure cylinders may be used in conjunction with a air control console to supply the breathing air. When diving deeper than 100 fsw or out side the no-decompression limits, the configuration of the cylinder bank(s) and air control console must be configured to assure that a reserve breathing gas supply is provided. This enables the team to operate without an air compressor and its accompanying bulk and noise. The number and size of the high-pressure cylinders required depend on the size of the boat and on operational requirements. For small boats, two or more sets of standard twin-cylinder scuba cylinders can be connected by a specially constructed manifold that is, in turn, connected to a high-pressure reduction regulator or small gas control panel. The umbilical is then connected to the pressure side of the pressure-reduction unit. In larger boats, air may be carried in a series of 240 or 300 ft^3 (6.8 or 8.5m^3) high-pressure cylinders. Regardless of the cylinder configuration used, all cylinders must be secured properly, and the valves, manifold, and regulator must be protected to prevent injury to personnel and equipment damage. The umbilical may be coiled on top of the air cylinders or in the bottom of the boat. For the convenience of the tender, the communication box is generally placed on a seat or platform. Communications equipment must be protected from weather and water spray. Because small boats can only be used to support relatively shallow water work, the umbilical from the boat to the diver is usually 100–150 ft. (30.5–45.7 m). Generally, it is wise to limit diving depths to less than 100 ft. (30.5 m) when working from a small boat.

The diving team for a surface-supplied dive from a small boat consist of a person-in-charge (diving supervisor), a diver, tender, and standby diver. The tender, who is a qualified diver, can also serve as the supervisor on such dives. If properly qualified, all personnel can alternate tasks to achieve maximum operational efficiency. The standby diver may be equipped with a second umbilical and mask, or can be equipped with scuba; he should be capable of donning scuba and entering the water in less than a minute. A standby using scuba should be fitted with a quick-release lifeline (readily releasable in the event of entanglement). Some divers use a heavy-duty communication cable as a lifeline, which allows the standby diver and tender to stay in communication. This line is also constructed so that it may be released readily in case of entanglement.

Many divers consider high-pressure cylinder air supply systems safer and more dependable than systems incorporating a small compressor and a volume or receiver tank. All divers should carry a small self-contained emergency scuba cylinder "bail-out cylinder" for use in the event of primary system failure. The bail-out cylinder is plumbed into the manifold block (see Figure 6.8). NOAA requires an emergency supply of this type for all surface-supplied diving operations.

FIGURE 6.8
Manifold Block Assembly

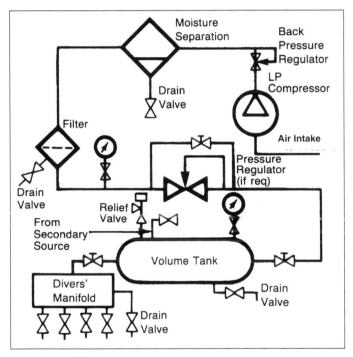

FIGURE 6.9
Schematic of a Low-Pressure Compressor-Equipped Air Supply System

6.1.9 Umbilical Diving from Ships

Prior to commencing surface-supplied diving operations, the ship must be secured in a multiple-point moor. The mooring must be observed to ensure functional stability before divers enter the water. All personnel, divers, and tenders should perform a thorough check of equipment. The ship's captain must be notified that divers are about to enter the water, and clearance should be obtained before the diving operation commences. The air-supply system,

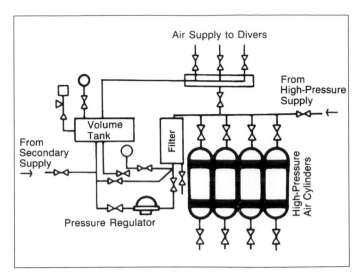

FIGURE 6.10
Schematic of a Typical High-Pressure Cylinder Bank Air Supply System

helmet or mask, and communications should be checked to ensure proper functioning. If not, corrections must be made before the diver enters the water.

The water should be entered using a ladder or diving stage lowered into the water. Jump entries are discouraged from heights more than 5–6 ft. feet (about 2.0 m) above the water. A descent line should be used. Descent rate will depend on the diver; generally, however, it should not exceed 75 ft. (22.9 m) per minute. If descending in a tideway or current, divers should keep their backs to the current so they will be forced against the descent line.

Divers and tenders should review thoroughly the line-pull signals described in Chapter 8. Although voice is the primary means of communication between divers and surface tenders when surface-supplied equipment is being used, line-pull signals are the backup form of communication if the voice system fails.

When the bottom is reached, the tender should be notified and the diver should proceed to the work site. The tender also should keep the diver constantly informed of bottom time. The diver should always be notified a few minutes in advance of termination times so that there is time to complete the task, getting breathing under control, and to prepare for ascent.

When work is completed, the diver should return to the ascent line and signal the tender that he is ready to ascend. The tender should pull in the excess umbilical line slowly and steadily. The diver should not release the ascent line, and should resist the temptation to assist the tender by climbing the line. The tender or divemaster must inform the diver of his decompression requirements well in advance of dive termination. Decompression stops can be made along the ascent line; however, a stage should be utilized for long decompresssions. When decompression is completed, the diver should return onboard ship via the ladder or diving stage, receiving assistance from his tender as required. If a ladder or diving stage is not available, access to and egress from the water can be via a small boat lowered over the side. Use of rope ladders is highly discouraged.

6.1.10 Basic Air Supply Systems

The two basic types of air supply systems used for surface-supplied diving are:

1. Air compressors and volume tanks
2. High-pressure cylinder banks

When properly configured, either of these air sources is able to supply breathing gas that is:

- Of specified purity
- Of adequate volume
- At the proper pressure
- Delivered at a sufficient flow rate to ensure adequate ventilation

Regardless of the type of system, it is imperative that it be in good repair, be serviced at regular intervals, and be monitored by trained personnel.

Air compressors are discussed in more detail in Chapter 5. When the air supply system for surface-supplied diving operations involves an air compressor, the general system configuration is similar to that shown in Figure 6.9. When surface-supplied diving operations utilize a high-pressure cylinder system for diver air supply, the general system configuration used is the one shown in Figure 6.10.

6.1.11 Rates of Air Flow

The rate at which air must flow from the air supply to diver depends on whether the breathing apparatus (helmet or mask) operates on a free-flow or demand principle. Demand masks and helmets are designed to operate in the demand mode even though many also have a free-flow capability. Normally the free-flow valve is intended for defogging the face plate, clearing water, or ventilating, and can also be used if the demand mode fails. Using a demand-mode helmet or mask in a free-flow mode is inefficient; it requires a continuous flow of gas rather than a flow strictly on demand. Most free-flow helmets and masks have no provisions for demand-mode diving, and operate only on a free-flow basis. With free-flow equipment, the primary requirement of the air supply system is that it must have a capacity (in acfm - actual cubic foot per minute) that will provide sufficient ventilation at depth to prevent the carbon dioxide level in the mask or helmet from exceeding safe limits at normal work levels, and during extremely hard work or emergencies. By ensuring that the apparatus is capable of supplying at least six acfm (170 liters) under all circumstances, divers can be reasonably certain that the inspired carbon dioxide will not exceed two percent.

To compute the ventilation rate necessary to control the level of inspired CO_2, the following equation should be used:

$$R = 6(Pa)(N)$$

where

R = ventilation flow rate in scfm
(standard cubic foot per minute)
Pa = absolute pressure at working depth in ata
N = number of divers to be supplied

Example:

What ventilation rate would be required for two divers using free-flow style helmets at 80 ft. (24.4 m)?

Solution:

$$R = 6acfm(Pa)(N)$$
$$R = 6acfm[(3.42ata)(2 \text{ divers})]$$
$$R = 41.04 \text{ scfm}$$

The flow requirement of 41.04 is expressed in standard cubic feet per minute (scfm).

To compute the flow rate required for demand systems, you must know what the anticipated work rate will be. For demand equipment, the rate of air flow should always be able to exceed the diver's consumption rate.

6.1.12 Supply Pressure Requirements—Free-Flow Systems

When using a free-flow mask or helmet, there are many factors that can influence air flow; length and inside diameter of umbilical, number of umbilical couplings, supply valve restrictions, and supply pressure. It is important that the diving umbilical in use is of good quality, with a smooth inner bore of at least 3/8" inside diameter. The number of umbilical connections or fittings between the supply console and the diver can severely restrict the flow of air to the diver. When diving to depths of 120 fsw (36.8 msw), it is recommended that the umbilical pressure be at least 50 psi over ambient pressure. When diving to depths in excess of 120 fsw (36.8 msw), it is recommended that the supply pressure be at least 100 psi over ambient pressure. Simple calculations give the supply pressures necessary for most free-flow diving.

For depths less than 120 fsw:

$$Ps = 0.445D + 65$$

where

Ps = supply air pressure in psig
D = depth in fsw
and 65 = absolute hose pressure (50 psi + 14.7 psi)

For depths greater than 120 ft. (36.6 msw):

$$Ps = 0.445D + 115 \text{ psia}$$

where
115 psia = absolute hose pressure (100 psi + 14.7 psi)

6.1.13 Supply Pressure Requirements—Demand Systems

Demand-mode diving generally requires higher pressures from the supply system, but the overall gas usage is less than that of free-flow diving. This means a smaller, lighter,

Surface-Supplied Diving

medium-pressure compressor can often be used where previously, if free-flow gear were used, only a large compressor would do. In addition, if high-pressure storage banks are used, the demand system allows for greater dive time due to more efficient use of gas. In demand-mode diving, the need to flow great quantities of air to ensure low levels of CO_2 is eliminated, due to the use of oral-nasal masks or very small oral cavities. Most regulators in demand helmets or masks are very similar to those used for open-circuit scuba diving. The actual supply pressure needed to allow the helmet or mask to work efficiently is dictated by the manufacturer; often, this pressure will be dependent on how deep the helmet or mask is worn. The basic formula for determining required air pressure is as follows:

(Depth in fsw × .445) + manufacturer's recommended pressure over ambient pressure setting = minimum supply pressure

where
> fsw = diver's depth
> .445 psig = the force exerted by one foot of salt water

Example:
If the manufacturer recommends a minimum supply pressure of 135 psig over ambient when diving to depths of 130 fsw, what would be the supply pressure setting on the console?

Solution:
> [(130 fsw × .445 psi) + 135 psig]
> (57 psi + 135 psig)
> 192.2 psig

Most demand-mode helmets and masks will have at least two recommended over-ambient supply pressures. This is usually the case because many demand regulators can be used with relatively low supply pressures when diving to depths of 60 fsw (18.4 msw) or less. However, as depth increases, so does the ambient pressure and the density of the breathing gas. This increase in ambient pressure makes it necessary to increase the supply pressure to maintain a driving force and to compensate for the increased gas density which causes a greater resistance to flow within the umbilical and gas-supply components.

For demand-mode diving, the air requirements for respiration are based on the maximum instantaneous peak flow rate under heavy work conditions. In order for the diver to have the required flow, the peak flow rate at the highest rate of work must be used. Computing the rate of flow that the air system must be able to deliver for demand-mode diving is essentially the same as calculating consumption rate at depth. However, due to variations and combinations of gas supply systems, as well as demand regulator performance characteristics, most manufacturers of demand-type helmets and masks will dictate supply pressure and gas flow requirements. In addition, some will also specify the umbilical lengths and number of umbilical couplings that may be used. The flow

requirement varies directly with the respiratory demands of the workload. Consequently, the rate at which air is consumed is always significantly lower than the peak inhalation flow rate.

It must be remembered that when computing the flow requirements, the actual flow will be influenced by certain mechanical restrictions within the system. As an example, the flow at the end of a single length umbilical, 300 ft. long, would be greater than the flow through two 150-ft. umbilicals coupled together. The most accurate way to validate the flow of a system is to do a flow test of the entire surface-supplied system from the outlet of the supply console to the end of the umbilical. Some manufacturers of surface-supplied consoles will list the flow capability of their system when used within certain guidelines. These guidelines will include supply pressure and the length, diameter, and number of umbilical connections consoles can accommodate. In addition, many manufacturers of helmets and masks also list breathing performance data; this is the measurement of volume-averaged pressure (resistive effort), usually expressed in joules/liter. Demand-mode consumption rates (actual gas being ventilated through the diver's lungs) are computed basically the same way as open-circuit scuba. To determine air consumption rates, two factors must be identified; anticipated highest work rate and depth of the dive.

The rate at which the diver is working is normally expressed in Respiratory Minute Volume (RMV). The final value can be converted to cubic feet in order to work bank storage formulas: one cubic foot = 28.316 liters. Before calculations can be made, values should be defined.

Average Working Breathing Rates:
> Light Work . . . . 0.8 ft³/min (22.5 liter)
> Moderate Work. . . . . 1.4 ft³/min (40.0 liter)
> Moderately Heavy . . . . 2.2 ft³/min (62.5 liter)
> Heavy . . . . 2.6 ft³/min (75.0 liter)
> Extremely Heavy . . . . 3.2 ft³/min (90.0 liter)

Formula for consumption rate at depth:
$$CD = RMV (PA)$$
where
> CD = consumption rate at depth
> RMV = total volume of air moved in and out of the lungs in one minute, measured in liters
> PA = pressure absolute, (depth + 33) ÷ 33

Example:
What would the rate of flow be for a diver using demand mask or helmet doing moderate work at 75 fsw (22.9 msw).

Solution:
Moderate Work = 1.4 ft³ × [(75 fsw + 33) ÷ 33]
> = (1.4 × 3.27)
> = 4.6 ft³/min

To change this value to liters multiply by 28.316:
> 4.6 × 28.316 = 130.8 l/min

Diver and Support Personnel Training

Diver and Support Personnel Training

7.0 GENERAL

This chapter describes the mission of NOAA diver training programs, the criteria for personnel selections, the training involved in preparing to dive under specialized circumstances, and basic approaches to diver training. It does not prescribe specific training procedures or attempt to teach divers how to perform specific underwater tasks.

Many organizations offer diver training. NOAA, the U.S. Navy, and other government organizations train divers to support mission requirements. Many colleges and universities offer diver training to students and faculty members who use diving as a research tool. Recreational diver training is also available from recreational diver certification agencies and local dive stores. Commercial diving schools offer training for divers in the commercial diving industry. These training organizations select students on the basis of their personal motivation, physical fitness, and basic swimming skills. Although this chapter emphasizes the training of NOAA divers and other support personnel, many of the principles described here can apply to the training of other divers.

7.1 MISSION AND PERSONNEL CERTIFICATION

As the nation's premier ocean science agency, NOAA has many programs that require work to be conducted below the ocean's surface. Underwater research and support activities are conducted by NOAA scientists, engineers, and technicians who are trained and certified to dive by the NOAA Diving Program (NDP). NDP, under the auspices of the Office of Marine and Aviation Operations (OMAO), is responsible for overseeing and managing NOAA diving personnel, equipment, and activities, ensuring that all diving is performed safely and efficiently. NOAA divers work in waters throughout the world in conditions that vary from the crystal clear water of a pristine marine sanctuary to the murky and polluted water of a congested harbor. On any given day, NOAA divers may be required to deploy and retrieve scientific instruments, document the behavior of fish and other marine animals, perform routine and emergency ship repair and maintenance, and locate and chart submerged objects.

Participation in diving activities under NOAA auspices requires certification by the NOAA Diving Program. Specific requirements for certification vary according to the certification category or training level and typically involve a combination of training and experience. The NOAA Diving Program offers a variety of dive and dive-support training courses which are open to NOAA personnel as well as employees of other governmental agencies on a space-available basis. Courses offered include:

- Working Diver
- Divemaster
- Diver Medical Technician
- Chamber Operator
- Surface-Supplied Diving
- Nitrox Diving
- Visual Cylinder Inspection
- Polluted-Water Diving Techniques

Diving certifications are awarded by the NOAA Diving Program in five categories based on an individual's training and experience level. These include:

- Trainee Diver
- Scientific Diver
- Working Diver
- Advanced Working Diver
- Master Diver

7.1.1 Selection Standards

NOAA divers are selected from volunteers on the basis of their psychological and physical fitness, and their water skills. The psychological evaluation consists of a personal interview, an assessment of motivation, and a general screening by experienced NOAA divers to identify individuals who are likely to be able to handle the stresses of diving. The evaluation interview helps to identify any misconceptions the candidate may have about training, requirements, conditions, and responsibilities of NOAA diving work.

7.1.2 Physical Examination

A physical examination is required to determine whether every candidate is medically qualified to dive. Ideally, the physician will be a certified diver and/or have training in hyperbaric medicine. Military, commercial, and scientific divers are evaluated according to standards set forth by their respective agencies or organizations. NOAA has developed and enforces its own medical standards for its divers.

NOTE
For more detailed information, or for a referral to a physician knowledgeable in diving medicine, contact medical services at DAN: (919) 684-2948.

Some medical conditions may disqualify a person from diving with compressed gas. Other conditions have been judged to increase the risk of serious injury or disability in the diving environment. In all instances, it shall be the decision of a trained hyperbaric medical examiner whether the condition disqualifies an individual from entering into or continuing to participate in diving duties.

The guidelines below present a framework for individual dive fitness evaluations. They are not established standards. These guidelines are organized in accordance with a systems approach, and no attempt is made to rank systems in terms of their relative importance.

7.1.2.1 Skin
These conditions should be disqualifying:

- Any chronic or acute dermatitis adversely affected by prolonged immersion
- Allergy to materials used in diving equipment that comes into contact with the skin
- History of sensitization or severe allergy to marine or waterborne allergens

7.1.2.2 Psychiatric
Careful attention should be paid to the maturity of prospective candidates, their ability to adapt to stressful situations, their motivation to pursue diving, and their cognitive learning ability. These conditions should be disqualifying:

- Acute psychosis
- Uncontrolled chronic or acute depression with suicidal tendencies
- Chronic psychosis in partial remission on medication
- Substance abuse, including abuse of alcohol or use of mood-altering drugs

7.1.2.3 Neurologic
A history of severe closed-head injury with prolonged unconsciousness or evidence of significant intracerebral trauma must be thoroughly investigated. There must be complete recovery. Diving after intracranial surgery should be evaluated individually; the candidate should not be at a greater risk of seizures post-operatively and should be physically able to participate in all aspects of diving. The following conditions should be considered:

- Any neurologic deficit, including abnormal EEG, behavioral-cognitive problems, or post-traumatic seizures should be disqualifying.
- Herniated nucleus pulposis of the lower back (if corrected) should be evaluated on an individual basis, according to the level of work anticipated.
- Any disorder that causes or results in loss of consciousness or any form of seizure disorder, including any form of seizure or prior cerebrovascular accident, should be absolutely disqualifying.

7.1.2.4 Ophthalmologic
Since a diver's vision is critical to his safety, it is important to review the following:

- Candidates should demonstrate adequate visual acuity to orient themselves in the water and on the surface. Corrective lenses, either fixed to the face mask or soft contact lenses (which allow for gas transfer), are acceptable.
- Narrow-angle glaucoma, aphakia with correction, motility disorder, cataract, and retinitis pigmentosa are relative disqualifications for diving; a skilled ophthalmologist should be consulted.
- Because color vision is required for certain diving tasks, deficiencies in color vision may be disqualifying.

7.1.2.5 Otolaryngologic
As a prerequisite to diving, candidates must have intact tympanic membranes and should be able to either autoinflate the tympanic membrane or demonstrate the ability to clear their ears in a hyperbaric chamber. These conditions may be disqualifying:

- Tympanic membrane perforations should be disqualifying (an opening in the tympanic membrane would allow water into the middle ear). If a tympanic membrane rupture is completely healed or has been surgically repaired and the candidate is able to autoinflate, he may be conditionally cleared for diving with the warning that the perforation may recur.
- Meniere's disease and other chronic conditions that are associated with vertigo.
- Extensive mastoid surgery, stapedectomy, or artificial cochlear implant.
- Barotitis should be temporarily disqualifying until all middle ear inflammation and fluid have resolved and tympanic membrane motility has returned to normal.
- Active ear infections should be temporarily disqualifying.
- Chronic or acute otitis externa should be disqualifying until healed.

7.1.2.6 Nose and Paranasal Sinuses

A patent nasal passage and the absence of sinus and nasal congestion are essential in diving. These conditions may be disqualifying:

- Nasal polyps, deviated nasal septum, and other obstructive nasal lesions
- Acute or chronic infection

A history of long-term decongestant use should trigger a search for the cause of the congestion, and candidates should be warned about the dangers of the chronic use of chemical agents while diving.

7.1.2.7 Oral and Dental

Candidates must be able to be fitted with and hold a scuba mouthpiece. These conditions should be disqualifying:

- Where there is a danger that trapped gas could get under a tooth and rupture it
- Badly decayed or broken teeth that impair the candidate's ability to hold a scuba mouthpiece

7.1.2.8 Pulmonary

Because any abnormality in pulmonary system function can cause arterial gas embolism, pneumothorax, or pneumomediastinum, all candidates should be given a screening chest x-ray. The following conditions are absolute disqualifications for diving:

- Exercise-induced reactive airway disease (RAD)
- History of spontaneous pneumothorax
- Previous penetrating chest trauma, surgery of the chest, or traumatic pneumothorax, unless careful evaluation shows no excessive scar formation or likelihood of air trapping
- Chronic obstructive pulmonary disease (COPD)
- Active pneumonia or lung infection, including active tuberculosis
- Mycotic (fungal) disease with cavity formation

7.1.2.9 Cardiovascular

Cardiovascular defects can be disqualifying because they predispose the individual to unacceptable risks. These conditions should be disqualifying:

- Cyanotic heart disease.
- Aortic stenosis or coaretation of the aorta.
- Prosthetic heart valves.
- Exercise-induced rhythm disorders, including disorders that manifest as paroxysmal tachycardias, despite control with drugs.
- Heart block, unless documented that it is not due to disease, and the cardiac response to exercise load is favorable.
- Cardiac or pulmonary A-V shunts.
- Candidates with pacemakers should be individually evaluated and, generally, should be disqualified.

- Coronary artery disease should be evaluated by an expert.
- Peripheral vascular disease (requires case-by-case evaluation).
- Candidates taking cardiovascular drugs (including blood pressure medication) should be evaluated on a case-by-case basis. The use of beta blockers increases the risk of bronchospasm and suppresses the stress response.
- Hypertension should be considered on a case-by-case basis. An EKG exam to evaluate a potential diver with any cardiovascular concerns should include an exercise stress test to 13 or 14 METS (Metabolic Exercise Tolerance Score) with no difficulty.

7.1.2.10 Hematological

These conditions should be disqualifying:

- Sickle-cell anemia
- Leukemia or pre-leukemia manifesting, as myelofibrosis and polycythemia
- Intoxication that has caused methemoglobinemia
- Anemia is relatively disqualifying and requires case-by-case evaluation

7.1.2.11 Gastrointestinal

These conditions should be disqualifying:

- Any active or chronic disorder that predisposes a diver to vomiting (including Meckel's diverticulum, acute gastroenteritis, and severe motion sickness)
- Unrepaired abdominal or inguinal hernia
- Active or uncontrolled peptic ulcer disease, pancreatitis, hepatitis, colitis, cholecystitis, or diverticulitis

7.1.2.12 Endocrinological

These conditions may be disqualifying:

- Diabetes mellitus should be disqualifying, unless it is diet-controlled.
- Other endocrine abnormalities should be evaluated on a case-by-case basis.

7.1.2.13 Musculoskeletal

These conditions should be disqualifying:

- Paralytic disorders
- Bone fractures that are incompletely healed and osteomyelitis that is actively draining
- Deformities, either congenital or acquired, that impair the candidate's ability to use scuba equipment or impair the candidate's ability to perform required tasks, including managing emergency situations
- Inadequate physical fitness to handle the physical work of diving

Diver and Support Personnel Training

7.1.2.14 Obstetric and Gynecological

Pregnancy is absolutely disqualifying because of the possible risk of bubble formation in the developing fetus during decompression and the risk of arterializing otherwise benign bubbles through patent foramen ovale and ductus arteriosis.

7.1.3 Swimming Skills

All applicants for NOAA scuba diver training shall perform the following swimming exercises without face masks, fins, or snorkels and with confidence and good watermanship:

- Swim 500 yards (457.2 meters) using the crawl, side-stroke, and breaststroke
- Swim under water for a distance of 25 yards (22.9 meters) without surfacing
- Stay afloat for 30 minutes

7.2 TRAINING PROGRAM REQUIREMENTS

7.2.1 Scuba Training

Although NOAA has its own diver training and certification program, NOAA personnel often receive basic scuba training before they become NOAA diver candidates. The primary course used to prepare and certify NOAA personnel for participation in diving operations is the NOAA Working Diver Course. The extensive, three-week program is designed to train NOAA employees in various facets of diving and underwater work techniques. During the course, students receive approximately 65 hours of classroom instruction and 75 hours of practical instruction aimed at exposing them to a variety of equipment, tasks, situations, and environments typically encountered as NOAA working divers. Students perform a variety of underwater projects to develop self-confidence and manual dexterity and to instill the team approach to underwater problem solving. Dives are conducted in several different locations (pool, training tank, confined, and open water) with visibility ranging from many feet to inches. The course also includes an orientation dive in a hyperbaric chamber, several deep dives (>100 ft. or > 30 m), and training in variable-volume dry suits. Students must successfully complete all water work and pass all written examinations in order to receive certification.

Regardless of the training organization, however, there are basic practices and procedures that should be included in any scuba training program. For example, any diver training program should produce:

- Divers who reach a level of competence that will permit safe open-water diving
- Divers who can respond to emergency situations and make appropriate decisions when faced with problems under water
- Divers who can execute assigned underwater tasks safely and efficiently

Diving procedures, particularly those of a lifesaving nature, should be practiced repeatedly to ensure automatic response in emergencies, and reduce the likelihood of the diver losing control and panicking (Bachrach and Egstrom 1986).

Training courses vary widely among organizations with respect to length, content, complexity, and water skills required. However, all courses should include both classroom sessions and in-water training (see Figure 7.1). The core elements of NOAA's training program for working divers are discussed in detail in the following sections.

7.2.1.1 Classroom

It is important for the candidate to develop a general understanding of diving principles, the diving environment, and the self-confidence (but not overconfidence) necessary to operate safely in the field.

Formal training courses are only the first step in becoming a safe and efficient diver. With this in mind, diver training should expose the trainee to a wide variety of diving-related experiences in addition to teaching the basics. Details of various diving systems and ancillary equipment will be learned as part of on-the-job training. Topics presented during the NOAA Working Diving Course include:

- Diving Physics: pressure, temperature, density, specific gravity, buoyancy, diving gases, and the gas laws and their practical application in diving; calculation of air consumption and supply, and buoyancy requirements
- Diving Physiology and Medicine: the anatomy and mechanics of circulation and respiration; the effects of immersion on the body, hypoxia; anoxia, hypercapnia, hypocapnia, hyperpnea, apnea, hyperthermia, hypothermia; the direct and indirect effects of pressure (squeeze and lung overpressure, including

FIGURE 7.1
Pool Used for Skin and Scuba Diving Skills

arterial gas embolism, decompression sickness, inert gas narcosis, and oxygen toxicity); breathing gas contaminants, drowning, near-drowning, overexertion, exhaustion, breathing resistance, "dead space," and psychological factors such as panic

- Equipment Care and Maintenance: selection, proper use, and care of diver-worn gear; variable-volume dry suits; operation and maintenance of air compressors and compressor systems; cylinder-filling procedures; requirements for testing and inspection of specific types of equipment (including scuba cylinders); and air purity standards and testing
- Diving Platforms: shore, small boat, and large vessel platforms; fixed structures; safety precautions and surface-support requirements in vessel diving; and water entry and exit
- Operations Planning: objectives, data collection, definition of tasks, selection of equipment, selection of dive team, emergency planning, special equipment requirements, and setup and check out of support platforms
- Recordkeeping: dive logs including diving profile, water conditions, work project, decompression, gas mixtures, dive equipment, incidents, etc.
- Introduction to Decompression Theory: definition of terms, structure and content of diving tables, single and repetitive diving principles and practical decompression table problems, dangers of diving at high altitude or flying after diving
- Diving Procedures: relationship of operations planning to diving procedures; warning signal requirements; hand and line signals; diver recall systems; water emergencies; buddy teams; tending; precautions required by special conditions (e.g., pollution, restricted visibility, currents); ship husbandry; boating safety; dive station setup and postdive procedures; procedures for search and recovery; salvage and object lifting; work techniques and tools; instrument deployment and maintenance; and underwater navigation methods
- Accident Prevention: management, basic principles of first aid and cardiopulmonary resuscitation (CPR); use of oxygen first aid equipment including positive-pressure/demand valves; development of accident-management plans; recovery of victims and boat evacuation procedures; recognition of pressure-related accident signs and symptoms; patient handling en route to treatment; introduction to recompression chambers and treatment procedures; and procedures for reporting accident investigations
- Diving Environment and Hazardous Marine Life: tides and currents (surf, thermoclines, arctic, temperate, and tropical conditions); waves and beaches; rip currents; and river, harbor, and marine life hazards

7.2.1.2 Pool and Open Water

A training program that progresses from pool to protected open water, and then to a variety of open-water situations is essential to diver training. Students should be exposed to open-water conditions while diving at night, and under conditions of reduced visibility. Individuals expected to conduct dives in cold water should be exposed to such conditions in a controlled training environment prior to performing working dives. To master skin (breath-hold) and scuba diving, an understanding is required of the proper use of mask, fins, and snorkel, surface swimming, surface dives, underwater swimming; pressure equalization; and rescue techniques.

Breath-hold or skin diving can be hazardous, and research divers using this technique must be competent swimmers in excellent physical condition. The skin diver is subject to barotrauma of the ears and sinuses, just as any other diver is; however, air embolism and related complications are a problem only if the skin diver breathes compressed gas from a scuba cylinder, a habitat, or even an underwater air/gas pocket. Because breath-holding can cause serious problems, divers should thoroughly understand the potential hazards of prolonged breath-holding under water.

Specific pool (see Figures 7.2, 7.3) and open-water skills evaluated/taught during the NOAA Working Diver Course include:

- Watermanship evaluation (NOAA swim test)
- Skin diving skills
  - Predive equipment assembly and inspection
  - Mask clearing
  - Snorkel clearing
  - Buoyancy control with swim vest (manual inflation/deflation)
  - Water entries
  - Kicks
  - Swimming with mask, fins, snorkel, and swim vest
  - Ear equalization during descent
  - Surface dives/descents/ascents
  - Rescues
- Scuba diving skills
  - Predive equipment assembly and inspection
  - Water entries and exits (shore, boats, piers)
  - Regulator clearing and recovery
  - Snorkel/regulator exchange
  - Buoyancy control with BC and variable-volume dry suits (descents/ascents/on-bottom/hovering)
  - Swimming with mask, fins, snorkel, wet suit, and scuba
  - Dry suit blow-up management and prevention
  - Mask, fins, and weight belt removal and replacement under water

FIGURE 7.2
Checking Scuba Diver's Equipment

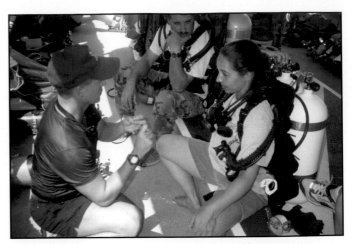

FIGURE 7.3
Predive Briefing

– Underwater communications (hand-signals)
– Air sharing (buddy-breathing, including octopus use and pony bottles)
– Controlled emergency swimming ascent
– Tired swimmer's carry
– Buddy transport (do-si-do, tank pull, tired swimmer push)
– Surfacing an unconscious diver
– Aquatic rescue breathing
– Dive profile information recording (depth, bottom time, cylinder air pressure)
– Underwater search and navigation
– Use of tools and equipment under water
  Light hand and pneumatic tools (wrenches, saws, pliers)
  Lift bags
  Acoustic listening devices (pinger locators)
  Wireless communications
  Hand held sonar units

During the NOAA Working Diver Course, students perform a minimum of six pool dives and 25 open-water dives.

Of the open-water dives, ten are performed using variable-volume dry suits with the remainder being made in wet suits. The instructor-to-student ratio during this training is 1:8 for pool dives and 1:4 for open-water dives.

7.2.2 Umbilical Dive Training

Umbilical diving is also referred to as surface-supplied diving. In umbilical diving, the diver's breathing gas is supplied via an umbilical from the surface, which provides the diver with an unlimited breathing gas supply.

Preliminary selection procedures and criteria for umbilical dive training are essentially the same as those for basic scuba. In NOAA, a diver applying for umbilical training should be certified as an advanced working diver, which requires the completion of at least 150 logged dives. Before qualifying as an umbilical diver, the trainee should receive instruction and training in:

• The general purpose and limitations of surface-supplied (umbilical) diving
• Equipment used in umbilical diving
• Assembling, disassembling, and operation of gas supply systems
• Use of accessory tools and equipment basic to umbilical procedures and specific to the particular tasks being contemplated
• Methods of achieving intelligible communication
• Equipment repair and maintenance
• Water entry, descent, ascent, and emergency procedures
• Tending umbilical divers

When initial training is completed, an open-water qualification test that includes both general diving techniques and actual working procedures should be given.

7.2.2.1 Qualification Test

To pass the qualification test, candidates must demonstrate the ability to:

- Plan and organize a surface-supplied air dive operation
- Demonstrate ability to rig all surface and underwater equipment properly, including air supply systems, mask/helmet, communications, and other support equipment
- Demonstrate proper procedures of dressing and undressing a diver, using the particular pieces of equipment needed for the working dive
- Tend a surface-supplied diver
- Demonstrate knowledge of the following emergency procedures: loss of voice communications, flooded masks and helmets, and entanglement
- Participate in at least two practice dives, as described below:
  - Properly enter water that is at least ten feet (3 m) deep and remain submerged for at least 30 minutes, demonstrating control of air flow, buoyancy, mobility, and familiarity with communication systems
  - Ascend and leave water in a prescribed manner
  - Properly enter water that is between 30 and 50 feet (9.1 and 15.2 m) deep and conduct work-related training tasks

After successful completion of this test, the instructor should evaluate the diver's performance and establish a phased depth-limited diving schedule to ensure a safe, gradual exposure to deeper working depths. Detailed descriptions of umbilical diving equipment and its use appear in Chapters 5 and 6.

7.2.3 Nitrox Training

Nitrox diving involves the use of a nitrogen-oxygen breathing mixture containing a higher fraction of oxygen than normally found in air.

The curriculum for NOAA's Nitrox Training Program includes coverage of the following topics:

- NOAA oxygen partial pressure limits
- NOAA NN32 and NN36 breathing mixtures
- Depth/time limits for oxygen during working dives
- Central nervous system and pulmonary oxygen toxicity
- Analysis of nitrox breathing mixtures
- Nitrox diving equipment (open-circuit systems)
- Equivalent air depth concept and calculation
- NOAA NN32 and NN36 decompression tables
- Safe handling of oxygen
- Introduction to gas mixing techniques
- Oxygen equipment cleaning

NOAA nitrox trainees attend classroom sessions and then progress to open-water dives. In order to receive the NOAA Nitrox Certification, students must pass a written examination and complete two open-water dives using nitrox breathing mixtures.

7.2.4 Saturation Training

This section introduces the basic components of training for saturation dives. See Chapter 17, Diving From Seafloor Habitats, for practices and procedures related to saturation diving.

Although the basic requirements for saturation diving are the same as those for surface-based diving, there are some important differences that need to be addressed during training. The diver's "home base" during saturation usually is either a seafloor habitat or a diving bell system. For this reason, the saturation diver needs a fundamental reorientation to his new underwater environment. For example, the saturation diver must constantly be aware that he cannot return to the surface in an emergency situation. This factor has specific implications with respect to the selection and use of certain pieces of saturation diving equipment. Saturation diving has special requirements including:

- Redundant air delivery systems:
  - These consist of double steel or aluminum cylinders using a manifold valve system with isolation capability, allowing the isolation of each cylinder in case of a critical equipment failure, such as an extruded cylinder neck o-ring or blown 'burst disc'. The use of steel cylinders (as opposed to aluminum) also eliminates the need for a separate weight system (i.e., weight belt). The use of weight belts during saturation diving adds an unnecessary potential point of failure. The sudden unexpected loss of ballast could result in an uncontrollable ascent to the surface.
  - The utilization of a redundant regulator system (two separate first and second stage regulators) provides an alternative regulator system in case of a complete failure of the diver's primary regulator.
  - The use of redundant pressure gauges (cylinder pressure) allows the monitoring of pressure within each individual cylinder, should isolation of the manifold be necessary.
- Line reels (cave or safety reels) must be used when divers are working away from the excursion lines (lines leading directly to the habitat). The inability to find one's way back to the habitat would constitute an emergency situation, since divers do not have the luxury of ascending to the surface to reorient themselves relative to the habitat location.
- Surface marker buoys (SMB) are used to mark either a surfaced diver or lost diver at depth.

- Personal strobe lights are carried by each diver to assist topside support personnel in locating a surfaced diver at night or during limited visibility.
- An emergency surface-communication device (UHF radio) is used by surface divers to communicate with shore-based personnel or emergency response vessels regarding their status and location.
- Saturation divers working outside the presence of trained medical personnel should be trained in the use of a simple otoscope, in order to detect ear barotrauma and external ear infections (otitis externa).
- Adequate thermal protection shall be worn because of the extended diving time involved in saturation which routinely causes chilling, even in tropical regions.
- A self-contained backup breathing gas supply shall be used when umbilical equipment is utilized.
- Extra precautions must be taken when filling scuba cylinders under water to prevent water from entering the cylinder.

Because the consequences of becoming lost are so serious, a saturation diving training program also should include training in underwater navigation techniques. Divers should be instructed in the use of navigational aids, such as grid lines, string highways, ripple marks, topographical features, and navigation by compass. Because compasses are not always accurate, divers should be trained to use the compass in combination with topographical and grid line information.

Training in habitat operations, emergency procedures, and local diving restrictions is usually conducted on site. Such training includes instruction in:

- Communication systems
- Use of special diving equipment
- Habitat support systems
- Emergency equipment
- Regional topography
- Underwater landmarks
- Navigational grid systems
- Depth and distance limitations for diver/scientists
- Operational and safety procedures used by the surface support team

Other features related to seafloor habitation also need to be identified during saturation training. Some of these relate to housekeeping chores inside the habitat. For example, water boils at a higher temperature under water than on the surface: 262°F (128 C) at 50.5 ft. (15.4 m) and 292°F (144 C) at 100 ft. (30.5 m); cooking procedures must be altered, because burned food not only constitutes a fire hazard but also produces toxic gases at depth. (For additional information on underwater habitation, see *Living and Working in the Sea* by Miller and Koblick 1995.)

A deviation from normal speech intelligibility may occur as a result of depth or the breathing mixture used in the habitat. The amount of speech distortion depends on the habitat breathing mixture and the depth. Other factors directly affecting the saturated diver or a habitat diving program include the necessity to pay special attention to personal hygiene, i.e., to take special care of the ears and skin. Because of the high humidity encountered in most habitats, the growth of certain pathogens and organisms is stimulated and recovery is prolonged. Proper washing, drying, and care of exposure suits is essential to prevent skin irritation or infections. Trainees should be aware that there are restrictions with respect to the use of toxic materials in a closed-environment system such as a habitat. These apply not only to the use of scientific preparations, but also to the use of normally harmless items such as rubber cement (used for the repair of wet suits) and aerosol sprays.

Training for saturation diving from underwater habitats should teach divers the procedures for making ascending and descending excursions from the storage depth. Special diving excursion tables have been developed for excursions from the saturation depth. These tables are designed to consider storage depth, oxygen and nitrogen partial pressures, and other factors. Trainees should become familiar with these tables and their limitations.

A unique feature of saturation diving is the diver's ability to make upward excursions; however, upward excursions constitute a decompression, and divers must be careful to remain within the prescribed excursion limits. This applies not only to the divers themselves, but also to certain types of equipment; for example, if a camera is opened and reloaded in a habitat, an upward excursion of 10–15 ft (3.0–4.6 m) can cause flooding because such equipment is not designed to resist internal pressure. Aquanaut candidates should be instructed to check all equipment to be used in a habitat to determine whether it is designed to withstand both internal and external pressures.

7.2.5 Research Diver Training

Approximately one-third of all dives conducted by NOAA personnel directly involve scientific research (i.e., observation or collection of data). Another one-third involve science-support tasks such as ship husbandry, lifting/moving heavy objects under water, underwater cutting, etc. The remaining one-third of dives performed involve training and proficiency. The objective of research-diving courses is to train divers in the techniques and methods of underwater work related to scientific investigations. Most research-diver training programs require that attendees be certified scuba divers with open-water diving experience prior to enrollment in the course. Typical programs involve approximately 100 hours of theoretical instruction and practical diver training. Theoretical aspects should include principles and activities appropriate to the intended area of scientific study and should be suitably tailored to the individual scientific diver, based on his or her academic background and research methodologies.

Suggested topics include:
- Data-gathering techniques
- Collecting techniques
- Installation of scientific apparatus
- Use of chemicals under water
- Site selection and relocation
- Animal and plant identification
- Tagging techniques
- Underwater photography or videography
- Dive planning

Each of these topics should be related to the problems faced by diving scientists and their impact on the conduct of underwater investigations. Diving safety should be emphasized throughout the course, so that upon completion of training, the divers feel completely comfortable in the water and are able to concentrate their energies on the scientific tasks at hand. This degree of competence can be achieved only if the basic diving skills are learned so thoroughly that routine operations and responses to emergencies become automatic.

In 1984, the Occupational Safety and Health Administration (OSHA), which had promulgated regulations in 1978 governing commercial diving operations, specifically exempted from these regulations those scientific and educational diving programs that could meet certain requirements. A research organization or educational entity wishing exemption from the Federal OSHA standard must have in place a diving program that has developed a diving manual, has a diving safety officer and diving control board, and has developed procedures for diving situations emergency.

The safety record of the research diving community reflects the effectiveness of current diver training and certification procedures. Individuals or organizations wishing information about scientific diving programs in the United States, should contact the American Academy of Underwater Sciences, 430 Nahant Road, Nahant, Maine 01908 USA or visit their website at: http://www.aaus.org.

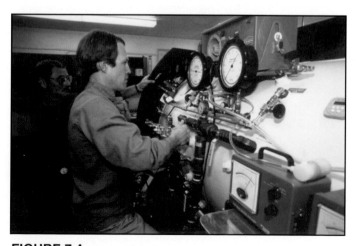

FIGURE 7.4
Diver Medical Technician (DMT) Pressurizing a Hyperbaric Chamber

7.2.6 Dive Leadership Training

Many organizations, including NOAA, the U.S. Navy, and commercial diving companies, designate certain experienced divers as supervisors. NOAA has four supervisory diving categories: Line Diving Officer, Unit Diving Supervisor, Diving Instructor, and Divemaster.

Each organization provides training that is specifically related to the goals of the organization; however, all diving supervisors are required to have a broad range of diving experience. In addition, every supervisor must have the working knowledge to plan diving projects, oversee diving activities, conduct inspections, and investigate accidents.

NOAA diving supervisors receive classroom and practical "hands on" training in the following leadership-oriented topics:

- NOAA diving leadership
- Techniques for conducting dive activities
- Dive planning
- Problem management and counseling
- Dive rescue
- Diving accident management
- Diving first aid
- Diving regulations (NOAA, OSHA, USCG)

Divemaster candidates are also evaluated on their ability to direct and supervise diving operations under normal and emergency conditions.

7.2.7 Chamber Operator Training

The operation and maintenance of hyperbaric chambers are a necessary part of many diving programs. Therefore, it is important to ensure that all personnel operating chambers are properly trained and certified as chamber operators (see Figure 7.4).

The NOAA training program for chamber operators includes the following topics:

- Introduction to hyperbaric chambers
- Chamber setup and subsystems
  - Predive and postdive procedures
  - Plumbing
  - Certifying and testing requirements
  - Internal mufflers and filters
  - Controls
  - Life-support and emergency procedures
  - Breathing and communication systems
  - Maintenance procedures
  - Overboard dump and BIBS (Built-in Breathing System)
- Recordkeeping
- Introduction to diving physics
- Decompression theory and decompression tables
- Recompression theory and treatment tables
- Barotrauma
- Examination and handling of patients
- Emergency management of decompression sickness and air embolism

Diver and Support Personnel Training

FIGURE 7.5
Hyperbaric Physician Setting up Intervenous Solution

FIGURE 7.6
Two DMTs Assessing an Injured Diver

- Inside tending procedures
- Chamber medical kit contents and use
- Review of case histories
- Hands-on experience with simulated treatments
- Chamber operation procedures
- Environmental control
- Gas analysis

7.2.8 Equipment Maintenance Training

Training in equipment maintenance is an important element in any diving program. Although fatal diving accident statistics rarely show that equipment failure is the cause of death, equipment malfunction does cause near-misses, lost time, inconvenience, and premature dive termination. Only trained and qualified personnel should perform maintenance and repair of diving equipment, especially regulators, scuba cylinders, and other life-support system components.

NOAA and other organizations have instituted a training and certification program for scuba-cylinder inspectors. The objective of these programs is to ensure that uniform minimum inspection standards are used at diving facilities. Students who successfully complete the course are certified as cylinder inspectors. The issuance of NOAA visual cylinder inspection stickers is tightly controlled.

The cylinder-inspection course covers the following topics:

- Reasons for cylinder inspection
- Frequency of inspection
- Types of inspection
- Analysis of cylinder structure and accessories
- Criteria of inspection (e.g., wall thickness, material and valve specifications)
- Evaluation of cylinder interior and exterior

- Use of inspection equipment (e.g., lights, probes, flushing solutions)
- Detailed inspection sequence
- Inspection of a minimum of ten cylinders under the supervision of an instructor

7.2.9 Diver Medical Technician Training

Although there are obvious advantages to having a qualified hyperbaric physician at a diving site, this is often not practical. As an alternative, a Diving Medical Technician (DMT) trained in the care of diving casualties can be assigned to the site (see Figures 7.5, 7.6). An individual so trained, can respond to emergency medical situations and can also communicate effectively with a physician located far from the diving site.

In the late 1970s, the need for medical technicians specializing in the emergency treatment of diving casualties was recognized. This specialized need arose because existing EMT training programs were heavily oriented toward urban ambulance-hospital emergency systems. The interest in diving medical technicians grew with the development of offshore drilling platforms. Experts determined that the most workable solution to this need was to cross-train working divers as medics, rather than to train medics to treat diving casualties. This choice to train working divers as medical technicians was also driven by economic considerations, since using a diver as a medic made it unnecessary to have an additional person standing by. The National Board of Diving and Hyperbaric Medical Technology (NBDHMT) was founded in 1981 and, by 1985, a number of training organizations were approved to provide DMT training.

NOAA follows the training standards of the NBDHMT for training and certification of DMT instructors and DMTs.

DMT instructors are required to submit course curricula to the NBDHMT for approval as well as evidence of their experience in emergency and diving medicine. NBDHMT approved DMT instructors are authorized to conduct board-sponsored DMT training programs. Upon successful completion of an approved DMT course, students may apply for certification by the NBDHMT. For more information on the DMT program, contact the NBDHMT at 1816 Industrial Blvd., Harvey, Louisiana 70058, Telephone (504) 328-8871.

The NBDHMT requires that DMT students have a background in commercial, scientific, or public safety diving, and have completed medical training prior to taking an approved DMT course. This level of training may be EMT-B, EMT-Paramedic, EMT-ACLS, or other advanced emergency medical skills.

There are two levels of DMT certifications: basic and advanced. Certified basic DMTs are protected under United States Law in the administration of basic life support. DMT-Basic training is based on the EMT-B program and consists of approximately 40 hours of lecture and practical training in the following areas:

- Pathophysiology of DCS and AGE
- Signs & symptoms of DCS and AGE
- Treatment of DCS and AGE
- Diving-related neurological exam
- Chamber safety and operation
- Charting and record keeping

DMT-Advanced training is also based on the EMT-B program, but includes a number of important additions. Because it may be hours or even days before medical help arrives in an emergency diving situation, the advanced DMT must be capable of delivering more support than a medical technician in an urban area. Accordingly, advanced DMTs receive training in parenteral drug administration, intravenous infusion techniques, airway management, pneumothorax stabilization, simple suture techniques, and other special procedures. DMT-Advanced training consists of approximately 60 hours of lecture and practical training. Advanced DMTs are legally allowed to use advanced life-support techniques only when operating under direct or standing orders from an employer and the employer's full-time or retained hyperbaric physician, or when in direct telephone contact with a Divers Alert Network-recognized hyperbaric physician.

All DMTs must be recertified every two years and must attend 24 hours of lectures and serve 24 hours in an ambulance/emergency room situation to maintain their certification.

7.2.10 Hyperbaric Physician Training

A hyperbaric physician is a medical doctor with special training in the treatment of medical problems related to diving and/or elevated atmospheric pressure. Such a physician may be a general practitioner or a specialist in any branch of medicine. In many cases, the personal impetus to become an expert in hyperbaric medicine derives from the fact that the physician is also a diver. Since conventional medical education includes very little training related to diving and hyperbaric medicine, special training in this area is necessary to ensure the diving community has medical personnel knowledgeable in the recognition and treatment of diving-related accidents and injuries. Historically, the U.S. Navy and U.S. Air Force have been the primary sources of expertise and trained personnel in hyperbaric medicine.

Because of the increase in the number of divers, however, the need for physicians trained to treat civilian diving casualties has increased. In response to this need, several organizations offer specialized training. These courses range from a series of lectures to more intensive courses lasting several weeks. The best source of information on the availability of courses in hyperbaric medicine is the Undersea and Hyperbaric Medical Society (UHMS), which is located at 10531 Metropolitan Avenue, Kensington, Maryland 20895 USA or website: http://www.uhms.org.

One of the most respected and comprehensive training courses in hyperbaric medicine in the United States is the program offered by NOAA, UHMS, and the Undersea Research Foundation. Started in 1977 with financial support from the Department of Energy and the cooperation of the U.S. Navy, this program has trained hundreds of physicians to date. The course includes training in the following areas:

- Physical and physiological effects of pressure
- Physiological effects of gases
- Life-support parameters and systems
- Fundamentals of inert gas exchange
- Decompression theory and procedures
- Recompression therapy
- Diagnosis and treatment of diving casualties
- Ear, nose, and throat problems
- Patent foramen ovale
- Hypothermia and hyperthermia in undersea and hyperbaric systems
- High pressure nervous syndrome
- Diving in polluted water
- Tunnel and caisson workers
- Oxygen toxicity
- Saturation diving
- Commercial diving
- Recreational diving
- Recompression chamber operation and safety procedures
- Pressure exposures in recompression chambers
- Orientation dives in commercial diving equipment
- Hyperbaric oxygen therapy

Physicians trained in hyperbaric medicine are an important resource for the diver. Every diver should obtain the name, address, and phone number of the nearest hyperbaric facility and/or hyperbaric physician in his area. In the event of a diving accident related to pressure, such as an arterial gas embolism or decompression sickness, discontinue diving and contact DAN on the emergency hotline (919) 684-8111 before returning to a hyperbaric environment. Hyperbaric chambers are described in Chapter 18, and the treatment of diving casualties is discussed in Appendix V.

7.2.11 Other Training Requirements

In addition to knowing how to use basic scuba diving equipment and techniques, NOAA divers may be called upon to use specialized equipment or procedures in the

FIGURE 7.7
Instructing Diver Trainees

performance of their duties. In such instances, training must be obtained from the NOAA Diving Center or sources approved by the NOAA Diving Program. Examples of types of specialized equipment and procedures requiring special training include:

- Variable-volume dry suits
- Equipment other than standard open-circuit scuba (i.e., surface-supplied, rebreathers, hookah, etc.)
- Special breathing mixtures other than air (i.e., nitrox, trimix, oxygen, heliox, etc.)
- Underwater tools (i.e., pneumatic-powered hand tools, cutting torches)
- In-water decompression techniques
- Special dive-support equipment (i.e., diver-propulsion vehicles, towed sleds, wet-submersibles, wireless communication systems, pinger/sonar locators, underwater video systems, contaminated-water gear, etc.)

The use of variable-volume dry suits, pingers/locators, and nitrox are core subjects included in the NOAA Working Diver Course (see Figure 7.7). Certification in the use of variable-volume dry suits by NOAA requires a minimum of five open-water training dives, resulting in a cumulative bottom time of at least 120 minutes.

Dive Planning

Dive Planning

8.0 GENERAL

Diving with air as the breathing gas is conducted using a variety of life-support equipment. The most frequently used mode is open-circuit scuba, where the diver carries the compressed air supply. Divers can also use umbilical-supplied air with a scuba regulator, and either a full-face mask or a lightweight diving helmet. This section deals with planning for air dives, operational methods of calculating air supply requirements, personnel requirements, and environmental conditions.

8.1 DIVE PLANNING

Careful and thorough planning are the keys to conducting an efficient diving operation and are imperative for diver safety as well. The nature of each dive operation determines the scope of the planning required. The dive plan should take into account the ability of the least qualified diver on the team and be flexible enough to allow for delays and unforeseen problems. It should include at least the following:

- Definition of Objectives
  - A clear statement of the purpose and goals of the operation
- Analysis of Pertinent Data
  - Surface conditions, such as sea state, air temperature, and wind chill factor
  - Underwater conditions, including water temperature, depth, type of bottom, tides and currents, visibility, extent of pollution, and hazards
  - Assistance and emergency information, including location, status, and contact procedures for the nearest recompression chamber, air evacuation team, U.S. Coast Guard, and nearest hospital
- Diving Team Selection
  - Divemaster
  - Medical personnel
  - Tenders/timekeeper
  - Coxswain/surface-support personnel
- Diving Mode Selection
  - Skin (snorkeling)

- Open-circuit scuba
- Rebreathers
- Surface-supplied
- Hookah
- Equipment and Supplies Selection
  - Breathing gas, including a backup supply
  - Dive platform and support equipment, including diver/crew shelter
  - Oxygen resuscitator and first aid kit
  - Backboard
  - Dive flag
  - Diving gear, tools, etc.
  - Water
  - Communications
- Schedule of Operational Tasks for All Phases
  - Transit to the site
  - Assembling dive gear and support equipment
  - Predive briefing
  - Calculating allowable/required bottom time
  - Recovery
  - Cleaning, inspection, repair, and storage of gear
  - Debriefing of divers and support personnel
- Final Preparations and Safety Checks
  - Review of dive plan, its effect, and all safety precautions
  - Outline diving assignments and sequence
  - Complete and post on-site emergency checklist
  - Review diver qualifications and conditions
  - Secure permission from command or boat captain for dive
- Briefing/Debriefing the Diving Team
  - The objective and scope of the operation
  - Conditions in the operating area
  - Diving techniques and equipment to be used
  - Personnel assignments
  - Specific assignments for each diver
  - Anticipated hazards
  - Normal safety precautions
  - Any special considerations
  - Group discussion period to answer questions by members of the diving team

8.1.1 Selection of Diving Equipment

The selection of the proper diving equipment depends on environmental conditions, qualifications of diving personnel, objectives of the operation, and diving procedures to be used. Although most diving is performed at depths less than 130 ft. (39.6 m) and often uses open-circuit scuba, some missions can be accomplished using only skin diving equipment. Other more complex assignments require surface-supplied or closed-circuit systems. Depth and duration of the dive, questions about the type of work to be accomplished (heavy work, light work, silent work), temperature of the water, velocity and nature of current, visibility, logistics, and the diver's experience and capabilities all influence the selection of diving equipment. Detailed descriptions of the various types of diving equipment are presented in Chapter 5. For planning purposes, the following guidelines may be used in selecting the appropriate diving equipment.

Breath-Hold Diving Equipment

Generally Used For:
- Scientific observation and specimen collection in shallow water in areas where more complex equipment is a disadvantage or is not available
- Shallow-water photography
- Scouting for diving sites

Major Advantages:
- Less physical work required to cover large surface areas
- Simplified logistics
- Fewer medical/physiological complications

Major Disadvantages:
- Extremely limited in depth and duration
- Requires diver to develop breath-holding techniques
- Can only be used in good sea conditions

Open-Circuit Scuba

Generally Used For:
- Scientific observation
- Light underwater work and recovery
- Sample collection
- Shallow-water research
- Ship inspection and light repair

Major Advantages:
- Minimum support requirements
- Mobility
- Accessibility and economy of equipment and breathing medium
- Portability
- Reliability

Major Disadvantages:
- Lack of efficient voice communication
- Limited depth and duration

Umbilical-Supplied Systems

Generally Used For:
- Scientific investigation
- Ship repair and inspection
- Salvage
- Long-duration scientific observation and data gathering
- Harsh environments (low visibility, strong currents, polluted water)

Major Advantages:
- Long duration
- Voice communication
- Protection of diver from environment

Major Disadvantages:
- Limited mobility
- Significant support requirements

Closed-Circuit Systems

Generally Used For:
- Observations of long duration

Major Advantages:
- Mixed-gas capability
- No noise or bubbles
- Conservation of breathing medium
- Long duration

Major Disadvantages:
- Complicated maintenance
- Extensive training requirements
- Cost of equipment

8.2 DIVE TEAM ORGANIZATION

8.2.1 Divemaster

NOAA Divemasters have complete responsibility for the safe and efficient conduct of all NOAA diving operations. In order to be a NOAA Divemaster, individuals must be certified NOAA Working Divers, or higher, and have completed the NOAA Divemaster training program. When no divemaster is present, diving should not be conducted. The divemaster's responsibilities include, but are not limited to:

- Overall responsibility for the diving operation
- Safe execution of all diving
- Preparation of a basic plan of operation, including evacuation and accident management plans
- Liaison with other organizations
- Inspection of equipment
- Proper maintenance, repair, and stowage of equipment
- Selection, evaluation, and briefing of divers and other personnel
- Monitoring progress of the operation, and updating requirements as necessary
- Maintaining the diving log
- Monitoring of decompression (when required)
- Coordination of boat operations when divers are in the water

The divemaster is responsible for assigning all divers to an operation and for ensuring that their qualifications are adequate for the requirements of the dive. The divemaster must ensure that all divers are briefed thoroughly about the mission and goals of the operation. Individual responsibilities are assigned to each diver by the divemaster. Where special tools or techniques are to be used, the divemaster must ensure that each diver is familiar with their application.

Training and proficiency dives should be made to ensure safe and efficient operations. During complex operations or those involving a large number of divers, divemasters should perform no diving, but should, instead, devote their efforts entirely to directing the operation.

The divemaster is in charge when divers are in the water during diving operations. Before any change is made to the boat's propulsion system (e.g., change in speed, direction, etc.), the boat captain must consult with the divemaster.

8.2.2 Diving Medical Officer/Diving Medical Technician

When it is not practical to have a qualified diving medical officer on site, a Diving Medical Technician trained in the care of diving casualties shall be assigned. The DMT is trained to respond to emergency medical situations and to communicate effectively with a physician not at the diving site. There are specialized courses available to train Diving Medical Technicians in the care of diving casualties.

In the event that neither a physician nor a trained technician is available, the divemaster should have available the names and phone numbers of at least three diving medical specialists who can be reached for advice in an emergency. Emergency consultation is available from the service centers listed below. Referred to as a "Bends Watch," each of these services is available to provide advice on the treatment of diving casualties:

- Divers Alert Network, Peter B. Bennett Center, 6 West Colony Place, Durham, North Carolina 27705, telephone (919) 684-8111 (ask for the Diving Accident Physician)
- Navy Experimental Diving Unit, Panama City, Florida 32407, telephone (850) 234-4351
- Brooks Air Force Base, San Antonio, Texas 78235, telephone (210) 536-3278 (before 7:00 a.m. and after 4:15 p.m. MST), emergency call (210) 536-3281 (Monday thru Friday between 7:00 a.m. and 4:15 p.m. MST)

All diving personnel shall have access to the phone numbers of these facilities, available at all times, especially if they will be diving in remote areas.

8.2.3 Science Coordinator

On missions where diving is performed in support of scientific programs, a chief scientist may be needed.

The chief scientist is the prime point of contact for all scientific aspects of the program, including scientific equipment, its use, calibration, and maintenance. Working with the divemaster, the chief scientist will brief divers on specific scientific tasks to be completed and supervise the debriefing and sample or data accumulation after a dive.

8.2.4 Divers

Although the divemaster is responsible for the overall diving operation, the diver is responsible for being in proper physical condition, for checking out personal equipment before the dive, and for thoroughly understanding the purpose and the procedures to be used for the dive. The diver is also responsible for refusing to dive when conditions are unsafe, when not in good mental or physical condition, or when diving would violate dictates of their training or applicable standards.

8.2.5 Support Divers and Other Support Personnel

In most diving operations, the number and types of support divers depend on the size of the operation and the type of diving equipment used. Ideally, those surface-support personnel working directly with the diver also should be qualified divers. Using unqualified personnel who do not understand diving techniques and terminology may cause confusion and can be dangerous. Persons not qualified as divers can be used when the need arises, but only after they have demonstrated that they understand procedures to the satisfaction of the divemaster.

8.3 ENVIRONMENTAL CONDITIONS

Environmental conditions at a dive site should be considered when planning a diving operation. Environmental conditions can be divided into surface conditions and underwater conditions. Surface conditions include weather, sea state, and amount of ship traffic. Underwater conditions include depth, bottom type, currents, water temperatures, and visibility. Regional and special diving conditions are discussed in Chapter 12.

8.3.1 Surface Environmental Conditions

When planning a dive, weather conditions are an important factor. Whenever possible, diving operations should be cancelled or delayed during bad weather. Current and historical weather data should be reviewed to determine if conditions are acceptable and are predicted to continue long enough to complete the mission. Continuous marine weather broadcasts are provided by NOAA on the following frequencies depending on the local area:

162.40 MHz, 162.475 MHz, or 162.55 MHz

These broadcasts can be heard in most areas of the United States and require only the purchase of a VHF radio receiver. Weather radios are designed to receive only NOAA radio broadcasts. Regular weather forecasts and

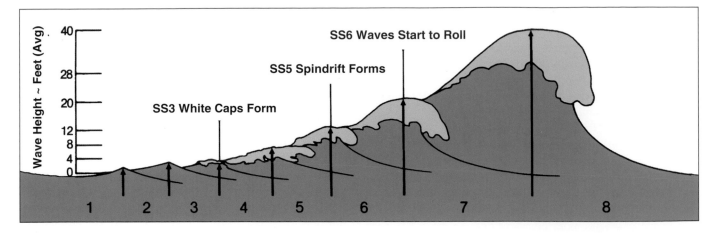

FIGURE 8.1
Sea States

special marine warnings are available any time of the day or night. Although both receivers pick up weather signals from approximately the same distance, the two-way systems have the advantage of transmission quality.

In some cases, surface weather conditions may influence the selection of diving equipment. For instance, even though water temperature may permit the use of standard wetsuits, cold air temperature and wind may dictate that a dry suit (or equivalent) should be worn when diving from an open or unheated platform.

Whenever possible, avoid or limit diving in moderate seas. Sea state limitations depend to a large degree on the type and size of the diving platform. Diving operations may be conducted in rougher seas from properly moored larger platforms such as diving barges, ocean-going ships, or fixed structures. When using self-contained equipment, divers should avoid entering the ocean in heavy seas or surf, as well as high, short-period swell. If bad weather sets in after a diving operation has commenced, all divers should be recalled. Except in an emergency, divers should not attempt scuba or surface-supplied diving in rough seas (see Figure 8.1 and Table 8.1).

Because many diving operations are conducted in harbors, rivers, or major shipping channels, the presence of ship traffic often presents serious problems. At times, it may be necessary to close off the area around the dive site or to limit the movement of ships in the vicinity of the dive site. Ship traffic should be considered during dive planning, and a local "Notice to Mariners" should be issued. Anytime diving operations are to be conducted in the vicinity of other ships, other vessels should be notified by message or signal that diving is taking place. Signal flags, shapes, and lights are shown in Table 8.2.

If the dive operation is to be conducted in the middle of an active fishing ground, divers must assume that people with various levels of experience and competence will be operating small boats in the vicinity and may not be acquainted with the meaning of diving signals.

Take the necessary precautions to ensure that they remain clear of the area.

Surface visibility is important. Reduced visibility may seriously hinder or force postponement of diving operations. If operations are to be conducted in a known fog bank, the diving schedule should allow for probable delays caused by low visibility. The safety of the diver and support crew is the prime consideration in determining whether surface visibility is adequate. For example, in low surface visibility conditions, a surfacing scuba diver might not be able to find the support craft or might be in danger of being struck by surface traffic.

8.3.2 Underwater Environmental Conditions

Dive depth is a basic consideration in the selection of personnel, equipment, and techniques. Depth should be determined as accurately as possible in the planning phases, and dive duration, air requirements, and decompression schedules should be planned accordingly.

The type of bottom affects divers ability to see and work. Mud (silt and clay) bottoms generally are the most limiting because the slightest movement will stir sediment into suspension, restricting visibility. The diver must orient himself so that any current will carry the suspended sediment away from the work area. Also, the diver should develop a mental picture of his surroundings so that his safe ascent to the surface is possible even in conditions of zero visibility.

Sand bottoms usually present little problem because visibility restrictions caused by suspended sediment are less severe than with mud bottoms. In addition, sandy bottoms provide firm footing.

Coral reefs are solid but contain many sharp protrusions. Divers should wear gloves and coveralls or a wetsuit for protection if the operation requires contact with the coral. Learn to identify and avoid corals and other marine organisms that might inflict injury. There's also the concern of not inflicting unnecessary damage to the environment during the process of studying it.

NOAA Diving Manual

TABLE 8.1
Sea State Chart

Sea-General		Wind			Sea						
Sea State	Description	(Beaufort) Wind Force	Description	Range (Knots)	Wind Velocity (Knots)	Wave Height Feet — Average	Wave Height Feet — Average 1/10 Highest	Significant Range of Periods (Seconds)	t (Average Period)	l (Average Wave Length)	Minimum Fetch (Nautical Miles)	Minimum Duration (Hours)
0	Sea like a mirror	U	Calm	Less than 1	0	0	0	–	–	–	–	–
1	Ripples with the appearance of scales are formed, but without foam crests.	1	Light Airs	1–3	2	0.05	0.10	up to 1.2 sec.	0.5	10 in.	5	18 min.
	Small wavelets still, but more pronounced; short crests have a glassy appearance, but do not break.	2	Light Breeze	4–6	5	0.18	0.37	0.4–2.8	1.4	6.7 ft.	8	39 min.
2	Large wavelets, crests begin to break. Foam of glassy appearance. Perhaps scattered white caps.	3	Gentle Breeze	7.10	8.5 / 10	0.6 / 0.88	1.2 / 1.8	0.8–5.0 / 1.0–6.0	2.4 / 2.9	20 / 27	9.8 / 10	1.7 / 2.4
3	Small waves, becoming larger, fairly frequent white caps.	4	Moderate Breeze	11–16	12 / 13.5 / 14 / 16	1.4 / 1.8 / 2.0 / 2.9	2.8 / 3.7 / 4.2 / 5.8	1.0–7.0 / 1.4–7.6 / 1.5–7.8 / 2.0–8.8	3.4 / 3.9 / 4.0 / 4.6	40 / 52 / 59 / 71	18 / 24 / 28 / 40	3.8 / 4.8 / 5.2 / 6.6
4	Moderate waves, taking a more pronounced long form; many white caps are formed. (Chance of some spray.)	5	Fresh Breeze	17–21	18 / 19 / 20	3.8 / 4.3 / 5.0	7.8 / 8.7 / 10	2.5–10.0 / 2.8–1.0.6 / 3.0–11.1	5.1 / 5.4 / 5.7	90 / 95 / 111	55 / 65 / 75	8.3 / 9.2 / 10
5	Large waves begin to form, the white foam crests are more extensive everywhere. (Probably some spray.)	6	Strong Breeze	22–27	22 / 24 / 24.5 / 26	6.4 / 7.9 / 8.2 / 9.6	13 / 16 / 17 / 20	3.4–12.2 / 3.7–13.5 / 3.8–13.6 / 4.0–14.5	6.3 / 6.8 / 7.0 / 7.4	134 / 160 / 164 / 188	100 / 130 / 140 / 180	12 / 14 / 15 / 17
6	Sea heaps up and white foam from breaking waves begins to be blown in streaks along the direction of the wind. (Spindrift begins to be seen.)	7	Moderate Gale	28–33	28 / 30 / 30.5 / 32	11 / 14 / 14 / 16	23 / 28 / 29 / 33	4.5–15.5 / 4.7–16.7 / 4.8–17.0 / 5.0–17.5	7.9 / 8.6 / 8.7 / 9.1	212 / 250 / 258 / 285	230 / 280 / 290 / 340	20 / 23 / 24 / 27

Dive Planning

TABLE 8.1
Sea State Chart (continued)

Sea State Description	(Beaufort) Wind Force	Description	Range (Knots)	Wind Velocity (Knots)	Wave Height Feet — Average	Wave Height Feet — Average 1/10 Highest	Significant Range of Periods (Seconds)	t (Average Period)	l (Average Wave Length)	Minimum Fetch (Nautical Miles)	Minimum Duration (Hours)
7 Moderately high waves of greater length; edges of crests break into spindrift. The foam is blown in well marked streaks along the direction of the wind. Spray affects visibility.	8	Fresh Gale	34–40	34 36 37 38 40	19 21 23 25 28	38 44 46.7 50 58	5.5–18.5 5.8–19.7 6–20.5 6.2–20.8 6.5–21.7	9.7 10.3 10.5 10.7 11.4	322 363 376 392 444	420 500 530 600 710	30 34 37 38 42
8 High waves. Dense streaks of foam along the direction of the wind. Sea begins to roll. Visibility affected.	9	Strong Gale	41–47	42 44 46	31 36 40	64 73 81	7–23 7–24.2 7–25	12.0 12.5 13.1	492 534 590	830 960 1110	47 52 57
Very high waves with long overhanging crests. The resulting foam is in great patches and is blown in dense white streaks along the direction of the wind. On the whole, the surface of the sea takes a white appearance. The rolling of the sea becomes heavy and shock-like. Visibility is affected.	10	Whole Gale	48–55	48 50 51.5 52 54	44 49 52 54 59	90 99 106 110 121	7.5–26 7.5–27 8–28.2 8–28.5 8–29.5	13.8 14.3 14.7 14.8 15.4	650 700 736 750 810	1250 1420 1560 1610 1800	63 69 73 75 81
9 Exceptionally high waves. (Small and medium-sized ships might be lost to view behind the waves for a long time.) The sea is completely covered with long white patches of foam lying along the direction of the wind. Everywhere the edges of the wave crests are blown into froth. Visibility affected.	11	Storm	56–63	56 59.5	64 73	130 148	8.5–31 10–32	16.3 17.0	910 985	2100 2500	88 101
Air filled with foam and spray. Sea completely white with driving spray; visibility very seriously affected.	12	Hurricane	64–71	>64	>80	>164	10–(35)	(18)			

TABLE 8.2
Signal Flags, Shapes, and Lights

Signal	Use	Meaning
White · Red · Red **Sport Diver Flag**	Displayed by civilian divers in the United States. May be used with code flag alpha (flag A), but cannot be used in lieu of flag A. The Coast Guard recommends that the red-and-white diver's flag be exhibited on a float marking the location of the divers.	"Divers are below. Boats should not operate within 100 feet." (Varies in accordance with individual state laws.)
White · Blue **International Code Flag "A"**	Must be displayed by all vessels operating either in international waters or on the navigable waters of the United States that are unable to exhibit three shapes (see last row of this table). Flag A means that the maneuverability of the vessel is restricted.	"My maneuverability is restricted because I have a diver down; keep well clear at slow speed."
"I" — Yellow, Black "R" — Yellow, Red **International Code Flags "I and R"**	Displayed by all vessels in international and foreign waters.	"I am engaged in submarine survey work (underwater operations); keep clear of me and go slow."
International Day Shapes and Lights Shapes/Day: Black Ball, Black Diamond, Black Ball Lights/Night: Red, White, Red	Displayed by all vessels in international and foreign waters engaged in underwater operations.	"This vessel is engaged in underwater operations and is unable to get out of the way of approaching vessels."

Currents must be considered when planning and executing a dive, particularly when using scuba. When a boat is anchored in a current, a buoyed safety line at least 100 ft. (30.5 m) in length should be trailed from the stern during diving operations. If, on entering the water, a diver is swept away from the boat by the current, the diver can use this safety line to keep from being carried down current.

Free-swimming descents should be avoided in currents, unless a means of retrieving the diver is available in case they miss their intended target. Descent from an anchored or fixed platform into water with currents should be made via a down line. A trail line also should be used unless a pickup boat is operating down current so that divers surfacing some distance from the entry point can be retrieved. A knowledge of changing tidal currents may allow the diver to drift down current and to return to the starting point on the return current.

Tidal changes often alter the direction of current and sometimes carry sediment-laden water and cause low visibility within a matter of minutes. Tidal currents may prevent diving at some locations except during slack tides. Because a slack tide may be followed by strong currents, divers should know the tides in the diving area and their effects.

Currents generally decrease in velocity with depth, and, therefore, it may be easier to swim close to the bottom when there are swift surface currents. Current direction may change with depth, however. When there are bottom currents, it is recommended, whenever possible, to start the swim into the current rather than with the current; this facilitates the return to the entry point at the end of the dive with the current. Divers should stay close to the bottom and use rocks (if present) to pull themselves along.

Water temperature has a significant effect on the type of equipment selected and, in some cases, determines the practical duration of the dive. A thermocline is a boundary layer between waters of different temperatures. Although thermoclines do not pose a direct hazard, their presence may affect the selection of diving dress, dive duration, or equipment. Thermoclines occur at various depths, including levels close to the surface and in deep water. Temperature may vary from layer to layer. As much as a 20°F (11C) variation has been recorded between the mixed layer (epilimnion) above the thermocline and the deeper waters (hypolimnion) beneath it.

Underwater visibility depends on time of day, locality, water conditions, season, bottom type, weather, and currents. Frequently, divers will be required to dive in water where visibility is minimal; sometimes, zero. Special precautions are needed. If scuba is used, a buddy line or other reference system, and float are recommended. A convenient way to attach a buddy line is to use a rubber loop that can be slipped on and off the wrist easily; this is preferable to tying a line that cannot be removed rapidly. The line should not slip off so easily, however, that it can be lost inadvertently.

Heavy concentrations of plankton often accumulate at the thermocline, especially during the summer and offshore of the mid-Atlantic states. Divers may find that plankton absorb most of the light at the thermocline and that even though the water below the thermocline is clear, a light is still necessary to see adequately. Thermoclines in clear water diffuse light within the area of greatest temperature change, causing a significant decrease in visibility.

WARNING

DIVERS SHOULD BE EXTREMELY CAUTIOUS AROUND UNDERWATER WRECKS OR OTHER STRUCTURES IN LOW VISIBILITY TO AVOID SWIMMING INADVERTENTLY INTO AN AREA WITH OVERHANGS.

A well-developed sense of touch is extremely important when working in low or zero underwater visibility. The ability to use touch cues when handling tools or instruments in a strange work environment is valuable to a diver in the dark. Rehearsing work functions on the surface while blindfolded will increase proficiency at underwater tasks.

Underwater, low-light-level, closed-circuit television has been used successfully when light levels are reduced, because a television camera "sees" more in these conditions than does the human eye. This is mainly true when the reduced visibility is caused by the absence of light; in cases where the problem is caused by high turbidity, a TV camera does not offer a significant advantage. When the purpose of the dive is inspection or observation and a closed-circuit television system is used, the diver serves essentially as a mobile underwater platform. The monitor is watched by surface support personnel who, in turn, direct diver movements. Underwater television cameras are available that are either hand held or mounted on the diver's helmet.

Often a diver will be required to dive in water that contains either waterborne or sediment-contained contaminants. The health hazards associated with polluted-water diving and the equipment to be used on such dives are described in Chapter 13.

8.4 DIVING SIGNALS
8.4.1 Hand Signals

Hand signals are used to convey basic information. There are various hand signalling systems presently in use. Divers in different parts of the country and the world use different signals or variations of signals to transmit the same message. A set of signals used by NOAA is shown in Figure 8.2 and Table 8.4. The signals consist of hand, instead of finger, motions so divers wearing mittens can also use them. To the extent possible, the signals were derived from those having similar meanings on land. Before the dive, the divemaster should review the signals shown with all of the divers. This review is particularly important when divers from different geographical areas constitute a dive team, or when divers from several organizations are

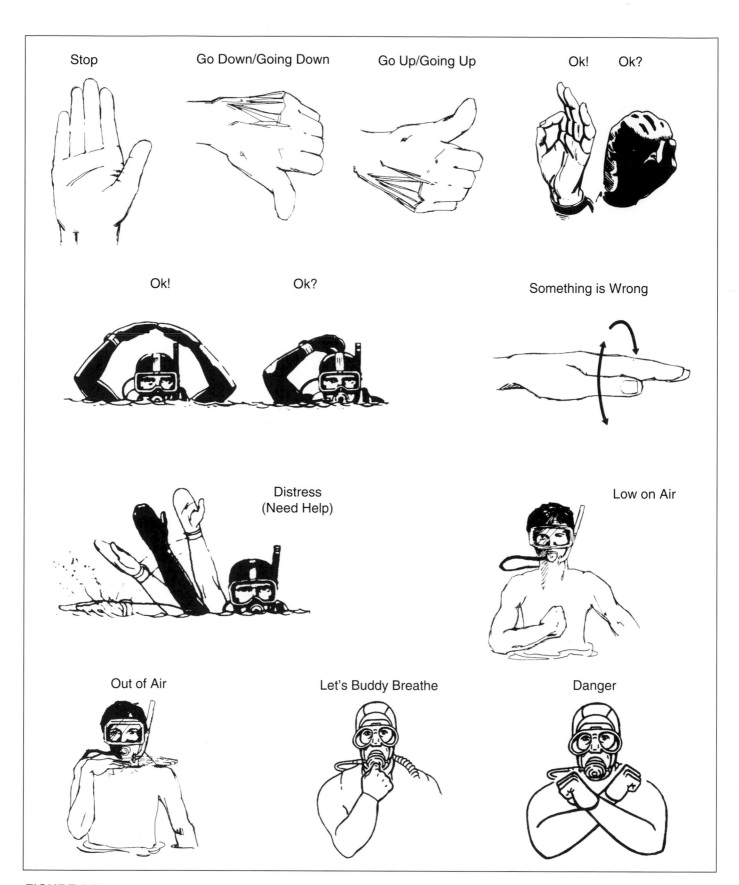

FIGURE 8.2
Hand Signals

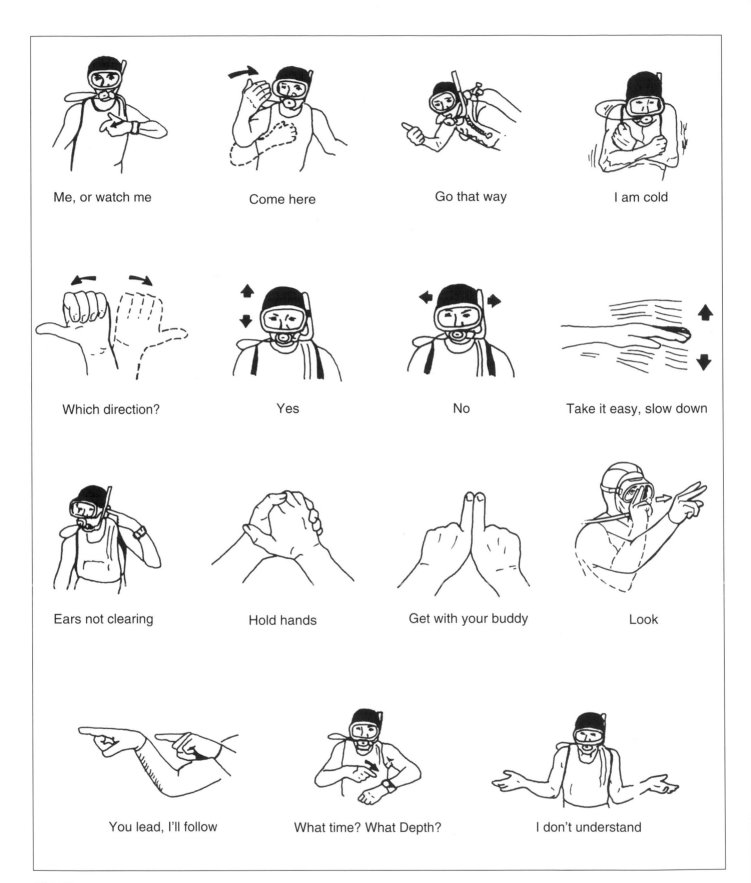

Me, or watch me | Come here | Go that way | I am cold

Which direction? | Yes | No | Take it easy, slow down

Ears not clearing | Hold hands | Get with your buddy | Look

You lead, I'll follow | What time? What Depth? | I don't understand

FIGURE 8.2
Hand Signals (continued)

cooperating in a dive. Signal systems other than hand signals have not been standardized. Whistle blasts, light flashes, cylinder taps, and hand squeezes generally are used for attracting attention and should be reserved for that purpose.

8.4.2 Surface-to-Diver Recall Signals

Unexpected situations often arise that require divers to be called from the water. When voice communication is not available, the following methods should be considered:

- Hammer—rapping four times on a steel hull or metal plate
- Bell—held under water and struck four times
- Hydrophone—underwater speaker or sound beacon
- Strobe—used at night; flashed four times

8.4.3 Line Signals

When using surface-supplied equipment, use line signals either as a backup to voice communications to the surface or as a primary form of communication. When using scuba, divers may use line signals in conditions of restricted visibility, for diver-to-diver communications or to communicate with the surface. Table 8.3 describes line signals commonly employed.

NOTE
Hand or line signals may vary by geographical area or among organizations. Divers should review signals before diving with new buddies or support personnel.

8.4.4 Surface Signals

If a diver needs to attract attention after surfacing and is beyond voice range, the following signaling devices/methods may be used:

- Whistle (diver or scuba air powered)
- Flare
- Flashing strobe
- Flags
- Hand/arm signals
- Throw water into the air

8.5 AIR CONSUMPTION RATES

When considering air consumption rates, three terms need definition:

- **Respiratory Minute Volume (RMV)** is the total volume of air moved in and out of the lungs in one minute.
- **Actual cubic feet (acf)** is the unit of measure that expresses actual gas volume in accordance with the General Gas Law.
- **Standard cubic feet (scf)** is the unit of measure expressing surface equivalent volume, under standard conditions,* for any given actual gas volume.

TABLE 8.3
Line Pull Signals for
Surface-to-Diver Communication

Emergency Signals
2-2-2 Pulls "I am fouled and need the assistance of another diver"
3-3-3 Pulls "I am fouled but can clear myself"
4-4-4 Pulls "Haul me up immediately"
All signals will be answered as given except for emergency signal 4-4-4

From tender to diver
1 Pull "Are you all right?"
When diver is descending, one pull means "stop"
2 Pulls "Going down"
During ascent, 2 pulls mean "You have come up too far, go back down until we stop you"
3 Pulls "Stand by to come up"
4 Pulls "Come up"
2-1 Pulls "I understand," or "Answer the telephone"

From diver to tender
1 Pull "I am all right" or "I am on the bottom"
2 Pulls "Lower" or "Give me slack"
3 Pulls "Take up my slack"
4 Pulls "Haul me up"
2-1 Pulls "I understand" or "Answer the telephone"
3-2 Pulls "More air"
4-3 Pulls "Less air"
Special signals from the diver to the tender should be devised as required by the situation

Searching Signals	Without circling line	With circling line
7 Pulls	"Go on (or off) searching signals"	Same
1 Pull	"Stop and search where you are"	Same
2 Pulls	"Move directly away from the tender if given slack, move toward the tender if strain is taken on the lifeline"	"Move away from the weight"
3 Pulls	"Go to your right"	"Face the weight and go right"
4 Pulls	"Go to your left"	"Face the weight and go left"

*Standard conditions for gases are defined as 32°F (0C), 1 ata pressure, and dry gas.

TABLE 8.4
Hand Signals

Signal	Meaning	Comment
Hand raised, fingers pointed up, palm to receiver	STOP	Transmitted in the same way as a Traffic Policeman's STOP
Thumb extended downward from clenched fist	GO DOWN or GOING DOWN	
Thumb extended upward from clenched fist	GO UP or GOING UP	
Thumb and forefinger making a circle with three remaining fingers extended (if possible)	OK! or OK?	Divers wearing mittens may not be able to extend three remaining fingers distinctly (see various drawings of signal)
Two arms extended overhead with fingertips touching above head to make a large "O" shape	OK! or OK?	A diver with only one free arm may make this signal by extending that arm overhead with fingertips touching top of head to make the "O" shape. Signal is for long-range use
Hand flat, fingers together, palm down, thumb sticking out, then hand rocking back and forth on axis of forearm	SOMETHING IS WRONG	This is the opposite of OK! The signal does not indicate an emergency
Hand waving over head (may also thrash hand on water)	DISTRESS	Indicated immediate aid required
Fist pounding on chest	LOW ON AIR	Indicates air supply is reduced to the quantity agreed upon in predive planning or air pressure is low and has activated reserve valve
Hand slashing or chopping throat	OUT OF AIR	Indicates that signaler cannot breathe
Fingers pointing to mouth	LET'S BUDDY BREATHE	The regulator may be either in or out of the mouth
Clenched fist, arms extended and forming a "X" in front of chest	DANGER	

In computing air consumption rate, the basic determinant is the respiratory minute volume, which is directly related to exertion level and which, because of individual variation in physiological response, differs among divers (Cardone 1982). See Table 8.5. Physiological research has yielded useful estimates of respiratory minute volumes for typical underwater situations likely to be encountered by most divers (U.S. Navy 1985). Table 8.6 shows these estimates. These estimates of respiratory minute volumes apply to any depth and are expressed in terms of actual cubic feet, or liters, per minute (acfm or alpm, respectively).

The consumption rate at depth can be estimated by determining the appropriate respiratory minute volume for the anticipated exertion level and the absolute pressure of the anticipated dive depth. This estimate, expressed in standard cubic feet per minute (scfm), is given by the equation:

$$Cd = RMV (Pa)$$

where

Cd = consumption rate at depth in scfm
RMV = respiratory minute volume in acfm
Pa = absolute pressure (ata) at dive depth

Problem:

Compute the air consumption rate for a 50 ft. (15.2 m) dive requiring moderate work, maximum walking speed, hard bottom.

Solution:

$$Cd = RMV (Pa)$$

RMV = 1.1 acfm (from Table 8.5)
Pa 50/33 + 1 = 2.51 ata
Cd = (1.1 acfm)(2.51 ata) = 2.76 scfm

TABLE 8.5
Respiratory Minute Volume (RMV) at Different Work Rates

Activity		Respiratory Minute Volume	
		Actual liters / min (STP)	Actual cubic ft / min (STP)
LIGHT WORK	SLOW WALKING ON HARD BOTTOM UNDER WATER	12	0.42
	SWIMMING, 0.5 KNOT (SLOW)	16	0.60
MODERATE WORK	SLOW WALKING ON MUD BOTTOM UNDER WATER	20	0.71
	SWIMMING, 0.85 knot (av. speed)	26	0.92
	MAX. WALKING SPEED, HARD BOTTOM U/W	30	1.1
HEAVY WORK	SWIMMING 1.0 KNOT	35	1.2
	MAX. WALKING SPEED, MUD BOTTOM U/W	35	1.2
SEVERE WORK	SWIMMING, 1.2 KNOTS	53	1.9

TABLE 8.6
Air Consumption Table at Depth

SURFACE AIR CONSUMPTION RATE (PSI PER MINUTE)

Surface	10	15	20	25	30	40	50	60	70	80	90	100	120	140	160
15	19	21	24	27	28	33	37	42	46	51	55	60	69	78	87
16	20	23	25	28	30	35	40	44	49	54	59	64	73	83	92
17	22	24	27	30	32	37	42	47	52	57	62	68	78	88	98
18	23	26	28	32	34	39	45	50	55	61	66	72	82	93	104
19	24	27	30	34	36	41	47	53	58	64	70	76	87	98	110
20	26	29	32	36	38	44	50	56	62	68	74	80	92	104	116
21	27	30	33	37	39	46	52	58	65	71	77	84	96	109	121
22	28	31	35	39	41	48	55	61	68	74	81	88	101	114	127
23	29	33	36	41	43	50	57	64	71	78	85	92	105	119	133
24	31	34	38	43	45	52	60	67	74	81	88	96	110	124	139
25	32	36	40	45	47	55	62	70	77	85	92	100	115	130	145
26	33	37	41	46	49	57	65	72	80	88	96	104	119	135	150
27	35	39	43	48	51	59	67	75	83	91	99	108	124	140	156
28	36	40	44	50	53	61	70	78	86	95	103	112	128	145	162
29	37	42	46	52	55	63	72	81	89	98	107	116	133	150	168
30	39	43	48	54	57	66	75	84	93	102	111	120	138	156	174
31	40	45	49	55	58	68	77	86	96	105	114	124	142	161	179
32	41	46	51	57	60	70	80	89	99	108	118	128	147	166	185
33	42	47	52	59	62	72	82	92	102	112	122	132	151	171	191
34	44	49	54	61	64	74	85	95	105	115	125	136	156	176	197
35	45	50	56	63	66	77	87	98	108	119	129	140	161	182	203
36	46	52	57	64	68	79	90	100	111	122	133	144	165	187	208
37	48	53	59	66	70	81	92	103	114	125	136	148	170	192	214
38	49	55	60	68	72	83	95	106	117	129	140	152	174	197	220
39	50	56	62	70	74	85	97	109	120	132	144	156	179	202	226
40	52	58	64	72	76	88	100	112	124	136	148	160	184	208	232

DEPTH (FEET)

8.5.1 Determining Individual Air Utilization Rates

An alternative approach that can be used expresses air utilization rates in terms of pressure drop in pounds per square inch (psi) rather than respiratory minute volume. Keep in mind that usable cylinder pressure is defined as the beginning cylinder pressure minus recommended air reserve (see Table 8.6). This technique allows divers to determine their Surface Air Consumption (SAC) rate which can be used to calculate estimated air consumption rate at any depth. To determine the rate, read the submersible pressure gauges at the beginning and end of a dive to a constant depth. These readings give the information needed to use the simple four-step procedure shown below:

1. Subtract ending psi (as read from the submersible pressure gauge) from the beginning psi to determine the amount of air used during the timed dive (Δ psi).

2. Using the following formula, determine the diver's surface air consumption (SAC) rate:

$$\text{psi per minute on the surface (SAC)} = \frac{\Delta \text{psi/time (min)}}{(\text{depth in ft} + 33)/33}$$

3. Find the psi per minute on the surface on the left side of the Air Consumption Table (Table 8.6) that is closest to the estimated psi per minute. Read across to the desired depth, which will give the estimated air consumption rate at depth.

4. To estimate how many minutes a cylinder of air will last at that depth, divide the number of usable psi in the cylinder (as shown on the submersible pressure gauge minus a reserve amount) by the psi per minute used at that depth.

Problem:

A diver swims a distance at 30 ft. (9.1 m) in ten minutes; the submersible pressure gauge reads 2,350 psi at the start and 2,050 at the end of the timed dive, showing that a total of 300 psi was consumed. What is the diver's SAC?

The basic equation is:

$$SAC = \frac{\Delta \text{psi/time (min)}}{(\text{depth in ft} + 33)/33}$$

Solution:

$$\frac{300 \text{ (psi)} \div 10 \text{ (mins)}}{(30 \text{ (depth)} + 33)/33} = \frac{30}{(63/33)} = \frac{30}{1.9} = 15.7 \text{ psi/min}$$

The diver would consume 15.7 psi per minute at the surface. Knowing the consumption rate at the surface allows the diver to use Table 8.6 to find the rate at any depth. The same information can be determined by multiplying the SAC figure times the depth of the planned dive in atmospheres absolute.

It is important to understand that individuals vary somewhat from day to day in their air consumption rates, and these calculations should thus be considered estimates only (Cardone 1982).

Problem:

Convert SAC to cubic feet per minute (CFM) by multiplying the diver's SAC times the cylinder constant (k) using formula:

$$RMV = SAC \times k$$

Solution:

The diver in this example had a SAC of 15.71 psi/min using a scuba cylinder with a k factor of 0.0267 ft³/psi.

$$RMV = SAC \times k$$
$$RMV = 15.71 \text{ psi/min} \times 0.0267 \text{ ft}^3/\text{psi}$$
$$RMV = 0.42 \text{ ft}^3/\text{min}$$

8.5.2 Scuba Duration

Knowing the probable duration of the scuba air supply is vital to proper dive planning. With scuba, the duration of the available air supply is directly dependent on the consumption rate. Scuba air supply duration can be estimated using the equation:

$$Da = \frac{Va}{Cd}$$

where

   Da = duration in minutes
   Va = available volume in scf
   Cd = consumption at depth in scfm

The available volume depends on the type (rated volume and rated pressure) and number of cylinders used, the gauge pressure measured, and the recommended minimum cylinder pressure. Consumption rate depends on the depth and the exertion level of the dive.

The "standard 80 cubic foot" aluminum cylinder has an internal volume of 0.399 cubic feet (11.3 liters) at one atmosphere. At its rated pressure of 3,000 psig, the cylinder contains a deliverable volume of 81.85 cubic feet (2,317.7 liters).

For a given scuba cylinder, the ratio of rated volume to rated pressure is a constant ($k = V_r/P_r$), meaning that a constant volume of air is delivered for each unit of cylinder pressure drop. Mathematically, this results in a linear relationship between gauge pressure and deliverable volume. Figure 8.3 shows this relationship for a 71.2 ft³ (2,016 liters) steel cylinder and an 80 ft³ (2,266 liters) aluminum cylinder. Deliverable volumes at any gauge pressure for these two cylinder types can be read directly from Figure 8.3, or they can be individually computed using the equation:

$$Vd = Pg \times k$$

where

Vd = deliverable volume in scf
Pg = gauge pressure in psig
k = cylinder constant

This equation can be used for any type of cylinder; see Table 8.7 for the appropriate cylinder constant.

For planning purposes, the available volume of air is the difference between the deliverable volume at a given cylinder pressure and the recommended minimum cylinder pressure. The recommended minimum cylinder pressures for the two most commonly used scuba cylinder types are shown in Table 8.8. The available volume of air in the diver's supply can be determined by the equation:

$$Va = N(Pg - Pm)k$$

where

Va = available volume in scf
N = number of cylinders
Pg = gauge pressure in psig
Pm = recommended minimum pressure in psig
k = cylinder constant

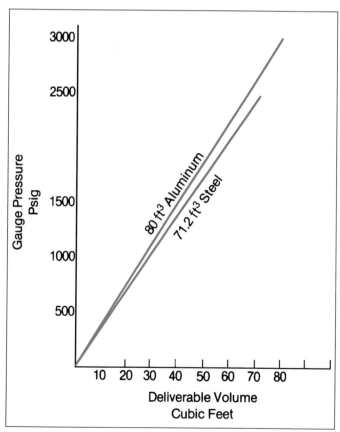

FIGURE 8.3
Deliverable Volumes at Various Gauge Pressures

For planning purposes, estimates of cylinder duration are based on available air volumes rather than deliverable air volumes.

Problem:

Estimate the duration of a set of twin 80 ft³ (2,318 liters) aluminum cylinders charged to 2,400 psig for a 70 ft. (21.3 m) dive for a diver with a RMV of 0.6 acfm.

Solution:

The basic equation for duration is:

$$Da = \frac{Va}{Cd}$$

where

Da = duration in minutes
Va = available volume in scf
Cd = consumption rate at depth in scfm

Step 1:
Determine Va using:

$$
\begin{aligned}
Va &= N(Pg - Pm)k \\
Va &= 2(2,400 \text{ psig} - 600 \text{ psig}) \, (0.0266 \text{ scf/psig}) \\
&= 2(1,800 \text{ psig}) \, (0.0266 \text{ scf/psig}) \\
&= 95.76 \text{ scf}
\end{aligned}
$$

Step 2:
Determine Cd using:

$$Cd = RMV (Pa)$$

where

RMV = respiratory minute volume in acfm
Pa = absolute pressure at dive depth

$$
\begin{aligned}
Cd &= 0.6 \ \text{acfm} \left(\frac{70}{33} + 1 \right) \\
&= 1.87 \text{ acfm}
\end{aligned}
$$

TABLE 8.7
Cylinder Constants

Rated Volume (scf)	Working Pressure (psig)	Rated Pressure (psig)	Cylinder Constant
Aluminum			
90	3000	3000	0.0300
80	3000	3000	0.0266
71.2	3000	3000	0.0237
50.0	3000	3000	0.0166
Steel			
100	2400	2640	0.0378
71.2	2250	2475	0.0288
52.8	1800	1980	0.0267
50.0	2250	2475	0.0202
42.0	1880	2068	0.0203
38.0	1800	1980	0.0192

Dive Planning

TABLE 8.8
Scuba Cylinder Pressure Data

Cylinder Type	Rated Pressure (psig)	Working Pressure (psig)	Reserve Pressure (psig)	Recommended Minimum Pressure (psig)
Steel 72	2475	2250	500	430
Aluminum 80	3000	3000	500	600

TABLE 8.9
Estimated Duration of 80 Ft^3 Aluminum Cylinder

Depth	ata	0.25 acfm At Rest*	0.7 acfm Light Work*	1.1 acfm Moderate Work*	1.5 acfm Heavy Work*	2.2 acfm Severe Work*
0	1.0	256.4	91.6	58.3	42.7	29.1
33	2.0	128.2	45.8	29.2	21.4	14.6
66	3.0	85.5	30.5	19.4	14.2	9.7
99	4.0	64.1	22.9	14.6	10.7	7.3
132	5.0	51.3	18.3	11.7	8.5	5.8
165	6.0	42.7	15.3	9.7	7.1	4.8

* Values are minutes.

Step 3:
Solve the basic equation for Da:

$$Da = \frac{Va}{Cd}$$

$$= \frac{95.76 \text{ scf}}{1.87 \text{ scfm}}$$

$$= 51.2 \text{ minutes}$$

Table 8.9 shows estimates of the duration of a single aluminum 80 ft^3 (2,318 l) cylinder at five exertion levels for various depths. These estimated durations are computed on the basis of an available air volume of 64.1 ft^3 (Va = 3,000 psig - 600 psig) (0.0267 ft^3/psig).

8.5.3 Scuba Air Requirements

Total air requirements should be estimated when planning scuba operations. Factors that influence the total air requirement are depth of the dive, anticipated bottom time, normal ascent time at 30 ft/min (9.1 m/min), any required stage decompression time, and consumption rate at depth. For dives in which direct ascent to the surface at 30 ft/min (9.1 m/min) is allowable, the total air requirement can be estimated using the equation:

$$TAR = tdt (Cd)$$

where
TAR = total air requirement in scf
tdt = total dive time in minutes
(bottom time plus ascent time at 30 ft/min)
Cd = consumption rate at depth in scfm

Problem 1:
Estimate the total air requirements for a 30-minute dive to 60 ft. (18.3 m) for a diver with a RMV of .92 acfm.

Solution:
Step 1:
Determine tdt. Total dive time is defined as the sum of the bottom time and normal ascent time at 30 ft/min (9.1 m/min):

$$tdt = 30 + 2 = 32 \text{ mins}$$

Step 2:
Determine Cd using the equation:

$$Cd = RMV (Pa)$$
$$RMV = 0.92 \text{ acfm}$$
$$Pa = \frac{60}{33} + 1 = 2.81 \text{ ata}$$
$$Cd = (0.92 \text{ acfm}) (2.81 \text{ ata})$$
$$= 2.59 \text{ scfm}$$

Step 3:
Determine TAR using the equation:

$$TAR = tdt\,(Cd)$$
$$= (32\ mins)\ (2.59\ acfm)$$
$$= 82.88\ scf$$

For dives in which stage decompression will be necessary, the total air requirement can be estimated using the equation:

$$TAR = Cd\,(BT + AT) + Cd_1T_1 + Cd_2T_2 + Cd_3T_3\ (etc.)$$

where Cd_1T_1, Cd_2T_2, are the air consumption rates and times at the respective decompression stops.

Problem 2:
Estimate the total air requirement for an 80-minute dive to 60 ft. (18.3 m) for a diver with a RMV of 0.6 acfm.

Solution:
Step 1:
Determine Cd and Cd_1 using the equation:

$$Cd = RMV\,(Pa)$$
$$= (0.6\ acfm)\ (2.8\ ata)$$
$$= 1.68\ scfm$$

Step 2:
Determine the total time for the dive, ascent, and decompression stops. For the dive and ascent to the surface, add the bottom time (BT) and the ascent time (AT) (to the nearest whole minute) at 30 ft/min (9.1 m/min).

$$BT + AT = 80 + 2 = 82\ mins$$

This dive requires a 10-ft. decompression stop. At an ascent rate of 30 ft/min, it will take two minutes to ascend from 60 ft. (18.3 m) to the surface.

The time required for decompression at 10 ft. (3 m) is 7 minutes, according to the USN Standard Air Decompression Table for a dive to 60 ft. for 80 minutes.

$$Cd_1 = 0.6 \left(\frac{10}{33} + 1 \right) = 0.78\ scfm$$

(Assume same RMV on decompression stop.)

Step 3:
Determine TAR using the equation for this case:

$$TAR = Cd\,(BT + AT) + Cd_1T_1$$
$$= (1.68\ scfm)\ (62\ mins) + (0.78\ scfm)\ (7\ mins)$$
$$= 104.2 + 5.5 = 109.7\ scf$$

Computation of these estimates during predive planning is useful to decide whether changes in assigned tasks, task planning, etc. are necessary to ensure that the dive can be conducted with the available air supply. However, positioning an auxiliary cylinder at the decompression stop is considered a safer practice than relying on calculations of the available air supply.

8.5.4 Surface-Supplied Air Requirements

Estimations of air supply requirements and duration of air supplies for surface-supplied divers are the same as those of scuba divers except when free-flow or free-flow/demand breathing systems are used; in these cases, the flow, in actual cubic feet per minute is used (in all calculations) instead of RMV (see Table 8.10). Also, the minimum bank pressure must be calculated to be equal to 220 psig plus the absolute pressure of the dive (expressed in psia).

Problem:
Estimate the air requirements for a 90 ft. (27.4 m) dive for 70 minutes with a demand/free-flow helmet. This dive requires decompression stops of seven minutes at 20 ft. (6.1 m) and 30 minutes at 10 ft. (3 m).

Solution:

$$TAR = Cd\,(BT + AT) + Cd_1T_1 + Cd_2T_2$$

where
 TAR = Total Air Requirement
  Cd = Consumption rate at depth (scfm)
  BT = Bottom time (mins)
  AT = Ascent time
  Pa = Pressure in ata

Step 1:
Determine Cd, Cd_1, Cd_2:

$$Cd = flow \times Pa$$
$$= (1.5\ acfm)(3.73\ ata) = 5.6\ scfm$$
$$Cd_1 = (1.5\ acfm)(1.61\ ata) = 2.4\ scfm$$
$$Cd_2 = (1.5\ acfm)(1.30\ ata) = 2.0\ scfm$$

Step 2:
$$TAR = Cd\,(BT + AT) + Cd_1\,T_1$$
$$= 5.6\ scf\,(70 + 3\ mins)$$
$$+ 2.4\ scf\,(7\ mins) + 2.0\ scf\,(30\ mins)$$
$$= 409\ scf + 17\ scf + 60\ scf$$
$$= 486\ scf$$

Cylinder constants for large high-pressure air/gas storage systems are determined in the same fashion as those for scuba cylinders, i.e., rated volume/rated pressure = k.

The procedure for determining available volume of air is also the same as for scuba. For example,

$$Va = N(Pg - Pm)\,k$$

Dive Planning

where
> V_a = available volume (scf)
> N = number of cylinders
> P_g = gauge pressure (psig)
> P_m = minimum reserve pressure (psig)
> k = cylinder constant

NOTE

If cylinder banks are used as a back-up to a compressor supply, the bank must be manifolded with the primary source so that an immediate switch from primary to secondary air is possible (see Figure 6.10).

Problem:

Determine the number of high-pressure air cylinders required to supply the air for the above dive (486 scf) if the rated volume equals 240 scf, rated pressure equals 2,400 psi, and beginning pressure equals 2,000 psi, using a minimum reserve pressure of 220 psi.

Solution:

Step 1:

How much air could be delivered from each cylinder?

$$V_a = N(P_g - P_m)k$$

$$k = \frac{240 \text{ scf}}{2,400 \text{ psi}} = 0.1 \text{ scf/psi}$$

$$P_m = 220 \text{ psi} + \left(\frac{90 + 33}{33}\right) \times 14.7 = 275 \text{ psi}$$

$$V_a = 1(2,000 - 275) \times 0.1$$
$$V_a = 172.5 \text{ scf/cylinder}$$

TABLE 8.10
Flow-Rate Requirements for
Surface-Supplied Equipment

Equipment Type	Flow Rate
Demand/freeflow	1.5 acfm
Free flow	6.0 acfm

NOTE: Significant variations in these values can occur, depending on the flow-valve set by the diver. Therefore, these values are minimum estimates.

Step 2:

How many cylinders would be required in the bank to supply the required amount of gas?

$$N = \frac{\text{vol. required}}{\text{vol/cyl}} = \frac{486 \text{ scf}}{172.5 \text{ scf/cyl}} = 2.8 \text{ or 3 cylinders}$$

NOTE

Calculations for gas supply requirements or scuba duration are for planning purposes only. The diver and tender must continuously monitor the gas supply throughout the dive.

Procedures for Scientific Dives

9

Procedures for Scientific Dives

9

9.0 GENERAL

Scientific diving has been widely performed since 1952 to observe underwater phenomena and to acquire scientific data. The use of diving has led to significant discoveries in the marine sciences. Placing the trained scientific eye under water is, in some instances, the only method that can be used to make valid observations and take accurate measurements. Scientific diving is occasionally also used to compliment submersible work, remote sensing, or surface ship surveys. Regardless of the project or the role that diving plays, marine research using diving as a tool has been important in understanding the ocean, its organisms, and its dynamic processes.

The scientific diver's working time is measured in minutes and seconds instead of hours (unless the saturation diving mode is used). The cost-effectiveness of scientific diving therefore depends on how efficiently scientists can perform their tasks. Efficiency under water requires good tools, reliable instruments that can be set up rapidly, and a well-thought-out dive plan. In the scientific community there is a fair amount of standardization of the equipment and methods used to perform research under water, yet in many cases, the instruments, tools, and techniques are improvised and advanced by individual scientists to meet the specific needs of the project. Through necessity, scientists who work under water must be proficient in their scientific discipline and as divers, inventors, and mechanics.

The purpose of this section is to describe some of the procedures used in scientific diving projects. These methods are intended as guidelines and should not be construed as the best or only way to perform underwater surveys or to gather data.

9.1 SITE LOCATION

To study any region carefully, it is necessary to plot on a base map the precise location from which data will be obtained (Holmes and McIntyre 1971). This is especially important if there is a need to return to the same location several times during a study. The scale of the base map depends on the detail of the study and the size of the area to be investigated. In geological mapping of the seafloor, a scale of 1 inch to 200 yards (2.5 cm to 183 m) is adequate for reconnaissance surveys. In archeological and some biological studies, a much more detailed base map, with a scale of 1 inch to 30 ft. (2.5 cm to 9 m), may be required. If existing charts do not contain the proper scale or sounding density, it may be necessary to use echosounder survey techniques to construct a bathymetric map of the bottom before starting the dive. Gross features can be delineated and bottom time used more efficiently if the diver has a good bathymetric map of the study area. If published topographic charts are inadequate, the sounding plotted on original survey boat sheets of a region (made by NOAA's National Ocean Service) can be contoured and will usually provide adequate bathymetric control for regional dive surveys. If the survey plan requires bottom traverses, it will be necessary to provide some means of locating the position of the diver's samples and observations on the base chart.

Techniques used to search for underwater sites fall into two general categories: visual search techniques and electronic search techniques. Divers must verify the results from the latter after the specific site has been located. Hand-held dive sonars or vessel fathometers are useful in determining water depth prior to initiating the dive.

9.1.1 Traditional Methods

Most scientific diving is carried out in nearshore waters where surface markers (fixed by divers over strategic points of the work site) may be surveyed from the shore using well-established land techniques, or from the sea using bearings from a magnetic gyro compass, Loran C, or Global Positioning System (GPS) coordinates.

At the other extreme in terms of complexity is a site relocation method used successfully by many scientists; in this method, landmarks on shore are sighted visually, without the use of artificial aids. Basically, once the site is located and the boat anchored over it, scientists take a number of sightings of various nearshore landmarks (such as trees, hills, and power poles) and align them visually so that when the site is revisited in the future, the landmarks

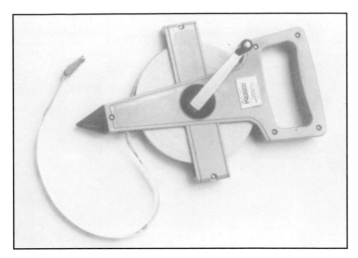

FIGURE 9.1
Fiberglass Measuring Tape

line up the same way. The only drawbacks to this method are that the work must be conducted near shore and the visibility must be good in order for the shoreside landmarks to be seen. When several lineups have been established and proven, they should be diagrammed in a notebook that is kept in the boat. These methods allow divers to establish the locations of major features in the working area accurately. If buoys are used for location, particular care is needed to ensure that the surface floats used during the initial survey be directly over the weights anchoring them to the selected underwater features; the best plan is to wait for a calm day at slack tide. Recognize that surface buoys may disappear at any time or may be repositioned over time.

In some cases it may be advisable to leave the seabed anchors in place after the floats have been cut away. If this is contemplated, the anchors should be constructed to rise slightly above the surrounding terrain so that they may be seen easily on the next visit. Small floats made of syntactic foam may be tied to the anchors below the surface with a short length of polypropylene line to aid in relocation. However, because biological fouling soon obscures any structure used, inexpensive, highly painted markers generally are cost effective. Floating markers, even if they are small and badly fouled, usually can be seen if they protrude a short distance above the surrounding substrate. Once the transect, grid, or other system of markers is established and fixed relative to permanent features on the shore, the diver should record the position of selected features within the working area in relation to the buoy array.

9.1.2 Electronic Methods

Satellite positioning equipment can position a scientist within a few meters of the desired location. GPS is readily available on most research vessels and low-cost handheld models exist for use in small boats. Loran equipment, although considered less accurate, can provide a general back-up.

9.2 UNDERWATER SURVEYS

A variety of methods are used to survey the underwater landscape; these include direct and indirect surveying methods. Direct methods require scientific divers to measure distances themselves, while indirect approaches use photography, underwater sonars, or acoustic means to determine distances, angles, and other features.

9.2.1 Direct Survey Methods

With the exception of long distance visual triangulation, many of the methods used in land surveying can also be used under water. A review of a standard college text on surveying will provide the scientist with some basic surveying concepts. Woods and Lythgoe (1971) give an excellent description and review of methods that have been devised specifically for work under water. In most diving surveys, distances are measured with a calibrated line or tape (the use of an expensive steel tape is unnecessary). Most ropes or lines will stretch and should be used only if the measurement error resulting from their use is acceptable. A fiberglass or vinyl measuring tape that has a minimum of stretch and is marked in feet and inches on one side and meters and centimeters on the other is commercially available (see Figure 9.1). If exact calibration is a concern, a steel tape is recommended. These tapes come in an open plastic frame with a large metal crank to wind the tape back onto the reel. They are ideal for most purposes and require no maintenance except for a freshwater rinse and lubrication of the metal crank. No matter what measuring method is used, especially if long distances are involved, the lines or tapes must be kept on reels to prevent tangling or fouling. In clear waters, optical instruments can and have been used to measure both distance (range finder) and angles between objects for triangulation.

The first step in surveying any area is to establish a horizontal and vertical control network of accurately located stations (benchmarks) in the region to be mapped. Horizontal control is the framework on which a map of features (topography, biology, or geology) is to be constructed; such a control provides a means of locating the detail that makes up the map. Vertical control gives the relief of the region and may be obtained by stadia distance and vertical angles or by spirit leveling. Comparing differences in depth using a diver's depth gauge or dive computer can make rough measurements, but measurements may be inaccurate if the irregular sea surface is used as the reference point.

One method that has worked well in areas of high relief where echosounders are not satisfactory is described below (Hubbard pers. com.):

1. Along a convenient axis (North/South, East/West, etc.), place two permanent poles, one on either end of the survey area. Stretch a line between them to serve as a fixed centerline.

2. At intervals prescribed by the size of the area and the irregularity of the terrain, place additional poles identified by some sort of coding. The use of a taut-line buoy may make the sites more visible.

3. Lay out the lines perpendicular to the centerline by using the centerline poles as tie-in points. If a permanent grid is desired, place poles at intervals comparable to those between the centerline poles. If the terrain has significant relief, horizontal changes can be measured by moving away from each centerline pole, as shown in Figure 9.2.

4. In areas of significant terrain, it is difficult to maintain an accurate horizontal measurement. Knowing the difference in depth (y) between the two points (from calibrated depth gauges or dive computers) and the measured slope distance (z), the horizontal distance (x) can be calculated easily using the formula:

$$x = \sqrt{z^2 - y^2}$$

When using a depth gauge or dive computer over a period of hours, tidal fluctuations must be taken into account. A reference staff or benchmark should be established at the beginning of the survey, and readings should be taken at the reference during the period over which depths are being measured in the survey area. By going in

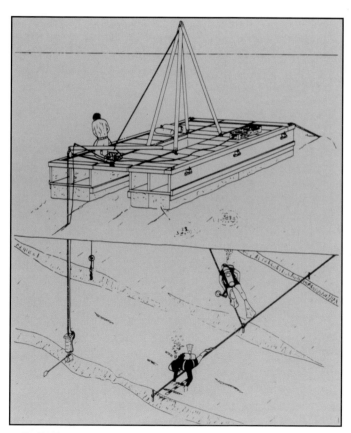

FIGURE 9.2
Bottom Survey in High-Relief Terrain

Procedures for Scientific Dives

either direction from each of the centerline poles, a complete bathymetric survey can be conducted with considerable accuracy.

Determining the two end points of the centerline by the methods described in Section 9.1.1 locates the site with respect to surface positions.

The detail to appear on the finished map is located by moving from the control networks (benchmarks) to the features to appear on the finished map. On some surveys, the control is located first and the detail is located in a separate operation after the control survey has been completed. On other surveys, the control and the detail are located at the same time. The former method is preferable if long-term observations are to be carried out in an area, for example, around a permanently established habitat. The latter technique is preferable if reconnaissance studies are being made in remote regions or in areas that will not require the re-establishment of stations.

9.2.2 Indirect Survey Methods

Indirect underwater surveying involves techniques that do not require the diver physically to measure angles and distances using tapes, lines, protractors, etc. Indirect underwater surveying currently is performed using either photographic or acoustic methods.

9.2.2.1 Underwater Photographic Survey

Reliable measurements can be obtained by means of photogrammetry. Though not as advanced under water as on land, this is a tool being used with increasing frequency. The possibility of poor visibility is a drawback in its application.

Photographs with appropriate scales in the field of view can be useful in measuring objects on the seafloor and in recording changes with time. Subtle changes often recorded on sequentially obtained exposures of the same area or station can be missed if memory alone is relied on.

Photographic transects are useful in showing variations over an area or changes that occur with depth. In the past, little true photogrammetry was conducted because of the technical difficulties in producing corrected lenses and maintaining altitude and constant depth and because of the high relative relief of many bottom features. However, improved techniques have been developed that allow increased accuracy and flexibility. Recent computerization of photogrammetric plotting equipment has reduced technical difficulties considerably.

To improve mapping for detailed archeological studies, photographic towers may be used (Bass 1964, 1968; Ryan and Bass 1962). The progress of excavation in each area can be recorded with grid photographs taken through a hole in the top of the tower. This approach produces a consistent series of photos that can be compared easily when analyzing the data. The tower ensures that each photo is taken from the same point of view, thus simplifying follow-on dark room procedures. A photograph is, however, a perspective view that requires correction for the difference in scale and position of objects.

A series of stereophoto-pair photographs may be taken of sites for three-dimensional viewing under a stereo-viewer. More important, it is possible to make three-dimensional measurements from such photos. Digital photography is a significant time-saving technology that allows images to be downloaded and analyzed by computer.

The use of wide-angle lenses, such as a 15 mm lens, permits detailed photographs to be taken that cover large areas from short distances. Bass (pers. com.) recommends that rigid metal grids be constructed and divided into 6.6 ft. (2 m) squares. These squares are then excavated and photographed individually.

9.2.2.2 Underwater Acoustic Surveys

Another method for conducting bottom surveys involves the use of sonic location beacons (pingers). These devices are particularly useful if there is a need to return to specific locations. The system may consist of small (the size of a roll of quarters) pingers, that can be placed at the site of interest, and a diver-held receiver. The pingers can be purchased with specific frequencies to differentiate between sites.

More complex and costly systems can be used to avoid some of the problems that arise with these simpler methods. A high-frequency sonic profiler (see Figure 9.3) can rapidly measure underwater sites (Dingler et al. 1977). Such a device, however, requires electronic and technical support beyond the means of most researchers. If cost is not a factor, the sonic profiling method is by far the best way of obtaining an accurate representation of small-scale subaqueous bed forms.

Acoustic Grid

This method of underwater survey is the acoustic equivalent of direct trilateration. In its simplest form, three acoustic transponders are placed at known positions on the sea bottom. These transponders are interrogated sequentially from within their established grid, and the time delay before each response occurs is measured and recorded. If the velocity of sound in seawater is known for that area and time, the delay in time can be related to the distance between the interrogator and each of the transponders.

Transponders are implanted and their positions are determined using direct underwater survey methods. The interrogator is a small, hand-held directional sonar device that has a digital readout of the time delay. The diver, positioned above the point to be surveyed, aims visually at the first transponder and takes three readings. The process is repeated for the other two transponders. Ideally, the data are sent to the surface via an underwater communications link. In the absence of this equipment, the data should be recorded on a writing slate attached directly to the interrogator. The accuracy of this system can be increased significantly by using four or five transponders.

Because so many variables affect the velocity of sound in seawater, errors in measurement can have a significant effect on the resulting mathematical analysis. For example,

FIGURE 9.3
High-Frequency Sonic Profiler

sound velocity measurements in very shallow water can be affected seriously by errors in recording temperature. Accurate results depend on keeping the salinity and temperature measurement errors small enough so that the errors in velocity are below the inherent equipment-introduced errors.

More sophisticated versions of the acoustic grid survey system are available, and many of these read out range directly. Although more convenient to use, system inaccuracy may still be created by variability in speed of sound. Compact sound velocimeters are now available that permit *in situ* measurements to be used immediately as survey system correctors.

The acoustic grid is particularly valuable when a site is visited repeatedly to measure features that vary over time, such as the motion of sand waves. Another advantage of this system is its internal completeness. If the geodetic location of the site is not important and only relative position and motion within the site are to be measured, the acoustic grid is an appropriate method. It is also possible to relate the grid measurements to a geodetic map at a later time.

Phase Measurement

Unlike the acoustic grid method, which determines the position of an object relative to a fixed network of transponders, phase measurement systems are contained within the support ship except for a single mobile transponder. Three receiving elements are located precisely with respect to each other on the underside of the support craft; they are usually attached to a mast extended over the side of the craft. A diver places a transponder on the object whose position is to be determined, and an interrogator located on the ship queries the transponder. A phase analysis is performed by the receiver on the return signal, which is displayed as deflection angle and line-of-sight range to the object with respect to the receiver element mast. The only variable is velocity of sound, which must be determined by the method discussed previously.

Small transponders are available that can be strapped to a scuba cylinder so that the position of the diver can be monitored continuously by personnel in the support craft. When continuous communication is available, the diver can be directed through a geodetically fixed survey pattern if the ship's position is known accurately.

This system is suited to applications where a large area must be surveyed or where there are only one or two sites of interest. Although the system has the disadvantage of requiring a surface-support platform, its inherent mobility and flexibility are distinct advantages except in situations where job requirements make the acoustic grid or one of the direct methods preferable.

Under certain conditions, the phase measurement system can be more fully utilized if diver-towing techniques are employed. In this case the position of the diver relative to the support ship must be monitored continuously, which increases both ease of operation and accuracy. Combining the phase measurement system with a good diver-to-surface communication system results in an excellent survey procedure.

9.3 UNDERWATER RECORDING METHODS

The simplest and most widely used method for recording data under water involves using a graphite pencil on a white, double-sided plastic board. These records are sufficiently permanent to withstand normal handling during a dive. Since most divers use abbreviations and shorthand in recording observations and species names, the notes should be transcribed as soon as possible. Wax pencils are usually not advisable because they become brittle and break in cold water, and pencil holders have metal parts that will corrode. Ordinary pencil lead can be cleaned off easily with scouring powder, but wax smears and often must be removed with a solvent. Mechanical pencils are also not recommended, since the metal parts will soon corrode. The best writing instrument is an off-the-shelf, readily available plastic pencil that uses bits of sharpened lead encased in plastic butts.

Slates can be made multipurpose by adding compasses, rulers, or inclinometers (see Figure 9.4). Because there is a risk of misinterpreting the often erratic notes made under water, a list of tasks to be undertaken and the form to be used for all measurements should be developed before the dive. These lists and tables may be inscribed on the plastic pads. In some cases, it is desirable to retain the original records (this is particularly important in the case of archeological drawings, for instance); drawings are then made with wax crayons on waterproof paper attached to the plastic board by screws or rubber bands. There are several types of underwater paper, including a fluorescent orange paper. Standard recording formats can be duplicated ahead of time to facilitate recording during a dive.

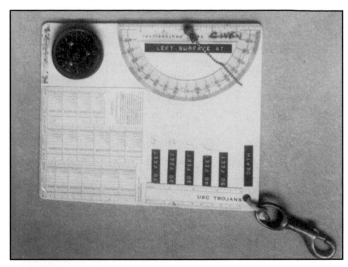

FIGURE 9.4
Multipurpose Slate

A simple and inexpensive technique for underwater data sheets is to prepare the sheets on regular typing paper and then have each sheet laminated in the same way that drivers' licenses and other important identification are preserved.

Where precise measurements are to be made, it is good practice for two observers to take independent measurements and to check them with each other for agreement before returning to the surface. If there is disagreement, the measurements should be repeated.

Tape recording is another useful, although somewhat specialized, method of documenting data under water. The most satisfactory and reliable system includes a cassette tape recorder as part of the hardwire two-way communication system used in umbilical diving; the alternative is a self-contained unit carried by a diver in the scuba mode. The position of the microphone and the way in which it is waterproofed is critical in determining the usefulness of an underwater tape recorder.

Low-cost commercial systems feature a special mouthpiece unit into which a microphone is built-in and to which the scuba regulator is attached. Coupled with this is a transponder and bone-phone (transmission of sounds through the bones in the skull). These systems allow diver-to-diver and diver-to-surface communications.

NOTE
The critical factor in a voice-recording system for data gathering is the ability of the diver to speak and enunciate clearly enough to be understood and transcribed accurately.

The best equipment configuration is a full-face mask, equipped with a microphone that is located away from the immediate mouth area. This position diminishes breathing noise and increases voice fidelity by picking up sounds from the resonating chamber formed by the mask rather than from the high-sibilant area in front of the lips. Several commercially available masks are equipped with demand regulators that can be used with standard scuba cylinders or with an umbilical supply. When an umbilical is used, most diver-tender communications systems can be wired to accept a tape recorder so that both diver and topside conversations can be recorded. Regardless of the unit selected, divers should practice using the system in shallow water until they can produce intelligible transcriptions routinely.

To optimize topside recording fidelity and minimize distortion and interference, cassette tapes of the highest quality should be used. Cassette tapes of 120 minutes of recording time are generally sufficient for most scuba missions. Maintenance is especially important for tape recorders in a salt-wet environment; special care must be taken at sea (checking O-rings, seals) to prevent corrosion.

9.4 BIOLOGICAL SURVEYS

Biological surveys generally have the same requirements and involve the same techniques as those described in Section 9.2; however, some specific aspects should be mentioned. Biological surveys are used for many purposes, including determining the environmental impact of placing man-made objects on the seafloor and assessing the effects of ocean dumping on marine resources. In most marine environments, it is not possible to evaluate the impact of man-made changes without performing special baseline surveys designed to obtain specific information about the biota and the physical environment. To be meaningful, these studies must be made before structures are emplaced on the seafloor or material is discharged into the area. When baseline information cannot be obtained before the natural undersea environment has been altered by human actions, biological surveys can be used to determine the incremental impacts of subsequent activities.

Baseline studies must be designed so that they can be monitored at prescribed intervals. Control stations placed outside the area being studied are necessary to provide data on environmental changes occurring naturally (e.g., seasonal effects).

The techniques of underwater biological surveying involve establishing a standardized methodology to make the results of the survey quantitatively meaningful and ecologically acceptable. This is done by choosing stations at specific depth intervals along a transect line and dropping an anchor at each station to serve as the center of a circle of study. Quantitative observations are then made within the circle; general bottom topography and biological features of the areas beyond the circles are also noted.

The amount of bottom area covered does not need to be the same for every station; water clarity and the complexity of the biota will affect the size of the study circle. The poorer the visibility, the more restricted the amount of bottom that can be surveyed. In West Coast regions and for sand stations having a limited macrobiota, a 10.2 ft. (3.1 m) line is generally used to produce a 323 ft^2 (30 m^2) area of study. In rocky areas, where the biota is more diverse, a 7.2 ft. (2.2 m) line can be used to define the radius of the circle of study. In addition, using tools such as plankton nets and bottom cores, scientists can estimate the number of plants and animals, take quantitative samples of life forms, and take photographs of general bottom conditions and of each quadrat.

Environmental factors that must be considered when surveying the establishment and growth of underwater communities include exposure to wave or swell action, type and slope of substrata, water temperature, dissolved oxygen and nutrient content, and extent of grazing. Variations in the intensity and spectral composition of light under water also have a significant effect on plant communities, but it is often difficult to obtain accurate light measurements. The illumination at or within a given plant community can be obtained with accuracy only by actual *in situ* light measurements; photographic light meters are not satisfactory for this purpose. Underwater spectroradiometers are probably the most effective means of measuring light in the sea and have been used in studies of photosynthesis and calcification rates of corals.

Most underwater investigators have used transect or simple quadrant methods for the analysis of benthic communities. A reasonable description of the change in biota relative to depth and other factors can be obtained by measuring the area of cover along a strip or band transect. Accurate quantitative data on standing crops can best be obtained by collecting the entire ground cover from a quadrat and sorting this into component species in the laboratory for subsequent analysis. Macrophotography and close-up digital video imaging are also viable tools for this purpose.

9.4.1 Estimating Population Densities

When estimating the biological content or density of a given region, it is necessary to take surface area into account. An irregular surface can greatly increase the area; to the extent that the surfaces sampled depart from the horizontal, area will be underestimated, which will cause density to be overstated. This bias becomes particularly important as the scale of the surface variation approaches the scale of the distribution being measured. Dahl (1973) describes a technique designed to quantify the estimation of irregular surfaces in the marine environment. Briefly, the technique consists of making some simple height, frequency, and surface length measurements and then applying a surface index formula to determine the surface area. The technique has been applied to coral reefs, benthic algal substrata, thalassa, sand and rubble zones, reef crests, and patch reefs.

A simple method for estimating populations of sessile organisms is described by Salsman and Tolbert (1965), who used it to survey and collect sand dollars (see Figure 9.5). At each location sampled, the authors spent 10–15 minutes making observations, taking photographs, and sampling population density. To facilitate counting and to

FIGURE 9.5
Counting Square for Determining Sand Dollar Density

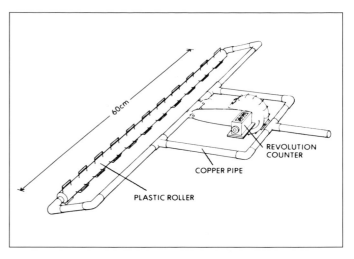

FIGURE 9.6
Diver-Operated Fishrake

ensure a random sample, a counting cell was constructed by bending an aluminum rod into a square 11.8 inches (30 cm) long on each side. Inexpensive counting squares also can be constructed using PVC tubing. As the divers approached the seafloor, they released the square, allowing it to fall to the bottom. The organisms within this square were counted and collected for later size determination; this procedure was then repeated at least two more times at each location sampled. The same method can be used to take a random sample of any sessile organism.

A device used for surveying epifauna is the diver-operated fishrake (see Figure 9.6). It has been used to obtain information on the small-scale distribution patterns and estimates of population densities of demersal fishes and invertebrates. The apparatus consists of a metal tubular frame fitted with a handle, a roller of rigid PVC tubing into which stainless steel wire "staples" are fixed, and an odometer made of a plastic tracking wheel and removable direct-drive revolution counter. It is pushed along the bottom by a diver who makes visual counts, size estimates, and other observations on animals that occur within the path traversed by the roller.

In some underwater situations involving observations of animal behavior, it is necessary to remain a reasonable distance from the subject so as not to interfere with normal behavior. Emery (1968) developed an underwater telescope for such situations by housing a rifle scope in PVC tubing with acrylic plastic ends. The underwater scope described by this author functioned satisfactorily at depths as great as 180 ft. (55 m). An underwater telephoto camera lens was used during the Tektite II experiments to avoid interfering with animal behavior (VanDerwalker and Littlehales 1971). Closed-circuit underwater breathing apparatus (rebreathers) can also be used for almost bubble-free behavioral observations. Video cameras on tripods allow the scientific diver to back away from animals that are difficult to approach (i.e., garden eel beds).

At the other end of the magnification continuum is an underwater magnifying system (Pratt 1976). This device, referred to as the Pratt Macrosnooper, has a magnification power of seven and permits the diver to study marine organisms too small to be comfortably observed with the naked eye. It is a three-element lens system designed specifically for use under water and consists of three lenses with appropriate spacers inserted into a 2-inch (5-cm) plastic pipe (see Figure 9.7). Holes are then drilled through the housing and the spacers to permit the entry of water for equalization at depth. When in use, the Macrosnooper is held against the mask faceplate. It should be cleaned and rinsed carefully, along with other diving equipment, after each use. Soap, mineral, or fungus deposits may be removed by an overnight soak in either diluted bleach, vinegar, or laundry detergent.

9.5 BIOLOGICAL SAMPLING

Although a discussion of research design for a sampling program is outside the scope of this manual, careful attention should be given to the implementation of sampling methods. Chapters on the design of sampling programs can be found in Holmes and Macintyre (1971) and planning of experiments in Cox (1958). As Fager and his colleagues have noted, underwater operations have several advantages over sampling from the surface for ecological studies involving quantitative sampling or observations of behavior (Fager et al. 1966). Probably the most important practical advantage is the ability to observe the sampling apparatus in operation, to make estimates of its effectiveness, and to improve the design or procedure *in situ*. In some cases, such as with small demersal fish, underwater sampling is considerably more effective than from the surface. Direct observation gives one a feeling for the types and magnitudes of the errors associated with the sampling and allows one to decide whether the sampling site is unusual or representative of a larger area. With the less

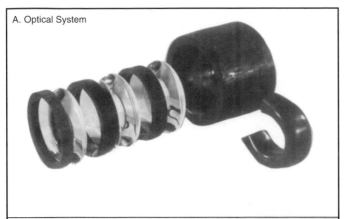

A. Optical System

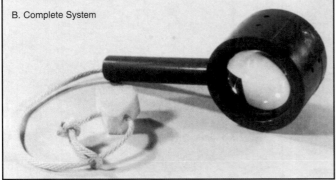

B. Complete System

FIGURE 9.7
Underwater Magnification System

FIGURE 9.8
Hensen Egg Nets Mounted on Propulsion Vehicle

common species, it may be particularly important to be able to make repeated population estimates without imposing unnatural mortality by the removal of individuals.

Because a diver using marker buoys, stakes, or pingers can return repeatedly to the same location, changes in both environment and the biota can be followed for considerable periods. In addition, changes can be imposed on the environment by selective removal of species, by alteration of substrata, and so on, and the effects of these experimental manipulations can be followed in detail.

9.5.1 Plankton Sampling

Planktonic organisms that live within 3.2 ft. (1 m) of the bottom can be sampled with a skid-mounted multilevel net apparatus that is pushed by a diver over a predetermined distance. Hand-operated butterfly valves are used to isolate the collection bottles located in the cod end of the net.

Plankton sampling nets 11.8 inches (30 cm) in diameter, with a mesh size of 0.08–0.12 inch (2–3 mm), are used to collect plankton selectively in reef areas. Air-filled bottles also can be inverted in appropriate areas to suck up plankton and water samples.

Several methods of sampling plankton have been developed. Ennis (1972) has employed a method using two diver propulsion vehicles to which a 19.7 inches (50 cm) plankton net was attached. A similar method was

used during a saturation dive in the Hydrolab habitat at Grand Bahama Island, when two 3.2 ft. (1 m) long Hensen egg nets were mounted on a single diver propulsion vehicle that was operated at a speed of about 2–3 knots (1–1.5m) (see Figure 9.8).

At the end of every run, each net should be washed separately and the sample should be concentrated into the cod end by holding the net up inside a trapped bubble of air under a plastic hemisphere having an 18 inches (45.8 cm) radius. The cod end should then be removed, and the contents of the net should be poured into a glass jar. The jar should be filled, except for a small volume at the top, with filtered seawater, and plastic wrap should be placed over the top of the jar to trap a small bubble of air. The jar is then removed from the hemisphere and carried to a work area. The work area should be deeper than the hemisphere so that hydrostatic pressure will help to keep the air bubble from escaping. A syringe filled with formalin is then pushed through the plastic wrap, the jar is capped, immediately secured, and labeled. When this procedure is carried out properly, there is no sample loss. Before a net is reused, it should be turned inside out and backflushed.

9.5.2 Benthic Organism Sampling

Quantitative sampling of the epifauna can be accomplished by counting the animals within a randomly located circle or square quadrat. A circle template, fixed center rod, and movable arm may be constructed of brass, with the center rod and movable arm marked with grooves at 0.4 inch (1 cm) intervals (see Figure 9.9). The position of an animal within the circle can be defined by three numbers: the distance along the center rod from a standard end; the distance from the center rod along the movable arm; and the half of the circle within which the animal was observed. To study details of the distribution pattern of individuals of sedentary species, the "distance of the nearest neighbor" technique can be used. This method involves preassembling a large, lightweight metal or PVC square

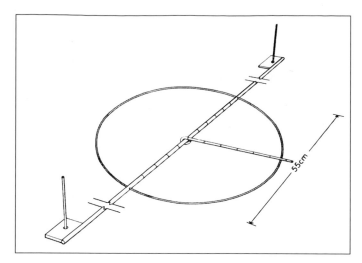

FIGURE 9.9
Circle Template

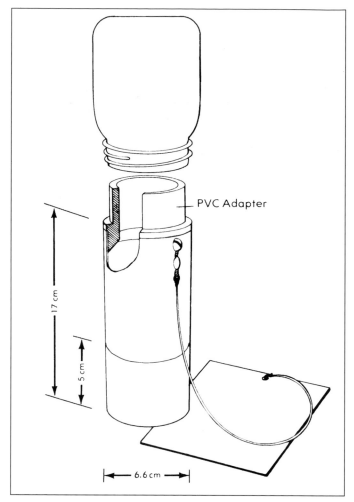

FIGURE 9.10
Coring Device with Widemouth Container

and dropping it at the appropriate location. Within the square, divers place short brass or plastic rods with fabric flags on them at predetermined positions in relation to the individuals of the species being examined. After the positions of all individuals have been marked, distances to nearest neighbors are measured, and reflexives are counted.

Samples of the substrate and infauna can be collected with no loss of sediment or organisms by using a simple coring device with a widemouth sample container (a jar) attached to the top (see Figure 9.10). The corer is pushed a given distance, e.g., 2 inches (5 cm), into the sand, tipped slightly, and an aluminum plate is slipped under it through the sand. The apparatus is inverted and the sediment is allowed to settle into the jar. Once all sediment and organisms are inside the jar, the coring attachment is removed and the jar is capped.

Another simple soft-bottom sampling device, especially good for small infauna and meiofauna, is a thin-walled coring tube of transparent plastic, the diameter of which is based on a predetermined sample designed to gather the desired substrate and organisms most efficiently. Most organisms obtained by this type of device will be found in the top 3.9 to 4.7 inches (10 to 12 cm) of the sample. For ease of handling, the tube should be at least 11.8 inches (30 cm) long and sealed with rubber corks, one of which has a small hole drilled through it. With both corks off, the tube should be rotated carefully into the sand to the desired depth, and the cork with the small hole should then be used to cap the tube. While gripping the tube for removal, the scientist's thumb should be held over the hole to create a suction that keeps the sediment from falling out. When the tube is free of the sediment, the bottom cork should be inserted. Samples accurate to any depth can be taken with this device, and depth lines can be marked on the outside of the tube. To remove the core, the scientist places a finger over the hole in the top cork, removes the bottom cork, and allows the plug to fall out. To remove discrete segments of the core, the plug may be

pushed out the end and cut into desired lengths or quick-frozen in dry ice immediately upon surfacing (to prevent migration of animals) and later cut with a hacksaw.

A multilevel corer is used for studying the depth distribution of infauna. This corer samples an area of about one inch square (2.54 cm²) to a depth of 2.4 inches (6 cm). The corer consists of a square brass box fitted with a funnel adapter at the top to accept widemouth sample containers. The front side of the corer is slotted to permit thin metal slide plates to be inserted to separate the sample into five separate layers, which can then be transferred under water to separate sample containers.

Another coring device for obtaining quantitative samples of the infauna is a square stainless steel box with handles and a screen covering one end (see Figure 9.11). Its rugged construction allows scientists to forcibly penetrate hard substrates, such as sand or vegetated bottoms, as well as softer sediments. The sampler, currently in use by NOAA/NMFS divers, can obtain a 0.17 square ft. (1/64 m²) sample to a depth of 9.1 inches (23 cm). After the corer is pushed into the substrate to the desired depth, one side of the device is excavated and the device is tilted over, after

Procedures for Scientific Dives

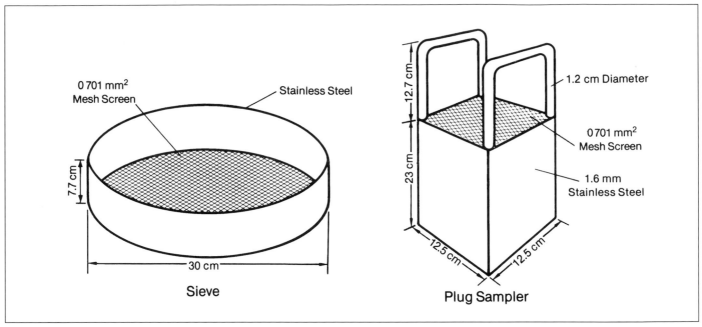

FIGURE 9.11
Infauna Sampling Box

which the corer and sample are pulled free. To prevent any sample loss, the diver holds the open end of the corer against his body while ascending. The contents are then placed in a sieve of appropriate mesh size (see Figure 9.11), washed free of most of the sediments, and the residue containing the organisms is placed in jars of preservative. A red dye (usually Rose Bengal) is added to the preservative to facilitate the sorting and identification process.

A multiple disk sampling apparatus for collecting epibenthic organisms has been developed by NOAA/NMFS divers. Each collecting unit consists of a disk 9.7 inches (24.6 cm) in diameter with a surface area of 0.54 square ft. (1/20 m²). Various kinds of material have been used in the construction of the disks (wood, glass, steel, rubber, cement). Rubber and cement generally are superior substrates for most sessile invertebrates. The disks are wired to a galvanized pipe frame placed on the bottom by divers. Individual disks are removed at intervals by divers who place a canvas collecting bag over the disk and cut the wire holding the disk to the frame. This procedure minimizes the loss of motile organisms. Individual bags containing the disks are filled with a narcotic solution (7.5 percent magnesium chloride mixed 1:1 with seawater) for one hour and the disks are then preserved in a ten percent formalin solution. Wiring disks rather than bolting them simplifies the operation and eliminates the problem of corroded fastenings. The experiment design (collecting frequency, substrate material to be tested, or other epifaunal survey requirements) dictates the number of disks to be used. Because of the large size of disks, the epifaunal assemblages that are collected by this method are more typical of those found on natural substrates. However, only a portion of each disk is examined and enumerated.

Some knowledge of geological techniques is helpful when sampling. For example, on rocky substrates it is important to know how to measure angles of inclines on overhangs or shelves, because this angle influences the orientation of many organisms (see Section 9.10.1). Similarly, knowing the composition of the rock is important in determining whether organisms can bore into it or merely attach to it, and the rock's composition will also determine its resistance to erosion over long periods. In soft bottoms, it is useful to describe sediment grain size and bottom configurations; determinations of grain size, chemical composition, and other physical characteristics are best done by scientists equipped to handle these tasks. Situations vary, and it may be helpful to consult geologists for recommendations on where to obtain the appropriate geological data.

9.5.3 Airlift Sampling

An airlift is a sampling device that consists of a long plastic pipe equipped with a device to supply air at the lower end. The airlift carries sediment and organisms to the top of the pipe in a stream of air and water, so that they can then be emptied into a mesh bag of a certain size. Large areas of soft bottom can be collected in a very short time with this device, and the samples can be screened through the bag in the process. When used with a diver-held scraping device, an airlift is also useful on hard substrates, especially to collect the small organisms that tend to escape when attempts are made to "scrape and grab."

9.5.4 Midwater Sampling

Although plastic bags have been used successfully to sample swarming copepods and small aspirators have been used to sample the protozoan *Noctiluca*, animals in midwater

FIGURE 9.12
Using a Container to Collect Zooplankton

must generally be collected using other techniques. It is difficult to sample even very small animals, such as the copepod *Oithona*, without disturbing them. Although small, copepods swim rapidly for short distances and readily dodge water bottles, nets, or aspirators. If nets must be used, they are deployed most effectively by divers swimming the nets by hand or by guiding diver-propulsion units to which the nets are attached (see Figure 9.8). No objects should obstruct the mouth of the net, because even monofilament bridles cause zooplankton to avoid nets.

The diver can easily capture larger, less motile zooplankton that range from several millimeters to a few centimeters in size, such as the gelatinous *medusae, ctenophores, salps, pteropods,* and *chaetognaths,* etc., by permitting the animals to swim into a hand-held container, preferably of clear plastic or glass (see Figure 9.12). This is the preferred method of data collection for all aspects of laboratory marine research, because it is the way to collect these delicate animals without the damage that normally occurs even with the most carefully handled net.

9.5.5 Estimating Density of Planktonic Aggregations

For many kinds of organisms, density and distribution can be determined photographically without disturbing the aggregation. The use of an 80 mm lens and extension tubes provides a small measured field of view of 11.8–15.7 inches (30–40 cm) from the camera. Depth of field varies systematically with f-stop (see Chapter 5). Instructions for some underwater cameras provide these calculations, but investigators can make them for their own cameras by photographing underwater targets at a series of known distances in front of the camera with different f-stops and determining the depth of field in the resulting photographs. Density of organisms such as copepods within swarms is determined by counting all of the animals in focus in the photograph, i.e., within a known volume determined by

area of field times depth of field. When the number of organisms in focus is large, density can be estimated by measuring the distance from one individual to its closest in-focus neighbor for each of some 20 individuals within a single plane. These distances are averaged and the density of the aggregation is estimated by entering this average into the formula for dose packing of spheres or of isohedronie arrays. Use of the formula:

$$1,000,000 \text{ cm}^3/0.589 \times (\text{average nearest neighbor's distance in cm})^3 = \text{Number of organisms per meter}^3$$

is preferred because isohedrons pack symmetrically along all three axis, whereas spheres do not.

Density measurements for animals sparsely distributed can be obtained more easily by swimming line transects between tethered buoys while counting the number of animals that pass through a grid of selected size (see Figure 9.13). Divers also may drift slowly on a tether with the ship and estimate densities by measuring the drift rate and counting the number of organisms that pass through a grid in a specified time.

Replicated measurements permit the application of most normal statistical procedures used in quantitative ecology. Some tests are of questionable validity because many statistics depend on presupposed patterns of normal distributions, patterns that may not apply to three-dimensional arrays. Nonetheless, many of the sampling procedures used by the terrestrial ecologist may be applied to underwater sampling. Biological oceanographers now use these new techniques frequently.

9.6 SHELLFISH STUDIES

The use of diving as a research tool to study lobsters, crabs, oysters, scallops, bivalves, snails, and other types of shellfish has increased as a result of both the commercial importance of these living resources and the difficulty of sampling these organisms effectively with conventional surface-oriented equipment. In general, shellfish studies have been directed toward the ecology of these organisms, their behavior in relation to sampling gear, the efficiency of sampling gear, and the potential effects of conventional sampling techniques on the bottom environment and its fauna. Historically, more underwater studies have been conducted on the American lobster of the New England coast (*Homarus*) than on any other single species of shellfish. In addition, extensive studies have been done in Florida and California on the spiny lobster (*Panulirus*) (Herrnkind and Engle 1977; Marx and Herrnkind 1985).

Direct *in situ* observation of lobsters is the most effective way to study lobster ecology and behavior. Comparative studies of lobsters in the laboratory-aquarium environment have shown that their behavior is altered significantly when they are in captivity. In addition, lobsters less than one-half pound (0.22 kg) in size generally are not

FIGURE 9.13
Plexiglas Reference Frame in Midwater

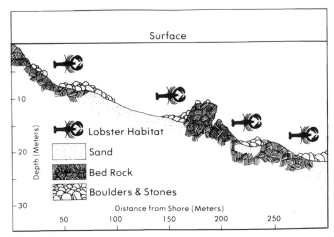

FIGURE 9.14
Benthic Environment of the American Lobster

nocturnally active in their natural environment, but are active at night in the confines of an aquarium tank. American lobsters spend most of their first three years of life in a labyrinth of tunnels projecting as many as three ft. (0.9 m) into the boulder-rock substrate of the ocean bottom (see Figure 9.14). Juvenile spiny lobster settle out and spend their initial years in surfgrass on the high-energy coast of California. Replicating both of these environments in an aquarium is difficult.

In the Chesapeake Bay, ecological studies of the commercially important blue crab (*Callinectes sapidus*) have been successful through the use of ultrasonic biotelemetry (Wolcott and Hines 1996). This powerful new research tool, in conjunction with scuba, affords researchers the opportunity to analyze movement, habitat utilization, physiological function and behavior of marine organisms.

9.6.1 Collecting Techniques

Many shellfish (crabs, lobsters, and clams) inhabit tunnels and burrows on the bottom. Others (scallops, oysters, and abalone) live in beds and reefs or creep across the seafloor and rocks. When collecting shellfish, divers should always wear gloves and carry catch bags. Gloves should also be used when handling specimens topside.

Lobsters inhabit burrows, tunnels, and caves in shallow coastal waters and in ocean depths that are beyond the range of surface-supplied diving. Those that are more than one-half pound in size are nocturnal in their movements; during daylight hours, they remain in their homes. When picked up, spiny lobsters and slipper lobsters should be held by the back; if grabbed around the abdomen (tail), the tail can cut a diver's fingers. The American lobster can be collected easily by grabbing it from the back, behind the claws. Lobsters can also be grabbed by their ripper claws and held for 1–2 seconds; if held longer, their crusher claws will be brought into action. Banding or pegging before the animal is put in a catch bag should inactivate lobster claws; this will prevent animals from crushing each other. Lobsters frequently will autotomize (drop) antennae and claws when handled; American lobsters do this especially during the winter months, when water temperatures range between 28.5° and 34.0°F (−1.94 and 1.1C).

The conventional method for commercial harvesting of the spiny and New England clawed lobster is the wire or wooden trap. Divers should assess the efficiency and design of this gear before using it, bearing in mind that spiny lobsters move much faster than American lobsters and are much more sensitive to being disturbed.

Commercial crabs are found in waters ranging from shallow estuaries to ocean depths that are beyond conventional diving limits. Gloved divers can catch them easily by hand with short-handled scoop nets and tongs. Caution should always be exercised when collecting crabs because they can pinch with their claws; depending on the size and species, such injuries can vary from a cut finger (Blue crab or Dungeness crab) to a broken finger (Stone crab or Alaskan King crab).

Blue crabs live in the shallow, temperate waters of estuaries, bays, and sounds in the Gulf of Mexico and Atlantic Ocean. When frightened, they will burrow quickly

NOAA Diving Manual

into the bottom or swim away with great speed. These fast-swimming, pugnacious crabs can be collected easily with a short-handled scoop net. They can be found partially buried and lying around shells and rocks or walking along the bottom.

Stone crabs inhabit burrows, depressions, and shell houses in the coastal waters along the South Atlantic and Gulf of Mexico states. An 18 inch (45.7 cm) pair of tongs is useful to extricate them from burrows and shell houses. Their claws can be brought into action quickly and can easily crush fingers, so they should be handled carefully. Stone crabs should be handled by their rear legs.

The Alaskan King crab lives in the cold waters of the North Pacific Ocean and the Bering and Okhotsk seas. Young crabs (2–3 years old) inhabit shallow waters in large "pods" of 2,000–3,000 individuals and migrate to deeper water as they mature (Drew 1988). Mature crabs (males range up to 6.6 ft. [2 m] and 22 lbs. [10 kg]) migrate seasonally between deep and shallow water to spawn. As the crabs walk across the bottom, divers can collect them by grabbing them cautiously from behind.

Dungeness crabs are found in shallow inshore, estuarine, and offshore waters from southern California to Alaska and the Aleutian Islands; they live in waters that are up to 328 ft. (100 m) deep. These large crabs, which range up to 9.4 inches (24 cm) across the back and up to 2.2 lbs. (1 kg) in weight, can move quickly, occasionally even faster than a diver can swim. Individual crabs can be captured from behind and placed in a mesh bag, if this is done cautiously.

Oysters inhabit relatively shallow waters in estuaries, bays, and sounds in the Gulf of Mexico, off the Atlantic coast states, and in the North Pacific. They occur individually, in clusters attached to rocks and pilings, and together in large beds of thousands of individuals. These sedentary shellfish are easy to collect by hand. A pry bar can be used to collect samples that are attached. Oysters can temporarily be piled loosely on the bottom during harvesting.

Scallops live in bays, sounds, and ocean bottoms in depths up to 328 ft. (100 m). Density varies from one or two individual scallops to dozens per square meter. They are collected easily by hand or scoop net. Loose piles of scallops should not be left on the bottom because the scallops may swim away. Getting one's fingers stuck in the shell of a live scallop is painful.

Abalone inhabit rocky coasts from Alaska to southern California. They are nocturnal foragers of algae and rest during the day at their "homespots" on a rock. An iron pry bar can be used to "pop" them loose, and they can sometimes be pried loose quite easily with a quick motion. Care must be taken to avoid cutting the animal's foot since these organisms are hemophiliacs.

9.7 TAGGING AND MARKING TECHNIQUES

Tagging aquatic organisms can provide information on many aspects of underwater life, including coastal migration, nearshore to offshore movement, seasonal distribution, and growth rate. Because tagging can damage the animal, the value of the information gained from a return should be carefully considered.

There are two different methods of tagging marine organisms: The animal can either be tagged *in situ* or be captured and brought to the surface for tagging. Figure 9.15 shows an electroshocking grid used to collect fish for tagging. Although more traumatic for the organism, the latter method has the advantage of allowing the animal to be weighed, measured, and examined in detail before release. Methods are available to take measurements *in situ* under water. Although body dimensions can be measured under water, a satisfactory method for determining body mass (weight) has not been developed.

Ebert (1964) described a fish-tagging gun that inserted a standard dart tag into bottom-dwelling fishes and which could be adjusted to account for skin or scale thickness. More recently, the plastic "T" tag, originally designed for marking clothing (see Figure 9.16), has been used. The needle of the tagging gun is placed against the organism and the tag is inserted into the body tissue. With practice, the depth of tag penetration can be controlled by the tagger. Because this particular gun has many metal parts, it must be washed and oiled carefully following inversion to avoid corrosion.

Lobsters have been tagged within their natural environments with short-term (lost at shedding) and long-term (retained at shedding) tags and marks. Lobster dens may be marked with styrofoam floats, numbered carefully to note specific locations. Color-coded tags may be inserted into the dorsal musculature between the abdomen and thorax of the lobster with the aid of a No.

FIGURE 9.15
Electroshock grid

FIGURE 9.16
Tagging a Spiny Lobster on the Surface

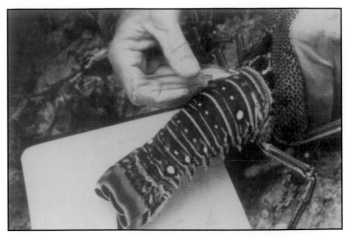

FIGURE 9.17
Tagging a Spiny Lobster *in Situ*

20 syringe needle (see Figure 9.17). Punching a small hole (0.16 inch or 4 mm) into one of the five tail fan sections may make a secondary mark; this mark will be retained through at least one molt and will permit recognition of a lobster that has lost its primary tag. Movements and locations of lobsters at night may be determined by using small sonic tags (pingers). These tags are small (about 1.2 x 2.0 x 0.4 inch or 3 x 5 x 1 cm) and weigh only a few grams. They operate in the general frequency range of 70 kHz and may be picked up as far away as 1,200 ft. (366 m) on an open bottom and 60 ft. (18.3 m) when the tagged lobster is in a crevice.

When conducting a survey of lobsters, it should be kept in mind that the very presence of the diver and the tagging procedures might affect overall behavior. In one study, a significant alteration of the population distribution was noted during the course of several weeks of capturing and tagging (Miller et al. 1971).

Long-term and short-term tags also have been used by divers in crab population studies. Long-term dart and spaghetti tags can be inserted at the isthmus of the carapace and abdomen, the point from which the crab exits when shedding. Short-term tags can be applied to the legs or carapace. Carapace tags for Blue crabs consist of an information-bearing plastic spaghetti tag with a loop of stainless leader wire at each end. A loop is put around each of the lateral spines of the carapace, adjusted, and then crimped with a leader sleeve. Other methods of short-term tagging include staining by injection or dipping with vital stains, fluorescent dyes, or phosphorescent dyes.

Tagging of oysters, scallops, and abalone can be accomplished by attaching Petersen tags with glue or a wire, painting the shell, using colored quick-setting cement, or staining the shell with vital stains. The excurrent holes on abalone shells are very convenient points of attachment for tags. A method for tagging abalone has been reported by Tutschulte (1968). This technique involves attaching a small battery-powered luminous beacon to the shell. During the night, the movements of the abalone with the light source on its shell are recorded on sensitive film by a camera fixed several meters above the seafloor. Movement of a marked animal may be recorded either as light streaks (in time exposures taken with a still camera) or as a moving point of light (in time-lapse cinematography). Animals studied by this method are subjected to a constant, low-intensity light and are not illuminated by the periodic flashes of high-intensity light required for direct observation in night diving; behavioral changes caused by unnatural light flashes are therefore probably eliminated with this method.

A technique has been developed for tagging echinoderms (Lees 1968). This method involves drilling a tiny hole completely through the sea urchin and inserting an inert filament (monofilament line or high-quality stainless steel line) that has been strung with small pieces of color-coded vinyl tubing. The urchin first is carefully removed from its hole or crevice and placed in a holding device made from a weighted plastic bowl lined with thick polyurethane foam; this enables the diver to press the urchin down into the foam to hold it still during the drilling operation. An ordinary hand drill fitted with an 18-gauge, 4 1/2 inches (11.4 cm) long hypodermic needle is used to drill completely through the body cavity. After the filament or wire has been threaded through the needle, the entire drill/needle assembly is slowly withdrawn, pulling the wire through the body cavity and leaving wire and tags in place on the urchin. The ends of the wire are then twisted together to form a loop, and the loose ends are trimmed.

The same technique can be used to tag sea cucumbers, except that the wire can be pushed through by hand instead of with a drill. Animals tagged in this fashion seem to be unaffected, and tags have been known to last for six to eight months. With sea cucumbers, trimming the tags short is important because fish may otherwise nibble on the long loose ends.

Tagging fin fish requires special skill and handling. The size of the fish must be sufficient so that the tag will not impair the ability of the fish to navigate, forage, or avoid predators. Lake (1983) lists several guidelines for tagging finfish:

- Use barbless hooks to catch the fish.
- Avoid the use of bait.
- Don't tag fish that have been tired by a long fight.
- Hold fish with a wet rag over their heads.
- Keep gills free of sand and dirt.
- Don't tag fish that are bleeding from the gills.
- Tag during cold water season whenever possible.
- During tagging, make sure that fish are not out of the water for more than 60 seconds.

A number of techniques have been used to tag fin fish. Three common methods involve Petersen disk tags, spaghetti tags, and dart tags. Disk tags are about 3/8–1/2 inch (0.95–1.27 cm) in diameter and come in a variety of colors. They can be attached to the back of the fish with monofilament line. This type of tag should not be used on fish that will grow to a large size because the tag will cause pressure on the fish as it grows (Randall 1961). Spaghetti tags are made of soft tubular-vinyl plastic about 1/16 inch (0.16 cm) in diameter, with monofilament nylon in the center. This type of tag can be attached by running the line through the fish's back beneath the rear of the dorsal fin. Because this type of tag can snag on rocks or coral, the method is not recommended for reef fishes. Dart tags consist of a vinyl plastic tube with a nylon tip and barb. They can be inserted into the back of the fish with a hollow needle so that the plastic streamer bearing the legend trails posteriorly, with a slight upward tilt. Although this technique permits fairly rapid tagging, these tags tend to come loose more easily than those implanted via the first two methods.

Another method of tagging fin fish involves injecting colored dyes subcutaneously (Thresher and Gronell 1978). This technique has been used successfully *in situ* for studying the behavior of reef fish. The dye can be injected via disposable plastic syringes and disposable needles. Although several different dyes have been used, plastic-based acrylic paints are the most satisfactory and apparently do not harm the fish or significantly affect their behavior. Two methods have been used, depending on the size of the species to be tagged. For small-scaled and scaleless species, the needle is inserted from the rear, parallel to the body surface, so that the tip enters the skin, runs underneath it for a short distance, and then emerges. This in-and-out technique ensures that the tag is placed immediately below the skin, the best position for producing a long-lasting tag. Slight pressure should be placed on the syringe to start the flow of dye (and ensure that the needle is not plugged), and then the needle should be pulled back under the skin and withdrawn. The smooth motion results in an even line of color below the skin. For large-scaled species, the needle should be inserted under the rear edge of a scale and moved gently from side to side while pressure is applied to the syringe, which causes a small pocket of dye to be deposited under the scale.

Acrylic paint tags inserted in this manner have lasted as long as 16 months; durability depends in part on the color of the paint.

Scallops have been marked successfully using a quick-setting calcium carbonate cement (Hudson 1972). This material meets four criteria: 1) it does not harm living tissue; 2) it is easy to apply and readily visible; 3) it adheres to a wet surface and hardens under water; and 4) it makes a durable mark. The recommended mixture for this purpose is:

- Seven parts Portland gray (or white) cement (Portland Type II is best because it is formulated especially for use in seawater)
- One part moulding paste
- Two parts builder's sand (fine grain)

This mixture will start to harden in 3–5 minutes (or sooner if less moulding paste is used). The materials should be thoroughly mixed while dry, and three parts of water should be added to 10 parts of dry mix. If colored cement is desired, no more than ten percent additive by volume should be used, so that the strength of the cement is not reduced. The final consistency should be similar to that of firm putty.

To apply cement to a scallop, the organism should be removed from the water and the upper valve should be pressed into a soft sponge to remove excess water. A small quantity of cement (about 1/2 cc for scallops 0.4–0.8 inch [10–20 mm] in shell height and one cc for scallops 1.2 inches [3 cm] or larger) is placed near the lip and then rubbed firmly across the shell at right angles to the ribs. This tightly grouts the depression between the ribs and leaves a thin coating of cement over the shell. Several quick thumb strokes are necessary to distribute cement evenly out to the lip so that new shell growth can be measured accurately. Only enough cement should be applied to fill the inter-rib areas; the upper surface of the ribs should be visible through the coating. Marked scallops can be returned immediately to the holding tank, where they should be held for several hours to allow further hardening. Scallops marked in this way have retained this marking material for 15 months or more.

The same type of cement has been used to transplant live coral in reef areas and to mark large marine gastropods and other delicate bivalve mollusks (Hudson, pers. com. 1978). Figure 9.18 shows a living elkhorn coral, *Acropora palmata*, implanted on a rocky outcrop. Another method for marking marine organisms involves the use of various dyes. Alizarin Red dye has traditionally been found useful for making permanent growth line marks in living corals and other invertebrates. The dye does not harm the coral, and subsequent growth can be measured after the coral is sliced with a saw. A tetracycline soak incorporates itself into an organisms $CaCO_3$ matrix, which later shows up as fluorescent lines under black light (e.g., purple urchin and coral studies).

FIGURE 9.18
Cement Used to Implant Elkhorn Coral

FIGURE 9.19
Algal Cover of Rock Substrate

9.8 BOTANICAL SAMPLING

Studies of benthic macroalgae and seagrasses in their natural environments focus on both subtidal and intertidal zones and depths. This is the region where sufficient light can penetrate the water to support the growth of diverse and often dense associations of photosynthetic organisms that grow attached to bottom substrates (see Figure 9.19). Benthic algae can occur at depths greater than 900 ft. (275 m), but few species occur in these relatively deep habitats. The sites where most research involving algal and angiosperm vegetation takes place are shallow enough to be accessible with scuba equipment.

Wherever stable rocky or sedimentary substrates occur, on beaches, in estuaries or bays, or on coral reefs, various forms of plants will develop. As with all underwater work, however, the questions posed and site-specific features limit and strongly influence the choice of sampling method. Large-scale biological studies may include samples or catalogues of plants, recorded with estimates of area covered. Data may sometimes be combined for forms or taxa (crusts, turfs, frondose, for example), depending on the need for taxonomic precision. Large discrete thalli, such as species of brown kelp, usually are counted. In some cases only indicator taxa, selected on the basis of economic value, dominance, or ease of identification or counting, are of interest. Sampling programs that are designed to record abundance and distribution patterns of plants and other sessile organisms are described in Sections 9.5.1 and 9.5.2.

Presence/absence of data or estimates of abundance are utilized for experimental studies as well as for descriptive investigations. The methods employed for these various objectives used to rely on sampling procedures that had largely been adapted from terrestrial or intertidal studies.

However, photographic and video sampling are newer underwater techniques. Their applicability to subtidal work is enhanced by their efficiency under conditions where time, mobility, and visibility are often severely limited.

9.8.1 Field Procedures

As with any ecological project, the objectives and constraints of the study and the features of underwater sites determine which techniques are appropriate. In recent years, subtidal biological methods have been summarized in books that draw on hundreds of scientific and technical publications (Littler and Littler 1985). These sources provide up-to-date reviews of methods, as well as discussions of their relative advantages and disadvantages. Accordingly, the following paragraphs represent only a brief review of botanical field procedures.

Generally, underwater botanical sampling, whether of data or specimens, depends on the use of transect lines, grids, and quadrats arranged in fixed, systematic, or haphazard ("random" is rarely practical) positions. Recently, circular sampling designs have been found useful in sites of heavy surge, rough water, or low visibility. In circular sampling, a radius-length line attached to a central fixture is used to partition the area and guide the diver. Underwater sites are usually located on the surface by sighting or buoys and on the bottom by a variety of fixed markers. Data can be recorded by notations on data sheets treated for underwater use, by collections of organisms, photography, voice recorder, or video camera (see Chapter 5).

Methods suitable for sessile animals are particularly appropriate for investigating marine plants. Studies that rely on these methods seek, in general, to differentiate and classify plant communities and to analyze the data to identify changes. As an index of productivity, standing crop data can be obtained by collecting the entire vegetation from a given area and sorting the material into component species in the laboratory. These specimens can then be dried, weighed, and reduced to ash for analysis of organic content.

For ecological studies or census data, the size and number of quadrats to be used must be determined by appropriate tests, such as species accumulation curves. Researchers often find it advisable to use an area somewhat larger than the minimal one to be confident of establishing statistically significant differences between samples.

Seasonal variations in the diversity and abundance of plants is very conspicuous in certain parts of the world. To get complete coverage of events in an area and to gain understanding of the natural cycles, it is necessary to sample repeatedly throughout the year. It is best to return to the same station to monitor changes over time using repeated measures statistical designs.

Some plants have narrow temperature tolerances, and may act as indicator species because their presence or absence suggests certain environmental characteristics. Northern latitude kelp taxa, for example, do not live in warm waters and are not found in tropical latitudes except where cold currents or deep cold water provide suitable circumstances.

9.8.2 Macro-Photogrammetric Method

Abundances of each algal group are determined following initial set-up and subsequently by detailed field estimates and taking 108 cm^2 macrophotographs (9 x 12 cm framer), projecting the images in the laboratory and scoring the percent cover of predominant taxa (Littler and Littler 1985). The high magnification afforded by macrophotography of the 108 cm^2 quadrats enhances the resolution, facilitating discrimination of turf species and crusts. Comparisons are made between treatments to detect changes in the relative abundances of the benthic producer groups that recruit, colonize and persist over a given experimental period.

9.8.3 Herbivory Assays

Natural levels of coral reef herbivory are assayed using the palatable red alga *Acanthophora spicifera*. This alga is a highly preferred food item by both parrotfishes and surgeonfishes, as well as by sea urchins. The alga is cut into 7.0 cm lengths and attached to ~3 x 10 cm dead coral-rubble fragments by thin (~1 mm thick x 5 cm long), dull-beige rubber bands. Fifteen replicates are placed haphazardly in each study zone for three hours. This technique avoids both pseudoreplication and novelty effects that could bias grazing patterns and rates. Percent eaten is determined by re-measuring the algal segments.

9.8.4 Palatability Experiments

Natural populations of reef fishes are used to assess the herbivore resistances of predominant macrophytes. Experiments are run on the fore-reef slope zone of high herbivory. The algae are collected while submerged and separated into approximately 10 cm^2 clumps to avoid bias arising from a size-based differential attractiveness to visual feeders. The 10 cm^2 clumps are attached to independent rubble fragments by thin dull-beige rubber bands and deployed at ~0.5 meter intervals in a randomized pattern (12 replicates per species). Surgeonfishes and parrotfishes usually show no wariness and begin feeding immediately, moving from clump to clump and feeding persistently as they locate a particularly palatable species. The clumps are photographed immediately after deployment and six hours later. Quantification of losses is determined digitally from the photographs.

9.8.5 Nutrient Enrichment Assays and Primary Productivity

Nutrient-enrichment bioassays are used to test the hypothesis that a given study site has had an oligotrophic or eutrophic antecedent history. This procedure assays the light-saturated net photosynthetic rate (Pmax) of the most common macrophytes in the study area in response to nitrogen and phosphorus enrichment (using the dissolved-O_2 technique), as an index to the long-term integration of ambient nutrient concentrations. Factorial treatments include overnight pulsing with nitrogen (as NH_4+, 16.0 µM) and phosphorus (as PO_43-, 1.6 µM), both N + P and a control (no nutrients added). The above concentrations were chosen to saturate the uptake rates in the small volumes used during nutrient pulsing (4-liter freezer bags). These concentrations represent realistic levels encountered in eutrophic reef environments (e.g., near bird islands). The bioassays are performed *in situ* in incubation jars under natural irradiance levels and water temperatures.

9.8.6 Collecting Techniques

Before beginning a study that requires the collection of plants, an investigator should survey local environmental conditions so that he will know where and how to sample. Most, but not all, macroalgae require a hard substrate for attachment, and the diversity of plants on rock surfaces usually is far greater than in soft sediment or sandy areas. Pilings, shells, dead corals, barnacles, shipwrecks, and mangrove roots are other places algae are likely to attach. Marine vascular plants (seagrasses) follow the reverse pattern; most species grow on soft or sandy substrates, although some, such as *Phyllospadix*, grow on the rocky shores of the western United States. Frequently, seagrasses and larger algae themselves provide substrates for a great array of smaller epiphytic plants.

Because benthic plants are attached to the substrate, a tool such as a putty knife, scraper, or knife is usually needed to remove entire plants if these are required for voucher specimens or for later study. Mesh bags, freezer bags, or small plastic vials with attached lids are useful for holding samples. If plant samples are necessary for identification, portions or selected branches are often adequate. If there is no reason for collecting material, a non-destructive sampling or experimental design can be implemented. If small thalli are needed for laboratory examination, it is often more efficient to collect pieces of rock or substrates than to remove and handle plants during the dive.

Procedures for Scientific Dives

When several divers are involved in a study, a system for incorporating "unknowns" (specimens that cannot be identified in the field) should be included in the planning stage. Vouchers for such data as well as for all critical taxa should be assembled and retained with the raw data.

If an investigator wishes to obtain a census of an area, collections from diverse substrates should be sampled. Because some plants live only in intertidal or shallow water, while others live only in deep water, collections should be made over a broad depth range. Data for large plants, such as the kelp *Macrocystis*, that may be 100 ft. (30 m) in length, with holdfasts 3 ft. (0.9 m) in diameter and as many as 400 or 500 stipes, are usually based on *in situ* observations and measurements. Care should be exercised when placing several types of marine plants in a common container, because plants that have extremely high acidic content may damage other forms of algae in the container.

A clipboard with waterproof paper and pencil for notes and a field notebook should be used to record data immediately after diving. Diving observations should be recorded as soon as possible. Ideal field data should include notes on depth, substrate, terrain, water temperature, current, visibility (clarity), conspicuous sessile animals, herbivores, the date, time, methods used, and the collector. If possible, information on available light, salinity, and other environmental factors should be obtained. Census data become more useful if the relative abundance of each species is at least estimated, i.e., whether common, occasional, or rare. Many marine species are inconspicuous, and these require careful microscopic examination and identification in follow-up work.

Accurate light measurements within a given plant community can be obtained by using small, self-contained light meters (see Figure 9.20). The use of photographic light meters that incorporate selenium photocells is unsatisfactory unless restricted spectral regions, isolated with colored filters, are measured. This is because a sensing system that responds differently to different wavelengths is being used to measure light that is becoming increasingly monochromatic with depth. The introduction of colored filters in front of the meter greatly reduces its sensitivity. An opal cosine collector can be added to make the system behave more like the plant's surface does in terms of light absorption, but such collectors can only be used in shallow, brightly lit waters. The apparatus needed to make such measurements generally incorporates a selenium photocell of increased surface area which augments the current output per unit of illumination, a system for easily changing the colored filters, and a sensitive ammeter whose range can be altered by current attenuation circuitry.

9.8.7 Specimen Preparation and Preservation

To determine the kinds of plants present, notes should be made on the collected specimens while they are still fresh. Herbarium and voucher specimens can be made from either fresh or preserved material.

FIGURE 9.20
Conducting Light Measurements

Although procedures for drying and mounting large algal and seagrass specimens are described in many easily obtained and standard guides, a few simple procedures are described here. Most marine algae have a glue-like substance on the outside of the cells that makes specimens more or less self-adherent to most kinds of paper. Standard herbarium paper will preserve a collection permanently, but this paper is not a prerequisite for making a useful set of voucher specimens. Formalin (2.5–5 percent) will preserve small or delicate forms, and permanent slides are useful for ongoing work.

There are standard herbarium methods for pressing plants and some special variations for marine algae. The usual approach is to float specimens in large, flat trays and to slide them carefully onto sheets of heavyweight herbarium paper. Using water, the plants are arranged on the paper; the paper is drained and placed on a sheet of blotting paper and topped with a square of muslin or other plain cloth or a piece of waxed paper. This is covered with another blotter, and a corrugated cardboard "ventilator" is placed on top. Another layer of blotter-paper-plant-cloth-blotter-cardboard is stacked on top. When 20 or 30 layers have been stacked, the pile should be compressed, using a weight or the pressure from heavy rocks or from straps wrapped around the plant press. The top and bottom pieces should be stiff; boards slightly larger than the herbarium paper and blotters are generally used. After several hours (or overnight), the stack should be taken apart, and the damp blotters should be replaced with dry ones. Many small algae dry in one day using this technique, but some, such as the large brown algae, may take a full week to dry completely, depending on humidity.

The usual method for preserving specimens for later detailed examination and herbarium preparation is simple and effective. For each station, one or more large plastic bags can be used to hold samples of larger plants. Small bags or vials should be used for selected fragile or rare plants. The best general preservative is a solution of three to four percent formalin in seawater buffered with one tablespoon of borax per gallon. Ethyl alcohol (70 percent, made up with freshwater) is recommended for longer storage. Plant and animal specimens should not be mixed.

Permanent slides may be made of microscopic species. One common method uses a solution of 80 percent clear corn syrup and four percent formalin. The slides should be allowed to dry slowly; as the syrup dries, more should be added. The edges of the slide can be sealed with clear nail polish.

Plants collected for histological study should be preserved in a manner that is appropriate for the particular technique to be used. In all cases, preserved specimens should be kept in a dark place, because exposure to light causes preserved plants to fade. Samples obtained from many stations can be kept in separate bags in a single large storage drum that can be sealed tightly to prevent formalin from leaking. For shipping, most of the preservative can be drained off, because the plants, once preserved, remain in good condition for several weeks if they are kept damp.

An alternative method for preserving whole large kelp involves soaking them for several hours or days in a solution consisting of ten percent carbolic acid and 30 percent each of water, alcohol, and glycerin. Specimens thus preserved may be dried and then rolled up for storage. The glycerin helps to keep the plants flexible indefinitely.

If possible, one wet preserved specimen should be kept for each pressed specimen. This is especially important for unidentified species, because taxonomic identification often depends on cell structure. Some small plants can be preserved with general collections, but delicate specimens should be isolated. Retaining small pieces of rock with encrusting algae attached helps keep the plants intact. Coralline algae and rock-encrusting species require special attention. Articulated corallines should be fixed in four percent formalin and ten percent glycerin before they are placed on paper and then brushed with a diluted solution of white glue as an alternative to older methods of storing in boxes.

Plants collected for particular purposes (electron microscopic study, chemical analysis, culture inocula) require special treatment. It is important to fix or preserve such specimens as soon as they are removed from seawater. Because algae are photosynthetic organisms and the deleterious effects of surface light on the pigment systems of specimens from subtidal habitats can affect other metabolic processes, they should be kept relatively cool and dark until placed in a killing (fixing) solution or used for physiological work.

9.9 ARTIFICIAL REEFS/HABITATS

Artificial reefs and habitats are manmade or natural objects intentionally placed in selected areas of marine, estuarine, or freshwater environments to provide or improve fish habitats. Much of the ocean, estuarine, and freshwater environment has a relatively barren, featureless bottom that does not provide the habitat that reef fish need. Natural reefs and rock outcrops are limited; less than ten percent of the continental shelf can be classified as reef habitat. Even if rough bottom consists of low-profile rock outcrops, it can provide a habitat for fish and invertebrates.

Properly sited and constructed artificial reefs can provide the same benefits as natural reefs. They can enhance fish habitat, provide more accessible and high-quality fishing grounds, benefit the anglers and economies of shore communities, and increase the total number of fish within a given area. Artificial reefs function in the same manner as natural reefs. They provide food, shelter, spawning and nursery habitat, and orientation in an otherwise relatively featureless environment.

Many non-toxic solid wastes or surplus materials have been used in the United States to build reefs such as junked automobiles and streetcars, scrap tires (see Figure 9.21), damaged concrete pipe and building rubble, surplus or derelict ships, and numerous other materials, including gas and oil structures. Rocks, tires, Christmas trees, and brush piles have been popular reef materials in freshwater. More recently, fabricated structures such as Japanese-style fish houses, concrete structures, and fiberglass-coated plastic units have been tested in the United States. Figure 9.22 shows an artificial reef complex. Fabricated units are commonly used in Japan and Taiwan. Fish aggregating devices (FAD's) also are becoming popular in the United States; these have been used for many years in the Western Pacific.

Although artificial reefs can enhance recreational and commercial fishing opportunities, creating a successful reef involves more than placing miscellaneous materials in ocean, estuarine, and freshwater environments. Planning is needed to ensure the success of artificial reefs. If materials are improperly placed or constructed, all or part of a reef can disappear or break apart and interfere with commercial fishing operations or damage natural reefs in the vicinity.

Divers can play a key role in documenting the success of an artificial reef. The charting of reef material on the site and any changes that occur over time are important pieces of information to researchers and managers. Also, diver estimates of reef fish populations can be made by direct counts of the number and species at the reef sites. Species, number of individuals, mean lengths, and behavioral observations should be recorded on waterproof data sheets (see Section 9.3). When visibility is 4 ft. (1.2 m) or more, these observations can be made by two or more divers. Each observer makes counts by species for sections of the reef, and these are then totaled for the entire reef. The totals obtained by all observers are averaged for a mean species count of territorial and schooling fish, such as black sea bass, Atlantic spadefish, snappers,

FIGURE 9.21
Tires as Underwater Habitats

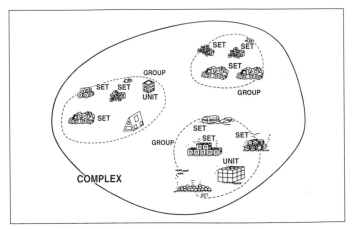

FIGURE 9.22
Diagram of an Artificial Reef Complex

grunts, and most porgies. For reclusive fish, such as cardinalfish, morays, and certain groupers, the highest count obtained by any one observer is used. Although the accuracy of fish population estimates varies with visibility, species, and time of day, it is assumed that, if conditions remain constant, the counts represent population density. Photographs taken at intervals from the same location also can be used to count and identify species. In this case, the photo print should be placed on a soft surface and a pin hole put through each identified fish; the print should then be turned over and the holes counted. Visibility should be measured after taking the picture to compare the areas covered by different photographs.

Scientific divers have used direct observation techniques to demonstrate that artificial reefs can be used to augment productive natural reef and rough bottom areas. They have also shown that these structures increase total biomass within a given area without detracting from biomass potential in other areas.

9.10 GEOLOGY

Most underwater geological research by divers has taken place in shallow marine waters, but the same techniques generally are applicable to research in lakes and rivers. The topics in this section are grouped into two general categories: characterization and experimentation. Geological characterization includes mapping, sampling, and testing parts of the underwater environment, while experimentation deals with the real-time analysis of specific geological processes. Experimental geological studies rely in part on information obtained from characterization studies, but they go much further in that they require extensive interplay between geology and other disciplines such as biology or fluid mechanics. Initially, underwater geological research primarily involved the characterization of existing conditions, but such studies now routinely entail experimentation as well.

Sophisticated methods have greatly expanded scientists' sampling abilities, yet careful observation is still the mainstay of most underwater geological studies. In some projects, observations may constitute the main data collected; in other cases, careful documentation may be important either to select sampling sites later or to place a chosen study site into the larger context of its surrounding environment. One of the most important elements of underwater geological research, therefore, is accurate note-taking, coupled with agreement on what was seen. It is advisable to supplement notes with a debriefing immediately after the dive and to record debriefing results along with the underwater notes.

Although most research projects require specific equipment, there are some basic tools that a diving geologist should carry routinely. These include a compass, inclinometer, depth gauge, noteboard, ruler, and collecting bag. These are small items, and many of them can be combined into a single tool. For example, a small, oil-filled plastic surveying compass with inclinometer can be cemented to a clipboard or to a plastic writing surface and a pencil can be attached with rubber tubing; a plastic ruler can also be mounted on the edge of the board (see Figure 9.23). Other useful equipment of a general nature might include an underwater or video camera, an assortment of small sampling bags or vials, lights, and small coring tubes.

9.10.1 Mapping

Three basic types of mapping can be accomplished under water: bathymetric, surficial, and geological. Bathymetric maps display the depth contour of the seafloor. Surficial maps show the two-dimensional character and distribution of the material that comprises the sea floor, and geological mapping projects a three-dimensional analysis of the rocks that crop out on the seafloor.

Bathymetric mapping is best done from a surface craft with echo-sounding equipment. Multibeam swath sonar systems are available in hull-mounted and towed fish configurations; although expensive, their accuracy is unsurpassed. A diver under water generally cannot match the range and efficiency, the accuracy of location, or the precision of depth determination and recording possible from a surface craft. However, in unnavigable water, or when taking precise measurements of a highly irregular bottom or of features too small to be resolved from the surface, underwater mapping may be the only practical means of compiling the bathymetry.

Bathymetric mapping can also be done in detail over a small bottom area to determine the area's microrelief. Small-scale bed forms are an example of an important geological feature too small to be resolved from surface craft. These forms develop in response to near-bottom currents, and their presence indicates aspects of the dynamics of the environment that otherwise may not be readily apparent. Moreover, such features may be preserved in the geological record, where they are of considerable use in deciphering ancient environments. Scaled photographs of bed forms provide important information on their shape and orientation. In mapping features such as sand ripples, however, the geologist needs to determine the average size of the bed forms over a section of seafloor. The small size of the bed forms, the nature of the sediment, and the fact that bed forms often are located in areas of strong wave-induced or unidirectional currents, create difficult sampling problems.

Peterson's Wheel-Meter Tape Triangulation Method

This triangulation method requires a wheel that is mounted on a vertical shaft and that has a rim marked in degrees. The shaft is driven into the bottom at selected locations. The 0° on the rim is aligned with magnetic North. A meter tape, pulled out from the top of the shaft, measures the distance to any point, with the direction read on the wheel rim where it is crossed by the tape.

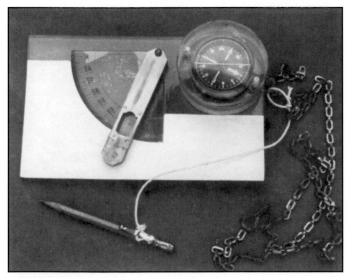

FIGURE 9.23
Underwater Geological Compass

A slightly larger wheel, mounted over and perpendicular to the first so that it can pivot around it, allows elevations to be calculated from simultaneous readings of upward or downward angles. This is a simple method of making measurements under limited visibility conditions, using two divers equipped with voice communication.

Meter Tape Triangulation Method

This triangulation method may be preferable to Peterson's wheel method when small areas need to be surveyed under conditions of reasonable visibility. Although this method is time consuming, it is inexpensive, requires little equipment and only a few divers, and is especially adaptable to level and uncomplicated sites. Control points at known distances from each other are selected and marked on the seafloor around the site. Horizontal measurements with a meter tape made from two of these control points to any object or point on the site provide the necessary information for plotting the position on a plane.

Plane Table Triangulation Method

This triangulation method may be used in clear water or on land, both for position triangulation and for taking elevations. Simple plane tables are necessary. They consist of a wooden table, three movable legs, and a weight. A simple alidade is constructed by combining a sighting device, a tube with cross hairs at each end, and a straightedge on a weighted base. Sheets of frosted plastic are then tacked to the table tops and the alidades are set on these. Two plane tables are placed on the bottom, one on each side of the site, and leveled. Initial sightings are made on a previously selected reference or primary fixed control point and across the site from one table to the other. Lines are inscribed on each plastic drawing surface with ordinary lead pencils and are then labeled. The resultant vectors, plus a measurement of the distance between the two points, establish the position of both tables on a horizontal plane. If the tables are not at the same elevation, the relationship is determined by placing a 19.7 ft. (6 m) long calibrated range pole, weighted at the lower end and buoyed at the top with a float, on the lower table. A sighting is made from the upper plane, and the distance between the sighted point on the length of the pole and the lower table provides the vertical elevation relationship.

A diver mans each of the two plane tables. A third diver moves the range pole from point to point on the site, and sightings are taken from each table and labeled consecutively. Elevations are measured by the third diver, who moves a marker up or down the pole until he or she receives a stop signal from the diver manning one of the plane tables. The distance is then measured from that point to the object being positioned. The plane table diver uses the horizontal element of the cross hairs for this measurement. The efficiency of this method is limited by the clarity of the water and the requirement that three divers record each point.

Dumas Measuring Frame Method

Archeologists have successfully used this method of precision mapping for small areas. A 16.4 ft. (5 m) square metal frame is fitted with four telescopic legs and extension couplings. The telescopic legs enable the frame to be leveled a few meters above a sloping site, and the extension couplings allow the size to be indefinitely doubled by fitting new sections into place. Using two sides of the frame as tracks, a horizontal crossbar mounted on wheels can be moved from one side of the frame to the other. This crossbar, in turn, is traversed by a yoke holding a vertical pole. The mobile crossbar, the vertical pole, and the frame are calibrated in centimeters. The vertical pole is adjusted to touch any object within the frame.

The coordinates of the point are recorded from three measurements read on the frame, the beam, and the elevation pole. The details around the point must be drawn by a diver hovering over portable 6.6 ft. (2 m) grids placed directly on the site materials. These simple grids are divided into 7.9-inch (20 cm) squares, which are designated by numbers and letters marked on the sides of the grids. The measuring frame is used to fix the positions of the corners of the grid. Although this method and the Dumas Measuring Frame method are no longer used extensively, they may be useful in certain circumstances.

Merifield-Rosencrantz Method

A simple method of determining the three-dimensional positions of a number of ground control reference marker stakes has been developed and tested by Merifield and Rosencrantz (1966). Two divers are used for the survey. The procedure consists of the following operations:

1. A rough sketch of the approximate locations of the points to be surveyed is drawn on a frosted plastic sheet for underwater recording. Using a tape measure, the slant distance between the various points is determined. A lattice work of measurements should be made, forming a triangular net (three sides of all triangles); this eliminates the need for making angle measurements. When possible, more than the minimum set of measurements should be taken. For example, if surveying a square that has a point at each corner, all four sides and both diagonals should be measured. One of these measurements is redundant, but it will enable the divers to check the accuracy of the measurements and to detect errors. (Errors can easily happen when a large number of points are being measured.)

2. The vertical height of each point is measured using a simple but extremely accurate level. A stake is driven into the ground in the middle of the array of points. A clear plastic hose with an inner diameter of 0.37 inch (0.94 cm) is fastened to the top of the central stake, with one end of the hose pointing down. The hose should be long enough to reach the farthest point to be measured. To set up the level, a diver first works all the air bubbles out of the hose.

The free end is held at the same level as the end attached to the stake. The diver then blows into the free end and fills the hose with air. As it fills, the hose will rise and form an inverted "u" in the water. The diver then swims to each point to be surveyed with the free end of the hose. A measuring stick is placed on the point and held vertically. The free end of the hose is placed alongside the stick and pulled down until bubbles are seen rising from the fixed end of the hose. When this occurs, the water level at the measuring stick is even with the mouth of the fixed end, and the vertical measurements can be read off the stick. If visibility conditions prevent seeing the fixed end, the hose at the free end should be pulled down slowly until the water level remains steady with respect to the measuring stick. When this occurs, bubbles will come out of the free end, even if poor visibility keeps them from being seen.

3. True horizontal survey distances and vertical heights are then calculated from these data using basic trigonometry and a hand-held scientific calculator. The microrelief of a small section of seafloor covered by unconsolidated sediment can be measured from one or a set of adjoining box cores (the basic box coring technique is shown in Figure 9.24). Because the surficial sediment in the box core may be modified during the coring process, additional steps must be taken when surface relief is desired. Newton (1968) covered the sediment surface with a layer of dyed sand followed by a layer of native sand to provide a protective covering before coring. After the core was impregnated with casting resin, the microrelief was obtained from slabs. This type of box coring is not only time consuming but is also extremely difficult to accomplish under the influence of strong currents.

Ripple height and wave length can be established under water and, where closely spaced, the resulting profiles can be used to create a three-dimensional map of a section of the seafloor. The sophistication of the equipment used to establish ripple profiles differs greatly, and the corresponding resolution of the data varies accordingly. Inman (1957) used a greased "comb" (see Figure 9.25) to obtain a profile of the large ripples that form in medium and coarse sand. In principle, this technique should give a fairly accurate profile of the ripples as long as the spacing of the comb elements is small compared with the ripple wave length. In practice, the comb is awkward to use because it has to be handled carefully to prevent grease from fouling divers and equipment and to ensure that the adhered grains are not lost before the trace can be measured. If visibility permits, photographing a scaled rod laid transverse to the ripples produces a quick but accurate measure of ripple wave length (see Figure 9.26). To measure the small ripples that form in fine sand, Inman (1957) laid a Plexiglas sheet on top of the ripples and marked off the crests with a grease pencil. Using this method, ripple heights could only be estimated, and the problem of ripple distortion

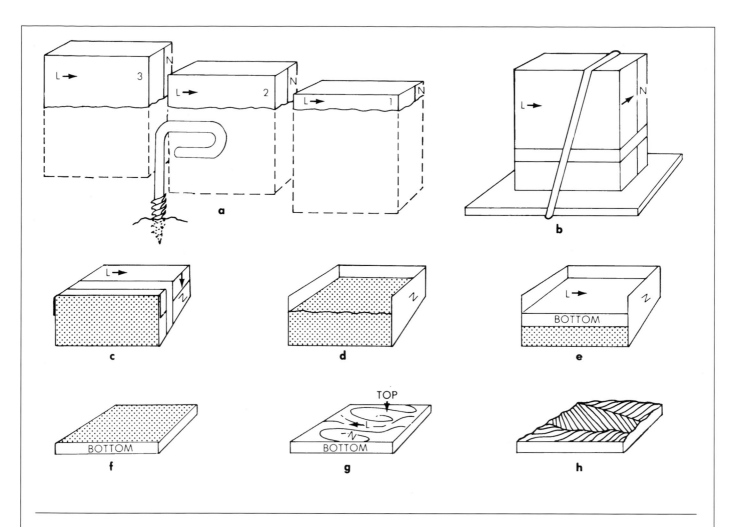

Taking and processing of sand box cores to identify internal structure: a–Senckenberg boxes, aligned in a series, shown here as normal to a northtrending shoreline (L). Box #1 is nearly completely emplaced, boxes #2 and 3 partly emplaced. Spiral anchor screwed in sand behind boxes provides stability and leverage for diver. b–Box filled with sand, bottom plate secured with elastic band. Both sides were taped together prior to sampling to prevent their spreading apart during emplacement. c–Box on side in laboratory, bottom plate removed. d–Upperside of box detached and uppermost 2–3 cm of sand removed by careful troweling. e–Metal tray inverted and pushed into sand surface. Orientation data transferred to tray. f–Tray removed and sand leveled and dried. Orientation data on underside of tray. g–Sand within tray impregnated with about 120 cc of epoxy resin. When resin has set, orientation data is transferred to the sand slab. h–Sand slab removed from tray, internal structure outlined by surface relief provided by preferential penetration of resin through individual beds. Orientation data on underside of slab.

FIGURE 9.24
Box cores (Senckenberg)

by the Plexiglas was always present. Furthermore, reliability decreases markedly when the current velocity increases because of scour around the sheet and the diver's inability to hold position long enough to mark the Plexiglas.

Underwater surficial mapping requires identification and delineation of the materials and features that compose the seafloor. In a small area, this can be accomplished more accurately by a diver at the underwater site than by instruments from a surface craft. Surficial features (such as rock outcrops, coral reefs, unconsolidated sediment, and textural and compositional variations in the sediment) must be identified, and their distribution must be traced and plotted to scale.

The problems of locating underwater features accurately and of covering a sufficiently large area can be minimized by towing the scientific diver who is in communication with a surface craft equipped for precise navigation. To ensure accurate location of features, the towed diver should mark the features with a float. In areas where the bottom can be seen clearly from above water, aerial photographs are useful to establish the general bottom configuration. The details can then be completed under water (see Figure 9.27). Geological mapping of the rocks that compose the seafloor is best accomplished by using seismic profiling techniques from a surface craft. If a specific question arises (such as the identification of a rock unit or the location of the surface trait of a

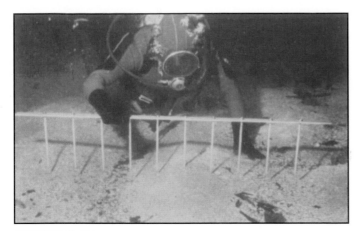

FIGURE 9.25
Greased Comb

FIGURE 9.26
Scaled Rod and Underwater Noteboard

fault) direct underwater observation must be used to answer it. For example, a geologist may need to know the attitude (strike and dip) of sedimentary strata or of fractures, joints, and faults in the rock. The strike of a rock bed is the compass direction that the bed would make when projected to a horizontal plane on the earth's surface. To fix the orientation of the bed, however, it is also necessary to know the dip. The dip is the angle in degrees between a horizontal plane and the inclined angle that the bed makes, measured down from horizontal in a plane perpendicular to the strike. Dip is measured with an inclinometer. These relationships are illustrated in Figure 9.28.

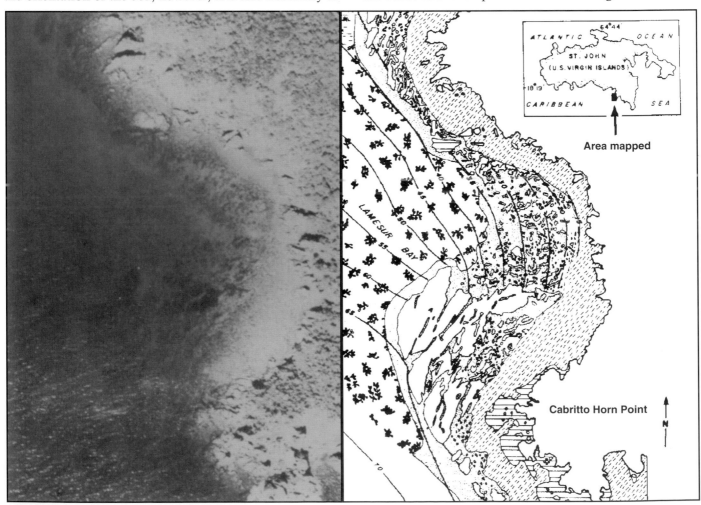

FIGURE 9.27
Aerial Photograph and Composite Map

NOAA Diving Manual

Rock outcrops on the seafloor may be located by noting irregularities in bottom profiles, anomalous shoals or reefs, or the presence of organisms such as kelp that normally grow on rocks. The rock outcrop may be so encrusted by bottom flora and fauna that recognition of features, such as stratification surfaces, fractures, and joint planes, is difficult. In such cases the diving geologist must clean off the encrustations, search for freshly scoured surfaces, or collect oriented samples in the hope of establishing the three-dimensional fabric of the rock in the laboratory. In some areas, differential weathering or erosion makes stratification surfaces and fractures more readily visible under water.

To measure the attitude of planar elements in the rocks, the diver needs an adequate compass with an inclinometer (see Figure 9.29). Underwater housings can be built for the relatively large surveying compasses commonly used on shore. A hollow plastic dish almost completely filled with fluid (plastic petri dishes work well) and marked with perpendicular crosshairs on the flat surfaces is a useful adjunct to underwater mapping. The dish is placed in the plane of the feature whose attitude is to be measured and rotated until the enclosed air bubble coincides with a crosshair. The other crosshair, which is now horizontal, defines the strike of the feature, and the downward direction of the crosshair coincident with the bubble defines the dip and dip bearing.

Some outcrops are located in water too deep to be sampled by these methods unless the diver is operating in the saturation mode. Where underwater sampling cannot be done, a photograph of the outcrop that includes a scale can yield a considerable amount of information.

For any kind of underwater mapping, it is useful to prepare a base map on which the outlines of previously established features are drawn in permanent marker on a sheet of plastic material. New features can be sketched in pencil on the base and, as they are confirmed, drawn onto the map.

9.10.2 Sampling

Diving geologists sample everything from unconsolidated sediments to surface and subsurface rock formations. Although standard land techniques can be used directly in a few underwater situations, they usually must be modified (or new techniques must be developed) to cope with the underwater environment. Diving allows selective sampling, which is not possible when using boat-based methods. The diver sees exactly what is collected and how it relates to other aspects of the submarine environment. Compromised samples can be discarded and easily replaced. Also, diving may be the only way of sampling the seafloor in areas, such as the high-energy surf zone, inaccessible to surface craft.

Rock sampling may be required in the compilation of an underwater geological map or to answer other questions. Samples broken directly from the outcrop are the most reliable, although talus fragments may be adequate if they can be traced to a particular outcrop. Breaking through the external weathered or encrusted rind of a submarine outcrop may be difficult because water makes swinging a hammer less effective than on the surface; a pry bar or geological pick can be used in existing fractures or can be driven against an outcrop with better effect. Explosives may be practical in some cases but must be used with extreme care (see Section 10.9). Pneumatic, electric, or hydraulic drills are available for underwater work (see Section 10.6).

Macintyre (1975, 1978) describes a hydraulically powered, diver-operated drill used in water depths up to 49 ft. (15 m). The drill consists of a Stanley® hydraulic impact wrench (modified for consistent rotation) that is powered by a hydraulic pump on the surface. The drill rotates at a maximum of 600 rpm and provides sufficient torque to core under any reasonable conditions. The unit will recover cores

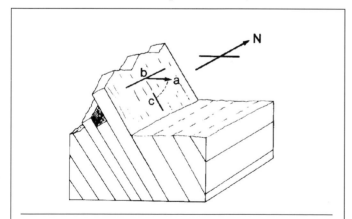

Block diagram illustrating dip and strike. Direction of dip due east, shown by arrow; amount of dip, angle abc. Notice that arrow extends horizontally as it would if placed flat on a map. Direction of strike is north-south, shown by cross-arm of symbol; it represents a horizontal or level line drawn on inclined bedding plane.

FIGURE 9.28
Dip and Strike of Rock Bed

FIGURE 9.29
Measuring Dip (Inclination) of a Rock Outcrop

FIGURE 9.30
Coring in a Deep Reef Environment with a Hydraulic Drill

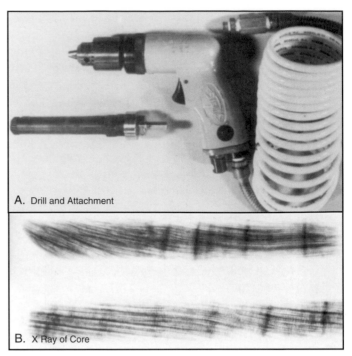

A. Drill and Attachment

B. X Ray of Core

FIGURE 9.31
Pneumatic Hand Drill

roughly 2–3.5 inches (5–9 cm) in diameter, using a double-walled core barrel. Such drilling operations are used to study the geological record of reef accumulation preserved in the subsurface of coral reefs (Macintyre and Glynn 1976).

Macintyre's original unit was powered by a Triumph 4-cylinder industrial motor, which limited the type of surface vessel used for support. Smaller units have been designed that utilize 5–10 hp motors. The result is a more portable unit, weighing about 350 lbs. (159 kg) that can be operated from a small boat. Although this approach reduces the flow rate over that of Macintyre's original design, cores over 82 ft. (25 m) in length have been retrieved with these newer systems (Halley et al. 1977; Hudson 1977; Macintyre et al. 1981; Shinn et al. 1977; Marshall and Davies 1982; Hubbard et al. 1985).

For use in water less than 6.6 ft. (2 m) deep or on exposed reefs, a tripod is required to support the drill (see Figure 9.30). In deeper water, a tripod is best used for control of the drilling operation. Using the habitat *Hydrolab* in the U.S. Virgin Islands as a base, Hubbard and his coworkers

(1985) were able to core horizontally into the reef face in water depths of 98 ft. (30 m). On such deep operations, bottom time is usually the limitation. In addition to tending the normal operation of the drill, a diver is needed to monitor the progress of the coring and to note anything that would be useful in logging the core at the surface. A submersible drilling frame can solve some of these problems when divers are working in deeper water. Adjustable legs allow deployment on an irregular, sloping bottom. The frame securely holds the drill in place, while a lift bag can be used either to place pressure on the drill or to lift it out of the hole. By using a video camera, the drill can be monitored remotely, and divers are needed only to set up and recover the cores.

The hydraulic drill is also useful in obtaining shorter samples through large coral heads for the purpose of examining internal growth bands. A larger diameter, single-walled barrel is fitted to the same drill and is used to remove a plug from the coral colony. Because this method is meant to be non-destructive, great care must be taken not to damage the surrounding colony. Some researchers have inserted a concrete plug into the hole they have drilled to promote overgrowth of the colony by algae.

The drill (see Figure 9.31A), which can operate at about 100 psi (7 kg/cm^2), is attached to a neoprene hose that is fitted to the low-pressure port of the first stage of a regulator, that is attached to a standard scuba cylinder. The drill bit is designed so that the core sample is forced up into the middle of a core barrel attached to the bit. This barrel, in turn, is designed to retain the core sample when the barrel is removed from the bit (see Figure 9.31B). The barrels containing the sample can be removed, and new barrels can be attached by the diver under water. The best cores can be obtained by running the drill at its maximum speed, with maximum pressure on the bit to make the hole quickly. When the full penetration of the bit is completed, a slight rocking motion of the bit in the hole will break the core free and permit it to be removed from the hole. Complete unfractured cores 0.39 inch (1 cm) in diameter and up to 33.5 inches (85 cm) long have been obtained with this method. A single 72 ft³ (2 m³) scuba cylinder is sufficient to drill four holes in the coral *Montastrea annularis* at depths up to 23 ft. (7 m). Because this equipment is not designed for use in salt water, extra care must be taken after use to rinse and clean it to avoid corrosion.

Sampling unconsolidated sediment generally is easier than sampling solid rock, but it may also present problems. The collection technique used depends on the purpose of the study. For example, if samples are collected for compositional or textural analysis, the primary concern is to obtain material representative of a larger entity. On the other hand, if internal structure or engineering properties are the goal, the sample should be as undisturbed as possible (see Section 9.10.2).

Collecting a representative sample creates a number of problems that must be resolved. For example, how deep below the surface should the sampler penetrate? The sediment beneath the seafloor may have been deposited under conditions markedly different from those producing the surface sediment; if so, its character will differ accordingly. How does one sample a sediment containing interlayered sand and mud? How large a sample is required to be representative of a specific particulate trace component, such as placer gold, without biasing the sample by the loss of some component, such as the finest or densest material? Many of these questions have been addressed in conjunction with subaerial sampling, and the techniques employed in this form of sampling are applicable to underwater sampling as well (Clifton et al. 1971).

Surficial samples taken with a small core tube circumvent many sampling problems and permit a highly consistent collection program. Plastic core tubes several centimeters in diameter with walls a millimeter or so thick are ideal and inexpensive. Cut into short tubes several centimeters long, they can be numbered and have rings drawn (or cut) on them 0.39–0.78 inch (1–2 cm) from the base and top (depending on the thickness of the sediment to be cored). Two plastic caps for each tube complete the assembly. The tubes are carried uncapped by the diver to the collection site. A tube is pushed into the sediment until the ring on the side coincides with the sediment surface, and a cap is placed carefully over the top of the tube. Its number is recorded, along with a description of the sample location. A trowel or rigid plate is slipped under the base of the tube, and the tube is then removed from the sediment and inverted. The second cap is placed on the base, and both caps are secured. This simple arrangement can be improved by adding a removable one-way valve to the top end and a

removable core catcher to the bottom. These items allow the diver to insert and remove the core without capping it. Capping is done at a convenient time, and the end pieces are then transferred to another tube for reuse.

An inexpensive alternative to a core tube is to cut one end off a 50-cc disposable syringe and to use it as a small piston core. The sampler is pushed into the sediment while the syringe plunger is being withdrawn slowly to keep the sampler at the sediment surface. The plunger provides enough suction to permit the small sampler to be removed quickly from the bottom without losing any sediment. The sample can then be extruded into a sample bag, or it can be kept in the core tube by capping the tube with a small rubber stopper.

Undisturbed samples of seafloor sediment are valuable for identifying internal structures, such as stratification or faunal burrows, and for making measurements of certain engineering properties. Compared with the brief view of the seafloor possible during a single dive, analysis of these structures provides a broader perspective on processes through time. Internal stratification, considered in light of sediment texture, can be used to infer the strength of prevailing currents during the time of deposition. The orientation of cross-stratification indicates the direction of the stronger currents in the system and may indicate the direction of sediment transport. The degree to which mixing by faunal burrowing disrupts these structures is indicative of the rate of production or stratification, which in turn reflects the rate of the occurrence of physical processes and/or the rate of sedimentation.

Internal structures of modern seafloor sediment also provide a basis for interpreting ancient sedimentary environments. Direct comparison of depositional features in a rock outcrop with those in an individual core may be difficult because of the limited view permitted by a core. This problem can be overcome, to a degree, by taking oriented cores in an aligned series, which yields a cross section that is comparable with that in the outcrop.

The collection of undisturbed samples from the seafloor requires special coring techniques. Diver-operated box cores have been used successfully to core the upper 3.9–7.8 inches (10–20 cm). Cans or similar containers from which the bottoms have been removed are useful in muddy sediments. With their tops off, they can be pushed easily into the mud until the top is at the sediment surface level (the surface layer can be lost if the container is pushed below the sediment surface). The opening at the top of the container is sealed by a screw cap or stopper after the can is emplaced in the sediment, and the sediment remains intact as the core is withdrawn. A wedge-shaped or spade corer permits the taking of somewhat larger surficial cores.

Cores can be taken in sandy sediment with a variety of devices, ranging in design from very simple to quite complex. Cores more than 6.6 ft. (2 m) long can be taken by driving thin-walled tubing several centimeters in diameter into the sediment. A simple apparatus consists of a removable collar that can be attached firmly to a 3 inch (7.6 cm) diameter thin-walled irrigation pipe. A pounding sleeve consisting of a 3-inch (7.6 cm) inside diameter pipe with two pipe handles welded to it is slipped over the irrigation pipe above the collar. By forcefully sliding the pounding sleeve down onto the collar, a 3.3–6.6 ft. (1–2 m) core can be taken (the core tube must be long enough to allow for the core and enough pipe above the collar to slide the pounding sleeve). Adding a removable piston attached to a stationary pole so that the piston remains at the sediment surface during coring can increase the penetration of this apparatus to several meters. Scientists have constructed a coring apparatus that used a hydraulic jack hammer. The jack hammer is attached to one end of a section of 3 inch (7.6 cm) diameter aluminum irrigation tubing cut into the necessary lengths. The attaching device is a slip-fit made by press-fitting a collar to a standard jack hammer chisel shaft. Slits are also cut into the upper six inches (15.2 cm) of the core tube to allow for the escape of water (Shinn et al. 1982). During operation, the entire device is suspended in the water with an air bag or air-filled plastic garbage can. Holding the core pipe in a vertical position, the diver releases air from the air bag and descends slowly until the tube makes contact with the bottom. After ascertaining that the core tube is oriented vertically, the trigger is pressed and the tube is jack-hammered into the bottom. Generally, 19.7 ft. (6 m) of penetration is attained in about 30 seconds. Experience has shown that loss due to compaction is less than ten percent. Cores up to 29.5 ft. (9 m) in length have been obtained using this method.

A different type of apparatus used for underwater coring is the vibracore, which relies on high-frequency vibrations rather than pounding to push the core tube through the sediments. The core tube is driven as deeply into the bottom as possible and is then extracted; during extraction, the vibration source is turned off. Several excellent but costly commercial units are available; a less-expensive unit can be constructed by attaching a simple concrete vibrator to the top of a 3-inch (7.6 cm) piece of irrigation pipe. This method works most efficiently in mud-rich deposits and peat (Macintyre et al. 1995). The unit can be powered by a small motor located in the support boat; cores 32.8 ft. (10 m) long have been taken with this type of unit.

Subaqueous cores are saturated with water when they are removed from the bottom and must be handled carefully to avoid destroying them. For example, unless great care is taken, the sediment may be washed from the corer as it is removed from the water, or liquefied by excessive agitation, or it will collapse during removal from the corer. The careful geologist avoids these frustrations by planning core retrieval and transport as an integral part of the coring system.

Divers can collect other types of geological samples. For example, gas escaping from seafloor seeps may be collected more easily by a diver/scientist operating at the seafloor site than by scientists working from a surface craft. Hydrocarbons in the sediment can be analyzed with greater precision when the samples have been taken by divers. These containers can be sealed immediately after sterilization, or opened under water, and then resealed with the sample inside before being returned to the surface.

9.10.3 Testing

In the context of this section, testing means determining some variable of the sediment *in situ* that cannot be identified accurately on the surface from a sample of the same sediment. For example, Dill and Moore (1965) modified a commercial torque screwdriver by adding a specially designed vane to the shaft. The vane was inserted carefully into the sediment, and torque was slowly and constantly increased until sediment failure occurred. From this simple test, these authors were able to determine the maximum shear strength of surface sediments. They also measured the "residual strength" of the sediment by continuing to twist the dial after initial shear occurred (see Figure 9.32). Use of this equipment generally is restricted to currentless locales because the diver has to remain motionless during the test to operate the apparatus correctly and accurately.

9.10.4 Experimentation

The underwater environment is a superb natural laboratory, and diving permits the geologist to study a number of processes in real-time experiments. Most studies of this type begin with a careful characterization of the study area, followed by an experiment (usually carried out over an extended period of time) designed to explore the interrelationships among geological, biological, physical, and chemical processes.

The experimental technique may be simple or sophisticated, depending on the nature of the phenomenon studied and the resources of the experimenters. Repeated observations at a selected site can produce much information on processes, such as bed-form migration or bed erosion and deposition. When visibility permits, real-time video, cinephotography, or time-lapse photography produces a permanent record of an ongoing process that can later be analyzed in great detail. Monitoring a site with sophisticated sensors can, for instance, yield quantitative information on the interaction of pertinent physical and geological variables.

Since many experimental studies in nature involve making serial observations of the same site, the experimental site may have to be reoccupied to continue the study or to service equipment. Relocating the site can be difficult and must be planned ahead of time. A buoy, stake, or prominent subaqueous landmark may suffice in clear, quiet water, while more sophisticated equipment such as sonic pingers (see Chapter 5) may be needed under adverse conditions. Surface buoys tend to arouse the curiosity of recreational boaters, who may tamper with or even remove

FIGURE 9.32
Taking a Vane Shear Measurement

them, and landmarks are seldom close enough to the actual site to be useful, especially when visibility is poor. Placing stakes at the actual site must be done carefully so as not to alter the current flow enough to compromise experimental results. GPS provides accurate coordinates for site relocation up to 10 meters under optimum conditions.

Some experiments involve the emplacement of unattended sensors that monitor conditions at specific times or whenever certain events occur. The data from such sensors are either recorded *in situ* or transmitted by cable or radio to a recording station. Relocation is necessary to maintain or recover the equipment used in such experiments.

Characterization studies will continue to be the mainstay of underwater geological research because most of them can be completed without elaborate equipment. *In situ* experimental studies, however, have become increasingly important as more geologists have discovered the advantages they offer in answering fundamental questions about the geological environment.

9.11 PHYSICAL OCEANOGRAPHY

Diving plays a critical role in the data collection process in a variety of physical oceanography studies. Certainly, the most important jobs performed by divers in oceanographic surveys are the deployment, inspection, maintenance and recovery of oceanographic instruments and instrument arrays. These tasks are most often conducted in shallow estuarine or coastal areas, and oil rigs are mostly shallow or in near-surface open-ocean

environments, but they are also performed in deeper environments. Divers have also been used to take readings from diver-operated instruments *in situ*, such as light meters or fluorometers (Dunton and Schell 1986; Mazel 1997), to measure water motion using a variety of methods (Muus 1968; Foster et al. 1985; Airoldi and Cenelli 1997), document flow patterns revealed by dye tracers (Woods and Lythgoe 1971), to take water or CTD samples at precise locations (Bozanic 1993), to study internal waves (Leichter et al. 1996) and the formation of bubbles in sound attenuation (LaFond and Dill 1957).

A description of how scuba is used in physical oceanography is provided in this section. It should be noted however, that because of the nature of this marine science discipline, diving has limited application for a number of reasons. Many physical oceanographers are interested in large-scale patterns and processes. These "blue water" scientists usually obtain their data through shipboard deployment of instruments or instrument arrays in deep water, or through attachment of instruments to manned submersibles or remotely-operated vehicles (ROVs). Even for those working in shallow estuarine and coastal areas, the use of scuba for making *in situ* measurements is generally impractical because the time scales over which most studies are conducted are usually much longer than divers can stay in the water. Scientists researching micro-scale processes, such as flow dynamics and turbulent cells, often conduct their studies under carefully controlled laboratory conditions (in water tunnels or flumes). However, divers can and do play important roles in the data collection process in physical oceanography.

9.11.1 Deployment, Inspection, Maintenance, and Recovery of Instruments

The emplacement, inspection, maintenance, and recovery of recording instruments and instrument arrays and the recovery of data *in situ* are jobs often performed by divers in support of oceanographic studies. Important physical parameters measured by various types of oceanographic instruments include current speed and direction, wave motions, temperature, conductivity, salinity, pressure, dissolved oxygen, light, fluorescence and sound. A description of oceanographic instrumentation is reviewed by Heine (1999).

Diving is usually the most practical and cost-effective method for surveying potential study sites to ensure their suitability for instrument deployment. Precise site selection is critical in most studies. Divers must take into account location, substrate, depth, and the exposure of instruments to a variety of environmental factors such as waves and surge, currents, sediment deposition, bio-fouling, ice and boat traffic. For example, scientists usually prefer to moor current meters on or over flat bottoms, well away from underwater obstructions (e.g., reefs or shoals) that disrupt the local flow field. During the deployment and recovery phases, proper assembly or disassembly of the various instrument mooring types (tautline, bottom-mounted) is

FIGURE 9.33
Deploying an Instrument Inside PVC Housing

FIGURE 9.34
Current Meter

FIGURE 9.35
Current Meter and Mooring

often best conducted underwater by divers (see Figure 9.33). Because most oceanographic instruments contain relatively fragile electronic components, divers are deployed to carefully attach and detach them from their moorings to prevent damage or loss that might occur if the instruments were deployed or recovered while coupled with their moorings (see Figure 9.34).

Instruments and moorings often become fouled, and sometimes damaged, by marine growth, movement of sediment or bottom debris. Corrosion and electrolysis also can be problematic, especially in marine environments. Divers are indispensable for inspection and cleaning of instruments and moorings *in situ* (see Figure 9.35). Inspections are not only important for assessing the condition of equipment, but also to confirm that instruments are properly positioned on the bottom or at certain levels in the water column. Some state-of-the-art equipment can be downloaded *in situ* by divers who run a cable to the instrument from a shipboard computer.

Of course, to inspect, clean, or recover instruments, scientists must first be able to find them. The most important aspect of the relocation process occurs during the deployment phase when scientists should take the proper steps to pinpoint the location of instruments being deployed as precisely as possible. The Global Positioning System (GPS), the sextant, and the use of range lines in nearshore regions are invaluable tools and procedures with which to facilitate this process. Once in the immediate vicinity of the mooring site during the maintenance or recovery phases, divers can relocate the instrument underwater by employing any number of search-and-recovery techniques (see Chapter 10). Circular search patterns have been found to be particularly effective in relocating moorings. Alternately, divers can use portable underwater acoustic receivers to home-in on pinger transponders attached to the moorings or instruments.

9.11.2 *In Situ* Sampling of Currents and Waves by Divers

In addition to deploying, maintaining and recovering recording instruments, divers can collect physical data underwater using a variety of techniques and devices. One of the first methods used to study currents on a small scale involved dye tracers (LaFond 1962; Zhukov et al. 1964). Water masses tagged with fluorescein dye can be tracked, timed and photographed or videographed to provide an accurate measurement of current speed and direction (see Figure 9.36). One advantage of using dye to measure current speed is that accurate measurements can be made at speeds slower than many current meters can resolve. Dyes are also ideal for investigating the turbulence occurring in various layers of the water column and can be used to study internal waves. This technique is particularly effective for characterizing turbulence within a thermocline. Woods and Lythgoe (1971) provide details of dye tracer methodology. The most important note of caution when conducting dye studies is the influence of diver motions on water column disturbance, particularly the creation of artificial vortices by finning.

Measurements of general water motion can be taken by using various diver-deployed/diver-monitored devices. Most of these techniques involve measuring the dissolution of some type of water-soluble material such as plaster of Paris (Muus 1968; Doty 1971), alabaster (Genovese and Witman 1997), or gypsum (Airoldi and Cinelli 1997). The dissolution of a given material, initially formed into spheres, slabs, or clods, is measured by weight loss or dimension reduction and then translated into water motion. Others researchers have used mechanical devices to measure wave motions or currents, including a shear-force dynamometer that records the magnitude and direction of the maximum force imposed on individual organisms by rapid water flow (Denny 1983). This diver-deployed device is described as rugged, simple to build, inexpensive and requires no external power. Foster et al. (1985) describe a method that divers can use to measure surge using a modified protractor and a buoyant tethered sphere. Heine (1999) reviewed these and other mechanical methods for measuring currents and water motion under water by divers.

9.11.3 Water Samples

The collection of water samples for determination of salinity, dissolved oxygen, dissolved nutrients, etc., is more often conducted using a variety of ship-operated samplers. Shipboard personnel can usually position and trigger these

FIGURE 9.36
Dye-Tagged Water Moved by the Bottom Current

devices to obtain samples at the desired locations. However, divers are sometimes employed to collect discrete samples at more precise locations. Bulk water samples can be obtained by swirling large plastic bags through the water until filled, sealing their mouths, and carrying them to the surface. Because large water samples are heavy, the bags should be put into rigid containers under water before lifting the samples onto the vessel. Smaller water samples can be obtained with more precision using a small plastic containers (e.g., soda bottle). If the desired sample is taken below approximately 20 meters, the air-filled container will compress and deform, but when opened at the desired depth the plastic can usually be manipulated by hand into its original shape. For deeper samples, the plastic container should be filled with surface water, then pumped out of the container by squeezing its sides at the desired sampling depth.

Divers also have used glass jars with a two hole stopper, one hole of which is fitted with a flexible sampling tube. At the desired depth, the diver inverts the unstopped jar, purges it with air, and then inserts the stopper. The jar is then righted and, as the air bubbles out of the open hole of the stopper, the diver manipulates the sampling tube to vacuum the water sample into the jar. After evacuating all the air, the diver seals the jar by inserting the tip of the sampling tube into the open hole of the stopper or by replacing the stopper with a cap.

It is difficult to obtain accurate measurements of dissolved oxygen in seawater because the changes in pressure to which a sample of seawater is subjected as it is brought to the surface affect the chemical nature of the solution. Liquids and solids are relatively insensitive to pressure effects, but dissolved gases are sensitive to pressure changes.

Procedures for Scientific Dives

FIGURE 9.37
Custom Dissolved Oxygen Water Sampler

Cratin et al. (1973) describe a portable, versatile, and inexpensive sampler, constructed of polyvinylchloride (PVC), which circumvents this problem (see Figure 9.37).

Conductivity, Temperature, and Depth (CTD)

As with water samples, CTD measurements are usually obtained by deploying the instrument from a ship. However, some models are portable enough to be handled by divers. A more sophisticated device that measures salinity, conductivity, dissolved oxygen, redox potential temperature and depth is mounted between double cylinders on a diver's back (Bozanic 1993). It should be noted that when taking measurements or samples in the water column, care should be taken to minimize the amount of activity around study sites to avoid unnecessary mixing of the water column. Vertical turbulence can occur through the action of a diver's exhalation bubbles; horizontal and vertical turbulence is created by a diver's finning motions. Water samples or CTD readings should be taken well away and upstream of all bubble activity.

Light and Fluorescence

Discrete sampling of light and fluorescence can be obtained using diver-carried/diver-operated instruments. Dean (1985) used divers to read digital counters associated with integrating quantum meters that measure photon flux densities. Instantaneous measurements of *in situ* illuminance have been made using an underwater photometer to obtain total illumination in foot-candles (Dunton and Schell 1986). Richardson and Carlton (1993) described a diver-operated irradiance meter that they used in a number of studies. The instrument recorded photosynthetically active radiation from 400–700 m. A similar type of irradiance meter has been used to make spot measurements of light penetration at various levels in the water column (Gittings et al. 1990).

Diver-operated instruments that can quantify the spectral reflectance and fluorescence excitation-emission spectrum of benthic organisms and substrates have recently been developed (Ackleson 1996; Mazel 1997). Using these state-of-the-art devices, divers can measure the fluorescence emitted by an object as discrete as a single coral polyp, view the data being recorded, store or discard the data, or change the instrument settings, all while under water.

9.11.4 Undersea Laboratories

Undersea laboratories have been of some advantage in experimental studies requiring the use of many instruments and dives of long duration. A diver-managed oceanographic instrumentation program was carried out during a Hydrolab underwater habitat mission (Schroeder 1975). The objective was to evaluate a continuously deployed shallow-water current and hydrographic monitoring system. Divers set up thermometers, current meters, pressure gauges for tidal measurements, and instruments for measuring depth, temperature, conductivity, salinity, dissolved oxygen, and pH using a tautline buoy array. Data were obtained by reading the instruments *in situ* and/or by remote display inside the habitat. When reading a vertical array of thermometers, the procedure was to approach the top thermometer at an angle, read and record it, then descend the buoy line to read the remaining instruments. This procedure prevented the aquanaut's exhalation bubbles from disrupting the thermal structure. Since 1987, the Aquarius undersea habitat has been active in conducting scientific studies. The effects of internal tidal bores on temperature, salinity and water velocities have been described from data collected through saturation missions from Aquarius (Leichter et al. 1996; Leichter et al. 1998). Other physical data collected from the undersea lab have been used in support of biological studies of the ocean (Sebens and Johnson 1991; Johnson and Sebens 1993).

9.12 ARCHEOLOGY

Diving for the purpose of studying the past has roots back to the early part of the twentieth century. A steep increase in activity took place after World War II, when the advent of scuba gear enabled terrestrial archeologists access to sites formerly beyond their reach. Materials have been salvaged from the depths since antiquity for non-scientific purposes and continue to be today, but such activities are not within the scope of this discussion. Presently, underwater archeological research is carried out by universities, and state and federal agencies. Comprehensive treatment of underwater archeology is provided by Delgado (1997), Gould (1983), and Green (1990).

Shipwrecks occupy a special niche in archeology, whether they are found under water or preserved in sand dunes or corn fields near shifting river beds. They demand research designs and strategies peculiar to their special nature as archeological and anthropological entities.

Typically, archeology conducted on inundated sites of former human activity, such as prehistoric sites in reservoirs or sinkholes and caves, simply involves an extension of land methodology to the underwater realm. Shipwrecks, due to their often discrete nature temporally and spatially, and because of the specialized material culture associated with them, demand the attention of maritime archeological specialists. (Muckelroy 1978, 1980).

There is often confusion over the use of the terms "underwater," "maritime," "nautical," and "marine" archeology. All are valid terms for different aspects of the discipline, but the term "underwater archeology" will be used here because it is most inclusive. Marine or treasure salvage are not scientific enterprises and should not be confused with archeology.

Typically, the underwater archeological process is divided into several stages that involve field work. There is the inventory and evaluation phase, which includes location and non-invasive documentation of sites; and the testing phase, which involves invasive techniques, partial site excavations, and full site excavations. For the diver, this translates to a series of procedures and specific techniques carried out by, or under the supervision of, a qualified underwater archeologist.

Generally, archeological research begins with formulation of a research design. Because it is not possible to collect "all the data," a design that incorporates specific questions and research domains and methodologies to address them provides a guiding framework that can be both efficient and effective in systematic archeological data recovery. In the case of any disturbance to archeological remains, the investigator must be clear about why the disturbance, is taking place, what is to be gained from the disturbance and what methods and techniques are to be employed. Sample analysis and artifact conservation must be in place prior to recovering any archeological materials.

9.12.1 Site Location

Broad-area survey for underwater archeological sites in marine environments usually involves systematic coverage with accurately positioned remote-sensing instruments (see Figure 9.38). Primary instruments used are the magnetometer (locates ferrous remains) and the side-scan sonar (images the seabed and objects above the seabed). Differentially-corrected Global Positioning System (DGPS) is usually the positioning system of choice for hydrographic surveys that require real-time positioning and high repeatability, and are available in any weather conditions. Accuracy depends upon the equipment and the nature of the corrections. DGPS accuracies vary from 1-10 m; archeological survey requirements are on the order of a 2-3 m circle of error.

Most underwater remote sensing carried out by resource management agencies is for the purpose of survey rather than search. The former indicates the intent to survey a block of submerged bottoms with the purpose of identifying and evaluating all significant cultural remains. A search is directed toward finding a particular site.

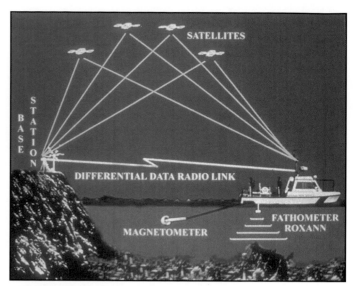

FIGURE 9.38
Remote Sensing

Remote-sensing survey parameters vary with instrument resolution, anticipated target size, and the level of desired coverage. Typically, transect spacing for magnetometer surveys for historical wrecks varies from ten meters in rivers to 30–50 m in marine environments.

The role of the diver in this phase is limited to ground-truthing through the visual confirmation of materials above the substrate and their first-level documentation. Divers must be closely supervised by a qualified archeologist. However, students and other support personnel taught to the level that they can confidently discriminate between cultural and natural remains in a given environment can carry out this task. They are expected to be able to reacquire remote-sensing targets, usually by using differential GPS units and coordinates provided by the survey director. They must establish a search area that will cover the zone of the magnetometer or side-scan sonar contact and identify anything man-made in the area, either above the substrate or within easy probing depth (up to a meter). Self-contained hand-held videos are often used to document what is found at any particular location. The images can then be reviewed by an archeologist who may return to the feature to further evaluate archeological significance.

Simple 360-degree circle searches from the center point of anomaly or contact as specified by the survey officer is a commonly used technique to examine an area. It requires only an anchor point (preferably from a swivel linked to a stationary pole two meters off the bottom), a line, and a compass. The compass is the best means of determining when a full circle has been completed. One notes the needle position at the beginning of the sweep and stops when the needle reaches or just passes the same point during the swim. The decision can then be made to extend the line and repeat the process. Even when visibility precludes seeing the anchor point, the compass will indicate when the full circle is completed. Some divers reverse course on each sweep to undo possible hang-ups on the bottom; others continue in the same direction. Their philosophy is that they will be able to ascertain if there has been an object impeding the search line when they reel back to the object, whereas changing directions could mask this problem.

9.12.2 Site Documentation

Usually these phases of the operation are (mapping, photography, videography, and sampling) diver-intensive. The only substitute is remote-operated vehicles, or in certain cases, submersibles.

Mapping

There is a good discussion of general mapping techniques in Section 9.10.1. Archeological mapping often demands a higher degree of accuracy simply because the features being mapped are usually smaller than geological landscapes, although the latter are often included in archeological site maps. Perhaps the most directly applicable technique to archeological mapping is baseline trilateration. This is a variation on triangulation techniques discussed elsewhere in this volume. The technique is taught in modified form by the Nautical Archeological Society (NAS) and described in their popular handbook (Dean et al. 1992). A detailed discussion of its application to large shipwrecks in the Great Lakes can be found in "Shipwrecks of Isle Royale National Park" (Lenihan 1994).

Baseline trilateration (see Figure 9.39) is a simple procedure that starts with a straight line being introduced into a concentration of shipwreck remains. This may be through the middle of the assemblage, down one side, and may include additional baselines to cover widely scattered wreckage fields. The size of the site is irrelevant. The procedure has been used successfully on comparatively intact portions of a wooden ship hull covering less than 30 m^2 of bottom and scattered wreckage that stretch more than a quarter of a mile. Once a scaled drawing of the baseline is transferred to paper, it becomes the backbone for all cultural material or natural features added to the map. One diver labels items to be mapped in and a team of support personnel measure the line itself, labeling set distances of 10 or 20-ft. increments. The line is measured and marked after being stretched on the bottom to avoid distortion from stretching a pre-marked line (see Figure 9.40). From this point, the process consists simply of measuring the distance to features of importance on the bottom from any two (or more) points on the baseline. Greatest accuracy is achieved when the section of baseline between the two chosen measuring points and the distance to each feature come as close as possible to forming an equilateral triangle. Note that archeologists tend to use feet and inches on shipwreck sites, because that is usually the numeric system used in building the ship. On the underwater remains of some sites, the metric system is frequently chosen by the archeologist.

FIGURE 9.39
Baseline Trilateration

FIGURE 9.40
Baseline Mapping

Another somewhat more sophisticated mapping system that was developed in 1980 for the *Mary Rose* excavation is the Direct Survey Method (DSM), that generates three-dimensional positions (Rule 1989). In this system, multiple tapes are used from survey datums to provide an x, y, and z coordinate for all points. A computer program has been developed to facilitate "best fit" computations. An advantage of this system is that the error of each measurement can be determined and minimized mathematically.

Photography

Underwater photographic surveys for general purposes are discussed in Section 9.2.2.1, but special considerations arise for underwater archeology. Underwater documentation of archeological sites with still photographs is an effective, time-tested method. However, the proper recording of the provenience of images is critical. Whether shooting over wide areas or smaller features, it is critical to have a point of reference in the photograph so that the image can be oriented to other forms of documentation, such as maps (see Figure 9.41). When artifacts are photographed, there must be some form of identification (a mug board) and a scale in the picture.

The most effective and user-friendly tool kit for archeological photography performed by scientists or technicians is an underwater 35 mm camera with the widest-angle lens available. A Nikonos with a 15–20 mm wide angle lens is ideal for archeological documentation. The ultra-wide-angle lens gives a tremendous depth of field, which translates to a large field of focus. Housed cameras also work well, but their use requires more maintenance and technical skills.

An ISO film speed should be used that will allow shooting at f-stops of f-8 to f-16 under the light conditions on the site. If one of the ultra-wide lenses is used, especially the Nikonos 15 mm, f-4.5 is adequate. Stops as low as f-4.5 provide a reasonable depth of field with this particular lens. If forced to use a longer focal length, pick a film speed that will keep the f-stop at f-8 or above.

If strobes are not used for shooting transparency films, a color-correcting filter (e.g., CC30R) over the lens should be used. Using a strobe often provides the best results, but it adds another level of complexity to the process. If housed cameras or strobes are used, an individual with photographic expertise must dedicate considerable energies to the photographic documentation phase of the project.

Videography

The underwater environment is perfectly suited for the use of video format. It has diffuse lighting with low contrast. The video format is also far less complicated than film (still or motion picture). Use of film requires a higher level of expertise to obtain consistently good results. A diver with little or no experience can get good, usable images with video (see Figure 9.42). Video is less expensive and easier to

FIGURE 9.41
Photographic Documentation

use than 16 mm motion picture film, and has a longer run time. The costs associated with the use of underwater video are about the same as 35 mm still photography. The still frames that can be taken from digital video are adequate for most uses. However, if high resolution is needed for large magnifications or high-quality reproduction and the project cannot afford the HD digital video, then 35 mm or medium-format stills are required. For most applications, lower-cost digital video will provide consistent, dependable results.

The chief problem that archeologists face in effectively using video for site documentation is the lack of adequate point of reference controls. For video to be used to its full advantage, it must be obtained in a systematic manner and be tightly referenced to a sketch or map of the site. The very ease of use sometimes results in overuse without proper controls. One way of increasing the value of video recording is to have the archeologist or technician use a full face-mask with a direct hard-wire link to the camera. This allows narration to be recorded directly on the tape, decreasing confusion about where images are being acquired. This also allows an informal type of audio note-taking, which has proved very valuable.

FIGURE 9.42
Video Documentation

Remote-Operated Vehicles (ROV)

In some situations involving deep water or other environmental constraints, underwater archeologists have increasingly relied on ROVs. The only relevance they have to diving operations is that they can prove to be either a hazard or a safety factor depending on how they are used. They may prove useful for monitoring the safety of dive teams and for bringing them tools from the surface, but their careless operation around divers can substantially interfere with operations. Electrical shock to the diver is unlikely because most ROVs employ sophisticated grounding systems, but any time an instrument utilizes AC from surface generators, divers should be aware of the potential risk.

9.12.3 Site Testing

Archeological sites under water may be tested using minimally invasive techniques to determine the nature and significance of the resource. Some degree of destruction is inevitable, so archeological standards require that the disruption of intact site materials is minimal and justified by returns in knowledge. One may dig to contact materials that are diagnostic, remove samples of cultural material or sediment matrix of the site, and determine depth and stability of cultural deposits. This stage of the archeological process must be conducted under direct control of a qualified archeologist and should follow completion of a rigorous nondestructive investigation. Several techniques are used for this purpose.

Hand-held Magnetometer

Before invasive techniques are used in archeological site testing, it is important to exhaust noninvasive measures. Intra-site magnetometry can define the boundaries of sediment-covered sites and indicate concentrations of ferrous material within an area, giving archeologists an idea of where to focus more invasive testing methods to achieve maximum results.

Intra-site magnetometry can be done in several ways. A traditional vessel-towed magnetometer can be used in multiple, high-resolution passes over a site, giving saturation-coverage. Another method is to employ a diver-held magnetometer. For shallow sites, the towfish can be floated and systematically maneuvered around the site's surface by a swimmer using buoys and directions from a spotter on the boat. For deeper sites, the magnetometer can be moved to set points on an established grid, or the diver maneuvering the towfish can be tracked using a sophisticated sonar-based diver tracking system. A third method is use of specially designed hand-held magnetometers.

Metal Detecting

Metal detectors (see Figure 9.43) are pulse-induction instruments that can locate both ferrous and non-ferrous materials. Their range is much more limited than a magnetometer, which detects ferrous objects by the disturbance they cause in the earth's magnetic field. Metal-detecting surveys are often conducted in conjunction with intra-site magnetometer surveys to differentiate large-mass, deeply

FIGURE 9.43
Metal Detecting

NOAA Diving Manual

buried ferrous materials found by magnetometer from smaller targets located by metal detecting. Metal-detecting surveys should be conducted systematically, either using a set grid over the site or a circle-search pattern. Instrument readings are plotted to indicate targets, directing subsequent excavation plans and/or establishing the site perimeter.

Probing

Probe surveys can be used to determine the extent of buried sites. Probes can be anything from a simple iron rod to tubular probes that are pumped with air or water to enable the probe to penetrate greater depths. Probing surveys plot where contact was made with something other than sediment; experienced operators are often able to distinguish contact with wood, ceramic, ferrous materials or stone. Annotation of depth reached at contact point also determines the amount of overburden on site.

Test Trenches and Pits

Test excavation locations are selected by the archeologist based on the cumulative data that has been generated from on-site investigations that include aspects of the environment that may affect site-formation processes (sometimes called "pre-disturbance" survey) and any historical documentation available. Locations are selected so as to obtain maximum information on the nature and extent of archeological deposits, with minimum impact to those remains. Test excavations record similar data as would be recorded during a site excavation, minimally to include precise horizontal and vertical (depth below seabed or datum) provenience, natural environmental variables, sedimentary matrix, and stratigraphy, as well as artifacts *in situ*. Typically, samples of natural and cultural materials are collected for laboratory analysis. Artifacts are often reburied in their find-locations after recording.

Test excavations can be done in either discrete pits or trenches; in either case, the disturbed area must be backfilled to minimize continued deterioration of archeological materials. Test pits are useful for determining the origin of metal-detector or magnetometer anomalies and for establishing the depth of overburden above the cultural layer necessary for excavation planning. Trenches can be useful in areas of deeper overburden that make sediment removal difficult. A trench is begun and moves along a prescribed line uncovering an area ahead while backfilling the area previously observed behind. This method is useful for establishing site boundaries with less spoil handling than is required by wide-area excavation techniques.

9.12.4 Partial and Full-Site Excavation

Full-site excavation is rarely opted for by responsible institutions or agencies. Entire shipwrecks are enormously difficult to preserve once removed from a stable environment, and they require extremely large budgets to ensure preservation and display in perpetuity. There are times,

however, when the financial and professional commitment is available to proceed. There have been excellent full-site excavations of classical vessels in the Mediterranean, but even those who advocate such excavations warn that it usually means that a 10–20-year commitment of the principal investigator is necessary to do the site justice. The tendency in the United States is to engage in partial site investigations governed by a problem-oriented research design. However, the excavation of *La Belle* recently by the Texas Antiquities Committee is a noteworthy exception. Regardless of the extent of the excavation, the following tools and techniques are most commonly used by divers engaged in such projects.

Air Lifts

Airlifts have been used by archeologists since the 1950s. An airlift is simply a tube into the deeper end of which air (usually surface-supplied) is injected through a diver-operated valve. The injected air and water mix, which is lighter than the surrounding water, rises in the tube, drawing more water and sediments into the airlift's mouth and exhausting them from the shallow end of the tube. Efficiency factors of airlift design include diameter of the tube, air pressure and volume, location of inlet valve, working depth, size and density of material being lifted and height of discharge. Some experimentation is usually necessary for determining the most effective combination of factors for any specific application. Refinements include an air chamber to distribute the injected air into the tube, a handle on the intake and either a reduced intake or a grid across the airlift's mouth to prevent intake of materials that could block the airlift. A blocked airlift quickly becomes buoyant and presents a potential safety hazard. Airlift sizes range from 8–60 cm or more in diameter, with air volume requirements ranging from 1.5 to more than 12 ft^3 per minute delivered at adequate over bottom pressure.

Large airlifts are for removing sterile overburden. Some means of horizontal displacement of sediments is usually desirable to prevent heavier sediments from falling back into the excavation. Airlifts do not work well in shallow water and can be difficult to control. Intake begins immediately upon injection of air, and large airlifts tend to bounce and dig soft sediments very rapidly. If not carefully controlled, large airlifts can decimate archeological sediments. Smaller airlifts can allow careful excavation after removal of sediment by hand fanning, trowels, brushes or other tools. Although no artifacts should ever be subjected to a trip through an airlift, a catch basket may be desirable for small materials missed by an excavator. Surface screening, desirable in some situations, is never a substitute for *in situ* documentation.

Injection Dredges

These dredges (see Figures 9.44 and 9.45) use water injected through a venturi tube or orifice to create a suction to draw water and sediments into the mouth of the device.

There are two basic configurations of a water dredge. The most common has about a short 30-degree angle in a tube. High-pressure water is directed through a smaller hose connected to the tube's angle. The venturi is created by water rushing through the longer straight section of the tube, which draws sediment into the shorter end of the angle. The second configuration, called a circle jet, uses a straight tube that has an adjustable orifice around the circumference of the tube. For efficient operation, both configurations require a jet pump delivering several hundred gallons per minute at more than 100 psi.

Injection dredges, once used as primary excavation devices, are, like airlifts, currently used only for the removal of sterile overburden. Dredges have some advantages over airlifts: they can operate in very shallow water and are more adjustable than airlifts. In addition, dredges move material horizontally, rather than vertically, as with the airlift, which retains more of the fine sediments. This makes trenching and backfilling much easier. Backfilling can be accomplished simply by turning the dredge around and replacing the spoil pile in its original position (see Figure 9.45).

Propwash Deflectors

These devices consist of a right-angled tube somewhat larger than a vessel's propeller designed to direct propwash of a moored vessel toward the bottom to displace sediments. The deflector is pivoted so that it can be removed when the vessel is underway. These devices, popularized by commercial treasure hunters, are very effective in shallow water. Depending on variables such as water depth, engine speed, propeller size and pitch, and bottom sediments, large holes several meters across and several meters deep can be dug in just a few minutes. These devices, appropriately nicknamed "blasters," while practical under some conditions for removing sterile overburden, can quickly destroy archeological materials and contextual information. Although some archeologists have used propwash deflectors productively, their application in commercial practices as the sole excavation tool for historic shipwrecks has been generally destructive, much like a bulldozer on a terrestrial site. However, under carefully controlled circumstances, propwash deflectors are useful for penetrating deep, sterile sediments and for keeping a hole open so that other tools, such as a water dredge, can be used for excavating cultural layers.

Cofferdams

These are water-tight containments constructed around a wreck or other site to be excavated. These allow the site to be de-watered and worked without diving apparatus. However, in some cases (notably a shipwreck excavated in Yorktown, Virginia) the containment acted as a stilling basin. Divers worked the site on compressed air, but without contending with currents and with much improved visibility.

FIGURE 9.44
Excavating with Injection Dredge

FIGURE 9.45
Backfilling with an Injection Dredge

9.13 ANIMAL CAPTURE TECHNIQUES

A wide variety of devices are used by scientists and commercial fishermen to aggregate, concentrate, or confine aquatic animals. Trawls, seines, traps, grabs, and dredges have all been evaluated and used successfully by scuba-equipped scientists interested in animal and gear behavior (Baldwin et al. 1996). Scientific divers who will be diving near such capture systems should train under simulated conditions before participating in open-water dives (High 1993). Marine scientists can help to improve the design of trawls and other such equipment by evaluating its underwater performance, observing how animals behave in relation to the gear, and then conveying this information to equipment designers.

In the FLARE and Hydrolab undersea programs, divers were able to observe fish near stationary traps 25–80 ft. (7.6–24.4 m) below the surface for up to eight hours per day (see Figure 9.46) and to devise methods to alter catch rates and the species captured (High and Ellis 1973). Divers from the National Marine Fisheries Service were also able to estimate accurately the populations of fish attracted to experimental submerged structures during studies designed to develop automated fishing platforms.

9.13.1 Nets

Nets vary in size, purpose, materials, and methods of use. Divers working close to an active net (one that is being towed) can interfere with its operation, especially if it is small, if they swim too near to it or touch it. Any net is considered large if direct diver contact does not appreciably influence its configuration or operation. Plankton nets typify small nets both in physical size and in the lightweight web required to retain micro-organisms. At the larger extreme, high-sea tuna seines often are 3,600 ft. (1,097 m) long, with 4.5 inches (11.4 cm) long meshes stretching 200 ft. (61 m) or more down into the water. Gill nets are designed to entangle fish attempting to push through the meshes; webbing mesh and thread size vary, as do net length and depth, in accordance with the size and species of fish sought. Gill nets use fine twine meshes hung vertically in the water between a corkline and a leadline. The net may be suspended at the surface or below the surface or be weighted to fish just above bottom and across the expected path of migratory fish. Divers and their equipment can easily become entangled in gill net webbing, which may be difficult to see in the water.

9.13.2 Seines

Seines are similar to gill nets in that a wall of web is held open vertically in the water by the opposing forces of a corkline and leadline; however, the seine is set in a circle to confine fish within the web rather than to entangle the fish (Clifton 1996). Seines often have rings along the lead-line through which a line or cable can be pulled to draw the bottom closed, which seals off the fish escape route.

9.13.3 Trawls

Trawls are nets constructed like flattened cones or wind socks typically towed by one or occasionally two vessels. The net target depth may be at the surface, in midwater, or across the seafloor. Specific designs and sizes vary widely, depending on the species sought and vessel used. A 9.8 ft. (3 m) long plankton net having a 1.6 ft. (0.5 m) mouth opening may be towed at speeds up to 3.5 knots (1.7 m/s), while a 202 ft. (61.6 m) long pelagic trawl with an opening 40.3 x 10.5 ft. (12.3 x 3.2 m) may filter water at three knots (0.5 m/s). Figure 9.47 shows a trawl diver. Trawls may be opened horizontally by towing each wingtip from a separate vessel, by spreading the net with a rigid wooden or metal beam, or by suspending paired otter-boards/trawl/doors in the water which are hydrostatically designed to shear horizontally out away from each other when towed at proper speed. NOAA divers frequently are called upon to observe and evaluate net operation while underway.

9.13.4 Diving on Stationary Gear

Diving on stationary gear such as traps, gill nets, and some seines presents few problems. Experienced divers can dive either inside or outside the net to observe animal behavior or to carry out work assignments. Divers must be alert to the entanglement hazard presented by loose diving gear, such as valves, mask rims, knives, vest inflator mechanisms, and

FIGURE 9.46
Fish Trap

FIGURE 9.47
Checking a Fish Trawl

Procedures for Scientific Dives

TABLE 9.1
Levels of Anesthesia for Fish

Stage	Description	Behavior
0	Unanesthetized	Normal for the species.
1	Sedation	Decreased reaction to visual stimuli and/or tapping on the tank; opercular rate reduced; locomotor activity reduced; color usually darker.
2	Partial loss of equilibrium	Fish has difficulty remaining in normal swimming position; opercular rate usually higher; swimming disrupted.
3	Total loss of equilibrium	Plane 1— Fish usually on side or back; can still propel itself; responds to tap on tank or other vibrations; opercular rate rapid. Plane 2— Locomotion ceases; fins may still move but ineffectively; responds to squeeze of peduncle or tail; opercular rate decreased.
4	Loss of reflex	Does not respond to peduncle squeeze; opercular rate slow—often may be erratic. This is the surgical level.
5	Respiratory collapse	Operculum ceases to move; cardiac arrest (death) will occur within one to several minutes unless fish revived in untreated water.

weight belt/fin buckles. A buddy diver can usually clear the entanglement more readily than the fouled diver can. Fouled divers must avoid turning or spinning around when in close proximity to net webbing, which will further entrap them in the web. It may be necessary for a fouled diver to remove the tank, disengage the caught mesh, and replace the tank assembly before continuing with the task at hand. It is recommended that divers carry a minimum of two knives when working around nets.

9.14 THE USE OF ANESTHETICS IN CAPTURING AND HANDLING FISH

Anesthesia has been defined as a state of reversible insensitivity of the cell, tissue, or organism. In connection with fish, the terms narcosis and anesthesia are often used interchangeably, although not all chemicals characterized as fish anesthetics also act as narcotics. Fish anesthetics have been used in conjunction with a multitude of operations, including capture, transport, tagging, artificial spawning, blood sampling, moving fish in aquarium, surgical intervention, and photographic sessions. There is a wealth of published information in the popular and scientific literature on a wide variety of chemicals and their applications.

The use of anesthetics does have an impact on the surrounding environment, and extreme care must be exercised to minimize this effect. The subsequent monitoring of an area in which anesthetics have been used must take this into account, because census and other data are affected by the use of anesthetics.

9.14.1 Response to Anesthetics

Fish anesthetics are administered most commonly by adding them to the water, which is then taken up by the gills. As the fish proceeds into anesthesia, it usually follows

a series of definable stages that are useful to know in evaluating the depth of the anesthesia. A simplified scheme defining the levels of anesthesia, which is devised largely from the work of McFarland (1959) and Schoettger and Julin (1967) is presented in Table 9.1.

The response of a particular fish to an anesthetic depends on a number of factors, including the species and size of fish, water temperature, salinity or hardness, pH, and state of excitability of the fish, as well as on the dosage and type of anesthetic. With some anesthetics, not all of the stages mentioned in Table 9.1 are observable; for example, with quinaldine there is generally no definitive sedation stage. Recovery begins when the fish is removed from the anesthetic bath and transferred to untreated water, where recovery then proceeds, usually in reverse order, through the stages shown in Table 9.1.

9.14.2 Selecting an Anesthetic

Factors to consider in choosing an anesthetic are purpose, toxicity, repellent action, ease of application, and cost. It may be helpful to refer to the literature to choose a suitable anesthetic for the species and purpose concerned. Table 9.2 lists some commonly used anesthetics, their qualities, purpose, and dosages. In the absence of applicable data, it is often advisable to conduct a preliminary experiment, since even closely related species may not respond to the same anesthetic in the same manner. Species-specific intolerance has been demonstrated with some anesthetics.

Many chemicals exhibit toxic effects that are unrelated to their anesthetic action, and these may be transitory or sustained. Some chemicals that exhibit toxic effects during long-term exposure may be satisfactory to use for short-term anesthesia.

The therapeutic ratio TR = LC50/EC is sometimes used in evaluating an anesthetic, where LC50 = the concentration lethal for 50 percent of the specimens and

TABLE 9.2
Fish Anesthetics

Anesthetic	Qualitites	Dosage (varies with species, temperature, etc.)	Common Use	Remarks	References
Benzocaine®	Powder, soluble in ethanol	25–100 mg/l	Immobilization, deep anesthesia	Widely used in human medicine; safe and effective with fish	Caldarelli 1986
Chloral hydrate	Solid, soluble, inexpensive	1–4 g/l	Sedation	Low potency; not widely used	McFarland 1959 McFarland 1960 Bell 1967
Cresols	Liquid; mix 50:50 with acetone to facilitate solution	20–40 mg/l for immobilization	Collection	Cresols have undesirable toxic effects; para-cresol is the most effective isomer	Howland 1969
Etomidate®	Make 1% solution in propylene glycol	2–10 mg/l	Immobilization	High potency; analog of Propoxate®; longer sedation times and safer than quinaldine and MS-222 mixture	Amend et al. 1982 Limsowan et al. 1983
Methylpentynol (Oblivon®, Dormison®)	Liquid, moderately soluble	0.5–2 ml/l 1500-8000 mg/l	Sedation or deep anesthesia	Widely used but less desirable than other anesthetics; low potency	Bell 1967 Klontz and Smith 1968 Howland and Schoettger 1969
Phenoxyethanol (2-phenoxyethanol)	Oily liquid	0.1–1 ml/l	Immobilization	Used frequently with salmonids	Klontz and Smith 1968 Bell 1967
Propoxate® (McNeil R7464)	Crystalline; soluble	1–4 mg/l	Collection, immobilization	Good collecting agent	Thienpoint and Niemegeers 1965 Howland 1969
Quinaldine (Practical grade)	Oily liquid, soluble with difficulty; dissolve in 10–50% acetone, ethanol, or isopropyl alcohol to facilitate solution	5–70 ml/l	Widely used for collection, immobilization	No sedation state; poor analgesic; efficacy varies widely with species and water characteristics; long exposures toxic	Schoettger and Julin 1969 Locke 1969 Moring 1970 Gibson 1967 Howland 1969

TABLE 9.2
Fish Anesthetics (continued)

Anesthetic	Qualities	Dosage (varies with species, temperature, etc.)	Common Use	Remarks	References
Quinaldine sulfate ($QdSO_4$)	Crystalline solid	15—70 mg/l	Collection, immobilization	Prepared from liquid quinaldine and has same properties	Allen and Sills 1973 Gilderhus, Berger, Sills, Harman 1973a
Rotenone®	Powder or emulsion	0.5 ppm	Ichthyocide; occasionally used for collecting	Used to salvage fish from freshwater ponds. Limited use in seawater for live collecting	Tate, Moen, Severson 1965
Sodium cyanide	Solid	DO NOT USE	Used in Philippines and elsewhere for collecting	Dangerous to humans; causes high mortality in fish	
Styrylpyridine (4-styrylpyridine)	White powder; soluble	20—50 mg/l	Immobilization, deep anesthesia	Not widely used but a successful anesthetic	Klontz and Smith 1968
Tricaine® (MS-222, tricaine methanesulfonate)	White crystalline powder; readily soluble	15—40 mg/l for sedation 40—100 mg/l for deep anesthesia 100—1000 mg/l for rapid immobilization	Immobilization, deep anesthesia; most widely used anesthetic	Expense bars its use for collecting; used extensively in surgery, fish handling, transport	Klontz and Smith 1968 Bell 1967
Urethane	Carcinogenic	DO NOT USE	Immobilization, deep anesthesia	Carcinogenic	Wood 1956
Mixtures of MS-222 and QdSO4	Powder, readily soluble	Various, e.g., 10:20 ppm QdSO4: MS-222 equals 25 ppm QdSO4 or 80—100 ppm MS-222	Immobilization, deep anesthesia	Combines desirable properties of each anesthetic; combination can be used in lower concentration than either anesthetic alone	Gilderhus, Berger, Sills, Harman 1973b

EC = the concentration necessary to provide the desired level of anesthesia. Generally, a TR of two or more is considered desirable, but since time of exposure and a variety of other factors affect the validity of the TR, its usefulness is somewhat limited.

The toxicity of the anesthetic to humans also must be considered. A given anesthetic may be dangerous to handle because of its acute toxicity or carcinogenic potential, or it may toxify fish flesh, rendering it dangerous or fatal to eat. This last consideration is important in cases where the fish will later be released to the wild, where fishermen might catch it.

In addition, the specific responses of fish to an anesthetic may be important, and the stages of anesthesia can vary with the anesthetic. As mentioned above, quinaldine generally cannot be used to induce the sedation stage, and some chemicals are much more repellent to fish than others. Other anesthetics may initially cause an increase in activity.

Several anesthetics have low solubility in water and must first be mixed with a carrier such as acetone or alcohol to increase their solubility. The need to premix may be inconvenient, particularly in field work. Finally, cost must be considered, especially when large field collections are concerned.

9.14.3 Application of Anesthetics

If an anesthetic is administered in high enough dosages, fish may be immobilized rapidly for capture or handling. The fish is then removed to untreated water for recovery. The chemical may be sprayed in the vicinity of the fish or added to a container holding the fish, or the fish may be removed to a separate bath, depending on the circumstances. Several anesthetics that are unsuitable for sustained anesthesia are satisfactory for rapid immobilization, provided the exposure is of short duration.

Sustained Anesthesia

Under suitable conditions, fish can be sustained safely under anesthesia for several days. Choosing the proper anesthetic with regard to toxicity and stability is critical. Before the anesthetic is administered, the fish should be starved for 24–48 hours to prevent regurgitation of food.

To perform surgery on captured fish, it is simplest to anesthetize the fish to the surgical level (Starr et al. 1998); the fish should then be placed in a trough or other restraining device, and its head should be immersed in an anesthetic bath for the duration of the procedure. For longer term surgery, more sophisticated procedures are required. One successful system employs two water baths, one containing untreated water and the other the anesthetic solution. The level of anesthesia can be controlled carefully by selectively recirculating water from the baths over the fish's gills. Steps should be taken to maintain the oxygen content near the saturation level and the ammonia concentration at the minimal level. Filtration may be required to maintain water quality (Klontz and Smith 1968).

Recovery

To revive fish in deep anesthesia, it may be necessary to move them gently to and fro in their normal swimming position. It is helpful to direct a gentle stream of water toward the fish's mouth, which provides a low-velocity current over the gills. It is not advisable to use a strong current or to insert a hose directly into the mouth because this may cause, rather than alleviate, hypoxia. The water in which the fish is being revived must be of good quality.

Some species recovering from certain anesthetics may undergo violent, uncontrolled swimming movements, and steps must be taken in such a situation to prevent self-inflicted injuries. For example, this is usually the case when the yellowtail *Seriola dorsalis* recovers from quinaldine anesthesia. Various physiological changes, some of which may persist for more than a week, have been observed in fish after anesthesia (Houston et al. 1971). During this post-treatment period, additional stress may result in mortality and should therefore be minimized.

NOTE
Anesthetics administered to food fish must be approved by the Food and Drug Administration, and those administering anesthetics are advised to be thoroughly familiar with all pertinent regulations. Violations of these regulations carry severe penalties.

Tidepools and Ponds

Anesthetics are useful when collecting fish in tidepools. The water volume in the pool must first be estimated, and then the desired dose of anesthetic is calculated and added to the pool. As the fish become immobilized, they are removed to untreated water as quickly as possible. It is desirable to collect fish from tidepools as the tide is rising, because a moderate amount of surge in the pool helps to flush anesthetized fish out of crevices, and diluting the pool water with incoming water will prevent the killing of specimens that are not going to be collected. With the proper anesthetic and dose, the mortality of uncollected specimens can be reduced to a negligible level (Gibson 1967; Moring 1970).

Reef and Shore

Many species of reef and shore fish can be collected with anesthetics. Quinaldine (1~20 percent) is used widely for this purpose. One-half to 1.05 quart (0.5 to 1 *l*) of the solution is generally used for each collection. Species susceptibility is highly variable. For example, angelfish and butterflyfish are highly susceptible, squirrelfish are moderately susceptible, and moray eels are highly resistant. The effectiveness of the anesthetic also varies with the physical situation as well as the skill and experience of the collector. Most anesthetics are at least somewhat repellent, and the fish usually need to be in a situation, e.g., in small caves, short crevices, or under rocks, where they can be confined within the anesthetic's influence for several seconds. The anesthetic is usually dispensed from a squeeze bottle in sufficient quantity to immobilize or partially immobilize specimens on the first application. The fish can then be collected with a hand net or, in the case of small specimens, with a manual "slurp" gun (see Figure 9.48).

A power syringe is available that allows oral anesthetics to be delivered through a probe. This device permits the diver to deliver the anesthetic at closer range to more species of fish than can be done using a squeeze bottle, and this delivery system may make the more expensive anesthetics practical to use for collecting.

Sedentary specimens can sometimes be collected by slowly trickling a light anesthetic dose downstream toward them. Fish in burrows are often difficult to collect with anesthetics because the burrows are so deep that the fish cannot be reached by discharging anesthetic from a squeeze bottle. Attaching tubing, such as a piece of aquarium air line, to the bottle may provide an adequate extension to reach into the burrow. The anesthetic should have repellent qualities that will cause the fish to emerge, because otherwise the fish might become anesthetized in the burrow and remain out of range. A noxious chemical can be added to some non-repellent anesthetics to ensure that the fish emerges.

Scientists at the Scripps Aquarium have developed a successful system for collecting garden eels of the *Taenioconger* species, which were previously difficult to collect. A piece of clear plastic, 6.6 ft. (2 m) square, is placed over the area of the eels' burrows and weighted down along the edges with sand. Approximately 1.05 qt. (1 liter) of 13 percent quinaldine solution in ethanol is applied under the plastic. The area is then left undisturbed for 20 minutes, after which the sedated and immobilized eels are gathered gently by hand. A single collection in a well-developed colony may yield more than 20 eels. This technique can be applied to other burrowing species, although the dosage and time of exposure may have to be varied.

Fish can also be anesthetized by injection. Although earlier attempts at collecting fish with projectile-mounted syringes were limited in their success, a recently developed technique utilizing Saffan®, a veterinary anesthetic, administered by a laser-sighted underwater dart gun, shows much promise. Harvey, Denny, Marliave, and Bruecker (1986) have successfully immobilized small sharks and ratfish with this technique, while Harvey (1986) has used it to collect moray eels and jacks.

Coral Heads

It usually is advantageous to enclose coral heads with a loose-fitting net before applying the anesthetic. Some species of fish such as wrasse and hawkfish reside in coral at night and can be collected easily at that time with the aid of anesthetics.

Large-Scale Collections

One technique used to collect fish over a large portion of a reef is to enclose the desired area with a seine and to administer a large enough quantity of anesthetic to immobilize the enclosed population rapidly. Divers should work as a team to recover the fish because of the danger of the divers becoming entangled in the net. Procedures to free entangled divers should be planned in advance.

Handling Large Fish

Sharks or other large fish captured by hook may be immobilized by spraying a strong anesthetic solution directly over their gills before bringing them aboard. Gilbert and Wood (1957) used a 1,000 ppm tricaine solution successfully in this situation.

Transportation

Anesthetics have been used, with conflicting results, to immobilize fish during transit. The effectiveness of this approach depends on a number of factors, including the type of anesthetic, species of fish, temperature, time in transit, preconditioning of fish, and water quality. Since most fish can be transported successfully without the use of anesthetics, information on the appropriateness of using anesthetics during transit should be obtained from the literature or by experimentation before attempting the procedure.

Summary

The use of anesthetics as collecting agents for aquarium fish is controversial, primarily because of concern about the delayed toxicity of the anesthetic agents. A survey of the literature indicates that, in the majority of species experimentally subjected to repeated anesthetization, delayed mortality is negligible. Professional aquarists at Scripps Aquarium, Steinhart Aquarium, and other institutions have also demonstrated that many other species that have not yet been subjected to formal experimentation can be collected safely and handled without significant mortality.

Most aquatic biologists concerned with collecting agree that judiciously applied anesthetics are useful collecting agents. However, the misuse of these chemicals, especially if

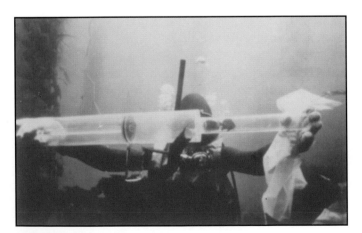

FIGURE 9.48
Slurp Gun Used to Collect Small Fish

widespread, can be very harmful. For example, the practice of using sodium cyanide to collect aquarium fish, which is sometimes done in under developed countries, is ill-advised and has resulted in human deaths, as well as high mortality among the fish and other organisms in the vicinity.

Recommendations

Tricaine® (MS-222) is a highly soluble and virtually odorless powder that is easy to use. It has proved to be a successful anesthetic in a wide variety of applications under a broad range of conditions in both freshwater and seawater, and there is an extensive literature on its properties and use. Tricaine® is a good choice where sustained sedation or surgical-level anesthesia is required, but high cost generally preludes its use as a collecting agent.

Quinaldine has been used widely to collect or handle fish. It is of low solubility in water and is generally dissolved in acetone, ethyl alcohol, or isopropyl alcohol before use in water. Quinaldine is not useful where sedation-level anesthesia is the goal, and it should not be used for major surgery or other painful procedures because it is a poor pain killer. Liquid quinaldine can be converted readily to a water-soluble salt, which greatly facilitates its use. When a mixture of the salt and Tricaine® is prepared in proper proportions, it combines the desirable properties of both chemicals and is effective at lower doses than either alone. Propoxate® and its analog Etomidate® are two relatively new and highly potent fish anesthetics that have potential as anesthetics for fish collection. Table 9.2 shows the commonly used fish anesthetics, including their recommended dosages.

9.14.4 Diver-Operated Devices

The capture of live fish poses no special problems for divers. Some fish are territorial and maintain discrete regions, while others live in schools and roam widely. Diurnal variations may also cause the fish to change their habitats during a 24-hour period.

Conventional methods of capture such as seining, trawling, and long-lining are not appropriate for capturing fish around coral reefs, and a number of special techniques must be used instead. An array of suction devices called slurp guns has been on the market for some time. These are powered either by rubber tubing, springs, or other means. After cornering a fish, the diver using a slurp gun (see Figure 9.48) pulls the trigger, drawing the plunger back and sucking a large volume of water in through a small opening and thus pulling small fish one–three inches (2.54–7.6 cm) into the gun. The fish are then moved into a holding container, and the gun is readied for another shot. The disadvantages of slurp guns are the limitation of the size of the fish that can be captured, the necessity for the diver to be very close to the fish, and the need to corner the fish, usually in a hole, to capture it.

Glass or plastic bottles also may be used to entrap small fish; however, fish may react to the pressure wave created by the moving jar and swim away. All bottles must be flooded fully with water before being submerged. A better technique than the bottle is the use of a piece of plastic core liner or plastic tube with a screen across one end, which can be slipped over fish more easily. Divers on the bottom can also use small gill nets. Animals such as sea urchins may be broken up and placed near the net to attract fish, or divers may herd fish into the net. Once entangled, fish may be withdrawn and placed in bags or wire cages.

As discussed earlier, fish traps may also be effective if baited appropriately and placed at a proper point either on the bottom or in the water column. Divers can then remove fish from the trap and rebait it while it remains on the bottom.

Deepwater fish can be caught on hook and line and reeled to 60 – 100 ft. (18.3 – 30.5 m), where divers can insert hypodermic needles into those with swim bladders and then decompress the fish. There is an 80 percent recovery rate on many species of rock fish when this technique is used. A dip net fastened to the end of a pole spear is useful in collecting fish near the bottom. The fish may be pinned against a rock or sand bottom, taken out of the net, and placed in an appropriate container; again, needle decompression may be helpful.

Many larger fish such as rays, skates, or harmless sharks may be caught either by hand or by a loop of heavy monofilament line an the end of a pole (such as a snake stick). Electric fish and rays should not be taken with metal poles or rods because of the shock potential (see Chapter 20).

Invertebrates may be collected by divers wearing gloves. A pry bar, screwdriver, putty knife, or diving knife may be useful in removing same specimens from their substrate. Delicate animals such as nudibranchs may be placed in separate plastic jars, vials, or Ziplock® bags. Vials and jars should be open at the beginning of the dive and completely filled with water before being returned to the surface.

Traps are effective for crabs, lobsters, and, occasionally, octopus. Nylon net bags are more easily used for collecting than bottles or plastic bags. Animals that are naturally buoyant will float out of the bottle or plastic bag when it is reopened to add another specimen.

Animals that live in the upper few centimeters of sediment or sandy bottom may be sampled by using either a scope, which has a line inscribed showing a given volume, or a cylinder made of plastic, stainless, aluminum, or other material that can be forced into the soft substrate. A simple cake server or spatula can be inserted from the side to provide a closure as the core of sediment is withdrawn from the bottom. The diameter of the cylinder should be such that it fits snugly over the mouth of the collecting bottle so the material can be forced into a labeled jar.

Nylon or other plastic screens can be obtained in a variety of mesh sizes. These may be tied over ends of plastic tubes as a sieve or be sewn into a bag to be used to hold sediment samples.

NOTES

Procedures for Working Dives

10

Procedures for Working Dives 10

10.1 SEARCH AND RECOVERY

All search techniques rely on one common element: the adoption and execution of a defined search pattern. The pattern should commence at a known point, cover a known area, and terminate at a known end point.

Search patterns are implemented by carrying out search sweeps that overlap. To be efficient, the overlap should be minimal. The initial step in a search is to define the general area and the limits to be searched. If the search is being conducted to locate a specific object, the last known position of the object is the starting point for defining the search area. The drift in the open sea resulting from sea and wind currents, the local wind condition at the time the object was lost, and the leeway (movement through the water from the force of the wind) should be studied. Sea currents can be estimated for a particular area using current NOAA Tidal Current Tables and Tidal Current Charts and the U.S. Navy Current Atlas of Surface Currents. Wind currents can be estimated using Table 10.1.

The leeway generally is calculated at zero to ten percent of the wind speed, depending on the area of the object exposed to the wind and the relative resistance of the object to sinking. The direction of leeway is downwind, except for boats that have a tendency to drift up to 40 percent off the wind vector. Calculation of the value and direction of leeway is highly subjective for objects that float or resist sinking; however, if the average wind velocity is relatively low (under five knots [2.5 m/s]), or the object is heavy enough to sink rapidly, the leeway has little or no effect on the calculation of a probable location.

After the vectors of water current, wind current, and leeway have been added and applied to the last known position of the object, a datum point is defined. The datum point is the most probable position of the object. Once the datum point has been defined, the search radius around the datum point is selected. The search radius, (r), is equal to the total probable error of position plus a safety factor, as defined by the following formula:

$$r = (1 + k) C$$

where

r = radius
k = safety factor (between 0 .1 and 1.5)
C = total probable error

The total probable error is a mathematical combination of the initial error of the object's position (x), the navigation error of the search craft (y), and the drift error (de). The drift error is assumed to be one-eighth of the total drift. The total probable error, (C), is:

$$C = (de^2+x^2+y^2)1/2$$

Each factor included in the total probable error is somewhat subjective. Selecting conservative values has the effect of enlarging the search radius; sometimes, a small search radius is selected and repeated expansions are made around the datum point until the object is located. Searching the area around the datum point can be implemented using a variety of patterns, depending on the search equipment, visibility, or number of search vehicles involved.

Systematic searching is the key to success. A good search technique ensures complete coverage of the area,

TABLE 10.1
Wind Speed and Current Estimations

Wind Speed, knots (m/s)	Wind Current, miles/day (km)
1 – 3 (0.5– 1.5)	2 (3.2)
4 – 6 (2.0– 3.0)	4 (6.4)
7 –10 (3.5– 5.0)	7 (11.3)
11–16 (5.5– 8.0)	11 (17.7)
17–21 (8.5–10.5)	16 (25.8)
22–27 (11.0–13.5)	21 (33.9)
28–33 (14.0–16.5)	26 (41.9)

clearly defines areas already searched, and identifies areas remaining to be searched. The visibility, bottom topography, number of available divers, and size of the object(s) to be located are prime factors in selecting the best method for a particular search.

There are two acoustic approaches to underwater object location. The first is to traverse the area being searched with a narrow beam fathometer, keeping track of the ship's position by normal surface survey methods. This approach is suitable for returning to the position of a known object that has high acoustic relief and is located in an otherwise relatively flat area, such as a wreck, significant rock outcrop, or a mount. The second acoustic method involves the use of side-scan sonar. When using side-scan sonar, a transponder receiver unit is towed from the surface. Acoustic beams are broadcast left and right, and the signals received are processed to present a picture of the bottom on both sides of the transponder-receiver unit. Approximate object position can be determined by knowing the ship's position, heading, and speed, and the approximate position of the transponder-receiver unit with respect to the ship.

Onboard microprocessors to control the range/gain necessary to produce optimum display contrast are beginning to replace manual adjustment of the gain; the use of microprocessors simplifies the task of the observer and increases the effectiveness of a search. If more precise determination is necessary, one of the acoustic surveying methods can be used. Underwater object location using acoustic techniques involves divers only after the object has been detected. The following diver search techniques have been useful for such applications.

10.1.1 Circular Search

In conditions where the bottom is free of projections, the visibility is good, the object to be located is reasonably large, and the area to be searched is small, use of the circular search technique is recommended. Under such favorable conditions, a floating search line is anchored to the bottom or tied with a bowline around the bottom of the descent line and is used to sweep the area. To determine when a 360-degree circle has been made, a marker line should also be laid out from the same anchor as the search line. This marker line should be highly visible and should be numbered with the radial distance from the anchor.

Where current is noticeable, the marker line should be placed in the down current position so that the diver always commences the search from the position having the least potential for entanglement. When more than one circle is to be made with tethered divers, the direction of travel should be changed at the end of each rotation to prevent the possibility of fouling lines.

The circular search has many modifications, depending on the number of divers and the thoroughness required. The standard technique is to station two divers along the search line close to the center of the search area. The marker line

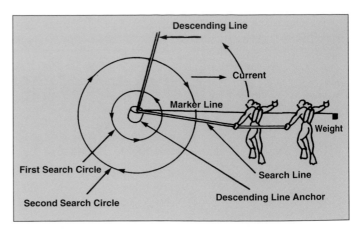

FIGURE 10.1
Circular Search Pattern

can be used to assign precise distances. The divers hold the search line and swim in a circle until they return to the marker line, which ensures that a full 360 degrees has been covered. The divers increase the radius for the next search, moving out a distance that permits good visual coverage. This procedure is continued until the outermost perimeter is reached (see Figure 10.1).

When two divers are searching, search effectiveness can be increased by having one diver hold the circling line taut and swim the outside perimeter of the area to be searched while another diver sweeps back and forth along the taut circling line. As shown in Figure 10.1, the first search will cover a full circle bounded by the outside diver's path. The search starts and finishes at the marker line. The search may be extended by the pattern, in which case the circling line is marked at the point where the outside diver was previously stationed. The outside diver then moves to a new position, farther out on the circling line, and the inside diver sweeps back and forth between the marker and the outside diver's new position. Positions may be changed at regular intervals if the divers become fatigued. Changing positions can be done at the end of each sweep by having the outside diver hold position after moving out one visibility length; the other diver then moves outside, taking up his position for the next sweep. If the search is conducted in murky water, using a weighted line may be advisable; if the lost object is shaped so that it will snag the moving line, a pull on the line will tell the diver that the object has been found.

Circular search techniques also may be used for diving through the ice in waters that have no current, such as inland lakes and quarries. The following procedure has been used successfully by the Michigan State Police Underwater Recovery Unit. When the ice is covered with snow, a circle is formed in the snow, using the ice entry hole as the center pivot point. The radius of the circle is determined by the length of line used to tend the diver. The circle on the ice indicates the area being searched and the approximate location of the diver who is searching under the ice.

If the object of the search is not recovered within the first marked-off area, a second circle that slightly overlaps the last circle is formed on the surface. This procedure is continued until the complete area has been searched. The circular pattern involves only one diver that is tethered, with a backup diver standing by; before entering the hole, the diver is secured by one end of the line, and the other end is held by the tender. The diver in search of an object will go directly below the hole and make a search of the immediate area. If the object is not found directly below, the diver returns to the surface and describes the underwater conditions. The diver then proceeds just under the ice to the full length of the line—approximately 75 ft. (23 m). With the use of rope signals, the diver begins circling, keeping the line taut and staying about 6–8 inches (15–20 cm) below the ice. After the diver completes one circle without encountering any resistance, the tender signals the diver to descend to the bottom. With the line taut, the diver begins the first circle on the bottom.

After the diver completes one circle, the tender signals the diver and pulls him to a new location (within the limits of visibility). The diver commences searching in a second circle, and the pattern is repeated until the diver again reaches the hole. If the diver's physical condition continues to be satisfactory, a second hole is cut in the ice and the procedure is repeated; otherwise, the standby diver takes over and a new standby diver is designated. Figure 10.2 illustrates this through-the-ice search technique.

10.1.2 Line-Tended (Fishtail) Search

The line-tended fishtail search is a simple method used to search identified areas that are relatively small and shallow, or hard to get to with open water techniques. The fishtail technique is shown in Figure 10.3. This technique

works well when diving in areas where there are vast amounts of debris and the diver could very easily become trapped under water. It is an excellent method to use when close coverage is required or there is zero visibility. The quality of coverage depends on the diver and his line tender working very close as a team. They must understand and react to the needs of each other.

The fishtail search is very effective in achieving thorough coverage under water; however, the searching diver must constantly be swimming, while at the same time maintaining a complete search of the bottom. This procedure can be physically exhausting as well as difficult. It is because of this that divers should not attempt to swim fishtail patterns in waters where there are moderate to strong currents. It is almost completely impossible to swim against moderate to strong currents under water while conducting search procedures. If it needs to be done, then the diver's time in the water will be very limited and the ability of the diver to be involved in a repetitive schedule may be nonexistent. Alternative search methods should be considered at this point, or a method modified to make the diver's job easier.

Although the diver is actually doing the swimming and searching, it is the responsibility of the line tender to insure that the area searched is complete and thorough. The tender must also be aware of what the diver is going through, based on his own experience at doing the same tasks. The tender must be able to communicate with the divers and get them to respond to specific directions. In most of the waters where this type of searching is done, the line tender is literally the diver's eyes.

Divers should automatically react to the instructions of the line tender, as conveyed to them through line signals or underwater voice communications. The diver should never have to worry about where they are going or when to stop, this is the responsibility of the line tender.

The following personnel and equipment items are needed for a fishtail search:

- One diver with basic scuba equipment
- One dive supervisor/line tender, with fishtail line, suggested length 50–75 ft. (15–23 m)
- One standby diver

The supervisor/tender will give the diver all information as to what the object of the search is, description, etc. The area will be reconnoitered and line signals reviewed, if underwater communication is not available. Once the diver has entered the water, he should inform the supervisor/tender of the diving conditions, visibility, silt, debris, etc. The supervisor/tender will determine from this information

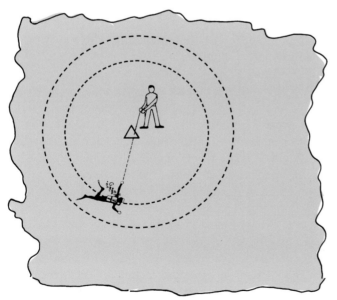

FIGURE 10.2
Circular Search Pattern Through Ice

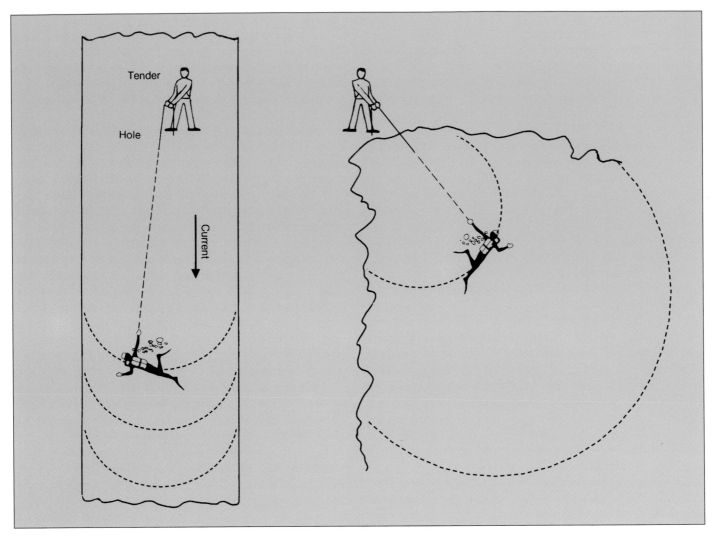

FIGURE 10.3
Arc (Fishtail) Search Pattern

exactly how the diver is to proceed and how far to bring the diver in on each subsequent pass. When directed, the diver should swim on the surface to the full length of the fishtail line, or until told to stop by the supervisor/tender. The diver will then descend to the bottom holding a taunt line on the fishtail line. If necessary, the line may be tied to the diver, thus eliminating the risk of the diver losing the line and having to return to the surface to retrieve it. However, the diver must be able to free himself from the fishtail line in case of an emergency, even if it means cutting the line.

In beginning the search, the diver should swim forward along the bottom, searching for the object being sought. It is important that the diver swim very slow and controlled, as energy may be quickly expended, completely exhausting the diver. At the conclusion of the fishtail arc, the supervisor/tender will signal the diver to reverse his direction and proceed back the other direction. This is accomplished by the diver placing the loop from the fishtail line in the opposite hand. If the diver swims off in the wrong direction, he will be signaled by the supervisor/tender of the error. At the end of each fishtail arc, the diver is pulled in until the designated area has been completely covered.

If the diver encounters vast amounts of debris and becomes trapped or confused, he can follow the fishtail line back toward the supervisor/tender. This should allow the diver a chance to orient himself and make the necessary adjustments. If the diver is unable to free himself, the diver should signal the line tender. The safety diver will be deployed and instructed to follow the fishtail line to the trapped diver and render assistance.

If the search area is in a river with a moderate to strong current, there is a possibility that the object being sought could be covered with sand. The diver and line tender should keep this in mind if they are unable to locate the object using the normal fishtail procedure. If the object is not located, the line tender may find it necessary to modify the search technique and search the area again using a modified search technique. The diver may have to use a

NOAA Diving Manual

tool to dig into the sand, such as a gardener's hand rake, or it may be necessary to use a metal detector. It will be up to the line tender in charge and the diver to determine which method will be best for their particular situation. In some cases it may even be necessary to use both a digging tool and a metal detector.

Once the object being sought has been located, the diver should retrieve it and bring it back to the surface. If the object is too big or heavy, the object can be marked by the diver using the fishtail line. Attaching the fishtail line to the object, will allow easy relocation of the object and the diver is then free to return to the surface and get what additional equipment he may need in retrieving the object.

The following signals may be used when conducting a fishtail search pattern if underwater communications are not used.

From Diver to the Line Tender:
- One pull—"Stop *or* I'm OK"
- Two pulls—"Give Me Slack"
- Three pulls—"Pull Me In"
- Four pulls—"Haul Me Up"

From the Line Tender to the Diver:
- One pull—"Stop *or* Are You OK?"
- Two pulls—"Change Direction"
- Three pulls—"Surface"

10.1.3 Jackstay Search Pattern

In the jackstay search pattern, a rectangular search area is laid out and buoyed (see Figure 10.4A). Buoy lines run from the bottom anchor weights to the surface, and a ground line is stretched along the bottom between the weights. Prior to descending, the diver takes compass bearings in the direction of the search pattern. The divers conducting the search descend on the buoy line and search along the ground line, beginning at one of the anchor weights. When the searching diver reaches the other anchor weight, the weight is moved in the direction of the search. The distance the weight is moved depends on visibility; if visibility is good, the weight is moved the distance the searching diver can comfortably see as he swims along the line. If visibility is poor, the line is moved only as far as the searching diver can reach. The searching diver then swims back toward the first anchor weight along the jackstay line (see Figure 10.4B). The length of the line determines the area to be covered. The jackstay search pattern is the most effective search technique in waters with poor visibility.

10.1.4 Searching a Large Area

Diving from an unanchored barge, small boat, or vessel can be an efficient method of covering a large area for search or survey purposes. When scuba divers are towed from a boat that is underway, the technique is referred to as tow diving. When a boat accompanies the diver, but the

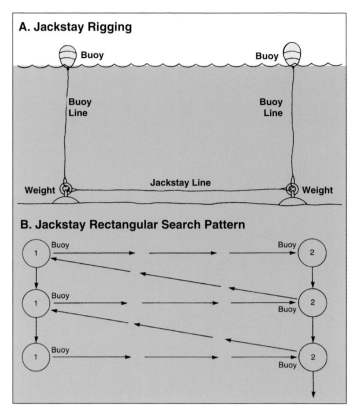

FIGURE 10.4
Jackstay Rigging and Rectangular Search Pattern

diver is not attached to the boat and is being propelled by current alone, the technique is called drift diving. There are procedures and safety precautions that apply to both kinds of diving; these are described below.

WARNING
WHEN DIVING FROM A VESSEL, THE ENGINES OF THE VESSEL SHOULD BE IN NEUTRAL POSITION WHEN THE DIVERS ARE CLOSE TO THE BOAT OR ARE ENTERING OR LEAVING THE WATER.

10.1.5 Tow Diving

Some underwater tasks require great distances to be covered in a minimum amount of time. These tasks include inspecting a pipeline, surveying a habitat site, searching for a lost instrument, observing fish populations over a wide area, or any number of similar operations. Free-swimming scuba divers are inefficient at carrying out such tasks, and quicker methods of search or survey are needed. Devices such as diver propulsion vehicles (DPV), wet subs, or towed sleds may be used to increase scuba diver efficiency.

Towing a scuba diver behind a small boat is another method of searching a large area. This technique is called tow diving; the scuba divers hold onto a line attached to the boat and vary their depth according to the contour of the bottom, which allows them to make a closeup search of the area over which the boat is traveling.

SCUBA DIVERS BEING TOWED MUST MONITOR AND CONTROL THEIR DEPTH TO AVOID BARO-TRAUMA.

When towing divers, the following safety precautions are recommended:

- If possible, the boat should be equipped with a "jet drive" propulsion system, which has no rudder or propeller.
- If the boat is equipped with a propeller, a propeller cage or shroud should be fabricated to protect the divers.
- A communications system should be set up between the divers and the boat, with signals agreed on and practiced prior to diving. A line separate from the tow or descent line may be employed as a safety line.
- Scuba divers being towed should carry signal devices (whistle, flare, surface marker buoys, etc.) especially in adverse weather conditions such as fog, in case they become separated from the boat and tow line.
- Unless there is danger of entanglement, the divers should carry a surface float to assist the boat crew in tracking them. The float line also can be used for signaling the divers while they are on the bottom.
- Two scuba divers should be towed together.
- All personnel on board should be thoroughly briefed on the dive plan.

One practical and inexpensive method of towing scuba divers involves the use of a single towline with loops, a tow bar, or a fluked anchor for the divers to hold. Divers using such an apparatus should be towed at a comfortable speed (one–two knots) that will not dislodge their masks. The height above the bottom at which the divers travel is controlled by the speed of the boat and the ability of the divers to arch their bodies and to plane up or down. A single towline, rather than a bridle, leading back to a yoke with a short line for each diver, works best. There should be two crew members in the tow boat, one to operate the vessel and the other to watch for surfacing divers and to keep the towline from fouling in the boat propeller.

The equipment necessary for towing scuba divers is normally available. The boat should have at least a 30-hp engine and should be large enough to accommodate four or more people and the diving equipment. A towline of 1/2 or 5/8 inch (1.3 or 1.6 cm) nylon line about 200 ft. (61 m) long used with about 75 lbs. (34 kg) of weight permits divers to reach depths of up to 90 fsw (28 msw). The towing weight should be made of two or three pieces of lead, steel, or concrete. Three 25-pound (11.3 kg) lead balls are ideal because there is less likelihood that a ball will hang up on submerged objects. A return line of 1/2 inch (1.3 cm) nylon 50 ft. (15 m) long should be tied to the towline at the weights. Polypropylene line should not be used because it is buoyant. The return line will trail behind the towed divers, who hang onto the towline at or near the weights.

Any time one diver leaves the towline, the partner should monitor the departing diver's actions until he returns and again makes contact with the towline. If the diver fails to regain the return line, the partner must abandon the towline and both divers must surface together.

Another towline method uses the aquaplane (see Figure 10.5). The simplest version is a board that, when tilted downward or sideways, provides a dynamic thrust to counter the corresponding pull on the towing line. The addition of a 'T' bar seat and proper balancing of the towing points permit one-handed control of the flight path. With an aquaplane, which can be made in a few hours from off-the-shelf materials, a team of divers can be towed behind a small boat. As with other towing methods, the maximum speed must be such that the diver's mask is not torn off (one–two knots). The dive team may operate either in tandem off the same board, which requires some practice and coordination, or each diver may have a separate board attached to a yoke.

In areas where entanglement is not a problem, divers may wish occasionally to drop off the towline during traverses to investigate objects of interest. A 50 ft. (15 m) return line attached to and trailing behind the aquaplane can be used to permit a diver who drops off the sled to grasp the line and return to the sled. It is important for those in the boat to know what the divers are doing, especially if they intend to drop off the line to observe the bottom. A sled or aquaplane released by a diver may continue planing downward by itself and crash into the bottom. Some tow rigs have a small wire built into the towline, with a waterproof push-button switch, so that the divers can communicate by buzzer with the tow boat.

One of the best methods of towing divers, especially if they intend to drop off the towline, is to equip each arm of the yoke with a large cork float, such as those used on fishing nets or mooring pickup poles. The diver merely straddles the cork and hangs onto the line ahead. The towing pull is then between the legs and not on the hands and arms. Maneuvering by body flexing is easy, and when the divers wish to leave the line they merely release their grip and spread their legs, allowing the cork to rise rapidly to the surface to let personnel in the boat know the divers are off the line. As soon as the cork breaks the surface, the boat stops, backs up along the line to the cork (the boat must not pull the cork and line to the boat), and hovers, with the engine in neutral, near the bubbles until the divers surface. The divers can then hand over samples,

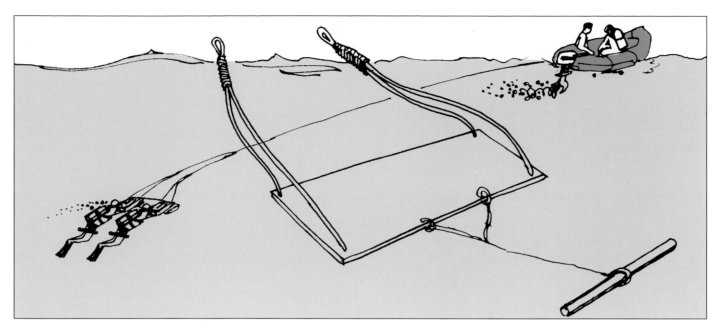

FIGURE 10.5
Aquaplane for Towing Divers

relate findings, and resume the tow. Experience has shown that there is little or no danger of losing the bubbles using this method, because the relatively slow towing speed of the boat allows the cork to surface within seconds of being released. The cork should surface at a point very close to the place where the divers dropped off the line. If this method is not used and if, after the divers drop off a tow, their bubbles cannot be seen from the tow boat, there is a chance that they are temporarily lost. In this case, a standby buoy with an adequate anchor should be ready to be lowered slowly and carefully overboard, so as not to hit the divers below. The tow boat should stand by at the buoy until the divers surface. This technique prevents the surface boat from being carried away from the survey area by current or wind.

The scope of the towline may be as much as 10-to-l, and in deep water this could place a diver far behind the tow boat. If a weighted line is used, as described earlier, the scope can be reduced to about 4-to-1. If the diver is a long distance behind the tow boat, a safety boat may be used to follow the towed divers to assist them if they become separated from the towline. Whenever a towing operation is planned, regardless of the equipment or method used, it is advisable to conduct a series of practice runs to determine the best combinations of boat speed, towline-yoke length, and diver-boat signals.

Although towing is a useful way to cover a great deal of terrain, there are limitations and drawbacks to this technique. It is difficult to take notes or photographs while under tow, unless enclosed sleds are used. There may be considerable drag on the body, so one should not carry bulky equipment either in the hands or on the weight belt. Until the diver leaves the towline, the hands should not be used for anything but holding on. Sample bags, cameras, etc., should be attached to the towline with quick-release snaps. The amount of work to be accomplished and the equipment to be carried can be determined in predive practice.

10.1.6 Drift Diving

Drift diving is used occasionally to cover a large area when there are strong currents. Divers are put into the water up stream and drift with the boat, which trails a buoy with a clearly visible diver's flag. The diver must carry a surface marker buoy to assist topside personnel in tracking the diver's position. If the operation must be conducted in heavy currents, divers should enter the water as far up current as necessary and drift with the current, holding onto a line attached to the drifting boat. If the drift involves a large vessel, a small boat should be used to track and retrieve the divers. As with towing scuba divers, drift divers should carry appropriate signaling devices.

During pickup, the boat operator should not (except in an emergency) approach the divers until the entire dive team is on the surface and has given the pickup signal. The boat's operator should bring the boat alongside the dive party on a downwind or down current side, and the dive tender should assist the divers aboard. In all cases, the boat's motor should be in idle during pickup, with the propeller in neutral.

10.1.7 Deepwater Towbar Search

The deepwater towbar search technique is used for searching large bodies of water when searching divers are required to locate relatively large objects. This method is most effective when searching divers have at least minimal visibility, however, it is still possible to be successful in zero visibility conditions. Using the towbar search method in zero visibility conditions requires careful planning and knowledge of debris which may interfere with a safe operation. Only experienced and knowledgeable divers should be used under these conditions.

The following equipment items are needed for a towbar search:

- Tow Vessel: The towing vessel should be large enough to comfortably handle the team of divers and their equipment. It should have a large open rear deck area which will allow freedom of movement for the line tender and safety divers. The vessel should be highly maneuverable, as well as having adequate power in case of rough seas. For best results the craft should not be less than 17 ft. in length.
- Vessel Propulsion: Regardless of the design of the craft being used as the tow vessel, the craft should be equipped with an engine rated no less than 80 hp.
- Towline: The towline used in this type of operation should be a minimum of 5/8 inch diameter braided non-stretch line. Either white or yellow line should be used for increased visibility. The length of the line may vary, but it should never be less than three times the depth of water in which the divers are working. The suggested lengths of towline are 50, 150, and 300 ft. (15, 46, and 91 m, respectively).
- Boat Tow Harness: The tow harness is a short line attached to each side of the vessel at the stern cleats of the towing rings. When attached to each side of the vessel, it must be long enough to extend around the engine and still remain free. This method can be used if a tow post is not available.
- Towline Pulley: If a tow post is not available and it is necessary to use a tow harness, then a towline pulley should also be used. The towline pulley moves freely along the tow harness while attached to the end of the towline. Movement of the pulley along

the tow harness allows the boat operator maximum maneuverability when towing.

- Towbar Harness: The towbar harness should attach to the towline at the diver's end. The towbar harness is also attached to the towbar at three separate locations. The harness is attached at both ends of the bar as well as in the middle of the towbar. It is important that the harness be attached in the middle to add strength to the towbar should debris be struck while towing. There should not be any slack in any of the three attachment lines, thus distributing the load equally between all three attachment points (see Figure 10.6).
- Towbar: The towbar is a device that the searching divers hang on to. The bar may be constructed of either metal pipe or schedule 80 plastic pipe (pvc). The bar should be constructed so that it protects the diver's hands should debris be encountered and struck by the towbar. Eye bolts should be used at the attachment points for the towbar harness. See Figure 10.6 for details on the towbar.
- Signal Line: A signal line should be tied to the towline approximately 3–5 inches from where the towline attaches to the towline pulley. If a tow post is used, the signal line may be attached approximately 3–5 inches from the tow post on the towline. A signal line should be attached even if underwater communication is used to serve as a backup should the underwater communications fail during towbar operations.

The search area is identified by positioning four buoy markers, one at each corner, to form a square or rectangle (see Figure 10.7). The towing vessel should then position itself just outside either side of the quadrant and the towbar is placed in the water and lowered to the bottom.

Divers should enter the water only after the engine(s) is in neutral or shut off. The divers will then follow the towline to the bottom where they will hang on to the towbar and wait to begin the search. After reaching the towbar, the divers should signal the surface, by voice communication or line signal, their readiness to begin the search. If line signals are used, the divers should give the line tender two hard tugs on the line. The boat operator will then begin towing the divers slowly (.5 knots), gradually increasing speed as directed by the divers. Generally, the maximum speed for such towing is 1–2 knots. The divers should establish neutral buoyancy, allowing them to stay off the bottom while still being able to see the bottom. This will help prevent "silt-out" conditions and allow divers to maintain visibility. In the event that the divers are working in zero visibility conditions, the divers should hang onto the bar with one hand and search the bottom with their free hand. The divers must maintain a position behind the shrouded handle of the towbar to help protect themselves from debris that might be struck during towbar operations.

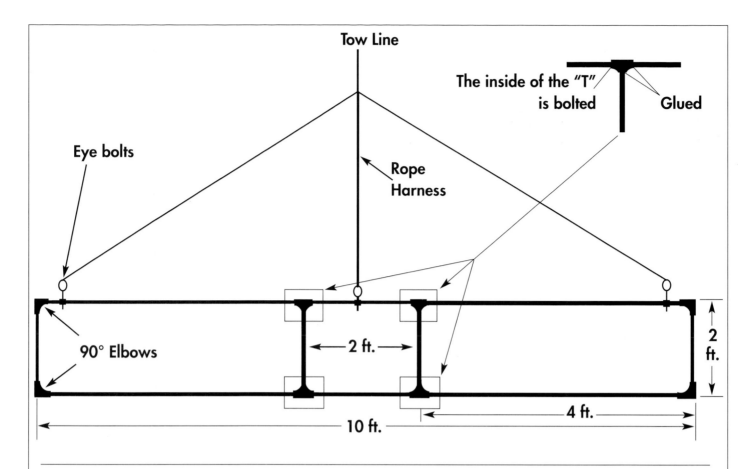

Schedule 80 PVC pipe is used throughout. All four corners are glued. At the "T" the two-foot sections are bolted allowing the tow-bar to be shortened if desired, the rest of the "T" is glued (see blow up of "T" section above). The rope harness is secured to the towbar with eye bolts. It is very important that the harness pulls equally on all three eye bolts. Weight can be added to the towbar, if needed, by pouring cement in the leading edge pipe, or securing weight to the center of the towbar near the center eye bolt. If in heavy current, a 20-inch piece of pipe can be placed between the divers legs and secured to the towbar with the appropriate length of rope, this should help relieve diver fatigue caused from hanging onto the towbar.

FIGURE 10.6
Towbar Construction

Once the tow vessel has reached the end of the search pattern, the boat operator will turn the vessel around by using a series of maneuvers that allow the boat to be placed in a position for the next pass. To accomplish this, the operator will have to back up the boat to give the line tender slack in the line. After enough slack is obtained, the operator will then go forward while turning the boat 180 degrees, allowing the boat to proceed in the opposite direction. While the boat is being backed up to obtain slack, the line tender must pull in excess line and keep it from becoming entangled in the propeller(s). When the vessel is turning on the surface, the divers should move out to the end of the towbar. While hanging onto the towbar with one hand, the other hand should hold onto the towbar harness. This position should be maintained until the towbar flips over and is positioned for the next pass. The divers should hang onto this line to help prevent the line from becoming entangled on the first stage of their scuba regulators. Once the vessel has been turned and is heading in the opposite direction for a new pass, the line tender must let the excess line back out to re-establish tension on the towline. At the end of each pass, the divers should signal each other to let one another know everything is okay. In limited visibility the divers will find it necessary to signal one another by grabbing the other diver's hand and shaking from side to side to let one another know everything is okay. If there is a problem, the diver should point the other diver's hand in the direction of the surface to let him know it is necessary to surface.

If one of the divers locates the object of the search, he should immediately signal the dive partner by shaking the bar. The partner should then give assistance in bringing the object back to the surface, if necessary.

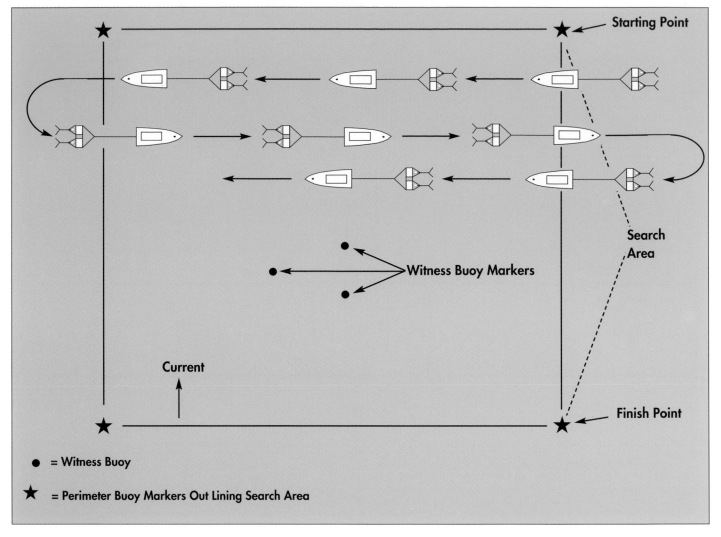

FIGURE 10.7
Towbar Search Method

In all cases, all divers should return to the surface together, even if the dive partner does not need assistance in bringing the object to the surface.

The following towline signals can be used when conducting a towbar search and voice communication is not used.

Divers to Surface:
- One pull—The boat is going too fast
- Two pulls—The boat is going too slow
- Three pulls—Stop
- Four pulls—Divers in trouble, send safety divers

Surface to Divers:
- Three pulls—From the line tender, divers are to surface

Divers on the towbar should conclude the dive or abort if any of the following circumstances occur:

- The object of the search is located
- When one of the divers' scuba cylinder reaches 500 psig pressure
- The diver or dive team experiences problems which they are not able to correct
- Either diver gets cold or fatigued
- There is an equipment malfunction

Additionally, either diver may terminate the dive for any condition, situation, or circumstance in which he is not comfortable or capable of performing the required skill or task.

10.1.8 Cable Cross Search

The cable cross search (see Figure 10.8) is intended to be used strictly for narrow waterways where there is a strong current which prevents a diver from swimming a designated pattern, or a towing vessel in a river from being able to hold position or maintain maneuverability.

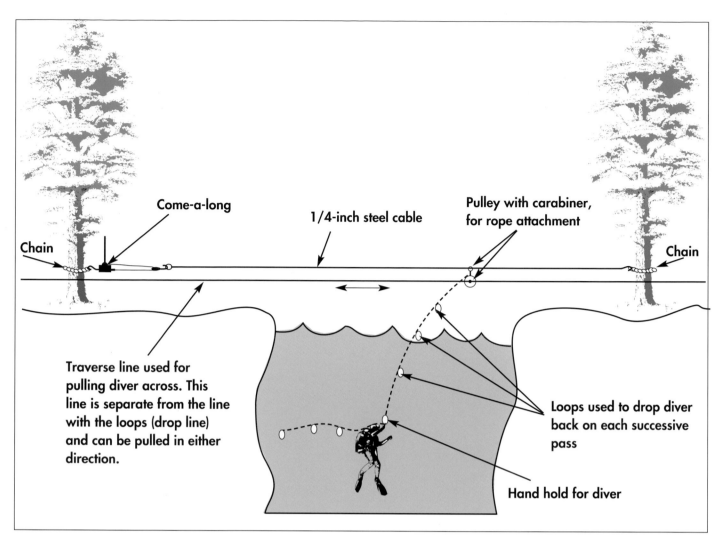

FIGURE 10.8
Cable Crossing Search Technique

The cable cross search technique is an extremely effective and dependable method for ensuring complete and accurate coverage. Although it does take a considerable amount of time to set up, with practice an experienced team can quickly set up the river area to be searched or change location with minimal delay. This search method is very flexible and can be modified to fit varying conditions, such as diving near water falls, hydroelectric dams, in and around heavy debris, strong currents, and waters with varying degrees of visibility.

The following equipment is necessary for a team of divers to conduct a cable cross search:

• Steel cable, 1/4 inch diameter with a minimum tensile strength of 2,300 lbs; this cable must be looped at each end around a cable thimble, then the cable is secured to itself with not less than three cable clamps. Depending upon the width of the river, a dive team should have cable in lengths of 50, 75, 100, 150, and 200 ft. available to them.

• At least one cable stretcher, commonly referred to as a "come-a-long;" the come-a-long should be equipped with 1/4-inch steel cable, with a tensile strength of 2,300 lbs.

• Two 36-inch lengths of 3/8-inch logging chain; one chain is used for each side of the river.

• One pulley wheel attached to the cable that will be crossing the river; it should be capable of withstanding a very heavy pull. This pulley must be capable of moving freely along the cable, from one side of the river to the other.

• A drop line from the pulley wheel to the water; the line should not be less than 5/8 inch diameter by 100 ft. in length. Hand hold loops (slipknot) should be placed in the line equal to the diver's visibility, but should not be more than 5 ft. apart.

• Traverse lines in two lengths of 5/8 inch diameter in lengths of 75, 150, or 300 ft. are suggested. One end of each line is secured to the pulley wheel, then each line is stretched to opposite sides of the river.

Procedures for Working Dives

- Depending on the diver and speed of the current, the diver may elect to add additional weight to his weight belt.

Once the area of the river to be searched has been identified, the steel cable is stretched across the river just slightly up stream. The steel cable should be secured on one side of the river by attaching it to some type of immovable object, such as a tree. The cable is then secured to the other side of the river, again attaching it to an immovable object. The come-a-long is used to draw the cable very taut. The pulley wheel is attached to the cable stretched across the river. The drop line is attached to the pulley wheel, with hand hold loops already placed in the drop line. The traverse pull line is stretched across the river.

Upon entering the water, the diver will be held steady against the rushing current by the drop line. The diver is then slowly pulled across the river by the team from the opposite side of the river. The team pulling the diver must do so slowly but consistently. This will enable the diver to scan the river bottom for the object. During the time that a diver is being pulled across the river, he should not drop down on the line to the next hand hold loop until the pass has been completed. At the end of the first pass, the diver should inform surface tenders of what he is finding and any other unusual problems that will be useful to the next diver. Once the diver has reached the last loop at the end of the drop line, the cable must be repositioned further down stream using the same techniques as described earlier.

10.1.9 Search Without Lines

When conditions are such that search lines cannot be used, a search can be conducted using an underwater compass. There are several search patterns that will ensure maximum coverage; however, simplicity of pattern is important. Divers should use the cardinal points North, East, South, West, and measure the length of a side in one-minute intervals or 50 kicks, and should turn the same way each time.

10.1.10 Recovery

The method chosen to recover a lost object depends on its size and weight. Small items can be carried directly to the surface by the diver, while larger items require lifting devices. When a lift is used, the diver must attach lifting straps and equipment to the item being recovered. A line that is not substantially longer than the depth of the water being searched and that has a small buoy attached should be carried to the spot to mark the located object.

10.2 UNDERWATER NAVIGATION

With the introduction of several new navigation systems in recent years, divers now have a choice of technologies ranging from precision navigation and survey systems to low cost homing devices. The key to a successful dive operation is the selection of a system or method of navigation that is appropriate for the task at hand (see Table 10.2). A list of some of the new systems available to divers follows:

- **Pingers and diver-operated pinger receivers** provide a simple and effective means of returning to a dive boat or habitat or finding an instrument or any other marked location (see Figures 10.9—10.11). The pinger emits sonar signals which are detected by the directional pinger receiver. The diver points the receiver around until the optical or audible receiver readout indicates the strongest signal. The pinger is located by swimming in that direction. Pinger systems may be optimized for specialized applications. Smart pingers extend battery life to several months or even years by pinging only during programmed time periods. Some pinger receivers convert signal strength to an approximate distance to target.
- **Diver-operated transponders and transponder interrogators** may be used where a more precise range to target is required (see Figure 10.9). The transponder interrogator measures signal run time to compute distance.
- **Long baseline acoustic positioning systems** are well suited for underwater surveys and other tasks requiring precise diver navigation. One meter positioning accuracy is routinely achieved and measurements down to a few centimeters resolution are possible in some cases. Prior to operations, acoustic transponders called baseline stations are deployed near the corners of a work site. A diver station interrogates these transponders, measuring signal run time and computing the distance to each baseline station. The diver station converts the distance data into a precise position which is displayed on a small data screen or signaled through a headset. AquaMap®, a commercial system optimized for scientific use, indicates the margin of error of a position fix and offers the ability to associate diver observations with position fixes. Other functions include tracking of diver movements from a surface station and the exchange of e-mail style messages between divers and the surface station.
- **Short baseline and ultra short baseline positioning systems** use shipboard-mounted sonar transducers instead of baseline stations. This simplifies system deployment but also results in reduced accuracy.
- **Diver-operated active sonar systems** provide a means for measuring distance to the sea floor or to other large obstacles (see Figures 10.10, 10.12). The diver sonar emits a signal which bounces off the obstacle. Signal run time indicates the distance of the obstacle which is displayed on a readout. Some diver sonars are equipped with a headset. By listening to the reflected signal, an experienced diver can discern the nature of the object. The maximum range of diver sonars varies from 100–650 ft., (31–198 m), depending on model, conditions and the size of the object.

- **GPS satellite navigation receivers** involve the use of non-acoustic approach to underwater navigation by divers. These receivers are equipped with a floating antenna on a thin cable. If the antenna is raised to within 2 inch of the surface, it can pick up the signals from GPS satellites. The position data is displayed on the diver station screen. The receivers are targeted to the military market where the use of a passive navigation receiver offers a stealth advantage over active sonar systems.

Despite the availability of many "high-tech" navigation systems, divers should be familiar with the principles of basic navigation using underwater landmarks as well as compass, watch, and depth gauge. These often will be the only tools needed for relatively short underwater excursions. In more extensive dive operations, basic navigation provides a valuable 'ground truthing' for other navigation methods which are always subject to failure.

TABLE 10.2
A Comparison Of Diver Navigation Technologies

Technology	Navigation Data	Advantages	Limitations	Typical Applications
Pingers and pinger receivers	Direction and approximate distance to pinger, range up to 1000 meters	Low cost, easy to use	Will only find marked objects or location, only rough distance data	Returning to boat or habitat, marking and finding equipment
Transponders and interrogators	Direction and precise range to target, one meter accuracy at up to 1000 meters	Simple way to measure distances, easy to use	Will only find marked objects or locations, higher cost than pingers	Marking and finding equipment, underwater measurements
Long baseline positioning	3-dimensional positions or range and bearing, 1 to 0.1 meter accuracy, range up to 1000 meter	High precision, diver navigation and tracking	Requires setup prior to operations	Precision survey, diver navigation, diver supervision
Short and ultra short baseline positioning	3-dimensional positions or range and bearing, range up to 1000 meters, precise distance but less precise direction	No setup prior to operations, diver navigation and tracking	Less accurate than long baseline	Rough survey, diver navigation, diver supervision
Active sonar	Distance and direction of obstacle, range up to 200 meters	Find and classify unmarked objects	Limited range smaller objects may be missed	Search and recovery, depth finding
Underwater GPS	3-dimensional positions, 10 meter accuracy with military version	Worldwide operation without setup	Limited accuracy, antenna must be raised within 5 cm of surface	Military, stealth
Doppler velocity log	Speed and heading, error about 1 percent of run distance	A form of dead reckoning, therefore unlimited range, stealth	Costly, must be mounted on sled, increasing error over time (drift)	Little or no diver use yet, interest primarily from military sector
Compass and watch	Range and bearing	Lowest cost, reliable	Limited accuracy, drift	Basic navigation backup to other systems

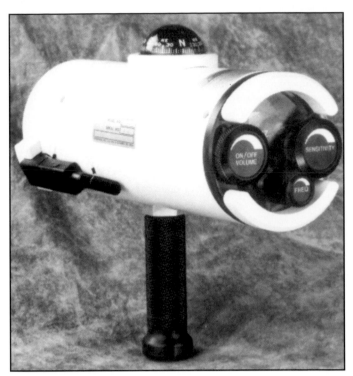

FIGURE 10.9
Diver-Operated Transponder and Transponder Interrogator

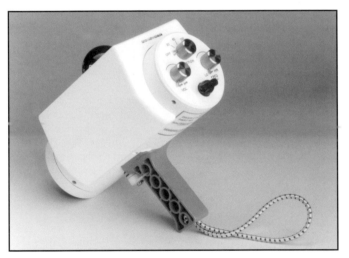

FIGURE 10.10
Diver-Operated Active Sonar System

10.2.1 Basic Underwater Navigation

Basic underwater navigation by means of simple observation or use of a compass and depth gauge remains a fundamental and essential skill for all divers. For most short excursions, these are the only instruments needed. Even when using advanced navigation instruments, basic navigation skills provide an important backup.

Much navigation can be accomplished by observing the environment. This is called natural navigation.

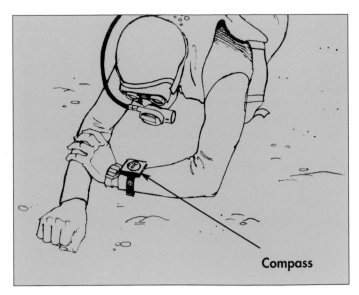

FIGURE 10.11
Proper Technique for Compass Navigation

Note the depth at the start of the dive along with the composition of the sea floor (rocky, sandy, etc.). Note important underwater landmarks such as boulders, big coral heads, patches of kelp and similar objects. Make a mental note of the time taken to swim from one landmark to the next. Notice the direction of the current. A basic knowledge of underwater features will help as well. For example, wave ripples in the sand typically run parallel to the shore and the sea floor normally slopes up toward the shore.

More precise navigation and even some basic measurements are possible by using a compass and watch. The diver starts by taking a compass bearing, then holding the compass in a horizontal position in front of him (note that compasses are prone to jamming if not kept horizontal). Be aware that metal items and dive instruments close to the compass may cause an incorrect compass reading.

The axis of the compass must be parallel to the direction of travel in order to swim an accurate compass course. A simple method of achieving this with a wrist mounted compass is for the diver to extend the arm that does not have the compass on it straight in front of them and then to grasp this arm with the other hand (see Figure 10.11). Swimming in this position will help the diver maintain a straight course and also provides a measure of protection against collision with objects in extremely poor visibility. When visibility allows it, the diver should note a point in the direction they wish to go, then swim towards it. A compass reading should be taken to the next point and so on. It is strongly recommended that the diver practice on land by walking compass courses prior to using a compass under water.

To measure a distance, the diver first finds his average swim speed by measuring the time it takes them to cover a

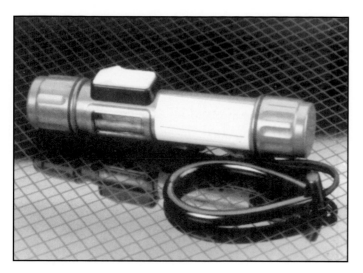

FIGURE 10.12
Sonar Receiver and Beacon

FIGURE 10.13
Diver Navigation Board

known distance at an easily maintained pace. Use this simple formula:

$$S = D / T$$

where
S = speed of advance in feet or meters per minute
D = distance covered in feet or meters
T = transit time in minutes

Next, use a timer or watch to note the time it takes to swim a measured distance. Use this formula to find the approximate distance:

$$D = S \times T$$

To navigate in poor visibility, the diver notes swimming times and directions. Using this technique and making only right angle turns will help a diver draw a mental map (or on a slate) showing current position relative to the start point. The diver should be able to navigate in a square and return close to the starting point by swimming four legs for the same amount of time, making a 90 degree right turn after each leg.

10.2.2 Water Depth/Underwater Distance

Sonar devices are available to determine water depth with a simple push of a button and are reliable and rugged. These handheld instrument also measures the distance under water from the diver position to any object, or how much further down the bottom is, or the distance up to the surface vessel (see Figure 10.12).

10.2.3 Diver Navigation Board

A navigational board may be used for divers who must navigate under water. This navigation system integrates a digital depth gauge, chronometer, and an underwater compass on a rugged and lightweight board (see Figure 10.13).

10.2.4 Precision Underwater Navigation

Precision navigation is of increasing importance in the marine sciences. Mapping an archeological site, studying populations of shell fish, or assessing the impact of an oil spill all require high positioning accuracy. Acoustic positioning technology, in particular long baseline systems, can achieve sub-meter accuracy over distances approaching one kilometer. Resolutions of better than 0.1 meters are possible for smaller survey grids. However, obtaining accurate and reliable survey data is not just a matter of reading numbers off a dive instrument. If the data is to withstand the scrutiny of scientific or legal opinion, the project leader must know navigation system. Careful attention must be paid to the planning and execution of the project as well as the interpretation of the data.

10.2.5 Choosing and Converting Between Coordinate Systems

Acoustic positioning systems generate position fixes that are relative to the location of their baseline network or transducer array. A coordinate of [X=201;Y=-40] for example, indicates the point 201 meters along and 40 meters to the right of the imaginary line originating at the first baseline station and extending towards the second baseline station. Baseline relative positioning will produce data sets that are consistent in themselves, i.e., the location of points *relative to each other* is accurate. Conversion of relative position fixes to latitude and longitude or a similar coordinate system is possible by surveying the point of origin and the orientation of the baseline network or transducer array. This is necessary and should be done only when operating from a moving boat (short and ultra short baseline systems), when assembling a composite of multiple data sets, or when data must be plotted on independently generated charts. Be aware that the error of the converted position fix will be the vector sum of the errors of the surface and the underwater position fixes. Thus a +/- 0.1 meter acoustic fix will easily be overshadowed by an associated +/- 1 meter DGPS fix.

10.2.6 Post-Mission or Real-Time Coordinate System Conversions

Acoustic positioning systems may be connected to a differential GPS receiver for automatic conversion of baseline relative position fixes into latitude and longitude. Such automatic conversion should be used to compensate for the movement of a vessel or platform on which a positioning system is established. Yet, it is inappropriate when a sea floor anchored long baseline network is used or when operating from a fixed platform. In these cases, the "jitter" inherent in any sequence of DGPS position fixes taken from the same point will be imposed on the survey data, reducing its repeatability. Instead, carefully survey the acoustic positioning system's point of origin and orientation once, then apply that same offset and orientation to all data points.

10.2.7 Installation

The baseline network or transducer array of an acoustic positioning system is its navigation reference. Baseline stations are small cylinders that are often anchored to the ocean floor by a line, then buoyed by a flotation collar to float in mid-water. If a baseline station moves due to surge or current, a corresponding error will appear in the data. Sufficient flotation should be used to minimize movement or mount baseline stations on rigid rods that are driven into the ocean floor. The geometry of the installation must also be considered. In long baseline systems, three baseline stations are located near the corners of a rectangular work site. This assures that at least two stations will always appear at an approximate right angle from the diver's viewpoint, optimizing accuracy. The separation of short baseline transducers should be maximized and the surface vessel positioned so that the diver will operate broadside to the longest baseline. When doing repeat studies in the same location, the baseline station must be marked on the first study and used on all follow-up studies.

10.2.8 Environmental Variables

Acoustic position fixes are only as accurate as a system's estimation of the speed of sound. Speed of sound depends on water temperature, salinity, and depth. Sound speed varies about seven percent from 0–30 degrees Celsius and about three percent from freshwater to seawater. Some positioning systems are configured to assume a certain water temperature and salinity, others measure these parameters. If a station measures temperature to estimate speed of sound, it must "see" the correct temperature. Sound speed estimation is not critical if the survey looks at the relative location of objects and not the exact distance between objects.

10.2.9 Raw Position Data

Acoustic long and short baseline positioning systems measure signal run times and depths which are then converted into X and Y coordinates. Several mathematical steps are involved in the conversion. By recording the raw components of a position fix, it is possible to retain the option of later correcting hidden errors. These may be caused by an unreliable range measurement, an incorrect sound speed estimation, or even a flaw in the mathematical conversion process.

10.2.10 Quality Control

A position fix is of little significance if the margin of error is not known. To verify positioning repeatability, multiple fixes should be taken at the same spot, then the typical error computed (some positioning systems will compute typical or RMS position errors automatically). If the error is too large, setup must be reverified. The choice of a poor baseline geometry or movement of baseline stations are some of several factors that will result in poor repeatability. To check positioning accuracy, position fixes generated with the acoustic system should be compared to measurements of the same positions generated by laser sighting, differential GPS, or other means. The characteristics of any discrepancy should be reviewed if it exceeds the expected amount. A wrong estimation of the speed of sound is the likely cause of the discrepancy if it increases proportional to the distance from the acoustic positioning system's point of origin. If the error is similar for all positions, then the point of origin of the acoustic system or the surface system (for example the differential GPS base station) may have been surveyed incorrectly. Signal path distortions seen by the surface or acoustic system may result in persistent or fluctuating position specific discrepancies.

10.3 INSTRUMENT IMPLANTATION

The proper implantation of scientific instruments is important to the success of underwater scientific investigations. Instruments that are implanted on the sea bottom include lights, cameras, positioning stakes, radiometers, recording current meters, thermistors, oxygen sensors, and acoustical devices. Factors affecting the success of implantation include:

- The instrument's size and weight, mounting dimensions, fragility, and attachment points
- The available power supply and instrument readout cables, or (if self-contained) the frequency with which the instrument's batteries must be changed or the instrument must be serviced or replaced

- The alignment of the instrument in position, its height above the bottom, and its sensitivity to misalignment
- Bottom conditions, the bearing strength of the bottom, anticipated currents, and the type of marine life
- The precise markings of instrument location and the methods used for recovery at completion of the mission

The size and weight of the instrument and its physical dimensions and fragility affect the type of anchor used and the techniques chosen to move the instrument to the site. For small instruments, a concrete block may be an appropriate anchor. The blocks can be predrilled, fitted with fasteners on the surface, and moved to the site as a unit and positioned. In other cases, the concrete block and instrument can be moved to the site separately, and a diver can then position and align the instrument in the water. A concrete block anchor can be lowered directly into position using a winch, or it may be fitted with flotation devices and guided into position by a diver, who removes the flotation device when the anchor is in position.

For large instrument packages, anchors can be made of metal rods that are driven into the bottom by a diver using a sledgehammer or pneumatic impact hammer. Steel rods create magnetic anomalies that can affect instrument readings; therefore, instruments should be used only after the effect of the anchoring system on the instrument's functioning has been calibrated. Anchoring pins or pilings may be grouted in place with concrete supplied from the surface. Embedment anchors can be used to stabilize an instrument installation and can be driven into the bottom to secure the lines. Chains or wires equipped with turnbuckles can be run over the instrument package between anchors to secure the installation further. The foundation package should be designed to accept the instrument package easily so that it is as easy as possible for the diver to attach the package. When the foundation is complete, a line or lines should be run to the surface to assist in lowering and guiding the instrument into place.

Many underwater instruments require outside power to operate and to transmit data to outside receivers. During the installation of instrument cables, a diver is usually required to anchor the cable at various points along the cable run. The first point of anchor should be near the instrument package. To reduce the possibility that the cable will topple the instrument or that movement of either the cable or instrument will break the cable connection, the diver should allow a loop (called a bight) of extra cable between the first anchor and the instrument. The diver should guide the instrument cable around any rocks or bottom debris that might abrade the cable covering. Anchors should be placed at frequent intervals along the length of the cable, wherever the cable turns, and on each side of the cable where it runs over an outcropping or rise in the bottom. Cable anchors can either be simple weights attached to the cable or special embedment anchors.

The alignment of the foundation is important to successful implantation. A simple technique to achieve alignment is to drive a nonferrous stake into the bottom that has a nonferrous wire or line attached, and then hang a compass from the line or wire. A second nonferrous stake is then driven into the bottom when the compass indicates that the alignment is correct. The two stakes and the attached line then act as the reference point for aligning the foundation or instrument. A tape is used to translate measurements from the reference stakes and line to the foundation or the instrument. Before selecting a location for an instrument, bottom conditions should be analyzed to identify the appropriate foundation. The instrument site should be reinspected at frequent intervals to monitor the condition of the instrument and to clear away sediment or marine growth that may affect instrument readings.

Unmanned instrumentation is increasingly used for long-term data gathering and environmental monitoring tasks. Because many unmanned instruments are self-contained and expensive, they must be equipped with reliable relocation devices. Although surface or subsurface buoys (used in combination with GPS satellite navigation systems) are the most common relocation devices, at least for short-term implantation, these buoys are subject to vandalism, fouling in ship propellers, and accidental release. Many users therefore equip these instruments with automatic pinger devices in addition to marker buoys.

If a pinger-equipped instrument is believed to be lost in the vicinity of implantation, a surface receiver unit operated from a boat can guide divers to the approximate location; they can then descend and search with a hand-held locator unit. This technique works especially well in murky water when the divers are surface supplied and use live-boating techniques, particularly if the pinger is weak and a long search is necessary.

10.4 HYDROGRAPHIC SUPPORT

In hydrographic operations, divers can be used to confirm the existence and/or location of hazards to navigation, locate and measure least depths, and resolve any sounding discrepancies identified by different surface-based measurement techniques. When using divers for this type of work, it is essential to consider the skills of the divers, water conditions, the nature of the work, special equipment requirements, and the availability of diver support. Because hydrographic operations are frequently conducted in open water, it is important to mark the dive site using buoys, electronic pingers, or fathometers; this precaution becomes increasingly important under conditions of reduced visibility and high currents.

10.4.1 Hazards to Navigation

A significant portion of hydrographic support diving is conducted to identify hazards to navigation. Once the general location of a navigational hazard has been identified, its precise location can be determined using underwater search techniques.

When the object has been found, it should be marked with a taut-line buoy and its geographic position should be noted. If the depth is shallower than about 50 ft. (15 m), a lead-line depth should be recorded, along with the time of notation.

Diving operations that are designed to prove that no navigational hazard exists in a particular area are extremely time consuming and require painstaking documentation of search procedures and location. The reported location and geographic position of the hazard should be marked precisely; a taut-line buoy should be used to mark the search control point. Any time the control point is moved, the move should be documented and the geographic position of the new control point should be noted. Documentation of the search should include the geographic position of control points, the type of search, the equipment used, water conditions, problems encountered, what was found or not found, and a statement describing the area that has been searched and any area that may have been missed.

10.4.2 Locating and Measuring Least Depths

Divers can be used to determine least depths accurately, especially in such areas as rocky shoals, coral reefs, and wreck sites. After the general location to be studied has been identified, a team of divers is sent down to mark precisely the least depth by tying off a line on the bottom so that a buoy floats directly overhead. Care must be taken to ensure that the lead line is plumb and that the time of marking is recorded. A taut-line buoy can be used to mark the geographic position of the least depth so that it can be noted and recorded by surface personnel.

Least depth measurements are obtained with a precise digital depth gauge that measures water pressure in pounds per square inch (psi). Divers carry the measuring device to the highest point on the underwater object and record the pressure reading.

10.4.3 Resolving Sounding Discrepancies

When measurements of undersea features do not agree, divers can be used to inspect the site, resolve the discrepancies, and mark the site correctly. Discrepant measurements are most likely to occur in areas such as rocky substrates, faulted or volcanic bottoms, and reefs.

10.5 WIRE DRAGGING

Wire dragging is a method of ensuring that surface ships can pass through an area safely. The method involves deploying a wire between two ships and holding it at depth with weights ranging from 50–250 lbs. (22–113 kg). The objective of this procedure is to tow the wire in such a manner that hydrodynamic forces induce an arc-shaped curve. As the ships move through the water, the wire will snag on obstructions protruding above the depth of the drag. Divers supporting wire-dragging operations are used to identify:

- The objects on which the wire hangs
- The least depth over the obstruction
- The highest protrusion that could be caught from any direction

Divers can also identify underwater features that pose a hazard to fishing nets and to trawling or ground tackle, and assist in the removal of minor obstructions. Another task performed by divers is assessing the scope of wreckage. If the least depth cannot be determined accurately, the approximate depth needed for clearance is sought.

Divers need to exercise extreme caution when working around wire drags because, in addition to the hazards associated with any wreck diving operation, the wire itself poses a hazard. For example, if the wire slips on an obstruction, it could pin a diver; if the strands of the wire are broken, the wire can cut a diver severely; and if a diver holds the wire and it pulls loose, it can sever the diver's fingers.

When an underwater obstruction needs to be investigated, the support boat must be tied off to the buoy nearest the obstruction. After agreeing on all procedures, the divers swim to the buoy and descend to the bottom wire. Depth gauges are checked, and the depth of the obstruction is noted on a slate.

Because of forces acting on both the wire and the upright to the buoy, the depth at the weight can vary from its setting by as much as 10 ft. (3 m). Once on the bottom, the divers proceed hand-over-hand along the wire, one behind the other, taking care to stay outside the bight of the wire. This may be difficult because most drags are run with the current, which tends to push the diver into the bight. The recommended procedure is to "crab" into the current, making every effort to stay as much above the wire as possible.

WARNING
DIVERS MUST BE EXTREMELY CAREFUL WHEN WORKING INSIDE THE BIGHT OF A GROUND WIRE.

After arriving at the obstruction, wire depth is recorded. The divers then try to find the least depth of the obstruction; this procedure requires the divers to leave the wire. If the obstruction is not substantial, the divers should be several feet above the obstruction's depth when they enter the bight. Once the least depth point is found, the divers record the depth and determine whether the high point could cause the ship to hang at any point. If the object is intact or is a candidate for recovery, the divers select a suitable place to tie off a small buoy. The buoy must be tied off inside the bight so as not to be torn away when the drag wire is recovered.

The depth information recorded is verified by a surface-tended pneumatic pressure gauge, or a portable, specifically designed depth gauge. Because the equipment involved is cumbersome, this technique is rarely used during the initial investigation. In relatively calm seas and slack current, a lead line may be used to verify depth information.

Because divers follow a wire in single file, it is easy for one diver to lose track of his buddy. A buddy-check should therefore be carried out every 50 ft. (15 m); this procedure also may prevent diver entanglement when there is poor visibility.

NOTE

Wire-drag support diving should be done only by experienced divers who are well trained in the techniques and fully aware of the hazards.

10.6 UNDERWATER TOOLS

A fundamental aspect of accomplishing work under water is the selection of proper tools and equipment. In all operations, the relative advantages and disadvantages of power tools and hand tools must be considered. The amount of effort that will have to be expended is an important consideration in underwater work, and power tools can reduce the amount of physical exertion needed. Having to supply tools with power and to transport them, however, may be a substantial disadvantage.

The performance of divers under water is degraded by several factors, including water resistance, diver buoyancy, equipment bulk, the confined space environment, time limitations, visibility restrictions, and a diver's inability to provide a proper amount of reaction force without adequate staging, hand grips, or bracing. A diver's performance may therefore decrease significantly compared with his performance on land. Even a relatively simple task like driving a nail can be difficult because of limited visibility, water viscosity, and other environmental factors; however, some tasks are easier to accomplish under water because of the diver's ability to move easily in three dimensions. Because diver safety is a primary consideration in any underwater operation, hazards such as electric shock, excessive noise, and other potential causes of injury must be taken into account when selecting underwater tools.

Table 10.3 lists some common tools used under water, along with their sources of power and available accessories. Many hydraulic tools can be bought off-the-shelf to perform under water. Information supplied by the manufacturer contains detailed specifications that should be carefully observed.

10.6.1 Hand Tools

Almost all standard hand tools can be used under water. Screwdrivers are generally available in three configurations: the machine (or straight-slotted) type, the phillips type, and the allen type. Of the three, the allen screwdriver is easiest for a diver to use, because only torque is required to operate it and the linear leverage necessary is minimum. Also, the allen type provides a longer lever arm. The other types of screwdriver have a tendency to slip out of the screw head and damage the screw when turning. A single multipurpose tool can

be made by welding a screwdriver blade and a pair of pliers to an adjustable wrench.

When using a hack saw under water, it is difficult to follow a straight line. An added complication is the tendency of the blade to flex, which increases the likelihood that the blade will break. Because it is easier for a diver to pull than push under water, it is useful to put the blade in the saw so that the sawteeth are oriented toward the diver and the cut is made on the draw rather than the push.

A 2–4-pound short-handled hammer is a commonly used underwater tool. Because considerably more effort is required to swing a hammer under water than on land, it is easier to develop force by pounding with the heavy weight of a sledge hammer than by swinging and hitting with a lighter hammer.

Because it is easy to lose or drop tools under water, they usually are carried to the work site in a canvas bag attached to the diver's arm with a line. They also can be attached to a descending line with a shackle to slide down the line to the job site from the surface. Tasks involving grinding, chipping, pounding, or reaming with hand equipment are arduous and time consuming, and the use of hand tools for these tasks is not practical unless the task is small. To protect hand tools after use, they should be rinsed with freshwater and lubricated with a protective water-displacing lubricant.

10.6.2 Pneumatic Tools

Although pneumatic tools are rarely designed specifically for use under water, they need little, if any, alteration to be used in this environment. According to Hackman and Caudy (1981), the power available in most air motors ranges from 1/8–25 hp, and loaded speeds range from 40–6,000 rpm; some of these tools have even higher speeds. Most pneumatic tools require 90 psig of air pressure to operate, and they exhaust into the water. A disadvantage of these tools is exhaust bubbles that may disturb divers or impair their visibility under water. In addition, the amount of pressure available for power decreases at depth. Pneumatic tools can be modified to include a hose attachment on the exhaust that is larger in diameter than the supply hose. Often, the exhaust hose is routed back to the surface, where it discharges to atmospheric pressure. Some pneumatic tools have rear exhausts. Even with these modifications, surface-supplied pneumatic power can be used only to depths of 100–150 ft. (31–46 m). After each day's diving, oil should be poured into the air inlet of the tool until it completely fills the motor section; the tool should then be submerged in an oil bath to displace any water trapped in the tool. All petroleum preservatives must be removed and the tool thoroughly cleaned prior to use under water to avoid polluting the surrounding water. Sections of the pneumatic hose where it attaches to the tool and air supply should be properly secured to prevent lashing of the tool in the event of a hose failure.

TABLE 10.3
Diver Power Tools

Tool	Type	Description/Function/Accessories
Drill	Hydraulic	Metal and wood bits to 3 inches; attachments for brushing, grinding, cutting, and trapping.
	Pneumatic	Metal and wood bits, star drills, and other accessories for heavy–duty work
Impact Wrench	Hydraulic	3/4 inch to 2 1/2-inch square or hex drives; 100 – 10,000 ft-lb. on bolts to 3 inches; also used to drill and tap; larger tools weigh 12 – 80 pounds
	Pneumatic	1/4 inch to 4 inches square drives; handles bolts to 12 inches; largest tool weighs 600 pounds
Cable Cutter	Hydraulic	Pressures to 10,000 psi over ambient; guillotine-type cuts cable to 2 1/2 inches
	Power velocity	Guillotine-type cuts cable to 1 1/2 inches
Stud Driver	Power velocity	Penetrates plate from 1/4 inch to 1 1/4 inch thick
Cutoff Saw	Hydraulic	4-inch cut; 6-inch to 10-inch wheels
	Pneumatic	4 1/2-inch cut
Grinder	Hydraulic	Hydraulic 9-inch wheel (7 inches max, recommended)
	Pneumatic	8-inch wheel
Chain Saw	Hydraulic	To 15 hp; bar length to 43 inches; used for wood only
Hole Cutter	Hydraulic	To 4 inches in diameter
	Pneumatic	
	Explosive	Shaped charge, cuts 4-inch hole in steel up to 2 inches thick
Milling Cutter	Hydraulic	Cuts large holes up to 72 inches in diameter in bulkheads
Hacksaw	Hydraulic	8 1/2-inch cut for wood; models also available for metal and pipe; 14-inch cut for wood; shorter for metal, pipe
	Pneumatic	
Hammer	Hydraulic	Used for hammering, chipping, punching, and chiseling; develops 40 ft-lb.; delivers 1 – 300 blows per minute
	Pneumatic	Standard paving breaker
Jack Hammer	Pneumatic	Turns and reciprocates
Spreader (Hurst Tool)	Hydraulic	Jaws open/close with six tons force, 32-inch spread
Band Saw	Hydraulic	Used for cutting soft metals and cables
Chisels	Hydraulic	Used for chiseling. Several accessory chisels are available
	Pneumatic	

10.6.3 Hydraulic Tools

Hydraulic tools are the most popular kind of tool with working divers because they provide consistent closed-cycle power, are safer to use under water, have little or no depth limitation, are much lighter per unit of power output, do not produce bubbles that obscure the diver's vision, and require relatively little maintenance. As with pneumatic motors, hydraulic systems have the capability to start and stop rapidly, and they can be operated at different speeds.

Tools such as drills (Figure 10.14A), impact wrenches (Figure 10.14B), chain saws, disc grinders (Figure 10.14C), and cable or pipe cutters usually are modified versions of hydraulic tools designed for use on land. To convert tools for underwater use, different seals are used, internal voids are compensated to withstand ambient pressure, external surfaces are painted or coated with a corrosion inhibitor, and dissimilar metals are insulated from each other.

To facilitate the field use of hydraulic tools in areas where hydraulic oil is not readily available or where environmental restrictions prohibit the discharge of oil, hydraulic tool systems are being developed that use seawater as the working fluid in place of oil.

Hydraulic tools require a power source at the surface or a submersible electrohydraulic power source that can be located under water at the work site near the diver. These power sources are compensated to operate at depth, but require built-in batteries or an electrical umbilical from the surface to run the pump. The tools normally operate at pressures from 1,000 – 3,000 psi. To use them, divers usually work standing on the bottom or on some structure. When working with these tools on the side of a structure or in the midwater column, a diver can use harnesses or a diver's stage for support.

A number of diver-operated hydraulic tools have been developed for underwater construction and salvage work. These tools include:

- A cutoff saw (2,000 psi, 6-14 gpm, 10 inch diameter by 1/8 inch thick blade)

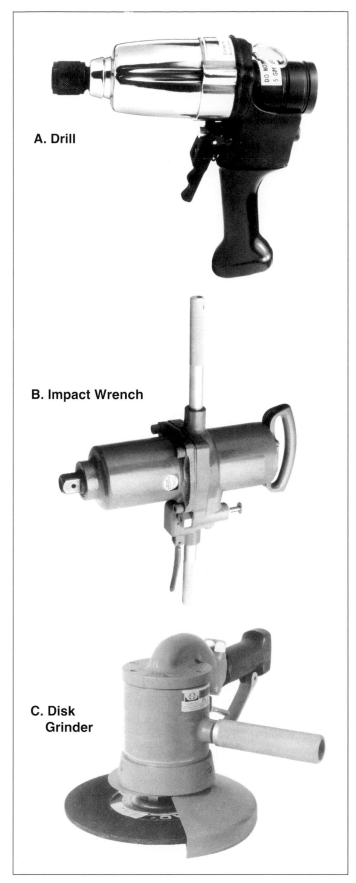

A. Drill

B. Impact Wrench

C. Disk Grinder

FIGURE 10.14
Underwater Hydraulic Tools

- A grinder (2,000 psi, 11 gpm, used with discs, cups, or wire brush)
- A come-along (1,500 psi, 2,000 lb. force, moves cable 1.5 inch per stroke, used as a rigging aid)
- A Hurst® tool (input of 5,000 psi and .07 gpm, jaws of tool open and close with force of six tons through a distance of 32 inches.)
- Impact wrenches (2,000 psi, five gpm, used for drilling, tapping, or to make/break of nuts and bolts)
- Linear actuators (10,000 psi rams, 8-ton pull-cylinders, 10,000 psi cutters or 2 1/2-inch wire rope, rebars, or splitting nuts)
- A pump (2,000 psi, five gpm hydraulic fluid; 100 psi, 400 gpm water flow, used for jetting, washing, and dredging)
- Hose reels and different hydraulic power supplies

An excellent source of information on the operation and maintenance of underwater hydraulic tools is the *U.S. Navy Diver Tool Manual*, NAVSEA #S9592-AJ-MMA-010, 1987. Some hydraulic tools have been designed solely for underwater use. There is, for example, a hydraulic hammer that operates on 2,000 psi, 0.5 – 3.0 gpm, and develops a 40 ft. pound force per blow; output speed ranges from 1 – 300 blows per minute. The unique design uses compressibility of the hydraulic fluid to generate and store the impact energy.

Hydraulic tools that minimize diver fatigue and discomfort should be selected. Most tools can be reconfigured or redesigned to increase diver comfort. More attention should be given to underwater human engineering principles in the design of new tools. Areas where progress could be made include weight reduction, special grips and triggers, placement of handles at the center of gravity or wherever they will best counteract torque, and reduction of vibration and reaction forces.

Hydraulic tools are easy to maintain. They should be rinsed thoroughly with freshwater after each use, and then sprayed with a protective lubricant such as WD-40®.

10.6.4 Electric Tools

Underwater tools that operate by electric power have been designed, developed, and manufactured, but they are seldom used. The AC motor, stator, and control electronics of such tools are potted in epoxy, and the motor is water cooled and lubricated. Electric tools require only a small umbilical, have no depth limitation, and are reasonably light in weight. Although ground-fault detector circuitry is provided, the fear of electric shock persists and constant electrical interruptions occur, most divers consequently prefer to use pneumatic or hydraulic tools despite their greater weight and support equipment requirements.

10.6.5 Power Velocity Tools

Power velocity tools are actuated by the firing of an explosive cartridge, which increases the pressure behind a piston to accelerate a stud or a cutter into the work piece.

Procedures for Working Dives

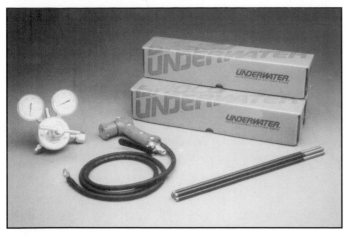

FIGURE 10.15
Ultrathermic Oxy-Arc Torch, Cutting Rods, and O$_2$ Regulator

FIGURE 10.16
Ultrathermic Oxy-Arc Process

Power velocity tools are used to attach padeyes, studs, and to make hollow penetrations in plate steel. Different configurations are used to cut cable, rebar, and hydraulic and electrical umbilicals. Studs are available to penetrate steel that is at least 1/4 inch thick (0.64 cm). The cutters can sever 1.5 inch (3.8 cm) in diameter cables or 2 inch (5.1 cm) in diameter composite umbilicals.

Power velocity tools are well suited to most underwater work. Their weight is comparable to that of hydraulic tools, but they require no umbilical or power line. Some models of underwater stud guns feature barrels that can be replaced easily by the diver. The heavier duty models, as well as most cutters, require that reloading be performed on the surface.

10.6.6 Cutting and Welding Tools

Cutting and welding are often required both in seawater and in underwater enclosures or habitats. Since habitat welding involves techniques and tools similar to those of atmospheric welding, this section addresses only cutting and welding tools that are used in seawater. Underwater cutting and welding processes emit toxic gases that rise to the surface and, since they are heavier than air, collect in any low-lying confined areas. Underwater cutting also produces potentially explosive gas mixtures. Ventilation of gases within the workpiece and at the surface during underwater cutting and welding is essential to protect both divers and surface personnel.

One of the most popular cutting method is ultrathermic, one of the oxy-arc processes (see Figures 10.15 and 10.16). Tubular steel cutting is the other. The oxy-arc process requires less training than oxy-hydrogen, oxy-acetylene, or shielded metal-arc cutting. The oxy-arc torch brings both oxygen and DC electric power to the cutting rod. The process uses electric power to heat the workpiece to ignition temperature; a jet of oxygen is then directed at the heated spot and the metal burns or oxidizes very rapidly. With Ultrathermic cutting, an electric arc is necessary only to start the cutting process. Once ignited, the ultrathermic cutting rod will continue to burn as long as oxygen is supplied. This feature, combined with the very high resultant temperature enables the diver to cut both ferrous and non-ferrous metals, burn rope, concrete, and rock. Additionally since the maintenance of an arc is not essential, precleaning of rust, paint, or marine growth is not required.

Electric current is not required for oxy-hydrogen, but an air hose is necessary to fill a shield cup around the tip to stabilize the flame and to hold water away from the area of metal being heated. The metal is brought to ignition temperature by the hydrogen/oxygen flame, then pure oxygen is directed at the heated spot to start the cutting action. Although acetylene is also used as a fuel gas for cutting, it is not recommended for under water use as it is unsafe at depths greater than 30 ft. (9 m). Shielded metal-arc cutting is a process in which metal is severed simply by melting and physically pushing the metal out of the kerf. An electric arc between the electrode and the workpiece provides the heat for melting. The process is used in situations where no oxygen is available. Although slow, shielded metal-arc cutting is suitable for metal less than 1/4 inch (0.64 cm) thick. The versatile ultrathermic oxy-arc process may be used for sections in excess of 10 inches (25.4 cm) in thickness.

Wet welding has grown in popularity due to its cost effectiveness and simplicity compared to habitat welding. The most widely used underwater welding process is shielded metal-arc welding. The weld is produced by heating with an electric arc between a flux-covered metal electrode and the workpiece. The heat developed by the arc causes the base metal parts, the core wire of the electrode, and some of the flux covering to melt and fuse. Other constituents of the flux decompose into gases and slag which shield the molten metals somewhat from contamination. When welding under water, technique is important and special training is required. Generally, underwater welds are not as ductile as surface welds because of water quench and contamination. The American Welding Society has produced a specification for underwater welding (AWS D3.6). Permanent welds are attainable with the use of proper procedures, underwater electrodes, good diver technique, and support equipment. Commercially produced underwater welding electrodes are recommended (see U.S. Department of Navy NAVSEA S0300-BB-MAN-010) for wet welding electrodes approved for Navy use and simple welding procedures. It is vitally important that the diver be aware at all times of the severe shock hazards and electrolysis associated with electric cutting and welding processes. Metal helmets must be insulated and anodes should be attached to all metal diving gear.

WARNING
SPECIAL DIVER TRAINING AND SUPERVISION ARE ESSENTIAL FOR UNDERWATER CUTTING OR WELDING OPERATIONS.

10.7 MAINTENANCE AND REPAIR TASKS

Maintaining and repairing equipment, structures, and instruments under water requires skill and an understanding of the task to be done. In addition, underwater maintenance and repair should be performed only when environmental conditions are acceptable.

If practical, divers should practice underwater tasks in shallow water before attempting them in deep water. The time that will be needed to accomplish the task must be known to enable the diver to complete the task (or a major portion of it) within the constraints of the air supply. For strenuous tasks, the task should be divided into sub-tasks and several divers should take turns carrying them out.

To accomplish underwater tasks, four task phases are involved:

1. Inspection of the site and determination of the condition of the equipment that needs maintenance or repair
2. Selection of appropriate tools
3. Performance of the repair or maintenance task
4. Reinspection to ensure that the task has been accomplished successfully

Many underwater maintenance and repair tasks performed by NOAA divers are associated with the inspection and repair of a ship's rudder, propeller, sea chest, or cathodic protection system. When a diver is working over the side of a ship to perform a maintenance task, the ship's propeller should be locked out and the rudder should be held in static position. The appropriate international code flag should be hoisted (code, alpha, rigid flag) or lights used.

Divers should be careful to avoid skin contact with the hull of the ship on which they are working, toxic paints are often used on the hull to inhibit marine growth (barnacles, algae). These paints retain their toxic qualities for months after the freshly painted ship has been returned to the water.

Maintenance and repair tasks can be accomplished more easily if a restraining system is used. Such a system can be as simple as a line for the diver to hold that is attached to a convenient point.

10.8 SALVAGE

Salvage of a ship or craft, its cargo, or its equipment requires a knowledge both of the technical aspects of recovery and the legal aspects of ownership of the salved items and claims for salvage. A salvor who recovers a ship or craft or its cargo without prior agreement with the owner must file a claim in the United States District Court nearest to the port in which the salved items are landed.

Salvage techniques vary considerably with the size, value, and condition of the item to be salved, the depth of the object and seafloor conditions, and the equipment available to conduct the salvage.

NOAA divers often salvage instruments or instrument arrays, small vessels, anchors, bottom samples, marine collections, or other small items. In the majority of these cases, the diver simply carries the small item to the surface with the limited aid of the BC. When an object weighs more than 10 lbs. (4 kg), a lift bag (or other appropriate lifting device) should be used or a line should be attached to the object that will facilitate a direct lift to the surface.

In some salvage operations such as archeological excavations, it may be necessary to clear bottom sediment from around the item before it can be recovered. This procedure is necessary to ensure that the item is free of entanglement. A water jet or air lift commonly is used to clear away entangling debris.

When working with heavy or overhead items with cables, lines, or chains under tension, divers must develop a sixth sense for safety. Divers should avoid positioning themselves or their umbilicals under heavy objects that might fall, or placing themselves above lines that are under tension. It is important to remember these safety rules for salvage recovery:

- Always use a separate air source other than that used for breathing by the diver to fill lift bags.
- Stay clear of the water column above and below a lift.
- If the lift goes out of control, let it go and get out from under it.
- Always place bags where lift is best balanced and the best leverage is attained.
- Always attach control lines and tow lines prior to lift.
- Make sure the surface is clear over the object prior to lift.
- The container should be vented to prevent excess air from rupturing it.
- The air will expand if the object is raised from the bottom before all the water has been displaced from the container; this will displace more water and may increase the speed of ascent to an uncontrollable rate.
- Plan the lifting job thoroughly, i.e., necessary air, lines, hardware, weather forecasts, towing and lifting procedures, etc.

10.8.1 Lifting Methods

When the operation calls for raising something from the bottom to the surface — or any point in between, basic principles of buoyancy can be used quite effectively. According to the Archimedes' Principle, any body wholly or partially submerged in a fluid is buoyed up by a force equal to the weight of the fluid displaced. The procedures following are four types of lifting methods using Archimedes' Principle:

- **Dead Lifting** using a winch or crane
- **Internal Buoyancy Lifts** using a device to compensate for the negative buoyancy
- **External Lift Bags**
- **Repairing and Restoring** the inherent buoyancy of the salvaged object itself

10.8.1.1 Dead Lifting

Dead lifting, although quite simple in design, can be extremely complicated and requires careful consideration and planning. Issues to be considered include:

- **Lift point of the object:** Lifting at the wrong point can cause damage to the object.
- **Lifting force needed:** Having a one ton lift crane to lift a 500 lb. object may be inadequate. The lift capacity of cranes is drastically reduced as the boom gets longer, or the reach needed is increased.
- **Weight of other objects in the lift:** The lift capacity of

cranes does not include the rigging attachments such as blocks, lifting slings and cable, hoods, and headache balls. These items may add hundreds of pounds to the weight of the object to be lifted.

- **Weather conditions:** High winds and seas can complicate the lifting scenario and substantially increase the dangers associated with the lift. Rain and snow that hampers visibility can also affect lifting.
- **Components of the lift:** As the temperature falls below freezing, metal becomes brittle. Hooks, cable, chain, and other rigging may fail prematurely.
- **Air/water interface:** Once the object reaches the surface, what about the water trapped in the object? Water trapped in an object can actually weigh more than the object itself. Mud and debris may be engulfed or hanging off of the object. There must be a plan for the arrival of the object once it reaches the surface.
- **Miscalculation of these items and others, can have disastrous results:** Rigging can come apart during lifts, booms can buckle, and entire cranes can flip over backwards as a result of a mistake, or an unplanned event. Dead lifts should be done under the supervision of a professional rigging team.

10.8.1.2 Internal Buoyancy Lifts

Internal buoyancy lifts are done by pumping air into voids or compartments of an object, displacing water with air to achieve positive buoyancy. Like dead lifting, internal buoyancy lifting can be complicated and dangerous. This method has many hidden factors involved in all phases of the lift:

- **The object may not withstand outward pressure.** Many objects, like boats and other floating items, are designed to take pressure in one direction. Pumping air into a compartment or into a flotation bag inside a compartment can overpressurize a compartment (as little as 5–8 pounds of pressure), causing a rupture or buckle and resulting in loss of compartment integrity.
- **Letting the water out.** As air is pumped into the compartment, water must have a means to escape. This can be done by using existing valves and plumbing contained in the object, or by cutting vent holes in the object. The question is where to put the holes, how many are needed, and how big should they be? Holes that are too small and too few in number may result in over pressurization of the object. Holes that are too large and too many in number, will allow water to come in faster than can be pumped out.
- **How much air pressure to use.** Too little air pressure and the water will not be forced out. Too much, and the object may overpressurize.
- **How much buoyancy is needed to lift the object, and how much water will be left in the compartment when the object begins to rise.** Moving water is a powerful force. If there is too much or too little

water in a compartment, and it begins to shift around as the object rises, it could generate enough force to roll the object over. This will put the vent holes for the water at the top, causing air to vent out, and the object to sink again. As in dead lifting, this method can be extremely dangerous, and should be undertaken with professional supervision only.

10.8.1.3 External Lift Bags

Lift bags are the most commonly used tool for raising submerged objects and are available in a wide variety of sizes and shapes (see Figures 10.17, 10.18). Generally speaking, it is recommended to use a commercially made lift bag rather than an improvised one for three reasons: 1) commercial bags are typically constructed from heavy-duty materials that can withstand the stress of raising a heavy object; 2) most commercial lift bags have exhaust valves, which are important for controlling ascents; and 3) commercial lift bags have loops, slings, and other convenient locations for rigging and securing the recovery object.

When selecting a commercial lift bag, try to pick one just large enough to handle the object's weight. The air in a lift bag expands during ascent; if the bag is nearly full before the ascent starts, the expanding air simply spills out of the bag. If the bag is too large and only partially full, it retains the expanding air, gaining buoyancy and speed as it rises. Some control is usually necessary when ascending with a lift bag, but a properly sized bag minimizes the likelihood of a runaway lift bag.

Lift bags range in capacity from a few pounds up to tens of thousands of pounds. Some lift bags are available with a variable-volume vent valve or an adaptable buoyancy control hose, which allows a diver to set the exact amount of air desired in the lift bag. This lets the diver lift, lower, or suspend the lift load automatically. The diver can also control ascent and descent rates by positioning the control hose at the appropriate location. This particular option gives any operation better buoyancy control. A bag that weighs only 26 lbs. can raise a ton of weight from the ocean bottom. These bags are made of high-strength synthetics like nylon and polyester and further protected by tough, chemically impervious coating of rubber and plastics. This synthetic fabric, called Kevlar®, is four times stronger than steel, with strengths from 750 – 1,300 psi.

Before an object can be raised, it must be secured to the lift bag with appropriate line, wire, rope, or chain. For lifting light objects, pre-stretched, nylon rope makes an ideal rigging rope; avoid polypropylene, which tends to slip loose more easily. There are three knots that are useful for rigging and tying. The **bowline** is normally used to tie line directly to an object. It is a strong, dependable knot that unties easily. The **sheet bend** is used to tie two lines of different diameter together, and **two half-hitches** is a quick way to attach line to an object (see Figure 10.19). Wire rope and chain should be used when lifting large, heavy items. Wire rope and chain have little or no stretch and can be attached with mechanical fasteners, (bolts, shackles, etc.). The additional weight of these materials must be included when determining lifting requirements.

With low visibility, a common situation in search and recovery, divers should be able to tie all three knots wearing gloves and with both eyes closed. Divers should practice tying the knots above water until they can tie them easily.

Once the object's rigged and ready to be raised, a marker line should be attached so that if the object comes

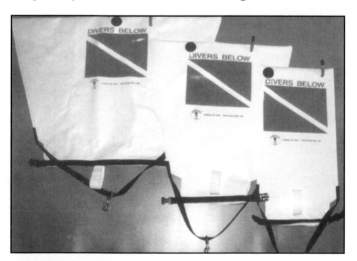

FIGURE 10.17
Various Sizes of Lift Bags

FIGURE 10.18
Salvages Using Flotation Bags

Procedures for Working Dives

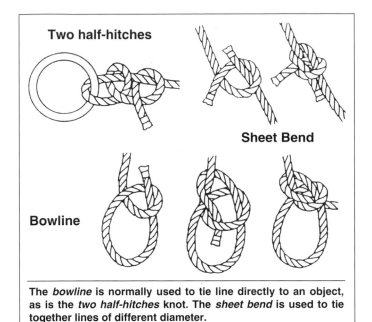

Two half-hitches

Sheet Bend

Bowline

The *bowline* is normally used to tie line directly to an object, as is the *two half-hitches* knot. The *sheet bend* is used to tie together lines of different diameter.

FIGURE 10.19
Three Methods of Line Attachment

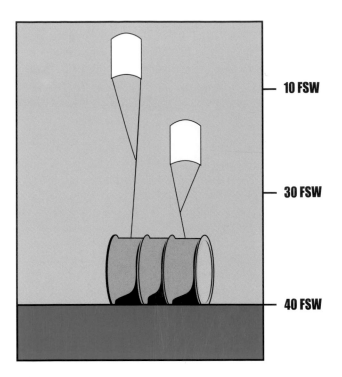

— 10 FSW

— 30 FSW

— 40 FSW

FIGURE 10.20
Lift Bag Staging

lose and sinks again, it can be relocated without another search. Air should be added slowly to the lift bag using an alternate air source, not the diver's primary breathing air, until all slack is out of the line leading between the lift bag and the object to be lifted. The diver must ensure that they are free and clear of all rigging lines prior to adding air to a lift bag.

Check the rigging. If it looks secure, add a little more air to the bag to put some strain on the rigging, especially all knots and check for slippage. If they are okay, all is ready to lift the object.

Add only enough air to make the object neutrally buoyant— not positively buoyant. Add a small amount of air to the bag, pause, and then pull-up on the rigging to see if it can raise the object. If not, repeat the process, adding a small burst of air each time, until it can lift the object. Raise the bag and object until they barely float just over the bottom.

On soft or muddy bottoms, suction must be overcome between the mud and the object. If the object is light, pull up firmly after each burst to break the suction.

WARNING
DO NOT OVER-INFLATE A LIFT BAG TO BREAK BOTTOM SUCTION. THIS MAY LEAD TO AN UNCONTROLLED ASCENT OF THE OBJECT.

Staging lift bags (see Figure 10.20) near the surface is a commonly used technique for overcoming bottom suction problems. Lift bags are located near the surface (10 ft.) and rigging is extended to the object requiring lift. Once the bags are filled and suction is broken, the object is off the bottom (10 ft.) and the lift bags are on the surface.

This procedure can be repeated to move an object to the surface.

At this point, if the object must be moved horizontally to be pulled from the water (to a dock, for example), swim it along the bottom, which is easier than towing it at the surface. Doing this usually depends on having a fairly level, unobstructed bottom (see Figure 10.21).

When ready to take the object up, simply pull it upward—do not add air. The expanding air will increase its buoyancy naturally. Depending upon the situation, the diver may either accompany the bag to the surface along side of it, or allow it to rise independently. In either case, the diver should position himself so that he is not under the lift bag and object, and will avoid being hit if the object slips loose or the lift bag spills.

If the diver ascends with the bag, he will need to control its ascent by exhausting air periodically. Be cautious not to exceed 30 feet per minute (9 m/min)—if difficulties develop and the lift bag begins to accelerate, let it go and get out from under it in case it topples and sinks when reaching surface. Remember, safety is more important than anything being recovered.

WARNING
DO NOT USE BUOYANCY COMPENSATORS OR DRY SUITS AS LIFTING DEVICES WHEN AN OBJECT WEIGHS MORE THAN TEN POUNDS.

In addition to the type of lift bags, special computer-controlled lifting systems have been developed for large salvage jobs. These systems are relatively insensitive to surface weather conditions and permit both ascent and descent velocities to be held constant, even for loads as great as 15 tons. Such systems can be used for emplacing and retrieving heavy instrumentation packages, as well as for salvage.

If the object cannot be lifted to the surface directly by winching or lift devices, the rise of the tide can be used if a large vessel or pontoon is available. At low tide, lines are connected tautly to the object and the surface platform; as the tide rises, the load rises with it.

Every salvage project must be planned and executed individually. Novice divers should not attempt underwater salvage tasks for which they are not properly trained or equipped.

10.8.1.4 Air Lifts

An air lift is used to lift mixtures of water, grain, sand, mud, and similar materials from the holds of ships during salvage operations. In some cases of stranding, an air lift may be used to clear away sand and mud from the side of the vessel or the bottom.

An air lift works on the pressure-differential principle. Air is introduced into the lower end of a partially submerged pipe. The combining of air bubbles with the liquid in the pipe forms a mixture that is less dense than the liquid outside the pipe. The lighter density results in less head pressure inside the pipe than outside, which causes the mixture to rise in the pipe. The amount of liquid lifted depends on the size of the air lift, submergence of the pipe, air pressure and volume used, and the discharge head.

An air lift consists of a discharge pipe and a foot piece or air chamber. The size of the discharge pipe ranges from approximately 3–14 inches (7.6–35.6 cm) in diameter, depending on the amount of work to be done and the service intended. The air chamber should be located approximately 20–30 inches (50.1–76.2 cm) from the end of the pipe. Table 10.4 may be used as a guide in selecting the size of discharge pipe and air line, taking into consideration the air available and the job to be done.

An air lift operates as follows: the discharge pipe is submerged in the mixture to be lifted to a depth of approximately 50–70 percent of the total length of the pipe. The air is turned on, and the lifting operation commences almost immediately. Occasionally, considerable experimentation is necessary to determine the amount of air required to operate the lift efficiently. The use of air lifts in archeological excavation is described in Chapter 9.

10.9 UNDERWATER DEMOLITION AND EXPLOSIVES

Many underwater tasks require the use of explosives. Several different types of explosives are available, and these can be applied in a variety of ways. Because explosives are powerful and dangerous tools, they should be used only by trained personnel. To achieve accurate results

FIGURE 10.21
Lift Bag Attached to a Shipwreck Artifact

in underwater applications, the explosive must be selected carefully and positioned properly.

Explosives are used under water to remove obstructions, to open new channels or widen existing ones, and to cut through steel, concrete, or wooden pilings, piers, or cables, or hole punching (see Figure 10.22). They are also used to trench through rock or coral.

Explosives suitable for underwater use include primacord, various gelatins, plastics, precast blocks, and some liquids. Such charges are relatively safe to use if the manufacturer's instructions are observed and general safety precautions for explosives handling are followed. Bulk explosives (main charges) generally are the most stable of the explosive groups; there is progressively less stability with the secondary (primers) and initiator (detonators/blasting caps) groups. Initiators and secondary explosives always should be physically separated from bulk explosives.

WARNING
ONLY PROPERLY TRAINED DIVERS AND CERTIFIED PERSONNEL ARE PERMITTED TO HANDLE EXPLOSIVES.

TABLE 10.4
Selection Guide for Discharge Pipe and Air Line

Diameter of Pipe, inches	Gallons per Minute	Diameter of Compressed Air Line, inches	Cubic Feet of Air
3	50–75	.50	15–40
4	90–150	.75	20–65
6	210–450	1.25	50–200
10	600–900	2.00	150–400

An underwater explosion creates a series of waves that propagate in the water as hydraulic shock waves (the so-called "water hammer") and in the seabed as seismic waves. The hydraulic shock wave of an underwater explosion consists of an initial wave followed by further pressure waves of diminishing intensity. The initial high-intensity shock wave is the result of the violent creation and liberation of a large volume of gas, in the form of a gas pocket, at high pressure and temperature. Subsequent pressure waves are caused by rapid gas expansion in a noncompressible environment, which causes a sequence of contractions and expansions as the gas pocket rises to the surface.

The initial high-intensity shock wave is the most dangerous; it travels outward from the source of the explosion, losing its intensity with distance. Less severe pressure waves follow the initial shock wave very closely. For an extended time after the detonation, there is considerable turbulence and movement of water in the area of the explosion. Many factors affect the intensity of the shock wave and pressure waves; each should be evaluated in terms of the particular circumstances in which the explosion occurs and the type of explosive involved. In all cases the diver should be out of the water, clear from charges before detonation.

FIGURE 10.22
Explosive Hole Punch

10.9.1 Types of Explosives

Some explosives have high brisance (shattering power in the immediate vicinity of the explosion) with less power at long range, while others have reduced brisance and increased power over a greater area. Those with high brisance are generally used for cutting or shattering purposes, while low-brisance (high-power) explosives are used in depth charges and sea mines, where the target may not be in immediate contact and the ability to inflict damage over a greater area is an advantage. The high-brisance explosives, therefore, create a high-level shock wave and pressure waves of short duration over a limited area. High-power explosives create a less intense shock and pressure waves of long duration over a greater area. The characteristics of the explosive to be utilized need to be evaluated carefully before use to estimate the type and duration of the resulting shock and pressure waves. The principal characteristics of the most commonly used explosives for demolition are shown in Table 10.5.

WARNING
BEFORE ANY UNDERWATER BLAST, ALL DIVERS SHOULD LEAVE THE WATER AND MOVE OUT OF RANGE OF THE BLAST.

If a diver must remain in the water, the pressure of the charge a diver experiences from an explosion must be limited to less than 50–70 pounds per square inch (3.5–4.9 kg/cm^2). To minimize pressure wave effects, a diver should also take up a position with feet pointing toward the explosion and head pointing directly away from it. The head and upper section of the body should be out of the water, or divers should float on their back with their head out of the water.

For scientific work, very low-order explosions are occasionally used to blast samples loose or to create pressure waves through substrata. Each use must be evaluated in terms of diver safety and protection. Bottom conditions, the degree of the diver's submersion, and the type of protection available to the diver can modify the effects of an explosion and must be considered in planning a dive involving the use of explosives. Divers also should be cautioned against diving in the vicinity when sub-bottom profiling using high-pressure air or high electrical discharges is being conducted.

NOAA Diving Manual

TABLE 10.5
Characteristics of Principal U.S. Explosives Used for Demolition Purposes

Name	Principal Uses	Velocity of Detonation (meters/sec)	Velocity of Detonation (feet/sec)	Relative Effectiveness as a Breaching Charge (TNT = 1.00)	Intensity of Poisonous Fumes	Water Resistance
Ammonium Nitrate	Demolition charge; composition explosives	2,700 mps	8,900 fps	—	Dangerous	None
PETN	Detonating cord; blasting caps; demolition charge	8,300 mps	27,200 fps	1.66	Slight	Excellent
RDX	Blasting caps; composition explosives	8,350 mps	27,400 fps	1.60	Dangerous	Excellent
TNT	Demolition charge; composition explosives	6,900 mps	22,600 fps	1.00	Dangerous	Excellent
Tetryl	Booster charge; composition explosives	7,100 mps	23,300 fps	1.25	Dangerous	Excellent
Nitroglycerin	Commercial dynamites	7,700 mps	25,200 fps	1.50	Dangerous	Good
Black powder	Time blasting fuse	400 mps	1,300 fps	0.55	Dangerous	Poor
Amatol 80/20	Bursting charge	4,900 mps	16,000 fps	1.17	Dangerous	Very poor
Composition A3	Booster charge; bursting charge	8,100 mps	26,500 fps	—	Dangerous	Good
Composition B	Bursting charge	7,800 mps	25,600 fps	1.35	Dangerous	Excellent
Composition C3	Demolition charge	7,625 mps	25,000 fps	1.34	Dangerous	Good
Composition C4	Demolition charge	8,040 mps	26,400 fps	1.34	Slight	Excellent
Tetrytol 75/25	Demolition charge	7,000 mps	23,000 fps	1.20	Dangerous	Excellent
Pentolite 50/50	Booster charge; bursting charge	7,450 mps	24,400 fps	—	Dangerous	Excellent

NOTES

Underwater Support Systems

SECTION	PAGE

Underwater Support Systems

11.0 GENERAL

Manned underwater support systems are used to improve a diver's productivity by increasing bottom time while submerged or under pressure and include seafloor habitats, surface-based saturation diving systems, and diving bells. During the last four decades, new technological developments and a greater understanding of the physiology of diving have improved the safety and usefulness of underwater support systems. Such systems help extend a diver's bottom time and provide expedient transportation to and from the worksite.

Looking back to the late 1960s and early to mid 1970s, there were upwards of 60 underwater habitats in use all over the world. Habitats were being constructed as fast as possible to join in the exploration of the earth's vast unknown oceans. Currently, there are only three scientific underwater habitats in use today, one of the three is the *Aquarius*, the technological showcase of NOAA's National Undersea Research Program. The large majority of habitats have been decommissioned and no longer performing the magnificent tasks for which they were designed. There are a few submersibles being used for scientific research, but they belong to a very small number of oceanographic institutions.

11.1 UNDERWATER HABITATS

Early underwater habitats were designed primarily to evaluate engineering feasibility or to demonstrate human capability to survive in the undersea environment for extended periods. They were not designed to accommodate the average scientific diver, nor could they be easily emplaced or moved. Since 1962, over 65 habitats have been utilized in 17 countries throughout the world (Miller and Koblick 1984, 1995). Habitats have been used for observation stations, seafloor laboratories, and as operational bases for working divers.

Underwater habitats provide diving scientists with unlimited access to defined areas of the marine environment, enabling them to make observations and to conduct experiments over long periods of time. Because habitats are open to the surrounding ambient water pressure, scientists/aquanauts living and working in habitats are subject to the same gas absorption problems as those individuals who dive and return to the surface on a per dive basis.

There are two types of underwater habitats, those designed for long-term habitation resulting in a diver becoming saturated, and those designed for short-term habitation, not involving saturation. Saturation occurs when a diver's body has absorbed all the inert gas it can for a given depth and gas mixture. Once in this state, the amount of time required to de-saturate to a normal condition remains constant whether the diver remains at depth one day, one week, or one month. First described by Dr. George F. Bond while serving as a U.S. Navy Diving Medical Officer, saturation diving is a technique used to maximize a diver's productivity by storing a diver at depth for the duration of a project, then decompressing him at the end of the saturation mission. This technique is in contrast to surface-based diving where a diver leaves from, and returns to the surface, decompressing as they ascend.

Habitats come in many sizes and shapes with accommodations ranging from spartan to luxurious. A University of New Hampshire survey describes those features of an underwater habitat that users consider desirable (see Table 11.1).

When designing and selecting habitats for marine science programs, technical, logistic, and habitability criteria must be applied if systems are to facilitate mission objectives. Important considerations include simplicity, functionality, and comfort. A scientist/aquanaut who is constantly wet, cold, crowded, and miserable for days at a time cannot be expected to perform efficiently or to produce scientific results of high quality.

TABLE 11.1
Desirable Features of Underwater Habitats

Overall Size About 8 ft x 38 ft (2.4 m x 11.6 m)	
SEPARATE WET ROOM:	**LIVING ROOM:**
Large entry trunk	Bunks
Wet-suit rack	Microwave
Hot shower	Food freezer & refrigerator
Hookah and built-in breathing system	Water heater
Scuba charging	Toilet
Wet lab bench	Individual desk & storage
Specimen freezer	Dry lab bench
Clothes dryer	Compactor
Diving equipment storage	Library
Rebreathers	Tapes, TV, radio
	Emergency breathing system
	Computer terminal
GENERAL:	
Hemispheric windows	External lights at trunk and viewports
Temperature and humidity control	External cylinder storage and charging
Separate double chambers	Habitat-to-diver communication
On-bottom and surface decompression capability	Diver-to-diver communication
Suitable entry height off bottom	Adjustable legs
Submersible decompression chamber for emergency escape	Mobility
External survival shelter	External or protective internal chemical hood

For a description of specific scientific projects accomplished to date using underwater habitats, contact the National Undersea Research Program, 1315 East-West Highway, Silver Spring, Maryland 20910.

11.1.1 Saturation Diving Habitats

The level of sophistication for habitats range from simple shelters to large systems designed for extended seafloor habitation. The habitats used most extensively were *Chernomor* (Soviet Union), *Helgoland* (West Germany), and *Tektite*, *Hydrolab*, *La Chalupa*, and *Aquarius* (USA). The habitats described in this section were selected because they represent a cross-section of those built to date, and the programs in which they were utilized include most U.S. marine scientific saturation programs. Saturation diving habitats differ from non-saturation habitats in the extent of support they offer. Non-saturation habitats are designed to provide an air space in which divers can enter to rest, converse, re-warm themselves, or take refuge in case of emergency. They have limited support capability and are intended for short exposures. Saturation habitats, on the other hand, can be quite complex in design and provide all support requirements to comfortably sustain a team of divers for extended periods of time under water. Decompression is

accomplished either inside the habitat or in a surface decompression chamber after an ascent is made with or without a diving bell.

Edelhab was designed and built by students from the University of New Hampshire as an engineering project in 1968. It was constructed mainly of salvaged and donated materials. The living quarters were enclosed in an 8 x 12 ft. (2.4 x 3.7 m) cylinder with a small viewing port at each end. The interior was insulated with 1.5 inch (3.8 cm) thick unicellular foam. Entry was made through a hatch centrally located in the floor. The interior had two permanent bunks (which folded to form a large seat) and a collapsible canvas cot. Communications, air, and power were provided from a support ship to the habitat through umbilicals. At the conclusion of the saturation mission, the divers returned to the surface and were quickly recompressed in a hyperbaric chamber to depth followed by a gradual ascent (decompression) back to sea level pressure. *Edelhab* had no dedicated amenities for scientific investigations, required a manned support ship, and was not easily relocated from site to site.

Hydrolab (see Figure 11.1) was designed to be simple and inexpensive to operate. The main structure was an 8 x 16 ft. (2.4 x 4.9 m) cylinder supported on four short legs and positioned 3 ft. (0.9 m) above a concrete base. It was submerged by venting and flooding ballast tanks and could be towed short distances for relocation in depths up to 100 ft. (30.5 m). Entry into the habitat was accomplished by means of a hatch at one end that also functioned as a lock when the chamber pressure was below ambient pressure. The single room was furnished with three bunks, folding chairs, a dehumidifier, an air conditioner, a sink, and a table surface (see Figure 11.2).

A self-contained, unmanned, 23-foot long (7-m) life-support barge floated at the surface above the habitat and supplied all life support, via an umbilical, including electrical power, high- and low-pressure air, and water. A small, stand-up shelter was provided nearby for emergencies and to serve as an air filling station. *Hydrolab* was decommissioned by NOAA in 1985, and resides at the NOAA campus in Silver Spring, Maryland.

Tektite (see Figure 11.3), used between 1969–70, was a four-person habitat consisting of two hulls attached to a base and connected by a crossover tunnel. The two cylinders were each divided into two compartments, containing the control center, living quarters, equipment room, and wet room.

The control center also served as a dry laboratory for scientists. The living quarters contained four bunks, a small galley, and storage and entertainment facilities. The equipment room contained the environmental control system, frozen food, and toilet facilities.

Air, water, electrical power, and communications were provided from the shore by means of umbilicals. The wet room was intended for scientific work; however, aquanauts had difficulty entering with specimens in hand and found

FIGURE 11.1
Hydrolab - Exterior

FIGURE 11.2
Hydrolab - Interior

FIGURE 11.3
Tektite

Underwater Support Systems

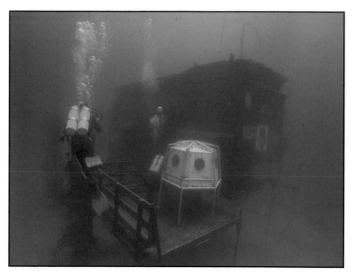

FIGURE 11.6
Aquarius **Under Water**

FIGURE 11.8
Aquarius **on a LRT Support Barge**

1990, when management of the system moved to the NURC/UNCW. After nearly two years worth of work refurbishing *Aquarius*, it was redeployed in March of 1992, at Conch Reef at a depth of 65 ft. (20 m), 5 miles offshore of the Florida Keys. The LRT vessel was reconfigured and moored overhead and provided high and low-pressure air, water, electricity, and environmental control. This "Mobile Support" Base (MSB) also served as a platform for a watch desk to allow staff to monitor life support and communications 24 hours a day during missions. The *Aquarius* supported scientific saturation diving, addressing marine environmental issues in the Florida Keys National Marine Sanctuary. A total of twenty-one scientific saturation missions were successfully completed from 1993 through 1996 (Shepard, Dinsmore, Miller, Cooper, and Wicklund 1996).

FIGURE 11.7
Aquarius **Undersea Research Laboratory**

FIGURE 11.9
Aquarius Mainlock System

FIGURE 11.10
Aquarius's Wet Porch

FIGURE 11.11
Life Support Buoy (LSB) for *Aquarius* 2000

FIGURE 11.12
Aquarius 2000

Before its recovery in 1996, plans were made to enhance the facility. In a unique partnership with industry, academia, and the U.S. Government, the *Aquarius* system was reconfigured to provide a more autonomous, offshore operational mode to allow for expanding technology and help reduce costs for continued scientific saturation missions. Partners in this refurbishment included the Harris Corporation, Harbor Branch Oceanographic Institute, NOAA, and NURC/UNCW. *Aquarius* 2000 was reployed in 1997 and commenced saturation diving operations in July 1998.

The *Aquarius* 2000 system replaced the barge with a large life-support and telemetry buoy, 33 ft. (10 m) in diameter, and containing the compressors and generators needed for air and power. The environmental control system (that cools and dehumidifies the habitat), storage for fresh water, and compressed air storage were relocated from the MSB to the *Aquarius* support frame under water. The watch desk, which receives crucial life-support information from the habitat and support buoy, was moved from the MSB to a shore-based location. Support personnel staff the watch

desk 24 hours a day during saturation missions and routinely visit the habitat for reprovisioning, maintenance, and to assist in decompression and aquanaut recovery.

The Life Support Buoy (LSB) (see Figure 11.11) also contains advanced telemetry and controls systems capable of transmitting real-time video, audio, and data from *Aquarius* and the surrounding seafloor back to the shorebase located approximately seven miles away. Continuous monitoring includes the status of life support equipment (compressors and generators) and parameters (temperature, oxygen, carbon dioxide), voice and video images of personnel and onboard equipment, and oceanographic and meteorological conditions.

The *La Chalupa* and *Marine Lab* habitats are also located in the Florida Keys. They are operated by the Marine Resource Development Foundation (MRDF), a private foundation with the goal of developing a better understanding of the earth's marine resources.

The MRDF facilities located in Key Largo, Florida, include a 30-foot deep (9.1-m), three acre, protected lagoon, which serves as home for these two habitats.

FIGURE 11.13
Marine Lab (MRDF)

Marine Lab was originally designed and constructed as an engineering project at the United States Naval Academy in 1974 (see Figures 11.13, 11.14). This 8 x 16 ft. (2.4 x 4.9 m) habitat, which was never used operationally, was obtained by MRDF in 1984. It has provided students and teachers an opportunity to live, work, and study from an undersea habitat for missions lasting from one to three days. Normally occupied by three to four persons, the habitat has housed over 200 persons in the first 18 months of operation. Because of the shallow depth, aquanauts do not have to decompress prior to surfacing at the conclusion of their stay in the habitat.

FIGURE 11.14
Marine Lab (MRDF)

Building upon the success of the *Marine Lab* program, MRDF helped develop *Jules Undersea Lodge* in 1986 (see Figure 11.15). This unique facility, converting the former *La Chalupa* habitat into a luxury undersea dwelling, created the world's first undersea hotel.

Although the lagoon depth is 30 ft. (9.1 m), the depth of these two systems (saturation depth) is 20.5 ft. (6.2 m).

11.1.2 Non-Saturation Habitats

Many diving projects require long periods of work or observation to be carried out in relatively shallow water. Simple underwater work shelters are useful on such projects; the primary function of these shelters is to allow divers to work for longer periods without surfacing, to protect them from the cold, and to serve as an emergency refuge and an underwater communication station. To be most effective, the shelter should be close to the diver's work site.

Underwater shelters vary in size and complexity, depending on the nature of the work and the funds available to provide support equipment and facilities. They can be made of materials such as steel, rubber, plastic, or fiberglass. Most of the shelters constructed to date consist of a shell designed to contain an air pocket, although some have been supplied with air from the surface or have used on-board auxiliary air cylinders.

Hardwire or acoustic communication systems have been used with some shelters. The decision to use work shelters should be based on considerations of ease of emplacement, operational preparation time, bottom working time, and cost-effectiveness.

The following are examples of three shelters that have been used successfully for scientific observation and studies.

FIGURE 11.15
Jules Undersea Lodge

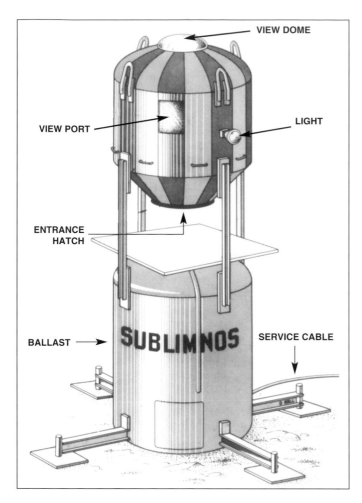

FIGURE 11.16
Sublimnos

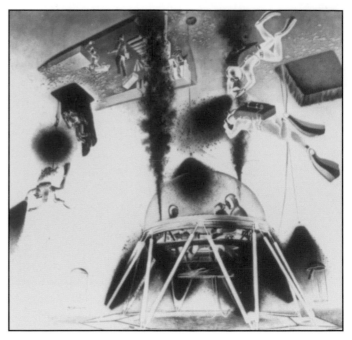

FIGURE 11.17
Subigloo

Sublimnos (see Figure 11.16) is a Canadian shallow-water shelter that was built for scientists operating on a tight budget. The shelter provided daylong underwater work capability for as many as four divers. The upper chamber was 9 ft. (2.7 m) tall and 8 ft. (2.4 m) in diameter. Entry was made through a 35-inch hatch (88.9-cm) in the floor of the living chamber.

Subigloo (see Figure 11.17), also Canadian, was used with great success in Arctic exploration programs in 1972 and 1974 and in the Caribbean in 1975. It consists of two 8 ft. (2.4-m) acrylic hemispheres on aluminum legs and permitted an unrestricted view, making it an excellent observational platform. *Subigloo* is now used daily by divers as a part of "The Living Seas" exhibit at Walt Disney's Epcot Center in Orlando, Florida.

Subigloo was designed to be operated continuously for 48 hours by two people and to be placed at depths of up to 30 ft. (9.1 m). As with the other shelters, decompression was accomplished by having the divers swim to the surface and immediately enter a deck decompression chamber.

11.2 SURFACE-BASED SATURATION DIVING SYSTEMS

Although most underwater habitats are fixed on the seabed and cannot be transported with divers inside, surface-based saturation diving systems, have proven their worth in several types of undersea tasks. On board the support ship or barge are the deck decompression chamber(s), control van (see Figure 11.18b), and other supporting machinery, such as electric generators, hydraulic power systems, and hot water generators. Normal living operations and decompression are carried out in the deck decompression chamber. Deck Decompression Chambers (DDC) are part of the integrated system (see Figure 11.18a). designed to provide divers with a dry, safe living environment that can be maintained for long periods at or near the pressure prevailing at the dive site itself. A diving bell (see Figure 11.18c) functions as a dry, pressurized, and sometimes heated elevator to transport divers between surface living quarters and underwater work sites. While the divers are on the bottom, the nearby diving bell functions as a tool storehouse and ready refuge. Most diving bells are capable of carrying and supporting two to four working divers.

When beginning a job, divers enter the bell and are lowered to the work site. After reaching the required depth, the divers equalize the bell pressure with the outside seawater pressure, open the lower hatch, and exit to start work. If necessary, the bell can be moved closer to the job site by maneuvering the ship. Upon completion of the task, the divers re-enter the bell and are raised to the surface, where the bell is mated to the deck decompression chamber.

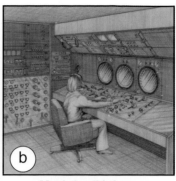

**Modular Diving
Control Van Console**

3-Man Diving Bell

**FIGURE 11.18
Saturation Diving Complex**

In the deck decompression chamber, the divers remain at depth and prepare for their next trip to the work site. With one or more teams, this cycle can continue 24 hours a day for days or weeks if necessary. Decompression is carried out after completion of the mission. Bell diving systems offer advantages over a sea floor habitat if a large bottom area is to be covered or if heavy tools and substantial surface support are required. Under saturated conditions, one or more teams of divers can live in relative comfort in the deck chambers. Hot meals can be passed in via small locks, and surface personnel can maintain direct contact with the divers. Commercial bell diving systems are designed to be operated between 165 and 1,500 fsw (50 and 460 msw), but can be operated at depths as shallow as 35 fsw (10.7 msw) when extended operations, such as a long bottom project must be carried out.

Today, most work done from surface-based saturation diving system is in support of the offshore oil industry. Additionally, the various navies of the world use bell diving systems for salvage, search and recovery, and instrument implantation.

11.3 OPEN-BOTTOM BELL SYSTEMS

11.3.1 Description

The open-bottom bell, referred to as a Class II or non-pressurized bell was developed as an in-water work platform and emergency way station. Unlike a diving stage, which serves only as an elevator between the surface and the work site, the open-bottom bell provides a semi-dry refuge, emergency breathing gases, and communications capability (see Figure 11-19). The bell consists of a rigid frame with an open grating on which the diver stands and an acrylic hemispheric dome that is open on the bottom. By adding suitable breathing gases to the inside of the dome, water is forced out, creating a dry gas bubble for the diver's head and shoulders. The acrylic dome is transparent, which affords the divers a full field of vision. Ballast is added to the bottom of the bell to make it negatively buoyant in the water (see Figure 11.20).

Emergency breathing gases may be supplied to the bell from two separate sources: one from a topside umbilical and another from high-pressure gas cylinders mounted on

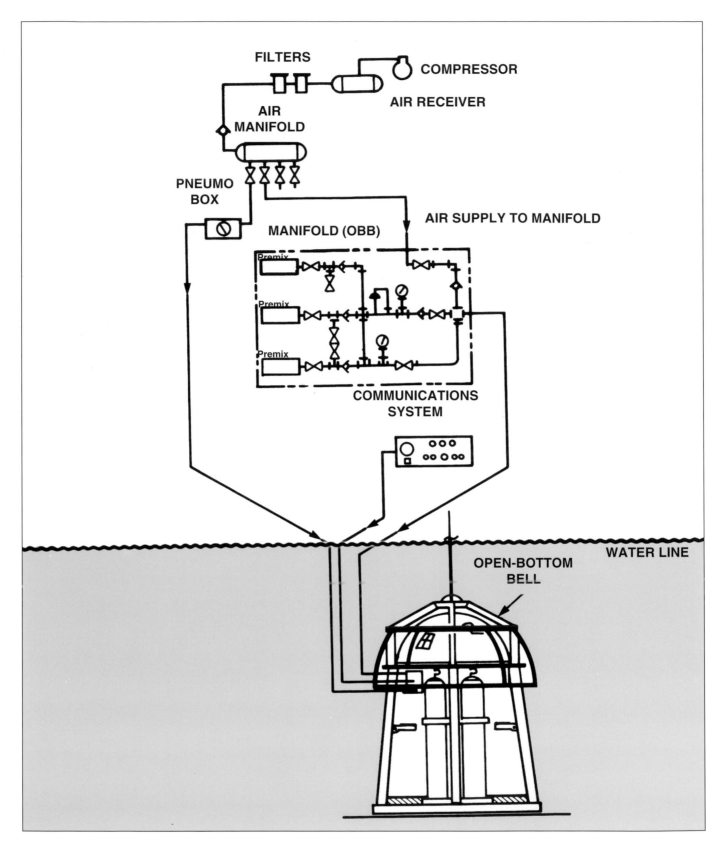

FIGURE 11.19
Open-Bottom Bell System

FIGURE 11.20
Open-Bottom Bell

FIGURE 11.21
Closed Diving Bell Used With a Saturation System

the outside of the bell. Both gases are routed to a manifold inside the dome and used for dewatering the bell dome and emergency breathing via built-in-breathing (BIB) masks or scuba regulators. A speaker mounted in the dome allows two-way voice communication with topside personnel.

The bell is raised and lowered by a wire cable from a crane, davit, or A-frame on the support vessel. A life support umbilical consists of a hardwire communication cable, gas supply hose routed from a surface control manifold, pneumofathometer hose providing continuous depth readouts at the surface, a strength member in case the primary lift cable breaks, and additional specialty components as required.

11.3.2 Operational Parameters

Although typically used in support of surface-supplied diving, the open bell may be used in conjunction with many types of diving operations. When supporting surface-supplied diving operations, the diver's umbilical is usually routed from the surface rather than from the bell. Most open bells can support two divers in normal operations and three divers in an emergency; however, they are often designed and built for specific purposes in various sizes and weights. Safe operation of an open bell requires a

stable support platform capable of holding its position in a variety of sea conditions.

OSHA and United States Coast Guard (U.S.C.G.) regulations require the use of an open bell on all dives deeper than 220 fsw (67 msw) or those involving more than 120 minutes of in-water decompression, except when a hard-hat diving outfit is used or when dives are being performed in a physically confining space. These regulations also allow open bell use to a depth of 300 fsw (92 msw) in helium-oxygen diving operations; in actual practice, however, the use of open bells is usually restricted to 225–250 fsw (69–77 msw) because of limited emergency support capabilities. Longer and deeper dives are more safely performed using a closed and pressurized diving bell (see Figure 11.21).

11.3.3 Operational Procedures

Operation of an open bell requires completion of a predive checklist of all major support systems, including the bell-handling, life-support, and communications systems. Positive control of the bell is essential during deployment and retrieval and requires the use of tag lines. The bell is lowered into the water, shackled into a separate downline to prevent the bell from turning during ascent and descent, and all control lines are removed. Divers enter the water, secure themselves on the outside of the bell, and prepare to descend. Riding the bell in this position rather than being transported inside the bell prevents the divers from being trapped inside if the lift cable breaks.

During ascent and descent, the bell and diver's depth and rate of travel are monitored and controlled by topside personnel via a control panel (see Figure 11.22). Compressed gases are added to the bell dome during descent to exclude water. Descent is stopped when the bell is 10 – 15 ft. (3 – 4.5 m) from the bottom, and the bell remains suspended in the water column while the divers are on the bottom. Whenever they leave the bell, the divers vent the dome to reduce the buildup of carbon dioxide, because an emergency return to the bell may require the divers to breathe the gas inside the dome while they don their emergency breathing equipment. The divers may pass their umbilicals through the frame of the bell to help to relocate the bell at the conclusion of the dive.

During ascent, the bell is raised at the appropriate rate of speed and is stopped at predetermined depths in accordance with the required decompression schedule. After the last in-water decompression stop, the bell is brought to the surface, the divers exit the bell and climb aboard the support platform, where further decompression may be completed on board.

Retrieval of the bell reverses the steps in the deployment procedure, except that a surface swimmer may have to enter the water to attach the tag lines and unshackle the bell from its downline. The bell is lifted aboard and secured to the deck. All systems are rechecked for proper operation, gas supplies are inventoried, gas banks are charged, and maintenance is performed in preparation for the next dive.

FIGURE 11.22
Diver/Open-Bottom Bell System Control Panel

Diving Under Special Conditions

12

Diving Under Special Conditions

12.0 GENERAL

The characteristics of underwater environments, such as temperature, visibility, and type of marine life, vary significantly from geographic region to region and influence the amount and type of diving work that can be carried out under water. The following paragraphs describe the diving conditions most typical of U.S. coastal and other areas and provide an overview of the diving characteristics of these regions.

WARNING

WHEN DIVING IN AN UNFAMILIAR REGION, OBTAIN INFORMATION ABOUT LOCAL CONDITIONS FROM DIVERS WHO ARE FAMILIAR WITH LOCAL WATERS. AN ORIENTATION DIVE SHOULD BE MADE WITH A DIVER FAMILIAR WITH THE AREA.

12.1 GEOGRAPHIC REGIONS

For the purpose of this chapter, the coastal regions are classified as shown in Table 12.1. The principal characteristics of each region are described in the following sections of this chapter.

TABLE 12.1
Definitions of Geographical Regions

Region	Area Encompassed
Northeast Coast	Maine to Rhode Island
Mid-Atlantic Coast	Rhode Island to Cape Hatteras
Southeast Coast	Cape Hatteras to Florida
Gulf of Mexico Coast	West Coast of Florida to Texas
Northwest Coast	Subarctic Alaska to Oregon
Mid-Pacific Coast	Northern and Central California
Southwest Coast	Point Conception to the Northern Baja Peninsula
Central Pacific Ocean	Hawaiian and Leeward Islands
Polar	Arctic and Antarctic
Tropics	Caribbean and Florida Keys

12.1.1 Northeast Coast

Diving in northeastern waters is an exciting and chilling experience. Generally, the best diving conditions in terms of water temperature, sea state, and underwater visibility occur from June through October. As one progresses north along the New England coast, water temperature decreases and underwater visibility increases.

Water temperatures near the surface during the spring and summer, when a substantial thermocline exists, range from 50–70°F (10–21C). Temperatures at 100 ft. (30.5 m) range from 48–54°F (9–12C). During the winter months, the temperature of the water column is essentially homogeneous, with temperatures reaching as low as 28.5°F (-2C) close to the surface. Subzero air temperatures and strong winds cause wind chill factors as low as -70–-80°F (-57–-62C). Dry suits have become standard for winter diving in the Northeast.

Underwater visibility is primarily a function of sea state and vertical turbulence in the water column. In the Northeast, horizontal visibility of 50–80 ft. (15.2–24.4 m) may occur occasionally throughout the year, usually in connection with calm seas. Proximity to a land mass or to estuaries or harbors is associated with a decrease in visibility because the load of suspended material in the runoff from the land mass and the processes associated with the mixing of fresh and salt water greatly elevate turbidity. During the summer, biologically caused "red tide" conditions may occur, lowering visibility to less than 1 ft. (0.3 m). Coastal waters within the Gulf of Maine have an average range in visibility of 25–35 ft. (7.6–10.7 m), while visibility in waters south of Cape Cod averages 10–15 ft. (3.0–4.6 m).

Several species of brown algae comprise the large kelp of the New England coast. Unlike the kelp of California, these kelp do not form surface canopies. New England kelp occasionally extend as much as 25 ft. (7.6 m) off the hard ocean bottom and, although they look impenetrable, they do not in fact present a significant entanglement hazard. Generally, these algal plants are sparsely distributed and seldom project more than 6–8 ft. (1.8–2.4 m) from the bottom.

The Gulf of Mexico coastline is characterized by a very gradual offshore slope resulting in relatively shallow diving depths for a long distance out from shore. The shallow coastline also means short period choppy wave conditions under moderate wind conditions. Shorelines accessible for beach entries are mostly of sand composition but may change to silt over sand or mud a short distance offshore, especially adjacent to river outlets. The offshore bottom is mostly featureless, but, in the northern and western Gulf, is interrupted by the limestone remains of prehistoric reefs, rock outcroppings and an increasing number of manmade artificial reefs and petroleum structures. Sponge bottom and small coral patch reefs occur off southwest Florida, and larger coral reef areas are located further offshore in the northwestern Gulf and off the west coast of Florida.

Hazardous Marine Animals: As in marine environments around the world, divers in the Gulf are most in danger of being cut, abraded or punctured by the small, sharp, shelled animals that adhere to and grow on almost every square inch of exposed rock and reef surface. The most notorious of the puncturing organisms is the sea urchin. Long and short-spined sea urchins are common throughout the Gulf. On the reefs, the unwary and unprotected diver is at risk of receiving deep and painful wounds from contact with coral.

Stinging organisms abound in the Gulf. Stinging hydrozoa including fire coral are common encounters in the south, and jellyfish occur throughout the Gulf. Most jellyfish are seasonal and are at their highest densities in the summer and early fall. The Portuguese man-of-war is an open ocean traveler, but may at times occur in large numbers near shore as a result of areal winds and currents. To avoid being stung, the diver should be alert, look before touching, and wear appropriate protective body covering.

There are also fishes inhabiting Gulf waters that can sting or shock divers. The stingers include scorpion fish and rays which are experts at concealing themselves from view of the unaware diver. Sting rays are especially problematic in the shallows where they are very hard to detect, and divers entering the water from the beach must shuffle their feet to avoid stepping on them. Electric rays and stargazers are capable of generating an electric charge and can shock an unsuspecting diver.

Gulf fishes that have the potential to bite divers fall into two categories, fishes that inhabit holes in the bottom and reef crevices, and those that occur in the water column. The bottom dwellers include eels (including moray eels) and toadfishes. These fishes normally do not present a threat unless the diver recklessly reaches into a hole without first checking for inhabitants. The off-bottom fishes include triggerfishes, barracuda, and sharks. The grey triggerfish has the worst reputation for biting and is responsible for missing finger tips and earlobes as well as scars on a number of Gulf divers. Although they are not thought of as a major threat, barracuda have attacked divers in the Gulf, but most of these were related to handling dead or dying fishes (spear fishing) or to diving in weather disturbed turbid water (which usually occurs after cyclonic activity).

The only marine mammal in the Gulf considered to be a potential threat to humans is the killer whale. These animals have only been observed well offshore where there is little chance that divers would encounter them.

12.1.5 Northwest Coast

Diving activities in the northwest take place off the coast of subarctic Alaska and extend to areas offshore from Oregon. Water temperatures in subarctic Alaska range from 34–38°F (1–3C) during the winter months and average 45–50°F (7–10C) during the summer. Divers in these waters must give serious consideration to their choice of thermal protection so that dive duration is not overly affected by the cold. During the winter, temperature and wind conditions may combine so that some bays, inlets, and near-shore waters freeze over. In these conditions, the hazard of icing of diving equipment must be considered.

Visibility in Alaskan waters varies drastically from place to place and from time to time. The best visibility occurs along coastlines and in the Aleutians, where it may range, at best, from 40–80 ft. (12.2–24.4 m). Visibility in the waters of bays and straits is usually 15–30 ft. (4.6–9.1 m). At any location, visibility may become temporarily limited by storms or phyto-plankton blooms. Late each spring in southeast Alaska, the visibility in the upper 30–40 ft. (9.1–12.2 m) of the water column may be near zero because of phyto-plankton, but below that layer the water may be very clear with a visibility of 40 ft. (12.2 m) or more. Although this deep, clear water is often dark because of the shading effect of the overriding low-visibility water, there is usually sufficient ambient light to see.

Currents and tides are strong and unpredictable in subarctic Alaskan waters. The large range of tidal exchanges can cause currents as high as 10 knots in certain narrows. Currents vary significantly with depth and have been observed to change direction within a period of minutes.

Much of the Alaskan coastline is steep and rocky; many areas are too steep to allow divers either to enter or exit the water. Such points must be carefully selected before a dive. Most sections of coastline are accessible only from boats. During times of heavy seas or swells, many near-shore diving locations become unsafe to dive.

Alaskan waters harbor relatively few hazardous marine organisms. Those that cause divers the most trouble are the urchins, barnacles, and jellyfish, with their potential to cause punctures, abrasions, and stings. Dense beds of floating kelp can cause some problems for divers, especially during surface swimming. Sharks and whales are common but are rarely, if ever, seen under water and generally do not influence diving activity. The presence of killer whales, which are common, is an exception to this general rule. Although no known diver/killer whale encounters have taken place in Alaska, general caution should keep divers out of the water if these animals are known to be near. Steller sea lions are very abundant in some areas of Alaska; although there are no reports that these animals have ever harmed divers in Alaska, California sea lions have been known to injure divers. Because sea lions are large, fast, and agile and are attracted to divers, they can disrupt an otherwise routine dive. In addition to being a psychological distraction, the activity of sea lions often causes serious movement of bottom sediments and a reduction of visibility.

Farther south, in the waters off Washington and Oregon, water temperatures range from about 43–60°F (6–16C) over the year in protected areas such as Puget Sound. In open-ocean waters, depending on the water masses moving through, temperatures ranging from 40–60°F (4–16C) may be encountered throughout the year. Visibility usually is low, ranging from 5–25 ft. (1.5–7.6 m) in coastal water near beaches and from 0–70 ft. (0–21.3 m) in protected Puget Sound waters.

Currents in certain areas are strong and unpredictable. This is especially true in river diving, where very low visibility can cause orientation problems. Logs, stumps, wrecked automobiles, fishing hooks and lines, and other bottom debris also pose distinct dangers to divers working in this region.

12.1.6 Mid-Pacific Coast

The mid-Pacific coastal region includes the waters of Northern and Central California. From San Francisco north, the best diving conditions in terms of underwater visibility as well as water temperatures generally occur from June through September. From San Francisco south to Point Conception, good diving conditions may continue through December.

From San Francisco north to the Oregon border, summer temperatures generally range from about 48–56°F (9–13C). A thermocline generally exists at depths from 20–40 ft. (6.1–12.2 m) during late spring and summer. The difference in surface and bottom temperatures during this period ranges between 2 and 5°F (1 and 3C). A full wet suit, including hood, boots, and gloves, is a necessity when diving in these waters and many divers use dry suits.

Underwater visibility varies quite drastically throughout the area from summer to winter. From Fort Bragg to the Oregon border, late spring and summer underwater visibility ranges between 10 and 15 ft. (3.0 and 4.6 m). In the late summer and fall, underwater visibility increases to about 15–25 ft. (4.6–7.6 m). During the winter and early spring, visibility decreases to 0–10 ft. (0–3.0 m). South of Fort Bragg to San Francisco, visibility ranges from 10–20 ft. (3.0–6.1 m), increasing to 30 ft. (9.1 m) in the fall. From Santa Cruz north to

San Francisco, visibility ranges from 5–15 ft. (1.5–4.6 m) in the early spring and summer, 10–25 ft. (3.0–7.6 m) in late summer and fall, and 0–10 ft. (0–3.0 m) during the winter and early spring. From Point Conception to Santa Cruz, visibility ranges from 15–25 ft. (4.6–7.6 m) during the late spring and summer and from 15–50 ft. (4.6–15.2 m) in the fall occasionally reaching 100 ft. (30.5 m) near Camel Bay. During winter and early spring, one can expect visibility to extend 5–20 ft. (1.5–6.1 m). The main factors controlling underwater visibility in this area are the huge plankton bloom, which occurs during upwelling in the spring and summer, and the dirty water conditions caused by rough seas and river runoffs during the winter and early spring.

Three species of surface-canopy-forming brown algae-kelp occur on the Pacific coast. From Monterey north, the dominant kelp is the bull kelp. This particular species forms large beds, but because of its structure, does not pose the same entanglement hazard to divers as the giant kelp. Kelp beds or forests are widely diversified both geographically and as a function of depth and temperature. Different varieties grow in different zones and support an incredible variety of sea life. Kelp will attach itself to practically any substrate (i.e., rock, concrete, steel, wreckage, etc.) and will often form a treelike structure, the base of which is a root-like hold-fast that provides a secure anchor and a home for many organisms. There is generally an area of open water between the stipes originating from one hold-fast.

North of Point Conception, surf conditions are probably the most important consideration in planning a dive. Divers can expect 2–3-ft. (0.6–0.9-m) surf in most areas even on calm days, and on rough days it is not uncommon to see waves 10 ft. (3.0 m) or more high. Divers should always scout the proposed dive area before going into the water to determine the safest area of entry and, in case conditions change, to choose alternate exit sites.

Long-shore currents and tidal currents are common and tend to be severe in northern and central California. On very windy days, divers should watch for strong currents around headlands, off rocky shores, and near reefs. Rip currents are common along beaches and in coves.

Hazardous Marine Animals: As in other areas, divers must watch for sea urchins, jellyfish, and rockfish. Fortunately, shark attacks in this area are not common. In the last fifteen to twenty years, fewer than two dozen shark attacks involving divers have been recorded. However, caution must be exercised when diving near seal breeding areas around Pt. Reyes, the Farallon Islands, Bodega Bay, Tomales Bay, and off San Francisco. Diving is not recommended except when underwater visibility is ideal. Stingrays and electric rays are also found in the mid-Pacific coastal region.

There are ecological reserves in this area, where all animals and plants are protected: Gulf of Farallon, Cordell Bank, and Monterey Bay National Marine Sanctuaries;

Point Lobos State Reserve; Point Reyes Seashore area; Salt Point State Park; Estero de Limantour Reserve in Marin County north of San Francisco; and Del Mar Landing in Sonoma County. Divers should consult with the sanctuary park authorities to determine the boundaries of these marine reserves and the restrictions that apply to them.

12.1.7 Southwest Coast

The waters of the Southwest include the area from Point Conception to the northern Baja Peninsula. Water temperatures range from 50–60°F (10–16C) in winter and 55–70°F (13–21C) in summer, with some localized areas made colder by upwelling. During much of the year, temperatures at depths below 100 ft. (30.5 m) are fairly stable in the 50° to the low 60°F (10–16C). In fall and winter there is a great deal of mixing in the upper layers and discrete temperature zones do not exist. However, a distinct summer thermocline at 40–60 ft. (12.2–18.3 m) causes a sharp temperature drop that should be considered in dive planning.

Horizontal visibility underwater ranges from 5–10 ft. (1.5–3.0 m) along much of the mainland coast to as much as 100 ft. (30.5 m) around the offshore islands. The best visibility conditions occur in the late summer and fall. During spring and early summer, underwater visibility is generally less than 30–50 ft. (9.1–15.2 m) around the islands, at least in part because of prevailing overcasts and heavy fogs. Winter storm conditions and rain runoff can reduce the visibility to zero for miles along the mainland coast, because the prevailing long-shore current distributes suspended material from storm drains and river mouths.

Shore conditions along the mainland coast of southern California range from sand beaches to high palisade cliffs. Ocean access from these areas is often impossible, and a careful check of charts and weather/surf forecasts, supplemented by a preliminary site visit, is highly recommended before initiating a dive. The offshore islands (i.e., Channel Islands) generally are accessible to divers only by boat. Moderate-to-heavy surf prevails along the entire mainland coast and on the windward sides of the offshore islands. Under certain weather conditions, the normally calm leeward sides also may present hazardous diving conditions.

Currents and tides are not of prime importance in the southwest coastal region, although there are local exceptions. Currents around the islands, especially during tidal changes, may attain speeds of 3–4 knots. The direction and relative strength of nearshore currents can be observed both topside and under water by watching the degree and direction of kelp layover.

Hazardous aquatic animals in this region include: sharks (especially around the offshore islands) such as the blue, horned, swell, angel, and leopard; whales (including killer whales); moray eels; sea urchins; and jellyfish. Divers should be aware of the habitats, appearance, and habits of these species.

Sewer outfalls are common along the mainland coast, and direct contact with sewer effluent should be avoided.

The outfall discharge point may occur from a few hundred feet to several miles offshore, in 60 to several hundred feet (18.3 to several hundred meters) of water. The effluent sometimes rises to the surface in a boil characterized by elevated temperatures, paper and other debris, and an unpleasant odor. If diving must be conducted in outfall areas, precautions such as immunization, use of full-face masks and dry suits, and scrupulous postdive hygiene must be observed (see Chapter 13 for polluted-water diving procedures). Most outfall discharge points are marked on charts and can be identified on the surface by a boil or by an orange-and-white striped spar buoy anchored near the pipe terminus.

As in Northern California, ecological reserves that have various restrictions have been established in the southwestern coastal region. The local office of the California Department of Fish and Game or National Park Service is the best source of information about the location of these reserves and any restrictions that pertain to them.

Diving in northern Mexican (upper Baja California) waters is similar to that in lower southern California. However, Mexico imposes heavy fines and impounds the boats of people diving in Mexican waters without proper permits; permits can be obtained through the Mexican government or from Mexican customs officials in San Diego, California.

12.1.8 Central Pacific Ocean

The most accessible diving in this area is around the Hawaiian Archipelago, which consists of the major Hawaiian Islands and the lesser-known Leeward Islands. The major islands are: Hawaii, Maui, Kahoolawe, Lanai, Molokai, Oahu, Kauai, and Niihau. The Leeward Islands are a group of rocks, shoals, and islets that are remnants of ancient islands and seamounts that extend from Kauai to Midway Island. They are all wildlife reserves and generally are inaccessible except to government personnel or authorized visitors.

The average water temperature around the major islands is 76°F (24C) with little change throughout the year. Underwater visibility is almost always excellent, ranging from 50–100 ft. (15.2–30.5 m) or more. Currents can sometimes be a problem in channels and near points and may reach speeds of up to 3 knots (1.5 m/s). High surf is also a potential hazard and may vary widely with the seasons.

It is possible to make shore entries from all the islands, but rocks, surge, and surf must always be considered when planning entries and exits. Since drop-offs occur very near shore and continue for several hundred feet, it is easy to get into deep water quickly after making a shore entry. Caution must always be exercised when diving in these areas to avoid exceeding depth limits.

Although most forms of dangerous marine life can be found in Hawaiian waters, they seldom pose a problem for divers. There have been a few recorded shark attacks, but they are extremely rare and usually involve swimmers or surfers.

Eel bites, sea urchin punctures, and coral abrasions are the most common types of injury. No license is needed to harvest fish or crustaceans for home consumption; however, game laws in most states place season and size limitations on some species.

12.1.9 Arctic and Antarctic

The two most important factors to be considered in arctic and antarctic environments are the effects of cold on the diver and the restricted access to the surface when diving under ice. These topics are covered in detail in section 12.10 which deals with diving in cold water and diving under ice.

Water temperature in arctic waters can be as low as 28°F (-2C), but the air temperature and its associated chill factor may be more limiting to divers than the cold water itself. Often, surface air temperatures as low as -40 – -50°F (-40 – -46C) are reached, with accompanying wind velocities that bring the chill factor to a temperature equivalent to -100°F (-73C) or less. In such conditions, protecting divers from the extreme cold is paramount both before and after the dive.

In polar regions the marine species of concern may include leopard seals, walrus, killer whales, and polar bears. A predive reconnaissance by an experienced observer will indicate if any of these animals are in the vicinity and are likely to cause a problem.

12.1.10 Tropics

Tropical waters provide an interesting environment for diving, because of the excellent underwater visibility and abundance of marine life. The visibility in tropical waters is generally 50 ft. (15.2 m) or more with little variation throughout the year. However, the waters may become murky and silty after a storm, during plankton blooms, or from silting near shore. Water temperatures hover around 70°F (21C) during the winter months and may be as high as 82°F (28C) in shallower waters during the summer.

Marine life is abundant, and many forms pose a danger to divers. Sharks often thrive in these waters and precautions should be taken when they are sighted. A wide variety of poisonous marine animals (jellyfish, scorpionfish, sea snakes) also abounds. Therefore, diving supervisors and divers should review area-specific guides to hazardous marine life.

12.1.11 Diving in Marine Sanctuaries or Underwater Parks

Divers may on occasion dive for recreation or work in sanctuaries or underwater parks. These marine sanctuaries have been set aside for the purpose of preserving or restoring recreational, ecological, or esthetic values. Examples include the NOAA National Marine Sanctuaries, and state and national parks.

Marine sanctuaries are built around distinctive marine resources whose protection and proper use require comprehensive, geographically-oriented planning and management, but do not necessarily exclude use by people. It is important when diving in these areas to follow the rules and regulations established for sanctuary management. Accordingly, when conducting working or scientific dives in designated marine sanctuaries and parks, it is important to check with local authorities before beginning operations.

12.2 DIVING FROM SHORE

A diver should expect to encounter a wide variety of conditions when entering the water from shore. Shorelines vary greatly, and diving from a particular shore requires individual preparation and planning (see Figure 12.1).

Before entering the water from shore, special attention should be given to determining a safe exit point. Since diving equipment is often placed on the ground near the water, extra care must be taken to ensure that diving equipment is kept free from dirt, which can cause regulator malfunction.

If the dive from shore is to be made to a precise underwater location, it is advisable to place a reference marker clearly at the water surface. This can be done by using a marker buoy or surface float. A small marker buoy floating on the surface, however, may be difficult for a diver to see; therefore, compass bearings, underwater contours or features, or triangulation methods using known shore positions should be used initially in locating a dive site.

When diving operations are being conducted from shore without a boat, a dive flag must be displayed at the dive location. If entry conditions permit, divers should carry and/or tow the flag with them during the dive. It is also advisable to equip each diver with a day/night signal flare or acoustical signaling device to alert shore personnel in an emergency. These devices provide a quick means of accurately locating a diver on the surface.

12.2.1 Through Surf

Entering the water even through moderate surf when burdened with diving equipment is a difficult and potentially hazardous operation. A careful analysis of surf conditions should be made and, if conditions are considered too severe to allow safe passage to open water, the dive should be postponed.

WARNING
BEFORE DIVING FROM AN UNFAMILIAR SHORE, LOCAL DIVERS SHOULD BE CONSULTED ABOUT LOCAL CONDITIONS.

Before entering the water, divers should observe the surf. By watching the surf for a short period of time, water entry can be timed to coincide with a small set of waves. On a steep sloping beach, the diver should approach the water fully dressed for diving. At the water's edge, the diver should don his fins, mask, and snorkel. With one hand on

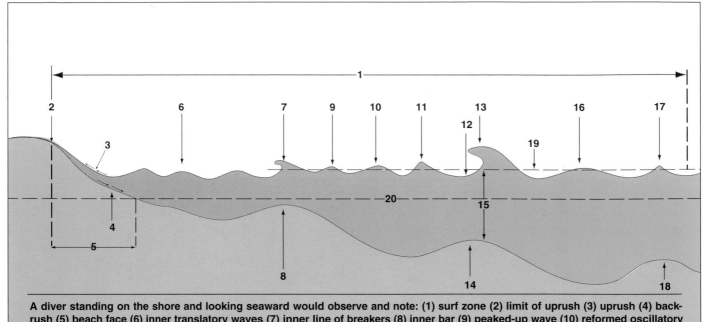

A diver standing on the shore and looking seaward would observe and note: (1) surf zone (2) limit of uprush (3) uprush (4) back-rush (5) beach face (6) inner translatory waves (7) inner line of breakers (8) inner bar (9) peaked-up wave (10) reformed oscillatory wave (11) outer translatory waves (12) plunge point (13) outer line of breakers (14) outer bar (inner at low tide) (15) breaker depth, 1.3 x breaker height (16) waves flatten again (17) waves peak up but do not break on this bar at high tide (18) deep bar (outer bar at low tide) (19) still-water level and (20) mean low water.

FIGURE 12.1
Diagram of Waves in the Breaker Zone

the mask, the diver should then turn around and back into the water with knees slightly bent and body leaning back into the waves, or face the waves and enter the water on their hands and knees.

When diving off beaches with gradual slopes and no surf, the diver should leave his fins off until he reaches waist-to-chest depth water. It is important to remember that sting ray encounters are not uncommon in shallow water, so the diver should shuffle his feet along the bottom rather than using a lifted step when traversing the shallows. Divers entering with a float should tow it behind them on 10–30 ft. (3.0–9.1 m) of line and should be aware of the possibility that turbulence may cause the line to wrap around an arm, leg, or equipment.

WARNING
DIVERS NEAR THE SURFACE SHOULD NOT HOLD THEIR BREATH WHEN A WAVE PASSES OVER-HEAD—THE RAPID PRESSURE DROP AT THE DIVER'S DEPTH AS THE WAVE TROUGH PASSES MAY CAUSE A LUNG OVERPRESSURE ACCIDENT.

When swimming through the surf zone, the diver's BC should not be inflated, and if possible, only the snorkel should be used. Swimming over breakers should not be attempted. As breakers approach, the diver should duck his head under and swim through them. Swimming into the base of the wave is advantageous because the circular motion of the entrained water will carry the diver up behind the wave. When waves are encountered in shallow water, the diver should turn his back toward and brace against them.

A group of divers may make a surf entry in buddy teams and meet beyond the surf zone. Once safely through the surf, all equipment should be checked prior to beginning descent.

Sand may have entered the mask, regulator, or fins as the diver passed through the surf. This should be removed before continuing with the dive. Sand in the regulator exhaust valve can cause it to seal improperly, permitting water, as well as air, to be inhaled. Sand in the fins, may be mildly irritating at first, but can cause painful abrasions by the end of a dive.

After successful entry, the diver can swim seaward on the surface using a snorkel if conditions are good, but may have to switch to scuba and swim as close to the bottom as possible if seas are rough. Sand ripples generally run parallel or somewhat oblique to shore and can be used, by swimming perpendicular to them, to navigate off shore. If the bottom is rocky, divers can pull themselves along by grasping the rocks. On a sandy bottom, a

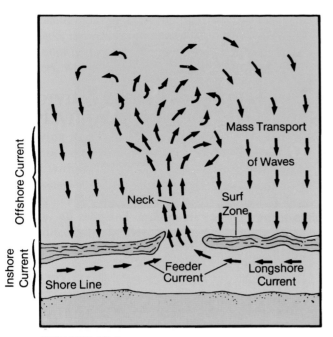

FIGURE 12.2
Near-Shore Current System

diver can accomplish the same by thrusting his knife into the bottom.

Exiting the water through the surf involves performing the same procedures used to enter, except in reverse order. The diver should wait just seaward of the surf for a small set or for a break in the sets of waves. When the time is right, the diver should begin swimming shoreward (keeping an eye on the incoming waves) immediately after the passage of the last of the larger waves. The smaller waves breaking behind will assist the diver's progress toward the beach. Using this assisting wave action, the diver should swim toward the beach. Divers should continue swimming, periodically checking for oncoming waves, until making contact with the bottom. Once bottom contact is made the divers should crawl out of the surf zone on hands and knees onto the beach.

When approaching a gradual sloping beach with no surf, the diver should remove his fins, stand and start walking (shuffling) toward the beach as soon as he reaches waist-deep water. When exiting with a float, divers should position them down current or push it ahead to avoid becoming entangled in the towline.

The following points concerning scuba equipment are highly recommended when entering through the surf:

- Keep equipment hydrodynamically streamlined.
- Minimize extraneous gear such as cameras, clipboards, etc.
- Secure all gear as tightly as possible, both personally and in boats.

- Overweight by at least six lbs. (2.24 kg) to stay on the seabed.
- Be prepared to have your face mask dislodged; hold on when necessary. The second-stage regulator is rarely pulled out of the mouth; fins are commonly pulled off one at a time. Items should not be tied to the weight belt because the weight belt may need to be ditched quickly if the diver gets into difficulties. Loss of weight belts is a common event in surf-zone diving.

12.2.2 Through Surf on a Rocky Shore

Before entering the surf from a rocky shore, divers should evaluate wave conditions and should not attempt to stand or walk on rocks located in the surf zone. Instead, divers should select the deepest backwash of the last large wave of a series and enter the water; the backwash should carry the diver between the larger rocks. Every effort should be made to swim around the rocks rather than over them. Divers should stay in the smaller, deeper channels between rocks and maintain a prone swimming position facing the next oncoming wave. They should kick or grasp a rock to keep from being carried back toward the shore and then kick seaward after the wave passes.

When exiting on a rocky shore, divers should stop outside the surf zone to evaluate wave conditions and should then exit toward the beach on the backside of the last large wave of a series. As momentum from the wave is lost, divers should kick or grasp a rock to avoid being carried seaward by the backwash. Divers should maintain their position, catch the next wave, and thus move shoreward, exercising caution over slippery rocks.

12.2.3 Through Shore Currents

In and adjacent to the surf zone, currents are generated by approaching waves (and surf), bottom contours and irregularities, shoreline geography, and tides. When waves approach the shore at an angle, a long-shore current is generated that flows parallel to the beach within the surf zone. Long-shore currents are most common along straight beaches. The current velocity increases with breaker height, increasing angle of the breaker to the shore, increasing beach slope, and decreasing wave period. The velocity of long-shore currents seldom exceeds 1 knot (0.5 m/s). Wave fronts advancing over non-parallel bottom contours are refracted to cause convergence or divergence of the energy of the waves. In areas of convergence, energy concentrations form barriers to the returning backwash, which is deflected along the beach to areas of less resistance. These currents turn seaward in concentrations at locations where there are "weak points," extremely large water accumulations, gaps in the bar or reef, or submarine depressions perpendicular to shore, and form a rip current through the surf (see Figure 12.2).

Diving Under Special Conditions

FIGURE 12.5
Back-Roll Method

• Manned while divers are in the water; an operator should be onboard and able to respond to an emergency at all times

Small boats used to tend divers can be anchored or unanchored. When anchored, the boat should be positioned downstream of the site for easy access when divers surface, and a surface float should be streamed off the stern. Even anchored boats need to be able to move immediately in case an incapacitated diver must be recovered; a buoyed anchor facilitates a quick getaway. The operator in the boat should keep a constant watch on the diver's bubbles, and great care should be taken to stay clear of divers if the engine is in gear. When tending without an anchor, the operator should drop divers off upstream of the site and remain downstream of the divers during operations. Drift diving with a surface float provides an effective method for keeping the boat in position for pickup.

12.4.1 Entering the Water

NOTE
Always examine the water below the point of entry just prior to entry.

Entering the water from a small boat can be accomplished safely by several methods. Sitting on the gunwale and rolling into the water is considered best if the distance is not greater than 3–4 ft. (0.9–1.2 m) as shown in Figure 12.5. The diver should sit on the gunwale facing the center of the boat with both feet inside, and lean forward to counterbalance the weight of the equipment. When ready to enter, the diver should hold his pressure gauge in one hand while ensuring that his mask and second-stage regulator are in place with the other hand, sit up, lean backward, and let the weight of the diving equipment carry him over the side.

A second method of entry is the "giant stride" (feet first) method, which is generally used when entering the water from a larger boat with an opening in the gunwale. Using this technique, the diver should look straight ahead or at the horizon and step off into the water. The intent is to hit the water feet first. Bending at the waist or looking down usually results in the diver landing on his face. If the diver must climb over or stand on the gunwale to enter the water, another individual should assist the diver.

When entering the water using these methods, the diver should always hold the face mask firmly in place. Also, any required equipment that cannot be carried easily and safely should be secured to a piece of line hung over the side, and retrieved after entry.

As a general rule, the diver should always enter the water slowly, using the method that will result in the least physical discomfort and disturbance to equipment. Each diver should determine the method best suited to various water conditions.

12.4.2 Exiting the Water

When preparing to exit the water into a boat, there are several general rules to follow. While ascending, divers should look upward continuously to ensure that the boat or other object is not directly overhead and that they will not strike it when surfacing. Holding an arm over the head with a closed fist while rotating 360 degrees during ascent is a good practice.

Upon surfacing, ensure that all divers are accounted for. Maintain contact with the boat, ladder, or trail/line, and begin an orderly exit, one diver at a time.

NOTE
Stay well clear of the area directly underneath or behind an exiting diver in case he falls back into the water.

Probably the most widely used method of returning to a small boat is via a diver ladder. Divers may choose to exit the water without removing any equipment. This should only be attempted if the ladder is strong enough to support the total weight. If equipment is removed prior to climbing the ladder, divers should be assisted in removing their cylinders and weight belts by someone in the boat or other divers in the water. Fins should be removed last and carried while climbing aboard.

A ladder may be built in many configurations, but every ladder should have these general characteristics:

- Extend below the surface of the water 3–4 ft. (0.9–1.2 m), providing a place for the diver to stand and hold on while removing equipment
- Strong, well built, and capable of being securely fastened to the side so it will not shift when subjected to the action of the seas and the diver's weight
- Wide enough to accommodate the diver comfortably
- Angled away from the boat to permit easier ascent
- Rungs that are flat and wide and side-rails above the water for hand-holds

Modifying conventional ladders to fit small boats is unsatisfactory because these ladders are closed on both sides by rung support shafts, are difficult to climb with equipment, and hang too close to the boat to provide sufficient toe space.

Figure 12.4 shows a ladder that is designed to allow a fully-equipped diver to re-enter a small boat without removing his fins. The most important features of the ladder are lack of side supports (open-step design), its slope, and its ability to be positioned on the transom of the boat. With a ladder of the open-step type, divers can use the inner sides of their feet to locate the ladder rungs and can then step onto the rung from the side.

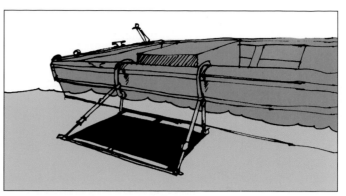

FIGURE 12.6
Side-Mounted Diver Platform

The angle between the shaft and the transom should be 35–40 degrees.

Positioning the ladder on the transom (the strongest part of the boat) is particularly important in current because the boat partially protects the diver from the force of the current and because the diver can climb out of the water parallel to the current. If conventional ladders positioned on the side of the boat are used, the current may push the boat ladder sideways.

The ladder should extend about 3–4 ft. (0.9–1.2 m) below the water's surface to allow diver access. The ladder should have a handle only on the side next to the motor, so the diver can pass unhampered on the other side.

Another method of assisting a diver into a small boat is the use of a platform rigged to the stern or the side of the boat and suspended just below the surface of the water. A diver can swim onto the platform, sit securely while removing equipment, and then stand up and step safely into the boat. A hand- or arm-hold should be provided. A portable, easily-stored platform (see Figure 12.6) can be constructed from either wood or metal.

12.5 FRESHWATER DIVING

There are thousands of square miles of freshwater in the United States. Basic techniques for diving in lakes, rivers and quarries are much like those used in ocean waters. However, some differences should be noted. For example, depth gauges that are calibrated for seawater density must be corrected to achieve accuracy in freshwater and vice versa. Buoyancy requirements also are different for fresh and salt water.

12.5.1 Great Lakes

Great Lakes divers need to be aware of the temperature changes that occur with depth and season. In a typical freshwater lake, the upper layer (epilimnion) temperature generally ranges between 55 and 75°F (13 and 24C) in late summer. However, the waters below the thermocline (hypolimnion) approach the temperature of maximum density for freshwater, 39°F (4C). Consequently, divers working below the thermocline, which averages 60 ft. (18.3 m) in these lakes in late summer, must adjust their buoyancy and use thermal protection.

During the winter months, the water temperature in the Great Lakes ranges between 32°F (0C) near the surface and 39°F (4C) on the bottom. During this period, a significant portion of the Great Lakes is ice-covered. Occasionally, divers are required to work under 2–16 inches (5.1–40.6 cm) of ice to make observations, collect samples, or to maintain scientific equipment. Diving under ice is particularly hazardous, requires special techniques and equipment, and should only be undertaken by divers with specialized training. Divers and surface-support personnel operating in the lakes may be subjected to atmospheric temperatures of ˉ30°F (ˉ34C), with wind-chill factors approaching ˉ100°F (ˉ73C).

Underwater visibility in the Great Lakes ranges from about 100 ft. (30.5 m) in Lake Superior to less than 1 ft. (0.3 m) in Lake Erie. Visibility is influenced by local precipitation and runoff, nutrient enrichment, biological activity, local bottom conditions, and diver activity. Significant seasonal variations also occur in these waters.

From September to December, storms and severe wave conditions can be expected in the Great Lakes. Divers working offshore at these times must use sturdy vessels and monitor weather forecasts. Because swift currents may be encountered in rivers and straits connecting with the lakes, Great Lakes divers must use considerable caution and be properly trained in the techniques of diving in currents.

12.5.2 Inland Lakes

Other lakes in the United States vary from clear mountain lakes with low sediment input to reservoirs, sediment-laden lakes, and glacial lakes, which usually have a milky appearance. When planning a lake dive, bottom terrain is as important a consideration as underwater visibility. Lakes may have vertical rocky sides, rocky outcrops, ledges, and talus slopes, or they may be sedimentary and composed primarily of old farm land. Algal blooms often occur in lakes during the warmer months and may completely block the light, even at shallow depths. Thermoclines also occur, and temperature and underwater visibility may vary greatly.

Old cables, heavy equipment, electric cables, rope, fishline, fishing lures, and even old cars are often found on lake bottoms. Many lakes have never been cleared of trees, barns, houses, water towers, and other objects. The bottom sediment of lakes is easily stirred up, as is sediment that has settled on lake-bottom trees or brush. Divers should stay off the bottom as much as possible and move slowly when forced to work on the bottom.

12.5.3 Quarries

Artificial water systems such as reservoirs and flooded strip mines, gravel pits, or stone quarries are popular spots for diving. In some areas, they represent the only place for diving, and in other regions they are used primarily for diver training. Quarries are usually deep; the

water originates from seepage in the surrounding water table. For this reason, the water is usually low in nutrients and significantly colder than water in areas primarily fed by runoff.

As the water near the surface warms during the summer months, a sharp thermocline is created that must be taken into account when dressing for a quarry dive. Quarries are used frequently as dump sites for old cars and a variety of junk, and quarry divers must be aware of becoming snagged on sharp metal or monofilament line, especially when the sediment is stirred up and visibility is reduced.

12.6 OPEN-OCEAN DIVING

Oceanographic research occasionally requires observing and sampling pelagic organisms directly in the open ocean instead of collecting specimens using such conventional techniques such as Niskin® bottles, grabs, or nets. However, because open-ocean (also termed blue-water) diving does not provide a fixed frame of reference, divers performing open-ocean dives may become disoriented because they have a reduced awareness of depth, buoyancy, current, surge, other divers, marine organisms, and occasionally, even of the direction to the surface (Heine 1985). Special techniques have been developed to aid the diver operating in the open ocean to carry out scientific tasks safely.

Open-ocean diving is usually done from a small boat to facilitate diver entry, exit, and maneuverability, and to minimize "sail" area, which reduces drift and the consequent dragging of divers through the water. Even when operations are being conducted from a large vessel, a small boat should be used to tend the divers because wind and surface currents often carry a larger boat away from the actual dive site.

Open-ocean dive teams generally consist of a boat operator (who remains in the boat), a safety diver, and as many as four or five divers. After reaching the dive site, a downline about 100 ft. (30.5 m) long, loaded with 5–10 pounds (1.9–3.7 kg) of weight and knotted at specific depths, is passed from the boat through a surface float and lowered to serve as a safety line for the divers (see Figure 12.7). This line is then secured to the surface float and to the small boat. A 4 ft. (1.2 m) sea anchor is frequently used to reduce drift caused by wind; the anchor can be attached to a loop in the downline at the surface float or to a separate float to keep it from collapsing and sinking if the wind dies. To mark the dive site, it is useful to drop a small open jar of fluorescein dye into the water. The vertical column of dye emitted as the jar ascends will be distorted by currents, giving a visual display of the current pattern in the water column.

Because of the absence of any visible reference and the inherent danger of drifting away or down, all open-ocean divers are tethered at all times to the safety line via an underwater trapeze. The trapeze can be configured from

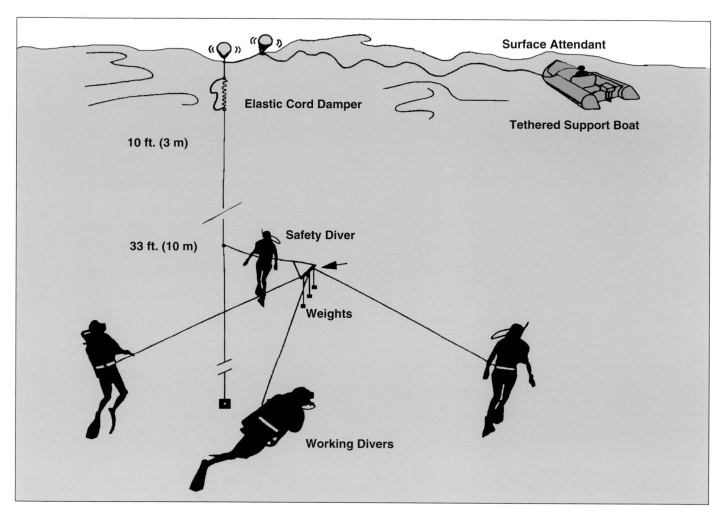

FIGURE 12.7
Down-Line Array for Open-Ocean Diving

any bar or ring that accepts clips and shackles easily. Figure 12.8 shows examples of four types of trapezes that have been used for this type of diving.

In conventional diving, buddy divers swim together; in open-ocean diving, however, the safety diver serves as the buddy diver for all of the divers on the team and vice versa. As shown in Figure 12.7, all divers are tethered to the trapeze by means of lines approximately 30–50 ft. (9.1–15.2 m) long; the length of the line depends on the underwater visibility and the task being undertaken. To avoid kinking, tethers should be braided lines. A good rule of thumb is to restrict the length of the tether to about 50–75 percent of the nominal underwater visibility distance (Heine 1985). The exception to this rule is the safety diver's tether, which should only be about 3 ft. (0.9 m) long.

Because tethers of a fixed length tend to droop and become tangled, they should be designed to remain taut at all times, which also facilitates line-pull signaling. This can be achieved by weighting the end nearest the safety diver with a 4–8-ounce fishing weight. The tether then passes

freely through the metal loop on the end of the swivel clip (see Figures 12.8, 12.9); these clips are attached to the trapeze, which is located near the safety diver. Thus, as a diver swims away from the safety diver, the tether pays out smoothly, and, when the diver returns, the tether retracts as the weight sinks. In conditions of low visibility, tether lines can be shortened by tying a knot on the weight side of the tether, thus shortening the length available to pay out. The other end of the tether should be connected to the diver's buoyancy compensator or to a separate harness. If the quick-release shackle is attached to the diver's buoyancy compensator or harness (rather than to the tether), it can be released by pulling it away from the diver's body, which ensures that it will release.

WARNING
TETHERS SHOULD NOT BE ATTACHED TO A DIVER'S WEIGHT BELT BECAUSE DITCHING OR LOSING THE BELT WOULD ADD EXCESSIVE WEIGHT TO THE TRAPEZE ARRAY.

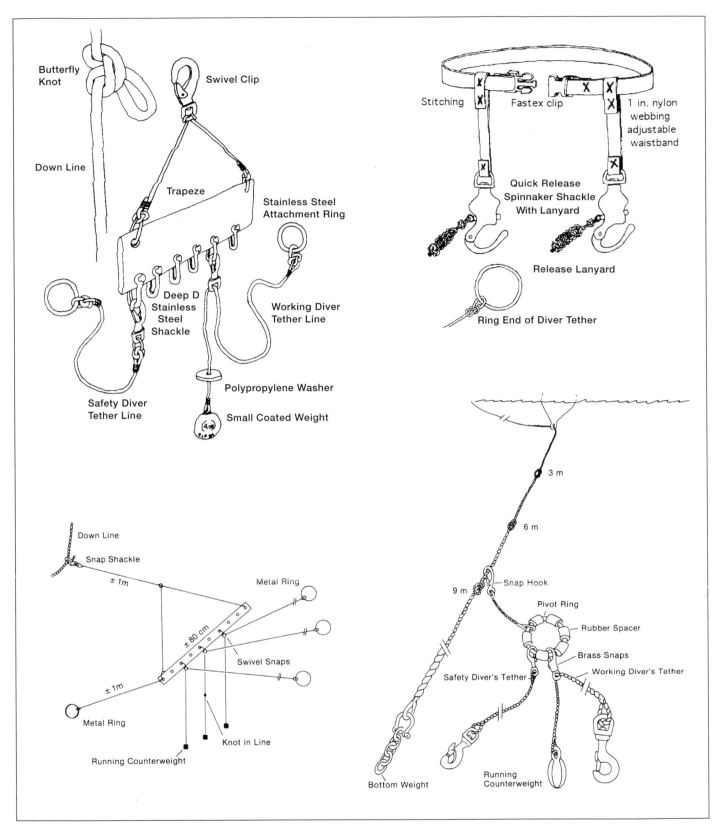

FIGURE 12.8
Four Multiple Tether Systems (Trapezes)

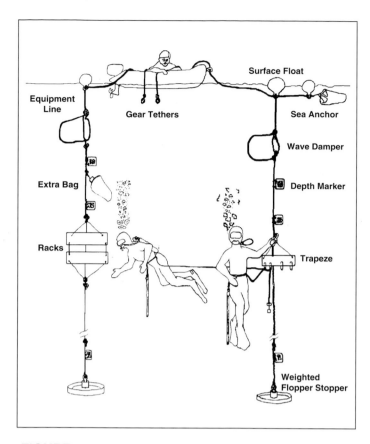

**FIGURE 12.9
Tethered Shot Lines**

Before starting a open-ocean dive, all equipment must be checked, and the divers must all be sure that they understand the diving signals, especially the line-pull signals, that will be used. The safety diver enters the water first, but all of the divers usually descend down the line together to connect the pivot ring to the vertical line and to prepare the tethers. During the dive, the safety diver monitors the tethers, keeps a lookout for hazards, and supervises the dive. The safety diver maintains visual contact with the other divers and can attract their attention by pulling on their tethers. The boat operator can signal the safety diver by pulling on the vertical line. In this way, the entire team can communicate and be alerted to ascend at any time during the dive. A good practice is to have each diver run the tether through the palm of one hand so that the line pulls can be detected easily. The safety diver can move the pivot ring up and down the vertical line to any of the knotted stops, as required, and can thus control the maximum depth of all the divers. The safety diver can also terminate the dive or send any diver up if the situation warrants such action. Divers can ascend at will by signaling their intent to the safety diver, unclipping their tethers at the pivot ring, and ascending the vertical line to the boat. It is important that the divers hold the downline when ascending so that they do not drift away from the boat.

If scientific or diving equipment is hung on the downline, it can be attached to the line at the appropriate depth as the line is deployed, which makes it unnecessary for the divers to carry the equipment. Any equipment hung on the downline should be positioned above the trapeze and safety diver, and the weight of the equipment must not be so great that it overweights the downline. Divers working below the trapeze must be careful to avoid entanglement in the weighted tethers, which would envelop the safety diver in a cloud of bubbles and reduce his ability to see. If a second line is deployed for equipment, it must be separated clearly from the safety line and should not be used as an attachment for tethers.

In addition to diving, safety, and scientific equipment, most open-ocean divers carry a shark billy. According to experienced open-ocean divers at the University of California at Santa Cruz:

> *Twenty percent of all open-ocean dives performed by our group in the central north and south Pacific gyre systems and the eastern tropical Pacific were aborted due to the persistent presence of sharks, specifically oceanic white tip sharks. In all cases they were spotted first by the safety diver. This underscores the value of the safety diver and a routine abort plan and the utility of the shark billy (Heine 1985).*

Divers generally work in an area upstream of the trapeze, which allows them to collect fresh, undisturbed samples, and to stay in a single area in sight of the safety diver. As they perform their tasks, the divers scan their surroundings and make visual contact with the safety diver. The safety diver constantly monitors the surroundings, checks for sharks, keeps an eye on the divers and the downline, and generally monitors the progress of the dive. During the course of the dive, the safety diver maintains contact with the divers by periodically tugging on the divers' tethers to ensure they are responding to pull signals appropriately. If a diver requires minor assistance, the safety diver signals another diver to go to his aid. Before the safety diver becomes involved in helping another diver, he must first signal another diver to act as the temporary safety diver. There must always be someone acting as safety diver (Heine 1985).

As with any specialized diving, open-ocean diving requires individualized training and practice. Dive masters should consult a specialized open-ocean diving manual for further details about this type of diving.

12.7 CORAL REEFS AND FRINGING REEFS

As part of dive planning from shore, small boat or large boat, access to a reef system, entry and exit conditions need to be considered. In areas of high tidal range, the changed tidal level between entry and exit time must be taken into account; divers can find themselves with a very long and difficult walk over jagged live coral at low tide.

During the course of the dive, visual contact should be maintained between divers because the use of tethering ropes in the coral environment is not always practical.

The seaward face of a coral atoll is a barrier or fringing reef containing all of the hazards attached to diving around coral elsewhere. In addition, there are several hazards particular to this environment. The primary danger is that of very rough seas suddenly rising up at the reef edge where an eroding margin gives way to a sudden vertical drop. This is because the face of a reef is characteristically steep, plunging away to great depths from the shallow coral reef bank. This steep slope, which is often undercut as a result of local changes in sea level, acts as a wall to the movement of water; and even without much wind, breakers can suddenly form on the reef margin with the impingement of swells that can otherwise be undetected on the open-sea surface. If divers are down on the reef face, they can become involved in the underwater surge associated with the disruption of sea swell at the reef face, in addition to becoming suddenly enmeshed in rough seas upon surfacing at the pick-up boat.

Most injuries around reefs involve cuts and abrasions from the extremely sharp surfaces of the growing coral; edge of shell can be as sharp as a knife. Dead coral is not as sharp or abrasive. Use of protective clothing and gloves is advised, regardless of the water temperature. A secondary hazard is that sharks are commonly found in the deeper water off the reef face. Reef sharks are attracted by the same rough water that is responsible for disturbing the coral at the margin of the reef and attracting an abundance of prey.

Many coral and fringing reefs are given a level of statutory protection by governments. This may take the form of protecting corals or other specific groups of organisms, and general permits are often required for scientific collection or research, imposing certain bag limits or prohibitions of certain collecting methods. An entire area may be contained within a marine park or sanctuary over which a range of rules and regulations applies. As part of dive planning, the nature of any restrictions or permit requirements applicable to this area should be ascertained prior to diving. Visual observation may be the only technique permitted in certain restricted areas.

12.8 FAST CURRENT

Water flow is considered to be extreme for divers when it is moving at a rate faster than a diver can comfortably swim into, commonly about one knot or less. Fast currents can cause some difficulties, but also allow drift diving, where the divers move with the current. Drift diving is particularly useful for surveying restricted sea lochs where tidal floods and ebbs allow divers to almost effortlessly achieve long dive tracks. Drift diving in currents should be tended by a maneuvering boat that monitors a float or series of floats carried along by each dive team. Where divers wish to remain at a particular location, rope techniques are essential. Diving down an anchored line is often necessary; however, heavy exertion may be required to maintain position against the current.

When diving into a current from an anchored boat, platform, or other fixed position, tethered divers face the risk of being swept to the surface due to additional drag on their umbilical or downline. Additional risks include being carried away from the dive site and topside support. Once on the surface, non-tethered divers should drift or swim with the current angling toward the shoreline or pick-up boat, rather than attempting to swim against the current.

Drifting along the surface in rivers is not necessarily dangerous, unless a hazard exists downstream as divers can usually be located quickly. Separation at sea, however, can present more significant problems as divers on the surface are hard to locate from a small boat. Divers working in open sea conditions should carry signaling devices such as flares and or a safety sausage or personal flotation and location device to increase their visibility. This can also be used as a lift bag or life ring for two persons (see Figure 12.10).

Water movement at sea can be complex for divers. The surface current may be quite different than current encountered at depth in both velocity and/or direction. Tracking divers from a boat by following bubbles is usually ineffective in areas of high current/waves; divers should tow or drift with a surface float to indicate their location. Support boats should be equipped with a diver recall device in addition to other safety-related gear.

Each diver should be as hydrodynamic as possible to be least affected by water drag. Masks should be low volume and snorkels should be held in a knife strap or pocket as the current drag on a snorkel affixed to the mask strap can pull a mask off. Short, broad fins are more manageable than long, speed-swimming

FIGURE 12.10
Personal Flotation and Location Device

fins, and adjustable heel strap fins are better than full-foot fins as they can be more easily refitted and secured. Instruments should be low profile and snag resistant as the diver is often swept into weeds and ropes. Diver-tending lines should be used on all dives in fast-moving waters.

12.9 CAVE DIVING

Cave diving is a specialized form of diving that can be performed in both inland freshwater and ocean "blue holes." To scientists, caves offer new laboratories for research. In cave diving, the emphasis should be placed on developing the proper psychological attitude, training in specialized techniques and life-support systems, dive planning, and the selection of an appropriately trained buddy diver.

WARNING
ONLY EXPERIENCED AND SPECIALLY TRAINED DIVERS SHOULD UNDERTAKE CAVE DIVING. OPEN-WATER EXPERIENCE IS NO SUBSTITUTE FOR CAVE-DIVING TRAINING.

The cave-diving environment is alien to humans, because it involves both the underwater environment and the limited access, limited visibility, confined-space environment typical of caves. It is sobering to realize that several hundred fatalities have occurred in underwater caves in the last decade. Examples of the special hazards that may be encountered in cave diving are:

- The absence of a direct and immediate ascent route to the surface
- The sometimes instantaneous loss of visibility because of silting or failure of the diver's light
- The entanglement and impact hazards associated with being in a confined, enclosed space

These and other factors all have an effect on the psychological composure of divers and their ability to cope with stressful situations. Improperly trained divers, unaware of the hazards unique to cave diving, often panic and drown when they encounter situations that are in fact normal for the cave-diving environment. It is imperative that divers develop the proper psychological attitude before they consider conducting a cave dive. Completion of a standard scuba-diving course does not prepare a diver for the special challenges faced in cave diving.

Before taking a course in cave diving, the diving student must have enough open-water experience to feel psychologically comfortable under water. Because their lives may one day depend on the quality of instruction received, anyone contemplating taking such a course should select one taught by an experienced and nationally certified, cave-diving instructor. A good cave-diving course should include pre-screening of potential divers, at least 100 hours of training in underwater work, and

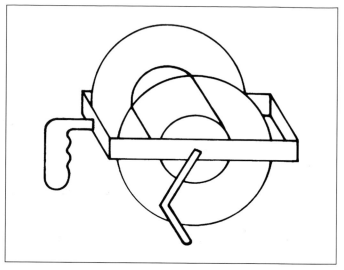

FIGURE 12.11
Typical Safety Reel

instruction in line safety, the elements of buoyancy control, buddymanship, dive planning, equipment handling, and dive theory. Four basic rules for cave-diving safety that must be followed by every diver are:

1. Always use a continuous guideline to the surface.
2. Save two-thirds of the total air supply for returning to the surface.
3. Carry at least three lights during the dive.
4. Carry a redundant scuba regulator and any other equipment the direct malfunction of which could cause a fatality.

A common hazard in cave diving is the presence of silt. To minimize silting, cave divers must be specially trained to swim horizontally and to maintain proper buoyancy at all times.

A safety reel and line are the diver's link to the surface and survival. Several kinds of line are used for safety and navigation. Temporary lines are the most commonly used and consist of a safety reel and line carried by the divers. A suitable safety reel should feature a line guide, drum, buoyancy chamber, a good turn ratio, and be capable of carrying approximately 400 ft. (122.0 m) of 1/16 inch (1.6 mm), 160-pound (59.7-kg) test to 1/8 inch (3.2 mm), 440-pound (164.3-kg) test, braided nylon line. The reel should be neutrally buoyant, compact, and rugged (see Figure 12.11). Large reels and lines create extra drag for the diver and require extra exertion.

When running a safety line, the diver with the reel should maintain tension. A light should be fastened to the line for easy recognition, and safety wraps should be made approximately every 25 ft. (7.6 m). The line should be centered in the cave as much as possible. The reel diver is first in and last out. The buddy is responsible for unwrapping the safety wraps on leaving the cave and for providing light for the diver tying and untying the line. Physical contact with the line should be avoided except when visibility decreases. In some cases, cave divers will use permanent lines for mapping or to permit a more complete exploration of a cave. Novices should use temporary lines and should not attempt to follow permanent lines unless they have a thorough knowledge of the cave. The technique for laying and retrieving a safety line is unique to cave diving and should be practiced until it becomes second nature because it could save one's life in a total silt-out, where there is a complete loss of visibility. It is important to remember that in cave diving the safety line is not to be used to pull one's self along the line, but only as visual and, if necessary, tactile aid during transit.

Standard cave diving life-support systems should include:

- Double cylinders
- Double manifolds with captured O-rings
- Two regulators
- Submersible pressure gauge
- Buoyancy compensator with power inflator hose
- Depth gauge
- Watch
- Decompression tables
- Wet or dry suit
- Safety reel with line
- Lights
- Compass
- Slate
- Pencil

The larger-capacity double-cylinder arrangement recommended for cave diving has an "ideal" or double-orifice manifold. This system manifolds two cylinders together with a common gas supply and uses two regulator adapters. If one regulator fails, that regulator may be secured while the second regulator continues to function without interruption and with access to both gas cylinders. One of the regulators also should have a 5-ft. (1.5-m) hose so that divers may share their gas supply when maneuvering out of tight situations.

Although the need for lighting in cave diving is obvious, the lighting taken on cave dives is often not adequate for safety. Each diver must carry at least three lights, with the brightest being at least 30 watts. Backup lights can be of lower wattage, but they must also be dependable and of high quality. All cave-diving equipment must be checked and rechecked by each member of the dive team before submersion to ensure proper functioning, ease of operation, and diver familiarity. During this time, the smooth operation of backup equipment should also be verified and the dive plan should be reviewed.

The maximum recommended number of cave divers per team is three. Larger groups may not be able to handle the integrated "buddymanship" necessary to maintain the

constant contact so essential in cave diving. For further information about cave diving, readers should write to the National Association of Cave Diving, Box 14492, Gainesville, Florida 32604, or the National Speleological Society's Cave Diving Section, 3508 Hollow Oak Place, Brandon, Florida 33511.
Websites: NACD (http://www.safecavediving.com)
NSS (http://www.caves.org)

12.10 COLD-WATER DIVING

Diving in cold water presents several equipment problems not found in warmer waters—the major difficulty involving the regulator. Many single-hose scuba regulators have a tendency to freeze in the free-flow position after approximately 20–30 minutes of extreme cold-water exposure. However, several models designed to resist freezing are available. The older double-hose regulators rarely developed this freezing problem.

NOTE
An early sign that freeze-up is about to occur is the presence of ice crystals on the tongue. Should this occur, the dive should be aborted immediately.

Second-stage freeze-up is generally caused by moisture in the exhaled breath, which then condenses and freezes on cold metal parts prior to entering the water.

First-stage demand regulators are also susceptible to freeze-up for the same reasons when used at temperatures below 39°F (4C). Freeze-up depends on the ambient temperature, rate of gas flow, relative pressure drop, the diameter and shape of the various passageways inside the demand valve, and the moisture in the breathing gas.

Another cold-water diving problem is that the diver's mask is more likely to fog in cold water. A non-irritating defogging agent applied to the mask before diving, or partially flooding the mask and flushing the faceplate will relieve this condition temporarily.

In practice, freeze-up problems normally start before entering the water when divers test their demand valves in a sub-zero environment. Ice crystals may form instantly inside the first stage valve and act as sites for further ice formation during the dive. Moisture in the diver's exhaled breath may produce instant second stage freeze-up. Water is either above or at the point of freezing and, if breathing from the regulator is postponed until under water, the high heat conductance of water will normally keep the demand valve above freezing.

NOTE
When diving in freezing or near freezing temperatures, it is highly recommended to submerge before breathing from or purging the demand valve.

Since rate of gas flow is crucial to determining whether the demand valve will freeze, a slow, normal breathing pattern should be adopted. Rapid inflation of dry suits and/or buoyancy compensators, in addition to free-flowing of regulators, must be avoided since they are likely to contribute to freeze-up. When freezing is likely, cylinders should be filled with breathing gas that is as dry as possible. Special dehydrating agents in the final filter cartridge can be employed.

If the first stage of the regulator has a chamber that communicates directly with the water, an anti-freezing cap can be used. This protective cap may be filled with an antifreeze solution to prevent freeze-up of the internal components. Many newer regulators utilize silicon-filled chambers on the first stage to prevent freeze-up. However, such preventative measures do not protect against freezing inside the second stage of the regulator.

A full-face mask has the inherent problem that a diver will necessarily commence breathing before entering the water, and, thereby, run the risk of initiating a freeze-up problem. It is good practice to avoid prolonged periods of breathing from the mask on land; it should be the last piece of equipment donned before the diver enters the water.

Many plastic and rubber components, especially seals and O-rings, become brittle at low temperatures. They may crack, shatter, or break easily, and are most susceptible when chilled or frozen. Equipment should be assembled, and seals seated, in a warm environment, prior to exposure to cold air or the dive. Following each dive, all equipment must be inspected carefully to ensure proper function.

Keeping the diver's body warm is the most important requirement in cold-water diving (see Figure 12.12). Although the standard foamed-neoprene wet suit has been used in 29°F (-2C) water for dives lasting longer than an hour, it is doubtful whether divers on these dives are comfortable or thermally safe. A major drawback of wet suits is that, when the dive is over, the diver is wet and will continue to lose body heat even after leaving the water. The loss of material thickness with depth drastically reduces the efficiency of any foam neoprene suit when diving much below 60 ft. (18.3 m).

Two types of diving dress have been used successfully under severe thermal conditions: the hot-water wet suit, which provides a continuous supply of preheated water to the diver, and the dry suit, which utilizes diver-controlled air and dry undergarments to provide insulating capability. Except for the hot-water wet suit, no dry or wet suit provides complete protection of the diver's hands for long periods. As the extremities become cold and dexterity is lost, the diver becomes less efficient, and the dive should be terminated. Hands should be protected with gloves or mittens with the fewest possible digits; the loss of manual dexterity associated with the use of gloves or mittens is overridden by the added warmth they provide. Rewarming chilled hands or filling the gloves or mittens with warm water just before the dive provides temporary comfort and warmth.

The use of heavy, insulating socks under the boots of a wet or dry suit will help keep the feet warm. Heat loss from the head can be reduced by wearing a second, well-fitted neoprene hood over the regular suit hood. With a properly fitted suit and all seals in place, a diver can usually be kept warm and dry, for short periods.

If divers and members of the surface-support crew follow certain procedures, the adverse effects of cold-water exposure can be greatly reduced. Suits should be maintained in the best possible condition, dry-suit underwear should be kept clean and dry, and all seals and zippers should be inspected and repaired (if necessary) before the dive. Protection from the elements should also be provided to prevent chilling and loss of body core temperature prior to entering the water. During the dive, divers should exercise as much as possible to generate body heat.

Dives should be terminated immediately if the diver begins to shiver involuntarily or experiences a serious loss of manual dexterity. Once involuntary shivering begins, the loss of dexterity, strength, and ability to function accelerates. After leaving the water, cold-water divers are often fatigued, and, because heat loss from the body continues even after removal from cold water, they are susceptible to hypothermia. Facilities must be provided that allow the diver to remove any wet clothes or suits, dry themselves, and don warm clothing, as soon as possible, to regain lost body heat. During cold water operations that require repetitive dives, the diver must be completely re-warmed between dives. Supervisors should be aware that an apparent feeling of warmth can be deceptive and should adjust dive schedules accordingly.

Adequate rest and nutrition are essential to providing cold-water divers with the energy necessary for this type of diving. A diver should have a minimum of 6–8 hours of sleep before a dive. Care must be taken to avoid dehydration, which can interfere with the body's thermal regulatory mechanism. Careful planning is of the utmost importance in all cold-water diving.

WARNING

IF A DIVER IS EXTREMELY COLD, ADJUST THE DECOMPRESSION SCHEDULE TO THE NEXT LONGER TIME.

12.11 DIVING UNDER ICE

In addition to the problems and limitations of diving in cold water, there are specific precautions that must be taken when diving under ice. Diving under ice is extremely hazardous and should be done only by experienced divers who have been specially trained.

Most ice diving is done from large and relatively flat surface-ice sheets that are stationary and firmly frozen to the shore. Even at locations many miles from the nearest land, these ice caps often offer a stable working platform. However, diving from drifting or broken ice is dangerous and should only be done as a last resort. When the ice cap is solid, there is no wave action to the water; however,

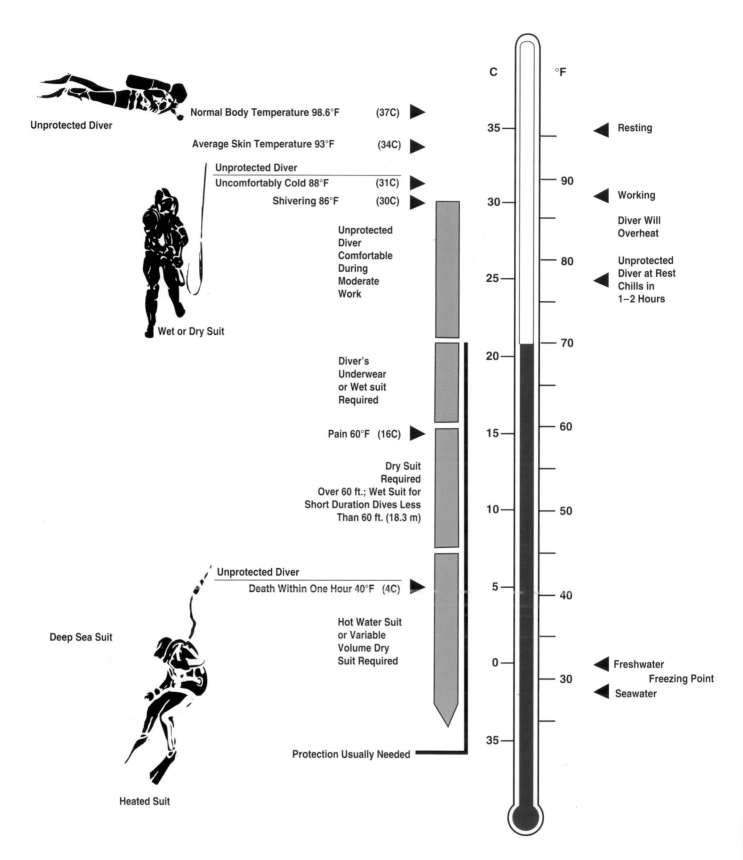

FIGURE 12.12
Water Temperature Protection Chart

FIGURE 12.13
Diver Tender and Standby Diver in Surface Shelter

line should be tied to the diver (not to the equipment) and the other end should be tied firmly to a large stationary object on the surface. Excursions under ice should be well planned, and the distance traveled under the ice away from the entry hole should be kept to a minimum; under normal circumstances, this distance should be limited to 90 ft. (27.4 m). Longer under-ice excursions make it difficult for the diver to get back to the entry hole in an emergency and increase the difficulty of searching for a lost diver. If divers must travel long distances under the ice, additional holes should be cut for emergency purposes.

Large marine mammals are very possessive about the breathing holes they use in the ice. Confrontation in such circumstances must be avoided at all costs, and marine mammals should generally be avoided, unless experiments or observations of them are being carried out under controlled conditions.

WARNING
DIVERS LOST UNDER THE ICE SHOULD ASCEND TO THE OVERHEAD ICE COVER IMMEDIATELY, MAINTAIN POSITIVE BUOYANCY, RELAX AS MUCH AS POSSIBLE TO CONSERVE AIR, AND WAIT FOR ASSISTANCE. DO NOT CONTINUE TO SEARCH FOR THE ENTRY HOLE.

To aid the diver to return to the entry hole, a bright light should be hung just beneath the surface. For night diving under ice, this light is a necessity; it is usually the only item required beyond those used in day-time operations. However, since cold water shortens the life of batteries, homing beacons and strobes should be checked before use. Because direct ascent to the surface is impossible when under the ice, a rapid means of determining direction often is critical. In shallow water, detours are often necessary to circumvent the "keels" (thickened areas) built up beneath the ice. Also, because of the absence of waves, there are no ripple patterns on the bottom to aid in orientation. For these reasons, the use of a tether is absolutely mandatory for under-ice diving.

If there is a failure in an ice diver's primary breathing system, the diver should switch to the backup system, notifying the buddy diver, and proceed immediately to the surface with the buddy diver. Because buddy breathing is difficult in cold water, all divers should practice buddy breathing before making excursions under the ice. Octopus regulators should not be used in cold water as substitutes for buddy breathing because the first stage of these regulators may freeze up. Special cylinder, valve, and regulator options are readily available and provide alternate buddy breathing options. Refer to Section 12.10 for additional tips on limited-access diving techniques.

If a diver's exposure suit tears or floods, the diver should surface immediately, regardless of the degree of flooding, because the chilling effects of frigid water can

divers must constantly be on guard because the current beneath the entry hole can change quickly and dramatically without producing any noticeable effect on the surface. In most cases, the absence of wave action produces good underwater visibility, although under ice-diving operations, conducted in areas characterized by river runoff or heavy plankton, may be associated with conditions of reduced visibility.

To enter the water through ice, divers should first drill a small hole through the ice at the site to determine ice thickness and water depth. If conditions are satisfactory, the area around the site should be cleared of snow and the size of the entry hole determined. A hole three by five ft. (0.9 by 1.5 m) allows three fully dressed divers to be accommodated at one time. If no shelter is used, a triangle-shaped hole works best.

In all diving operations under ice, there should be one surface tender for each diver and at least one standby diver (see Figure 12.13). While the diver is in the water, the tender must be attentive both to the diver and to the surface conditions, such as deteriorating weather, or moving ice. Tenders should be briefed on the diver's tasks, so that they will understand the diver's movements and be able to respond quickly in an emergency. A safety cause thermal shock within minutes. Surface-supplied diving is becoming more popular in under-ice operations because it eliminates the need for safety lines, navigation lights, and provides unlimited air. The full-face masks or helmets of most surface-supplied diving systems provide additional protection for the diver's face and also provide the capability for diver-to-diver and diver-to-surface communication. These added features must be weighed carefully against the burden of added logistical support required to support surface-supplied diving. Using dry suits and new thermal underwear now available, the surface-supplied diver can spend long periods under the ice in relative safety and comfort.

If an ice dive operation is scheduled to last for more than one to two days, a tent or shed should be constructed over the entry hole (see Figure 12.13). Such a shelter will protect both surface-support personnel and divers from the wind and, together with a small portable heater, can provide relative comfort in the severest of diving conditions.

12.12 KELP DIVING

Kelp is found in dense beds along many of the colder and temperate coasts of the world. In the United States, these plants are found along the shore regions of the west coast. Kelp beds or forests are widely diversified, both geographically and as a function of depth and temperature. Different varieties grow in different zones and support an incredible variety of sea life. Kelp will attach itself to practically any substrate (i.e., rock, concrete, steel, wreckage, etc.) and will often form a tree-like structure, the base of which is a rootlike holdfast that provides a secure anchor and a home for many organisms. Hollow floats or pneumatocysts are found at the base of the blades and fronds on many of the larger, longer kelp plants. These floats cause the fronds to float up and keep the stipes relatively upright. The floating fronds form a canopy when they have grown sufficiently to reach the surface. In many instances, this rapidly growing canopy becomes very dense and can be several feet thick on and near the surface. The canopy will usually have thin spots or openings located randomly throughout the area, and these thin spots or openings provide entry and exit points for divers. These thinner areas are easily seen from below the surface because the light penetration is greater; in addition, as a diver positioned under such a light area exhales, the rising bubbles usually float the kelp outward to form an opening that is sufficiently large to enable the diver to surface. Care should be exercised when the diver's head is out of the water, because the kelp may float back and fill the hole surrounding the diver. Although the kelp will not actually wrap itself around the diver, divers who twist around and struggle may become entangled.

Equipment that is not relatively streamlined can snag and tangle in the kelp and cause problems. If the diver becomes entangled, it is important to remember that kelp is designed to withstand the pulling forces of wind, wave, and currents and, consequently, the tensile or stretching strength of the plant is very great. Divers wishing to break a strand of kelp should fold it to develop a sharp angle in the stipe. Nicking the kelp with a sharp object will separate the kelp easily; however, caution must be exercised when using sharp objects such as knives to avoid inadvertently cutting other critical equipment items. The easiest way to get free is to remain calm and to pull the strands away carefully with a minimum of movement.

When working from a boat, it is best to anchor in an opening so that the wind or current will drift the boat back on the anchor line to a second opening in the kelp. Divers may also anchor outside the kelp and swim in to do their work. If the boat is anchored in the kelp, the anchor will be full of kelp that must later be removed.

Training in kelp diving is necessary to master entry and exit skills. Entry through the kelp is best accomplished by finding a thin area and making a feet-first, feet-together entry, rather than a headfirst, or backroll entry that could easily lead to entanglement. It is important to get through the canopy and into the open water between the stipes. Once through the surface canopy, the diver can swim with comfort in the forest-like environment. As the diver swims along, it is important to watch for the light areas that signal the thinner areas of the kelp bed. Surfacing slowly permits a diver's exhaust bubbles to assist in making an opening. When the diver approaches the surface, the arms should be raised over head so that any kelp that may be encountered may be moved to the side easily as the diver moves upward into the hole that has been opened. Once on the surface, the diver should stay in the vertical position and should not turn around; this helps avoid entanglement.

The diver who wishes to travel on the surface of a kelp bed to get back to the shore or to the boat has several choices. If the diver is sufficiently skilled, it is easy to use a series of breath-hold dives to move in steps to the desired location. Each step requires the diver to surface through an opening in the kelp and to take a breath or two in preparation for the next step. Another useful technique, often called the Kelp Crawl, resembles the "Dog Paddle" and involves keeping the body on the surface above the kelp canopy. This technique involves reaching across the kelp in an extended position and grasping the kelp. Using a narrow flutter kick, the diver presses himself down as his body is pulled over the kelp canopy. It is important to present a streamlined surface to the kelp, since anything that extends out from the body will probably snag. Swim fins with adjustable heel straps should have the loose end of the strap inside rather than outside of the buckle. Taping the loose end of a strap to the main portion of the strap is also a good solution. Wearing a diving knife on the inside of the calf rather than anywhere on the outside of the body is also a snag reducer. Kelp divers should remember that they want to move through or over the kelp in a stream-lined fashion and that inflated buoyancy compensators, game bags, and tools of all kinds should be organized to present minimal interference.

Divers should also remember that because kelp floats, it may be used as flotation if needed. In windy conditions, divers should approach a small boat from downwind to avoid being pressed against the boat by the kelp and becoming entangled.

Various forms of kelp may grow together so that the taller kelp, such as *Macrocystis,* may be found growing over a forest of *Pelagophycus* (elk kelp). This second, lower canopy of kelp will further reduce the light level, but will be easier to swim through than the surface canopy. All kelp beds are influenced by wind, currents, and surge, and major beds may disappear from surface view in a swift current because they are held down at an angle. This has its advantages because the kelp will stream with the current and thus may be used as a navigational aid during the dive. Achieving comfort and efficiency in kelp diving is the result of training and practice. Having a buddy diver along who is equally well trained is also extremely important.

12.13 WRECK DIVING

Wreck diving subjects the diver to many of the same hazards as those found in cave or ice diving (see Sections 12.9, 12.11). In the past 20 years, wreck diving has evolved into an activity requiring both specialized equipment and training, particularly in the case of deep-wreck diving. Regardless of purpose (harvesting, artifact collecting, photography, or exploring), wreck diving may involve the diver entering the wreck. The act of penetrating the enclosed space of the wreck necessitates additional equipment and training.

Most intact wrecks are at depths in excess of 80 ft. (24.4 m), because those in shallower water have been destroyed either by storms or removed by humans because they were navigational hazards.

After arriving on the bottom at the wreck site, the first team of divers must check the anchor of the support boat for security and then ensure that the anchor line will not chafe. The path into a wreck usually has fair to good visibility. On the return trip, however, visibility may be reduced dramatically because the divers have stirred up silt and ferrous oxide (rust) from the walls and exposed steel plates. The reduced visibility and the confusion and anxiety caused by the many passageways, entrances, chambers, bulkheads, and tight spaces require that wreck divers use a penetration line such as a braided, 1/8 inch (3.2 mm) nylon line on a reel. The line should be tied off at the wreck's entrance, payed out during entry, and reeled in during return. If the line is lost or cut, the diver should pause, allow the silt to settle, and regain his composure before attempting to return to the surface. Placing the faceplate of the underwater light into the silt will reduce the ambient light level and allow the diver's eyes to adapt

partially to the darkness. This will facilitate the detection of any surface light coming into the passageways and thus aid in the identification of possible exit paths.

Because of depth, twin scuba cylinders, together with a pony bottle with a separate regulator, are recommended as standard wreck-diving equipment. In some instances, a spare air supply and regulator should be placed outside the wreck. These precautions are necessary in case the diver becomes entangled, or if unplanned decompression is needed. During wreck diving, entanglement may be caused by objects such as monofilament fishing line, fish nets, collapsed bulkheads, overheads, or narrow spaces. The amount of equipment carried by the diver should be kept to a minimum. As in other confined space environments, gauges, lights, and other support items must be secured to prevent snagging on obstacles, but readily available when needed. Although a diver inside a wreck may be tempted to breathe in the air pockets produced by previous divers, this practice should be avoided because the partial pressure of oxygen in these pockets is usually quite low, and hydrogen sulfide may be present.

Diving dress should be appropriate for the ambient temperature. In temperate conditions, dive skins or coveralls are recommended as protection from scratches, scrapes and/or stinging organisms. Extreme caution must be taken not to snag the suit or equipment on the sharp objects commonly found in wrecks, such as decayed wooden decks or corroded metal bulkheads; these are frequently overgrown by algae, coral, barnacles, or other marine growth, and may not be readily visible. Divers must not remove or disturb historical artifacts unless authorized.

12.14 NIGHT DIVING

Night diving exposes the diver to an entirely different aspect of the underwater world. Marine life may be more or less abundant and appear to be different colors than is the case during the day. Areas that are familiar to the diver during the day may appear changed to the extent that orientation and locating familiar landmarks may be difficult even with good artificial light. Accordingly, special precautions and extra planning are required for night dives.

Anchoring is especially critical at night. The boat must be secure before the diver enters the water (except when liveboating, in which case other steps are appropriate). It is also important at night to have correct marking lights that are clearly visible to other vessels, in addition to a light the divers can see under water. A chemical light (cylume) or small strobe light attached to the anchor line or downline is recommended.

The boat should not be left unattended with personnel in the water. An operator should be onboard and able to respond to an emergency immediately. Predive checks are particularly important at night, because the limited visibility precludes even a cursory inspection of equipment once in the water. Night diving in fog or heavy rain should be avoided because it is easy for the diver to lose sight of the lights on the dive boat or those carried by other divers.

Each diver should carry a reliable diving light with a charge sufficient to last longer than the time anticipated for the dive. A second light is advisable, because light failure is common. The light should be secured to the diver in a manner that permits the illumination of watches, gauges, or navigational aids. A chemical light should be taped to the snorkel or cylinder valve for underwater and surface visibility, in case the dive lights fail. The entire night-dive team should be careful to maintain dark adaptation before and during the dive. Every effort should be made to avoid shining diving lights directly into the eyes of fellow divers or crew members, both before and during the dive. Once in the water, it is easy to keep track of a buddy's light at night; however, one diver may occasionally lose another because the glare of the light being held prevents seeing the buddy's light. In this case, the divers should turn off or otherwise shield their lights momentarily, adjust their eyes, locate the buddy's light, and then immediately turn their lights back on.

If a team is left with only one light, the dive should be terminated. Lights may also be used to signal the surface; sweeping the light in a wide arc over the head is the standard "pick me up" signal. At night, a whistle or chemical flare should also be carried in case of light failure.

Shore entries are more hazardous at night because such features as rocks, algae, holes, waves, and rip currents are not easily seen. Entries from boats, piers, and other surface platforms require special caution so that the diver avoids hitting objects on or below the surface.

If a shore exit requires a particular approach because of in-water obstacles, two shore lights in a line can serve as a navigational aid for divers. When possible, experienced night divers should be buddied with novice night divers. Making the entry at dusk rather than at night reduces some of the problems of night diving. Whenever possible, the area to be dived by night should first be dived by day to provide the divers with entry and exit experience.

Predive

Lights: Adequate light should be available for the surface team to safely achieve their objectives. Lights carried by the divers and lights used to mark entry and exit points, provide position and range, and mark the surface cover boat. When using flashlights, avoid shining them around as it upsets night vision. Be sure that lights used in the course of the dive are not confused with navigational markers.

Markers: Jack stays, marker panels, and guides should be rigged to aid the diver in complex situations. For less complicated operations, a simple shot-line or mainline leading directly to the site will often suffice.

Briefing: The diving team should be briefed thoroughly on the task, including routes to and from the site, leaving and entering diving platforms, and safety procedures. Briefing is more important than on day dives as the dive-team members must be able to anticipate the actions of other divers without being able to observe them.

Dive

Safety: The decision whether to use a lifeline to the surface will depend on the circumstances. A lifeline can be very effective for scientific diving at night. It gives the diver a psychological boost and, more importantly, it gives him a line of communication with topside. In the event of difficulties, it gives support personnel a direct route to the diver.

Light: Many divers are surprised, the first time they dive at night, at the amount of light under water. The moon and stars are the main source of this light and, once the diver has obtained night vision, visibility can be quite good without artificial light. Despite the possibility of good underwater vision, each diver must still carry at least one underwater light. Good quality, lightweight underwater lights are readily available. Excellent emergency lights are the chemical "Cyalume®" or "cool lite" light stick, as well as battery-powered lights. These work equally well under water and topside, and are unaffected by pressure at least to 165 ft. (50.3 m) depth.

Postdive

Safety: Locating and recovering divers at night is not always easy. Extra care should be taken, especially if decompression is involved. Thought should be given to rehearsing diver-recovery procedures during the day.

Clothing: Adequate windproof protection should be available for divers leaving the water to keep the chill away and to allow them to continue participating in the scientific aspects of the project.

NOTE

Decompression diving is more hazardous at night than during the day and should be avoided. To be conducted safely, night decompression dives need considerable advance planning.

In night decompression diving, lights marking the decompression line are necessary to ensure that the divers conduct their in-water decompression near the dive boat or other platform. Divers operating in a decompression mode should not swim out of sight of lines or lights that will guide them back to the decompression line and dive platform.

12.15 DIVING IN DAMS AND RESERVOIRS

Hydroelectric dams across rivers in the northwest United States incorporate bypass and collection systems for the protection of migrating fish species such as salmon and steelhead trout (see Figure 12.14). Because fish-passage research is conducted at many of these dams, NOAA and other scientist/divers are often required to inspect, maintain, install, or retrieve research gear such as flow meters, and fish-guidance and passage devices. If time and circumstances permit,

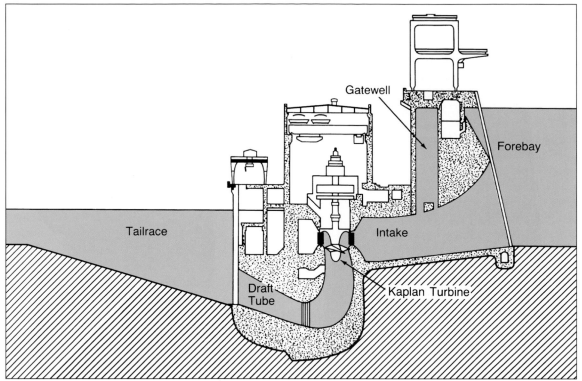

FIGURE 12.14
Cross Section of a Typical Hydroelectric Dam

a shutdown and de-watering of turbine intakes, gatewells, and fish ladders is the safest and most efficient manner for performing work on dam bypass and collection facilities. However, safe and efficient diving operations can be performed within and on the upstream and downstream faces of dams, even when these are still operating. The agency operating the dam typically supplies a diving inspector to coordinate such dives, because strict coordination between divers and the powerhouse operations staff is mandatory to ensure proper clearances for turbine shutdown and flow-gate closures.

12.15.1 Diving at Dams

The safety aspects of diving at dams are comparable to those involved in cave, wreck, and over-bottom diving, and many of the same procedures are used in dam diving. Predive planning by the dive team with dam personnel will help ensure a safe diving operation. If such operations are undertaken at altitudes in excess of 300 feet for dives deeper than 145 fsw (actual depth) or 1,000 feet for all dives, special altitude diving procedures must be instituted.

Four major conditions must be considered when planning dives at dams are:

1. Depth
2. Water temperature
3. Visibility
4. Flow velocities

Depth is always a primary factor in diving and clearly must be considered when diving in and around dams. Depending on where the dives are to be performed at dams, depths can vary greatly and can be quite deep.

Water temperatures may vary from slightly above freezing in winter to almost 80°F (27C) in summer. Divers should be protected from the elements before diving and during surface intervals in both warm and cold seasons, because of the potential for heat exhaustion or hypothermia. Most research diving at dams occurs during the spring overflow when rivers swell from rains and melting snow and fish migrations occur. The spring runoff produces low underwater visibility, i.e., 0–2 ft. (0–0.6 m), from silt carried by flooding waters. In warmer months, algae blooms may also cause low underwater visibility. Even in clear water, the sediment disturbed by divers reduces visibility so that the small amount of natural light penetrating the gatewells is reduced. Although diving lights are only minimally effective, the problems associated with low visibility at dams can be overcome by careful planning, studies of the blueprints and plans of the dam, and familiarization with the research devices to be used during the dive. Objects can be recognized by touch and orientation can be maintained, even in zero underwater visibility, if the diver is familiar both with the gear and with the dam's structures. The velocity of the flow and the force of the suction through screens or orifices at dams can be eliminated or controlled by coordinating the diver's actions carefully with dam-operations personnel before the dive.

When bypass systems become fouled or clogged by river debris, divers sometimes are required to enter dam gatewells to clear the system's orifices. The hazards of gatewell diving can be reduced by taking adequate precautions to ensure that the influence of suction, caused by the large hydrostatic head, is avoided at the orifice. Diving procedures are much the same as those for umbilical diving, whether the diver is using surface-supplied air or scuba cylinders. At a minimum, a tender line to the diver should be used for contact and signals, although hardwire communication is preferred. A diver cage should be provided to transport the diver to and from the orifice level and the intake deck of the dam, and a safety diver is required. Figure 12.15 shows a diver ready to be lowered into a dam gatewell. Procedures to shut down the bypass system immediately, in the event of an emergency, should be coordinated with the dam-operations controller, before the dive.

Work on fish ladders (see Figure 12.16) should be performed during off-season when the number of upstream adult fish runs is low and the water flows can be cut off for a period of time, which permits the task to be completed in the open air. On rare occasions, this is impractical and diving is the only way to complete the task. Flows in fish ladders appear quite turbulent when viewed from above; however, baffles or weir walls are regularly spaced perpendicular to the flow, and the water flows either over the top of each weir or through large rectangular orifices located at the base of the baffle wall. When diving in pools between baffle walls, flows as high as 8 feet per second (fps) (2.4 mps) may be encountered in areas directly in line with the orifices, but may be as low as 1 fps (0.3 mps) to either side or above the line of the orifice. By using safety lines and exercising caution, diving tasks may be performed in much the same manner as they are conducted when diving amid pools and boulders in rivers with relatively fast currents.

<u>**WARNING**</u>
WHEN DIVING TASKS MUST BE PERFORMED ON THE UPSTREAM FACE OF A DAM, TURBINES AND/OR SPILLWAY GATES MUST BE SHUT DOWN.

Adjacent units should also be shut down for safety and to reduce flows near a work station. Divers can be transported to and from the level of work and to the intake deck of the dam by means of a diver cage and crane. A boat or floating platform is also useful for the standby diver and equipment. Diving on the downstream face of a dam is handled similarly; flows are shut off to avoid sweeping the diver downstream.

Divers should avoid water contaminants, such as spilled petroleum or lubrication products used in the

FIGURE 12.15
Line-Tended Diver Lowered into Dam Gatewell

FIGURE 12.16
Fish Ladder

routine operation and maintenance of dams, or gaseous by-products generated by underwater cutting and welding. These contaminants can become concentrated in confined areas such as gatewells, where the water level may be 15–20 ft. (4.6–6.1 m) below the deck of the dam. Before starting or continuing a dive, any contaminant discovered should be eliminated from the dive site.

12.15.2 Diving at Water Withdrawal and Pumping Sites

The impact of water withdrawal on populations of juvenile fish in the Columbia Basin of the northwest United States is a major concern to fisheries agencies. Water is withdrawn from the Columbia and Snake rivers via pumps and siphons, and is then used for irrigation, industrial applications, drinking water, thermal cooling, fish and wildlife propagation, and other domestic needs. Before water can be withdrawn from these rivers, the U.S. Army Corps of Engineers requires that those seeking permits to install and operate water withdrawals must install fish-protective facilities. Periodically, divers are required to inspect fish screens at water-withdrawal sites to monitor the condition of the screening and the status of compliance with established screening criteria.

Several basic types of water-withdrawal sites are common:

- A vault-like structure with a screened underwater opening; some vault-like structures may have trash-rack bars in front of the fish screening
- A pier-like structure set out from the shoreline that supports turbine pumps
- A combination pier/vault created by closing in the area under a pier with driven sheet piling or other material
- A simple arrangement of a pump or siphon with a single intake line extending below the low-water elevation

A stable work boat serves as the best diving platform for accessing most withdrawal sites. Some sites with enclosed fish screens must be accessed by ladder or small crane. For such a diving task, weight belts, masks, and fins are lowered by lines to the divers once they are in the water; this procedure is reversed after the dive.

Diving in and around pump intakes can be performed safely if certain hazards are recognized and the necessary precautions are taken. In general, intake velocities are not high enough to present a suction hazard, although pumps should be shut down, if possible. To perform an inspection during the pumping season, however, the approach velocities may have to be measured while the pumps are operating. Surface-supplied equipment should only be used when diving on sites with operating pumps, when the tender or another diver can tend the umbilical or line to keep them away from the pump. Loose lines, hoses, straps, cylinder pressure gauges, and other gear should not be used or should be well secured to avoid being sucked into unscreened pumps or wound around impeller shafts. Because of the need for mobility in and around a pump site, a buddy team with scuba gear is the preferred method of diving at pump intakes. Low underwater visibility, ranging from 0–6 ft. (0–1.8 m), is found in the lower Columbia and Snake rivers, and this distance increases to 15 ft. (4.6 m) in the upper Columbia River. If large pumps are operating and the visibility is exceptionally low, the dive should be aborted.

Divers should enter the water carefully feet first, because pump sites are notorious for the presence of debris, rocks, snags, and pieces of sharp metal, all of which present a hazard to divers, their suits, and any loose equipment. In addition, because there is less scuba diving activity in inland waters than in oceans, inland boaters tend to be less familiar with "diver down" signal flags and their meaning. Pump-site divers should descend and ascend close to the pump-site structure or the shoreline. Surface personnel should watch for boating traffic and hail it with a loudspeaker to inform boaters that divers are operating under water.

12.16 RIVER DIVING

Rivers throughout the world vary in size, turbidity, and in the terrain through which they flow; diving conditions vary with the river. Any river should be studied thoroughly and conditions known before the dive is planned. Current velocities vary across a river. Near the inner bank of a meander the water can be almost slack, whereas on the outer bank, water flow can be very rapid. Lateral turbid water shear zones occur. Log jams may be a hazard, as are submerged objects such as sharp rocks, trees, limbs, old cars, barbed wire, and the ever-present monofilament fishing lines, nets, and lures. Rapids or steep profiles are hazardous because a diver may be slammed against a rock or other submerged object and sustain serious injury or be held by the current.

River diving has a number of special aspects for which the diver should be prepared. For example, divers who grab the bottom to stop and look at an object should hold their face masks to prevent them from being torn off by the current. Divers should be aware that more weights are required when diving in currents than in quiescent water, and they should plan their dives accordingly. Where there is considerable surface current, diving in large holes may be done by dropping directly to the bottom. At some distance below the surface, the diver may be surprised to find either no current or one flowing slightly toward the head of the hole. Divers should also remember when working with lines, tethers, or umbilicals in any type of current that the drag on these lines greatly hampers a diver's ability to travel and may carry the diver to the surface. They also create an entanglement hazard.

In a swift river current, entering the water can be difficult. One technique is to attach a line about 20 ft. (6.1 m) long to the anchor with a handle (similar to those used by water skiers) on the other end. The divers can grasp the handle and descend by making appropriate changes in body position, which lets the current do most of the work. Descent can also be made by using the anchor line, but this requires considerably more effort. Divers always need something to hold onto because of the difficulty of moving across the bottom in fast currents. One helpful device is shown in Figure 12.17 (Gale 1977). This device, referred to as a creeper, is used by lifting and moving the corners forward at alternate turns, as shown; it can also serve as a diver's anchor. Large rocks or sharp drop-offs along river bottoms may create enough turbulence downstream to disorient a diver. In such a situation, the diver should move hand-over-hand along the bottom, or use a creeper, because the current is less on the bottom. This technique can be used even on sand or gravel bottoms.

Another difficulty sometimes encountered in fast-flowing streams or rivers is the blocking of light by bubbles. In or under white water, it may be almost dark. Rivers carrying large amounts of sediment, either normally or as a result of recent rains, are also extremely dark. Using underwater lights is not much help in turbid waters because the light is reflected or blocked by the particles suspended in the water. When working in rivers where the waters are reasonably clear, but the bottom is easily stirred up, divers should work upstream against the flow. Any sediment that is disturbed will flow downstream, away from the direction of travel, which allows the diver to work in much greater visibility.

River diving near low-headed dams presents additional hazards because the hydraulic action created by such dams creates currents with the potential to pull boats and swimmers back toward the dam from downstream. River divers who are required to work without lines in waters near low-head dams, waterfalls, or rapids with significant dropoffs should work on the bottom and stay as clear of the affected area as possible.

12.17 DIVING FROM A SHIP

As in all diving operations, diving from a large ship requires comprehensive planning before the dive or series of dives. Because operating a ship represents a significant investment, all logistical factors involving personnel, equipment, weather, etc., should be thoroughly considered in dive planning.

NOTE

When diving from NOAA ships and the ship is being used as a surface-support diving platform, the ship's captain has the final decision in any matter pertaining to the vessel; however, the divemaster has the final decision in matters concerning diving.

12.17.1 Personnel

It is imperative that close communication between the divemaster, the captain, and the science coordinator be

A. Closeup View of a Creeper

B. Creeper in Use

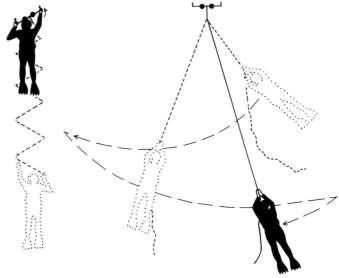

FIGURE 12.17
Creeper

initiated and maintained so that the intent of the diving operations is well understood and can be carried out as safely as possible.

It is highly desirable for the captain to have prior knowledge of diving techniques and procedures, although this may not always be the case. When diving from a ship, the following personnel requirements should be considered before beginning a cruise.

Divemaster: Divemasters are responsible for all aspects of the diving operation. They schedule all dives, designate divers, and dive teams. They discuss the operational necessities with the captain and, as required, work as a diver under the supervision of a temporary dive master.

Science Coordinator: In conjunction with the divemaster and the captain, the science coordinator formulates and ensures that the scientific goals of the diving mission are achieved. On a regular basis throughout the cruise, these goals are re-evaluated and, when necessary, revised.

12.17.2 Use and Storage of Diving and Related Equipment

A suitable diving locker should be designated and used for storing diving equipment. The designated area should be clean, well ventilated, adequate in size, and equipped so that diving equipment can be hung up to dry. The diving locker should be kept locked when not in use, and the key should be kept with the divemaster.

During predive planning, the stock of backup diving gear should be assessed. Equipment easily lost, such as knives, weight belts, etc., should be stocked in excess so divers can be re-equipped quickly. Spare replacements for critical life-support items such as regulators should be available on board.

Air compressors play an important role in a shipboard diving operation. The compressor should be positioned with intake toward the bow of the ship, which will swing into the wind while at anchor, away from engine exhausts of main, auxiliary, and/or any other engines. In addition, compressor intakes must be free of fume contamination from paint lockers, gasoline, solvents, and preservatives being used by scientists.

Cool running of the compressor requires good ventilation; in hot climates, the compressor should be run at night. Oil-lubricated compressors should have some type of oil/water separator built into the system. It is also desirable to have a filtration system column that eliminates CO, CO_2, hydrocarbons, oil, water, and other contaminants, in accordance with breathing air specifications. All NOAA diving air compressors are tested for air quality every six months.

12.17.3 Safety Considerations

When a large ship is selected for a diving platform, it is generally because the diving must be conducted at a considerable distance from shore or in a remote region. When the distance is beyond the range of rapid emergency assistance or transport, the divemaster should have preplanned procedures for prompt, adequate treatment onboard ship and, when necessary, evacuation to a destination where further treatment can be obtained.

The divemaster should contact all sources of emergency assistance and rapid transport close to the dive site and should determine the round-trip range of emergency transport vehicles, including distances and times from shore to the dive site and back to the nearest recompression chamber. On cruises out of the rapid emergency assistance or transport range, especially where decompression or repetitive diving is scheduled, a recompression chamber and trained, qualified chamber personnel should be onboard the ship. The possibility of decompression sickness, gas embolism, or an emergency free ascent requiring immediate surface recompression cannot be discounted. Depending on the complexity of the dive operation and

remoteness of the dive location, a portable double-lock chamber may need to be located at the immediate dive site.

<u>NOTE</u>
Dives conducted in remote areas without any recompression capability should closely adhere to conservative profiles.

Safe execution of the dive depends upon the proper handling of the mother ship before, during, and after the dive (Coale, Michaels, and Pinto, as cited in Heine 1985). Typically, any object remaining in one place for a period of time, such as sediment trap arrays, productivity arrays, or ships, will attract sharks. For this reason, open-ocean diving near such objects is not recommended. The bridge and the mess-deck personnel should be instructed to refrain from dumping garbage or pumping bilges in the vicinity of the dive; fishing is also not permitted near the site. If the ship has been on station for some time before initiation of a dive, the ship should steam away from the station for a distance of at least 5 miles (8 km) so that the boat can be launched in cleaner water. To minimize the sonic attraction of sharks to the divers, the mother ship should be instructed not to come closer than 1/2 mile (0.8 km) to the dive location.

12.17.4 Diving While Under Way

Divers may occasionally be required to make underwater observations on towed equipment or instruments that can not be made from a stationary platform or the surface. Because this type of operation is inherently more dangerous than other diving operations, only divers trained in the unique aspects of diving under tow should participate.

The safest way to dive on towed systems is with the use of a small dive-support boat. The boat is loaded with equipment and personnel and separated from the towing vessel before the start of the tow. After the system is deployed, the small boat moves the divers in position to enter ahead of the towing cable. The divers, after entering, should take a position to either side of the projected path of the approaching cable and submerge as it nears. They should drift back and maintain visual or hand contact with the cable until the equipment is reached. The small boat should take a position behind and just to the side of the towed system where the operator can maintain a watch for exhaled bubbles, signal floats, and surfacing divers.

Another way to make this type of dive is to enter from the towing vessel. It is essential that great care be taken when entering from a moving ship. A spot should be selected on the side of the ship well aft and, if possible, aft of the ship's propeller(s). The diver should never enter the water directly off the stern, because the propeller(s) and the ship's movement through the water cause turbulence that could result in diver disorientation or equipment problems.

Diving Under Special Conditions

attached between the cylinder and the back pack or buoyancy compensator. Loose ends of fin straps should be inside of the strap, next to the ankle, to prevent the flopping strap or buckles from entangling in the towed gear. Wherever possible, straps that do not have to be adjusted for each dive should be securely taped to prevent them from pulling out.

Regulators with second-stage breathing resistance adjustments work best for diving under tow. Non-adjustable second stages often free-flow as a result of increased water flow through ambient ports and increased pressure on the diaphragm. With an adjustable second stage, the diver can adjust for the increased diaphragm pressure without compromising breathing comfort.

Because of the possibility of regulator mouthpiece damage or separation and the awkwardness of buddy breathing under tow, an octopus second stage should be included as standard equipment for towed diving. Either an in-line octopus that attaches between the BC inflator and the low-pressure inflator hose or a combination octopus/inflator works best. These alternate breathing systems provide the towed diver easy access and reduced entanglement potential over a separate octopus that might end up dangling at the diver's side. Because of the increased likelihood of sand and debris entering into the towed diver's octopus, a thorough cleaning, possibly including partial disassembly, is recommended after diving.

Other equipment and hoses should be securely attached and stowed away. The diver's gauge console should be easily accessible, but tucked away so that it does not become entangled when not being checked. If snorkels are deemed necessary, they should not be worn on the mask strap, but should be stowed in such a way that they do not become an entanglement problem.

The knife is a very important piece of safety equipment for the towed diver especially when diving on trawls. Knife selection is partly dependent on intended use, but should include a good cutting edge as the main selection criteria. Since stainless steel blades do not hold a sharp edge well; a sharp serrated edge may better serve the purpose. How the knife is attached to the diver is dependent on its size. Larger knives are worn on the diver's calf and should be strapped to the inside of the calf to reduce entanglement problems. Smaller knives can be attached to the forearm or to the BC where they may be more easily accessed. A folding knife that can be stored away in the sleeve of a wet suit or the accessory pocket of a BC is a nice back-up to the primary knife.

Towed divers must have exposure suits with thermal qualities superior to those necessary for regular dives. Rapid movement through cold water will quickly chill divers, reducing their efficiency and exposing them to the dangers of hypothermia. Dry suits are excellent for use in water temperatures below 60°F (16C); however, additional drag on towed divers may preclude the use of these suits when high mobility is desired.

12.17.4.2 Communications for Diving While Under Way

Trawl divers rely on standard hand signals plus a few specialized signs to communicate with each other; but, communications with the surface, while necessary, are much more challenging than in other types of diving operations. Hard-wire communications can be established when a dive sled is used, but are nearly impossible to set up when divers descend directly to the towed system. Wireless communication systems have improved over recent years and may be applicable for some towed diver operations. Regardless of whether other communication methods are used, simple color-coded float communications should be included on all towed dives. At a minimum, there should be one color-coded float to signal an emergency and another to signal divers ascending attached to the towed system. Additional floats can be added to signal the vessel to make changes in speed, direction, system depth, etc. The vessel can communicate to the divers with changes in towing speed or course direction. It is absolutely essential that the response to an emergency float signal be preplanned and understood by all personnel engaged in the project.

Towed divers can use a lift bag and reel as an ascent signal. This is advisable on deeper dives where a slow ascent and a safety stop can create a large separation between divers and the towing vessel. The towed diver should also carry an acoustic signalling device attached in-line to their low-pressure inflator hose for signaling the diver support boat at the surface. Other surface signaling devices that may be necessary for some towed diving operations include signal flares, smoke canisters, signaling mirrors, and marker dye.

12.18 PINNACLE AND SEAMOUNT DIVING

Pinnacles are ocean features found worldwide in both coastal and oceanic situations. They are characterized by their relatively flat tops and steep sides. They include rocks of both sedimentary and igneous origin, often possessing coral heads of particular interest to physical and chemical oceanographers, geologists, and biologists. Their isolated situations offer interesting community and genetic studies.

Steep sides, often rugged topography, and swirling currents hinder anchoring or establishing a downline on pinnacles. Care must be taken to ensure the anchor finds bottom and is not dragged over the edge.

In oceanic operations, divers can be swept from view very quickly. Large ships tend to swing at anchor and are generally unsuitable as a diving platform. Divers must be tended from a small boat, and lookouts should be posted on the larger vessel as currents increase the uncertainty of where a diver will surface.

Water clarity in the vicinity of seamounts is usually extremely good; however, judgment of depth can be deceptive. To assist and maintain proper depth, the downline may be marked for depth reference.

Pinnacles, and particularly seamounts in deep water areas, usually attract sharks. Divers are advised to carry a shark billie, during open-ocean diving, and to exercise extreme caution.

12.19 DIVING IN REMOTE LOCATIONS AND ON COASTS OF DIFFICULT ACCESS

A remote area is one where the population density and boat traffic is so low that the occupant of a diving boat stranded away from the main base would have little chance of being picked up or receiving assistance of any kind. Equally, a base camp is regarded as isolated when it would take days rather than hours to get an injured person to a medical treatment facility. Under these conditions, forward planning and anticipation of problems are of the utmost importance.

Even when a dive site is not remote from human habitation in a geographical sense, it may have difficult or limited access from the landward side due to cliffs, dune fields, desert, strong currents, or wave action. The main concern of a divemaster is the ability to deal with an emergency situation involving an injured diver. With difficult or restricted landward access, a diving operation is usually undertaken from the seaward side by boat. Should seaward access be restricted as well, emergency planning must be carried out in advance. Arrangements should be made in advance with government agencies or private interests that may provide logistical support in an emergency. Even in very remote locations, radio, and/or satellite communication can be established with a diving-support center.

A member of the team should have specific responsibility to ensure that the boats contain working flares, dye markers, a hand-held compass, survival packs, drinking water, and other items as determined for the region and logistics. There should always be a stock of food on board. It is now standard operating procedure to include portable VHF radios, portable telephones, and a GPS on even the smallest boats and inflatables.

There should be at least two serviceable boats on the dive site, except when operating close to base. When operating a single boat, a spare engine should be carried. For longer trips, two boats should travel in convoy. Radio contact should be maintained between boats and the base camp at predetermined intervals, in addition to potential emergency calls.

Keep within anchor depth wherever feasible, especially when there is an off-shore wind or tide, and carry a sea anchor. When anchoring on reefs, remember that a fouled anchor is likely, and plan for enough spare diving time to allow a diver to free the anchor.

The inventory of medical supplies should be far more extensive than would normally be the case for a project in an area less remote. At least one member of the team at each dive site should be trained and qualified as a diver-medic (DMT).

All equipment should be kept as simple as possible to reduce potential problems of breakdown and maintenance. If complex equipment is essential, the fullest possible inventory of replacement parts and repair tools should be on hand, and members of the team should be able to make the repairs.

In remote areas, backup medical, rescue, and recompression facilities are generally unavailable. Therefore, the diving operation must be conducted with a unrelenting concern for safety to ensure that these emergency services will not be required. The risk and consequences of decompression sickness (DCS), and the reduced availability of therapy, are a vital consideration and dictate conservative diving practice. In order to respond effectively to potential DCS incidents, detailed plans must be established in advance. Prior to the commencement of any remote diving operation, it is recommended that the emergency response plan be proven by a dry run to test communications, transport availability, and every other aspect of the emergency procedures.

Portable recompression facilities are desirable, but the cost and logistics requirements may be prohibitive. In-water recompression therapy is not advisable. NOAA and the U.S. Navy have developed treatment tables and techniques for in-water recompression with 100% oxygen. This technique is only allowed under certain circumstances and requires specific equipment and training. When diving without recompression facilities, surface oxygen therapy for suspected DCS is advised.

12.20 DIVING IN LOW AND ZERO VISIBILITY

The diver's ability to navigate accurately is reduced in low-and zero-visibility conditions. There is a danger that the diver will, unknowingly, put himself in a hazardous situation from which extrication will be difficult without assistance from another diver or from the surface. Specimen collecting in these conditions can also introduce hazards to divers and their assistants (e.g., geologists with hammers, and biologists with nets or core samplers). The presence of potentially dangerous marine animals can also increase hazards in low-visibility situations.

In addition to the presence of a standby diver, it is recommended that there be, instantly available, fully rigged emergency breathing gear (i.e., scuba cylinder and regulator). Divers may become fouled and are, thus, in danger of exhausting their air supply before they can be removed to safety.

Conservative planning relative to bottom time and air consumption should be considered. Lifelines are useful in quiet water, or where an unencumbered ascent can be made. The presence of a shot line, sampling gear, and currents, all contribute to the risk of snagging the lifeline.

Divers must proceed with caution and maintain contact with the lifeline. In extreme conditions, the lifeline may be surface-tended to permit signaling to and from the diver. In currents with poor bottom visibility, divers should structures moored in open water, such as spar buoys, which can be several tens of meters long. In this case, the best technique is for divers to fix the measuring equipment in the supporting structure on site, utilizing an adjustable buoyancy apparatus to provide for "weightless" techniques. Small, commercially available buoyancy compensators for light-weight instruments, and lifting bags for heavy objects, are commonly used. However, weightless assembly techniques are sensitive to depth changes and are difficult for even experienced divers to control in operations where heavy loads can have significant depth variation. Specially constructed, automatic, constant-volume buoyancy compensators have been developed to provide precise control and better safety. Divers involved in these operations must have demonstrated excellent buoyancy control during training before attempting to handle oceanographic equipment under water. Where it is necessary for divers to be untethered, a safety diver with no other project responsibilities should be positioned with an unobstructed view and tethered, similar to an open-ocean diver, with sufficient lateral line to reach any of the active divers. Signals or communications between the safety diver and the surface should be established before the dive so that the safety diver can inform surface support personnel immediately of any emergency situation.

Subsurface buoys in shallow water also can be designed to allow divers to check conditions of the measuring systems under water, and recover and replace the data-acquisition unit, or carry out servicing with a minimum interruption of measurement recording. Precise operations of lifting equipment by divers are also commonly necessary, especially where other equipment is present in the water. The use of diving operations can remove the need for shipboard recovery and replacement of scientific equipment.

Sea deployment of bottom-mounted structures is frequently required. Divers can observe descent, impact, and at-rest orientation characteristics of remotely-employed equipment during tests, often using cameras and video equipment placed near rapidly descending apparatus. In order to avoid potential injury to divers, these tests should be carried out only in excellent visibility, with perfect communication between divers and the surface. The direct observation of equipment placement can be used to improve deployment technique, and to allow prediction of the manner of placement in deeper water, where direct observation is limited.

Additional References

For information on extreme cold weather conditions and the polar environment, refer to:

- *A Guide to Extreme Cold Weather Operations* (Naval Safety Center, July 1986)
- *Polar Operations Manual* S0300-A5-MAN-010 (Naval Coastal Systems Center) (NCSC)
- *Guide to Polar Diving* (Office of Naval Research, June 1976
- *UCT Artic Operation Manual* NAVFAC P-992 (To obtain a copy of this manual, contact NCSC, Code 5110.)

Polluted-Water Diving

Polluted-Water Diving

13.0 GENERAL

During the last three decades, as the number of scientific diving operations in polluted water has increased, the spectrum of materials to which divers are exposed has grown as well. At first, little consideration was given to the possible effects of these materials on the divers themselves. In the early 1970s, for example, diver services were used in studies that examined the fate and effect of sewage and chemicals introduced into the sea. Immunizations against certain pathogenic microorganisms were given in some cases, but illness was still reported in some divers who were exposed to sewage. As the list of dangerous substances to which divers were being exposed increased and as the substances became more hazardous, attention was focused on the potential threat to diving and support personnel and on the effectiveness of available diving apparatus in protecting divers.

Many divers are unaware of the dangers of diving in polluted water. While some bodies of water do not appear polluted, they may have high levels of biological or chemical contamination. Additionally, divers may mistakenly believe that the water itself will dilute the hazard to a low level while ignoring the possible cumulative effect of multiple exposures.

The same hazardous materials that would concern a person topside must concern divers under water. These hazards include biohazards, toxic chemicals, and radiation. However, the situations in which divers encounter these underwater hazards are very different from those on the surface. The main difference in dealing with a hazardous material under water is that, in most cases, the hazardous material is suspended or dissolved in the water around the diver. This means that unless the diver equips himself properly, the material may enter the diver's mouth through the regulator or mask. For this reason, ordinary scuba equipment is not considered acceptable for this type of diving. Contaminants may also get into a diver's eyes, even if he wears a full-face mask or helmet, and they can touch his skin through his wet suit. Compare this situation to a liquid spill topside, where the chemical puddles in the street, and it's easy to appreciate the increased risks. In addition, some materials that present only a minor concern on the surface create a major exposure hazard under water. This is why even full coverage diving helmets must be specially rigged for dives of this nature.

Toxins that float on top of the water, such as gasoline, also present a serious hazard to the diver. The diver must pass through them to enter or exit the water. Substances that sink in water are those most likely to collect as pockets of pure chemical substance on the bottom. Concentrated chemicals are obviously very hazardous.

Diving supervisors should attempt to identify the nature and severity of contaminants in waters at proposed dive sites by contacting local, state, and federal water quality agencies.

13.1 HAZARDS

13.1.1 Biological Pollutants

Biological pollutants are probably the most common form of hazardous materials encountered by divers. Three main classes of biological contaminants are of concern to divers. *Bacteria* are single-celled creatures that exhibit characteristics common to both plants and animals. *Protozoans* are single-celled animals. *Viruses* are organisms that take over the chemistry of a host cell in living creatures to reproduce themselves.

Fecal coliforms are a disease-producing bacteria found in human and animal feces. They are universally present in the water wherever there is raw sewage, or inadequate sewage treatment. Swallowing water that contains fecal coliforms can produce severe, disabling diarrhea. It might not kill the diver, but it will result in lost time from work.

In the Hudson River, New York, fecal coliform counts as high as 100 times the maximum level considered safe for human contact have been recorded. In the New River, along the California–Mexico border, fecal coliform counts as high as 700,000 per 100 milliliters have been registered.

The Hudson and New Rivers are sites that one would suspect as polluted just from the appearance and smell of the water. Yet, even rivers and streams that appear to be clear and clean may contain high levels of coliforms and other organisms.

Other examples of sites where unacceptable levels of fecal coliforms have been identified include waterways located near cattle ranching or feed lot operations. Most bodies of water near agricultural areas face similar problems.

Santa Monica Bay, off Los Angeles, is sometimes closed to water sports due to spills of untreated sewage. This occurs whenever heavy rains fill the storm drains and cause the waste treatment plants to exceed their capacity. In February of 1990, eight million gallons of raw sewage spilled into Santa Monica Bay, closing beaches there for several weeks. Similar occurrences are common throughout the United States.

A diver who dives in a waterway that contains high numbers of fecal coliforms must be equipped with the right equipment. Ordinary surface-supplied diving gear is usually not enough. In New York City and in Imperial County, California, even the public safety divers (fire, sheriff, police) now wear special dry suits and full-face masks or diving helmets (Hackett 1988).

If fecal coliforms are present, there are probably several other forms of biological pollution as well. Other dangerous bacteria include *Cholera, Vibrio vulnificus,* and *Aeromonas hydrophilla.*

Vibrio vulnificus is an extremely potent marine bacteria that can cause death. It enters the body through the mouth or raw wounds.

Aeromonas hydrophilla infects open cuts in the body and is commonly found in harbor waters. For example, *Aeromonas* was isolated from the nose and throat of scuba diving scientists after dives in the harbor at Norfolk, Virginia. *Aeromonas* infections have been fatal if not properly treated.

Like bacteria, many *protozoans* occur as a result of pollution. For example, eight different species of *Acanthamoeba* occur in polluted waters. This dangerous single-celled organism causes inflammation of the spinal chord, with death as the end result.

Giardia lamblia, another *protozoan*, causes intestinal pain, diarrhea, and high fever. *Giardia* has been positively identified in stool samples taken from the New York City Fire Department dive team members. Today, there are almost no streams in the Sierra Nevada mountains that do not contain *Giardia*. This comes as a result of the high number of animals, including humans, in these areas. In general, it is unwise to drink water from lakes or streams unless it is treated.

In Florida, levels of *protozoans* in the inland waterways may create dangerous conditions for divers. For heavily contaminated waters, public safety divers have been banned from entering the water there unless they are totally encapsulated.

One of the most commonly known viruses, Hepatitis type A, survives outside the body in both fresh and salt water. In Hepatitis A, the subject's liver becomes inflamed. Like other disease-producing organisms that spread through contact with raw sewage, hepatitis can be found in fecal matter.

Another recently identified hazard is the dinoflagelate, *Pfiesteria piscicida*, which has been found in the coastal waters of Florida and as far north as Chesapeake Bay (Barker 1998). *Pfiesteria* causes skin lesions on fish and humans. Other documented human effects include vertigo and disorientation which occurs after exposure, as well as neurological problems and extreme mood swings.

13.1.2 Toxic Chemicals

When most people think of hazardous materials emergencies, they usually think about accidental spills of toxic chemicals. However, in many situations, divers also face serious threats from low-level, long-term pollution of waterways. This long-term pollution continues to occur in waterways as diverse as the harbors of the East coast, the Mississippi River, and the waters of San Diego's Mission Bay.

A dramatic example of a toxic "spill" occurred on Earth Day, 1980, when a chemical waste storage site in Elizabeth, New Jersey, exploded. More than 20,000 drums of acids, solvents, pesticides, explosives, and carcinogens were involved in the fire. Water used to fight this fire drained from the storage yard and carried many of the contaminants into Bayonne Bay. A third of the firefighters who fought the blaze reported symptoms of illness for up to ten days after the incident. They complained of skin rashes, nausea, throat irritation, and tingling sensations in the limbs. Consequently, the New Jersey Department of Environmental Protection banned commercial fishing downstream of the incident. Three months after the New Jersey spill, NOAA divers were conducting underwater experiments 22 miles from the site of the explosion. Equipped with full-face masks and vulcanized rubber dry suits, their dives were made with no apparent ill effects. Yet at the same time, only a few miles away, two sport divers surfaced, reporting burning sensations around their necks and mouths. Both divers were hospitalized.

San Diego's Mission Bay is a popular water sports location on the west coast of the United States. In 1987, an electronics firm was cited by the Environmental Protection Agency (EPA) for dumping PCBs (polychlorinated biphenyls) into the bay (LaRue 1986). PCBs are used in the manufacture of electronics components. A level of 50 parts per million (ppm) of PCBs results in a hazardous classification for solid wastes. Levels as high as 3,000 ppm were found in a culvert which emptied from the violator's storm drain into the bay. Divers from the San Diego Port District conducted training dives in a lagoon where the drain emptied into the bay. Levels of PCBs as high as 34 (ppm) were detected in the area where the divers trained. PCBs, which tend to accumulate in the mud on the bottom, do not break down for many years. Three of the San Diego divers developed lymphoma, a form of cancer. One diver died from the disease and another developed anemia. While it has not been possible to establish a direct link between the divers' conditions and the PCBs, the divers filed law suits against the electronic firm in question.

PCBs released in accidental spills in other parts of the country also pose serious potential threats to divers. In January 1990, a manufacturing plant in Virginia spilled approximately one million gallons of PCB-contaminated water into the Shenandoah River.

In Puget Sound, Washington, three different marine regions were declared toxic hazard sites by the EPA in 1988. The two most dramatic were Commencement Bay and Eagle Harbor; both were listed on the EPA Superfund cleanup list. Commencement Bay is bordered by refineries, chemical plants, pulp mills, and a defunct copper smelting plant. Samples of the mud on the bottom have revealed high levels of petrochemicals, copper, lead, zinc, and arsenic. Eagle Harbor has very high levels of PAHs, resulting from a now-closed wood treatment operation.

Another hazard commonly found in most harbors and marinas is the variety of residues from boat bottom paints that have been used on both large and small vessels. These bottom paints were designed to kill or inhibit the growth of marine life. The same chemicals that discourage marine growth may also be hazardous to humans.

One of the primary components of these anti-fouling paints is an organotin compound known as tributyltin, more commonly known as "TBT." There are 20 TBT compounds; nine are used in boat bottom paints.

TBTs dissolve into fats, giving them the ability to move across the membranes of living cells. This trait makes them effective in killing marine organisms, such as barnacles. Like PCBs, TBTs tend to collect in the silt found on the bottom of harbors. Almost all the research that has been done on TBTs has concentrated on the effect of these chemicals on marine creatures. However, chemicals in this class have toxic effects on the human central nervous system, blood, liver, kidneys, heart, and skin. More alarming, is the fact that while people react to a single acute dose of TBTs, repeated sub-toxic doses also produce adverse reactions. This suggests a cumulative effect, where low doses keep adding up in a diver's body after repeated exposures.

Since some scientific dives take place in harbors, TBTs must be of concern to divers and diving safety officers. A scientist for the EPA has labeled TBTs as the "most toxic chemicals ever deliberately added to the marine environment."

Tribytyltin use is restricted in some states and countries. In 1988, U.S. President Ronald W. Reagan signed the Organotin Antifouling Paint Control Act which prohibited the use of TBT on non-aluminum vessels less than 83 feet (25 meters) in length; EPA subsequently instituted this ban via federal regulations. High levels of TBTs have been found in San Diego Bay, San Francisco Bay, Honolulu Harbor, Long Beach Harbor (California), Narraganset Bay, Thames River (Connecticut), and Mayport, Florida. All of these ports see traffic from Navy ships, a prime user of TBT anti-fouling paints.

Although tributyltin breaks down in clear waters, it persists much longer in murky harbor waters. The by-products of TBT's decay are also harmful. It may be years after TBT is banned worldwide before it can no longer be detected in the marine environment.

Divers who work around wooden piers and wharves must also beware of the dangers of creosote. Most wooden pilings are treated with creosote to prevent wood decay. Creosote also discourages marine worms from boring holes in the pilings. Unprotected divers can get chemical burns from brushing against pilings that are coated with creosote.

Certain chemicals are so dangerous that no diver should consider working around them. These chemicals include, but are not limited to, the following:

- Acetic anhydride
- Acrylonitrile
- Carbon tetrachloride
- Cresol
- Chlordane
- Dichloropropane
- Epichlorohydrin
- Ethylbenzene
- Methyl chloride
- Methyl parathion
- Perchloroethylene
- Styrene
- Trichloroethylene
- Xylene

Programs for monitoring the effects of hazardous chemicals on divers must be maintained for divers engaged in dealing with acute exposures. Blood, urine, and stool samples are recommended predive and postdive when divers expose themselves to specific known chemical toxins. In addition, tests of the divers' lung capacities are merited in cases where chemicals are known to affect the divers' breathing ability.

13.1.3 Radioactive Substances

Radioactive substances are most likely to enter the marine environment through industrial accidents. Protecting divers from this hazard is a matter of limiting the time they are exposed, ensuring the divers maintain an adequate distance from the material, and using proper shielding. In situations where this type of hazard exists, dive activities should be deferred to military or commercial diving organizations who have the experience to deal with this type of emergency.

13.1.4 Thermal Conditions

Aside from the risks of exposure to hazardous materials, dry suits and masks/helmets also create thermal hazards for the diver. These hazards, which are similar to those faced by hazardous-material ("HAZ-MAT") personnel topside, include fluid loss, heat cramps, and heat exhaustion. From the time that the diver dresses-in before the dive until completion of decontamination at the end of the dive, heat stress can be a severe problem. If the diver works in cold water, some of the heat stress will be relieved during the dive. Moving from very warm surface climates into cold water, and back to hot surface temperatures, is stressful in itself. If the diver works in warm water, there is no relief from heat stress. Overheating may be a very real danger. Divers who work in warm waters must carefully evaluate these conditions and plan dives accordingly.

In the early 1980s, NOAA and the Environmental Protection Agency (EPA) developed a "suit-under-suit" system (SUS) to deal with two problems associated with contaminated water diving; thermoregulation and leakage. The SUS consists of a thin inner suit (foam neoprene neck-entry dry suit with attached booties) covered by a conventional dry suit (vulcanized rubber with ankle exhaust valves and an adjustable-pressure arm-mounted exhaust valve) (see Figure 13.1). A "neck dam" installed in the outer suit is clamped to the entrance hoke of the inner suit, creating a closed cavity between the two suits and separating the diver's head from the suits. An outer chafing/restraining garment is worn over the outer suit. Clean water of the desired temperature (hot or cold) is pumped into the area between the two suits to warm or cool the diver. Since the entire volume of the suit is filled with water under a pressure slightly greater than the outside water, a puncture or leak in the suit results in clean water leaking out, rather than outside water coming in, as is the case with air-filled suits. The insulation quality of the inner suit provides a buffer layer when cooling is necessary and helps prevent burning of the diver in the event very hot water is accidentally sent to the diver via the umbilical from the surface. Today, an adaptation of the SUS is used by divers working in nuclear power plants to reduce hyperthermia and prevent exposure to any potential contaminants.

In extended contaminated water diving operations in warm weather, the diver's physiology must be monitored. These include heart rate, body temperature, and weight. Measurements of these vital functions should be taken before and after diving. Experiments have been conducted at the Swedish National Institute of Occupational Health on the effectiveness of diver cooling using an ice filled vest (Holmer 1989). The divers in the study wore dry suits, similar to the SUS mentioned above, fitted with vests containing 46 small pockets filled with blocks of ice in plastic bags. At water temperatures of 107°F (41.7C), the divers were able to complete dives that were 15–30 minutes longer when equipped with the ice-filled vest. Further tests will need to be performed to determine maximum safe exposure times for using such systems.

13.2 TRAINING

Training for contaminated water diving operations requires the combined talents of many people. Ideally, the staff for a training course in contaminated water diving

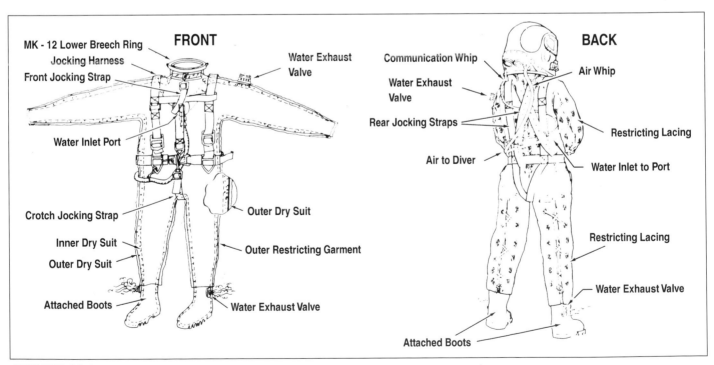

FIGURE 13.1
Suit Under Suit (SUS)

would include a biologist, a chemist, a HAZ-MAT specialist, and a diving safety officer intimately familiar with appropriate diving equipment and procedures.

As a minimum, polluted-water diving training should include the following topics along with hands-on and in-water scenarios:

- Hazard recognition and evaluation
- Go/No-Go decision making
- Equipment selection
- Dive planning
- Dress-in procedures
- Diving procedures
- Emergency procedures
- Postdive decontamination

13.3 EQUIPMENT

13.3.1 General

Polluted-water diving operations require specialized equipment. Both the divers in the water and the support personnel topside must be properly equipped. Although equipment used topside is essentially the same as that used by personnel for HAZ-MAT operations, special consideration must be given to splash-back protection and the amount of water required to decontaminate the divers. Equipment used for polluted-water diving is somewhat different from standard "off the shelf" scuba or surface-supplied diving equipment.

There are several characteristics of commonly used diving equipment that make it unacceptable for diving in contaminated water: foam neoprene dry suits are difficult to impossible to adequately decontaminate; the numerous "breakable" seals on masks, helmets, and suits increase potential for leaks; and reliable, dry-glove arrangements are scarce. Moreover, exhaust valves in demand regulators allow a few small droplets of water to enter during the exhaust cycle. When the demand valve is activated during inhalation, the jet of incoming air breaks up the droplets into a mist which is then inhaled by the diver.

It is essential to keep in mind that accidents which occur when diving in polluted water may require additional procedures prior to initiating standard diving accident management. The combination of top-quality, well-maintained equipment, coupled with proper training, safety consciousness, and common sense can go a long way to reduce the likelihood of accidents. There is no such thing as 100 percent safe contaminated-water diving.

Just as there are different levels of protection for HAZ-MAT situations topside, there are different types of diving equipment to be selected according to the hazard level under water. Unfortunately, no standards currently exist for diving equipment that can be selected based upon the potential effects/risks of the hazard to the divers.

After evaluating actual and potential contaminants in the dive planning process, three options are available:

1. Diving is not an option when unacceptable exposure conditions exist or when the water contains chemicals in which a diver should never be allowed to operate. In this case, other means (i.e., remotely operated vehicles, surface sampling devices, etc.) must be used to obtain required data.
2. For less severe but still hazardous exposures where it is absolutely necessary to have a diver enter the water, total encapsulation (i.e., full-coverage helmet mated to a dry suit with dry gloves) should be required.
3. In less polluted environments (i.e., where contaminants are bound to sediments or the waters carry low levels of biological contamination) a full-face mask can often be used with a dry suit and dry gloves. This system offers a lesser degree of protection than a helmet but far more protection than a half mask with scuba regulator.

13.3.2 Full-Face Masks

Full-face masks can be supplied with breathing gas from a variety of sources including open-circuit scuba, surface-supplied systems, or a rebreather. When used in the open circuit mode, full-face masks should be equipped with a series non-return valve to prevent a backflow of contaminants into the breathing system. In addition, the mask should have separate inhalation and exhalation chambers. This will help to further reduce the possibility of inhaling a spray of contaminants if leakage occurs on the exhaust side of the breathing system.

Since a full-face mask can leak if a strap breaks or becomes loose, another desirable feature is a positive pressure regulator. Scuba full-face masks normally operate in the demand mode, but masks with positive pressure are designed to free flow if the face seal is broken. This very important feature can help prevent contaminants from entering the mask in the event of a leak. Positive pressure masks also clear water automatically if the mask completely floods. Conservative calculation of breathing gas supply requirements is absolutely essential when using full-face masks with open-circuit scuba equipment. Unfortunately, buoyancy can be a problem with some full-face masks. Depending on the individual, some masks with high internal volumes may be buoyant producing jaw fatigue and generally making the mask uncomfortable to wear. Selecting a mask with the lowest volume available is advisable, assuming it meets the other important criteria for the specific polluted-water application (see Figure 13.2).

It is possible to use a full-face mask with a fully closed-circuit rebreather, however, the cost involved with purchasing and maintaining the system, plus the additional training requirements for personnel, may make the use of such systems for polluted-water application prohibitive.

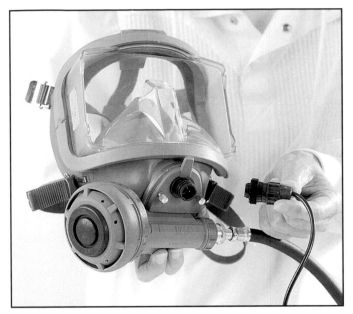

FIGURE 13.2
Full-Face Masks for Use in Contaminated Water

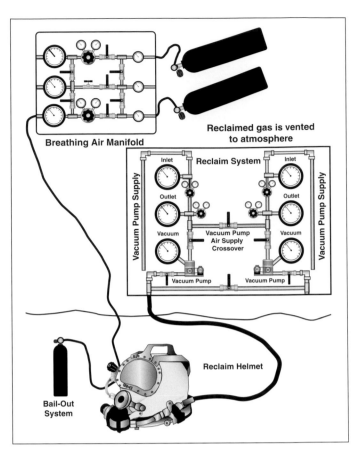

FIGURE 13.3
Schematic of Reclaim System with Topside Supply

13.3.3 Diving Helmets

For exposure to chemical or biological hazards that can produce severe illness or death, divers should be equipped with a full coverage helmet, a dry suit with a mating yoke for the helmet, and mating dry gloves. The advantage of a diving helmet over a full-face mask is that the diver's entire head is encapsulated in a dry environment. Diving helmets are also less likely to be accidentally pulled-off a diver's head and they are less prone to leak.

The typical mode for supplying breathing gas to a full-coverage helmet is from a surface-supplied source. Such sources consist of either a low-pressure air compressor or a high-pressure gas storage system that is reduced to low pressure. Another, more sophisticated mode of supplying gas to a diving helmet is a "reclaim" gas system. A reclaim system, also referred to as a "push-pull" system, routes the helmet's exhaust to the surface, by means of a separate hose, where it is either recycled or exhausted to the surrounding atmosphere (see Figure 13.3). The advantage of this type of system is that it reduces the possibility of contaminants entering the helmet via a back-flow through the exhaust valve (see Figure 13.4), and protects the tender from volatile contaminants being released from the sediment and transported to the surface with exhaust bubbles. The disadvantage is that they are more expensive and not easily deployed on a small boat. Special reclaim systems have been developed specifically for polluted-water diving (Divex 1997).

Diving helmets that are equipped with demand regulators, without reclaim systems, are subject to the same exhaust "splash-back" problems experienced with open-circuit scuba regulators. To reduce the possibility of this happening, NOAA developed the "series exhaust valve" (SEV)

(see Figure 13.4). The SEV helps prevent a back-flow of water into the helmet. Both the regulator exhaust and the main helmet exhaust are linked together with a special tube, and a third external exhaust valve is added to the system. Any water that manages to sneak past this outer exhaust valve is unlikely to make it past either of the two other valves. Testing by NOAA using dye tracers revealed the presence of occasional droplets of water behind the outer-most valve, however, none were detected inside the second valve.

13.3.4 Umbilicals

One of the big problems with umbilicals for surface-supplied diving in the past has been that they have traditionally been assembled with duct tape, which can absorb contaminants or even disintegrate when used in contaminated water. New umbilicals are available today made from chemically resistant hoses that are manufactured in a spiral and require no tape to hold the components together (see Figure 13.5). These are preferred for many polluted-water diving scenarios.

13.3.5 Dry Suits

If a dry suit is to be used with a full-face mask, the dry suit must be equipped with a latex or vulcanized rubber

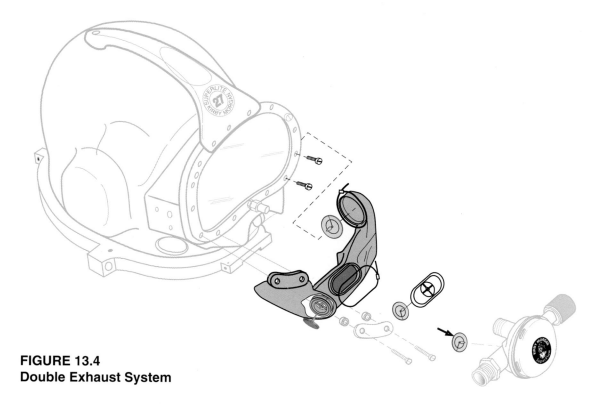

FIGURE 13.4
Double Exhaust System

dry hood which is attached directly to the suit (see Figure 13.6). The full-face mask must seal on the hood without leakage. If the diver is using a full-coverage helmet (see Figure 13.7), the interface between the diving helmet and the dry suit is extremely critical. Ideally, the helmet should mate directly to the suit, quickly and easily. Yet, the connection must be positive and secure. The system should be designed so that few, if any, contaminants are trapped between the helmet and the suit when the two are separated after the dive.

Dry suits for contaminated water diving should be made from a material that has a smooth, non-porous outer surface. The material must not absorb or trap contaminants. For diving in biologically polluted water, vulcanized rubber dry suits are the most popular choice.

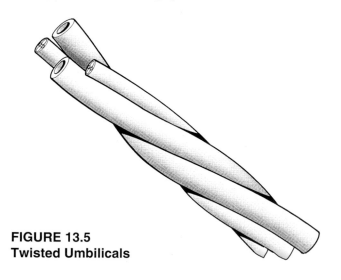

FIGURE 13.5
Twisted Umbilicals

NOAA and the EPA conducted tests in the 1970s with different types of dry suits in several biologically contaminated rivers. After decontamination, it was determined that suits with a nylon fabric exterior showed signs of bacteria for several days after the dive. In contrast, vulcanized rubber dry suits displayed almost no evidence of bacteria after proper wash down. Based upon these tests, vulcanized rubber dry suits have become the most widely used type of suits for diving in polluted water. While vulcanized rubber dry suits help protect the diver from most biological contamination, they do not protect him from all types of chemicals or radiation.

NOTE
No type of diving helmet/mask or suit can guarantee complete protection from exposure to contaminants under water.

Dry suits used in a contaminated environment must also be equipped with attached boots. Suits with thin latex socks are unacceptable, due to the ease with which the material can be punctured, especially when walking on the bottom of a garbage littered harbor.

Dry glove systems consisting of a set of cuff rings and gloves (or mittens) should also be used for polluted-water diving operations. Cuff rings come in pairs of inner and outer rings. The inner ring, which is machined from hard plastic, goes inside the sleeve of the dry suit where the sleeve attaches to the wrist seal. The outer ring, which is made from rubber, slips over the sleeve and compresses the suit over the inner ring. Take care not to tighten the clamp too much or it will cut the glove. Tape should be used over

FIGURE 13.6
Full-Face Mask with Dry Suit

FIGURE 13.7
Full-Coverage Helmet with Dry Suit

the clamp to prevent it from snagging, or tape may be used alone to hold the gloves in position. The dry gloves or mittens snap into position over the outer ring (see Figure 13.8).

It is essential to remember that any individual piece of diving gear will not be compatible with all chemical environments. In 1983, the U.S. Navy's Surface Weapons Center commissioned a study on the effects of a variety of hazardous chemicals on diving equipment (Glowe 1983). The tests, which were performed by the TRI Environmental, Inc., covered a wide variety of military and commercial diving equipment. The results of immersion tests of selected suit and helmet components and Gates C3 diving hose to chemical exposure are available from the NOAA Diving Center (NDC), Seattle, Washington. In 1998, Trelleborg Viking conducted permeability and resistance tests on their vulcanized rubber dry suits, zippers, latex seals, and gloves for various chemical exposures. These results are also available from NDC.

In addition to protecting the diver, the diver's tenders, who aid him in dressing and handle the diving hose, must also be properly protected. The tenders will be in the "hot zone" while they tend the diver at the water's edge (see Figure 13.9). They must also accompany and assist the diver through the decontamination procedure. Tenders must wear the appropriate protection according to the hazard level (Barsky 1999). Besides dressing the diver, they must keep a firm grip on the diver's umbilical at all times. Since they cannot leave the diver's hose unattended, they must be provided with a sufficient air supply, if the situation warrants it. The air supply must last for the anticipated duration of the dive, as well as including a reserve. Tenders must also be protected from heat stress.

13.4 POLLUTED-WATER DIVING TECHNIQUES

Diving in contaminated water is not much different than diving under ordinary conditions. The procedures and techniques used under water are basically the same as they are for any surface-supplied dive. The real differences in diving in contaminated water are the procedures and techniques that take place before and after the dive. Gear set-up, dress-in procedures, air supply systems, and decontamination are quite different when diving in contaminated water as compared to diving in less hostile environments.

The preparation for a contaminated water dive actually starts with team training. Even though the diver may be very experienced, the extra equipment required for contaminated water diving usually requires extra training for personnel. The diver must become thoroughly familiar with the dry suit, full-face mask or helmet, and any other gear to be utilized. Both the diver and tenders must be familiar with the decontamination procedures. A difficult and important part of contaminated water diving is dressing the diver quickly and efficiently so that he does not become overheated.

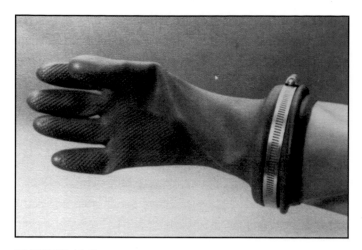

FIGURE 13.8
Hose Clamp on Dry Glove

FIGURE 13.9
Protected Dive Tender

Inoculations will usually be in order if the diver will be diving in biologically contaminated water. Hepatitis vaccination is considered essential if the diver will be exposed to fecal coliforms. Other inoculations, including polio and typhoid, may be needed depending upon the location of the dive. The integration of a HAZ-MAT team with the dive team is desirable whenever possible. The tender must be trained in the use of SCBAs (Self-Contained Breathing Apparatus) and HAZ-MAT suits and be prepared to tend the diver while totally encapsulated.

The first step in planning a contaminated water dive is determining what equipment should be used. To do this, the dive team must know what contaminants are present at the dive site. This is the cardinal rule of contaminated water diving; if the diver doesn't know what's in the water, he should not dive.

Plans for decontamination should include making sure the right equipment is on hand before the diver enters the water. This means that the dive team must have the proper decontamination solutions and wash down gear prepared prior to the dive.

Generally, the diver should select the highest level of protection available, unless there is some good reason why this is not possible. The justification for this is that even though he may think he knows what hazards are present, there may be additional hazards under water that have not been anticipated. For example, if the diver is working in a biologically contaminated river, it is possible for people to dump chemicals upstream from the dive site with no notice given.

When the dive team actually arrives at an incident, as with any HAZ-MAT scenario, they must determine the center of the contaminated site. The location of the "hot zone" as well as the adjacent "contamination reduction zone" and the "support zone" will greatly influence the placement of the surface support gear. The hot zone is the area that contains the spill or other contamination.

The contamination reduction zone is where the process of decontamination occurs. The support zone is where all personnel and equipment are stationed that are not equipped to be exposed to the contaminants. The division of the dive site into these separate zones is known as the "zone management system" (see Figure 13.10).

The diver's life support equipment will usually be placed as close to the contamination reduction corridor as possible. Ideally, the diver's air manifold operator should be able to see the dive site and have visual contact with the tender at the water's edge. If this is not possible, they must at least have audio communications between both areas.

The diver's topside air manifold operator should not be encapsulated. An encapsulated air manifold operator will be unable to communicate clearly with the diver without special communications equipment. In addition, the air manifold operator cannot leave the manifold unattended to change his own SCBA. Finally, if the manifold operator is located where there is the possibility of contacting contaminated material, it might be possible for contaminated air to be introduced into the diver's breathing system. As with any hazardous materials incident, the dive station and incident command supervisor should be located up-wind of any potential source of chemical fumes.

WARNING
SINCE WIND DIRECTION AND/OR AIRBORNE CONTAMINATES CAN NOT BE CONTROLLED, UTILIZATION OF AIR COMPRESSORS COULD PRESENT SERIOUS COMPLICATIONS. FILLING OF ALL HIGH-PRESSURE CYLINDERS, SCBA, AND SCUBA CYLINDERS SHOULD BE FILLED WELL CLEAR OF POSSIBLE CONTAMINATION.

Exposure levels that are tolerable at the surface may be highly toxic at elevated partial pressures under water.

During the set up of equipment, thoughtful attention must be given to the routing of the diver's umbilical. For example, in an inland hazardous materials spill, the surface-supplied diver's umbilical may often need to cross a street to reach a drainage canal or lake. While the street may be cordoned off to local traffic, the diver's breathing air umbilical must still be protected from emergency vehicles that might accidentally run over the hose. A truck that runs over a diving hose could cause it to fail immediately. A truck that parks on top of a diver's hose could leave a diver with no air. Obviously, either situation must be avoided since this jeopardizes the diver's lifeline.

The best protection for the dive hose is to route the traffic around it with traffic cones or crowd control tape. If this is impossible it may be necessary to build some sort of simple protective shield to cover the hose, such as several wooden two by four beams, nailed together, with a channel between them for the hose to fit inside.

During set-up, all equipment must be thoroughly inspected. Although each piece of gear should have been tagged after its last cleaning and use, it should all be completely inspected again. Particular attention should be given to the seals on the suit, the valves, and the rubber parts on the helmet. Although a piece of gear may have been in good condition when it was last stored, it may have deteriorated over time.

Divers should always personally test the non-return valve on any surface-supplied diving helmet to make sure it is operating properly. The diver must not be able to suck any air back through the valve. If a non-return valve fails the diver can be seriously injured. Do not dive unless the non-return valve on the helmet is operating properly.

Whether dressing the diver or the standby diver, both crew members should be provided with a chair or other place to sit. Both divers will be wearing a lot of equipment and a sturdy bench, chair, or stool will be a necessity. In addition, if the weather is at all warm, there must be some type of shade and cooling for the divers. Overheating is a major problem in contaminated water diving, as it is in all HAZ-MAT operations.

Dive team organization must be completely discussed prior to every dive so that each person understands their responsibilities. Additional team members will be needed to assist during the wash down of the diver and the tender. Contaminated water diving requires a great deal of logistical support.

Divers must ultimately understand that they are responsible for making the decision whether or not it is safe to dive. Divers must never be forced to dive when they feel conditions are unsafe.

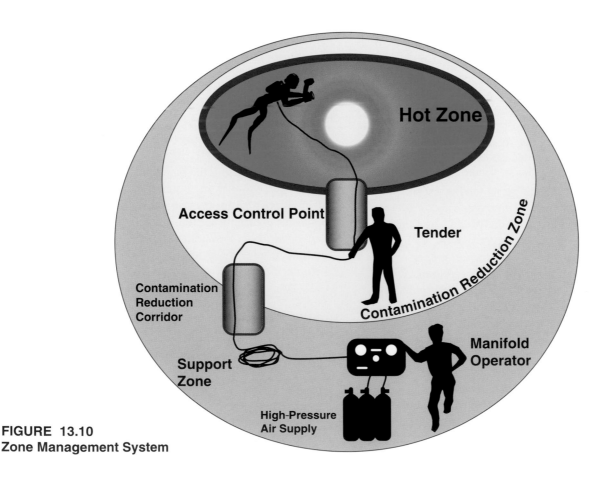

**FIGURE 13.10
Zone Management System**

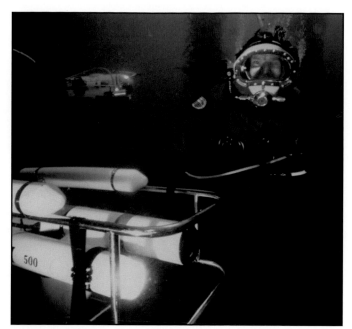

FIGURE 13.11
Remotely Operated Vehicle (ROV)

outside of the gloves to help hold them in place. Caution should be used whenever the diver works around wreckage or other debris to avoid damaging the connection between the gloves and the suit. If latex dry gloves are worn, the diver may need to wear additional disposable work gloves over them to protect the dry gloves from puncture.

After the diver is dressed in, but prior to him entering the water, the entire diving system worn by the diver must be leak tested. The best way to accomplish this is to submerge the diver in a vat of clear, clean water. Carefully observe the system for leaks. If a test tank is not available, then the diver's suit should be inflated and the diver should be sprayed with a solution of soapy water.

During a contaminated water dive, the diver must be constantly alert to feelings of wetness inside his suit, or unusual smells inside the diving helmet. If the diver even suspects there is a leak in his diving system he must exit the water immediately and proceed to decontamination. In an out-of-air situation, the diver must never remove a full-face mask or helmet. Aside from the danger of exposing himself to contaminants, he will not be able to see underwater. In the surface-supplied mode, he should be able to switch to his bail-out reserve with no interruption of his breathing air supply. Training for other emergencies, such as entanglement and regulator failure, should be a regular part of each dive team's program.

13.5 DECONTAMINATION PROCEDURES

Decontamination should start as the diver exits the water (Traver 1982). When the diver first mounts the ladder to exit the water the tenders can hose the diver off as part of the gross decontamination process.

During the gross decontamination process the diver will still be wearing all his equipment. Considering the weight of most diving helmets, and the other equipment the diver will be wearing, it is very important for the tenders to perform their duties as quickly as possible. The diver is apt to be extremely fatigued after a hard dive and the heat build-up inside the dry suit can be extreme during decontamination. If a diver were to pass out during decontamination, this would pose a serious emergency for the dive team.

Of special concern during the decontamination procedures is the area where the diving helmet mates to the dry suit. This is one location where most diving systems will trap contaminants. Extra care must be taken to ensure that there is no trace of contaminants left in the collar of the suit when the helmet is removed. If this area is not scrupulously cleaned, any remaining contaminants will run down inside the collar towards the diver's neck. This area must be scrubbed and rinsed with large amounts of water.

Decontamination solutions should be specific to the hazard encountered. For biological contamination, commonly used solutions include Betadine, Zeppamine, and tincture green soap. For chemical solutions, the appropriate

At the dive site, the diving supervisor and divers will need to evaluate all the conditions affecting the dive. Important aspects to consider include the depth, any physical underwater hazards (aside from the contaminant), topside weather conditions, underwater visibility, currents, etc. If the decision is made not to dive, it may be preferable to use a remotely operated vehicle (ROV). Many commercial diving companies have ROVs available that can be used for this type of work and some dive teams are using this type of equipment regularly (see Figure 13.11).

Once the zone management system is in place, and the hazard has been identified, it is time to start dressing the diver. During the dress-in for a contaminated water dive, the diver should allow the tender to adjust the neck seal and other pieces of equipment as much as possible. There are two principle reasons for this: the tender can see things that may be wrong with the equipment that the diver may not be able to determine by feel alone, and the tender is less likely to tear or damage a neck seal or other piece of equipment than a diver working by himself.

Surface-supplied divers wearing a diving helmet should be assisted in mating the helmet to the dry suit yoke. Tenders who assist in mating the helmet to the suit must take care not to injure the diver's neck. The weight of the helmet itself, combined with careless handling by the tenders, can produce discomfort and possible injury.

While many scientific divers use dry gloves for cold water diving, using dry gloves in contaminated water requires extra care. Dry gloves should be kept separate from the internal pressure inside the suit. In cases where the gloves leak, they will compromise the diver's entire dry suit system. Clamps or waterproof tape should be used on the neutralizing agents must be employed. When the chemicals present are very toxic or hazardous, or where decontamination procedures are complex, the equipment is usually containerized for safe handling and transport. Gear used in wash-down may include hoses, brushes, showers, and equipment to capture and transport the used decontamination solution and equipment (see Figure 13.12). In cases of simple biological contamination, a child's wading pool may be sufficient in which to wash down the diver's equipment. All water used during the decontamination process, which normally involves fairly large quantities, must be captured. Recovery drums must be available to transport the spent decontamination fluids.

As the diver removes each piece of his equipment, it should be placed in a marked container or bag. There should be a tag attached to the container listing the date, the exposure time, the contaminants, the level of decontamination achieved, and what piece of gear is inside. Equipment that has been damaged or cannot be effectively decontaminated may need to be destroyed. Dive teams should remember to budget for replacing one-third of their equipment on an annual basis.

It is especially important to clean items such as dry suits and helmets as soon as possible after the dive. If the suit is damp inside from the diver's sweat, the suit will grow mold inside if it is not properly cleaned and dried. This final cleaning will take place during the definitive decontamination.

NOTE
Personal hygiene is the number one priority when diving in contaminated water.

Procedures required for major decontamination exposure are generally well recognized. A prudent decontamination, immunization, and monitoring protocol has been established following HAZ-MAT and medical authorities. Unfortunately, divers and support personnel exposed to mild or moderate contamination often disregard possible consequences of the exposure and fail to maintain personal hygiene as a minimum. Definitive decontamination for the diver includes a minimum 5 minute shower, during which he scrubs vigorously with a brush and appropriate decontamination solution, rinse,

FIGURE 13.12
Decontamination of Diver

and a second scrub, after removal of all dry suit undergarments and his bathing suit. The diver then towels himself dry, disposes of the towel, and enters a second shower. A mobile decontamination facility is the best location for these showers. Any cuts or scratches the diver receives during the course of the dive should be examined by a doctor, particularly if the injury occurs in biologically contaminated water. Biological contaminants can cause serious infections; therefore, divers must report any post-dive illness or other problems to the appropriate supervisory and medical personnel.

Definitive decontamination of diving equipment usually takes place at a dedicated facility. At a minimum, the valves in diving helmets and dry suits need to be completely disassembled and checked for any sign of damage. If the contaminants encountered during the dive are beyond the scope of the dive team, the manufacturer of the equipment should be contacted for further instructions. Dive equipment should never be returned to a manufacturer without contacting them first. All equipment used in contaminated water diving operations should have a use log and a maintenance log to record the information on the history of the gear. At the completion of maintenance, each piece of gear should be tagged and dated to indicate it is ready for the next operation. Any piece of equipment that is not operational should have a red tag clearly affixed to it indicating any problems with the gear.

13.6 ADDITIONAL RESOURCES
13.6.1 Resources for Consultation
The following resources are available for consultation regarding diving in contaminated water:

- NOAA Hazardous Materials and Assessment
   Division
   7600 Sand Point Way NE
   Seattle, WA 98115
   Telephone: (206) 526-6943 (Voice)
           (206) 526-6329 (Fax)
   E-mail: Nir.Barnea@noaa.gov

- U.S. Environmental Protection Agency
   Nation Health and Environmental
      Effects Research Laboratory
   1 Sabine Island
   Gulf Breeze, FL 32561-5299
   Telephone: (850) 934-9242 (Voice)
           (850) 934-9201 (Fax)

Rebreathers

Rebreathers 14

14.0 GENERAL

A rebreather is a type of self-contained underwater breathing apparatus that "recycles" most or all of each breath a diver takes, cleanses the carbon dioxide from it, and replenishes the oxygen. Although rebreathers were around before the 1880s, it is only in the last ten years that rebreathers have become a regularly accepted piece of equipment in the non-military communities.

The popularity of rebreathers has increased with the greater availability of nitrox breathing gas and the proliferation of computer chips. Where at one time rebreathers were rarely used outside of the military, today rebreathers are increasingly being used by recreational, technical, and scientific divers.

NOTE
Use of rebreathers by NOAA personnel requires special training and certification by the NOAA Diving Program.

14.1 TYPES OF REBREATHERS

There are three main categories of rebreathers, as well as some variations within these categories. The three principle types of rebreathers are:

1. Closed-Circuit Oxygen Systems
2. Semiclosed-Circuit Mixed-Gas Systems
3. Closed-Circuit Mixed-Gas Systems

14.1.1 Closed-Circuit Oxygen Systems

Closed-circuit oxygen systems, as their name implies, are designed to use pure oxygen as the breathing gas (see Figures 14.1, 14.2). They have a depth limitation of 25–30 fsw (8–10 msw) due to the oxygen partial pressure (see Chapter 3) and are among the simplest of rebreathers. This type of rebreather emits no bubbles during normal operation, except when the diver is ascending.

14.1.2 Semiclosed-Circuit Mixed-Gas Systems

Semiclosed-circuit mixed-gas systems are designed to recirculate most, but not all, of each exhalation from the

FIGURE 14.1
"Oxy-lung" Closed-Circuit Oxygen System

diver (see Figures 14.3–14.5). Semiclosed-circuit systems may either use pre-mixed gas or are "self-mixing." If the system uses pre-mixed gas (with a constant oxygen percentage), prior to diving the diver must select the proper mixture for his planned maximum operating depth and workload.

Semiclosed-circuit mixed-gas systems recirculate a mixture of nitrogen and oxygen (nitrox), or helium and oxygen (heliox) for deeper applications, by way of a breathing loop similar to that used on a closed-circuit oxygen system.

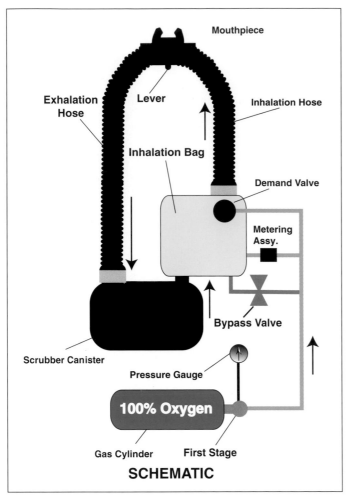

FIGURE 14.2
Closed-Circuit Oxygen System

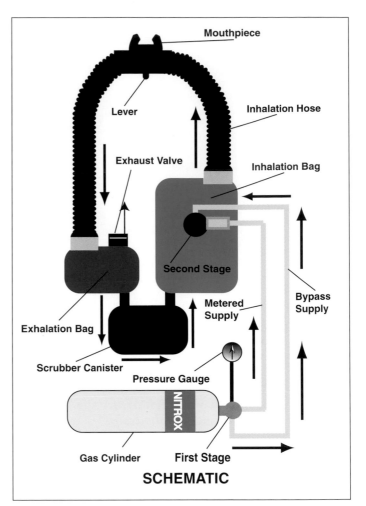

FIGURE 14.3
Semiclosed-Circuit Nitrox System

FIGURE 14.4
SIVA® Plus
Semiclosed
System

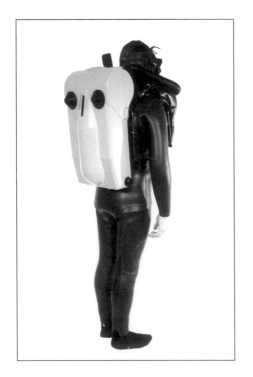

FIGURE 14.5
SIVA® Plus Semiclosed System with Shroud Removed

A small volume of fresh, oxygen-rich supply gas is injected into the breathing loop to compensate for the oxygen that the diver consumes during respiration. A corresponding volume of gas is exhausted from the breathing loop to maintain a near-constant volume of gas in the system. Semiclosed-circuit systems can be used to deeper depths than closed-circuit oxygen rebreathers, and conserve more gas than standard open-circuit scuba systems. No single semiclosed-system design has the capability of providing the diver with a safe system for all depths and workloads (Nuckols et al, 1998).

There are two basic design approaches used to control the injection of fresh make-up gas for semiclosed-circuit systems. The first uses one or more critical flow orifices or nozzles to maintain a constant mass injection rate of gas into the breathing loop. The oxygen concentration and the pre-set, fixed injection rate for the make-up gas must be selected to meet the oxygen demands of the diver during maximum expected activity levels. This is extremely important to help prevent hypoxia at shallow depths and hyperoxia at deeper depths.

The second design approach couples the injection of make-up gas with the diver's respiratory rate. These "respiratory-coupled" systems are based on the well-known fact that a diver's respiratory rate is roughly proportional to his metabolic oxygen requirement. These systems usually use some type of mechanical coupling device with the counter-lung, or breathing bag(s), to control either the injection rate of fresh make-up gas, or the rate at which gas is exhausted from the breathing circuit loop.

14.1.3 Closed-Circuit Mixed-Gas Systems

The closed-circuit system uses either pure gases or gas mixtures as the diluent with oxygen to provide nitrox or heliox. This type of system is very versatile with the deepest depth capability of all rebreathers (see Figures 14.6—14.8). These systems usually are dependent on electronics and battery power to control the gas mixture being supplied to the diver. These systems are generally the most complex types of rebreathers and have no inherent depth limitation.

In addition, closed and semiclosed-systems contain, or should contain, oxygen sensors. The use of separate high-pressure diluent and oxygen gas supplies is also unique to the closed-circuit mixed-gas system.

14.2 REBREATHER DESIGN

To work properly, a rebreather must meet a number of criteria, including the following:

- It must provide a reliable means for removing carbon dioxide from the diver's exhalations. This can be done chemically or electro-mechanically.
- It must supply a sufficient amount of oxygen to compensate for the oxygen the diver metabolizes with each breath. Too little oxygen and the diver will pass out from hypoxia; too much oxygen and the diver can suffer from oxygen toxicity (hyperoxia).

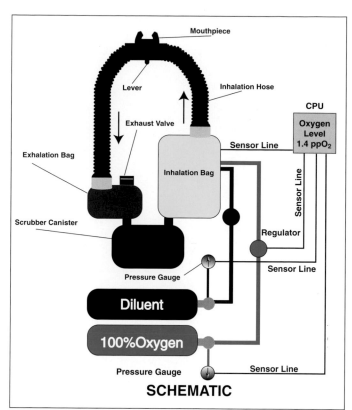

FIGURE 14.6
Closed-Circuit Mixed-Gas System

- The breathing "loop" must be adequately sealed to prevent water intrusion.
- The system must have as low a breathing resistance as possible, since the movement of the gas through the system is dependent on the diver's lung power to push the gas around the "loop." Breathing resistance is a critical issue in rebreather design (Clarke 1996), and dives where high work rates are expected are generally not recommended with this type of equipment.
- It is strongly recommended that all rebreathers have some type of oxygen monitoring system to measure the partial pressure of oxygen in the breathing loop.

All rebreathers contain the following minimum elements:

- Pressure reducing regulator(s)
- At least one flexible inhalation bag (breathing bag)
- Large diameter, low-pressure breathing hoses
- Scrubber canister and some type of carbon dioxide-absorbent system (either a chemical or mechanical device)

Another highly desirable element for rebreathers is a carbon dioxide sensor. The inability to monitor carbon

FIGURE 14.7
MK 16 Closed-Circuit System

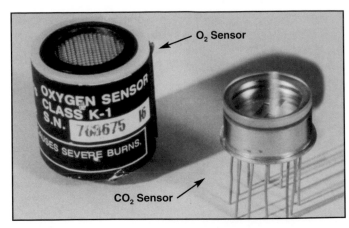

FIGURE 14.9
Oxygen Galvanic Sensor and Carbon Dioxide Sensor

dioxide in rebreathers has been a significant problem in the design of rebreathers to date. A carbon dioxide sensor allows direct monitoring of the CO_2 level in the breathing loop and provides valuable information for the calculation of a diver's decompression profile. Recent advances in carbon dioxide sensor design may someday allow such sensors to be a standard component of all rebreathers (see Figure 14.9).

FIGURE 14.8
MK 16 Closed-Circuit System with Shroud Removed

14.3 HOW REBREATHERS WORK

Although normal air contains 20.9 percent oxygen, the body does not consume all of the oxygen inhaled. How much oxygen is used in each breath depends primarily on how hard the diver is working.

As the diver moves into deeper water and the partial pressure of oxygen increases, the actual percentage of oxygen in the gas mixture needs to be reduced. For example, a saturation diver working at 400 fsw (122 msw) might be breathing a gas mixture of 96% helium and only 4% oxygen. By reusing the inert gas in the mixture and replacing the small amount of oxygen that is metabolically consumed, a diver using a closed-circuit system can stay under water for a significant period of time.

Most rebreathers use a chemical absorbent that is based upon a substance known as "soda lime" (see Figure 14.10). The chemical reaction of combining the carbon dioxide in the diver's exhaled breath with the absorbent produces heat and moisture as by-products, both of which are generally beneficial to the diver. The heat can be useful in helping to keep the diver's core temperature warm while the moisture helps prevent dehydration.

FIGURE 14.10
Chemical Absorbent

NOAA Diving Manual

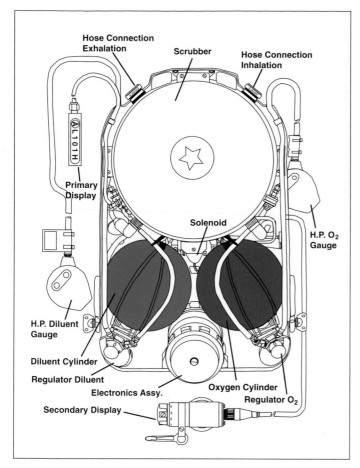

FIGURE 14.11
Components of Closed-Circuit Mixed-Gas System

Soda lime is a mixture of caustic soda (NaOH, sodium hydroxide) and lime (Ca(OH)$_2$, calcium hydroxide). Potassium hydroxide (KOH) is also usually included in the group (Stolp, Moon 1993). This same absorbent is used in research submersibles, underwater habitats, hyperbaric chambers, and diving bells.

While the absorbent material is housed in a canister that varies with different rebreather designs, canisters usually fall into one of two categories: radial flow or axial flow. In the radial flow design, the gas enters through an opening at one end of the canister and is dispersed out the sides. With axial flow, the gas enters through an opening at one end of the canister and exits at the other end, after traveling through the entire length of the canister. In either design, the canister must allow all gas to flow through it easily while ensuring that carbon dioxide is efficiently removed.

In a closed-circuit oxygen system, the gas flow is controlled by the actual volume of the gas in the breathing loop via a simple mechanical system that may consist of nothing more than a lever and a needle valve. When the volume in the breathing loop is depleted to a specific volume, the lever triggers the opening of the needle

valve, allowing the addition of oxygen which refills the inhalation bag (breathing bag). These systems are compact and lightweight, yet offer long bottom times within their limited depth range.

In a semiclosed-circuit system, there is a constant flow of breathing gas flowing into the unit at a controlled rate. As long as the gas supply to the system is turned on, gas flows through the rebreather and a portion of it flows out the exhaust valve.

In a closed-circuit mixed gas system the gas flow is frequently controlled by a solenoid valve that is controlled by the onboard electronics. The electronics will be one of two architectures: analog (older designs) or microprocessor. Redundant oxygen sensors are used to measure the amount of oxygen in the system and communicate with the electronics that control the solenoid's injection of oxygen (see Figure 14.11). It should be noted that there are still some older systems that have analog instead of digital electronics. Although these systems are designed to function automatically, they can all be operated in the manual mode by the diver in the event of electronic failure.

Some of the most sophisticated rebreathers today have computers built into them that control all functions. They also may be integrated with a dive computer to provide decompression calculations in real time. Several have the ability to download complete dive information to a PC so that the entire dive may be logged and reviewed.

The gas flow through the rebreather is simple. Oxygen and diluent gas from high-pressure cylinders are mixed with the remaining gas in the breathing loop prior to inhalation. The gas is supplied to the diver through a corrugated hose (right side), a one-way valve, and a mouthpiece with a shut-off valve (see Figure 14.12).

When the diver exhales, the gas travels into the mouthpiece, through a one-way valve on the exhaust side (left side), and into another corrugated hose. The gas passes into an exhalation bag or directly into the scrubber where the carbon dioxide is removed. From the scrubber, the gas flows back into the inhalation bag, or directly to the corrugated hose on the supply side. The gas travels around the loop based solely upon the diver's inhalation s and exhalations. There is no mechanical assist like there is with a demand scuba regulator.

Semiclosed and closed-circuit systems are relatively sophisticated and complex, and should only be used by properly trained and extremely competent divers. Rebreathers must be given the utmost respect because their use can easily lead to a diving accident if not scrupulously maintained and used properly.

14.4 ADVANTAGES OF REBREATHERS

There are a number of advantages to using rebreathers (Crosson and Youngblood 1996). These advantages can usually be classified as either physiological or operational.

FIGURE 14.12
Full-Face Mask with a Closed-Circuit Rebreather

The closed-circuit oxygen system utilizes 100 percent oxygen, thus no inert gas is absorbed in the tissues requiring staged decompression. This is the only physiological advantage of the oxygen rebreather. From an operational standpoint, the system allows bubble-free dives and has relatively low maintenance requirements.

Semiclosed-circuit mixed-gas systems have no real physiological advantage over open-circuit scuba systems. Operationally, however, they allow for a greater bottom time (due to the increased duration of the gas supply) when compared with open-circuit systems with an equal amount of available breathing gas.

There are several distinct advantages in closed-circuit mixed gas systems as compared with open-circuit scuba. From a physiological perspective, the diver's body can maintain the highest oxygen level practical thanks to a constant partial-pressure of oxygen. Since the oxygen level is maximized, the inert gas uptake is minimized and decompression time is typically reduced. Even if a diver is not using a higher oxygen concentration during the decompression phases of the dive, at minimum a constant level is maintained. When using open or semiclosed-circuit systems, the use of a fixed mixture causes the oxygen partial pressure to be lowered during the ascent, including

decompression stops. Reducing the oxygen concentration during the ascent phase of the dive is not a safe practice and should be avoided, since it is detrimental to decompression and may lead to hypoxia. Additional cylinders of oxygen can be carried by the diver, specifically for decompression; however, this increases the overall amount of equipment that must be carried by the diver throughout the entire dive. From an operational standpoint, the closed-circuit mixed-gas system has a number of advantages as compared with open-circuit systems: the duration of the closed-circuit system's gas supply is independent of depth, and a higher partial pressure of oxygen can be used during decompression without carrying extra gas cylinders.

Oxygen rebreathers have been used by scientific divers working for the California Department of Fish and Game (Wendell et al. 1996) and the U.S. Fish and Wildlife Service in their research and control programs with sea otters (*Enhydra lutris*). The oxygen rebreather is a good choice for this type of work because its compact size allows the divers to move quickly while releasing no bubbles. Since the otters are normally captured on the surface, there is no need for the divers to dive deep and the depth limitation of this type of gear is not a major concern.

For photography and close visual observations, rebreathers often allow the diver to get closer to certain animals than might normally be possible, due to the lack of bubbles and noise (see Figure 14.13). However, this isn't necessarily true with all creatures in all situations. To many species of fish, a diver still appears as a large, imposing predator, whether they produce bubbles or not.

For deep diving and overhead environments, a closed-circuit mixed-gas system is an ideal system. By using a

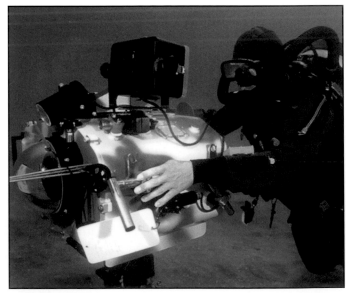

FIGURE 14.13
Advanced Underwater Photography System

rebreather, the need for multiple gas cylinders is eliminated and the total amount of weight and bulk the diver must carry is generally less. In addition, since the diver can control the amount of oxygen in the system, there is the added benefit of being able to increase the percentage of oxygen to almost 100 percent during precautionary decompression stops (safety stops) or actual decompression.

In polluted water, a rebreather used in conjunction with a full-face mask may be a better choice than open-circuit scuba with a full-face mask. By using a closed-circuit system, the chance of contaminants entering the breathing system through the exhaust valve is greatly reduced. See Chapter 13 on polluted-water diving.

Rebreathers can be tremendously helpful for scientific divers who must work from small boats. With a rebreather, divers have the ability to make very long dives without the need to carry a large number of cylinders. This is particularly advantageous for diving from an inflatable or other small vessel.

14.5 DISADVANTAGES OF REBREATHERS

Despite their many advantages, rebreathers also have some serious limitations and disadvantages that restrict their use to specific applications. These disadvantages relate to their costs, training, and risks.

Rebreathers are more expensive to purchase, operate, and maintain than open-circuit scuba. Even the least expensive semiclosed-circuit system is considerably more than the price of open-circuit scuba.

In addition to purchasing the rebreather itself, there are several essential and desirable accessories that should be part of any rebreather system. These accessories include an oxygen analyzer for checking gas mixtures, flow check apparatus for testing semiclosed-circuit systems, and bailout systems. Another accessory would be a full-face mask. The application of a full-face mask is certainly of value in polluted water, but when discussing the pros and cons, it should be noted that an open-circuit system can provide a constant positive pressure while the closed-circuit system cannot.

Full-face masks are suggested for use with rebreathers because they give the diver some protection in the event the diver passes out either due to hypoxia or hyperoxia (Barsky et al. 1998). A full-face mask will help prevent the inhalation of water and drowning during unconsciousness or an oxygen convulsion. Of course, it is still essential to get the victim back to the surface as quickly as possible if either of these events occur. If a full-face mask is to be used, a "switchover block" should be used to facilitate the use of an open-circuit bailout while keeping the mask in place.

Rebreather divers should be nitrox qualified prior to starting a rebreather training course. Candidates for rebreather training should have demonstrated the discipline required to dive nitrox mixtures within their limits.

Because there are no two rebreathers that are identical, rebreather training is system specific. Even though divers may have extensive experience diving with a particular unit, if they switch to another rebreather, they will need to complete a training course for the new rebreather. While the principles of rebreather diving will be the same for all units, the actual operation and mechanics will almost always be extremely different.

The pre-diving preparation for a rebreather dive is more time consuming than the predive preparation for an open-circuit dive. For a semiclosed-circuit system it might take 15–20 minutes to set up the gear. It might take anywhere from half an hour to an hour to completely prep a closed-circuit mixed-gas system for a dive. Similarly, postdive maintenance is also time consuming.

Rebreathers typically use nitrox for shallow diving and helium-oxygen mixtures for deeper work. All of these gas mixtures are more expensive to produce than ordinary compressed air. In addition, rebreathers require the use of carbon dioxide absorbent which costs additional money, and closed-circuit mixed-gas rigs also use batteries.

Aside from the initial costs of purchasing the rebreather and the consumables that are used on each dive, maintenance of a rebreather is a time consuming and expensive task. Each diver who uses a rebreather must be fully trained in the maintenance and basic repairs for that system.

Most rebreathers have more components than a typical open circuit scuba system; consequently there are higher annual maintenance costs for replacement of parts. Replacement parts may include hoses, O-rings, sensors, valves, and breathing bags. Since rebreathers are not manufactured in large quantities, the cost for these parts will generally be higher than what they would be for open-circuit scuba parts.

While closed-circuit mixed-gas systems offer tremendous depth capabilities, there is a danger associated with this capability since the diver can incur an extreme decompression obligation. For this reason, it is essential that appropriate back-up systems be in place and that meticulous dive planning occur prior to the dive (Pyle 1996). Extended deep dives with rebreathers may be beyond the scope of what most scientific diving organizations' risk management will allow.

14.6 RISKS ASSOCIATED WITH REBREATHER DIVING

Aside from the normal risks of diving, there are four areas which must be of special concern to rebreather divers. These include hypoxia (insufficient oxygen), hyperoxia (oxygen toxicity), hypercapnia (CO_2 poisoning), and exposure to caustic mixtures which occur when chemical absorbents are exposed to water.

14.6.1 Hypoxia

There are several ways in which hypoxia can occur with a semiclosed-circuit system. These include failure to activate the cylinder, inadequate maintenance, failure to select the appropriate orifice for the gas mix used, or hypoxia during ascent due to lack of flushing of the breathing bags prior to ascent. Since hypoxia gives very little or no warning, these incidents are almost always fatal unless there is another diver immediately available to assist the disabled victim.

Unlike open-circuit scuba, if the diver fails to turn a rebreather's gas cylinder(s) on, he can still breathe the gas within the system. Should the diver further fail to check his oxygen monitoring display there is nothing to warn the diver of the falling level of oxygen in the system.

Selecting the wrong metering orifice or setting for the gas mixture in use can also lead to a hypoxic episode if the flow rate is too slow for a particular gas mixture. Although gas will be flowing into the rebreather, the diver will be using oxygen faster than the system supplies it, leading to black-out. This is why the projected workload must be considered when selecting the correct orifice size in semiclosed-circuit systems.

14.6.2 Oxygen Toxicity

Oxygen toxicity is always a possibility when a diver is using gas mixtures with an oxygen level outside established limits. Using a rebreather, the risks of oxygen toxicity may be greater depending upon the type of rebreather and how it is used.

For example, with a semiclosed-circuit system using pre-mixed gas, if the diver is working hard and his oxygen uptake is high, it is possible to exceed the maximum operating depth (MOD) for the mix without getting a high oxygen alarm. However, once the diver rests or vents the system, the oxygen level will climb rapidly and the diver could be exposed to a PO_2 high enough to cause oxygen toxicity.

If the diver is using a closed-circuit mixed-gas system and has deliberately flooded the system with oxygen for purposes of decompression, the risk of CNS oxygen toxicity is high if the diver fails to maintain the proper depth. Since the level of oxygen can be varied by the diver while using this type of equipment, the risk of oxygen poisoning is always present. Given that the symptoms of oxygen toxicity can occur without warning (Donald 1992), only the most conscientious and safety conscious candidates should be selected for rebreather training. There is little margin of error with this type of gear.

14.6.3 Hypercapnia

Carbon dioxide poisoning will occur any time the absorbent material is used beyond the point at which it can effectively remove CO_2 from the diver's exhaled breath. The onset of carbon dioxide poisoning usually occurs more slowly than oxygen poisoning, but must not be ignored. When planning deeper dives with a significant decompression obligation, the canister duration must be considered. If the decompression time exceeds the canister life, the diver must plan on switching to an "off-board," open-circuit decompression gas delivery system.

Carbon dioxide poisoning can also be the result of an improperly filled scrubber canister. If the canister is not properly packed with absorbent, a phenomenon known as "channeling" can take place. Channeling is defined as the movement of gas through a canister without exposure to active absorbent. Since gas flow takes the path of least resistance, it bypasses the absorbent material and flows through the open channel.

14.6.4 Caustic Mix

When a rebreather floods, one of the most serious hazards from this type of accident occurs when the carbon dioxide absorbent used in the scrubber canister becomes wet. The reaction between most absorbents and water can produce a caustic solution that causes severe chemical burns. This is more commonly referred to as a "caustic cocktail." Some of the more recent CO_2 absorbent agents do not cause chemical burns.

14.7 GENERAL PROCEDURES FOR REBREATHER DIVING

While the procedures for diving with different types of rebreathers are system specific, there are general procedures that are recommended for all rebreathers. Aside from some of the factors that have already been discussed, other critical issues include the maintenance of a rebreather log, dive planning, buoyancy control, and emergency procedures.

Every rebreather diver needs to keep a "maintenance and use log" for their rebreather so they can track the remaining time on batteries, oxygen sensors, and absorbent. Without an accurate log, it is impossible to know when components need to be replaced or service needs to be performed.

Dive planning is even more critical with a rebreather than it is with open-circuit scuba. Divers using semiclosed-circuit systems with pre-mixed gas must observe the depth limits for the mix selected. Divers using closed-circuit mixed-gas systems must plan their dive based upon their mission as well as allowing for an ample gas reserve to cover contingencies.

As with all diving, proper buoyancy control is essential to productivity and safety. Most rebreathers require some additional weight to counteract the buoyancy of the breathing bags (see Figure 14.14). The placement of this weight is critical to good trim and ease of swimming and working under water. Different rebreathers will require the placement of additional weights in varying locations according to the design of the rebreather, desired swim attitude, and other factors.

During the dive, it is essential to monitor the rebreather regularly for any malfunction. With a rebreather, problems are usually not immediately obvious like they are with open-circuit scuba. Careful rebreather divers make it a habit to check critical gauges and displays regularly, and keep an eye on their partner's rig for leaks or other problems.

In most cases of rebreather failure, the response to the emergency will be the same; i.e., the diver switches to open circuit bail-out and terminates the dive. While most closed-circuit electronic systems have ways to operate the rebreather in the manual mode if the electronics fail, the diver must always be prepared to switch to open circuit bail-out and terminate the dive.

Prior to any direct ascent, it is always prudent for the diver to check gauges, locate buoyancy compensator hoses, and stabilize breathing. With a semiclosed-circuit system, the diver must always completely flush the breathing system in order to avoid the possibility of ascent hypoxia. If this is not done and the diver has been working hard, it is possible for the diver to pass out during ascent as the partial pressure of oxygen in the breathing loop falls. If the oxygen content in the breathing loop is not at the desired level, or at least at an acceptable level, there will be a further reduction in the oxygen partial-pressure during ascent. The resulting level may be dangerously hypoxic, depending on the PO_2 prior to leaving the bottom and the distance to the surface.

During ascent, it is also essential for the diver to carefully monitor his buoyancy as the gas expanding in the breathing bags can cause an increase in buoyancy. The diver must be prepared to vent additional gas from his dry suit or buoyancy compensator to cope with this change in buoyancy.

Postdive maintenance must be performed as soon as possible after the diving day is completed. Rebreathers are not as tolerant as open-circuit equipment when maintenance is neglected. Due to the closed nature of the breathing loop, it is very easy for bacteria and fungus to grow in the breathing bags and hoses if these are not thoroughly cleaned and dried after diving.

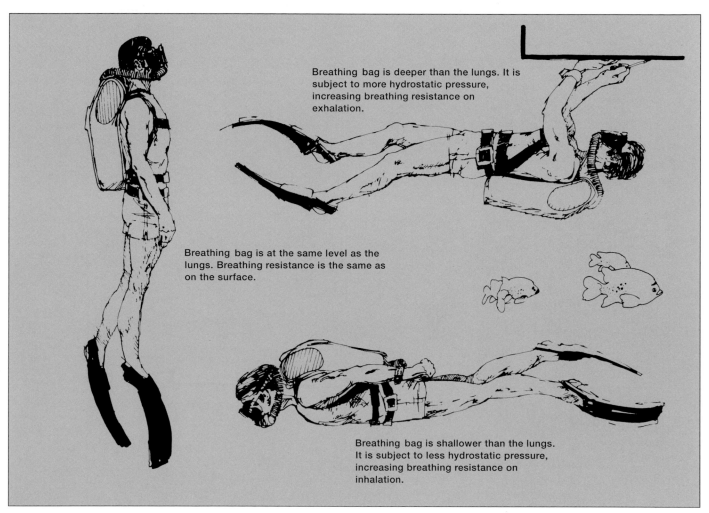

Breathing bag is deeper than the lungs. It is subject to more hydrostatic pressure, increasing breathing resistance on exhalation.

Breathing bag is at the same level as the lungs. Breathing resistance is the same as on the surface.

Breathing bag is shallower than the lungs. It is subject to less hydrostatic pressure, increasing breathing resistance on inhalation.

FIGURE 14.14
Effects of Hydrostatic Pressure on Location of Breathing Bags

Nitrox Diving

Nitrox Diving

15.1 NITROGEN-OXYGEN BREATHING MIXTURES

Divers have used air as a breathing gas since the beginning of diving. Its principal advantage is that it is readily available and inexpensive to compress into cylinders or use directly from compressors with surface-supplied diving equipment. Air is not the "ideal" breathing mixture for diving because of the effects of nitrogen narcosis at deeper depths and the decompression liability it imposes. Since decompression obligation is dependent on exposure to inspired nitrogen partial pressure, this obligation can be reduced by replacing a portion of the nitrogen content of divers' breathing gas with oxygen, which is metabolized by the body. This is the fundamental benefit of nitrogen-oxygen diving (Wells 1989).

The two most commonly used nitrogen-oxygen mixtures in NOAA are 32% and 36% oxygen, called NOAA Nitrox 32 (NN32) and NOAA Nitrox 36 (NN36). The remainder, the other gas in nitrox mixes, is nitrogen. Other mixes can be used with permission from the NOAA Diving Office. "Nitrox" is a generic term that can be used for any gaseous mixture of nitrogen and oxygen, but in the context of this chapter, the implication is that nitrox is a mixture with more oxygen than that in air. Using NN32 or NN36 versus air can significantly increase the amount of time a diver can spend at depth without incurring additional decompression.

Table 15.1, which is a comparison of air and the NOAA nitrox mixes for no-stop dive times measured in minutes, clearly indicates why oxygen-rich mixtures are a preferred choice for diving in the 50–130 fsw (15–40 msw) depth range.

A diver making a 90 fsw (28 msw) dive using one of these mixtures can increase the air no-stop dive time from 30 minutes to as much as 50 minutes. Assuming a diver uses a 30-foot-per-minute rate of descent, a diver using air will have only 27 minutes on the bottom, whereas the diver breathing NN36 will have 47 minutes. This is a 74 percent increase in bottom time.

But the increased bottom time does not come without an operational price tag. Nitrox diving comes with limits and safety procedures. This chapter explains why nitrox works

TABLE 15.1
No-Stop Dive Times

Depth (fsw)	(msw)	USN Air 21%	NN32 32%	NN36 36%
50	15	100	200	310
60	18	60	100	100
70	22	50	60	60
80	25	40	50	60
90	28	30	40	50
100	31	25	30	40
110	34	20	25	30
120	37	15	25	
130	40	10	20	

and describes how NOAA divers take advantage of this principle for their scientific underwater work.

15.1.1 Early Use of Nitrogen-Oxygen Breathing Mixtures

The use of oxygen-rich breathing gases for diving is not a new concept. References to such gas mixes go back to the 19th century. The eminent American physicist and chemist, Elihu Thompson (1853–1936), first proposed the breathing of hydrogen and oxygen (Davis 1962). The U.S. Navy has used nitrox effectively with semiclosed rebreathers since the 1950s when it was studied intensively by Dr. Edward H. Lanphier, and also by Dr. Christian J. Lambertsen.

Commercial application of nitrogen-oxygen mixtures was practiced from the late 1950s, particularly by André Galerne at International Underwater Contractors (IUC) of New York (Galerne 1989). These techniques were used to a limited extent by IUC and other commercial companies. When equipment for on-line mixing of oxygen and air was developed, nitrox techniques became more popular and were used more extensively by a few commercial diving companies.

15.1.2 NOAA Use of Nitrox Breathing Mixtures

NOAA's involvement with nitrox breathing mixtures began in the mid-1970s in an effort to increase the efficiency of diving operations. The cost per hour of bottom time for diving operations can be quite expensive considering all the various direct and indirect costs involved with extended at-sea operations (i.e., vessel operating costs, salaries of personnel, diving equipment, etc.). The increase in useful bottom time provided by the use of nitrox mixtures results in a reduction of dives or divers required to accomplish a given amount of work; thus, it is a very cost-effective way to reduce the cost per hour of bottom time.

In early 1977, Dr. J. Morgan Wells, then Director of the NOAA Diving Program, proposed using nitrox breathing mixtures with open-circuit diving equipment (scuba or surface-supplied) for NOAA diving operations. The proposal was based on a fixed nitrogen and oxygen mixture containing 32% oxygen. This gas mixture, which was designated "NOAA Nitrox I," (now called NN32) was selected based on two parameters: 1) a maximum operating depth of 130 fsw (40 msw), which also corresponded to the maximum depth limit for NOAA scuba diving, and 2) a maximum partial pressure of oxygen of 1.6 ata, which was, and still is, the maximum PO_2 authorized for normal diving operations within NOAA. Decompression tables were developed for both no-stop and decompression diving operations. The original Nitrox Tables were identical to the U.S. Navy Standard Air Decompression Tables in format and use.

The proposal was approved by NOAA's Diving Safety Board and Diving Medical Review Board in late 1977 and a series of tests were conducted to verify the validity of the decompression tables using Doppler bubble-monitoring techniques. Following successful test results, NN32 was approved for NOAA-wide use in early 1978. The NN32 decompression tables were subsequently published in the second edition of the *NOAA Diving Manual* in 1979.

In 1984, Dr. Wells and the NOAA Diving Program (NDP) developed a system for mixing air and oxygen and compressing it to pressures of over 3,000 psig. The system, designated the "NOAA Continuous Nitrox Mixer," involved injecting low-pressure oxygen into the intake of a compressor that does not allow oil to come in contact with the air being compressed (oil-free or oil-less). The oxygen was combined with air in a mixing coil prior to entering the compressor. The result was a high-pressure mix containing a higher fraction of oxygen than found in normal atmospheric air. The gas could then be used to fill storage cylinders or individual scuba cylinders. The system significantly reduced the cost and time required to prepare nitrogen-oxygen gas mixes. NOAA continuous nitrox mixing systems were installed at several NOAA diving units and on-site training was conducted by NDP personnel.

Meanwhile, at approximately the same time, the NOAA National Undersea Research Center at the University of North Carolina in Wilmington (NURC/UNCW) developed a comprehensive nitrox diving program to support undersea research efforts in the South Atlantic Bight and Gulf of Mexico. With the assistance of Dr. Wells, the NURC/UNCW program developed standards and procedures for using nitrox, a mixing system (which eventually progressed from a simple partial pressure system to a continuous mixer using an oxygen generator), a nitrox diver training program, and decompression tables for oxygen-enriched mixtures between 30–40% oxygen content.

To date, NURC/UNCW has conducted over 25,000 nitrox dives, making their program one of the most active in the United States. Besides using nitrox mixtures in support of field operations, the NURC/UNCW program also actively promoted nitrox in the scientific diving community by publishing and presenting numerous technical papers at various symposia and conferences, conducting workshops and training sessions, and assisting other organizations in the development of similar diving programs. Much of the credit for the widespread acceptance of nitrox in the scientific diving community belongs to NURC/UNCW.

Later NOAA authorized a second mix for use by NOAA divers. Designated then as "NOAA Nitrox II," (now called NN36) this mixture contained 36% oxygen. The mixture was designed to maximize bottom time at or near 100 fsw (31 msw). Both the 32% and 36% nitrox decompression tables are included in this fourth edition of the manual. See Appendix VII.

In 1988, the National Undersea Research Program (NURP) and Harbor Branch Oceanographic Institution (HBOI) sponsored a workshop on the use of nitrox mixtures for diving. Leading experts in the fields of decompression, oxygen physiology, dive computers, gas logistics, and rebreathers from the scientific, military, and commercial diving community assembled at the HBOI facility in Fort Pierce, Florida to discuss the subject. The consensus of the workshop was that the concepts and approaches being used were sound, and basically endorsed the use of nitrox for diving applications. A report titled, "Workshop on Enriched-Air Nitrox Diving" (Hamilton et al. 1989), known informally as the Harbor Branch Nitrox Workshop, was generated and presented the state-of-the-art information on nitrox diving at the time.

NOAA's development of a continuous blending system increased the safety and effectiveness of the preparation of nitrox mixtures. The original and widely used version of this apparatus used pure, high-pressure oxygen. In 1989, the NOAA Experimental Diving Unit began investigating alternative methods of supplying oxygen to the blending system. The system utilized gas separation devices ("oxygen generators") which essentially extract oxygen from atmospheric air. Two fundamentally different gas separators were investigated: a pressure swing adsorption system (PSA) and a membrane separation system. The PSA system utilized the selective adsorption-desorption characteristics of nitrogen on molecular sieve material (clay-like) during pressurization and depressurization with air. The membrane-based system depends on the differential rates of diffusion of gases through the walls of hollow fibers pressurized with air. Both systems utilize compressed air as a gas source and produce streams of high oxygen/low nitrogen and low oxygen/high nitrogen gases. The high oxygen/low nitrogen function is used with the NOAA Continuous Nitrox Mixer to produce nitrox mixtures for diving. This new system offers the advantage of providing high oxygen mixtures without the problems associated with the purchase, transportation, storage, and handling of high pressure or liquid oxygen. The system has proven to be particularly useful in remote areas where oxygen availability is limited and expensive, or aboard ships where space for storage of cylinders is limited.

Nitrox was not confined to only NOAA, NURC, and a few commercial diving companies. In 1985, Dick Rutkowski, retired Training Director of the NOAA Diving Program, developed a training and certification program for the recreational diver. Today, 20 years after its formal introduction to NOAA's diving program, most recreational scuba training agencies have some type of nitrox diver-training program and the mixes are used widely among recreational and technical divers.

Although nitrox diving has become fashionable in the civilian community, it is important to realize that using gases other than air (be it heliox, trimix, or nitrox) requires the diver and support personnel to maintain a high level of training and proficiency in order to maximize safety.

15.2 MISCONCEPTIONS

Nitrox is safer than air. "Safe" to most people means without risk, and all diving contains a level of risk. Nitrox has significant decompression advantages over air, but to take advantage of those benefits other risks must be managed. The risks include oxygen toxicity, conforming to the required depth and time limits, ensuring that the right mix is used, the need for special equipment maintenance, a requirement for gas analysis, and the risks involved in gas mixing. When all are managed properly, the risks are minimal, just as for air diving in the same depth ranges.

Nitrox is for deep diving. Quite the contrary, nitrox has very stringent depth limits because of the higher concentration of oxygen in the mixture. The greatest advantages for no-stop diving are in the 50–110 fsw (15–34 msw) diving range. The two standard mixtures of 32% and 36% oxygen have maximum operational depths of 130 fsw (40 msw) and 110 fsw (34 msw) respectively (at a PO_2 of 1.6 ata). There are other applications for using oxygen or high-oxygen mixtures to accelerate decompression and for supplementing decompression to build in an additional safety margin, but those particular mixes are used only in the shallow part of the dive.

Nitrox eliminates the risk of decompression sickness. No gas or diving table can absolutely ensure that a diver will not get decompression sickness. Using nitrox provides significant decompression advantages over air, but with all diving there is a risk of decompression sickness. The procedures and techniques in this chapter can help minimize those risks while maximizing diving time.

Nitrox makes treatment for decompression sickness impossible. In the event that a diver who was breathing nitrox develops decompression sickness, the treatment is conducted in the same manner as an air diver incident, taking into account the possibility of extra oxygen exposure. An early misconception was that the extra oxygen exposure would compromise a hyperbaric treatment, and this was extended to mean the diver could not be treated at all.

Nitrox reduces narcosis. Initially it would seem logical that with reduced nitrogen in the breathing mix there would be reduced nitrogen narcosis at depth. Although this has not been adequately studied, oxygen's properties suggest that it can also be a narcotic gas under pressure. The result is that one should not expect a significant change in narcosis when diving nitrox as compared to air (Bennett 1970; Linnarsson, Ostlund, Sporrong, Lind, and Hamilton 1990).

15.3 TERMINOLOGY

A number of terms are introduced and used in this chapter. These mainly address names for the gas mixtures and type of diving.

The early terms for nitrogen-oxygen mixtures as used by the U.S. Navy were called just that, nitrogen-oxygen mixtures, or nitrox. As with any other breathing gas mixtures, because of the different ways it can be expressed, it is important always to specify all the major component gases as well as the percentages.

Other terms often used to describe oxygen-rich mixtures, called "nitrox" in this chapter, include oxygen-enriched air (OEA) and enriched-air nitrox (EAN). From the latter of these have evolved the terms "EAN or "EANx." The "x" was originally the "x" in nitrox, but in some usage it has become a subscript showing the oxygen percentage, as in EAN32 for 32% oxygen. Historically, NOAA had referred to the 32% and 36% mixtures as "NOAA Nitrox I" and "NOAA Nitrox II," respectively. To more clearly identify the oxygen content in these two mixes, NOAA has redesignated them as NN32 and NN36.

15.4 ADVANTAGES OF NITROX

Nitrox breathing mixtures are beneficial in helping to prevent decompression sickness (DCS). Using a gas mixture with less nitrogen in it effectively lowers this risk. This does not mean that a diver will never get decompression sickness; it means with proper management, the already small risk of DCS can be even smaller when diving with oxygen-rich mixtures.

Nitrox mixtures are of special value in the multi-day, repetitive-dive series. No-stop dive incident statistics show that almost 80 percent of recreational cases of decompression sickness are a result of repetitive air dives (Divers Alert Network 2000). If a diver were to dive the same time and depth profiles with nitrox instead of air, not only would the decompression be less, but there would also be an overall reduction of nitrogen in the body, thereby lowering the risk of decompression sickness.

15.4.1 Repetitive Dive Example

The following examples compare two dives, one using NN36 and the other air (see Figure 15.1). Notice that NN36 provides twice as much bottom time on the second dive as the air dive (36 minutes instead of 17 minutes).

Example 1:

A diver breathing air completes the first dive to 90 fsw (28 msw) for 20 minutes, waits one hour between dives, and then is allowed a repetitive no-stop dive to 80 fsw (25 msw) for 17 minutes. Maximum bottom time for 80 fsw with no-decompression stops is 40 minutes minus 23 minutes residual nitrogen time resulting in 17 minutes (using U.S. Navy Dive Tables).

Example 2:

A diver breathing NN36 does the same first dive to 90 fsw (28 msw) for 20 minutes, waits one hour between dives and then can do a repetitive dive to 80 fsw (25 msw) for 36 minutes. This is over twice the no-stop time as is allowed when using air.

The diver using NN36 in this example has a 19-minute no-stop time advantage over the diver doing a similar profile with air. The air diver would have to complete a 17-minute decompression stop at 10 fsw (3 msw) to do a 30-minute, second dive. This becomes significant when scientists have multiple dives to do over multiple days. By replacing some of the nitrogen with oxygen in the breathing mixture, the divers can conduct their work with minimal or no required decompression stops.

Example 1: Air
First Dive   90 fsw/20 mins no-stop
       One hour surface interval, Group F ——> E
Second Dive   80 fsw/17 mins no-stop
Example 2: NN36
First Dive   90 fsw/20 mins no-stop
       One hour surface interval, Group E ——> D
Second Dive   80 fsw/36 mins no-stop

FIGURE 15.1
Comparison of Air Versus NN36

15.5 SELECTING A NITROX MIX

Diving with nitrox gas mixtures requires the completion of a variety of critical predive tasks. They include choosing an appropriate mix, planning operating depths, managing oxygen exposure, and choosing the appropriate decompression table. As with all types of diving, there is a planning process; with nitrox diving it is essential that each component be examined carefully, as each will affect the others. With time and practice most divers become familiar with the planning process and it becomes automatic.

This section deals with selecting the most appropriate mix based on the partial pressure of the gas for the depth of the dive. It is important to remember that all time spent on a dive may not be at one constant depth, but may be at many different depths throughout the dive. For purposes of oxygen management for dive planning, nitrox divers should not exceed an oxygen partial pressure of 1.6 ata under any conditions and may want to further limit exposure when doing other than light work or exertion (see Chapter 3).

15.5.1 Concerns of the Mix

The most important concern is that the mix chosen is the most appropriate for the dive planned. Too much oxygen in the mix increases risk of oxygen toxicity; while too much nitrogen, shortens the no-stop time. Using the wrong mix with the wrong table could lead to decompression sickness. It is important that only the appropriate mix be used with the correct decompression table.

Oxygen in high doses becomes toxic and can cause central nervous system problems if the dose is too high for too long (see Chapter 3). The partial pressure of oxygen at depth is the depth limiting factor for any nitrox mixture. A key facet in nitrox dive planning is to optimize the oxygen level by displacing as much nitrogen as possible while remaining within the oxygen exposure limits.

The two standard NOAA nitrox mixes, 32% and 36% oxygen content, are considered the best all around gas mixes for dives in the 50–130 fsw (15–40 msw) depth range (Mastro 1989). Other mixes can be used for specific depths; they are determined by selecting the mix based upon a partial pressure at depth and dive time desired.

15.5.2 Oxygen Exposure Time

In choosing the appropriate mix, the diver should refer to the NOAA Oxygen Exposure Limits (see Table 15.2). The lower the PO_2, the longer the dive can be conducted from an oxygen tolerance perspective. However, reducing the oxygen exposure limits also reduces the depth at which certain mixtures may be used. For example, using NN32 at a depth of 130 fsw (40 msw) results in a PO_2 to 1.58 ata, which limits exposure time to 45 minutes. Using the same mixture, but limiting the PO_2 to 1.4 ata, the exposure time would be increased to 150 minutes, but the mixture could not be used deeper than 111 fsw (34 msw).

Nitrox dives are planned with PO_2 levels not exceeding 1.6 ata, though a slightly lower level provides less oxygen exposure risk. These levels provide significant single exposure bottom time with a relativity low risk of oxygen toxicity.

TABLE 15.2
NOAA Oxygen Exposure Limits

PO2 (atm)	Maximum Single Exposure (minutes)	Maximum per 24 hr (minutes)
1.60	45	150
1.55	83	165
1.50	120	180
1.45	135	180
1.40	150	180
1.35	165	195
1.30	180	210
1.25	195	225
1.20	210	240
1.10	240	270
1.00	300	300
0.90	360	360
0.80	450	450
0.70	570	570
0.60	720	720

15.5.3 Maximum Operating Depth

The Maximum Operating Depth (MOD) is the maximum depth that should be dived routinely with a given nitrox mixture. The MOD is determined by the limits of oxygen exposure. NOAA considers the maximum operating PO2 for dives to be 1.6 ata; this limits dives to 45 minutes. A lower PO2 would result in a longer dive with a lower oxygen exposure and may be warranted under certain circumstances. Higher than 1.6 ata, the risk of CNS oxygen toxicity increases dramatically and becomes unacceptable.

NOAA requires that the MOD be displayed prominently on the diver's cylinder. Typically, it is displayed on a tag attached to the cylinder valve.

To calculate the maximum depth for a given mix, find out how many atmospheres of a mix it takes to produce a PO2 at a given level, and then convert the figure back to fsw. First, determine the fraction of an atmosphere of oxygen (FO2) in each atmosphere of the mix, then divide the PO2 limit by this value. Next convert this number from absolute units back to depth units by subtracting one atmosphere and multiplying the number of atmospheres remaining by 33, the number of fsw per atm.

$$MOD, \text{fsw} = \left(\frac{(PO_2 \text{ limit}, ata)}{(FO_2 \text{ mix}, ata)} - 1 \text{ ata} \right) \times 33 \text{ fsw/atm}$$

Or, the conversion back to fsw can be done by multiplying by 33 first, then subtracting the number of fsw in one atmosphere.

$$MOD, \text{fsw} = \left(\frac{(PO_2 \text{ limit}, ata)}{(FO_2 \text{ mix}, ata)} \times 33 \text{ fsw/atm} \right) - 33 \text{ fsw}$$

For example, to determine the MOD for 36% oxygen, which has an FO2 of 0.36, at a limit of 1.6 ata, divide 1.6 ata by 0.36, then subtract 1 and multiply the results by 33.

$$MOD, \text{fsw} = \left(\frac{(1.6 \text{ ata})}{(0.36)} - 1 \text{ ata} \right) \times 33 \text{ fsw/atm} = 113 \text{ fsw}$$

15.5.4 Partial Pressure of Oxygen Chart

The calculation of partial pressure can be made easier using the Partial Pressure of Oxygen, Table 15.3. To use the chart to find the depth for a given PO2 with a specific mix, enter from the top under the percentage of oxygen in the mix, then slide down that column to the number that is closest to but does not exceed the desired PO2, then move to the left to the fsw/msw column to read the depth. Chart calculations were created by first converting fsw to ata, then multiplying the fraction of oxygen by that number.

15.5.5 Fraction of Oxygen for the Mix

Once the diver has determined the PO2 level for the dive, the next step is to find the correct fraction of oxygen needed to prepare the mix. This calculation is based on the final partial pressure of the oxygen that is desired.

For most nitrox diving operations, the standard 32% and 36% oxygen mixes are normally sufficient. There may be times, however, when a dive calls for the most no-stop dive time for a specific depth. This would be achieved by determining the fraction or percentage of oxygen needed for that depth and having a specific mix blended for that dive.

Table 15.4 provides oxygen percentages for PO2 levels from 1.3–1.6 ata and depths to 130 fsw (40 msw). One can also make these calculations by formula. Select the desired PO2 and divide by the depth of the dive converted to atmospheres absolute. This will result in the fraction of the gas needed to be mixed which may be converted to percentage by multiplying by 100.

This is another application of the basic formula for partial pressure. Remember to convert fsw to ata.

$$FO_2 \text{ Fraction} = \frac{PO_2 \text{ (ata)}}{\text{Depth (ata)}}$$

For example, if the PO2 is to be 1.6 ata, the best mix for a dive at 85 fsw (3.58 ata) is 1.6 ata /3.58 ata, or 44.6% oxygen (rounded down to 44%), and 56% nitrogen so as not to exceed the 1.6 PO2 limit. It is important that rounding of values be in the direction of prudence.

The planning process can also be done in reverse, as is shown with the maximum operating depth of a given mix (see Figure 15.2). For example, how deep can a 32%

Nitrox Diving

TABLE 15.3
Partial Pressure of Oxygen

Depth (fsw)	(msw)	atm abs	21%	28%	29%	30%	31%	32%	33%	34%	35%	36%	37%	38%	39%	40%
0	0	1.00	0.21	0.28	0.29	0.30	0.31	0.32	0.33	0.34	0.35	0.36	0.37	0.38	0.39	0.40
35	11	2.05	0.43	0.57	0.59	0.62	0.64	0.66	0.68	0.70	0.72	0.74	0.76	0.78	0.80	0.82
40	12	2.21	0.46	0.62	0.64	0.66	0.69	0.71	0.73	0.75	0.77	0.80	0.82	0.84	0.86	0.88
50	15	2.52	0.53	0.71	0.73	0.76	0.78	0.81	0.83	0.86	0.88	0.91	0.93	0.96	0.98	1.01
60	18	2.82	0.59	0.79	0.82	0.85	0.87	0.90	0.93	0.96	0.99	1.02	1.04	1.07	1.10	1.13
70	22	3.12	0.66	0.87	0.90	0.94	0.97	1.00	1.03	1.06	1.09	1.12	1.15	1.19	1.22	1.25
80	25	3.42	0.72	0.96	0.99	1.03	1.06	1.09	1.13	1.16	1.20	1.23	1.27	1.30	1.33	1.37
90	28	3.73	0.78	1.04	1.08	1.12	1.16	1.19	1.23	1.27	1.31	1.34	1.38	1.42	1.45	1.49
100	31	4.03	0.85	1.13	1.17	1.21	1.25	1.29	1.33	1.37	1.41	1.45	1.49	1.53	1.57	1.61
110	34	4.33	0.91	1.21	1.26	1.30	1.34	1.39	1.43	1.47	1.52	1.56	1.60	1.65	1.69	1.73
120	37	4.64	0.97	1.30	1.35	1.39	1.44	1.48	1.53	1.58	1.62	1.67	1.72	1.76	1.81	1.86
130	40	4.94	1.04	1.38	1.43	1.48	1.53	1.58	1.63	1.68	1.73	1.78	1.83	1.88	1.93	1.98
140	43	5.24	1.10	1.47	1.52	1.57	1.62	1.68	1.73	1.78	1.83	1.89	1.94	1.99		
150	46	5.55	1.17	1.55	1.61	1.67	1.72	1.78	1.83	1.89	1.94	2.00				
160	49	5.85	1.23	1.64	1.70	1.76	1.81	1.87	1.93	1.99						
170	52	6.15	1.29	1.72	1.78	1.85	1.91	1.97								

PO$_2$ (atm) based on depth and percentage of oxygen. The body of the chart has PO$_2$ values for various mixes at a range of depths. Standard 32% and 36% mixes are in light grey. PO$_2$ levels higher than 1.6 ata are in dark grey and considered exceptional exposures and should be avoided.

nitrox mix be used without exceeding an operating PO$_2$ of 1.6 ata? Divide 1.6 ata by 0.32, the result is 5 ata. Next, convert 5 ata into depth units by multiplying by 33, then subtracting 33, and the result is 132 fsw (41 msw).

From the steps just applied, the diver can take the desired mix and choose the appropriate diving table.

MAXIMUM DEPTH FOR A MIX

ata = PO$_2$ (ata) / FO$_2$

ata = 1.6 ata / 0.32 = 5 ata

5 ata = 5 ata x 33 fsw = 165 fsw - 33 fsw = 132 fsw

FIGURE 15.2
Maximum Operating Depth at 1.6 ata PO$_2$

15.6 DIVING TABLES

This section discusses the NOAA Nitrox Decompression Tables and techniques needed for diving with mixtures other than air.

15.6.1 NOAA Nitrox Diving Tables

In 1979, NOAA introduced diving procedures and decompression tables for a standard nitrox mixture of 32% oxygen, 68% nitrogen. The decompression tables were calculated using what has become known as the "equivalent air depth" concept, which is simply to decompress from a non-air dive using air decompression tables that have the same nitrogen partial pressure (PN$_2$). Later, NOAA introduced 36% oxygen, which is even more beneficial for the 50–90 fsw (15–28 msw) range. The full nitrox decompression tables (see Appendix VII) are in the same format as the U.S. Navy Dive Tables.

This edition of the *NOAA Diving Manual* introduces a new abbreviated decompression table format, more precisely named NOAA Nitrox 32 and 36 Decompression Tables–Abbreviated Format (NN32-A and NN36-A). The format includes all the information needed to conduct no-stop repetitive dives, as well as dives that require only one level of required decompression stop at

TABLE 15.4
Percentage of Oxygen at Various PO₂ Levels

fsw	msw	atm	PO₂ 1.3	1.4	1.5	1.6
40	12	2.21	58%	63%	67%	72%
45	14	2.36	55%	59%	63%	67%
50	15	2.52	51%	55%	59%	63%
55	17	2.67	48%	52%	56%	59%
60	18	2.82	46%	49%	53%	56%
65	20	2.97	43%	47%	50%	53%
70	22	3.12	41%	44%	48%	51%
75	23	3.27	39%	42%	45%	48%
80	25	3.42	38%	40%	43%	46%
85	26	3.58	36%	39%	41%	44%
90	28	3.73	34%	37%	40%	42%
95	29	3.88	33%	36%	38%	41%
100	31	4.03	32%	34%	37%	39%
105	32	4.18	31%	33%	35%	38%
110	34	4.33	30%	32%	34%	36%
115	35	4.48	29%	31%	33%	35%
120	37	4.64	28%	30%	32%	34%
125	38	4.79	27%	29%	31%	33%
130	40	4.94	26%	28%	30%	32%

the 10 fsw (3 msw) depth. This new format makes it easier for divers and their supervisors to plan both single and repetitive dives using the standard NOAA nitrox gas mixes.

The new NOAA Nitrox Decompression Tables fall within the NOAA oxygen exposure limits. Normal exposures to 130 fsw (40 msw) can be done with NN32, and to 110 fsw (34 msw) with NN36. The allowed times are sufficiently generous that the oxygen exposure time limits are not likely to be exceeded in normal no-stop scuba diving. That is to say, it is difficult for the average diver using single scuba cylinders to carry enough breathing gas to stay on the bottom long enough to reach the oxygen exposure time limit. If, however, the diver uses larger capacity cylinders, or uses surface-supplied equipment, or conducts decompression dives using the nitrox decompression tables, then the oxygen exposure time limits can be reached and in some cases exceeded in normal operations.

15.6.2 Equivalent Air Depth Principle

The equivalent air depth (EAD) is the depth based on the partial pressure of nitrogen in the gas mixture to be breathed, rather than the actual depth of the dive. For a breathing mixture with less nitrogen than air, the equivalent depth is shallower than if air were being breathed (see Table 15.5). Although a diver is physically at a specific depth, physiologically the body is absorbing nitrogen equivalent to a shallower depth, since it is the partial pressure of the breathing gas that determines gas loading.

EAD decompression is based not on the actual depth of the dive, but on the equivalent inert gas exposure depth experienced by the diver. Once the EAD has been determined, the diver can use the "equivalent air depth" with any air diving table to find the resulting no-stop and decompression stop dive times, and the repetitive criteria. The EAD may be calculated using a formula, or tabulated using a look-up table. Table 15.6 provides equivalent air depths for oxygen percentages between 28–40%. To use the table, locate the oxygen percent for the nitrox mixture to be used. Moving down the column locate the exact or next greater depth of the dive. Move horizontally on the same row to the column at the far left labeled "EAD." This is the EAD for the dive. An exceptional exposure depth (dark gray) is included for each mix illustrated for emergency purposes only.

15.6.3 Custom Tables

There may be situations where a table for a specific mix and depth are needed for a special diving project. In these cases, the diver has two choices. The first option is to select a table using the EAD technique. Here the diver determines the equivalent air depth for the specific depths and mixes, either selected from a table or calculated using the formulas, then selects the desired air diving tables based on the equivalent depths. The second option is to have special tables developed specifically for the project.

TABLE 15.5
Equivalent Air Depth Comparison

AIR DEPTH (fsw)	EAD for	
	NN32	NN36
60	47	42
80	64	59
90	73	67
110	90	83
130	107	

TABLE 15.6
Equivalent Air Depth Conversion Table
Fraction of Oxygen and Actual Depths (fsw)

EAD (fsw)	28% ↓	29% ↓	30% ↓	31% ↓	32% ↓	33% ↓	34% ↓	35% ↓	36% ↓	37% ↓	38% ↓	39% ↓	40% ↓
30	36	37	38	39	40	41	42	43	44	46	47	49	50
40	47	48	49	50	51	53	54	55	57	58	60	62	63
50	58	59	61	62	63	64	66	67	69	71	72	74	76
60	69	70	72	73	75	76	78	80	81	83	85	87	89
70	80	81	83	84	86	88	90	92	94	96	98	100	102
80	90	92	95	96	98	100	102	104	106	108	110	113	
90	101	103	106	107	109	112	114	116	118	121			
100	112	114	117	119	121	123	126	128					
110	123	126	128	130	133	135							
120	134	137	139	142									
130	145	148	150										
140	156	159											
150	167												

From time to time, NOAA will have special tables developed for specific projects, but for the most part the EAD application to the U.S. Navy Dive Tables works well and meets NOAA's needs.

15.6.4 Repetitive Dives

Repetitive diving is quite common in NOAA diving. In fact, repetitive diving is one of the primary reasons nitrox breathing gases are used in the NOAA diving program.

NOAA defines a repetitive dive as one that begins within 12 hours of a previous dive. This means that the tables assume that a diver is clear of inert gas (for practical purposes) after 12 hours. If the second dive starts less than 10 minutes after the first dive, it is considered an extension of the previous dive. NOAA nitrox decompression tables utilize the same rules and procedures on repetitive dives.

15.6.5 Using Repetitive Procedures

The procedure for using repetitive adjustments is straightforward and reasonably simple. Basically, the diver determines from the first (or previous) dive its "residual" effect, then applies that to the next dive. For a first dive, read the "repetitive group letter" directly off the table. This group letter depends on the actual bottom time of the dive, for both no-stop and decompression dives. Then the time spent at the surface between this dive and the next one is used to determine the new repetitive group letter. Once this is determined, select the new group letter designation to be in effect after the surface interval. Follow that to the depth of the next dive and read the "penalty time" for the second dive in minutes to be added to the actual bottom time to use in selecting the correct decompression table for the second dive. This method works the same for both U.S. Navy Air and NOAA Nitrox Decompression Tables, although the charts and tables are configured differently.

Once the second dive is complete, re-enter the table with a new repetitive group letter designation and repeat the process. For surface intervals of less than 10 minutes, add the entire time of the first (or previous) dive to the actual time for the second (or following) dive to get the corrected repetitive dive time, and use this for selecting the correct schedule.

15.6.6 Diving at Altitude

Details on diving at altitude are found in Chapter 4. Altitude tables may be prepared by performing altitude "corrections" to standard air or nitrox tables.

The NOAA Dive Tables are authorized for use to an altitude of 1,000 ft. A number of factors must be considered when diving at altitude. The water in a mountain lake will be fresh water, which has a lower density than sea water. An effective way to deal with this is to use sea water gauges, since the tables are for sea water pressure (some gauges and dive computers are already calibrated to fresh water). The reference pressure of the pressure gauge (zero depth) should be set to zero at the surface of the lake or otherwise taken into account.

For diving at elevations above 1,000 feet, it is necessary to use tables designed or adapted for altitude. The Equivalent Air Depth principle will work for altitude diving with nitrox, but should be done with air tables that are already adjusted for altitude. Nitrox is well suited for diving at altitude. The primary benefits are to decompression; these become even more valuable at altitude to help offset the reduced dive time due to altitude adjustments.

15.6.7 Dive Computers and Nitrox

A dive computer performs the same sort of calculations mentioned above for tables, but does them in real time. Whereas decompression tables display decompression stops at 10 fsw (3 msw) increments, the computer shows the "ceiling"—the depth to which the diver can ascend without violating the computer's ascent limits. This has been called the "safe ascent depth," but for the same reason decompression tables are not described as "safe," the term "ceiling" is preferred.

There are two options for using dive computers with nitrox. The best is to use a computer designed for the proper mixes. Early computers were limited to one or two specific mixes, but more recently dive computers have become available that allow the percentage of oxygen to be set in 1% increments (see Figure 15.3). The recorded data can also be downloaded to a PC for logging and analysis. Some computers even allow for multiple nitrox mixes to be used during advanced types of decompression dives. Nitrox computers monitor the diver's exposure to oxygen, based on the mixture used, and signals when limits are approached or exceeded. For these computers, divers should refer to the manufacturer's instructions and to the specific training required for the particular unit.

As a second option, a common application is a nitrox mixture used with a dive computer designed for air to reduce the risk of DCS. In using an air computer with nitrox, it should be possible to use the computer to its full limits without the need for as much added conservatism as when using air. Even so, ascent rates should be performed according to recommendations; the benefit of the extra oxygen is not enough to compensate for too fast an ascent

rate. **The oxygen limits of the mixture must be heeded; since the computer "thinks" the diver is using air, it will not warn when oxygen limits have been exceeded.** It is also mandatory to observe the maximum operating depth of the gas being used.

15.7 USING NOAA NITROX DECOMPRESSION TABLES

This section discusses the procedures for using NOAA Nitrox Tables, and other air tables utilizing the equivalent air depth concept.

15.7.1 Using Fixed Tables

The most expedient method for determining decompression information is to use the NOAA NN32 and NN36 Decompression Tables (see Appendix VII). However, by using the EAD principle, any nitrox dive can be planned using the EAD formula and U.S. Navy Air Dive Tables.

As discussed in detail in Chapter 3, divers have certain single and cumulative time limits for oxygen exposure, depending on the partial pressure of the oxygen at the maximum depth of the dive. For example, for a dive with a maximum operating partial pressure of 1.5 ata, the time limit is 120 minutes. However, dives that place

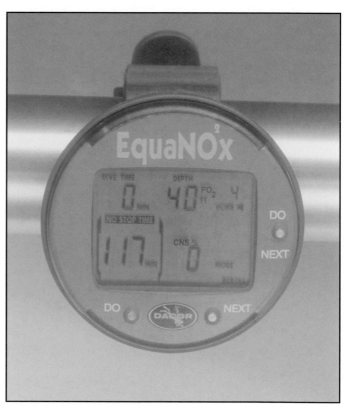

FIGURE 15.3
Nitrox Dive Computer

the partial pressure of oxygen at a 1.6 ata level provide only 45 minutes of oxygen exposure time. Oxygen exposure level and time need to be monitored carefully. If a single planned dive is to be longer than 45 minutes, the PO_2 level will have to be reduced by choosing a mix with a lower oxygen content.

Other considerations include having enough gas to breathe, repetitive diving procedures, and verifying the actual mix in the cylinder. For most NOAA diving operations, the mix will be prepared in advance based upon the dive plan. The mix must fall within the tolerance limits, ±1 percentage unit from the nominal value. When using the EAD principle, calculation should be based on the **exact mix** in the cylinder.

15.7.2 NOAA Nitrox 32% and 36% Decompression Tables

The NN32 and NN36 Decompression Tables make planning dives that use 32% and 36% oxygen relatively simple. The *Abbreviated* (NN32-A & NN36-A) format has been designed to accommodate all no-stop dives and decompression dives requiring a 10-ft. decompression stop. The fully expanded nitrox decompression tables are included in Appendix VII.

The procedures for using the NOAA Nitrox Decompression Tables–*Extended* are essentially no different from conducting decompression dives with the U.S. Navy Dive Tables, except that the diver must also take oxygen exposure time into consideration. For example, a 130 fsw (40 msw) dive using NN32 can be done for 40 minutes, requiring stops at 20 and 10 fsw for 2 and 21 minutes respectively and to remain within the normal range of oxygen exposure time (1.6 ata PO_2 / 45 minutes); however, a 50-minute dive would place the diver beyond the normal exposure range of oxygen partial pressure. It is critical, whenever decompression dives are planned, that both oxygen exposure and decompression obligation be considered.

The NN32–A (see Table 15.7) and NN36–A (see Table 15.8) Tables are designed for diving with the two nitrox mixes in the range 40–130 fsw (12–40 msw). Each depth/time schedule has information for completing required decompression stops, if they are needed, for dives that exceed the no-stop limit. The NN32–A Table has a useable depth range to 130 fsw (40 msw) and the NN36–A Table has a range to 110 fsw (34 msw). The tables have a maximum operating depth based on an oxygen partial pressure exposure of 1.6 ata.

The NN32–A and NN36–A Tables are divided into three charts that interact with each other.

Figure 15.4 shows Chart 1, the No-stop Time and End-of-Dive Group Letter. It shows the no-stop dive times for the various depths with a circle around the maximum no-stop time for each depth. For dives of less than the maximum time, the times are shown in the body of the chart and the End-of-Dive group letter is shown at the bottom for each of these times. Dive times that require decompression are shown as a double entry, with the upper figure the time

CHART 1 - DIVE TIMES WITH END-OF-DIVE GROUP LETTER

(00) MAXIMUM NO-STOP TIME — DIVE TIME REQUIRING DECOMPRESSION 00 / MINUTES REQUIRED AT 10 fsw STOP (3*msw*) 00

PO_2	START DEPTH *msw*	fsw															
0.8	*12*	40➤	15	30	45	60	75	95	120	145	170	205	250	310	344	(405)	
0.9	*15*	50➤	5	15	25	30	40	50	70	80	100	110	130	150	170	(200)	250 / 11
1.0	*18*	60➤		10	15	25	30	40	50	60	70	80	90	(100)	120 / 5	160 / 21	180 / 29
1.0	*22*	70➤		10	15	20	25	30	40	50	55	(60)	70 / 2	80 / 7	100 / 14		
1.1	*25*	80➤		5	10	15	20	30	35	40	45	(50)	60 / 8	70 / 14	80 / 18		
1.2	*28*	90➤		5	10	15	20	25	30	35	(40)		50 / 10	60 / 17	70 / 23		
1.3	*31*	100➤		5	10	12	15	20	25	(30)		40 / 7		50 / 18	60 / 25		
1.4	*34*	110➤		5	10	12	15	20	25	(30)		40 / 7		50 / 18	60 / 25		
1.5	*37*	120➤		5	7	10	15	20	22	(25)	30 / 3		40 / 15				
1.6	*40*	130➤			5	10	13	15	(20)	25 / 3		30 / 7					
			A	B	C	D	E	F	G	H	I	J	K	L	M	N	O

Figure 15.4
Part of the NN32–A, Chart 1

at depth, and the lower figure, in a dark box, the stop time. Stop time is to be taken at a depth of 10 fsw, as measured at the diver's mouth.

Chart 1 (see Figure 15.4) has a PO_2 level indicator for each depth. The PO_2 levels have been rounded to the next highest level for conservatism. For exact PO_2 use the formula or use Table 15.3. Chart 1 also provides information necessary for the planning and execution of a nitrox dive. For example, if a diver wants to dive to 90 fsw using a 32% mix, the maximum no stop time is 40 minutes. The schedule shows an end-of-dive group letter of I, at the bottom of the column that contains 40 minutes in the 90 fsw row. The PO_2 is shown at the left end of the 90 fsw row as 1.2 ata for this dive.

Figure 15.5 is Chart 2—Surface Interval Time. This chart is used to determine a new group letter after a surface interval following a previous dive. Enter this chart from the top, following down from the group letter to the appropriate interval time. Times are shown as ranges, so select the range that will include the actual interval time from surfacing from the first dive until beginning descent for the next. For example for a 1:25 surface interval, enter the chart in the J column, move down to the box containing 1:47/1:20, indicating a surface interval time between 1 hour 20 minutes and 1 hour 47 minutes. From here, move to the left to find the new group letter at the end of that interval, which in this example is the letter G.

Figure 15.6 is Chart 3—Repetitive Dive Time. The amount of "residual nitrogen time" is a function of the next dive. In the body of the chart, in each column below the depth headings, the entries each have two numbers. The upper number is the *Residual Nitrogen Time* (RNT) from the previous dive, the lower number is the *Adjusted No-stop Dive Time* that can be used for the repetitive dive to the depth at the top of the column. The lower numbers are the adjusted no-stop repetitive dive times which were calculated by subtracting the RNT from the maximum allowable bottom time for that depth.

TABLE 15.7
NOAA Nitrox 32 No-Decompression Dive Table –Abbreviated

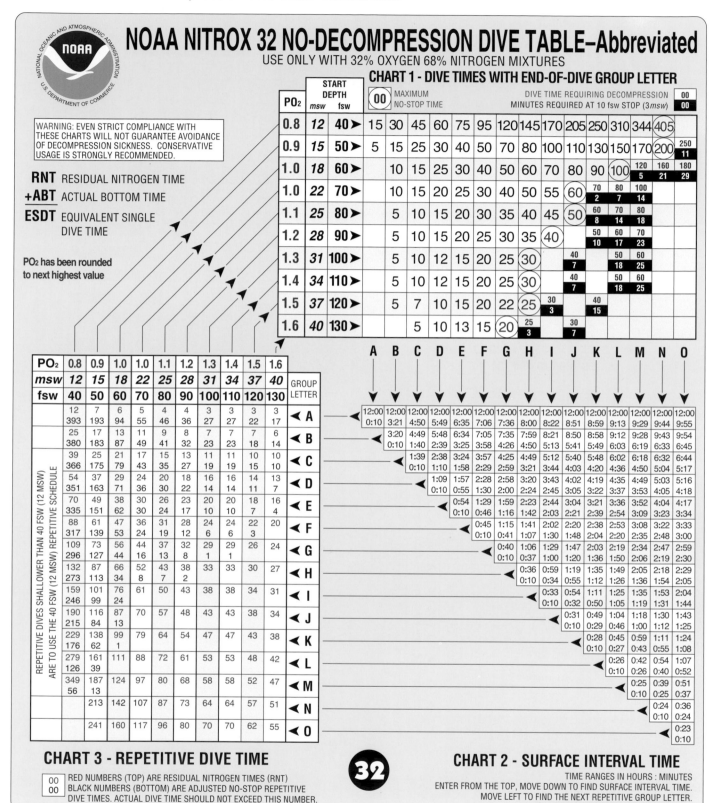

NOAA NITROX 32 NO-DECOMPRESSION DIVE TABLE–Abbreviated
USE ONLY WITH 32% OXYGEN 68% NITROGEN MIXTURES

WARNING: EVEN STRICT COMPLIANCE WITH THESE CHARTS WILL NOT GUARANTEE AVOIDANCE OF DECOMPRESSION SICKNESS. CONSERVATIVE USAGE IS STRONGLY RECOMMENDED.

RNT RESIDUAL NITROGEN TIME
+ABT ACTUAL BOTTOM TIME
ESDT EQUIVALENT SINGLE DIVE TIME

PO₂ has been rounded to next highest value

CHART 1 - DIVE TIMES WITH END-OF-DIVE GROUP LETTER

CHART 3 - REPETITIVE DIVE TIME

00 / 00 RED NUMBERS (TOP) ARE RESIDUAL NITROGEN TIMES (RNT)
BLACK NUMBERS (BOTTOM) ARE ADJUSTED NO-STOP REPETITIVE DIVE TIMES. ACTUAL DIVE TIME SHOULD NOT EXCEED THIS NUMBER.

32

CHART 2 - SURFACE INTERVAL TIME
TIME RANGES IN HOURS : MINUTES
ENTER FROM THE TOP, MOVE DOWN TO FIND SURFACE INTERVAL TIME.
MOVE LEFT TO FIND THE NEXT REPETITIVE GROUP LETTER.
Copyright © 2000 Best Publishing Company

TABLE 15.8
NOAA Nitrox 36 No-Decompression Dive Table–Abbreviated

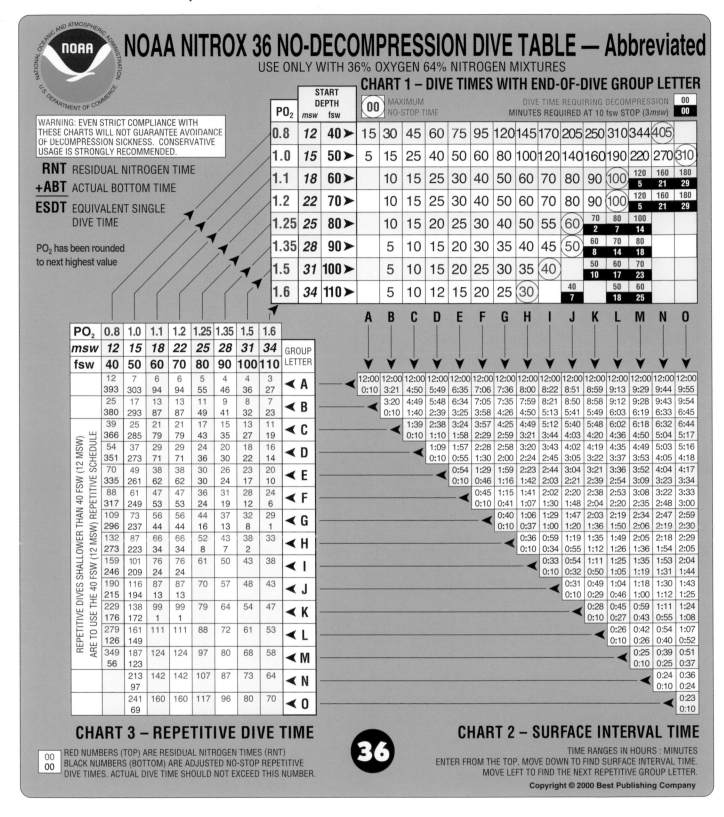

NOAA NITROX 36 NO-DECOMPRESSION DIVE TABLE — Abbreviated
USE ONLY WITH 36% OXYGEN 64% NITROGEN MIXTURES

WARNING: EVEN STRICT COMPLIANCE WITH THESE CHARTS WILL NOT GUARANTEE AVOIDANCE OF DECOMPRESSION SICKNESS. CONSERVATIVE USAGE IS STRONGLY RECOMMENDED.

RNT RESIDUAL NITROGEN TIME
+ABT ACTUAL BOTTOM TIME
ESDT EQUIVALENT SINGLE DIVE TIME

PO_2 has been rounded to next highest value

CHART 1 – DIVE TIMES WITH END-OF-DIVE GROUP LETTER

PO_2	START DEPTH msw	fsw														
0.8	12	40 ➤	15	30	45	60	75	95	120	145	170	205	250	310	344	(405)
1.0	15	50 ➤	5	15	25	40	50	60	80	100	120	140	160	190	220	270	310
1.1	18	60 ➤		10	15	25	30	40	50	60	70	80	90	(100)	120/5	160/21	180/29
1.2	22	70 ➤		10	15	25	30	40	50	60	70	80	90	(100)	120/5	160/21	180/29
1.25	25	80 ➤		10	15	20	25	30	40	50	55	(60)	70/2	80/7	100/14		
1.35	28	90 ➤		5	10	15	20	30	35	40	45	(50)	60/8	70/14	80/18		
1.5	31	100 ➤		5	10	15	20	25	30	35	(40)	50/10	60/17	70/23			
1.6	34	110 ➤		5	10	12	15	20	25	(30)	40/7	50/18	60/25				

00 MAXIMUM NO-STOP TIME
00/00 DIVE TIME REQUIRING DECOMPRESSION MINUTES REQUIRED AT 10 fsw STOP (3msw)

A B C D E F G H I J K L M N O

CHART 3 – REPETITIVE DIVE TIME

PO_2	0.8	1.0	1.1	1.2	1.25	1.35	1.5	1.6	GROUP LETTER
msw	12	15	18	22	25	28	31	34	
fsw	40	50	60	70	80	90	100	110	
	12/393	7/303	6/94	6/94	5/55	4/46	4/36	3/27	◄ A
	25/380	17/293	13/87	13/87	11/49	9/41	8/32	7/23	◄ B
	39/366	25/285	21/79	21/79	17/43	15/35	13/27	11/19	◄ C
	54/351	37/273	29/71	29/71	24/36	20/30	18/22	16/14	◄ D
	70/335	49/261	38/62	38/62	30/30	26/24	23/17	20/10	◄ E
	88/317	61/249	47/53	47/53	36/24	31/19	28/12	24/6	◄ F
	109/296	73/237	56/44	56/44	44/16	37/13	32/8	29/1	◄ G
	132/273	87/223	66/34	66/34	52/8	43/7	38/2	33	◄ H
	159/246	101/209	76/24	76/24	61	50	43	38	◄ I
	190/215	116/194	87/13	87/13	70	57	48	43	◄ J
	229/176	138/172	99/1	99/1	79	64	54	47	◄ K
	279/126	161/149	111	111	88	72	61	53	◄ L
	349/56	187/123	124	124	97	80	68	58	◄ M
		213/97	142	142	107	87	73	64	◄ N
		241/69	160	160	117	96	80	70	◄ O

REPETITIVE DIVES SHALLOWER THAN 40 FSW (12 MSW) REPETITIVE SCHEDULE ARE TO USE THE 40 FSW (12 MSW) REPETITIVE SCHEDULE

CHART 2 – SURFACE INTERVAL TIME

	A	B	C	D	E	F	G	H	I	J	K	L	M	N	O
A	12:00/0:10	12:00/3:21	12:00/4:50	12:00/5:49	12:00/6:35	12:00/7:06	12:00/7:36	12:00/8:00	12:00/8:22	12:00/8:51	12:00/8:59	12:00/9:13	12:00/9:29	12:00/9:44	12:00/9:55
B		3:20/0:10	4:49/1:40	5:48/2:39	6:34/3:25	7:05/3:58	7:35/4:26	7:59/4:50	8:21/5:13	8:50/5:41	8:58/5:49	9:12/6:03	9:28/6:19	9:43/6:33	9:54/6:45
C			1:39/0:10	2:38/1:10	3:24/1:58	3:57/2:29	4:25/2:59	4:49/3:21	5:12/3:44	5:40/4:03	5:48/4:20	6:02/4:36	6:18/4:50	6:32/5:04	6:44/5:17
D				1:09/0:10	1:57/0:55	2:28/1:30	2:58/2:00	3:20/2:24	3:43/2:45	4:02/3:05	4:19/3:22	4:35/3:37	4:49/3:53	5:03/4:05	5:16/4:18
E					0:54/0:10	1:29/0:46	1:59/1:16	2:23/1:42	2:44/2:03	3:04/2:21	3:21/2:39	3:36/2:54	3:52/3:09	4:04/3:23	4:17/3:34
F						0:45/0:10	1:15/0:41	1:41/1:07	2:02/1:30	2:20/1:48	2:38/2:04	2:53/2:20	3:08/2:35	3:22/2:48	3:33/3:00
G							0:40/0:10	1:06/0:37	1:29/1:00	1:47/1:20	2:03/1:36	2:19/1:50	2:34/2:06	2:47/2:19	2:59/2:30
H								0:36/0:10	0:59/0:34	1:19/0:55	1:35/1:12	1:49/1:26	2:05/1:36	2:18/1:54	2:29/2:05
I									0:33/0:10	0:54/0:31	1:11/0:50	1:25/1:05	1:35/1:19	1:53/1:31	2:04/1:44
J										0:31/0:10	0:49/0:29	1:04/0:46	1:18/1:00	1:30/1:12	1:43/1:25
K											0:28/0:10	0:45/0:27	0:59/0:43	1:11/0:55	1:24/1:08
L												0:26/0:10	0:42/0:26	0:54/0:40	1:07/0:52
M													0:25/0:10	0:39/0:25	0:51/0:37
N														0:24/0:10	0:36/0:24
O															0:23/0:10

00/00 RED NUMBERS (TOP) ARE RESIDUAL NITROGEN TIMES (RNT) BLACK NUMBERS (BOTTOM) ARE ADJUSTED NO-STOP REPETITIVE DIVE TIMES. ACTUAL DIVE TIME SHOULD NOT EXCEED THIS NUMBER.

36

TIME RANGES IN HOURS : MINUTES
ENTER FROM THE TOP, MOVE DOWN TO FIND SURFACE INTERVAL TIME.
MOVE LEFT TO FIND THE NEXT REPETITIVE GROUP LETTER.

Copyright © 2000 Best Publishing Company

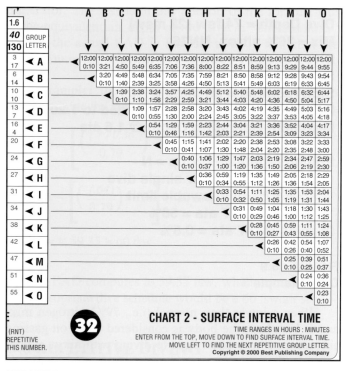

CHART 2 - SURFACE INTERVAL TIME

TIME RANGES IN HOURS : MINUTES
ENTER FROM THE TOP, MOVE DOWN TO FIND SURFACE INTERVAL TIME.
MOVE LEFT TO FIND THE NEXT REPETITIVE GROUP LETTER.
Copyright © 2000 Best Publishing Company

FIGURE 15.5
Part of the NN32–A, Chart 2

REPETITIVE DIVES SHALLOWER THAN 40 FSW (12 MSW) ARE TO USE THE 40 FSW (12 MSW) REPETITIVE SCHEDULE

PO_2	0.8	0.9	1.0	1.0	1.1	1.2	1.3	1.4	1.5	1.6	GROUP LETTER
msw	12	15	18	22	25	28	31	34	37	40	
fsw	40	50	60	70	80	90	100	110	120	130	
	12/393	7/193	6/94	5/55	4/46	4/36	3/27	3/27	3/22	3/17	A
	25/380	17/183	13/87	11/49	9/41	8/32	7/23	7/23	7/18	6/14	B
	39/366	25/175	21/79	17/43	15/35	13/27	11/19	11/19	10/15	10/10	C
	54/351	37/163	29/71	24/36	20/30	18/22	16/14	16/14	14/11	13/7	D
	70/335	49/151	38/62	30/30	26/24	23/17	20/10	20/10	18/7	16/4	E
	88/317	61/139	47/53	36/24	31/19	28/12	24/6	24/6	22/3	20	F
	109/296	73/127	56/44	44/16	37/13	32/8	29/1	29/1	26	24	G
	132/273	87/113	66/34	52/8	43/7	38/2	33	30	27		H
	159/246	101/99	76/24	61	50	43	38	38	34	31	I
	190/215	116/84	87/13	70	57	48	43	43	38	34	J
	229/176	138/62	99/1	79	64	54	47	47	43	38	K
	279/126	161/39	111	88	72	61	53	53	48	42	L
	349/56	187/13	124	97	80	68	58	58	52	47	M
		213	142	107	87	73	64	64	57	51	N
		241	160	117	96	80	70	70	62	55	O

CHART 3 - REPETITIVE DIVE TIME

- 00 (top) RED NUMBERS (TOP) ARE RESIDUAL NITROGEN TIMES (RNT)
- 00 (bottom) BLACK NUMBERS (BOTTOM) ARE ADJUSTED NO-STOP REPETITIVE DIVE TIMES. ACTUAL DIVE TIME SHOULD NOT EXCEED THIS NUMBER.

FIGURE 15.6
Part of the NN32–A, Chart 3

To use Chart 3, enter on the right with the group letter designation from Chart 2 (which is G from the above example) and move to the left to the column that has the depth of the next dive at the top. Continuing with a repetitive dive to 60 fsw (18 msw), intersect row G with the 60 fsw column and the resulting no-stop dive time is 44 minutes, the residual nitrogen time from the previous dive is 56 minutes.

Example 1:

In this example (see Figure 15.7), the diver uses a 36% mix for a no-stop dive to 90 fsw (28 msw), using either the abbreviated or expanded table for a bottom time of 50 minutes. PO_2 level is 1.35 ata at 90 fsw. According to Table 15.2, a diver can breathe a PO_2 of 1.35 ata for up to 165 minutes, which places the 50 minute maximum bottom time well within the NOAA oxygen exposure limits.

Example 2:

In this example (see Figure 15.8), the diver uses a 32% mix for a dive to 90 fsw (28 msw) using either the abbreviated or expanded table for a bottom time of 50 minutes. The PO_2 level is 1.2 ata at 90 fsw, so the oxygen exposure of 50 minutes at 1.2 ata is applied for calculation of the CNS "clock."

If the dive is extended to 50 minutes, the diver is required to complete a 10 minute decompression stop at 10 fsw (3 msw). The oxygen exposure becomes 50 minutes at 1.2 ata, and thus rises to 24% of the single exposure limit (see Chapter 3).

Example 3:

In this example (see Figure 15.9), the diver uses a 36% mix for a dive to 74 fsw (23 msw) for 117 minutes. Here the diver will use the NN36 No-Decompression Table–Expanded format, since the time is too long for the abbreviated format, and must be planned as a decompression dive using the NN36 Decompression Table. The schedule used will be the 80 fsw/120 minute line, which requires a 10 fsw stop for 26 minutes. Oxygen exposure needs to be calculated for both the bottom time and the decompression time. The ending repetitive pressure group letter is N and the total oxygen exposure is approximately 56% of the limit (117 min out of a possible 210 min).

To calculate the oxygen exposure fraction "oxygen clock," find the PO_2 limit on the NOAA Oxygen Exposure Normal Limits Table (see Figure 15.2) and divide the dive time at that PO_2 level by the Oxygen Exposure Limit. For the example, in Figure 15.9 the PO_2 level is 1.17 ata; using the 1.20 limit divide 117 minutes by 210 minutes, resulting in 0.5571 or 56% rounded up. Next calculate the exposure than the previous dive, although it will calculate correctly, will provide shorter no-stop dive time. For that reason, it is best to plan repetitive dives with progressively higher oxygen-content mixtures.

15.8.3 Omitted Decompression

Should a nitrox diver surface with a decompression obligation, for whatever reason, or upon surfacing discover that some required decompression has been omitted, the diver should be observed and/or treated in accordance with omitted decompression procedures outlined in Chapter 4 for air diving.

15.9 PROCEDURES FOR USING NOAA NITROX DIVING TABLES

The NOAA nitrox diving tables and charts have certain procedures for maximizing their effectiveness while minimizing risks. These are standard procedures to be used when diving with NOAA nitrox tables and charts.

Maximum Descent Rate:	75 fsw per min (23 msw/min)
Maximum Ascent Rate:	30 fsw per min (9 msw/min)
Travel Rate Exceeded:	If the ascent rate is faster than 30 fpm, STOP THE ASCENT, allow dive timers to catch up, and then continue the ascent. If the stop is reached early, start the stop time after the timers catch up.
Delayed Ascent:	*With no-decompression stops* If delayed more than one minute during ascent and no-decompression stops were planned, add the time of the delay to the actual bottom time of the dive and recompute the dive schedule *With decompression stops* Follow procedures outlined in the *U.S. Navy Dive Manual*, Rev 4, 1999.
No-Stop Bottom Time:	Bottom time is measured from the time a diver leaves the surface to the time the diver leaves the bottom for a direct ascent to the surface.
Safety Stop:	A safety stop of 3–5 minutes at 10–20 fsw (3–6 msw) is recommended on all dives deeper than 60 fsw (18 msw) and on all repetitive dives at any depth. This time is not "counted" in bottom time and is not considered a required decompression stop.
Decompression Stops:	Stops are to be taken at the specified depth and measured at the diver's mouth.
Cold or Strenuous Dives:	If a diver is particularly cold or has been doing strenuous work the diver should use the next greater bottom time when determining their decompression schedule. For example, a dive to 90 fsw (28 msw) for 20 minutes would be considered a dive to 90 fsw for 25 minutes. This puts the diver in a higher repetitive group letter.
Repetitive Dives:	A repetitive dive is any dive that has been made less than 12 hours after a previous dive. Although no-stop repetitive dives are typically conducted to successively shallower depths for operational reasons, they may be conducted to depths up to 40 fsw (12 msw) deeper than the previous dive.
Short Surface Interval:	Whenever a surface interval of less than 10 minutes occurs the two dives are to be considered as one single dive and the dive schedule for the deepest dive for the total time is to be used.
Flying After Diving:	Requires surface interval before ascent to altitude after diving. See Chapter 4 to determine minimum required time before flying.
Altitude Diving:	The NOAA nitrox diving tables are usable to 1,000 ft. (305 m) elevation. For diving at higher elevations, use EAD with altitude tables or a dive computer that has altitude capability.

15.10 OUT OF GAS EMERGENCIES

There may be situations where divers who need to share gas have been breathing different gas mixtures. Since the important issue is to have something to breathe, the choice of gas is not a matter of great concern, but some procedures should be followed.

15.10.1 Diver Within No-stop Limits

A nitrox diver who has not yet exceeded the no-stop time, can breathe air or any nitrox mix for an immediate ascent. This will have trivial decompression consequences. A safety stop should be made at 10–20 fsw (3–6 msw) for three to five minutes, gas supply permitting. If the situation is reversed and an air diver needs to breathe an oxygen-rich mix, this is also permitted; a safety stop should be made, has supply permitting.

15.10.2 Shifting to Air During a Decompression Stop

If a diver breathing nitrox is required to switch to air during a decompression stop, the stop time(s) listed in the dive table can be completed without deviation or adjustment. This is because the decompression stop times listed in the table are based on the U.S. Navy Air Decompression Table, which assumes the diver is breathing air. If the decompression must be shortened because of depletion of the air supply, omitted decompression procedures must be followed upon surfacing.

15.11 PREPARATION OF NITROX GAS MIXTURES

The commonly used methods for creating gas mixes are discussed in this chapter, each with its own advantages and disadvantages. It is important for the diver using oxygen-rich mixtures to have an understanding of how mixtures are prepared and the cleanliness requirements of mixing systems and diving equipment.

15.11.1 Oxygen Handling

In the process of gas mixing, the object is to obtain the correct percentage of oxygen in the high-pressure mix. This can be done by mixing pure oxygen with nitrogen or air, or by removing nitrogen from air. One of the main problems when mixing with high-pressure oxygen is the risk of fire (Mastro and Butler 1990). Everything that is not already completely oxidized, which means virtually everything, will burn in high-pressure oxygen when there is a source of ignition. The diver using nitrox mixtures may not need to handle pure oxygen, but some understanding of its hazards is essential.

15.11.2 The Fire Triangle

Fire is a rapid chemical reaction between a **fuel** and an **oxidizer** (oxygen), and it can only take place if there is a source of **ignition** (heat) to start it. Oxidation can occur without fire, as in rusting, but fire requires heat to initiate burning. After ignition, the chemical reaction releases energy as heat, and this heat sustains the reaction. If any one of the ingredients (fuel, oxygen, or ignition) is removed, there cannot be a fire. If all three are not present at the same time, fire is prevented. If a fire does exist, removing any one of the ingredients will extinguish the fire. This is the basic theory of fire protection.

Fuel: At high pressures of oxygen, once a fire is started, the gas system itself can become the fuel, but it takes something flammable to start a fire in a gas system. This can be any sort of particulate matter, lubricants, solvents, and "soft goods" like rubber and plastic that may be part of the system.

Some types of "fuels" found in diving systems that normally are of little fire concern, in air can become quite flammable in an oxygen-enriched environment. These include silicone grease, silicone rubber, neoprene, compressor lubricants, plastic shavings, metal shavings, organic material, dust from a variety of sources, and even body oils. Lubricants are probably the worst offender in practice. There is a

misconception that silicone lubricants are safe with oxygen; they are not. Oxygen-compatible lubricants such as Christo-Lube®, Krytox®, and Halocarbon® 25-5 S should be used (Mastro and Butler 1990).

Oxidizer: In all the mixing systems presented in this chapter, oxygen is present by intent at levels greater than in air; the oxidizing agent in the fire triangle is there by default and cannot be removed from the equation. Under the right circumstances, the oxygen in air can participate vigorously in combustion, so increased levels of oxygen can only increase the hazard. Further, recalling the main theme of this chapter, as oxygen is increased in a mix, the inert nitrogen background gas is reduced; for this and other reasons combustion does not follow the oxygen fraction in a linear way. The rate of combustion increases as both the fraction and the partial pressure of oxygen increase. Both are important.

Ignition: A source of energy is required to initiate a fire in an oxygen-rich environment. Three main sources of ignition inside a gas system are: 1) particle impact; 2) friction; and 3) pneumatic impact or compression heating. Ignition by particle impact can occur when particulate matter (i.e. dirt, sand, metal shavings, etc.), carried by flowing gas in the oxygen system, strikes various surfaces and components in the system. The kinetic energy of the moving particles converted to thermal energy (heat) on impact, and can ignite the particle itself or the surrounding material (ASTM 1995). Localized friction heating of combustible materials can occur in system components subject to high gas velocities. Ball valve designs used in high differential pressure throttling applications are particularly susceptible to seat and seal material frictional heating (Mastro and Butler 1990). Another phenomenon, the heat of compression that causes a gas cylinder to heat up when compressed, may produce enough heat to raise the temperature to the point of combustion; this is the same effect that causes fuel to ignite in the cylinders of a diesel engine without a spark plug. This is especially true if the compression is abrupt.

The compression in a gas line when a valve is opened or closed abruptly can cause ignition temperatures to develop. If there are contaminants in the line a fire can result. For this reason, oxygen systems do not use quick-opening valves such as ball valves.

15.11.3 Air to be Mixed with Oxygen

Some methods of preparing nitrox involve air being mixed with oxygen. It is extremely important that the air be clean and free of oil mist and particulate matter. Ordinary compressed air is not clean enough for mixing with oxygen. Standards for breathing air allow an amount of oil mist or hydrocarbons that is tolerable physiologically, but has too much oil in it to be safe for use with high-pressure oxygen. For example, one set of standards for divers' breathing air allow 5 mg/m³ of oil mist. With this amount of oil in the air, oil can accumulate in equipment which may pose a problem when exposed to oxygen-rich breathing mixtures. Currently none of the existing standard "grades" of air adequately addresses allowable oil mist or hydrocarbon—they either do not address oil, imply that none can be present, or allow too much.

To deal with this dilemma, leaders in the industry supplying oxygen-rich mixtures for recreational diving and the U.S. Navy (*U.S. Navy Diving Manual*, Rev. 4, 1999) specify that a condensable hydrocarbon level of 0.1 mg/m^3 is acceptable for "air to be mixed with oxygen." This is low enough to avoid oil buildup in equipment, but high enough to be measured. It is just at the lower limit of detectability by ordinary test methods, and is now attainable by filtration, as well as by using compressors that are not lubricated with oil.

Compressors that do not expose the air to lubrication in the first place can produce oil-free air, and these are used most frequently by the NOAA Diving Program. The terms "oil-free" and "oil-less" have been used to describe two different types of compressors; those that are non-oil lubricated thus producing a product containing no oil, and those that are oil lubricated but which also produce a product that is free of oil as a result of hyper-filtration. For the purposes of this text, the terms "oil-free" and "oil-less" refer to those compressors which are non-oil lubricated.

In addition to reducing the oil mist, particulate matter needs to be filtered. Most hyper-filtration systems remove large particulates while removing oil mist at the same time. Since the introduction of nitrox mixing systems in the late 1980s, new filtration systems have become available that can process clean compressed breathing grade air to meet the stringent requirements for air to mixed with oxygen.

While this filtration process may work well enough for preparing air prior to mixing it with oxygen, it is not acceptable practice to add oxygen to oily air and then filter the oil out of a mix after the oxygen has been added. The air must be filtered prior to being mixed with oxygen.

15.11.4 Cleaning for Oxygen Service

It has become well established that equipment used for handling oxygen has to be made of oxygen-compatible materials and has to be clean, free of hydrocarbons, particulate matter, and other materials that can burn in the presence of oxygen. One step in meeting these requirements is oxygen cleaning.

NOAA Standards for Oxygen Service

NOAA, as well as, several other agencies including OSHA (29 CFR 1910.430) and U.S. Coast Guard (46 CFR 197.452) allow gas mixes with oxygen up to 40% to be handled as if they were air. This "40%" approach separates the handling of nitrox mixtures and equipment used for preparing and using these mixes into two separate and distinct categories: one follows procedures for air and the other for oxygen. NOAA has adopted this approach for its nitrox and mixed gas diving operations, with some exceptions discussed later in this section. NOAA has used the "40% rule" on scuba equipment and gas distribution systems since the introduction of nitrox into its diving program without any problem.

The NOAA policy states that any equipment used for 100% oxygen or an oxygen level above 40% at high pressure (above 200 psi) must be oxygen compatible, use oxygen-compatible lubricants, and be formally cleaned for oxygen service. This includes scuba cylinders and valves, first stage regulators, and any high-pressure hoses. NOAA recognizes two levels of oxygen cleaning, a formal procedure according to industry practice, and an "informal" method that meets essentially the same criteria, but lacks the formal certification and documentation procedures.

Formal Oxygen Cleaning

Formal oxygen cleaning requires strict procedures to be followed by trained technicians, and all steps must be documented in detail (see Figure 15.10). The Compressed Gas Association (CGA), American Society for Testing and Materials (ASTM), National Fire Protection Association (NFPA), NASA, U.S. Navy (MIL-STD 1330D 1996), and numerous other organizations publish formal procedures for oxygen cleaning. Formal oxygen cleaning has to be done by technicians trained and authorized in those procedures. The details of how to do formal oxygen cleaning are beyond the scope of this manual.

Just cleaning the apparatus for oxygen service is not the whole picture, since the equipment has to be kept clean. According to most specifications, once an oxygen system is cleaned and assembled it is necessary to use special procedures to "open" an oxygen system to ensure that the system does not become contaminated.

Informal Oxygen Cleaning

"Informal" oxygen cleaning is intended to clean equipment as clean as formal oxygen cleaning, but without the certification and documentation.

Generally, equipment should be cleaned of any visible debris and lubricants, then scrubbed or cleaned ultrasonically with a strong detergent in hot water, then rinsed several times in clean hot water. Good detergents are Crystal®, Simple Green®, Navy Oxygen Cleaner® (NOC), Alconox®, and liquid detergents such as Joy® or Dawn®. When dry, the soft components are replaced and the equipment is lubricated as necessary with oxygen-compatible lubricant.

Once cleaned, the equipment should be dedicated for use only with nitrox mixtures and not used with air from an oil-lubricated compressor without proper hyper-filtration. If it is, it should be cleaned again prior to use with gas mixtures containing more than 40% oxygen content. Equipment removed from a system should be protected from recontamination.

Scuba regulators, cylinder valves, high-pressure gauges, and cylinders that will be used with mixtures

FIGURE 15.10
Preparation of Regulator Parts for Oxygen Service

The following may be informally cleaned for use with oxygen:

- Cylinders, valves, hoses, etc., that will be in contact with high-pressure pre-mixed gases greater than 21% and 40% or less oxygen content
- Gas storage cylinders, valves, and piping that will only be filled with pre-mixed gas mixes of 40% or less oxygen content

Diving equipment that will only be used with air may be cleaned using ordinary cleaning procedures.

15.11.5 Design and Technique in Using Oxygen Systems

The risk of fire in a system working with high oxygen levels can be minimized by proper design and technique. Design includes avoiding sharp corners and quick-opening valves, and using the right materials. The metals used for standard diving equipment are acceptable for oxygen use. The "soft goods," which includes seals, flexible tubing, diaphragms, etc., might have to be replaced with "oxygen-compatible" components. In some cases these are less likely to burn in oxygen; in other cases such materials are chosen because they are more durable when exposed to high-pressure oxygen. Specific "oxygen-compatible" replacement part kits are available from each respective manufacturer for converting standard scuba gear to nitrox compatible.

Proper techniques for using oxygen systems include cleaning systems properly and keeping them clean, using proper lubricants, and handling gases so as to avoid causing rapid gas movement by opening valves slowly.

15.12 EQUIPMENT CONSIDERATIONS
15.12.1 Scuba Cylinders

Scuba cylinders that will be used for nitrox are to be properly "dedicated" for nitrox to avoid mistaking a nitrox cylinder with an air cylinder. In addition they need to be cleaned properly as outlined previously.

In the commercial gas world, different gases (helium, oxygen, argon, air, propane) are placed in cylinders with unique valve connections to prevent misidentification. Each gas is assigned a unique valve connection and a cylinder content label is also required.

The U.S. scuba industry currently has two valve configurations (see Figure 15.11); one is for the standard "yoke" regulator, and the other for the DIN-threaded connector with a captive O-ring. At this time, neither of these connectors can prevent a scuba regulator that has not been cleaned from being placed on a nitrox cylinder. Because any scuba regulator can fit onto any cylinder despite contents, it is most important that identification procedures be strictly followed.

There is a third valve type, the EIN 144. This valve is used in parts of Europe for nitrox cylinders. It is different from the standard U.S. valves in that is has an external reverse

containing 40% or less oxygen content may also be informally cleaned for use with oxygen. Cylinders can be marked as clean, but should only be marked as cleaned for oxygen service when that is the case. They should be marked so that only premixed nitrox up to 40% oxygen content can be introduced. As a reminder, the lubricant is believed to be the weak spot; only oxygen-compatible lubricants should be used with mixtures having an oxygen content greater than 40%. Use the following checklists to ensure proper safety.

The following must be cleaned for oxygen service (either formally or informally):

- Gas mixing and blending systems, and any equipment containing 100% oxygen
- Cylinders and valves that will be in contact with high pressure oxygen or oxygen mixes greater than 40% oxygen content
- Diving equipment that will come in contact with oxygen fractions greater than 40% oxygen content at high pressure (including regulators, valves, hoses, cylinders, gauges, etc.)

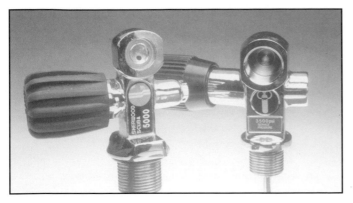

FIGURE 15.11
Yoke and DIN Style Scuba Valves

thread configuration requiring a dedicated scuba regulator. This special valve is used to prevent regular "air" scuba regulators and filling devices from being placed on nitrox cylinders. The concept is a sound one and falls in line with the way CGA differentiates gas valves on storage cylinders.

A label on a nitrox cylinder distinguishes it from other scuba cylinders. The label has become an international standard for identifying nitrox cylinders, their level of cleanliness, and their contents.

15.12.2 Identification of Nitrox Cylinders

One method of identifying nitrox cylinders is the use of a yellow cylinder with the top painted green down four inches from the shoulder of the cylinder. Stenciled on the body of the cylinder in two-inch high letters is the word "Nitrox."

Another acceptable method is to use a commercially available label that surrounds the top of the cylinder. On yellow cylinders a four-inch green band with the words "Nitrox," "Oxygen-Enriched Air," "Enriched Air," or "Enriched Air Nitrox" or the equivalent are printed in yellow or white letters and placed just below the shoulder of the cylinder. (see Figure 15.12)

For cylinders that are not yellow, the same green band will have a one-inch yellow band on both top and bottom. A cylinder that is properly prepared and labeled should not be filled with any mixture other than Nitrox.

15.12.3 Cylinder Label for Oxygen Cleaning

This label (see Figure 15.13) or a MIL STD 1330 label is applied to the cylinder after it has been cleaned and placed into oxygen service. These labels indicate when the cylinder was cleaned and its level of cleanliness. Some nitrox filling systems require a cylinder to be cleaned for oxygen service before being filled since high-pressure oxygen is in contact with the valve and the cylinder when it is being filled. Other systems do not use oxygen for filling. The label distinguishes whether the cylinder has been cleaned for oxygen service. A cylinder that does not have an "oxygen service" certification should not be filled by partial pressure methods because during the mixing procedure the cylinder would be exposed to 100% oxygen.

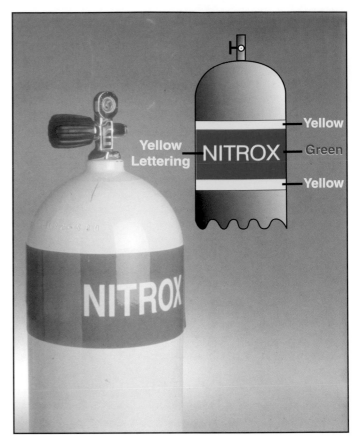

FIGURE 15.12
Single Tank with Nitrox Tank Wrap

The label only certifies that the cylinder has been cleaned for the date indicated. If the cylinder has been contaminated any time after the inspection date, it should be immediately marked "CONTAMINATED." After cleaning it should be re-labeled. Contamination can occur by having the cylinder filled with air from an oil-lubricated compressor. It is prudent to inspect and re-clean scuba cylinders annually. NOAA requires annual visual inspection of all scuba cylinders.

15.12.4 Cylinder Labeling

Every nitrox cylinder must be properly labeled as to its contents and fill data (see Figure 15.14). In some cases, once a cylinder has been analyzed at the fill station it is likely that it will not be analyzed again. Unless analyzed again immediately before use, the cylinder-contents label is the only way to know what gas is in the cylinder before diving. The data include fill date, cylinder pressure, oxygen percentage, maximum operating depth, the name or identification of the person completing the label, and the user's initials verifying that it was analyzed. The contents label or tag should be attached to the cylinder or valve. Plastic re-useable contents tags can be written on in pencil and erased for the next use. Non-reusable labels should be ascribed with a permanent marker, not with a grease pencil which may come off, and should only be removed by a gas-blending technician before the next fill.

FIGURE 15.13
NOAA Oxygen Service Label

NITROX Contents Data

Fill Date	
Oxygen %	
Pressure	
Max. Depth	
Analyzed by	
User	

Caution: This cylinder contains gas other than air. Observe maximum operation depth limit. Use only with appropriate procedures for the mix indicated. Failure to heed proper use may result in serious injury or death.

FIGURE 15.14
Cylinder Contents Label

<u>NOTE</u>
Pre-mix does not ensure correct mix. The safest method is to do an analysis prior to dive.

15.12.5 Fill Station Log

Once a cylinder has been filled and analyzed, a permanent record is kept at the filling center in a fill station log. In the log, the diver prints their name, the date, cylinder serial number, cylinder pressure, oxygen percentage, maximum operating depth, and then signs the log. The cylinder log is used to help keep track of cylinders and helps ensure that a technician can verify the last fill should a contents tag or label somehow get removed from the cylinder. A cylinder that loses its label must be re-analyzed to properly ensure its contents. The log also verifies, by the diver's signature, that the diver has personally analyzed the cylinder being received.

It is generally accepted practice that a mix within ±1% of the desired mix is acceptable. The NOAA nitrox tables use the ±1% range, thus NN32 can be 31–33 oxygen content, and NN36 can be 35–37 oxygen content. However, if the mix is off by more than 1% in either direction of the desired mix, the mixture will need to be adjusted or totally re-mixed. If time is a factor on a diving operation, the mix may be used as long as its oxygen limit (MOD) is not exceeded and proper decompression procedures (such as EAD) are applied.

15.13 PREPARING NITROX MIXTURES

Nitrox blending systems have traditionally involved adding oxygen to air in some manner. Recently, two new methods have become available that enrich air in a different way, by removing some of the nitrogen. This section reviews three "oxygen addition" methods: commercial mixing by weight, partial pressure mixing, and continuous flow blending. It also reviews two nitrogen removal methods: pressure-swing adsorption and membrane separation.

15.13.1 Commercial Pre-Mix

The simplest and most straightforward method of obtaining precisely mixed-gases is to purchase them from a commercial supplier. This method of obtaining nitrox may be preferred when logistics and project costs are appropriate.

The gases are normally mixed by weight; this avoids any anomalies due to "non-ideal" behavior of the gases and allows mixes to be quite precise. It also eliminates complications resulting from temperature changes during mixing. Mixing can be in cylinders, small banks of cylinders known as "quads," or large tube trailers. It is necessary to have appropriate scales, which are somewhat expensive because they measure a small change in a heavy weight. Because of the use of precision scales, mixing by weight is generally considered a shore-based technique. This is by far the most accurate method of obtaining mixed gases with a reliable analysis. Although premix requires oxygen handling by the commercial gas company, it does not require oxygen handling by the end user.

15.13.2 Partial-Pressure Mixing

As its name implies, partial-pressure mixing sets the proportions of the mix by partial-pressure. The technician puts a measured amount of oxygen (by pressure) into a cylinder and then fills the cylinder to a specific final pressure with another gas. For nitrox, it is typically ultra-pure air (see Figure 15.15). Oxygen is added first so that it need not be handled at the full cylinder pressure. Because high-pressure oxygen is added, the entire system, including the cylinder being filled, must be cleaned for oxygen service. Since pressure is influenced by temperature and the cylinder can get warm during compression, it is necessary to let the cylinder cool before making the pressure determinations. Because the proportions often need to be adjusted after cooling and/or analyzing, the overall process can be fairly time consuming.

Recently developed computerized partial-pressure mixing systems streamline the process by using microprocessors, pressure transducers, and temperature sensors, combined with sophisticated valve systems, making partial-pressure mixing relatively easy. Available systems are capable of filling upwards of 100 cylinders a day.

Partial-pressure mixing is also used to "top off" a cylinder when the oxygen content and pressure are already known, to the same or a different mix.

To make partial-pressure mixing effective, air needs to be supplied at a pressure high enough to fill the scuba cylinders completely. To get maximum utilization of pressure from a bank of supply cylinders, they are often used in bank configuration using a "cascade" fill technique. The supply cylinder with the lowest pressure is used first, and others follow one at a time in sequence, progressing to the one with the highest remaining pressure.

Compressors are often used with partial-pressure mixing. Compressors may be oil-free or used with ultra filtration systems that can supply air suitable for mixing with oxygen. Another way to boost gas to scuba cylinder pressure is with a "boost pump." Such systems are available that are cleaned for oxygen service. They use electricity or low-pressure air for power, amplifying pressure by means of different sized pistons.

Partial-pressure blending allows mixing a variety of mixtures for different diving operations. This method is not limited to any oxygen percentage and is good for mixing in remote locations. **The cylinders, valves, and the mixing system must always be cleaned for oxygen service when using this method.**

It is important that oxygen or nitrox mixtures not be introduced into oil-lubricated compressors.

Partial-pressure gas mixing is one of the simpler methods of mixing nitrox, but is also one of the more challenging. Handling pure oxygen and managing flow rates requires care and skill. However, because it is of frequently used in the field, this brief section on technique is included. This section assumes that there is a properly designed and oxygen-clean filling system available, supplied with either hyper-filtered air or air from an oil-free compressor, and either medical grade or aviator's grade oxygen. For purposes of safety, partial-pressure mixing should not be started until there is no doubt as to the cleanliness of any part of the mixing systems, including valves, scuba cylinders, or air quality.

The fill rate for introducing oxygen should be 60 psi per minute or less, and the cylinder should not get overly warm to the touch. A metered needle valve or oxygen flow regulator should be used to help regulate the oxygen flow. Once the oxygen has been introduced and the pressure gauge stabilizes, air is added to the cylinder at a flow rate not to exceed 400 psi per minute. The air flow rate can also be regulated with a metering needle valve. Filling from a compressor at a rate of 10 cfm or less is sufficient to maintain slow air fill rate. Higher capacity compressors should bank air prior to mixing or mix multiple cylinders at a time to slow the fill rate. The cylinder is best filled dry and slow enough that it remains close to ambient room temperature. There may be slight variations in the final mix if the temperature is either too high or too low; this can be adjusted after a final analysis. In any case the final pressures in all cylinders should be taken with the cylinders at room temperature, otherwise the pressure will have to be adjusted to account for the temperature difference. Filling an empty cylinder is usually the desired choice, but at times a partially filled cylinder will be refilled with the same or different mix.

15.13.3 Oxygen Fill Formula

Mixing with pure gases (oxygen and nitrogen) to make a nitrox mix is rarely done except by industrial gas companies. Blending technicians will normally use air and oxygen. The oxygen already in air must be considered when mixing nitrox using air. To determine the amount of oxygen to add to a cylinder for a desired mix the technician will use known values in a fill formula. Target FO_2 is the desired oxygen percentage in decimal form, 0.21 is the oxygen component in air, 0.79 is the nitrogen component in air, and FP is the final pressure (psi) of the cylinder.

Filling an Empty Cylinder

O_2 psi to add $=[(\text{target } FO_2 - 0.21) \div 0.79] \times FP$

Example: Desired mix of NN36 at 3,000 psi, filling an empty cylinder. To simplify the arithmetic, it is handy to use a dimensionless factor.

Step 1: Determine a conversion factor for this target mix, and air:

FIGURE 15.15
Filling Nitrox Cylinder

Conversion factor = [(target FO_2-0.21) ÷ 0.79]

NN36 conversion factor = [(0.36-0.21) ÷ 0.79] = 0.1898

Step 2: O_2 psi to add = conversion factor × FP

O_2 psi to add = 0.1898 × 3,000 psi = 569.6 psi

Step 3: Finish fill with ultra-pure air to final pressure (at room temperature).

This method ignores the ambient pressure (14.7 psi) of air that exists in an "empty" scuba cylinder. The amount of oxygen in it is trivial to the final mix.

Filling a Partially Filled Cylinder

At times, it may be advantageous to blend a nitrox mix in a cylinder that already contains a known mixture. This can be done for economy of gas, or to change a mix that has been made for a different dive.

In this situation the technician completes the "oxygen to add" calculation in two steps: 1) determine the amount of oxygen (in psi) in the existing mix, and 2) determine the

amount of oxygen needed for the desired mix, then find the difference. This difference is the new amount of oxygen to add to make the new mix.

Example: Divers have returned from a diving operation with some gas remaining in their cylinders and need to refill them with the same mix.

A returned cylinder is analyzed and contains 550 psi of NN36.

Step 1: Determine how much oxygen has been added to make 550 psi of 36% nitrox.
Conversion factor = [(target FO_2-0.21) ÷ 0.79]

NN36 conversion factor = [(0.36-0.21) ÷ 0.79] = 0.1898

Step 2: O_2 psi to add = conversion factor × FP

O_2 psi to add = 0.1898 x 550 psi = 104.4 psi

Step 3: Determine how much oxygen would be needed to make 3,000 psi of 36% nitrox.

Step 3a: Conversion factor = [(target FO_2-0.21) ÷ 0.79]

NN36 conversion factor = [(0.36-0.21) ÷ 0.79] = 0.1898

Step 4: O_2 psi to add = conversion factor × FP

O_2 psi to add = 0.1898 × 3,000 psi = 569.6 psi

Step 5: Subtract the existing oxygen from the total oxygen needed.

569.6 psi – 104.4 psi = 465.17 psi of oxygen is needed

Step 6: Add the needed oxygen of 465.17 psi to the existing mixture of 550 psi:

456.17 psi + 550 psi = 1,015 psi

Step 7: Add oxygen to the cylinder until the pressure reaches 1,015 psi, then add air to reach the final desired pressure of 3,000 psi (at room temperature).

The oxygen supply pressure needs to be sufficient to enable the partially-filled cylinder to be topped up.

Because of the potential for mathematical error in this process, all gas mixtures must be analyzed prior to use.

Changing a Mix

There are times where a particular mix has been made and it needs to be changed to either a higher or lower oxygen content mix. In these situations, the technician can predict what will need to be done. For example if an existing mix contains 32% oxygen and the new desired mix is 36% then oxygen will need to be added. If a mix of 40% exists and a 32% mix is needed then air will be added. In either case the technician must analyze the mix after adjustment to verify the contents, before tagging and releasing the cylinder.

Using Premix

It is common on some dive operations to premix a bank of gas for later mixing with air to make lower oxygen content nitrox mixes. This can be done either with the NOAA Continuous Nitrox Mixer or a membrane separation system. Typically a high oxygen content mix will be made, such as a 36% or 40% mix. Lower oxygen content mixes are then made by introducing the premix into the scuba cylinder and topping-off with compatible air. It may be necessary to use a gas booster to maximize the premix gas transfer.

Premix Filling Formula

Premix psi to add =

[(target FO_2 - 0.21) ÷ (premix FO_2 - 0.21)] × desired pressure

Example: Desired mix is NN32 at 3,000 psi. The storage bank contains 40% oxygen.

Premix to add =

$$= [(0.32-0.21) \div (0.40-0.21)] \times 3,000 \text{ psi}$$

$$= [0.11 \div 0.19] \times 3,000 \text{ psi}$$

$$= 0.5789 \times 3,000 \text{ psi}$$

$$= 1,736.94 \text{ psi of } 40\% \text{ O}_2$$

Top with air to 3,000 psi and analyze

15.13.3.1 Oxygen to Add Charts

For ease of use and to help minimize calculation errors an Oxygen Mixing Table is provided for five common nitrox gas mixes (see Table 15.9).

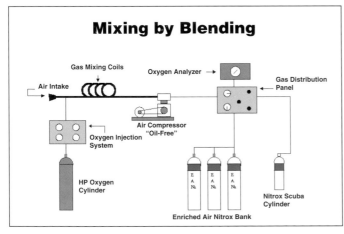

Mixing by Blending

FIGURE 15.16
Illustration of NOAA Continuous Nitrox Mixer

TABLE 15.9
Oxygen Mixing Table

Final Nitrox psi	OXYGEN PRESSURE (psi) TO ADD				
	Oxygen Percentage Desired				
	30%	32%	36%	40%	50%
4000	456	557	760	962	1468
3900	444	543	741	938	1432
3800	433	529	722	914	1395
3700	422	515	703	890	1358
3600	410	501	684	866	1322
3500	399	487	665	842	1285
3400	387	473	646	818	1248
3300	376	460	627	794	1211
3200	365	446	608	770	1175
3100	353	432	589	745	1138
3000	342	418	570	722	1101
2900	330	404	551	697	1065
2800	319	390	532	673	1028
2700	308	376	513	649	991
2600	296	362	494	625	954
2500	285	348	475	601	918
2400	273	334	456	577	881
2300	262	320	437	553	844
2200	251	306	418	529	808
2100	239	292	399	505	771
2000	228	279	380	481	734
1900	216	265	361	457	697
1800	205	251	342	433	661
1700	194	237	323	409	624
1600	182	223	304	385	587
1500	171	209	285	361	551
1400	160	195	266	336	514
1300	148	181	247	313	477
1200	137	167	228	289	441
1100	125	153	209	265	404
1000	114	139	190	241	367
900	103	125	171	216	330
800	91	111	152	192	294
700	80	97	133	168	257
600	68	84	114	144	220
500	57	70	95	120	184
400	46	56	76	96	147
300	34	42	57	72	110
200	23	28	38	48	73
100	11	14	19	24	37

Select final cylinder pressure in left column, intersect with desired oxygen mix. Add this amount of oxygen to empty cylinder at 60 psi per minute, add oxygen compatible air to cylinder at no more than 400 psi per minute to final pressure. Let cylinder stand, then analyze. Adjust mix if necessary.

Filling an empty cylinder:
- Find the desired mix and final pressure
- Add oxygen to the cylinder to the specified amount, let the pressure gauge stabilize
- Continue filling with compatible air to the final pressure

Select final cylinder pressure in left column, intersect with desired oxygen mix. Add this amount of oxygen to empty cylinder at 60 psi per minute, add oxygen compatible air to cylinder at no more than 400 psi per minute to final pressure. Let cylinder stand, then analyze. Adjust mix if necessary.

Filling a partially-filled cylinder:
- Look up the existing pressure and oxygen content
- Look up the desired mix and pressure
- Subtract the existing oxygen from the desired oxygen
- Add the differential amount of oxygen to the cylinder
- Continue filling with compatible air to the final pressure

It is important that the cylinder not get hot during the filling process. Upon completion let the cylinder stand for 30 minutes to mix and stabilize then analyze.

15.13.4 Continuous Flow Mixing

The NOAA Continuous Nitrox Mixer, developed by Dr. Morgan Wells in 1989, is one of the most user-friendly methods for mixing oxygen with air (see Figure 15.16). With this method, oxygen is metered into the intake stream of an oil-free compressor. The resulting mixture is compressed and routed to a gas distribution panel. The mixture is analyzed continuously, and this analysis is used to adjust the input oxygen flow. Oxygen-enriched air is vented from the distribution panel to the atmosphere until the desired mixture is obtained. With a scuba cylinder attached to the system, both the storage bank and scuba cylinder valves are open. Thus, nitrox enters the scuba cylinder from both the compressor and storage bank. When pressure in the scuba cylinder reaches that of the storage bank, the bank valve is closed, and all gas from the compressor enters the scuba cylinder. When the pressure of the scuba cylinder reaches the desired pressure, the fill valve is closed and the bank valve is opened, thus diverting the gas from the compressor to the storage bank. The above cycle is repeated with a new empty scuba cylinder. The point at which the bank pressure and scuba cylinder pressure are equal is obvious from the slowed increase in pressure at the scuba cylinder fill gauge. If the cylinder to be filled contains nitrox at a pressure greater than the storage bank, the bank valve is left closed, and gas is added only from the compressor. When all scuba cylinders are filled, the storage bank valve is opened, and the storage bank is filled to capacity. This significantly reduces the time required for the next filling operation, and allows the filling of some scuba cylinders without operating the "mixer." The above procedure also eliminates the requirement for an additional booster pump.

Numerous sources of gaseous oxygen are available for metering into the NOAA Continuous Nitrox Mixer. Compressed gaseous oxygen is normally used if the nitrox requirement is small or irregular. Liquid oxygen is generally a good source when large quantities of oxygen are used on a regular basis. The oxygen source does not have to be "pure" oxygen, since the system will function effectively when mixing air

with nitrox mixtures containing a fraction of oxygen greater than that of the desired final mixture. NOAA Experimental Diving Unit Report 93-04 (Wells and Moroz 1993) describes modifications of the basic "mixer" which incorporates such gas separation technologies as "pressure swing absorption," and differential permeability "membrane" systems. Such systems are currently available from commercial sources. Systems utilizing gas separation units and the NOAA Continuous Nitrox Mixer are of particular value when nitrox preparation is required in areas where pure oxygen is difficult to obtain, or expensive.

15.13.5 Pressure Swing Adsorption

The pressure swing adsorption (PSA) system is based on a material called "molecular sieve," a synthetic clay-like substance with pores that give it a very high surface area that adsorbs gases ("adsorb" means to absorb on the surface). Nitrogen is adsorbed more readily than oxygen; so, air that passes through the adsorbent bed emerges richer in oxygen. Two beds of adsorbent are normally used, and the gas stream is selectively alternated between them. While one is adsorbing, the other is being purged. Control of the cycling and pressures enables different levels of oxygen to be produced. The maximum oxygen such a system can deliver is approximately 95%, with the balance argon. Argon behaves much like oxygen in this type of adsorbent bed, so it will be present in the product gas in about the same ratio to oxygen as it is in air. The presence of argon at this level is not harmful to a diver.

This system does not require high-pressure oxygen, but is somewhat complicated and moderately expensive to acquire and maintain. The output gas can be fed directly into the NOAA Continuous Nitrox Mixer at atmospheric pressure.

15.13.6 Membrane Separation

The membrane separation system works by forcing clean low-pressure air through a membrane that allows oxygen to pass more readily than nitrogen. The "membrane" is in the form of thousands of tiny hair-like hollow tubules. The output gas is richer in oxygen than air, and the level of oxygen can be controlled by varying the input flow rate. The maximum effective oxygen level in commercial membrane systems is about 50%. This technique is used commercially to separate helium from natural gas, and for other gas separation processes.

Like the PSA system, no oxygen is needed to prepare nitrox mixes with the membrane system and the output gas can be used as the feed gas for the NOAA Continuous Nitrox Mixer. The membrane system is relatively sturdy and needs little maintenance. The input gas has to be properly filtered.

15.13.7 Boosting Pressure to Scuba Cylinders

The 40% rule only applies to the introduction of completed nitrox mixes into scuba cylinders and for use with scuba regulators and storage banks. Introducing a nitrox mixture with an oxygen content greater than air into an oil-lubricated compressor places all at risk of explosion. The NOAA continuous nitrox mixing method is used only with oil-free compressors.

It is common to use a gas booster to complete the filling process of a scuba cylinder, either for scavenging oxygen supply or for boosting premix to final pressure in the scuba cylinder. It is important that gas boosters used with high oxygen content mixes be prepared and appropriately labeled for oxygen service. Using a gas booster that has been contaminated or has not been prepared properly can result in explosion.

15.14 PERFORMING GAS ANALYSIS

All divers who use gas mixes need to know how to properly analyze the gas they will be using. Before discussing the procedures of how to analyze gas, a short discussion of how oxygen analyzers work is in order.

15.14.1 Oxygen Analyzers

Oxygen analyzers are available from many manufacturers, in different sizes and types; some have a digital display, and others use an analog (needle) read-out. See Figure 15.17 for various models. Either type can be used successfully for analyzing breathing gas mixtures. Ideally, an oxygen analyzer should have a resolution to a fraction of 0.001 or 0.1% (one-tenth of a percent). For example, the digital read-out should be able to read 32.4% instead of 32% or 35.8% instead of 36%. Divers should refer to the manufacturer's instructions to insure sufficient accuracy of their analyzer.

The heart of an oxygen analyzer is its detection method. There are two primary types of oxygen analyzers generally used for breathing gases; paramagnetic and electrochemical.

Paramagnetic analyzers are primarily used in research laboratories; the traditional ones are accurate, stable, relatively expensive, and somewhat delicate, and intolerant of vibration.

The other category of oxygen analyzer available in portable units comprises those that are electrochemical. The electrochemical cell breaks oxygen into ions and electrons and measures the current generated; this current is proportional to the partial pressure of oxygen to which the sensor is exposed. Electrochemical oxygen analyzers use two electrodes made of different metals; these are immersed in an electrolyte solution that is contained by a thin, oxygen-permeable membrane. Oxygen diffuses through the membrane to the cathode, where it is reduced, generating a very small current. This current is linearly proportional to the PO_2; it is measured by the unit's electronic circuit and the results are displayed.

The electrochemical analyzers are of two types—polargraphic and fuel cell. The function of these is the same to the user and the difference is not relevant here. These are also used in laboratories and industrial settings.

Electrochemical analyzers are relatively inexpensive, can be made portable and rugged, and show little interference from other gases. However, they tend to be unstable and may need frequent calibration, especially as the cell begins to age. Cell life depending on manufacturer and use can be anywhere from 6 to 18 months.

15.14.2 The Analysis Process

The process of analyzing a cylinder of gas mix involves calibrating the analyzer with a "standard gas" or "calibrating gas," then repeating with the "unknown" or "sample" mix. Both the calibrating gas and the sample mix should be passed through the analyzer at the same flow rate.

No matter what the method or mechanism of a gas analyzer, the analysis is no better than the calibration of the analyzer. An electrochemical cell tends to be quite linear. Some types of analyzers are not linear, and these can be a great deal more trouble to use. Being linear, it needs to be calibrated in only two places to give reliable readings. This is called "zeroing" and "spanning." In effect this sets the slope and the intercept of the calibration curve. Oxygen analyzers can be "zeroed" with an inert gas such as argon, nitrogen, or helium; the gas type does not matter with this mechanism. Some analyzers rely on an electrical zero, but this may not be quite as reliable, since this method does not account for drift of the sensor cell.

Ideally it is best to calibrate or "span" an analyzer with a "standard" gas that is close in oxygen level to the sample. For analyzing oxygen levels in the range of 21–40% oxygen, it is satisfactory to calibrate with fresh outside air, using the value 20.95% oxygen. Since values above this level are "extrapolations," if an analyzer is spanned but not zeroed properly it may be off by a percentage point or two at 40%. The best method is to "bracket" the unknown with calibration gases.

15.14.3 Analyzing Gas

It is standard procedure for NOAA divers to analyze the gas before accepting or signing out a nitrox cylinder for use. In addition, the diver will want to analyze the gas again just before diving with it. The procedures for analysis are simple to follow, but must be done carefully to maintain the integrity of the resulting analysis. The diver will choose diving tables and oxygen limits based on this analysis.

One properly calibrated analyzer, used correctly, is adequate for checking scuba cylinders. Repeated analysis with the same unit properly calibrated helps build the confidence in the tool. If in doubt as to the accuracy of the analyzer, a second properly calibrated unit may be utilized for comparative purposes.

15.14.3.1 Calibrating Gas

The best calibration gases are normally obtained from a commercial gas supplier, and should be in the range of or slightly higher than the sample to be analyzed. As an alternative, atmospheric air has a uniform composition everywhere, at a level of 20.95%, or 21% for practical purposes. Industrial "air" obtained in cylinders might vary from this value, so only compressed atmospheric air should be used.

15.14.3.2 Flow Rate

Proper analysis depends not only on the analyzer itself, but on the flow rate of the gas passing in front of the sensor cell. The sample should be read at the same flow rate as is used for the calibration. A flow meter or flow controller should be used. Different tools are available to regulate the gas flow for analyzing (see Figure 15.18). One type uses a special regulator fitted with a flow valve capable of adjusting the flow rate from zero to ten liters per minute (the upper end of this device is much higher than needed). Ideally, the flow should be between one-half and one liter per minute. One type of special fitting is available that connects to the low-pressure inflation hose of a buoyancy compensator and acts as a flow meter that is either adjustable or preset to two liters per minute. Although it is possible to analyze the gas without a flow meter, readings can be inaccurate and this is not recommended practice.

15.14.3.3 Calibration

Before performing an analysis the analyzer should be calibrated to a known gas. The flow rate regulating device is attached to the source of calibrating gas or compressed atmospheric air. Turn on the oxygen analyzer, set the flow rate at (nominally) one liter per minute and let the gas flow through the sensor for approximately one minute or until the reading is stable. Once settled, make sure the reading is set to the value of the calibrating gas, or 20.9% (see Figure 15.19) if air is used; adjust the calibration setting on the analyzer if necessary.

If adjustments are needed too often during re-calibration, it may be time to replace the sensor.

15.14.3.4 Analyzing the Nitrox Cylinder

Once the meter has been calibrated, leave it turned on and move the sampling device onto the cylinder that needs analysis. The reading shown in Figure 15.20 (31.8%) is appropriate for use as NN32. Remember that the flow rate should be the same as that to which the unit was calibrated. The meter should read the new gas for at least one minute or until stable. If the sampling hose between the cylinder and the analyzer is more than 24 inches in length, the flow should be allowed to continue for at least two minutes. The resultant reading is the oxygen fraction in the mixture. At sea level, this is equal to the oxygen fraction. Transfer this number immediately to the cylinder contents label, fill out the rest of the data, and attach it to the cylinder. This information should also be entered in a permanent log book.

FIGURE 15.17
[From left] Analox Mini-Ox, OMS Professional, Teledyne 320B, Miniox (Catalyst Research)

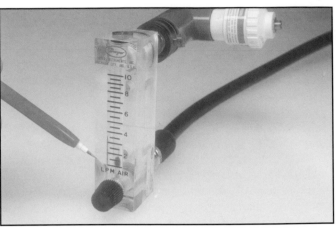

FIGURE 15.18
Flow Meter Connected to Low-Pressure Inflator Hose

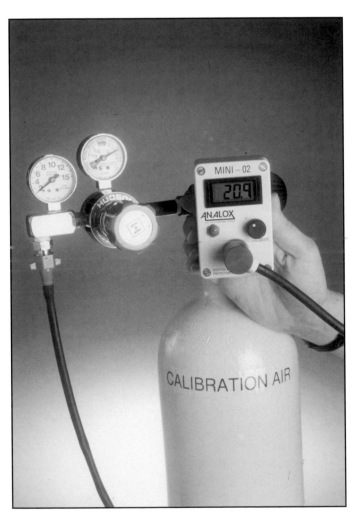

FIGURE 15.19
Oxygen Analyzer, with Flow Meter Set to 2 lpm

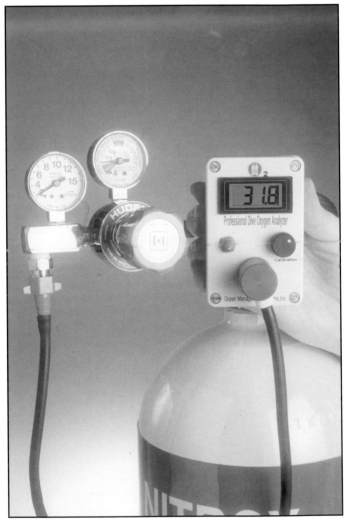

FIGURE 15.20
Oxygen Analyzer Analyzing a Nitrox Cylinder

Mixed-Gas and Oxygen Diving

16

is air, which can be used effectively from sea level to approximately 150 fsw (46.1 msw). At depths greater than this, nitrogen narcosis (covered in detail in Chapter 3) is the dominant limiting factor in the use of nitrogen-based breathing mixtures.

For circumstances that require clear thinking and quick response to solve a problem, deep diving with air can be dangerous. It is the reason NOAA limits the use of air to 170 fsw (52.2 msw).

Other gases can cause narcosis. See Chapter 3, Diving Physiology, Section 3.3.3.1, Inert Gas Narcosis.

16.1.2 Helium

Helium has not been known to produce narcotic effects on divers at any depth at which it has been used (Lambertsen, Gelfand, Peterson, Strauss, Wright, Dickson, Puglia, and Hamilton 1977). Its lower density makes it much easier to breathe than nitrogen, and in some cases (long exposures) it improves decompression. Helium's use is limited by its cost and more limited availability than air. However for deeper dives where attention to detail is paramount, helium is usually well worth its extra cost if it avoids an accident caused by narcosis rendering a diver unable to cope with a problem.

Another drawback associated with the use of helium is the loss of body heat, which is caused in part by the fact that the thermal conductivity of helium is approximately six times that of air. Helium has a higher thermal conductivity than nitrogen; its thermal properties make it unfavorable in cases where the diver is immersed in a helium gas mixture, or if it is used inside a diving suit. Helium is a very poor insulator. Helium properties with respect to High Pressure Nervous Syndrome (HPNS) and hyperbaric arthralgia are relevant in surface-oriented diving.

Mixtures containing helium feel colder for the diver to breathe, but because helium is a lighter gas with less thermal capacity, breathing a helium mixture may actually remove less heat from the diver than an equivalent nitrogen-based mixture. It has been determined that in order to avoid hypothermia, breathing gas has to be heated for divers working at depths deeper than approximately 500 fsw (153.5 msw). Heat loss in the breathing gas relies on a combination of both heat capacity and conductivity, but definitive research to partition the relative importance of these two effects in breathing gas heat loss has yet to be done.

Another well-known property of helium is its tendency to distort human speech. This can make voice communication difficult or impossible at great depths. The effect can be corrected with electronic "unscramblers," but they are generally not needed in the range of surface-oriented diving.

Yet another gas-related deep diving problem not likely to be encountered by NOAA surface-oriented divers is isobaric inert gas counterdiffusion. This phenomenon can occur when a person saturated with a nitrogen gas load (or other soluble, slow-moving gas) is switched into a helium-rich environment (or other rapidly diffusing gas). The helium diffuses into the skin faster than the nitrogen diffuses out, leading to a local supersaturation manifested as severe itching and rashes. This can also predispose a diver to vestibular (inner ear) decompression sickness. Switching to air or another nitrogen-based gas during decompression from a dive with helium mixtures does not cause counterdiffusion problems because the helium off-gases faster than the nitrogen can on-gas.

16.1.3 Other Inert Gases (Hydrogen, Neon, Argon)

As mentioned, several other gases have been studied as replacements for the helium component. Neon, argon, and hydrogen have been used operationally, but mainly on an experimental basis. All three carry with them some significant disadvantages. Still other gases, including sulfur hexafluoride, nitrous oxide, and carbon tetrafluoride, have been used as experimental gases to vary the properties of breathing mixtures.

Neon offers some advantages over helium. Although evidence is weak, it appears to have some decompression advantages for certain profiles. Neon is not narcotic, and it has lower thermal conductivity and distorts speech less than helium (Lambertsen, Gelfand, Peterson, Strauss, Wright, Dickson, Puglia, and Hamilton 1977). However, neon's density causes it to create more breathing resistance than helium, a problem as depth increases beyond approximately 500 fsw (153.5 msw). Pure neon is too expensive to use for diving. However, a mixture of neon and helium produced as a by-product in the cryogenic distillation of air (about 75% neon and 25% helium, called "crude neon" or "neon 75") could be economically feasible under the right circumstances and has been used in several commercial and recreational diving operations.

Hydrogen is not easily used as a diver's breathing gas because of its explosive qualities. However, by keeping the oxygen concentration in the mixture below the limit of combustion, non-explosive hydrogen-oxygen mixtures can be used. The lower flammability limit of hydrogen is 4% oxygen, and this can be attained in a gas that will have enough PO_2 for breathing deeper than about 200 fsw (61.4 msw). Special techniques are used to prepare the mixtures. Hydrogen has some distinct advantages in its low density and more favorable HPNS properties, but these are only relevant in very deep diving. Hydrogen is narcotic, is unfavorable during decompression, and counterdiffuses against helium. One interesting new prospect for hydrogen is that microbial enzymes are being studied that enable laboratory animals to "digest" this gas and remove it from the blood circulation.

16.1.4 Decompression with Special Gas Mixtures

The fraction of inert gas in a breathing mixture (or conversely, the fraction of oxygen) is an important factor in determining a diver's decompression requirements. Breathing a nitrox mixture that contains a higher fraction of oxygen than air will clearly reduce the need for decompression. The situation is not so clear when helium is used as an inert gas. In fact, when both helium and nitrogen are involved the role of the inert gases may seem paradoxical.

For short dives ("bounce dives") the predominant factor for decompression is the oxygen level, with the nature of the inert gas or gases a secondary factor. In such dives with a trimix of oxygen, helium, and nitrogen, helium appears to be less favorable in decompression. When comparing decompression obligation for heliox and trimix gases containing equal amounts of oxygen, the mixture with the highest percent of helium will result in the greatest decompression requirement. Table 16.1 illustrates how a heliox mix results in significantly more decompression time over a trimix with nitrogen in the mix. Note that if the diver were only to decompress using the "bottom mix," the trimix decompression is 136 minutes less than the heliox decompression which results in a significant time savings. Additionally, the heliox mixture produces no narcosis whereas the trimix has an equivalent air narcotic effect at 52 fsw (16 msw).

For longer exposures, saturation and exposures approaching saturation, the situation is reversed. It takes roughly three times as long to decompress from a saturation exposure in a nitrox environment than in a heliox environment. Oxygen plays a major role in saturation also, with the rate of decompression directly related to the PO_2.

16.2 OXYGEN PHYSIOLOGY

A certain amount of oxygen is needed to sustain life every minute, and this value is a measure of the activity level of the individual, among other factors. A normal or "average" individual at rest needs about 300 ml of oxygen per minute, and during heavy work this level can be as high as three liters or more. Moderate activity takes about one liter/minute. This oxygen is normally extracted from the air being breathed. The value of oxygen consumption does not change when pure oxygen is being breathed. The rate of oxygen consumption is used as an indirect measure of energy production by the body.

The physiological and toxic boundaries of oxygen partial pressures as a function of ambient pressure (depth) and percentage of oxygen are summarized in Figure 16.1, which shows the relations between mix composition, pressure (depth), and partial pressure limits. Pressure is shown on the horizontal axis, in atmospheres at the top and depth in feet of sea water at the bottom. The percentage of oxygen in mixes is shown on the left vertical axis, partial pressures on the right, and the curved isopleths that show effects of different PO_2s are labeled on the right vertical axis. This diagram shows that many mixtures can be breathed over a wide range of pressures.

16.2.1 Oxygen Toxicity

The major concern of oxygen toxicity to a diver is a convulsion, the epileptic-like seizure that can follow oxygen exposure beyond a certain limit. A convulsion in the water for a diver breathing by scuba mouthpiece can readily lead to drowning. There are other less dramatic CNS symptoms, widely taught and covered in detail in Chapter 3. These symptoms represent a toxic response to oxygen exposure, and may serve as a warning about an impending convulsion; however, a convulsion can occur without any warning.

16.2.2 Managing Oxygen Exposure

The core of countermeasures for avoiding oxygen toxicity rests with dose limits, exposure times, and PO_2 levels above which the risk of toxicity becomes unacceptable. In addition, controlling certain "environmental" factors can reduce the risk. For specific information on how to monitor and manage oxygen exposures see Chapter 3.

16.3 DIVING WITH SPECIAL GAS MIXES

This section deals with the methods for using mixed gases operationally, with special attention to decompression.

TABLE 16.1
Decompression Comparison

Heliox		Trimix	
21% O_2 79% HE		21% O_2 50% HE 29% N_2	
Depth fsw	Minutes	Depth fsw	Minutes
200	30	200	30
Decompression Stops		Decompression Stops	
80	3		
70	5	70	2
60	6	60	3
50	10	50	6
40	17	40	10
30	30	30	16
20	61	20	30
10	139	10	68
Total Runtime	305		169
Decompression Time	271		135

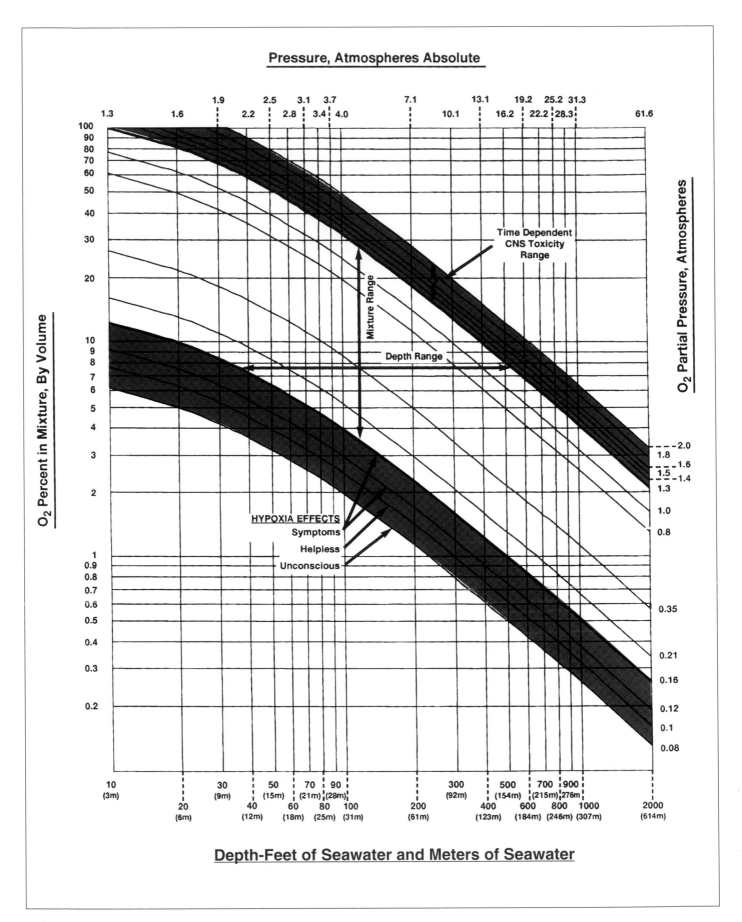

FIGURE 16.1
Effect of Oxygen with Various Pressures and Mixtures

16.3.1 Technical Diving

Beginning in the late 1980s, a new category of diving began to develop in the United States, known as "technical diving." Whereas traditional scientific diving involves no-stop scuba diving with air or nitrox to 130 fsw (39.9 msw), standard technical diving practice entails diving with self-contained diving equipment in the range from about 170 fsw (52.2 msw) to as deep as 350 fsw (107.5 msw) using trimixes of oxygen, helium, and nitrogen.

A "technical dive" is an untethered dive that involves a change of breathing mix during the dive (or a dive with a rebreather, which has been called technical diving in Great Britain for half a century).

16.3.1.1 Accelerated Decompression

It has long been known in commercial and military diving that using oxygen during decompression for air and heliox dives not only makes the decompression shorter but more efficient (Hamilton 1980, Vann 1989, Flynn, Maurer, and Latson 1999). The downside of using the bottom mix (air or heliox) for decompression is that the partial pressure of the oxygen in the mix is too low at the shallower depths where decompression stops occur for it to assist in eliminating inert gas loading. If the diver can shift gas during the ascent phase of the dive from a bottom mix to a high oxygen content mix (i.e. nitrox or 100% oxygen) then the decompression can be shortened. For traditional surface-supplied diving this is relatively simple to do, the gas switch is made on the surface and the diver has the proper gas delivered to his helmet or mask at depth via an umbilical. For open-circuit scuba diving the diver needs to carry the decompression gas with him and physically switch (remove one regulator and insert another) from one gas supply to another. The advantages of accelerating the decompression include less immersion time, more efficient decompression, and the ability to obtain increased bottom time with reasonable decompression. When necessary, oxygen alone can be used to decrease decompression time when an oxygen-rich nitrox is not available.

Table 16.2 illustrates the advantages of gas shifting for a dive to 130 fsw (39.9 msw) using air as the bottom mix.

16.3.1.2 Diving with Trimixes of Nitrogen, Helium, and Oxygen

Helium has been used to avoid nitrogen narcosis since the 1930s for diving beyond the traditional air range (approximately 190 fsw (58.3 msw), or shallower in many situations). Traditionally, such diving has been conducted with helium-oxygen mixtures, "heliox," but lately "trimixes" of nitrogen, helium, and oxygen have been used for diving in the surface-oriented range to about 350 fsw (107.5 msw). The term "trimix" has also been applied to very deep saturation diving mixtures with 5–10% nitrogen added to relieve HPNS (see Chapter 3).

TABLE 16.2
Accelerated Decompression Comparison

Depth		Air Only	Air+NN36	Air+ Nitrox 50	Air + Oxygen	Air + Nitrox 50 + Oxygen
fsw	msw	Time/min	Time/min	Time/min	Time/min	Time/min
130	40	60	60	60	60	60
110	34		shift to NN36			
70	22			shift to Nitrox 50		shift to Nitrox 50
Stop Depth		********* Stop Times *********				
40	12	8	6	5	8	5
30	9	15	12	10	15	10
					**** shift to 100% oxygen ****	
20	6	27	19	15	11	9
10	3	48	34	27	17	16
Total Time		161	134	120	114	103
Total Decompression Time		98 min	71 min	57 min	51 min	40 min
% CNS Limit		23%	27%	37%	60%	60%
OTU's		66	82	105	115	127

16.3.1.2.1 Rationale and Need for Using Trimix

The rationale for using trimix is to allow divers to function more normally at depths where air becomes too narcotic. This is accomplished by adding helium to air or nitrox mixtures to produce complex trimixes. In order to do this, it is necessary to have unique and dedicated decompression procedures. Custom trimix decompression tables have been developed and several computer software programs have become available that allowed divers to compute their own trimix (and other) decompression tables. Original trimix decompression tables were based on algorithms developed by Professor Alfred A. Bühlmann, which were published and available to the general public. Dive equipment was first customized by individual divers and later developed by specialty manufacturers; operational and emergency procedures evolved, and technical diving matured into a reasonably well-defined practice.

16.3.1.2.2 Selecting an Appropriate Trimix

The purpose of using trimix is to control both the oxygen fraction and the narcotic effects of nitrogen. Once the depth of a dive site has been determined, the gas mixture for that depth can be created. This is done by first determining the oxygen exposure level to be used, then choosing an acceptable level of narcosis. For most trimix dives the oxygen exposure is set so the working portion of the dive has a PO_2 of 1.6 ata or less. This is similar to selecting the oxygen fraction for nitrox diving. The narcosis level is set somewhere between 70 and 120 fsw (21.5 and 36.8 msw). This is called the "equivalent narcotic depth" or "END." The END is normally set at 4.0 PN_2 or less depending on the dive operation. By adjusting the amount of helium in the mix the nitrogen is diluted, thus reducing the overall narcotic effect of the mixture at depth.

For example, when planning NOAA research dives to the Monitor National Marine Sanctuary (MNMS) at a depth of 230 fsw (70.6 msw), the parameters called for a maximum PO_2 of 1.5 and an END of 75 fsw (23.0 msw) or less. The following steps were involved in determining the best trimix to use for the dives:

Step 1 Find the oxygen fraction:

- Determine the total pressure (in ata) at 230 fsw:

  230 fsw / 33 + 1 ata = 7.97 ata

- Determine the maximum oxygen percent allowed without exceeding a 1.5 PO_2 at a depth of 230 fsw:

  1.5 ata PO_2 / 7.97 ata = 0.188 = 18% O_2

Step 2 Find the nitrogen fraction:

- Determine the total pressure (in ata) at 230 fsw:

  230 fsw / 33 + 1 ata = 7.97 ata

- Determine the total pressure (in ata) at 75 fsw:

  75 fsw / 33 fsw + 1 ata = 3.27 ata

- Determine the PN_2 at a depth of 75 fsw:

  3.27 ata × 0.79 = 2.58 ata

- Determine the maximum nitrogen percentage allowed without exceeding a 2.58 ata PN_2 at a depth of 230 fsw:

  2.58 ata / 7.97 ata = 0.324 = 32% N_2

Step 3 Find the helium fraction:

- Add the oxygen and the nitrogen together:

  0.18 O_2 + 0.32 N_2 = 0.50

- Subtract the total from 1.0 to find helium fraction needed:

  1.0 - 0.50 = 0.50 = 50% He

The final mix selected for dives to the MNMS was 18% oxygen, 50% helium, and 32% nitrogen. The mix is written as 18/50 trimix and has since been designated NOAA Trimix 18/50.

16.3.1.2.3 Mixture Adjustment for Operational Considerations

Choosing a trimix is not strictly a "by the numbers" decision. The dive supervisor will make decisions on a mix based upon decompression time, mixing logistics, and operational simplicity. Variable mix tables make the supervisor's decisions easier. The NOAA Trimix 18/50 tables are variable mix tables which allow for using a range of mixes with one set of tables. The tables allow for 17–19% oxygen and 40–50% helium. These tables allow for optimization of the mix for the given site or allow for general use over a range of depths. Other trimix tables have an even wider range such as 16–21% oxygen and 17–50% helium. There are also trimix tables that are generated for a specific mix. It is important to plan for the maximum depth from an oxygen standpoint first, then select the helium fraction, especially when using mixes with less than 16% oxygen.

16.3.1.2.4 Equivalent Narcotic Depth

Because the nitrogen partial pressure in a given trimix will be lower than that in air, the narcotic effect produced will be less than it would be breathing air to the equivalent depth. It is reasonable to assume that when the nitrogen is replaced in part with helium that only the nitrogen plays a role in narcosis. However, since oxygen has some narcotic properties, it is appropriate to include the oxygen fraction in the END calculation when using trimixes (Lambersten et al. 1977, 1978). The non-helium portion (i.e., the sum of the oxygen and the nitrogen) is to be regarded as having the same narcotic potency as an equivalent partial pressure of nitrogen in air, regardless of the proportions of oxygen and nitrogen.

Table 16.3 illustrates helium fractions used to create trimixes with various END levels. It is possible, however, to calculate the amount of helium required to achieve a specific END at a particular depth by using the formula:

$$FHe = (Pd - PEND) / Pd$$

where
  FHe = fraction of helium in the mixture
  Pd = depth of the dive in ata
PEND = depth in ata of the desired END

Example:
Determine the amount of helium required to achieve an END of 90 fsw for a trimix dive to 200 fsw.

Solution:
Determine the total pressure at 200 fsw (P_d):

(200 fsw + 33)/33 or (200 fsw/33) + 1 = 7.06 ata

Determine the total pressure at 90 fsw (P_{END}):

(90 fsw + 33)/33 or (90 fsw/33) + 1 = 3.73 ata

Solve (P_d - P_{END}) / P_d =

(7.06 ata - 3.73 ata) / 7.06 ata = 0.472 = 47% FHe

16.3.1.2.5 Trimix Dive Profile

The typical trimix dive profile consists of descent to and work on the bottom breathing trimix, referred to as "bottom mix," followed by ascent to the first decompression stop also on bottom mix. At the first decompression stop there is normally a switch to an intermediate decompression mix, usually nitrox. For many trimix dives an intermediate mix such as the NOAA Nitrox 36 (NN36) is appropriate. The switch is made at a depth that will not produce a PO_2 level greater than 1.6 ata, in the case of NOAA Trimix 18/50, the switch to NN36 is made at 110 fsw (33.8 msw). The depth at which the diver switches from bottom mix to decompression gas is specified in the trimix decompression tables. The diver remains on nitrox during ascent until reaching 20 fsw (6.1 msw) at which point the breathing gas is switched to oxygen. The diver continues to breath oxygen until cleared to ascend to the 10 fsw (3.1 msw) stop and then to the surface. Should sea conditions make it difficult to maintain a 10 fsw (3.1 msw) stop position, the stop can be completed for the 20 fsw (6.1 msw) and 10 fsw stop times.

Planning includes making sure that the diver will not be exposed to a toxic level of oxygen during any phase of the dive. It may be advantageous to insert "air breaks" during oxygen decompression stops. This technique of breath-ing air for 5 minutes after every 20 minutes on oxygen, has proven beneficial in reducing the chances of CNS oxygen toxicity, especially at 20 ft. where the PO_2 on 100% oxygen is high (1.6 ata). Planning also requires consideration of narcosis due to the nitrogen in the mix, to calculate for the "equivalent narcotic depth." As mentioned earlier, the suggested practice is to consider the total partial pressure of both the oxygen and nitrogen components as if it were air, then relate that to a narcotic level not to exceed a maximum "air equivalent" of 130 fsw (139.9 msw).

16.3.1.2.6 Trimix Decompression Tables

In preparation for archeological dives to the Monitor National Marine Sanctuary, the NOAA Experimental Diving Unit developed a standard trimix, designated NOAA Trimix I (NTI), and a simple method for its preparation. NTI consisted of a nominal 18% oxygen (17-19%), 40-50% helium, and the balance nitrogen. NOAA Nitrox 36 (NN36) was used both as a decompression gas and as a "stock" mixture for the preparation of the NTI. NN36 can be prepared by an air separation device (PSA or membrane) coupled with the NOAA Continuous Nitrox Mixer. This procedure significantly reduces the quantity of pure oxygen that must be transported to the dive site for the preparation of gas mixtures used to support trimix diving operations. (Wells and Phoel 1995). When used with 18% oxygen, this mixture has a maximum operating depth of 260 fsw (79.8 msw), that falls within NOAA's maximum oxygen exposure limit of 1.6 ata for a maximum of 45 minutes (see Table 16-4). This mixture is most effective in the range of 170-240 fsw (52.2-73.7 msw). The NOAA Trimix decompression tables were originally created in 1993, by Hamilton Research Ltd. In 1998, the tables were revised by the same company and re-designated "NOAA Trimix 18/50." These decompression tables have been used on several deep diving research projects sponsored by NOAA.

The NOAA Trimix 18/50 Decompression Tables were published in two formats. One is a detailed format for a single depth and bottom time and the other a condensed format with several bottom times for a single dive. A sample of a detailed format is shown in Table 16.4. Note the table identification DH58T0.H00 at the upper left; each table set is uniquely identified so that calculation parameters can be tracked. Each column is labeled. The tables allow the divers to descend at their own rate, and the time of descent is considered part of the bottom time. The tables require a fixed stop at 110 fsw, even if not required for the decompression. This "forced" stop was inserted to provide time for the diver to shift breathing gas from the bottom mix to the intermediate decompression gas at a fixed depth (i.e., while stopped) instead of performing the shift while ascending. The column "Dec time" is the elapsed decompression time from leaving bottom, and "Run time" is elapsed time since leaving the surface. The diver need not keep track of the time of individual stops, but only has to leave each stop when the decompression time is up, as shown in the "Dec time" column. That is, the diver leaves

TABLE 16.3
Helium Selection Based Upon Equivalent Air Narcotic Depth

fsw	msw	atm abs	END 85 fsw % Helium	END 100 fsw % Helium	END 110 fsw % Helium	END 120 fsw % Helium
130	40	4.94	0.28	0.18	0.12	0.06
140	43	5.24	0.32	0.23	0.17	0.11
150	46	5.55	0.35	0.27	0.22	0.16
160	49	5.85	0.39	0.31	0.26	0.21
170	52	6.15	0.42	0.34	0.30	0.25
180	55	6.45	0.45	0.38	0.33	0.28
190	58	6.76	0.47	0.40	0.36	0.31
200	61	7.06	0.49	0.43	0.39	0.34
210	64	7.36	0.51	0.45	0.41	0.37
220	67	7.67	0.53	0.47	0.44	0.39
230	71	7.97	0.55	0.49	0.46	0.42
240	74	8.27	0.57	0.51	0.48	0.44
250	77	8.58	0.58	0.53	0.50	0.46
260	80	8.88	0.60	0.55	0.51	0.48
270	83	9.18	0.61	0.56	0.53	0.49
280	86	9.48	0.62	0.58	0.54	0.51
290	89	9.79	0.63	0.59	0.56	0.53
300	92	10.09	0.65	0.60	0.57	0.54

To find helium needed for the trimix, select maximum dive depth, then intersect with desired END. The resulting number is the helium fraction needed in the mix. The 40−50% helium range has been highlighted as the range for NOAA Trimix 18/50. Use of helium shallower than depths indicated will always produce a lesser narcotic effect.

Mixed-Gas and Oxygen Diving

TABLE 16.4
Sample Trimix Table

```
NOAA Trimix 18/50 Tables; inwater; 18/50+36+O₂   DEPTH        230 FSW
rwh/dd                  98May12                  BOTTOM TIME  25 Mins
DH58T0.H00              mf11f6.dcp               BOTTOM MIX   18TX50
                                                 BOTTOM PO2   1.43 ATM

Depth Stop Dec  Run        HiPO2                 Times in minutes
 FSW  time time time  Mix  ATM                   Comments
------------------------------------------------------------------
 00   00   00   00   Air   0.21 Descent optional; included in bottom t.
      00   00   00   18TX50 0.19 Breathe trimix 18%O2, 50%He from sfc
230   25   00   25   18TX50 1.51 Ascend to 110 fsw or 1st stop at 60 f/min.
                                 Fixed stop at 110, change gas and rate
110   01   03   28   36EANx 1.60 Stop 1 m at 110 fsw; switch to 36% EANx
                                 Ascent rate 30 fsw/min after 110 fsw stop.
\\\\\\\\\\\\\\\\\\\\\\\\\\\\\\\\\\ Some stops deleted for manual
 70   02   09   34   36EANx 1.15
 60   02   12   37   36EANx 1.04
 50   05   17   42   36EANx 0.93
 40   06   23   48   36EANx 0.82
 30   16   40   65   36EANx 0.71
 20   13   53   78   Oxygen 1.61 Breathe 100% O2 at 20 fsw, to surface
 10   24   77  102   Oxygen 1.30
 00   00   78  103   Air   0.21 Reach surface
                                 Total time = 01:43 hr:mn OTU   140 units
                                 Decom time = 01:18 hr:mn VC Drop = -0.8%
                                 Max O2 Fract= 0.50 Mix used(Tx;EA):  205   46
```

This table shows detailed display of stops and gas switches, as well as a summary of dive information. VC is estimated reduction in vital capacity. The "mix used" entries, here 205 and 46, are an estimate for gas consumed in cubic feet. This table is for illustrative purposes only and is not complete, do not use for actual diving.

the 110 fsw stop 3 minutes after leaving bottom. The "Max O₂ Fract" is 0.50, which means the diver has used 0.5 or 50% of the allowable exposure limit. The two numbers on the lower right are estimates of gas consumed, in cubic feet at approximately one cubic foot of gas per minute.

Other trimix tables are available through technical training organizations, decompression specialists, and dive computational software programs. Dive computers are also becoming available for use with trimixes. Only decompression tables approved by the NOAA Diving Safety Board may be used on NOAA projects.

16.3.1.2.7 Management and Supervision During Trimix Diving

There is another less tangible aspect of trimix diving that must be considered, the human factor. Individuals considering this type of diving must be physically fit, properly trained and equipped, and extremely comfortable and competent in the water. While individual divers have to be self sufficient, there should also be strong supervision and a support system for divers in the water. The support team should know the divers' plan and be ready to provide whatever help is needed, from providing extra gas to full rescue if necessary. Divers working as a buddy pair need to be extremely well coordinated and have the right equipment for the buddy operation. A good team plan is to have all divers use similar equipment and wear it configured the same way; this greatly facilitates one diver helping another in the water.

NOAA diving operations require that divers who will be using trimix be fully trained and certified (NAO 209–123). In addition, all divers must be cleared for diving by an approved medical physician and show proof of recent proficiency in trimix diving under similar conditions and to similar depths as those to be conducted. NOAA also requires that a detailed operations plan be prepared for each trimix diving operation to be conducted. A typical operation plans includes the following information:

- Overview of operating area and environment
- Description of site
- Expedition goals and objectives
- Contingency plans
- Potential adverse conditions
- Documentation (permits, dive certificates,etc)
- Budget and financial considerations
- Personnel and responsibilities
- Chain of command
- Schedule
- Methodology to be used
- Equipment and facilities
- Logistics and support
- Advance and emergency notification
- Search and rescue facility availability
- Dive accident management plan

Fatal accidents in technical diving can almost all be placed into two categories. The first is the familiar pattern for all self-contained, open-circuit diving of running out of gas, either as the terminal event or as the trigger for a sequence of events leading to an accident. The second is breathing the wrong gas at the wrong time, usually resulting in a toxic or inadequate level of oxygen.

16.3.1.3 Diving with Helium-Oxygen Mixtures

Although NOAA and other scientific diving programs use trimix effectively, commercial and military diving in the same depth range is almost universally carried out with helium-oxygen, "heliox" mixtures. Trimix has some small advantages over heliox in decompression, voice distortion and insulating properties. When mixing costs can be ignored, trimixes may also be less expensive. However, there are compensating factors in favor of heliox, most notably reduced breathing resistance and narcosis. Depending on the volume required, heliox may be less expensive than trimix because of the extra costs of mixing and analyzing trimix.

Traditional heliox diving, the practice known as "mixed-gas diving" or just "gas diving" is well established. Although most commercial diving companies jealously guard their proprietary mixed-gas decompression tables, some such tables are published in the *U.S. Navy Diving Manual*.

The dive profile for heliox is similar to that using trimix. Descent may be started with bottom mix or with air if the bottom mix contains less than 16% oxygen. If air is used, the diver will be shifted to the bottom mix at a predetermined depth during descent and will remain on bottom mix while on the bottom and through all or a portion of the ascent. The diver is typically switched to an intermediate decompression mixture of nitrox and/or 100% oxygen during ascent. Most surface-supplied heliox diving conducted by commercial diving companies and the U.S. Navy utilizes surface decompression with oxygen, "Sur-D/O₂," whereby the diver exits the water from 40 or 30 fsw (12.3 or 9.2 msw), enters a chamber, is recompressed to a predetermined depth (typically 40 fsw or 12.3 msw), and completes decompression breathing oxygen in the chamber.

16.3.1.4 Diving with Pure Oxygen

Certain research investigations and military applications call for the use of closed-circuit oxygen systems. Use of this equipment requires a thorough understanding of the principles and hazards involved, the major concern being CNS oxygen toxicity (see Chapter 3).

The U.S. Navy has recently performed research on pure oxygen diving in exercising human volunteers. These investigations have shown, in a limited number of exposures, that substantially longer times appear to be possible for pure oxygen working dives than those given in Table 16.5, without the occurrence of oxygen convulsions (Butler and Thalmann 1984; Butler and Thalmann 1986; Butler 1986; Walters, Gould, Bachrach and Butler 2000); however, NOAA finds that the conservative limits established in this table are satisfactory for NOAA diving operations.

Except for certain special operations, NOAA divers do not commonly use closed-circuit oxygen systems. Those

TABLE 16.5
NOAA Oxygen Exposure Limits

PO₂ (atm)	Maximum Single Exposure (minutes)	Maximum per 24 hr (minutes)
1.60	45	150
1.55	83	165
1.50	120	180
1.45	135	180
1.40	150	180
1.35	165	195
1.30	180	210
1.25	195	225
1.20	210	240
1.10	240	270
1.00	300	300
0.90	360	360
0.80	450	450
0.70	570	570
0.60	720	720

needing detailed procedures for this type of diving are referred to the *U.S. Navy Diving Manual* and manufacturer's literature.

16.4 MIXED-GAS DIVING EQUIPMENT

Surface-oriented mixed-gas diving can be performed with a variety of equipment, mostly of two general categories: self-contained and surface-supplied. Included within the self-contained category are open-circuit scuba systems and rebreathers. The surface-supplied category includes the same equipment that is used for air diving as covered in Chapter 6. Since surface-supplied mixed-gas diving is rare within NOAA, such equipment is not covered in this manual. Rebreathers are an integral part of mixed-gas diving and are covered in Chapter 14.

This section describes equipment that has become the standard for mixed-gas scuba diving. It addresses the specific reasons for the components and how the equipment is configured for different environments and diving operations. Many recreational trimix divers operate as individuals, and each may select the specific components and configure them according to their own preference, although the trend has been to standardize most major items. However, as mentioned above, a professional diving team should standardize components, rigging, and procedures.

The open-circuit trimix diver is required to be self-contained; the diver must not only carry a sufficient gas supply to conduct the working portion of the dive, but also sufficient gas to conduct the sometimes lengthy decompression.

The typical scuba trimix diving rig described here is considered adequate for both open-ocean and cave exploration in the range 100–350 fsw (30.7–107.5 msw). An experienced mixed gas diver will usually use the same diving rig regardless of breathing mixtures. The familiar rig becomes the most comfortable one to the diver and, therefore, the safest.

The rig consists of cylinders and their mounting system, manifolds, regulators, buoyancy device, pressure gauge, timing device, emergency equipment, lighting, mask, and fins. The equipment described here is available from a variety of manufacturers (see Figure 16.2).

16.4.1 Backplate, Harness, and Buoyancy Compensator

A technical diving harness provides a sturdy frame to which cylinders and other equipment are attached. The harness is typically made of two inch nylon webbing, and is threaded through a backplate made of stainless steel, aluminum, or structural plastic. The cylinders, normally two, are bolted to the backplate. Between the cylinders and the backplate a buoyancy compensator, in the fashion of a wing, is sandwiched. The buoyancy compensator should have between 45 and 65 lbs. (17 and 24 kg) of lift for twin cylinder sets. Some systems have a built-in redundant back-up bladder. This is especially important when wearing only a wet suit. Caution is advised when diving with steel cylinders and a wet suit; the cylinders are negatively buoyant when empty and cannot be dropped, a situation that can mean the diver's life may depend on the

FIGURE 16.2
Properly Dressed Trimix Diver

buoyancy compensator. NOAA requires redundant flotation capability on all trimix dives. Examples of redundant buoyancy capability are twin air bladders within a single BC; two separate, single-bladder BCs, or a single-bladder BC used in combination with a variable-volume dry suit.

16.4.2 Gas Cylinders and Manifolds

Scuba cylinders are available in a variety of sizes, materials, and working pressures. A typical technical diving rig utilizes twin cylinders with a minimum working volume of 160 ft³ of gas, with the average capacity 200–300 ft³ (5,000–8,000 liters) per set of doubles.

The cylinders are joined with stainless steel bands and a dual-outlet isolation manifold. The manifold allows the diver to draw all the gas from both cylinders through either regulator with the manifold open. The isolation valve allows the diver to close either cylinder in the event of a leak, ruptured hose, or regulator failure.

The isolation manifold uses a captured O-ring or DIN-threaded valve system which provides a secure method for mounting the regulator first stage; it also allows for working pressures up to 4,500 psi (300 bars). The isolation manifold system allows a level of redundancy if a regulator fails. These cylinders are commonly called "back gas" because they are mounted on the diver's back.

Besides back gas the trimix diver will also carry one or more additional cylinders, typically 40–80 ft³ (1,000–2,000 liters) in size for intermediate and final decompression gases, usually a nitrox mixture and 100% oxygen. These decompression cylinders are called "stage/sling bottles," or "wing tanks." The cylinders are clipped to the diving harness, and each has its own breathing regulator. For open-ocean diving the decompression cylinders typically remain with the diver, whereas in cave diving the stage bottles are routinely deposited ("staged") at various points during the penetration for use later during exiting.

16.4.3 Regulators, Hoses, and Masks

Breathing regulators for trimix diving should provide high gas flow with a minimum of CO_2 build up (i.e., low breathing resistance). It is recommended that both back gas regulators be of the same manufacture and model for standardization.

The regulator on the right post of the manifold is fitted with a 5–7 ft. (1.5–2 m) "long hose" which simplifies gas sharing. This is the diver's primary regulator; it has the long hose because that is the regulator to be given to another diver who needs gas. The right post regulator may also be fitted with a low-pressure inflation hose for a dry suit. The left post regulator is fitted with a short hose and is secured to the diver with a rubber necklace allowing it to rest under the diver's chin. In this position, this backup regulator is readily available to be used should the diver need to donate their primary regulator to another diver. A submersible pressure gauge is also fitted to the left post regulator, and a low-pressure inflation hose for the buoyancy compensator.

For dives involving an exposure to high oxygen or long exposures to oxygen breathing for decompression, some consider it advisable to wear a full-face mask. This is to reduce the likelihood of drowning in case of an oxygen-induced convulsion. Full-face masks also allow the use of through-water communications. Unfortunately, full-face masks cause higher gas consumption, especially when using positive-pressure masks. Further, they result in a larger dead space volume, which may cause a slight rise in CO_2.

16.4.4 Depth and Timing Devices

Trimix and accelerated decompression diving uses special diving tables that require specific stops, so depth and time information is critical; an electronic depth/time gauge is normally used. Some dives can be managed with a dive computer (such as when diving with air and nitrox) with the units serving as the primary depth and timing device. Trimix computers are also becoming available which can manage multiple gas shifting. A dive computer that covers the depth range of the dive may be used for time and depth information only, and for the purposes of recording the dive for future analysis even though it does not compute decompression for a trimix dive. Depth and timing devices are normally worn on the diver's wrist, with a back up unit stored in an accessories pouch.

16.4.5 Tools and Emergency Equipment

Cutting tools are carried on all dives; typically a small, very sharp knife is mounted on the harness or BC inflation hose, and sometimes a larger knife that can be used to pry or cut. A pair of EMS (bandage) scissors or shears is better for cutting monofilament fishing line and netting. The open-sea trimix diver will also carry safety equipment for assisting them in being located on the surface, such as flares, smoke, dye markers, signal mirrors, surface location aids (a "diving sausage"), electronic positioning beacons, pingers, and strobe lights. These may be needed if the diver loses contact with the boat, or even if he surfaces a short distance from the boat in a choppy sea. Also needed are two line reels, one to be used as an ascent line, working with a diver-deployed surface marker buoy and/or lift bag, and the other as a back up. Line reels enable the diver to manage decompression even if the anchor/down line cannot be found or if the line has been severed.

16.5 MANAGING SPECIAL BREATHING GAS MIXTURES

16.5.1 Gas Purity Issues

As is true for any breathing mixture, the quality of the breathing gas is vitally important. In general, few purity problems are associated with gases obtained in cylinders from commercial vendors. The problems that do occur are usually caused by factors such as improper mixing or analysis, incorrect labeling or color-coding, contamination resulting from improper handling or a poorly maintained compressor, or solvent residue left in storage containers or hoses. The importance of ensuring that any mixture used for breathing is the correct one, correctly mixed and analyzed, cannot be overemphasized.

16.5.1.1 Air to be Mixed with Oxygen

Specifications for the purity of breathing air are covered in Chapter 2. For air purity, avoiding carbon monoxide and limiting the "oil mist" or "condensable hydrocarbons" is almost uniquely important. Air compatibility and cleaning requirements are addressed in more detail in Chapter 15.

16.5.1.2 Oxygen Gas Purity

Table 16.6 outlines the specifications for purity of oxygen. Cylinder identification is covered in Chapter 15 and Section 16.8.

The purity standards for oxygen and the specification are in three grades:

1. Grade A Aviator's oxygen
2. Grade B Industrial, medical oxygen
3. Grade C Technical oxygen

The difference between Grades A and B is in the moisture content. Grade A, used by aviators, must be extremely dry to prevent freezing at the low temperatures associated with high altitudes. Grade B is allowed to contain a maximum of 5 ml free water per cylinder. Grades A and B oxygen are suitable for use in a breathing medium for divers. Both Grades A and B are required to be 99.5% pure oxygen, and must pass tests for acidity or alkalinity, carbon dioxide, carbon monoxide, halogens, and other oxidizing substances as specified in the U. S. Pharmocopia. Grade C, technical oxygen, is safe to breathe but it may have an objectionable odor and for that reason should not be used for routine diving.

16.5.1.3 Inert Gas Purity

Helium is produced in several quality verification levels, but all are suitable for use in diving (except "balloon grade" helium that is essentially leftover gas, which meets no purity standards). Nitrogen, oxygen, argon, and neon are produced by the fractional distillation of atmospheric air. Nitrogen is not likely to be needed except for nitrox saturation diving. In some areas it has been possible to get nitrogen compressed with oil lubricated compressors ("oil-pumped nitrogen"); this grade should not be used for diving because of the possible oil contamination.

Industrial "air" supplied in cylinders is usually made by recombining oxygen and nitrogen from the fractionation process. Although it will be oil-free "air," as defined by the Compressed Gas Association, the oxygen content can vary between 19.5% and 23.5% by volume. For additional information on gas purity, see the *U.S. Navy Diving Manual* or the *Compressed Gas Association Handbook of Compressed Gases*.

TABLE 16.6
Diver's Oxygen Breathing Purity Requirements

Constituent	Specification
Oxygen (percent by volume)	99.5%
Carbon Dioxide (by volume)	10 ppm (max)
Methane (CH_4 by volume)	50 ppm (max)
Acetylene (C_2H_2)	0.1 ppm (max)
Ethylene (C_2H_4) Ethane (C_2H_6 and other hydrocarbons)	0.4 ppm (max) 6.0 ppm (max)
Nitrous Oxide (N_2O) by volume Refrigerants Solvents	 2.0 ppm (max) 0.2 ppm (max)
Moisture (water vapor measured by ppm or measured by dew point)	7 ppm (max) > -83°F
Odor	Odor free

General Note: Gaseous and liquid oxygen shall contain not less that 99.5% by volume. The remainder, except for moisture and minor constituents specified shall be argon and nitrogen.

16.6 GAS MIXING

Two or more pure gases or gas mixtures may be combined by a variety of techniques to form a final mixture of predetermined composition. This section reviews the concepts of gas mixing and covers some of the methods used for mixing gases of interest to NOAA divers. See Chapter 15 for more information on gas mixing procedures.

The simplest and most straightforward method of obtaining precisely mixed gases is to purchase them from a commercial supplier. This is also one of the most expensive methods. Mixing can be accomplished in cylinders, small groups of cylinders known as "quads" or "banks," or tube trailers. Although premix requires oxygen handling by the commercial gas company, it does not require handling of oxygen by the divers themselves. In all cases the gas must be analyzed for proper oxygen content prior to use.

16.6.1 Mixing Trimixes and Heliox

Most heliox mixtures (helium-oxygen, usually with less than 21% oxygen) used by the commercial diving industry is prepared by commercial vendors. This may also make sense for scientific diving as well, depending on the project budgets and logistical concerns. On-line mixing for surface-supplied divers using a "mixmaker" system is also used for helium-based breathing mixtures. Trimixes are normally made by partial pressure mixing methods.

The accuracy of the oxygen component of trimix and heliox mixtures is more critical than with nitrox mixtures. Since trimix and heliox are used for diving in the 150–350 fsw (46.1–107.5 msw) depth range, the oxygen fraction is usually lower than 21%, and the hazards induced by the wrong oxygen level may be fatal. However, there can be fairly wide latitude in the helium and nitrogen proportions of a trimix. Small differences of 2–3% make a trivial difference in the decompression, narcotic, and thermal properties of such mixtures.

16.6.1.1 Non-Ideal Gas Behavior in Partial Pressure Mixing

Some gases compress more or less than other gases. "Compressibility" is a physical property of gases; oxygen compresses more easily than helium and this difference becomes greater at higher pressures. For example, if an empty cylinder is filled to 1,000 psi with oxygen and then topped-off to 2,000 psi with helium, the resulting mixture will contain more oxygen than helium. To get equal amounts of each gas the cylinder would first be filled to 954 psi of oxygen and then topped with 1,046 psi of helium to 2,000 psi.

"Real gas" corrections for certain specific mixtures are covered in the *U.S. Navy Diving Gas Manual* (1971). A variety of commercial and shareware software programs are available for mixing gases. These programs allow for creating mixtures starting with empty or partially-filled cylinders (topping-up), for changes in mixtures, and take into consideration non-ideal compressibility factors and temperature changes.

16.6.1.2 Use of Air for Mixing Trimix

Most trimixes currently used for diving are composed of oxygen, helium, and air. As an example, a typical trimix for open-circuit scuba diving in the 200–250 fsw (61.4–76.8 msw) range is NOAA Trimix 18/50 (18% oxygen, 50% helium, and 32% nitrogen and trace gases). To mix NT 18/50 to a final cylinder pressure of 3,500 psi, an empty (evacuated and cleaned) cylinder is first filled with oxygen to 305 psi, then helium is added until the total pressure reaches 2,032 psi. After the cylinder cools the intermediate oxygen analysis should read 16%. Ultra-filtered air can then be used to bring the final pressure to 3,500 psi. Final oxygen analysis should show 18% oxygen content.

In some situations where oxygen is not available, suitable diving mixtures can be made using only helium and air, a mix that has been called "heliair." This method avoids the hazards of handling and mixing with pure oxygen, but has the disadvantage that the range of mixes is limited and one must be careful to keep track of the components. It is relatively easy to end up with a mix with oxygen too low to sustain life. For example if a helium fraction of 0.50 were desired, 50% of the cylinder would be filled with helium, then air would be added. The resulting oxygen fraction would be 10.5%; far too low for most mixed-gas scuba dives. The helium "dilutes" the oxygen in air when mixed, thus lowering the final amount of oxygen in the mixture. In order to keep the oxygen fraction at a higher level (16–18%), the helium fraction must be quite low, usually less than 25% making the use of "heliair" unattractive for the 180–250 fsw (55.3–76.8 msw) depth range. This method of mixing does work well when using nitrox mixes for the "top-up" gas.

Air is also used for topping-up partially used trimix cylinders. It is common for trimix divers to return with cylinders that are 1/3 to 1/2 full. Trimix can be topped-up, analyzed and used again for another dive to a shallower depth. For example: trimix 18/50/32 at 1,500 psi can be topped-up with air to 3,100 psi, with a resulting mix of 19/26/55 (O_2, He, N_2), a suitable mix for diving to 185 fsw (56.8 msw) with an END of 120 fsw (36.8 msw). Air used for trimixes should be of the purity of "air to be mixed with oxygen," mentioned in Chapter 15.

16.6.1.3 Use of Nitrox for Mixing Trimix

NOAA Trimix 18/50 is an attractive mix, not only for its operational characteristics but also for its simple method of preparation. By utilizing a stock mix of NN36 (36% oxygen, 64% nitrogen) both the trimix and the intermediate decompression mix can be made without the need for oxygen and in some cases can eliminate the need of a gas booster. The NN36 can be prepared either with commercial premix, continuous blending, pressure swing adsorption, or by membrane separation methods (see Chapter 15).

To mix NOAA Trimix 18/50 an empty cylinder is filled to one half the final desired pressure with helium, is allowed to cool and then adjusted for exact pressure.

TABLE 16.7
Trimix By Mixing NN36 with Helium

MOD 1.6 atm PO$_2$ fsw	MOD 1.4 atm PO$_2$ fsw	% Helium to add	% of NN36	Final FO$_2$	Final Helium Factor	Trimix
150	126	0.20	0.802	0.29	0.20	29/20/51
200	168	0.37	0.629	0.23	0.37	23/37/40
250	210	0.48	0.518	0.19	0.48	19/48/33
260	223	0.50	0.500	0.18	0.50	18/50/32
300	255	0.56	0.440	0.16	0.56	16/5628
350	297	0.62	0.383	0.14	0.62	14/62/14*
400	352	0.66	0.339	0.12	0.66	12/66/12*

Multiply final cylinder pressure by helium factor. Fill empty cylinders to indicated psi, let cool, adjust helium if necessary. Top up to desired final pressure with NN36. Analyze and label. *Caution: final mix hypoxic on the surface and to a depth of 10 feet.

Premixed NN36 is then added to the cylinder until the final desired pressure is achieved. The resulting gas analysis should show an oxygen level of 18%.

The "stock mixture" procedure can be used for other mixes as well. Table 16.7 illustrates the factors needed to create a variety of mixes using only NN36 and helium. All of the mixes result in an END of approximately 85 fsw (26.1 msw) for their maximum operating depth.

To use the chart, identify the desired oxygen percent in the mix then multiply the final desired cylinder pressure by the helium factor to find the amount of helium to add in psi. For example, NOAA Trimix 18/50 (18% oxygen–50% helium) is needed at 2,600 psi. Multiply 2,600 psi by 0.50 resulting in 1,300 psi of helium needed in an empty cylinder, then top with NN36 to the final pressure. To make a trimix 29/20 (29% oxygen–20% helium) for a dive in the 130–150 fsw (39.9–46.1 msw)range, less helium would be needed. For a final cylinder pressure of 3,000 psi, multiply 3,000 psi by 0.20 resulting in 600 psi of helium needed in the empty cylinder, then top with NN36 to the final pressure.

Refilling cylinders with the same mix as that already in the cylinder can be done by using the same mixing methods but requires a little more care. For example, a NOAA trimix 18/50 cylinder has 1,500 psi remaining after a dive. The cylinder needs to be refilled with the same mix to 3,500 psi, thus requiring an additional 2,000 psi of trimix be added to the cylinder. Multiply 2,000 psi by 0.50 results in 1,000 psi of helium needed to be added bringing the total pressure to 2,500 psi, (intermediate oxygen analysis of 11.2%). NN36 is used to top-off the cylinder to the final pressure of 3,500 psi. The final oxygen analysis will be 18%. A gas booster may be needed to bring the helium up to the intermediate pressure, but in any event the handling of high-pressure oxygen has been avoided.

16.6.1.4 Mixing and Stratification

For both trimix and heliox, stratification of the gases during mixing in a cylinder is a concern because of the different densities of the gases. Helium stratified over air or oxygen in a cylinder may take weeks to diffuse if there is no agitation. Stratification can be prevented by having a mixing tube inside the cylinder receiving the gas. A mixing tube will channel the incoming gas into a forceful stream that will flow deeper into the cylinder thus facilitating mixing with the existing gas in the cylinder. One method to correct stratification is to roll cylinders continuously for an hour in the sun or under a heat lamp. Or, a more practical approach is to lay the cylinders on their side and then turned them occasionally for 24 hours. Another method is for the final few hundred psi to be added into the cylinder at a very high flow rate to stir the gases. Once the gases are thoroughly mixed they stay mixed and do not separate. If an analysis seems to change over time, it is probably due to the fact that the gas was not completely mixed before the first analysis.

16.7 BREATHING GAS ANALYSIS

Gas analysis is essential in mixed-gas diving, mainly because of the very real hazards of both high and low oxygen. Virtually all gas analysis done in mixed-gas diving is for oxygen. The process of analyzing oxygen in trimix and heliox mixtures is same as that used for analyzing oxygen in nitrox mixtures. Refer to Chapter 15, for specific information on various types of oxygen analyzers and their calibrating and operating requirements and procedures.

16.7.1 Analysis for Gases Other Than Oxygen

Overwhelmingly, the need for sophisticated gas analysis for gases other than oxygen is for contaminants

Mixed-Gas and Oxygen Diving

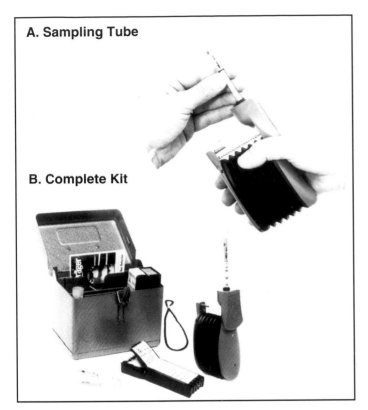

A. Sampling Tube

B. Complete Kit

FIGURE 16.3
Colorimetric Gas Sampler

TRIMIX Contents Data

Fill Date	
Oxygen %	
Helium %	
Nitrogen %	
PSI/Bar	
Max. Depth	
Analyzed by	
User	

Caution: This cylinder contains gas other than air. Observe maximum operation depth limit. Use only with appropriate procedures for the mix indicated. Failure to heed proper use may result in serious injury or death.

NOAA
NATIONAL OCEANIC AND ATMOSPHERIC ADMINISTRATION
U.S. DEPARTMENT OF COMMERCE

FIGURE 16.4
Cylinder Contents Label for Trimix Cylinder

in compressed air. If analysis is needed for gas mixes purchased in cylinders, the simplest approach is to obtain this information from the company supplying the gas. Certified analysis results for each cylinder are available when purchasing gas from a commercial vendor. Active trace gases (as opposed to inert gases) can be analyzed with colorimetric tubes. Except for potential contaminants, the only other gas for which an analysis may be needed is helium.

16.7.1.1 Colorimetric Tubes

Field instruments that operate on the colorimetric principle are available to measure a large number of chemically active gases (e.g., oxygen, hydrocarbons, carbon monoxide, carbon dioxide, nitrous oxide, etc., but not inert gases). Each consists of a small sealed glass tube containing chemicals sensitive to the specific gas, marked with a scale. A measured amount of gas is drawn through the tube, and the material in the tube changes color based on the amount of the test gas that is pulled through the tube, and the level can be read on the scale (see Figure 16.3). A wide variety of tubes can be obtained for these devices, each specific for a particular gas or group of gases and for a given range. The precision is quite adequate for most diving applications, but it requires a fairly large sample, takes a few minutes, and the tubes are not reusable. For frequent analysis this can be expensive, but this is the method of choice when a specific gas analysis is needed

only occasionally. One common application is for testing for carbon monoxide in compressed air.

16.7.1.2 Helium Analysis

There is no need to analyze for helium in mixes of only oxygen and helium if the oxygen can be measured. For trimixes, this need is rarely great enough to justify purchase of a helium analyzer, for several reasons. First, if a trimix is being prepared with proper care, the helium fraction can be determined with considerable confidence by keeping records of the mixing process. Second, whereas oxygen fractions have to be accurately known and reasonably precise, the helium content can vary within fairly broad limits in a trimix without creating significant physiological problems (Hamilton 1997). The major factors for consideration are decompression, narcosis, and heat loss. For short duration, non-saturation diving, the helium/nitrogen ratio has a relatively small effect on decompression time, narcosis and thermal limits.

It may be desirable to have a helium analyzer in situations where diving gases are being reclaimed, or where it is necessary to top-off half-full cylinders on a regular basis.

Special helium analyzers that work on the principle of thermal conductivity are the least expensive. These analyzers are quite reliable if the background gases are oxygen and nitrogen, but usually need correction factors if neon and argon are to be measured. Mass spectrometers and gas chromatographs are more complex, accurate, and expensive, and are generally not appropriate for field applications.

16.8 CYLINDER IDENTIFICATION AND LABELING

Gas analysis is of no value unless the results are documented and used. A high number of fatalities in self-contained diving with mixed-gas breathing mixtures are caused by divers breathing the wrong gas (or a proper gas at the wrong time). This may be due to breathing from the wrong regulator or an improperly labeled cylinder.

All scuba cylinders with non-air mixtures must have a durable, dated label (initialed by the user) giving the composition or analysis of the mixture inside (see Figure 16.4). The data should include fill date, cylinder pressure, oxygen and helium percentages, MOD, the name or identification of the person who filled the cylinder and/or filled out the label, and initials verifying the analysis. It is not sufficient to use abbreviated names such as "NT18/50," the actual composition

should be recorded. In addition, there are some color and labeling conventions, but these do not replace the cylinder contents label. Cylinders to be transported for commercial purposes must also meet Department of Transportation requirements.

Nitrox scuba cylinders have their own unique labeling system that has been universally accepted. See Chapter 15 for details.

Oxygen scuba cylinders are usually white or green in color and identified simply with the word OXYGEN stenciled on the cylinder. The number "20" may be stenciled near the bottom of the cylinder indicating the maximum operating depth for oxygen.

There is currently no standardized labeling or color coding for trimix or heliox scuba cylinders or banks other than the actual content label. Some groups have developed cylinder wraps similar to that used on nitrox cylinders with the words "Special Mix" or "Trimix" on them, but no convention has been established.

During mixed-gas diving operations, it is advisable to mark in 2–3 inch letters horizontally on the cylinder near the bottom the MOD. This clearly identifies the diver's cylinder to another diver, and is used as a visual safety precaution for other divers to see what gas is being breathed.

NOTES

Diving From Seafloor Habitats

Diving From Seafloor Habitats

17.0 GENERAL

As interest in the oceans and divers' ability to work increases, techniques and facilities are needed that will enable the scientist or working diver to remain at depth for longer periods of time. An approach that has proved useful in underwater scientific research is nitrox and air saturation-excursion diving from habitats positioned on the seafloor. Although habitat-based diving has been used since the 1960s, new techniques for this type of diving are still developing.

Saturation is the term used to describe the state that occurs when a diver's tissues have absorbed all the nitrogen or other inert gas they can hold at any given depth (U.S. Navy Diving Manual 1999). Once tissue saturation has occurred, the length of the decompression that will be required at the end of the dive will not increase with additional time spent at that depth.

Under saturation conditions, the diver works out of a pressure facility the atmosphere of which is maintained at approximately the same pressure as that of the surrounding water. The saturation facility may be an ocean floor installation, a pressurized chamber on board a surface vessel, or a diver lockout submersible.

The term "habitat" usually is applied to a pressure or ambient-pressure vessel that is placed on the floor of the ocean and that provides basic life support, comfort, and a base of operation for the diver and the necessary support equipment. Habitats are maintained at a pressure that is equivalent to the pressure of the sea water at the habitat's entrance hatch. Thus this practice is usually called "habitat diving."

A surface-based saturation diving system consists of a deck decompression chamber (DDC) that is located on a surface support platform and a pressurized diving bell that the saturation diver uses to commute to and from the underwater worksite. The DDC, which provides facilities for the life support and comfort of the saturated diver, may be maintained at a pressure that is close to that of the working depth. The personnel transfer capsule (PTC), which can be either a diving bell or a lockout submersible, is also maintained at a pressure close to that of the working depth. During transfer from one chamber to another, the PTC is mated to the DDC to enable the diver to remain at pressure at all times.

A diver lockout submersible is a vehicle designed with at least two separate compartments; these compartments enable the divers to enter and exit the water while submerged. Usually the pilot's compartment stays at one atmosphere.

Regardless of the system used, the saturation diver undergoes decompression only on completion of the total dive sequence rather than at the end of each dive (unless an excursion dive has been made to deeper than the storage depth, requiring decompression).

Saturation diving is an essential technique for the scientist who needs to spend long periods on the bottom and for the working diver who wishes to extend the working portion of the dive. Since 1958, when Captain George Bond, U.S.N., conducted the laboratory experiments leading to the development of saturation diving (Bond 1964), saturation diving programs have been carried out by a variety of organizations from many nations, using both land-based hyperbaric chambers (simulated dives) and open sea systems. Although the military and commercial diving industries have devoted substantial effort to developing practical saturation diving techniques involving helium-oxygen gas mixtures for use at depths to 1,000 fsw (307 msw) and deeper, NOAA has concentrated on saturation diving in shallower waters 40–300 fsw (12–92 msw) utilizing more readily available and less costly nitrogen-based gases, particularly air. NOAA owns the Aquarius Undersea Laboratory, currently the only underwater laboratory operating in the U.S. It is operated by the National Undersea Research Center at the University of North Carolina at Wilmington and is deployed in the Florida Keys.

This chapter discusses various aspects of saturation diving and provides, for historical interest, summaries of some air and nitrogen-oxygen exposures in underwater habitats only (see Table 17.1).

17.1 PRINCIPLES OF SATURATION DIVING

A diver's body absorbs inert gases as a function of the depth and duration of the dive, the type of breathing mixture used, the characteristics of the individual diver's tissues, and

TABLE 17.1
Summary Information About Nitrogen-Oxygen Exposures

Date	Project	Data Source	Breathing Gas or PO$_2$	Depth, fsw	Duration, Days	Team Size/Total No. Participants	Comments Concerning Period of Saturation Exposure
1962	Conshelf I	Chouteau 1969	Air	35	7	2	Some adaptive responses
1962	Conshelf II	Chouteau 1969	Air	35	30	5	
1965	Glaucus	Miller and Koblick 1984	Air	35	7	2	
1966	Bubble	Miller and Koblick 1984	Air	31	.50	14-21	No decompression sickness on direct ascent to surface
				31	1	4-6	Decompression sickness on direct ascent to surface
1966-67	Ikhtiandr	Miller and Koblick 1984	Air	39.4	1-2	3	
			Air	40	7	12	
1967	U.S.N.	Larsen and Mazzone 1967	Air	35	1.25	13	
1967	Meduza-I	Miller and Koblick 1984	Air	78.7	6	3	
1967	Meduza-II	Miller and Koblick 1984	Air	85	8	3	
1967-68	Hebros	Miller and Koblick 1984	Air	23	7	5	
1968	Malter-I	Miller and Koblick 1984	Air	26	2	2	
1968-74	Chernomor	Miller and Koblick 1984	0.40	45.9	2.5-6.5	28	Descending excursions to 295 fsw
			0.36	82	3.5-16.5	13	
			0.30-0.425	49.5	53	5	Symptoms of pulmonary oxygen toxicity during excursions until habitat
			0.23-0.27	65.6	16	3	PO$_2$ reduced for final 12 days in saturation
				98.4	12	3	
			0.20-0.22	131.2	16+	3	
			0.20-0.33	101.7	23	5	
			0.20-0.33	101.7	27-28	4-5	
1968-74	Chernomor	Miller and Koblick 1984	0.23-0.34	60.7	15.5	5	
			0.24-0.34	65.6	17.5	5	
1969	TEKTITE I	Pauli and Cole 1970	0.21	42	60	4	
1969	Helgoland	Miller and Koblick 1984	0.25	75.4	6-12	8	
1970	Predictive Studies II	Lambertson and Wright 1973	0.21	100	14	6	No serious toxic, narcotic, or physiological effects; some adaptive responses
1970	TEKTITE II	Beckman and Smith 1972	0.21	50	5-20	56	
1970	LS-I	Miller and Koblick 1984	Air	33	32	3	
1970	Shelf-I	Miller and Koblick 1984	Air	65.6	4.5-6	6	
1970	EDALHAB I	Miller 1976	Air	26	2	4	
1971	EDALHAB II	Miller 1976	Air	43	4	2	
1971	Tonofond	Miller 1976	0.33	49	3-10	14	
			0.33	65	3-10	12	
			0.33	81	3-10	12	
1971	Hydrolab	Miller and Koblick 1984	Air	50	2-8	24	
1972	FLARE	Miller 1976	Air	42-45	5	25	
1972	Pre-SHAD I	Miller 1976	Air	50	2	2	Intolerance to oxygen during treatment of decompression sickness
1972	NOAA-Ops I	Hamilton et al. 1973	0.21	30	7	3	
			0.21	90	7	3	
1972	NOAA-Ops II	Hamilton et al. 1973	0.21	60	7	2	
			0.21	120	7	3	One diver sick (relationship to pressure exposure uncertain); no gross impairment due to narcosis
1972-74	La Chalupa	Miller and Koblick 1984	0.23, 0.25	50, 60	15	36	
1972-75	Hydrolab	Miller 1976	Air	42, 60	2-14	317	
1973-75	Lora	Miller 1976	Air	26	1	7	
1973	PRUNE I	Miller 1976	0.16-0.39	95	14	4	
1973	SHAD I	Miller 1976	Air	50	29	2	12.5% decrease in red blood cell mass
1973	Helgoland	Miller and Koblick 1984	0.25	75	5	3	
1973-75	Hydrolab	Miller and Koblick 1984	Air	42, 45, 60	2-14	164	
1974	SHAD II	Miller 1976	Air	60	27	2	19.3% decrease in red blood cell mass
1974	SHAD III	Miller 1976	Air	50	7	3	Intolerance to oxygen during treatment of decompression sickness
1974	PRUNE II	Miller 1976	0.17-0.42	106	11	4	
1975	SCORE I	Miller 1976	Air	60	5	8	Significant reduction in vital capacity in some subjects, decreased O$_2$ tolerance in air excursion, significant decrease in red blood cell mass

Date	Project	Data Source	Breathing Gas or PO$_2$	Depth, fsw	Duration, Days	Team Size/Total No. Participants	Comments Concerning Period of Saturation Exposure
1975	**SCORE II**	Miller 1976	Air	60	5	16	13.3% decrease in red blood cell mass
1975	Helgoland		0.36-0.50	112	3-16	14	Narcosis in some individuals
1975	**NISAT I**	Hamilton et al. 1982	0.21-0.3	198	7+7 for decompression	3	Vertigo and nausea in two divers during initial hours of dive; PO$_2$ raised to 0.3 ata
1975	**NISAT II**	Hamilton et al. 1982	0.3	66	8	3	Isobaric switch from nitrogen to helium on dive day three; mild pruritus in two divers. Decompression on helium
1976	**NISAT III**	Hamilton et al. 1982	0.3	99	8	3	Isobaric switch from nitrogen to helium on day three; all divers experienced severe pruritus and urticaria; after change of inert gases, one diver developed isobaric decompression sickness that required therapy consisting of increasing depth to 129 fsw and breathing increased oxygen. Decompression on helium
1976	**AIRSAT I**	Eckenhoff and Vann 1985	Air	60	8	11	Three dives, daily 8-hour no-decompression excursions to 100 fsw. Significant vital capacity reduction in one diver
1977	**Neritica**	Miller and Koblick 1984	Air	29	0.5-17	82	
1977-79	**AIRSAT II**	Eckenhoff and Vann 1985	Air	60	10	12	Three dives, daily 2-hour excursions to 150 fsw with 160 min. decompression back to storage depth
1978-85	**Hydrolab**	NOAA	Air	47	7	357	
1979	**Commercial Welder Training**	Peterson et al. 1980	Air	45	4	10	Air saturation with both air and heliox excursions; no problems
			He-15%O$_2$	79	8-10 hours	6	
			Air	79	4-12 hours	9	
			Air	65	4-13 hours	4	
1979	**Facilities Test**	Swedish Naval Diving Center	0.3-0.4	98	5	3	
1979-80	**Diver Exercise Studies**	Norwegian Underwater Institute	0.3-0.4	98-121	12	12	
1979-81	**AIRSAT III**	U.S.N. Sub Med Res Lab	0.21	132	7	12	
1981-83	**SUREX**	Eckenhoff and Parker 1984	Air	45, 55, 65	7	18	Study of no-stop excursions to surface
			Air	65, 75	7	6	
1982	**NISAHEX**	Muren et al. 1984	0.42	197	11	6	Adaption to narcosis observed. Heliox and trimix excursions conducted
1982	**Duke-NOAA-Oceaneering Dive**	Miller and Koblick 1984	0.4	165	9	10	Adaptation to narcosis observed
1982-83	**AIRSAT IV**	U.S.N. Sub Med Res Lab	0.21	132	5	18	
1984	**MINISAT I**	Eckenhoff et al. 1986	Air	25.5	2	19	
1984	**MINISAT II**	Eckenhoff et al. 1986	Air	29.5	2	15	
1985-86	**AIRSAT V**	U.S.N. Sub Med Res Lab	0.4	111, 70	5	6	Study of no-stop ascent distances in saturation
			0.4	111, 60	5	6	
			0.4	111, 55	5	4	Bends in three divers following steep ascent from saturation depth
			0.4	111, 60	5	8	Bends in three divers following steep ascent from saturation depth
			0.4	111, 65	5	5	
1986	**REPEX I**	Hamilton et al. 1988a	0.3	50	6.5	4	
1986	**REPEX II**	Hamilton et al. 1988a	0.3	80	6.5	4	
1986	**REPEX III**	Hamilton et al. 1988a	0.3	110	8.5	4	
1986-87	**AIRSAT VI**	U.S.N. Sub Med Res Lab	0.4 Air	111, 132, 74	6	6	Study of no-stop ascent distances in saturation
1988-89	**Aquarius**	NURC/FDU	Air	47	3-14	6	First deployment of Aquarius, St. Croix, U.S. V.I. (12 missions completed)
1993-96	**Aquarius**	NURC/UNCW	Air	47	5-14	6	First deployment of Aquarius in the Florida Keys (Conch reef) (22 missions completed)
1998-Present	**Aquarius 2000**	NURC/UNCW	Air	47	4-10	6	Second deployment of Aquarius in the Florida Keys (Conch reef) in semi-autonomous mode (ten missions completed)

factors affecting the diver's condition at the time of the dive, such as temperature and work rate. In long-duration dives, a diver's body becomes saturated with the inert gases in the breathing mixture at the partial pressure of each inert gas component in the mixture. For practical purposes, the state of saturation is reached in 12–24 hours. The techniques of saturation diving make use of the fact that, once the body reaches this equilibrium, they can safely remain saturated for long periods without increasing the diver's decompression obligation.

From an operational standpoint, there are two principal factors in saturation diving, the depth at which the diver's tissues become saturated (called the storage depth), and the vertical range of depths over which the diver can move (termed the excursion depths). The storage depth determines the breathing mixtures that can be used, the possible range of vertical excursions the diver can undertake, and the decompression schedule to be followed. The storage depth should be selected to maximize the diver's effectiveness in the working depth range. When selecting a storage depth, both ascending and descending excursions should be considered.

17.2 BREATHING GASES

Several different breathing mixtures have been used successfully in saturation diving, including: air, nitrogen-oxygen, helium-oxygen and trimix; nitrogen-helium-oxygen. These mixtures may be used singularly or in combination, both as the habitat gas at storage depth and as the breathing gas for excursions from the habitat.

NOTE
Because of the gas exchange characteristics of nitrogen and helium, saturation and saturation-excursion diving involving switches from one inert gas to another should not be attempted without the advice of a qualified hyperbaric physiologist.

Air has been used extensively as a breathing gas in saturation diving. Its use as a habitat gas is limited to relatively shallow depths of 50 fsw (15 msw), because of oxygen toxicity (Adams et al. 1978). Short excursion dives from the storage depth have been conducted successfully to depths as great as 250 fsw (77 msw) using air as the breathing gas. Because oxygen toxicity and nitrogen narcosis are both concerns on air dives to such depths, excursions using this breathing gas must be planned carefully. Several successful laboratory and at-sea saturation programs have been carried out at storage depths of 60 fsw (18 msw) using air as the breathing gas. These dives have revealed physiological responses that, although apparently normal and reversible adaptations, suggest that operational air-saturations should be limited to 50 fsw (15 msw) (see Table 17.1). There is also some indication that habitation at this oxygen partial pressure (PO$_2$) level (i.e., that of air at 60 fsw (18 msw);

PO$_2$ = 0.59 ata) may predispose divers to pulmonary oxygen toxicity (Miller 1976) and that such an oxygen partial pressure may reduce a diver's tolerance for oxygen during any subsequent treatment for decompression sickness (Adams et al. 1978). Because the use of air has obvious decompression advantages, research on its use as a breathing gas at depth will continue.

Shallow-water saturation diving has also been conducted using **nitrogen-oxygen** (nitrox) mixtures. The proportions of nitrogen and oxygen in nitrox mixtures are selected to provide a partial pressure of oxygen within a range from 0.21 ata (close to the normal atmospheric value) to 0.50 ata. Such mixtures can be used for habitat depths equal to or shallower than 50 fsw (15 msw) and should be used for habitat depths greater than 50 fsw. Based on extensive military and commercial saturation diving experience with helium-oxygen gas mixtures, the optimal saturation oxygen partial pressure range is 0.30 to 0.40 ata, with a nominal value of 0.35 ata considered acceptable for all applications.

If the oxygen partial pressure of air at the saturation depth is too high, it can be adjusted by adding either nitrogen or low-oxygen nitrox mixtures or by allowing the oxygen in the habitat to be "breathed down" by the divers. If the oxygen partial pressure is above the recommended maximum level, care must be taken to ensure that the divers do not experience oxygen toxicity as a result of breathing hyperoxic gas in the habitat and during their air excursion dives. Consequently, breathing down the oxygen concentration is not acceptable in many situations and can best be used with very small habitats.

Divers engaged in excursion diving using air as the breathing gas must continuously be aware of the danger of oxygen toxicity. They must know the maximum amount of time that can be spent safely at various depths without incurring problems related to oxygen exposure. As with other toxicities, oxygen poisoning is a function of dose, duration of exposure, and exertion level.

Although neurological symptoms, such as convulsions, are the most serious consequence of oxygen poisoning, the symptoms most likely to be associated with over exposure in saturation-excursion diving are pulmonary. Accordingly, pulmonary tolerance limits that are safe for repeated daily exposures have been incorporated into the limits discussed in Chapter 3 and have also been applied (where appropriate) to the tables in this section on saturation diving.

The degree of oxygen exposure can be quantified by using a system that permits pulmonary oxygen toxicity to be correlated with reduced vital capacity. The oxygen dose that causes a ten percent reduction in vital capacity is considered the maximum safe cumulative oxygen dose. Diving operations should be planned so that every diver has a safety margin that will allow him to be treated for decompression sickness with oxygen without exceeding this ten percent level.

Nitrox breathing mixtures have been used to depths of 198 fsw (61 msw) in the laboratory and nitrox saturation dives have been conducted in the open sea to depths as great as 111.5 fsw (34 msw). To date, open-sea saturation dives that have used nitrogen-oxygen mixtures as the storage gas have employed air as the breathing gas for excursion dives. A review of the data gathered during these exposures reveals that:

- The limiting factor when air is used as the saturation storage gas is oxygen partial pressure.
- The limiting factor when a nitrogen-oxygen mixture is used as the storage gas is nitrogen narcosis.
- Extended exposure (for as long as 14 days) to air at 50 fsw (15 msw; 0.5 ata PO_2) has not produced irreversible or deleterious effects on human volunteers (Adams et al. 1978).
- Extended exposure (27 days) to air at 60 fsw (18 msw; 0.589 ata PO_2) has caused significant decreases in red blood cell mass and, in some, but not all individuals, a significant decrease in lung vital capacity, which indicates pulmonary oxygen toxicity (Miller et al. 1976).
- The degree of nitrogen narcosis varies among individuals.
- Partial acclimation to narcosis may occur in some individuals after continued exposure.
- Prolonged exposure to normoxic nitrogen at depths to 120 fsw (37 msw) has not produced a significant decrement in diver performance.

Based on this information, the following recommendations can be made for air and nitrox saturation dives:

- Air saturation should be limited to a depth of 50 fsw (15 msw).
- The oxygen partial pressure of nitrogen-oxygen mixtures used in saturation storage gases should be kept within the range of 0.3–0.5 ata.
- The operational use of nitrogen-oxygen as a storage gas should be limited to a depth of 120 fsw (37 msw).

Helium-oxygen has been used widely as a breathing gas by the U.S. Navy and the commercial diving industry for saturation and excursion diving (readers should refer to the *U.S. Navy Diving Manual* (1999), and other diving physiology literature for information on this type of diving). In general, helium-oxygen, and occasionally **tri-mixes**, are selected as a breathing gas in surface-oriented diving when the job to be done requires that work be performed at a depth of 220 fsw (68 msw) or more. NOAA typically use these gases at 170 fsw or greater. The principal reason for using these mixtures is the avoidance of nitrogen narcosis and oxygen toxicity. Helium mixtures have rarely been used as a breathing gas for excursions from air or nitrogen/oxygen saturation exposures; under some circumstances, isobaric bubble disease (the counterdiffusion phenomenon) could occur when these two gases are used (D' Aoust 1977).

17.3 LIFE SUPPORT CONSIDERATIONS

Excursion diving from a saturation system or habitat is usually performed with standard diving equipment, i.e., scuba, umbilical, or closed-circuit systems. Because this equipment is described elsewhere in this manual, the following discussion describes the life support features of the saturation system itself.

Life support equipment and techniques vary greatly from one system to another. Some systems require complicated gas mixing and monitoring equipment on a surface support vessel, while others can be supported by equipment that supplies compressed gas, power, and environmental control from an autonomous buoy. Other systems, such as lockout submersibles, require a self-contained life support system.

The characteristics that a particular saturation diving life support system must have depend on the depth, mission duration, water temperature, sea surface condition, requirements for mobility, type of equipment to be used for excursions, rescue potential, and, in many cases, the nature of the work or scientific program to be carried out. Regardless of the system and its peculiarities, all divers must become familiar with the function of each system component, the system's maintenance requirements, and all emergency procedures. Training programs usually provide this information and offer an opportunity for such familiarization. However, all saturation systems have some features in common that relate directly to the health and safety of divers.

In saturation diving, the oxygen pressure for storage should be maintained between 0.30–0.50 ata. Carbon dioxide levels should not exceed a sea level equivalent of 0.5% by volume (5,000 ppm) (U.S. Navy). Carbon monoxide should not exceed a partial pressure that is equivalent to 0.002% by volume (20 ppm) at sea level. If air is the breathing gas, safe partial pressures of carbon dioxide can be maintained by constantly venting the interior atmosphere at a rate of two cfm for each diver at rest and four cfm for each diver not at rest (U.S. Navy). Control of the oxygen partial pressure usually is not a problem at shallow depths when air is used as both the storage and excursion diving gas.

In closed-circuit life support systems and diver-carried rebreathers, which usually use mixed gases, carbon dioxide buildup is a significant problem, and a carbon dioxide scrubbing system is necessary. The active ingredient in scrubbing systems is a chemical, usually composed predominantly of soda lime (Sodasorb®, Sofnolime® or other trade name), that will absorb the carbon dioxide. The length of the absorbent's active life depends on the CO_2 output of the divers, the ambient temperature, and the relative humidity. The man-hour rating of a particular absorbent is provided by the manufacturer. Table 17.2 summarizes the characteristics of barium hydroxide, lithium hydroxide, and soda lime. Because carbon dioxide absorption is influenced by temperature, less CO_2 is

TABLE 17.2
Characteristics of Three Carbon Dioxide Absorbents

Characteristics	Carbon Dioxide Absorbents		
	Soda Lime	Lithium Hydroxide	Barium Hydroxide
Absorbent Density, lb/ft^3	55.4	28.0	65.4
Theoretical CO_2 Absorption, lb CO_2/lb	0.49	0.92	0.39
Theoretical Water Generated, lb/lb CO_2	0.41	0.41	0.41
Theoretical Heat of Absorption, BTU/lb CO_2	670[2]	875[1]	670[1]
Useful CO_2 Absorption, lb CO_2/lb (based on 50 percent efficiency)	0.245	0.46	0.195
Absorbent Weight, lb per diver hour (0.71 lb CO_2)	2.90	1.55	3.65
Absorbent Volume, ft^3 per diver hour	0.0533	0.0552	0.0558

[1] Based on calcium hydroxide reaction only
[2] Based on generating gaseous H2O

absorbed at 40°F (4.4C) than at 70°F (21.1C). Some scrubbers sized for adequate performance at 70°F may have only one-third of their absorbing capacity at 40°F.

Providing external insulation and heating scrubbers that are to be used in cold water are ways of minimizing the size of the canister that must be carried and ensuring that the absorbent achieves its design efficiency. Insulation and heating also minimize moisture condensation.

The efficiency of CO_2 absorbents also is influenced by relative humidity. Barium hydroxide and soda lime absorbents can only achieve their rated capacity when the relative humidity is above 70%. Lower humidity levels reduce absorbent capacity. Under conditions of high gas humidity and low scrubber surface temperature, water may condense on the walls of the canister or in the absorbent, which reduces absorptive capacity and increases pressure drop through the canister.

Backup auxiliary habitat scrubbing systems are frequently used in case the primary system fails. If no backup scrubber system is available, the chamber should be ventilated as described earlier. Divers must remain alert for symptoms of carbon dioxide poisoning (changes in breathing rate or shortness of breath, headache, sweating, nausea, or weakness); the onset of such symptoms is sometimes difficult to detect over a long period. Divers also may not be aware of CO_2 buildup because they associate minor breathing difficulties with the greater density typical of breathing gases under pressure.

In addition to atmospheric control, a satisfactory life support system must have adequate controls for temperature and humidity. At shallow depths, comfortable temperature and humidity ranges in air or nitrogen/oxygen environments are 78–83°F (25.6–28.3C) and

50–75%, respectively. At deeper depths or in helium-oxygen saturation atmospheres, temperatures as high as 92°F (33.3C) and a relative humidity between 40–60% may be necessary for comfort.

The atmosphere's relative humidity affects both the comfort and safety of chamber inhabitants. Habitat humidity is controlled by air conditioning and the use of dehumidifiers or moisture absorbers. Excessive humidity not only decreases scientific productivity but encourages the growth of fungus or bacteria that cause infections. On the other hand, humidity that is too low can be a fire hazard.

17.4 OPERATIONAL CONSIDERATIONS

Use of the saturation mode greatly extends a diver's bottom time or working time because it reduces the relative amount of time that divers must spend compressing and decompressing. Saturation divers also find this mode psychologically advantageous because it is convenient and reassuring to have a dry chamber close at hand.

17.4.1 General Procedures

A diver undergoing saturation on the seafloor for the first time has much to learn. First and foremost, the diver must learn that the surface is not a haven in an emergency; instead, refuge must be found at the working depth. Also, saturated divers must:

- Learn to rely on themselves for support when needed
- Be aware that the entire saturation, from predive preparation to the long decompression at the end of the mission, demands substantial commitment

- Become familiar with the saturation system, its operation, all emergency procedures, and all fire safety rules
- Become familiar with the diving equipment and its limitations
- Become familiar with the surrounding area of the seafloor, the transect lines (see Figure 17.1), and any other orientation markers
- Learn the limits and procedures for making vertical excursions
- Plan all missions and excursions in advance, taking into account the equipment, saturation system, depth, excursion profiles, and the saturation experience of other team members
- Assume responsibility both for their own and their buddy's safety during excursions

Figure 17.1
Diver Following Transect Line

17.4.2 Emergency Procedures (Habitats)

All well-conceived saturation operations should have contingency plans that chart a course of action in case a primary life support system fails or another emergency arises. Any contingency plan should give first priority to diver safety. In a habitat, any emergency, however minor, threatens diver safety. The following emergency procedures are intended to serve as general guidelines that apply to all habitats and personnel transfer capsules. However, because most habitats are one-of-a-kind systems, certain differences in hardware and design will dictate specific procedures that should be followed for each.

WARNING
COMPLETE EMERGENCY PROCEDURES SHOULD BE DEVELOPED FOR EACH SYSTEM AND ALL SURFACE SUPPORT PERSONNEL AND DIVERS SHOULD BECOME FAMILIAR WITH THEM.

Fire Safety: Fire is probably the most critical emergency that can threaten divers using a saturation system. Habitats using air as the storage gas are susceptible to fire because air supports combustion more readily under increased pressure. Burning rates under hyperbaric conditions are primarily a function of the percentage of oxygen present (Shilling et al. 1976). Atmospheres that have less than 6% oxygen will not support combustion. A normoxic nitrogen-oxygen habitat atmosphere contains a lower percentage of oxygen than an air-filled habitat and therefore presents a lesser fire hazard. Care must be taken, however, when oxygen is used during decompression or treatment for decompression sickness.

For diving operations conducted outside the zone of no combustion, avoid placing highly combustible materials in the habitat. Mattresses, pillows, and bed linen should be covered in fire-retardant material. In the event of fire, divers should follow the general procedures below, although their order may vary:

- Make a quick assessment of the source of the smoke or flame (if the source is a movable item, remove it from the habitat immediately, if possible).
- Don emergency breathing masks.
- Shut off all power except lights and emergency communications.
- Notify surface personnel.
- Attempt to extinguish the fire with water and/or pressurized water extinguishers.
- Attempt to remove all flammable materials from the immediate area of the flames. Also attempt to remove smoldering material from the chamber.
- Leave the chamber after donning diving gear unless you are directly involved in fighting the fire.
- If the fire gets out of control, notify surface personnel of this action and evacuate if conditions permit.
- Proceed to available underwater stations and await surface support. Emergency evacuation tables with O_2 prebreathing periods will be provided before transport to a shore-based recompression chamber.

Loss of Power: Most shallow water habitat systems have a primary power source and an emergency or standby power source. Primary power is usually 110 volts AC; emergency power is usually 24 volts DC, stored in external battery pods. In some systems, the emergency power is designed to activate automatically if the primary source fails. Typically, backup DC batteries will power emergency lights, communications, O_2 & CO_2 sensors, and CO_2 scrubbers. Battery duration usually has a safety factor of five to cover decompression times.

In a power emergency, divers should perform the following procedures:

- Activate the emergency power source, if this system is not automatically activated
- Notify surface support personnel and stand-by to assist in isolating and remedying the cause of the failure

Loss of Communication: Most saturation systems have a backup communication system. Sound-powered phones that require no external power often are used. In some cases, communication over diver communication circuits may be possible. When a communication failure occurs, communication should be established immediately on a secondary system, the surface should be notified of primary system failure, and attempts should be made to reactivate the primary system.

Surfacing: Ascending to the surface, whether intentionally or not, is a serious hazard facing saturated divers, especially when they are using self-contained equipment and are not physically attached to a habitat by an umbilical or tether. Saturated divers who are away from the habitat must be careful to avoid any circumstance that would require them to make an emergency ascent to the surface or that might result in accidental surfacing.

If a diver does surface accidentally, however, the buddy diver must:

- Immediately return the diver to the saturation depth. If the accidental surfacing was caused by equipment failure, the diver's buddy should swim immediately to the surface and bring the surfaced diver down, using the emergency octopus regulator, and should then proceed to the closest refuge which may be a way-station or the habitat itself.
- Notify surface support personnel immediately.
- At storage depths of 60 fsw (18 msw) or less, have the diver begin breathing pure oxygen while awaiting instructions from surface support; if deeper, an enriched oxygen mixture should be used to provide an oxygen partial pressure between 1.5–2.5 ata.
- Make preparation for emergency recompression, if directed to do so by surface support personnel.

NOTE
A diver who accidentally surfaces or becomes lost is in great danger. The best assurance against such emergencies is strict adherence to carefully planned preventive measures.

Lost Diver: A saturated diver working away from a habitat or PTC should be continuously aware of his dependence on that facility for life support. Any excursion should be planned carefully so that the return to the chamber is known and assured. As in all diving, buddy divers are a necessity. In the saturated condition, it is especially necessary for diving buddies to stay close together and to be aware at all times of their location, significant landmarks, and the distance and direction back to the habitat. Many habitats, particularly those permanently fixed and continually used, have navigation lines extending to various underwater areas. Divers should become familiar with these navigation aids and use them as reference points during excursions. Divers are also trained in the use of cave diving reels and are required to use them when working away from navigation lines. Saturation divers should place primary reliance for orientation on established navigation lines. A compass should be used only to provide a backup orientation system.

If a diver becomes lost, he should take the following actions:

- Begin signaling by banging on his scuba cylinder with a knife, rock, or other hard object.
- To conserve breathing gas, ascend to the maximum upward excursion depth limit that still permits the bottom to be seen clearly (in murky water or at night, this will not be possible).
- If lost at night, turn off dive light momentarily to look for the habitat or buddy's light. Activate emergency U/W strobe.
- Begin making slow circular search patterns, looking for familiar landmarks or transect lines.

Divers hopelessly lost at saturation depths shallower than 100 fsw (31 msw) should ascend slowly to the surface while they still have sufficient air. On reaching the surface, the diver should take a quick (less than 30 seconds) compass sighting on the support system or buoy over the habitat and should then return to the bottom, rejoin his buddy, and proceed directly to the habitat or nearest underwater way-station.

Night Diving: Night excursions from habitats are common, particularly for scientific divers wishing to observe marine life. Divers must take special care not to become lost during these excursions. Every diver must be equipped with two well-maintained lights that are in good working condition and are equipped with fresh batteries. Every diver should also have an emergency light, preferably a flashing strobe. In emergencies, the strobe can be used for navigation if the diver shields his eyes from the flash. To assist divers back to the habitat if their lights have failed, a flashing strobe should be located on the habitat.

Decompression Sickness After Excursions: Although excursions from a habitat are not likely to cause decompression sickness, habitat operational plans should include procedures for treating decompression sickness. Specific procedures will vary from one habitat program to another, but the following general guidelines can be used if decompression sickness occurs after an excursion dive.

Therapy will typically be conducted in the habitat rather than bringing the affected diver to the surface. The treatment of choice, as always, is recompression and the breathing of enriched oxygen mixtures (PO_2 1.5–2.5 ata). If recompression is not possible, treatment using oxygen breathing and the administration of fluids and drugs should be attempted under medical supervision. Recompression in the water should be used only as a last resort. Decompression from saturation should be delayed for at least 36 hours after a diver has been treated for decompression sickness.

Habitat Evacuation: In the event that the aquanauts have to be evacuated from the habitat before the end of a planned mission, whether for an emergency situation such as a fire, or loss of an essential service, or due to an injury, or as a precaution because of an impending storm, there might not be sufficient time for a normal decompression. One plan is to have the aquanauts prepare for ascent by "prebreathing," oxygen to reduce their nitrogen loading while a fast boat proceeds from shore. Upon arrival, the boat picks up the crew and transfers them to a shoreside chamber where decompression can be completed. Such procedures were developed for the Aquarius Undersea Laboratory in the Florida Keys. Specific information concerning these procedures may be obtained from the National Undersea Research Program.

17.4.3 General Health Practices

The health and welfare of aquanauts living in an open, semiclosed, or closed environmental system are of prime importance to maintaining an effective undersea research program. The micro organisms that are associated with habitat living may impair the performance of divers to the point where the divers must be removed from the program; therefore, it is essential to maintain a proper balance among the indigenous microflora. To maintain this balance, certain health practices should be followed. Although different programs may require different practices, depending on the habitat and local conditions, observance of the general procedures that follow will help to maintain the health of saturation divers:

- Do not allow a person with a cold, ear infection, severe skin problem, or contagious disease to go into the habitat or to have contact with any diver who is to go into the habitat.
- Do not allow any medicines into the habitat that have not been approved by the responsible physician.
- Maintain the habitat's humidity and temperature at proper levels.
- Ensure that divers wash thoroughly with soap and fresh water after each excursion.
- Have the divers wash the inside of their wet suits daily with soap and water.
- Treat ears after each dive or minimally, twice daily, irrigating each ear with 2% acetic acid in aluminum acetate solution (i.e., Domeboro®) for five minutes by the clock.
- Treat any cut, abrasion, etc., no matter how small.
- Keep the living quarters as clean and dry as possible.
- Ensure that any food that has fallen into crevices, where it might decay, is cleaned up immediately.
- Remove garbage from the habitat daily, because it is both a health and fire hazard.
- Change bed linens and towels in the habitat at least twice a week.
- Prevent divers from staying in the water without proper thermal protection, because body temperatures can drop significantly even in tropical waters.

TABLE 17.3
Medications Approved for Habitat Diving

Decongestants	Antibiotics
Sudafed	Cortisporin ear drops
Afrin	Dicloxacillin
Claritin D	Pen VK
Entex	Amoxicillin
Becanase	Doxycyclin
Chlorpheniramine	Augmentin
Bromfed	Unasyn
Humibid	Cipro
Novafed	Fortaz
Dimetapp	Diflucan
Neosynephrine	(anti-fungal for Candidiasis)
	Gris Peg
	(anti-fungal)
Anti-diarrhea	Keflex
Immodium	Unasyn
	Anti-hypertensives
Analgesics	Lisinopril
Motrin	Kosar
Tylenol	Tenormin
Aspirin	
Naprosyn	**Cough Suppressants**
CAMA	Guifenesin Syrup
Susprin	Azithromy
Fexeril	Mytussin

Many of the above are registered trade names

- When inside the habitat, ensure that divers wear warm, clean, and dry clothing (including footwear).
- Wash the interior of the habitat thoroughly after each mission with a solution of non-ionic detergent or other comparable disinfectant.
- Wash the habitat's sanitary facilities and surrounding walls and floor thoroughly every day with a suitable disinfectant solution.

Table 17.3 is a list of medications that have been used successfully in the Ocean Simulation Facility by the U.S. Navy during various saturation diving exposures to a maximum depth of 1,000 fsw (307 msw).

17.4.4 Hazardous Materials

To avoid atmospheric contamination, fires, and diver disability, equipment and materials that could be hazardous must be excluded from the habitat. Such hazardous materials fall into five general categories:

- Volatile materials, both liquids and solids
- Flammables
- Medications whose pharmacologic effects may be altered by pressure
- Objects that cannot withstand increased pressure
- Ungrounded or otherwise hazardous electrical equipment

Before beginning a habitat mission, all personal diving and scientific equipment should be approved for use inside

Diving From Seafloor Habitats

TABLE 17.4
Hazardous Materials for Habitat Operations

Flammables (Volatile)	Explosion/ Implosion Hazards	Volatile Poisons	Metals, Metalloids, and their Salts	Mood-Altering Drugs	Miscellaneous Materials
Acetones	Pressurized aerosol cans	Mercury	Mercury	Ethanol	Tobacco smoking materials of any kind
Gasoline		Ammonia	Fluorides	Marijuana	Matches or lighters
Ethers	Flares of any kind or ignitables	Chlorine	Selenium	Sedatives	Newly made (un-aired) vinyl or styrofoam materials (their solvents, vinyl chloride and isocyanate, respectively, are very toxic)
Naphtha		Sulfur dioxide		Hallucinogens	
Alcohols	Signaling devices	Hydrogen sulfide		Tranquilizers Ataractics	
		Halogenated hydro-carbons		Hypnotics	
				Anti-Depressants Stimulants	Cosmetics or perfumed materials (deodorants)
		Aromatic hydro-carbons			Concentrated acids or bases
		Formalin			Adhesives, including wet-suit cement

the habitat and then recorded. To avoid difficulties, aquanauts should provide documentation for any equipment or materials whose safety is likely to be questioned. Table 17.4 presents a list of materials that are hazardous in habitat operations. This list is not exhaustive, and any doubtful materials should be screened carefully by qualified personnel before being allowed inside a habitat; factors such as mission duration and the habitat's scrubbing capability should be taken into account during this process. If substances that are necessary also have the potential to affect divers in the habitat adversely, safe levels, control methods, and monitoring procedures for the use of these materials should be established. In addition, all divers and topside staff should be made aware of the signs and symptoms of any potentially exposure-related effects associated with the use of these substances.

17.5 EXCURSION DIVING

Excursion diving while saturated in a habitat requires special preparation and strict adherence to excursion diving tables. A diver who is saturated at one atmosphere (i.e., at surface pressure) can make dives (excursions) to depth and return directly to the surface without decompression as long as his body has not absorbed more gas during the dive than it can safely tolerate at surface pressure. Similarly, a diver who

is saturated at a pressure greater than one atmosphere (i.e., at the ambient pressure) can make excursions either to greater depths (downward) or lesser depths (upward) by following the depth/time limits of excursion tables. Many factors change the conditions of excursions (i.e., temperature, work load, equipment, the diver's experience); these factors must be considered when planning any excursion dive or decompression.

WARNING
DIVERS SHOULD START THEIR RETURN TO THE HABITAT FROM EXCURSION DIVES WELL BEFORE THE PRESSURE IN THEIR CYLINDER FALLS BELOW THE AMOUNT THAT WILL SUPPORT THEM DURING THEIR RETURN.

17.5.1 Descending Excursions

In a descending excursion, the bottom time is counted from departure from the saturation depth. The rate of descent may be the same as for dives from the surface (60 fsw/minute). Descending excursions should be made in accordance with the times shown in Table 17.5. Table 17.6 represents no-decompression excursion limits determined

TABLE 17.5
No-stop Descending Excursion Times Incorporating NOAA 1991 Oxygen Limits

Habitat Storage Depth (fsw)

Depth	80	85	90	95	100	105	110	115	120	125	130	135	140	145	150	155	160	165	170	175	180	185	190	195	200	205	210	215	220	225	230	235	240	245	250
PO_2	.72	.75	.78	.81	.84	.88	.91	.94	.97	1.01	1.03	1.07	1.10	1.13	1.16	1.19	1.22	1.26	1.29	1.32	1.36	1.38	1.42	1.45	1.48	1.51	1.54	1.57	1.61	1.64	1.67	1.71	1.73	1.76	1.80
35	350	267	156	113	91	78	68	60	55	50	45	40	36	32	28	24	22	18	15	13	12	11	10	9	8	8	7	7	6	6	5	5	5	5	
40	*	*	283	229	143	108	89	77	68	61	54	46	41	37	34	31	28	25	22	20	16	14	13	11	10	9	9	8	7	7	6	6	6	5	5
45	*	*	*	301	240	202	147	112	92	80	70	59	50	44	39	35	32	30	28	25	23	21	17	15	13	12	11	10	9	8	8	7	7	6	6
50	*	*	*	*	323	253	210	181	137	108	91	69	56	48	42	38	34	31	29	27	25	23	22	21	18	16	14	12	11	10	9	9	8	7	7
55	*	*	*	*	*	350	267	219	187	164	140	86	64	53	45	40	36	33	30	28	26	24	22	21	20	19	18	16	14	13	12	11	10	8	8
60	*	*	*	*	*	*	314	245	203	174	153	137	86	63	52	45	40	36	32	30	27	25	24	22	21	20	19	18	17	15	13	12	11	9	9
65	*	*	*	*	*	*	*	284	224	187	161	142	127	85	63	52	44	39	35	32	29	27	25	23	22	21	19	18	17	17	15	13	12	10	10
70	*	*	*	*	*	*	*	*	236	191	162	145	128	111	85	63	51	44	39	35	32	29	27	25	23	22	20	19	18	17	16	16	14	11	11
75	*	*	*	*	*	*	*	*	*	213	174	148	129	114	103	84	62	51	44	39	35	31	29	26	25	23	21	20	19	18	17	16	15	12	13
80	*	*	*	*	*	*	*	*	*	*	288	228	191	165	145	95	70	66	53	45	41	36	35	32	29	27	25	23	22	20	19	18	17	16	15
85	*	*	*	*	*	*	*	*	*	*	*	*	*	*	317	145	103	84	70	54	48	41	36	32	29	27	25	23	22	20	19	18	17	16	15
90	*	*	*	*	*	*	*	*	*	*	*	*	*	*	*	225	145	103	84	70	62	54	46	40	36	32	29	27	25	22	22	22	19	18	17
95	*	*	*	*	*	*	*	*	*	*	*	*	*	*	*	*	328	225	168	143	113	97	68	55	47	41	37	33	30	26	26	24	23	21	20
100	*	*	*	*	*	*	*	*	*	*	*	*	*	*	*	*	*	*	*	*	306	227	143	113	80	62	52	46	40	37	33	31	28	26	25
105	*	*	*	*	*	*	*	*	*	*	*	*	*	*	*	*	*	*	*	*	*	341	281	193	135	109	93	72	59	50	44	40	36	33	31
110	*	*	*	*	*	*	*	*	*	*	*	*	*	*	*	*	*	*	*	*	*	*	354	308	262	174	129	107	77	62	53	46	41	38	35
115	*	*	*	*	*	*	*	*	*	*	*	*	*	*	*	*	*	*	*	*	*	*	*	*	334	294	257	176	132	83	65	55	48	43	39
120	*	*	*	*	*	*	*	*	*	*	*	*	*	*	*	*	*	*	*	*	*	*	*	*	*	347	303	270	243	163	91	68	57	49	44
125	*	*	*	*	*	*	*	*	*	*	*	*	*	*	*	*	*	*	*	*	*	*	*	*	*	*	*	329	291	261	237	101	72	59	51

Note: Values are in minutes

* No time limit (up to 6 hours) for that depth-time combination

Allowable excursion times in minutes breathing air from an air or normoxic nitrogen-oxygen saturation, taking into account the oxygen limits from the *1991 NOAA Diving Manual*, Table 15-1. Shaded areas show exposures where oxygen exceeds NOAA 1991 limits. Intermediate values should use the next shallower habitat depth. (This table is equivalent to Table 12-5 of the *1979 NOAA Diving Manual*, but with updated oxygen limits.)

Diving From Seafloor Habitats

17-11

TABLE 17.6
No-stop Limits for Descending Excursions Based on Gas Loading Alone

Habitat Storage Depth (fsw)

Depth	80	85	90	95	100	105	110	115	120	125	130	135	140	145	150	155	160	165	170	175	180	185	190	195	200	205	210	215
PO₂	.72	.75	.78	.81	.84	.88	.91	.94	.97	1.01	1.03	1.07	1.10	1.13	1.16	1.19	1.22	1.26	1.29	1.32	1.36	1.38	1.42	1.45	1.48	1.51	1.54	1.57
35	350	267	156	113	91	78	68	60	55	50	45	40	36	32	28	24	22	18	15	13	12	11	10	9	8	8	7	7
40	*	*	283	229	143	108	89	77	68	61	54	46	41	37	34	31	28	25	22	20	16	14	13	11	10	9	9	8
45	*	*	*	301	240	202	147	112	92	80	70	59	50	44	39	35	32	30	28	25	23	21	17	15	13	12	11	10
50	*	*	*	*	323	253	210	181	137	108	91	69	56	48	42	38	34	31	29	27	25	23	22	21	18	16	14	12
55	*	*	*	*	*	350	267	219	187	164	140	86	64	53	45	40	36	33	30	28	26	24	22	21	20	19	18	16
60	*	*	*	*	*	*	314	245	203	174	153	137	86	63	52	45	40	36	32	30	27	25	24	22	21	20	19	18
65	*	*	*	*	*	*	*	284	224	187	161	142	127	85	63	52	45	39	35	32	29	27	25	23	22	21	19	18
70	*	*	*	*	*	*	*	315	236	191	162	145	128	111	85	63	51	44	39	35	32	29	27	25	23	22	20	19
75	*	*	*	*	*	*	*	*	279	213	174	148	129	114	103	84	62	51	44	39	35	31	29	26	25	23	21	20
80	*	*	*	*	*	*	*	*	*	270	240	240	228	191	165	145	95	66	53	45	40	35	32	29	27	25	23	22
85		*	*	*	*	*	*	*	*	*	270	240	240	225	210	210	195	122	70	55	47	41	36	32	29	27	25	23
90			*	*	*	*	*	*	*	*	*	240	240	225	210	210	195	180	180	95	66	54	46	40	36	32	29	27
95				*	*	*	*	*	*	*	*	*	240	225	210	210	195	180	180	165	150	97	68	55	47	41	37	33
100					*	*	*	*	*	*	*	*	*	225	210	210	195	180	180	165	150	150	135	113	80	62	52	45
105						*	*	*	*	*	*	*	*	*	210	210	195	180	180	165	150	150	135	135	120	83	83	45
110							*	*	*	*	*	*	*	*	*	210	195	180	180	165	150	150	135	135	120	83	83	45
115								*	*	*	*	*	*	*	*	*	195	180	180	165	150	150	135	135	120	83	83	45
120									*	*	*	*	*	*	*	*	*	180	180	165	150	150	135	135	120	83	83	45

Note: Values are in minutes
* No time limit (up to 6 hours) for that depth - time combination

Allowable excursion times in minutes breathing air from an air or normoxic nitrogen-oxygen saturation without regard to oxygen tolerance limits. (Derived from Table 12-4 of the 1979 Second Edition of the *NOAA Diving Manual*)

NOAA Diving Manual

by computation of inert gas exchange rates without regard for oxygen exposure limits. Because oxygen tolerance limits are important in the deeper and longer excursions, existing guidelines for oxygen tolerance have been superimposed to provide Table 17.5. Table 17.6 is included in the manual for reference only and should not be used without considering oxygen tolerance limits.

In descending excursions, the following guidelines should be observed:

- The breathing gas for all excursions described in Tables 17.5 and 17.6 is air.
- The maximum recommended depth for any air-breathing excursion is 215 fsw (66 msw).
- Descending excursions conducted in accordance with Tables 17.5 and 17.6 are no-decompression excursions (no-stop).
- A descending excursion may be made at any time after an ascending excursion.
- The ascent rate back to the storage depth after a descending excursion should be 30 fsw/minute.
- If the no-decompression time for a descending excursion is exceeded for any reason, the diver must be decompressed before returning to the saturation depth. The schedule that should be followed is a U.S. Navy air schedule, used on a differential basis. The schedule should be determined by subtracting the saturation depth from the excursion depth, and then using that value to select the appropriate table. The bottom time should be the actual bottom time of the excursion (the time between departing the habitat depth and beginning ascent). The schedule should be followed by adding the stop depths called for in the table to the saturation depth to determine actual stop depths. Alternative procedures for managing a decompression excursion can be found in Hamilton et al. 1988a and 1988b.
- Short descending excursions have only a slight effect on subsequent ascending excursions, short or long (after a 4-hour interval).
- Long descending excursions may seriously prejudice subsequent ascending excursions. After a 6-hour excursion at 30 fsw or deeper than the storage depth, a subsequent ascending excursion that approaches the limits should not be performed for 36-hours. If an ascending excursion is necessary between 18 – 36 hours after such a dive, use 50 percent of the time allowed by the Ascending No-stop Excursion Table, or follow the procedure described in the first paragraph of 17.5.3.
- Partial pressure conversions should not be used in determining descending excursion limits. Regardless of breathing gas, determine these limits as if saturated on a normoxic mixture at the actual saturation depth.

When planning a diving schedule for saturated divers, it is recommended that ascending excursions be made before descending excursions. This will maximize diving efficiency and reduce the probability of decompression sickness. When determining descending excursion times using Tables 17.5 and 17.6, the saturation storage depth should be rounded to the nearest five fsw interval *shallower* than the actual depth.

Descending Excursions
Example 1:
The storage depth is 50 fsw (15 msw), the mixture is air, and the diver is to dive to a depth of 140 fsw (43 msw). How long can he stay at 140 fsw without exceeding the normal oxygen tolerance limits?

Solution:
- Find the 50 fsw depth in Table 17.5 (column one) and read across to the 140 fsw column.
- He may stay at 140 fsw for 56 minutes.

Example 2:
The storage depth is 83 fsw (25 msw), the mixture is normoxic, and the diver is to make a dive to 160 fsw (49 msw) to collect specimens. How long can he stay at 160 fsw without exceeding the normal oxygen tolerance limits?

Solution:
- Find the 80 fsw depth in Table 17.5 (column one) and read across to the 160 fsw column.
- He may stay at 160 fsw for 95 minutes.

Example 3:
The storage depth is 50 fsw (15 msw), the mixture in the habitat is air (PO_2 = 0.5 ata), and the diver makes an excursion to a depth of 125 fsw (38 msw) for two hours (120 minutes). What will be the diver's decompression obligation time in order to return to the habitat's storage depth of 50 fsw (15 msw)?

Solution:
- Subtract the habitat storage depth from the maximum depth achieved during the excursion.

  125 fsw - 50 fsw = 75 fsw

- Using the U.S. Navy Dive Tables, determine the decompression schedule required for a dive to 75 fsw for 120 minutes. The following decompression stops are required:

  20 feet for 17 minutes
  10 feet for 56 minutes

- Add the habitat storage depth to each decompression stop to determine actual depth at which to perform decompression stops.

  20 feet + 50 = 70 fsw for 17 minutes
  10 feet + 50 = 60 fsw for 56 minutes

Diving From Seafloor Habitats

Tables 17.5 and 17.6 may also be used for an air environment in the habitat because the divers start with less nitrogen than when breathing normoxic mixtures; therefore, the excursion times are more conservative and thus have lower risk in terms of decompression sickness.

17.5.2 Repetitive and Continuation Excursions

For continuation downward excursions (excursions made within four hours of returning to habitat storage depth from previous downward excursions) to a depth equal to or shallower than the previous downward excursion, use the following procedures to calculate allowable bottom time at the new depth:

- Calculate the ratio of time used on the first downward excursion to time allowed and determine the unused portion by subtracting the fraction from 1.0, then multiply by the maximum allowable bottom time at the depth of the second downward excursion.

Formula: Allowable Excursion Time=

$$\left[1.0 - \left(\frac{\text{Time Used (mins)}}{\text{Time Allowed (mins)}}\right)\right] \times \begin{array}{c}\text{Max. Allowable Time (mins)}\\ \text{(at repetitive depth)}\end{array}$$

- Use the allowable dive time as the maximum allowable bottom time for the continuation dive (be sure to allow adequate time for ascents and descents from storage depth).

Example:

First excursion from a habitat depth of 45 fsw was to 110 fsw for 90 minutes. After 2 hours and 30 minutes in the habitat, the aquanauts want to dive to 85 fsw. What is their allowable excursion time at 85 fsw?

1st excursion = 110 fsw / 90 minutes

Solution:

$$\left[1.0 - \left(\frac{90 \text{ mins}}{147 \text{ mins}}\right)\right] = .39 \times 360 \text{ mins} = 140 \text{ mins at 85 fsw}$$

where
    90 = time used on 1st excursion to 110 fsw
   147 = allowable time to 110 fsw
   .39 = decimal ratio of remaining time
   360 = max allowable at 85 fsw (depth of 2nd
        excursion) (see Table 17.5)

Continuation downward excursion = Storage depth interval < 4 hours: For continuation downward excursions to a depth greater than all previous downward excursions, the total sum of bottom time for all excursions shall be the allowable time for the deepest excursion shown in Table 17.5.

Repetitive downward excursion = Storage depth interval > 4 hours: One repetitive downward excursion (excursions begun at least four hours after return to habitat depth from a previous downward excursion) may be made to a depth equal to or shallower than the previous downward excursion. The time limit for the second downward excursion should be half that shown in Table 17.5. Note the following parameters:

- If the total time in Table 17.5 is desired for a proposed excursion, a period of 12 hours at storage depth must have elapsed following completion of the previous dive.
- After having utilized 1.5 times the maximum allowable time from the Table 17.5 excursion time (with any combination of continuation dives or a repetitive dive) a period of 12 hours at storage depth must elapse prior to a subsequent dive.
- Ascent rates from all downward excursions should not exceed 30 fsw per minute.
- No downward excursions will be made in the six hours prior to beginning scheduled decompression.
- A surface support boat may or may not accompany the aquanauts, and they will be tracked so that in the event of an emergency, their location will be known.

NOTE
When conducting a repetitive dive (> 4-hour storage depth interval) and the first excursion occurring after 12-hour storage depth interval utilizes less than 50 percent of maximum allowable bottom time, consider this repetitive dive to be a continuation dive and calculate allowable excursion time using the continuation dive formula.

17.5.3 Ascending Excursions

Ascending excursions are short decompressions in themselves and should not prejudice subsequent descending excursions. After a long excursion (over one hour) only a few feet deeper than the storage depth, subsequent ascending excursions should be safe if they are calculated on the basis of the depth of the long excursion rather than on the storage depth. To determine ascending excursion times using Table 17.7, the saturation depth should be rounded to the nearest five fsw interval **deeper** than the actual storage depth.

Example 1:

The habitat depth is 55 fsw (17 msw) and a 120 minute excursion is made to a depth of 80 fsw (24 msw). The oxygen environment in the habitat is normoxic. Three and one-half hours later an excursion is made to 25 fsw (8 msw). What would be the maximum allowable time of the upward excursion?

Solution:

Read over from the 80 fsw habitat depth row (column one normoxic) to the 25 fsw (8 msw) column in Table 17.7. The maximum time is nine minutes.

TABLE 17.7
Ascending No-Stop Excursions From Air or Normoxic Nitrogen-Oxygen Saturation

Habitat Depth (fsw) **	Habitat Depth (fsw) ***	Excursion Depth (fsw) 0	5	10	15	20	25	30	35	40	45	50	55	60	65	70	75	80	85	90
30	38	36	48	60	*	*	*	*												
35	45	30	37	48	60	*	*	*	*											
40	51	24	31	40	52	60	*	*	*	*										
45	57	17	24	31	40	52	60	*	*	*	*									
50	64	12	18	25	32	42	60	*	*	*	*	*								
55	70	7	13	18	25	32	42	60	*	*	*	*	*							
60	76	0	7	13	18	25	32	42	60	*	*	*	*	*						
65		0	0	8	14	20	27	34	44	60	*	*	*	*	*					
70		0	0	0	8	14	20	27	34	44	60	*	*	*	*	*				
75		0	0	0	0	9	15	21	28	36	47	60	*	*	*	*	*			
80		0	0	0	0	0	9	15	21	28	36	47	60	*	*	*	*	*		
85		0	0	0	0	0	5	10	16	23	30	37	48	60	*	*	*	*	*	
90		0	0	0	0	0	0	5	10	16	23	30	37	48	60	*	*	*	*	*
95		0	0	0	0	0	0	0	6	12	18	24	31	40	52	60	*	*	*	*
100		0	0	0	0	0	0	0	0	6	12	18	24	31	40	52	60	*	*	*
105		0	0	0	0	0	0	0	0	0	7	13	18	25	32	42	60	*	*	*
110		0	0	0	0	0	0	0	0	0	0	7	13	18	25	32	42	60	*	*
115		0	0	0	0	0	0	0	0	0	0	0	7	13	18	25	32	42	60	*
120		0	0	0	0	0	0	0	0	0	0	0	0	7	13	18	25	32	42	60

Note: Values are in minutes
* No time limit for that depth-time combination
** Column for Normoxic Depth
*** Column for Air Depth

In ascending excursions, the following guidelines should be observed:

- Begin timing the excursion upon departure from saturation storage depth and plan the dive so as to be **back at the habitat depth by the end of the allowed excursion time.**
- The ascent rate should be 10–30 fsw/minute.
- The descent rate back to the storage depth should be 30–75 fsw/minute.
- If decompression sickness symptoms occur, descend immediately to storage depth.
- If the descent is momentarily delayed because of ear problems, it is preferable to discontinue descent (or even temporarily to ascend a short distance) and clear the ear, rather than to risk incurring ear barotrauma by adhering strictly to the table.
- Ascending excursions can be figured using an equivalent normoxic depth for the habitat if the breathing gas is air instead of a normoxic nitrogen-oxygen mixture (see second example).

Example 2:
The habitat depth is 97 fsw, the mixture is normoxic, and the diver is to make an ascending excursion to a depth of 47 fsw to work on an instrument package.

Solution:
- Enter Table 17.7 at 100 fsw (column one normoxic) and read across to the 45 fsw column.
- The excursion to 47 fsw should last no more than 12 minutes from start of ascent until returning to storage depth.

Example 3:
The habitat depth is 49 fsw, the mixture is air, and the diver wants to ascend to a depth of 20 fsw.

Solution:
- Enter Table 17.7 using 51 fsw (column two air) and read across to the 20 fsw column.
- The diver may stay at 20 fsw for 60 minutes.

Excursion information contained in this manual was derived from material included in the 1975 and 1979 editions, and updated with new oxygen limits published in the 1991 edition. Additional procedures for both ascending and descending excursions from air or nitrogen-oxygen saturation can be found in Hamilton et al. (1988a, 1988b).

17.6 DECOMPRESSION AFTER AN AIR OR NITROGEN-OXYGEN SATURATION DIVE
The operational procedures for decompression after a saturation dive vary among systems. In some systems

(50 fsw or less), the divers may swim to the surface, immediately enter a recompression chamber, recompress to the saturation depth, and begin decompression. This method is possible if the surface interval is less than five minutes and the depth less than 50 fsw (Edel 1969; Weeks 1972; Walden and Rainnie 1971). Other systems are designed to decompress divers in the habitat on the bottom and then have the divers swim to the surface upon completion of decompression (Wicklund 1973). In other cases, the habitat can be raised to the surface and towed to a shore base where decompression is completed and standby facilities may be available (Koblick et al. 1974). These procedures are all discussed in detail in Miller et al. (1976).

In deep diving systems, the divers usually are transferred to a surface decompression chamber in a personnel transfer capsule that remains at the storage depth pressure. Decompression is then accomplished in accordance with standard procedures for the depth, duration, and breathing gas.

The following paragraphs contain decompression procedures and tables for saturation dives in which air and or normoxic mixtures of nitrogen and oxygen are used as the breathing gas. The decompression tables are based on computer models, hyperbaric chamber experiments, and open-sea saturation diving experience.

Descending excursions will prejudice a subsequent saturation decompression. It is necessary, therefore, to delay the start of saturation decompression after the last descending excursion, no matter which decompression schedule is used.

TABLE 17.8
Time Intervals Between Final Descending Excursion and Start of Decompression From Saturation Storage Depth

Final Descending Excursion		
Excursion Depth (fsw)	Duration of Excursion (hr)	Delay Before Beginning Saturation Decompression (hr)
Any depth	< 2	12
< 50	2–4	24
< 50	> 4	16
< 50	1–2	36
50–100	> 2	30
50–100	1–2	48
> 100	> 2	
> 100	4	
< 1	4	

This table also applies to excursions requiring decompression; if bends occurred as a result of an excursion, a delay of at least 48 hours is recommended prior to beginning saturation decompression.

Table 17.8 shows the required time intervals between the final descending excursion and the start of decompression. Another approach that may be quicker than waiting after long excursions for the times shown in Table 17.8 would be to compress the habitat to the depth of the last excursion and to decompress from that depth. This procedure provides the same margin of safety as using Table 17.8.

Example:
The storage depth is 45 fsw (14 msw) and the diver makes a final descending excursion to a depth of 110 fsw (34 msw) for three hours. Because this excursion is 65 fsw (20 msw) below the storage depth for longer than two hours, he has to wait 36 hours before beginning saturation decompression.

Decompression tables and procedures for saturation dives using helium and oxygen are not included in this Manual; the reader is referred to the *U.S. Navy Diving Manual* (1999) for further information on such dives.

17.6.1 Decompression After Nitrogen-Oxygen or Air Saturation Exposures

Since the publication of the first edition of this manual in 1975, a significant amount of experience has accumulated in air and nitrogen-oxygen saturation decompression. The procedures described in the following paragraphs are based on or derived from the best accumulated experience available.

Several factors influence the choice of a decompression profile: the depth of saturation, the gas mixture breathed, and the depth and duration of the last excursion prior to commencing decompression. Four different saturation decompression schedules have been used by NOAA since 1976 on various operations. The first, Table 17.9, was used in the NOAA SCORE project. This schedule was developed originally for the NOAA Diving Program and has been used both in the laboratory and in the field (Miller et al. 1976). Table 17.9 was designed for use with air saturation at 60 fsw (18 msw) but has been modified to be consistent with the recommended maximum air saturation depth of 50 fsw (15 msw). See Table 17.13 for summary information about nitrogen-oxygen saturation decompression tables 17.9 through 17.12.

Table 17.10 has been used for over 300 decompressions after saturation in the Hydrolab habitat. On only one occasion has decompression sickness been documented after its use, and on this occasion the incident occurred during flight following saturation. In other instances, precautionary recompression treatment was given to four aquanauts (Miller et al. 1976).

Two additional saturation decompression schedules are shown in Tables 17.11 and 17.12. These tables were contained in the 1975 edition of this manual. In that edition (1975), Table 17.11 (formerly 12-7) was referred to as an "emergency" table and Table 17.12 (formerly Table 12-5) was referred to as a "standard" table. These terms were used deliberately but are now considered to be misleading and have been changed.

Table 17.11 (now referred to as "standard") is appropriate when a more rapid ascent is desired and extensive oxygen breathing is acceptable. Table 17.12 (now referred to as "conservative") is recommended for use when special circumstances suggest that the risk of decompression sickness may be greater than usual (Miller et al. 1976).

Table 17.13 provides summary information about all of the decompression schedules contained in Tables 17.9 through 17.12 and provides criteria for choosing the optimal table.

17.6.2 Emergency Recompression in the Habitat

In the event that an aquanaut experiences symptoms of decompression sickness either following return to the habitat from an excursion or at the end of the mission decompression, the diver should be thoroughly evaluated by a Diving Medical Officer (DMO) or Diver Medical Technician (DMT) and then placed on 100% oxygen. If DCS is suspected, treatment should be initiated immediately.

Decompression sickness following an excursion: If symptoms of DCS occur following a downward excursion, the victim and a DMT will move to the entry lock for recompression therapy. The other aquanauts will remain in the main lock at storage depth for the duration of the treatment. Once the entry lock has been isolated from the main lock, the DMT will commence treatment in accordance with treatment tables provided in Appendix VI. After treatment is completed and the DMT and the aquanaut are at surface pressure, they will lock-out of the habitat and return to the surface. If the DCS incident occurs close to the end of the mission, the decision may be made to decompress all occupants on the appropriate treatment table and terminate the saturation mission.

Decompression sickness during normal saturation decompression: If symptoms of DCS occur during the decompression phase of the mission, the victim will be placed on 100% oxygen and the main lock, containing all occupants, will be pressurized to the appropriate treatment depth. A chamber operator will be locked-in the chamber to conduct the treatment in accordance with the prescribed treatment tables (see Appendix VI).

Selection of appropriate treatment tables: The decision as to which treatment table to use for treatment of DCS depends on several factors including the condition of the patient and entire aquanaut team, impending weather conditions, availability of support personnel and supplies, and condition of equipment. Table 17.14 lists the various treatment tables that are available and the conditions and considerations for their use. Table 17.15 provides a decision flow chart for selection of the appropriate treatment table based on the condition of the patient.

17.6.3 Diving After Decompression from Saturation Exposure

Divers who have completed a saturation decompression may be resaturated immediately. However, if a diver wishes to make non-saturation dives soon after completion of a saturation decompression, he must wait six hours before qualifying for a repetitive Group Z of the Residual Nitrogen Timetable for Repetitive Air Dives (see Appendix IV). The Residual Nitrogen Timetable for Repetitive Air Dives should then be followed as directed, with the diver moving to successively lower repetitive groups after the intervals specified in the tables. Any dives undertaken within 36 hours after an air or nitrogen-oxygen saturation dive should be limited to a depth of 50 fsw (15 msw) or shallower for a maximum exposure of 1 hour.

Example:

Time

0800 A diver surfaces from a completed decompression; however, more coral specimens located at 50 fsw (15 msw) are needed. How long must the diver wait before he may go to 50 fsw (15 msw) for 30 minutes without incurring a decompression obligation?

1200 After waiting six hours, the diver is in repetitive Group Z. The Residual Nitrogen Time-table for Repetitive Air Dives specifies that 2 hours and 18 minutes must be spent at the surface for the tissues to have released sufficient nitrogen to permit a 34-minute dive to 50 fsw (15 msw) (which will place the diver in repetitive Group H prior to the dive).

1418 The diver dives to 50 fsw (15 msw) for 30 minutes and surfaces without decompressing.

A diver who has just completed saturation decompression may be resaturated immediately.

17.6.4 Flying After a Saturation Decompression

After a saturation decompression, divers should wait at least 48 hours before flying. Observance of this rule greatly reduces the likelihood that such divers will experience decompression sickness.

TABLE 17.9
NOAA Air Decompression Table
for Air Saturation at 50 fsw

Depth (fsw)	Rate of Decompression	Time (min)
50 to 30	6 min/ft	120
30 to 28	22 min/ft	44
28 to 26	23 min/ft	46
26 to 24	24 min/ft	48
24 to 22	25 min/ft	50
22 to 20	26 min/lt	52
20 to 18	27 min/ft	54
18 to 16	28 min/ft	56
16 to 13	29 min/ft	87
13 to 10	30 min/ft	90
10 to 8	31 min/ft	62
8 to 6	32 min/lt	64
6 to 4	33 min/ft	66
4 to 2	34 min/ft	68
Time at 1 fsw	**68 min**	**68**

Total time   975 min
16:15 hr:min

No oxygen

Depart the saturation depth at the rate specified for that depth in the schedule and follow the schedule to the surface. If the hatch seal of the chamber cannot be maintained as pressure approaches sea level, stop ascent, and hold at the lowest pressure which can be maintained for the remainder of the time indicated for the decompression. Breathe air throughout the decompression.

TABLE 17.10
NOAA Air/Oxygen Decompression Table
for Air Saturation at 42 fsw

Depth (fsw)	Rate of Ascent (fsw per min)	Time (min)	Breathing Gas
42 to 24	2	9	Air
24 stop	—	180	Air
24 to 20	1	4	Air
20 stop	—	180	Air
20 to 16	1	4	Air
16 stop	—	180	Air
16 to 12	1	4	Air
12 stop	—	75	Oxygen
12 to 8	1	4	Air
8 stop	—	80	Oxygen
8 to 4	1	4	Air
4 stop	—	90	Oxygen
4 to surface	1	4	Air

Total time   418 min
13:38 hr:min

Oxygen time   4.1 hr

Decompression may be carried out inside the habitat. At the end of decompression, divers compress the habitat to ambient pressure, lock out and swim to the surface. The compression rate should be approximately 30 fsw/min. After decompression, divers should remain in the vicinity of a recompression chamber for 24 hours.

TABLE 17.11

NOAA Air/Oxygen Decompression Table For Air/Normoxic
Saturation Between 0-100 fsw Standard (Formerly Table 12-7, 1975 Edition, Table 12-12, 1979 Edition)

	First Stop			Subsequent Stops		
A	**B**			**C**		
Saturation Depth Range (fsw)	**Depth (fsw)**	**Gas**	**Time at Stop (hr:min)**	**Depth (fsw)**	**Gas**	**Time at Stop (hr:min)**
96-100	80	Air	1:30	75	Air	2:15
91-95	75	Air	1:30	70	Air	2:25
86-90	70	Air	1:30	65	Air	2:30
81-85	65	Air	1:35	60	Air	2:35
76-80	60	Air	1:40	55	Air	2:40
71-75	55	Air	1:40	50	Air	2:45
66-70	50	Air	1:45	45	Air	2:45
61-65	45	Air	1:45	40	Air	2:00
56-60	40	Air	0:30	40	Oxygen	0:30
				35	Oxygen	1:00
51-55	35	Oxygen	0:45	30	Air	0:30
				30	Oxygen	1:00
46-50	30	Oxygen	0:45	25	Air	2:00
				25	Oxygen	1:00
41-45	25	Oxygen	1:00	20	Air	0:30
				20	Oxygen	1:00
36-40	20	Oxygen	1:00	15	Air	2:00
31-35	15	Oxygen	0:30	15	Oxygen	1:00
26-30	10	Oxygen	0:30	10	Air	0:30
				10	Oxygen	1:00
				5	Air	0:30
				5	Oxygen	0:30
22-25	5	Oxygen	0:30	30	Oxygen	0:30
0-21	No-Decompression			Surface		

Choose the appropriate saturation range from column A; move horizontally to the column B to determine the first stop; move horizontally to column C for the second stop; then move down the column vertically for the rest of the schedule.

Example — To determine the decompression schedule for a saturation exposure at 50 fsw:

- Locate 50 fsw in column A, i.e., 46 to 50 fsw Saturation Depth Range.
- Move horizontally to column B to determine the depth, gas, and time for the first stop, at 30 ft., breathing oxygen for 45 minutes.

- Move horizontally to the column C for the first subsequent stop (the second stop), i.e., at 25 ft., breathing air for two hours.
- Subsequent stops are determined by reading vertically down the column C, i.e., the third stop is again at 25 ft. breathing oxygen for one hour, the fourth stop is at 20 ft., breathing air for 30 minutes, etc., to the bottom of the column and surface.
- For the final stop recompress the chamber to 30 fsw.

Ascent rate is not critical (1 to 30 fpm). Stop times include time to ascend from the preceding stop. Final ascent, after 30 minutes oxygen breathing at 30 fsw, should be 10 fpm or slower, and oxygen or air may be breathed to the surface.

TABLE 17.12
NOAA Air/Oxygen Decompression Table
For Air/Normoxic Saturation Between 0–100 fsw
Conservative (Formerly Standard Table 12‑5, 1975 Edition, Table 12-13, 1979 Edition)

Decompression using Air and Oxygen after N_2O_2 Saturations from 0–100 fsw						
	First Stop			**Subsequent Stages**		
A	**B**			**C**		
Saturation Depth Range (fsw)	Depth (fsw)	Gas	Time at Stop (hr:min)	Depth (fsw)	Gas	Time, at Stop (hr:min)
96-100	80	Air	3:00	75	Air	4:00
91-95	75	Air	3:00	70	Air	4:00
86-90	70	Air	3:00	65	Air	4:30
81-85	65	Air	3:00	60	Air	4:30
76-80	60	Air	3:00	55	Air	5:00
71-75	55	Air	3:30	50	Air	5:00
66-70	50	Air	3:30	45	Air	5:00
61-65	45	Air	3:30	40	Air	5:00
56-60	40	Air	4:00	35	Air	0:30
				35	Oxygen	1:00
51-55	35	Oxygen	1:00	35	Air	0:30
				35	Oxygen	1:00
				30	Air	2:00
46-50	30	Air	2:00	30	Oxygen	1:00
				25	Air	0:30
				25	Oxygen	1:00
41-45	25	Oxygen	0:30	25	Air	0:30
				25	Oxygen	1:00
				20	Air	3:00
36-40	20	Air	1:30	20	Oxygen	1:00
				15	Air	0:30
				15	Oxygen	1:00
31-35	15	Oxygen	1:00	15	Air	0:30
				15	Oxygen	1:00
				10	Air	4:00
26-30	10	Air	2:00	10	Oxygen	1:00
				5	Air	0:30
				5	Oxygen	1:00
				5	Air	0:30
				5	Oxygen	1:00
22-25	5	Oxygen	0:30	30	Oxygen	0:30
0-21	No-Decompression			Surface		

Decompression procedures are the same as those used for Table 17.11.

TABLE 17.13
Summary Information About Nitrogen-Oxygen
Saturation Decompression Tables 17.9 Through 17.12

Schedule	Maximum Saturation Depth (fsw)	Time From Max. Depth (hr:min)	Hours from Intermediate Depths (fsw)				Oxygen (time, hr)
			100	80	60	40	
Table 17.9	50	16:15	—	—	—	15.3	none
Table 17.10	42	13:38	—	—	—	13.6	4.1
Table 17.11 Standard	100	34:55	36	25.3	14	7	7.5
Table 17.12 Conservative	100	64:30	64.5	47.5	28.5	14	11.5

These are approximate times for comparison. The times may differ as a function of the starting depth and method of starting ascent.

Selection of Air or Nitrogen-Oxygen Saturation Decompression Procedures

Schedule	Depth Range (fsw)	Oxygen Required	Conditions and Considerations for Use
No-Decompression	0-26	No	When N_2 partial pressure does not exceed 47 fsw, (i.e., air at 26 fsw).
Table 17.9	26-50	No	Schedule of choice for air saturation at 50 fsw and shallower.
Table 17.10	42	Yes	Dependable for air saturation close to, but not deeper than 42 fsw.
Table 17.11 Standard	22-100	Yes	Designed for normoxic exposures from 22-100 fsw and N_2 partial pressure equivalents. Recommended when most rapid ascent is required and oxygen breathing can be tolerated.
Table 17.12 Conservative	22-100	Yes	Designed for normoxic exposures from 22-100 fsw and partial pressure equivalents. Recommended when decompression complications are likely. Extensive oxygen breathing required.

TABLE 17.14
Selection of Air or Nitrogen-Oxygen
Saturation Recompression Treatment Tables

Treatment Table	Depth (fsw)	Oxygen Required	Conditions and Considerations for Use
Saturation 5	60	Yes	Emergency evacuation from storage depth.
Saturation 5 Emergency	60	Yes	Contingency treatment table when forced to reduce treatment time due to impending storm or equipment failure, etc.
Saturation 6 Conservative	60	Yes	Decompression sickness following a downward excursion.
Saturation 6 Emergency	60	Yes	Contingency treatment table when forced to reduce treatment time due to impending storm or equipment failure, etc.
Saturation 6-A	165	Yes	Symptoms consistent with an air embolism or serious neurological impairment.

See Appendix VI for Tables

TABLE 17.15
Saturation Recompression Treatment Flow Chart

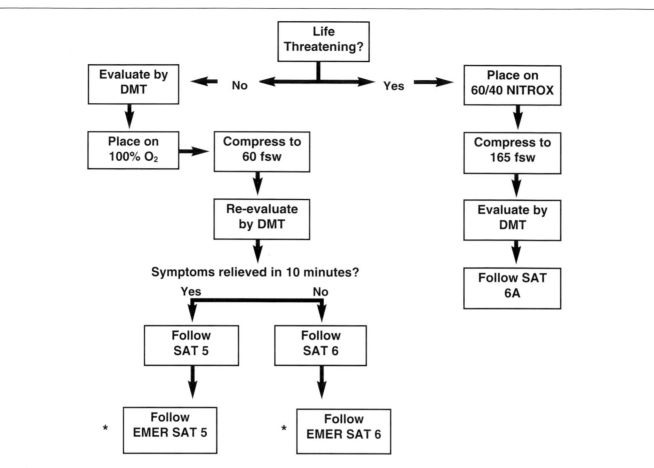

* *Contingency Tables (use if treatment time needs to be reduced, otherwise use normal treatment tables)*

Saturation Recompression Treatment Table Usage

SAT 5

Emergency evacuation from storage depth

Symptoms of decompression sickness relieved after 10 minutes at 60 fsw for occurrence of decompression sickness following a downward excursion

Emergency evacuation from normal saturation

SAT 6

Decompression sickness following a downward excursion

Disabled aquanaut on surface requiring recompression and unable to return to storage depth via the water column

Decompression sickness during normal saturation decompression

SAT 6A

Symptoms consistent with an air embolism or serious neurological impairment

Emergency SAT 5

Contingency treatment table when forced to reduce treatment time due to impending storm or equipment failure, etc.

Emergency SAT 6

Contingency treatment table when forced to reduce treatment time due to impending storm or equipment failure, etc.

Hyperbaric Chambers and Support Equipment

18

SECTION	PAGE

FIGURE 18.2
Multiplace Hyperbaric Chamber

- **Hyperbaric chamber** literally means "high pressure chamber." The term hyperbaric is derived from it's two halves. The first, *hyper-*, refers to higher than ambient pressure or more pressure than is found in the normal environment. The second, *baric*, refers to pressure. Hence, "high pressure chamber."

The history of modern hyperbarics goes back to the invention of the air compressor, about 300 years ago. But the history of using chambers for the treatment of diving illnesses begins just a little more than 100 years ago, even though reasonable descriptions of decompression illness were recorded as early as 1840 with the salvage of the *HMS Royal George*. The advent of air compressors, coupled with the development of boiler technology, has brought us to where we are today.

Pressure Vessels for Human Occupancy (PVHO) is the official nomenclature of the American Society for Mechanical

---

ASME PVHO-1

Certified by _____

_____
(Name of manufacturer)

_____ psi internal _____ psi external
(Max. allowable working pressures)

_____ °F maximum _____ °F maximum
(Max. allowable working pressures)

_____   _____
(Manufacturer's serial number)   (Year Built)

Figure 18.3
Nameplate for Hyperbaric Chamber

Engineering (ASME) for a pressure chamber that is built with the intention of compressing people. This standard (ASME PVHO-1) deals with the materials, design, and manufacturing of the pressure vessel (see Figure 18.3). The National Fire Protection Association also publishes guidelines (NFPA 99, Health Care Facilities, Chapter 19–Hyperbaric Facilities) that deal primarily with a hyperbaric chamber in health care facilities, but it also applies to chambers installed for training purposes.

The Association of Diving Contractors International (ADCI) publishes a Consensus Standard which addresses how chambers should be outfitted, when they need to be deployed, and how they should be utilized for commercial diving operations.

Codes are comprehensive where the structural integrity of the pressure vessel is concerned and include all aspects of material selection, welding, penetrations into the vessel walls, flanges for egress, and testing. Only high quality pressure gauges and ancillary equipment should be used in outfitting a hyperbaric chamber (see Table 18.1). All such equipment should be tested and calibrated before a diving operation.

TABLE 18.1
Hyperbaric Chamber Piping Guide

Function	Designation	Color Code
Helium	HE	Buff
Oxygen	OX	Green
Helium-Oxygen Mix	HE-OX	Buff & Green
Nitrogen	N	Light Gray
Nitrogen-Oxygen Mix	N-OX	Light Gray & Green
Exhaust	E	Silver
Air (Low Pressure)	ALP	Black
Air (High Pressure)	AHP	Black
Chilled Water	CW	Blue & White
Hot Water	HW	Red & White
Potable Water	PW	Blue
Fire Fighting Material	FP	Red

If structural modifications such as those involving welding or drilling are made, the chamber must be re-certified before further use. An ASME "U" stamp can be found on the Certification Plate for newly certified hulls. An ASME "R" stamp will also be present on hulls that have been modified and re-certified.

18.1 HYPERBARIC CHAMBERS

Hyperbaric chambers rated for human occupancy come under the control and auspices of the ASME PVHO regardless of its pressure rating. Additionally, hyperbaric chambers have been classified by NFPA as the following:

- **CLASS A**, or multiplace chambers are built for occupancy by more than one person and carry special

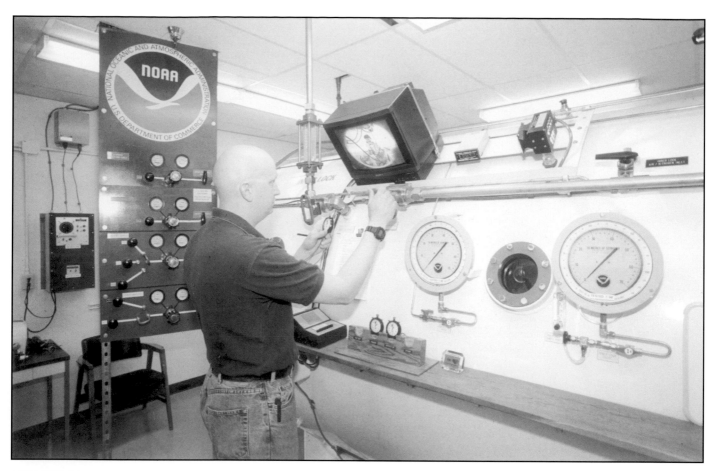

FIGURE 18.4
Multiplace Hyperbaric Chamber—Exterior View

requirements for construction and installation. This includes all multiplace chambers where separate parts of the chamber can be pressurized differentially.
- **CLASS B**, or monoplace chambers are built for occupancy by only one person. In the 1960s, many monoplace chambers were built and deployed to dive sites, but have generally been replaced by multiplace chambers. Class B chambers are typically used in clinical settings such as hospitals.
- **CLASS C**, or animal chambers are built for conducting research or treating animals and should not be used for pressurizing human beings.

Chambers can also be monoplace (single compartment) and multiplace (multi-compartment) which fall into the CLASS A category. Any chamber constructed to accommodate at least one diver and one tender (or attendant) is considered a multiplace chamber. A monoplace chamber that has more than one person in it (patient, tender, passenger, etc.) is a multiplace or CLASS A chamber, regardless of what was intended when it was built, and must conform to the appropriate requirements.

Chambers that have more than one compartment (multiplace) (see Figure 18.4) permit one compartment to be pressurized to depth while another compartment

(or more) can be left at the surface, or where needed. In the case of medical treatment, this allows tenders, physicians, etc. to be pressurized into the main compartment to attend to the patient (or other duties) and then lock back out to the surface as needed.

Another feature found on many, multiplace chambers is a medical lock. This is a relatively small extension of the main compartment which can also be pressurized separately. Often these compartments are no more than 9–12 inches in diameter and 12–18 inches deep with a sealable hatch on both ends. One end protrudes into the main compartment while the other is accessible to the outside. Small items, meals, fluids, etc. can be sent through the medical lock as needed.

Due to the uniqueness of decompression illness, and the hands-on necessity of evaluating patients during the course of the treatment, most diving casualties should be treated in multiplace chambers. This allows for good access to the patient and the capability to send needed items to depth.

Modern deck chambers are usually 54–60 inches in diameter, although NOAA has several 42 inch diameter chambers for use on-board ships where deck space may be limited. Multiplace hyperbaric treatment chambers used in hospital settings are generally larger; 8–10 ft. in diameter. Large chambers used to house and decompress saturation

Hyperbaric Chambers and Support Equipment

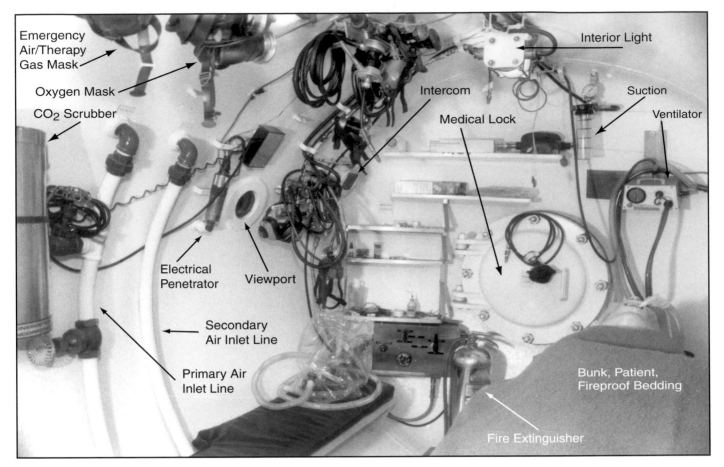

FIGURE 18.5
Multiplace Hyperbaric Chamber—Interior View

divers for long exposures are outfitted with toilet facilities, beds, and showers; but such comfortable chambers are usually found only at sites where large-scale diving operations or experimental dives are conducted.

At a minimum, chambers should be equipped with the following (see Figure 18.5):

- Pressurization and exhaust systems
- Viewports
- Depth control gauges and control manifolds
- A two-way communication system
- Built-in-breathing system (BIBS) for the delivery of oxygen or other treatment gas (N_2O_2), including connections for demand-type oxygen inhalators or a ventilation hood system for constant flow delivery
- Gas monitoring ports
- Stop watches, or some system of tracking the passage of elapsed time
- Illumination system, generally consists of an external lighting source illuminating the interior via light pipes or by shining light through an observation port, but may include specially designed internal lighting
- Fire suppression system—may be water based, including a deluge system and a hand line

Other equipment that may be needed and is highly desirable include:

- Environmental control systems for heating and cooling the environment

18.2 TRANSPORTABLE CHAMBERS

Small, lightweight, portable chambers have been available since the early 1960s. Varying designs of these chambers have been outfitted for both single- and dual-occupancy (generally one patient and one tender). Gas requirements in small chambers are minimal. A few scuba cylinders of air and an adequate supply of oxygen are generally sufficient to initiate a treatment using this type of chamber.

Currently, available transportable chambers have been produced using a host of modern materials including Kevlar®, stainless steel, and titanium. A couple of the designs that have been developed during the past decade have found acceptance.

One design, called a Parasal® or Tup-Mate® (depending on the fabricator), and Transportable Recompression Chamber by the U.S. military, is relatively lightweight and has a unique shape, allowing head-to-foot access to the patient by a tender.

The chamber is designed with a "standard" NATO flange (locking device) which allows the transportable lock to be mated with another appropriately equipped chamber. When combined with its optional Transfer Lock, it is referred to as a Transportable Recompression Chamber System (TRCS). This was originally designed as a fly-away chamber for loading into small aircraft or medium-size helicopters and is fully compressible to 165 fsw (51 msw) in the field. Depending on features and materials, this unit weights in at 600–1,100 lbs.

A second type of transportable chamber is referred to as a "hyperbaric stretcher" (see Figure 18.6). This is a low-cost monoplace chamber made principally out of Kevlar® which collapses into two footlocker size boxes and can be deployed as needed. Depth is limited in this type of chamber, but it will handle all but the most critical diving casualties. The disadvantages here are the inability to examine a patient during treatment, and the inability to monitor anything other than a fully-conscious patient.

18.3 OPERATIONS

The specific operation of any given chamber will vary from organization to organization and from installation to installation. Variables include the equipment provided, the personnel available, and the likelihood of need.

18.3.1 Staffing

The minimum team for conducting any recompression operation consists of a chamber supervisor, an inside tender, an outside tender and, depending on the circumstances, a diving physician. The responsibilities of each of these team members are described below.

18.3.1.1 Chamber Supervisor

The supervisor has overall responsibility for all aspects of hyperbaric treatment including the crew, and the operation of the chamber. Responsibility also includes all movement of the chamber and personnel changes during the course of a treatment.

The diving supervisor must be familiar with all phases of chamber operation, treatment procedures, and must ensure that communication, logging, and all phases of treatment are carried out according to prescribed procedures.

18.3.1.2 Inside Tender

The inside tender, who must be familiar with the diagnosis of diving-related injuries and illnesses, monitors and cares for the patient during treatment.

Other responsibilities of the inside tender include:

- Releasing the door latches (dogs) after a seal is made
- Communicating with outside personnel
- Providing first aid as required by the patient
- Administering oxygen or nitrogen-oxygen to the patient
- Providing normal assistance to the patient as required

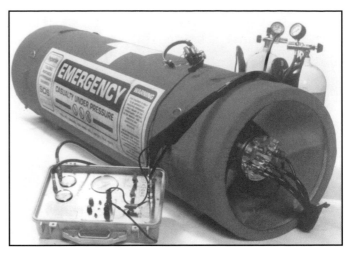

FIGURE 18.6
Portable Hyperbaric Stretcher Inflated

- Ensuring that ear protection sound attenuators are worn during compression and ventilation
- Maintaining a clean chamber and transferring body waste as required
- Ensuring proper switch from air to O_2 on air breaks and O_2 periods

During the early phases of treatment, the inside tender must constantly watch for signs of change in the patient's symptoms. The patient should not be given drugs that will mask the signs of injury. Observing these signs is the principal method of diagnosing the patient's condition, and the depth and time of symptom relief determine the treatment table to be used. The final decision as to which treatment table to use must be made by the chamber supervisor on the recommendation of the attending physician.

18.3.1.3 Outside Tender

The outside tender is responsible for:

- Maintaining and controlling the air supply to the chamber
- Keeping the dive log
- Communicating with inside personnel
- Decompressing any inside tending personnel leaving the chamber before patient treatment is complete
- Pressurizing, ventilating, and exhausting the chamber

18.3.1.4 Diving Physician

The diving physician is trained in the treatment of diving injuries. Although it may not be possible to have a diving physician present during all treatments, it is essential that the chamber supervisor be able to consult by telephone or radio with a qualified diving physician.

When a diver is being recompressed, all attending personnel must work as a team for the benefit of the patient. If the patient has symptoms of serious decompression illness

- The size of the chamber does not influence the rate (acfm) required for ventilation.
- Increasing depth increases the actual mass of air required for ventilation; but when the amount of air is expressed in volumes as measured at chamber pressure, increasing depth does not change the number of actual cubic feet (acfm) required.
- If high-pressure air banks are being used for the chamber supply, pressure changes in the cylinders can be used to check the amount of ventilation being provided.

18.3.5 Built-In-Breathing System (BIBS)

The BIBS, or mask breathing system, provides breathing gas to the chamber occupant when wearing the mask. Usually this gas will be oxygen, but may also be some other mixture (i.e., Nitrox 50). Emergency air is a third gas that is often plumbed to the chamber BIBS providing a known source of clean air in cases where the air in the chamber becomes contaminated.

BIBS can either dump its exhaust into the chamber, or be plumbed for overboard dump. Overboard dump BIBS evacuate the exhaled gases through a regulated exhaust and provide a safe means of delivering high oxygen concentration breathing gases to a patient or decompressing diver in the chamber. Non-overboard dump BIBS can rapidly cause extreme increases in the ambient oxygen levels in side the chamber, but are quite adequate for delivering emergency air when needed.

Very simply, a BIBS mask is an oral-nasal mask providing breathing gas on demand. Its purpose is to obstruct the exchange of gas with the surrounding air and maintain an enclosed breathing medium. A control knob on the inlet regulator allows for fine control of gas delivery pressure. This should be set to minimize breathing effort without allowing freeflow. The oral-nasal mask is attached to a breathing gas supply line via a hose and (usually) an oxygen quick-connect. The exhaust regulator is attached to an evacuation line via a hose and a quick-connect. Although a check-valve is normally found in the inlet connector, the exhaust connector generally does not have any additional obstructions in the gas pathway and must be plugged when not in use.

With the overboard discharge unit, the diver's exhalation is removed through a regulator mounted on the side of the mask. For chambers anticipating pressurization deeper than 60 fsw (18 msw), a back pressure regulator must be installed on the exhaust line (usually outside of the hull) to regulate the maximum negative pressure being applied in the mask.

The mask must be cleaned with an antiseptic solution between uses by different individuals. A mixture of antibacterial soap and hot water, alcohol, and a sterilizing agent is recommended. Bleach mixtures, although very effective at sanitizing the masks, will cause premature aging and deterioration of the rubber mask parts. Routine inspection of the mask parts is necessary. Cracking or brittleness in the sealing surfaces of the oral-nasal mask or hoses indicate that replacement is necessary. Routine inspection and preventive maintenance are required annually, or sooner if a unit malfunctions. Generally, inspection and repair service is provided by the manufacturer or distributor, although many companies and organizations, including NOAA, have qualified technicians to perform these tasks. Consult the appropriate manufacturer's instruction manual for further information.

18.3.6 Oxygen Analyzers

Oxygen analyzers are useful for monitoring oxygen concentrations in chambers where oxygen is used for therapy, surface decompression, or research. The oxygen level in a hyperbaric chamber should be maintained between 21–23% to reduce the danger of fire. An upper limit of 23.5% should be observed in accordance with current National Fire Protection Association recommendations.

Oxygen analyzers are also useful in monitoring the breathing gas being supplied to the BIBS. Analyzing gas cylinders upon arrival at the site and again prior to attaching to the gas panel ensures that the gas being delivered to the panel valve is the correct gas. Analyzing the BIBS gas as it is being delivered ensures that the breathing gas is what is intended and helps monitor for leaks in the system where multiple gases are plumbed into the BIBS.

Several models and types of oxygen analyzers are available on the market. Some are intended for use at depth resulting in a partial pressure reading, or at least the remote sensor is at depth even though the electronics are outside. Most analyzers are designed to be used outside the chamber. Increased pressure on the sensor as gas passes the fuel cell results in artificially high readings (see Chapters 16 and 17).

18.3.7 Carbon Monoxide (CO) Analyzers

In recent years, it has become more common for carbon monoxide analyzers to be mounted on the air supply to ensure the quality of the air supply. These may or may not be wired into the supply compressor. Some newer systems monitor CO concentrations downstream in the delivery system and have automatic shutdowns on the compressor in cases where high CO concentrations are detected.

18.3.8 Electrical Systems

Chamber electrical support systems vary in complexity, depending on the capability and size of the system. Whenever possible, it is best to keep all electricity outside of the chamber.

Lights can usually be provided through fiber optics or port windows, but may be housed in special spark-proof fixtures. Light housings inside chambers must never be covered with clothing, blankets, or other articles that could heat up and ignite.

Increasingly, low level electronics are finding their way into chambers, ranging from battery-powered communications to cameras, ECG leads to defibrillation pads.

NOAA HYPERBARIC CHAMBER PRESSURE TEST

NOTE

A pressure test must be conducted on every NOAA hyperbaric chamber:

1. When initially installed
2. When moved and reinstalled
3. After repairs / overhaul
4. At two-year intervals when in place at a given location

The test is to be conducted as follows:

1. Pressurize the innermost lock to 100 ft. (45 psig). Using soapy water or an equivalent solution, leak test all shell penetration fittings, viewports, dog seals, door dogs (where applicable), valve connections, pipe joints, and shell weldments.

2. Mark all leaks. Depressurize the lock and adjust, repair, or replace components as necessary to eliminate leaks.

   a. Viewport leaks—Remove the viewport gasket (replace if necessary), wipe clean.

   CAUTION

   Acrylic viewports should not be lubricated or come in contact with any lubricant, volatile detergent, or leak detector. (Non-ionic detergent is to be used for leak test.) When reinstalling viewport, take up retaining ring bolts until the gasket just compresses the viewport. Do not overcompress the gasket.

   b. Weldment Leaks—Contact appropriate technical authority for guidance on corrective action.

3. Repeat Steps 1 and 2 until all the leaks have been eliminated.

4. Pressurize the lock to 165 ft. (73.4 psig), and locate and mark leaks. Depressurize chamber and repair leaks in accordance with Step 2 above. Repeat this procedure until final pressure maintains a minimum depth of 145 ft. (65 psig) following a 60-minute hold.

6. Repeat Steps 1 through 5, leaving inner door open and the outer door closed. Leak test only those portions of the chamber not previously tested.

FIGURE 18.9
Pressure Test Procedures for NOAA Chambers

Chambers must always be electrically grounded. Even systems that do not have any electrical components must be provided with a path for electrical discharge.

Whenever practical, 110 vac (voltage alternating current) should be isolated from contact with any chamber component; higher voltages of alternating current should be avoided. Twelve or 24 volts-DC systems are preferable.

18.4 CHAMBER MAINTENANCE

Proper care of a hyperbaric chamber requires both routine and periodic maintenance. After every use, or no less than once a month, whichever comes first, the chamber should be maintained routinely. During these checks, minor repairs should be made and supplies restocked. At least twice a year, the chamber should be inspected inside and out. Any deposits of grease, dust, or other dirt should be removed and the affected areas repainted as appropriate.

Usually, only steel chambers are painted. Aluminum chamber are normally a dull, uneven gray color that permits corrosion to be easily recognized.

Corrosion is best removed by hand-sanding or by using a slender pointed tool, being careful not to gouge or otherwise damage the base metal. The corroded area and a small area surrounding it should be cleaned to remove any remaining paint or corrosion. Steel chambers should then be painted with an appropriate non-toxic, flame-retardant paint.

All NOAA chambers must be pneumatically pressure tested annually (see Figure 18.9).

18.5 FIRE PREVENTION

Hyperbaric chambers pose a special, but not unmanageable fire hazard because of the increased flammability of materials in compressed air, i.e., an environment otherwise oxygen enriched. Chamber fire safety basically requires the same basic practices that would apply anywhere else. The chamber environment, however, does involve two special considerations:

- The chamber atmosphere is an artificial one
- People are confined with the fire in a relatively small space with no realistic place to escape

The traditional trio of conditions necessary for a fire (see Figure 18.10), in a chamber or anywhere else are:

- A source of ignition
- Combustible materials
- Oxygen

In chambers, the oxidizer is present in an enriched state in the form of oxygen as part of the pressurized air.

Combustible materials must be limited. Limit the combustible material and minimize the potential for combustion.

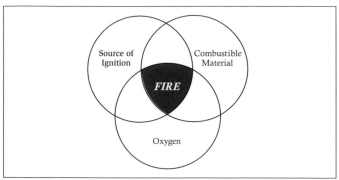

FIGURE 18.10
Conditions Required For A Fire

All combustible materials should be kept in a closed stainless steel container.

Sources of combustion are probably the most controllable of the trio. Matches, lighters, and gas hand warmers are definitely inappropriate for use inside of chambers. Frayed wiring as a source of ignition can be completely avoided through the application of good preventative maintenance and friction can be avoided through good operational practices.

There are four steps in chamber fire safety in addition to preventive measures:

   1. Detect the fire
   2. Extinguish it
   3. Use a mask for breathing
   4. If possible, escape

A safe chamber begins in the design stage. Various codes and design handbooks address the issues of safe chamber design. After safe design, the manner in which a chamber is used is next in importance. This section reviews chamber fire safety, covering both basic principles and operational techniques.

18.5.1 Ignition

Possible sources of ignition in a hyperbaric chamber include:

   • Electrical wiring or apparatus
   • Cigarettes or other smoking materials
   • Heat of compression
   • Electrostatic sparks

The most common sources of chamber fires in the past have been lighted cigarettes, faulty electrical wiring, and sparks from electrically-powered devices. Electrical fires, however, can start either from overheating caused by a defective component, a short circuit, a jammed rotor in a motor, sparks produced by making or breaking a load-carrying circuit, or from a device with arcing brushes.

The safe use of electrical devices in a chamber is primarily a design factor, requiring proper installation of the supply wiring and properly designed devices. Wiring should be insulated with mineral materials or Teflon® and be shielded in metal conduit. The housings of electrical devices, such as instruments, can be purged with an oxygen-free inert gas (usually 100% nitrogen) during operation and may or may not be pressure proof. Lights may be enclosed and purged, or they may be external to the chamber and have the light directed inside with a "light pipe" or fiber optic shaft. Even an enclosed light can generate enough heat to start a fire, a fact to be considered at both the design and operational stages. A fire protection plan should include the capability to disconnect all electrical power instantaneously. Auxiliary lighting must be available.

At some installations, control of the electrical hazard is achieved by allowing no electricity in the chamber at all. When electricity is used, however, it requires protection of the occupants from electrical shock. This may be accomplished by employing protective devices such as ground fault detectors and interrupters. Use of low voltage direct current (e.g., 12 and 24 volts) avoids this hazard, but it is a dangerous misunderstanding to think such voltages cannot start a fire if high-current flow is possible. Devices tolerant of pressure and qualifying as intrinsically safe may be used. Low-current, low-voltage devices such as headsets and microphones are generally considered safe. There is a fundamental difference between the concepts behind "explosion proof" and those required for chamber safety. Explosion-proof housings are made to prevent the ignition of flammable gases or vapors by sparks generated by electrical equipment. This is not an expected problem in a hyperbaric chamber. Junction boxes and other equipment made to explosion-proof standards may provide the kind of protection afforded by mechanical housings, but this equipment is designed for a purpose different from the enriched-oxygen environment common to hyperbaric chambers, and may, in fact, be inadequate.

Although static sparks should be avoided, the atmosphere in a chamber is usually humid enough to suppress sparks. Also, static sparks are only a hazard with vapors, gases, or dry, finely divided materials. None of these should be present in a chamber's atmosphere. Static sparks can usually be prevented by using conductive materials and by grounding everything possible. In some medical hyperbaric chambers, the patient is grounded using a wrist or ankle strap not unlike the ones used in computer repair shops.

Although the heat of compression is more of a problem in the piping of oxygen-rich gases, it is also a factor in chamber safety. Because gases heat up when compressed, the sudden opening of a valve, which allows an oxygen mixture to compress in the pipes, can cause a miniature explosion. A different, but related hazard is the gas flow through a filter or muffler in the air supply. If the air is produced by an oil-lubricated compressor, some oil may collect on the filter or muffler and be ignited by compression or sparks generated by flowing gas.

Smoking is off-limits in chambers. Far too many chamber fires and subsequent injury were reported in past years as a result of cigarettes.

18.5.2 Combustion

The primary factor increasing the risk of fire in a hyperbaric chamber is the increased combustibility caused by the enriched oxygen atmosphere. Such an environment is defined as one that either has a partial pressure or an oxygen percentage that is greater then that of air at sea level pressure. The burning rate of material (determined in a laboratory with paper strips) when the pressure is equivalent to 75 fsw (23 msw) is twice that of sea level air, and is 2.5 times as fast at 165 fsw (51 msw).

An additional hazard is introduced when the gas mixture in the chamber also has an increased partial pressure of oxygen. The relationships among flammability, partial pressure, and oxygen fraction are complex and non-linear, but show a consistent trend toward faster burning with increased oxygen percentage or with an increasing pressure at the same oxygen percentage. The nature of the background gas is important, too, with helium requiring higher ignition temperatures, but allowing faster burning.

Because of the greatly increased risk when oxygen is added to the chamber atmosphere, it is now considered essential to use an overboard dump system for exhaled gas when divers are breathing oxygen by mask during decompression or treatment. It is also considered advisable in purging the chamber with air to maintain a low oxygen level. It takes high flows to keep the oxygen within accepted limits, and high flows may be accompanied by excessive noise and compressor wear and tear.

The "zone of no combustion" concept is helpful in the management of fire safety in chambers. This concept takes into account the fact that, although changes in pressure at a constant oxygen percentage affect the burning rate, changes in the percentage of oxygen have a greater effect. As a result, there is a "zone of pressure: an oxygen percentage that provides adequate oxygen for respiration, but that will not support combustion" (Shilling, Werts, and Schandelmeier 1976).

18.5.3 Materials

The third element required to make a fire is fuel (i.e., something to burn). Chamber fire safety requires that all combustible materials in a chamber be kept to a minimum. And, where possible, materials that are not flammable in enriched oxygen be used. Some materials regarded as non-flammable in air will burn in a high oxygen mixture, so it is best to rely on materials known to be safe or relatively safe in oxygen.

Metals are safe, as are ceramics. For wiring insulation, TFE (Teflon®) is probably the best all-around material. Some fluorine-based elastomers are relatively safe in high oxygen mixtures, but their conductive properties are poor and they are expensive. For clothing, the popular choice is Durette Gold®, but Nomex® is also a good choice. One hundred percent cotton that has been washed in a simple soap compound is also an adequate, and relatively inexpensive solution to bedding and clothing issues.

Although chamber design is important to fire safety, even the well-designed chamber needs to be used properly. Good housekeeping is mandatory; all loose clothing, papers, and other flammable materials must be stowed or removed from the chamber when it is being operated beyond the fire-safe zone. Particularly important to eliminate are fuzzy, powdered, or finely divided materials and flammable liquids and gases.

One flammable gas that may come into increasing use in diving is hydrogen, especially outside of North America where helium is not plentiful and comparatively expensive. The use of this gas is being explored for deep diving because of its physiological properties (primarily its low density and lack of narcotic effect). Hydrogen can be used without danger of explosion (once it is mixed) when the mixture contains less than 4% oxygen, making it unsuitable for breathing shallower than 100 fsw (31 msw). Most of the safety problems associated with the use of hydrogen as a diving gas occur during handling and mixing.

WARNING
MATCHES, LIGHTERS, FLAMMABLE MATERIALS, AND ELECTRICAL APPLIANCES ARE NOT PERMITTED IN THE CHAMBER.

18.5.4 Management of a Fire

The preceding sections addressed the prevention of chamber fires. Another component of fire safety requires that the people involved be able to deal with a fire once it starts. Although some past chamber fires have spread rapidly (NFPA 1979), many others have been extinguished without loss of life. It is essential that chamber personnel be trained in fire safety techniques.

18.5.5 Detection

Numerous fire detection mechanisms are available for routine fire protection. Many of these systems are usable in hyperbaric chambers, particularly ones operating at the relatively low pressures used with compressed air. The detection mechanisms most suitable for chamber use infrared or ultraviolet technology. Ionization, or smoke detectors, may also be of value.

There are two problems with fire detection systems: false alarms and failure to detect a fire quickly enough. Any detection system needs to be studied thoroughly in the context of the uses and needs of the particular installation. Most experts feel, for example, that clinical hyperbaric chambers treating patients with open wounds should have an alarm system only, rather than one that would automatically deluge the chamber. A preferred approach is to have both a hand-held directable fire hose inside and switches to activate a general deluge system easily available to both chamber occupants and the topside crew.

Whether a deluge or alarm system is used, it should be thoroughly tested at the time of installation. It should also be tested periodically and the manning crew kept proficient in its use. The best protection against fire is an alert chamber crew backed up by detectors.

18.5.6 Extinguishment

Fire extinguishment is accomplished by physical actions involving three basic mechanisms:

- The combustible material can be cooled to a temperature below that required for ignition or the evolution of flammable vapors.
- The fire can be smothered by reducing the oxygen or fuel concentration to a level that will not support combustion.
- The fuel can be separated from the oxidizer by removing either the fuel of the oxidizer or by mechanically separating the two. Mechanical protein foams operate in this fashion by blanketing the fuel and separating it from the oxidizers.

At present, the best fire extinguishing agent for use in hyperbaric chambers is water. Water extinguishes primarily by cooling and works best if it strikes the base of the flame or wets the fire in spray form. The pressure at the spray nozzle must be at least 50 psi greater than the chamber pressure to produce the desired degree of atomization and droplet velocities. Simultaneous with the discharge of water, all electrical power to the chamber should be shut off to prevent shorting and electrical shocks to chamber occupants. A 1/2 inch (ID) hand-held fire hose will adequately permit trained chamber occupants to control small localized fires. The fire suppression system should be tested periodically under chamber operating conditions.

18.5.7 Breathing Masks and Escape

Most fire fatalities are caused by smoke inhalation rather than burns. Accordingly, the first thing the occupants of a chamber with a fire should do, unless immediate escape is possible, is to don a breathing mask. The masks should be handy and should have a breathable gas on-line at all times. If it is possible for occupants to move quickly to another chamber or compartment that can be sealed off from the fire, they should do so rather than donning masks and trying to extinguish the fire.

Summary of Fire Protection Precautions

A summary of chamber fire precautions follows:

- Maintain oxygen concentration and partial pressure as low as possible, preferably within the region of non-combustion. Use an overboard dump system whenever high PO_2 mixtures are being employed.
- Eliminate ignition sources.
- Minimize combustibles, with the complete exclusion of flammable liquids and gases.
- If combustible materials must be employed, the type and quantity, and their arrangement in the chamber must be carefully controlled.
- The extinguishment system must be water-based and include not only a deluge system, but a hand-line as well. The deluge should be controllable from both inside and outside of the chamber.
- A BIBS mask, with a breathable gas on-line, should be available for every chamber occupant. In addition, at least one spare mask should be mounted in case of an initial failure.
- Escape to another chamber or directly into the sea should be the first option in the fire safety operations plan, whenever feasible.

Summary of Safety Precautions

- Do not use oil on any oxygen fitting, air fitting, or piece of equipment.
- Do not allow oxygen supply tanks to be depleted below 100 psig.
- Ensure hatch dogs (securing mechanism) are in good operating condition and seals are tight.
- Do not leave doors dogged (locked) after pressurization.
- Do not allow open flames, smoking materials, or any flammables to be carried into the chamber.
- Do not permit electrical appliances to be used in the chamber unless approved by a NOAA official.
- Do not perform unauthorized repairs or modifications on the chamber support systems.
- Do not permit products in the chamber that may contaminate or off-gas into the chamber atmosphere.

Hazardous Aquatic Animals

SECTION	PAGE

Hazardous Aquatic Animals

19.0 GENERAL

Many aquatic animals are potentially hazardous to divers. Although only a few present serious physical threats, several animals can inflict pain, precipitate an allergic reaction, or instantaneously create another disability that can seriously impair a diver's effectiveness. The ubiquity of hazardous creatures and their inclination to appear at inopportune times make it imperative to be aware of them, to respect their territorial rights, and to avoid needless unpleasant contact with them. This chapter discusses some of these animals and these unpleasant interactions. For convenience, hazardous aquatic life can be classified as those creatures that:

- Abrade, Lacerate, or Puncture (some of which may have an associated venom)
- Sting (envenomate)
- Bite
- Shock (electrical)
- Poison if eaten

19.1 GENERAL MEDICAL PROCEDURES

When rescuing a diver suffering from an injury due to an encounter with marine life and envenomation, the rescuer should anticipate near drowning, immersion hypothermia, decompression sickness, or arterial air embolism. The general principles of first aid (airway, breathing, circulation, and signs of shock) must be monitored. Appropriate treatment should be instituted immediately. Meticulous attention to basic wound management is necessary to minimize post-traumatic infection.

Seawater is not the most favorable irrigator as it carries a significant infection risk. Sterile water or saline are acceptable. Irrigation should be performed before and after debridement to maximize the benefits.

If a wound acquired in the natural aquatic environment (i.e., from an aquatic animal or contaminated with seawater or natural freshwater) becomes infected, seek immediate medical attention. The victim should be started on an antibiotic to cover *Vibrio* species of micro-organisms (marine) or *Aeromonas* species of bacteria (freshwater). Use ciprofloxacin 500 mg, trimethoprim-sulfamethoxazole, one double strength tablet, or doxycycline 100 mg, giving any of these drugs in a dose, twice a day, orally.

Wounds should be thoroughly cleaned twice a day with soap and water or with a dilute antiseptic, such as povidone-iodine (10% maximum concentration), then rinsed with clean fresh (tap) water. Apply a thin coating of an antiseptic ointment, such as bacitracin or mupirocin, and cover with a non-adherent dressing, which should then be covered by an absorbent dressing. Any wound which disrupts the skin can become contaminated with *Clostridium tetani*. A proper anti-tetanus booster or immunization update should be administered. Tetanus has caused death following penetrating marine wounds.

Marine envenomations, such as those by the box-jellyfish, stonefish, and certain sea snakes may require the administration of specific antivenom. The rationale for administering antivenom is to provide early and adequate neutralization of the toxin at the tissue site before it gains systemic dominance.

19.2 ANIMALS THAT ABRADE, LACERATE, OR PUNCTURE

The bodies of many aquatic animals are enclosed in sharp, spiny or abrasive "armor" that can wound the exposed areas of a diver's body that may come into forceful contact with these creatures. Included in this group of animals are mussels, barnacles, sea urchins, and stony corals. The wounding effect caused by human contact with these animals is enhanced in aquatic habitats because human skin is softened by immersion. Wounds continuously exposed to water become macerated and resist healing. Wounds will be aggravated when exposed to tropical humidity or repetitive abrasion. Careless divers may, in time, become incapacitated by an accumulation of ulcerating sores. The chance of primary infections are due to unique bacteria which thrive in the salt-laden marine environment. Compounding the problem,

FIGURE 19.1
Sea Urchin

FIGURE 19.2
Sea Urchin

secondary infections in such wounds are not uncommon. Long-term diving projects may be jeopardized if participants fail to avoid and sufficiently care for these injuries, however minor they may initially seem. By wearing proper skin protection offered by immersion suits and diving gloves, divers will reduce their susceptibility to these injuries.

19.2.1 Sea Urchins

Among the more troublesome animals for divers working near tropical reefs are venomous sea urchins. This concern applies especially after sunset when visibility is reduced and many of the noxious sea urchins migrate out of crevices and are more prevalent than during the day. Sea urchins (see Figures 19.1, 19.2) may also be a problem in temperate waters, but the species in these regions lack the potent venom found in the tropical species, and offer only a puncture rather than poisoning hazard.

Most difficulties with venomous sea urchins result from accidental contact with certain long-spined species (*Diadema*). With sufficient contact, the friable spines invariably break off in the wound and, being quite brittle, frequently cannot be completely removed. Gloves and protective clothing afford some protection against minor brushes with these animals, but may be limited when a diver strikes forcefully against them. In order to avoid painful injury, divers should avoid contact working close to venomous sea urchins. Divers should practice good buoyancy control, be observant, and avoid contact.

Some short-spined tropical urchin species called *pedicellariae*, are hazardous because of tiny pincer-like seizing organs, that are found among their spines. Although some *pedicellariae* hold receptacles for the urchin's potent venom, they are very small structures and usually do not pose a threat to divers who incidentally come into contact with them. It is prudent for a diver to be aware of the hazard found in *pedicel-*

lariae, but when a diver is wearing gloves these urchins can be safely handled. The *Pacific Tripneustes* urchin carries a neurotoxin with a predilection for facial and cranial nerves.

Signs and Symptoms:
- Immediate sharp, burning pain
- Intense muscle aching and spasm
- Redness and swelling
- Spines sticking out of skin or black dots where they have broken off
- Purple discoloration of skin around the place spines entered (this is caused by retention of spine dye and does not necessarily indicate retention of a spine)
- Numbness
- Nausea and vomiting

Treatment:
Immerse the wound in non-scalding, hot water to tolerance 110–114°F (43.3–45C). This frequently provides pain relief. Administer appropriate pain medicine. Spines that can be grasped, without crushing them, should be removed with tweezers. Spines that have been broken off flush with the skin are nearly impossible to remove; probing around with a needle will only break the spines into little pieces and further traumatize the area. Some spines will be dissolved by the body; others may fester and rise to the point where they can be removed with tweezers. Others will be surrounded by scar tissue and remain as minute nodules under the surface of the skin.

19.2.2 Starfish

The Crown-of-Thorns starfish, (see Figure 19.3) *Acanthaster planci*, is a particularly venomous starfish found in tropical oceans worldwide. It carries sharp and rigid ice-pick like spines which may grow to three inches in length. The cutting edges may easily penetrate most diving gloves and create a painful puncture wound with copious bleeding and slight swelling and numbness. Multiple puncture wounds may lead to vomiting, swollen lymph glands, and brief muscular paralysis.

Signs and Symptoms:
- Pain is moderate with remission over one to three hours.
- Wound can become dusky or discolored.
- Multiple wounds may result in paraesthesia, nausea, and vomiting.

Treatment:

The treatment is similar to that for a sea urchin puncture. Immerse the wound in non-scalding, hot water to tolerance 110–114°F (43.3–45C) for 30–90 minutes. This frequently provides pain relief. Unfortunately, with many of these wounds, the area is anaesthetized and the victim is able to tolerate quite high temperatures, well in excess of 114°F temperature. Therefore, always include an unaffected part of the body in the hot water to "sense" the temperature. This will avoid situations which can occur from hot water treatments causing further significant damage and necrosis in the wound area. Administer appropriate pain medicine. Carefully remove any readily visible spines. If there is a question of a retained spine or fragment, seek the assistance of a physician.

Handling other starfish, such as the sun or rose star, can cause a skin rash. This may be treated with topical calamine lotion with 1% menthol or 1% topical hydrocortisone lotion.

FIGURE 19.3
Crown-of-Thorns Starfish

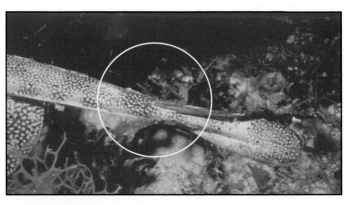

FIGURE 19.4
Stingray Tail with Spine

19.2.3 Rays and Fishes

More than 1,000 species of fish are either poisonous to eat or venomous. The latter inflict these wounds more for protection than prey capture. Spines may be concealed in such locations as dorsal or tail spines, pectorally, on their heads, or elsewhere on their bodies. Generally, these fish injure only divers who deliberately handle or provoke them; however, some wound divers who have unintentionally touched them.

Stingrays: Stingrays are responsible for more human stings than any other group of fishes. The stingray is non-aggressive, but is capable of protecting itself against intruders. They have been recognized as venomous since ancient times, and were known as "demons of the deep" and "devil fishes." Stingrays carry one or more spike-like spines near the base of their flexible tails which they can use effectively against persons who come in contact with them (see Figure 19.4). These spines can inflict venomous puncture wounds or a painful broad laceration. Humans are most vulnerable when wading along a sandy bottom in shallow water or swimming close to the ocean floor. Walking with a shuffling motion tends to frighten stingrays away. If the "wing" of a ray is significantly disturbed (i.e., stepped upon), the tail is whipped upwards as a reflex action. Compared to those of other stingrays, species of the family *Dasyatidae* (see Figure 19.5), present the greatest danger, as

FIGURE 19.5
Stingray (*Dasyatidae*)

FIGURE 19.6
Stingray (*Myliobatidae*)

they combine large size, the habit of lying immobile on the seafloor covered with sand, and a large spine that is carried relatively far back on a whip-like tail. Large rays of this type can drive their spines through the planks of a small boat or deeply into a human appendage. Swimmers coming into contact with the bottom and a stingray lying unseen in the sand have been mortally wounded when struck in the abdomen or chest, causing a pneumothorax. *Urolophid*, or round, stingrays have a short muscular caudal appendage with the spine attached and are able to deliver severe stings with a whip of their tail.

Less dangerous are stingrays of the family *Myliobatidae*, which includes the bat rays and eagle rays, even though these animals can be large and have long venomous spines on their tails (see Figure 19.6). The spine of this species is at the base of the tail rather than farther back and is a less effective weapon than the spine of the *Dasyatid* or *Urolophid* ray. Rather than lying immobile on the bottom most of the

FIGURE 19.7
Manta Ray

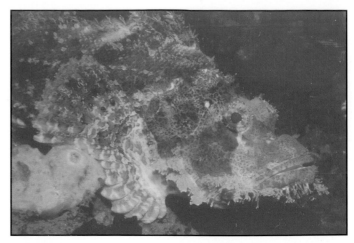

FIGURE 19.8
Scorpionfish

time, they more often swim through the midwaters, with their greatly expanded pectoral fins flapping gently like the wings of a large bird. When on the seafloor, *myliobatid* rays usually root actively in the sand for their shelled prey and are readily seen. Manta rays (see Figure 19.7) usually carry vestigial spines that pose little threat to the diver. Divers hitching a ride on this two-ton animal are more likely to be injured by falling off, or by ascending too rapidly.

Scorpionfishes: Scorpionfishes (see Figure 19.8) are among the most widespread family of venomous fishes and second to stingrays in envenomation incidents. The *Scorpaenidae* family, which numbers several hundred nearshore species, has representatives in all of the world's seas; the most dangerous forms are found in tropical areas. Many scorpionfishes are sedentary creatures that lie immobile and unseen on the seafloor. The family has three distinct groups, based upon their venom organ structure, and toxicity (see Figure 19.9). Lionfish, zebrafish, and butterfly cod of the *Pterois* type have long slender spines with

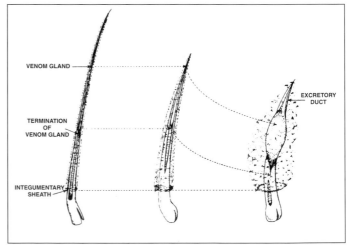

FIGURE 19.9
Three Types of Scorpionfish Dorsal Stings

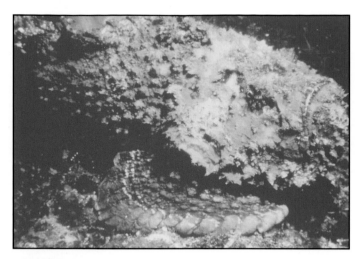

FIGURE 19.10
Stonefish

FIGURE 19.12
Surgeonfish

small venom glands and a less potent sting. *Scorpaena* such as scorpionfish, bullrout, and sculpin (a common, nearshore scorpionfish species of Southern California), have shorter, thicker spines with large venom glands and more of a sting. Scorpionfish usually inject their venom with their dorsal fin spines and less often do so with the spines of their anal and pelvic fins. The *Synanceia* represented by the stonefish, (see Figure 19.10), common to the shallow, tropical waters of the western Pacific and Indian Oceans, have stout, powerful spines with highly developed venom glands and a potentially fatal sting which requires antivenom treatment. Although stonefish are not aggressive toward divers, their camouflage makes it easy to accidentally step on them unless special care is taken.

In contrast to the cryptic sculpin and stonefish, another group of scorpionfishes, the brilliantly hued lionfishes,

FIGURE 19.11
Lionfish

stand out strikingly against their surroundings (see Figure 19.11). Because lionfishes are beautiful animals that make little effort to avoid humans, an inexperienced diver or unwary marine aquarist may be tempted to grasp one. This will prove a painful mistake because lionfish venom is fairly potent.

Surgeonfishes: Some surgeonfishes, a member of the family *Scorpaenidae* (see Figure 19.12) can inflict venomous puncture wounds with their fin spines similar to those wounds produced by scorpionfishes and other similarly armed fishes. Many surgeonfishes can also inflict deep lacerations with knifelike spines (epidermal appendages) they carry on either side of their bodies, just forward of their tails. Some of the species have venomous spines. The more dangerous surgeonfishes, which belong to the genus *Acanthurus*, usually carry these spines flat against their bodies in integumentary sheaths. When threatened, the fish erect their spines at right angles to the bodies and attack adversaries with quick, lashing movements of their tails. Divers injured by surgeonfishes have usually been hurt while trying to spear or otherwise molest them.

Other fishes armed with venomous spines include the spiny dogfish, family *Squalidae*; weever fishes, family *Trachinidae*; toadfishes, family *Batrachoididae*; stargazers, family *Uranoscopidae*; freshwater and marine catfishes, family *Ariidae*; and rabbitfishes, family *Siganidae*. These fishes do not usually "attack" to drive their venom apparatus into their victims; instead, the force is supplied by the victims themselves who handle, step upon, or otherwise come into contact with these fishes.

Needlefish, slender, lightning-quick surface swimmers found in tropical seas, often leap out of the water in fear or when attracted to lights. On occasion, they have leaped and collided with people, spearing them in the chest, abdomen, extremities, head, and in one case causing a brain injury by penetrating the eye. Death may occur from chest or abdominal penetration. "Flying" fishes pose less risk, as they have blunt heads.

Signs and Symptoms:
- Severe, localized pain at the wound site, which may spread to involve the entire limb peaking around 60–90 minutes and lasting up to 12 hours if untreated.
- Wound will be discolored by a surrounding ring of cyanotic "bluish" tissue.
- Localized vasoconstriction, swelling, may be accompanied by an ashen appearance.
- Fainting, weakness, nausea, vomiting, headache, restlessness, limb paralysis.
- Respiratory distress, shock.
- Cardiac arrhythmias, cardiac arrest.

Recognize symptoms of diving-related disorder in the event of a fast ascent precipitated by painful envenomation at depth.

Treatment:
Because fainting is common after a poisonous wound, particularly if there is severe pain, the victim should be removed from the water as soon as possible. The wound should be soaked in nonscalding, hot water to tolerance 110–114°F (43.3–50C) for a period of at least 30 minutes. Remember to include an unaffected part of the body in the hot water to "sense" temperature. Administer appropriate pain medicine. In the treatment of fish and ray injuries, it should be noted that any puncture wound that involves body cavities (chest, abdomen) deserves immediate medical treatment, even if there is little clinical problem evident. Fatal complications can be either immediate or delayed; thus, investigation and hospitalization is required for these wounds.

The victim should be observed for any sign of difficulty breathing, profound weakness, or an abnormal pulse (heart) rate. The pain rarely lasts for more than 24 hours, unless there is a bit of fish spine retained in the wound, or if an infection has intervened. If the spine has penetrated to the bone then osteomyelitus may occur. Swelling may persist for up to a few weeks and may be associated with a clear watery discharge. Considerable local tissue necrosis, which may be best treated by excision, also may result. Medical assistance should be obtained as quickly as possible. An antivenom is available for administration in the event of a sting from the dreaded stonefish.

19.3 ANIMALS THAT STING

A diverse array of otherwise unrelated primitive and extremely sophisticated animals is considered together in this section because their ability to inject venom into other organisms poses a threat to divers in the water. The instrument of injection varies from the microscopic stinging cells of the coelenterates (hydroids, corals, anemones, and jellyfishes) to the rigid spines on the bodies of Crown-of-Thorns starfish, sea urchins, and fishes. There are also the harpoon-like radular teeth of cone shells, beaks of octopuses, bristles of annelid worms, and fangs of sea snakes. Mere contact with the surface of some sponges can produce severe dermatitis. The toxicity of the venom and the amount of venom introduced vary from species to species and sometimes among individuals of the same species. Furthermore, humans may differ in their sensitivity to a given venom. The reactions of humans to marine animal stings may range from no noticeable reaction to mild irritation to sudden death (usually from an allergic reaction, but occasionally due to a direct toxic effect). It is wise to be aware of and avoid injury by all marine organisms known to be venomous. Occasional contact may be inevitable, even among the most experienced divers.

19.3.1 Sponges
Sponges handled directly from the ocean can cause two types of skin reaction. The first is an allergic type similar to that caused by poison oak, the difference being that the reaction generally occurs immediately after the sponge is handled. The skin becomes red, with burning, itching, and occasional blistering. A typical offender is the West Indian Fire Sponge found off the Hawaiian Islands and Florida Keys. The second type of reaction is caused by small spicules of silica from the sponges, which are broken off and embedded in the outermost layers of the skin. The red moss sponge (found in the northeastern U.S.) is a known culprit for this type of sting. All divers should wear proper gloves. To avoid unnecessary reactions, sponges should not be broken, crumbled or crushed with bare hands.

Signs and Symptoms:
- Itching and burning skin a few hours after contact.
- Local joint swelling, stiffness.
- Redness, mottled skin.
- When large areas are involved, the victim may complain of fatigue, fever, chills, dizziness, and muscle cramps.
- Severe cases result in skin scaling off.

Treatment:
Because it is difficult to tell which precise type of skin reaction has occurred, if a person develops a rash after handling a sponge, the following therapy should be undertaken: Soak the affected skin with white vinegar (5% acetic acid) for 15 minutes. This may be done by wetting a gauze pad or cloth with vinegar and laying it on the skin. Then dry the skin; apply the sticky side of adhesive tape to the skin and peel it off. This will remove most sponge fragments. An alternative is to apply a thin

FIGURE 19.13
Stinging Hydroid

venomous thread that, in some species, can penetrate human skin. The reactions of humans to the stings of hazardous coelenterates range from mild skin irritation to major organ failure and death.

Stinging hydroids (see Figure 19.13) occur on many reefs in tropical and temperate-zone seas. Typically, they are feather-like colonies of coelenterates armed, like jellyfish (see Figure 19.14), with nematocysts. Because colonies of these animals may be inconspicuous (they often extend only a few inches high), they may go unnoticed. Except to the occasional person who is hypersensitive to their stings, hydroids generally are more of a nuisance than a hazard. Divers are most likely to be affected on the more sensitive parts of their bodies, such as the inner surfaces of their wrists and arms. Although a diveskin or wet suit protects most of the body from the stings of hydroids, it will not protect against stings on the hands and face. Following a storm, the branches may be fragmented and disperse through the water, such that exposure will occur by just being in the vicinity.

The Atlantic Portuguese Man-of-War, and the smaller Pacific Bluebottle, grouped together in the genus *Physalia*, are colonial hydroids known as polymorphic

layer of rubber cement or a commercial facial peel; let it dry and adhere to the skin, then peel it off. Repeat the vinegar soak for 15 minutes or apply rubbing (40% isopropyl) alcohol for one minute. Once again, dry the skin, then apply hydrocortisone lotion (0.5 to 1%) thinly twice a day until the irritation is gone. If the rash worsens (blistering, increasing redness or pain, swollen lymph glands), this may indicate an infection. The victim should be started on an antibiotic to oppose *Vibrio* bacteria (ciprofloxacin, trimethoprim-sulfamethoxazole, or doxycycline). Proper tetanus immunization should be a part of sponge dermatitis therapy.

19.3.2 Hydroids, Jellyfishes, and Sea Anemones

Grouped here are a variety of organisms that drift or swim slowly at the water's surface or at mid-depths, as well as sessile bottom dwellers attached to rocks or coral outcroppings. Floating forms have gelatinous, semi-transparent, and often bell-shaped bodies with trailing tentacles armed with stinging cells, called nematocysts. In large specimens, these stinging tentacles may trail down as far as 100 ft. (30 m) into the water.

Nematocysts are characteristic of a large group of related, though superficially very diverse, marine animals known as coelenterates. In addition to the jellyfishes, the coelenterates also include the hydroids and stinging corals considered below. Different coelenterates have different types of nematocysts, but all function similarly. When the animal is disturbed, the nematocyst forcefully discharges a

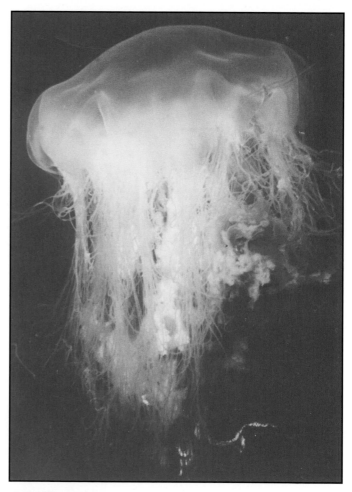

FIGURE 19.14
Common Medusa Jellyfish

colonial siphonophores. Siphonophores differ from the other forms, considered here as jellyfish, in that each organism is actually a colony of diverse individuals. These "individuals" each perform for the entire colony a specialized function, such as swimming or capturing prey. A gelatinous, gas-filled (carbon dioxide and nitrogen) float, which may be six inch or more in diameter, buoys the man-of-war at the surface; from this float trail tentacles as long as 45 ft. (15 m) laden with nematocysts. The *Physaliae* depend upon winds, currents, and tides for movement, travelling as individuals or in colonies resembling flotillas. Man-of-war stings can be dangerous to humans, so divers should stay well clear of these animals (see Figure 19.15). Unfortunately, even the most careful diver can become entangled in a man-of-war tentacle because these nearly transparent structures trail so far below the more visible float. It is especially difficult to detect fragments of tentacles that have been torn from the colony and are drifting free. The nematocysts on these nearly invisible fragments can be as potent as those on an intact organism. Dermatitis can result from contact with water containing venom that has already been released from nematocysts. In addition, a tentacle fragment washed up on the beach can retain its stinging potency for months, even in a semi-dried state. A Mediterranean octopus, *Tremoctopus*, stores intact segments in its suckers for later use.

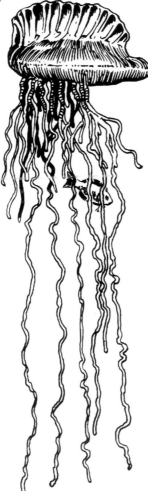

More properly regarded as jellyfish are a group of carnivorous coelenterates known as scyphozoans; each individual is an independent, actively swimming animal adapted to deal rapidly with prey. These include the common jellyfishes encountered by divers in all oceans. Although many can sting, relatively few are lethal. The true giant jellyfish, typified by the genus *Cyanea* is often encountered by divers in temperate and arctic coastal waters of both the Atlantic and Pacific oceans. Tentacles of larger lion's mane or other specimens may exceed 100 ft. (30 m) in length. Divers should be aware that there is a chance of being stung even after they leave

FIGURE 19.15
Portuguese Man-of-War

the water because segments of the tentacles of these animals may adhere to the diver's gloves. Touching the glove to bare skin, especially on the face, will produce a sting as painful as any received from the intact animal. Coelenterate dermatitis can develop under clothing as well where small pieces of tentacle are trapped and cause skin lesions. In Florida, thimble jellyfish larvae have caused extensive injuries when congregated in surface layers.

The most dangerous of the jellyfishes, *Chironex fleckeri*, belongs to a tropical subgroup of scyphozoans known as *cubomedusae*, often misnomered as "sea wasps." The *Chironex* or box jellyfish of the Indo-Pacific possess an extremely virulent and potentially fatal sting that has caused deaths in humans (see Figure 19.16). Death within five minutes is possible, mostly from acute respiratory failure. An adult *Chironex* has enough venom (in excess of 10 ml) to kill three adults. These creatures prefer quiet, protected, and shallow areas off northern Queensland, Australia, but can be found in the open ocean. Fortunately for divers, the most dangerous species are usually encountered by unprotected ocean bathers.

The class *Anthozoa* includes the sea anemones, stony corals and soft corals. They are treated here because they envenom. *Anthozoa* of various species are capable of inflicting painful wounds with their stinging cells. Anemones frequently look like beautiful flowers immersed in tidal pools, deceiving people into touching them. The reason for the name "Hell's Fire" sea anemone (*Actinodendron*) found in the Indo-Pacific region is apparent after contact. Sponge fisherman's (sponge diver's) disease is caused by contact with an anemone (*Sagartia* or *Actinia*) that attaches itself symbiotically to the base of a sponge. Exposure to the planktonic larvae of sea anemones has also caused outbreaks of coelenterate dermatitis.

Signs and Symptoms:
These vary depending on species, extent, and location of sting and a person's reaction:

- Pain ranging from a mild prickly sensation to an intense throbbing, shooting pain
- Reddening of the area (welts, blisters, swelling)
- "Frosted" (silvery) cross-hatched skin irritation, leading to necrosis (box jellyfish, see Figures 19.17, 19.18)
- Pieces of tentacle on affected area
- Cramps, nausea, vomiting
- Decreased touch and temperature sensation
- Severe backache
- Loss of speech
- Frothing at the mouth
- Constriction of the throat
- Respiratory difficulty
- Paralysis
- Delirium
- Convulsions
- Shock

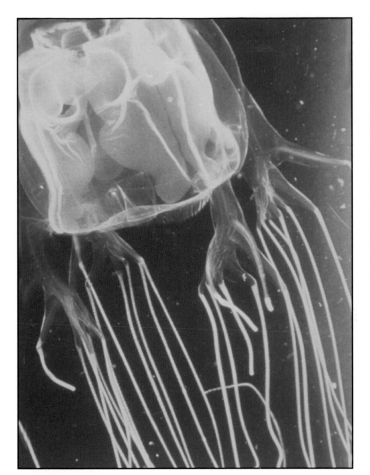

FIGURE 19.16
Box Jellyfish

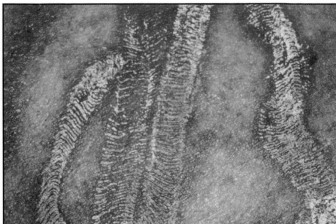

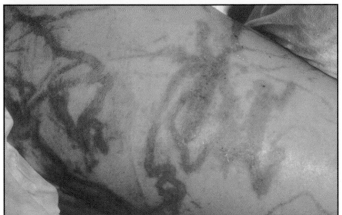

FIGURES 19.17, 19.18
Top — Box Jellyfish Tentacles
Bottom — Sting/Skin Reaction

Treatment:

A diver who has been stung by a jellyfish should be removed from the water as quickly as possible. The rescuer should remove any tentacles, taking care not to come into contact with them. The wound area should be rinsed with 5% acetic acid or household vinegar (this is absolutely recommended for a box jellyfish sting prior to any attempt to remove tentacles adhering to the victim), sodium bicarbonate solution, or household ammonia solution to prevent untriggered nematocysts from discharging. Irrigating with vinegar is the most common recommended first-aid for most jellyfish stings, such as the *Cubomeducae* (*Cubozoan*) injuries. Alternative decontaminants include isopropyl (rubbing) alcohol or papain paste/powder (unseasoned meat tenderizer) or, for *Chrysaora* stings, administer a very strong mixture of baking soda in a slush. The area should **not** be rinsed with freshwater or rubbed with sand to remove any tentacles because this will cause increased stinging. A rinse under a freshwater shower of sufficient force to physically remove nematocysts, however, has been anecdotally reported to be helpful for east coast U.S. "jellyfish" stings. For treatment of jellyfish stings other than

Cubozoan, by far the most common treatments currently are ice or cold packs, anti-burn preparations, or anaesthetic preparations. The victim should be kept lying down with feet elevated, and monitored for signs of shock. CPR and oxygen should be administered if required. If signs of an allergic reaction are present, the victim should be injected with (subcutaneous) aqueous epinephrine 1:1000 (adult dose 0.3 to 0.5 ml) from an allergy kit (i.e., EpiPen®). If the allergic reaction is mild, an oral antihistamine (i.e., diphenydramine 50 mg) can be administered.

Other treatments for a box jellyfish sting recommended by experts include application of a pressure-immobilization dressing and/or intramuscular injection of specific antivenom, which is available from Commonwealth Serum Laboratory of Melbourne, Australia. Early administration of box jellyfish antivenom is often associated with an immediate improvement in pain and other signs and symptoms.

After the skin surface is "decontaminated" and the nematocysts inactivated, the skin should be lightly shaved using a sharp-edged razor and shaving foam or a slimy paste of soap. Following this, the skin may be

Hazardous Aquatic Animals

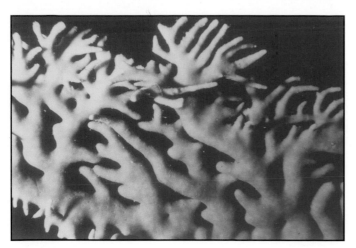

FIGURE 19.19
Stinging or Fire Coral

NOTE
When a diver comes in contact with coral, in addition to the risk of personal injury, there is an environmental impact. Even an accidental brush against coral can wipe off the protective mucus coating of a reef-building coral, leaving it vulnerable to disease and infestation by marauding bacteria.

Signs and Symptoms:
- Itchy, red, swollen area or wound
- Lingering, infected and oozing wound
- Lacerations or abrasions with bleeding

Treatment:
The wound should be cleansed with soap and water to remove bacteria and foreign matter. An antiseptic ointment (i.e, mupirocin or bacitracin) should then be thinly applied and the wound covered with an absorbent sterile dressing which is changed daily. The victim should be started on an antibiotic to cover *Vibrio* species of micro-organisms (marine) or *Aeromonas* species of bacteria (freshwater). Use ciprofloxacin 500 mg, trimethoprimsulfa-methoxazole, one double-strength tablet, or doxycycline 100 mg, giving any of these drugs in a dose, twice a day, orally. Aspirin or another mild analgesic may be used if the wound is painful; if severe, medical attention should be sought.

19.3.4 Marine Worms

Marine worms, which divers should avoid contact with, are classified in a class known as *polychaetes*. Two types that reportedly inflict stinging wounds are bristle worms and blood worms.

Bristleworms (see Figure 19.20), which divers often encounter when overturning rocks or amongst sponges, have tufts of sharp chitinous bristles along their segmented bodies that, in many species, can be erected when the animal is irritated. Easily detached, they penetrate the skin like cactus spines and are difficult to remove. Blood worms burrow in mud or sand. Their jaws contain venomous teeth and are able to inflict painful bites.

The bite or sting of a marine worm induces an immediate intense inflammation typified by a burning sensation with a raised, red, and itchy rash, most frequently on the hands and fingers. Untreated, the pain is generally self-limited over the course of a few hours, but the redness and itching may last for two to three days. With multiple punctures, there may be marked swelling.

Signs and Symptoms:
- Intense burning inflammation with urticarial rash on hands and fingers
- Sensation of pricking and abrasion

rinsed with freshwater. If the residual inflammation is significant, the victim may benefit from the administration of 1% topical hydrocortisone lotion.

19.3.3 Coral

Coral is common in most tropical waters. True corals are capable of inflicting serious wounds with their razor-sharp, calcareous outer skeletons. Because coral cuts are some of the most common injuries inflicted on divers in tropical waters, contact with corals should be carefully avoided. Divers should wear adequate hand, elbow and knee protection and insure their skin is completely protected when working among corals. Coral cuts tend to take a long time to heal; even if promptly and properly treated, they can lead to prolonged disability and skin infections. In extreme cases, the victim will develop celluitis and wound necrosis. Some corals have stinging cells similar to those of jellyfish and produce a sting that rapidly disappears, but may leave red itchy welts.

Stinging corals, often called fire corals, belong to a group of colonial coelenterates known as millepores (see Figure 19.19). They are a widespread component in the development of tropical reefs among the more familiar stony corals, which they superficially resemble. Contact with the nematocysts of millepores affects humans in much the same way as contact with the nematocysts of stinging hydroids. Common Florida and Bahamas species have a characteristic tan-colored, blade-type growth, with lighter (almost white) upper portions. *Millepora* outcroppings assume upright, clavate, bladed, or branching calcareous encrustations over coral rock surfaces, or on the branches of soft corals such as alcyonarians. The *Millepora* zone of the outer Florida Keys ranges from 10–40 ft. deep (3–12 m). Unprotected and unwary divers handle, kneel, or lean upon this marine stinger regularly.

FIGURE 19.21
Cone Snail Shells

end of their shells, persons handling these animals should grasp them at the wide end. Nevertheless, extreme caution should be exercised as the proboscis can be extended to reach around to the opposite end of the animal.

Signs and Symptoms:
- Stinging or burning at wound site
- Numbness or tingling at wound site that spreads to the rest of the body
- Muscular paralysis
- Difficulty in swallowing and speaking
- Respiratory distress

Treatment:
A constricting band such as an elastic (Ace®) wrap or belt should be placed above the sting to prevent drainage from the wound but should not be tight enough to stop arterial flow. Loosen this constriction bandage for 90 seconds every ten minutes. An alternative is to apply the pressure-immobilization technique (see Figure 19.22). To do this, place a 2 x 4 inch cloth pad (1/4 inch thick) over the bite, and apply an elastic wrap firmly around the involved limb directly over the padded bite site. Allow a margin of at least four to six inches on either side of the wound, taking care to check for adequate circulation in the fingers and toes (normal feeling and color). Immediate medical attention should be sought. Careful observation is required in case of cardiac or respiratory failure. Be prepared to administer CPR.

19.4 ANIMALS THAT BITE

Serious injuries caused by the bites of non-venomous marine animals are rare. The possibility of such injury is psychologically threatening, however, because this hazard has been so widely publicized that many divers are distracted by it. It is important that working divers view this hazard realistically.

19.4.1 Fishes

Moray Eels: Moray eels, a member of the family *Muraenidae* (see Figure 19.23), are potential hazards of

FIGURE 19.20
Bristleworm

Treatment:
Remove all large visible bristles with tweezers. Gently dry the skin, taking care to avoid breaking or embedding the spines further into the skin. Apply a layer of adhesive tape, non-caustic glue, or a facial peel to remove the residual smaller spines. Apply 5% acetic acid (vinegar), rubbing (40% isopropyl) alcohol, dilute ammonia, or a paste of unseasoned meat tenderizer (papain) for 10–15 minutes. If the residual inflammation is significant, the victim may benefit from the administration of topical 1% hydrocortisone lotion.

19.3.5 Cone Snails ("Shells")

Certain tropical marine snails which inhabit cone-shaped shells are hazardous to divers. The shells are an especially attractive hazard because collectors are drawn to the colorful natural domicile of the most dangerous species (see Figure 19.21). There are more than 400 kinds of cone shells, each with a highly developed venom apparatus used to stun the small animals that are its prey. The weapon of cone shells is, thus, an offensive rather than defensive one. This fact helps to reduce the number of times people handling these shells are stung. Although only a relatively few of the cone shells are dangerous to divers, the stings of some can be deadly. Because cone shells inject their venom with a harpoon-like structure located at the narrow

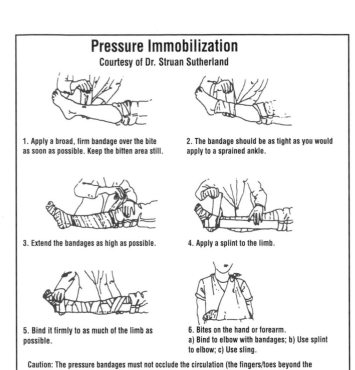

Pressure Immobilization
Courtesy of Dr. Struan Sutherland

1. Apply a broad, firm bandage over the bite as soon as possible. Keep the bitten area still.

2. The bandage should be as tight as you would apply to a sprained ankle.

3. Extend the bandages as high as possible.

4. Apply a splint to the limb.

5. Bind it firmly to as much of the limb as possible.

6. Bites on the hand or forearm.
a) Bind to elbow with bandages; b) Use splint to elbow; c) Use sling.

Caution: The pressure bandages must not occlude the circulation (the fingers/toes beyond the bandage should remain pink and with normal sensation). The bandage should be left in place until proper medical support is available.

FIGURE 19.22
Pressure Immobilization

tropical reefs, and a few species live in the warmer temperate regions of California and Europe. Morays are bottom dwellers and can be found in and around crevices as well as in holes and under rocks or corals. They are rarely seen free swimming or on the reef top. Although relatively few eels grow large enough to threaten a diver seriously, some attain a size greater than 10 ft. (3 m). The tenacious moray with powerful jaws and long needlelike teeth, can seriously injure a human.

Divers injured by morays have usually been bitten when they are reaching into a reef crevice in order to grasp an object. An aggressive eel probably felt threatened or mistook the diver's hand for prey. Elderly, vision-impaired

FIGURE 19.23
Moray Eel

eels may attack without provocation, particularly at night. The moray will usually release its grip when it recognizes that it has taken hold of something unfamiliar. If a diver can resist the impulse to pull free, he may escape with no more than a series of puncture wounds. But presence of mind is rare in such a situation, and a diver usually receives a severe laceration(s) when wrenching his hand from the backward-pointing teeth of the eel.

Barracudas: Barracudas, a member of the family *Sphyraenidae*, (see Figure 19.24) are potentially dangerous fishes that occur widely in the coastal waters of tropical and subtropical seas. A barracuda can reach 6 – 8 ft. (1.8 – 2.3 m) in length, and can weigh up to 110 pounds. With long, canine-like teeth in a large mouth, these fishes have the size and dentition to injure humans severely. The barracuda's teeth are adapted for seizing and holding prey.

FIGURE 19.24
Barracuda

FIGURE 19.25
Great White Shark

The teeth are particularly sharp on both edges, and produce a smooth cutting wound which may not cause much pain at the time, but bleeds copiously. Although barracudas seldom attack divers, they do so rapidly and fiercely, often out of confusion in murky waters. Where visibility is limited, for example, the barracuda may see only a moving hand or foot which may be mistaken for prey. Occasionally, a barracuda will be attracted to a diver (possibly out of curiosity), often at a distance of only a few meters, and sometimes into water no more than knee deep. An attack may also occur when a diver jumps into the water, as when entering the sea from a boat. To a nearby barracuda, the diver's splash may simulate the splash of an animal in difficulty—and hence vulnerable—and the barracuda may strike without realizing what made the splash. Thus, one should be especially alert in murky water to avoid unnecessary splashing when large barracudas may be present. The most common scenario leading to a barracuda bite involves attraction to the luring flash of metal, such as ankle jewelry on the dangling legs of a boater or the abnormal movements of speared fish.

Sharks: Sharks, more than any other animal, have generated sensational publicity as a threat to divers, even though shark bites are among the most infrequent injuries that divers sustain in the sea. Only a few of the many species of sharks threaten humans. Out of some 350 species of sharks known to ichthyologists, only 27 species have been incriminated in attacks on humans. The most frequent implicated offenders are the larger animals, such as the great white, blue, mako, bull, dusky, hammerhead, tiger, and grey reef sharks. Most sharks are non-offensive animals and do not threaten divers. Some generally docile

sharks, such as nurse and swell sharks, however, will bite divers who molest them. Although any large animal with sharp teeth should be left alone, the sharks discussed below may initiate unprovoked attacks on divers.

The great white shark (*Carcharadon carcharis*) shown in Figure 19.25 is responsible for more attacks on humans than any other species, particularly in the waters of southern Australia, the east coast of South Africa, the middle Atlantic coast of North America, and the coast north of Point Conception, California. The gray reef shark, numerous on tropical Pacific reefs, is a typical, potentially dangerous species (see Figure 19.26). This shark's unparalleled potential for destruction has repeatedly been incriminated in human attacks.

Sharks are carnivorous. The danger to humans is a combination of size, aggression, and dentition. Any creature over 3 ft. long that generally resembles this animal should be regarded cautiously, and if over 8 ft. long, should be avoided even if this requires that the diver leave the water. For example, grey reef sharks that range between 3 and 7 ft. (0.9-2.1 m) in length are numerous in shallow tropical waters, and diving operations often cannot be performed unless the presence of sharks in the area is tolerated. When such sharks are in the vicinity, divers should avoid making sudden or erratic movements. Common sense dictates that no injured or distressed animals should be in the water because these are known to precipitate shark attacks. When operations are conducted in the presence of sharks, each group of divers should include one diver who keeps the sharks in view and is alert for changes in their behavior. The chances of trouble are minimal as long as the sharks swim slowly and move naturally. The situation may become dangerous, however, if the sharks assume agitated postures, such as pointing their pectoral fins downward, arching their backs, or elevating their heads (snouts). In a mob frenzy, sharks become fearless and savagely snap at anything and everything, including each other. Most victims are attacked violently and without warning by single sharks. The first contact may be a "bumping" or an attempt by the shark to wound the victim prior to the definitive strike. Severe skin abrasions and lacerations from the shark skin (shagreen) denticles can be engendered in this manner.

The following are recommendations for avoiding and/or protecting one's self from potentially dangerous encounters with sharks:

- Avoid shark-infested waters, particularly at dusk and after dark. Do not dive in known shark feeding grounds.
- Swim in groups. Sharks tend to attack single swimmers.
- When diving, avoid deep drop-offs, murky, turbid water, or areas near sewage outlets.
- Maintain constant vigilance.
- Do not tether captured (i.e., speared) fish to your body.
- Do not corner or provoke sharks.

FIGURE 19.26
Gray Reef Shark

- If a shark appears, leave the water with slow, purposeful movements. DO NOT PANIC OR SPLASH. If the shark approaches a diver in deep water, he should attempt to move to defensive terrain so that he is protected from the rear. If a shark moves in, attempt to strike a firm blow to the snout.
- If stranded at sea, and a rescue helicopter arrives, cautiously exit the water at the earliest opportunity. Surface chop and sounds created by rotor wash attract sharks.

Treatment:

The internationally agreed treatment for shark attack, once the diver has been rescued, is to:

1. Stop blood flow
2. Immobilize the wound
3. Ensure that no further hemorrhage is permitted, and that fluid replacement is adequate, prior to transportation to medical facilities

The jaws of a shark are crescent-shaped and contain a series of razor-sharp rip-saw teeth. The biting force of some sharks is estimated at 18 tons/square inch, and can inflict catastrophic wounds. Severe shark bites result acutely in massive tissue loss. In most cases, the immediate threat to life is hypovolemic shock. It may be necessary to compress the wounds or manually constrict arterial bleeding while the victim is in the water. As soon as the victim is out of the water, all means available

must be used to control bleeding. However, injudicious use of pressure points or tourniquets should be avoided. The patient will need intravascular volume replaced and should be kept well-oxygenated. Even if a shark bite appears minor, the wound should be washed out and bandaged and the victim taken to a doctor. Often the wound will contain pieces of shark teeth, seaweed, sand debris, and shark mouth flora which must be removed in order to avoid an infection. Like other animal bites, shark bites should not be sewn or taped tightly shut in order to allow drainage. This helps to prevent serious infection. The victim should be started on an antibiotic to oppose Vibrio bacteria (ciprofloxacin, trimethoprim-sulfamethoxazole, or doxycycline).

A bad scrape from the a shark's skin must be thoroughly cleaned and antiseptic ointment (i.e., mupirocin or bacitracin) with an absorbent dressing/bandage applied.

Other fish that bite: Any large fish with sharp teeth or powerful jaws can inflict a damaging bite. Generally, however, such fish are hazardous to divers only when they are handled. Pufferfish, wolffish, and triggerfish can be especially troublesome in this respect. These fishes have teeth and jaws adapted to feeding on heavily armored prey, and large specimens are quite capable of biting off a human finger. Triggerfishes (see Figure 19.27) are territorial and should be avoided if they seem aggressive.

In the tropics, some of the larger sea basses can grow to more than 10 ft. (3.0 m). These giant fish, including certain

FIGURE 19.27
Triggerfish

FIGURE 19.28
Sea Snake

groupers and jewfishes, are commonly seen by divers in tropical waters. Groupers are extremely curious, bold, voracious feeders which usually lurk around rocks, caves, caverns, and shipwrecks.

19.4.2 Reptiles

Venomous snakes (see Figure 19.28) are a more widespread hazard in freshwater than in the sea. The cottonmouth (water moccasin) snake, which has a bite known to have been fatal to humans, may be the most dangerous animal hazard divers face in freshwater. This species, which is difficult to identify because of its highly variable coloration, does not show the fear of humans that is characteristic of most aquatic snakes. In regions inhabited by the cottonmouth, divers should avoid any snake that does not retreat. Wet suits afford reasonably good protection, but can be penetrated by the fangs of larger specimens. The diver should not attempt to strike back because this practice may result in multiple bites. Although the evidence is not conclusive, the cottonmouth is believed not to dive deeper than about 6 ft.. Another species to avoid is the timber rattlesnake, an excellent swimmer at the surface.

Venomous sea snakes of the genus *Astrotia fischer* occur only in tropical regions of the Pacific and Indian oceans. These reptiles have highly virulent venoms; fortunately, they generally do not bite humans unless handled. Sometimes a sea snake caught amid a netload of fishes will bite a fisherman. Generally, they are not aggressive toward divers who meet them under water except infrequently during mating season or if guarding an egg nest. Sea snakes are the most numerous of all reptiles and are sometimes seen in large numbers in the open ocean. Divers most often observe them amid rocks and coral where they prey on small fishes. They are agile underwater swimmers, and divers should not lose respect for their deadly bite simply because they are usually docile.

Signs and Symptoms:

Signs and symptoms of sea snake envenomation, listed below, may be delayed for up to a few hours:

- Generalized malaise, anxiety, or, possibly, a feeling of well-being
- Difficulty with speech and swallowing
- Vomiting
- Aching or pain on movement
- Weakness, progressing within 1–2 hours to an inability to move, beginning in the legs
- Muscle spasm
- Droopy eyelids
- Thirst, burning dryness of throat
- Shock
- Respiratory distress
- Fang marks (two small punctures approximately one inch [1.3 centimeters] apart) and, possibly, a fang left in the wound

Treatment:

The victim must remain as calm and inactive as possible. The neurotoxic components of the venom are potent and act on neuromuscular transmission. If possible, apply the firm pressure-immobilization technique. Alternatively, a constricting bandage should be placed above the wound but should not be drawn so tightly as to interrupt arterial flow. The band should be periodically loosened, but not removed until the victim is in a suitable hospital. The victim should be transported immediately to the nearest medical facility for antivenom treatments. Serious envenomation occurs in approximately 25 percent of humans bitten by sea snakes. As the bite is a defensive act, the dose of venom injected is usually small. Therefore, sea snake antivenom is only indicated in those victims who show signs of serious envenomation. If one hour has elapsed since the bite and distinct muscle groups are not painful in passive movement, serious poisoning can be excluded. Antivenom has been proven effective even 7 or 8 hours after the bite, so it is desirable to wait until there is evidence of systemic poisoning before giving antivenom.

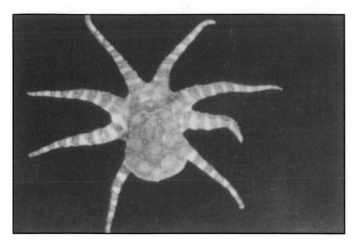

**FIGURE 19.29
Blue-Ringed Octopus**

If possible, capture the snake for identification purposes, but take care not to become another victim.

19.4.3 Octopi

Octopi are timid and highly intelligent creatures able to change color to match the slightest variation in the environment. The octopus has a beak capable of piercing shellfish, suction pads which are strong enough to pry open bi-valves and oysters, and defensive ink which can be used as a distracting escape decoy. There have been reported cases in which an octopus has actually attacked a diver when provoked or when retaliating against a spear or knife. Most species are harmless except for the blue-ringed octopus found in tidal rock pools around Australia (see Figure 19.29). The blue-ringed octopus bites prey with its parrot-like beak, secreting a salivary venom that enters the wound and subdues the prey. Most bites to humans are caused by people picking up or accidentally treading upon the octopus rather than it "attacking" humans. At least 14 cases of humans being bitten by octopus are recorded, one diver in Australia who allowed a blue-ringed octopus to crawl over his bare skin was bitten on the neck and died within two hours. The injected tetrodotoxin venom has a selective effect on nerve action potentials which induces paralysis and can be lethal. One average size octopus (weighing 26 grams) has enough venom to paralyze up to ten adult human beings.

Signs and Symptoms:
- Toxin has a short duration of action; complete onset of paralysis may be under ten minutes
- Difficulty in breathing, respiratory failure
- Fixed dilated pupils
- Weakness, paraesthesia, numbness, tightness in the chest

Treatment:
If the bite is from a blue-ringed or spotted octopus, apply the pressure-immobilization technique. An alternative method is to simply wrap the entire limb at the described tightness with an elastic bandage. The wrap is meant to impede absorption of venom into the general circulation by containing it within the compressed tissue and microscopic blood and lymphatic vessels near the limb surface. The limb should be splinted to prevent motion. If the bite is on the hand or arm, also apply a sling. Be prepared to provide breathing assistance, if respiratory failure develops, until immediate medical attention is secured. For non-venomous bites, clean the wound with soap and water and apply antiseptic ointment and a bandage.

19.4.4 Other Reptiles

Reptiles that bite, including turtles, alligators, and crocodiles are potential hazards to divers, both in freshwater and in the sea.

Turtles are frequently encountered by divers. Although the larger individuals of some species can injure divers with their bites, these animals are not generally threatening. The larger marine turtles have occasionally inflicted minor injuries, but several freshwater species are far more vicious and aggressive. These include the alligator snapping turtle and common snapping turtle of American freshwaters. The softshell turtle also may inflict a wound.

Alligators that have been encountered by divers, including the American alligator, have not proved threatening. Nevertheless, the potential for serious injury exists, and divers should be cautious. Any animal over 3 ft. (1 m) is likely to be dangerous.

Crocodiles are more dangerous than alligators. A species in the tropical western Pacific which enters coastal marine waters is feared far more than sharks by the natives. Crocodilians can move fast on land and in water, with recorded attacks including victims in boats, on dry land, and free swimming in deep water.

19.4.5 Aquatic Mammals

Juvenile and female seals and sea lions frequently frolic in the water near divers. Underwater encounters with sea lions can be expected if the animals are nearby during a dive. Their activity can be distracting or even frightening, but it is rarely dangerous. Large bull seals and sea lions, although aggressive on the above-water rocks on their breeding rookery, apparently do not constitute a serious threat underwater. Divers have been seriously bitten and, therefore, should avoid ill-tempered and abnormally aggressive animals. A potentially greater danger when swimming with seals is being mistaken for a seal by a great white shark. Similarly, the infamous leopard seal of Antarctic waters is a threat that must be respected. If a leopard seal is sighted, diving should be suspended. If under water at the time, divers should not surface in open water, but follow the sea bed to the shore or to direct exit below the boat before ascending. If bitten by a seal or sea lion, the diver should consult a physician because of the potential for unusual wound infections.

Common sense dictates that divers avoid large whales underwater. The killer whale can generate enough crushing power to bite a seal or porpoise in half with a single bite. Usually, whales stay clear of divers, so most incidents occur when divers put themselves in jeopardy by provoking the whales. A whale may be startled when a diver approaches too close and may strike a diver accidentally in a sudden surge of evasive action.

Muskrats are potential hazards in freshwater. Usually they attack only if they believe they are being threatened and their bites produce only minor wounds. There is a danger that rabies can be contracted from a muskrat bite, however, so in addition to seeking immediate medical advice, a diver who is bitten should make every effort to capture or kill the animal for examination.

The hippopotamus is a frequent killer in Africa. Unpredictable and bad-tempered, hippos have attacked boats and people in the water.

19.5 ANIMALS THAT SHOCK

The electric ray can be found in the temperate and tropical oceans of the world. The torpedo ray of California can grow to 6 ft. in length and weigh up to 200 pounds (see Figure 19.30). This ray is shaped somewhat like a stingray, except its "wings" are thick and heavy and the tail is flattened for swimming. Electric rays are slow-moving animals; alert divers should have little trouble avoiding them. As is true of so many undersea hazards, these animals threaten only those divers who molest them. The electric ray's shock dose, which can be as high as 200 volts, is generated by modified muscles in the forward part of the animal's disc-shaped body. Generally, the ventral side of the ray is negative and the dorsal side is positive. The shock, enough to electrocute a large fish, can stun a diver and induce drowning.

FIGURE 19.30
Torpedo Ray

19.6 ANIMALS THAT ARE POISONOUS TO EAT

Most seafoods are edible and nourishing; however, several of the most toxic substances known are sometimes found in marine organisms. Mollusk shellfish, such as clams, mussels, and oysters are sometimes poisonous to eat when exposed to red tide blooms. These shellfish become poisonous because they feed on toxic dinoflagellates, which are microscopic plankton. Most of these episodes of poisoning have occurred along the Pacific coast from California to Alaska; the northeast coast from Massachusetts to Nova Scotia, New Brunswick and Quebec; and in the North Sea countries of Britain and West Germany. It is advisable to check with local authorities to determine what periods of the year are safe for eating mollusk shellfish. Violent intoxications and fatalities have also been reported from eating tropical reef crabs; these should not be eaten without first checking with the local inhabitants. Numerous species of tropical reef fishes are known to be poisonous to eat because they cause a disease known as ciguatera. An edible fish in one locality may be deadly in another. In addition, most pufferfish contain a deadly poison known as tetrodotoxin; puffers and related species should not be eaten. Improperly preserved fish, such as tuna, can generate toxins and become scombrotoxic, causing an allergic-type reaction in someone who ingests the toxic seafood.

19.6.1 Ciguatera

Ciguatera poisoning is caused by eating fish containing toxins (ciguatoxins), the products of certain species of algae eaten by the fish. Ciguatoxic fish are rarely identified out of the tropical reef zone identified by 35 north and south latitudes. About 800 species of fish have been known to carry ciguatera; the most common types being predaceous species; barracudas, groupers, snappers, jacks, wrasses, parrotfishes, and surgeonfishes. Currently it is impossible to distinguish toxic fish from harmless fish except by laboratory analysis or by feeding the suspected fish to animals and watching for a reaction. The occurrence of fish containing ciguatoxin is unpredictable and can occur in a fish species that was harmless the day before. The toxins are not destroyed by cooking. Because the concentration of toxins builds up over time, oversized fish of a given species are more likely to be toxic than smaller ones. The internal organs and roe of afflicted fish are particularly toxic. Severe ciguatera poisoning may cause severe disability or even death in humans.

Signs and Symptoms: (reported in over 150 cases) include:

- Numbness and tingling of the lips, tongue, and throat
- Abdominal cramps
- Nausea and vomiting

- Diarrhea
- Weakness, prostration
- Reversal of thermal sensitivity (hot feels cold and cold feels hot)
- Muscle and joint aching
- Nervousness
- Metallic taste in mouth
- Visual disturbances
- Extreme fatigue
- Muscle paralysis
- Convulsions
- Headache, dizziness and imbalance
- Heart failure

Treatment:

There is no definitive, first-aid field therapy available for ciguatera poisoning. If symptoms occur within four hours of eating fish, vomiting should be induced. Medical attention should be sought as soon as possible because the hospital treatment team may be able to administer mannitol through an intravenous route to treat severe neurological or cardiac symptoms. Other drugs may be helpful for certain severe symptoms, such as an antihistamine for itching or anti-nausea drug for nausea and vomiting. Rapid death is extremely rare. If paralysis of the respiratory system occurs, be prepared to assist respiration and if necessary administer CPR.

During recovery from ciguatera poisoning, the victim should exclude the following from their diet: fish, fish sauces, shellfish, shellfish sauces, alcoholic beverages, nuts, and nut oils. It should be noted that ciguatera poisoning has a 12 percent fatality rate, and that complete recovery may require many months, even years.

19.6.2 Scombroid Poisoning

Some scombroid (mostly dark-fleshed) fish (i.e., tuna, bonito, mackerel, bluefish) that have been exposed to sunlight or been left standing at room temperature for several hours may develop a toxin that is a type of histamine (the chemical perpetrator of allergic reactions). Such fish may have a peppery or sharp taste or may be completely normal in color, taste, or appearance. Within a few minutes of consumption, symptoms of this type of poisoning develop. The symptoms usually clear within 8–12 hours, although fatigue and headache may persist for a few days.

Signs and Symptoms:
- Nausea, vomiting, burning of throat
- Flushing of the face
- Diarrhea
- Abdominal pain
- Severe headache
- Dizziness
- Massive red welts
- Severe itching

- Severe dehydration (thirst)
- Shortness of breath and wheezing
- Bronchospasm, severe respiratory distress
- Cardiac palpitation
- Inability to swallow
- Shock

Treatment:

The victim should seek medical aid as soon as possible. Vomiting should be induced if it does not occur spontaneously. If the victim is short of breath or extremely weak, treat as if for an allergic reaction. Use epinephrine (adrenaline) (injected from an allergy kit, such as an EpiPen®, in an adult dose of 0.3 to 0.5 ml subcutaneously) and/or an oral antihistamine (i.e., diphenydramine [Benadryl®] 50 mg or fexofenadine [Allegra®] 60 mg). The itching, rash, and headache usually respond to an oral antihistamine.

19.6.3 Paralytic Shellfish Poisoning

Paralytic shellfish poisoning can be linked to a dinoflagellate *Protogonyaulaux* species. During the summer months, many shellfish which inhabit waters along the Pacific coast, Northeast Atlantic, or Gulf of Mexico may become poisonous. This lethal condition is caused by the ingestion of poisonous phytoplankton which contain different types of toxins that do not affect the shellfish but which can be poisonous to humans. Saxitoxin is the most frequently identified toxin. If a single dinoflagellate predominates, it can discolor the water creating a "colored" tide, of which red is commonly recognized. To the old axiom "don't eat shellfish in the Northern hemisphere in months that do not contain the letter 'r'" should be added "it doesn't matter how you spell the month if the shellfish have been dining in *Gonyaulax*." The poison works directly on the central nervous system so the usual symptoms of "food poisoning," such as nausea and vomiting, are not generally present. The poison impairs breathing and may also affect the heart and circulation of the blood. Death, which occurs in severe cases, results from respiratory paralysis. Onset of symptoms is variable but may occur within 20 minutes of ingestion.

Signs and Symptoms:
- Tingling or burning sensation of the lips, mouth, tongue or face that spreads to other parts of the body
- Numbness
- Muscle weakness and paralysis
- Respiratory failure
- Infrequent nausea, vomiting, and other gastrointestinal ailments

Treatment:

Vomiting should be induced as quickly as possible, and immediate medical attention should be sought. Rescuers should be prepared to provide mouth-to-mouth resuscitation or CPR.

19.6.4 Tetrodotoxin "Puffer" Fish Poisoning

Certain puffers (blowfish, globefish, swellfish, porcupinefish) contain tetrodotoxin, one of the most potent poisons in nature (see Figure 19.31). These fish are prepared as a delicacy ("fugu") in Japan by specially trained and licensed chefs. The toxin is found in the entire fish with greatest concentration in the liver, intestines, reproductive organs, and skin. After the victim has eaten the fish, symptoms can occur as quickly as ten minutes later or be delayed by a few hours. Because tetrodotoxin poisoning can be fatal to humans, it is wise to avoid eating puffers.

Signs and Symptoms:
- Numbness and tingling around the mouth
- Lightheadedness
- Drooling
- Sweating
- Vomiting
- Diarrhea, abdominal pain
- Weakness, difficulty walking
- Paralysis
- Difficulty breathing
- Collapse

FIGURE 19.31
Pufferfish

Treatment:

If a person suffers from puffer poisoning, transport immediately to a hospital. Continually monitor the victims breathing, and assist if necessary. Unfortunately, there is no antidote; the victim will need sophisticated medical management until the toxin is metabolized.

NOTES

Emergency Medical Care

20

Emergency Medical Care

20

20.0 GENERAL

First aid is classically defined as the immediate, temporary assistance provided to a victim of injury or illness before the services of emergency medical personnel or a physician can be obtained. The purpose of first aid is to prevent further injury or worsening of the victim's condition. When an accident occurs, the proper response can mean the difference between life and death, temporary or permanent disability, and short or long-term hospitalization.

In the diving environment, due to time delays inherent in the distances traveled when diving, either professionally or as a recreational diver, the classic definition of first aid is frequently obscured by circumstances.

It is for this reason that everyone involved in diving operations should have more than just a cursory understanding of the basics of first aid. At a minimum, all NOAA divers should complete a comprehensive first aid and cardiopulmonary resuscitation course. More appropriately, a certain number must be trained as caregivers, Emergency Medical Technicians, or take the diving-focused Diver Medical Technician course. The Dive/First Responder® program, available through colleges and universities, community colleges, vocational-technical schools, or through private companies providing such training and education, is also an option for non-professional/recreational divers. Typically, these programs are endorsed or sponsored by the American National Red Cross, National Safety Council, American Heart Association, Divers Alert Network and other similar, nationally recognized organizations.

20.1 EMERGENCY MEDICAL RESPONSE

In anticipating both the routine and unusual medical problems that may arise in the course of diving, all diving operations should have a diving accident management plan. Such a plan should cover assignment of individual responsibilities in an emergency, the location of equipment and supplies necessary for medical treatment, the availability of a trained hyperbaric physician, and procedures for ensuring adequate patient transport to recompression or medical facilities, if necessary. In addition, emergency kits should be available that can be used at the scene of a diving injury. These kits should contain the equipment and supplies necessary to treat victims of diving injuries and to maintain life support measures until an emergency medical team can arrive, or until transportation to a definitive treatment facility can be arranged.

20.1.1 Medical Equipment and Supplies

Before a diving operation begins, it is important to consider what medical items would be needed in a diving accident. These items should then be separated into those kits that can be used in a hyperbaric chamber and those that will be kept at the surface. An excellent way to handle this requirement is to establish medical kits small enough to carry on a diving operation or to take into the recompression facility. One suggestion, in accordance with a diving accident management plan, is to place the necessary medical items into three kits, each having a different purpose:

- Diving operations medical (first aid) kit
- Primary medical treatment kit, containing diagnostic and therapeutic equipment to be available when required and to be inside the chamber during all treatments
- Secondary medical treatment kit, including equipment and medical supplies that need not be immediately available within the chamber but that could be locked in separately when required

20.1.2 Diving Operations Medical (First Aid) Kit

The following items are recommended for a diving operations medical kit that would be available at all diving sites:

- **General:**
  — Bandaids®
  — Tube of disinfectant (antibiotic cream)
  — Aspirin tablets
  — Dramamine® or other over-the counter (OTC) sea sickness medication

- **Diagnostic Equipment:**
  — Flashlight
  — Stethoscope
  — Otoscope-ophthalmoscope
  — Sphygmomanometer (aneroid type only)
  — Thermometer
  — Reflex hammer
  — Tuning fork (500, 1,000, and 2,000 hertz)
  — Pin and brush for sensory testing
  — Tongue depressors
  — Bandage scissors
  — Non-sterile exam gloves
  — Surgical masks or protective goggles

- **Bandages:**
  — Topper sponges
  — Adhesive tape (1/2, 1, and 2-inch rolls)
  — Adhesive compress (1-inch)
  — Bandage compress (4-inch)
  — Eye dressing packet
  — Gauze pads, sterile (4 x 4-inch)
  — Curlex® roller bandage (1, 2, and 4-inch)
  — Triangular bandages (40-inch)
  — Trauma dressing

- **Emergency Treatment Equipment:**
  — Oropharyngeal airway (large, medium, and small)
  — Tongue depressor taped and padded as a bite pad in case of seizures
  — Oxygen resuscitator (capable of ventilating an unconscious victim)
  — Oxygen first aid equipment for emergency resuscitation
  — Flexible rubber suction catheter
  — Suction equipment
  — Plastic non-flexible suction tips (Yankauer® suction tip)
  — Asepto® syringe
  — Tourniquet
  — Tweezers
  — Artery forceps (5 and 8-inch)
  — Splinting boards (4 x 12-inch)
  — Splinting boards (4 x 24-inch)
  — Wire ladder splints
  — Liquid/crystal ice packs
  — Blanket
  — Pocket mask with oxygen inlet
  — Non-rebreather masks

20.1.3 Primary Medical Treatment Kit

The suggested contents for a medical treatment kit to be available in the recompression chamber during every treatment:

- **Diagnostic Equipment:**
  — Flashlight
  — Stethoscope

— Otoscope-ophthalmoscope
— Sphygmomanometer (aneroid type only)
— Thermometer
— Reflex hammer
— Tuning fork (500, 1,000, and 2,000 hertz)
— Pin and brush for sensory testing
— Tongue depressors

- **Emergency Airway Equipment:**
  — Large-bore needle and catheter (12 or 14 gauge) for cricothyroidotomy or relief of tension pneumothorax
  — Small Penrose® drain or Heimlich® valve for adaption to a thoracentesis needle to provide a one-way flow of gas out of the chest
  — Laryngoscope with extra batteries and bulbs
  — Laryngoscope blades
  — Cuffed endotracheal tubes with adapters (8.0, 8.5, and 9.5 mm)
  — Syringe and sterile water for cuff inflation (10 ml) saline
  — Malleable stylet (approximately 12-inch long)
  — Sterile lubricant
  — Soft rubber suction catheters
  — Exam glove
  — Face masks or protective goggles

- **Miscellaneous:**
  — Bandage scissors
  — Tourniquet
  — Adhesive tape
  — Automated external defibrillator (AED)

- **Drugs:**
  — Lactated Ringers® solution, 500 and 1,000 ml bags
  — Normal saline, 500 and 1,000 ml bags
  — Atropine for injection
  — Sodium bicarbonate for injection
  — Calcium chloride for injection
  — Decongestant nasal spray
  — Dexainethasone for injection
  — Epinephrine for injection (1:10,000 and 1:1,000)
  — Lidocaine® for injection
  — Diphenhydramine hydrochloride for injection
  — Phenytoin sodium for injection
  — Tylenol® or Motrin®
  — Codeine tablets, 30 mg
  — Aspirin tablets, 325 mg
  — Sterile water for injection
  — Injection methyl prednisolone (40 mg/ml in 5 ml) or Decadron® shock pack (dexainethasone)
  — Injection Valium® (10 mg in 2 ml)
  — Sterets® injection swabs

When possible, pre-loaded syringes should be available to avoid the need for venting the vial to prevent implosion during pressure change within the chamber. If necessary, vials can be vented with a needle inserted through the rubber stopper for pressure equalization during descent and ascent, but the sterility of such vials should then be considered to have been violated and the vial should be discarded and replaced.

20.1.4 Secondary Medical Treatment Kit

The following additional medical supplies are recommended for a kit to be kept near the recompression chamber for use inside the chamber:

- Drugs:
  — Lactated Ringers® solution, 500 and 1,000 ml bags
  — 5% dextrose in normal saline
  — 5% dextrose in water
  — Dextran 70 in saline, 500 ml
  — Normal saline, 500 and 1,000 ml bags
- Intravenous infusion sets
- Intravenous infusion extension sets
- Three-way stopcocks
- Syringes (2, 5, 10, and 30 ml)
- Sterile needles (18, 20, and 22 gauge)
- Nasogastric tube
- Catheterization set, urethral
- Myringotomy knife
- Wound closure instrument tray, disposable
- Sterile scalpel and blade assortment
- Assorted suture material
- Surgical soap
- Sterile towels
- Sterile gloves, surgical (sizes 6–8)
- Gauze pads, sterile (4 x 4-inch)
- Gauze roller bandage, sterile (1 and 2 inch)
- Bandaids®
- Cotton balls
- Splints
- Eye patches
- Medicut® cannula

20.1.5 Use of the Kits

Because conditions differ on board ship, at land-based diving operations, and at diver training sites, the responsible physician should modify the contents of the medical kits to suit the operation's needs. All three kits should be taken to the recompression chamber or scene of the accident. Sterile supplies should be produced in duplicate. Any sterile supplies not sealed adequately against changes in atmospheric pressure should be sterilized after each pressure exposure or, if not exposed in the interim, at six-month intervals. All drug ampules will not withstand pressure, and bottle stoppers may be pushed in by increased pressure. Bottles with stoppers

may be vented with a needle during pressurization and can then be discarded if not used.

The emergency kit should be sealed in such a way that it can be opened readily when needed; the condition of the seal should indicate that it has been opened. Each kit should contain a list of contents, and each time it is opened, the contents should be verified against the inventory and the condition of all items checked.

Use of the primary or secondary medical treatment kits should be restricted to the physician in charge or to a trained and certified diving medical technician (DMT). Concise instructions for administration of each drug should be provided in the kit. In untrained hands, many of these items can be lethal.

20.2 BASIC PRINCIPLES OF EMERGENCY MEDICAL CARE

The first step in administering first aid is to evaluate the victim's condition quickly and accurately and to elect an appropriate course of action. This evaluation must be done systematically, quickly, and comprehensively. In caring for the victim of a medical or trauma emergency, there are several steps involved in immediate assessment and intervention. Too often these have been viewed as separate components. In reality, assessment and care constitute a continuum:

Scene Safety Assessment: Quick examination of the victim to identify those problems that may present an immediate life-threat. The survey may have to be interrupted as problems are encountered that must be corrected. As shown on the next page, Airway-Breathing-Circulation constitute the core elements of the scene safety assessment. At any point along the way, this process may be halted in order to provide appropriate correction of a problem or resuscitation as needed.

Initial Assessment: Once immediate threats to a victim's life have been corrected or eliminated a more comprehensive examination is carried out. In a trauma victim, this is a thorough head-to-toe evaluation of all body parts and systems. In a medical emergency, the secondary survey may be more focused on those body parts and systems that have the greatest likelihood of being involved based on the victim's chief complaint. It is possible that during the secondary survey, the rescuer may identify problems that, if left unchecked, might develop into life threatening circumstances. During this phase of the care continuum, additional treatment and stabilization may be provided beyond that initiated during the scene safety assessment.

Detailed Assessment: Although generally not viewed as a part of out-of-hospital emergency medical care, it is possible that even though the rescuer is not a medical professional, he may be called upon to deliver definitive care in the diving setting.

20.3 INFECTION CONTROL

While it was once felt that caregivers were under no threat from victims when it came to delivering emergency care, new threats have emerged in the past 20 years that have significantly changed the way care is rendered to a stranger. Virulent forms of hepatitis and tuberculosis are present in significant numbers of individuals. And, there is evidence to suggest that a vast percentage of the American population may be suffering from subclinical (no signs or symptoms) Hepatitis C. The current thinking is that many of those who contract Hepatitis C may some day have more serious consequences with the development of cirrhosis of the liver or, even worse, liver cancer.

In addition to these problems, the rescuer must be aware of the human immunodeficiency virus (HIV), the virus that causes AIDS. This virus, though extremely fragile, is carried in bodily fluids, blood, lymph and semen, but the real threat from the virus is the likelihood that there are hundreds of thousands of people in the U.S. who are carrying the virus and don't even know it. So, treat all victims as though they present a risk of infection.

First, it is important to eliminate direct contact with blood or other bodily fluids, mucous membranes, wounds, or burns. The tools that the rescuer should employ to protect himself include the following:

- Good quality, disposable latex, nitrile, or vinyl gloves. Fit is not as critical as protection. If gloves are too big, that shouldn't be a problem. But, if gloves are too small, there is the risk of having the gloves tear when being applied or during use, an event that must be avoided at all costs.
- A pocket mask with a one-way valve should it be necessary to provide artificial ventilation to the victim using the mouth and lungs as the means for restoring or supplementing the victim's breathing.
- Eye protection in the form of eyeglasses that are wide enough to prevent fluids from becoming splashed in the eyes. More appropriately, medical kits used in the diving environment should contain inexpensive goggles designed for emergency medical care. As a last resort, in the diving environment, the rescuer might even employ a dive mask for this purpose, though it's likely to be cumbersome.
- A disposable, medical face mask will prevent the inhalation of infectious organisms in airborne droplets. Though in the marine setting the rescuer is unlikely to encounter such situations, there are certain infections for which a face mask may also be appropriately put on the victim as well as the rescuer—meningitis and tuberculosis, for example.

Each of these items is relatively inexpensive and should be a part of a personal kit or the medical kit carried on board every boat.

20.4 PRIMARY SURVEY—A DETAILED LOOK

If the body loses its ability to take in oxygen and release carbon dioxide through the respiratory system or can no longer move life-sustaining oxygen through the circulatory system, then tissues and organs and, eventually, the person will die. Therefore, the main purpose of the scene safety assessment is the establishment and/or maintenance of an adequate airway, to assure that the victim is breathing and that adequate circulation is present. Thus, there are the ABC's of the scene safety assessment:

- **Airway:** Assurance that the victim is conscious enough to maintain his own airway or manually opening the airway to make certain it is maintained. If it is suspected that there might be injury to the victim's cervical spine, a special method for opening the airway should be employed. This is discussed in detail later in the chapter.
- **Breathing:** Once an adequate airway has been established, then breathing must be evaluated and either restored or aided. Ideally, all victims should receive supplemental oxygen as part of breathing restoration, but this is particularly true when dealing with a diving emergency.
- **Circulation:** As soon as it has been determined that the airway is patent or maintained and that there is adequate breathing, the last phase of the scene safety assessment assesses the circulation. First, determine that there is a heartbeat. Without spontaneous heartbeat, the oxygen being supplied through the lungs cannot reach the body's tissues and organs. Next, it is vital to determine whether there is life-threatening bleeding; if such bleeding is found, it must be stopped.

Once it has been observed that a conscious victim can talk clearly and seems to be properly oriented to his surroundings, the scene safety assessment is completed, so long as there is not any obvious life-threatening bleeding.

20.4.1 Airway Assessment and Management

The first step is to determine whether the victim has simply fainted. Assuming there are no signs/symptoms of injury to suggest spinal trauma, roll the victim into a face-up position on a firm surface like the deck of a boat or the firm sand on a beach. Gently shake the victim and shout, "Are you OK?" Should trauma be a possibility, as discussed below, relative to spinal stabilization, then do not shake the victim, but simply tap on the victim's shoulder firmly and shout. If the victim has simply fainted, he will usually regain consciousness immediately or soon after lying down. If the victim doesn't respond or regain consciousness, ask bystanders to notify whatever emergency medical services are available (assign a specific bystander to call 911, or have someone on the boat notify the authorities by marine radio), and then continue with the process of caring for the victim.

If the victim regains consciousness and is breathing adequately, as explained below, then continue to the initial assessment, again provided that no life-threatening bleeding is present.

By performing these steps, the first step has been taken in the performance of cardiopulmonary resuscitation (CPR).

In the unresponsive victim, the second step is to open the victim's airway to enable breathing. Do this with the head-tilt, chin-lift method which puts a hand (the one closest to the victim's head) on the victim's forehead, while two or three fingers of the other hand are placed under the victim's jaw. By lifting with the fingers under the jaw and, at the same time, pressing gently on the victim's forehead, the head is tilted back into a hyperextended position. This lifts the tongue and keeps it from blocking the airway of the victim. Sometimes, opening the airway is enough to start the victim breathing spontaneously.

If it is suspected that the victim may have sustained a spinal injury, then the technique used for opening the airway is called the jaw thrust maneuver. This process is accomplished by taking both thumbs and placing them pointing downward on the large bones under each of the victim's eyes—the "cheek" bones. With the thumbs in this position, the rescuer should be able to get his fingers behind the victim's jaw at the point where he can feel the bend in the lower jaw. This bone is called the mandible. With the thumbs and fingers in this position, and using the opposing forces of the thumb against the fingers, the rescuer will be able to move the lower jaw forward. This will lift the tongue off the back of the throat and establish an open airway. All of this must be done without any manipulation of the spine, which must be maintained in a neutral position.

With the victim's airway now open, put an ear very close to the victim's mouth and nose while watching the victim's chest for the rise and fall of breathing for three to five seconds. Listen and feel for the noise and movement of air through the victim's mouth and nose. Remember to LOOK-LISTEN-FEEL for breathing.

If the victim is breathing but bubbling, gurgling, or crowing sounds come with each breath, then it's likely that the airway is partially blocked or that there is foreign matter in the airway. If this is the case, suction should be utilized. Though many oxygen systems sold to the diving community employ a suction unit that is oxygen-driven, manual suction devices are just as effective and they do not waste preciously needed oxygen. When using a suction device, remember that the use of suction should be intermittent and brief. Suction not only removes foreign matter from the victim's airway, but also removes life-giving air from the victim's airway as well. Therefore, when using a suction device, suction should be applied for no more than 15 seconds at a time, and periods of ventilation should be permitted between suction efforts. In addition, no suction device should be inserted into the airway any farther than can be seen.

Ideally, the person who performed the jaw thrust maneuver to open the airway should maintain that position while another caregiver assesses the victim's breathing.

If the victim is not breathing, initiate mouth-to-mask breathing, cover the victim's mouth and nose with the pocket mask and give the victim two full ventilations, or rescue breaths. These breaths are slow, full ventilations taking 1 1/2 to 2 seconds per breath. After each of these breaths, pause long enough between breaths to allow the victim to exhale passively. Following delivery of the two rescue breaths described here, evaluate the unresponsive victim immediately to determine if a pulse is present. The pocket mask device will reduce the possibility of contamination from the victim.

In this situation, make the OK sign to demonstrate the preferred hand position for the hand grasping the mask device. The thumb and index finger circle the port through which the rescuer ventilates the victim while the remaining fingers are used to assist in maintaining the seal of the mask over the victim's face.

The circular device appearing above the thumb and index finger is the one-way valve incorporated in the mask which prevents the victim's exhaled air or other expired or regurgitated matter from entering the caregiver's mouth or airway. Use of these one-way valves is consistent with the concept of self-protection when providing care to a victim.

This particular mask device is an oro-nasal mask and is placed over the victim's mouth and nose, with the opening of the breathing tube directly over the victim's mouth. The fingers of the right hand are used to lift the jaw, while the left hand is on the forehead. Even with the pocket mask device, the head-tilt, chin lift technique must be utilized to maintain an open airway.

With the left and right hands in proper position, the caregiver ventilates the victim for 1 1/2 to 2 seconds per ventilation and allows the victim to exhale passively between breaths. Using peripheral vision, the caregiver can also monitor chest rise with each ventilation to be certain that the breaths are properly entering the victim's lungs. If chest rise is not observed during efforts to ventilate, the head-tilt, chin lift maneuver should be repeated, since the airway may be blocked by the victim's tongue or other anatomic structures. If such repositioning does not result in successful ventilation of the victim, then there may be an airway obstruction that cannot be corrected simply by repositioning. In these cases the foreign-body-airway-obstruction technique learned in formal CPR training should be employed.

20.4.2 Managing the Victim with Suspected Spinal Injury

Always consider the possibility that in-water trauma may have caused injury to the victim's spinal cord. Some mechanisms of injury where such injury may be suspected include: victim hitting his head on the bottom of a boat or diving platform; victim has been struck by a boat; victim who hit his head on the bottom while diving into shallow water; or a victim has been thrown around uncontrollably in the surf. These examples presume a spinal cord injury has taken place, and inappropriate management of the victim may lead to further, permanently disabling, injury.

The section of the spinal cord that is most frequently injured in such accidents is the cervical spine, the section of the spinal column in the neck.

The most critical aspect of managing such victims is maintaining the cervical spine in a neutral in-line position. Quite simply, this means that a rescuer should try to keep the victim's neck in a position that approximates the normal position that the neck is in when the victim is standing upright with the head looking straight forward.

When moving a victim in the water, manual support to keep the head in that position is supplemented by the buoyant effect of the water. In essence, the water can provide some of the splinting effect necessary. In the water, cradle the victim's head in your hand and forearm to provide such support. It is important that the rescuer get assistance in managing such a victim at the earliest moment, since maintaining a victim in this position, while keeping the body aligned, is extremely difficult to do alone. In wading water, the victim needs to be towed with one arm being utilized to stabilize the spine itself, while the other hand is used to maintain the head in a neutral position. Again, assistance of other trained individuals or bystanders should be enlisted as soon as possible. If the victim is otherwise stable, he should be maintained in the water until additional assistance arrives with appropriate equipment for removing the victim from the water, and replacing the manual stabilization technique being employed.

Removing such a victim from the water to a boat is always a difficult process, particularly if the victim needs to be lifted over a gunwale or transom. After getting the maximum amount of help, an effort should be made to stabilize the victim onto something rigid and long enough to support, at a minimum, the victim's torso, neck, and head before being removed from the water. A backboard or basket litter, even a door from one of the boat's hatches might be removed from its hinges and used for this purpose. Once the victim is stabilized appropriately while still in the water, a lifting device may be fashioned from lines to aid in lifting the victim from the water. If the boat is equipped with a diving platform, it will simplify the procedure if the stabilized victim is first lifted to the diving platform and then to the deck of the boat. The ideal boat for diving and diving rescues should be equipped with a water-level door which not only eases handling of victims in emergencies, but makes the recovery of divers in rough water conditions both easier and safer. Many boats utilized for diving and fishing have such doors built into the transom or the side of the boat.

In a beach environment, provided the beach is sandy, the victim can be manually stabilized and carefully brought far enough up the beach to be clear of the water that might enter his airway. Once moved to the beach, provided there are no other hazards present, the victim should be left on the beach until properly trained emergency medical services personnel arrive and transport the victim to a medical facility.

20.4.3 In-Water Artificial Ventilation

Mouth-to-mouth resuscitation can be started in the water. In some cases, it might be better to establish the airway for the victim, provide the two initial slow, full ventilations that might stimulate a return of spontaneous breathing, and then concentrate on moving the victim to the boat or shore for further care. On the other hand, in the water, the presence or absence of a pulse may be difficult to ascertain (cold water, gloves, etc.) and if the victim is not breathing, but does have heart activity, mouth-to-mask ventilation may be all that is required. Additionally, since pulses at the carotid artery are not generally palpable at very low blood pressures, there may still be circulation that simply cannot be felt.

20.4.4 Emergency Airway Management and Artificial Ventilation

It is most desirable to have the victim's airway maintenance supplemented by using an oropharyngeal airway, if, as a part of the life support provided, mouth-to-mask ventilation or ventilation utilizing a manually triggered, oxygen-powered positive pressure/demand valve is used.

If the victim is breathing, then a decision must be made whether the breathing is adequate, or if some supplemental ventilation is required, either using mouth-to-mask ventilation or an oxygen unit.

Most victims of serious illness or injury will be breathing relatively rapidly. In some cases, this is a positive finding, but if the victim is breathing too rapidly, there may not be enough air moving in and out of the lungs with each breath. In such cases, manage the breathing.

Using a watch, count the number of breaths the victim takes during 15 seconds and multiply by four, to determine the number of times the victim is breathing each minute. If the victim is breathing at a rate over 30 times per minute, observe the breathing for another minute and if the rate does not slow, provide mouth-to-mask ventilation and try to provide deep breaths into the victim at a rate of 12 per minute. If supplemental oxygen is available, it should be used.

If the victim is breathing at a rate of less than ten breaths per minute, then supplement the victim's breathing to the extent that the victim will have a total of not less than 12 breaths per minute, counting their own breathing and the supplemental breaths.

20.4.5 Circulatory Status Assessment and Management
20.4.5.1 Adult One-Rescuer CPR

Artificial ventilation is done by mouth-to-mouth resuscitation, or utilizing a supplemental device as described above, while artificial circulation is done by external cardiac massage. Together, they are called cardiopulmonary resuscitation (CPR). What has been described thus far as part of the scene safety assessment and intervention is, in fact, the initial phase of CPR.

Though the material presented here is quite thorough, every diver should complete a CPR course from a recognized training agency. Some of those include the American National Red Cross, American Heart Association, or National Safety Council First Aid Institute.

CPR, as discussed to this point, is aimed at supplying the victim's body with oxygen and ridding his body of excess carbon dioxide. The purpose of CPR may also include the establishment and maintenance of the victim's circulation until more advanced life support can be initiated, or until normal breathing and heart beat are restored. Once begun, CPR is continued until relieved by emergency medical services personnel, or until the rescuer is unable to continue.

For the sake of simplicity, this discussion deals exclusively with one-rescuer CPR. In the event that CPR is required for an extended period of time, other divers can continue one-rescuer CPR should the rescuer become overly fatigued. Instead of attempting to utilize a variety of CPR methods typically needed only by health care professionals, focus on performing optimal CPR, utilizing the one-rescuer method only and switching off as needed.

Immediately after delivering two rescue breaths, check the victim's pulse to determine if the heart is still beating. Do this by sliding two fingertips gently into the groove-like indentation between the trachea (windpipe) and the large muscle (sternocleidomastoid) running down the side of the victim's neck. If the heart is beating adequately, a pulse may be felt in a major artery found in this anatomic landmark—the carotid artery. Take five to ten seconds to detect the victim's pulse before going any further. The five to ten second delay serves two purposes. First, it may take a few seconds to discern a weak pulse. Second, if the victim's heart is beating extremely slowly, but still beating spontaneously, it may take that long to feel more than one pulse beat. This would be particularly true in cases of severe hypothermia and certain depressant drug overdose. If there is a pulse, then the victim's heart is still beating, and chest compressions are not needed. However, if the victim is still not breathing, then give the victim rescue breaths at a rate of one breath every five seconds (12 breaths per minute).

Recheck the pulse every few minutes to be certain the victim's heart is still beating. It is generally believed that, in an adult, the presence of a pulse in the carotid artery is consistent with a blood pressure adequate to keep the brain sufficiently perfused. In a sense, if a pulse is present, the victim has blood pressure sufficient to sustain life.

If no pulse is felt, then the victim's heart is probably not beating, or it is not beating adequately. Another possibility is that the victim's heart is not beating in an organized fashion and may require defibrillation. In any event, chest compressions are necessary. Initiate chest compressions along with mouth-to-mask resuscitation. Expose the victim's chest, if it is not already bared. Take two fingertips from the hand closest to the victim's feet and draw those finger tips along the lower border of the victim's rib cage, until they rest at the V-shaped bottom of the victim's sternum (breastbone) in the mid-line of the body. Those two finger tips are left in that position (on the xiphoid process, the lowest segment of the sternum). The heel of the other hand, which is closest to the victim's head, is placed on the sternum adjacent to the two fingers resting on the xiphoid process.

Now the hand closest to the victim's feet is placed on top of the hand already resting on the sternum. It helps to interlock your fingers to avoid putting pressure on the ribs. Compress the sternum at a rate of 80 to 100 strokes per minute. Each stroke should compress the chest at least 1 1/2 inch, but not more than 2 inches.

NOTE
During CPR, depths of compression are reduced for children and infants.

After compressing the victim's chest for 15 strokes, ventilate the victim two more times and then continue alternating 15 chest compressions with one ventilation. After four cycles of compressions and ventilations, recheck the pulse. If the pulse has returned, then stop chest compressions, but continue artificial ventilations as needed. If there has been no return of pulse, then the victim should be ventilated and chest compressions and artificial ventilation should continue in the same 15:2 ratio.

CPR is continued as above until the victim begins to breathe spontaneously, or the rescuer is too weak to continue, or is relieved by someone else who knows how to do cardiopulmonary resuscitation, or until the victim is placed in the care of emergency medical services personnel.

20.4.5.2 Early Defibrillation

It is now evident that CPR by itself may not be adequate to save lives in cardiac arrest. The 1992 National Conference on Cardiopulmonary Resuscitation (CPR) and Emergency Cardiac Care (ECC) concluded that there was the need for more widespread use of early defibrillation intervention. While basic CPR prolongs the life of the victim for a few minutes, most victims of sudden cardiac arrest will not ultimately survive unless there is further intervention.

Sudden death secondary to cardiac disease is a leading cause of death in the United States. Estimates are that if all the links in what is called the "chain of survival" are intact, upwards of 49 percent of all victims of sudden cardiac death might survive to discharge. This contrasts to rather dismal survival to discharge rates that occur at present in the United States with the system as it exists in most parts of the country. The critical links in the chain of survival include:

- Early recognition of the problem and mobilization of the EMS response
- Early CPR intervention
- Early defibrillation
- Early advanced cardiac life support

A diver trained in CPR can be instrumental in performing the key functions in the first three links in the chain (Guidelines 2000).

Certain heart rhythm abnormalities respond very favorably to the delivery of a direct current shock through the heart muscle. One of these rhythms is called ventricular fibrillation. When the heart is behaving in that manner, the heart simply quivers without any blood being pumped. According to the report of the committee mentioned above, "the majority of adults (80–90 percent) with sudden, non-traumatic, cardiac arrest are found to be in ventricular fibrillation when the initial electrocardiogram is obtained" (Guidelines 2000).

Most survivors of ventricular fibrillation receive early defibrillation. Survival dramatically falls if the first defibrillation effort is not delivered within eight to ten minutes of the initial arrest. The emphasis on early defibrillation is so great that the implication of the 1992 report is that, optimally, automated external defibrillators should be available to deal with sudden cardiac death.

The automated external defibrillator (AED) is a medical device that not only analyzes a victim's cardiac rhythm, but also guides the rescuer through the steps to deliver the potentially life-saving shock. Automated external defibrillators sold today are described as semi-automatic in their method of operation. The semi-automatic defibrillator analyzes the cardiac rhythm and determines if a shock is warranted. The shock cannot be delivered without some physical action by the rescuer. The material below, very briefly, shows the steps in the utilization of one such device. **As with most material in this section, it is important to recognize that the brief presentation here does not constitute training, but simply provides material to supplement appropriate training by the agencies previously cited.**

Automated defibrillators are remarkable devices in that they not only analyze cardiac rhythms, but also provide voice prompts to the caregiver. For example, some of the "spoken," computer-generated, commands that may be heard from the automated defibrilator's speaker include: "stand-clear," "analyzing," "charging," "press to shock," "check pulse," "start CPR," "stop CPR," "check victim," etc.

As in basic CPR described above, the victim is checked for responsiveness, breathing, and pulse. In the non-breathing and pulseless victim, insure that someone has activated the emergency medical services agencies and, at the same time, have someone bring the automatic defibrillator to the victim and place it beside the victim. If there is more than a momentary delay until the automated defibrillator is deployed, perform basic CPR and, if possible, the victim's breathing should be supported with supplemental oxygen.

The automated defibrillator, due to its sophisticated computer technology, is typically not the sort of device that a diver will purchase for himself. However, it has largely been established as a standard of care that should be present, along with adequate oxygen and oxygen delivery devices, on large boats, party boats, dive boats, research vessels, land-based research diving facilities, and live-aboard dive vessels.

20.5 STOPPING LIFE-THREATENING BLEEDING

Once the presence of a patent airway, breathing, and adequate circulation are assured, the last phase of the scene safety assessment/intervention is control of any visible, life-threatening, or severe bleeding.

It is unusual that any external bleeding will require care beyond direct pressure to the site of the bleeding and, if the injury is to an extremity, lifting it above the level of the heart. It is important, particularly when bleeding is present, to be especially cognizant of the infection risks and take the steps necessary for protection.

Remove the disposable gloves from their packaging and put gloves on before proceeding.

Provided there is time, a sterile dressing should be removed from its packaging in a manner that the sterility of the dressing is maintained to the maximum extent.

The sterile dressing should be firmly held against the wound with a gloved hand and, if the wound is in an extremity, the extremity should be lifted above the level of the victim's heart. The force of gravity working against the movement of blood will, in a small part, contribute to the slowing of the rate of bleeding.

If direct pressure with the dressing substantially slows, but does not entirely stop the bleeding, do not remove the dressing. Instead, apply another dressing on top of the blood-soaked dressing and continue this process until the soaking of the dressings subsides, or until it is determined that more aggressive methods must be employed to stop the bleeding.

If direct pressure and elevation, if applicable, do not significantly reduce the rate of the flow of blood, then it may be necessary to use alternative means to stop the bleeding. If the uncontrolled bleeding is in the upper arm, pressure should be applied to the brachial artery, found on the inside of the upper arm. Apply pressure where there is a pulse.

This will compress the artery against the bone of the upper arm.

The pressure point to use for bleeding in the leg is the femoral artery. Feel along the crease in the groin on the inside of the upper leg to find a pulse. Use the heel of one hand to compress the artery against the bone.

A tourniquet is the absolute last resort in an effort to control bleeding from an extremity. The "litmus test" applied to the use of the tourniquet should be that the risk of the loss of a portion of the limb is an appropriate trade-off for the stopping of the bleeding that cannot be stopped by any other means. In a situation where there are many victims in need of care and some of those victims have severe extremity bleeding, the tourniquet can be utilized as a stop-gap measure when victims vastly outnumber care-givers. Tourniquets used in such a setting will likely be replaced with direct pressure and/or pressure points when the number of caregivers become sufficient to provide one caregiver per victim.

A three to four inch band of cloth makes a good tourniquet. This is usually a triangular bandage folded into what is known as a cravat. The cravat should be placed between the victim's heart and the wound, about one inch above the wound. The cravat is wrapped around the extremity and an over-hand knot is tied in the cravat to hold it in place (see Figure 20.1).

A stout stick is needed, or on a boat, a wrench is usually readily available, at least six inches in length. Place it over the overhand knot and then tie it in place with a square knot. Twist the stick in circles until the bleeding stops. Once the bleeding has stopped, take another cravat and use it to tie the stick in place.

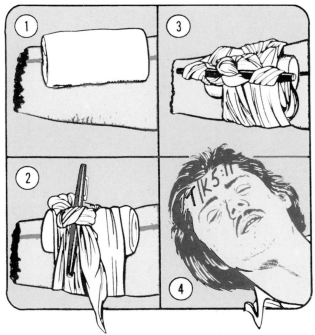

FIGURE 20.1
Application of a Tourniquet

Remember, the tourniquet is truly a last-ditch effort to stop bleeding that cannot be stopped by direct pressure, elevation, or the use of pressure points. Be certain that the direct pressure and elevation method or pressure on an arterial pressure point have been given adequate time before making the decision to apply a tourniquet.

If the tourniquet is used as other than a short-term, stop-gap measure, take a marking device of some kind and write the initials "TK" on the victim's forehead as well as the time the tourniquet was applied. Finally, in preparing the victim for transport, never allow the tourniquet to be covered since it may be missed or accidentally dislodged. Keeping the tourniquet in sight will make all those involved in the care or handling of the victim aware of the tourniquet's presence.

20.6 USE OF SUPPLEMENTAL OXYGEN

With the knowledge available today relative to the need for oxygen in the ill or injured victim, especially for diving accident victims, it is absolutely mandatory to have adequate supplemental medical oxygen supplies present at all diving operations.

One of the most effective oxygen systems providing high concentrations of oxygen to the victim is a positive pressure/demand valve. The essentials of this type of system will be easy for the scuba diver to identify with since the parts have very similar parallels in diving.

The oxygen cylinder for most portable systems is the aluminum or steel D, aluminum Jumbo D, or aluminum or steel E size. Like the scuba cylinder, this is the source of the gas to deliver to the victim, but unlike the scuba cylinder, these cylinders contain pure oxygen. At the top of the cylinder, there is either a handle or wrench-operated metal stem for turning the cylinder supply on and off. The essential information for each of these popular portable oxygen cylinders for both steel and aluminum cylinders is listed in Table 20.1.

In order to select the appropriate system for the setting in which the oxygen may be utilized, determine the maximum time that oxygen might be required under the worst of circumstances. For example, if activities might take the vessel as far as 30 minutes from the dock, assume that an emergency might require 15 to 20 minutes of oxygen prior to getting under way. Next, assume there might be an additional delay of 15 minutes awaiting emergency medical service's arrival at the dock. So, at the outside, the caregiver will need a 65-minute supply. Two D cylinders would probably be adequate for this situation, but a third cylinder might be a good idea.

The oxygen delivery system has a regulator that is similar to the first stage of the scuba system. This regulator reduces the pressure of the oxygen from cylinder pressures to a usable pressure of approximately 50 lbs. per square inch (psi). Also included on the better regulators

TABLE 20.1
A Comparison of Oxygen
Storage Cylinders Commonly in Use

Cylinder Type	Fill Pressure (psi)	Capacity in Liters	Duration at 15 Liters per Minute
Aluminum D	2015	424.7	Approx. 28 min.
Steel D	2015	410.4	Approx. 27 min.
Jumbo D	2216	648.3	Approx. 43 min.
Aluminum E	2015	679.4	Approx. 45 min.
Steel E	2015	682.0	Approx. 45 min.

is a gauge indicating the remaining oxygen in the cylinder in psi. The outlets on the regulator are one or two DISS (threaded, high-pressure) outlets and, typically, a nipple-type outlet. The nipple outlet is used to deliver oxygen using supply tubing and a face mask or nasal cannula (These methods of delivery will not be dealt with since a simpler approach is available). With the device described below and this type of regulator, the only thing to do in order to be ready to administer oxygen to a victim is turn on the cylinder valve.

Manually triggered, oxygen-powered positive pressure/demand valve delivery systems are used by the NOAA diving program. It may be used with a breathing victim who can initiate a flow of oxygen by simply inhaling through a well-sealed mask (demand mode). Or, can be used in non-breathing victims by applying pressure to the appropriate button on the valve itself while maintaining an adequate mask seal (manually triggered mode).

In a breathing victim, oxygen administration with the demand valve is as simple as turning the cylinder valve on and allowing the victim to hold the mask. The victim needs to hold the mask firmly to his face and be reassured that each time he inhales, oxygen will be delivered. In a spontaneously breathing person, there is no other action required in order for the victim to get oxygen. All that has to be done is for the mask seal to be maintained. In the same vein, there is no reason for the victim to remove the mask from the face to exhale, since there is a valve system within the device to permit exhalation.

It is important to monitor the victim to be sure that he is maintaining a good seal on the mask and that oxygen is flowing with each inhalation. It is also important to monitor the remaining oxygen in the cylinder and change cylinders as needed.

If the victim is conscious and breathing, but too unstable to manage the mask himself, then the caregiver should hold the mask in place. It is most important to maintain the mask seal so that oxygen will flow each time the victim inhales.

In the same manner as described above, constantly monitor the oxygen supply in order to be prepared to change the oxygen cylinder with little delay, if it should become necessary.

As mentioned, a combination positive pressure/demand valve delivery system is the preferred system for ventilating an unresponsive and non-breathing victim. The first step is to turn on the oxygen supply at the cylinder. That will immediately provide a supply of oxygen to the positive-pressure/demand valve. At the same time, if help is available, another caregiver may be able to maintain the airway and provide assistance.

Next, properly adjust the mask to fit the victim, insuring that mask seal is adequate and minimizing the risk of leaks. With the type of mask discussed previously, mask seal is fairly easy to maintain. If a more typical oro-nasal mask is used, similar to the mask normally supplied with an oxygen unit, then establishing and maintaining the mask seal may be more difficult. In addition, with the oro-nasal mask, it might be necessary to maintain the mask seal while a second caregiver performs the ventilations.

Using the same hand position on the mask as described under mouth-to-mask ventilation, the mask seal is maintained by the rescuer with one hand. With his other hand, oxygen is released into the victim's lungs. Due to the high pressures and volumes that can be delivered by the positive-pressure/demand valve, there is a technique that will enable the rescuer to give the victim just the right amount of oxygen. With the thumb just at the edge of the button that initiates the oxygen flow, gently roll the thumb up onto that button. This will cause a slow release of oxygen through the valve. As soon as the victim's chest rises in response to the flowing oxygen, thumb pressure is released from the button and the victim exhales passively. Done properly, even with the substantial oxygen flow potential through the demand valve, the ventilations can be delivered over the desired one to two seconds with the victim being able to exhale passively after each ventilation. There is no need to remove the mask in order for the victim to exhale, since there is a valve system built into the demand valve to allow for exhalation.

The frequency of ventilations and the cycle of ventilations to compressions remains the same using the positive pressure/demand valve as it would be if mouth-to-mask resuscitation were employed. The significant advantage is that instead of delivering a FiO_2 (fraction of inspired oxygen) of $0.16-0.21$ ($16-21\%$ oxygen concentration), it is likely that the rescuer will be delivering a FiO_2 of 1.00 (100% oxygen). This is beneficial for any trauma or medical victim, but is especially helpful when dealing with a diving emergency where excess nitrogen is the culprit and the objective is to adjust partial pressures of gases in the victim's circulating blood and tissues.

Using oxygen-delivery equipment requires two very important components—familiarity with the equipment and competence in using it. During an emergency, when oxygen is needed most desperately, is not the time to learn to use the equipment. In addition to receiving training in how the equipment is assembled, how to change the oxygen cylinder, and how to trouble shoot problems, it is important to have adequate experience ventilating a mannequin so that the process will be natural in time of crisis. Like scuba diving, providing emergency care requires proper training and practice to maintain one's level of competence.

20.7 A COMPLETE VICTIM ASSESSMENT — THE SECONDARY SURVEY

20.7.1 The Head-To-Toe Examination

The secondary survey is initiated after completing primary victim care—having identified and managed those problems which might be life threatening.

In the process of this further evaluation, a rescuer reevaluates the victim to be certain that no potentially life-threatening problems were missed during primary victim care. He is also identifying those problems that may not be life threatening, but should be managed, or at the very least, noted at the conclusion of the secondary survey. During this integrated process, he will also interview the victim to learn any significant facts regarding the victim's medical history and exactly what brought on the problem.

For a victim suffering an illness, the secondary survey may take on a little different pattern than for the victim suffering from injury (trauma). The trauma victim truly requires a complete head-to-toe check, as described in detail below.

In illness emergency surveys, a rescuer will generally focus on those parts of the body about which the victim is complaining. In order not to confuse the issue, this discussion will explain the secondary survey as it relates to a trauma victim. To use these techniques on a illness victim, simply use those procedures described below that would apply to the part of the body about which the victim is complaining. In both injury and illness, the medical history interview that is described in the next section is essentially the same.

Eyes and hands are the tools every rescuer will need to conduct a secondary survey. Visualization and recognition of abnormalities, as well as touching the victim, are the major methods used by every caregiver, including physicians.

The secondary survey is performed from head to toe. Particularly in the case of a trauma victim, it is necessary to remove unnecessary body covering so that the victim's body surfaces can be seen and touched. In all cases, this is done with discretion and concern for the victim's emotional, as well as physical, welfare. If it is necessary to remove a woman's clothing, for example, be careful to cover her breasts with a sheet or towel in the interest of modesty. The same sensitivity applies when the genital area of either sex is exposed.

If a wet suit must be removed, start by cutting at the neck of the suit down the sleeve. Removal of coverings to expose the victim begins at the upper body since there is greater risk to the victim from injuries to the neck, chest, and abdomen than from injuries to the lower extremities. As much as possible cut apparel at or near the seams so that the wet suit or garment may possibly be repaired later. However, never jeopardize the victim for the sake of a garment. As garments are removed, constantly scan the victim's exposed body for signs of injury.

Rather than exposing a little of the victim and assessing, it will keep the process more organized and less likely to miss something important to expose the victim all at once. Then return to the victim's head to begin the thorough head-to-toe evaluation.

Remember, by this point, primary victim care has been completed and the rescuer can be relatively confident that all obvious life-threatening injuries have been identified and treated.

Taking precautions against the risk of infection, begin the secondary assessment of the victim by gently palpating (feeling) the victim's scalp and noting any deformities or places where fluid that may be blood is present. External bleeding hidden by the hair will be evident from the appearance of blood on the gloved fingers. Note any reaction the victim may have to being touched that appears to indicate feeling pain. Examine the ears for any bleeding or discharge.

Next, slide both hands to the back of the victim's neck to feel if there are any noticeable deformities and any indication that pain is present. If, during the scene safety assessment, it appears that an injury mechanism may have caused injury to the spine, or if neck pain response is elicited, stabilize the neck. Enlist the assistance of another caregiver or a bystander to hold the victim's head in a neutral position. Additionally, if the victim is conscious and oriented, caution the victim that it is important that no head movement take place since it might lead to further injury.

Take a hand and shade one of the victim's eyes. While doing so, watch the pupil (black, central portion of the eye) to observe if it dilated (got larger) while it was shaded. If it did not, it may indicate some serious problems either to the eye itself or the brain. When the hand shading the eye is removed, the pupil should constrict (get smaller). This procedure should be repeated with the other eye. Again, failure to react in this fashion is a sign of trouble—make a note of it.

Move the fingers down to the prominent bones under the eyes and press gently. Feel for deformity and watch the victim for a response to pain when these bones are pressed. While doing this segment of the assessment, also examine the nostrils for the discharge of blood-like fluid. Do one side of the victim's face and then the other, so as to specifically identify an area where an injury has occurred.

The victim's mouth should be opened either voluntarily or by the rescuer. Note any pain when the victim's mouth is opened and examine inside the mouth for any debris, broken teeth, blood clots, etc. If any loose or foreign matter is noticed, carefully remove it with your fingers. Be careful not to push such material deeper into the victim's airway, and don't reach too far back into the victim's throat to remove the object, or vomiting may be stimulated.

Examine the front portion of the neck visually for open wounds or signs of injury, such as abrasions or discoloration. The entire neck should be gently palpated with the finger tips, particularly in diving accidents. If little "blister pack" like bubbles are felt under the skin or noises that sound like Rice Krispies® are heard when pressing on the tissues, it probably indicates the presence of subcutaneous emphysema. This indicates the presence of free air bubbles under the skin and is usually found in severe lung injuries where air has actually escaped from the lungs and chest cavity and has migrated under the skin to the neck region.

A visual scan of the skin over the collarbone (clavicle) is performed to identify injuries or discoloration, usually bruising, consistent with injury. Use fingers to press gently along the length of each collarbone, the most commonly fractured bone in the body. By doing these bones and others separately rather that using both hands and doing them simultaneously, the rescuer only has to elicit a painful response from the victim once, since it is evident when palpating a victim unilaterally which side the injury is on. If both bones are palpated at the same time and the victim is not completely lucid, a painful response may be difficult to isolate relative to location without repeating the stimulation that caused pain.

Re-examine the chest. Remember that it was visually scanned at the time the garments were removed. If any open wounds are noted that look like they are through the chest wall or are bubbling, have someone place a gloved hand over the wound to prevent further passage of air in and out. Later, after the examination is complete, the bystander's hand can be replaced with some form of dressing which will prevent air from entering the chest. The Asherman Chest Seal®, developed by a U.S. Navy Seal, is a device specifically designed for rapid treatment of such chest injuries.

Use one hand to stabilize the chest on the side opposite the section of the chest that will be palpated. Use fingers to feel for each rib that can be palpated. On finding a rib, pressure should be applied and the rib evaluated for stability—does it feel loose or are there pieces of a broken rib rubbing against neighboring, damaged bone? This process is repeated for every rib that can be felt, and then is done in exactly the same fashion on the other side. In addition to feeling for lack of stability as described above, also watch for a painful response from the victim.

Imagine that there are two lines drawn on the front of the victim's body. One of these lines goes from the chin down to the victim's crotch through the belly button and the other imaginary line goes perpendicular to the first through the belly button. These two imaginary lines subdivide the

victim's abdomen into four quadrants. First visually scan the abdomen for signs of injury, and then palpate each of these four quadrants separately, noting if it is hard, is stiffened by the victim when pressed upon, or causes a painful response from the victim when pressed on. Each quadrant of the abdomen is palpated separately. Mentally note the findings. Other than managing any open wounds found on the abdomen, the rescuers only role in this phase of the assessment is to identify anything abnormal.

When reporting the findings to emergency medical services personnel, describe in which of the four areas of the abdomen the findings were present. Going back to the imaginary lines from above, the abdomen is separated into four quadrants described as the right upper quadrant (RUQ), left upper quadrant (LUQ), right lower quadrant (RLQ), and left lower quadrant (LLQ). Left and right in this regard, as in all other descriptions relative to left and right on a victim, refer to the victim's right and left. Though it will not do anything different to a victim knowing what may be injured or ailing in a particular quadrant, it may be of interest to know the major abdominal organs found in each of the four quadrants. The major organs of the RUQ are the liver and the gall bladder. The LUQ contains the stomach and the spleen. Small intestines and the appendix are found in the RLQ and the large intestine is the major structure in the LLQ. The urinary bladder is located in the middle of the bottom of the abdomen as is a woman's uterus. The female reproductive organs, the ovaries are found in both the RLQ and the LLQ.

Now place both palms on the "wings" of the pelvis (anatomically described as the superior iliac crests). With hands in this position, push them toward each other and "squeeze" the pelvis toward the middle of the victim's body, noting any feeling of instability or any painful response.

If the above evaluation did not elicit any response from the victim, shift position slightly so that your body is over the victim's pelvis, and shift hand position slightly. With the hands in this position, apply body weight on both sides of the pelvis simultaneously, as though trying to push the victim's pelvis into the ground. Again, try to note any instability of the pelvis and any painful response on the part of the victim.

Visually examine each leg, looking for any obvious deformity of the legs and joints, unevenness in size indicating swelling, open wounds, abrasions, or bruising. With both hands, palpate the entire length of each leg separately. This palpation should be fairly deep since the objective is to feel for the bones underneath, or at least press deeply enough to stimulate a painful response to pressure from the victim, if injury is present.

Having completed the visual and manual evaluation of each leg, use one hand to stabilize the bottom of the leg and, if the victim is conscious, ask the victim to wiggle their toes on the leg being held. Then stroke the foot with fingertips and ask the victim if that touch was felt. This procedure is then repeated on the opposite leg. This method is how to determine if the nerves to the leg are functioning properly from a sensory standpoint, and whether or not the victim is capable of voluntarily moving the lower extremities, also a nerve-involved assessment step.

Now evaluate the victim's arms. As with all other parts of the body, the first step is to visually scan the arms for obvious deformities or injuries. Next, in a fashion similar to the procedure used with the legs, the bones of the arms are palpated, checking one arm at a time.

Finally, the arm is stabilized with one hand in a fashion similar to the procedure described with the leg above. Ask the victim to wiggle the fingers first and then stroke the hand with their fingers and ask the victim if the touch can be felt. This procedure is performed on both arms. Similar to the steps used for the legs, this procedure determines if the nerve pathways to and from the arms are intact.

When reaching the victim's wrist, feel for the presence of a radial pulse. This pulse is found on the under side of the arm at the same side of the wrist where the thumb is on the hand. If a pulse is present, it is a pretty good sign that the victim's blood pressure is probably not dangerously low. If a watch is available, count the pulse beats in 15 seconds. Taking that number and multiplying by four will yield the victim's heart rate for one minute. If mentally multiplying times four is not simple enough, count the pulses for 30 seconds and double the result. If no pulse is felt at the wrist on either arm, the rescuer needs to consider the possibility that the victim is very ill due to what is called shock. If that is the case, oxygen needs to be administered as soon as possible, as well as measures taken to conserve the victim's body heat.

If there are no injuries to the lower extremities, it may be appropriate to elevate the lower extremities. This allows gravity to assist with the shifting of some of the victim's blood from the legs to the body core. If the victim complains of increased discomfort in the head or the victim finds it more difficult to breathe with the legs in this position, then the victim should be maintained in a flat position.

In this section an attempt has been made to concentrate on recognition and management of problems, but it is necessary to briefly examine the concept of shock. The technical definition of shock is inadequate tissue perfusion. This means that the circulatory system is incapable of delivering adequate oxygen and nutrients to the tissues, most significantly the vital organs. At the same time, potentially toxic by-products of the body's metabolism are no longer being removed adequately. The grave results of this process, without appropriate recognition and intervention, may be death to tissues, organs, or in the most extreme cases, the victim. The simplest means of identifying impending or present shock is usually the appearance of the victim or a drop in blood pressure.

The body's natural defenses against shock will cause the victim to appear pale and feel cool to the touch. At the same time, the victim's skin surface will usually be extremely moist (often described as clammy). Without further understanding of the complex details of shock, rescuers need to recognize that a victim who is pale, cool, clammy, and has either a weak or absent pulse at the wrist may be in very grave condition. This victim needs immediate aggressive care which, for the most part, is beyond the scope of the basic caregiver. The principal steps to take may include:

- Keeping the victim lying down
- Preventing the loss of body heat, and in the diving environment, making sure the victim is dry to limit evaporative heat loss
- Administering oxygen to the victim as soon as these signs of shock are recognized or before

In these situations, the pulse should be felt at the neck in the same fashion used during primary victim care and the heart rate determined by counting those pulses for 15 or 30 seconds and multiplying as described above.

Now, gently place a palm on the victim's chest and count the number of inhalations in 15 or 30 seconds. Multiplying in the same way as with the pulse, the victim's breathing rate has now been assessed.

The last step in the secondary assessment or survey is to record the findings. In the diving environment, a dive slate is probably the most convenient device on which to record the information and is impervious to water, so the notes won't disintegrate if they get wet or the ink won't smear as might happen if pen and paper are utilized.

The information is recorded from head to toe with all injuries noted. The presence or absence of moving and feeling in the four limbs is recorded. Finally, the presence or absence of a radial pulse is noted, along with the heart rate and breathing rate. Also, in this part of the note taking process, record observations relative to "what happened" to cause the victim's condition.

20.7.2 Taking the Necessary History

Aside from the immediate medical or injury problems (medically referred to as acute conditions), it is also important for all medical caregivers to know something about the victim's medical history that might have some relevance to the current problem. If, during the secondary survey, problems have been identified that require treatment quickly, then the performing of the medical history interview can be delayed until those conditions are cared for.

Some examples of problems that might need immediate attention include:

- The victim's airway or breathing deteriorating
- Recognition that the victim's overall condition is failing, consistent with shock
- Wounds that need to have bleeding stopped and dressings applied

- Injuries to the bones or joints that need to be splinted
- Diving illnesses that need the immediate administration of oxygen
- Painful marine life injuries that need immediate treatment in order to relieve significant victim discomfort

Otherwise, the victim history-taking interview should follow immediately after recording the findings from the primary and secondary assessments.

First explain to the victim that it is important to learn something about his medical history so that those who will be caring for him will know about everything that is important in making treatment decisions for them.

Use a very simple grouping of letters, called a mnemonic, to easily learn the necessary components of the complete medical history interview.

The mnemonic in this case is A-M-P-L-E. In the dictionary ample is defined as meaning abundant, sufficient, or adequate. Remember that as a caregiver it is important to take an AMPLE medical history! Each of the letters in the word represents a component of the victim's medical history:

A - Allergies
M - Medications
P - Past illnesses or injuries, past medical history
L - Last meal or last oral intake
E - Events leading up to the injury or illness

Allergies are important as some acute allergic reactions, called anaphylactic responses, may trigger breathing difficulties and may also lead to the victim slipping into a severe shock state. Sometimes, people have such reactions from the consumption of certain seafood. At other times, stinging insects may precipitate allergic reactions in people. In the marine setting, though quite rare, true anaphylactic reactions have been observed after a victim has sustained a marine life sting. If the victim does have an allergic history from bites and stings or past allergic reactions to certain foods, it is important to monitor his condition closely. Be on the alert for breathing difficulties or severe deterioration of the victim, since this may be the early signs of a major crisis.

A rescuer is not expected to know what certain medications do when he hears the names of the medications, but victims can usually tell why they may be taking certain medications. If a victim says he is taking "water" or "pressure" pills he may very well have a history of heart or high blood pressure problems which may have caused the present medical emergency. If the victim takes "sugar" pills or medication for "sugar" they are probably diabetic. People with seizure disorders, typically epilepsy, take medications such as Dilantin®, Tegretol®, or phenobarbital. A more extensive discussion of medications is unnecessary for the basic caregiver, but any time a victim is taking prescription medications it may indicate that there is a disease process which caused the victim's difficulty or contributed to it. Divers who have trouble clearing their ears while diving sometimes use decongestants. These medications have a finite effect, and if they wear off while a victim was diving "rebound effect," they may have precipitated a diving-related injury.

When discussing past illnesses with a victim, concentrate on major illnesses that might cause or contribute to a victim's difficulties or precipitate a victim becoming unstable enough to sustain injury. In the diving and marine environment, the illnesses that may lead to serious problems include heart disease, respiratory diseases including asthma, high blood pressure (hypertension), diabetes, and seizure disorders.

What a victim has ingested orally may be a cause of a victim's difficulty. In the marine setting, ingestion of certain marine life can lead to various illnesses. Dehydration has been implicated as a contributing factor to diving injuries. Question a diving injury victim relative to adequate non-alcoholic fluid intake during the prior 24 hours. Alcohol or other drugs of abuse may be contributors to a victim's injuries. Query the victim relative to the use of alcohol or drugs during the period of time coincident with the injury or illness. Low blood sugar (hypoglycemia) may be a cause of instability in both diabetics and non-diabetics alike. Determine whether the victim has eaten within a reasonable period of time prior to the illness or injury. Basically, any information relative to any ingestion that may have contributed to the problem should be noted and reported to the medical care professionals who assume the victim's care.

Perhaps the most significant part of the medical history interview has to do with the events which led up to the injury or illness. In the simplest terms, this is the "what happened" part of the interview. In diving accidents, it is important to learn the dive profile. If the victim's buddy had the same profile, prudence would suggest that the buddy should be evaluated at the same medical facility as the victim. Also, the victim's dive equipment should be brought together in one place and transported with the victim for evaluation at a later date. In the case of non-diving-related trauma, it is significant to ask the victim if everything was normal before the injury. What to discover here is whether the injury was purely an accident, or if there was some medical problem that precipitated the victim hurting himself. In the case of injuries, it may be useful to learn what caused the accident resulting in the trauma in order to prevent future similar accidents. As much as possible, record in the victim's own words what took place before an accident. If the problem is medical, have the victim describe what was taking place before the symptoms of the problem were first noticed. Specifically, what activity was the victim involved with? Was the victim at rest or performing some specific strenuous activity? What had the victim been doing for the hours immediately preceding the onset of illness? Did the victim notice any unusual feelings during those hours that were not quite normal, but didn't seem like they were too severe?

As a final part of the medical history-taking interview, have the victim describe his symptoms. In the victim's own words, if pain is present, what does it feel like? Does anything make the pain worse or better? How long has the pain been present and has its intensity changed during that period? Does the pain remain in one place or does it seem to radiate to other parts of the body?

All information learned during this part of the interview should be recorded in the same fashion as the findings during the primary and secondary assessment and subsequently related to medical care personnel who assume responsibility for the victim.

20.8 ELECTROCUTION

Electrocution may result from the careless handling, poor design, or poor maintenance of power equipment, such as welding and cutting equipment, or electric underwater lights. All electrical equipment used under water should be well insulated. In addition, divers should be properly insulated from any possible source of electrical current. Another source of electrocution and electrical burns is lightning.

Prevention of electrocution from lightning is simply a matter of divers not permitting themselves to remain out in the open, particularly on a boat, when there is obviously the threat of lightning from thunderstorms. When seeking shelter from storms, it is important to avoid those places and structures where one might reasonably expect lightning to strike (i.e., under trees or in structures that stand alone in an open area).

When leaving the water to enter a boat or habitat, divers should not carry a connected light or electric tool. Victims may not be able to separate themselves from the source of the shock. Before intervening, the rescuer must first be certain that he too is not being exposed to an electrocution hazard. When attempting to separate the electrocution victim from the source of the electricity, make certain that a non-conducting material is used to effect the separation. Non-metallic poles, long pieces of dry lumber, or wooden oars are objects that might be found in the diving environment suitable for separating the victim from an electrical source. If an electrical extension cord is involved, it might be most effective to find the plug and disconnect the cord.

Signs and Symptoms:
- Unconsciousness
- Seizures
- Cardiopulmonary arrest
- Burns—though electrical burns rarely appear as severe as the real tissue damage that has occurred

The victim, if unresponsive after being separated from the electrical source, must have a scene safety assessment performed and may likely require CPR. Since many electrocutions place the victim into ventricular fibrillation, rapid deployment of the semi-automatic defibrillator is a prudent action. Even if an electrocution victim seems to be normal after the event, they must be evaluated at a medical care institution. Potentially lethal side effects of electrical injury include heart dysrhythmias, kidney abnormalities and failure, and methemoglobinemia, a severe and life-threatening condition that is precipitated by the unseen breakdown of tissues following serious injury.

20.9 WOUNDS

Open wounds, most often lacerations, are frequently encountered in the marine environment. The primary concern is to stop the bleeding and to prevent any further contamination of the wound.

Since blood will undoubtedly be present, caregivers must don disposable gloves for protection. Dressing packages should be opened in a manner that will minimize contamination of the dressing. Carefully examine any package for visual cues how to effectively remove the dressing or bandage from the package.

The dressing is placed over the victim's wound and pressure is applied until all bleeding has stopped. Bleeding extremities are also elevated while direct pressure is applied. Both pressure and gravity are used to slow bleeding. If the bleeding continues and soaks through the first dressing applied, simply apply an additional dressing on top of the first. This process of adding dressings continues until the bleeding stops with blood-soaked dressings remaining in place.

With the bleeding stopped, apply a self-conforming bandage to hold the dressing in place. The first step in this process is to utilize some technique to keep the bandage from "spinning" around the victim's arm as it is applied. By wrapping one corner of the end of the bandage and "locking" it under the first wrap of the bandage, the conforming bandage can be stabilized on any body part.

Most bandaging techniques employ the open-spiral/closed-spiral technique. The open spiral is simply wrapping the bandage so that the dressing held in place but is not overlapped sequentially. That will be executed during the closed-spiral phase. When holding a roll of conforming bandage, it is held in such a way that the additional material is released from "under" the bandage roll rather than from the "top." This method makes it a bit easier to maintain appropriate tension on the bandage as well as make it less likely that the bandage will "get away."

After securing the dressing in place with the open spiral, wrap the bandage in the opposite direction utilizing the closed spiral technique. In this wrapping of the bandage, each wrap overlaps the previous wrap so that the dressing is completely covered by the bandage.

When applying a bandage to a victim, several options are available at the end of the procedure to secure the bandage in place. Tape the bandage in place. The bandage may be split along its length with an overhand knot tied in the resulting "tails" and these tail pieces being used to tie the bandage in place by encircling the extremity and tying a square knot in the opposite tails. Finally, one of the fastest techniques extends a large loop of the bandaging material away from the extremity at the end of the bandaging process. A loop is taken over a finger and the bandage is taken back in the opposite direction. The result is the loop ends up on one side of the extremity and the balance of the conforming bandaging material in the hand on the opposite side of the extremity. Bringing the opposing ends together, an overhand knot is first tied in the bandage, and this is then made into a square knot by making a second tic. Be certain that the knot is not made so tight that the circulation is impaired. A finger should fit under the tied part of the bandage without too much effort.

After the bandage is tied, trim excess bandaging material from the ends so that these pieces will not become entangled in anything and compromise the management of the victim. With the dressing tied in place by the bandaging method chosen, periodically touch the victim's hand or foot, depending upon the extremity bandaged, to make sure it is remaining as warm as the opposite extremity. If it is not, then there is a possibility that the bandage has impaired the victim's circulation or swelling has caused such impairment. The bandage should be untied and re-tied more loosely.

If treating smaller wounds and unable to get the victim to medical assistance immediately, the small wounds may be washed with soap and water and then dressed in the same manner as above. The only difference is that there will not be any substantial bleeding that needs to be stopped.

20.10 BURNS

When one is exposed to boats, there are many sources of heat that may cause burns. Manifolds, stuffing boxes, generators, compressors, and gas or alcohol stoves are just a few of the heat sources that may cause such burns.

Burns can be particularly insidious injuries leading to infection, severe scarring, and partial disability of the burned area.

There are three generally accepted classifications of burns with which you should have some familiarity.

Superficial: Classified as a burn only involving the epidermis. Often referred to as superficial burns, they redden the skin but initially cause no other damage. Treat such burns by immersing the effected body part in cool water. The objective is to reduce the temperature of the affected tissues to limit the damage and reduce the victim's discomfort. If on board a boat and looking for some immediate relief for minor burns, Burn Gel® or other similar products can be used. This is a gel material that may be spread on minor burns, but most significantly, it contains 2% Lidocaine HCl, a topical anesthetic.

Partial Thickness: Classified as a burn involving the epidermis and the dermis, but not penetrating the dermis. Sometimes called partial thickness burns, they are more severe than first degree burns as there is more extensive tissue damage. Blistering is a strong indication of a second degree burn. For small burns of this classification, the same type of treatment as for first degree burns may be initially utilized. This should be followed with the application of sterile dressings or specialized burn dressings, discussed below. Though blisters may not be attractive, care should be taken to keep the blisters intact since they are a natural "bandage" covering injured tissue below.

Full Thickness: Classified as a full thickness burn with all layers of the skin receiving damage. While they are sometimes confused with second degree burns, a strong indicator are areas that are dry and white or even charred black. The patient may complain of severe pain or no pain at all, which indicates severe nerve damage (although there will usually be pain around the periphery of the third degree burn). Third degree burns may involve permanent nerve damage, respiratory arrest, and other major complications and victims should be transported immediately to a medical facility.

There has been a tendency among first-aid providers over the years to want to put something on burns. A very simple rule is DON'T! First, most topical substances that are commonly used do nothing to enhance healing. Second, most are suspended in material which has limited bacteriostatic strength, but can provide an excellent "glue" for particulate matter that may come into contact with the victim. Finally, since all serious burns should be assessed medically, these substances will have to be removed anyway so that the burn may be appropriately evaluated and treated.

All but the most minor superficial burns should be evaluated at a hospital emergency department. In addition, there are several types of burn situations that need to be treated in hospitals designated as burn centers. Local emergency medical services personnel should be aware which facilities are designated burn centers. If there is any doubt, the victim should be transported to the nearest trauma center. Those burn injuries which require such special attention include:

- Partial thickness burns covering more than 15% of body surface area
- Full thickness burns covering more than 5% of body surface area
- Any significant burns involving the hands, face, feet, or genital area
- Any high-voltage electrical burns
- Any inhalation or airway burns
- Any chemical burns from chemicals that may continue to destroy tissues
- Any burns which occurred with associated significant other injuries

Reference to the percentage of the body surface area burned is made above and there are several methods for making such determinations. However, the simplest procedure is a method of estimation based on the surface area of the victim's palm. As a rough estimating tool, each "palm" is equal to 1% of the victim's body surface. Visually estimate the surface area of the victim's palm and then make an estimate how many of those palm surface areas would cover the area injured by burn. So, if the estimate is that ten of the victim's palms might cover the burned area, that would equal a 10% burn.

20.11 FRACTURES AND SPRAINS

"Slip and fall" injuries are a problem, particularly when wet boat decks come into play. Detailed diagnosis of bone and joint injuries typically are left to trained medical personnel. All a rescuer really needs to do is to recognize that there has been an injury that may involve the bones and joints.

If a victim has suffered a falling or twisting injury and complains of severe pain in a bone or joint, the initial presumption should be that injury has taken place. Swelling and discoloration may confirm such injuries. Injuries like this need to be evaluated by a physician, preferably in a hospital emergency room, and should be x-rayed to determine the severity of injury. Even if there is no fracture present, there may be significant injury to the tissues surrounding a joint and the injury needs to be managed as a fracture.

Principles of bone and joint injury management are universal in that the primary objective is to immobilize the bones and joints immediately above and immediately below the site of the injury. If a long bone is involved, the bones and joints both above and below the possibly injured bone should be immobilized.

The ankle is a commonly injured joint in the marine environment and management can take advantage of some available materials. For an injured ankle, one may use a wet suit, blanket, or two large beach towels for splinting.

The folded wet suit (or alternate materials mentioned) is pulled up the victim's leg to be certain that the area covered is adequate to immobilize the ankle. The cravat (triangular bandages) is first brought under the victim's foot that has been wrapped in the folded wet suit. In larger victims, two cravats may have to be tied together to have sufficient length for application of the bandage. Take the long ends and cross them behind the victim's leg then bring the ends around and across the victim's instep. The "tails" are now slipped through the material originally taken behind the victim's leg. With the long ends pulled through the "stirrups" formed by the material and with steady upward pressure, the ankle and foot are secured with the cravat and wet suit material. The ends of the cravats are tied off on top of the victim's foot.

Though not as rigid as a cast, this method immobilizes an injured ankle adequately and will enable the victim to be moved from the boat or beach with limited additional risk of further injury.

The forearm bones are commonly fractured either by falls or having heavy objects falling upon them. Managing such an injury ideally requires the assistance of a bystander or another caregiver during the initial stages so that any additional movement of the injured extremity is minimized.

The victim's upper arm, elbow, wrist, and hand are stabilized manually first. Due to the interconnections between the hand and the arm, it is important to be certain that the hand is immobilized. This will prevent unnecessary pain and further injury to the victim. The hand should be immobilized in what is described as the position of function. One of the simplest methods of doing this is by placing a roll of self-conforming bandage gently into the victim's grip while the support of the arm is manually maintained.

Another caregiver or bystander can manage the manual support of the injured extremity while the rescuer shapes a SAM splint to the victim's arm. The SAM splint was developed by an orthopedic surgeon (Sam Scheinberg) and is an ideal device for the marine environment, since it is essentially impervious to the environment, light in weight, and when rolled up takes up very little space. This splint can also be re-used and is suitable for bone and joint injuries of the arm and wrist, shoulder, and, when two splints are used together, can be used to splint the leg or ankle. The splint is secured in place using a self-conforming bandage in the same manner as discussed in wound management.

For upper extremity injuries, the splint is only the first part of care and the arm should be further supported and immobilized using a sling and swathe.

To prepare a sling for the victim, tie an overhand knot in the point of the triangular bandage that will be used as the splint. If a triangular bandage is laid out on the beach or boat deck, two "long arms" and one "short arm" will be noticed. The knot should be tied at the very end of the short arm as indicated in Figure 20.2. This knot will help to form the "cup" at the victim's elbow when the sling is applied.

In applying the sling to the victim, take the portion of the triangular bandage closest to the victim's body and pass it around the side of the neck on the same side as the injury. The other end of the triangular bandage, the portion which is on the outside of the victim's arm, is passed

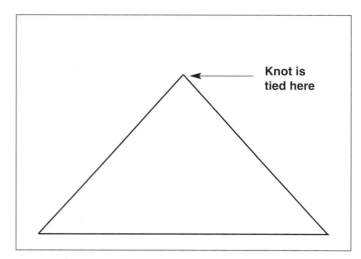

Knot is
tied here

FIGURE 20.2
Placement of Knot for a Sling

over the shoulder opposite the victim's injured arm. The sling is tied behind the victim's neck with a square knot, but the knot should rest to the side of the neck in the interest of the victim's comfort.

As a final safeguard, take another triangular bandage and bring it over the outside of the upper arm and tie it off under the victim's opposite arm. This is described as the swathe and yields a full immobilization of the injured arm. With slight modifications, this same sling and swathe technique is useful for the management of upper arm, shoulder, and collar bone injuries.

20.12 POSSIBLE MEDICAL PROBLEMS

Though most people encountered in the diving environment are generally healthy, it is possible that on board a boat, divers may be exposed to certain medical emergencies. None of these will be discussed in great detail, but some thoughts are offered relative to the initial management of some illnesses that may be encountered.

20.12.1 Respiratory Emergencies

The simplest way to classify respiratory problems is those victims breathing too fast, those breathing too slow, or those whose breathing is impaired due to some internal obstruction.

20.12.1.1 Hyperventilation

Breathing too fast, hyperventilating, may be a natural response to injuries or to blood loss and need not be treated. Instead, deal with the underlying problems in a manner previously discussed. Hyperventilation may also be a result of diabetes or other metabolic emergencies and needs the attention of medical professionals, as it may be a sign of a very serious medical condition.

However, hyperventilation syndrome can be a problem, as it may lead to an imbalance of respiratory gases in the body that need to maintain a relatively delicate balance. It is usually precipitated from some emotional response, but once started, appears to be self-sustaining and beyond the voluntary control of the victim.

The victim will usually breathe from 35 to 50 times per minute and may complain of numbness and tingling around the mouth and nose. The victim is anxious and appears to be suffering from air hunger and may also exhibit cramping of the hands and forearms.

Management of this type of hyperventilation is directed at getting the victim's respiratory gases back into balance. Take two immediate actions:

1. Continue to reassure the victim that everything is OK, and that they need to concentrate on trying to slow their breathing.
2. Using either a paper bag or an oxygen mask not connected to any oxygen, have the victim re-breathe their own exhaled air. This will increase the level of carbon dioxide in their blood, the gas that has been over-depleted via hyperventilation, and bring their respiratory rate back under control.

If the victim's breathing does not quickly come under control, the victim needs to be treated by more advanced emergency medical personnel.

20.12.1.2 Inadequate Breathing (Hypoventilation)

This type of problem can be the result of a disease process, extreme weakness, or some injuries that cause the victim to limit chest wall movement. In any case, the problem leads to an inadequate volume of gas being exchanged each minute, with too little oxygen being taken into the system, and too little carbon dioxide being exhaled.

The rescuer may notice the problem by observing a very slow breathing rate of less than ten breaths per minute. Very shallow breathing or cyanosis (a bluish color change seen in the nail beds and around the lips) may be present. Any of these findings should be treated by administering oxygen and providing ventilatory support to the victim in the manner discussed earlier under Section 20.4.4.

20.12.1.3 Obstructive Problems

Diseases such as chronic bronchitis, emphysema, and asthma all result in some degree of blockage or impairment of normal gas exchange. If a victim has one of these diseases and such a person is in respiratory difficulty and in obvious distress, oxygen should be administered and supplementary ventilation should be considered. Such victims are almost always more comfortable if maintained in a sitting position.

These are emergencies that need to be transferred immediately to the emergency medical services system for care.

20.12.2 Cardiovascular Emergencies

In the course of discussing primary victim care, the procedures to follow in the event of cardiac arrest were examined. Even if the condition being treated is essentially self-limiting, like angina, the victim needs to be transferred to the emergency medical services system for ongoing care and ultimate disposition. It has been recognized that one of the leading causes of unnecessary deaths from heart disease occurs because of delay in reaching appropriate care. Do not contribute to the problem.

Certain chronic cardiac problems, the most common of which is called chronic or congestive heart failure, will usually involve a victim in respiratory distress and needing appropriate care, along with immediate transfer to the emergency medical services system.

Other heart conditions usually present with a victim having any one of the following signs and symptoms:

- Chest pain (this pain will usually be described by the victim as crushing or squeezing and will not be relieved by any change of position or with breathing)
- Respiratory distress
- Nausea or vomiting
- Unusual fatigue
- Skin color and quality that may be shock-like as previously described or cyanotic

Angina is a condition where a victim usually has the chest pain precipitated by either physical or emotional stress. The pain of angina is brought on by inadequate blood flow to the heart muscle and might be compared to a cramp of the heart muscle. However, it is often difficult to distinguish the pain of angina from that of a more serious cardiac problem.

The rescuer should take several steps if initially it appears that angina is the victim's problem:

1. Calm and reassure the victim and keep the victim in a position in which they are most comfortable, often a sitting position.
2. Administer oxygen to the victim.
3. If the victim has medication for angina, assist the victim in taking the medication. If the medication is nitroglycerin in tablet form, wear disposable gloves when handling the medication, since it can be absorbed through the skin and give the caregiver a severe headache.

Very often, the symptoms of the angina will quickly disappear when the victim has been calmed, oxygen has been administered, and the victim's own medication has been taken.

If the victim's pain and discomfort does not quickly subside, it must be presumed that angina is not the problem, but that the victim is having an acute myocardial infarction (heart attack) and may be in imminent threat of death. Treatment for the heart attack victim is essentially the same as that for the angina victim at the basic level, except that the victim must be cautioned not to assist in his movement in any way and allow you to move the victim at all times. If the victim is in a tight-fitting wet suit or similar garment, these restricting garments must be loosened in order to allow the victim to breathe with as little effort as possible. The semi-automatic defibrillator should be immediately accessible, in the event the victim becomes unresponsive.

20.12.3 Stroke (Cerebrovascular Accident)

Strokes are usually precipitated by either a blockage of a blood vessel leading to the brain or a rupture of a vessel in the brain. Most often, victims of these problems have a history of high blood pressure. On occasion, a stroke may occur, as in the case of heart attacks, without any prior medical history or warning.

A victim suffering from a stroke will exhibit one or more of the following signs and symptoms:

- Headache (sometimes described as the worst headache the victim has ever had)
- Visual disturbances (the victim will tell the caregiver that their vision is distorted or that they are blind in one or both eyes)
- Abnormalities of speech
- Inability to move one side of the body or weakness or loss of feeling to one side of the body

- Memory loss or disorientation
- Seizures
- Loss of consciousness

With recognition of any of these signs or symptoms, activate emergency medical service resources. Next, immediate care must be given to the victim:

- The victim's breathing status needs to be monitored since stroke victims sometimes have difficulty protecting their own airway. If any difficulty is noticed, position the victim in a way that breathing is unobstructed.
- Keep the victim calm and reassured. If the victim is still responsive, place them in a position in which they are most comfortable with constant attention to their airway. The recovery position is recommended.
- Administer oxygen.
- Make sure that the victim's body temperature is maintained and that no additional body heat will be lost.
- If the victim is unresponsive, place the victim on his side in such a way that any saliva or vomit will tend to drain out of the mouth rather than being inhaled.

This care and vigilant monitoring should continue until the victim is transferred to emergency medical services personnel.

20.12.4 Convulsions (Seizure)

Seizures might be simply described as a short-circuit in the victim's brain which may result in involuntary action of an isolated segment of the victim's body. Generalized motor seizures or convulsions are a major medical emergency and require intervention beyond the basic level. Contact local emergency medical services personnel.

With a seizing victim, certain essential care must be performed while awaiting the arrival of emergency care personnel:

- Do not try to restrain the victim in any way.
- Move any objects away from the victim that might cause injury.
- Make sure that the victim's airway is maintained. This is particularly important after the active seizing stops. Most seizures are followed by a period of unconsciousness, and it is during that period that the airway may become impaired. Position the victim in a manner similar to the unconscious stroke victim.
- After the active seizure, do not try to arouse the victim if they seem to be sleeping. This is a natural aftermath to a major seizure.

Take notes relative to the progression of the seizure (what part of the body it started in) and the duration of the active seizing. This information, along with any other known medical history, should be given to emergency medical services personnel upon their arrival.

20.12.5 Diabetic Emergencies

The disease processes involved with diabetes are extremely complex, with one of the principle problems being known as microangiopathy (loosely interpreted, meaning a disease caused by blood vessels being small). This, as well as some of the other manifestations of diabetes, has been the basis for the controversy surrounding diabetics and scuba diving. The two camps in the controversy contend that diabetics should not be permitted to scuba dive, while the opponents of this view hold that diabetes should not be a condition warranting the disqualification from sport diving. Currently, diabetes may not disqualify an individual from diving. Whatever the marine or freshwater environment, it is possible that diabetic emergencies will be encountered.

The disease tends to be rather complicated in the way it manifests itself, but the problems typically encountered will have to do with insulin, glucose, or both. Insulin is a chemical produced by the body that enables the body to utilize glucose, a sugar that serves as the body's primary energy source. If an individual does not have enough insulin, the glucose present cannot be utilized. At the other extreme, if the individual has enough insulin but no glucose, other problems will arise.

The two significant diabetes-related emergencies the rescuer may encounter are hypoglycemia (low blood sugar) and diabetic ketoacidosis, at one time called diabetic coma.

Hypoglycemia usually develops rather rapidly due to a quick drop in the blood sugar level (glucose). It may be precipitated by strenuous activity beyond the diabetic victim's normal activity level: scuba diving, snorkeling, or swimming. The blood's sugar level drops and the body, particularly the brain, is precipitately deprived of the primary source of energy. Notice the following signs and symptoms:

- The victim's mental status may be altered with confusion, bizarre behavior, combativeness, and irritability being some of the leading results.
- The victim may have cold, clammy skin like that described for shock.
- The victim will complain of being weak and uncoordinated, if still responsive.
- The pulse will be rapid, but may be bounding since there has been no loss of blood .
- Finally, in the worst cases, the victim may be seizing.

If the victim is still conscious enough to protect his own airway, administer sugar to the victim. Simple sources include non-diet soft drinks, sugar and water syrup, and fruit juices. Other sources made particularly for emergency care include very thick sugar gels that are contained in tubes and can be expelled under the victim's tongue. This allows the glucose to be quickly absorbed by the numerous blood vessels under the tongue.

In addition to this care specifically addressing hypoglycemia, monitor the victim's airway, and in the event of seizure precipitated by this problem, the victim must be protected from further injury.

In most cases, the victim will quickly respond to this type of care, but any delay in response to oral sugar administration requires immediate notification of emergency medical services for assistance.

Diabetic ketoacidosis is a far more serious diabetic emergency, since a simple dose of glucose will not provide any "quick-fix" for the victim. Instead, the victim needs immediate, sophisticated medical intervention that is only available at a hospital. Expediency in getting the emergency medical services mobilized is critical for the victim's well being and needs to take the highest priority.

The victim of diabetic ketoacidosis usually admits to a history of diabetes and typically have the following signs and symptoms:

- The victim may be confused and complaining of a headache.
- The victim will complain of thirst and be producing excess amounts of urine.
- The victim will appear dehydrated with warm, dry skin.
- The victim may have deep, sighing breathing with a fruity odor to the breath.
- If able to take a victim history, it will usually be determined that the victim hasn't been "feeling well" for a period of days, and that the problem has been gradually developing, rather than a sudden onset typical of hypoglycemia.

Management of these victims is a matter of keeping them as comfortable as possible until emergency medical services personnel can take over care. The victim's airway must be monitored, since a comatose victim may be unable to maintain a clear airway. Oxygen administration is desirable and, if the victim is conscious and able to protect the airway, small quantities of water (no more than 8 ounces every 15–30 minutes) may be helpful to relieve some of the dehydration the victim has experienced. If in doubt whether the victim is suffering from diabetic ketoacidosis or is hypoglycemic, oral administration of sugar as in hypoglycemia will do little harm to the victim and if the victim is hypoglycemic, the oral sugar administration may assist the victim.

20.13 HEAT ILLNESSES

The two serious heat emergencies that may be encountered in diving are heat exhaustion and heat stroke.

Prevention of these injuries is probably one area where every diver can play a part. When individuals are working in a heated environment (i.e., below decks on a boat), be certain that everyone takes frequent breaks to cool themselves, and make sure that adequate fluid consumption is continuing throughout the work day. Despite the availability of numerous commercially available beverages, water remains the best fluid for hydration.

In the diving environment, on particularly warm days, do not let divers spend too much time in wet or dry suits while not in the water. These garments retain body heat and divers can sustain a significant rise in body temperature while so attired.

20.13.1 Heat Exhaustion

Heat exhaustion is caused by excessive fluid loss from the body, as well as loss of sodium, most often due to profuse sweating. This problem can be made worse by vomiting, diarrhea, and heavy alcohol consumption.

The victim of heat exhaustion may have the following signs and symptoms:

- Rapid pulse
- Dizziness, anxiety, irritability, headache, and vision problems
- Normal to slightly elevated body temperature
- Cold and clammy skin with pallor, similar to shock
- Mild cramps, nausea, and sometimes vomiting

The treatment of this emergency includes keeping the victim calm and removing unnecessary clothing. The purpose is to lower the victim's body temperature. If the victim is conscious and capable of protecting his own airway, it is advisable to give the victim a solution consisting of one teaspoon of salt dissolved in eight fluid ounces of water. Have the victim drink this slowly over a period of 15 minutes to avoid precipitating vomiting.

As it may be difficult to determine if the victim is suffering from heat exhaustion or heat stroke, discussed below, it is important to remove the victim from the source of excessive heat, as well as to remove any body covering that may be causing any additional internal heat build-up. If in doubt relative to the heat-related problem from which the victim is suffering, treat for heat stroke.

20.13.2 Heat Stroke

This is a truly life-threatening heat-related emergency. The victim's core temperature has risen to a potentially deadly level and the body's natural "thermostat" has failed.

The signs and symptoms of heat stroke may look very much like heat exhaustion, or the victim may present the classic heat stroke signs and symptoms:

- Very rapid pulse and respirations
- Red, hot, and dry skin—but this may not be as evident in those who are in excellent physical condition

- Headache, weakness, dizziness
- Anxiety and fatigue
- Sweating will usually have ceased

Treatment of the victim of heat stroke requires immediate, aggressive intervention in order to save the victim's life! The rescuer should have someone else, if possible, immediately initiate the mobilization of emergency medical services, while he turns attention to the victim. The top priority for the care of a victim with heat stroke is the lowering of the victim's body core temperature. Actions that should take place include:

- Remove all of the victim's clothing and cover the victim with a cool-water-soaked sheet.
- Place the victim in an air-conditioned area if available.
- Administer oxygen while maintaining the victim's airway.
- Place chemical cold packs or bags of ice under the victim's arm pits, at the groin, around the head and neck, and anywhere else the source of cold can be placed near a major supply of moving blood.
- Be prepared to manage the victim in the event convulsing begins.

The need for rapid cooling of these victims cannot be over emphasized. Without rapid cooling, the victim of heat stroke will either die or, if they survive, suffer permanent, debilitating brain injury.

20.14 HYPOTHERMIA MANAGEMENT

Water possesses the physical property of drawing heat from the human body at a rate far in excess of air. Body heat is lost 25 times faster in water than in air of the same temperature.

With that basic understanding of the physics of heat loss, it is evident that there is a risk of significant body heat loss even in temperate exposures. As an example, though 70°F (21C) water is not typically viewed as terribly frigid, an individual tossed into such water for a period of four hours has experienced an environmental exposure equivalent to standing naked in 70°F (21C) air for 100 hours! Taking the normal temperatures in the 50°F range in the Great Lakes during the typical diving/boating season and similar temperatures along the Pacific coast year-round, it becomes evident that a rescuer may care for individuals who have been subject to significant exposures to the cold.

Hypothermia is a drop in the body's core temperature to less than 95°F (35C) (Normal body temperature is 98.6°F (37C)). Any time a victim has been subject to immersion, the victim should be cared for as though hypothermia is present. Hypothermia is classified as mild, moderate, and severe based upon core temperature. Some of the signs and symptoms of the varying classes of hypothermia include the following:

Mild Hypothermia: The victim will be shivering, appear apathetic, have motor difficulties (wobbling gait, awkward manual control), and may have memory loss (amnesia).

Moderate Hypothermia: Shivering will have stopped by the time the core temperature reaches approximately 88°F (31C) so the victim may no longer be shivering. The victim will appear to be in a stupor. Heart beat and respirations may slow at the lower temperatures within the moderate range, and pupils of the eyes may be dilated.

Severe Hypothermia: At this point, the core temperature is down to nearly 80°F (27C). The victim has lost voluntary movement capabilities and most reflexes are gone. Respiratory difficulties may become more severe due to accumulation of fluid in the lungs brought on by the hypothermia. These victims are also at great risk for cardiac arrest.

First prevent any further heat loss to the victim. Most hypothermia victims encountered in diving will have suffered extended immersions. The victim's clothing must be removed and the victim must be dried. Be careful to handle these victims gently, since rough handling may bring on cardiac arrest in the moderate to severely hypothermic victim.

Additional required care includes:

- Maintain the victim's airway and, if trauma is suspected, provide immobilization of the cervical spine while maintaining the airway.
- If necessary, all normal basic life support procedures must be carried out, including CPR. The basic tenet in caring for dead hypothermic victims is that the "victim is not dead until they are warm and dead." Simply put, this means that the rescuer and emergency medical services personnel must continue resuscitative efforts until the victim has been transferred to a hospital.
- If there will be any significant delay in getting the victim to advanced care, the victim should be wrapped in blankets and rewarmed utilizing chemical hot packs, similar to those utilized to treat marine life envenomation. However, if the transfer to emergency medical services personnel will be quickly accomplished, then the aggressive rewarming should be delayed until the victim is in the hospital. The reason for this is that in a hospital setting, the victim will be rewarmed from the inside out using sophisticated medical interventions. Rewarming a hypothermia victim from the outside-in presents a risk of a problem called "after-drop" where colder blood from the body's surface and extremities moves into the body's core and may actually drop the body core temperature further.
- The victim can be rewarmed by wrapping the naked victim in a blanket with a naked companion. The non-hypothermic person's body heat will help rewarm the victim.
- If the victim does not have an impaired gag reflex, they can then be given warmed fluids by mouth. Warm juices, water, and thin soups are appropriate.

Any fluids containing caffeine (coffee, tea, hot chocolate) and any beverages containing alcohol should not be given to the victim.

- Unless basic life support is required, oxygen should probably be avoided, since it will tend to reduce the victim's core temperature further because oxygen is cold relative to normal body temperature.

The keys to keep in mind in managing these victims is that the victim must be handled gently, needs to be rewarmed, and must be transferred to a hospital as soon as possible for further care.

NOTE

To rewarm the victim, it may be possible on a vessel to utilize warm water from either the compressor or engine in a bath container.

20.15 SEASICKNESS (MOTION SICKNESS)

Seasickness can be a distinct hazard to a diver. Diving should not be attempted when a diver is seasick: vomiting while submerged can cause respiratory obstruction and death.

Signs and Symptoms:
- Nausea
- Dizziness
- Feelings of withdrawal, fatigue
- Pallor or a sickly complexion
- Slurred speech
- Vomiting

There is no effective treatment for seasickness except to return the stricken diver to a stable platform, preferably shore. All efforts are therefore directed at prevention. Some people are more susceptible than others, but repeated exposures tend to decrease sensitivity. The susceptible person should eat lightly just before exposure and avoid diving with an alcohol hangover. Seasick individuals should be isolated to avoid affecting others on board adversely. Drug therapy is of questionable value and must be used with caution, because most motion sickness preparations contain antihistamines that make the diver drowsy and could affect a diver's judgment. The use of scopolamine by means of a skin patch has been shown to be useful in preventing seasickness, but this drug has been known to cause psychotic behavior in sensitive persons. Those choosing to use the scopolamine patch are cautioned not to touch the patch followed by touching their eyes as this will cause dilation of the pupil of the affected eye. Drugs should be used only under the direction of a physician who understands diving, and then only after a test dose on non-diving days has been shown not to affect the individual adversely.

One side effect of seasickness is dehydration. Divers should be aware of the role dehydration plays in decompression sickness and rehydrate accordingly before diving.

Diving Accident Management and Emergency Procedures

21

Diving Accident Management and Emergency Procedures

21.0 GENERAL

Accident management has a broader meaning than the term implies; it includes many activities, ranging from accident prevention to selection of personnel, equipment, and procedures, and the emergency care of victims after an accident. Prevention through proper training, dive planning, and the on-scene management of casualties as they pertain to open-water accidents is the emphasis of this chapter.

Reports of scuba fatalities indicate that proper accident management procedures frequently could have prevented the accident or saved a life once an accident occurred. Divers killed accidentally are usually found with intact equipment, weight belts on, functioning regulators, cylinders containing some air, and uninflated buoyancy control devices (Wachholz 2000).

Instances in which equipment failure led to the death of a diver are extremely rare. Human error and inadequate diver performance seem to be the major contributing factors in many fatal accidents, and panic is probably the initiating cause in most instances (Bachrach and Egstrom 1986). In some cases, a feeling of apprehension may precede panic and in itself may produce problems leading to a diving accident. Many divers are apprehensive, and even experienced ones may be disturbed by certain kinds of water conditions or other circumstances associated with a particular dive. The competent diver is one who gains as much information as possible about the dive site, boat, equipment, and other features of the dive. Planning prepares the diver to meet unexpected situations; a thorough knowledge of the dive site, including currents, marine hazards, and sea states is essential for proper planning (see Chapter 8).

21.1 PANIC

Panic is different from apprehension. Apprehension implies a sense of foreboding, and awareness of danger. Panic implies unreasoning and overmastering fear causing hysterical activity (Bachrach and Egstrom 1986). One kind of panic involves the belief that an individual is losing control of his own performance and the situation. Panic is accompanied by severe physiological changes that may, in turn, contribute to further loss of control. For example, a diver taking rapid, shallow breaths because of panic will suffer a buildup of carbon dioxide as a result of inadequate ventilatory exchange. Lowered air intake also can result in a loss of buoyancy and lead to inefficient swimming movements, which further aggravates the diver's sense of panic.

Another kind of panic involves stereotypical behavior. For example, a diver discovering that he is low on air, or out of air, should respond properly either by releasing his weight belt, or by asking a buddy for assistance. On the other hand, the stereotypical response is panic that causes the diver to rush or accelerate his ascent to the surface, causing even greater panic and loss of control. In many cases, the diver delays releasing his weight belt or asking for assistance until panic strikes; by that time, he has lost the necessary motor coordination and presence of mind to act effectively.

Before a diver reaches the point of panic, warning signs appear that should alert the divemaster and/or the dive partners to the possibility of problems. Warning signs of panic in the water include:

- Indications of anxiety (primarily a "wide-eyed" look and a change in breathing rate and pattern from smooth and regular to rapid and shallow)
- Changes in swimming movements (generally, a shift from smooth and regular movements to jerky and irregular)

The panicking diver frequently goes through desperate motions, such as "clawing" to the surface, trying to hold his head way above water, removing his mask, and spitting out his mouthpiece; all of which only compound the problem.

Training is the best means of preventing panic, especially in emergency procedures such as ditching a weight belt and operating the buoyancy compensator. Every diver needs to be well equipped, in good physical condition and well informed about dive conditions and the purpose of the dive. The following paragraphs describe these aspects of dive planning.

21.2 ANTICIPATION OF A PROBLEM

Every diver should develop skill in recognizing the warning signs, either in himself, another diver, or in the dive situation, that foreshadow a diving accident. This ability can significantly increase the chance of averting a fatality and thus enhance the safety of both victim and rescuer. Danger signs exhibited by divers are both varied and subtle and may be apparent before or during the dive. However, a diver's ego may cause him to disguise incompetence, anxiety, illness, or other distress before a dive, and, once the dive has begun, features of the environment, such as difficulty in communication, may make it nearly impossible to observe such signs.

21.2.1 During Training

The management of diving accidents should begin when a candidate expresses an interest in learning to dive. The process of screening applicants before admitting them as candidates to a diving training program should include obtaining a diving physical and evaluating swimming and watermanship. During the in-water evaluation, the candidate should be required to demonstrate endurance and confidence in the water so that the instructor can assess whether the candidate is comfortable in the aquatic environment. Candidates should be encouraged to obtain breath-hold diving experience before beginning scuba lessons to enhance their ability and confidence in the use of mask, snorkel, fins, and other equipment, and to maintain those skills throughout their diving careers. Points for the instructor to observe include such things as breathing through the snorkel with the candidate's face in the water (without a mask), surface diving to retrieve an object in about 20 ft. (6.1m) of water, and clearing the snorkel easily. Another good test of aquatic ability is having an unequipped swimmer catch his breath and rest while unsupported in deep water after a strenuous swim.

Throughout the preliminary training and evaluation, the instructor should estimate how the diver-candidate is likely to handle an emergency or react under stress, and should identify the areas in which the candidate needs special attention and extra training. An area of training often neglected is learning the proper procedures for dressing and attachment of gear such as weights, buoyancy compensator, gauges, etc. These procedures should be overlearned to the extent that they become second nature, which ensures that equipment will be properly positioned in the event of an emergency.

Because panic is frequently involved in diving accidents, it is important that the candidate learn to feel confident and at ease in the water at the outset of training. Signs of anxiety or a lack of confidence in the water include:

- Evidence of claustrophobia
- Expressed fear of and difficulty with underwater swimming
- Difficulty adapting to mouth breathing
- Difficulty in adapting to underwater breathing using scuba apparatus
- Poor watermanship without swimming or flotation aids
- Complaints about the regulator's breathing resistance
- Constant fidgeting with dive equipment
- Obvious under weighting
- Constant interest in swimming to the surface
- Rapid and/or shallow breathing
- Stiff and uncoordinated movements
- Reluctance to exhale fully when requested to do so by the instructor
- Hanging onto the instructor's hand too tightly when being escorted
- Becoming anxious when minor equipment problems occur on the bottom
- Lack of acknowledgment when the instructor looks directly into the eyes
- Constantly being "wide-eyed"
- Complaints of inability to clear the ears, especially during early open-water training
- Removal of the mask and/or the regulator immediately when the diver reaches the surface

Many other signs that reveal anxiety, fear, or incompetence can be observed. Although in most instances these problems can be overcome by proper training, some individuals, even with excellent training, are better advised not to pursue diving.

Experienced divers sometimes can anticipate another diver's problems during open-water training. In such cases, the experienced diver should observe the extent of the other diver's familiarity with equipment, ease in donning it, and ability to correct a leaking mask or put a regulator in the mouth under water. The experienced diver also should note whether the inexperienced diver swims off alone, oblivious to his buddy, and whether there is difficulty in breathing from the regulator with the mask off. Each of these occurrences may be a clue indicating that the candidate may subsequently panic easily or become overconfident. Even the best divers are concerned about becoming overconfident and seek advanced training.

21.2.2 During Dive Preparation

Although individuals suffering from serious illnesses or injuries usually make no attempt to dive, many divers enter the water with minor discomforts that may have adverse consequences, particularly if an emergency develops. Examples of such minor maladies are ear or sinus infections, headaches, lung congestion, seasickness, cramps, and the side effects of medication. Divers should assess not only their own condition but also that of other divers in the group.

Before entering the water, each diver should note the configuration, condition, and completeness of the buddy diver's equipment. The over-equipped diver encumbered with more equipment than can be handled safely in the water should be advised to leave non-essential items on the shore or in the boat. During predive preparations, every diver should be alert to signs of dive ineptness or error, such as lack of knowledge of procedures, nervousness, or mistakes made assembling equipment.

Other signs of potential problems are more subtle and psychological in nature; included in this category are changes in personal characteristics, such as an increase in the pitch of voice, incessant chattering, procrastinating before actually entering the water, and withdrawal. Signs of overheating or chilling, such as excessive sweating or shivering, also should be noted. These signs should be addressed before entering the water, either by providing direct assistance (if the problem is mechanical), by giving reassurance, by practicing a particular skill, or by suggesting that individual not dive (if circumstances warrant). Although some divers might be embarrassed by the latter suggestion, others might welcome it with relief.

21.2.3 During Entry and Descent

Failure to use proper entry techniques or forgetting essential equipment such as fins, mask, weight belt, or forgetting to turn their air on, may be signs that the diver requires watching. Other hints that the diver may be under stress or uncomfortable in the water are failure to surface properly or to check with the buddy before descent and excessive "high treading." High treading means that the diver treads with his arms and/or fins with vigor sufficient to lift the major portion of his body out of the water without using buoyancy compensation. When this activity is accompanied by dog paddling and using the arms excessively, it is a sign that a potentially serious problem is in the making. Rejecting the mask or other essential equipment in the water is also a portent of problems, as is the tendency to cling to or clamber onto objects above the surface (not to be confused with the normal practice of using a float or some other object for temporary support).

Once the descent begins, there may be other signs that a problem is developing. Although anyone can have occasional difficulty with ear clearing or buoyancy control, chronic problems or overconcern may indicate an uneasy diver who needs watching. Ear equalization problems at depths below 50 ft. (15.2 m) are particularly indicative of a potential problem. Sudden changes in descent rate also should be noted because they may indicate either over confidence or a desire to return to the surface. Throughout the descent and initial phase of the dive, every diver should observe his buddy for signs of erratic behavior, such as abrupt changes in swimming speed, fiddling with equipment, lack of stability, or difficulty with buoyancy control. Sudden or unnecessary use of the hands and arms for propulsion or buoyancy often is a sign of anxiety and impending difficulty. The diver exhibiting any or all of these signs may be unaware that anything is out of the ordinary, but experienced divers should be sensitive to such behavior before a problem develops.

21.2.4 During the Dive

Once entry and descent has been achieved, the alert diver continues to watch for signs that suggest an approaching problem. The things to watch for are basically the same as those during descent (i.e., general uneasiness, fast breathing, straying from the buddy, erratic behavior, or equipment problems). Any deviation from good diving practice, such as failure to check the air supply, depth, and time, should be mentally noted. Diving accidents are particularly likely to happen either in the first three minutes of a dive (because of lack of preparedness) or in the final five minutes (because the dive has been extended too long). Photographer-divers should be watched especially carefully because it is easy to become preoccupied with the task at hand and to forget to keep track of time, depth, and air supply. It is also important to keep track of significant changes in surface conditions or currents that might affect ascent or exit from the water. In conditions of poor visibility or during night dives, extra care must be taken to ensure that lights are functioning properly and that divers stay close together. In addition, at least one diver should watch for potentially dangerous marine animals if they are known to exist in the area.

At the end of the dive, divers should surface in buddy pairs. Prior arrangements about when and where the dive will be terminated should have been made before beginning the dive.

21.2.5 During Ascent and Exit

It is especially important to maintain a continual awareness of potential problems at the end of a dive. Several factors can contribute to carelessness and accidents, such as fatigue, cold, equipment malfunction, and overconfidence. In observing a buddy diver during ascent, it is essential to note the following:

- No-decompression time has been exceeded.
- Rate of ascent is too rapid, especially during the last 10 ft. (3 m).
- Distance between divers is too great.
- Surfacing will take place either where there are obstacles (kelp, active boat channels, rip current, breaking waves) or down current from the support platform.

Diving Accident Management and Emergency Procedures

Proper attention also must be given to ensuring an adequate air supply and that the buddy is breathing properly during ascent. Expanding air in the BC (buoyancy compensator device) during ascent can lead to a ballistic (or uncontrolled) ascent, and failure to make a safety stop can increase decompression risk.

Each diver should ensure that the buddy does not exit from the wrong place in the surf line, exit to an unsafe surface in a heavy surge, get too close to a dive ladder/platform in a heavy swell, or hang on tightly to a line attached to the bottom during a heavy swell. Because divers are often fatigued at the end of a dive, extra caution must be paid to the routine handling of equipment while climbing up a ladder or into a boat. In particular, divers should avoid coming up to a ladder or in the falling zone of an exiting diver.

WARNING
UNLESS A DIVER EXHALES WHEN THE TROUGH OF A WAVE PASSES OVERHEAD, HANGING ONTO A LINE ATTACHED TO THE BOTTOM IN HEAVY SWELLS IS DANGEROUS BECAUSE THE PRESSURE CHANGE MAY CAUSE A LUNG OVEREXPANSION INJURY.

21.3 CAUSES OF EMERGENCIES

Diving emergencies can arise from an almost infinite number of causes, including exhaustion, embolism, decompression sickness, nitrogen narcosis, heart attacks, high currents, marine animals or creature encounters, entanglement, heavy surf, out-of-air emergencies, equipment failure, and panic. In general, diving accidents are overwhelmingly caused by human error than by equipment failure (Wachholz, pers. comm. 2000).

In the planning stages of a dive, contingency plans should be made, and all divers should be briefed and familiarized with those plans. New or unfamiliar equipment should be understood thoroughly by all divers, and practice sessions should be held before the dive.

Before initiating a dive, experienced divemasters visualize the worst incident scenarios and mentally rehearse the management of these hypothetical accidents. It is even more effective to sketch an accident management flow diagram. In planning, it is essential to assess the capabilities of the dive team to ensure that, in the event of an accident, novice divers are not unnecessarily exposed to risks.

No matter how well-planned the dive or how well-trained the diver, emergency situations occasionally arise, usually as a result of failure to observe some safety precaution. In most instances, taking a few seconds to assess the situation accurately and determine the actions necessary can keep the emergency from becoming an accident. Instinctive reactions seldom are correct and may prove to be blind impulses brought on by panic (Smith and Allen 1978). Adequate training should prepare the diver for most emergencies, provided that panic does not intervene.

The following paragraphs describe some of the more common causes of diving emergencies and methods of avoiding and managing emergencies if they do occur.

21.3.1 Loss of Air Supply

The first step in evaluating an out-of-air situation should be to confirm that the apparent air loss is real. Before reacting precipitously, the diver should stop, think, attempt to breathe, and, if it is possible to do so, proceed with a normal ascent. Divers should be taught that many out-of-air situations are related to the diver or the situation rather than to the equipment or actual loss of air supply.

If a diver determines that his air supply is depleted, the suggested order for managing loss of air supply is:

- Normal ascent
- Alternate air source ascent
- Controlled emergency swimming ascent
- Buddy breathing ascent
- Emergency buoyant ascent

Many divers choose to equip their scuba cylinders with two second-stage hoses to use for emergency buddy breathing. The use of an alternative second stage is considered a desirable option in out-of-air situations. If this technique is used, the alternative second stage hose should be at least 12 inches (30.5cm) longer than the primary hose, be marked for easy identification, and be oriented so that it will always be right side up when used. When using an alternative second stage system, the distressed diver should notify his buddy that air is needed and should then proceed to breathe from the extra regulator. Since the air supply of the buddy also is likely to be low, ascent should begin immediately after a brief stabilization period. Two persons breathing from a cylinder with low air volume through a single scuba regulator can quickly deplete the air supply. Also, in cold water, the extra flow caused by simultaneous breathing of the divers may cause the regulator to freeze. The divers should maintain physical contact by holding onto each other's straps.

WARNING
WHEN ONE DIVER RUNS OUT OF AIR, THE BUDDY'S SUPPLY IS ALSO USUALLY LOW AND WITH DOUBLE CONSUMPTION, THE AVAILABLE AIR CAN BE DEPLETED QUICKLY. THEREFORE, BUDDY BREATHING (ALTERNATE AIR SOURCE) ASCENT SHOULD BEGIN IMMEDIATELY.

Auxiliary scuba cylinders attached to the primary cylinder can be used as an emergency air source. Such cylinders can be obtained in sizes ranging from 1.7–15 cubic feet (0.05–0.4 cubic meter) and are normally used with a separate regulator. They are designed as an emergency system only. For example, a 4 ft^3 (0.11 cm^3) cylinder provides about 14–16 breaths at a depth of 100 ft. (30.5 m) and about 80 breaths in shallow water.

If loss of air is sudden and unexpected and no auxiliary air sources are available, buddy breathing using a single regulator may be necessary. Often, the distressed diver will begin to cough or choke. Until the diver's condition is stabilized, both the diver and buddy should maintain their depth while continuing to buddy breathe. Air donors should allow the victim to use their air supply as much as possible without jeopardizing their own supply. When the distressed diver's condition has stabilized, a safe ascent can be made.

The most efficient method of buddy breathing is for the two divers to face each other, each alternately breathing from the same mouthpiece while ascending (see Figure 21.1). During the exchange of the mouthpiece, the exhaust valve on single-hose regulators must be positioned below the mouthpiece so that water can be eliminated from the second stage; this position can be

FIGURE 21.1
Buddy Breathing

achieved conveniently if the divers are side by side, with the diver in distress on the left. The donor controls the air, and both divers exhale between exchanges. Contact should be maintained by having each diver hold the straps or belt of the other diver.

WARNING
DURING BUDDY BREATHING, ONE DIVER SHOULD BE BREATHING FROM THE REGULATOR WHILE THE OTHER DIVER IS EXHALING.

When using dry suits or large buoyancy compensators, extra precautions should be taken to prevent uncontrolled ascent caused by air expansion of the suit/BC as the diver rises in the water column. For example, the normal procedure of dropping the weight belt should not be followed when a constant-volume dry suit is used unless the suit is flooded. During ascent, the amount of air in the dry suit or partially-inflated buoyancy compensator should be controlled by the exhaust valves or use another venting method such as opening a cuff or neck seal.

If it is necessary to cover a horizontal distance while buddy breathing, a number of different methods can be used. The two most common are for the divers to swim side by side (about halfway on their sides), facing each other, or to swim one above the other. In this manner, the mouthpiece can easily be passed back and forth between divers.

If buddy breathing is not possible, the diver can make an emergency buoyant ascent to the surface while **venting air continuously**. Unless the breathing apparatus is entangled, however, a diver should not abandon it. The reduction of ambient pressure as the diver rises to the surface increases the pressure differential, possibly providing additional air for breathing from the scuba and allowing the diver to make a controlled ascent, but divers must remember **not to hold their breaths** while employing these procedures.

WARNING
EMERGENCY BUOYANT ASCENTS ARE DIFFICULT AND HAZARDOUS AND SHOULD BE USED ONLY AS A LAST RESORT TO RESOLVE AN EMERGENCY SITUATION.

Should a diver find himself in an uncontrollable ascent, he should spread his arms and legs, thus increasing drag and stability and slowing the rate of ascent. The diver must continue to exhale throughout the ascent. The head should be extended back, allowing maximal opening of the throat and a good overhead view. The diver should swim to the surface, staying constantly aware of possible entanglements or obstructions and the consequences of breathholding. The mouthpiece should be left in place.

WARNING
A DIVER HAVING DIFFICULTY ASCENDING SHOULD RELEASE HIS WEIGHT BELT IMMEDIATELY. MAKE SURE NO OTHER DIVERS ARE BELOW BEFORE DROPPING THE BELT.

At night or when visibility is low, the diver should exert extra care to hold his extended arm over his head during ascent to avoid hitting a boat or other object on the way up.

WARNING
DISCARDING SELF-CONTAINED EQUIPMENT AND MAKING A FREE ASCENT SHOULD BE THE LAST OPTION. WHEN THIS PROCEDURE MUST BE USED, EXHALE ALL THE WAY TO THE SURFACE.

Regardless of the out-of-air emergency response system used, certain criteria should be met. Egstrom (1984) has listed the essential ones:

1. Standardized procedure
2. Simple
3. Require only a minimal amount of skill to implement
4. Reliable and effective
5. Involve a minimum amount of retraining
6. Inexpensive

All of these emergency techniques require learning of skills and must be practiced to the point of overlearning. For example, a study conducted by the staff of the University of California, Los Angeles, Diving Safety Research Project found that students who practiced buddy breathing on successful trials were able to perform without errors (Egstrom 1984). Practice while swimming was more effective than practicing while sitting on the bottom of the pool. When diving with a familiar partner and equipment, buddy breathing should be practiced periodically. This is even more important when either partner or the equipment is unfamiliar.

21.3.2. Loss or Flooding of Equipment

Flooding of a face mask may be caused by another diver inadvertently kicking the mask loose with a fin, by high currents, or by turning the head and striking a rock, net, or other obstruction. The mask can be cleared by tilting the head back, pressing the top of the mask against the forehead, and blowing into the mask through the nose. The air will displace the water, forcing it out the bottom of the mask. If the mask is lost, the diver should fix his position, wave one hand over his head, and have his dive buddy come to him.

When the second stage of the regulator is lost, the hose generally remains lying over the diver's right shoulder. If it is not, it can be located by reaching back over the right shoulder with the right hand, grasping the first stage of the regulator at the cylinder's valve to locate the hose where it joins the first stage, and then following the hose out to the mouthpiece. The mouthpiece probably will be flooded, but it can be cleared by a sharp exhalation or by pushing the purge button.

21.3.3 Fouling and Entanglement

When a diver becomes trapped, entangled, or fouled, it is important to make a calm assessment of the situation. Struggling generally results in even deeper entanglement and damage to, or loss of, diving equipment. Divers using scuba should be more concerned about entanglement than when using other types of diving gear, because their air supply is limited and communication with the surface may not be possible. Maintaining a cool head, using common sense, notifying a nearby buddy diver, and using a diving knife usually suffice to gain freedom from entanglement. Emergency free ascent should be used only as a last resort. When using surface-supplied diving equipment, the diver should notify surface personnel as soon as entanglement occurs. If the diver cannot become untangled promptly, the assistance of a standby diver should be requested.

21.3.4 Near Drowning

The most common antecedent to drowning is panic, which occurs when divers find themselves in a position for which they are mentally or physically unprepared. The majority of drownings can be avoided if the diver is trained properly, is in good physical condition, and is using reliable, well-maintained equipment.

The most important step in the immediate treatment of a near-drowning victim is to restore breathing. The most effective means of artificial resuscitation (when used by trained personnel) is a mechanical resuscitator. If one is not available, artificial resuscitation is required. The most effective form is mouth-to-mouth resuscitation. This method is simple and can be administered to a victim still in the water. Victims of near drowning in water at a temperature of less than 70°F (20C) may appear to be dead and yet have a significant chance of survival if cardiopulmonary resuscitation (CPR) is started immediately. Recovery has occurred even after submersion in cold water for periods of up to 40 minutes. The chances of recovery increase if the victim is young and the water is colder.

21.4 ASSESSING A PROBLEM

Obvious indicators of diver distress that most swimmers and rescuers recognize easily include cries for help, arm or whistle signals, an actively struggling diver, or one who appears ill or unconscious. Because scuba divers should always dive in pairs, finding one drowned or distressed diver may mean that the buddy has also succumbed or is in distress. In some cases, there is no forewarning of serious trouble. For example, an exhausted swimmer may simply slip quietly and suddenly beneath the surface without a sound. Indications of anxiety or difficulty may be suppressed because of ego (unwillingness to admit having a problem) or may actually be hidden by the face mask or other diving equipment. As discussed earlier, high treading, clinging, clambering, and removing equipment are all signs of impending trouble.

Regardless of how the rescuer becomes aware that a diver is in distress or whether the emergency occurs on the surface or under water, the first step is a rapid, but thorough, assessment of the situation. Factors that should be considered at the outset are location and distance to the victim, ability to establish and maintain visual contact, and the availability of additional assistance (personnel and equipment). It is not advisable even for a trained rescuer to attempt to rescue a diver without the appropriate equipment. For example, rescue in the surf should not be made without fins. Dive boats usually have readily accessible life-saving floats, seat cushions, and ring-buoys that can be thrown. There may also be surfboards, floats, buoys, and rescue boards on the beach. Rescuers should assess their ability to carry out a rescue. The rescue hierarchy is reach-throw-row-go; that is, the first strategy of choice should be to reach for the victim with your arm, a pole, or other device, followed by throwing a lifeline or ring buoy, and so on, to the last alternative, which involves a rescuer entering the water to render assistance to the victim. If more than one person is in a group, the individual or individuals best suited to perform a rescue should be selected immediately, while others are assigned to stay with the boat, obtain flotation equipment, and perform other necessary tasks, which are particularly important if there are adverse environmental conditions, such as poor visibility, strong currents, or poor surface conditions. If the victim is under water, overhead obstructions may further complicate the situation.

As the victim is approached, the rescuer should try to determine the cause of the problem (i.e., entanglement, a strong current, rough sea, or some other environmental factor). Other possible causes of distress include nausea, decompression sickness, embolism, contact with poisonous marine life, or equipment problems. Being familiar with the victim's equipment is an important part of the overall assessment. If the weights are to be released, care must be taken to ensure that the weights fall clear of both the victim and the rescuer and that the waist strap of the scuba and/or BC are not confused with the weight belt.

WARNING
DIVERS EXPERIENCING STRESS AT THE WATER'S SURFACE SHOULD DROP THE WEIGHT BELT IMMEDIATELY TO ENSURE THAT THEY WILL FLOAT.

The rescuer should immediately note the location of the oral or power inflator of the BC and activate the appropriate mechanism or begin oral inflation.

Of primary importance is the state of the victim. If unconscious and under water, the victim must be brought to the surface quickly. If unconscious and on the surface, the method of handling differs from that used with a conscious victim. If the victim is conscious, the rescuer must assess the victim's mental state and then proceed in a manner that does not increase the victim's pain, induce panic, or complicate existing injuries or the rescue process. Finally, the rescuer must assess the victim's state of buoyancy. If the victim is not positive, the rescuer must take immediate action to establish positive buoyancy. An additional factor that must be assessed is the method of transporting the victim to shore. For example, returning the victim to the starting point of the dive may not be the best procedure because other locations may be more accessible, have essential lifesaving equipment, or be more suitable for administering first aid.

NOTE
Water safety authorities strongly advocate that the rescuer avoid direct physical contact with an unstabilized victim, if possible.

During a swimming rescue, the rescuer should continue trying to enlist help as long as possible. The victim should be observed continuously at all times because the victim may sink, become unconscious, panicky, or stop breathing. When a rescuer is approaching a submerged victim, especially in water with poor visibility, two observers stationed at fixed points (boat or shore) pointing at the place of the victim's submergence provide a bearing for the rescuer.

If the victim is conscious and on the surface, the rescuer should explain what is going to happen and make every effort to calm the victim. If the victim is submerged and conscious, conventional hand signals should be used and the rescuer should demonstrate exactly what the victim is expected to do. Positive buoyancy should be established for the victim immediately. If the victim's equipment is to be ditched, it is recommended that it be handed to the rescuer rather than dropped, because this makes it more likely that it will fall clear of the body. Depending on the situation, rescuers also may have to remove their own equipment, such as the weight belt or scuba unit, to facilitate rescue. Upon reaching the victim, the rescuer should pause momentarily to reassess the situation and to rest briefly before proceeding further

21.5 RESCUE PROCEDURES

Although certain rescue procedures should be considered standard, the trained rescuer must still use common sense because no two emergencies are identical. The following procedures are not intended to be an exhaustive treatment of scuba lifesaving techniques, but rather to alert the reader to these rescue procedures.

When attempting any of the rescue procedures described in the following paragraphs, the diver should be careful not to become entrapped by the victim, or the result may be a double casualty. The first concern of rescuers when they are seized by a struggling victim must be their own safety. One way to escape from a victim's grasp is to inflate the victim's or his own buoyancy system, which will push the divers apart.

21.5.1 Victim Submerged and Unconscious

An unconscious, non-breathing victim, whether submerged or on the surface, is in imminent danger of death. Virtually all of the rescuer's efforts must be directed at initiating and maintaining artificial resuscitation. Since resuscitation cannot be administered under water, the first consideration of the rescuer should be to get the victim to the surface.

WARNING
NO RESUSCITATIVE EFFORTS SHOULD BE ATTEMPTED WHILE SUBMERGED.

The rescuer should establish positive buoyancy as soon as possible and bring the victim to the surface in a controlled, buoyant ascent. The rescuer should approach the victim and remove the weight belt. If this is not possible, the BC should be inflated to achieve a slight positive buoyancy. Rescuers may need to remove their own weight belts and adjust their BC's to ensure that they are not more buoyant than the victim. As described by Seiff (1985), the victim should then be placed in a left-sided "do-si-do" position with the head tilted back and be brought to the surface at a normal rate of ascent. In this position, expanding gases in the victim's lungs should escape without difficulty. The "do-si-do" is a swimming position that affords the rescuer maximum mobility while controlling the victim (see Figure 21.2). The left upper arms are interlocked so that the rescuer can increase his control over the victim by squeezing the victim's arm between the rescuer's arm and chest. The rescuer should always be on the left side of the victim to facilitate control of the power inflator hoses on both the victim's and the rescuer's BCs.

WARNING
RESCUERS SHOULD BE CAREFUL NOT TO RISK EMBOLISM BY ASCENDING TOO FAST WITH AN UNCONSCIOUS VICTIM.

Once the unconscious diver is on the surface (weight belt already removed, buoyancy compensator inflated, and mask off) and it has been determined that the diver is not

FIGURE 21.2
Do-Si-Do Position for Administering In-Water Mouth-to-Mouth Artificial Resuscitation

breathing, the rescuer should be positioned for mouth-to-mouth or mouth-to-mask resuscitation. Based on in-water tests, it is recommended that the rescuer's mask be left on to retain optimal visual capabilities (Orr 1981). Removal of the victim's mask may be enough to start the victim breathing again. The best method for controlling the victim's position in the water while performing mouth-to-mouth or mouth-to-mask resuscitation is the "do-si-do" position shown in Figure 21.2.

The procedure for in-water mouth-to-mouth or mouth-to-mask resuscitation is as follows:

1. With the victim in a face-up position, the rescuer slides an arm between the body and the same arm of the victim. Rescuer remains on the victim's left side for ease in controlling BC power inflators.
2. Grasp the victim's hair, hood, or buoyancy compensator, and pull back to place the victim in a level position and to tilt his head to open his airway.
3. The rescuer places the heel of his free hand on the victim's forehead and seals the victim's nose by pinching it closed with thumb and forefinger (see Figure 21.3).
4. Rescuer seals his mouth over the mouth of victim and gives slow, deep exhalations to re-establish an adequate oxygen level. Do not pull up over the victim to start resuscitation; this will tend to force the victim's head under water. Instead, simply roll the victim's head over to a position that permits sealing the victim's mouth with a minimum amount of kicking effort.
5. If there is resistance to lung inflation, pull the victim's head back further and try again. If that doesn't work, check the airway for blockage. If a foreign object or vomit is present, use fingers to remove the obstruction quickly before continuing attempts to inflate the victim's lungs.
6. After successfully completing the two inflations, continue ventilating the victim's lungs at approximately 12 breaths per minute.
7. After filling the victim's lungs, allow the air to escape. Although the chest cannot be seen to rise and fall, the rescuer can hear the air passing through or can feel it with his cheek.
8. Continue to verify that an adequate seal is maintained. A perfect seal is not essential, but an effort should be made to minimize escaping air.
9. Check the victim continually to insure that he is not choking or vomiting.
10. Continue to ventilate the victim's lungs during the tow to the beach or boat. The victim's lungs should be filled with each breath to ensure that fresh air, rather than stale, is being provided. If the rescuer begins to feel dizzy because of hyperventilation, the rescue breathing rate should be slowed.

Sea conditions may override a controlled ventilation rate and will force the rescuer to modify the rate to match the seas' rhythm. This is accomplished by timing the ventilation to occur when the waves are washing over the victim's face. While continuing to resuscitate the victim, the rescuer, should start swimming toward the beach or boat at a comfortable pace. The rescuer should be careful not to overexert himself during the rescue attempt. If it is necessary to use one arm for swimming, the rescuer can achieve a nose seal by pressing his cheek against the victim's nose. If two rescuers are present, one should be stationed at the victim's head and one at his feet. The rescuer at the head is in charge. If three rescuers are available, two should be at

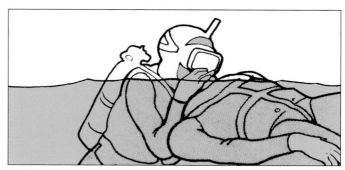

FIGURE 21.3
Artificial Resuscitation on Unconscious Victim

the head and one at the feet to push. The cylinder, BC, and weight belt, if still attached, should be removed from both the victim and the rescuers prior to bringing the victim on board a vessel.

<u>NOTE</u>
A single rescuer should angle the kick downward and toward the victim's feet. This not only provides some momentum toward shore or a boat, but also tends to keep the faces of both victim and rescuer out of the water. Care must be taken not to over-inflate the buoyancy compensators because the bulk created may prevent the rescuer from getting close enough to permit a good mouth-to-mouth seal.

Mouth-to-mouth resuscitation requires no equipment and can be started immediately, but it is difficult to sustain for any length of time, especially in rough water. In addition, because the victim's mouth is open during exhalation, water may enter and further complicate resuscitation efforts.

If the submerged victim is unconscious, but still breathing, the rescuer should hold the victim's mouthpiece in place to maintain a good seal, achieve positive buoyancy, and proceed with a controlled ascent to the surface. The victim should be kept in a vertical position with his head in a normal, straight forward, but not hyperextended attitude.

21.5.2 Victim Submerged and Conscious

An assessment of the condition of a submerged victim may reveal any one of a variety of situations, each requiring a different form of contact and handling. When approaching a conscious submerged victim, eye contact should be established immediately and the victim should be signaled to stop swimming and hold onto a solid object, if one is available.

If both the victim and the rescuer are suspended in the water column, the rescuer should immediately stabilize the victim's buoyancy and drop the victim's weight belt or stabilize the buoyancy by appropriate means if the victim is wearing a dry suit. The rescuer should then stabilize his own buoyancy. When making physical contact with the victim, the rescuer should be alert for sudden grasping motions or rapid ascents; initially the rescuer should offer a hand only. If at all possible, only highly trained rescue divers should attempt a mid-water rescue.

Stabilizing the victim may be enough to rectify the problem, assuming that the anxiety or distress was not caused by a problem such as entanglement or injury. Attempts to ascend with the victim before stabilization are not advised because the situation may continue to deteriorate. After stabilization, the rescuer should signal and initiate a controlled ascent while maintaining both eye and physical contact with the distressed diver. If, after reaching the surface, the victim shows signs of anxiety or stress, the dive should be terminated. If the submerged victim is entangled, the first action of the rescuer is to provide a source of air (if needed), calm the victim, and communicate to the victim what will be done next. Knives and other tools should be used with great caution, and the rescuer should remain alert for renewed struggling on the part of the victim during disentanglement. Except in cases of a minor snag, the victim and buddy should return to the surface and, at least temporarily, terminate the dive. Reassessment of both the victim and his equipment should be made by the divemaster on shore or on the support vessel.

An injured or ill diver should be taken to the surface at a reasonable rate of speed, with care taken to maintain breathing. Depending on the severity of the injury or illness, the victim may have to be assisted by buoyancy control or propulsion during ascent. The ascent should be interrupted only if breathing is impaired by vomiting or other aspects of the injury or illness, and should be continued as soon as breathing has been restored. Limited first aid or treatment of a particularly serious injury (i.e., hand pressure on a severe laceration) can be performed during ascent, but should not be allowed to interfere with the victim's breathing or with continuing ascent. In an injury involving serious bleeding, the rescuer should stay alert for predators in the water, both during ascent and after surfacing.

An uncontrolled descent caused by loss of buoyancy can create problems for the diver and rescuer even in relatively shallow waters, because of the danger of barotrauma or impact with bottom features. Uncontrolled descents in deep water may be complicated by nitrogen narcosis and can involve very serious problems of oxygen poisoning, rapid air consumption, and subsequent drowning. In this situation, a rescuer must quickly assess the risk and make a decision. In shallow water, for example, it may not seem prudent to risk ear squeeze to rescue a diver who is certain to come to rest on a shallow bottom and who will almost certainly be rescued by a conservative rescue procedure. However, a diver descending uncontrollably in very deep water presents a serious dilemma for the would-be rescuer. Variables to be assessed quickly include not only the victim's situation, but the rescuer's capabilities, air supply, susceptibility to narcosis, and so forth. Only the rescuer can make this personal decision. A wrong decision can mean the loss of two divers instead of one. In such situations, the possibility of a rescue without physical contact should be considered. An attempt should be made to get the attention of the descending diver by banging on a cylinder or possibly even dropping an object passed the descending diver's line of vision. Then, the diver can be motioned to the surface if the problem has simply been a lack of attention or concern. Visual contact serves at least to slow the victim's descent long enough for a pursuing rescuer to reach that depth.

If pursuit of a descending diver is successful, the first contact should almost always be made from behind the victim. This allows the rescuer to grasp the cylinder valve of a diver dropping in a vertical feet-first position or in a horizontal plane. A diver dropping in a head-first position should first be grabbed by a fin(s) to slow descent and to arrest any propulsive action. In such cases, the rescuer should quickly "climb" down the descending diver to grasp the cylinder valve. In situations where narcosis may be a factor for either party, the rescuer should remain behind the victim while slowing his descent and initiating ascent. Before establishing contact with the victim and inflating his buoyancy device, the rescuer should establish his own buoyancy. This ensures the rescuer's safety and permits him to use his oral inflator to add additional buoyancy rather than attempting to use the victim's inflation device.

If the descending victim is struggling or appears otherwise irrational, the rescuer should remain above and behind the victim to ensure his own safety. Divers not directly involved in handling the victim of uncontrolled descent should be sensitive to both the decompression and air supply needs of both the rescuer and the victim. The other divers can pre-position additional scuba equipment or obtain other resources that might be necessary.

An uncontrolled ascent may be caused by a loss of buoyancy control or panic. Although rescue of such a victim requires an extremely rapid response, rescuers must first ensure that their own ventilation will be adequate for the rescue. The rescuer also should be aware of the fact that a rapidly ascending diver may be making a calculated emergency swimming ascent. "Rescuing" such a diver may create more problems than it solves.

Where obvious breath-holding is a factor, the main objective is to arrest the ascent quickly. The rescuer should grab the most accessible part of the victim, which, on a rapidly ascending individual, may be the fins. This will serve not only to maintain contact, but also will stop the propulsive motion. The rescuer should shift his grasp immediately to the victim's ankle or leg because the victim can easily swim right out of his fins.

Victims who are not overly buoyant may be stopped simply by physical contact with a slightly negative buoyant rescuer. As soon as possible in a rescue procedure, the rescuer should establish a position above the ascending victim. The most effective position is face to face, maintained by keeping a grip on the victim's buoyancy compensator. Panicky ascending victims often claw desperately, and a rescuer must be alert to the possibility of losing his mask during contact with a desperate victim.

During attempts to arrest uncontrolled ascent in deep water, the rescuer must also recognize that an ascent that is initially non-buoyant may become buoyant near the surface because of air expanding in the buoyancy compensators of both the victim and the rescuer. Attempts to use signals, demonstrations, and if necessary squeezes, pushes, or other more vigorous thoracic pressers directly at the diaphragm should be made to make the victim exhale during uncontrolled ascent. Applying steady pressure may be safer and more effective than using a jab or punch.

21.5.3 Convulsions in the Water

A convulsion in itself rarely causes injury, but the secondary consequences for a scuba diver can be disastrous. First, the intense muscle contraction of the neck and jaw can cause the diver to spit out the mouthpiece, which is difficult to reinsert. Consequently, the diver is likely to drown unless rescued quickly. There is a risk of pulmonary barotrauma leading to arterial gas embolism if a diver ascends too rapidly or out of control; however, the threat of drowning out-weighs that of AGE.

The rescue of a convulsing diver is a complex subject. This is only a brief guide that discusses just a few of the considerations.

If a full-face mask is being used, it should be possible for the affected diver to breathe. However, if the diver is breathing from a standard scuba regulator, it is usually not worthwhile to attempt to reinsert the diver's mouthpiece. As soon as the initial phase of the convulsion is over, the diver should be taken to the surface using a controlled ascent rate, without unnecessary delay. The trade-offs are a risk of embolism from too fast an ascent, or certain drowning if ascent is delayed. The risk of embolism is the better option and the diver should be taken to the surface. At the surface, treat for near drowning according to signs and symptoms. Use surface oxygen as first aid. A diver who has a significant decompression obligation or is exhibiting signs and symptoms of DCS or AGE should be transported to the nearest medical facility and, when possible, directly to a recompression chamber.

21.5.4 Victim on the Surface and Unconscious

When confronted with an unconscious victim on the surface, speed is of the utmost importance. A surface approach is recommended because it affords continuous eye contact with the victim. Although some degree of positive buoyancy on the part of the victim may be assumed, many buoyancy compensators currently in use do not ensure that the face of a helpless victim will be maintained out of the water.

When approaching the victim, the rescuer should have positive buoyancy and the BC should be inflated as needed. The victim should be pulled to the face-up position, and his weights and scuba cylinder should be dropped. It may be necessary for the rescuer to drop his weights and cylinder, as well. If the equipment is not dropped at the outset, the rescuer may forget to do so, thus making the rescue more difficult and hazardous. While maintaining contact with the victim, the rescuer should place the victim in a left-sided, "do-si-do" position. Mouth-to-mouth or mouth-to-mask resuscitation should be started as soon as possible, and should be continued at a rate of twelve breaths per minute (or one breath every 5 seconds) while the victim is being transported to the dive vessel or to shore.

The procedure for rescuing an unconscious diver on the surface is outlined in the following steps:

1. Approach
2. Arousal
3. Call for assistance
4. Establish buoyancy-drop weights/cylinder
5. If face-down, turn victim to face-up position
6. Lock into rescuer position (Do-si-do, head cradle, etc.)
7. Remove victim's mask and regulator
8. Open airway look, listen, and feel for breathing
9. If not breathing, give victim two rescue breaths
10. Continue rescue breathing
11. Line up your point of exit and start your tow
12. Commence towing while continuing rescue breathing

NOTE
To date, the administration of in-water cardiopulmonary resuscitation (CPR) is not recommended (Kizer 1984). The effectiveness, even in a swimming pool, has not been demonstrated. To attempt it in the open water will delay getting the victim to a place where CPR can be administered properly.

21.5.5 Victim on the Surface and Conscious

When approaching a conscious victim on the surface, every effort should be made to utilize an extension rescue technique and to obtain help. The rescuer also must carefully assess the victim's mental state. If the victim is rational and coherent and no alternative rescue technique is available, the approach should probably be made from the front and on the surface; this approach allows continuous eye contact and reassures the victim because it allows him to observe the rescuer's actions.

If the victim is panicky or struggling, a different approach is required. One technique requires the rescuer to approach the victim from the front while submerged. This is generally a safe method because the victim will be extremely reluctant to go under water. Another technique involves a surface approach from the rear of the victim. Some prefer this approach because an unexpected wave or buoyancy problem for the rescuer is unlikely to bring the rescuer within the grasp of the victim. An approach from the rear facilitates the rescuer's grabbing the victim's cylinder valve, permits the rescuer to reach and activate the victim's buoyancy device, to release the victim's weight belt, and to disconnect the low-pressure inflator hose going to the buoyancy compensator. The rescuer is also in good position to tow the victim and can release the cylinder from the backpack, if necessary. However, it is better not to surprise the victim. In most cases, the rescuer will be seen or heard even when approaching from the rear. Thus the rear approach frequently will become a frontal approach because the victim will turn to face the rescuer.

Once physical contact has been made between rescuer and victim, the first action of the rescuer should be to establish the victim's buoyancy by releasing his weight belt and inflating his buoyancy compensator. When releasing a weight belt, care must be taken not to mistake the cylinder strap for the weight belt-release mechanism, and to ensure that the weight belt does not become entangled with other equipment in the drop path.

It is important for the rescuer to be aware of the head position of the victim. It is natural for an anxious or frightened diver to lift his head from the water. Because the human head weighs about 17 lbs., it takes significant effort on the part of the victim to raise it and keep it out of the water. Therefore, if the rescuer can induce the victim to keep his head above water, the rescue effort will be simplified. Even without using a snorkel or regulator, the rescuer should keep the victim in a head-back position with the nose and mouth clear of the water; most people can float with little effort if their head is partially or completely submerged.

Once contact and buoyancy have been established, the rescuer may consider removing the victim's mask. This will facilitate breathing, ease some of the psychological stress, and improve eye contact. If the victim is calm, however, the mask can remain in place to keep water out of the nose. Generally, to facilitate towing it is desirable to remove the backpack and cylinder. This is essential if a long, unassisted tow is anticipated, if the tow must pass through kelp, or if exit from the water must be made through surf or rocks. Throughout the process of removing

equipment the procedures followed should be explained and the assistance of the victim obtained, if possible.

21.5.6 Towing a Victim in the Water

After the victim has been stabilized at the surface, the cause of the original incident may still be present. The victim should be checked immediately to confirm that his face is not in the water, that his mask has not been pulled down over his mouth, and that his airway is clear. The regulator (if functioning properly) may need to be returned to the victim's mouth. In calm water, it may be useful to leave a snorkel in the victim's mouth; however, if the victim is being towed on his back, water may enter his snorkel and mouth.

Towing a victim should not be attempted if the victim is panicky or struggling, or if the safety of the rescuer is otherwise in jeopardy. If the victim is conscious and breathing and help is on the way, then the rescuer should wait until help arrives before attempting the tow. Distance, chop, swells, currents, surf, kelp, and the strength of the rescuer should be evaluated.

To tow a victim effectively, the rescuer must remain mobile, which may require the removal of such equipment as the weight belt or cylinder. The victim's body should be in a position (usually floating on his back) that will not impede the tow (see Figure 21.4). If the victim does not have a functioning regulator, his buoyancy compensator should be inflated just enough to keep his face out of the water (see Figure 21.5).

FIGURE 21.4
Fin to Either Side for Greatest Effect

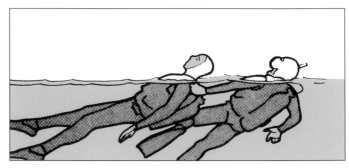

FIGURE 21.5
Towing a Conscious Casualty

The rescuer should use a towing technique that allows him to observe the victim. With a conscious victim, if possible, the rescuer should maintain continuous eye contact.

Towing a Line

Whenever possible, a towline or rescue throw bag should be used. This method is less fatiguing for the rescuer, reduces the need to ditch equipment, and may permit the rescuer to minimize physical contact with a struggling victim.

A *conscious victim* should grasp the line, which may have a buoyant object attached to it. After grasping the line, the conscious victim should be instructed to roll over onto his back to avoid being pulled under water during the tow. Once the victim has the line and is in position, the tow can commence slowly; haste could result in pulling the line loose or in swamping the victim. If the victim is unconscious, the line should be attached by the rescuer so that it can be detached easily. As long as it can be released easily, the line can also be attached to the rescuer.

Cylinder-Tow Method

Although many towing techniques require physical contact between rescuer and victim, it is generally recommended that divers learn the cylinder-tow method. Using this technique, the rescuer grasps the victim's cylinder with his right hand from his position at the victim's left side, being certain to maintain visual and verbal contact . This method allows the rescuer to commence mouth-to-mouth or mouth-to-mask resuscitation in the "do-si-do" position described earlier. It should be kept in mind, however, that although the victim's cylinder provides a convenient handle, towing is faster if the cylinder is removed. Circumstances such as surface conditions, towing distance, and the relative size of rescuer and victim dictate whether equipment should be left intact or dropped. Regardless of these circumstances, the cylinders of the rescuer and victim must be removed if the tow is through kelp or heavy surf.

Towing with Two Rescuers

Two rescuers may efficiently tow a victim on the surface. After the victim has been stabilized on his back with his weight belt removed, buoyancy compensator inflated, and mouthpiece removed, rescuers position themselves on both sides of the victim. The rescuer on the victim's right supports the victim's head with his left hand and grasps the victim's elbow or upper arm with his right hand in a palm-down position. The second rescuer grasps the victim's lower left arm firmly. The tow is made with both rescuers swimming on their backs.

Another method that may be used by two rescuers is to place the victim on his back with a rescuer on each side. Each rescuer grasps a wrist of the victim with the outside hand and places the inside hand on the victim's upper arm or in the armpit. When using this tow, the rescuers swim in a snorkel position.

21.5.7 Leaving the Water with a Victim

Removing the victim from the water may be the most difficult part of the rescue. It can be exceedingly difficult to transport a victim through heavy surf, coral formations, or mud, or to lift a victim onto a pier, dock, or boat. The situation may be complicated further if the victim requires continuous artificial resuscitation. Regardless of the point of exit, any encumbering equipment belonging to either the victim or the rescuer should be removed before leaving the water. Victims requiring artificial resuscitation should be placed on a flat hard surface as quickly as possible, because CPR should not be attempted in the water.

If the victim is unconscious, the head and chest should be tilted downward during removal from the water; this position will help drain water from the victim's airway (see Figure 21.6). In cases where a back or neck injury are suspected, care should be taken to avoid any twisting, bending, flexing, or extending of the victim. In such cases, the victim should be secured to a back board before being removed from the water. These special precautions should not delay removing the victim from the water if he is not breathing because CPR must be started as soon as possible.

NOTE
When attempting to remove a victim from the water, every effort should be made to obtain help by shouting, lighting flares, using a radio, or any other means at hand.

FIGURE 21.6
Boat Crew Assisting Casualty From Water

FIGURE 21.7
Rescuers Working as a Team

The following scenarios should be used to rescue divers:

Into Small Boats: A single rescuer will have considerable difficulty getting an incapacitated diver into a small boat, particularly if the victim is unconscious. If the boat is properly equipped with a ladder, the rescuer should climb in first and then assist the victim. If there is no ladder, the hands of the victim may have to be secured to the anchor line or some part of the boat to keep his face out of the water while the rescuer climbs into the boat. Once aboard, the rescuer can untie the victim's hands and pull him aboard. If the victim can climb aboard a boat with no ladder, the rescuer's shoulders may be used as a step. It is important during efforts to get into a small boat to keep the victim between the rescuer and the boat in order to maintain control.

Onto Larger Boats, Piers, and Cliffs: Lifting an incapacitated victim into a large boat, onto a high dock, or up a wall or cliff presents a serious problem for a rescuer, even if help is available. If the boat's gunwales are too high to reach over, a line with a bowline in it may be slipped under the victim's arms, with the knot in the middle of his back. If help is available, one or more lines can be attached to the loop so that the weight of the victim can be divided among the members of the rescue team (see Figure 21.7).

Through Surf: Exiting through the surf with an injured diver is very difficult and exposes the victim and the rescuer to the possibility of serious injury. As the surf zone is approached from open water, the rescuer must continually watch the approaching waves. Large waves generally come

in "sets" or groups of three to six waves about 10 to 15 seconds apart, with two to three minutes of smaller waves between sets. It is advisable to leave the surf zone during the lull between sets of larger waves, waiting outside the surf zone for a lull. If the victim is apprehensive or panicky, it may be necessary to pause seaward of the surf zone to calm him down.

WARNING
NEVER ATTEMPT TO TOW A PANICKY VICTIM THROUGH SURF TO SHORE.

To permit continued observation of the surf, the rescuer may tow the victim from the back toward shore. If it appears that large breaking waves may catch them, it is advisable to move seaward again to wait for the next lull. As a breaking wave approaches, the rescuer should turn toward shore, hold the victim firmly, cover the victim's mouth and nose, and let the wave strike from behind. Surf is often accompanied by rip currents, and the rescuer must be cautious to avoid being swept seaward. The use of more than one rescuer is highly desirable when exiting through surf. If two rescuers are available, the victim should be transported with one rescuer on each side towing the victim by the arms. Once ashore, the victim should be treated in accordance with the injuries sustained.

Onto a Rocky Shore: When going from deep water onto an adjacent rock or reef, the rescuer should tow the victim as close to the rocks as possible, then attempt to ride a swell up onto the rock with the buoyant victim turned sideways and held in front of the prone rescuer. The wave may serve as a kind of cushion because the leading edge precedes the victim and rebounds off the rocks, helping to prevent the victim from striking the rocks. The rescuer must brace himself on the rocks as soon as contact is made and hold on until the swell has receded. The victim then can be rolled higher onto the rocks. Once on solid ground, a standard fireman's or

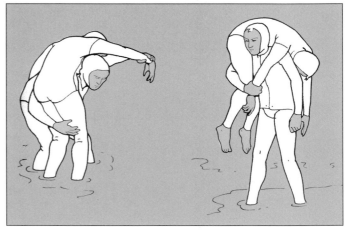

FIGURE 21.8
A Fireman's Lift

shoulder carry can be used to move the victim further ashore (see Figure 21.8). As with other resuscitation techniques, CPR, if needed, should be started as soon as possible.

21.6 ACCIDENT MANAGEMENT

Once the victim has been removed from the water and is on a solid platform such as a boat, pier, or beach, reassessment of the situation must be made immediately. Check first for life-threatening conditions such as airway obstruction, cessation of breathing, reduced circulation, bleeding, and shock. Every effort should be made to summon outside help using telephones, radios, runners, flags, or any other available means.

When divers retrieved from the water are unconscious or collapse soon after surfacing, they should be treated for arterial gas embolism unless another cause is clearly indicated. The many possible causes of unconsciousness include arterial gas embolism, decompression sickness, cardiac arrest, carbon monoxide poisoning, head injury, near-drowning, convulsion, insulin reaction (a diabetic on insulin), hyperventilation, or hypoventilation. Regardless of the cause, the immediate priority if the patient is not breathing is cardiopulmonary resuscitation. Clearing of the airway, mouth-to-mouth ventilation (or ventilation using of barrier devices, such as a pocket masks, are recommended), and chest compressions (CPR) may also be required. Because the unconsciousness must be assumed to have been caused by an embolism, the diver must be transported immediately to the nearest available medical facility. Divers Alert Network (DAN) should be contacted for assistance in case the victim must be transferred to a recompression chamber. During transportation, the diver should be positioned supine or in the recovery position. Cardiopulmonary resuscitation should be continued if necessary, and supplemental oxygen should be administered. Resuscitation should continue until the victim recovers or is pronounced dead by a physician. Prompt recompression is necessary for an unconscious diver under all conditions except when:

- Arterial gas embolism or decompression sickness has been completely ruled out
- Another lifesaving measure that makes recompression impossible, such as a thoracostomy, is essential

21.6.1 Summoning Aid

Because many divers and boaters are not familiar with the procedures for summoning aid in emergencies, critical time is lost, causing needless suffering and, perhaps, loss of life. The nature of the aid and the procedures to obtain it obviously vary with the situation, (i.e., on land in a populated area, on land in a remote area, or at sea). When on land in a populated area, local police, fire, and rescue services should be notified, as in any kind of accident. On a boat, the best procedure is to seek assistance from the U.S. Coast Guard.

Many signals have been devised over the years to signal distress or other emergency status. The most common signals are listed below. These have been accepted by international agreement, or national custom, or may be used occasionally by Coast Guard Search and Rescue units (U.S. Coast Guard 1973).

International Distress Signals:
- A voice signal consisting of the spoken word "Mayday"
- A gun or other explosive signal fired at intervals of about a minute
- A continuous sounding with any fog-signaling apparatus
- Rockets or shells throwing red stars fired one at a time at short intervals
- A signal made by radiotelegraphy or by any other signaling method consisting of the group S-O-S in the Morse Code
- The International Code Signal of distress indicated by the code group NC
- A signal consisting of a square flag having above or below it a ball or anything resembling a ball
- Flames on a vessel (as from a burning tar barrel, oil barrel, etc.)
- A rocket parachute flare or a hand flare showing a red light
- A smoke signal giving off a volume of orange-colored smoke
- Slowly and repeatedly raising and lowering arms outstretched to each side
- The radiotelegraph alarm signal, which is designed to actuate the radiotelegraph auto alarms of vessels so fitted, consisting of a series of 12 dashes, sent in one minute, with the duration of the interval between consecutive dashes being one second
- The radiotelephone alarm signal consisting of two tones transmitted alternately over periods from 30 seconds to one minute

Table 21.1 summarizes the procedures for obtaining emergency aid, evacuation of casualties, and diving medical advice. Only national information has been included because local numbers and procedures vary from location to location, and radio call numbers and telephone numbers are changed frequently.

When contact is made by radio or telephone, the caller should declare that the situation is an emergency and state the nature of that emergency. For example, "This is an emergency. I have a diving accident victim needing treatment in a recompression chamber." The caller should be prepared to provide information on the location, including direction and distance from prominent landmarks, environmental conditions relating to seas state, roads, wind, etc., and the status of the victim. Unusual circumstances should be described and the number of victims identified. If the victim's location changes, all individuals involved in the rescue should be

TABLE 21.1
Sources of Emergency Assistance

<table>
<tr><td colspan="2" align="center">**Medical Advice—Nearest Operable Chamber Location**</td></tr>
<tr><td>U.S. Navy Experimental Diving Unit
Panama City, Florida (904) 234-4355</td><td>Divers Alert Network
The Peter B. Bennett Center
6 W. Colony Place
Durham, North Carolina 27705
(919) 684-8111</td></tr>
</table>

Emergency Communications Frequencies

500 kHz	International CW/MCW distress and calling
2182 kHz	International voice distress, safety and calling (particularly useful for communications between aircraft and vessels)
156.8 MHz	FM, U.S. voice distress and international voice safety and calling marine radio (Channel 16)

Continuous Broadcast NOAA Weather Frequencies
(When weather affects emergency operations)
162.550 MHz
162.475 MHZ
162.400 MHz

advised of the new location and of any planned moves or changes.

In 1980, Divers Alert Network (DAN) was established at Duke University Medical Center in Durham, North Carolina, as the country's medical advisory service for sport divers. Divers, as well as non-divers, physicians and other allied healthcare professionals may receive assistance with emergency and non-emergency issues related to diving and diving safety.

Access to DAN's non-emergency services is available 9:00 a.m. to 5:00 p.m., eastern time, Monday through Friday, by calling (919) 684-2948 ext. 222.

Access to DAN's 24-hour diving emergency services is available by contacting (919) 684-8111 or (919) 684-4326 (collect in an emergency). When the call is answered and the caller identifies the situation as a diving emergency, he will be placed in contact with a DAN medical professional (physician, nurse, paramedic, or medical technician) trained in diving medicine and available 24 hours a day. The caller may be advised directly or referred to a local physician trained in diving medicine or to a medical facility for evaluation. If necessary, DAN will assist with referral or emergency evacuation to an appropriate medical facility.

If other boats are not immediately available, proceed to the nearest inhabited dock and telephone local emergency medical services (EMS), U.S.C.G. facility or Divers Alert Network (DAN). Advise them of a diving accident, state the need for transportation, and give the exact location. Have someone remain at the telephone for further assistance.

If symptoms occur on land after diving, contact local medical personnel. These individuals should be able to assist or give the location of the nearest recompression chamber.

There are a number of miscellaneous distress signals that may alert rescue aircraft:

- Inverted U.S. flag; used as a distress signal by marine craft in the United States
- A cloth of international orange color (United States)
- A cloth of international orange color with a black square and ball inscribed thereon (United States and Canada)
- A cloth of red color (Caribbean territories)
- Green fluorescent dye marker
- Flashes (as from a signal mirror)
- Smoke from signal fires (three signal fires arranged in a triangular pattern are a positive sign of distress)

Occasionally, divers in a small boat may be called on to render assistance in an emergency situation. If the emergency call is by radio or telephone, the procedures will be obvious. If, however, a rescue craft is seeking assistance from a boat in the area of an emergency, it is important that those in the boat understand some simple air-to-surface signals. The maneuvers used in this situation by the U.S. Coast Guard Search and Rescue System are described below.

International Aircraft to Ground Craft Signals

The following maneuvers performed in sequence by an aircraft means that an aircraft wishes to direct a surface craft toward an aircraft or a surface craft in distress:

- Circling the surface craft at least once
- Crossing the projected course of the surface craft close ahead at low altitude and rocking the wings, opening and closing the throttle, changing the propeller pitch
- Heading in the direction in which the surface craft is to be directed

The following maneuver by an aircraft means that the assistance of the surface craft is no longer required:

- Crossing the wake of the surface craft close astern at a low altitude and rocking the wings, opening and closing the throttle, changing the propeller pitch

NOTE
Opening and closing the throttle and changing the propeller pitch are alternative signals to rocking the wings.

21.6.2 On-Site Care of the Diving Casualty

Two life-threatening conditions may occur as a result of a diving accident: air embolism and decompression sickness. They are sometimes grouped together as decompression illness (DCI).

Successful treatment depends on early recognition of the frequently confusing symptoms of DCI. Divers, instructors, emergency personnel, and physicians must be able to recognize decompression illness and begin the proper early treatment while arranging entry into the hyperbaric trauma system.

It is important to provide early treatment for DCI. It is not necessary to distinguish between air embolism and decompression sickness, as the initial management of both conditions is the same.

Once DCI symptoms have been detected, the field delivery of emergency oxygen is essential. Why oxygen? By excluding nitrogen from the lungs of the injured diver, he will more quickly eliminate excess nitrogen accumulated from his dive. Oxygen may also reduce nitrogen bubble size, increase oxygenated blood flow to the body's tissues and reduce blood sludging (a thickening of blood resulting from excess nitrogen). Oxygen can also help reduce tissue swelling, and for those divers in respiratory distress, it may ease breathing.

WARNING
EVEN IF SYMPTOMS ARE RELIEVED WITH EMERGENCY OXYGEN, THE INJURED DIVER STILL REQUIRES A FURTHER MEDICAL EVALUATION.

21.6.2.1 General Procedures of Accident Management
(see Figure 21.9)

1. First priority always goes to the airway.
2. Every injured person in respiratory distress should receive oxygen.
3. Every injured person whose illness or injury suggests the possibility of oxygen deficiency should receive oxygen.
4. Every unresponsive person should be assumed to have a respiratory insufficiency and needs:
   - Protection of airway
   - Careful monitoring to determine whether assisted ventilation or CPR is required
   - Oxygen
5. When in doubt, administer oxygen.

21.6.2.2 Immediate Care Protocol

1. ABC-establish a clear Airway, check Breathing and Circulation (pulse).
2. If necessary, commence rescue breathing.
3. Check for pulse, commence cardiopulmonary resuscitation (CPR) if needed.
4. Confirm whether the diver had a source of compressed air or other breathing gas under water.

IF NO:

Probably not a diving related accident. Administer appropriate first aid. Call for help if needed.

IF YES:

Embolism and decompression illness must be considered as a cause. Call for help in management and evacuation. Follow this protocol and give appropriate first aid:

5. Did symptoms begin while diver was under water?
   - Always serious
   - Begin treatment for serious symptoms
6. Are the symptoms mild?
   - Itching not related to marine or aquatic life
   - Non-painful joint "awareness"
7. If only mild symptoms are present:
   - Place diver in lateral recumbent (recovery position)
   - Make brief neurological assessment (do not allow to interfere with urgent first aid measures)
   - Begin oxygen first aid. Use 100% oxygen delivered by positive pressure/demand valve system or non-rebreather mask
   - Protect diver from heat, cold, further injury
   - Evaluate for other illness or injury in addition to DCI
8. If mild symptoms are present:
   - Observe carefully for improvement or deterioration
   - Continue oxygen for 30 minutes

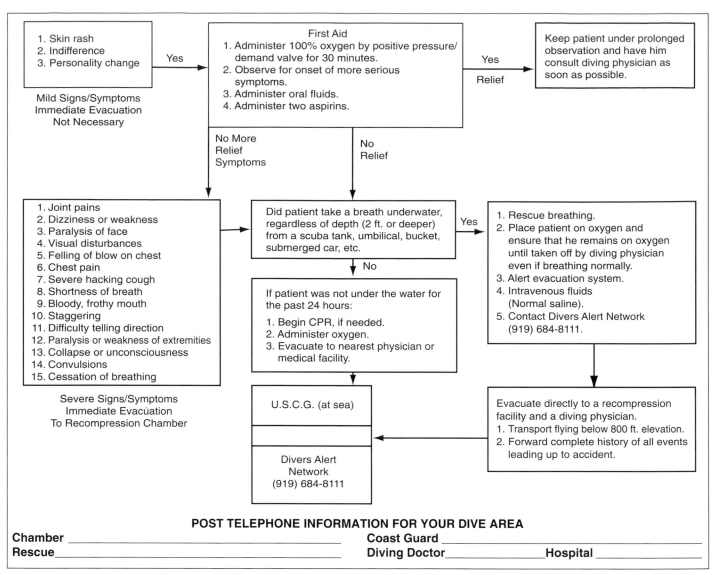

FIGURE 21.9
Diving Accident Management Flow Chart

- If symptoms are still present treat as serious
- If symptoms are gone, observe
- Contact DAN or EMS for assistance

9. If serious symptoms are present:
  - Maintain appropriate position
  - Continue oxygen as long as available
  - Constant observation and periodic neurological evaluation
  - Maintain contact with Coast Guard, EMS, or other emergency agency
  - Contact DAN when possible

10. If serious symptoms improve or clear completely:
  - Continue oxygen and other measures
  - Evacuate to medical facility as soon as possible for evaluation

11. If serious symptoms are not improving or are getting worse:

- Carefully recheck techniques of first aid and make any corrections needed
- Notify emergency agency of situation
- Make an urgent evacuation consistent with safety

21.6.2.3 Additional Advanced Life Support (ALS)

This procedure is for personnel who are ALS-qualified and under medical direction. The following procedures should be done by trained personnel only:

- Cardiac monitor.
- Intubation if needed.
- 100% oxygen by non-rebreather mask, bag-valve-mask or positive pressure/demand valve as indicated.
- Intravenous access with normal saline, keep at open rate until directed by medical control.
- Do not use intravenous fluids containing dextrose.

- If air evacuation is used, cabin pressure must be maintained near sea level and not exceed 800 ft. (244 m) unless aircraft safety is compromised.
- Maintain custody of diving equipment for testing.

21.6.2.4 In-Water Recompression Treatment

WARNING

DO NOT ATTEMPT TREATMENT BY IN-WATER RECOMPRESSION WITH COMPRESSED AIR.

In-water recompression treatment of the diver usually ends with the diver being forced to the surface by cold water or an inadequate air supply. Other problems can include panic, seasickness, drowning, and hypothermia. Incomplete treatment and further nitrogen uptake by the diver often occur. When treatment is incomplete and a victim has mild signs and symptoms of decompression illness, the usual result is a much more seriously injured diver. If the initial symptoms are serious, the results may be disastrous.

First aid treatment on the surface with 100% oxygen is effective in stabilizing the injured diver while being transported to a medical facility.

21.6.2.5 Neurological Assessment and Examination

A common problem in the management of diving cases is that such cases are often misdiagnosed initially, either by divers at the scene or by a physician untrained in diving medicine. To minimize the likelihood of overlooking serious symptoms of decompression illness, an attending physician should give a neurological examination before, during, and after treatment. Such an examination usually takes about 30 minutes and requires certain diagnostic equipment and training to interpret the results.

Since a physician is rarely at the scene of a diving accident, a 5-minute neurological examination has been developed that can be administered by non-medical personnel.

Examination of an injured diver's central nervous system soon after an accident may provide valuable information to the physician responsible for treatment. The "Neuro" exam is easy to learn and can be done by individuals with minimal medical experience (See Appendix III).

21.7 EVACUATION BY AIR

Each helicopter evacuation presents unique problems. Knowing what to expect and the procedures to follow, however, can save time, effort, and perhaps a life. The following information is applicable to U.S. Coast Guard (U.S.C.G.) helicopter evacuation by sea (see Figure 21.10), but the same rules also apply to most helicopter evacuations:

- Try to establish communications with the helicopter. If the boat does not have the necessary frequency, try to work through another boat.
- Maintain speed of 10–15 knots (5–7.5 m/s); do not slow down or stop.
- Maintain course into wind about 20 degrees on port bow.
- Lower all antennas, if possible, without losing communications.
- Secure all loose objects on or around the decks, because the helicopter will create strong winds.
- Make sure the patient is ready in advance of the transfer, because time is critical both to the victim and the hovering aircraft.
- Signal the helicopter pilot when all is ready, using hand signals by day and flashlight by night.
- If a trail line is dropped by the aircraft, guide the basket to the deck with the line.
- To prevent electric shock, allow the lifting device (stretcher) to touch the boat before handling it.
- Do not secure any lines/wires from the boat to the stretcher.
- Place a personal flotation device on the patient.
- Tie the patient into the stretcher, face up.
- If the patient cannot communicate, attach personal information such as name, age, address, what happened, results of neuro exam (if completed), and what medication has been administered.
- If the patient is a diving accident victim, ensure that the flight crew has a copy of, or is instructed in, medical procedures for diving accidents.
- If the patient is a diving accident victim, ensure that the flight crew delivers the patient to a hyperbaric trauma center (recompression chamber complex).
- If the patient is dead, inform the flight crew so they do not take unnecessary risks.
- Helicopter transfers should not be made if the victim is being given CPR because the chest compression should not be stopped for the time required to transfer the victim. In addition, the helicopter crew may not include an individual trained in CPR.

FIGURE 21.10
Evacuation by Air

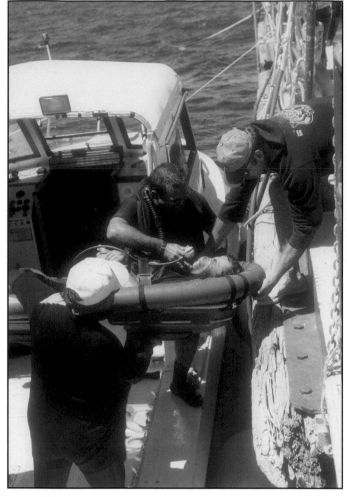

FIGURE 21.11
Emergency Evacuation

21.8 GUIDELINES FOR EMERGENCY EVACUATION

Regardless of the means of evacuation (see Figure 21.11), certain factors must be followed to minimize additional injury to the patient. These factors include providing the maximum amount of advance information to the rescuing organization and the emergency-receiving facility and advising the rescue crew in the proper procedures for transporting a diving casualty.

The following medical evacuation information should be forwarded with the patient. If possible, take time to explain the following steps to the physician or paramedic. Do not assume that they understand the reasons why oxygen should be administered to a diving accident victim. If a patient is breathing normally, a physician may stop the oxygen breathing because he does not realize that the patient must continue to breathe oxygen to off-load inert gases.

The following steps should be taken:

- Maintain breathing and heart functions; ensure the airway remains open.
- Keep patient on 100% oxygen.
- Ensure paramedics/physicians understand why the patient needs to be taken to a recompression chamber instead of a hospital.
- Do not stop giving oxygen to a diving accident patient even if the patient is breathing normally.
- Keep patient out of the hot sun and watch for shock.
- Do not give any pain-killing drugs (including aspirin); intravenous injections can be given to prevent vascular collapse or dehydration.
- Instruct flight crews to fly or pressurize the aircraft below 800 ft. (244 m).
- Provided the aircraft can handle the extra weight, the diving buddy should be transported with the patient because he also may need recompression or he can provide information about the incident.
- A complete history of all events leading up to the accident and evacuation must be forwarded with the patient.
- Depth gauges, cylinders, regulators, and other diving equipment should be maintained in the condition in which they were found, pending any accident investigation.

21.9 ACCIDENT REPORTING PROCEDURES

All diving accidents involving NOAA personnel, whether fatal or non-fatal, must be reported promptly. The procedures for reporting accidents are contained in the NOAA Diving Regulations (NOAA Administrative Order 209-123).

Accidents, both fatal and non-fatal, should also be reported to DAN. In addition to providing medical advice during diving emergencies, DAN serves as a clearing house for information on diving accidents and their treatment. Information (without identifying data) is collected on the victims to be studied on a national level. It is then made available to those participating groups, such as certifying agencies and equipment manufacturers, who are responsible for training and equipping divers.

Reporting accidents is more than a legal responsibility; it permits an investigation and compilation of accident statistics. From this information, all concerned can learn to improve diving techniques, which will result in fewer diving accidents in the future.

Appendix
Dive Planning

SECTION	PAGE

NOAA DIVING OPERATIONS PLAN
DEVELOPMENT GUIDELINES

I. Introduction to the NOAA Dive Operations Plan
    The purpose of preparing a dive plan is to ensure that NOAA diving operations are thoroughly planned so as to maximize the chances of safely and successfully achieving the objectives of the dive project. This document provides a generic dive plan template from which a project-specific plan can be prepared. Not all the information listed in this document may be required for each diving operation, nor is this template intended to encompass all information that may be needed for each diving project. The NOAA Diving Supervisor and the Project Manager/Chief Scientist must use their judgement in determining which sections of the dive plan should be completed.

II. For single day or simple diving projects, the NOAA Diving Supervisor and the Project Manager/Chief Scientist should plan diving operations using the list of information in this Appendix.

III. For multiple day or complex diving projects, the NOAA Divemaster and the Project Manager/Chief Scientist should work together to complete the following sections:

   - **Section I: Overview of Diving Project Activities**
   - **Section II: Schedule of Diving Operations**
   - **Section III: Specific Dive Plan Information**
   - **Section IV: Estimated Budget**
   - **Dive Safety and Planning: Predive Checklist and Postdive Checklist**
   - **Diving Accident Management Plan**

   A. **Section I: Overview of Diving Activities**
   - Project objective(s) and question(s) to be answered by the project.
   - Mailing addresses, telephone number, fax numbers and e-mail addresses for key participants.
   - Significance of project or benefit to the (Name of NOAA Unit, Ship, or Party).
   - General location of diving operations, dive vessel(s) to be used, and a map of all potential dive sites.
   - Dates of diving project and list of participants, including both NOAA and non-NOAA divers.
   - General overview of diving techniques or procedures to be used, including illustrations of techniques or references to publications explaining procedures in greater detail if necessary.
   - Statement regarding compliance with OSHA/USCG Commercial Diving Regulations (Are operations subject to or exempt?).

   B. **Section II: Schedule of Diving Operations**
   Provide the following information concerning schedules and timing of events:
   - [Date(s)]: Mobilization activities to prepare for the diving project.
   - [Date(s)]: Testing or training to prepare for diving activities.
   - [Date(s)]: Dive times and diving activities planned for the project, including daily briefings and debriefings.
   - [Date(s)]: Planned day(s) off, if applicable.
   - [Date(s)]: Demobilization activities to complete the diving project.
   - [Date(s)]: Report on the results of the diving project prepared by NOAA Divemaster in consultation with Project Manager/Chief Scientist.

   C. **Section III: Specific Dive Plan Information**
   Provide the following information:
   - Names, agency affiliations, certification levels, and roles or functions for all diving participants.
   - Underwater tasks to be completed (in order of priority), the estimated time to accomplish each task, and whether the task falls under the USCG/OSHA Commercial Diving Regulations or is exempt due to its scientific nature.
   - Dive sites by name (if applicable), location (LAT/LONG), and depth (FSW).
   - Equipment required to accomplish the underwater tasks and the agency responsible for supplying the equipment.
   - Any special permits (i.e., collection permits in marine sanctuaries) or chemicals (i.e., Rotenone) that may be required or used during the operation.
   - The following statement should be included in Section III: *"All diving operations will comply with the NOAA Diving Regulations (NOAA Administrative Order 209–123, 1999), current policies of the NOAA Diving Center, and applicable reciprocity agreements."*

   D. **Section IV: Estimated Budget**
   Provide the following estimates:
   - Salaries (including overtime) and dive pay
   - Travel and per diem
   - Contractual services
   - Equipment and/or facilities
   - Expendable supplies and materials

DIVE SAFETY AND PLANNING
PREDIVE CHECKLIST

The Dive Safety and Planning Predive Checklist is to be completed by the assigned NOAA Divemaster prior to NOAA dive activities.

I. Mission Safety
- ☐ Dive operations are planned in accordance with NOAA Diving regulations.
- ☐ NOAA Unit Diving Supervisor, or assigned Divemaster, approves planned dive operations.
- ☐ A certified NOAA Divemaster is in-charge of the diving operation.
- ☐ All divers are on active dive status with the NOAA Diving Program.
- ☐ The Diving Accident Management Plan is posted, coordinated, and reviewed (i.e., chamber availability, evacuation route, etc.), and all personnel informed of their duties.
- ☐ Predive briefing conducted.
- ☐ Dive mission, objectives, and goals are defined, reviewed, and understood by dive team and support personnel.

II. Identify, Analyze, and Prepare for Potential Hazards
- ☐ Identify dive site entry procedures and exit access point(s).
- ☐ Define depth, bottom time, and minimum breathing gas pressure limits for the planned dives.
- ☐ Define next deeper and next longer bottom time limits in case planned limits are exceeded accidentally.
- ☐ Evaluate and discuss potential for entrapment, entanglement, or other physical or mechanical hazards.
- ☐ Evaluate and discuss potential for bottom obstructions or dangerous bottom conditions.
- ☐ Evaluate and discuss potential for dangerous marine life.
- ☐ Evaluate and discuss potential for strong current, low visibility, thermoclines, surge, etc.
- ☐ Evaluate and discuss potential for contamination or exposure to pollution (i.e., petroleum products, biological or chemical hazards, etc.).
- ☐ Evaluate and discuss local marine traffic hazards (notify vessel traffic of diving operations).
- ☐ Complete Dive Safe Ship Operations (NOAA Form 64-3) if applicable.
- ☐ Ensure that Material Safety Data Sheets (MSDS) available for all chemicals being used.

III. Diving and Support Personnel
- ☐ Ensure that all divers are authorized to perform their assigned duties according to their NOAA certification levels (i.e., Working Diver, Scientific Diver, Trainee Diver, or Observational Diver).
- ☐ Ensure that all divers are qualified (i.e., proper training and experience) to safely complete assigned underwater tasks.
- ☐ Verify that all divers are physically and mentally fit to conduct dive.
- ☐ Ensure that dive physicals are available for each diver in case of an emergency.
- ☐ Ensure that support personnel understand all diver hand signals and can offer immediate assistance in case of an emergency.
- ☐ Brief the dive team and support personnel.

IV. Equipment
- ☐ Ensure all dive gear and techniques are appropriate and authorized.
- ☐ Ensure all diver gear is on-hand, inspected, and found fully functional prior to the divers entering the water.
- ☐ Ensure all emergency and support equipment/supplies are available, inspected and found fully functional prior to commencing dive operations:
  - ☐ Drinking water
  - ☐ Means of communication (i.e., radio, cellular telephone, landline telephone, SATCOM, etc.)
  - ☐ Oxygen resuscitator, first aid kit, and backboard
  - ☐ Divemaster kit, including a complete set of USN Decompression Tables
- ☐ Ensure dive platform is stable, seaworthy, and outfitted with required safety equipment.
- ☐ Ensure appropriate dive flags (sport and/or code alpha) are prominently displayed.

NOTES

DIVE SAFETY AND PLANNING
POSTDIVE CHECKLIST

The Dive Safety and Planning Postdive Checklist is to be completed by the assigned NOAA Divemaster following NOAA dive activities.

- ☐ Notify vessel bridge when diving operations are completed.
- ☐ Strike the dive flags.
- ☐ Ensure dive team buddies stay together for a minimum of 30 minutes after each dive.
- ☐ Recover and stow all support equipment.
- ☐ Ensure that all dive equipment is thoroughly cleaned and properly stowed.
- ☐ Refill all scuba cylinders.
- ☐ Log all dives and topside activities.
- ☐ Conduct a dive debrief.
- ☐ Monitor divers for signs and symptoms of pressure-related illnesses or injuries for a minimum of 2 hours after each dive.
- ☐ Provide contact numbers for nearest chamber, transportation to chamber, and Divemaster.
- ☐ File a final dive report.

DIVING ACCIDENT MANAGEMENT PLAN

A Diving Accident Management Plan is prepared for each diving locale and operation. The Plan is to be implemented in the event of a diving emergency.

I. **Dive Accident Plan: <u>Conscious and Alert Diving Accident Victim</u>**
   A. Evaluate victim's Airway, Breathing, and Circulation (ABC).
   B. Put the victim on 100% oxygen using a positive-pressure/demand oxygen resuscitator.
   C. Call 911 (local EMS) and the U.S. Coast Guard at [LOCATION] at [USCG TELEPHONE NUMBER], or hail them on VHF radio, channel 16, to report the diving accident. The EMS dispatcher will notify land transportation, [NAME OF LOCAL HOSPITAL], and the [NAME OF THE CLOSEST RECOMPRESSION CHAMBER].
   D. Evaluate the victim and gather additional information about the incident:
      • Perform a 5-minute field neurological examination on the stricken diver
      • Gather as much information about the dive as possible
      • Interview the victim's dive buddy for additional information
      • Secure victim's dive gear for examination (DO NOT DISASSEMBLE GEAR OR EXHAUST ANY AIR FROM THE SYSTEM)
   E. If decompression sickness is suspected, or any other type of pressure-related injury (arterial gas embolism, pneumothorax, etc.) keep the victim on his back (DO NOT RAISE THE VICTIM'S LEGS). Place the victim on his side if nauseated or vomiting–keep the airway clear.
   F. The victim should be transported to [NAME OF LOCAL HOSPITAL] for evaluation. The [NAME OF CLOSEST RECOMPRESSION CHAMBER] is the closest available recompression chamber.
      • If not nauseated and not experiencing altered level of consciousness, give the victim water to drink during transportation to the [NAME OF LOCAL HOSPITAL].
      • Continue oxygen administration.
      • Send any and all information about the dive with the victim to the hospital including results of field neurological examination.
      • Keep victim comfortable and observe for shock or change in condition.
   G. Based on the evaluation by the doctor at [NAME OF LOCAL HOSPITAL], the victim may be transported to the [NAME OF CLOSEST RECOMPRESSION CHAMBER] for treatment.

II. **Dive Accident Plan: <u>Unconscious and Non-Responsive Dive Accident Victim</u>**
   A. Evaluate victim's Airway, Breathing, and Circulation (ABC).
   B. Start cardio-pulmonary resuscitation, or rescue breathing using a positive-pressure/demand oxygen resuscitator.
   C. Call 911 (local EMS) and the U.S. Coast Guard at [LOCATION] at [U.S.C.G. TELEPHONE NUMBER], or hail them on VHF radio, channel 16, to report the diving accident. The EMS dispatcher will notify land transportation, [NAME OF LOCAL HOSPITAL], and the [NAME OF THE CLOSEST RECOMPRESSION CHAMBER].
   D. Evaluate the victim and gather additional information about the incident:
      • Gather as much information about the dive as possible
      • Interview the victim's dive buddy for additional information
      • Secure victim's dive gear for examination (DO NOT DISASSEMBLE GEAR OR EXHAUST ANY AIR FROM THE SYSTEM)
   E. Transport the victim to the harbor that is the closest to the dive site [NAME OF NEAREST HARBOR OR EVACUATION SITE] where a local ambulance should be standing-by to evacuate the victim to [NAME OF LOCAL HOSPITAL].
   F. If there is a problem transporting the victim to the nearest harbor or if the time delay is significant (>2 hours), call or radio the U.S.C.G. at [U.S.C.G. TELEPHONE NUMBER] or VHF channel 16, to arrange air evacuation of the victim. The U.S.C.G. air evacuation team will coordinate with [NAME OF LOCAL HOSPITAL].

III. **Medical Assistance and Recompression Chamber Contact Information**
   A. Before commencing dive operations, the Divemaster will contact the primary recompression chamber to ensure that the chamber is operational and available to receive patients. If the primary chamber is not operational, alternate facilities should be contacted.
   B. Primary recompression chamber facility:
      • LOCATION
      • ADDRESS
      • TELEPHONE NUMBER DURING NORMAL BUSINESS HOURS
      • TELEPHONE NUMBER AFTER HOURS
   C. Alternate telephone numbers for recompression chambers and medical advice are:
      • [FIRST ALTERNATE and TELEPHONE NUMBER]
      • [SECOND ALTERNATIVE and TELEPHONE NUMBER]
   D. **Divers Alert Network**
      • The Peter B. Bennett Center, 6 West Colony Place, Durham, North Carolina 27705, U.S.A
      • (919) 684-8111 (24 hour emergency telephone number)

NOTES

Appendix
Field Neurological Assessment

SECTION	PAGE

Field Neurological Assessment II

GENERAL

The neurological exam is a very straightforward non-invasive procedure that can be done by a non-physician in field conditions, with just simple tests of cognition, motor, sensory, and coordination functions.

The exam covers the following areas:

- Mental Status
- Coordination/Motor
- Cranial Nerves
- Sensory Function
- Deep Tendon Reflexes

Mental Status: This is best determined from first interactions with the individual and should include observations of their alertness, orientation, and thought process.

Obtain a good history which includes the dive profile, present symptoms, and changes in symptoms with time. The patient's responses during the neurological examination will give the examiner a good indication of the patient's mental status. Most important, determine if the patient knows the time and place, can recognize familiar people, and understands the present situation. Check for appropriate mood reactions. Memory can be tested by asking the name of their dive buddy, or what they had for their most recent meal.

Cognitive function involves intellectual processes of perception, awareness, comprehension of ideas, and all aspects of perception, thinking, reasoning, and remembering. Simple tests may include: asking the patient to remember something such as a list of objects, bat, golf ball, mask, snorkel, and fins, and have them repeat the list later; spelling a word such as "universe" backwards; counting backwards from 100 by "sevens;" and recalling the information at the end of the examination. Most diving casualties have normal mental status.

Coordination: (cerebellar/inner ear function): The first indicator of muscle strength and general coordination is to observe how the patient walks. A normal gait indicates that many muscle groups and general brain functions are normal. More thorough examination includes tests of brain and inner ear. As always, all neurological tests are to be done bilaterally and results compared.

1. Heels-to-Toe Test: The tandem walk is the standard "drunk driver" test. While looking straight ahead, the patient must walk a straight line, placing the heel of one foot directly in front of the toes of the opposite foot. Deficits to notice are whether the patient limps or the patient staggers to one side.

2. Romberg Test: With eyes closed, the patient stands with feet together and arms extended to the front, palms up. Note whether the patient can maintain his balance or if he immediately falls to one side. Some examiners recommend giving the patient a small shove from either side with the fingertips.

3. Finger-to-Nose Test: The patient stands with eyes closed and head back, arms extended to the side. Bending the arm at the elbow, the patient touches his nose with an extended forefinger, alternating arms. An extension of this test is to have the patient, with eyes open, alternately touch his nose with his fingertip and then touch the fingertip of the examiner. The examiner will change the position of his fingertip each time the patient touches his nose. In this version speed is not crucial, but accuracy is important.

4. Heel-Shin Slide Test: While standing, the patient touches the heel of one foot to the knee of the opposite leg, foot pointing forward. While maintaining this contact, he runs his heel down the shin to the ankle. Each leg should be tested.

5. Rapid Alternating Movement Test: The patient slaps one hand on the palm of the other, alternating palm up and then palm down. Any exercise requiring rapidly changing movement will suffice. Again, both sides should be tested.

Motor: A diver with decompression sickness may experience disturbances in the muscle system. The range of symptoms can be from a mild twitching of a muscle to weakness and paralysis. No matter how slight the abnormality, symptoms involving the motor system shall be treated.

Extremity Strength: It is common to find deficits in muscle strength in a diver with a severe central nervous system decompression illness incident. All muscle groups need to be tested and compared with the same muscle group on the other side, also known as bilateral testing and comparison. One-sided muscle weakness is known as a hemiparesis. The scale is graded from a low of 1 to normal of 6:

1. *Paralysis*: No motion possible.
2. *Profound Weakness*: Flicker or trace of muscle contraction.
3. *Severe Weakness*: Able to contract muscle but cannot move joint against gravity.
4. *Moderate Weakness*: Able to overcome the force of gravity but not the resistance of the examiner.
5. *Mild Weakness*: Able to resist slight force of examiner.
6. *Normal*: Equal strength bilaterally (both sides), and able to resist examiner. The testing of extremity strength is divided into two parts: upper body and lower body. Each muscle group is compared to the same group in the opposite limb. There are six muscle groups tested in the upper extremity: deltoids, latissimus, biceps, triceps, forearm muscles, and hand muscles (see Table II.1). These muscles are tested with resistance provided by the examiner. The patient should overcome force applied by the examiner which is tailored to the patient's strength. A table is included to describe the tests (see Table II.2). The lower extremity strength is assessed by watching the patient walk on his heels for a short distance and then on his toes. The patient should then walk while squatting (duck walk). These tests adequately assess lower extremity strength as well as balance and coordination. If a more detailed examination of the lower extremity strength is desired, testing should be accomplished at each joint.

Cranial Nerves: These include 12 pairs of nerves that emanate from the skull and are organized as they originate from the front centerline of the head, named by numerals. Each can be assessed with simple tests.

1. *Olfactory nerves* can be tested with an ammonia ampule or some non-toxic irritant to test for smell.
2. *Optic nerves* carry all the visual signals from the two eyes. One eye should be tested at a time. Test for light and dark, perception of objects, and reading ability. Ask for any symptoms of blurring of vision, loss of vision, spots in the visual field, or peripheral vision loss (tunnel vision). More detailed testing can be done by standing in front of the patient and asking him to cover one eye and look straight at you. In a plane midway between yourself and the casualty slowly bring your fingertip in turn from above, below, to the right, and to the left of the direction of gaze until the patient can see it. Compare this with the earliest that you can see it with the equivalent eye. If a deficit is present, roughly map out the positions of the blind spots by passing the fingertip across the visual field.

3. *Oculomotor nerve*
4. *Troclear nerve*
5. *Abducens nerve*
   These three nerves control eye movement. The simplest way to test for proper function is to have the subject track the tip of you finger while you move it through the person's visual field, and bringing it to the tip of his nose until he looks cross-eyed. Also test the oculomotor nerve by shining a penlight into each eye, one at a time to test for normal constriction of the iris. Both should constrict and in following, return to nearly equal size.

6. *Trigeminal nerve* governs sensation of the forehead and face and the clenching of the jaw. It also supplies the muscle of the ear (tensor tympani) necessary for normal hearing. Sensation is tested by lightly stroking the forehead, face, and jaw on each side with a finger or wisp of cotton wool.

7. *Facial nerve* controls the face muscles. It is tested by having the patient smile, show his teeth, whistle, wrinkle his forehead, and close his eyes tightly. The two sides should perform symmetrically. Symmetry for the nasoabial folds (lines from nose to outside corners of the mouth) should be observed.

8. *Acoustic nerve* controls hearing and balance. Test this nerve by whispering to the patient, rubbing your finger together next to the patient's ears, or putting a tuning fork near the patient's ears.

9. *Glossopharyngeal nerves* transmit sensation from the upper mouth and throat area. It supplies the sensory component to the gag reflex and constriction of the pharyngeal wall when saying "aah." This nerve is tested by touching the back of the patient's throat with a tongue depressor. This should cause a gagging response. This nerve is normally not tested.

10. *Vagus nerve* has many functions, including control of the roof of the mouth and vocal cords. The examiner can test this nerve by having the patient say "aah" while watching for the palate to rise. Note the tone of the voice, hoarseness may also indicate vagus nerve involvement.

11. *Spinal accessory nerve* controls the turning of the body from side to side and shrugging the shoulders. This nerve is tested by having the patient turn his head from side to side. Resistance is provided by placing one hand against the side of the patient's head. The examiner should note that an injury to the nerve on one side will cause an inability to turn the head to the opposite side or weakness/absence of the shoulder shrug on the affected side.

TABLE II.1
Extremity Strength Tests

Test	Procedure
Deltoid Muscles	The patient raises his arm to the side at the shoulder joint. The examiner places a hand on the patient's wrist and exerts a downward force that the patient resists.
Latissimus Group	The patient raises his arm to the side. The examiner places a hand on the underside of the patient's wrist and resists the patient's attempt to lower his arm.
Biceps	The patient bends his arm at the elbow, toward his chest. The examiner then grasps the patient's wrist and exerts a force to straighten the patient's arm.
Triceps	The patient bends his arm at the elbow, toward his chest. The examiner then places his hand on the patient's forearm and the patient tries to straighten his arm.
Forearm Muscles	The patient makes a fist. The examiner grips the patient's fist and resists while the patient tries to bend his wrist upward and downward.
Hand Muscles	The patient strongly grips the examiner's extended fingers. The patient extends his hand with the finger widespread. The examiner grips two of the extended fingers with two of his own fingers and tries to squeeze the patient's two finger together, noting the patient's strength of resistance.
Lower Extremity Strength	The patient walks on his heels for a short distance. The patient then turns around and walks back on his toes. The patient walks while squatting (duck walk). These tests adequately assess lower extremity strength as well as balance and coordination. If a more detailed examination of lower extremity strength is desired, testing should be accomplished at each joint as in the upper arm.

In the following tests, the patient sits on a solid surface such as a desk, with feet off the deck.

Test	Procedure
Hip Flexion	The examiner places his hand on the patient's thigh to resist as the patient tries to raise his thigh.
Hip Extension	The examiner places his hand on the underside of the patient's thigh to resist as the patient tries to lower his thigh.
Hip Abduction	The patient sits as above, with knees together. The examiner places a hand on the outside of each of the patient's knees to provide resistance. The patient tries to open his knees.
Hip Adduction	The patient sits as above, with knees apart. The examiner places a hand on the inside of each of the patient's knees to provide resistance. The patient tries to bring his knees together.
Knee Extension	The examiner places a hand on the patient's shin to resist as the patient tries to straighten his leg.
Knee Flexion	The examiner places a hand on the back of the patient's lower leg to resist as the patient tries to pull his lower leg to the rear by flexing his knee.
Ankle Dorsiflexion (ability to flex the foot toward the rear)	The examiner places a hand on top of the patient's foot to resist as the patient tries to raise his foot by flexing it at the ankle.
Ankle Plantarflexion (ability to flex the foot downward)	The examiner places a hand on the bottom of the patient's foot to resist as the patient tries to lower his foot by flexing it at the ankle.
Toes	The patient stands on tip toes for 15 seconds. The patient flexes his toes with resistance provided by the examiner.

12. *Hypoglossal nerve* governs the muscle activity of the tongue. An injury to one of the hypoglossal nerves causes the tongue to twist to that side when stuck out of the mouth.

Sensory Function: In addition, test sensory function. Common symptoms of decompression sickness in a diver that may indicate spinal cord dysfunction are pain, numbness, paralysis, and tingling (pins and needles feeling, also called paresthesia). An examination of the patient's sensory faculties should be performed. We have included diagrams of the dermatomal (sensory) areas of the skin sensations that correlate with each spinal cord segment. Note that the dermatomal areas of the trunk run in a circular pattern around the trunk. The dermatomal areas in the arms and legs run in a more lengthwise pattern. In a complete examination, each of the spinal segments should be checked for loss of sensation. Sensations easily recognized by most normal people are sharp/dull discrimination (to perceive as separate) and light touch. It is possible to test pressure, temperature, and vibration in special cases. The likelihood of DCS affecting only one sense, however, is very small.

An ideal instrument for testing changes in sensation is a sharp object such as the Wartenberg pinwheel or a tooth pick or safety pin. Light point depression without scratching or breaking the skin is the intent of this test. Pain is not the objective. The pinwheel or other sharp object should be moved from the top of the shoulder slowly down the front of the torso to the groin area. Another method is to run it down the rear of the torso to just below the buttocks. The patient should be asked if he felt the sharp/dull instrument while going down the trunk on each side of his body. The neck area is tested in similar fashion.

In testing the limbs, a circular pattern of testing is best. Each limb is tested in at least three locations and any difference in sensation on each side of the body is noted. On the arms, the elbow, and at the wrist. In testing the legs, the upper thigh is circled just below the knee and at the ankle.

The hand is tested by running the sharp object across the back and palm of the hand and then across the fingertips.

If an area of abnormality is found, the area is marked for use as a reference point in assessment using a marking pen to trace the areas of decreased or increased sensitivity on the body of the patient. These areas are used as a reference to determine whether the area is improving. An example of improvement is an area of numbness getting smaller.

Deep Tendon Reflexes: The purpose of the deep tendon reflexes is to determine if the patient's response is normal, nonexistent, hypoactive (deficient), or hyperactive (excessive). The patient's response should be compared to responses the examiner has observed earlier. Notation should be made of whether the responses are equal bilaterally (meaning same on both sides) and if the upper and lower reflexes are similar. If any difference in the reflexes is noticed, the patient should be asked if there is a prior medical condition injury that would cause the difference. Isolated differences should not be treated because it is extremely difficult to get symmetrical responses bilaterally. To get the best response, each tendon is struck with an equal, light force and with sharp, quick taps. Usually, if a deep tendon reflex is abnormal due to decompression sickness, there will be other abnormal signs present. The biceps, triceps, knee, and ankle reflexes should be tested by striking the tendon as described in Table II.2.

TABLE II.2
Reflexes

Test	Procedure
Biceps	The examiner holds the patient's elbow with the patient's hand resting on the examiner's forearm. The patient's elbow should be slightly bent and his arm relaxed. The examiner places his thumb on the patient's biceps tendon, located in the bend of the patient's elbow. The examiner taps his thumb with the percussion hammer, feeling for the patient's muscle to contract.
Triceps	The examiner supports the patient's arm at the biceps. The patient's arm hangs with the elbow bent. The examiner taps the back of the patient's arm just above the elbow with the percussion hammer, feeling for the muscle to contract.
Knee	The patient sits on a table or bench with his feet off the deck. The examiner taps the patient's knee just below the kneecap, on the tendon. The examiner looks for the contraction of quadriceps (thigh muscle) and movement of the lower leg.
Ankle	The patient sits as above. The examiner places slight pressure on the patient's toes to stretch the Achilles' tendon, feeling for the toes to contract as the Achilles' tendon shortens (contracts).

NOAA Diving Manual

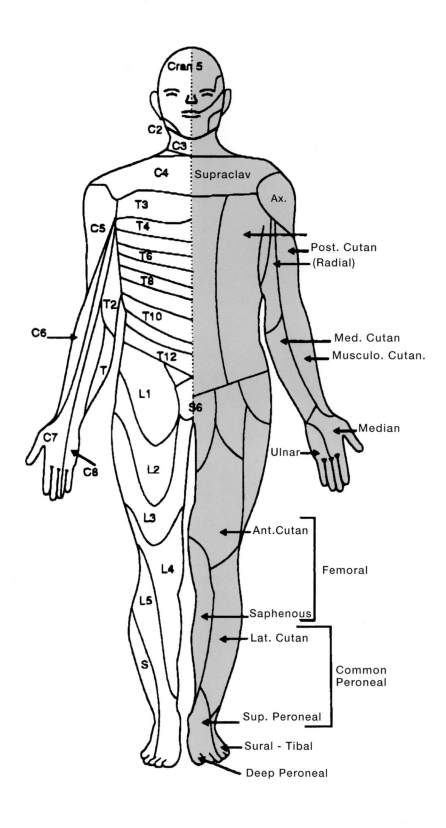

FIGURE II.1
Dematomal Areas Correlated to Spinal Cord Segment (sheet 1 of 2)

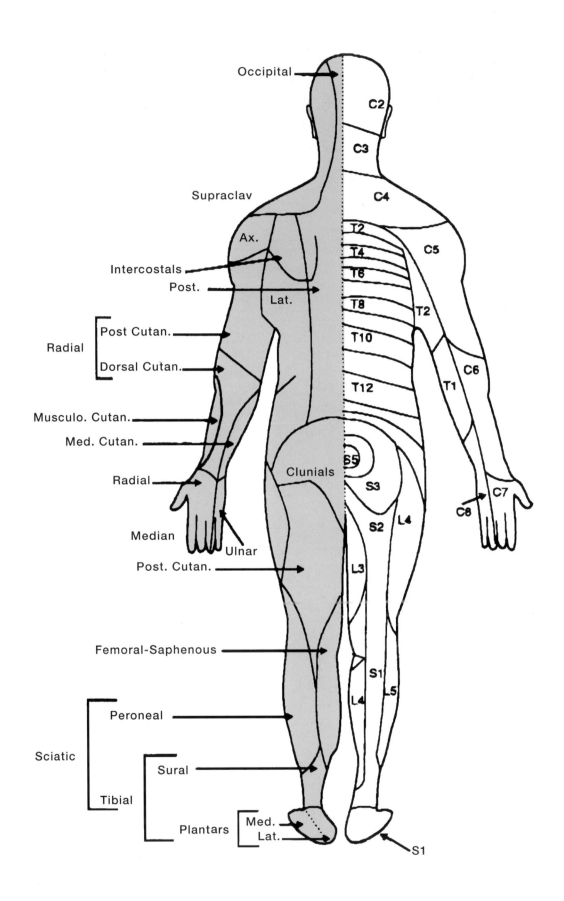

FIGURE II.1 (continued)
Dematomal Areas Correlated to Spinal Cord Segment (sheet 2 of 2)

Neurological Examination Checklist

(sheet 1 of 2)

Patient's Name: _____   Date/Time: _____

Describe pain/numbness: _____

HISTORY

Type of dive last performed: _____

Depth: _____ How long: _____ Number of dives in last 24 hours: _____

Was symptom noticed before, during, or after the dive? _____

If during, was it while descending, on the bottom, or ascending? _____

Has symptom increased or decreased since it was first noticed? _____

Have any other symptoms occurred since the first one was noticed? _____

Describe: _____

Has patient ever had a similar symptom before? _____ When: _____

Has patient ever had decompression sickness or an air embolism before? _____ When: _____

MENTAL STATUS/STATE OF CONSCIOUSNESS

Coordination

Walk: _____
Heel-to-Toe: _____
Romberg: _____
Finger-to-Nose: _____
Heel Shin Slide: _____
Rapid Movement: _____

Cranial Nerves

Sense of Smell (I) _____
Vision/Visual Fld (II) _____
Eye Movements, Pupils (III, IV, VI) _____
Facial Sensation, Chewing (V) _____
Facial Expression Muscles (VII) _____
Hearing (VIII) _____
Upper Mouth, Throat Sensation (IX) _____
Gag & Voice (X) _____
Shoulder Shrug (XI) _____
Tongue (XII) _____

Strength   (Grade 0 to 5)

Upper Body

Deltoids   L _____ R _____
Latissimus L _____ R _____
Biceps   L _____ R _____
Triceps   L _____ R _____
Forearms   L _____ R _____
Hands   L _____ R _____

Lower Body

Hips
Flexion   L _____ R _____
Extension   L _____ R _____
Abduction   L _____ R _____
Adduction   L _____ R _____

Knees

Flexion   L _____ R _____
Extension   L _____ R _____

FIGURE II.2
Neurological Examination Checklist (sheet 1 of 2)

Neurological Examination Checklist

(sheet 2 of 2)

Reflexes

(Grade: Normal, Hypoactive, Hyperactive, Absent)

<u>Ankles</u>

Biceps	L _____	R _____
Triceps	L _____	R _____
Knees	L _____	R _____
Ankles	L _____	R _____

Dorsiflexion	L _____	R _____
Plantarflexion	L _____	R _____

<u>Toes</u> L _____ R _____

Sensory Examination for Skin Sensation

(Use diagram to record location of sensory abnormalities—numbness, tingling, etc.)

Location

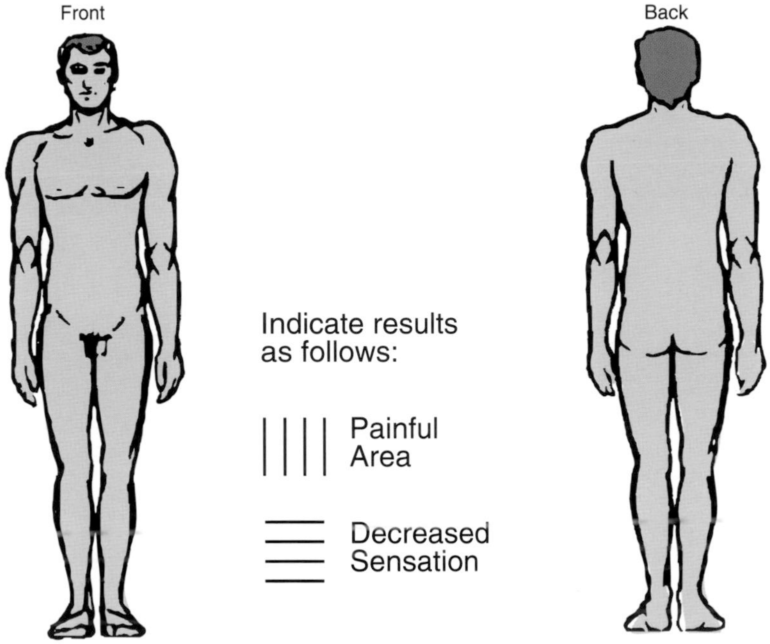

Front

Back

Indicate results
as follows:

| | | Painful
Area

— — Decreased
Sensation

Comments

_____

_____

_____

_____

_____

_____

_____

Examination Performed By:_____

FIGURE II.2 (continued)
Neurological Examination Checklist (sheet 2 of 2)

Appendix
No-Decompression
Air Dive Table

NOAA NO-DECOMPRESSION AIR DIVE TABLE

National Oceanic and Atmospheric Administration — NOAA — U.S. Department of Commerce

WARNING: EVEN STRICT COMPLIANCE WITH THESE CHARTS WILL NOT GUARANTEE AVOIDANCE OF DECOMPRESSION SICKNESS. CONSERVATIVE USAGE IS STRONGLY RECOMMENDED.

RNT RESIDUAL NITROGEN TIME
+ ABT ACTUAL BOTTOM TIME
ESDT EQUIVALENT SINGLE DIVE TIME

(USE ESDT TO DETERMINE END-OF-DIVE LETTER GROUP)

CHART 1 — DIVE TIMES WITH END-OF-DIVE GROUP LETTER

00	MAXIMUM NO-STOP TIME

DIVE TIME REQUIRING DECOMPRESSION MINUTES REQUIRED AT 10 fsw STOP (3 msw)	00 / 00

DEPTH msw	fsw														
12	40 ▶	5	15	25	30	40	50	70	80	100	110	130	150	170	(200)
15	50 ▶		10	15	25	30	40	50	60	70	80	90	(100)	120 / 5	160 / 21
18	60 ▶		10	15	20	25	30	40	50	55	(60)	70 / 2	80 / 7	100 / 14	
22	70 ▶		5	10	15	20	30	35	40	45	(50)	60 / 8	70 / 14	80 / 18	
25	80 ▶		5	10	15	20	25	30	35	(40)		50 / 10	60 / 17	70 / 23	
28	90 ▶		5	10	12	15	20	25	(30)		40 / 7		50 / 18	60 / 25	
31	100 ▶		5	7	10	15	20	22	(25)	30 / 3		40 / 15			
34	110 ▶			5	10	13	15	(20)	25 / 3		30 / 7				
37	120 ▶			5	10	12	(15)	20 / 2	25 / 6	30 / 14					
40	130 ▶			5	8	(10)	15 / 1		20 / 4		25 / 10				

CHART 2 — SURFACE INTERVAL TIME

GROUP LETTER	A	B	C	D	E	F	G	H	I	J	K	L	M	N
◀A	12:00 / 0:10	12:00 / 3:21	12:00 / 4:50	12:00 / 5:49	12:00 / 6:35	12:00 / 7:06	12:00 / 7:36	12:00 / 8:00	12:00 / 8:22	12:00 / 8:51	12:00 / 8:59	12:00 / 9:13	12:00 / 9:29	12:00 / 9:44
◀B		3:20 / 0:10	4:49 / 1:40	5:48 / 2:39	6:34 / 3:25	7:05 / 3:58	7:35 / 4:26	7:59 / 4:50	8:21 / 5:13	8:50 / 5:41	8:59 / 5:49	9:12 / 6:03	9:28 / 6:19	9:43 / 6:33
◀C			1:39 / 0:10	2:38 / 1:10	3:24 / 1:58	3:57 / 2:29	4:25 / 2:59	4:49 / 3:21	5:12 / 3:44	5:40 / 4:03	5:48 / 4:20	6:02 / 4:36	6:18 / 4:50	6:32 / 5:04
◀D				1:09 / 0:10	1:57 / 0:55	2:28 / 1:30	2:58 / 2:00	3:20 / 2:24	3:43 / 2:45	4:02 / 3:05	4:19 / 3:22	4:35 / 3:37	4:49 / 3:53	5:03 / 4:05
◀E					0:54 / 0:10	1:29 / 0:46	1:59 / 1:16	2:23 / 1:42	2:44 / 2:03	3:04 / 2:21	3:21 / 2:39	3:36 / 2:54	3:52 / 3:09	4:04 / 3:23
◀F						0:45 / 0:10	1:15 / 0:41	1:41 / 1:07	2:02 / 1:30	2:20 / 1:48	2:38 / 2:04	2:53 / 2:20	3:08 / 2:35	3:22 / 2:48
◀G							0:40 / 0:10	1:06 / 0:37	1:29 / 1:00	1:47 / 1:20	2:03 / 1:36	2:19 / 1:50	2:34 / 2:06	2:47 / 2:19
◀H								0:36 / 0:10	0:59 / 0:34	1:19 / 0:55	1:35 / 1:12	1:49 / 1:26	2:05 / 1:36	2:18 / 1:54
◀I									0:33 / 0:10	0:54 / 0:32	1:11 / 0:50	1:25 / 1:05	1:35 / 1:19	1:53 / 1:31
◀J										0:31 / 0:10	0:49 / 0:29	1:04 / 0:46	1:18 / 1:00	1:30 / 1:12
◀K											0:28 / 0:10	0:45 / 0:27	0:59 / 0:43	1:11 / 0:55
◀L												0:26 / 0:10	0:42 / 0:26	0:54 / 0:40
◀M													0:25 / 0:10	0:39 / 0:25
◀N														0:24 / 0:10

CHART 3 — REPETITIVE DIVE TIME

40	50	60	70	80	90	100	110	120	130	GROUP LETTER
7 / 193	6 / 94	5 / 55	4 / 46	4 / 36	3 / 27	3 / 22	3 / 17	3 / 12	3 / 7	◀A
17 / 183	13 / 87	11 / 49	9 / 41	8 / 32	7 / 23	7 / 18	6 / 14	6 / 9	6 / 4	◀B
25 / 175	21 / 79	17 / 43	15 / 35	13 / 27	11 / 19	10 / 15	10 / 10	9 / 6	8 / 2	◀C
37 / 163	29 / 71	24 / 36	20 / 30	18 / 22	16 / 14	14 / 11	13 / 7	12 / 3		◀D
49 / 151	38 / 62	30 / 30	26 / 24	23 / 17	20 / 10	18 / 7	16 / 4			◀E
61 / 139	47 / 53	36 / 24	31 / 19	28 / 12	24 / 6	22 / 3				◀F
73 / 127	56 / 44	44 / 16	37 / 13	32 / 8	29 / 1					◀G
87 / 113	66 / 34	52 / 8	43 / 7	38 / 2						◀H
101 / 99	76 / 24									◀I
116 / 84	87 / 13									◀J
138 / 62	99 / 1									◀K
161 / 39										◀L
187 / 13										◀M
										◀N

00 / 00	TOP NUMBERS (RED) ARE RESIDUAL NITROGEN TIMES, RNT

BOTTOM NUMBERS (BLACK) ARE ADJUSTED MAXIMUM DIVE TIME FOR A REPETITIVE DIVE WITH NO DECOMPRESSION
BLACK AREA: REQUIRES DECOMPRESSION

Appendix

U.S. Navy
Dive Tables

SECTION	PAGE

U.S. Navy Dive Tables

U.S. Navy Dive Table 3

Unlimited/No-Decompression Limits and Repetitive Group Designation Table for Unlimited/No-Decompression Air Dives–1999

Depth (feet/meters)		No-Decompression Limits (min)	A	B	C	D	E	F	G	H	I	J	K	L	M	N	O
10	3.0	unlimited	60	120	210	300	797	★									
15	4.6	unlimited	35	70	110	160	225	350	452	★							
20	6.1	unlimited	25	50	75	100	135	180	240	325	390	917	★				
25	7.6	595	20	35	55	75	100	125	160	195	245	315	361	540	595		
30	9.1	405	15	30	45	60	75	95	120	145	170	205	250	310	344	405	
35	10.7	310	5	15	25	40	50	60	80	100	120	140	160	190	220	270	310
40	12.2	200	5	15	25	30	40	50	70	80	100	110	130	150	170	200	
50	15.2	100		10	15	25	30	40	50	60	70	80	90	100			
60	18.2	60		10	15	20	25	30	40	50	55	60					
70	21.3	50		5	10	15	20	30	35	40	45	50					
80	24.4	40		5	10	15	20	25	30	35	40						
90	27.4	30		5	10	12	15	20	25	30							
100	30.5	25		5	7	10	15	20	22	25							
110	33.5	20			5	10	13	15	20								
120	36.6	15			5	10	12	15									
130	39.6	10			5	8	10										
140	42.7	10			5	7	10										
150	45.7	5			5												
160	48.8	5				5											
170	51.8	5				5											
180	54.8	5				5											
190	59.9	5				5											

★Highest repetitive group that can be achieved at this depth regardless of bottom time

U.S. Navy Dive Table 4

Residual Nitrogen Timetable for Repetitive Air Dives – 1999

Locate the diver's repetitive group designation from his previous dive along the diagonal line above the table. Read horizontally to the interval in which the diver's surface interval lies.

Next, read vertically downward to the new repetitive group designation. Continue downward in this same column to the row which represents the depth of the repetitive dive. The time given at the intersection is residual nitrogen time, in minutes, to be applied to the repetitive dive.

* Dives following surface intervals of more than 12 hours are not repetitive dives. Use actual bottom times in the Standard Air Decompression Tables to compute decompression for such dives.

** If no Residual Nitrogen Time is given, then the repetitive group does not change.

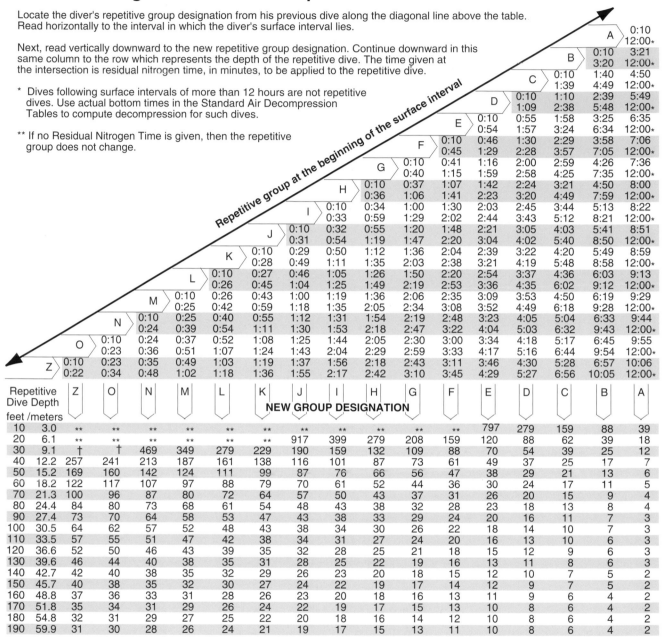

Repetitive Dive Depth feet /meters	Z	O	N	M	L	K	J	I	H	G	F	E	D	C	B	A
							NEW GROUP DESIGNATION									
10 3.0	**	**	**	**	**	**	**	**	**	**	**	797	279	159	88	39
20 6.1	**	**	**	**	**	**	917	399	279	208	159	120	88	62	39	18
30 9.1	†	†	469	349	279	229	190	159	132	109	88	70	54	39	25	12
40 12.2	257	241	213	187	161	138	116	101	87	73	61	49	37	25	17	7
50 15.2	169	160	142	124	111	99	87	76	66	56	47	38	29	21	13	6
60 18.2	122	117	107	97	88	79	70	61	52	44	36	30	24	17	11	5
70 21.3	100	96	87	80	72	64	57	50	43	37	31	26	20	15	9	4
80 24.4	84	80	73	68	61	54	48	43	38	32	28	23	18	13	8	4
90 27.4	73	70	64	58	53	47	43	38	33	29	24	20	16	11	7	3
100 30.5	64	62	57	52	48	43	38	34	30	26	22	18	14	10	7	3
110 33.5	57	55	51	47	42	38	34	31	27	24	20	16	13	10	6	3
120 36.6	52	50	46	43	39	35	32	28	25	21	18	15	12	9	6	3
130 39.6	46	44	40	38	35	31	28	25	22	19	16	13	11	8	6	3
140 42.7	42	40	38	35	32	29	26	23	20	18	15	12	10	7	5	2
150 45.7	40	38	35	32	30	27	24	22	19	17	14	12	9	7	5	2
160 48.8	37	36	33	31	28	26	23	20	18	16	13	11	9	6	4	2
170 51.8	35	34	31	29	26	24	22	19	17	15	13	10	8	6	4	2
180 54.8	32	31	29	27	25	22	20	18	16	14	12	10	8	6	4	2
190 59.9	31	30	28	26	24	21	19	17	15	13	11	10	8	6	4	2

Residual Nitrogen Times (Minutes)

† Read vertically downward to the 40/12.2 (feet/meter) repetitive dive depth. Use the corresponding residual nitrogen times (minutes) to compute the equivalent single dive time. Decompress using the 40/12.2 (feet/meter) standard air decompression table.

U.S. Navy Dive Table 5

Standard Air Decompression Table – 1999

Depth feet/meters	Bottom time (min)	Time first stop (min:sec)	50 15.2	40 12.1	30 9.1	20 6.0	10 3.0	Total decompression time (min:sec)	Repetitive group
40 12.1	200						0	1:20	*
	210	1:00					2	3:20	N
	230	1:00					7	8:20	N
	250	1:00					11	12:20	O
	270	1:00					15	16:20	O
	300	1:00					19	20:20	Z
					Exceptional Exposure				
	360	1:00					23	24:20	**
	480	1:00					41	42:20	**
	720	1:00					69	70:20	**
50 15.2	100						0	1:40	*
	110	1:20					3	4:40	L
	120	1:20					5	6:40	M
	140	1:20					10	11:40	M
	160	1:20					21	22:40	N
	180	1:20					29	30:40	O
	200	1:20					35	36:40	O
	220	1:20					40	41:40	Z
	240	1:20					47	48:40	Z
60 18.2	60						0	2:00	*
	70	1:40					2	4:00	K
	80	1:40					7	9:00	L
	100	1:40					14	16:00	M
	120	1:40					26	28:00	N
	140	1:40					39	41:00	O
	160	1:40					48	50:00	Z
	180	1:40					56	58:00	Z
	200	1:20				1	69	72:00	Z
					Exceptional Exposure				
	240	1:20				2	79	83:00	**
	360	1:20				20	119	141:00	**
	480	1:20				44	148	194:00	**
	720	1:20				78	187	267:00	**
70 21.3	50						0	2:20	*
	60	2:00					8	10:20	K
	70	2:00					14	16:20	L
	80	2:00					18	20:20	M
	90	2:00					23	25:20	N
	100	2:00					33	35:20	N
	110	1:40				2	41	45:20	O
	120	1:40				4	47	53:20	O
	130	1:40				6	52	60:20	O
	140	1:40				8	56	66:20	Z
	150	1:40				9	61	72:20	Z
	160	1:40				13	72	87:20	Z
	170	1:40				19	79	100:20	Z

* See No Decompression Table for repetitive groups
** Repetitive dives may not follow exceptional exposure dives

U.S. Navy Dive Table 5

Standard Air Decompression Table – 1999 (Continued)

Depth feet/meters	Bottom time (min)	Time first stop (min:sec)	50 15.2	40 12.1	30 9.1	20 6.0	10 3.0	Total decompression time (min:sec)	Repetitive group
80 24.3	40						0	2:40	*
	50	2:20					10	12:40	K
	60	2:20					17	19:40	L
	70	2:20					23	25:40	M
	80	2:00				2	31	35:40	N
	90	2:00				7	39	48:40	N
	100	2:00				11	46	59:40	O
	110	2:00				13	53	68:40	O
	120	2:00				17	56	75:40	Z
	130	2:00				19	63	84:40	Z
	140	2:00				26	69	97:40	Z
	150	2:00				32	77	111:40	Z
					Exceptional Exposure				
	180	2:00				35	85	122:40	**
	240	1:40			6	52	120	180:40	**
	360	1:40			29	90	160	281:40	**
	480	1:40			59	107	187	355:40	**
	720	1:20		17	108	142	187	456:40	**
90 28.7	30						0	3:00	*
	40	2:40					7	10:00	J
	50	2:40					18	21:00	L
	60	2:40					25	28:00	M
	70	2:20				7	30	40:00	N
	80	2:20				13	40	56:00	N
	90	2:20				18	48	69:00	O
	100	2:20				21	54	78:00	Z
	110	2:20				24	61	88:00	Z
	120	2:20				32	68	103:00	Z
	130	2:00			5	36	74	118:00	Z
100 30.4	25						0	3:20	*
	30	3:00					3	6:20	I
	40	3:00					15	18:20	K
	50	2:40				2	24	29:20	L
	60	2:40				9	28	40:20	N
	70	2:40				17	39	59:20	O
	80	2:40				23	48	74:20	O
	90	2:20			3	23	57	86:20	Z
	100	2:20			7	23	66	99:20	Z
	110	2:20			10	34	72	119:20	Z
	120	2:20			12	41	78	134:20	Z
					Exceptional Exposure				
	180	2:00		1	29	53	118	204:20	**
	240	2:00		14	42	84	142	285:20	**
	360	1:40	2	42	73	111	187	418:20	**
	480	1:40	21	61	91	142	187	505:20	**
	720	1:40	55	106	122	142	187	615:20	**

* See No Decompression Table for repetitive groups
** Repetitive dives may not follow exceptional exposure dives

U.S. Navy Dive Table 5

Standard Air Decompression Table – 1999 (Continued)

Depth feet/meters	Bottom time (min)	Time first stop (min:sec)	Decompression stops (feet/meters) 50 15.2	40 12.1	30 9.1	20 6.0	10 3.0	Total decompression time (min:sec)	Repetitive group
110 33.1	20						0	3:40	*
	25	3:20					3	6:40	H
	30	3:20					7	10:40	J
	40	3:00				2	21	26:40	L
	50	3:00				8	26	37:40	M
	60	3:00				18	36	57:40	N
	70	2:40			1	23	48	75:40	O
	80	2:40			7	23	57	90:40	Z
	90	2:40			12	30	64	109:40	Z
	100	2:40			15	37	72	127:40	Z

Depth feet/meters	Bottom time (min)	Time first stop (min:sec)	Decompression stops (feet/meters) 70 21.3	60 18.2	50 15.2	40 12.1	30 9.1	20 6.0	10 3.0	Total decompression time (min:sec)	Repetitive group
120 36.5	15								0	4:00	*
	20	3:40							2	6:00	H
	25	3:40							6	10:00	I
	30	3:40							14	18:00	J
	40	3:20						5	25	34:00	L
	50	3:20						15	31	50:00	N
	60	3:00					2	22	45	73:00	O
	70	3:00					9	23	55	91:00	O
	80	3:00					15	27	63	109:00	Z
	90	3:00					19	37	74	134:00	Z
	100	3:00					23	45	80	152:00	Z
	Exceptional Exposure										
	120	2:40				10	19	47	98	178:00	**
	180	2:20			5	27	37	76	137	286:00	**
	240	2:20			23	35	60	97	179	398:00	**
	360	2:00		18	45	64	93	142	187	553:00	**
	480	1:40	3	41	64	93	122	142	187	656:00	**
	720	1:40	32	74	100	114	122	142	187	775:00	**

Depth feet/meters	Bottom time (min)	Time first stop (min:sec)	70 21.3	60 18.2	50 15.2	40 12.1	30 9.1	20 6.0	10 3.0	Total decompression time (min:sec)	Repetitive group
130 39.6	10								0	4:20	*
	15	4:00							1	5:20	F
	20	4:00							4	8:20	H
	25	4:00							10	14:20	J
	30	3:40						3	18	25:20	M
	40	3:40						10	25	39:20	N
	50	3:20					3	21	37	65:20	O
	60	3:20					9	23	52	88:20	Z
	70	3:20					16	24	61	105:20	Z
	80	3:00				3	19	35	72	133:20	Z
	90	3:00				8	19	45	80	156:20	Z

* See No Decompression Table for repetitive groups
** Repetitive dives may not follow exceptional exposure dives

U.S. Navy Dive Table 5

Standard Air Decompression Table – 1999 (Continued)

Depth 200 feet / 60.9 meters — Exceptional Exposure

Bottom time (min)	Time first stop (min:sec)	130 / 39.6	120 / 36.5	110 / 33.5	100 / 30.4	90 / 27.4	80 / 24.3	70 / 21.3	60 / 18.2	50 / 15.2	40 / 12.1	30 / 9.1	20 / 6.0	10 / 3.0	Total decompression time (min:sec)
5	6:20													1	7:40
10	6:00												1	4	11:40
15	5:40											1	4	10	21:40
20	5:40											3	7	27	43:40
25	5:40											7	14	25	52:40
30	5:20										2	9	22	37	76:40
40	5:00									2	8	17	23	59	115:40
50	5:00									6	16	22	39	75	164:40
60	4:40								2	13	17	24	51	89	202:40
90	3:40					1	10	10	12	12	30	38	74	134	327:40
120	3:20				6	10	10	10	24	28	40	64	98	180	476:40
180	2:40		1	10	10	18	24	24	42	48	70	106	142	187	688:40
240	2:40		6	20	24	24	36	42	54	68	114	122	142	187	845:40
360	2:20	12	22	36	40	44	56	82	98	100	114	122	142	187	1061:40

Depth 210 feet / 64.0 meters — Exceptional Exposure

Bottom time (min)	Time first stop (min:sec)	130 / 39.6	120 / 36.5	110 / 33.5	100 / 30.4	90 / 27.4	80 / 24.3	70 / 21.3	60 / 18.2	50 / 15.2	40 / 12.1	30 / 9.1	20 / 6.0	10 / 3.0	Total decompression time (min:sec)
5	6:40													1	8:00
10	6:20												2	4	13:00
15	6:00											1	5	13	26:00
20	6:00											4	10	23	44:00
25	5:40										2	7	17	27	60:00
30	5:40										4	9	24	41	85:00
40	5:20									4	9	19	26	63	128:00
50	5:20								1	9	17	19	45	80	178:00

Depth 220 feet / 67.0 meters — Exceptional Exposure

Bottom time (min)	Time first stop (min:sec)	130 / 39.6	120 / 36.5	110 / 33.5	100 / 30.4	90 / 27.4	80 / 24.3	70 / 21.3	60 / 18.2	50 / 15.2	40 / 12.1	30 / 9.1	20 / 6.0	10 / 3.0	Total decompression time (min:sec)
5	7:00													1	8:20
10	6:40												2	5	14:20
15	6:20											2	5	16	30:20
20	6:00										1	3	11	24	46:20
25	6:00										3	8	19	33	70:20
30	5:40									1	7	10	23	47	95:20
40	5:40									6	12	22	29	68	144:20
50	5:20								3	12	17	18	51	86	194:20

Depth 230 feet / 70.1 meters — Exceptional Exposure

Bottom time (min)	Time first stop (min:sec)	130 / 39.6	120 / 36.5	110 / 33.5	100 / 30.4	90 / 27.4	80 / 24.3	70 / 21.3	60 / 18.2	50 / 15.2	40 / 12.1	30 / 9.1	20 / 6.0	10 / 3.0	Total decompression time (min:sec)
5	7:20													2	9:40
10	6:20											1	2	6	16:40
15	6:20											3	6	18	34:40
20	6:20										2	5	12	26	52:40
25	6:20										4	8	22	37	78:40
30	6:00									2	8	12	23	51	103:40
40	5:40								1	7	15	22	34	74	160:40
50	5:40								5	14	16	24	51	89	206:40

Depth 240 feet / 73.1 meters — Exceptional Exposure

Bottom time (min)	Time first stop (min:sec)	130 / 39.6	120 / 36.5	110 / 33.5	100 / 30.4	90 / 27.4	80 / 24.3	70 / 21.3	60 / 18.2	50 / 15.2	40 / 12.1	30 / 9.1	20 / 6.0	10 / 3.0	Total decompression time (min:sec)
5	7:40													2	10:00
10	7:00											1	3	6	18:00
15	7:00											4	6	21	39:00
20	6:40										3	6	15	25	57:00
25	6:20										4	9	24	40	86:00
30	6:20									1	4	8	15	22	56	113:00
40	6:00								3	7	17	22	39	75	171:00
50	5:40							1	8	15	16	29	51	94	222:00

* See No Decompression Table for repetitive groups
** Repetitive dives may not follow exceptional exposure dives

U.S. Navy Dive Table 5

Standard Air Decompression Table – 1999 (Continued)

Decompression stop depths (feet / meters): 200/60.9, 190/57.9, 180/54.8, 170/51.8, 160/48.7, 150/45.7, 140/42.6, 130/39.6, 120/36.5, 110/33.5, 100/30.4, 90/27.4, 80/24.3, 70/21.3, 60/18.2, 50/15.2, 40/12.1, 30/9.1, 20/6.0, 10/3.0

250 / 76.2 — Exceptional Exposure

Bottom time (min)	Time first stop (min:sec)	200	190	180	170	160	150	140	130	120	110	100	90	80	70	60	50	40	30	20	10	Total decompression time (min:sec)
5	7:40																			1	2	11:20
10	7:20																		1	4	7	20:20
15	7:00																	1	4	7	22	42:20
20	7:00																	4	7	17	27	63:20
25	6:40																2	7	10	24	45	96:20
30	6:40																6	7	17	23	59	120:20
40	6:20															5	9	17	19	45	79	182:20
60	5:20												4	10	10	10	12	22	36	64	126	302:20
90	4:20									8	10	10	10	10	10	28	28	44	68	98	186	518:20
120	3:40						5	10	10	10	10	10	16	24	24	36	48	64	94	142	187	688:20
180	3:00					4	8	8	10	22	24	24	32	42	44	60	84	114	122	142	187	935:20
240	3:00					9	14	21	22	22	40	40	42	56	76	98	100	114	122	142	187	1113:20

260 / 79.2 — Exceptional Exposure

Bottom time (min)	Time first stop (min:sec)	200	190	180	170	160	150	140	130	120	110	100	90	80	70	60	50	40	30	20	10	Total decompression time (min:sec)
5	8:00																			1	2	11:40
10	7:40																		2	4	9	23:40
15	7:20																	2	4	10	22	46:40
20	7:00																1	4	7	20	31	71:40
25	7:00																3	8	11	23	50	103:40
30	6:40															2	6	8	19	26	61	130:40
40	6:20														1	6	11	16	19	49	84	194:40

270 / 82.3 — Exceptional Exposure

Bottom time (min)	Time first stop (min:sec)	200	190	180	170	160	150	140	130	120	110	100	90	80	70	60	50	40	30	20	10	Total decompression time (min:sec)
5	8:20																			1	3	13:00
10	8:00																		2	5	11	27:00
15	7:40																	3	4	11	24	51:00
20	7:20																2	3	9	21	35	79:00
25	7:00															2	3	8	13	23	53	111:00
30	7:00															3	6	12	22	27	64	143:00
40	6:40														5	6	11	17	22	51	88	209:00

280 / 85.3 — Exceptional Exposure

Bottom time (min)	Time first stop (min:sec)	200	190	180	170	160	150	140	130	120	110	100	90	80	70	60	50	40	30	20	10	Total decompression time (min:sec)
5	8:40																			2	2	13:20
10	8:00																	1	2	5	13	30:20
15	7:40																1	3	4	11	26	54:20
20	7:40																3	4	8	23	39	86:20
25	7:20															2	5	7	16	23	56	118:20
30	7:00														1	3	7	13	22	30	70	155:20
40	6:40													1	6	6	13	17	27	51	93	223:20

290 / 88.4 — Exceptional Exposure

Bottom time (min)	Time first stop (min:sec)	200	190	180	170	160	150	140	130	120	110	100	90	80	70	60	50	40	30	20	10	Total decompression time (min:sec)
5	9:00																			2	3	14:40
10	8:20																	1	3	5	16	34:40
15	8:00																1	3	6	12	26	57:40
20	8:00																3	7	9	23	43	94:40
25	7:40															3	5	8	17	23	60	125:40
30	7:20														1	5	6	16	22	36	72	167:40
40	7:00													3	5	7	15	16	32	51	95	233:40

300 / 91.4 — Exceptional Exposure

Bottom time (min)	Time first stop (min:sec)	200	190	180	170	160	150	140	130	120	110	100	90	80	70	60	50	40	30	20	10	Total decompression time (min:sec)
5	9:20																			3	3	16:00
10	8:40																	1	3	6	17	37:00
15	8:20																2	3	6	15	26	62:00
20	8:00															2	3	7	10	23	47	102:00
25	7:40														1	3	6	8	19	26	61	134:00
30	7:40														2	5	7	17	22	39	75	177:00
40	7:20													4	6	9	15	17	34	51	90	236:00
60	6:00									4	10	10	10	10	10	14	28	32	50	90	187	465:00
90	4:40					3	8	8	10	10	10	10	16	24	24	34	48	64	90	142	187	698:00
120	4:00			4	8	8	8	8	10	14	24	24	24	34	42	58	66	102	122	142	187	895:00
180	3:30	6	8	8	8	14	20	21	21	28	40	40	48	56	82	98	100	114	122	142	187	1173:00

NOTES

Appendix
Flow Charts and Treatment Tables

SECTION	PAGE

Flow Charts and Treatment Tables

GENERAL

This appendix contains the diving accident treatment flow charts and a number of U.S. Navy Treatment Tables used to recompress divers who have experienced decompression sickness or arterial gas embolism as a result of their diving activities. The information in this appendix reflects treatment procedures recommended by the NOAA Diving Program and taught in the NOAA training program. All of the tables in this appendix have been widely used in the field and have been shown to be safe and effective.

Diving Accident Treatment Flow Charts

The flow charts shown are decision trees designed to aid dive supervisors, diving physicians, Diving Medical Technicians, chamber operators, and other health care professionals who must decide how best to treat stricken divers. Use of the decision tree requires only that the diver's condition be observed; a medical diagnosis is not required for treatment to begin.

Recompression Treatment Tables

The recompression treatment tables recommended by NOAA are shown on the following pages. Instructions for the use of these tables appear with each table and should be followed precisely.

RECOMPRESSION TREATMENTS WHEN CHAMBER IS AVAILABLE

Oxygen Treatment Tables are more effective and, therefore, preferable over Air Treatment Tables. Treatment Table 4 can be used with or without oxygen but should always be used with oxygen if it is available.

Symptoms During Decompression and Surface Decompression: If symptoms of decompression sickness occur in the water during decompression, follow Flow Chart 1. After completing recompression treatment, observe the diver for at least 6 hours. If any symptoms recur, treat as a recurrence of Type II symptoms. As an option, the on-site Diving Supervisor may elect not to recompress the diver 10 feet in the water, but to remove the diver from the water when decompression risks are unacceptable and treat him in the chamber. When this is done, the surface interval should be 5 minutes or less, with the diver always treated as having Type II symptoms.

Treatment of Symptoms During Sur-D Surface Interval: If surface decompression procedures are used, symptoms of decompression sickness may occur during the surface interval. Because neurological symptoms cannot be ruled out during this short period, the symptomatic diver is treated as having Type II symptoms, even if the only complaint is pain.

Treating for Exceeded Sur-D Surface Interval: If the prescribed surface interval is exceeded but the diver remains asymptomatic, the diver is treated with Treatment Table 5, or Treatment Table lA if no oxygen is available. If the diver becomes symptomatic, the diver is treated as if Type II symptoms were present. Any symptoms occurring during the chamber stops are treated as recurrences in accordance with Flow Chart 3.

Recompression Treatments When Oxygen Is Not Available: If no oxygen is available, select the appropriate Air Treatment Table in accordance with Table 1A, Table 2A, Table 3, and Table 4.

Use Table 1A if pain is relieved at a depth less than 66 feet. If pain is relieved at a depth greater than 66 feet, use Table 2A. Table 3 is used for treatment of serious symptoms where oxygen cannot be used. Use Table 3 if symptoms are relieved within 30 minutes at 165 feet. If symptoms are not relieved in less than 30 minutes at 165 feet, use Table 4.

Descent/Ascent Rates for Air Treatment Tables: The Air Treatment Tables (1A, 2A, 3, and 4 using air) are used when no oxygen is available. They are not as effective as the Oxygen Treatment Tables. The descent rate is 20 feet per minute; the ascent rate is not to exceed 1 foot per minute.

Recompression Treatments When Oxygen Is Available: Use Oxygen Treatment Tables 5, 6, 6A, 4, or 7, according to Flow Charts 2, 3, and 4. The descent rate is 20 feet per minute. Upon reaching treatment depth not to exceed 60 fsw, place the patient on oxygen. For depth deeper than 60 fsw, use treatment gas if available. Additional guidelines for each treatment table are given below.

Treatment Table 5: Treatment Table 5 may be used for the following:

- Type I (except for cutis-marmorata) symptoms when a complete neurological examination has revealed no abnormality
- Asymptomatic omitted decompression of shallow surfacing (20 fsw or less)
- Asymptomatic omitted decompression of rapid ascent (from deeper than 20 fsw) if the missed decompression is less than 30 minutes
- Asymptomatic divers who have exceeded surface interval limits following a Sur-D dive
- Treatment of resolved symptoms following in-water recompression
- Follow-up treatments for residual symptoms

Performance of Neurological Exam at 60 fsw: After arrival at 60 fsw a neurological exam shall be performed (see Appendix II) to ensure that no overt neurological symptoms (e.g., weakness, numbness, incoordination) are present. If any abnormalities are found, the stricken diver should be treated using Treatment Table 6.

Extending Oxygen Breathing Periods on Treatment Table 5: Treatment Table 5 may be extended by two oxygen breathing periods at 30 fsw. Air breaks are not required prior to an extension, between extensions, or prior to surfacing. In other words, the Diving Supervisor may have the diver breathe oxygen continuously for 60 minutes at 30 fsw and travel to the surface while breathing oxygen. If the Diving Supervisor elects to extend this treatment table, the tender does not require additional oxygen breathing than currently prescribed.

When Use of Treatment Table 6 is Mandatory: Treatment Table 6 is mandatory if:

- Type I pain is severe and immediate recompression must be instituted before a neurological examination can be performed, or
- A complete neurological examination cannot be performed, or
- Any neurological symptom is present.

These rules apply no matter how rapidly or completely the symptoms resolve once recompression begins.

Complete Relief after 10 Minutes: If complete relief of Type I symptoms is not obtained within 10 minutes at 60 feet, Table 6 is required.

Musculoskeletal Pain Due to Orthopedic Injury: Symptoms of musculoskeletal pain that have shown absolutely no change after the second oxygen breathing period at 60 feet may be due to orthopedic injury rather than decompression sickness. If, after reviewing the patient's history, the Diving Medical Doctor feels that the pain can be related to specific orthopedic trauma or injury, Treatment Table 5 may be completed. If no Diving Medical Doctor is on site, Treatment Table 6 shall be used.

NOTE
Once recompression to 60 feet is done, Treatment Table 5 shall be used even if it was decided symptoms were probably not decompression sickness. Direct ascent to the surface is done only in emergencies.

Treatment Table 6: Treatment Table 6 is used for the following:

- Type I symptoms where relief is not complete within 10 minutes at 60 feet or where a neurological exam is not complete
- Type II symptoms
- Cutis marmorata
- Arterial gas embolism
- Symptomatic uncontrolled ascent
- Asymptomatic divers with omitted decompression greater than 30 minutes
- Treatment of unresolved symptoms following in-water treatment
- Recurrence of symptoms shallower than 60 fsw

Treating Arterial Gas Embolism: Arterial gas embolism is treated by initial compression to 60 fsw. If symptoms are improved within the first oxygen breathing period, then treatment is continued using Treatment Table 6. Treatment Table 6 may be extended for two oxygen breathing periods at 60 fsw (20 minutes on oxygen, then 5 minutes on air, then 20 minutes on oxygen) and two oxygen breathing periods at 30 fsw (15 minutes on air, then 60 minutes on oxygen, then 15 minutes on air, then 60 minutes on oxygen). If there has been more than one extension, the tenders' oxygen breathing period is extended 60 minutes at 30 feet.

Treatment Table 6A: Arterial gas embolism or severe decompression symptoms are treated by initial compression to 60 fsw. If symptoms improve, complete Treatment Table 6. If symptoms are unchanged or worsen, assess the patient upon descent and compress to depth of relief (significant improvement), not to exceed 165 fsw. Once at the depth of relief, begin treatment gas (N_2O_2,

HeO$_2$) if available. Stay there for 30 minutes. A breathing period of 25 minutes on treatment gas, interrupted by 5 minutes of air, is recommended at depth to simplify time keeping. The patient may remain on treatment gas during ascent from treatment depth to 60 fsw since the P0$_2$ will continually decrease during ascent. Decompress to 60 fsw at a travel rate not to exceed 3 ft/min. Upon arrival at 60 fsw, complete Treatment Table 6. Consult with a Diving Medical Doctor at the earliest opportunity. The Diving Medical Doctor may recommend a Treatment Table 4. Treatment Table 6A may be extended for two oxygen breathing periods at 60 fsw and two oxygen breathing periods at 30 fsw. If deterioration is noted during ascent to 60 feet, treat as a recurrence of symptoms (Flow Chart 4).

Treatment Table 4: If a shift from Treatment Table 6A to Treatment Table 4 is contemplated, a Diving Medical Doctor shall be consulted before the shift is made. Treatment Table 4 is used when it is determined that the patient would receive additional benefit at depth of significant relief, not to exceed 165 fsw. The time at depth shall be between 30 to 120 minutes, based on the patient's response.

Recurrence of Symptoms: If deterioration is noted during ascent to 60 feet, treat as a recurrence of symptoms (Flow Chart 4).

Oxygen Breathing Periods: If oxygen is available, the patient should begin oxygen breathing periods immediately upon arrival at the 60-foot stop. Breathing periods of 25 minutes on oxygen, interrupted by 5 minutes of air, are recommended. This simplifies timekeeping. Immediately upon arrival at 60 feet, a minimum of four oxygen breathing periods (for a total time of 2 hours) should be administered. After that, oxygen breathing should be administered to suit the patient's individual needs and operational conditions. Both the patient and tender must breathe oxygen for at least 4 hours (eight 25-minute oxygen, 5-minute air periods), beginning no later than 2 hours before ascent from 30 feet is begun. These oxygen-breathing periods may be divided up as convenient, but at least 2 hours' worth of oxygen breathing periods should be completed at 30 feet.

Treatment Table 7: Treatment Table 7 is considered an heroic measure for treating non-responding severe gas embolism or life-threatening decompression sickness. Committing a patient to Treatment Table 7 involves isolating the patient and having to minister to his medical needs in the recompression chamber for 48 hours or longer. Experienced diving medical personnel must be available before committing to Treatment Table 7.

Considerations: A Diving Medical Doctor shall be consulted before shifting to a Treatment Table 7 and careful consideration shall be given to life support capability. In addition, it must be realized that the recompression facility will be committed for 48 hours or more.

Indications: Treatment Table 7 is an extension at 60 feet of Treatment Tables 6, 6A, or 4 (or any other nonstandard treatment table). This means that considerable treatment has already been administered. Treatment Table 7 is not designed to treat all residual symptoms that do not improve at 60 feet and should never be used to treat residual pain. Treatment Table 7 should be used only when loss of life may result if the currently prescribed decompression from 60 feet is undertaken.

Time at Depth: When using Treatment Table 7, a minimum of 12 hours should be spent at 60 feet, including time spent at 60 feet from Treatment Table 4, 6, or 6A. Severe Type II decompression sickness and/or arterial gas embolism cases may continue to deteriorate significantly over the first several hours. This should not be cause for premature changes in depth. Do not begin decompression from 60 feet for at least 12 hours. At completion of the 12-hour stay, the decision must be made whether to decompress or spend additional time at 60 feet. If no improvement was noted during the first 12 hours, benefit from additional time at 60 feet is unlikely and decompression should be started. If the patient is improving but significant residual symptoms remain (e.g., limb paralysis, abnormal or absent respiration), additional time at 60 feet may be warranted. While the actual time that can be spent at 60 feet is unlimited, the actual additional amount of time beyond 12 hours that should be spent can only be determined by a Diving Medical Doctor (in consultation with on-site supervisory personnel), based on the patient's response to therapy and operational factors. When the patient has progressed to the point of consciousness, can breathe independently, and can move all extremities, decompression can be started and maintained as long as improvement continues. Solid evidence of continued benefit should be established for stays longer than 18 hours at 60 feet. Regardless of the duration at the recompression below 60 feet, at least 12 hours must be spent at 60 feet and then Table 7 followed to the surface. Additional recompression below 60 feet in these cases should not be undertaken unless adequate life support capability is available.

Decompression: When using Treatment Table 7, tenders breathe chamber atmosphere. Chamber oxygen should be kept above 19% and carbon dioxide below 1.5% surface equivalent (sev) (11.4 mmHg). Decompression on

Treatment Table 7 is begun with an upward excursion at time zero from 60 to 58 feet. Subsequent 2-foot upward excursions are made at time intervals appropriate to the rate of decompression:

Depth	Rate	Time Interval
58-40 feet	3 ft/hr	40 min
40-20 feet	2 ft/hr	60 min
20-4 feet	1 ft/hr	120 min

Preventing Inadvertent Early Surfacing: Upon arrival at 4 feet, decompression should be stopped for 4 hours. At the end of 4 hours at 4 feet, decompress to the surface at 1 foot per minute. This procedure prevents inadvertent early surfacing.

Time Intervals: The travel time between subsequent stops is considered as part of the time interval for the next shallower stop. The time intervals shown above begin when ascent to the next shallower stop has begun.

Oxygen Breathing: On a Treatment Table 7, patients should begin oxygen breathing periods as soon as possible at 60 feet. Oxygen breathing periods of 25 minutes on 100% oxygen, followed by 5 minutes breathing chamber atmosphere, should be used. Normally, four oxygen breathing periods are alternated with 2 hours of continuous air breathing. In conscious patients, this cycle should be continued until a minimum of eight oxygen breathing periods have been administered (previous 100% oxygen breathing periods may be counted against these eight periods). Beyond that, oxygen breathing periods should be continued as recommended by the Diving Medical Doctor, as long as improvement is noted and the oxygen is tolerated by the patient. If oxygen breathing causes significant pain on inspiration, it should be discontinued unless it is felt that significant benefit from oxygen breathing is being obtained. In unconscious patients, oxygen breathing should be stopped after a maximum of 24 oxygen breathing periods have been administered. The actual number and length of oxygen breathing periods should be adjusted by the Diving Medical Doctor to suit the individual patient's clinical condition and response to oxygen toxicity.

Sleeping, Resting, and Eating: At least two tenders should be available when using Treatment Table 7, and three may be necessary for severely ill patients. Not all tenders are required to be in the chamber, and they may be locked in and out as required following appropriate decompression tables. The patient may sleep anytime except when breathing oxygen deeper than 30 feet. While asleep, the patient's pulse, respiration, and blood pressure should be monitored and recorded at intervals appropriate to the patient's condition. Food may be taken at any time and fluid intake should be maintained.

Ancillary Care: Patients on Treatment Table 7 requiring intravenous and/or drug therapy should have these administered in accordance with a Diving Medical Doctor.

Abort Procedures: In some cases, a Treatment Table 7 may have to be terminated early. If extenuating circumstances dictate early decompression and less than 12 hours have elapsed since treatment was begun, decompression may be accomplished using the appropriate 60-foot Air Decompression Table as modified. The 60-foot Air Decompression Tables may be used even if time was spent between 60 and 165 feet (e.g., on Table 4 or 6A), as long as at least 3 hours have elapsed since the last excursion below 60 feet. If less than 3 hours have elapsed, or if any time was spent below 165 feet, use the Air Decompression Table appropriate to the maximum depth attained during treatment. All stops and times in the Air Decompression Table should be followed, but oxygen-breathing periods should be started for all chamber occupants as soon as a depth of 30 feet is reached. All chamber occupants should continue oxygen-breathing periods of 25 minutes on 100% oxygen, followed by 5 minutes on air, until the total time breathing oxygen is one-half or more of the total decompression time.

If more than 12 hours have elapsed since treatment was begun, the decompression schedule of Treatment Table 7 shall be used. In extreme emergencies, the abort recommendations may be used if more than 12 hours have elapsed since beginning treatment.

Treatment Table 8: Treatment Table 8 is an adaptation of a Royal Navy Treatment Table 65 mainly for treating deep uncontrolled ascents when more than 60 minutes of decompression have been missed. Compress symptomatic patient to depth of relief not to exceed 225 fsw. Initiate Treatment Table 8 from depth of relief. The Table 8 schedule from 60 feet is the same as Treatment Table 7.

Treatment Table 9: Treatment Table 9 is a hyperbaric oxygen treatment table using 90 minutes of oxygen at 45 feet. This table is recommended by the Diving Medical Doctor cognizant of the patient's medical condition. Treatment Table 9 is used for the following:

• Residual symptoms from AGE/DCS

This table may also be recommended by the cognizant Diving Medical Doctor when initially treating a severely injured patient whose medical condition precludes long absences from definitive medical care.

Flow Chart 1

Treatment of Decompression Sickness Occurring While at a Decompression Stop in the Water

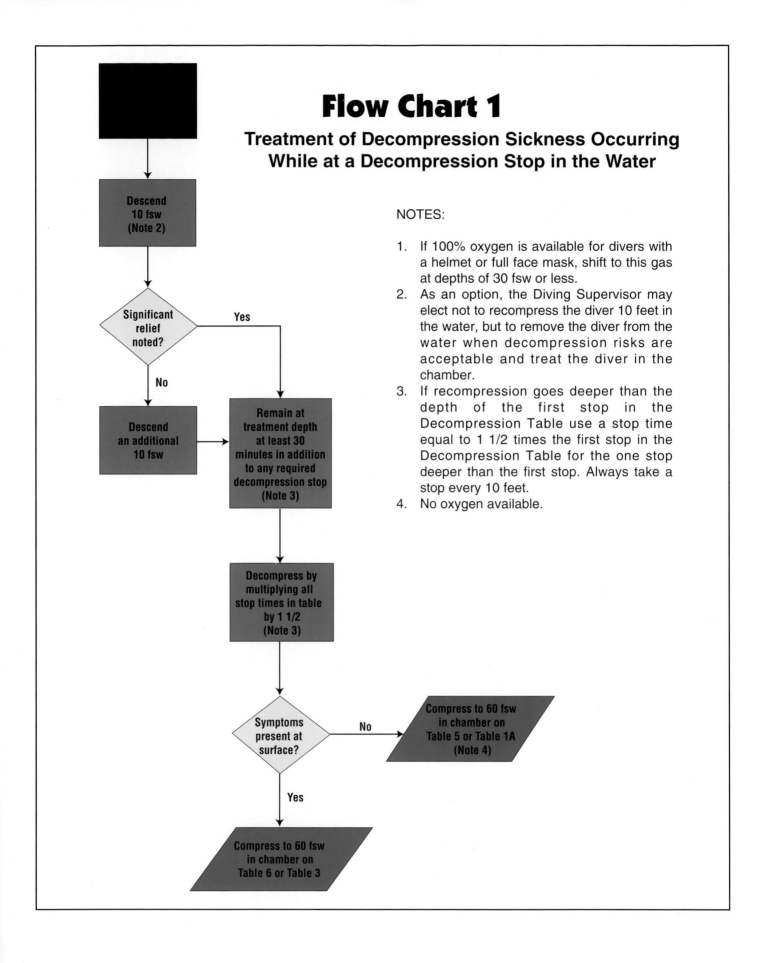

Descend 10 fsw (Note 2)

Significant relief noted?

— Yes →

— No →

Descend an additional 10 fsw

Remain at treatment depth at least 30 minutes in addition to any required decompression stop (Note 3)

Decompress by multiplying all stop times in table by 1 1/2 (Note 3)

Symptoms present at surface?

— No → **Compress to 60 fsw in chamber on Table 5 or Table 1A (Note 4)**

— Yes → **Compress to 60 fsw in chamber on Table 6 or Table 3**

NOTES:

1. If 100% oxygen is available for divers with a helmet or full face mask, shift to this gas at depths of 30 fsw or less.
2. As an option, the Diving Supervisor may elect not to recompress the diver 10 feet in the water, but to remove the diver from the water when decompression risks are acceptable and treat the diver in the chamber.
3. If recompression goes deeper than the depth of the first stop in the Decompression Table use a stop time equal to 1 1/2 times the first stop in the Decompression Table for the one stop deeper than the first stop. Always take a stop every 10 feet.
4. No oxygen available.

Flow Chart 2

Treatment of Type I
Decompression Sickness
Treatment from Diving or Altitude Exposures

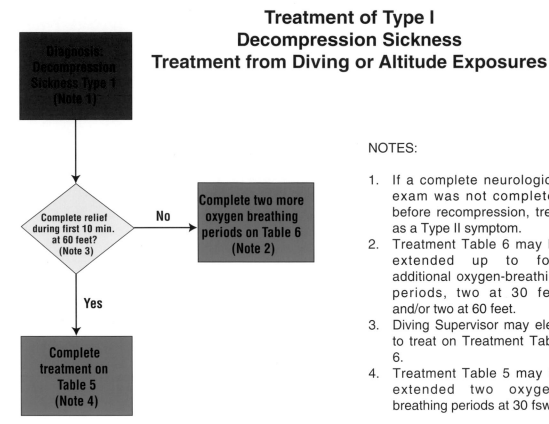

NOTES:

1. If a complete neurological exam was not completed before recompression, treat as a Type II symptom.
2. Treatment Table 6 may be extended up to four additional oxygen-breathing periods, two at 30 feet and/or two at 60 feet.
3. Diving Supervisor may elect to treat on Treatment Table 6.
4. Treatment Table 5 may be extended two oxygen-breathing periods at 30 fsw.

Flow Chart 3

Treatment of Arterial Gas Embolism or Decompression Sickness

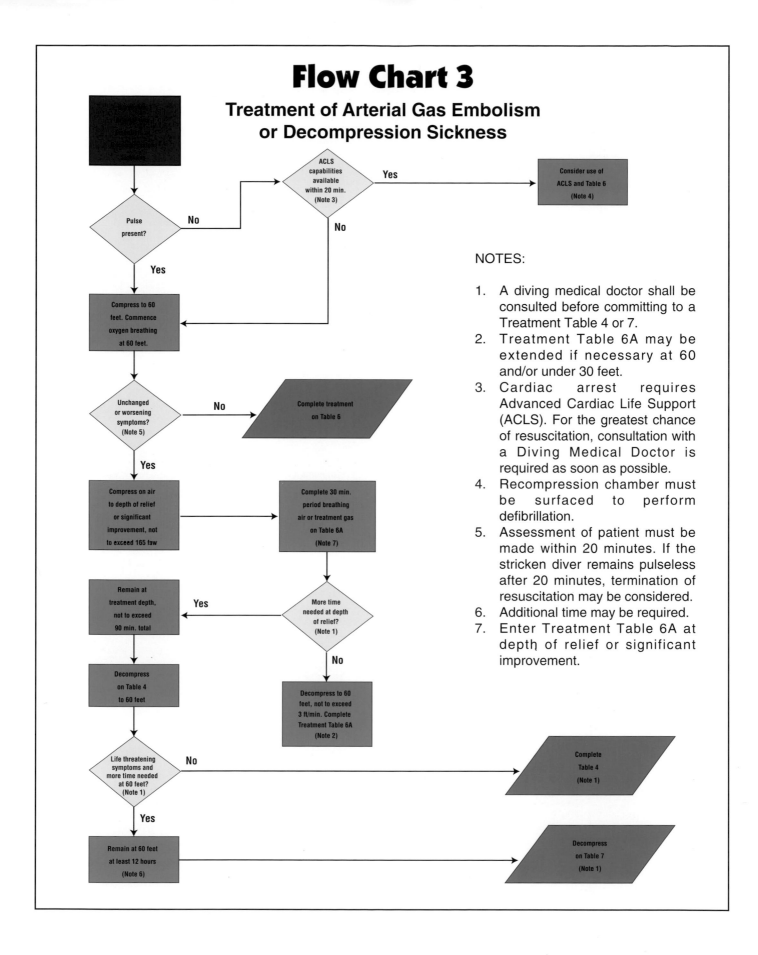

NOTES:

1. A diving medical doctor shall be consulted before committing to a Treatment Table 4 or 7.
2. Treatment Table 6A may be extended if necessary at 60 and/or under 30 feet.
3. Cardiac arrest requires Advanced Cardiac Life Support (ACLS). For the greatest chance of resuscitation, consultation with a Diving Medical Doctor is required as soon as possible.
4. Recompression chamber must be surfaced to perform defibrillation.
5. Assessment of patient must be made within 20 minutes. If the stricken diver remains pulseless after 20 minutes, termination of resuscitation may be considered.
6. Additional time may be required.
7. Enter Treatment Table 6A at depth of relief or significant improvement.

Flow Chart 4
Treatment of
Symptom Recurrence

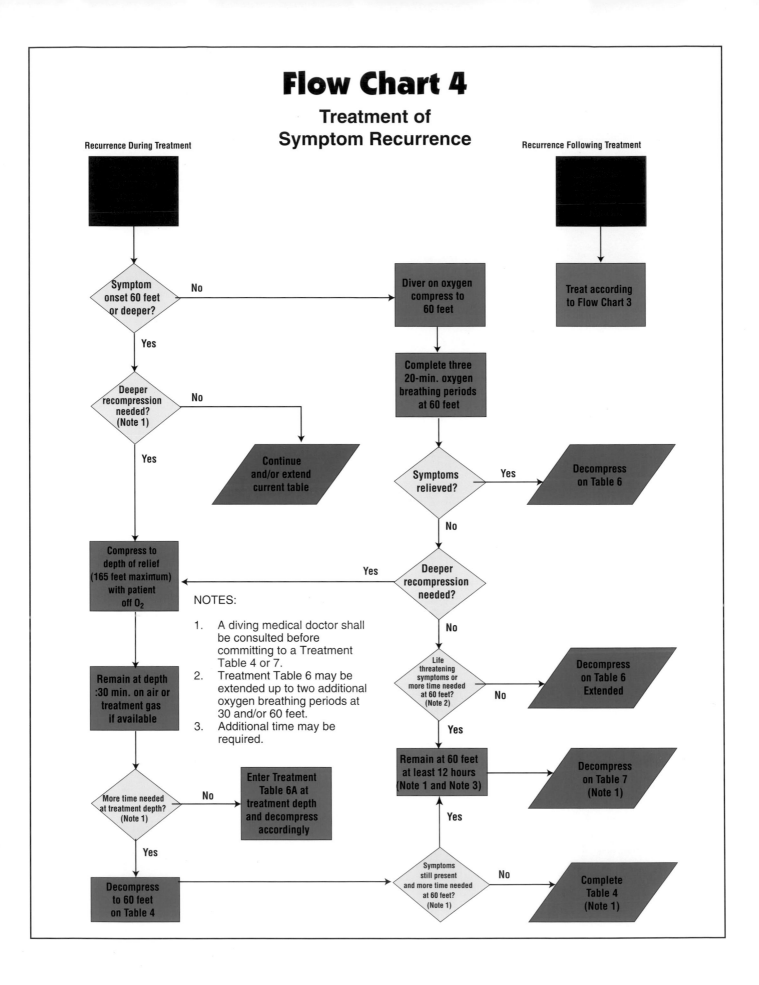

Recurrence During Treatment

Symptom onset 60 feet or deeper? — No →

Yes ↓

Deeper recompression needed? (Note 1) — No →

Yes ↓

Continue and/or extend current table

Compress to depth of relief (165 feet maximum) with patient off O₂

Remain at depth :30 min. on air or treatment gas if available

More time needed at treatment depth? (Note 1) — No → Enter Treatment Table 6A at treatment depth and decompress accordingly

Yes ↓

Decompress to 60 feet on Table 4

Diver on oxygen compress to 60 feet

Complete three 20-min. oxygen breathing periods at 60 feet

Symptoms relieved? — Yes → Decompress on Table 6

No ↓

Deeper recompression needed? — Yes → (to Compress to depth of relief)

No ↓

Life threatening symptoms or more time needed at 60 feet? (Note 2) — No → Decompress on Table 6 Extended

Yes ↓

Remain at 60 feet at least 12 hours (Note 1 and Note 3) → Decompress on Table 7 (Note 1)

Yes ↑

Symptoms still present and more time needed at 60 feet? (Note 1) — No → Complete Table 4 (Note 1)

Recurrence Following Treatment

Treat according to Flow Chart 3

NOTES:

1. A diving medical doctor shall be consulted before committing to a Treatment Table 4 or 7.
2. Treatment Table 6 may be extended up to two additional oxygen breathing periods at 30 and/or 60 feet.
3. Additional time may be required.

Air Treatment Table 1A

1. Descent rate — 20 ft/min.
2. Ascent rate — 1 ft/min.

3. Time at 100 feet includes time from the surface.

Depth/Time Profile

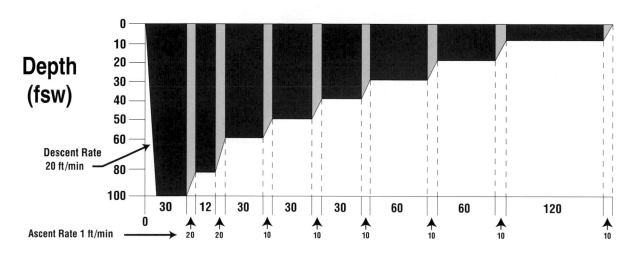

Depth (fsw)

Descent Rate 20 ft/min

Ascent Rate 1 ft/min →

Time at Depth (minutes)

Total Elapsed Time: 472 Minutes (7 hours 52 minutes)

Depth (feet)	Stop Time (minutes)	Ascent Time (minutes)	Breathing Media	Total Elapsed Time (hrs:min.)
100	30		Air	0:30
80	12	20	Air	1:02
60	30	20	Air	1:52
50	30	10	Air	2:32
40	30	10	Air	3:12
30	60	10	Air	4:22
20	60	10	Air	5:32
10	120	10	Air	7:42
0		10	Air	7:52

Treatment Table 4

1. Descent rate — 20 ft/min.
2. Ascent rate — 1 ft/min.
3. Time at 165 feet includes time from the surface.
4. If only air is available, decompress on air. If oxygen is available, patient begins oxygen breathing upon arrival at 60 feet with appropriate air breaks. Both tender and patient breathe oxygen beginning two hours before leaving 30 feet.
5. Ensure life support considerations can be met before committing to Table 4. Internal chamber temperature should be below 85° F.
6. If oxygen breathing is interrupted, no compensatory lengthening of the table is required.
7. If switching from Treatment Table 6A or 3 at 165 feet, stay a maximum of two hours at 165 feet before decompressing.
8. If the chamber is equipped with a high-O_2 treatment gas, it may be administered at 165 fsw, not to exceed 2.8 ata O_2. Treatment gas is administered for 25 minutes interrupted by 5 minutes of air.

Depth/Time Profile

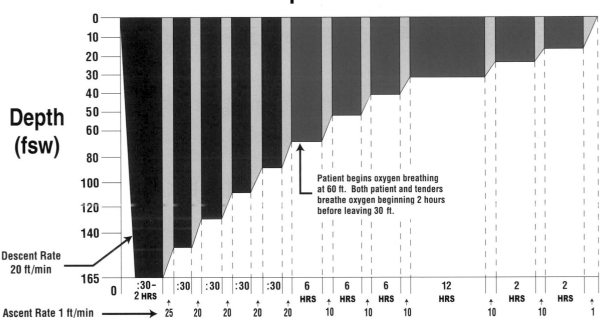

Depth (fsw)

Descent Rate 20 ft/min

Patient begins oxygen breathing at 60 ft. Both patient and tenders breathe oxygen beginning 2 hours before leaving 30 ft.

Ascent Rate 1 ft/min

Time at Depth (minutes)

Total Elapsed Time:
39 Hours 6 Minutes
(30 minutes at 165 fsw)
to 40 hours 36 minutes
(2 hours at 165 fsw)

Breathing Media

■ = Oxygen   ■ = Air

Treatment Table 5

1. Descent rate — 20 ft/min.
2. Ascent rate — Not to exceed 1 ft/min. Do not compensate for slower ascent rates. Compensate for faster rates by halting the ascent.
3. Time on oxygen begins on arrival at 60 feet.
4. If oxygen breathing must be interrupted because of CNS Oxygen Toxicity, allow 15 minutes after the reaction has entirely subsided and resume schedule at point of interruption. *

5. Treatment Table may be extended two oxygen-breathing periods at the 30-foot stop. No air break required between oxygen-breathing periods or prior to ascent.
6. Tender breathes 100% O_2 during ascent from the 30-foot stop to the surface. If the tender had a previous hyperbaric exposure in the previous 12 hours, an additional 20 minutes of oxygen breathing is required prior to ascent.

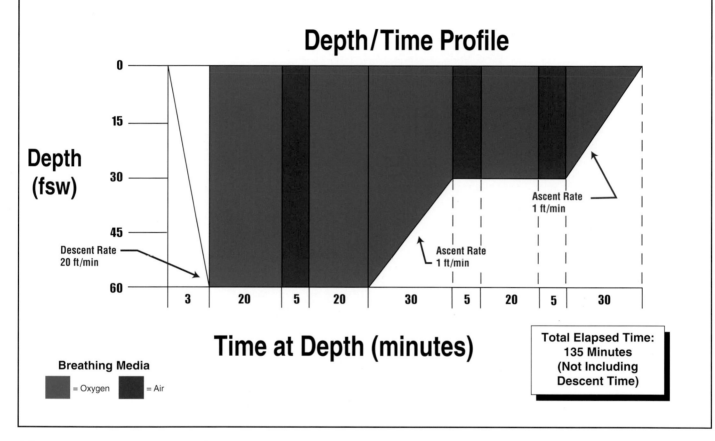

Depth/Time Profile

Depth (fsw)

Descent Rate 20 ft/min

Ascent Rate 1 ft/min

Ascent Rate 1 ft/min

Time at depth (minutes): 3 | 20 | 5 | 20 | 30 | 5 | 20 | 5 | 30

Time at Depth (minutes)

Breathing Media
■ = Oxygen   ■ = Air

Total Elapsed Time: 135 Minutes (Not Including Descent Time)

* Procedures In the Event of Oxygen Toxicity. At the first sign of CNS oxygen toxicity, the patient should be removed from oxygen and allowed to breathe chamber air. Oxygen breathing may be restarted 15 minutes after all symptoms have subsided. If symptoms of CNS oxygen toxicity develop again, interrupt oxygen breathing for another 15 minutes. If CNS oxygen toxicity develops a third time, contact a Diving Medical Doctor as soon as possible to modify oxygen breathing periods to meet requirements.

Treatment Table 6

1. Descent rate — 20 ft / min.
2. Ascent rate — Not to exceed 1 ft/min. Do not compensate for slower ascent rates. Compensate for faster rates by halting the ascent.
3. Time on oxygen begins on arrival at 60 feet.
4. If oxygen breathing must be interrupted because of CNS Oxygen Toxicity, allow 15 minutes after the reaction has entirely subsided and resume schedule at point of interruption. *
5. Table 6 can be lengthened up to two additional 25 – minute periods at 60 feet (20 minutes on oxygen and five minutes on air), or up to two additional 75 – minute periods at 30 feet (15 minutes on air and 60 minutes on oxygen), or both.
6. Tender breathes 100% O₂ during the last 30 minutes at 30 fsw and during ascent to the surface for an unmodified table or where there has been only a single extension at 30 or 60 feet. If there has been more than one extension, the O₂ breathing at 30 feet is increased to 60 minutes. If the tender has had a hyperbaric exposure within the past 12 hours, an additional 60 – minute O₂ period is taken at 30 feet.

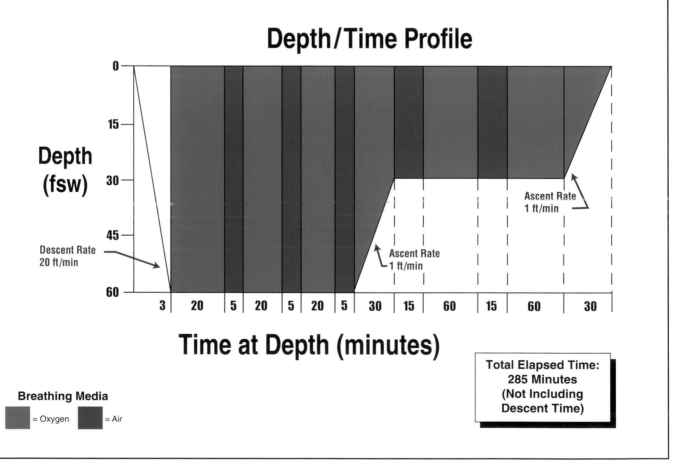

Depth/Time Profile

Depth (fsw)

Descent Rate 20 ft/min

Ascent Rate 1 ft/min

Ascent Rate 1 ft/min

3 | 20 | 5 | 20 | 5 | 20 | 5 | 30 | 15 | 60 | 15 | 60 | 30

Time at Depth (minutes)

Total Elapsed Time: 285 Minutes (Not Including Descent Time)

Breathing Media

= Oxygen   = Air

* **Procedures In the Event of Oxygen Toxicity.** At the first sign of CNS oxygen toxicity, the patient should be removed from oxygen and allowed to breathe chamber air. Oxygen breathing may be restarted 15 minutes after all symptoms have subsided. If symptoms of CNS oxygen toxicity develop again, interrupt oxygen breathing for another 15 minutes. If CNS oxygen toxicity develops a third time, contact a Diving Medical Doctor as soon as possible to modify oxygen breathing periods to meet requirements.

Treatment Table 6A

1. Descent rate — 20 ft/min.
2. Ascent rate — 165 fsw to 60 fsw, not to exceed 3 ft/min, 60 fsw and shallower, not to exceed 1 ft/min. Do not compensate for slower ascent rates. Compensate for faster rates by halting the ascent.
3. Time at treatment depth does not include compression time.
4. Table begins with initial compression to depth of 60 fsw. If initial treatment was at 60 feet, up to 20 minutes may be spent at 60 feet before compression to 165 fsw. Contact a Diving Medical Doctor.
5. If a chamber is equipped with a high-O_2 treatment gas, it may be administered at 165 fsw and shallower, not to exceed 2.8 ata O_2. Treatment gas is administered for 25 minutes interrupted by five minutes of air. Treatment gas is breathed during ascent from the treatment depth to 60 fsw.
6. Deeper than 60 feet, if treatment gas must be interrupted because of CNS oxygen toxicity, allow 15 minutes after the reaction has entirely subsided and resume schedule at point of interruption. *
7. Table 6A can be lengthened up to two additional 25-minute periods at 60 feet (20 minutes on oxygen and five minutes on air), or up to two additional 75-minute periods at 30 feet (60 minutes on oxygen and 15 minutes on air), or both.
8. Tender breathes 100% oxygen during the last 60 minutes at 30 fsw and during ascent to the surface for an unmodified table or where there has been only a single extension at 30 or 60 fsw. If there has been more than one extension, the O_2 breathing at 30 fsw is increased to 90 minutes. If the tender had a hyperbaric exposure within the past 12 hours, an additional 60 minute O_2 breathing period is taken at 30 fsw.
9. If significant improvement is not obtained within 30 minutes at 165 feet, consult with a Diving Medical Doctor before switching to Treatment Table 4.

Depth/Time Profile

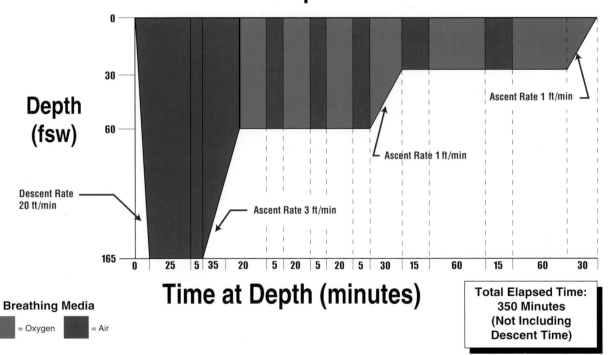

Depth (fsw)

Descent Rate 20 ft/min

Ascent Rate 3 ft/min

Ascent Rate 1 ft/min

Ascent Rate 1 ft/min

Time at Depth (minutes)

0 | 25 | 5 | 35 | 20 | 5 | 20 | 5 | 20 | 5 | 30 | 15 | 60 | 15 | 60 | 30

Breathing Media

= Oxygen   = Air

Total Elapsed Time: 350 Minutes (Not Including Descent Time)

* **Procedures In the Event of Oxygen Toxicity.** At the first sign of CNS oxygen toxicity, the patient should be removed from oxygen and allowed to breathe chamber air. Oxygen breathing may be restarted 15 minutes after all symptoms have subsided. If symptoms of CNS oxygen toxicity develop again, interrupt oxygen breathing for another 15 minutes. If CNS oxygen toxicity develops a third time, contact a Diving Medical Doctor as soon as possible to modify oxygen breathing periods to meet requirements.

Treatment Table 7

1. Table begins upon arrival at 60 feet. Arrival at 60 feet is accomplished by initial treatment on Table 6, 6A, or 4. If initial treatment has progressed to a depth shallower than 60 feet, compress to 60 feet at 20 ft/min to begin Table 7.
2. Maximum duration at 60 feet is unlimited. Remain at 60 feet a minimum of 12 hours unless overriding circumstances dictate earlier decompression.
3. Patient begins oxygen breathing periods at 60 feet. Tender should breathe only chamber atmosphere throughout. If oxygen breathing is interrupted, no lengthening of the table is required.
4. Minimum chamber O_2 concentration is 19%.
5. Maximum CO_2 concentration is 1.5% SEV (11.4 mmHg). Maximum chamber internal temperature is 85° F.
6. Decompression starts with a 2-foot upward excursion from 60 to 58 feet. Decompress with stops every two feet for times shown in profile below. Ascent time between stops is approximately 30 seconds. Stop time begins with ascent from deeper to next shallower step. Stop at four feet for four hours and then ascend to the surface at 1 ft/min.
7. Ensure chamber life-support requirements can be met before committing to Treatment Table 7.
8. A Diving Medical Doctor shall be consulted before committing to this treatment table.

Depth/Time Profile

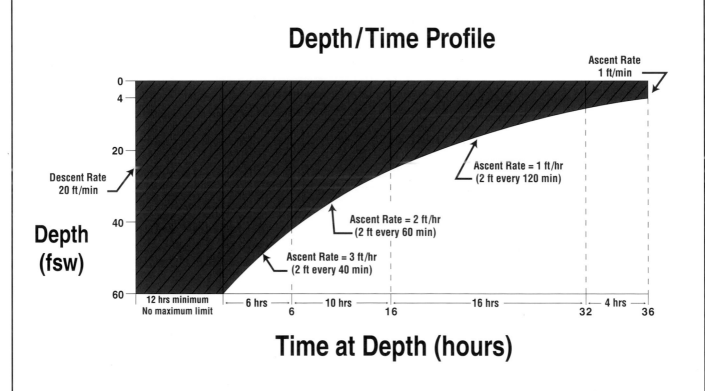

Depth (fsw)

Time at Depth (hours)

Treatment Table 8

1. Enter the table at the depth which is exactly equal to or next greater than the deepest depth attained in the recompression. The descent rate is as fast as tolerable.

2. The maximum time that can be spent at the deepest depth is shown in the second column. The maximum time for 225 fsw is 30 minutes; for 165 fsw, 3 hours. For an asymptomatic diver, the maximum time at depth is 30 minutes for depths exceeding 165 fsw and 2 hours for depths equal to or shallower than 165 fsw.

3. Decompression is begun with a 2-fsw reduction in pressure if the depth is an even number. Decompression is begun with a 3-fsw reduction in pressure if the depth is an odd number. Subsequent stops are carried out every two fsw. Stop times are given in column three. The stop time begins when leaving the previous depth. Ascend to the next stop in approximately 30 seconds.

4. Stop times apply to all stops within the band up to the next quoted depth. For example, for ascent from 165 fsw, stops for 12 minutes are made at 162 fsw, and at every two-foot interval to 140 fsw. At 140 fsw, the stop time becomes 15 minutes. When traveling from 225 fsw, the 166 foot stop is 5 minutes; the 164−foot stop is 12 minutes. Once begun, decompression is continuous. For example, when decompressing from 225 feet, ascent is not halted at 165 fsw for 3 hours. However, ascent maybe halted at 60 fsw and shallower for any desired period of time.

5. While deeper than 165 fsw, a helium-oxygen mixture with 16−21% oxygen may be breathed by mask to reduce narcosis. At 165 fsw and shallower, a heliox mix with a PO_2 not to exceed 2.8 ata may be given to the diver as a treatment gas. At 60 fsw and shallower, pure oxygen may be given to the diver as a treatment gas. For all treatment gases (HeO_2, N_2O_2, and O_2), a schedule of 25 minutes on gas and 5 minutes on chamber air should be followed for a total of four cycles. Additional oxygen may be given at 60 fsw after a 2-hour interval of chamber air. See Treatment Table 7 for guidance.

6. A high-O_2 treatment mix can be used at treatment depth and during decompression. If high O_2 breathing is interrupted, no lengthening of the table is required.

7. To avoid loss of the chamber seal, ascent may be halted at four fsw and the total remaining stop time of 240 minutes taken at this depth. Ascend directly to the surface upon completion of the required time.

8. Total ascent time from 225 fsw is 56 hours, 29 minutes. For a 165-fsw recompression, total ascent time is 53 hours, 52 minutes, and for a 60-fsw recompression, 36 hours, 0 minutes.

Depth (fsw)	Max Time at Initial Treatment Depth (hours)	2-fsw Stop Times (minutes)
225	0.5	5
165	3	12
140	5	15
120	8	20
100	11	25
80	15	30
60	Unlimited	40
40	Unlimited	60
20	Unlimited	120

Treatment Table 9

1. Descent rate — 20 ft/min.
2. Ascent rate — 20 ft/min. Rate may be slowed to 1 ft/min depending upon the patient's medical condition.
3. Time at 45 feet begins on arrival at 45 feet.
4. If oxygen breathing must be interrupted because of CNS Oxygen Toxicity, oxygen breathing may be restarted 15 minutes after all symptoms have subsided. Resume schedule at point of interruption. *

5. Tender breathes 100% O_2 during last 15 minutes at 45 feet and during ascent to the surface regardless of ascent rate used.
6. If patient cannot tolerate oxygen at 45 feet, this table can be modified to allow a treatment depth of 30 feet. The oxygen breathing time can be extended to a maximum of three to four hours.

Depth/Time Profile

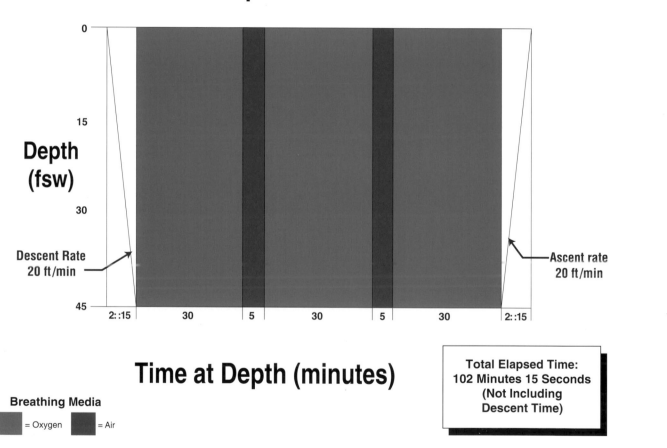

Depth (fsw)

Descent Rate 20 ft/min

Ascent rate 20 ft/min

| 2::15 | 30 | 5 | 30 | 5 | 30 | 2::15 |

Time at Depth (minutes)

**Total Elapsed Time:
102 Minutes 15 Seconds
(Not Including
Descent Time)**

Breathing Media

■ = Oxygen   ■ = Air

---

* Procedures in the Event of Oxygen Toxicity. At the first sign of CNS oxygen toxicity, the patient should be removed from oxygen and allowed to breathe chamber air. Oxygen breathing may be restarted 15 minutes after all symptoms have subsided. If symptoms of CNS oxygen toxicity develop again, interrupt oxygen breathing for another 15 minutes. If CNS oxygen toxicity develops a third time, contact a Diving Medical Doctor as soon as possible to modify oxygen breathing periods to meet requirements.

Appendix

Saturation Treatment Tables

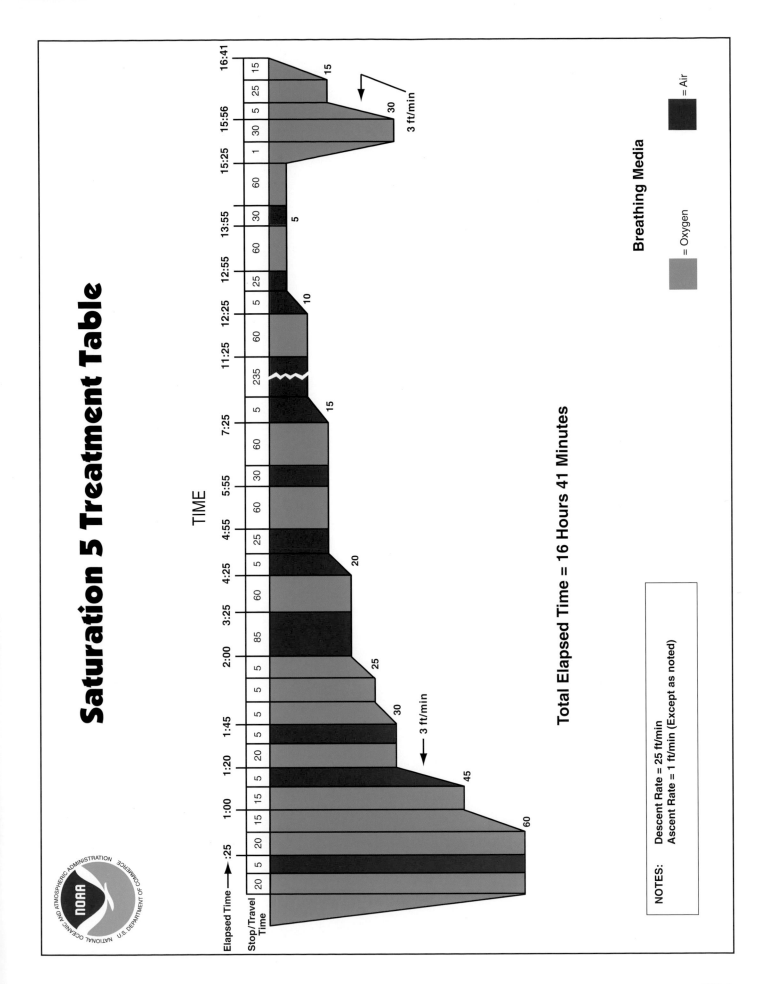

Saturation 5 Treatment Table

TIME

Total Elapsed Time = 16 Hours 41 Minutes

NOTES: Descent Rate = 25 ft/min
Ascent Rate = 1 ft/min (Except as noted)

Breathing Media

= Oxygen   = Air

NOTES

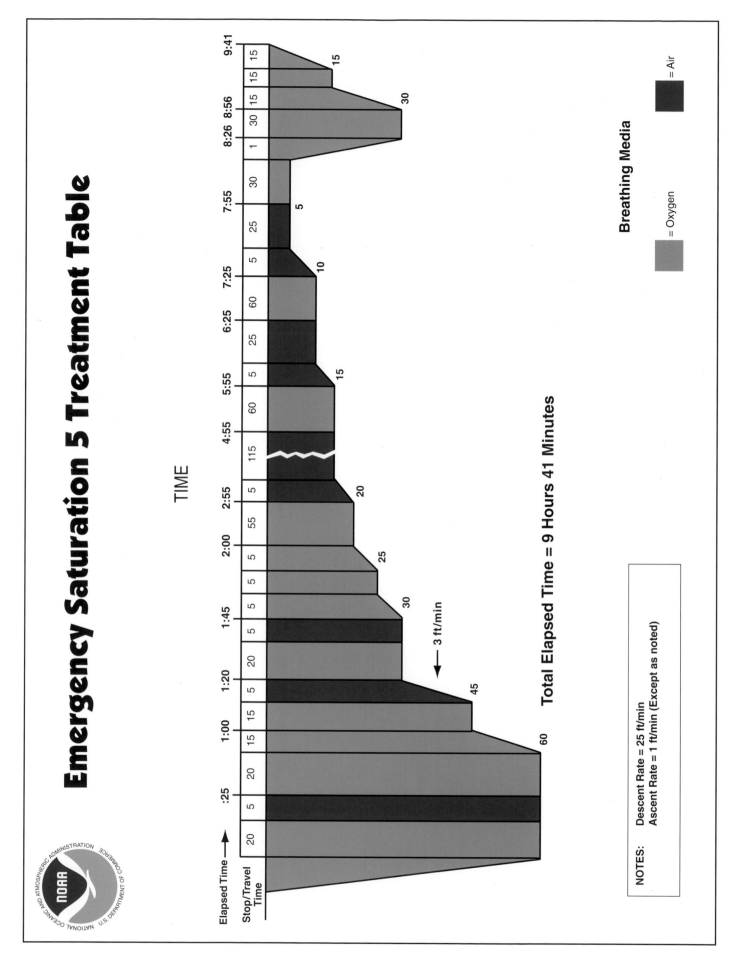

Emergency Saturation 5 Treatment Table

TIME

Total Elapsed Time = 9 Hours 41 Minutes

Elapsed Time ⟶

			:25	1:00	1:20	1:45	2:00	2:55	4:55	5:55	6:25	7:25	7:55	8:26 8:56		9:41

Stop/Travel Time

| 20 | 5 | 20 | 15 | 5 | 20 | 5 | 5 | 5 | 55 | 5 | 115 | 60 | 5 | 25 | 60 | 5 | 25 | 5 | 30 | 1 | 30 | 15 | 15 | 15 |

60

45

3 ft/min ↓

30

25

20

15

10

5

15

30

15

Breathing Media

= Oxygen ■ = Air

NOTES: Descent Rate = 25 ft/min
Ascent Rate = 1 ft/min (Except as noted)

NOAA Diving Manual

VI-3

NOTES

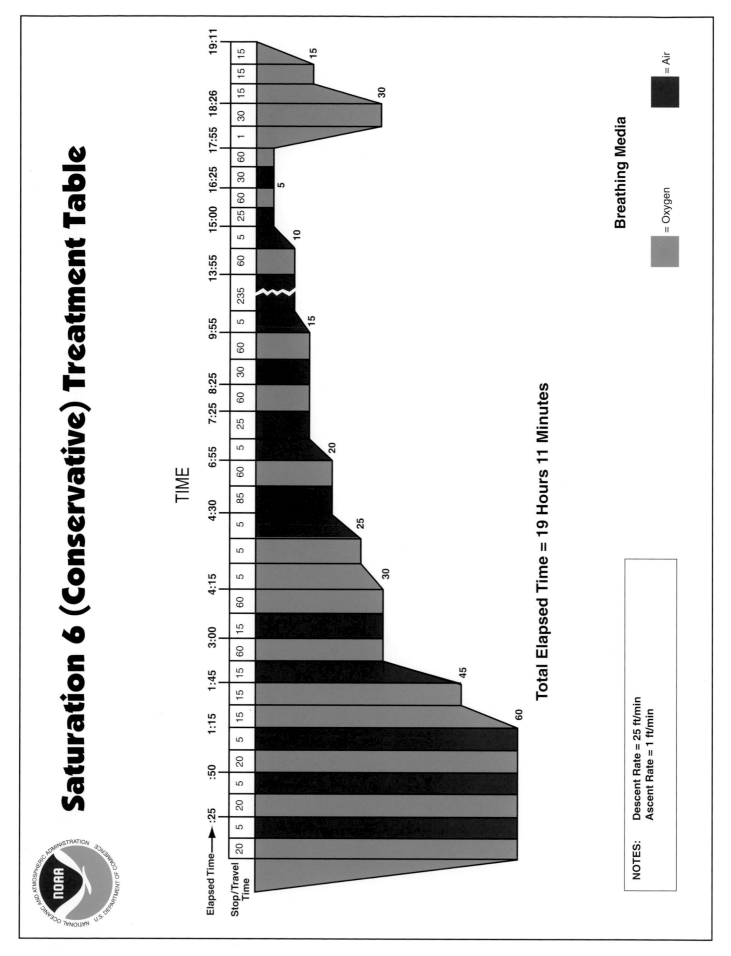

Saturation 6 (Conservative) Treatment Table

TIME

Total Elapsed Time = 19 Hours 11 Minutes

Breathing Media

= Oxygen

= Air

NOTES: Descent Rate = 25 ft/min
Ascent Rate = 1 ft/min

NOTES

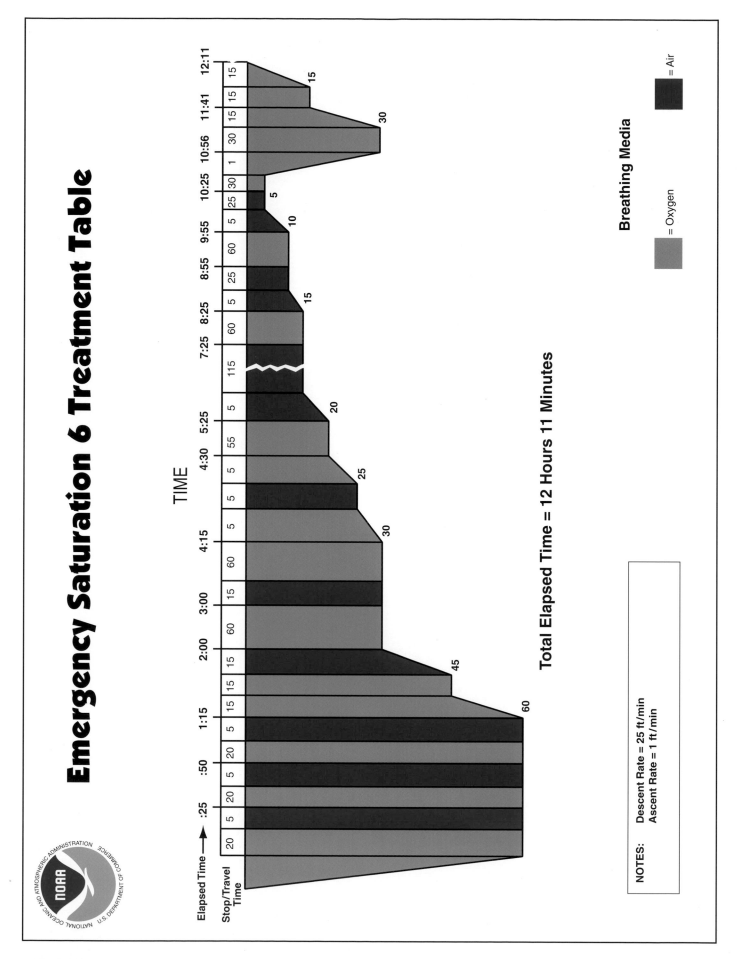

Emergency Saturation 6 Treatment Table

TIME

Total Elapsed Time = 12 Hours 11 Minutes

Breathing Media

= Oxygen

= Air

NOTES: Descent Rate = 25 ft/min
Ascent Rate = 1 ft/min

NOTES

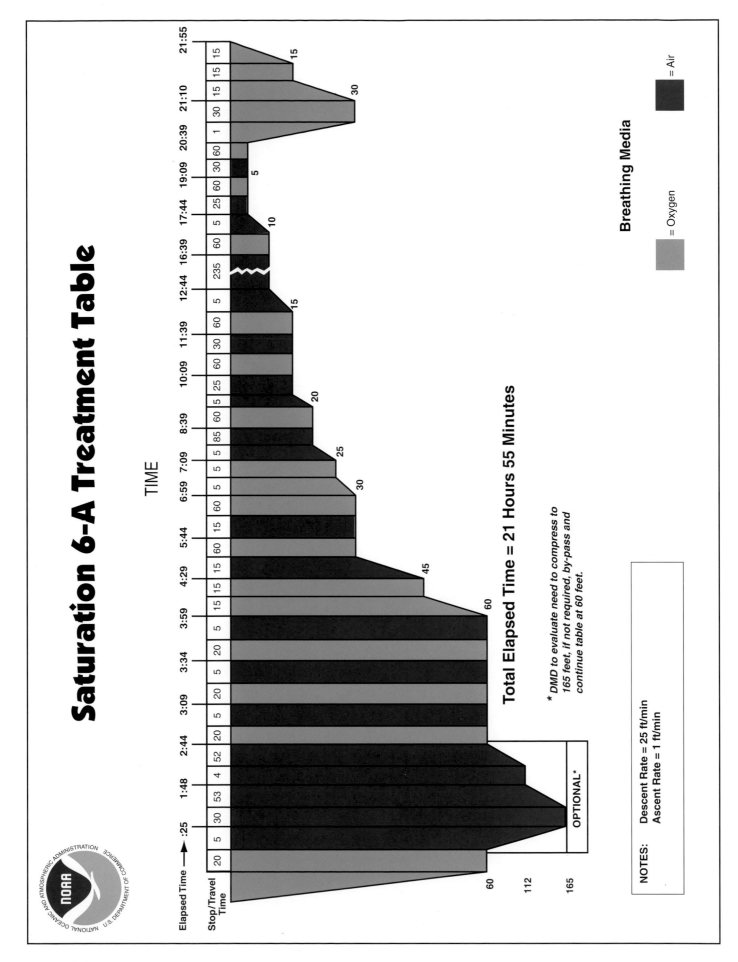

Saturation 6-A Treatment Table

TIME

Total Elapsed Time = 21 Hours 55 Minutes

* *DMD to evaluate need to compress to 165 feet, if not required, by-pass and continue table at 60 feet.*

OPTIONAL*

Breathing Media

= Oxygen   = Air

NOTES: Descent Rate = 25 ft/min
Ascent Rate = 1 ft/min

NOTES

Appendix

Nitrox Dive Tables

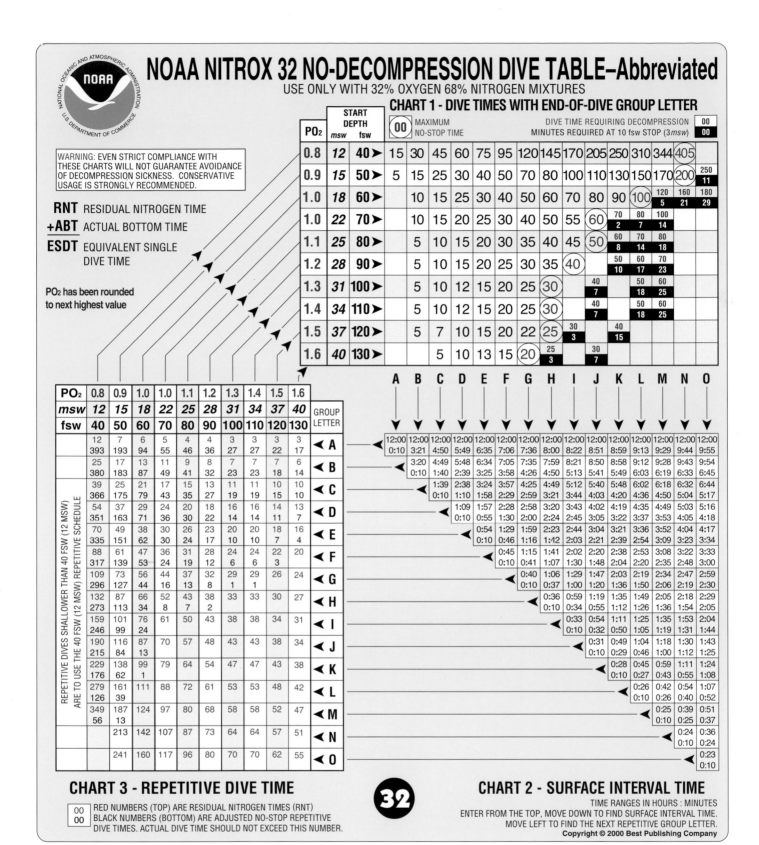

NOAA NITROX 32 NO-DECOMPRESSION DIVE TABLE–Abbreviated
USE ONLY WITH 32% OXYGEN 68% NITROGEN MIXTURES

CHART 1 - DIVE TIMES WITH END-OF-DIVE GROUP LETTER

WARNING: EVEN STRICT COMPLIANCE WITH THESE CHARTS WILL NOT GUARANTEE AVOIDANCE OF DECOMPRESSION SICKNESS. CONSERVATIVE USAGE IS STRONGLY RECOMMENDED.

RNT RESIDUAL NITROGEN TIME
+ABT ACTUAL BOTTOM TIME
ESDT EQUIVALENT SINGLE DIVE TIME

PO_2 has been rounded to next highest value

CHART 3 - REPETITIVE DIVE TIME

REPETITIVE DIVES SHALLOWER THAN 40 FSW (12 MSW) ARE TO USE THE 40 FSW (12 MSW) REPETITIVE SCHEDULE

RED NUMBERS (TOP) ARE RESIDUAL NITROGEN TIMES (RNT)
BLACK NUMBERS (BOTTOM) ARE ADJUSTED NO-STOP REPETITIVE DIVE TIMES. ACTUAL DIVE TIME SHOULD NOT EXCEED THIS NUMBER.

CHART 2 - SURFACE INTERVAL TIME

TIME RANGES IN HOURS : MINUTES
ENTER FROM THE TOP, MOVE DOWN TO FIND SURFACE INTERVAL TIME.
MOVE LEFT TO FIND THE NEXT REPETITIVE GROUP LETTER.
Copyright © 2000 Best Publishing Company

NOTES

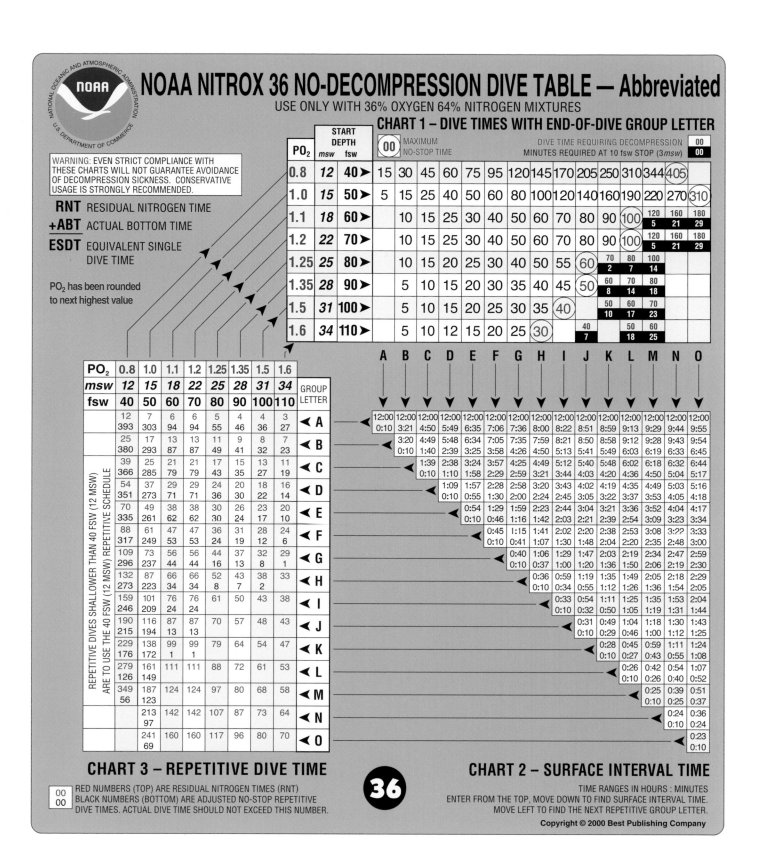

NITROX DIVE PLANNING
WORKSHEET

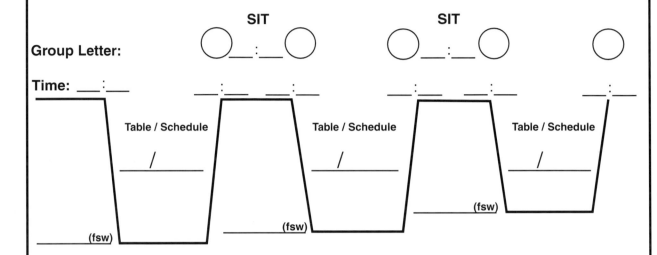

Group Letter:

SIT ___:___   SIT ___:___

Time: ___:___   ___:___ ___:___   ___:___ ___:___   ___:___

Table / Schedule
_____ / _____

Table / Schedule
_____ / _____

Table / Schedule
_____ / _____

(fsw)

(fsw)

(fsw)

RNT = 0   PO$_2$ _____
ABT = _____
            % Limit ___
ESDT = _____

RNT = _____   PO$_2$ _____
ABT = _____
            % Limit ___
ESDT = _____

RNT = _____   PO$_2$ _____
ABT = _____
            % Limit ___
ESDT = _____

ABT – Actual Bottom Time — The time from the moment of descent until beginning a direct ascent to surface.

ESDT – Equivalent Single Dive Time — The sum of the RNT and ABT. This figure is used to obtain a group letter on Chart 1 for a repetitive dive.

Group Letter – A letter symbol for the Residual Nitrogen remaining in the body from a previous dive. Place in circle.

Oxygen Exposure Percent Limit – Maximum time on a single dive that the diver can be exposed to a certain partial pressure of oxygen.

PO$_2$ – Partial pressure of oxygen for the maximum depth obtained.

Repetitive Dive – Any dive made within 12 hours of a previous dive.

RNT – Residual Nitrogen Time – The time to be considered in planning a repetitive dive due to nitrogen remaining in the body from previous dives within the last 12 hours.

Safety Stop – A 3–5 minute safety stop at 15–20 fsw (4.6–6.1 msw) is strongly recommended for all dives deeper than 60 fsw (18.4 msw) and all repetitive dives.

SIT – Surface Interval Time – The time spent at the surface between dives.

Single Dive Oxygen Exposure Limits	
PO$_2$ atm	Minutes
1.60	45
1.55	83
1.50	120
1.45	135
1.40	150
1.35	165
1.30	180
1.25	195
1.20	210

Remember

• Ascend no faster than 30 feet per minute (1 foot every 2 seconds).

No-Decompression Limits and Repetitive Group Designation Table for No-Decompression Dive

Depth (feet/*meters*)	No-Decompression Limits (min)	A	B	C	D	E	F	G	H	I	J	K	L	M	N	O
15 *5*	unlimited	60	120	210	300	797	★									
20 *6*	unlimited	35	70	110	160	225	350	452	★							
25 *8*	unlimited	25	50	75	100	135	180	240	325	390	917	★				
30 *9*	595	20	35	55	75	100	125	160	195	245	315	361	540	595		
40 *12*	405	15	30	45	60	75	95	120	145	170	205	250	310	344	405	
45 *14*	310	5	15	25	40	50	60	80	100	120	140	160	190	220	270	310
50 *15*	200	5	15	25	30	40	50	70	80	100	110	130	150	170	200	
60 *18*	100		10	15	25	30	40	50	60	70	80	90	100			
70 *22*	60		10	15	20	25	30	40	50	55	60					
80 *25*	50			5	10	15	20	30	35	40	45	50				
90 *28*	40			5	10	15	20	25	30	35	40					
100 *31*	30			5	10	12	15	20	25	30						
110 *34*	30			5	10	12	15	20	25	30						
120 *37*	25			5	7	10	15	20	22	25						
130 *40*	20				5	10	13	15	20							
★★ 140 *43*	15				5	10	12	15								
★★ 150 *46*	10				5	8	10									

★★ Oxygen Exceptional Exposures
★ Highest repetitive group that can be achieved at this depth regardless of bottom time

Residual Nitrogen Time

Repetitive Dive Depth (fsw)	Z	O	N	M	L	K	J	I	H	G	F	E	D	C	B	A
10	**	**	**	**	**	**	**	**	**	**	**	797	279	159	88	39
20	**	**	**	**	**	**	917	399	279	208	159	120	88	62	39	18
30	+	+	+	349	279	229	190	159	132	109	88	70	54	39	25	12
40	+	+	+	349	279	229	190	159	132	109	88	70	54	39	25	12
50	257	241	213	187	161	138	116	101	87	73	61	49	37	25	17	7
60	169	160	142	124	111	99	87	76	66	56	47	38	29	21	13	6
70	122	117	107	97	88	79	70	61	52	44	36	30	24	17	11	5
80	100	96	87	80	72	64	57	50	43	37	31	26	20	15	9	4
90	84	80	73	68	61	54	48	43	38	32	28	23	18	13	8	4
100	73	70	64	58	53	47	43	38	33	29	24	20	16	11	7	3
110	73	70	64	58	53	47	43	38	33	29	24	20	16	11	7	3
120	64	62	57	52	48	43	38	34	30	26	22	18	14	10	7	3
130	57	55	51	47	42	38	34	31	27	24	20	16	13	10	6	3
140	52	50	46	43	39	35	32	28	25	21	18	15	12	9	6	3
150	46	44	40	38	35	31	28	25	22	19	16	13	11	8	6	3

Values are in Minutes

** If no Repetitive Nitrogen Time is given, then the Repetitive Group Letter does not change.
+ Read vertically downward to 50 Repetitive Dive Depth. Use the corresponding residual nitrogen time (minutes) to compute the equivalent single dive time. Decompress using the 50 NN32 Decompression Schedule Table 5.

NOTES

NOAA NITROX **32** DECOMPRESSION DIVE TABLE

DEPTH fsw (msw)	PO₂ (atm)	BOTTOM TIME (min)	TIME TO FIRST STOP (min:sec)	DECOMPRESSION STOPS 40 (fsw)	30	20	10	TOTAL ASCENT TIME (min:sec)	REPETITIVE GROUP LETTER
50 (15)	0.9	200					0	1:40	*
		210	1:20				2	3:40	N
		230	1:20				7	8:40	N
		250	1:20				11	12:40	O
		270	1:20				15	16:40	O
60 (18)	1.0	100					0	2:00	*
		110	1:40				3	5:00	L
		120	1:40				5	7:00	M
		140	1:40				10	12:00	M
		160	1:40				21	23:00	N
		180	1:40				29	31:00	O
		200	1:40				35	37:00	O
70 (22)	1.0	60					0	2:20	*
		70	2:00				2	4:20	K
		80	2:00				7	9:20	L
		100	2:00				14	16:20	M
		120	2:00				26	28:20	N
		140	2:00				39	41:20	O
80 (25)	1.1	50					0	2:40	*
		60	2:20				8	10:40	K
		70	2:20				14	16:40	L
		80	2:20				18	20:40	M
		90	2:20				23	25:40	N
		100	2:20				33	35:40	N
		110	2:00			2	41	45:40	O
		120	2:00			4	47	53:40	O
		130	2:00			6	52	60:40	O
90 (28)	1.2	40					0	3:00	*
		50	2:40				10	13:00	K
		60	2:40				17	20:00	L
		70	2:40				23	26:00	M
		80	2:20			2	31	36:00	N
		90	2:20			7	39	49:00	N
		100	2:20			11	46	60:00	O
		110	2:20			13	53	69:00	O
100 (31)	1.3	30					0	3:20	*
		40	3:00				7	10:20	J
		50	3:00				18	21:20	L
		60	3:00				25	28:20	M
		70	2:40			7	30	40:20	N
		80	2:40			13	40	56:20	N
		90	2:40			18	48	69:20	O
110 (34)	1.4	30					0	3:40	*
		40	3:20				7	10:40	J
		50	3:20				18	21:40	L
		60	3:20				25	28:40	M
		70	3:00			7	30	40:40	N
		80	3:00			13	40	56:40	N
		90	3:00			18	48	69:40	O
120 (37)	1.5	25					0	4:00	*
		30	3:40				3	7:00	I
		40	3:40				15	19:00	K
		50	3:20			2	24	30:00	L
		60	3:20			9	28	41:00	N
130 (40)	1.6	20					0	4:20	*
		25	4:00				3	7:20	H
		30	4:00				7	11:20	J
		40	4:00			2	21	27:20	L
		Exceptional Exposure							
		50	3:40			8	26	38:20	M**
		60	3:40			18	36	58:20	N**

* See No Decompression Table 3 for Repetitive Group Letter
** Time Exceeds Recommended Oxygen Partial Pressure Limits for Routine Diving Operations

NOTES

No-Decompression Limits and Repetitive Group Designation Table for No-Decompression Dive

Depth (feet/meters)		No-Decompression Limits (min)	A	B	C	D	E	F	G	H	I	J	K	L	M	N	O
15	5	unlimited	60	120	210	300	797	★									
20	6	unlimited	60	120	210	300	797	★									
25	8	unlimited	35	70	110	160	225	350	452	★							
30	9	unlimited	25	50	75	100	135	180	240	325	390	917	★				
40	12	405	15	30	45	60	75	95	120	145	170	205	250	310	344	405	
45	14	405	15	30	45	60	75	95	120	145	170	205	250	310	344	405	
50	15	310	5	15	25	40	50	60	80	100	120	140	160	190	220	270	310
60	18	100		10	15	25	30	40	50	60	70	80	90	100			
70	22	100		10	15	25	30	40	50	60	70	80	90	100			
80	25	60		10	15	20	25	30	40	50	55	60					
90	28	50			5	10	15	20	30	35	40	45	50				
100	31	40			5	10	15	20	25	30	35	40					
110	34	30			5	10	12	15	20	25	30						
★★ 120	37	25			5	7	10	15	20	22	25						
★★ 130	40	25			5	7	10	15	20	22	25						

★★ Oxygen Exceptional Exposures
★ Highest repetitive group that can be achieved at this depth regardless of bottom time

Residual Nitrogen Time

Repetitive Dive Depth (fsw)	Z	O	N	M	L	K	J	I	H	G	F	E	D	C	B	A
10	**	**	**	**	**	**	**	**	**	**	**	797	279	159	88	39
20	**	**	**	**	**	**	**	**	**	**	**	797	279	159	88	39
30	**	**	**	**	**	**	917	399	279	208	159	120	88	62	39	18
40	+	+	+	349	279	229	190	159	132	109	88	70	54	39	25	12
50	257	241	213	187	161	138	116	101	87	73	61	49	37	25	17	7
60	169	160	142	124	111	99	87	76	66	56	47	38	29	21	13	6
70	169	160	142	124	111	99	87	76	66	56	47	38	29	21	13	6
80	122	117	107	97	88	79	70	61	52	44	36	30	24	17	11	5
90	100	96	87	80	72	64	57	50	43	37	31	26	20	15	9	4
100	84	80	73	68	61	54	48	43	38	32	28	23	18	13	8	4
110	73	70	64	58	53	47	43	38	33	29	24	20	16	11	7	3
120	64	62	57	52	48	43	38	34	30	26	22	18	14	10	7	3
130	64	62	57	52	48	43	38	34	30	26	22	18	14	10	7	3

Values are in Minutes

** If no Repetitive Nitrogen Time is given, then the Repetitive Group Letter does not change.
+ Read vertically downward to 50 Repetitive Dive Depth. Use the corresponding residual nitrogen time (minutes) to compute the equivalent single dive time. Decompress using the 50 NN32 Decompression Schedule Table 5.

NOTES

DEPTH fsw (msw)	PO₂ (atm)	BOTTOM TIME (min)	TIME TO FIRST STOP (min:sec)	\<40\> DECOMPRESSION STOPS	30	20	10 (fsw)	TOTAL ASCENT TIME (min:sec)	REPETITIVE GROUP LETTER
60 (18)	1.1	100					0	2:00	*
		110	1:40				3	5:00	L
		120	1:40				5	7:00	M
		140	1:40				10	12:00	M
		160	1:40				21	23:00	N
		180	1:40				29	31:00	O
		200	1:40				35	37:00	O
70 (22)	1.2	100					0	2:20	*
		110	2:00				3	5:20	L
		120	2:00				5	7:20	M
		140	2:00				10	12:20	M
		160	2:00				21	23:20	N
		180	2:00				29	31:20	O
		200	2:00				35	37:20	O
80 (25)	1.25	60					0	2:40	*
		70	2:20				2	4:40	K
		80	2:20				7	9:40	L
		100	2:20				14	16:40	M
		120	2:20				26	28:40	N
		140	2:20				39	41:40	O
90 (28)	1.35	50					0	3:00	*
		60	2:40				8	11:00	K
		70	2:40				14	17:00	L
		80	2:40				18	21:00	M
		90	2:40				23	26:00	N
		100	2:40				33	36:00	N
		110	2:20			2	41	46:00	O
		120	2:20			4	47	54:00	O
100 (31)	1.5	40					0	3:20	*
		50	3:00				10	13:20	K
		60	3:00				17	20:20	L
		70	3:00				23	26:20	M
		80	2:40			2	31	36:20	N
		90	2:40			7	39	49:20	N
		100	2:40			11	46	60:20	O
		110	2:40			13	53	69:20	O
110 (34)	1.6	30					0	3:40	*
		40	3:20				7	10:40	J
		50	3:20				18	21:40	L**
		60	3:20				25	28:40	M**
		70	3:00			7	30	40:40	N**
		80	3:00			13	40	56:40	N**

Exceptional Exposure (for the 110 fsw rows 50–80)

* See No Decompression Table 3 for Repetitive Group Letter
** Time Exceeds Recommended Oxygen Partial Pressure Limits for Routine Diving Operations

NOTES

Appendix
Diving Glossary

Diving Glossary

A

abdomen [**ab**•doe•mun]
The part of the body located between the diaphragm and the pelvis; the cavity that contains the abdominal organs (viscera).

abducens nerve [ab•**dyu**•senz nurv]
The sixth cranial nerve; controls the external rectus muscles of the eye.

abort [uh•**bort**]
To terminate a dive task or procedure ahead of schedule or before completion.

abort profile [uh•**bort** pro•fyle]
Decompression schedule used to bring a diver safely to the surface when a dive must be aborted.

absorption [ab•**zorp**•shun]
Taking in, as through pores; soaking in or up.

acfm
Actual cubic feet per minute.

acidosis [ass•uh•**dose**•us]
Clinical term indicating an increase in the acidity of the blood.

acoustic (auditory) nerve [uh•**koo**•stik •(**ah**•di•tor•ee) nurv]
The eight cranial nerve; controls hearing.

acoustic relief [uh•**koo**•stik ree•**leef**]
A discontinuity, such as a wreck or rock outcrop on the seafloor, that alters the reflection of an acoustic signal in a way that makes the object distinguishable from the surrounding area.

adsorption [ad•**zorp**•shun]
The assimilation of gas or vapor by the surface of a solid.

aerobic [air•**oh**•bik]
1. Of the nature of an aerobe; 2. Of or produced by aerobes.

air [air]
A naturally occurring gas mixture comprising approximately four-fifths nitrogen, one-fifth oxygen, and various trace gases.

air embolism [air **em**•bo•liz•um]
A pathologic condition occurring in the body when bubbles of air are forced into the circulation and gain access to the arterial system, causing blockage of blood flow and leading to local hypoxia and cellular death.

air lock [air lahk]
A small chamber with outer and inner hatches that allow divers to swim out by equalizing chamber pressure with ambient sea pressure.

alidade [**al**•i•dayd]
An indicator or sighting instrument used to determine direction and range for topographic surveying and mapping.

alimentary canal [**al**•i•men•tree kuh•nal]
The muscular-membranous tube, about 30 feet in length, that extends in animals and humans from the mouth to the anus.

alternobaric vertigo [al•tur•no•**bear**•ik **ver**•tee•go]
Dizziness caused by asymmetric clearing of the middle ear during ascent or descent.

altitude correction [**al**•tuh•tood kur•**rek**•shun]
Adjustment to decompression schedules necessitated by the reduced barometric pressure prevailing at altitude.

alveolar [al•vee•**oh**•lur]
A small depression or pertinent to an alveolus.

alveoli [al•vee•**oh**•lee]
A cluster of air sacs at the end of the bronchial trees; sockets for the teeth or any small hollows or cavities; singular form, alveolus.

alveolus [al•vee•**oh**•lus]
A small membranous sac in the lungs in which gas exchange takes place.

Ama divers [**ah**•muh dy•vurz]
Female pearl divers of Japan known for their ability to make deep and long breath-hold dives and to tolerate cold water.

ambient [**am**•bee•unt]
Pertaining to the surrounding environment.

ambient pressure [**am**•bee•unt **presh**•ur]
The pressure of fluid (usually water plus air pressure) upon objects placed in it; usually expressed in terms of absolute pressure.

amniotic fluid [**am**•nee•ah•tik flu•id]
The serous fluid within the sac that encloses a fetus.

analgesic [an•ul•**gee**•zik]
A medication that reduces or eliminates pain.

anatomy [uh•**nat**•uh•mee]
The science of the structure of the body and the relationship of its parts to one another.

anesthesia [an•us•**thee**•zee•uh]
The loss of feeling or sensation, particularly the sensation of pain.

aneurysm [**an**•yoor•iz•um]
A saclike enlargement of a blood vessel caused by a weakening of the vessel wall.

anorexia [an•o•**reks**•ee•uh]
The absence of appetite.

anoxia [uh•**nox**•ee•uh]
The absence of oxygen. (see: hypoxia)

antigen [**an**•tee•jen]
Any bacterium or substance which, when injected into an organism, is capable of causing the formation of an antibody.

aortic stenosis [a•**or**•tik stuh•**no**•sis]
Constriction or narrowing of the aortic artery.

aperture [**ap**•uh•chur]
In photography, the opening that regulates the amount of light passing through a camera lens.

aphakia [af•**a**•kee•uh]
The absence of a lens in the eye.

aphasia [uh•**faz**•ee•uh]
Partial or complete loss of the ability to express ideas in speech or writing.

apnea [**ap**•nee•uh]
A temporary cessation of breathing.

apoplexy [ap•uh•pleks•ee]

The name given to the complex of symptoms and signs caused by hemorrhage or blockage of the brain or spinal cord. This term is also applied to the signs and symptoms resulting from bursting of a vessel in the lungs, liver, etc.

aqualung [ah•kwuh•lung]

A self-contained underwater breathing apparatus in which air from a cylinder is supplied to the diver at surrounding pressure; also, scuba.

aquanaut [ah•kwuh•not]

A person trained to live and work in the water.

argon [ahr•gon]

A colorless, odorless gas which does not react chemically under standard conditions; used occasionally as a diluent gas in diving.

arrhythmia [uh•rith•me•uh]

A lack of normal rhythm, especially of the heart beat.

arteriole [ahr•teer•ee•ole]

The smallest artery, one that branches into the microscopic capillaries.

arthralgia [ahr•thral•jee•uh]

Pain in the joints of the body.

artificial respiration [ahrt•uh•fish•ul res•purr•ay•shun]

Any means by which an alternating increase and decrease in chest volume is created, while maintaining an open airway in mouth and nose passages.

ASA film speed (ASA ISO)

In photography, a number referring to a film's sensitivity to light. This number can be used, along with the readout from an exposure meter, to determine camera settings for aperture and shutter speed.

ascent [uh•sent]

Movement in the direction of reduced pressure whether simulated or due to actual elevation in water or air.

aseptic [ass•sep•tik]

Free from any infectious or septic material.

asphyxia [ass•fik•see•uh]

Condition characterized by decreased oxygen and increased carbon dioxide in the body as a result of interference with respiration.

aspirator [ass•pur•a•tor]

A device used to remove liquids or gases from a space by suction.

atherosclerosis [ath•ur•o•sklur•o•sis]

Thickening of the outer layers of an artery and degeneration of the artery's elastic layer.

atmospheres absolute [at•mus•feerz ab•so•loot]

The sum of barometric and hydrostatic pressures.

atmospheric diving system [at•mus•feer•ik dyv•ing sis•tem]

A pressure-resistant one-man diving system that has articulated arms and sometimes legs and is both equipped with life support capability and designed to operate at an internal pressure of one atmosphere.

atmospheric pressure [at•mus•feer•ik presh•ur]

Pressure exerted by the earth's atmosphere, which varies with altitude above sea level.

atom [at•um]

A unit of matter; the smallest unit of an element, consisting of a nucleus surrounded by a system of electrons equal in number to the number of nuclear protons.

attended diving [uh•ten•dud dyv•ing]

Diving with a lifeline and a tender.

audiometer [odd•ee•ahm•i•tur]

An instrument used to measure hearing thresholds for pure tones at normal frequencies.

aural [a•ral]

Pertaining to the ear.

aural barotrauma [a•ral barotrauma]

Damage of one eardrum or both, caused by changes in ambient pressure.

auricle [ore•uh•cul]

The projecting part of the ear.

autonomic dysreflexia [aw•toe•nahm•ik dis•ree•fleks•ee•uh]

A physiologic response that may occur in a person with certain spinal cord injuries and that can be triggered by any irritating stimulus, such as a full bladder; autonomic dysreflexia can lead to elevated blood pressure, reduced heart rate, seizures, unconsciousness, and death.

autonomic nervous system [aw•toe•nahm•ik nur•vus sis•tum]

That part of the nervous system not under conscious control.

A-V (arteriovenous) shunt

A link between an artery and a vein that may be congenital, occur spontaneously, or be created surgically. It can cause blood to flow prematurely from one vessel to another.

B

Babinski reflex [buh•bin•skee ree•fleks]

A reflex characterized by extension of the big toe and flexion of the other toes; the existence of the Babinski reflex indicates spinal cord involvement.

back pressure [back presh•ur]

Pressure resulting from restricting the full natural flow of gas.

backscatter

In photography, light that is reflected back toward the camera lens by particles suspended in the water.

ballast [bal•ust]

Weight in the form of water, lead, iron pigs or shot, used to change the displacement of a submersible or vessel.

bar [bahr]

An offshore ridge or, mound of sand, gravel or other material submerged at least at high tide, especially at the mouth of a river or estuary or lying a short distance from a beach; also a unit of measurement: 0.98692 atm.

barodontalgia [bair•oh•dahn•tahl•jia]

Acute pain in a tooth, caused by pressure.

barometer [bur•ahm•uh•tur]

An instrument for measuring atmospheric pressure.

barometric pressure [bair•uh•met•rick presh•ur]

Air or atmospheric pressure.

barotitis media [bear•oh•tie•tus meed•ee•uh]

See middle ear squeeze.

barotrauma [bair•oh•trahm•uh]

Physiological injury or damage to the tissues caused by unequal pressures.

bathymetry [bath•thim•uh•tree]

The art or science of determining or measuring depths of water.

bed forms [bed formz]

A geologic feature of the seafloor caused by environmental dynamics, such as near-bottom or wave-induced currents.

bell [bell]

A tethered underwater support system providing life-support services and used to transport divers.

bends [bendz]

An imprecise colloquial term usually denoting decompression sickness with pain in the extremities. (See: decompression sickness)

benthic [ben•thik]

An adjective referring to the benthos, or seafloor. Plants and animals that live on the seafloor are benthic organisms.

beta blockers [bay•tuh blok•urs]

Drugs used to treat a variety of conditions, including cardiovascular problems. A prominent effect of these drugs is a reduction in heart rate, which causes, in turn, a reduction in cardiac output and oxygen consumption by the heart muscles.

biomass [by•o•mas]

The amount of organic matter per given volume.

bleeding [bleed•ing]

The appearance of fresh blood at the nose, ears or mouth, or from a wound; the reduction of pressure in a linear chamber by slightly opening a valve.

blowup [bloe•up]

The uncontrolled ascent of a diver wearing a deep-sea diving suit or a variable-volume dry suit.

body squeeze [bod•ee skweez]

Squeeze caused by excessive external pressure when the diver is wearing a variable-volume dry suit with a rigid helmet, most commonly caused by falling through the water at a rapid rate, or failure of the non-return valve in the helmet exhaust system and resulting loss of air supply.

bottle [baht•ul]

A hollow metal cylinder equipped with a narrow neck opening and retaining valve; used to contain compressed breathing gases.

bottom time [baht•um tyme]

The duration of elapsed time from leaving the surface to begin a dive until beginning a direct ascent to the surface.

bounce dive [bowns dyv]

A rapid dive with a very short bottom time to minimize the time required for decompression.

boundary layer [bown•dree lay•ur]

The thin layer of higher viscosity or drag around a stationary body or in a stationary conduit that is created by the motion of a fluid of low viscosity, such as air or water.

Boyle's law [Boylz law]

At a constant temperature, the volume of gas varies inversely with the pressure.

bradycardia [bray•duh•kahrd•ee•uh]

Slow heart beat, evidenced by a pulse of 60 or less beats per minute.

breathhold dive [breth•hold dyv]

A dive without breathing equipment, performed by holding the breath while underwater.

breathing air [bree•thing air]

Commercially prepared or machine-compressed air which is free of contaminants that would be injurious to a diver operating under pressure.

breathing apparatus [bree•thing ap•ur•at•us]

A device for delivering respirable breathing mixture, enabling the diver to breathe underwater; also called a breathing device.

breathing gas [bree•thing gas]

Oxygen, or a mixture of oxygen and other gases, breathed through a supply system in diving, hyperbaric chambers, and in medical treatment.

breathing resistance [bree•thing re•zis•tuns]

The sum of resistance to flow within the airways and breathing apparatus.

brisance [bri•zahnts]

The shattering effect of a sudden release of energy, such as occurs in an explosion.

bronchi [brong•kye]

Large tubes leading from the trachea and branching to connect to the bronchioles.

bronchiole [brong•kee•ol]

A very small subdivision of the lung tubes; a microscopic bronchial tube leading to the alveoli.

bronchospasm [brong•ko•spaz•um]

A sudden and involuntary contraction of the bronchial tubes.

C

caisson [kay•sahn]

A water-tight pressure chamber used for underwater construction.

calorie [kal•ur•ee]

A unit of heat, the amount required to raise the temperature of 1 gram of water 1 degree centigrade.

carapace [kare•uh•payce]

A hard bony or chitinous outer covering; examples of carapaces are the fused dorsal plates of a turtle or the portion of the exoskeleton covering the head and the thorax of a crustacean.

carbon dioxide [kar•bun dy•ahks•yd]

CO_2, a colorless, odorless and tasteless gas produced by the body's metabolism, which is harmful when breathed in excessive amounts.

carbon monoxide [kar•bun mun•ahks•yd]

CO, a colorless, odorless and tasteless gas produced by partial combustion; cumulative and leading to asphyxiation when breathed.

carbon monoxide poisoning [kar•bun mun•ahks•yd poy•sun•ing]

Insufficient oxygen reaching the tissues, caused by carbon monoxide combining with hemoglobin in the blood and preventing the blood from carrying oxygen.

carboxy-hemoglobin [kar•box•ee•heem•o•glow•bin]

The compound of carbon monoxide (CO) and hemoglobin that is formed when CO is present in the blood.

cardia [car•dya]

The cardiac orifice of the stomach, the point where it is entered by the esophagus, being to the left and in the vicinity of the heart.

cardiac [kar•dee•ak]

Pertaining to the heart.

cardiopulmonary [car•dyo•pul•ma•neri]

Of the heart and lungs as a unified body system.

cardiovascular [ca r•dyo•vas•kyr•ler]

Of the heart and blood vessels as a unified body system.

carotid [kur•aht•ud]

Relating to the principal artery extending up through the neck to the head.

carrier wave [kair•ee•ur wayv]

An electric wave that can be modulated to transmit signals in radio, telephonic, or telegraphic systems.

cathodic protection [kath•awd•ik pro•tek•shun]

A technique designed to reduce the corrosion that occurs in seawater as a result of the presence of dissimilar metals; when cathodic protection is used, a sacrificial metal is introduced to serve as the anode (site of corrosion), which protects nearby metal parts.

cell [sell]

A mass of protoplasm in the body, containing a nucleus.

centigrade (C) temperature [sen•tuh•grayd tem•pur•uh•choor]

Thermometric scale on which the interval between the freezing point and the boiling point of water is divided into 100 degrees with 0 degrees representing the freezing point and 100 degrees the boiling point.

cerebellum [sair•uh•bell•um]

The part of the hindbrain that lies below the occipital part of the cerebrum on each side, concerned with the coordination of movement.

cerebrovascular [sair•uh•bro•vas•kyoo•lur]

Pertaining to the blood vessels of the brain.

cerebrum [sair•ee•brum]

The largest part of the brain located in the upper portion of the cranium, consisting of two cerebral hemispheres divided into lobes.

cervical spine [surv•i•kul spyn]

The upper seven vertebrae of the spine.

Charles' law [Charlz law]

At a constant pressure, the volume of an ideal gas varies directly with the absolute temperature.

cholecystitis [ko•lee•sis•tyt•us]

Inflammation of the gall bladder.

chokes [choaks]

Slang for the pulmonary symptoms of decompression sickness.

circulatory system [su•kyoo•luh•tor•ee sis•tum]

All the arteries and veins through which blood is pumped through the body by the heart.

clavicle [klav•uh•kul]

The collar bone.

closed-circuit breathing system [klozd sur•kit bree•thing sis•tum]

A breathing apparatus in which the breathing gas is recycled, carbon dioxide is removed, and oxygen is added to replenish the supply as needed.

CO

(See: carbon monoxide)

CO_2

(See: carbon dioxide)

coarctation [ko•ark•tay•shun]

Compression of the walls of a vessel or canal.

cochlea [kohk•lee•uh]

A snail-shaped cavity in the temporal bone of the inner ear that contains the organ of hearing.

coelenterata [si•len•tur•aw•tuh]

A phylum of the animal kingdom comprised of hydroids, jellyfish, sea anemones, corals, and related animals. Most species are marine and all are aquatic.

colitis [ko•ly•tus]

Inflammation of the colon.

combustion [kum•bus•chun]

The process of burning.

compressed air [kum•**prest** air]
   Air under pressure; may be used as a breathing mixture if free from contaminants.
compression [kum•**press**•un]
   That part of a dive involving an increase in pressure upon the diver, either due to the admission of compressed gas in a chamber or to descend in the water.
compression arthralgia [kum•**presh**•un ahr•**thrall**•juh]
   Pain in the joints during compression, particularly during rapid compression to pressures greater than 10 atmospheres.
compression chamber [kum•**presh**•un **chaym**•bur]
   A chamber used for compression.
compression stage [kum•**presh**•un stayj]
   One of the steps taken to pressurize air.
condensation [kahn•den•**say**•shun]
   The physical process by which a vapor becomes a liquid or solid.
conductive hearing loss [kun•**duk**•tiv **heer**•ing laws]
   A type of auditory defect caused by impairment of the conductive mechanism of the ear; such impairments can occur when the eardrum is damaged, air passages are blocked, or movement of the bones of the inner ear is impaired.
conjunctivitis [kun•**junk**•uh•**vyt**•us]
   Inflammation of the conjunctiva (mucus membrane) of the eye.
constant-volume dry suit [**kahn**•stunt **vawl**•yoom dry•soot]
   A dry diving suit designed to be partially inflated to prevent squeeze and to provide insulation against cold.
copepod [**ko**•puh•pawd]
   A small planktonic crustacean that is usually less than 2 millimeters in length.
cornea [**kohr**•nee•uh]
   The transparent anterior portion of the eyeball.
coronary [**kor**•uh•nair•ee]
   Refers to structures that encircle a part or organ in a crownlike manner; for example, the coronary arteries encircling the base of the heart.
counterdiffusion [**kownt**•ur•duh•**fyooz**•shun]
   The movement of two inert gases in opposing directions through a semipermeable membrane.
cricothyroidotomy [kry•koh•**thy**•royd•awt•toe•me]
   Incision through the ring-shaped cartilage of the larynx.
cryogenics [**kry**•o•jen•iks]
   The production of low temperatures.
cyanosis [**sigh**•uh•**no**•sus]
   A bluish discoloration of the skin, lips, and nail beds caused by insufficient oxygen in the blood.

D

Dalton's law [**dahl**•tunz law]
   The partial pressure of a given quantity of gas is the pressure it would exert if it alone occupied the same volume; the total pressure of a mixture of gases is the sum of the partial pressures of the components of the mixture.
day vision [day **viz**•zhun]
   Normal vision which includes color perception.
dead air space [ded air spays]
   Space in diving equipment and in the human respiratory system that receives minimum ventilation.
debridement [di•**breed**•ment]
   Surgical removal of tissue.
decibel [**des**•uh•bul]
   A unit for measuring the relative loudness of sound.
deck decompression chamber [dek de•kum•**presh**• un **chaym**•bur]
   A hyperbaric chamber which is an integral part of a deep diving system, located on a surface platform from which diving is conducted.
decompression [de•kum•**presh**•un]
   Releasing from pressure or compression; following a specific decompression table or procedure during ascent; ascending in the water or experiencing decreasing pressure in the chamber.

decompression accident [de•kum•**presh**•un ak•suh•dent]
   An occurrence of decompression sickness; colloquially, a hit.
decompression arthralgia [de•kum•**presh**•un ahr•**thral**•juh]
   Pain in the joints during decompression.
decompression chamber [de•kum•**presh**•un **chaym**•bur]
   An enclosed space used to gradually decrease pressure to which a diver is exposed, from ambient underwater pressure back to 1 atmosphere.
decompression dive [de•kum•**presh**•un dyv]
   Any dive deep enough or long enough to require controlled decompression; i.e., any dive in which an ascent must include decompression stops.
decompression schedule [de•kum•**presh**•un **sked**•jool]
   A set of depth-time relationships and instructions for controlling pressure reduction.
decompression sickness [de•kum•**presh**•un **sik**•nus]
   A condition caused by the formulation of inert gas bubbles in the tissues and circulatory system as a result of releasing pressure too rapidly.
decompression stop [**de**•kum•**presh**•un stop]
   The designated depth and time at which a diver must stop and wait during an ascent from a decompression dive. The depth and time are specified by the decompression table in use.
decompression table [de•kum•**presh**•un **tay**•bul]
   A tabulation of decompression schedules.
dehydration [de•hy•**dray**•shun]
   A condition due to excessive water loss from the body or its parts.
demand mask [de•**mand** mask]
   A diving mask having a demand regulator which activates the gas supply by the negative pressure associated with inhalation.
demand system [de•mand **sis**•tum]
   Diver life support equipment in which gas flows only during diver's inhalation and exhalation.
demersal fish [duh•**mur**•sul fish]
   Bottom-living fish, such as plaice or flounder.
density [**den**•suh•tee]
   The ratio of the mass of any object to the volume of the object; in oceanography, equivalent to specific gravity.
depth [depth]
   The vertical distance from a specified sea level to the sea floor.
depth gauge [depth gayj]
   A pressure-sensitive meter used to determine depth.
depth of field
   Term used in photography to denote the distance between the nearest and most distant objects that will be in focus.
dermatitis [dur•muh•**ty**•tus]
   Inflammation of the skin.
diaphragm [**dy**•uh•fram]
   A large muscle separating the chest from the abdomen; when breathing, the diaphragm pushes the intestines down to create more potential volume, thus decreasing the pressure so air from outside enters to equalize the pressure.
diastole [**dy**•uh•stole]
   The period of relaxed dilatation of the heart muscle, especially of the ventricles; adjective: diastolic.
diffraction [di•**frak**•shun]
   The process which allows sound waves to bend around obstacles in their path.
diffusion [di•**fyoo**•zhun]
   The process in which particles of liquids, gases or solids intermingle as the result of spontaneous movement caused by thermal agitation and, in dissolved substances, move from a region of higher to lower concentration.
digestive system [di•**jest**•uv **sis**•tum]
   The organs of the body that accomplish the assimilation of food.
dip
   A geological term for the angle in degrees between a horizontal plane and the inclined angle of a rockbed, as measured down from the horizontal in a plane perpendicular to the strike.
displacement [dis•**plays**•munt]
   The weight of water displaced by a body floating in it, this weight being equal to the weight of the body.

dive [dyv]

An exposure to increased pressure whether under water or in a hyperbaric chamber.

diver's palsy [**dyv**·urz **pahl**·zee]

Paralysis associated with serious decompression sickness. (See: decompression sickness)

diverticulitis [dy·vur·**tik**·yoo·**ly**·tus]

Inflammation of a diverticulum, an outpouching of the colon that may occur in humans.

diving system [**dyv**·ing **sis**·tum]

A system composed of three basic subsystems which can be used in various combinations: (1) a surface support ship or platform; (2) a deck decompression chamber used to decompress divers on the surface; (3) a tethered capsule used to transport divers from the surface to the underwater work site.

Donald Duck effect [**Dahn**·uld Duk uh·fect]

Changes in the quality of the voice caused by breathing light gases, such as helium.

doppler bubble monitor [**daw**·plur **buh**·buhl **mon**·uh·tur]

A device that detects moving bubbles in the circulatory system by picking up changes in the frequency of sound reflected by moving objects.

do-si-do position [doe·see·doe puh·**zi**·shun]

A position used in diver rescues on the surface that enables the rescuer to administer mouth-to-mouth resuscitation to an unconscious victim.

double lock chamber [**dub**·ul lahk **chaym**·bur]

A chamber with two compartments that can be pressurized independently.

drowning [**drown**·ing]

Suffocation or strangulation in water or other liquid.

dry suit [dry soot]

Protective diving garment which is completely sealed to prevent water entry.

dysbarism [**dis**·bur·izm]

A general term applied to any clinical condition caused by a difference between the surrounding atmospheric pressure and the total gas pressure in the various tissues and cavities in the body.

dyspnea [**disp**·nee·uh]

Shortness of breath out of proportion to physical exertion.

E

ear drum

(See: tympanic membrane)

ear squeeze [eer·skweez]

A symptom complex resulting from pressure imbalance, causing symptoms ranging from pain to hemorrhage and/or rupture of the tympanic membrane of the ear.

edema [uh·**deem**·uh]

Swelling caused by fluid buildup in tissue.

effusion [e·**fyoo**·shun]

The escape of fluid into a space or part; also, the fluid that has escaped.

elastomer [ee·**lass**·toe·mur]

A rubberlike material, such as neoprene or silicone rubber.

electrocardiogram [e·**lek**·tro·**kahr**·dee·uh·gram]

The tracing of the electric current produced by heart muscle activity; the record produced by an electrocardiograph.

electrocardiograph [e·**lek**·tro·**kahr**·dee·uh·graf]

An instrument used for making records of the heart's electric currents.

electroencephalogram [e·**lek**·tro·en·**sef**·uh·luh·gram]

A graphic record of the electrical activity of the brain. Also, EEG.

electron [e·**lek**·trahn]

One of the three basic particles of atoms which has a negative charge.

element [**el**·uh·munt]

A fundamental and irreducible constituent of a composite entity.

embolism, air or gas [**em**·buh·liz·um, air or gas]

Gas bubbles in the circulatory system caused by gas or air passing into the pulmonary veins after rupture of the alveolar vaculature.

embolus [**em**·bo·lus]

A foreign or abnormal object carried by the blood stream into a smaller vessel, causing its obstruction.

emergency ascent [e·**mur**·jun·see uh·sent]

Unplanned ascent to the surface under stressful conditions.

emergency buoyant ascent [e·**mur**·jun·see **booy**·unt uh·**sent**]

Rapid ascent to the surface caused by dropping the weight belt or inflating the flotation device; the diver continuously exhales in order to avoid pulmonary barotrauma.

emergency controlled ascent [e·**mur**·j un·see kun·**trold** uh·sent]

A little-used term meaning ascent to the surface, using breathing apparatus, at a rate which ignores standard ascent rates or decompression stops.

emphysema [em·fuh·**see**·muh]

A pulmonary condition characterized by loss of lung elasticity and restriction of air movement.

emphysema, interstitial [em·fuh·**see**·muh, in·tur·**stee**·shul]

The thinning and loss of elasticity in a space in body tissue or structure.

emphysema, mediastinal [em·fuh·**see**·muh, mee·dee·**ass**·tu·nul]

Presence of air in tissues in the vicinity of the heart, lungs, and the large blood vessels in the middle of the chest.

emphysema, subcutaneous [em·fuh·**see**·muh, sub·kyoo·**tayn**·ee·us]

Swelling or inflation due to abnormal presence of air in tissues just under the skin; usually appears in or near the neck.

emphysematous bullae [em·fuh·see·muh·tus byu·lye]

Blebs or air-filled blisters in the lungs caused by emphysema.

EMS

Emergency medical system.

endocardium [en·do·**kahr**·dee·um]

The membrane which lines the heart chambers.

envenom [en·ven·um]

To poison or put venom into or onto something.

epicardium [ep·uh·**kahrd**·ee·um]

The membrane that forms the outer layer of the heart wall and is continuous with the lining of the sac that encloses the heart.

epidermis [ep·uh·**durm**·us]

The outer epithelial layer of the skin, which contains no blood vessels.

epifauna [ep·i·**fawn**·uh]

Marine animals that live on the surface of the seafloor.

epilimnion [ep·uh·**lim**·nee·um]

The layer of water above a thermocline.

epiphytic plants [ep·i·**fit**·ik]

Plants that are attached to or are supported by another plant but that obtain their food independently.

equivalent air depth [e·**kwiv**·uh·lunt air depth]

The air breathing depth which has a nitrogen partial pressure equivalent to that at the diving depth.

equivalent bottom time [e·**kwiv**·uh·lunt **baht**·um tym]

A hypothetical period of time taken to represent residual gas elimination time, and which is added to the bottom time of one dive to determine the decompression obligation for comparable dives.

erythema [air·uh·**thee**·muh]

Skin redness usually due to congestion of the blood in the capillaries.

esophageal [uh·**sahf**·uh·jee·ul]

Relating to the gullet.

esophagus [uh·**sahf**·uh·gus]

The gullet; a tubular passage extending from the pharynx to the stomach.

ester [**es**·tur]

A compound that reacts with water, acid, or alkali to form an alcohol plus an acid.

euphoria [yoo·**for**·ee·a]

1. a feeling of well being, 2. an abnormal feeling of buoyant vigor and health.

eustachian tube [yoo·**stay**·shun toob]

The canal connecting the middle ear and the throat; permits the equilibration of pressure between the external and middle ears.

exceptional exposure dive [eks·**sep**·shun·ul eks·**po**·zhur dyv]

Any dive in which the diver is exposed to higher partial pressures, with bottom times that are considered extreme.

excursion dive [eks•**kur**•zhun dyv]
Movement of a diver either upward or downward from saturation depth; the permissible safe distance and time of the excursion dive depend on the saturation depth.

experimental diving unit [eks•peer•uh•**men**•tul **dyv**•ing **yoo**•nut]
U.S. Navy diving research center, Washington, D.C.; also, EDU.

expiration [eks•pur•**ay**•shun]
The act of breathing out or emitting air from the lungs; also, exhaling.

expiratory reserve volume [eks•**pyr**•uh•tor•ee re• zurv **vahl**•yoom]
Maximum amount of air that can be breathed out after normal exhalation.

exposure meter
A meter that indicates the correct aperture and shutter speed combination for film exposure.

external auditory canal [eks•**turn**•ul **aw**•duh•tor• ee kuh•**nal**]
The canal leading from the outer ear to the eardrum.

external ear squeeze [eks•**turn**•ul ear skweez]
Squeeze caused by the sealing of the space between the external ear and the eardrum during compression; can be caused by tightly fitting hood, bathing cap, or ear plugs.

externa otitis [eks•**turn**•ah oh•**ty**•fus]
A superficial infection of the auditory canal; a common occurence in habitat living, wet pot and open-sea diving; usually caused by a mold or bacterium.

exudation [x•yu•**day**•shun]
The passing of material, i.e., serum or pus, through the wall of a vessel and into adjacent tissues.

eye squeeze [aye skweez]
Squeeze of the eyes caused by using nonpressure-compensated goggles.

F

f number
(See f stop).

f stop
A number used in photography to refer to the relative diameter of the aperture; the higher the number, the smaller the aperture. Each consecutively higher-numbered stop admits half as much light as the previously numbered stop.

face plate [fays playt]
Glass or plastic window in a diving helmet, constructed to provide an air space between the eyes and the water and to permit both eyes to see in the same plane; the skirt makes contour contact with the face, preserving air space; pressure may be equalized by breathing into the mask.

face plate squeeze [fays playt skweez]
Pressure building up in the mask on descent; also, mask squeeze.

face squeeze [fays skweez]
Squeeze of the face caused by failure to compensate for increased ambient pressure.

facial nerve [**fay**•shul nurv]
The seventh cranial nerve; controls motion of the face, ear, palate, and tongue.

fahrenheit
(See: temperature - Fahrenheit)

fathom [**fath**•um]
The term for the unit of measurement of depth in the ocean, for countries using the English system of units; equal to six feet (1.83 meters).

fathometer [fath•**ahm**•uh•tur]
A device used to determine water depth by means of echoes reflecting off the bottom.

fenestrated [**fen**•es•**trait**•ud]
Perforated, as in a fenestrated contact lens.

fins [finz]
Device attached to the feet of a diver to increase area and thrust power, speed and control in the water, also called swim fins.

flapper (flutter) valve [**flap**•pur valv]
A soft rubber tube collapsed at one end. When the ambient water pressure is greater than the air pressure within the valve, the valve remains collapsed. When the air pressure within the valve is greater than the ambient water pressure, the valve opens.

flotation device [flo•**tay**•shun de•vys]
An inflatable vest used to assist ascent or to provide positive buoyancy; used for fine buoyancy control while submerged.

fluid [**floo**•ud]
A substance having particles which easily move and change their relative position; both liquids and gases are fluids.

forced expiration reserve volume [**for**•sd eks•py•**ray**•shun ree•**serv** vol•yoom]
The rate of flow of air per second that can be forcefully expired after the end of the normal tidal volume.

forced expiratory volume [**for**•sd eks•py•ra•tor•ee **vol**•yoom]
The volume (of the forced vital capacity) which can be forcibly exhaled in one second (of importance in submarine escape).

free diving [free **dyv**•ing]
Diving without tether, umbilical or marking device; also breathhold diving.

full face mask [full fays mask]
A diving mask, either supplied with breathing gas on demand or continuously and independent of respiration, which covers the eyes, nose and mouth of the diver.

functional residual capacity [**funk**•shun•ul ree• **zid**•yul ka•**pas**•i•tee]
The volume of gas remaining in the lung after a normal expiration.

G

gangrene [**gang**•green]
Death of a mass of tissue, accompanied by bacterial invasion and putrefaction; usually due to blood vessel obstruction.

gas [gas]
In diving, any respirable mixture breathed by the diver.

gas chromatograph [gas kro•**mat**•uh•graf]
A laboratory instrument used to identify and measure closely related chemical substances.

gas laws [gas lawz]
Mathematical descriptions of the relations of pressure, temperature and volume under ideal conditions.

gastric [**gast**•rik]
Of, in, or near the stomach.

gastritis [gas•**try**•tus]
Inflammation of the stomach, usually of the lining mucosa.

gastroenteritis [gas•tro•en•**try**•tus]
Inflammation of the stomach and intestines.

general gas law [**jen**•rul gas law]
Boyle's and Charles' laws combined.

geodesy [jee•awd•uh•see]
The science of describing the size and the shape of the earth in mathematical terms.

glaucoma [glah•**ko**•muh]
A disease of the eye caused by intense intraocular pressure due to an excess of fluid within the eye.

glossopharyngeal nerve [glohs•o•fair•un•jeel nurv]
The ninth cranial nerve; controls sensation, motion, and taste associated with the tonsils, pharynx, middle ear, and tongue.

grand mal seizure [grand mawl **see**•zhur]
A major convulsion that involves unconsciousness, loss of motor control, jerking of the extremities, and biting of the tongue.

ground fault interrupter [grownd fawlt in•tur•up•tor]
An electronic device that detects electrical leakage by comparing the current in a hot wire with the current in an accompanying neutral wire.

H

habitat [**hab**•uh•tat]
A seafloor structure, either movable or fixed, in which divers can live for extended periods and from which they make excursion dives.

half time [haf tym]

In diving, a half time is the time required for a tissue to absorb or eliminate 50 percent of the equilibrium amount of inert gas.

hard hat [hahrd hat]

Common term for diving helmet, also, protective hat worn by riggers, etc.

hardwire phone [hard•wyr fon]

A communication link through a wire.

harness assembly [har•nus uh•sem•blee]

The combination of straps used to attach diving equipment to the diver.

heat conduction [heet kun•duk•shun]

The transfer of heat from one part of a body to another, or from one body to another.

heliox [hee•lee•ahks]

A breathing mixture of helium and oxygen used at depth because it has little narcotic effect; also, oxyhelium.

heliox diving [hee•lee•ahks dyv•ing]

Mixed gas diving using oxygen with helium as an inert diluent.

helium [hee•lee•um]

A colorless, odorless gas used as a replacement for nitrogen in the gas mixture for deep-sea divers; breathing helium mixtures causes speech distortion which hinders communication.

helmet [hel•mut]

A device worn over the head of a diver, designed to furnish breathing gas, allow visibility through viewports, enable two-way communication, and be compatible with dry suit and wet suit.

hematoma [hee•muh•to•muh]

A tumor or swelling filled with blood.

hematopoietic tissues [hi•mat•uh•poy•et•ik ti•shuz]

Blood-producing tissues, such as the bone marrow.

hemiplegia [hee•muh•plee•juh]

Paralysis of one side of the body.

hemo- [hee•mo]

Combining form denoting a relationship to blood.

hemoglobin [hee•mo•glo•bun]

The oxygen-carrying colored compound in the red blood cells; it combines with oxygen, carbon dioxide and carbon monoxide.

hemoptysis [hi•mawp•tuh•sis]

Spitting of blood from the larynx, trachea, bronchi, or lungs.

hemorrhage [hem•ur•uj]

Any discharge of blood from the blood vessels.

Henry's law [hen•reez law]

At a constant temperature the amount of a gas which dissolves in a liquid with which it is in contact is proportional to the partial pressure of that gas.

hepatitis [hep•uh•tie•tus]

Inflammation of the liver.

herbarium [ur•bare•ee•um]

A collection of dried plants that are mounted and labeled in preparation for scientific use.

herniated nucleus pulposis [hur•nee•ate•ud new•kle•us puhl•po•sis]

A rupture of a disk in the spinal cord that is caused by degenerative changes or a trauma that compresses a nerve root or the cord itself.

high pressure nervous syndrome [hy presh•ur nur•vus sin•drohm]

Neurological and physiological dysfunction that is caused by hyperbaric exposure, usually to helium.

holdfast

The rootlike structure at the base of a kelp that anchors the plant to the seafloor.

hopcalite [hop•kuh•lyt]

A catalyst used in air compressors and breathing apparatus filters to remove carbon monoxide or other gases.

hose [hoz]

Flexible pipe for conveying fluid or gas.

hydraulic [hy•draw•lik]

Moved or worked by fluid pressure.

hydrostatic [hy•dro•stat•ik]

Of or relating to liquids at rest or to the pressures they exert or transmit.

hydrostatic pressure [hy•dro•stat•ik presh•ur]

The pressure of a column of water acting upon a body immersed in the water, equal in all directions at a specific depth.

hyperbaric [hy•pur•bair•ik]

1. of or having a pressure or specific gravity greater than that within the body tissues of fluids, 2. designating or of a pressurized (usually oxygenated) chamber, used in diving or treatment of various diseases and conditions.

hyperbaric arthralgia [hy•pur•bair•ik ahr•thral•juh]

A general term describing decompression arthralgia; sometimes described by divers as "no joint juice."

hyperbaric chamber [hy•pur•bair•ik chaym•bur]

A chamber designed to withstand high internal pressure; used in hyperbaric experimentation, diving simulations, and medical treatment.

hyperbaric facility [hy•pur•bair•ik fuh•sil•uh•tee]

The entire group of systems and subsystems used to support a high pressure chamber or chambers; may include a wet pot or compartment to simulate an actual underwater environment.

hyperbaric oxygenation [hy•pur•bair•ik akhs•uh•jun•ay•shun]

The inhalation of oxygen at pressures above one atmosphere.

hypercapnia [hy•pur•kap•nee•uh]

An excess of carbon dioxide in the body's tissues; elevated carbon dioxide levels may occur in a habitat or other closed space, in a diving suit, or in breathing equipment; also, hypercarbia.

hypercarbia

(See: hypercapnia)

hyperoxia [hy•pur•akhs•ee•uh]

An excess of oxygen in the body tissues produced by breathing a mixture in which the inspired oxygen pressure is greater than its partial pressure in air.

hyperpnea [hy•pur•pnee•a]

An increased respiratory rate or breathing which is deeper than that seen in resting subjects. A certain degree of hyperpnea is normal after exercise.

hypertension [hy•pur•ten•shun]

High blood pressure.

hyperthermia [hy•pur•thur•mee•uh]

The elevation of body temperature above normal; in diving, may occur in hyperbaric chambers as a result of environmental exposure to heat or failure of the body's thermoregulatory system.

hyperventilation [hy•pur•ven•tuh•lay•shun]

Increase in rate and/or volume of respiration above normal; may lead to hypocapnia; also called overbreathing.

hypoallergenic [hy•po•al•ur•gen•ik]

An adjective given to materials that are not likely to cause allergic responses in contact with the skin.

hypocapnia [hy•po•kap•nee•uh]

A physiological state in which the systemic arterial carbon dioxide pressure is low; symptoms may include finger tingling, muscle spasms, dizziness, loss of consciousness; commonly caused by hyperventilation (overbreathing).

hypoglossal nerve [hy•po•glos•ul nurv]

The twelfth cranial nerve; controls movement of the tongue.

hypolimnion [hy•po•lim•nee•un]

The layer of water below a thermocline.

hypotension [hy•po•ten•shun]

Lower than normal blood pressure.

hypothalamus [hy•po•thal•uh•mus]

The nerve center in the brain that influences certain bodily functions, such as metabolism, temperature, regulation, and sleep.

hypothermia [hy•po•thurm•ee•uh]

Reduction of body temperature as a result of environmental exposure to cold or failure of the body's thermoregulatory system; some hypothermia accompanies most dives; unless a diver is suitably protected, it may result in reduced performance; if exposure is prolonged or extreme, it can be fatal.

hypovolemic shock [hypo•vo•leem•ic shawk]

A physiological condition that is caused by a reduction in the volume of intravascular fluid and that may cause a decrease in cardiac output.

hypoxemia [hy•pok•**see**•mya]
Insufficient oxygenation of the blood.

hypoxia [hy•**pahks**•ee•uh]
Tissue oxygen pressure below normal; may be produced by breathing mixtures deficient in oxygen, by disease states, or by gases such as carbon dioxide. (see: anoxia)

I

ideal gas [ay•**deel** gas]
A term denoting a gas which would exactly obey the gas laws.

ideal gas law [ay•**deel** gas law]
A law that defines the relationships among pressure, temperature, volume and quantities of substance of any ideal gas.

inclinometer [in•kli•**nom**•uh•tur]
In geology, an instrument for measuring the angle of slope.

inert gases [in•**urt** gas•uz]
Gases that exhibit stability and extremely low reaction rates; examples of inert gases are helium, argon, krypton, xenon, and sometimes, radon. These gases are called inert because they are not biologically or chemically active.

inert gas elimination [in•**urt** gas e•lim•uh•**nay**•shun]
The transfer of inert gas (nitrogen, helium, etc) under the influence of a pressure gradient from the tissues to the blood to the lungs, from which it is exhaled; also called gas washout.

infauna [in•**fawn**•uh]
Marine animals living within the seafloor sediment, such as worms and some clams.

inguinal [in•**gwyn**•ul]
In mammals, pertaining to the groin.

inhalation [in•hul•**ay**•shun]
The process of bringing air into the lungs.

inner ear [**inn**•ur eer]
That portion of the ear that is located within the confines of the temporal bone and that contains the organs of equilibrium and hearing.

in situ [in **sit**•too]
A physiological term meaning in the natural or normal place or position; confined to the site of origin without invasion of neighboring tissues.

inspiration [in•spur•**ay**•shun]
The act of breathing air into the lungs.

inspiratory capacity [in•**spir**•a•tor•ee ka•**pas**•i•tee]
The volume by which the lung can be increased by a maximum inspiratory effort following a normal expiration.

inspiratory reserve volume [in•**spir**•uh•tor•ee re•**zurv** **vahl**•yoom]
The maximum amount of air that can be breathed in after normal inspiration.

intercooler [in•tur•**koo**•lur]
A component of an air compressor that is designed to cool the air and to cause water and oil vapors to condense and collect as the air passes through the air/liquid separator.

internal waves [in•**tur**•ul wayvz]
Waves arising at an internal boundary that is formed between layers of water that have different densities; such as internal boundary occurs when a layer of warm surface water from a river runoff overlays a layer of salty or cold water.

intracranial surgery [in•truh•**kra**•nee•ul **sur**•jur•ee]
Surgery within the skull.

intrapleural pressure [in•truh•**ploor**•ul **presh**•ur]
Pressure within the space between the chest wall and the lungs (pleural space).

ischemia [is•**kee**•me•uh]
A lack of sufficient blood to a part of the body usually due to the obstruction of an artery.

isobaric [ay•so•**bair**•ik]
Relating to process taking place without change of ambient pressure.

J

jocking belt (jockstrap) [jawk•ing bellt]
A strap worn by divers to prevent the diving helmet from being lifted off the shoulders, especially during entry into the water. The strap passes between the diver's legs and is attached to the front and back of the weight belt, which in turn, is linked to the helmet.

jugular [**jug**•yoo•lur]
Referring to the veins of the neck which drain the areas supplied by the carotid arteries.

K

kelp [kelp]
Various varieties of large brown sea weeds.

Kelvin temperature [**kel**•vun **tem**•pur•uh•choor]
A thermometric scale on which the unit of measurement equals the centigrade degree.

keratitis [kair•uh•tie•tus]
Inflammation of the cornea of the eye.

kerf [kurf]
A groove or notch made by a saw, ax, cutting torch, etc.

L

laminar flow [lam•i•nur floe]
Nonturbulent flow of a fluid.

laryngospasm [lar•**in**•joh•spasm]
Reflex closure of the airway.

larynx [**lair**•inks]
The voice box; covered by two membranes, the vocal cords.

leeway
Movement of an object through the water as a result of the force of the wind.

lifeline [**lyf**•lyn]
A line between the diver and tender, used to signal and supply the diver, to assist in normal ascent, and retrieve the diver in an emergency; usually part of the umbilical.

life support system [lyf suh•**port** sis•tum]
A system designed to produce a controlled environment for chamber occupants; may include capability to supply metabolic oxygen, control temperature and humidity, and remove carbon dioxide.

lightweight diving mask [**lyt**•wayt **dyv**•ing mask]
A full face cover through which surface-supplied breathing gases are delivered to a diver; gases may flow freely through the mask or may be delivered through an oronasal demand assembly.

liquid [**lik**•wud]
Any substance which assumes the shape of the vessel in which it is placed without changing volume.

live boating [**lyv**•**bot**•ing]
Diving from a vessel which is underway.

lockout submersible [**lok**•owt sub•**merz**•uh•bul]
A submersible that has one compartment for the pilot and/or observer that is maintained at one atmosphere and another compartment that can be pressurized to ambient pressure so that divers can enter and exit while under water.

longshore current [lawng•shor kur•unt]
A current that is generated by waves that are deflected by the shore at an angle. Such currents run roughly parallel to the shoreline.

LORAN-C
A long range, high-precision navigation system in which hyperbolic lines of position are determined by measuring the difference in the time at which synchronized pulse signals are received from two fixed transmitters.

lungs [lungz]
Two sponge-like breathing organs consisting of approximately 750 million alveoli.

lymph [limpf]

A slightly yellow watery fluid found in the lymphatic vessels; any clear watery fluid resembling true lymph.

lymphatic system [lim·fat·ik sis·tum]

A system of vessels and glands, accessory to the blood vascular system, which conveys the lymph fluid throughout the body.

M

manometer [muh·nom·uh·tur]

An instrument for measuring the pressure of liquids and gases. In its simplest form, a manometer consists of a U-tube, one end of which is open to the atmosphere and the other end of which is open to the region where the pressure is to be measured. If the pressure in the two areas is different, the liquid will be higher in one leg of the tube than in the other.

mask [mask]

Diving equipment worn over the face to provide an air pocket for better vision; also may have a breathing valve.

mask squeeze

(See: face plate squeeze)

mass spectrometer [mass spek·trom·uh·tur]

A laboratory instrument that uses the masses of compounds to identify and quantitate them. The principle of spectrometry involves ionizing the substance and separating the resulting molecular and fragment ions by means of electric and magnetic fields.

maximal breathing capacity [maks·uh·mul breeth·ing kuh·pas·uh·tee]

The greatest respiratory minute volume which a person can produce during a short period of extremely forceful breathing. (See: minute volume)

maximum expiratory flow rate [mak·si·mum ek·spy·ra·toh·ree flho rayt]

The rate of flow of expirate at maximum voluntary effort on the part of the subject.

maximum inspiratory flow rate [mak·si·mum in·spy·ra·toh·ree floh rayt]

The rate of flow of inspirate at maximum voluntary effort on the part of the subject.

Meckels diverticulum [mek·uhls dy·vur·tik·yu·lum]

A congenital sac, resembling the appendix, that occurs naturally in 1-2 percent of the population. This sac is located in the lower intestine and can ulcerate, hemorrhage, or develop obstructions or infections.

media otitis [mee·dee·uh oh·tyt·us]

Inflammation or infection of the middle ear; in diving, often used to describe a condition in which the middle ear fills with fluid.

mediastinal emphysema [mee·dee·ass·tun·ul em· fuh·see·muh]

(See: emphysema)

mediastinum [mee·dee·ass·tie·num]

The space between the lungs and chest wall, under the breastbone where the heart is located.

medical lock [med·uh·kul lahk]

Located in the inner lock in the hyperbaric chamber to facilitate the transfer of medical supplies, food or other articles between occupants of the chamber and the outside support crew.

medullary osteonecrosis [med·joo·lair·ee ahs·tee· oh·neh·kro·sus]

Osteonecrosis occurring in the shaft of the bone; usually symptomless and unaffected by x-ray.

Meniere's disease [muh·neers duh·zees]

A disease of the middle ear that is characterized by vertigo, sudden deafness, and symptoms of apoplexy.

metabolism [muh·tab·uh·liz·um]

The physical and chemical changes or processes by which living substance is maintained and energy produced. Adjective: metabolic.

methemoglobinemia [met·hee·muh·glow·buh·nee·mee·uh]

The presence of methemoglobin in the blood; this condition can be caused by toxic agents that are ingested, inhaled, or absorbed.

microbe [my·krob]

A living organism of very small size; the term is often used synonymously with bacterium.

middle ear squeeze [mid·'ul eer skweez]

Squeeze caused by the inability to equalize the pressure in the middle ear through the Eustachian tube as the external pressure builds up against the eardrum; results in bleeding between the tympanic membrane and the middle ear spaces.

minute volume [mi·nut vol·yoom]

The total volume of air passing in and out of the lungs in one minute.

mixed gas [mikst gas]

A breathing medium consisting of oxygen and one or more inert gases, synthetically mixed.

mixed gas dive [mikst gas dyv]

A dive using a mixture of gases as a breathing medium; the ratio of diluent gas to oxygen is changed to keep the partial pressure of oxygen at or near the normal 1-atmosphere level.

modulation [mawd·u·lay·shun]

The process of varying a characteristic of one wave in accordance with that of another wave. Modulation can be achieved by varying the amplitude, frequency, or phase of the carrier wave.

molecule [mahl·uh·kyool]

A stable grouping of atomic nuclei and electrons bound together by electrostatic and electromagnetic forces.

monoplace chamber [mahn·oh·plays chaym·bur]

A portable one-person hyperbaric chamber used for therapy in a hospital setting and for transport.

morbidity [moor·bid·i·tee]

A scientific term meaning disease or sickness.

mouthpiece [mowth·pees]

A relatively watertight channel for the flow of breathing gas between the life-support system and the diver; consists of a flange which fits between the lips and teeth and two bits, one on either side of the mouthpiece opening, which serve to hold the teeth comfortably apart; held in place by slight pressure of the lips and teeth.

mucosa or mucous membranes [myu·ko·sa; myu·kus mem·braynz]

The tissues lining those body cavities and canals that are exposed to air.

multiplace chamber [mul·tuh·p'l chaym·bur]

A pressure vessel designed to be used by more than one person at a time; usually a double lock chamber.

mushroom valve

A type of poppet valve that has a disk-like head attached to a stem. The stem reciprocates in a valve guide under the action of a cam that bears against the end of the stem or that operates a tappet that, in turn, bears against the valve stem.

myalgia [my·al·jee·uh]

Muscle pain or aching.

myelofibrosis [my·uh·low·fy·bro·sis]

A disease state in which the marrow is replaced by fibroplastic cells.

myocardium [my·oh·kahrd·ee·um]

The muscular substance of the heart.

myoclonic jerking [my·uh·klawn·ik jur·king]

A series of involuntary movements characterized by alternating contraction and relaxation of muscles.

myringotomy [meer·in·got·um·ee]

Incision of the tympanic membrane (ear drum).

N

narcosis [nahr·ko·sus]

A state of altered mental function ranging from mild impairment of judgment or euphoria (false sense of well-being), to complete loss of consciousness; resembles alcoholic intoxication; produced by exposure to increased partial pressure of nitrogen and certain other gases.

nasal passages [nay·zul pas·uh·juz]

Openings where air enters the body as it is breathed in; nose hairs collect dust, moist walls filter the air, and the air is warmed as it moves through the passages.

nasal septum [nay•zulo sep•tum]
The partition between the two nasal cavities in humans.

nausea [naw•zhuh]
An unpleasant sensation, vaguely referred to the stomach, often culminating in vomiting.

nautical mile [naw•tik•ul myl]
A unit of distance designed to equal approximately 1 minute of arc of latitude; according to the National Bureau of Standards, its length is 6,080.20 feet, or approximately 1.15 times as long as the statute mile of 5,280 feet; also known as a geographical mile.

neat's-foot oil [neetz•foot oyl]
A light yellow oil obtained from the feet and shinbones of cattle.

neck dam (seal)
A rubber skirt that is attached to some lightweight helmets instead of a breastplate. A neck dam is tapered to fit tightly around the neck like a collar.

necrosis [nih•kroe•sis]
The localized death or decay of living tissue in a part of the body, as bone; it is the result of loss of blood supply, burning or other severe injuries.

negative buoyancy [neg•uh•tiv booy•yun•see]
State in which the weight of the submerged body is greater than the weight of the displaced liquid, causing the body to sink.

negative-pressure breathing [NPB]
Breathing from a mask, helmet, or the like, where the pressure of the gaseous mixture being breathed is less than the ambient pressure thus requiring an additional conscious effort to inhale.

nematocyst [nem•ut•uh•sist]
A structure consisting of a flask-shaped body bearing barbs and a long slender filament that can be discharged by the stinging cells of coelenterates.

neon [nee•ahn]
A colorless, odorless gas found in air (1 part in about 65,000 parts of ordinary air); has been used as a breathing gas for divers because it has minimal narcotic effect.

neoprene [nee•uh•preen]
An oil-resistant synthetic rubber; because of its insulation properties, it is used for diver wet suits.

nervous system [nur•vus sis•tum]
Brain, spinal cord, and nerves of the body.

neuralgia [nyoor•al•juh]
An aching or spasmodic pain along the course of nerves.

neuritis [nyoor•eye•tus]
Inflammation of a nerve, usually accompanied by pain, tenderness, and possibly loss of sensation.

neuromuscular [noo•roh•mus•kyoo•lar]
Intermediate in nature between nerve and muscle; pertaining both to nerve and muscle, as neuromuscular cells.

neuron [nyoor•ahn]
The nerve cell body plus its processes; the structural unit of nerve tissue.

neuropathy [nyu•rawp•uh•thee]
Any disease of the nervous system.

neutral buoyancy [noo•trul booy•un•see]
The state in which the weight of the body is equal to the weight of the displaced liquid, so the body remains suspended in the liquid.

niggle [nig•'ul]
Mild, transient and poorly localized symptoms of decompression sickness not requiring treatment.

night vision [nyt vi•zhun]
The natural adaptation to darkness as a diver descends; includes no color perception; when a diver remains on the bottom for a period of time, it will seem as if the light has increased.

niskin bottle [nis•kin baw•tul]
A water-sampling device that is designed to collect water samples in amounts ranging routinely from 1.8 quart (1.7 liter) to 31.7 quarts (30 liters). Niskin bottles also can be used in conjunction with reversing thermometers to record temperature and depth concurrently.

nitrogen [ny•truh•jun]
A colorless, odorless, tasteless, nontoxic inert gas found in great abundance in the atmosphere; nitrogen is commonly used as a diluent with oxygen in diving gas mixtures; when breathed under pressure, has narcotic effect.

nitrogen narcosis [ny•truh•jun nahr•ko•sus]
Narcotic effect resulting from breathing the nitrogen in compressed air at depths greater than 100 feet; also called air narcosis and "rapture of the deep."

nitrox [ny•trahks]
A breathing mixture containing nitrogen and oxygen in various proportions.

noble gases [no•bul gas•uz]
Gases whose chemical structure is characterized by closed shells or subshells of electrons. These gases are also called inert gases.

no-decompression dive [no-de•kum•presh•un dyv]
A dive from which a diver can return directly to the surface at a controlled rate without stopping at shallower depths to allow inert gas to be eliminated from the body; also called a no-stop dive.

no-decompression limits [no-de•kum•presh•un lim•uts]
Specified times at given depths from which no decompression stops are required on return to the surface; also referred to as a no-stop curve and no-stop limits.

nomogram [nawm•uh•gram]
A graphic representation of mathematical relationships or laws.

normal ascent rate [nor•muhl uh•sent rayt]
The ascent rate used under conventional or routine conditions; this rate is 30 feet per minute.

normoxic [nor•mahk•sik]
Relating to normal partial pressures of oxygen equivalent to those found in air at one atmosphere.

nucleus [nyoo•klee•us]
A small spherical body within a cell; in chemistry, the central part of an atom.

nystagmus [nis•tag•mus]
A physiological condition characterized by repeated, involuntary, rapid movements of the eyes, usually in the horizontal plane but sometimes also in the vertical plane.

O

occipital [ahk•sip•uh•ul]
Relating to the back part of the head.

oceanography [oh•shun•nag•ra•fee]
The study of the sea including physical boundaries, the chemistry and physics of sea water, and marine biology.

octopus rig [ahk•tuh•poos rig]
A single-hose regulator with an extra low-pressure port to which an additional second stage has been fitted; double regulator is for emergency shared-air breathing or in case of failure of the primary regulator.

oculomotor nerve [awk•yuh•luh•moe•tor nurv]
The third cranial nerve; controls the movement of the eyes.

olfactory [ol•fak•tur•ee]
Pertaining to the sense of smell.

omitted decompression [oh•mit•ud de•kum•presh•uh]
An ascent in which a diver comes to the surface at a rate greater than 30 feet per minute, and without one or more decompression stops.

operculum [oh•pur•kyu•lum]
The plate covering the gills of a bony fish.

optic nerve [op•tik nurv]
The second cranial nerve; controls sight.

oronasal mask [or•oh•nay•zul mask]
A breathing mask that covers and allows breathing through both nose and mouth.

oropharyngeal airway [or•o•fair•un•jeel air•way]
That part of the airway in humans that consists of the mouth and the pharynx

osmosis [ahs•**mo**•sus]

The passage of a pure solvent, such as water, from a solution of lesser concentration to one of greater concentration, through a semipermeable membrane.

osseous [**ahs**•see•us]

Bony; resembling or having the quality of bone.

ostalgia [as•**tal**•ja]

Pain in a bone.

osteitis [as•tee•**y**•tis]

Inflammation the bone or bony tissue.

osteomyelitis [aws•tee•a•**my**•ly•tis]

Inflammation of the bone marrow.

osteonecrosis

(See: dysbaric osteonecrosis, juxta-articular osteonecrosis, medullary osteonecrosis)

osteoneuralgia [a•stee•oh•noo•**ral**•ja]

Pain of a bone.

otitis [oh•**tyt**•us]

Inflammation of the ear which may be marked by pain, fever, abnormalities of hearing, tinnitus and vertigo; a very common problem in diving.

otterboards [**awt**•tur•bordz]

Door-shaped boards that are attached to trawling nets to keep the nets open during trawling.

outgassing [**owt**•gas•ing]

In vacuum terminology, the vaporization of contaminants within a vacuum system as pressure is decreased; commonly refers to the decompression of a diver back to normal condition; the process of gas elimination.

oval window [oh•vahl **win**•doe]

The upper of two membrane-covered openings in the cochlea of the inner ear.\

overboard dump (discharge system) [o•vur•bord dump]

A system built into a hyperbaric chamber and that transfers exhaled gas out of the chamber.

overexertion [oh•vur•eg•**zur**•shun]

Physical condition characterized by a feeling of suffocation, inability to breathe deeply enough for comfort; working beyond the limits of fitness; also called exhaustion.

oxidation [ahks•uh•**day**•shun]

Induction of chemical reaction or reactions in which oxygen is added to a substance; rust.

oxygen [**ahks**•uh•jun]

A colorless, odorless, tasteless and, under normal conditions, non toxic gas; found free in the atmosphere; the most abundant element in the ocean; essential in cellular respiration of all animals and man, but may be toxic at elevated partial pressures.

oxygen breathing [ahks•uh•jun **breeth**•ing]

The breathing of 100 percent oxygen; in diving, used in some closed-circuit scuba and in the treatment of diving injuries, also to enhance the elimination of inert gas during the final stages of decompression.

oxygen cleaning [ahks•uh•jun **kleen**•ing]

A method of cleaning a diving gas supply system in which high percentages of oxygen are to be used ensure elimination of all hydrocarbons and other potentially combustible contaminants.

oxygen high pressure (OHP) [ahks•uh•jun hy **presh**•ur]

In diving, higher than normal partial pressure of oxygen within the body.

oxygen poisoning

(See: oxygen toxicity)

oxygen toxicity [ahks•uh•jun tahk•**sis**•uh•tee]

Deleterious effects caused by breathing high partial pressures of oxygen; prolonged exposure can result in effects which become progressively more severe as the inspired partial pressure and or the duration of exposure increases; depending on level and length of exposure, may cause lung damage, involvement of the central nervous system or convulsions.

oxyhemoglobin [awx•hi•hee•moe•glow•bin]

Oxidized hemoglobin in the arterial blood.

P

pancreatitis [pan•kree•uh•**tie**•tis]

Inflammation of the pancreas.

paradoxical shivering [pair•uh•**dahk**•suhkul **shiv**•ur•ing]

Uncontrollable shivering under conditions of high helium partial pressures, accompanied by a subjective feeling of warmth.

paranasal sinuses [pair•uh•nay•zal sy•nuh•suz]

The air-filled cavities in the cranial bones accessory to the nose; the paranasal sinuses comprise the frontal, sphenoidal, ethmoidal, and maxillary sinuses.

paraparesis [pair•u•puh•**rees**•is]

Partial paraplegia.

paraplegia [pair•uh•**plee**•juh]

Loss of function, and occasionally of sensation, in the lower body.

parenteral drug administration [puh•**rent**•ul•rul drug ad•min•us•tray•shun]

Administration of drugs by a route other than oral, i.e., by subcutaneous or intravenous injection.

paresthesia [par•es•**thee**•zha]

Abnormal sensation without objective cause, such as numbness, pricking, etc.; heightened sensitivity.

paroxysmal tachycardias [puhr•awk•**siz**•mul tak•uh•kard•ee•uh]

Periodic bouts of fast heart beats.

partial pressure [**pahr**•shul **presh**•ur]

Pressure exerted by one component in a gaseous system, described by Dalton's law; the partial pressure of a gas is equal to the product of the ambient pressure and that fraction of the total pressure in a mixture which can be ascribed to that gas.

patent [**pay**•tunt]

Open, as in "a patent airway."

pathogenic organisms [path•uh•jen•ik or•gun•iz•umz]

Organisms that produce disease.

peduncle [**pee**•dun•kul]

Any stalklike structure that supports another structure or organ.

pelagic organisms [puh•laj•ik or•gun•iz•umz]

Plants and animals that live in the open sea and that are not associated with the shore or sea floor.

perception of color underwater [pur•sep•shun uv kul•ur un•dur•wah•tur]

Conditions of lighting and water color may cause red and blue to appear black; in clear ocean water, however, yellow and dark blue retain their color and, in green water, red and bluegreen retain theirs, to a considerable depth; proceeding toward depth, red is filtered out first, then orange, then yellow, then green, then blue; factors other than depth affecting color underwater include salinity, turbidity and the degree of pollution of the water.

perfusion [pur•**fyoo**•zhun]

The flow of blood or lymph through an organ or tissue, by which gases and chemical substances are distributed and exchanged.

pericardium [pair•uh•**kahr**•dee•um]

The serous membrane that lines the sac enclosing the heart.

perilymph fistula [pair•uh•limf fis•tyoo•luh]

A round or oval window rupture allowing the fluid (perilymph) surrounding the middle ear to escape into the inner ear; rupture of the round or oval windows is caused by stretching them beyond capacity or by a sudden reversal in position, usually occurring during a forceful attempt to clear the ears. (See: alternobaric)

pH

Measure of relative acidity and alkalinity based on a 0 to 14 scale; seven is pH of pure water and represents neutrality; below 7 acidity increases as hydrogen ions increase, above 7 alkalinity increases as ions decrease.

pharyngeal [fur•**in**•jee•ul]

Referring to the pharynx.

pharynx [**fair**•ingks]

The saclike tube extending from the nose and mouth to the larynx and esophagus; also, the throat.

phase measurement system [faze mez•ur•ment sis•tum]

A method for determining the position of an object on the seafloor that uses a single transponder placed on the object and three receiving elements located on the underside of the surface support platform.

phoria [for•ee•uh]

Any tendency of deviation of the eyes from normal.

photogrammetry [foe•toe•**gram**•uh•tree]

The application of photographic principles to the science of mapping; photogrammetry involves the use of special cameras to photograph the earth's surface to produce mosaic pictures or scale maps.

photon [foe•tawn]

The basic unit (quantum) of the electromagnetic field; photons have zero mass, no electric charge, and an indefinitely long lifetime.

photophobia [foe•toe•foe•bee•uh]

Literally, a fear of light; in practice, a disinclination or inability to use the eyes in strong light.

photosensitive [fo•to•**sen**•suh•tiv]

Affected by light; also refers to photographic emulsions.

physics of diving [**fiz**•iks uv **dyv**•ing]

The application of physical laws and principles to underwater activities.

physiology [fiz•ee•**ahl**•uh•jee]

The science which deals with the activities or functions of the body and its parts.

physiology of diving [fiz•ee•**ahl**•uh•;ee•uv **dyv**•ing] The organic processes and phenomena dealing with life and the functions of organs of human beings while in a water environment.

phytoplankton [fy•toe•plank•ton]

Minute marine plants that drift in the sea and are usually microscopic; phytoplankton are either single-celled or loose aggregates of a few cells.

pinger [peeng•ur]

An underwater locating device that emits an acoustic signal.

pituitary [pih•too•i•tare•ee]

A gland, located in humans at the base of the brain, that influences growth, metabolism, sexual cycles, and many other bodily functions.

plane table

A surveying instrument used to locate and map topographical features.

plankton

Plant and animal organisms (usually microscopic) that float or drift in fresh or salt water.

plasma [**plaz**•muh]

The fluid portion of the blood.

platelet [**playt**•lut]

A small, non-nucleated cell found in the blood of all animals, concerned with blood coagulation and contraction of a clot; platelet loss often occurs after decompression; also thrombocyte.

pleura [**ploo**•ra]

A thin watery membrane which covers the inside of the thorax and also envelopes the lungs separately, forming two closed sacs. The two layers covering the lungs and inner chest wall are held in opposition by surface tension and by positive barometric pressure inflating the lungs. These overcome the elastic recoil of the lungs.

pleurisy [**ploor**•uh•see]

Inflammation of the thin, watery membrane covering the lungs and lining of the chest cavity; also, pleuritis.

pneumatocysts [new•**mat**•tuh•sistz]

Hollow floats found at the base of the blades or fronds of certain kelp plants and that cause the fronds to flat up to form a canopy.

pneumofathometer [noo•mo•fath•**ahm**•uh•tur]

A hollow tube, connected at the surface end to a gauge, and open at the diver's end under the surface; used to measure the water pressure at the diver's end of the tube.

pneumogauge hose [**noo**•mo•gayj hos]

A durable, lightweight, flexible hose attached to a low-pressure air supply source on the surface and open at the diver's end; used to monitor the diver's depth; usually attached to the umbilical with the open end terminating at the diver's chest.

pneumomediastinum

(see emphysema)

pneumonia [noo•**mon**•yuh]

Inflammation of the lungs.

pneumopericardium [noo•mo•pair•uh•**kar**•dee•um]

A condition in which gas is present in the membrane sac which contains the heart.

pneumothorax [noo•mo•**thor**•aks]

The presence of air between the lungs and the chest wall; possible collapse of lung tissues and corresponding respiratory compromise; specifically, the result of rupture of cysts on the lung surface or dissection of gas along fascial planes to the mediastinum and thence around a lung to produce collapse.

polycythemia [pawl•ee•sy•**thee**•mee•uh]

A condition characterized by an excessive number of corpuscles (usually red) in the blood.

port

When facing the bow, the left side of a vessel, marked by red lights at night.

positive buoyancy [**pahz**•uh•tiv **booy**•yun•see]

The state in which the weight of the displaced liquid is greater than the weight of the submerged body, s.o the body will float or be buoyed upward. (See: buoyancy, negative buoyancy, neutral buoyancy)

pressure [**presh**•ur]

The force distributed upon a surface, usually expressed in pounds per square inch (p.s.i). (See: absolute pressure, ambient pressure, atmospheric pressure, design pressure, gauge pressure, hydrostatic pressure, partial pressure, standard atmospheric pressure, working pressure)

profile [**pro**•fyl]

In diving, a graphic presentation of the depth-time relationships during a dive.

prognosis [prahg•**no**•sus]

A forecast of the probable results of a disorder; the outlook for recovery.

prosthesis [pross•**thee**•sis]

A man-made replacement for a missing body part.

protozoa [proe•toe•zoa]

One of the lowest classes of the animal kingdom, the protozoa are organisms that consist of simple cells or colonies of cells and that possess no nervous or circulatory system.

provenance data [prawv•uh•nuns day•tuh]

The original data.

psig

Abbreviation for pounds per square inch gauge; a term used to express the difference between absolute pressure and the specific pressure being measured.

psychosis [sie•**koh**•sis]

A disease of the mind characterized by loss of contact with reality.

pulmonary [**pool**•mun•air•ee]

Pertaining to the lung (e.g., designating the artery conveying blood from the heart to the lungs, and the vein conveying blood from the lungs to the heart).

pulmonary barotrauma [**pul**•mun•air•ee bair•uh•**trah**•muh]

Damage to the lung alveoli due to changes in pressure; usually a result of increased internal pressure; may result in air embolism, pneumothorax or emphysema, and probably is second only to drowning as a cause of death in diving.

pulmonary edema [puhl•mun•**air**•ee uh•**deem**•uh]

An accumulation of fluid in the lungs.

pulmonary function [**pool**•mun•air•ee funk•shun]

The factors included in the act of breathing, including ventilatory mechanics (mechanics of breathing), alveolar ventilation, and gas exchange between the alveoli and the blood.

pulmonary ventilation [**pul**•mun•air•ee ven•tuh•**lay**•shun]

Movement of air or respirable gas in and out of the lungs and, by extension, the movement of the inspired gas into the blood through the alveolar wall.

pulmonic [pul•**mahn**•ik]

Referring or relating to the lungs or the pulmonary artery.

purse seine [purs sayn]

A fishing net that is made to hang vertically in the water by weights at the lower edge and floats at the top and that is pursed or drawn into the shape of a bag to enclose the catch.

pyrolytic decomposition [pie•roe•li•tik dee•kom•po•zi•shun]

Chemical change caused by heat or fire.

Q

quadrat [**kwodd**•rut]
A device, which is usually a square of polyvinyl chloride tubing, that is placed on the seafloor and used to estimate the density of marine plants or animals in a defined area.

quadriparesis [kwodd•ruh•puh•**ree**•sus]
Partial quadriplegia.

quadriplegia [kwodd•ruh•plee•juh]
Loss of function, and occasionally sensation, from the neck or chest down.

R

radiometer [ray•dee•awm•uh•tur]
An instrument, which is essentially a heat flow meter, that is used to detect and measure long wave radiation and solar radiation.

radular teeth [ra•dyu•lur teeth]
Minute teeth that are imbedded in a horny strip on the floor of the mouth of a snail and that are used to scrape up food.

Rankine temperature [**rang**•kun tem•pu r•uh•choor]
(See: temperature, Rankine)

rapture of the deep [**rap**•chur uv thu deep]
Euphemism for nitrogen narcosis. (See: nitrogen narcosis)

rebreather [re•**bree**•thur]
A closed-circuit or semi-closed-circuit underwater breathing apparatus.

recompression [re•cum•**presh**•un]
Returning a diver to the highest pressure experienced (or greater if necessary) for the purpose of minimizing and eliminating the effects of decompression sickness or air embolism; also, for treatment of these; accomplished in a chamber rather than return to depth underwater.

recompression chamber [re•cum•**presh**•un **chaym**•bur]
An enclosed space used to rapidly increase the pressure to which a diver has been exposed, to return the diver to the ambient underwater pressure; also, used when treating a diver for air embolism or decompression sickness.

refraction [re•**frak**•shun]
The effect of the bending of light rays underwater, due to the fact that water is of a different density than air; causes objects to appear larger or smaller than they are, or to be in a position other than where they are actually located.

regulator, demand [**reg**•yoo•lay•tur, duh•**mand**]
An apparatus in which the gas supply is activated by the negative pressure associated with inhalation.

remotely operated vehicle
An unmanned, tethered or untethered vehicle that is designed for underwater observation, work, or sample collection.

repetitive group designation [ruh•**peh**•ti•tive grup **dez**•ig•**nay**•shun]
A letter that is used in decompression tables to designate the amount of nitrogen remaining in a diver's body for 12 hours after the completion of a dive.

repetitive dive [ree•**pet**•uh•tiv dyv]
A dive following another dive within 12 hours but more than 10 minutes.

residual air [reh•**zid**•u•ul air]
The amount of air that remains in the lungs after a person voluntarily expels all of the air possible.

residual nitrogen [re•**zij**•oo•ul **nite**•roe•jun]
Denoting a concept which describes the amount of nitrogen remaining in a diver's tissues following a hyperbaric exposure.

residual nitrogen time [re•**zij**•oo•ul **nite**•roe•j un time]
Time added to actual bottom time for calculating a decompression schedule for a repetitive dive; based on the concept of residual nitrogen.

residual volume [re•**zij**•oo•ul **vahl**•yoom]
The volume of air which remains in the lungs after the most forceful exhalation.

respiration [**res**•pur•ay•shun]
The act or function of breathing; the oxidation reduction process by which energy in food is transformed to other kinds of energy for the continuance of life.

respiratory minute volume [**res**•pur•uh•tore•ee **min**•ut **vahl**•yoom]
The amount of air inhaled and exhaled per minute to maintain proper body function; variable, depending on the individual and the degree of exertion.

respiratory rate [**res**•pur•uh•tore•ee rate]
The rate of breathing: normal range, 10 to 20 breath per minute (6 quarts of air); under exertion, approximately 20 times the individual's normal breath rate; an index of the degree of exertion.

retina [**ret**•'n•uh]
The innermost coating of the eyeball; the nerve coat of the eye, made of nerve cells and fibers.

retinitis pigmentosa [reh•tin•**eye**•tis pig•munn•**toe**•sa]
An inflammation of the retina that involves all layers of the retina.

ribs [ribz]
Bone and cartilage that form the chest cavity and protect its contents; tissue between ribs allows for expansion of the chest cavity.

rip current [rip **kur**•unt]
A strong surface current that flows seaward from the shore.

roentgen [**ren**(t)•jun]
The international unit of radiation; a standard quantity of x or gamma radiation.

Romberg's sign [**rom**•burgz sine]
A swaying of the body and an inability to stand when the eyes are closed and the feet are placed close together; the presence of this sign indicates neurological impairment.

round window [rownd **win**•doe]
The lower of two membrane-covered openings in the cochlea of the inner ear.

rubber suit [**rub**•ur soot]
Partial or complete covering for a diver, primarily to insulate and preserve body heat; classified as wet and dry; wet suits, usually of foam neoprene, permit a thin layer of water to contact the diver's skin; dry, a rubber sheet prevents contact with the water, but requires the additional insulation afforded by cloth underclothing or a wet suit.

rupture [**rup**•chur]
The breaking apart or bursting under unequalized pressure of, for example, an ear drum.

S

saturation [sach•ur•ay•shun]
The condition in which the partial pressure of a gas dissolved in a fluid is equal to its maximum possible partial pressure, under the existing ambient conditions of temperature and pressure.

saturation depth [sach•ur•ay•shun depth]
The depth or pressure at which a diver's tissues are saturated; also called storage depth.

saturation dive [sach•ur•ay•shun dyv]
An exposure of sufficient duration so that the diver's tissue gases reach equilibrium with the pressure environment; once this occurs, the decompression time required at the end of a dive does not increase with additional time spent at any depth; the diver works out of a habitat or other pressurized chamber.

saturation diving system [sach•ur•ay•shun **dyv**•ing **sis**•tum]
A pressurized diving system that incorporates a life support system for long term saturation dives.

scfm
Standard Cubic Feet per Minute, defined as cubic feet per minute at standard conditions at one atmosphere and 0C.

schedule, decompression
(See: decompression schedule)

scuba [**skoo**•buh]
Derived from the acronym for self-contained underwater breathing apparatus, now the word used to describe apparatus in which the inspired gas is delivered by demand regulator and exhaled into the surrounding water (open-circuit). and the gas supply is carried on the diver's back.

sea [see]

Denoting that all seas (except inland seas) are physically interconnected parts of the earth's total salt water system.

sea level pressure [see **lev•**ul **presh•**ur]

Atmosphere pressure at mean sea level, either directly measured or determined from observed station pressure.

seborrheic dermatitis [seb•uh•ree•ik dur•muh•tie•tis]

An inflammatory scaling disease of the scalp, face, and, occasionally, of other areas of the body.

seismic profiling [syz•mik pro•fyl•ing]

A method for obtaining a profile of the seafloor or of the layers of sediment and rock below the seafloor; seismic profiling uses a strong energy source from the surface and then measures the strength of the reflected energy.

seismic waves [syz•mik wayvz]

Shock waves caused by earthquakes or explosions that travel inside the earth or on its surface.

self-contained diving

(See: scuba)

semi-closed circuit scuba [sem•ee-klozed sur•kut skoo•ba]

A self-contained underwater breathing apparatus in which the breathing gas is recirculated through purifying and oxygen replenishing systems; oxygen levels are maintained by regulating the flow of the gas; a portion of the exhaled gas is lost into the surrounding water.

semi-submersible rig [sem•ee-sub•mur•shu•bul rig]

A large offshore drilling rig built on huge caissons; some self-propelled, ballasted to drill depth, held by anchors; allows drilling to greater depths in areas of severe wave conditions.

separated gas [sep•ur•ay•tud gas]

Describing the presence of gas in the body in joints and between muscles where the word bubble would not be appropriate; also used by extension to describe all unspecified collections of gas, including bubbles.

sepsis [sep•sis]

Poisoned state due to absorption of pathogenic bacteria and their products into the blood stream, blood poisoning.

sepsis gas [sep•sis•gas]

Poisoning due to gas bacillicus.

sepsis intestinal [sep•sis intestinal]

Poisoning due to ingestion of decaying food.

sessile [sess•uhl]

Permanently attached or fixed; not free-moving.

sextant [seks•tunt]

A navigational instrument that is used to measure the altitude of celestial bodies.

shear [sheer]

A force that lies in the plane of an area or a parallel plane and that tends to cause the plane of an area to slide on the adjacent planes.

shutter speed

In photography, the amount of time a camera shutter exposes a film to light.

side-scan sonar [syd•skan soe•nar]

A search system in which acoustic beams are directed laterally and downward in planes perpendicular to the line of the advance of a towed transponder-receiver unit. Return signals are then processed to present a picture of the seafloor on both sides of the towed unit.

silent bubbles [sigh•lunt bubb•ulz]

Gas bubbles which may be detected in the blood vessels or tissues, but which cause no signs or symptoms of decompression sickness; may be demonstrated by ultrasonic flow techniques such as Doppler; also called covert bubbles.

single hose unit [sing•gul hoze yoo•nut]

Open-circuit scuba having a single intermediate pressure hose with first-stage pressure reduction at the yoke (cylinder attachment), and second or ambient reduction at the mouthpiece; the exhaust is at the mouthpiece.

single lock chamber [sing•gul lahk chaym•bur]

A pressure chamber with only one pressurized compartment; usually having a small lock for the passage of supplies, poses a compromising restriction where interchange of personnel is required, as in treatment of decompression sickness.

sinus [sigh•nus]

A cavity or hollow space in the skull connecting with ear, nose or throat.

sinusitis [sigh•nus•eye•tus]

Inflammation of the membranes lining the sinuses. (See: sinus)

sinus squeeze [sigh•nus skweez]

A squeeze caused by blockage of the opening between one of the sinuses and the nose; may be due to a common cold or sinusitis; or, due to a failure to equalize sinus pressure with ambient pressure, usually due to the presence of sinusitis accompanying the common cold.

skeletal system [skell•uh•tul sis•tum]

The bones of the body.

snorkel [snor•kul]

A tube in the mouth with the open end above the surface of the water, allowing the swimmer or diver to breathe comfortably without turning the head.

solid [sahl•ud]

Distinct from liquid or gaseous; of definite shape and volume.

solubility coefficient of gases [sohl•yu•bill•uh•tee koh•ee•fish•unt uv gas•uz]

Under experimental conditions of pressure and temperature, the volume of gas dissolved by a unit volume of solvent.

sonar [so•nahr]

Previously an acronym, now the word for sound navigation and ranging; the method or equipment for determining by underwater sound techniques the presence, location, or nature of objects in the sea.

sound [sownd]

The perception of vibrations transported to the ear through some form of matter; travels more rapidly through denser substances such as water; underwater hearing is affected by reverberations off the bottom, heat and salinity of the water, microorganisms, noises from the surface, and the diver's head covering; to measure depth with a line and weight.

sound velocity [sownd vu•loss•uh•tee]

The rate of travel at which sound energy moves through a medium, usually expressed in feet per second.

specific gravity [spuh•siff•ik gra•vuh•tee]

The relative weight of a substance as compared to water.

specific heat [spuh•siff•ik heet]

The amount of heat required to raise the temperature of a unit mass of a substance by one unit of temperature compared to the amount of heat required to raise a similar mass of water by the same amount.

spectrometer [spek•trom•uh•tur]

An instrument used to measure spectra or to determine the wavelengths of various kinds of radiation from infrared to gamma.

spectroradiometer [spek•tro•ray•dee•awm•uh•tur]

An instrument used to measure the spectral distribution of radiant energy.

sphygmomanometer [sfig•moe•man•ahm•uh• tur]

An instrument for measuring arterial blood pressure.

spina bifida [spy•nuh bif•uh•duh]

A congenital anomaly in which the spinal membranes protrude through a congenital cleft (split) in the lower part of the vertebral column.

spirit level [spear•ut lev•ul]

A level that is used in combination with a telescope to compute the difference in elevation between two points.

spontaneous pneumothorax [spahn•tayn•ee•us noo•moe•thor•aks]

Pnemothorax without known cause. (See: pneumothorax)

sport diver [sport dyv•ur]

One who dives (with or without scuba) for recreation.

squeeze [skweez]

An injury caused by a difference in pressure in an enclosed space within the body.

stadia [stay•dee•uh]

A method of surveying distances that involves the use of two parallel lines to intercept intervals on a calibrated rod; the intervals are proportional to the intervening distance.

stage decompression [stayg·dee·kom·**presh**·un]
A decompression procedure involving decompression stops of specific durations at given depths.

staggers [**stag**·urz]
A descriptive term referring to the dysequilibrium of decompression sickness when the inner ear is involved.

standby diver [**stand**·by dyv·ur]
A suited or partially suited diver, ready to assist the working diver should an emergency arise.

stapedectomy [stay·pih·**dek**·tah·mee]
Removal of the stirrup-shaped bone in the middle ear.

starboard [**star**·burd]
When facing the bow, the right side of a vessel, marked by green lights at night.

statute mile [**stach**·oot myle]
4,280 ft. or 1.6093 km., or 0.869 nautical miles.

stipe [styp]
The flexible stemlike structure of seaweeds, such as kelp, that serves as the shock absorber between the upper leafy parts of the plant and the anchored holdfast at the bottom.

stratigraphy [struh·**teeg**·ruh·fee]
The study of rock strata, and especially of their distribution, deposition, and age.

strike [stryk]
In geology, the compass direction that a rockbed would take if it were projected to a horizontal plane on the earth's surface.

sub-bottom profile
See seismic profiling.

subcutaneous [sub·kyoo·**tane**·ee·us]
Occurring or located beneath the skin.

subcutaneous emphysema [sub·kyoo·**tain**·ee·us em·fuh·**zee**·muh]
(See: emphysema, sucutaneous)

submersible [sub·**mur**·suh·b'l]
A one-atmosphere vehicle for underwater operation.

submersible decompression chamber [sub·**mur**·suh·b'l de·kum·**presh**·un **chaym**·bur]
A chamber that can be lowered into the water to transport divers between the surface and the work site; can be mated to the deck decompression chamber.

submersible work chamber (SWC) [sub·**mur**·suh·b'l wurk **chaym**·bur]
A single-wall, pressure-proof, helium-tight tank of steel mounted on a support frame, designed to accommodate two divers.

substernal [sub·**stur**·nul]
An adjective meaning beneath the breast-bone.

suits, diving [soots, dyv·ing]
Specialized protective clothing used by divers underwater.

suit squeeze [soot skweez]
Injury resulting from unequal ambient pressure in a diving suit.

supersaturated solution [soo·pur·sat·chur·a·tud so·lu·shun]
A solution that holds more gas than would be possible at the same temperature and pressure at equilibrium.

surface decompression [sur·fuss de·kum·presh·un]
The procedure in which a portion of the in-water decompression is omitted, and the diver is brought to the surface and recompressed in a chamber to complete the decompression; sometimes confused with decanting.

surface interval [sur·fuss **in**·tur·vul]
The elapsed time between surfacing from a dive and the moment when the diver leaves the surface for the next dive.

surface supplied [sur·fuss suh·**plyd**]
A form of diving in which the breathing gas is supplied from a compressor or cylinder(s) on the surface.

surficial maps [sur·**fish**·ul mapz]
Maps showing the two-dimensional character and distribution of material comprising the seafloor of an area.

swim fins [swim finz]
Devices worn on the feet of a diver or swimmer to increase the propulsive force of the legs.

swimmer delivery vehicle (SDV) [**swim**·ur de·**liv**·ur·ee **ve·hik**·ul]
A type of wet submersible used for the underwater transport of divers.

symbiosis [sim·bee·oh·sus]
The living together of two or more organisms in an association which is mutually advantageous.

symptoms [**simp**·tums]
Perceptible changes in body state or function that may be indicative of disease or injury; the word applies to changes perceptible to the individual himself, but is often used to include signs which are abnormalities that can be detected by an observer or examiner.

synchronization [sin·kro·niz·**a**·shun]
In photography, the interval between the opening of the shutter and the burst of light from the strobe.

syndrome [**sin**·drome]
A group of symptoms that indicate a specific disorder; a complex of symptoms and signs that occur together.

systemic [sis·**tem**·ik]
Affecting the whole body; generalized.

systole [sis·**tole**·ee]
The period of heart muscle contraction, especially that of the ventricles; adjective: systolic.

systolic blood pressure
The blood pressure recorded during systole (contraction of the heart).

T

tachycardia [tack·uh·**kahrd**·ee·uh]
A rapid heart beat; the term usually applies to a resting pulse rate above 100 per minute.

talus [**tay**·luhs]
The mass or coarse rock fragments that accumulates at the foot of a cliff as a result of weathering and gravity.

taxa [taks·uh]
In taxonomy, a category, such as a species or genus.

telemetry [tuh·**lem**·uh·tree]
The science and technology of the measurement and transmission of data by wire, radio, acoustic, or other means.

temperature [tem·pur·uh ·choor]
The degree of hotness or coldness measured on a definite scale; may be measured in Celsius, centigrade, Fahrenheit, Kelvin or Rankine temperature scale.

temperature, absolute [tem·p'ruh·choor, ab·so·loot]
Temperature measured or calculated on a scale having absolute zero as the minimum and scale units equal in magnitude to celsius degrees. Absolute zero is the lowest temperature that could possibly be reached at which all molecular motion would cease.

temperature, Celsius [tem·p'ruh·choor, sell·see· us]
Thermometer scale in which water boils at 100C and freezes at 0C (absolute zero is 273° below Celsius zero).

temperature, Fahrenheit [tem·p'ruh·choor, Fair·un·hite]
Thermometer scale where water boils at 212° F, and freezes at 32° F above Fahrenheit zero, and where absolute zero is 459.6° below Fahrenheit zero.

temperature, Rankine [tem·p'ruh·choor, Rang·kun]
The Rankine scale is another absolute temperature scale, which has the same size degrees as the Fahrenheit scale. The freezing point of water is 492°R and the boiling point of water is 672 °R.

temporal mandibular joint (TMJ) pain [tem·puh·rul man·dibu·lur joint]
Pain in the area of the temple and the jaws; TMJ pain is often caused by grinding the teeth or by gripping a mouthpiece too firmly.

tender [ten·dur]
The individual responsible for seeing that the diver receives care both topside and underwater; also called the attendant; a support vessel.

tethered diving [teth·urd dyv·ing]
Diving with a lifeline and a tender.

thallus [thal·us]
A plant that has a body that is not differentiated into root, stem, or leaf.

theodolite [thee•**awd**•ul•eyet]

An optical instrument used to measure angles and distances.

thermal balance [**thur**•mul **bal**•uns]

A state characterized by stable body temperature in which heat gain equals heat loss.

thermal stress [**thur**•mul stress]

A condition in which the body attempts to maintain normal temperature when the surrounding temperature is either higher or lower than that of the body.

thermistor [**thur**•miss•tur]

An electrical resistor made of a material whose resistance varies sharply with temperature in a known manner.

thermocline [**thur**•mo•klyne]

An abrupt change in temperature encountered at varying depths.

thoracentesis [thor•uh•sen•**tee**•sis]

A medical procedure involving puncturing of the thorax to remove accumulated fluid.

thoracic squeeze [thor•**ass**•ik skweez]

Injury to the lung due to chest air spaces not being equalized to ambient pressure.

thorax [**thor**•aks]

That portion of the body between the head and the abdomen; enclosed by the ribs in vertebrates.

thrombosis [throm•**boh**•sis]

Coagulation of the blood in some part of the circularly system, forming a clot that obstructs circulation in that part.

thrombus [**throm**•bus]

A stationary plug or clot in a blood vessel or in one of the cavities of the heart.

tidal air

The volume of air inspired and expired by a person during rest.

tidal volume [**tide**•ul **vahl**•yoom]

The amount of gas exchanged in respiration cycle, measured by averaging over several breaths.

tinnitus [ti•**ny**•tus]

A ringing, roaring, or hissing sound in the ears.

tissue half time

(See: half time)

topographic chart [taw•puh•**graf**•ik chart]

A chart that graphically represents the exact physical configuration of a place or region.

torr [toar]

A unit of pressure equal to 1/760 of an atmosphere and very nearly equal to the pressure of a column of mercury 1 millimeter high at 0• C (32• F) and standard gravity.

total bottom time

(See: bottom time)

toxemia [tahk•**see**•me•uh]

A general toxic condition in which poisonous products are present into the blood stream.

toxic [**tahk**•sik]

Poisonous.

Toynbee maneuver [**Toyn**•bee mah•**new**•ver]

The act of swallowing while the mouth and nose are closed.

trachea [**tray**•kee•uh]

The wind pipe, formed of cartilage rings to maintain an open airway; carries air to the bronchial tubes.

tracheobronchial [**tray**•kee•oh•brahng•kyul]

Relating to the trachea and the bronchi. (See: bronchi, trachea)

tracheobronchitis [**tray**•kee•o•brawn•**ky**•tus]

Inflammation of the trachea and bronchi.

tracheostomy [**tray**•kee•ahs•tuh•mee]

A surgical opening into the trachea, for the introduction of a tube through which the patient may breathe.

transect [tran•**sekt**]

In diving, a reference line attached to the seafloor and designed to provide directional orientation or to serve as a base line for scientific observations or surveys.

transmural pressure [trans•**myoo**•rul **pre**•shur]

The differential between the pressure acting on the inside and outside of a surface; e.g., the tubes in the lungs, or the chambers of the heart.

transponder [tranz•**pawn**•dur]

An electronic device consisting of a receiver of signal impulses and a responder that automatically returns signal impulses to the interrogator-responder.

transpulmonary pressure [trans•**pool**•mun•air•ee **pre**•shur]

The difference between the oral pressure and the pressure exerted on the visceral pleural cavity of the lung.

trauma [**traw**•muh]

An injury or wound which may be produced by external force or by shock.

treatment depth [**treet**•munt depth]

The depth (pressure) to which a patient is compressed during decompression treatment.

treatment mix, gas [**treet**•munt miks, gas]

The breathing gas mixture used in the treatment of decompression sickness.

treatment table [**treet**•munt **tay**•bul]

A collection of decompression schedules used to treat decompression sickness or air embolism; sometimes loosely used as a synonym for an individual schedule.

trigeminal nerve [try•**jem**•un•ul nurv]

The fifth cranial nerve; controls motion and sensation of the face, teeth, and tongue.

trilateration [try•lat•ur•**a**•shun]

A method of determining the relative positions of three or more points and that involves treating these points as vertices of a triangle and then measuring their angles and sides.

trimix [**try**•miks]

A gas mixture involving three gases; usually oxygen, helium, and nitrogen

trochlear nerve [**trawk**•lee•ur nurv]

The fourth cranial nerve; controls the superior oblique muscles of the eye.

tunnel vision [**tun**•ul **vizh**•un]

The narrowing of the field of vision; in diving, most commonly encountered in connection with oxygen toxicity.

turbidity [tur•**bid**•uh•tee]

Reduced water clarity resulting from the presence of suspended matter.

turbulence [**tur**•byoo•luns]

A disturbed or disordered, irregular motion of fluids or gases.

turbulent flow [**tur**•bu•lunt floe]

A type of flow in which the fluid velocity at a fixed point fluctuates with time in nearly random way; contrasts with laminar flow.

tympanic membrane [tim•**pan**•ik **mem**•brayn]

The membrane separating the external auditory canal from the middle ear; also called the ear drum.

U

ulcer [**ul**•sir]

An open lesion upon the skin or mucous membrane of the body.

ulcer duodenal [**ul**•sir duodenal]

An ulcer in the first section of the small intestine, between the stomach and the jejunum. due to the action of the gastric juice.

umbilical [um•**bill**•uh•cull]

The composite of hoses and lines supplying life support to the diver.

undertow [**un**•dur•toe]

An often misused term meaning a seaward current near the bottom of a sloping beach; caused by the return, under the action of gravity, of the water carried up to the shore by wave action.

unit pulmonary toxicity dose [**you**•nut **pull**•mun• air•ee tok•**sis**•uh•tee dose]

A unit of measure devised by the Institute for Environmental Medicine at the University of Pennsylvania; used for calculating the total oxygen exposure incurred during all phases of a dive, including decompression.

upwelling

In coastal areas, the replacement of surface waters by deeper waters; upwelling is caused by winds that transport surface waters offshore.

V

vaccine [vack•**seen**]
A substance inoculated into the body, used to cause antibody formation in order to prevent a specific disease.

vagus nerve [**vay**•gus nurv]
The tenth cranial nerve; controls sensation and motion of the ear, pharynx, larynx, heart, lungs, esophagus, and other parts of the body.

Valsalva maneuver [Val•**sal**•vuh muh•**noo**•vur]
A maneuver to equalize the pressure in the middle ear with the ambient pressure against the outer surface of the eardrum; the nose is compressed shut, the mouth is shut, the glottis is open, and an attempt is made to exhale through the nose; results in forcing air through the eustachian tube into the middle ear, but also causes increased pulmonary pressure which has been known to cause rupture of lung tissues and the round window of the ear.

valve [valv]
A device that starts, stops or regulates the flow of gas or air in diving equipment.

valve, non-return [valv, nahn-re•**turn**]
A valve which prevents reverse flow through the gas supply umbilical.

variable volume dry suit [**vair**•ee•uh•bul **vahl**• yoom dry soot]
A dry suit with both an inlet gas valve and an exhaust valve; together with a weighted belt, the diver can maintain buoyancy control.

vascular [**vas**•kyoo•lur]
Pertaining to or composed of blood vessels.

vascular system [**vas**•kyoo•lur **sis**•tum]
The heart, blood vessels, lymphatics and their parts considered collectively. It includes the pulmonary and portal system.

vasoconstriction [**vas**•oh•kun•**strik**•chun]
A decrease in the diameter of blood vessels, especially constriction of arterioles; leads to decreased blood flow to a part of the body.

vasodilation [**vas**•oh•dye•**lay**•shun]
An increase in the diameter of blood vessels, especially the dilation of the smallest arteries (arterioles) resulting in an increase of the blood to a part of the body.

vasomotor control [vaz•uh•**mo**•tur kun•**trol**]
Regulation of the tension of blood vessel walls.

vasovagal effects [faz•o•**vay**•jul e•**fekz**]
A group of physiological effects caused by fright, trauma, pain, and other stress-inducing situations; vasovagal effects include nausea, sweating, paleness, decreased cardiac output, and related symptoms.

vector [**vek**•tur]
A quantity completely specified by a magnitude and direction.

velocity [vuh•**loss**•uh•tee]
In blasting, the rate of the detonation wave traveling through a column of explosive material.

vena cava [**vee**•nuh **kah**•vuh]
Either of the two large veins that enter into and return blood to the right atrium of the heart.

ventilate [**ven**•tuh•late]
Procedure in which a diver increases gas flow to ventilate or flush the life-support system.

ventilatory capacity [**ven**•til•a•tor•ee ka•**pas**•i•tee]
A function of maximum breathing capacity, timed vital capacity, and maximum expiratory flow rate, all of which are maximum - effort dynamic ventilatory measures and all reflect the work limits of the anatomical respiratory apparatus.

ventricle [**ven**•trik•ul]
The two lower chambers of the heart.

ventricular fibrillation [ven•**trik**•yu•lur fib•bri•**lay**•shun]
A condition in which the ventricles of the heart develop an irregular and chaotic rhythm and the electrical activity of the heart becomes disorganized. If ventricular fibrillation is not stopped immediately, it is fatal.

venturi effect [ven•**tur**•ee ee•**fect**]
A type of flow in which the flow rate is higher and the relative pressure is lower; venturi effects are caused by a smooth constriction in a pipe or by a restriction of an area through which gas or liquid flows.

venule [**ven**•yul]
A small vein.

vertebra [**vur**•tuh•brah]
Any one of the bones of the spinal column.

vertigo [**vur**•ti•go]
A disoriented state in which the individual or the surrounding seems to rotate dizzily; objective vertigo: the sensation that the external world is revolving around one, subjective vertigo: the sensation that one is revolving in space.

vestibular decompression sickness [ves•**tib**•yoo•lur]
Decompression sickness involving the inner ear; often associated with vertigo.

vestibular system [ves•**tib**•yoo•lur **sis**•tum]
That part of the inner ear concerned with balance.

vestibule [**ves**•ti•byool]
Any cavity or space serving as an entrance to another cavity or space, as the vestibule of the inner ear leading into the cochlea.

virtual image [**vur**•tyu•uhl **im**•uge]
An image from which rays of reflected or refracted light appear to diverge, as from an image seen in a plane mirror.

viscera [**vis**•sur•uh]
The organs in the three large body cavities, such as the stomach and the liver in the abdominal cavity.

visceral [**vis**•sur•ul]
Pertaining to the internal organs.

viscosity [vis•**kahs**•uh•tee]
The property of a fluid or gas that resists change in the shape or arrangement of its elements during flow; thickness.

vital capacity [**vye**•tul kuh•**pass**•uh•tee]
The maximum volume of air that can be expired after a maximum inspiration.

vortex [**vor**•teks]
A type of flow that involves rotation about an axis, such as occurs in a whirlpool.

voucher specimen [**vow**•chur **spes**•uh•mun]
A specimen collected to provide species identification or evidence that a given species was collected from a certain place.

W

weight [wayt]
A measure of the heaviness or mass of an object.

weir [weer]
A dam or bulkhead over which water flows, or a bulkhead containing a notch through which water flows; weirs can be used to measure volume in a flow of water.

wet submersible [wet sub•**merz**•uh•bul]
A underwater vehicle designed so that its occupants are exposed to the ambient environment.

wet suit [wet soot]
A closed cell, synthetic rubber diving suit which provides a thermal barrier by trapping a thin layer of body-warmed water next to the diver's skin.

working pressure [**wurk**•ing **presh**•ur]
The approximate pressure required to operate a system over its intended mission range.

work of breathing [wurk uv **bree**•thing]
The amount of effort a diver must exert to breathe through the equipment; the work of breathing depends on depth, type of equipment, gas mixture and the condition of the lungs.

Y

yoke [yoke]
A device for attaching regulators to cylinders in order to make a leak-proof seal.

Z

zooplankton [zoo•**plank**•ton]
Drifting marine animals that range in size and complexity from microscopic single-celled animals to large multicellular ones.

PREFIXES AND SUFFIXES

a: means without, none, or nothing

aero: air

algia: pain

baro or baric: relating to air pressure

capnia: refers to carbon dioxide or smoke without fire

cardio: refers to the heart

don: refers to the teeth

dys: difficult

hyper: more than

hypo: less than

ia: condition of

itis: inflamation

media: middle

necro: dead

osis: condition of

osteo: refers to bones

oto: refers to the ear

ox: oxygen

pnea: refers to breathing

septic: refers to germs

vaso: refers to blood vessels

ABBREVIATIONS

A	argon
ABT	actual bottom time
ac	alternating current
acfm	actual cubic feet per minute
AED	automated external defibrillator
AGE	arterial gas embolism
ALS	advanced life support
AM	amplitude modulation
ASA	American Standards Association
ASME	American Society for Mechanical Engineering
ata	atmospheres absolute
atm	atmosphere
A-V	arteriovenous
BCF	Bureau of Commercial Fisheries
BIBS	built-in-breathing system
BTU	British thermal unit
C	degrees centigrade
cm^3	cubic centimeter
cfm	cubic feet per minute
cm	centimeter
cmH_2O	centimeter of water
cm^2	square centimeter
cm^3	cubic centimeter
cmHg	centimeter of mercury
CNS	central nervous system
CO	carbon monoxide
CO_2	carbon dioxide
CPR	cardiopulmonary resuscitation
CPTD	cumulative pulmonary toxicity dose
CTD	conductivity, temperature, and depth
D	depth
DAN	Divers Alert Network
dc	direct current
DCI	decompression illness
DCS	decompression sickness
DDC	deck decompression chamber
DGPS	Differentially-corrected Global Positioning System
DIN	Deutsches Institut fuer Normung
DMT	diving medical technician
DOT	Department of Transportation
DPV	diver propulsion vehicle
EAD	equivalent air depth
EAN	enriched-air nitrox
°F	degrees Fahrenheit
fl oz	fluid ounce
fpm	feet per minute
fsw	feet of seawater
ft.	foot
ft^2	square foot
ft^3	cubic foot
GI	gastrointestinal
gm	gram
gm/cm^3	grams per cubic centimeter
gm/liter	grams per liter
gm/cm^2	grams per square centimeter
H_2	hydrogen

HAZ-MAT	hazardous-material
HBOI	Harbor Branch Oceanographic Institution
He	helium
Hg	mercury
hp	horsepower
HP	high pressure
HPNS	High Pressure Nervous Syndrome
Hz	Hertz—cycles per second
ICC	Interstate Commerce Commission
i.d.	inside diameter
in.	inch
in^2	square inch
in^3	cubic inch
inHg	inches of mercury
K	Kelvin
kg	kilogram
kg/cm^2	kilogram per square centimeter
kHz	kiloHertz—one thousand cycles per second
km^2	square kilometer
kw	kilowatt
l	liters
lb	pound
lb/ft^3	pound per cubic foot
lb/in^2	pound per square inch
liters/min	liters per minute
lpm	liters per minute
LSB	life support bouy
m	meters
m^2	square meter
m^3	cubic meter
mb	millibar
mg/liter	milligrams per cubic meter
min	minute
ml	milliliter
ml/liter	milliliters per liter
mm	millimeter
mmHg	millimeters of mercury
MNMS	Monitor National Marine Sanctuary
MOD	maximum operating depth
MP	mid-pressure
MRDF	Marine Resource Development Foundation
MSB	mobile support base
MTBE	methyl tertiary butyl ether
N/m^2	Newton per square meter
N_2	nitrogen
$NaHCO_3$	sodium bicarbonate
NEDU	Navy Experimental Diving Unit
NBDHMT	National Board of Diving and Hyperbaric Medical Technology
NBS	National Bureau of Standards
NDP	NOAA Diving Program
Ne	neon
NOAA	National Oceanic and Atmospheric Administration
NURC	National Undersea Research Center
O_2	oxygen
o.d.	outside diameter

OEA	oxygen-enriched air	SAM	registered trademark (Dr. Sam Scheinberg)
OMAO	Office of Marine and Aviation Operations	scf	standard cubic feet
OSHA	Occupational Safety and Health Administration	scfm	standard cubic feet per minute
OUR	Office of Undersea Research	SCBA	self-contained breathing apparatus
oz	ounce	scuba	self-contained underwater breathing apparatus
Pa	pascal (SI unit of pressure)	SDC	submersible decompression chamber
PCB	Polychlorinated Biphenyls	SEV	series exhaust valve
PFLD	personal flotation and location device	SI	International system of Units
pH	hydrogen-ion concentration	SMB	surface marker bouy
PO_2	partial pressure of oxygen	STPD	standard temperature and pressure, dry
pp	partial pressure	SUS	suit-under-suit
ppm	parts per million	TBT	tributyltin
PSA	pressure swing adsorption	TMJ	temporal mandibular joint
psi	pounds per square inch	TNT	trinitrotoluene
psia	pounds per square inch absolute	TRCS	transportable recompression chamber system
psig	pounds per square inch gauge	UBA	underwater breathing apparatus
PTC	personnel transfer capsule	UHMS	Undersea and Hyperbaric Medical Society
PVC	polyvinyl chloride	UNCW	University of North Carolina in Wilmington
PVHO	pressure vessels for human occupancy	UPTD	unit pulmonary toxicity dose
R	Rankine	URI	upper respiratory infection
RMV	respiratory minute volume	USC&GS	United States Coast and Geodetic Survey
RNT	residual nitrogen time	v	volt
ROV	remotely operated vehicle	V	volume
rpm	revolutions per minute	VC	vital capacity
SAC	surface air consumption	vac	voltage alternating current
SAE	Standard Average European	VOX	voice

Appendix
References

Bond, G. 1964. New Developments in High Pressure Living. *U.S. Naval Submarine Medical Center Report No. 442.* Groton, Conn.: U.S. Naval Submarine Medical Center.

Bond, G. 1964. *NOAA Diving Manual*, 1991, Rockville, MD: NOAA, U.S. Department of Commerce, R-2.

Boni, M.R., R. Schibli, P. Nussberger, and A.A. Büehlmann. 1976. Diving at diminished atmospheric pressure. *Undersea Biomed. Res.* 3(3):189-204.

Bookspan, J. 1995. *Diving Physiology in Plain English.* Kensington, MD: Undersea and Hyperbaric Medical Society, Inc.

Bove, A. 1984. Rx for divers. *Skin Diver* 33(8):29, 30, 112.

Bove, A. 1985. Buoyancy compensator rebreathing. *Skin Diver* 34(1):60.

Bove, A. 1985. Physiology of diving I. *NAUI News.* pp. 21-22.

Bove, A. 1997. Diving Medicine 3rd Ed. W.B. Saunders Company.

Boyd, E. 1980. Dive knife roundup. *Skin Diver* 29(1):63-64.

Bozanic, J. 1993. Preliminary investigations in anchialine caves of Cuba. In: Heine, J.N., and N.L. Crane, eds. Diving for Science.1993, *Proc. of AAUS Scientific Diving Symp.* Monterey, CA. pp. 33-41.

Burgess, R.F. 1980. *Man: 12,000 Years Under the Sea.* New York: Dodd, Mead & Co.

Butler, F.K., Jr., and E.D. Thalmann. 1984. CNS Oxygen Toxicity in Closed-Circuit Scuba Divers. In: Bachrach, A.J., and M.M. Matzen, eds. *Underwater Physiology VIII.* Bethesda, MD: Undersea Medical Society, pp. 15-30.

Butler, F.K., Jr. 1986. Central Nervous System Oxygen Toxicity in Closed-Circuit Scuba Divers III. *Rept. 5-86.* Panama City, FL: U.S. Navy Experimental Diving Unit.

Butler, F.K., Jr., and E.D. Thalmann. 1986. Central nervous system oxygen toxicity in closed circuit scuba divers II. *Undersea Biomed. Res.* 13(2):193-223.

Calderelli, K.A. 1986. The use of benzocaine in recirculation anesthesia of laboratory and ornamental fish. In: Dierauf, L.A., ed. *Proceedings of the 17th Annual IAAAM Conference and Workshop,* Biloxi, MS.

Cardone, B.J. 1982. Air consumption tables. *Skin Diver* 31(7).

Chen, V. 1974. The prophylactic/therapeutic treatment of decompression sickness by heparin and aspirin. *Unpublished Master's Thesis* (Zoology). Texas A&M University, College Station, Tex.

Chouteau, J. 1969. Saturation diving: The Conshelf experiments. In: Bennett, P.B., and D.H. Elliott, eds. *The Physiology and Medicine of Diving and Compressed Air Work.* London: Bailliere Tindall.

Church, R. 1971. Beginner's Guide to Photography Underwater. Available from Ron Church Publications, P.O. Box 1163, La Jolla, CA.

Clark, J.M., and C.J. Lambertsen. 1971. Pulmonary oxygen toxicity: a review. *Pharmacol. Rev.* 23:37-133.

Clark, J.M., and C.J. Lambertsen. 1971. Rate of development of pulmonary O_2 toxicity in man during O_2 breathing at 2.0 ATA. *J. Appl. Physiol.* 30:739-752.

Clark, J.M. 1983. Oxygen toxicity. In: Bennett, P.B., and D.H. Elliott, eds. *The Physiology and Medicine of Diving and Compressed Air Work.* (3rd Ed.) London: Bailliere Tindall.

Clark, J.M., R. Gelfand, N.D. Flores, C.J. Lambertsen, and J.B. Pisarello. 1987. Pulmonary tolerance in man to continuous oxygen exposure at 3.0, 2.5, 2.0, and 1.5 ATA. In: Bove, A.A., A.J. Bachrach, and L.J. Greenbaum, eds. *Underwater and Hyperbaric Physiology.* Bethesda, MD.: Undersea and Hyperbaric Medical Society.

Clarke, J. 1996. Measurement of average resistance in underwater breathing apparatus. *Proceedings of the ASME Conference.* Houston, Texas.

Clarke, J. 1996. Work of Breathing in Underwater Breathing Apparatus and CO_2 Buildup. In: *Proceeding of the Rebreather Forum 2.0,* Diving Science and Technology, Santa Ana, CA pp. 69-75.

Clausen, C. 1975. Florida spring confirmed as 10,000 year old early man site. *Florida Anthropol.* 28(3): Part 2.

Clifton, H., R. Hunter, and R. Phillips. 1971. Depositional structures and processes in the non-barred high energy nearshore. *J. Sediment. Petrol.* 41: 651-670. (Note: detailed figure captions were published in J. Sediment. Petrol. 41(4):1 163-1164.)

Clifton, K.E. 1996. Field methods for the behavioral study of foraging ecology and life history of herbivorous coral-reef fishes. In: Lang, M.A., and C.C. Baldwin, eds. 1996. Methods and Techniques of Underwater Research. *Proc. of AAUS Scientific Diving Symp.* Smithsonian Institution, Washington, D.C. pp. 75-82.

Cockrell, W.A. 1978. Pleistocene man in Florida. *Archeol. East. North Am.* 6: Summer.

Colwell, R.R., ed. 1981. Special issue on microbial hazards of diving in polluted water. *Marine Technol. Soc. J.* 15(2).

Colwell, R.R. 1982. Microbial Hazards of Diving in Polluted Waters: a Proceedings. *Publication UM-SG-TS-82-01,* University of Maryland Sea Grant Program. College Park, MD.: University of Maryland.

Colwell, R.R., and D.J. Grimes. 1983. Microbiological/chemical hazards to divers in polluted waters. In: Lotz W.E., ed. *Protection of Divers in Water Containing Hazardous Chemicals, Pathogenic Organisms, and Radioactive Material.* Bethesda, MD.: Undersea Medical Society.

Comroe, J.H., Jr., R.D. Dripps, P.R. Durnke, and M. Deming. 1945. Oxygen toxicity for twenty-four hours in normal men at sea level and at a simulated altitude of 18,000 feet. *JAMA* 128:710-717.

Coolbaugh, J.C. 1983. Protection of divers in biologically polluted waters. In: Lotz, W.E., ed. *Protection of Divers in Water Containing Hazardous Chemicals, Pathogenic Organisms, and Radioactive Material.* Bethesda, MD.: Undersea Medical Society.

Cotter, J. 1981. Soft contact lens testing on fresh water scuba divers. *Contact Lens* 7:323-326.

Cox, D.R. 1958. *Planning of Experiments.* Wiley and Sons. p. 308

Cozens, G. 1980. Regulator roundup. *Skin Diver* 29:33-48.

Cozens, G. 1981a. Submersible pressure gauges. *Skin Diver* 30(3):49-58.

Cozens, G. 1981b. Shine on–an illuminating report on U/W handlights. *Skin Diver* 30(6):49-58.

Cramer, J.L. 1975. Comparative analysis of unaided emmetropic and unaided noncorrected myopic underwater visual acuity. *Res. Q. Am. Assoc. Health Phys. Ed.* 46:100-109.

Cratin, P., J. Warriner, M. Wert, T. DeGrow, and A. Bryson. 1973. Preliminary *in situ* physicochemical studies of oxygen in seawater. *Hydro-Lab J.* 2(1): 5-8.

Cross, E. 1967. Technifacts from a master diver. *Skin Diver* 16(12):60.

Cross, E. 1970. Technifacts: high altitude decompression. *Skin Diver* 19(11):17.

Crosson, D. 1989. Closed-circuit diving systems for science. *Proceedings of the 10th Meeting of the United States-Japan Cooperative Program in Natural Resources Panel on Diving Physiology and Technology.* Kaui, Hawaii; pp. 179-182.

Crosson, D. 1991. Human-technology integration as applied to advanced diving systems. *Proceedings of the 11th Meeting of the United States-Japan Cooperative Program in Natural Resources Panel on Diving Physiology and Technology.* Hakone, Shizuoka, Japan; pp. 409-413.

Crosson, D., and D. Youngblood. 1996. Current status of closed-circuit underwater breathing apparatus. *Life Support & Biosphere Science.* 2: pp. 111-115.

Dahl, A. 1973. Surface area in ecological analysis: quantification of benthic coral-reef algae. *Marine Biol.* 23(4): 239-249.

D'Aoust, B.G. 1977. *NOAA Diving Manual*, 1991, Rockville, MD: NOAA, U.S. Department of Commerce, R-3.

D'Aoust, B.G., K.H. Smith, H.T. Swanson, R. White, C.A. Harvey, W.D. Hunter, T.S. Neuman, and R.F. Goad. 1977. Venous gas bubbles: production by transient deep isobaric counter-diffusion of helium against nitrogen. *Science* 197:889-891.

D'Aoust, B.G., and C.J. Lambertsen. 1982. Isobaric gas exchange and supersaturation by counterdiffusion. In: Bennett, P.B., and D.H. Elliott, eds. *The Physiology and Medicine of Diving.* (3rd Ed.) London: Bailliere Tindall.

Daugherty, C.G. 1983. *Field Guide for the Diving Medic.* Flagstaff, AZ.: Best Publishing Co. (Distributed by National Association of Diver Medical Technicians.)

Davis, R.W. 1962. *Deep Diving and Submarine Operations.* (7th Ed.) Chessington, Surrey, U.K.: Siebe Gorman.

Dean, M. et al. 1992. Archeology Underwater: *The Nautical Archaeological Guide to Principles and Practice.* London.

Dean, T.A. 1985. The temporal and spatial distribution of underwater quantum irradiation in a Southern California kelp forest. *Estuar. Coast. Shelf Sci.* 21: 835-844.

Delgado, J.P., ed. 1997. *Encyclopedia of Underwater and Maritime Archaeology.* Yale University Press, New Haven.

Dembert, M.L., G.J. Beck, J.F. Jekel, and L.W. Mooney. 1984. Relations of smoking and diving experience to pulmonary function among U.S. Navy divers. *Undersea Biomed. Res.* 11(3):299-304.

Denny, M.W. 1983. A simple device for recording the maximum force exerted on intertidal organisms. *Limnol. Oceanogr.* 28: 1269-1274.

Dick, A. 1982. Diving Accident Network: immediate medical assistance for dive emergencies. *Skin Diver* 31(l0):33.

Dill, R., and D. Moore. 1965. A diver-held vane-shear apparatus. *Marine Geol.* 3: 323-327.

Dingler, J., J. Boylls, and R. Lowe. 1977. A high-frequency sonar for profiling small-scale subaqueous bedforms. *Marine Geol.* 24: 279-288.

Dinsmore, D.A. 1988. Use of optimal enriched air breathing mixtures to maximize dive time and operational flexibility. In: Lang, M.A., ed. Advances in Underwater Science. *Proceedings of the American Academy of Underwater Sciences, Eighth Annual Scientific Diving Symposium.* AAUS, 947 Newhall St., Costa Mesa, CA 92627. (NURC/UNCW R-88-05). pp. 33-40.

Dinsmore, D.A. 1989. Enriched air diving safety considerations. In: *Oceans '89 Proceedings.* The IEEE Service Center, 445 Hoes Lane, Piscataway, NJ 08854. (NURC/UNCW R-89-11). pp. 1695-1697.

Dinsmore, D.A. 1989. NURC/UNCW nitrox diving program. In: Hamilton, R.W., D. Crosson and A.W. Hulbert, eds. *Workshop on Enriched Air Nitrox Diving.* National Undersea Research Program Research Report 89(1), September 1989. (NURC/UNCW R-89-20). pp. 75-84.

Divers Alert Network (DAN). 2000. *Report on Decompression Illness and Diving Fatalities*. (Based on 1998 data). Durham, NC: Divers Alert Network.

Divers Alert Network (DAN). 2000. Report on Decompression Illness and Diving Fatalities. DAN (Publisher) Durham, NC. pp. 62, 63.

Divex 1997. Dirty Harry: *A Diving System for Use in Contaminated Waters*. Aberdeen, Scotland

Donald K. 1992. *Oxygen and the Diver*. The SPA Ltd., Worcestshire, England. pp. 237.

Dorr, V.A. 1971. Combustion Tests of Prototype Decompression Chamber Clothing. *Final Report. ONR Contract N00024-69-C-0201, Task 71-3*. Tarrytown, N.Y., Ocean Systems, Inc.

Doty, M.S. 1971. Measurement of water movement in reference to benthic algal growth. *Bot. Mar*. 14: 32-35.

Drew, C.B. 1988. Behavioral Ecology of Podded Red King Crabs Paralithodes camtschatica. In: Lang, M.A., ed. Advances in Underwater Science. *Proc. of AAUS Scientific Diving Symposium*. Scripps Institution of Oceanography, La Jolla, CA. pp. 13-26.

Dunford, R., and J. Hayford. 1981. Venous gas bubble production following cold stress during a no-decompression dive. *Undersea Biomed. Res.* 8(l):41-49.

Duntley, S.Q. 1963. Light in the sea. *J. Opt. Soc. Am*. 53:214-233.

Duntley, S.Q. 1976. Underwater vision. In: Adolfson, J., ed. Underwater 75. *Proceedings of the Fourth World Congress of Underwater Activities*. Vol. 2. Stockholm: Almqvist & Wiksell International.

Dunton, K.H. and D.M. Schell 1986. A Seasonal Carbon Budget for the Kelp Laminaria Solidungula in the Alaskan High Arctic. Mar. Ecol. Prog. Ser. 31: 57-66.

Ebert, E.E. 1964. Underwater tagging gun. *Cal. Fish Game* 50(l): 29-32.

Eckenhoff, R.G., and J.W. Parker. 1984. Latency in the onset of decompression sickness on direct ascent from air saturation. *J. App.I. Physiol.* 56:1070-1075.

Eckenhoff, R.G., and R.D. Vann. 1985. Air and nitrox saturation decompression: a report of 4 schedules and 77 subjects. *Undersea Biomed. Res.* 12(l):41-52.

Eckenhoff, R.G., S.F. Osborne, J.W. Parker, and K.R. Bondi. 1986. Direct ascent from shallow air saturation exposures. *Undersea Biomed. Res.* 13(3):305-316.

Edel, P. 1969. *NOAA Diving Manual*, 1991, Rockville, MD: NOAA, U.S. Department of Commerce, R-3.

Edel, P. 1969. Delineation of Emergency Surface Decompression and Treatment Procedures for Project Tektite Aquanauts. *Internal Report*. Pasadena, Tex.: J., and J. Marine Diving Co., Inc.

Edmonds, C., C. Lowry, and J. Pennefather. 1976. Nitrogen narcosis. In: *Diving and Subaquatic Medicine*. Mosman, Australia: Diving Medical Centre.

Edmonds, C., C. Lowry, and J. Pennefather. 1981. *Diving and Subaquatic Medicine*. (2nd Ed.) Mosman, Australia: Diving Medical Centre.

Edmonds, C., C. Lowry, and J. Pennefather. 1992. *Diving and Subaquatic Medicine* 3rd Ed. Butterworth Heinemann.

Egstrom, G.H. 1974. *Underwater Work Performance and Work Tolerance*. Bio-Technology Report, Department of Kinesiology, University of California at Los Angeles.

Egstrom, G.H. 1982. SCUBA diving practice and equipment. In: Bennett, P.B., and D.H. Elliott, eds. *The Physiology and Medicine of Diving*. (3rd. Ed.) London: Bailliere Tindall.

Egstrom, G.H. 1984. Emergency procedure: air sharing. *NAUI News*, May.

Elliott, D.H., and E.P. Kindwall. 1982. Manifestations of the decompression disorders. In: Bennett, P.B., and D.H. Elliott, eds. *The Physiology and Medicine of Diving*. (3rd. Ed.) London: Bailliere Tindall.

Emery, A. 1968. Underwater telescope. *Copeia* 3: 627-628.

Ennis, G. 1972. A diver-operated plankton collector. *J. Fish. Res. Board* (Canada) 29(3):341-343.

Fager, E., A. Fleichsig, R. Ford, R. Clutter, and R. Ghelardi. 1966. Equipment for use in ecological studies using scuba. *Limnol. Oceanography*. 11(4): 503-509.

Farmer, J., Jr. 1976. Inner ear decompression sickness. *Laryngoscope* 86(9):1315-1327.

Federal Register. 1984. *United States Code of Federal Regulations*. OSHA Commercial Diving Operations, 29 CFR 1910 subpart T,pp. 752-763.

Federal Register. 1984. *United States Code of Federal Regulations*. USCG Commercial Diving Operations, 46 CFR 197 subpart B.

Ferris, S.H. 1972. Magnitude estimation of absolute distance underwater. *Percept. Mot. Skills* 35:961-971.

Ferris, S.H. 1973. Improving distance estimation in clear and in turbid water. *Percept. Mot. Skills* 36:771-776.

Flynn, E.T., J. Maurer, and G.W. Latson. 1999. Acceleration of Saturation Decompression with 100% Oxygen. *Undersea Hyperbaric Med 26* (Suppl):pp. 46-47.

Foster, M.S., T.A. Dean and L.E. Deysher. 1985. Subtidal techniques,pp. 189-232. In: Littler, M.M., and D.S. Littler, eds. *Handbook of Phycological Methods. Ecological Field Methods: Macroalgae*. Cambridge Univ. Press. p.617

Fowler, B., K.N. Ackles, and G. Porlier. 1985. Effects of inert gas narcosis on behavior - a critical review. *Undersea Biomed. Res.* 12(4):369-402.

Frankenhaeuser, M., V. Graff-Lonnevig, and C.M. Hesser. 1960. Psychomotor performance in man as affected by high oxygen pressure (3 ATA). *Acta Physiol. Scand.* 50:1.

Gale, W.F. 1977. River diving devices. *Skin Diver* 26(10).

Galerne, A. 1989. The use of nitrox in the diving industry. In: Hamilton, R.W., D. Crosson, and A.W. Hulbert, eds. *Workshop on Enriched Air Nitrox Diving*. National Undersea Research Report Program Research Report 89(1), September 1989.pp. 43-50.

Genovese, S.J., and J.D. Witman. 1997. Particle flux measurement in deep (25-40m) suspension-feeding communities in the Gulf of Maine. In: Maney, E.J. Jr., and C.H. Ellis, Jr., eds., Diving for Science. 1997. *Proc. of AAUS Scientific Diving Symp*. Boston, MA.pp. 59-69.

Gibson, R. 1967. The use of the anesthetic quinaldine in fish ecology. *J. Animal Ecol.* 36(2): 295-301.

Gilbert, P.W., and F. Wood. 1957. Method of anesthetizing large sharks and rays safely and rapidly. *Science* 126(1266): 212-213.

Gilderhus, P., B. Berger, J. Sills, and P. Harman. 1973a. The efficacy of quinaldine sulfate as an anesthetic for freshwater fish. *Investigations in Fish Control. Report No. 49*. LaCrosse, Wis.: Bureau of Sport Fisheries and Wildlife.

Gilderhus, P., B. Berger, J. Sills, and P. Harman. 1973b. The efficacy of quinaldine sulfate:MS-222 mixtures for the anesthetization of freshwater fish. *Investigations in Fish Control. Report No. 54*. LaCrosse, Wis.: Bureau of Sport Fisheries and Wildlife.

Gittings, S.R., K.J.P. Deslarzes, B.S. Holland, and G.S. Boland. 1990. Ecological monitoring on the Flower Gardens Banks: Study design and field methods. In: Jaap, W.C., ed. Diving for Science. 1990, Proc. of *AAUS Scientific Diving Symposium*. St. Petersburg, FL. pp. 107-118.

Glowe, D. 1983. *Final Report Chemical Compatibility Testing of Diving Related Material*. Texas Research Institute. Austin, TX.

Gould, R.A., ed., 1983. *Shipwreck Anthropology*. University of New Mexico Press, Albuquerque.

Graver, D. 1985. The octopus. *Skin Diver* 34(3):11.

Graver, D. 1987. Scuba quiz, diving out of air ascents. *Skin Diver* 36(l):15-16.

Green, J. 1990. *Maritime Archaeology: A Technical Handbook*. Academic Press, London.

Grove, R.S., and C. Sonu. 1985. Fishing reef planning in Japan. In: D'Itri, F.M., ed. *Artificial Reefs: Marine and Freshwater Applications*. Chelsea, Mich.: Lew Publishers, Inc.

Guidelines 2000 for Cardiopulmonary Resuscitation and Emergency Cardiovascular Care, American Heart Association, Part 1, p. 3.

Hackett, M. 1988. Desert Diving: The ICSURT Story. *The Backup: Official Publication of the California Reserve Peace Officers Association*. Santa Ana, CA: Trident Media, (Sept./Oct.) 8(4):10-15.

Hackman, D.J., and D.W. Caudy. 1981. *Underwater Tools*. Columbus, Ohio: Battelle Press.

Hall, H. 1980a. Professional dive mask roundup. *Skin Diver* 29(2):59-70.

Hall, H. 1980b. Pro dive final roundup. *Skin Diver* 29(3):47-58.

Hall, H. 1980c. Dry suit roundup. *Skin Diver* 29(12):33-42.

Hall, H. 1982. Morrow's dive ray gives you super vision up to 99 feet away. *Skin Diver* 31(2).

Halley, R.B., E.A. Shinn, J.H. Hudson, and B. Lidz. 1977. Recent and relict topography of boo bee patch reef, Belize. In: *Proceedings of the Third International Coral Reef Symposium*. Miami, FL.

Hamilton, R.W., D.J. Kenyon, M. Freitag, and H.R. Schreiner. 1973. NOAA OPS I and II: Formulation of Excursion Procedures for Shallow Undersea Habitats. *Internal Memorandum UCRI-731*. Tarrytown, NY.: Union Carbide Corp.

Hamilton, R.W., D.J. Kenyon, and R.E. Peterson. 1980. Effect of Duration of Exposure to M-Values on Their Validity. In: Berghage, T.E., ed. *Decompression Theory*, 29WS(DT)6-25-80. Bethesda, MD: Undersea Medical Society.

Hamilton, R.W., G.M. Adams, C.A. Harvey, and D.R. Knight. 1982. SHAD-Nisat: A Composite Study of Simulated Shallow Saturation Diving. *Report 985*. Groton, Conn.: Naval Submarine Medical Research Laboratory.

Hamilton, R.W., T.C. Schmidt, and S.D. Reimers. 1983. Fire safety: welding in hyperbaric air. In: Ackles, K.N., ed. *Proceedings of the Second Canadian Ocean Technology Congress*. Toronto, Canada: Association of Diving Contractors.

Hamilton, R.W., D.J. Kenyon, R.E. Peterson, G.J. Butler, and D.M. Beers. 1988. Repex: Development of Repetitive Excursions, Surfacing Techniques, and Oxygen Procedures for Habitat Diving. *National Undersea Research Program Technical Report 88-lA*. Rockville, MD: NOAA, U.S. Department of Commerce.

Hamilton, R.W., D.J. Kenyon, and R.E. Peterson. 1988. Repex Habitat Diving Procedures: Repetitive Vertical Excursions, Oxygen Limits, and Surfacing Techniques. *National Undersea Research Program Technical Report 88-lB*. Rockville, MD: NOAA, U.S. Department of Commerce.

References

Hamilton, R.W. 1989 Dec. Tolerating exposure to high oxygen levels: Repex and other methods. *Marine Tech Soc J* 23(4):19-25.

Hamilton, R.W. 1997. Mixed-Gas Diving. In: Bove, A.A., ed. *Diving Medicine*, (3rd Ed.) Philadelphia: WB Saunders.

Hamner, W.M. 1975. Underwater observations of blue-water plankton: logistics, techniques and safety procedures for divers at sea. *Limnol. Oceanogr.* 20:1045-1051.

Harvey, B., C. Denny, J. Marliave, and P. Bruecker. 1986. *New Sedation Techniques for Sharks: Saffan Administered by Underwater Dart Gun.* Unpubl. Ms.

Heine, J.N. 1999. *Scientific Diving Techniques: A Practical Guide for the Research Diver.* Flagstaff, AZ: Best Publishing Co., p.225

Heine, J.N. 1985. *Blue Water Diving Guidelines.* Moss Landing: California State University.

Hendricks, P.L., D.A. Hall, W.L. Hunter, Jr., and P.J. Haley. 1977. Extension of pulmonary oxygen tolerance in man at 2 ATA by intermittent oxygen exposure. *J. Appl. Physiol.* 42:593-599.

Herrnkind, W., and J. Engle. 1977. Personal Communication.

Hesser, C.M. 1963. Measurement of inert gas narcosis in man. In: Lambertsen, C.J., and L.J. Greenbaum, eds. *Underwater Physiology II. Proceedings of the Second Symposium on Underwater Physiology.* Washington, D.C.: National Academy of Sciences.

Hesser, C.M., J. Adolfson, and L. Fagraeus. 1971. Role of CO_2 in compressed air narcosis. *Aerosp. Med.* 42:163-168.

High, W.L. 1967. *Scuba Diving, A Valuable Tool for Investigating the Behavior of Fish Within the Influence of Fishing Gear.* Paper presented at the FAO Conference on Fish Behavior in Relation to Fishing Techniques and Tactics. Bergen, Norway: Food and Agriculture Organization of the United Nations.

High, W.L., and I.E. Ellis. 1973. Underwater observations of fish behavior in traps. *Helgol. Wiss. Meeresunters* 24: 341-347.

High, W.L. 1986a. Significance of scuba cylinder codes. *NDA News.* (Jan./Feb.) Montclair, CA.: NAUI Diving Association.

High, W.L. 1986b. Cylinder codes. *NDA News.* (Mar./Apr.) Montclair, CA.: NAUI Diving Association.

High, W.L. 1987. *A Guide for Visual Inspection of Scuba and Scuba Cylinders.* Montclair, CA.: National Association of Underwater Instructors.

High, W.L. 1987. Compressor filters corrode too. *NDA News.* (Jan./Feb.) Montclair, CA.: NAUI Diving Association.

High, W.L. 1993. Observations of a scientist-diver on fishing technology and fisheries biology. Resource Assessment and Conservation Engineering Division, *Alaska Fisheries Science Center,* Seattle, WA. p.48

Hollien, H., and H. Rothman. 1976. Diver communication. In: *Research Underwater.* London: Academic Press.

Hollien, H., and J.W. Hicks, Jr. 1983. Diver navigation by sound beacon. *Sea Grant Today* 13(l):10-1 1.

Holmer, I. 1989. Body cooling with ice for warm-water diving operation. In: *Undersea Biomedical Research,* Bethesda, MD. Vol. 16, No. 6. pp. 471-479.

Holmes, C.D. 1962. Introduction to College Geology. New York: Macmillan Co.

Holmes, N.A., and A.D. McIntyre. 1971. *Methods for Study of Marine Benthos.* IBP Handbook No. 16. Philadelphia: F.A. Davis Company.

Houston, A., R. Madden, R. Woods, and H. Miles. 1971. Some physiological effects of handling and tricaine methanesulphonate anesthetization upon the brook trout, Salvelinus fontinalis. *J. Fisheries Res. Board* (Canada) 28(5): 625-633.

Howland, R. 1969. Laboratory studies of possible fish collecting aids with some toxicities for the isomers of cresol. *Investigations in Fish Control.* Report No. 34. LaCrosse, Wis.: Bureau of Sport Fisheries and Wildlife.

Howland, R., and R. Schoettger. 1969. Efficacy of methylpentynol as an anesthetic on four salmonids. *Investigations in Fish Control.* Report No. 29. LaCrosse, Wis.: Bureau of Sport Fisheries and Wildlife.

Hubbard, D.K., R.B. Burke, and I.P. Gill. 1985. Accretion in deep, shelf-edge reefs, St. Croix, USVI. In: Crevello, P.D., and P.M. Harris, eds. *Deep-Water Carbonates, A Core Workshop.* SEPM Workshop No. 6, pp. 491-527.

Hudson, J.H. 1972. Marking scallops with quick-setting cement. In: *Proc. Nat. Shellfisheries Assoc.* 62.

Hudson, J.H. 1977. Long-term bioerosion rates on a Florida reef: a new method. In: *Proceedings of the Third International Coral Reef Symposium* 2: 492-497.

Hunter, W.L., Jr., R.J. Biersner, R. Spahr, and C. Harvey. 1978. Aseptic bone necrosis among U.S. Navy divers: survey of 934 nonrandomly selected personnel. *Undersea Biomed. Res.* 5(1):25-36.

Hunter, W.L., Jr., and R.J. Biersner. 1982. Comparison of long-bone radiographs between U.S. Navy divers and matched controls. *Undersea Biomed. Res.* 9 (2):147-159.

Inman, D. 1957. *Wave-Generated Ripples in Nearshore Sands.* Beach Erosion Board, U.S. Army Corps of Engineers, Tech. Memo No. 100.

Jeppesen Open Water Sport Diver Manual. 1989. (4th Ed.) Englewood, Colo.: Jeppesen Sanderson, Inc. (Copyrighted by Mosby Year Book, Inc., St. Louis)

Jerlov, N.G. 1976. Marine optics. In: *Oceanographic Series No. 14.* Amsterdam: Elsevier.

Johnson, A.S., and K.P. Sebens. 1993. Consequences of a flattened morphology: Effects of flow on feeding rates of the scleractinian coral Meandrina meandrites. *Mar. Ecol. Prog. Series* 99(1-2): 99-114.

Kall, C.H. 1984. A computer controlled air-bag lift system. In: *Underwater Syst. Design,* (Oct./Nov.): pp. 24-26.

Kent, M.B., ed. 1979. Emergency Ascent Training. *Undersea Medical Society Workshop Report. UMS Publication No. 32,* WS (EAT) 10-31-79. Bethesda MD.: Undersea Medical Society.

Kesling, D. and R. Berey 1989. Training, Equipment and Operational Procedures for Conducting Scientific Saturation Diving Activities. In: Lang, M.A. and W.C. Jaap, eds. Proceedings of American Academy of Underwater Sciences, Ninth Annual Scientific Diving Symposium. Costa Mesa, CA. pp. 199-211.

Kesling, D. 1998. The Age of Aquarius. In: Lang, M.A. ed. Proceedings of American Academy of Underwater Sciences. Eighth Annual American Academy of Underwater Sciences, Scientific Diving Symposium. Costa Mesa, CA. pp. 89-92.

Kindwall, E.P. 1972. Aseptic bone necrosis in persons who work under pressure. Occupational safety and health problems of the diving industry. In: *Offshore Petroleum Production. Medical Research Report No. EA 7104.* Washington, D.C.: American Petroleum Institute.

Kindwall, E.P. 1976. Medical examination of divers. In: Strauss, R.H., ed. *Diving Medicine.* New York: Grune and Stratton.

Kindwall, E.P. 1999. Hyperbaric Oxygen Therapy. In: *The Merck Manual,* 17th Ed. Merck Sharp End Dohue Research Laboratories. Raway, N.J. Merck and Co.

Kinney, J.A.S., S.M. Luria, and D.O. Weitzman. 1967. Visibility of colors underwater. *J. Opt. Soc. Am.* 57:802-809.

Kinney, J.A.S., S.M. Luria, and D.O. Weitzman. 1969. Visibility of colors underwater using artificial illumination. *J. Opt. Soc. Am.* 59:624-628.

Kinney, J.A.S. 1985. *Human Underwater Vision: Physiology and Physics.* Bethesda, MD.: Undersea Medical Society.

Kinney, J.A.S., and J.W. Miller. 1974. Judgments of the Visibility of Colors Made from an Underwater Habitat. *Naval Submarine Medical Research Laboratory Report No. 777.* Groton, Conn.: Naval Submarine Medical Research Laboratory.

Kirk, J. 1998. Proposed minimum requirements for the operational characteristics and testing of closed-circuit life support system control electronics. *Life Support & Biosphere Science* 5(1): pp. 97-105.

Kizer, K.W. 1984. Aquatic rescue and in-water CPR. *NAUI News,* Jan.

Klontz, G., and L. Smith. 1968. Methods of using fish as biological research subjects. In: Gay, W.L., ed. *Methods of Animal Experimentation.* New York: Academic Press.

Koblick, I. et al. 1974. *NOAA Diving Manual,* 1991, Rockville, MD: NOAA, U.S. Department of Commerce, R-5.

Koblick, I., J. Biaggi, D. Olsen, and E. Geiger. 1974. Undersea labs for marine resource inventory. *Marine Technol. Soc. J.* 8(l):12-18.

Kollias, J., L. Barlett, V. Bergsteinova, J.S. Skinner, E.R. Buskirk, and W.C. Nicholas. 1974. Metabolic and thermal responses of women during cooling in water. *J. Appl. Physiol.* 36:577-580.

LaFond, E.C., and R. Dill. 1957. Do bubbles exist in the sea? *USNEL Technical Memorandum* 259. San Diego: US Navy Electronics Lab.

LaFond, E.C. 1962. Internal waves. In: Hill, M.N., ed. *The Sea, Interscience,* New York.

Lake, T. 1983. How to tag fish. *Bull. Am. Littoral Soc.* 14(3):16-19.

Lambertsen, C.J. 1967. Origins of saturation diving. In: Lambertsen, C.J., ed. Underwater Physiology III. *Proceedings of the Third Symposium on Underwater Physiology.* Baltimore, MD.: Williams & Wilkins.

Lambertsen, C.J., and W.B. Wright. 1973. Multiday exposure of men to high nitrogen pressure and increased airway resistance at natural inspired oxygen tension: a 14-day continuous exposure to 5.2% O_2 in N_2 at 4 ATA pressure. *Aerosp. Med.* 44(7):821-869.

Lambertsen, C.J., R. Gelfand, R. Peterson, R. Strauss, W.B. Wright, J.G. Dickson, Jr., C. Puglia, and R.W. Hamilton. 1977. *Human Tolerance to He, Ne, and N2 at Respiratory Gas Densities Equivalent to He-O2 Breathing at Depth to 1,200, 2,000, 3,000, 4,000 and 5,000 feet of Sea Water. (Predictive Studies III). Aviation, Space, and Environmental Medicine.*

Lambertsen, C.J. 1978. Effects of hyperoxia on organs and their tissues. In: Robin, E., ed. *Extrapulmonary Manifestations of Respiratory Disease.* New York: Marcel Dekker.

Lambertsen, C.J., J.M. Clark, R. Gelfand, J.B. Pisarello, W.H. Cobbs, J.E. Bevilacqua, D.M. Schwartz, D.J. Montabana, C.S. Leachy, P.C. Johnson, and D.E. Fletcher. 1987. Definition of tolerance to continuous hyperoxia in man. In: Bove, A.A., A.J. Bachrach, and L.J. Greenbaum, eds. Underwater and Hyperbaric Physiology IX. *Proceedings of the Ninth International Symposium on Underwater and Hyperbaric Physiology*. Bethesda, MD.: Undersea and Hyperbaric Medical Society.

Lang, M.A., and R.W. Hamilton, eds. 1989. *Proceedings of Dive Computer Workshop*, USC Catalina Marine Science Center. Costa Mesa, CA: AAUS

Langley, T.D., and R.W. Hamilton, Jr. 1975. Somatic-evoked brain responses as indicators of adaptation to nitrogen narcosis. *Aviat. Space Environ. Med.* 46:147-151.

Lanphier, E.H. 1983. Should women dive? In: Shiraki, K., and S. Matsuda, eds. *Hyperbaric Medicine and Underwater Physiology*. Bethesda, MD.: Undersea Medical Society.

Larsen, R.T., and W.F. Mazzone. 1967. Excursion diving from saturation exposures at depth. In: Lambertsen, C.J., ed. Underwater Physiology III: *Proceedings of the Third Underwater Physiology Symposium*. Baltimore, MD.: Williams & Wilkins.

Larson, H.E. 1959. *A History of Self-Contained Diving and Underwater Swimming.* Washington, D.C.: National Academy of Sciences–National Research Council.

LaRue, S. 1986. Teledyne Accused of Dumping PCB's into San Diego Bay. *San Diego Union*, July 24th, pp. B-1, D-7.

Lees, D.C. 1968. Tagging subtidal echinoderms. Underwater Natural. *Bull. Am. Littoral Soc.* 5(3): 16-19.

Lehner, C.E., C. Rynning, M.E. Bolton, and E.H. Lanphier. 1982. *Fetal Death During Decompression Studies in Sheep*. Poster sessions presented at the University of Wisconsin. Sea Grant Institute.

Leichter, J.J., S.R. Wing, S.L. Miller and M.W. Denny. 1996. Pulsed delivery of subthermocline water to Conch Reef (Florida Keys) by internal tidal bores. *Limnol. Oceanogr.* 41(7): 1490-1501.

Leichter, J.J., G. Shellenbarger, S.J. Genovese and S.R. Wing. 1998. Breaking waves on a Florida (USA) coral reef: a plankton pump at work? *Mar. Ecol. Prog. Ser.* 166: 83-97.

Lenihan, D.J. 1994. *Shipwrecks of Isle Royale National Park.* Lake Superior Port Cities, Duluth.

Limsowan, C., J.M. Grissle, and J.A. Plumb. 1983. Etomidate as an anesthetic for fish: its toxicity and efficacy. *Trans. Am. Fish. Soc.* 112: 544-550.

Linnarsson, D., A. Ostlund, A. Sporrong, F. Lind, and R.W. Hamilton. 1990. Does Oxygen Contribute to the Narcotic Action of Hyperbaric Air? In: Sterk, W., and L. Geeraedts, eds. *Proceedings XVIth Meeting of the European Undersea Biomedical Society*. Amsterdam: Foundation for Hyperbaric Medicine.

Littler, M.M., and D.S. Littler. 1985. Nondestructive Sampling. In: Littler, M.M., and D.S. Littler, eds. *Handbook of Phycological Methods, Ecological Field Methods: Macroalgae*. Cambridge University Press. pp. 162-175.

Locke, D. 1969. Quinaldine as an anesthetic for brook trout, lake trout and Atlantic salmon. In: *Investigations in Fish Control*. Report No. 24. LaCrosse, Wis.: Bureau of Sport Fisheries and Wildlife.

Lotz, W.E., ed. 1982. *Protection of Divers in Water Containing Hazardous Chemicals, Pathogenic Organisms and Radioactive Material*. Undersea and Hyperbaric Medical Society, 10531 Metropolitan Ave., Kensington, MD, 20895: UMS Pub# CR 60(CW) 2-1-83.

Luria, S.M., and J.A.S. Kinney. 1969. Visual Acuity Under Water Without a Face Mask. Naval *Submarine Medical Research Laboratory Report No. 581.* Groton, Conn.: Naval Submarine Medical Research Laboratory.

Luria, S.M., and J.A.S. Kinney. 1974a. Visibility of Colored Targets in Free-Swimming Scuba Search. *Naval Submarine Medical Research Laboratory Report No. 769.* Groton, Conn.: Naval Submarine Medical Research Laboratory.

Luria, S.M., and J.A.S. Kinney. 1974b. Vision in the Water Without a Face Mask. *Naval Submarine Medical Research Laboratory Report No. 795.* Groton, Conn.: Naval Submarine Medical Research Laboratory.

Lyne, A.J. 1978. Ocular effects of hyperbaric oxygen. Trans. *Ophthalmol. Soc.* U.K. 98(l):66-68.

McAniff, J.J. 1986. U.S. *Underwater Diving Fatality Statistics 1983-1984*. Kingston, R.I.: University of Rhode Island.

McCallum, R.I., and J.A.B. Harrison. 1982. Dysbaric osteonecrosis: aseptic necrosis of bone. In: Bennett, P.B., and D.H. Elliott, eds. *The Physiology and Medicine of Diving*. (3rd Ed.) London: Bailliere Tindall.

McClellan. 1982. *Analysis of Material Release Data to Determine the "Typical" Spill Environment.* Paper presented at Undersea Medical Society Workshop on Protection of Divers in Interior Waters. Bethesda, MD.: Undersea Medical Society.

McFarland, W. 1959. A study of the effects of anesthetics on the behavior and physiology of fishes. *Inst. Marine Sci.* 6:23-55.

McFarland, W. 1960. The use of anesthetics for the handling and transport of fishes. *Cal. Fish Game* 46(4):407-431.

Mclver, R.G. 1968. Bends resistance in the fetus. Abstract Only. In: *Preprint of the Scientific Program for the Annual Scientific Meeting of the Aerospace Medical Association,* May 1968.

Macintyre, I.G. 1975. A diver-operated hydraulic drill for coring submerged substrates. *Atoll Research Bulletin* 185: 21-26.

Macintyre, I.G., and P.W. Glynn. 1976. Evolution of modern Caribbean fringing reefs. *Bull. Am. Assoc. Petrol. Geol.* 60:1054-1072.

Macintyre, I.G. 1977. Distribution of submarine cements in a modern Caribbean fringing reef. *J. Sed. Petrol.* 57:503- 516.

Macintyre, I.G. 1978. A hand-operated submersible drill for coring reef substrata. In: Stoddart, D.R., and R.E. Johannes, eds. Coral Reefs: Research Methods. *UNESCO Monographs on Oceanographic Methodology.*

Macintyre, I.G., R.B. Burke and R. Stuckenrath. 1981. Core holes in the outer fore reef off Carrie Bow Cay, Belize: A Key to the Holocene History of the Belizean Barrier Reef Complex. *Proc. Fourth Int'l Coral Reef Symp.*, Manila 1: 567-574.

Macintyre, I.G., M.M. Littler and D.S. Littler. 1995. Holocene history of Tobacco Range, Belize, Central America. *Atoll Research Bulletin*. No. 430. p. 18

Marshall, J., and P.J. Davies. 1982. Internal structure and holocene evolution of One Tree Reef, Southern Great Barrier Reef. *Coral Reefs* 1:21-28.

Marx, J., and W. Herrnkind. 1985. Factors regulating microhabitat use by young juvenile spiny lobsters, Panulirus argus: food and shelter. *J. Crustac. Biol.* 5:650-657.

Mastro, S.J. 1989. Use of two primary breathing mixtures for enriched air diving operations. In: Lang, M.A., and W.C. Jaap, eds. Diving for Science . 89. *Proceedings of the American Academy of Underwater Sciences Ninth Annual Scientific Diving Symposium*. AAUS, 947 Newhall St., Costa Mesa, CA 92627. pp. 241-247.

Mastro, S.J., and D.A. Dinsmore. 1989. The operational advantages of Enriched Air Nitrox versus air for research diving. *MTS Journal* 23(4):42-46. (NURC/UNCW J-89-09).

Mastro, S.J., and G. Butler. 1990. Air quality requirements for the on-site production of oxygen enriched breathing mixtures. In: *Oceans '90 Proceedings*. The IEEE Service Center, 445 Hoes Lane, Piscataway, NJ 08854.

Mathewson, R.D., III. 1977. *Method and Theory in New World Historic Wreck Archaeology: Hypothesis Testing on the Site of Nuestra Senora de Atocha, Marquesas Keys, Florida.* Unpublished Master's Thesis. Florida Atlantic University, Boca Raton, FL.

Mathewson, R.D., III. 1981. *A Cultural Resource Survey of the Continental Shelf From Cape Hatteras to Key West.* New Orleans, LA.: Bureau of Land Management.

Mathewson, R.D., III. 1983. *Archaeological Treasure: The Search for Nuestra Senora de Atocha.* Woodstock Vt.: Seafarers Heritage Library.

Mathewson, R.D., III. 1986. *Treasure of the Atocha.* New York: Pisces Books.

Mazel, C.H. 1997. Diver-operated instrument for *in situ* measurement of spectral fluorescence and reflectance of benthic marine organisms and substrates. *Optical Engineering* 36(9): 2612-2617.

Mebane, G., and A. Dick. 1985. DAN *Underwater Diving Accident Manual*. (Rev. Ed.) Durham, NC.: Duke University Medical Center.

Merifield, P., and D. Rosencrantz. 1966. A simple method for surveying a small area underwater. *Limnol. Oceanogr.* 11(3):408-409.

Mertens, L. 1970. *In-Water Photography: Theory and Practice.* New York: Wiley-Interscience.

Miller, J.W., J. VanDerwalder, and R. Waller, eds. 1971. *Tektite II, Scientists-in-the-Sea.* Washington: U.S. Government Printing Office.

Miller, J.W. 1976. *NOAA Diving Manual*, 1991, Rockville, MD: NOAA, U.S. Department of Commerce, R-7.

Miller, J.W., ed. 1976. *Vertical Excursions Breathing Air from Nitrogen-Oxygen or Air Saturation Exposures.* U.S. Dept. of Commerce, National Oceanic and Atmospheric Administration.

Miller, J.W., and I.G. Koblick. eds. 1984, 1995. *Living and Working in the Sea.* New York: Van Nostrand Reinhold.

Moring, J. 1970. Use of the anesthetic quinaldine for handling Pacific Coast intertidal fishes. *Trans. Am. Fish. Soc.* 99(4): 803-806.

Morrison, J., and S. Reimers. 1982. Design principles of underwater breathing apparatus. In: Bennett, P.B., and D.H. Elliott, eds. *The Physiology and Medicine of Diving*. (3rd Ed.) London: Bailliere Tindall: pp. 55-95.

Muckelroy, K. 1978. Maritime Archaeology. *New Studies in Archaeology.* Cambridge.

Muckelroy, K. 1980. *Archaeology Under Water: An Atlas of the World's Submerged Sites.* New York.

References

Muren, A., J.A. Adolfson, H.C. Ornhagen, M. Gennser, and R.W. Hamilton. 1984. Nisahex: excursions with nitrox and trimix from deep nitrox saturation. In: Bachrach, A.J., and M.M. Matzen, eds. *Underwater Physiology VIII. Proceedings of the Eighth Symposium on Underwater Physiology.* Bethesda, MD.: Undersea Medical Society.

Murphy, G. 1980. Snorkel roundup. *Skin Diver* 29(9):37-48.

Murphy, G. 1987. The whale sharpeye: underwater color without flash. *Skin Diver* 36(5):46-47.

Murphy, G. 1987-1988. Nikonos photo course. *Skin Diver* pp. 36-37.

Murphy, R. 1985. Artifact preservation. *Skin Diver* 34(4):97-102. 119.

Muus, B.J. 1968. A field method for measuring "exposure" by means of plaster balls. *Sarsia* 34:61-68.

Nadel, E.R. 1984. Energy exchanges in water. *Undersea Biomed. Res.* 11(2):149-158.

National Aeronautics and Space Administration. 1973. J. Parker and V. West, eds. *Bioastronautics Data Book.* (2nd Ed.) Washington: U.S. Government Printing Office.

National Fire Protection Association. 1979. Fire Hazards in Oxygen-Enriched Atmospheres. *NFPA Report No. 53M.* Boston, Mass.: National Fire Protection Association.

National Fire Protection Association. 1984. *99 Health Care Facilities.* Quincy, Mass.: National Fire Protection Association.

Naval Facilities Engineering Command. 1972. Design Manual, Hyperbaric Facilities. *Report NAVFAC DM-39,* Washington, D.C.: Department of the Navy.

NAVSEA (see U.S. Department of the Navy)

Nemiroff, M.J., J.R. Willson, and T.H. Kirschbaum. 1981. Multiple hyperbaric exposures during pregnancy in sheep. *Am. J. Obstet. Gynecol.* 140(6):651-655.

Newton, R. 1968. Internal structure of wave-formed ripple marks in the nearshore zone. *Sedimentol.* 11:275-292.

NOAA Diving Manual. 1979. (2nd Ed.) Washington, D.C.: U.S. Government Printing Office.

Nuckols, M.L., J. Clarke and C. Grupe. 1998. Maintaining safe oxygen levels in semiclosed underwater breathing apparatus. *Life Support & Biosphere Science* 5(1): pp. 87-95.

Nuckols, M.L., J. Clarke and W.J. Marr. Future date. Assessment of oxygen levels in alternative designs of semiclosed underwater breathing apparatus. *Life Support & Biosphere Science.*

Orr, D. 1981. Viable alternatives for the scuba rescuer. *NAUI News,* (May/June).

Palmer, R. 1994. *An Introduction to Technical Diving.* Underwater World Publications.

Pauli, D., and H. Cole, eds. 1970. Project Tektite I. U.S. Dept. of the Navy, *ONR Report DR 153.* Washington, D.C.: U.S. Government Printing Office.

Pegnato, P.E. 1986. Recent developments in equipment and procedures for diving in waters containing hazardous substances. In: *Proceedings of the Eighth Meeting of the UJNR Panel on Diving Physiology and Technology.* Symposium Series for Undersea Research 4(1). Rockville, MD.: Undersea Research Program, National Oceanic and Atmospheric Administration.

Penzias, W., and M. Goodman. 1973. *Man Beneath the Sea, A Review of Underwater Ocean Engineering.* New York: John Wiley and Sons.

Peterson, R.E., R.W. Hamilton, and I. Curtsell. 1980. Control of Counterdiffusion Problems in Underwater Dry Welding. Paper presented at Association of Diving Contractors. *International Diving Symposium '80.* Gretna, LA.

Phoel, W. 1981. NOAA's requirements and capabilities for diving in polluted waters. *Mar. Technol. Soc. J.* 15(2):4-9.

Photosea Systems Inc. 1984. 'Time-lapse' stereo photogrammetry system. *Int. Underwater Sys. Des.* 6:6.

Pierce, A.L. 1977. Mouth to Mouth vs. Mouth to Snorkel: Shouldn't We Be Able to Give Air Both Ways? *Private Publication.* 663 Parkview Blvd., Yeadon, PA.

Pierce, A.L. 1983. Your buoyancy compensator: an emergency source of breathable air. *NAUI News,* (Sept/Oct).

Pierce, A.L. 1985. *Scuba Life Saving.* Royal Life Saving Society, 64 Charles Street East, Toronto, Canada.

Pisarello, J.B., J.M. Clark, C.J. Lambertsen, and R. Gelfand. 1987. Human circulatory responses to prolonged hyperbaric hyperoxia in Predictive Studies V. In: Bove, A.A., A.J. Bachrach, and L.J. Greenbaum, eds. Underwater and Hyperbaric Physiology IX. *Proceedings of the Ninth International Symposium on Underwater and Hyperbaric Physiology.* Bethesda, MD.: Undersea and Hyperbaric Medical Society.

Plueckhahn, V.D. 1984. Alcohol and Accidental drowning. Medical Journal of Australia 2. pp. 22-25.

Powell, M.R., and M.T. Smith. 1985. Fetal and maternal bubbles detected noninvasively in sheep and goats following hyperbaric decompression. *Undersea Biomed. Res.* 12:59-67.

Pratt, H.W. 1976. The Pratt Macrosnooper, a 7X Under water Magnifying System. *National Marine Fisheries Service, Northeast Fisheries Center,* National Oceanic and Atmospheric Administration.

Pyle, R.A. 1996. Lerner's Guide to Closed Circuit Rebreather Operations. In: *Proceedings of the Rebreather Forum 2.0,* Diving Science and Technology, Santa Ana, CA. pp. 49-67.

Randall, J. 1961. Tagging reef fishes in the Virgin Islands. In: *Proceedings of the Fourteenth Annual Session of the Gulf and Caribbean Fisheries Institute.*

Richardson, L.L., and R.G. Carlton. 1993. Behavioral and chemical aspects of black band disease of corals: An *in situ* field and laboratory study. In: Heine, J.N., and N.L. Crane, eds. Diving for Science. 1993, *Proc. of AAUS Scientific Diving Symposium.* Monterey, CA. pp. 107-116.

Rodwell, M.H., and R.J. Moulton. 1985. Fabric Flammability Under Hyperbaric Conditions. *Report No. OT.0.85009.* Cambridge, U.K.: The Welding Institute.

Ross, H., and M.H. Rejman. 1972. Adaptation to speed distortions under water. Br. *J. Psychol.* 63:257-264.

Rottman, K. 1982. Barodontalgia–it must be tooth squeeze. *Skin Diver* 31(2):6.

Rule, N. 1989. The Direct Survey Method (DSM) of Underwater Survey and its Application Underwater. *International Journal of Nautical Archaeology* 18(2): 157-162.

Rutkowski, R. 1985. *Diving Accident Manual,* National Oceanic and Atmospheric Administration.

Ryan, E., and J.F. Bass. 1962. Underwater surveying and draughting: a technique. *Antiquity* 36(144): 252-261.

Salsman, G., and W. Tolbert. 1965. Observations on the sand dollar, Mellita quinquiesperforata. *Limnol. Oceanogr.* 10(1): 152-155.

Schmidt, T.C., R.W. Hamilton, Jr., C. Moeller, and C.P. Chattin. 1974. Cognitive and Psychomotor Performance During NOAA OPS I and II. Tech. Memo. Report CRL-T-799, 23. Tarrytown, N.Y.: Union Carbide Corporation.

Schoettger, R., and A. Julin. 1967. Efficacy of MS-222 as an anesthetic on four salmonids. *Investigations in Fish Control.* Report No. 13. LaCrosse, Wis.: Bureau of Sport Fisheries and Wildlife.

Schoettger, R., and A. Julin. 1969. Efficacy of quinaldine as an anesthetic for seven species of fish. *Investigations in Fish Control.* Report No. 22. LaCrosse, Wis.: Bureau of Sport Fisheries and Wildlife.

Schroeder, W., F. Ferrari, and J. Snider. 1973. Preliminary findings of a zooplankton study on the southern coast of Grand Bahama Island. *Hydro-Lab J.* 2(l):85-92.

Schroeder, W. 1974. Collecting and handling zoo-plankton and epibenthic organisms underwater. *Mar. Technol. Soc. J.* 8(5):40-43.

Schroeder, W. 1975. Hydrographic and current observations on the southern coast of Grand Bahama Island. *Hydro-Lab J.* 3(1): 48-66.

Sebens, K.P., and A.S. Johnson. 1991. Effects of water movement on prey capture and distribution of coral reefs. *Hydrobiologia* pp. 216-217, 247-248.

Seiff, S.R. 1985. Diver rescue techniques in California. *NAUI News,* Apr.

Shepard, A.N., D.A. Dinsmore, S.L. Miller, C.B. Cooper, and R.I. Wicklund 1996. Aquarius Undersea Laboratory: The Next Generation. Proceeding of the American Academy of Underwater Sciences, Sixteenth Annual Scientific Diving Symposium, Methods and Techniques of Underwater Research.

Shilling, C.W. 1965. *The Human Machine.* Annapolis, MD: U.S. Naval Institute.

Shilling, C.W., M.F. Werts, and N.R. Schandelmeier, eds. 1976. *The Underwater Handbook: A Guide to Physiology and Performance for the Engineer.* New York: Plenum Press.

Shilling, C.W., C.B. Carlston, and R.A. Mathias. 1984. *The Physician's Guide to Diving Medicine.* New York: Plenum Press.

Shilling, C.W., et al. 1976. *NOAA Diving Manual,* 1991, Rockville, MD: NOAA, U.S. Department of Commerce, R-8.

Shinn, E.A., J.H. Hudson, R.B. Halley, and B. Lidz. 1977. Topographic control and accumulation rate of some holocene coral reefs: South Florida and Dry Tortugas. In: *Proceedings of the Third International Coral Reef Symposium,* Miami, FL.

Shinn, E.A., J.H. Hudson, R.B. Halley, B. Litz, D.M. Robbin and I.G. Macintyre. 1982. Geology and sediment accumulation rates at Carrie Bow Cay, Belize. In: Ruetzler, K., and I.G. Macintyre, eds. *The Atlantic Barrier Reef Ecosystem at Carrie Bow cay, Belize.* I: Structure and Communities. Smithsonian Contribution to the Marine Sciences, Washington, D.C. Smithsonian Institution Press. p. 539

Simon, D.R., and M.E. Bradley. 1978. Corneal edema in divers wearing hard contact lenses. *Am. J. Ophthalmol.* 85:462-464.

Simon, D.R., and M.E. Bradley. 1980. Adverse effects of contact lens wear during decompression. *JAMA* 244:1213-1214.

Simon, D.R., and M.E. Bradley. 1981. Adverse effects of contact lens wear during decompression. *Institute of Diving Newsletter,* Summer.

Smith, R., and C. Allen. 1978. *Scuba Lifesaving and Accident Management.* Young Men's Christian Association (YMCA), Key West, FL.

Snyderman, M. 1980a. Horsecollar B.C. roundup. *Skin Diver* 29(10):33-44.

Snyderman, M. 1980b. Horsecollar B.C. roundup, Part II: 21 tankmounted and wraparound compensators. *Skin Diver* 29(11):49-58.

Somers, L.H. 1972. *Research Diver's Manual.* (1st Rev. Ed.) Technical Report 16. Ann Arbor: Sea Grant Program, University of Michigan.

Somers, L.H. 1986. *Diver Education Series: Physiology of Breath-Hold Diving.* Sea Grant College Program, University of Michigan, Ann Arbor, Mich.

Somers, L.H. 1986. *Diver Education Series: The First Responder.* Sea Grant College Program, University of Michigan, Ann Arbor, Mich.

Somers, L.H. 1986. Thermal Stress and the Diver. *NAUI News,* (Sept/Oct).

Standard Practice for Precision Cleaning and Testing of Shipboard Oxygen, Helium, Helium-Oxygen, Nitrogen, and Hydrogen Systems. 1996. MIL-STDD-1330D(SH), United States Department of Defense.

Starr, R.M., J.N. Heine and K.A. Johnson. 1998. A novel approach to tagging deepwater rockfishes *in situ*. In: Hartwick, B., E. Banister and G. Morariu, eds. 1998. Diving for Science 1998. *Proc. of AAUS Scientific Diving Symp.* Vancouver, British Columbia.pp. 83-102.

Stolp, B., and R. Moon. 1993. Soda Lime Reactivity. In: Grace, W.R., *The Sodasorb Manual*, pp. M17-M20.

Stolp, B., and R. Moon. 1993. Physiological Factors in Carbon Dioxide Removal. In: Grace, W.R., *The Sodasorb Manual*, pp. M6-M16.

Strauss, M.B., and W.S. Vaughan. 1981. Rewarming experiences with hypothermic scuba divers. *Undersea Biomed. Res.* 8(l):25.

Surgeon General. 1986. U.S. Department of Health and Human Services, Public Health Service, Centers for Disease Control, 1986. The Health Consequences of Involuntary Smoking: A Report of the Surgeon General.

Tate, B., T. Moen, and B. Severson. 1965. The use of rotenone for the recovery of live fish. *Progress. Fish Cultur.* 27(3): 156-160.

Thienpoint, D., and C. Niemegeers. 1965. R7464A, new potent anesthetic in fish. *Int. Zoo. Yearbook* 5: 202-205.

Thresher, RE., and A.M. Gronell. 1978. Subcutaneous tagging of small reef fishes. *Copeia* 2: 352-353.

Tutschulte, T.C. 1968. Monitoring the nocturnal movement of abalones. *Bull. Am. Littoral Soc.* 4(3): 12-15.

Traver, R.P. 1984. Introduction to Personnel Safety Equipment and Decontamination Operations. In: Lotz, W.E., ed. *Protection of Divers in Water Containing Hazardous Chemicals, Pathogenic Organisms and Radioactive Material.* Bethesda, MD: Undersea Medical Society, pp. 311-339.

Traver, R.P. 1985. *Manual of Practice for Marine Safety Officers and On-Scene Coordinators Involved in Chemically and/or Biologically-Contaminated Underwater Operations.* Edison, NJ: U.S. Environmental Protection Agency, EPA/NOAA IAG AD-13-F-2-826-0.

Trelleborg Viking, Inc. 1998. *Diving in Contaminated Water.* Portsmouth, NH. pp. 24.

Tzimoulis, P. 1982. Divers don't do drugs. *Skin Diver* 31(2):4.

U.S. Army Corp of Engineers. 1984. *Shore Protection Manual, Volume II.* Coastal Engineering Research Center, Department of the Army, Waterways Experiment Station, Corps of Engineers, Vicksburg, Miss.

U.S. Coast Guard. 1973. *National Search and Rescue Manual.* Department of Transportation. Washington, D.C.: U.S. Government Printing Office.

U.S. Coast Guard. 1975. *A Pocket Guide to Cold Water Survival.* Department of Transportation. Washington D.C.: U.S. Government Printing Office.

U.S. Department of Navy. 1971. *U.S. Navy Diving-Gas Manual.* (2nd Ed.) NAVSHIPS 00994-009-6010. Washington, D.C.: U.S. Government Printing Office.

U.S. Department of the Navy, NAVSEA. 1982. Operation and Maintenance Instructions, Diver Tools. Vols. I and II. *NAVSEA Report S9592-AJ-MMA-0l0.* Washington, D.C.: U. S. Department of the Navy, Naval Sea Systems Command.

U.S. Department of the Navy. 1985. *U.S. Navy Diving Manual,* NAVSEA 0994-LP-00l-9010, Revision 1. Washington, D.C.: U.S. Government Printing Office.

U.S. Department of the Navy. *NAVSEA S0300-BB-MAN-010.* 2531 Jefferson Davis Hwy., Arlington, VA, 22242-5160: Naval Sea Systems Command.

U.S. Department of the Navy. 1986. *Operations Publication OP-5.* Vol. 1, Change 14. Washington, D.C.: U.S. Government Printing Office.

U.S. Department of the Navy. 1987. *U.S. Navy Diving Manual, Volume 2, Mixed-Gas Diving.* Revision 2. Washington, D.C.: U.S. Government Printing Office.

U.S. Department of the Navy. 1988. *U.S. Navy Diving Manual, Volume 1, Air Diving.* Revision 2. Washington, D.C.: U.S. Government Printing Office.

U.S. Department of the Navy. 1999. *U.S. Navy Diving Manual*, Revision 4. NAVSEA 0910-LP-708-8000. Naval Sea Systems Command, 2531 Jefferson Davis Hwy. Arlington, VA 22242-5160.

U.S. Navy Diving Manual - see U.S. Department of the Navy (year)

University of New Hampshire. 1972. *Manned Underwater Platforms.* U.S. Department of Commerce Technical Report No. 111. Durham, N.H.: University of New Hampshire.

VanDerwalker, J., and B. Littlehales. 1971. Tektite II: Part I. Science's window on the sea. *National Geograph.* 140(2): 256-289.

Vann, R.D. 1989. *Physiology of Nitrox Diving.* In: Hamilton, R.W., A.W. Hulbert, and D.J. Crosson, eds. Harbor Branch workshop on enriched air nitrox diving. Technical Report 89-1. Rockville, MD: NOAA Undersea Research Program.

Vaughan, W.S., and J.A.S. Kinney. 1980. Vision-Perception Research and Analysis Relevant to Display Design for Underwater Applications. *Office of Naval Research Technical Report No. N00014-74-C-0602; NR 196-157.*

Vaughan, W.S., and J.A.S. Kinney. 1981. Human Engineering Guides to Design of Displays for Underwater Applications. *Office of Naval Research Technical Report No. N00014-74-C-0602;* NR 196-157.

Wachholz, C. 1986. The high cost of diving injuries–the need for diver insurance. *Ascent Lines.* Young Men's Christian Association (YMCA) Scuba Program, Norcross, Georgia.

Wachholz, C. 2000. Dan Personnal Communication.

Walden, B., and W. Rainnie. 1971. *NOAA Diving Manual,* 1991, Rockville, MD: NOAA, U.S. Department of Commerce, R-9.

Walden, B., and W. Rainnie. 1971. *Project FLARE.* Florida Aquanaut Research Expedition Program Plan. Woods Hole, Mass.: Woods Hole Oceanographic Institution.

Walsh, J.M. 1980. Interaction of drugs in the hyperbaric environment. *Undersea Medical Society Workshop Report No. 21 (DR), 10-1-80.* Bethesda, MD.: Undersea Medical Society.

Walsh, J.M., and H.M. Ginzburg. 1984. Use of drugs and related substances under diving conditions in: Shilling, C.W., C.B. Carlston, and R.A. Mathias, eds. *The Physician's Guide to Diving Medicine.* New York: Plenum Press.

Walters, K.C., M.T. Gould, E.A. Bachrach, and F.K. Butler, Jr. 2000. Screening for Oxygen Sensitivity in U.S. Navy Combat Swimmers. *Undersea Hyperbaric Med Soc* 27(1):21-26.

Webb, P., ed. 1985. Prolonged and repeated work in cold water. *Undersea Medical Society Workshop Report No. 68.* Bethesda, MD: Undersea Medical Society.

Weeks, A. 1972. FLARE. *Exploring the Coral Reefs.* National Oceanic and Atmospheric Administration, Washington, D.C.

Weeks, A. 1972. *NOAA Diving Manual,* 1991, Rockville, MD: NOAA, U.S. Department of Commerce, R-9.

Wells, J.M. 1986. Diving operations in heated/contaminated water. In: *Proceedings of the Eighth Meeting of the UJNR Panel of Diving Physiology and Technology.* Rockville, MD.: NOAA Undersea Research Program.

Wells, J.M. 1988. The use of nitrogen oxygen mixtures as divers breathing gas. In: *Proceedings: Oceans '88.* The Institute of Electrical & Electronic Engineers, Ocean Engineering Society, pp. 1305-1308.

Wells, J.M. 1989. Nitrox diving within NOAA: History, Applications, and Future. In: Hamilton, R.W., D. Crosson, and A.W. Hulbert, eds. Workshop on Enriched Air Nitrox Diving. *National Undersea Research Program Research Report 89(1),* September 1989. pp. 31-35.

Wells, J.M., and L. Moroz. 1993. Applications of gas separation technology in the preparation of diver's breathing gases and hyperbaric atmospheres. *MTS '93 Conference Proceedings,* Washington, D.C., pp. 568-571.

Wells, J.M., and L. Moroz. 1994. Applications of differential permeability gas separation technology in the preparation of breathing gas for diving and hyperbaric therapy. In: *Undersea and Hyperbaric Medicine,* 1994, Vol. 21 supplement.

Wells, J.M., and W.C. Phoel. 1995. Recent developments in the preparation of mixed gas breathing media - nitrox, heliox, and trimix. In: Naraki, N., Y. Taya, and M. Mohri eds., *Proceedings of the 13th Meeting of the UJNR Panel on Diving Physiology,* Oct 23-25, 1995, Miura, Kanagaw, Japan. Published by JAMSTEC (Japan Marine Science & Technology Center), Yokosuka. pp. 115-122.

Wells, J.M. 1998. Potential applications of differential permeability membranes in the control of gas composition in closed circuit atmospheres. *Life Support & Biosphere Science* 5(3): pp. 271-277.

Wells, J.M. Equipment Innovations cut risks for divers in polluted water. Inn: *Sea Technology.* 25(12): pp.22-23.

Wendall, F., Pattison, C., and Harris, M. 1996. Sea Otter, *Enhydra Lutris.* Containment Management: Field Studies and Feaseibility Assessment. California Dept. of Fish and Game, Marine Resources Division Administrative Report 96-5, pp. 10.

Wickham, D.A., and J.W. Watson, Jr. 1976. SCUBA diving methods for fishing systems evaluation. *Marine Fish. Rev.* 38(7):15-23.

References

Wicklund, R., G. Wenz, and R. Clarke. 1972, 1973, 1975. *Bulletin of the Hydro-Lab Underwater Research Program*. Vols. 1, 2, and 3. Riviera Beach, FL.: Perry Foundation.

Wicklund, R. et al. 1973. *NOAA Diving Manual*, 1991, Rockville, MD: NOAA, U.S. Department of Commerce, R-10.

Wolcott, T.G., and A.H. Hines. 1996. Advances in ultrasonic biotelemetry for animal movement and behavior: The blue crab case study. In: Lang, M.A., and C.C. Baldwin, eds. Methods and Techniques of Underwater Research. *Proc. of AAUS Scientific Diving Symp.*, Smithsonian Institution, Washington, D.C. pp. 229-236.

Wood, E. 1956. Urethane as a carcinogen. *Progress. Fish Cultur.* 18(3): 135-136.

Woods, J., and J. Lythgoe, eds. 1971. *Underwater Science.* London: Oxford University Press.

Woodward, R. 1982. Microprocessor-controlled diver navigation. *Underwater Sys. Des.* 4(2).

Wright, W.L. 1982. Scuba diver's delayed toxic epithelial keratopathy from commerical mask defogging agents. *Am. J. Ophthalmol.* 93: 470-472.

Zhukov, L.A., A.V. Mayer and G.R. Rekhtzamer. 1964. Use of underwater photo and movie survey for investigation of turbulence in the sea. *Mat. 11 Konf. Probl.* Vzaimodeystviye Atmos Gidros Severn Chasti Atlantich Okeana, pp.151-155.

Zumrick, J. 1985. A comparison of the insulating properties of two commercially available dry suit undergarment combinations. In: Webb, P., ed. Prolonged and Repeated Work in Cold Water. *Undersea Medical Society Workshop Report No. 68.* Bethesda, MD.: Undersea Medical Society.

Appendix
Index

Index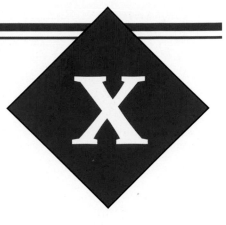

D

Index

T

X

Y

Z